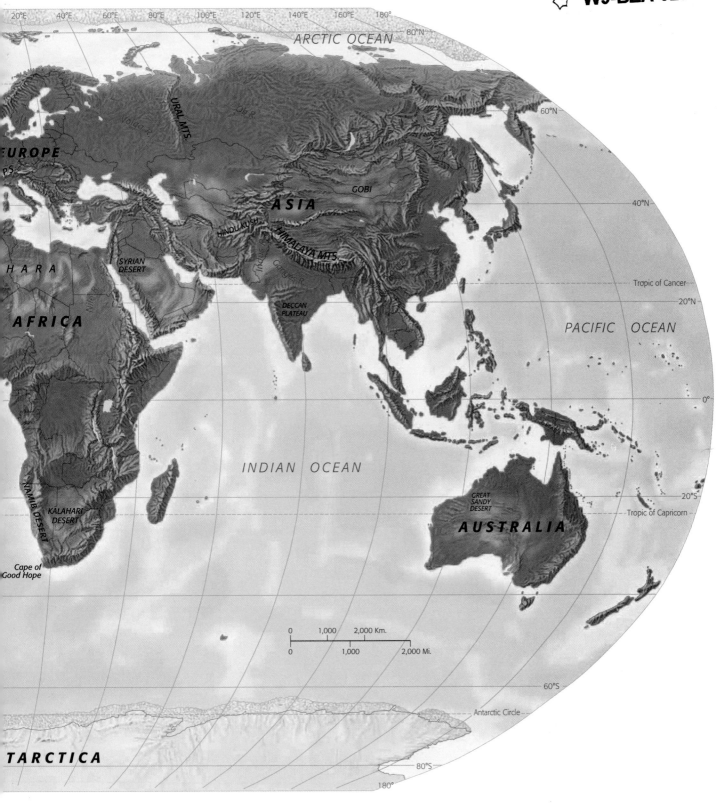

ARCTIC OCEAN

80°N

60°N

URAL MTS.

Volga R.

Ob R.

EUROPE

GOBI

40°N

ASIA

HINDU KUSH

HIMALAYA MTS.

SYRIAN
DESERT

Indus R.

Ganges R.

Tropic of Cancer

20°N

HARA

Nile R.

DECCAN
PLATEAU

AFRICA

PACIFIC OCEAN

0°

INDIAN OCEAN

NAMIB DESERT

KALAHARI
DESERT

GREAT
SANDY
DESERT

20°S

Tropic of Capricorn

Cape of
Good Hope

AUSTRALIA

0	1,000	2,000 Km.
0	1,000	2,000 Mi.

60°S

Antarctic Circle

TARCTICA

80°S

180°

A·HISTORY·OF
WORLD·SOCIETIES

A·HISTORY·OF WORLD·SOCIETIES

eighth edition

John P. McKay
University of Illinois at Urbana-Champaign

Bennett D. Hill
Late of Georgetown University

John Buckler
University of Illinois at Urbana-Champaign

Patricia Buckley Ebrey
University of Washington

Roger B. Beck
Eastern Illinois University

Clare Haru Crowston
University of Illinois at Urbana-Champaign

Merry E. Wiesner-Hanks
University of Wisconsin–Milwaukee

BEDFORD / ST. MARTIN'S
Boston • New York

FOR BEDFORD/ST. MARTIN'S

Publisher for History: Mary Dougherty
Executive Editor for History: Traci Mueller
Director of Development for History: Jane Knetzger
Executive Marketing Manager: Jenna Bookin Barry
Copyeditor: Sybil Sosin
Proofreader: Angela Hoover Morrison
Text Design and Page Layout: Janet Theurer
Photo Research: Carole Frohlich
Indexer: Leoni McVey
Cover Design: Donna Lee Dennison
Cover Art: Portrait of Yintang, Prince Yi, looking through a window. China, Qing dynasty, 18th century. Hanging scroll. Ink and color on silk. Arthur M. Sackler Gallery, Smithsonian Institution, Washington, D.C. Purchase from Smithsonian Collections Acquisition Program, and partial gift of Richard G. Pritzlaff, S1991.64.
Cartography: Charlotte Miller/GeoNova
Composition: NK Graphics
Printing and Binding: R.R. Donnelley & Sons Company

President: Joan E. Feinberg
Editorial Director: Denise B. Wydra
Director of Marketing: Karen R. Soeltz
Director of Editing, Design, and Production: Marcia Cohen
Assistant Director of Editing, Design, and Production: Elise S. Kaiser
Managing Editor: Elizabeth M. Schaaf

Library of Congress Control Number: 2008933879

Manufactured in the United States of America.

3 2 1 0 9 8
f   e   d   c   b   a

For information, write: Bedford/St. Martin's, 75 Arlington Street, Boston, MA 02116 (617-399-4000)

ISBN-10: 0–312–68293–X   ISBN-13: 978-0–312–68293–4   (combined edition)
ISBN-10: 0–312–68294–8   ISBN-13: 978-0–312–68294–1   (Vol. I)
ISBN-10: 0–312–68295–6   ISBN-13: 978-0–312–68295–8   (Vol. II)
ISBN-10: 0–312–68296–4   ISBN-13: 978-0–312–68296–5   (Vol. A)
ISBN-10: 0–312–68297–2   ISBN-13: 978-0–312–68297–2   (Vol. B)
ISBN-10: 0–312–68298–0   ISBN-13: 978-0–312–68298–9   (Vol. C)

Preface

In this age of a global environment and global warming, of a global economy and global banking, of global migration and rapid global travel, of global sports and global popular culture, the study of world history becomes more urgent. Surely, an appreciation of other, and earlier, societies helps us to understand better our own and to cope more effectively in pluralistic cultures worldwide. The large numbers of Turks living in Germany, of Italians, Hungarians, and Slavic peoples living in Australia, of Japanese living in Peru and Argentina, and of Arabs, Mexicans, Chinese, and Filipinos living in the United States—to mention just a few obvious examples—represent diversity on a global scale. The movement of large numbers of peoples from one continent to another goes back thousands of years, at least as far back as the time when peoples migrated from Asia into the Americas. Swift air travel and the Internet have accelerated these movements, and they testify to the incredible technological changes the world has experienced in the last half of the twentieth century and beginning of the twenty-first.

For most peoples, the study of history has traditionally meant the study of their own national, regional, and ethnic pasts. Fully appreciating the great differences among various societies and the complexity of the historical problems surrounding these cultures, we have wondered if the study of local or national history is sufficient for people who will spend their lives in the twenty-first century on one small interconnected planet. The authors of this book believe the study of world history in a broad and comparative context is an exciting, important, and highly practical pursuit. It is our conviction, based on considerable experience in introducing large numbers of students to the broad sweep of world history, that a book reflecting current trends can excite readers and inspire an enduring interest in the long human experience. Our strategy has been twofold.

First, we have made social history the core element of our work. We not only incorporate recent research by social historians but also seek to re-create the life of ordinary people in appealing human terms. A strong social element seems especially appropriate in a world history text, for identification with ordinary men and women of the past allows today's reader to reach an empathetic understanding of different cultures. At the same time we have been mindful of the need to give great economic, political, intellectual, and cultural developments the attention they deserve. We want to give individual students and instructors a balanced, integrated perspective so that they can pursue on their own or in the classroom those themes and questions that they find particularly exciting and significant.

Second, we have made every effort to strike an effective global balance. We are acutely aware of the great drama of our times—the passing of the era of Western dominance and the increasing complexity in lines of political, economic, and cultural power and influence. Today the whole world interacts, and to understand that interaction and what it means for today's citizens, we must study the whole world's history. Thus we have adopted a comprehensive yet manageable global perspective. We study all geographical areas, conscious of the separate histories of many parts of the world, particularly in the earliest millennia of human development. We also stress the links among cultures, political units, and economic systems, for it is these connections and interactions that have made the world what it is today.

Changes in the Eighth Edition

In preparing the Eighth Edition of this book, we have worked hard to keep our book up-to-date and to strengthen our distinctive yet balanced approach.

Organizational Changes

Responding to the wishes of many of the faculty who use this book, we have shortened the text significantly. The narrative has been tightened in each chapter, and the consolidations improve the overall global balance of our work.

In addition, several chapters have been extensively reorganized. Merry Wiesner-Hanks from the University of Wisconsin-Milwaukee and Clare Crowston from the University of Illinois joined the author team with this edition, taking responsibility for Chapters 7, 10, 13, and 14 and Chapters 15–17 and 21, respectively. Chapter 7, "Europe and Western Asia, ca. 350–850," has a broader geographic focus, with more material on the Byzantine Empire and the various migrating peoples. Former Chapter 13 on the Americas has been brought into the story earlier as new Chapter 10, and the chapter has been rewritten to reflect the newest scholarship on early cultures of North America, Mesoamerica, and South America. Discussion of the Thirty Years' War has been integrated into Chapter 16, allowing a better assessment of its impact on state-building, along with broader coverage of economic and demographic trends. Other chapters have been restructured as well. Chapter 19, "The Islamic World Powers, ca. 1400–1800," has been completely reorganized to highlight parallels among the Ottoman, Safavid, and Mughal Empires in terms of political, cultural, and economic developments. Reflecting current understandings of the connections around the Atlantic world, Chapter 21 includes extensive discussion of the Haitian Revolution along with the American and French Revolutions. Chapter 26, "Nation Building in the Western Hemisphere and Australia," contains a new section that places the nations in comparative perspective. In addition, former chapters 33 and 34 are now combined as a new and streamlined Chapter 33, "A New Era in World History." The new chapter focuses on global political and economic issues (such as the United Nations, terrorism, globalization and its consequences, and vital resources), plus global issues that affect individuals (such as poverty, disease, urbanization, and education), and shows how they evolved over the course of the twentieth century. "The Middle East in Today's World," a supplement to later printings of the seventh edition, has been updated to reflect recent developments in the Middle East, and is now the Epilogue.

Geographical and Gender Issues

In previous editions we added significantly more discussion of groups and regions that are often shortchanged in the general histories of world civilizations, and we have continued to do so in this new revision. This expanded scope reflects the renewed awareness within the historical profession of the enormous diversity of the world's peoples. Examples include more material on the Etruscans in Chapter 5, the Huns in Chapter 7, and the Turks in Chapter 8. Chapter 10 includes increased discussion of the Hohokam, Hopewell, and Mississippian peoples in North America and of pre-Inca cultures in Peru. Study of the Mongols and other peoples of Central Asia has exploded in the past several years, which has shaped the changes in Chapter 11. Chapter 17 includes a new discussion of new ideas about race during the Enlightenment. Chapter 21 has considerable new material on the Haitian Revolution. Overall, an expanded treatment of non-European societies and cultures has been achieved.

In addition, we have continued to include updated and expanded material relating to gender in nearly every chapter, incorporating insights from women's history, the history of sexuality, the history of the family, and the new history of masculinities. Chapter 4 includes revised coverage of Greek sexuality and the family, with new focus in Chapter 7 on the role of women in barbarian society, Chapter 8 on women in classical Islamic society, Chapter 12 on women's lives in Song China, Chapter 14 on gender hierarchies in Renaissance Europe and on the Reformation and marriage, Chapter 18 on women, marriage, and work in early modern Africa, Chapter 22 on the sexual division of labor in the Industrial Revolution, and Chapter 33 on women's rights and feminist movements. In addition to "Individuals in Society" features from previous editions that focus on the lives of specific women, several new ones have been added: the feature in Chapter 1 focuses on the Egyptian monarch Nefertiti, in Chapter 7 on Empress Theodora of Constantinople, in Chapter 13 on the Christian abbess Hildegard of Bingen, and in Chapter 16 on the Jewish merchant and diarist Glückel of Hameln. Chapter 8 includes a new "Listening to the Past" feature on the etiquette of marriage in the Islamic world.

Cross-Cultural Comparisons and Connections

In this edition we have continued to expand our comparative coverage to help students see and understand the cross-cultural connections of world history. Chapter 2 offers expanded discussion of trading networks in early India, and both Chapters 5 and 6 provide enhanced discussion of the Silk Road. Chapter 7 includes a reframed discussion of the barbarian migrations into Europe. Chapter 8 addresses new questions such as "How were the Muslim lands governed and what new challenges did they face?" and "What social distinctions were important in Muslim society?" Updated treatment of the trans-Saharan trade appears in Chapter 9, and Chapter 10 now discusses trade along the rivers and lakes of North America. Chapter 15 has been extensively rewritten, with a new section on global economies, forced migrations, and cultural encounters. Chapter 24 addresses the important question "What were the global consequences of European industrialization between 1800 and 1914?"

Incorporation of Recent Scholarship

As in previous revisions we have made a serious effort to keep our book fresh and up-to-date by incorporating new and important scholarship throughout the Eighth Edition. Chapter 4 includes new findings about the role of women in religious movements in the ancient world, including Christianity. Chapter 7 highlights the continuing significance of the Byzantines and the transformations brought through barbarian migrations. Chapter 10 features innovative research on agricultural communities in the Americas and the connections among them. New sections on popular religion and social hierarchies appear in Chapters 13 and 14. Chapters 14 and 17 include sections derived from the new scholarship on changing conceptions of race. Chapter 17 also draws upon new work about the emergence of the public sphere in Enlightenment Europe to discuss the political and social implications of intellectual change. Chapter 20 features new treatment of maritime East Asia. Chapter 26 includes a new comparative discussion of the incorporation of the nations of the Americas into the world economy. Material in the final three chapters and the Epilogue has been updated to ensure a clear account of contemporary world history. Thus, the text includes discussion of such events as the unfolding war in Iraq, the worsening crisis in Afghanistan, Hezbollah's revival in Lebanon, moves toward peace in Israel, elections in Zimbabwe, charges of genocide against the Sudanese president, China and Tibet and the 2008 Olympics, and North Korea's dismantling of its nuclear facilities. In sum, we have tried hard to bring new research and interpretation into our global history, believing it essential to keep our book stimulating, accurate, and current for students and instructors.

Revised Full-Color Art and Map Program

Finally, the illustrative component of our work has been carefully revised. We have added many new illustrations to our extensive art program, which includes over three hundred color reproductions, thus highlighting the connections among art, material culture, events, and social changes. Illustrations have been selected to support and complement the text, and, wherever possible, illustrations are contemporaneous with the textual material discussed. Considerable research went into many of the captions in order to make them as informative as possible. We have reflected on the observation that "there are more valid facts and details in works of art than there are in history books," and we would modify it to say that art is "a history book." Artwork remains an integral part of our book; the past can speak in pictures as well as in words. The maps have been completely redesigned and revised in this edition to be more dynamic, engaging, and relevant than ever before. The use of full color serves to clarify the maps and graphs and to enrich the textual material. The maps and map captions have been updated to correlate directly to the text.

Distinctive Features

Distinctive features from earlier editions guide the reader in the process of historical understanding. Many of these features also show how historians sift through and evaluate evidence. Our goal is to suggest how historians actually work and think. We want the reader to think critically and to realize that history is neither a list of cut-and-dried facts nor a senseless jumble of conflicting opinions.

"Individuals in Society" Feature

The Eighth Edition presents eight new short studies of a fascinating woman or man, which are carefully integrated into the main discussion of the text. This "Individuals in Society" feature grew out of our long-standing focus on people's lives and the varieties of historical experience, and we believe that readers will empathize with these flesh-and-blood human beings as they themselves seek to define their own identities today. The spotlighting of individuals, both famous and obscure, carries forward the greater attention to cultural and intellectual developments that we have used to invigorate our social history, and it reflects changing interests within the historical profession as well as the development of "micro history."

The men and women included in the Eighth Edition represent a wide range of careers and personalities. Several are renowned historical or present-day figures, such as Plutarch, the Greek historian and biographer (Chapter 5); Amda Siyon, probably the most important ruler of Ethiopia's Solomonic dynasty (Chapter 9); Giuseppe Garibaldi, the flamboyant, incorruptible popular hero of Italy's national unification (Chapter 23); and the Dalai Lama, exiled spiritual leader of a captive nation (Chapter 33). Two individuals were brilliant writers who testified to tragedy and calamitous destruction: Vera Brittain, an English nurse on the frontlines in World War I (Chapter 27); and Primo Levi, an Italian Jewish chemist who survived the Holocaust and probed the horrors of the death camps (Chapter 30). Others are lesser-known individuals, yet highly accomplished in their own societies and time, such as the Ban family from China, who were influential in the military, government, and literary fields (Chapter 6); Bhaskara, the Indian astronomer and mathematician who published many books in those fields (Chapter 11); Tan Yunxian, a Chinese female doctor who devoted her practice to the treatment of women (Chapter 20); and José Rizal, a Philippine nationalist and author (Chapter 25).

"Listening to the Past" Feature

A two-page excerpt from a primary source concludes each chapter. This signature feature, entitled "Listening to the Past," extends and illuminates a major historical issue considered in the chapter. Each primary source opens with a problem-setting introduction and closes with "Questions for Analysis" that invite students to evaluate the evidence as historians would. Drawn from a range of writings addressing a variety of social, cultural, political, and intellectual issues, these sources promote active involvement and critical interpretation. Selected for their interest and importance and carefully fitted into their historical context, these sources do indeed allow the student to "listen to the past" and to observe how history has been shaped by individual men and women, some of them great aristocrats, others ordinary folk.

"Global Trade" Feature

In the form of two-page essays that focus on a particular commodity, this popular feature explores the world trade, social and economic impact, and cultural influence of that commodity. Each essay is accompanied by a detailed map showing the trade routes of the commodity. Retaining the seven essays of the previous edition on pottery, silk, tea, slaves, indigo, oil, and arms, we added one on spices in Chapter 11. We believe that careful attention to all of these essays will enable the student to appreciate the complex ways in which trade has connected and influenced the various parts of the world.

Improved Pedagogy

To help make the narrative accessible to students, we have put a number of pedagogical features in the text. At the start of each chapter, an outline of the major section titles provides students with a brief preview of the chapter coverage. Also at the beginning of each chapter, we pose specific historical questions to help guide the reader toward understanding. These questions are then answered in the course of the chapter, and each chapter concludes with a concise summary of its findings. All of the questions and summaries have been re-examined and frequently revised in order to maximize their usefulness.

Throughout the chapter we have highlighted in boldface the major terms with which a student should become familiar. These Key Terms are then listed at the conclusion of the chapter. The student may use these terms to test his or her understanding of the chapter's material. A complete list of the Key Terms and definitions is also provided on the student website, along with electronic flashcards that allow students to quiz themselves on their mastery of the terms.

In addition to posing chapter-opening questions and presenting more problems in historical interpretation, we have quoted extensively from a wide variety of primary sources in the narrative, demonstrating in our use of these quotations how historians evaluate evidence. Thus primary sources are examined as an integral part of the narrative as well as presented in extended form in the "Listening to the Past" chapter feature. We believe that such an extensive program of both integrated and separate primary source excerpts will help readers learn to interpret and think critically.

Each chapter concludes with a Summary section and carefully selected suggestions for further reading. These suggestions are briefly described to help readers know where to turn to continue thinking and learning about the world. Also, chapter bibliographies have been thoroughly revised and updated to keep them current with the vast amount of new work being done in many fields.

Revised Timelines

To better present the flow of critical developments, the comparative timelines of earlier editions have been converted into chapter chronologies in each chapter. The extended comparative timeline has been moved to the front of the book and is now a perforated foldout poster. Comprehensive and easy to locate, this useful timeline poster allows students to compare simultaneous political, economic, social, cultural, intellectual, and scientific developments over the centuries.

Flexible Format

World history courses differ widely in chronological structure from one campus to another. To accommodate the various divisions of historical time into intervals that fit a two-quarter, three-quarter, or two-semester period, *A History of World Societies* is published in three versions that embrace the complete work:

- One-volume hardcover edition: *A History of World Societies* (Chapters 1–33 and Epilogue)
- Two-volume paperback edition: *Volume I: To 1715* (Chapters 1–16); and *Volume II: Since 1500* (Chapters 15–33 and Epilogue)
- Three-volume paperback edition: *Volume A: From Antiquity to 1500* (Chapters 1–13); *Volume B: From 800 to 1815* (Chapters 10–21); and *Volume C: From 1775 to the Present* (Chapters 21–33 and Epilogue)

Overlapping chapters in two-volume and three-volume editions facilitate matching the appropriate volume with the opening and closing dates of a specific course. In addition, this title is available as an e-Book.

Ancillaries

We are pleased to introduce a full ancillary package that will help students in learning and instructors in teaching:

- *Student website*
- *Instructor website*
- *Electronic Testing (powered by Diploma™)*
- *Online Instructor's Resource Manual*
- *PowerPoint maps and images*
- *PowerPoint questions for personal response systems*
- *Blackboard® and WebCT® course cartridges*

The student website features a wide array of resources to help students master the subject matter including learning objectives, chapter outlines, pre-class quizzes and other self-testing material like interactive flashcards, chronological ordering exercises, and more. Students can also find additional text resources such as an online glossary, audio chapter summaries, and an audio pronunciation guide.

The instructor website features all of the material on the student site plus additional password-protected resources for teaching the course such as an electronic version of the *Instructor's Resource Manual* and *PowerPoint* slides.

Electronic Testing (powered by *Diploma*) offers instructors a flexible and powerful tool for test generation and test management. Supported by the Brownstone Research Group's market-leading *Diploma* software, this new version of *Electronic Testing* significantly improves on functionality and ease of use by offering all of the tools needed to create, author, deliver, and customize multiple types of tests. *Diploma* is currently in use at thousands of college and university campuses throughout the United States and Canada.

The online *Instructor's Resource Manual,* prepared by John Reisbord of Vassar College and updated for the Eighth Edition by Jason Stratton of Bakersfield College, contains advice on teaching the world history course, instructional objectives, chapter outlines, lecture suggestions, paper and class activity topics, primary source and map activities, and suggestions for cooperative learning.

We are pleased to offer a collection of world history *PowerPoint* maps and images for use in classroom presentations. This collection includes all of the photos and maps in the text, as well as numerous other images from our world history titles. *PowerPoint* questions and answers for use with personal response system software are also offered to adopters free of charge.

Graded homework questions have been developed to work with the *Blackboard* and *WebCT* course management systems. Instructors can choose to use the content as is, modify it, or even add their own.

In addition, instructors have numerous options for packaging Bedford/St. Martin's titles with *A History of World Societies.* Based on the popular "World History Matters" websites produced by the Center for History and New Media at George Mason University, the print resource *World History Matters: A Student Guide to World History Online* provides an illustrated and annotated guide to 150 of the most useful and reliable websites for student research in world history as well as advice on evaluating and using Internet sources. This title, edited by Kristin Lehner, Kelly Schrum, and T. Mills Kelly, is available free when packaged with the textbook. Over 100 titles in the *Bedford Series in History and Culture* combine first-rate scholarship, historical narrative, and important primary documents for undergraduate courses. Each book is brief, inexpensive, and focused on a specific topic or period. Package discounts are available. Trade books published by sister companies Farrar, Straus and Giroux; Henry Holt and Company; Hill and Wang;

Picador; St. Martin's Press; and Palgrave Macmillan are available at a 50 percent discount when packaged with Bedford/St. Martin's textbooks. For more information, visit **bedfordstmartins.com/tradeup**.

Acknowledgments

It is a pleasure to thank the many instructors who have read and critiqued the manuscript throughout its development:

Wayne Ackerson
Salisbury University

Edward M. Anson
University of Arkansas at Little Rock

Beau Bowers
Central Piedmont Community College

Eric Dorn Brose
Drexel University

Erwin F. Erhardt III
Thomas More College

Dolores Grapsas
New River Community College

Candace Gregory-Abbott
California State University, Sacramento

Roger Hall
Allan Hancock College

John Jovan Markovic
Andrews University

Christopher E. Mauriello
Salem State College

Michael G. Murdock
Brigham Young University

Phyllis E. Pobst
Arkansas State University

Thomas Saylor
Concordia University

Jason M. Stratton
Bakersfield College

Ruth Smith Truss
University of Montevallo

Claude Welch
State University of New York at Buffalo

It is also a pleasure to thank our editors for their efforts over many years. To Christina Horn, who guided production, and to Tonya Lobato, our development editor, we express our admiration and special appreciation. And we thank Carole Frohlich for her contributions in photo research and selection.

Many of our colleagues at the University of Illinois, University of Washington, Eastern Illinois University, and the University of Wisconsin–Milwaukee continue to provide information and stimulation, often without even knowing it. We thank them for it.

Each of us has benefited from the criticism of his or her coauthors, although each of us assumes responsibility for what he or she has written. John Buckler has written Chapters 1, 4, and 5. Patricia Buckley Ebrey has written or updated Chapters 2–3, 6, 8, 11–12, 19–20, and 25–26. Bennett Hill originally conceived the narrative for Chapters 7–9, 12–15, 18–20, and 26; since his untimely death his coauthors have taken on his chapters. In this edition new coauthor Merry Wiesner-Hanks handled Chapters 7, 10, 13, and 14; and new coauthor Clare Crowston handled Chapters 15–17 and 21. Roger Beck contributed to Chapters 9 and 18 and handled Chapters 27–33 in this edition. Roger Beck also wrote the Epilogue. John McKay originally wrote the narrative for Chapters 16–17, 21–24, and 27–30, and he continues to take responsibility for Chapters 22–24 in this edition. Finally, we continue to welcome the many comments and suggestions that have come from our readers, for they have helped us greatly in this ongoing endeavor.

J.P.M.

J.B.

P.B.E.

R.B.B.

C.H.C.

M.W-H.

Brief Contents

Contents

Chapter 14

EUROPE IN THE RENAISSANCE
AND REFORMATION, 1350–1600   386

Chapter 15

THE ACCELERATION OF
GLOBAL CONTACT   426

Chapter 16

ABSOLUTISM AND CONSTITUTIONALISM IN EUROPE, CA. 1589–1725   460

Chapter 17

TOWARD A NEW WORLDVIEW IN THE WEST, 1540–1789   492

Chapter 18

AFRICA AND THE WORLD, CA. 1400–1800   516

Epilogue

Maps

Listening to the Past

Individuals in Society

About the Authors

JOHN P. MCKAY Born in St. Louis, John P. McKay received his B.A. from Wesleyan University (1961), his M.A. from the Fletcher School of Law and Diplomacy (1962), and his Ph.D. from the University of California, Berkeley (1968). He began teaching history at the University of Illinois in 1966 and became a Professor there in 1976. John won the Herbert Baxter Adams Prize for his book *Pioneers for Profit: Foreign Entrepreneurship and Russian Industrialization, 1885–1913* (1970). He has also written *Tramways and Trolleys: The Rise of Urban Mass Transport in Europe* (1976) and has translated Jules Michelet's *The People* (1973). His research has been supported by fellowships from the Ford Foundation, the Guggenheim Foundation, the National Endowment for the Humanities, and IREX. He has written well over a hundred articles, book chapters, and reviews, which have appeared in numerous publications, including *The American Historical Review, Business History Review, The Journal of Economic History,* and *Slavic Review.* He contributed extensively to C. Stewart and P. Fritzsche, eds., *Imagining the Twentieth Century* (1997).

BENNETT D. HILL A native of Philadelphia, Bennett D. Hill earned an A.B. from Princeton (1956) and advanced degrees from Harvard (A.M., 1958) and Princeton (Ph.D., 1963). He taught history at the University of Illinois, where he was department chair from 1978 to 1981. He published *English Cistercian Monasteries and Their Patrons in the Twelfth Century* (1968), *Church and State in the Middle Ages* (1970), and articles in *Analecta Cisterciensia, The New Catholic Encyclopaedia, The American Benedictine Review,* and *The Dictionary of the Middle Ages.* His reviews appeared in *The American Historical Review, Speculum, The Historian,* the *Journal of World History,* and *Library Journal.* He was one of the contributing editors to *The Encyclopedia of World History* (2001). He was a Fellow of the American Council of Learned Societies and served on the editorial board of *The American Benedictine Review,* on committees of the National Endowment for the Humanities, and as vice president of the American Catholic Historical Association (1995–1996). A Benedictine monk of St. Anselm's Abbey in Washington, D.C., he was also a Visiting Professor at Georgetown University.

JOHN BUCKLER Born in Louisville, Kentucky, John Buckler received his Ph.D. from Harvard University in 1973. In 1980 Harvard University Press published his *Theban Hegemony, 371–362 B.C.* He published *Philip II and the Sacred War* (Leiden 1989) and also edited *BOIOTIKA: Vorträge vom 5. Internationalen Böotien-Kolloquium* (Munich 1989). In 2003 he published *Aegean Greece in the Fourth Century B.C.* In the following year appeared his editions of W. M. Leake, *Travels in the Morea* (three volumes), and Leake's *Peloponnesiaca.* Cambridge University Press published his *Central Greece and the Politics of Power in the Fourth Century BC,* edited by Hans Beck, in 2008.

PATRICIA BUCKLEY EBREY Born in Hasbrouck Heights, New Jersey, Patricia Ebrey received her A.B. from the University of Chicago in 1968 and her Ph.D. from Columbia University in 1975. She taught Asian history and culture at the University of Illinois for twenty years before moving to the University of Washington in 1997. Her research has been supported by fellowships from the American Council of Learned Societies, the National Endowment for the Humanities, the Guggenheim Foundation, and the Chiang Ching-Kuo Foundation. Probably the best known of her many books are *Chinese Civilization: A Sourcebook* (1981, 1993), *The Inner Quarters: Marriage and the Lives of Chinese Women in the Sung Period* (1993) (which won the Levenson Prize of the Association for Asian Studies), and *The Cambridge Illustrated History of China* (1996). *East Asia: A Cultural, Social, and Political History,* coauthored with Anne Walthall and James Palais, is now in its second edition.

ROGER B. BECK An Indiana native, Roger B. Beck received his B.A. from the University of Evansville (1969), and an M.S. in social studies education (1977), M.A. in history (1979), and Ph.D. in African history (1987) from Indiana University. He taught history at international schools in Paris, Tokyo, and London for six years and was a visiting lecturer at the University of Cape Town in 1981. He has taught at Eastern Illinois University since 1987, where he is Distinguished Professor of African, World, and Twentieth-century World History. His publications include *The History of South Africa* (2000), a translation of P. J. van der Merwe's *The Migrant Farmer in the History of the Cape Colony, 1657–1842,* and more than seventy-five articles, book chapters, and reviews. He is a senior consultant to McDougal Littell's widely used high school text *World History: Patterns of Interaction,* now in its third edition. He is the recipient of two Fulbright fellowships. He has been an active member of the World Hisvtory Association for nearly twenty years, including serving a term on the executive council and as treasurer for six years.

CLARE HARU CROWSTON Born in Cambridge, Massachusetts, and raised in Toronto, Clare Haru Crowston received her B.A. in 1985 from McGill University and her Ph.D. in 1996 from Cornell University. Since 1996, she has taught at the University of Illinois, where she has served as associate chair and Director of Graduate Studies, and is currently Associate Professor of history. She is the author of *Fabricating Women: The Seamstresses of Old Regime France, 1675–1791* (Duke University Press, 2001), which won two awards, the Berkshire Prize and the Hagley Prize. She edited two special issues of the *Journal of Women's History* (vol. 18, nos. 3 and 4) and has published numerous articles and reviews in journals such as *Annales: Histoire, Sciences Sociales, French Historical Studies, Gender and History,* and the *Journal of Economic History.* Her research has been supported with grants from the National Endowment for the Humanities, the Mellon Foundation, and the Bourse Châteaubriand of the French government. She is a past president of the Society for French Historical Studies and a former chair of the Pinkney Prize Committee.

MERRY E. WIESNER-HANKS Having grown up in Minneapolis, Merry E. Wiesner-Hanks received her B.A. from Grinnell College in 1973 (as well as an honorary doctorate some years later), and her Ph.D. from the University of Wisconsin–Madison in 1979. She taught first at Augustana College in Illinois, and since 1985 at the University of Wisconsin–Milwaukee, where she is currently UWM Distinguished Professor in the department of history. She is the co-editor of the *Sixteenth Century Journal* and the author or editor of nineteen books and many articles that have appeared in English, German, Italian, Spanish, and Chinese. These include *Early Modern Europe, 1450–1789* (Cambridge, 2006), *Women and Gender in Early Modern Europe* (Cambridge, 3d ed., 2008), and *Gender in History* (Blackwell, 2001). She currently serves as the Chief Reader for Advanced Placement World History and has also written a number of source books for use in the college classroom, including *Discovering the Western Past* (Houghton Mifflin, 6th ed, 2007) and *Discovering the Global Past* (Houghton Mifflin, 3d. ed., 2006), and a book for young adults, *An Age of Voyages, 1350–1600* (Oxford 2005).

A·HISTORY·OF
WORLD·SOCIETIES

Peace Panel, Standard of Ur. This scene depicts the royal family on the upper band, and various conquered peoples bringing the king tribute on the lower bands. *(Courtesy of the Trustees of the British Museum)*

chapter

1

EARLY CIVILIZATION IN AFROEURASIA, TO 450 B.C.E.

Chapter Preview

Mesopotamian Civilization from Sumer to Babylon (ca. 3000–1595 B.C.E.)
• How did the Sumerians lay the foundations of a flourishing civilization in the hard land of Mesopotamia?

Egypt, the Land of the Pharaohs (3100–1200 B.C.E.)
• How did geography enable the Egyptians easily to form a cohesive, prosperous society?

The Rise of the Hittites (ca. 1650–ca. 1200 B.C.E.)
• How did the Hittites affect the life of the ancient Near East?

The Children of Israel (ca. 950–538 B.C.E.)
• How did the Hebrews form a small kingdom after the fall of larger neighboring empires?

Assyria, the Military Monarchy (859–612 B.C.E.)
• What enabled the Assyrians to conquer their neighbors, and how did they doom themselves by their cruelty?

The Empire of the Persian Kings (ca. 1000–464 B.C.E.)
• How did Iranian nomads create the Persian Empire that ultimately embraced all of these earlier peoples?

Human beings began the long road from their origins to the contemporary world in numerous places and under various circumstances. Although conditions were sometimes similar in all of them, their paths were unique. None fits into a tidy pattern. This chapter begins with the events that shaped the history of one of those places, the ancient **Near East,** or what is today often called the Middle East. Chapter 2 traces the origins of civilization in India, and Chapter 3 in China.

The ancient Near East includes parts of northeastern Africa, western Asia, and Mesopotamia, modern Iraq. It thus forms part of the larger Eurasia, the area from modern England in the west to Japan in the east. Within a small part of Eurasia, ancient Mesopotamian people invented writing, which allowed them to preserve knowledge of their achievements. They recorded their past and spread their learning, lore, and literature to posterity. Their innovations and those of the Egyptians laid the foundations of civilization in the region.

MESOPOTAMIAN CIVILIZATION FROM SUMER TO BABYLON (CA. 3000–1595 B.C.E.)

How did the Sumerians lay the foundations of a flourishing civilization in the hard land of Mesopotamia?

A good place from which to see the long path from nomadic hunters to urban folk is Mesopotamia, the Greek name for the land between the Euphrates and Tigris Rivers. Settled life in this region began only between 7000 and 3000 B.C.E., an era known as the Neolithic period. The term *Neolithic*, which means "neio stone age," comes from the new stone tools that people used to create a life of farming and animal husbandry. By ca. 3000 B.C.E. they had invented the wheel. Sustained agriculture resulted in a more stable life. Larger populations made possible the division of labor. These developments led to the evolution of towns and a new way of life (see Map 1.1). The growth and

● **Stonehenge** Seen in regal isolation, Stonehenge sits among the stars and in April 1997 along the path of the comet Hale-Bopp. Long before Druids existed, a Neolithic society laboriously built this circle to mark the passing of the seasons. *(Jim Burgess)*

Near East *The region between the eastern coast of the Mediterranean Sea and the Tigris and Euphrates Rivers.*

Neolithic period *The period between 7000 and 3000 B.C.E. that serves as the dividing line between anthropology and history. The term itself refers to the new stone tools that came into use at this time.*

diversity of the population created the need for the earliest governments that transcended families. Towns functioned and prospered through a recognized central authority governed by laws. Stable, strong populations organized themselves for peace and war, with the result that towns became the most successful feature of the **Neolithic period**.

The Invention of Writing and Intellectual Advances (ca. 3000–2331 B.C.E.)

By ca. 3000 B.C.E. the Sumerians, whose origins are mysterious, had established a number of towns in the southernmost part of Mesopotamia, which became known as Sumer. Towns grew into cities, and one of the Sumerian's many advances was the invention of writing. This momentous innovation helped unify Sumerian society by making communications much easier and opening Sumerian society to a broader world.

The Sumerians started by drawing pictures of objects, pictographs, from which they developed the style of writing known as cuneiform. The name comes from the Latin term for "wedge-shaped" used to describe the strokes making up the signs. The next step was to simplify the system. Instead of drawing pictures, the scribe made *ideograms*: conventionalized signs that were generally understood to represent ideas. The sign for star could also be used to indicate heaven, sky, or even god. (See line A in Figure 1.1.) The real breakthrough came when the scribe learned to use signs to represent sounds. For instance, the scribe drew two parallel wavy lines to indicate the word *a* or "water" (line E). Besides water, the word *a* in Sumerian also meant "in." The word *in* expresses a relationship that is very difficult to represent pictorially. Instead of trying to invent a sign to mean "in," some clever scribe used the sign for water because the two

● FIGURE 1.1 **Sumerian Writing** *(Source: Excerpted from S. N. Kramer, The Sumerians, University of Chicago Press, Chicago, 1963, pp. 302–306. Reprinted by permission of the publisher.)*

	MEANING	PICTOGRAPH	IDEOGRAM	PHONETIC SIGN
A	Star			
B	Woman			
C	Mountain			
D	Slave woman			
E	Water In			

words sounded alike. This phonetic use of signs made possible the combining of signs to convey abstract ideas.

The Sumerian system of writing was so complicated that only professional scribes mastered it after many years of study. By 2500 B.C.E. scribal schools flourished throughout Sumer. Most students came from wealthy families and were male. Each school had a master, a teacher, and monitors. Discipline was strict, and students were caned for sloppy work and misbehavior. One graduate of a scribal school had few fond memories of the joy of learning:

My headmaster read my tablet, said:
"There is something missing," caned me.
. . . .
The fellow in charge of silence said:
"Why did you talk without permission," caned me.
The fellow in charge of the assembly said:
"Why did you stand at ease without permission," caned me.[1]

Although Sumerian education was primarily intended to produce scribes for administrative work, schools were also centers of culture and scholarship.

Sumerian Thought and Religion

The building of cities, palaces, temples, and canals demanded practical knowledge of geometry and trigonometry. The Sumerians and later Mesopotamians made significant advances in mathematics using a numerical system based on units of sixty, ten, and six. They also developed the concept of place value—that the value of a number depends on where it stands in relation to other numbers.

Sumerian medicine was a combination of magic, prescriptions, and surgery. Sumerians believed that demons and evil spirits caused sickness and that magic spells and prescriptions could drive them out. Over time some prescriptions worked, and in this slow but empirical fashion medical understanding grew.

The Sumerians originated many religious beliefs, and their successors added to them. The Mesopotamians were polytheists—that is, they believed that many gods run the world. They did not, however, consider all gods and goddesses equal. Some deities had very important jobs taking care of music, victory, law, and sex, while others had lesser tasks, overseeing leatherworking and basketweaving. Mesopotamian gods were powerful and immortal and could make themselves invisible. Otherwise, they were very human: they celebrated with food and drink and they raised families. They enjoyed their own "Garden of Eden," a green and fertile paradise. They could be irritable, vindictive, and irresponsible. Nor were the motives of the gods always clear. In times of affliction one could only pray and offer sacrifices to appease them. Encouraged and directed by the traditional priesthood, which was dedicated to understanding the ways of the gods, the people erected shrines in the center of each city around which they built their houses. The best way to honor the gods was to make the shrine as grand and as impressive as possible, for gods who had a splendid temple might think twice about sending floods to destroy the city.

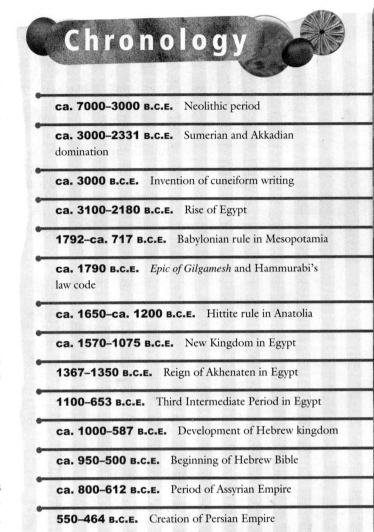

Chronology

ca. 7000–3000 B.C.E.	Neolithic period
ca. 3000–2331 B.C.E.	Sumerian and Akkadian domination
ca. 3000 B.C.E.	Invention of cuneiform writing
ca. 3100–2180 B.C.E.	Rise of Egypt
1792–ca. 717 B.C.E.	Babylonian rule in Mesopotamia
ca. 1790 B.C.E.	*Epic of Gilgamesh* and Hammurabi's law code
ca. 1650–ca. 1200 B.C.E.	Hittite rule in Anatolia
ca. 1570–1075 B.C.E.	New Kingdom in Egypt
1367–1350 B.C.E.	Reign of Akhenaten in Egypt
1100–653 B.C.E.	Third Intermediate Period in Egypt
ca. 1000–587 B.C.E.	Development of Hebrew kingdom
ca. 950–500 B.C.E.	Beginning of Hebrew Bible
ca. 800–612 B.C.E.	Period of Assyrian Empire
550–464 B.C.E.	Creation of Persian Empire
ca. 600–500 B.C.E.	Spread of Zoroastrianism

The Sumerians had many myths to account for the creation of the universe. According to one (echoed in Genesis, the first book of the Hebrew Bible), only the primeval sea existed at first. The sea produced heaven and earth, which were united. Heaven and earth gave birth to Enlil, who separated them and made possible the creation of the other gods. Myths are the earliest known attempts to answer the question "How did it all begin?"

In addition to myths, the Sumerians produced the first epic poem, the *Epic of Gilgamesh*. An epic poem is a narration of the achievements, the labors, and sometimes the failures of heroes that embodies a people's or a nation's conception of its own past. The Sumerian epic recounts the wanderings of Gilgamesh, the semihistorical king of Uruk, and his search for eternal life. He learns that life after death is so dreary that he returns to Uruk, where he ends his life. The *Epic of Gilgamesh* shows the Sumerians grappling with such enduring questions as life and death, people and deity, and immortality. (See the feature "Listening to the Past: A Quest for Immortality on pages 26–27.)

> **Primary Source:**
> **The Epic of Gilgamesh**
> *Find out how Gilgamesh's friend Enkidu propels him on a quest for immortality, and whether that quest is successful.*

Sumerian Society

Sumerian society was a complex arrangement of freedom and dependence, and its members were divided into four categories: nobles, clients, commoners, and slaves. **Nobles** consisted of the king and his family, the chief priests, and high palace officials. The king generally rose to power as a war leader, elected by the citizenry, who established a regular army, trained it, and led it into battle. The might of the king and the

> **nobles** *The top level of Sumerian society: the king and his family, the chief priests, and high palace officials.*

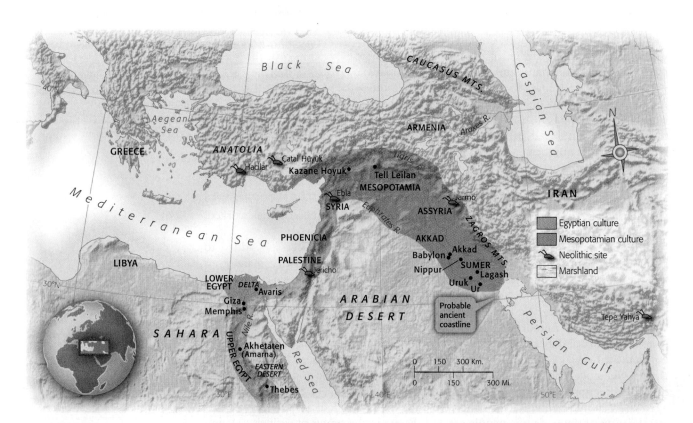

MAP 1.1 **Spread of Cultures in the Ancient Near East** This map illustrates the spread of the Mesopotamian and Egyptian cultures through a semicircular stretch of land often called the Fertile Crescent. From this area, knowledge and use of agriculture spread throughout western Asia.

frequency of warfare quickly made him the supreme figure in the city, and kingship soon became hereditary. The symbol of royal status was the palace, which rivaled the temple in its grandeur.

The king and the lesser nobility held extensive tracts of land that were, like the estates of the temple, worked by clients and slaves. Slaves were prisoners of war, convicts, and debtors. While they were subject to any treatment their owners might mete out, they could engage in trade, make profits, and even buy their freedom. **Clients** were free people who were dependent on the nobility. In return for their labor, they received small plots of land to work for themselves. Although this arrangement assured the clients of a livelihood, the land they worked remained the possession of the nobility or the temple. Commoners were free and could own land in their own right. Male commoners had a voice in the political affairs of the city and full protection under the law. Each of these social categories included both men and women, but Sumerian society also made clear distinctions based on gender. Sumerian society was *patriarchal,* that is, most power was held by older adult men.

● **Ziggurat** The ziggurat is a stepped tower that dominated the landscape of the Sumerian city. Surrounded by a walled enclosure, it stood as a monument to the gods. Monumental stairs led to the top, where sacrifices were offered for the welfare of the community. *(Charles & Josette Lenars/Corbis)*

clients *Free men and women who were dependent on the nobility; in return for their labor, they received small plots of land to work for themselves.*

The Triumph of Babylon and the Spread of Mesopotamian Civilization (2331–ca. 1595 B.C.E.)

Although the Sumerians established the basic social, economic, and intellectual patterns of Mesopotamia, the Semites played a large part in spreading Sumerian culture far beyond the boundaries of Mesopotamia. Semites are people related by the Semitic language spoken by Jews, Arabs, Phoenicians, Assyrians, and others. In 2331 B.C.E. the Semitic chieftain Sargon conquered Sumer and created a new empire. The symbol of his triumph was a new capital, the city of Akkad. Sargon led his armies to the Mediterranean Sea, spreading Mesopotamian culture throughout the Fertile Crescent (see Map 1.1). Though extensive, Sargon's empire soon fell to the Babylonians, who united Mesopotamia politically and culturally.

Hammurabi (r. 1792–1750 B.C.E.), king of the Amorites, another Semitic people, won control of the region and established his capital at Babylon. He accomplished three things: he made his kingdom secure, unified Mesopotamia, and joined together the Sumerian idea of urban kingship and the Semitic concept of tribal chieftain. He succeeded culturally in making Marduk, the god of Babylon, the sovereign of all other Mesopotamian deities. Hammurabi's most memorable achievement was the code that

Primary Source: The State Regulates Health Care: Hammurabi's Code and Surgeons
Consider the various rewards and punishments for surgeons who either succeed or fail at their jobs in 1800 B.C.E.

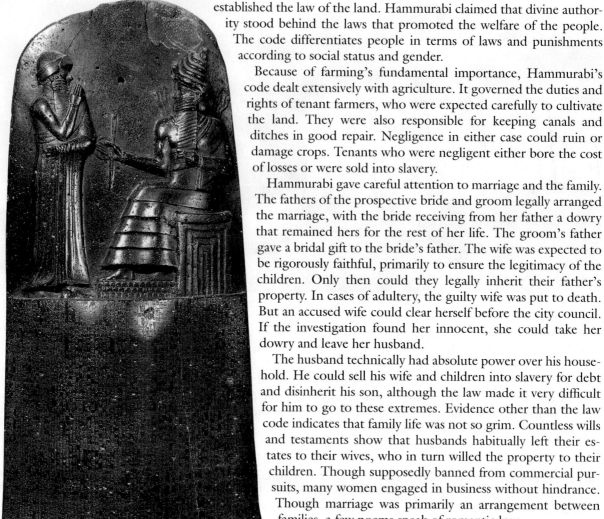

established the law of the land. Hammurabi claimed that divine authority stood behind the laws that promoted the welfare of the people. The code differentiates people in terms of laws and punishments according to social status and gender.

Because of farming's fundamental importance, Hammurabi's code dealt extensively with agriculture. It governed the duties and rights of tenant farmers, who were expected carefully to cultivate the land. They were also responsible for keeping canals and ditches in good repair. Negligence in either case could ruin or damage crops. Tenants who were negligent either bore the cost of losses or were sold into slavery.

Hammurabi gave careful attention to marriage and the family. The fathers of the prospective bride and groom legally arranged the marriage, with the bride receiving from her father a dowry that remained hers for the rest of her life. The groom's father gave a bridal gift to the bride's father. The wife was expected to be rigorously faithful, primarily to ensure the legitimacy of the children. Only then could they legally inherit their father's property. In cases of adultery, the guilty wife was put to death. But an accused wife could clear herself before the city council. If the investigation found her innocent, she could take her dowry and leave her husband.

The husband technically had absolute power over his household. He could sell his wife and children into slavery for debt and disinherit his son, although the law made it very difficult for him to go to these extremes. Evidence other than the law code indicates that family life was not so grim. Countless wills and testaments show that husbands habitually left their estates to their wives, who in turn willed the property to their children. Though supposedly banned from commercial pursuits, many women engaged in business without hindrance. Though marriage was primarily an arrangement between families, a few poems speak of romantic love.

● **Law Code of Hammurabi**
Hammurabi ordered his code to be inscribed on a stone pillar and set up in public. At the top of the pillar Hammurabi is depicted receiving the scepter of authority from the god Shamash. *(Hirmer Verlag München)*

EGYPT, THE LAND OF THE PHARAOHS (3100–1200 B.C.E.)

How did geography enable the Egyptians easily to form a cohesive, prosperous society?

The Greek historian and traveler Herodotus in the fifth century B.C.E. called Egypt the "gift of the Nile." No other single geographical factor had such a fundamental and profound impact on the shaping of Egyptian life, society, and history as the Nile (see Map 1.2). The Egyptians praised the Nile primarily as a creative and comforting force:

Primary Source:
The Hymn to the Nile
Discover the degree to which the Nile River is viewed as godlike, and the perceived power it has over the survival of the people of Egypt.

Hail to thee, O Nile, that issues from the earth and comes to keep Egypt alive! . . .
He that waters the meadows which Ra created,
He that makes to drink the desert . . .
He who makes barley and brings emmer [wheat] into being . . .
He who brings grass into being for the cattle . . .
He who makes every beloved tree to grow . . .
O Nile, verdant art thou, who makest man and cattle to live.[2]

To the Egyptians, the Nile was the source of life.

Egypt was also nearly self-sufficient. Besides the fertility of its soil, Egypt possessed enormous quantities of stone, which served as the raw material of architecture and sculpture. Abundant clay was available for pottery, as was gold for jewelry and ornaments. The raw materials that Egypt lacked were close at hand. The Egyptians obtained copper from Sinai and timber from Lebanon. They had little cause to look to the outside world for their necessities, a fact that helps to explain the insular quality of Egyptian life.

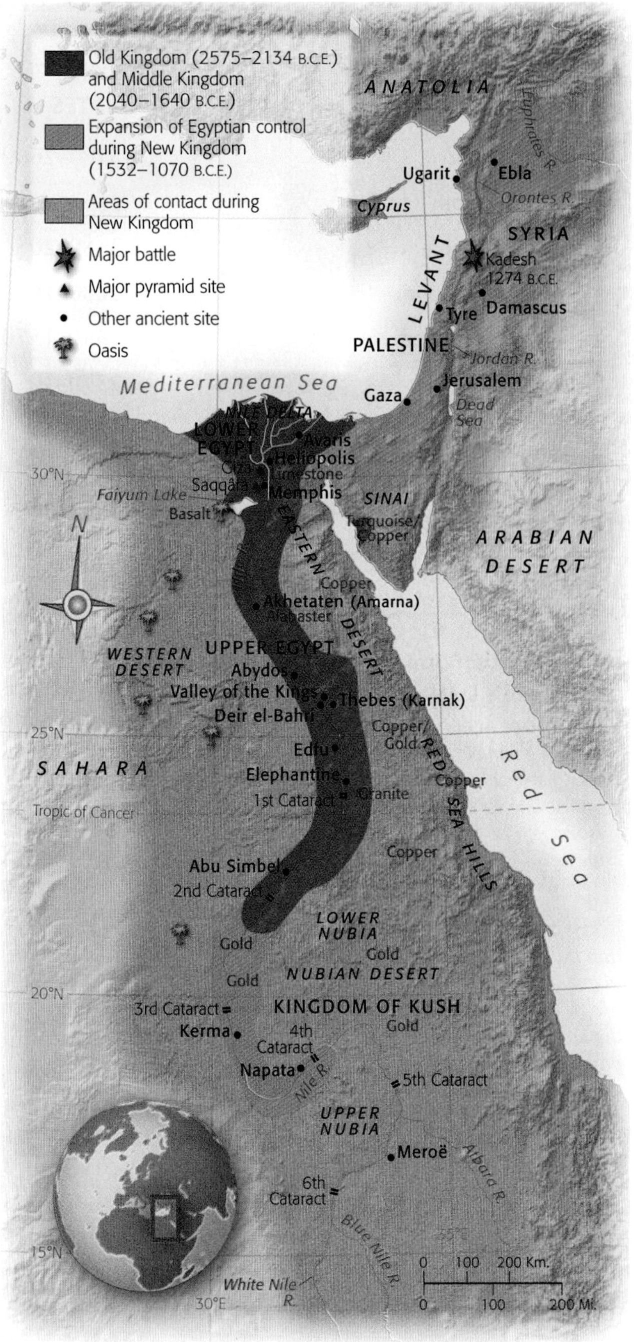

The God-King of Egypt

Geographical unity quickly gave rise to political unification of the country under the authority of a king whom the Egyptians called **"pharaoh."** The precise details of this process have been lost. The Egyptians themselves told of a great king, Menes, who united Upper and Lower Egypt into a single kingdom around 3100 B.C.E. Thereafter, they divided their history into dynasties, or families, of kings. For modern historical purposes, however, it is useful to divide Egyptian history into periods (see page 10). The political unification of Egypt ushered in the period known as the Old Kingdom (2660–2180 B.C.E.), an era remarkable for prosperity, artistic flowering, and the evolution of religious beliefs.

In religion, the Egyptians developed complex, often contradictory, ideas of their gods. They were polytheistic in that they worshiped many gods, some mightier than others. Their beliefs were rooted in the environment and human ecology. The most powerful of the gods were Amon, a primeval sky-god, and Ra, the sun-god. Amon created the entire cosmos by his thoughts. He brought life to the land and its people, and he sustained both. The Egyptians cherished Amon because he championed fairness and honesty, especially for the common people. The Egyptians considered Ra the creator of life. He commanded the sky, earth, and the underworld. Ra was associated with the falcon-god Horus, the "lord of the sky," who served as the symbol of divine kingship. Horus united Egypt and bestowed divinity on the pharaoh. The obvious similarities between Amon and Ra eventually led the Egyptians to combine them into one god, **Amon-Ra.** Yet the Egyptians never fashioned a formal theology to resolve the differences. Instead, they worshiped these gods as different aspects of the same celestial phenomena.

The Egyptians likewise developed views of an afterlife that reflected the world around them. The dry air of Egypt preserves much that would decay in other climates. The dependable rhythm of the seasons also shaped the fate of the dead. According to the Egyptians, Osiris, a fertility god associated with the Nile, died each year, and each year his wife, Isis, brought him back to life. Osiris eventually became king of the dead, and he weighed human beings' hearts to determine whether they had lived justly enough to deserve everlasting life. Osiris's care of the dead was shared

MAP 1.2 **Ancient Egypt** Geography and natural resources provided Egypt with centuries of peace and abundance.

pharaoh *The leader of religious and political life in the Old Kingdom, he commanded the wealth, the resources, and the people of Egypt.*

Amon-Ra *An Egyptian god, consisting of Amon, a primeval sky-god, and Ra, the sun-god.*

Periods of Egyptian History

PERIOD	DATES	SIGNIFICANT EVENTS
Archaic	3100–2660 B.C.E.	Unification of Egypt
Old Kingdom	2660–2180 B.C.E.	Construction of the pyramids
First Intermediate	2180–2080 B.C.E.	Political chaos
Middle Kingdom	2080–1640 B.C.E.	Recovery and political stability
Second Intermediate	1640–1570 B.C.E.	Hyksos "invasion"
New Kingdom	1570–1075 B.C.E.	Creation of an Egyptian empire Akhenaten's religious policy
Third Intermediate	1100–653 B.C.E.	Political fragmentation

Primary Source:
The Egyptian Book of the Dead's Declaration of Innocence
Read the number of potential sins that would likely tarnish a journeying spirit and prevent entrance into the realm of the blessed.

Book of the Dead *An Egyptian book that preserved their ideas about death and the afterlife; it explains that after death, the soul leaves the body to become part of the divine.*

pyramid *The burial place of a pharaoh; a massive tomb that contained all things needed for the afterlife. It also symbolized the king's power and his connection with the sun-god.*

by Anubis, the jackal-headed god who annually helped Isis resuscitate Osiris. Anubis was the god of mummification, essential to Egyptian funerary rites. The Egyptians preserved these ideas in the ***Book of the Dead,*** which explained that after death the soul and the body became part of the divine. They entered gladly through the gate of heaven where they remained in the presence of Aton (a sun-god) and the stars. Thus for the Egyptians life did not end with death.

The focal point of religious and political life in the Old Kingdom was the pharaoh, who commanded the wealth, resources, and people of all Egypt. The Egyptians considered him to be Horus in human form. In Egyptian religion Horus was the son of Isis and Osiris, which meant that the pharaoh, a living god on earth, became one with Osiris after death. The pharaoh was the power that achieved the integration between gods and human beings, a pledge that the gods of Egypt (strikingly unlike those of Mesopotamia) cared for their people.

The king's surroundings had to be worthy of a god. Only a magnificent palace was suitable for his home. In fact, the very word *pharaoh* means "great house." Just as the pharaoh occupied a great house in life, so he reposed in a great **pyramid** after death. The massive tomb contained everything the pharaoh needed in his afterlife. The walls of the burial chamber were inscribed with religious texts and spells relating to the king's journeys after death. The pyramid also symbolized the king's power and his connection with the sun-god. To this day the great pyramids at Giza near Cairo bear silent but magnificent testimony to the god-kings of Egypt.

The Pharaoh's People

Because the common folk stood at the bottom of the social and economic scale, they were always at the mercy of grasping officials. Taxes might amount to 20 percent of the harvest, and tax collection could be brutal.

The regularity of the climate meant that the agricultural year was routine and dependable, so farmers seldom suffered from foul weather and damaged crops. Farmers sowed wheat and nurtured a large variety of trees, vegetables, and vines. They tended cattle and poultry, and when time permitted they hunted and fished in the marshlands of the Nile.

Egyptian society seems to have been a curious mixture of freedom and constraint. Slavery did not become widespread until the New Kingdom (1570–1075 B.C.E.). There was neither a caste system nor a color bar, and humble people could rise to the highest positions if they possessed talent. On the other hand, most ordinary folk were probably little more than serfs who could not easily leave the land of their own free will. Peasants were also subject to forced labor, including work on the pyramids and canals. Young men were drafted into the pharaoh's army, which served both as a fighting force and as a labor corps.

To ancient Egyptians the pharaoh embodied justice and order—harmony among people, nature, and the divine. If the pharaoh was weak or allowed anyone to challenge his unique position, he opened the way to chaos. Twice in Egyptian history the pharaoh failed to maintain rigid centralization. During those two eras, known as the First and Second Intermediate Periods, Egypt was exposed to civil war and invasion. Yet the monarchy survived, and in each period a strong pharaoh arose to crush the rebels or expel the invaders and restore order.

The Hyksos in Egypt (1640–1570 B.C.E.)

While Egyptian civilization flourished behind its bulwark of sand and sea, momentous changes were taking place around it that would leave their mark even on rich, insular Egypt. These changes involved vast and remarkable movements, especially of peoples who spoke Semitic tongues.

The original home of the Semites was perhaps the Arabian peninsula. Some tribes moved into northern Mesopotamia, others into Syria and Palestine, and still others into Egypt. Shortly after 1800 B.C.E., people whom the Egyptians called **Hyksos,** which means "rulers of the uplands," began to settle in the Nile Delta. The movements of the Hyksos were part of a larger pattern of migration of peoples during this period. Such nomads normally settled in and accommodated themselves with the native cultures. The process was mutual, for each group had something to give and to learn from the other.

Primary Source: Advice to Ambitious Young Egyptians
This interesting piece of propaganda serves to convince potential scribes that the job of scribe is the best of all possible occupations.

Hyksos *Called "rulers of the uplands" by the Egyptians, these people began to settle in the Nile Delta shortly after 1800 B.C.E.*

● **Pyramids of Giza** Giza was the burial place of the pharaohs of the Old Kingdom and of their aristocracy, whose smaller rectangular tombs surround the two foremost pyramids. The small pyramid probably belonged to a pharaoh's wife. *(Jose Fuste Raga/Corbis)*

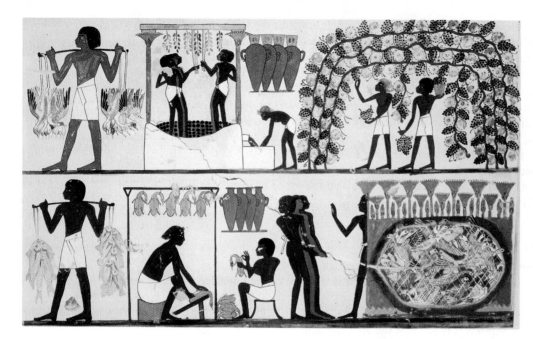

● **Egyptian Harvest Scene** This cheerful wall painting depicts two aspects of the harvest. Workers at the top right pick bunches of ripe grapes for winemaking. Their colleagues in the center stamp the grapes, and the large pottery jars store the wine. *(Louvre/Réunion des Musées Nationaux/Art Resource, NY)*

So too in Egypt, where bands of Hyksos entered the delta looking for good land. Their success led them to settle and to establish a capital city at Avaris in the northeastern Nile Delta. They probably exercised direct control no farther south. The Hyksos brought with them the method of making bronze and casting it into tools and weapons that became standard in Egypt. They thereby brought Egypt fully into the **Bronze Age** culture of the Mediterranean world. Bronze tools made farming more efficient than ever before because they were sharper and more durable than the copper tools they replaced. The Hyksos's use of bronze armor and weapons as well as horse-drawn chariots and the composite bow revolutionized Egyptian warfare. Yet the newcomers also absorbed Egyptian culture. The Hyksos came to worship Egyptian gods and modeled their monarchy on the pharaonic system.

Bronze Age *The period in which the production and use of bronze implements became basic to society; bronze made farming more efficient and revolutionized warfare.*

The New Kingdom: Revival and Empire (1570–1075 B.C.E.)

The pharaohs of the Eighteenth Dynasty arose to challenge the Hyksos. These pharaohs pushed the Hyksos out of the delta, subdued Nubia in the south, and conquered Palestine and parts of Syria in the northeast. Egyptian warrior-pharaohs thereby inaugurated the New Kingdom—a period characterized by enormous wealth and conscious imperialism. They created the first Egyptian empire, which they celebrated with monuments on a scale unparalleled since the pyramids of the Old Kingdom. Also during this period, probably for the first time, widespread slavery became a feature of Egyptian life. The pharaoh's armies returned home leading hordes of slaves who constituted a new labor force for imperial building projects.

One pharaoh of this period, Akhenaten (r. 1367–1350 B.C.E.), was more concerned with religion than with conquest. Nefertiti, his wife and queen, encouraged his religious bent (see the feature "Individuals in Society: Nefertiti, the 'Perfect Woman'"). They worshiped the sun-god Aton as universal, the only god, whereas the Egyptian people were polytheistic—they believed in many gods. Akhenaten considered all these and other deities frauds and so suppressed their worship. Although the precise nature of Akhenaten's religious beliefs remain debatable, most historians agree that the royal pair were monotheists: they believed in only one god. Yet this **monotheism,** imposed from above and enforced by intolerance, failed to find a place among the people. Akhenaten's religion died with him.

monotheism *The belief in one god; when applied to Egypt, it means that only Aton among the traditional Egyptian deities was god.*

Nefertiti, the "Perfect Woman"

Egyptians understood the pharaoh to be the living embodiment of the god Horus, the source of law and morality, and the mediator between gods and humans. His connection with the divine stretched to members of his family, so that his siblings and children were also viewed as in some ways divine. Because of this, a pharaoh often took his sister or half-sister as one of his wives. This concentrated divine blood set the pharaonic family apart from other Egyptians (who did not marry close relatives) and allowed the pharaohs to imitate the gods, who in Egyptian mythology often married their siblings. A pharaoh chose one of his wives to be the "Great Royal Wife," or principal queen. Often this was a relative, though sometimes it was one of the foreign princesses who married pharaohs to establish political alliances.

The familial connection with the divine allowed a handful of women to rule in their own right in Egypt's long history. We know the names of four female pharaohs, of whom the most famous was Hatshepsut (r. 1479–1458 B.C.). She was the sister and wife of Thutmose II and, after he died, served as regent for her young stepson Thutmose III, who was actually the son of another woman. Hatshepsut sent trading expeditions and sponsored artists and architects, ushering in a period of artistic creativity and economic prosperity. She built one of the world's great buildings, an elaborate terraced temple at Deir el Bahri, which eventually served as her tomb. Hatshepsut's status as a powerful female ruler was difficult for Egyptians to conceptualize, and she is often depicted in male dress or with a false beard, thus looking more like the male rulers who were the norm. After her death, Thutmose III tried to destroy all evidence that she had ever ruled, smashing statues and scratching her name off inscriptions, perhaps because of personal animosity and perhaps because he wanted to erase the fact that a woman had once been pharaoh. Only within the last decades have historians and archaeologists begun to (literally) piece together her story.

Though female pharaohs were very rare, many royal women had power through their position as "Great Royal Wives." The most famous of these was Nefertiti, the wife of Akhenaten. Her name means "the perfect (or beautiful) woman has come," and inscriptions also give her many other titles. Nefertiti used her position to spread the new religion of the sun-god Aton. Together she and Akhenaten built a new palace at Akhetaten, the present Amarna, away from the old centers of power. There they developed the cult of Aton to the exclusion of the traditional deities. Nearly the only literary survival of their religious belief is the "Hymn to Aton," which declares Aton to be the only god. It describes Nefertiti as "the great royal consort whom he! Akhenaten! Loves, the mistress of the Two Lands! Upper and Lower Egypt!"

Nefertiti is often shown the same size as her husband, and in some inscriptions she is performing religious rituals that would normally have been done only by the pharaoh. The exact details of her power are hard to determine, however. An older theory held that her husband removed her from power, though there is also speculation that she may have ruled secretly in her own right after his death. Her tomb has long since disappeared, though in 2003 an enormous controversy developed over her possible remains. There is no controversy that the bust shown above, now in a Berlin museum, represents Nefertiti, nor that it has become an icon of female beauty since it was first discovered in the early twentieth century.

Nefertiti, queen of Egypt.
(Bildarchiv Preussischer Kulturbesitz/ Art Resource, NY)

Questions for Analysis

1. Why might it have been difficult for Egyptians to accept a female ruler?

2. What opportunities do hereditary monarchies such as that of ancient Egypt provide for women? How does this fit with gender hierarchies in which men are understood as superior?

THE RISE OF THE HITTITES
(CA. 1650–CA. 1200 B.C.E.)

How did the Hittites affect the life of the ancient Near East?

Indo-European *Refers to a large family of languages that includes English, most of the languages of modern Europe, Greek, Latin, Persian, and Sanskrit, the sacred tongue of ancient India.*

Around 1650 B.C.E. the Hittites, who had long been settled in Anatolia (modern Turkey), became a major power in that region and began to expand east and south (see Map 1.3). The Hittites were an Indo-European people. The term **Indo-European** refers to a large family of languages that includes English, most of the languages of modern Europe, Greek, Latin, Persian, and Sanskrit, the sacred tongue of ancient India. The Hittite king Hattusilis I built a hill citadel at Hattusas, the modern Boghazköy, from which he led his people against neighboring kingdoms. His grandson and successor, Mursilis I (r. ca. 1595 B.C.E.), extended the Hittite conquests as far as Babylon. Upon his return home, the victorious Mursilis was assassinated by members of his own family, which opened the door to foreign invasion. Only when the Hittites were united behind a strong king were they a power to be reckoned with. Unshaken, the Hittites produced an energetic line of kings who built a powerful empire. Their major technological contribution was the introduction of iron into war and agriculture in the form of weapons and tools.

Around 1300 B.C.E. the Hittites stopped the Egyptian army of Rameses II (r. ca. 1290–1224 B.C.E.) at the Battle of Kadesh in Syria. Having fought each other to a standstill, the Hittites and Egyptians first made peace and then an alliance. The two greatest powers of the Near East thus tried to make war between them impossible.

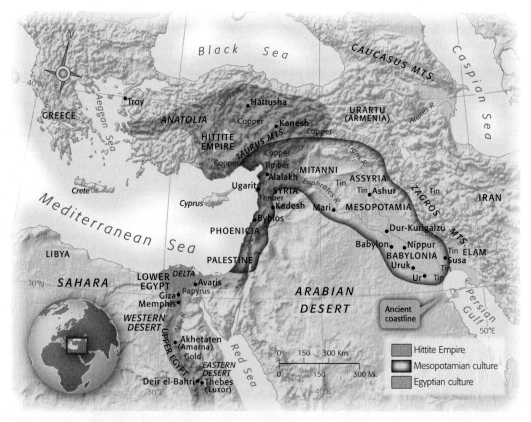

MAP 1.3 **Balance of Power in the Near East** This map shows the regions controlled by the Hittites and Egyptians at the height of their power. The Hittites conquered part of Mesopotamia during their expansion eastward.

● **Hittite Solar Disk** This cult standard represents Hittite concepts of fertility and prosperity. The circle surrounding the animals is the sun, beneath which stands a stag flanked by two bulls. Stylized bull's horns spread from the base of the disk. The symbol is also one of might and protection from outside harm. *(Museum of Anatolian Civilizations, Ankara)*

The Hittites and Egyptians next included the Babylonians in their diplomacy. They all made alliance for offensive and defensive protection, and swore to uphold one another's authority. These contacts facilitated the exchange of ideas throughout western Asia. The Hittites also passed much knowledge from the east to the newly arrived Greeks in Europe. Like the Hittite kings, Rameses II used the peace after the Battle of Kadesh to promote prosperity and concentrate the income from the natural wealth and the foreign trade of Egypt on internal affairs. In many ways, he was the last great pharaoh of Egypt.

This peaceful situation lasted until the late thirteenth century B.C.E., when both the Hittite and Egyptian empires fell to invaders. The most famous of these marauders, the **Sea Peoples**, remain one of the puzzles of ancient history. The Sea Peoples were a collection of peoples who went their own individual ways after their attacks on the Hittites and Egyptians. They dealt both the Hittites and the Egyptians hard blows, making the Hittites vulnerable to overland invasion from the north and driving the Egyptians back to the Nile Delta. The Hittites fell under these attacks, but the battered Egyptians managed to retreat to the delta and hold on.

Sea Peoples *Invaders who destroyed the Egyptian empire in the late thirteenth century; they are otherwise unidentifiable because they went their own ways after their attacks on Egypt.*

A Shattered Egypt and a Rising Phoenicia

The invasions of the Sea Peoples brought the great days of Egyptian power to an end. The long wars against invaders weakened and impoverished Egypt, causing political upheaval and economic chaos. Egypt suffered a four-hundred-year period of political fragmentation, a new dark age known to Egyptian specialists as the Third Intermediate Period (ca. 1100–653 B.C.E.).

In southern Egypt, meanwhile, the pharaoh's decline opened the way for the energetic Nubians to extend their authority northward throughout the Nile Valley. Since the imperial days of the Eighteenth Dynasty, the Nubians, too, had adopted many features of Egyptian culture. Now they embraced Egyptian culture wholesale.

The reunification of Egypt occurred late and unexpectedly. With Egypt disorganized, an independent African state, the kingdom of Kush, grew up in the region of

HIEROGLYPHIC	REPRESENTS	UGARITIC	PHOENICIAN	GREEK	ROMAN
	Throw stick	T	⟨	Γ	G
	Man with raised arms		⇂	E	E
	Basket with handle		↓	K	K
	Water		⟋⟍	M	M
	Snake		⟍	N	N
	Eye	◁	O	O	O
	Mouth		?	Π	P
	Head		9	P	R
	Pool with lotus flowers		W	Σ	S
	House		9	B	B
	Ox-head		K	A	A

modern Sudan with its capital at Nepata. Like the Libyans, the Kushites worshiped Egyptian gods and used Egyptian hieroglyphs. In the eighth century B.C.E., their king Piankhy swept through the entire Nile Valley from Nepata in the south to the delta in the north. United once again, Egypt enjoyed a brief period of peace during which the Egyptians continued to assimilate their conquerors. Nonetheless, reunification of Egypt did not lead to a new empire.

Yet Egypt's legacy to its African neighbors remained rich. By trading and exploring southward along the coast of the Red Sea, the Egyptians introduced their goods and ideas as far south as the land of Punt, probably a region on the Somali coast. Egypt was the primary civilizing force in Nubia, which became another version of the pharaoh's realm, complete with royal pyramids and Egyptian deities. Egyptian religion penetrated as far south as Ethiopia.

Among the sturdy peoples who rose to prominence were the Phoenicians, a Semitic-speaking people who had long inhabited several cities along the coast of modern Lebanon. Phoenicians took to the sea to become outstanding explorers and merchants. They played a predominant role in international trade, in which they exported their manufactured goods. Their most valued products were purple and blue textiles, from which originated their Greek name, Phoenicians, meaning **"Purple People."** They also worked metals, which they shipped processed or as ore. They imported rare goods and materials from Persia in the east and from their neighbors to the south. Their exported wares went to Egypt, as far as North Africa and Spain, and even into the Atlantic. The variety and quality of their exports generally made them welcome visitors. Although their goal was trade, not colonization, they nevertheless founded Carthage in 813 B.C.E., a city that would one day struggle with Rome for domination of the western Mediterranean. Their voyages naturally brought them into contact with the Greeks, to whom they introduced the older cultures of the Near East. Indeed, their enduring significance lay in their spreading the experiences of the Near East throughout the western Mediterranean.

Phoenician culture was urban, based on the prosperous commercial centers of Tyre, Sidon, and Byblos. The Phoenicians' overwhelming cultural legacy was the develop-

Purple People *The Greek name for the Phoenicians, a culture that inhabited the eastern coast of the Mediterranean Sea, so called because of the remarkable purple dye they produced from certain sea snails.*

ment of an alphabet (see Figure 1.2). Unlike other literate peoples, they used one letter to designate one sound, a system that vastly simplified writing and reading. The Greeks modified this alphabet and then used it to write their own language. We still use it today.

THE CHILDREN OF ISRAEL (CA. 950–538 B.C.E.)

How did the Hebrews form a small kingdom after the fall of larger neighboring empires?

Baal *An ancient Semitic fertility god represented as a golden calf.*

Babylonian Captivity *The period of Jewish history between 586 and 537 B.C.E. during which the political and spiritual leaders of the kingdom of Judah were deported to Babylon following the defeat of Judah by Nebuchadnezzer.*

The fall of the Hittite Empire and Egypt's collapse allowed the rise of numerous small states. South of Phoenicia arose a small kingdom, the land of the ancient Jews or Hebrews. It is difficult to say precisely who the Hebrews were because virtually the only source for much of their history is the Hebrew Bible, a religious document that contains many myths and legends as well as historical material. Like the earlier Hyksos, they probably migrated into the Nile Delta seeking good land. There, according to the Bible, the Egyptians enslaved them. The Hebrews followed their leader Moses out of Egypt, and in the thirteenth century B.C.E. they settled in Palestine. There they encountered the Philistines; the Amorites, relatives of Hammurabi's Babylonians; and the Semitic-speaking Canaanites. Despite numerous wars, contact between the Hebrews and their new neighbors was not always hostile. They freely mingled with the Canaanites, and some went so far as to worship Baal, an ancient Semitic fertility-god represented as a golden calf. Only later did the Hebrews consider Yahweh the only god. Despite the anger expressed in the Bible over Hebrew worship of **Baal**, there is nothing surprising about the phenomenon. Once again, newcomers adapted themselves to the culture of an older, well-established people.

The greatest danger to the Hebrews came from the Philistines, whose superior technology and military organization at first made them invincible. The Hebrew leader Saul (ca. 1000 B.C.E.), while keeping the Philistines at bay, established a monarchy over the twelve Hebrew tribes. David of Bethlehem continued Saul's work and captured the city of Jerusalem, which he enlarged and made the religious center of the realm. His work is consolidating the monarchy and enlarging the kingdom paved the way for his son Solomon (ca. 965–925 B.C.E.). Solomon created a nation by dividing it into twelve territorial districts cutting across the old tribal borders. He also launched a building program that included cities, palaces, fortresses, and roads. The most symbolic of these projects was the Temple of Jerusalem, which became the home of the Ark of the Covenant, the chest that contained the holiest of Hebrew religious articles. The temple in Jerusalem was intended to be the religious heart of the kingdom and the symbol of Hebrew unity.

At Solomon's death his kingdom broke into political halves. The northern part became Israel, with its capital at Samaria. The southern half was Judah, and Jerusalem remained its center. With political division went religious rift: Israel established rival sanctuaries for gods other than Yahweh. Although the Assyrians later wiped out the northern kingdom of Israel, Judah survived numerous calamities until the Babylonians crushed it in 587 B.C.E. The survivors were sent into exile in Babylonia, a period commonly known as the **Babylonian Captivity**. In 538 B.C.E. the Persian king Cyrus the Great permitted some forty thousand exiles to

● **The Golden Calf** According to the Bible, Moses descended from Mount Sinai, where he had received the Ten Commandments, to find the Hebrews worshiping a golden calf, which was against Yahweh's laws. In July 1990 an American archaeological team found this model of a gilded calf inside a pot. The figurine, which dates to about 1550 B.C.E., is strong evidence for the existence of the cult represented by the calf in Palestine. *(Courtesy of the Leon Levy Expedition to Ashkelon. Photo: Carl Andrews)*

Primary Source:
Moses Descends
Mount Sinai with the
Ten Commandments
Find out why the God of the Hebrew Bible issued the Ten Commandments, and what he promised Moses's people in return for keeping—or violating—them.

return to Jerusalem. During and especially after the Babylonian Captivity, the exiles redefined their beliefs and practices, thereby establishing what they believed was the law of Yahweh. Those who lived by these precepts came to be called Jews.

Daily Life in Israel

Marriage and the nuclear family were fundamentally important in Jewish life; celibacy was frowned upon and almost all major Jewish thinkers and priests were married. With parents making all the arrangements, boys and girls were often married while little more than children. They were expected to begin their own families at once. Sons were especially desired because they maintained the family bloodline, while keeping ancestral property in the family. A firstborn son became the head of the household at his father's death. Daughters were less highly valued because they would eventually leave the family after marriage. Unlike other cultures, Jews forbade infanticide because Yahweh prohibited it.

Mothers oversaw the early education of the children, but as boys grew older, their fathers gave them more of their education. The most important task for observant Jews was studying religious texts, an activity limited to men until the twentieth century. Women were obliged to provide for men's physical needs while they were studying, so Jewish women were often more active economically than their contemporaries of other religions.

The Hebrews were originally nomadic, but they adopted settled agriculture in Palestine. The development of urban life among Jews created new economic opportunities, especially in crafts and trade. Jewish merchants began to participate in maritime and caravan trade, and in the process entered the mainstream of Near Eastern life. Yet they always faithfully retained their unique religion and culture.

MAP 1.4 **The Assyrian and Persian Empires** The Assyrian Empire at its height (ca. 650 B.C.E.) included almost all of the old centers of power in the ancient Near East. By 513 B.C.E., however, the Persian Empire not only included more of that area but also extended as far east as western India. With the rise of the Medes and Persians, the balance of power in the Near East shifted east of Mesopotamia for the first time.

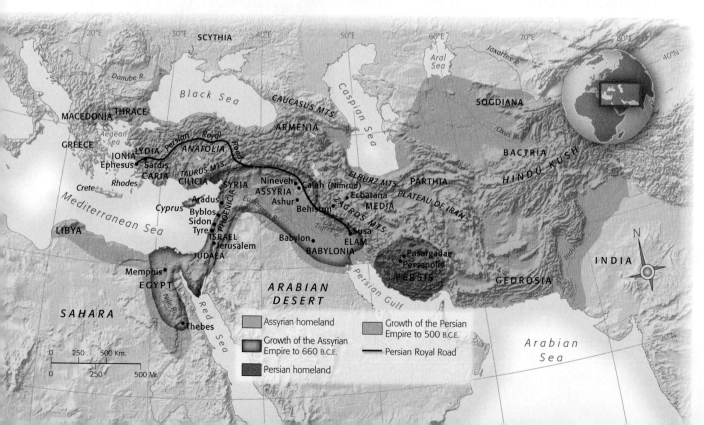

● **Siege of a City** Art here serves to glorify horror. The Assyrian king Tiglath-pileser III launches an assault on a fortified city. The impaled bodies shown at center demonstrate the cruelty of Assyrian warfare. Also noticeable are the various weapons and means of attack used against the city. *(Courtesy of the Trustees of the British Museum)*

ASSYRIA, THE MILITARY MONARCHY (859–612 B.C.E.)

What enabled the Assyrians to conquer their neighbors, and how did they doom themselves by their cruelty?

Small kingdoms like those of the Phoenicians and the Jews could exist only in the absence of a major power. The beginning of the ninth century B.C.E. saw the rise of such a power in Assyria. The Assyrians dominated northern Mesopotamia with their chief capital at Nineveh on the Tigris River. The Assyrians were a Semitic people heavily influenced by the Babylonian culture to the south. They were also one of the most warlike people in history, and for over two hundred years they fought to dominate the Near East. The Assyrian kings Tiglath-pileser III (r. 774–727 B.C.E.) and Sargon II (r. 721–705 B.C.E.) conquered Syria, Palestine, and the two Jewish kingdoms, and in ca. 717 B.C.E. Sargon defeated the Egyptians before turning against Babylon. By almost constant warfare the two kings carved out an empire that stretched from east and north of the Tigris River to central Egypt (see Map 1.4).

Although atrocity and terrorism struck unspeakable fear into Assyria's subjects, Assyria's success was also due to sophisticated, farsighted, and effective military organization. Assyrian military genius was remarkable for the development of a wide variety of siege machinery and techniques, including excavations to undermine city walls and battering rams to knock down walls and gates. Never before in the Near East had anyone applied such technical knowledge to warfare. The Assyrians even invented the concept of a corps of engineers who bridged rivers with pontoons or provided soldiers with inflatable skins for swimming. The Assyrians also knew how to coordinate their efforts both in open battle and in siege warfare.

Not only did the Assyrians know how to win battles, but they also knew how to use their victories. As early as the reign of Tiglath-pileser III, the Assyrian kings began to organize their conquered territories into an empire. The lands closest to Assyria became provinces governed by Assyrian officials. Kingdoms beyond the provinces were not annexed but became dependent states that followed Assyria's lead. The Assyrian king chose their rulers either by regulating the succession of native kings or by supporting native kings who appealed to him. Against more distant states the Assyrian

Primary Source:

An Assyrian Emperor's Résumé
Read the inscription left behind by Ashur-Nasir-Pal, in which he promotes himself as an especially effective—and brutal—military leader.

kings waged frequent war in order to conquer them outright or make the dependent states secure.

In the seventh century B.C.E. Assyrian power seemed firmly established. Yet the downfall of Assyria was swift and complete. Babylon finally won its independence in 626 B.C.E. and joined forces with a new people, the Medes, an Indo-European-speaking folk from Iran. Together the Babylonians and the Medes destroyed the Assyrian Empire in 612 B.C.E., paving the way for the rise of the Persians. The Hebrew prophet Nahum spoke for many when he asked: "Nineveh is laid waste: who will bemoan her?"[3] Their cities destroyed and their power shattered, the Assyrians disappeared from history, remembered only as a cruel people of the Bible. Two hundred years later, when the Greek adventurer and historian Xenophon passed by the ruins of Nineveh, he marveled at the extent of the former city but knew nothing of the Assyrians. The glory of their empire was forgotten.

THE EMPIRE OF THE PERSIAN KINGS (CA. 1000–464 B.C.E.)

How did Iranian nomads create the Persian Empire that ultimately embraced all of these earlier peoples?

The Iranians were Indo-Europeans from central Europe and southern Russia. They migrated into the land to which they have given their name, the area between the Caspian Sea and the Persian Gulf. They then fell under the spell of the more sophisticated cultures of their Mesopotamian neighbors. The Persians, the most important of the Iranian peoples, went on to create one of the greatest empires of the ancient Near East. Though as conquerors they willingly used force to accomplish their ends, they normally preferred to depend on diplomacy to rule. They usually respected their sub-

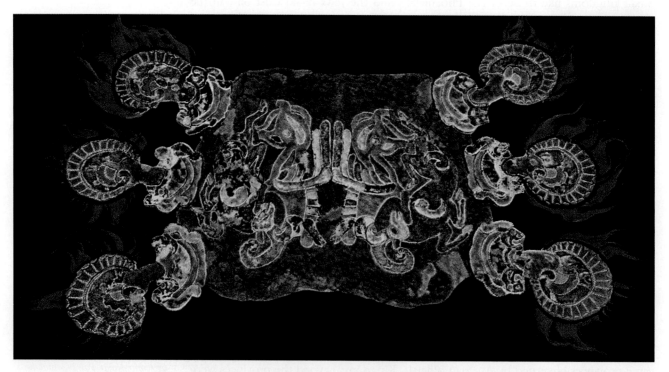

● **Persian Saddle-Cloth** This elaborately painted piece of leather, dating from the fourth or third centuries B.C.E., served a ceremonial rather than a practical function. *(© The State Hermitage Museum, St. Petersburg)*

jects and allowed them to practice their native customs and religions. Thus the Persians gave the Near East both political unity and cultural diversity.

Persia, modern Iran, is a stark land of towering mountains and flaming deserts, with a broad central plateau in the heart of the country (see Map 1.4). Between the Tigris-Euphrates Valley in the west and the Indus Valley in the east rises an immense plateau surrounded on all sides by lofty mountains that cut off the interior from the sea.

Iran's geographical position and topography explain its traditional role as the highway between western and eastern Asia. Throughout history wild nomadic peoples migrating from the broad steppes of Russia and Central Asia have streamed into Iran. Confronting the uncrossable salt deserts, most have turned either westward or eastward, moving on until they reached the advanced and wealthy urban centers of Mesopotamia and India. When cities emerged along the natural lines of east-west communication, Iran became the area where nomads met urban dwellers, a meeting ground of unique significance for the civilizations of both east and west.

The Coming of the Medes and Persians

The Iranians entered this land around 1000 B.C.E. as nomads who migrated with their flocks and herds. Like their kinsmen the Aryans, who moved into India, they were also horse breeders, and the horse gave them a decisive military advantage over the prehistoric peoples of Iran. The Iranians rode into battle in horse-drawn chariots or on horseback and easily swept the natives before them. Yet, because the influx of Iranians went on for centuries, there continued to be constant cultural interchange between conquering newcomers and conquered natives.

Gradually two groups of Iranians began coalescing into larger units. The Persians had settled in Persia, the modern region of Fars, in southern Iran. Their kinsmen the Medes occupied Media in the north, with their capital at Ecbatana, the modern Hamadan. Even though distracted by grave pressures from their neighbors, the Medes united under one king around 710 B.C.E. and extended their control over the Persians in the south. In 612 B.C.E. the Medes joined the Babylonians in overthrowing the Assyrian Empire. With the rise of the Medes, the balance of power in western Asia shifted for the first time east of Mesopotamia.

The Creation of the Persian Empire (550–464 B.C.E.)

In 550 B.C.E. Cyrus the Great (r. 559–530 B.C.E.), king of the Persians and one of the most remarkable statesmen of antiquity, conquered the Medes. His conquest resulted not in slavery and slaughter but in the union of the Iranian peoples. Having united Iran, Cyrus set out to achieve two goals. First, he wanted to win control of the west and thus of the terminal ports of the great trade routes that crossed Iran and Anatolia (modern western Turkey). Second, he strove to secure eastern Iran from the pressure of nomadic invaders. In a series of major campaigns Cyrus achieved both goals. He swept into Anatolia, easily overthrowing the young kingdom of Lydia. His generals subdued the Greek cities along the coast of Anatolia, thus gaining him flourishing ports on the Mediterranean. From Lydia Cyrus, marching to the far eastern corners of Iran, conquered

● **Funeral Pyre of Croesus** This scene, an excellent example of the precision and charm of ancient Greek vase painting, depicts the Lydian king Croesus on his funeral pyre. He pours a libation to the gods while his slave lights the fire. Herodotus has a happier ending, when he says that Cyrus the Great set fire to the pyre, but that Apollo sent rain to put it out. *(Louvre/ Réunion de Musées Nationaux/Art Resource, NY)*

● **The Impact of Zoroastrianism** The Persian kings embraced Zoroastrianism as the religion of the realm. This rock carving at Behistun records the bond. King Darius I is seen trampling on one rebel with others behind him. Above is the sign of Ahuramazda, the god of truth and guardian of the Persian king. *(Robert Harding World Imagery)*

the regions of Parthia and Bactria. The Babylonians welcomed him as a liberator when his soldiers moved into their kingdom.

With these victories Cyrus demonstrated to the world his benevolence as well as his military might. He spared the life of Croesus, the conquered king of Lydia, to serve him as friend and adviser. He allowed the Greeks to live according to their customs, thus making possible the spread of Greek culture farther east. Cyrus's humanity likewise extended to the Jews, whom he found enslaved in Babylonia. He restored their sacred objects to them and returned them to Jerusalem, where he helped them rebuild their temple.

The Religion of Zoroaster

Around 600 B.C.E. Zoroaster, a religious thinker and preacher, introduced new spiritual concepts to the Iranian people. He taught that life is a constant battleground for the two opposing forces of good and evil. The Iranian god **Ahuramazda** embodied good and truth but was opposed by Ahriman, a hateful spirit who stood for evil and lies. Ahuramazda and Ahriman were locked together in a cosmic battle for the human race, a battle that stretched over thousands of years.

Zoroaster emphasized the individual's responsibility to choose between good and evil. He taught that people possessed the free will to decide between Ahuramazda and Ahriman and that they must rely on their own conscience to guide them through life. Their decisions were crucial, Zoroaster warned, for there would come a time of reckoning. The victorious Ahuramazda, like the Egyptian god Osiris, would preside over a last judgment to determine each person's eternal fate.

Zoroaster's teachings converted Darius, who did not, however, impose it on others. Under the protection of the Persian kings, **Zoroastrianism** won converts throughout Iran. It survived the fall of the Persian Empire to influence Judaism, Christianity, and early Islam. Good behavior in the world, even though unrecognized at the time, would receive ample reward in the hereafter. Evil, no matter how powerful in life,

Ahuramazda *The chief Iranian god, who was the creator and benefactor of all living creatures; unlike Yahweh, he was not a lone god.*

Zoroastrianism *The religion based on the teachings of Zoroaster, who emphasized the individual's responsibility to choose between good and evil. Though Zoroaster's teachings often met with opposition, the Persian ruler Darius was a convert.*

would be punished after death. In some form or another, Zoroastrian concepts still pervade many modern religions.

The Span of the Persian Empire

Cyrus's successors rounded out the Persian conquest of the ancient Near East. In 525 B.C.E. his son Cambyses (r. 530–522 B.C.E.) subdued Egypt. Darius (r. 521–486 B.C.E.) and his son Xerxes (r. 486–464 B.C.E.) unsuccessfully invaded Greece, but Darius in about 513 B.C.E. conquered western India. He created the Persian satrapy of Hindush, which included the valley of the Indus River. Thus, within thirty-seven years (550–513 B.C.E.) the Persians transformed themselves from a subject people to the rulers of an empire that included Asia Minor, Mesopotamia, Iran, and western India. They had created a vast empire encompassing all of the oldest and most honored kingdoms and peoples of these regions (see Map 1.4).

The Persians also knew how to preserve the peace they had won on the battlefield. Unlike the Assyrians, they did not resort to royal terrorism to maintain order. The Persians instead built an efficient administrative system to govern the empire based in their capital city of Persepolis near modern Schiras, Iran. From Persepolis they sent directions to the provinces and received reports back from their officials. To do so they built and maintained a sophisticated system of roads linking the empire. The main highway, the famous **Royal Road,** spanned some 1,677 miles (see Map 1.4). Other roads branched out to link all parts of the empire from the coast of Asia Minor to the valley of the Indus River. These highways meant that the king was usually in close touch with officials and subjects. The roads simplified the defense of the empire by making it easier to move Persian armies. The system also allowed the easy flow of trade. In all, these roads enabled the Persian kings to translate the concepts of right, justice, and good government into a practical reality.

Royal Road *The main highway created by the Persians; it spanned 1,677 miles from western Turkey to Iran.*

● **The Royal Palace at Persepolis**   King Darius began and King Xerxes finished building a grand palace worthy of the glory of the Persian Empire. Pictured here is the monumental audience hall, where the king dealt with ministers of state and foreign envoys. *(George Holton/Photo Researchers)*

Chapter Summary

Key Terms

Near East
Neolithic period
nobles
clients
pharaoh
Amon-Ra
Book of the Dead
pyramid
Hyksos
Bronze Age
monotheism
Indo-European
Sea Peoples
Purple People
Baal
Babylonian Captivity
Ahuramazda
Zoroastrianism
Royal Road

To assess your mastery of this chapter, go to
bedfordstmartins.com/mckayworld

• How did the Sumerians lay the foundations of a flourishing civilization in the hard land of Mesopotamia?

During the Neolithic period peoples used their new stone tools to create lives centered on towns. In Mesopotamia the Sumerians established the basic social, economic, and intellectual patterns that defined civilized life. These developments brought order and prosperity and led to the unification of Mesopotamia by Hammurabi and the Babylonians. They in turn nurtured and encouraged the spread of this rich life beyond Mesopotamia.

• How did geography enable the Egyptians easily to form a cohesive, prosperous society?

In Egypt, meanwhile, other peoples turned the fertile Nile Valley into the home of a rich, sophisticated society that lived harmoniously under the rule of kings, the pharaohs. This era saw the building of the pyramids, political stability, and long years of prosperity. During a period of internal weakness the Hyksos, a nomadic people, introduced Bronze Age technology into Egypt when they settled in the Nile Delta. Egyptian pharaohs, however, rallied to drive out the Hyksos and establish the rich period of the New Kingdom. A complex polytheistic mythology underlay Egyptian culture, and the pharaoh Akhenaten failed in his attempt to introduce Aton as the only true god.

• How did the Hittites affect the life of the ancient Near East?

From the northern fringes of this sphere came the Hittites, an Indo-European people who introduced iron tools and weapons. After establishing their own empire, they promoted a general alliance with the Egyptians and Babylonians that led to an era of peace.

• How did the Hebrews form a small kingdom after the fall of larger neighboring empires?

In the thirteenth century B.C.E. hostile invaders, the Sea Peoples, disrupted this stable world, which also allowed lesser native folk to become prominent. The Nubians of Africa adopted and preserved the old Egyptian civilization. The Phoenicians built small trading kingdoms that linked the Near East to the broader Mediterranean world. The Hebrews benefited from the absence of major powers to create a minor kingdom. They developed religious beliefs and a code of life that still flourish today.

• What enabled the Assyrians to conquer their neighbors, and how did they doom themselves by their cruelty?

In this world rose the Assyrians, another Semitic people who had lived on its periphery. Through effective military techniques and brutal aggression, they conquered the entire region, until a coalition of peoples utterly destroyed them.

• How did Iranian nomads create the Persian Empire that ultimately embraced all of these earlier peoples?

The Persians, one of the peoples instrumental in overthrowing the Assyrians, were also Indo-Europeans—Iranians from the north. They too created an empire, one that stretched from the eastern Mediterranean to western India. They introduced law, justice, and toleration into their imperial rule. They encouraged political unity and cultural diversity. Through their religion Zoroastrianism they fostered the concept of life as a battleground between good and evil.

Suggested Reading

Brosius, M. *The Persians: An Introduction.* 2006. Covers all of Persian history.

Edwards, D. N. *The Nubian Past.* 2004. Examines the history of Nubia and Sudan.

Hawass, Z. *Silent Images: Women in Pharaonic Egypt.* 2000. Blends texts and pictures to depict the history of Egyptian women.

Herzfeld, E. *Iran in the Ancient Near East.* 1987. Puts Persian history in a broad context.

Kuhrt, A. *The Ancient Near East,* 2 vols. 1995. Covers the region from the earliest times to Alexander's conquest.

Leick, G. *The Babylonians.* 2002. Introduces all aspects of Babylonian life and culture.

Marokoe, G. *The Phoenicians.* 2000. Presents these seafarers at home and abroad in the Mediterranean.

Oren, E. D. *The Hyksos.* 1997. Concentrates on the archaeological evidence for the Hyksos.

Rice, M. *Egypt's Early Making: The Origins of Ancient Egypt.* 2004. Treats the earliest periods of Egyptian history.

Visicato, C. *The Power of Writing.* 2000. Studies the practical importance of early Mesopotamian scribes.

Notes

1. Quoted in S. N. Kramer, *The Sumerians* (Chicago: University of Chicago Press, 1963), p. 238.
2. J.B. Pritchard, ed., *Ancient Near Eastern Texts,* 3d ed., p. 372. Copyright © 1969 by Princeton University Press. Reprinted by permission of Princeton University Press.
3. Nahum 3:7.

Listening to the PAST

A Quest for Immortality

The human desire to escape the grip of death, to achieve immortality, is one of the oldest wishes of all peoples. The Sumerian Epic of Gilgamesh is the earliest recorded treatment of this topic. The oldest elements of the epic go back at least to the third millennium B.C.E. According to tradition, Gilgamesh was a king of Uruk whom the Sumerians, Babylonians, and Assyrians considered a hero-king and a god. In the story Gilgamesh and his friend Enkidu set out to attain immortality and join the ranks of the gods. They attempt to do so by performing wondrous feats against fearsome agents of the gods, who are determined to thwart them.

During their quest Enkidu dies. Gilgamesh, more determined than ever to become immortal, begins seeking anyone who might tell him how to do so. His journey involves the effort not only to escape from death but also to reach an understanding of the meaning of life.

The passage begins with Enkidu speaking of a dream that foretells his own death.

Listen, my friend [Gilgamesh], this is the dream I dreamed last night. The heavens roared, and earth rumbled back an answer; between them I stood before an awful being, the sombre-faced man-bird; he had directed on me his purpose. His was a vampire face, his foot was a lion's foot, his hand was an eagle's talon. He fell on me and his claws were in my hair, he held me fast and I smothered; then he transformed me so that my arms became wings covered with feathers. He turned his stare towards me, and he led me away to the palace of Irkalla, the Queen of Darkness [the goddess of the underworld; in other words, an agent of death], to the house from which none who enters ever returns, down the road from which there is no coming back.

At this point Enkidu dies, whereupon Gilgamesh sets off on his quest for the secret of immortality. During his travels he meets with Siduri, the wise and good-natured goddess of wine, who gives him the following advice.

Gilgamesh, where are you hurrying to? You will never find that life for which you are looking. When the gods created man they allotted to him death, but life they retained in their own keeping. As for you, Gilgamesh, fill your belly with good things; day and night, night and day, dance and be merry, feast and rejoice. Let your clothes be fresh, bathe yourself in water, cherish the little child that holds your hand, and make your wife happy in your embrace; for this too is the lot of man.

Ignoring Siduri's advice, Gilgamesh continues his journey, until he finds Utnapishtim. Meeting Utnapishtim is especially important because, like Gilgamesh, he was once a mortal, but the gods so favored him that they put him in an eternal paradise. Gilgamesh puts to Utnapishtim the question that is the reason for his quest.

Oh, father Utnapishtim, you who have entered the assembly of the gods, I wish to question you concerning the living and the dead, how shall I find the life for which I am searching?

Utnapishtim said, "There is no permanence. Do we build a house to stand forever, do we seal a contract to hold for all time? Do brothers divide an inheritance to keep forever, does the flood-time of rivers endure? . . . What is there between the master and the servant when both have fulfilled their doom? When the Anunnaki [the gods of the underworld], the judges, come together, and Mammetun [the goddess of fate] the mother of destinies, together they decree the fates of men. Life and death they allot but the day of death they do not disclose.

Then Gilgamesh said to Utnapishtim the Faraway, "I look at you now, Utnapishtim, and your appearance is no different from mine; there is nothing strange in your features. I thought I should find you like a hero prepared for battle, but you lie here taking your ease on your back. Tell me truly, how was it that you came to enter the company of the gods and to possess everlasting life?" Utnapishtim said to Gilgamesh, "I shall reveal to you a mystery, I shall tell you a secret of the gods."

Utnapishtim then tells Gilgamesh of a time when the great god Enlil had become angered with the Sumerians and encouraged the other gods to wipe out humanity. The god

Gilgamesh, from decorative panel of a lyre unearthed at Ur. *(The University Museum, University of Pennsylvania, neg. T4-108)*

Ea, however, warned Utnapishtim about the gods' decision to send a great flood to destroy the Sumerians. He commanded Utnapishtim to build a boat big enough to hold his family, various artisans, and all animals in order to survive the flood that was to come. Although Enlil was infuriated by the Sumerians' survival, Ea rebuked him. Then Enlil relented and blessed Utnapishtim with eternal paradise. After telling the story, Utnapishtim foretells Gilgamesh's fate.

Utnapishtim said, ". . . The destiny was fulfilled which the father of the gods, Enlil of the mountain, had decreed for Gilgamesh: In nether-earth the darkness will show him a light: of mankind, all that are known, none will leave a monument for generations to compare with his. The heroes, the wise men, like the new moon have their waxing and waning. Men will say, Who has ever ruled with might and power like his? As in the dark month, the month of shadows, so without him there is no light. O Gilgamesh, this was the meaning of your dream [of immortality]. You were given the kingship, such was your destiny, everlasting life was not your destiny. Because of this do not be sad at heart, do not be grieved or oppressed; he [Enlil] has given you power to bind and to loose, to be the darkness and the light of mankind. He has given unexampled supremacy over the people, victory in battle from which no fugitive returns, in forays and assaults from which there is no going back. But do not abuse this power, deal justly with your servants in the palace, deal justly before the face of the Sun."

Questions for Analysis

1. What does the *Epic of Gilgamesh* reveal about Sumerian attitudes toward the gods and human beings?

2. At the end of his quest, did Gilgamesh achieve immortality? If so, what was the nature of that immortality?

3. What does the epic tell us about Sumerian views of the nature of human life? Where do human beings fit into the cosmic world?

Source: The Epic of Gilgamesh, translated by N. K. Sanders. Penguin Classics 1960, Second revised edition, 1972, pp. 91–119. Copyright © N. K. Sanders, 1960, 1964, 1972. Reproduced by permission of Penguin Books Ltd.

The North Gate at Sanchi, Madhya Pradesh. One of four ornately carved gates guarding this Buddhist memorial shrine, second century B.C.E. *(Jean-Louis Nou/akg-images)*

2 THE FOUNDATION OF INDIAN SOCIETY, TO 300 C.E.

Chapter Preview

**The Land and Its First Settlers
(ca. 3000–1500 B.C.E.)**
• What does archaeology tell us about the earliest civilization in India?

**The Aryans and the Vedic Age
(ca. 1500–500 B.C.E.)**
• What kind of society and culture did the Indo-European Aryans create?

India's Great Religions
• What ideas and practices were taught by the founders of Jainism, Buddhism, and Hinduism?

**India and the West
(ca. 513–298 B.C.E.)**
• How did India respond to the expansion of the Persian and Greek empires?

**The Mauryan Empire
(ca. 322–185 B.C.E.)**
• What were the consequences of the unification of much of India by Chandragupta and Ashoka?

**Small States and Trading Networks
(200 B.C.E.–300 C.E.)**
• How was India shaped by political disunity and contacts with other cultures?

During the centuries when the peoples of ancient Mesopotamia and Egypt were developing urban civilizations, people in India were wrestling with the same challenges—making the land yield food, building cities and urban cultures, grappling with the political administration of large tracts of land, and asking basic questions about human life and the cosmos.

Like the civilizations of the Near East, the earliest Indian civilization centered on a great river, the Indus. From about 2800 to 1800 B.C.E., this Indus Valley, or Harappan, culture thrived, and numerous cities were built over a huge area. A very different Indian society emerged after the decline of this civilization. It was dominated by the Aryans, warriors who spoke an early version of Sanskrit. The Indian caste system and the Hindu religion, key features of Indian society into modern times, had their origins in early Aryan society. The earliest Indian literature consists of the epics and religious texts of these Aryan tribes.

By the middle of the first millennium B.C.E., the Aryans had set up numerous small kingdoms throughout north India. This was the great age of Indian religious creativity, when Buddhism and Jainism were founded and the early Brahmanic religion of the Aryans developed into Hinduism. Alexander the Great invaded north India in 326 B.C.E., and after his army withdrew, the first major Indian empire was created by the Mauryan dynasty (ca. 322–ca. 185 B.C.E.), which unified most of north India. This dynasty reached its peak under the great king Ashoka (r. ca. 269–232 B.C.E.), who actively promoted Buddhism both within his realm and beyond it. Not long afterward, however, the empire broke up, and for several centuries India was politically divided.

Although India never had a single language and only periodically had a centralized government, cultural elements dating back to the ancient period—the core ideas of Brahmanism, the caste system, and the early epics—gave India cultural identity. These cultural elements spread through trade and other contact, even when the subcontinent was divided into hostile kingdoms.

THE LAND AND ITS FIRST SETTLERS (CA. 3000–1500 B.C.E.)

What does archaeology tell us about the earliest civilization in India?

The subcontinent of India, a landmass as large as western Europe, juts southward into the warm waters of the Indian Ocean. Today this region is divided into the separate countries of Pakistan, Nepal, India, Bangladesh, and Sri Lanka, but these divisions are recent, and for premodern times the entire subcontinent will be called India here.

In India, as elsewhere, the possibilities for both agriculture and communication have always been strongly shaped by geography (see Map 2.1). Some regions are among the wettest on earth; others are arid deserts and scrubland. Most areas in India are warm all year, with temperatures over 100°F common. Average temperatures range from 79°F in the north to 85°F in the south. Monsoon rains sweep northward from the Indian Ocean each summer. The lower reaches of the Himalaya Mountains in the northeast are covered by dense forests, sustained by heavy rainfall. Immediately to the south are the fertile valleys of the Indus and Ganges Rivers. These lowland plains, which stretch all the way across the subcontinent, over time were tamed for agriculture, and India's great empires were centered there. To their west are the great deserts of Rajasthan and southeastern Pakistan, historically important in part because their flat terrain enabled invaders to sweep into India from the northwest. South of the great river valleys rise the jungle-clad Vindhya Mountains and the dry, hilly Deccan Plateau. In this part of India, only along the coasts do the hills give way to narrow plains where crop agriculture flourished. India's long coastlines and predictable winds fostered maritime trade with other countries bordering the Indian Ocean.

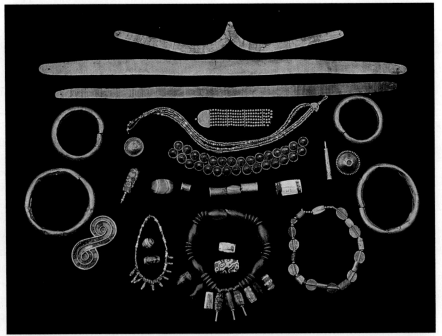

● **Harappan Artifacts** Small objects like seals and jewelry found at Harappan sites provide glimpses of early Indian religious imagination and daily life. The molded tablet shown on the left depicts a female deity battling two tigers. She stands above an elephant. The jewelry found at these sites, such as those pieces shown on the right, makes much use of gold and precious stones. *(J. M. Kenoyer/Courtesy Department of Archaeology and Museums, Government of Pakistan)*

Neolithic settlement of the Indian subcontinent occurred somewhat later than in the Middle East, but agriculture was well established by about 7000 B.C.E. Wheat and barley were the early crops, probably having spread in their domesticated form from the Middle East. Farmers also domesticated cattle, sheep, and goats and learned to make pottery.

The story of the first civilization in India is one of the most dramatic in the ancient world. From the Bible, Europeans knew about ancient Egypt and Ur, but no one knew about the ancient cities of the Indus Valley until 1921, when archaeologists found astonishing evidence of a thriving and sophisticated Bronze Age urban culture dating to about 2500 B.C.E. at Mohenjo-daro in what is now Pakistan.

This civilization is known today as the Indus Valley or the **Harappan** civilization, from the modern names of the river and a major city, respectively. Archaeologists have discovered some three hundred Harappan cities and many more towns and villages in both Pakistan and India, making it possible to see both the vast regional extent of the Harappan civilization and its evolution over a period of nearly a millennium. It was a literate civilization, like those of Egypt and Mesopotamia, but no one has been able to decipher the more than four hundred symbols inscribed on stone seals and copper tablets. Its most flourishing period was 2500 to 2000 B.C.E.

The Indus civilization extended over nearly five hundred thousand square miles in the Indus Valley, making it more than twice as large as the territories of the ancient Egyptian and Sumerian civilizations. Yet Harappan civilization was marked by a striking uniformity. Throughout the region, for instance, even in small villages, bricks were made to standard proportions of 4:2:1. Figurines of pregnant women have been found throughout the area, suggesting common religious ideas and practices.

Like Mesopotamian cities, Harappan cities were centers for crafts and trade surrounded by extensive farmland. Fine ceramics were made on the potter's wheel and decorated with geometric designs. Cotton was used to make cloth (the earliest anywhere) and was so abundant that goods were wrapped in it for shipment. Trade was extensive. As early as the reign of Sargon of Akkad in the third millennium B.C.E., trade between India and Mesopotamia carried goods and ideas between the two cultures, probably by way of the Persian Gulf. The port of Lothal had a stone dock seven hundred feet long, next to which were massive granaries and bead-making factories. Hundreds of seals were found there, some of Persian Gulf origin, indicating that Lothal was a major port of exit and entry.

Both Mohenjo-daro, in southern Pakistan, and Harappa, some four hundred miles to the north, were huge, more than three miles in circumference, and housed populations estimated at thirty-five thousand to forty thousand. They were both defended by great citadels that towered forty to fifty feet above the surrounding plain. Both cities had obviously been planned and built before being settled; they were not the

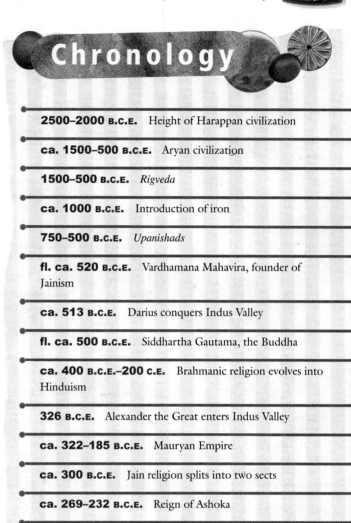

Chronology

2500–2000 B.C.E.	Height of Harappan civilization
ca. 1500–500 B.C.E.	Aryan civilization
1500–500 B.C.E.	*Rigveda*
ca. 1000 B.C.E.	Introduction of iron
750–500 B.C.E.	*Upanishads*
fl. ca. 520 B.C.E.	Vardhamana Mahavira, founder of Jainism
ca. 513 B.C.E.	Darius conquers Indus Valley
fl. ca. 500 B.C.E.	Siddhartha Gautama, the Buddha
ca. 400 B.C.E.–200 C.E.	Brahmanic religion evolves into Hinduism
326 B.C.E.	Alexander the Great enters Indus Valley
ca. 322–185 B.C.E.	Mauryan Empire
ca. 300 B.C.E.	Jain religion splits into two sects
ca. 269–232 B.C.E.	Reign of Ashoka
ca. 200 B.C.E.–200 C.E.	Classical period of Tamil culture
fl. ca. 100 C.E.	Nagarjuna, theorist of Mahayana Buddhism
ca. 200 C.E.	Code of Manu

Harappan *The first Indian civilization; it is also known as the Indus Valley civilization.*

outcomes of villages that grew and sprawled haphazardly. Streets were straight and varied from nine to thirty-four feet in width. The houses were substantial, many two stories tall, some perhaps three. The focal point of a house was a central courtyard onto which the rooms opened, much like many houses today in both rural and urban India.

Perhaps the most surprising aspect of the elaborate planning of these cities is their complex system of drainage, well preserved at Mohenjo-daro. Each house had a bathroom with a drain connected to brick-lined sewers located under the major streets. Openings allowed the refuse to be collected, probably to be used as fertilizer on nearby fields. No other ancient city had such an advanced sanitation system.

Both cities also contained numerous large structures, which excavators think were public buildings. One of the most important was the large ventilated storehouse for the community's grain. Mohenjo-daro also had a marketplace or place of assembly, a palace, and a huge pool some thirty-nine feet long by twenty-three feet wide and eight feet deep. Like the later Roman baths, it had spacious dressing rooms for the bathers. Because the Great Bath at Mohenjo-daro resembles the ritual purification pools of later India, some scholars have speculated that power was in the hands of a priest-king and that the Great Bath played a role in the religious rituals of the city.

The prosperity of the Indus civilization depended on constant and intensive cultivation of the rich river valley. Although rainfall seems to have been greater then than in recent times, the Indus, like the Nile, flowed through a relatively dry region made fertile by annual floods and irrigation. And as in Egypt, agriculture was aided by a long, hot growing season and near constant sunshine.

Because the written language of the Harappan people has not been deciphered, their political, intellectual, and religious life is largely unknown. There clearly was a political structure with the authority to organize city planning and facilitate trade, but we do not even know whether there were hereditary kings. There are clear connections between Harappan and Sumerian civilization, but just as clear differences. For instance, the Harappan script, like the Sumerian, was incised on clay tablets and seals, but it has no connection to Sumerian cuneiform, and the artistic style of the Harappan seals also is distinct. There are many signs of continuity with later Indian civilization, ranging from the sorts of pottery ovens used to some of the images of gods. Some scholars think that the people of Harappa were the ancestors of the Dravidian-speaking peoples of modern south India. Analysis of skeletons, however, indicates that the population of the Indus Valley in ancient times was very similar to the modern population of the same region.

The decline of Harappan civilization, which began soon after 2000 B.C.E., cannot be attributed to the arrival of powerful invaders, as was once thought. Rather the decline was internally generated. The port of Lothal was abandoned by about 1900 B.C.E., and other major centers came to house only a fraction of their earlier populations. Scholars have offered many explanations for the mystery of the abandonment of these cities. Perhaps an earthquake led to a shift in the

● **Mohenjo-daro** Mohenjo-daro was a planned city built of fired mud brick. Its streets were straight, and covered drain-pipes were installed to carry away waste. From sites like this, we know that the early Indian political elite had the power and technical expertise to organize large, coordinated building projects. *(Josephine Powell)*

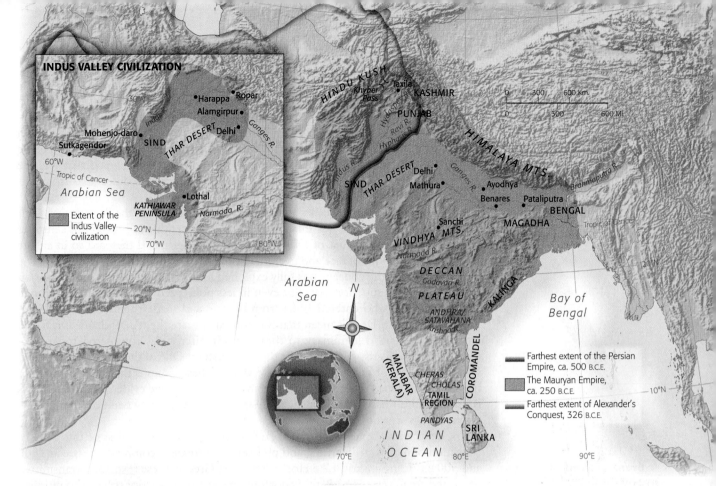

MAP 2.1 **India from ca. 2500 B.C.E. to 300 C.E.** The earliest civilization in India developed in the Indus River valley in the west of the subcontinent. The Ganges River valley was the heart of the later Mauryan Empire. Although India is protected from the cold by mountains in the north, mountain passes in the northwest allowed both migration and invasion.

course of the river, or perhaps rainfall and snowmelt decreased and the rivers dried up. Perhaps the long-term practice of irrigation led to the buildup of salts and alkalines in the soil until they reached levels toxic to plants. Perhaps long-distance commerce collapsed, leading to an economic depression. Perhaps the population fell prey to diseases, such as malaria, that led people to flee the cities. Even though the Harappan people apparently lived on after scattering to villages, they were not able to retain key features of the high culture of the Indus civilization. For the next thousand years, India had no large cities, no kiln-fired bricks, and no written language.

THE ARYANS AND THE VEDIC AGE
(CA. 1500–500 B.C.E.)

What kind of society and culture did the Indo-European Aryans create?

After the decline of the Indus Valley civilization, a people who called themselves **Aryans** became dominant in north India. They were speakers of an early form of Sanskrit, which was an Indo-European language closely related to ancient Persian and more distantly related to Latin, Greek, Celtic, and their modern descendants, such as English. The Sanskrit *nava,* "ship," is related to the English word *naval; deva,* "god," to *divine; raja,* "ruler," to *regal;* and so on. The word *Aryan* itself comes from *Arya,* "noble" or "pure" in Sanskrit, and has the same root as *Iran* and *Ireland.*

Until relatively recently, the dominant theory was that the Aryans came into India from outside, perhaps as part of the same movements of people that led to the Hittites

> **Aryans** *The dominant people in North India after the decline of the Indus Valley civilization; they spoke an early form of Sanskrit.*

● **Bronze Sword**   A striking example of the quality of Aryan arms is this bronze sword, with its rib in the middle of the blade for strength. Superior weapons gave the Aryans military advantage. *(Courtesy of the Trustees of the British Museum)*

Rigveda   *The earliest collection of hymns, ritual texts, and philosophical treatises, it is the central source of information on early Aryans.*

raja   *From an ancient Indo-European word meaning "to rule," and related to the modern English "royal," raja refers to an Aryan tribal chieftain who led his people into battle and governed them during peacetime.*

occupying parts of Anatolia, the Achaeans entering Greece, and the Kassites conquering Sumer—all in the period from about 1900 to 1750 B.C.E. Some scholars, however, have proposed that the Indo-European languages spread to this area much earlier; to them it seems possible that the Harappan people were speakers of an early Indo-European language. If that was the case, the Aryans would be one of the groups descended from this early population.

Modern politics complicates analysis of the appearance of the Aryans and their role in India's history. It was Europeans in the eighteenth and nineteenth centuries who developed the concept of Indo-European languages, and they did so in an age both highly conscious of race and in the habit of identifying races with languages. The racist potential of the concept was fully exploited by the Nazis, with their glorification of the Aryans as a superior race. But even in less politicized contexts, the notion of a group of people who entered India from outside and made themselves its rulers is troubling to many. Does it mean that the non-Aryans are the true Indians? Or, to the contrary, does it add legitimacy to those who in later times conquered India from outside? Does it justify or undermine the caste system? One of the difficulties faced by scholars who wish to take a dispassionate view of these issues is that the evidence for the earlier Harappan culture is entirely archaeological and the evidence for the Aryans is almost entirely based on linguistic analysis of modern languages and orally transmitted texts of uncertain date.

The central source for the early Aryans is the **Rigveda**, the earliest of the Vedas, a collection of hymns, ritual texts, and philosophical treatises composed between 1500 and 500 B.C.E. in Sanskrit. Like Homer's epics in Greece, these texts were transmitted orally and are in verse. The *Rigveda* portrays the Aryans as warrior tribes who glorified military skill and heroism; loved to drink, hunt, race, and dance; and counted their wealth in cattle. The Aryans did not sweep across India in a quick campaign, nor were they a disciplined army led by one conqueror. Rather they were a collection of tribes who frequently fought with each other and only over the course of several centuries came to dominate north India.

Those the Aryans fought often lived in fortified towns and put up a strong defense against them. The key to the Aryans' success probably lay in their superior military technology: they had fast two-wheeled chariots, horses, and bronze swords and spears. Their epics, however, present the struggle in religious terms: their chiefs were godlike heroes, and their opponents irreligious savages who did not perform the proper sacrifices. In time, however, the Aryans clearly absorbed much from those they conquered.

At the head of each Aryan tribe was a chief, or **raja**, who led his followers in battle and ruled them in peacetime. The warriors in the tribe elected the chief for his military skills. Next in importance to the chief was the priest. In time, priests evolved into a distinct class possessing precise knowledge of the complex rituals and of the invocations and formulas that accompanied them, rather like the priest classes in ancient Egypt, Mesopotamia, and Persia. The warrior nobility rode into battle in chariots and perhaps on horseback; they met at assemblies to reach decisions and advise the raja. The common tribesmen tended herds and in time worked the land. To the conquered non-Aryans fell the drudgery of menial tasks. It is difficult to define precisely their social status. Though probably not slaves, they were certainly subordinate to the Aryans and worked for them in return for protection.

Over the course of several centuries, the Aryans pushed farther east into the valley of the Ganges River, at that time a land of thick jungle populated by aboriginal forest peoples. The tremendous challenge of clearing the jungle was made somewhat easier by the introduction of iron around 1000 B.C.E. Iron made it possible to produce strong axes and knives relatively cheaply.

The Aryans did not gain dominance over the entire Indian subcontinent. South of the Vindhya range, people speaking Dravidian languages maintained their control. In the great Aryan epics the *Ramayana* and *Mahabharata*, the people of the south and Sri

Lanka are spoken of as dark-skinned savages and demons who resisted the Aryans' conquests. Still, in time these epics became part of the common cultural heritage of all of India.

Early Indian Society (1000–500 B.C.E.)

As Aryan rulers came to dominate large settled populations, the style of political organization changed from tribal chieftainship to territorial kingship. In other words, the ruler controlled an area whose people might change, not a nomadic tribe that moved as a group. Moreover, kings no longer needed to be elected by the tribe; it was enough to be invested by priests and to perform the splendid royal ceremonies they designed. The priests, or **Brahmans,** supported the growth of royal power in return for royal confirmation of their own power and status. The Brahmans also served as advisers to the kings. In the face of this royal-priestly alliance, the old tribal assemblies of warriors withered away. By the time Persian armies reached the Indus around 513 B.C.E., there were sixteen major kingdoms in north India.

Early Aryan society had distinguished among the warrior elite, the priests, ordinary tribesmen, and conquered subjects. These distinctions gradually evolved into the **caste system.** Society was conceived in terms of four hierarchical strata whose members do not eat with or marry each other. These strata (called **varna**) are *Brahman* (priests), *Kshatriya* (warriors and officials), *Vaishya* (merchants and artisans), and *Shudra* (peasants and laborers). The lowest level probably evolved out of the efforts of the numerically outnumbered Aryans to maintain their dominance over their subjects and not be absorbed by them. The three upper varnas probably accounted for no more than 30 percent of the population. Social and religious attitudes entered into these distinctions as well. Aryans considered the work of artisans impure. They left all such work to the local people, who were probably superior to them in these arts anyway. Trade, by contrast, was not viewed as demeaning. Brahmanic texts of the period refer to trade as equal in value to farming, serving the king, or serving as a priest.

Those without places in this tidy social division—that is, those who entered it later than the others or who had lost their caste status through violations of ritual—were **outcastes.** That simply meant that they belonged to no caste. In time, some of these people became "untouchables," because they were "impure." They were scorned because they earned their living by performing such "polluting" jobs as slaughtering animals and dressing skins.

Slavery was a feature of early social life in India, as it was in Egypt, Mesopotamia, and elsewhere in antiquity. Those captured in battle often became slaves, but captives could also be ransomed by their families. Later, slavery was less connected with warfare and became more of an economic and social institution. As in ancient Mesopotamia, a free man might sell himself and his family into slavery because he could not pay his debts. And, as in Hammurabi's Mesopotamia, he could, if clever, hard-working, or fortunate, buy his and his family's way out of slavery. At birth, slave children automatically became the slaves of their parents' masters. Indian slaves could be bought, used as collateral, or given away.

Women's lives in early India varied according to their social status, much as men's did. Like most nomadic tribes, the Aryans were patrilineal and patriarchal (tracing descent through males and placing power over family members in the senior men of the family). Thus women in Aryan society probably had more subordinate roles than did women among local Dravidian groups, many of whom were matrilineal. But even in Aryan society, women were treated somewhat more favorably than in later Indian society. They were not yet given in child-marriage, and widows had the right to remarry. In the epics such as the *Ramayana,* women are often portrayed as forceful personalities, able to achieve their goals both by feminine ploys of cajoling men and by more direct action. (See the feature "Listening to the Past: Rama and Sita" on pages 50–51.)

Brahmans *Priests of the Aryans. They supported the growth of royal power in return for royal confirmation of their own religious rights, power, and status.*

caste system *The Indian system of dividing society into hereditary groups that limited interaction with each other, especially marriage to each other.*

varna *The four strata into which Indian society was divided under the caste system.*

outcastes *People not belonging to a caste; they were often scorned and sometimes deemed "untouchables."*

Brahmanism

The gods of the Aryans shared some features with the gods of other early Indo-European societies such as the Persians and Greeks. Some of them were great brawling figures, such as Agni, the god of fire; Indra, wielder of the thunderbolt and god of war, who each year slew a dragon to release the monsoon rains; and Rudra, the divine archer who spread disaster and disease by firing his arrows at people. Varuna, the god of order in the universe, was a hard god, quick to punish those who sinned and thus upset the balance of nature. Ushas, the goddess of dawn, was a gentle deity who welcomed the birds, gave delight to human beings, and warded off evil spirits.

The core of the Aryans' religion was its focus on sacrifice. By giving valued things to the gods, people strengthened them and established relationships with them. Gradually, under the priestly monopoly of the Brahmans, correct sacrifice and proper ritual became so important that most Brahmans believed that a properly performed ritual would force a god to grant a worshiper's wish.

The *Upanishads*, composed between 750 and 500 B.C.E., record speculations about the mystical meaning of sacrificial rites and about cosmological questions of man's relationship to the universe. They document a gradual shift from the mythical worldview of the early Vedic age to a deeply philosophical one. Associated with this shift was a movement toward *asceticism—severe self-discipline and self-denial.* In search of wisdom, some men retreated to the forests. These ascetics concluded that disciplined meditation on the ritual sacrifice could produce the same results as the physical ritual itself. Thus they reinterpreted ritual sacrifices as symbolic gestures with mystical meanings.

Ancient Indian cosmology focused not on a creator who made the universe out of nothing, but rather on endlessly repeating cycles. Key ideas were **samsara,** the transmigration of souls by a continual process of rebirth, and **karma,** the tally of good and bad deeds that determined the status of an individual's next life. Good deeds led to better future lives, evil deeds to worse future lives—even to reincarnation as an animal. Thus gradually arose the concept of a wheel of life that included human beings, animals, and even gods. Reward and punishment worked automatically; there was no all-knowing god who judged people and could be petitioned to forgive a sin, and each individual was responsible for his or her own destiny in a just and impartial world.

To most people, especially those on the low end of the economic and social scale, these ideas were attractive. By living righteously and doing good deeds, people could improve their lot in the next life. Yet there was another side to these ideas: the wheel of life could be seen as a treadmill, giving rise to a yearning for release from the relentless cycle of birth and death. One solution offered in the *Upanishads* was **moksha,** or release from the wheel of life. Brahmanic mystics claimed that life in the world was actually an illusion and that the only way to escape the wheel of life was to realize that ultimate reality was unchanging.

This unchanging, ultimate reality was called **brahman.** The multitude of things in the world is fleeting; the only true reality is brahman. Even the individual soul or self is ultimately the same substance as the universal brahman, in the same way that each spark is in substance the same as a large fire. Equating the individual self with the ultimate reality suggested that the apparent duality in the world is in some sense unreal. At the same time it conveyed that all people had in themselves an eternal truth that corresponded to an identical but greater all-encompassing reality.

The *Upanishads* gave the Brahmans a high status to which the poor and lowly could aspire in a future life. Consequently, the Brahmans greeted the concepts presented in these works and those who taught them with tolerance and understanding and made a place for them in traditional religious practice. The rulers of Indian society also encouraged the new trends, since the doctrines of samsara and karma encouraged the poor and oppressed to labor peacefully and dutifully. In other words, although the

---

samsara *The transmigration of souls by a continual process of rebirth.*

karma *The tally of good and bad deeds that determines the status of an individual's next life.*

moksha *Release from the wheel of life.*

brahman *The unchanging, ultimate reality, according to the Upanishads.*

new doctrines were intellectually revolutionary, in social and political terms they supported the existing power structure.

INDIA'S GREAT RELIGIONS

What ideas and practices were taught by the founders of Jainism, Buddhism, and Hinduism?

By the sixth and fifth centuries B.C.E., cities had reappeared in India, and merchants and trade were thriving. Bricks were again baked in kilns and used to build ramparts around cities. One particular kingdom, Magadha, had become much more powerful than any of the other states in the Ganges plain, defeating its enemies by using war elephants and catapults for hurling stones. Written language had by this point reappeared.

This was a period of intellectual ferment throughout Eurasia—the period of the early Greek philosophers, the Hebrew prophets, Zoroaster in Persia, and Confucius and the early Daoists in China. In India it led to numerous sects that rejected various elements of Brahmanic teachings. (See the feature "Individuals in Society: Gosala.") The two most important in world-historical terms were Jainism and Buddhism. Their founders were contemporaries living in east India in minor states of the Ganges plain. Hinduism emerged in response to these new religions but at the same time was the most direct descendant of the old Brahmanic religion.

Jainism

The key figure of Jainism, Vardhamana Mahavira (fl. ca. 520 B.C.E.), was the son of the chief of a petty state. Like many ascetics of the period, he left home to become a wandering holy man. For twelve years, from ages thirty to forty-two, he traveled through the Ganges Valley until he found enlightenment and became a "completed soul." Mahavira taught his doctrines for about thirty years, founding a disciplined order of monks and gaining the support of many lay followers, male and female.

Mahavira accepted the doctrines of karma and rebirth but developed these ideas in new directions. He argued that human beings, animals, plants, and even inanimate objects all have living souls enmeshed in matter, accumulated through the workings of karma. Even a rock has a soul locked inside it, enchained by matter but capable of suffering if someone kicks it. The souls conceived by the Jains have finite dimensions. They float or sink depending on the amount of matter with which they are enmeshed. The ascetic, who willingly undertakes suffering, can dissipate some of the accumulated karma and make progress toward liberation. If a soul at last escapes from all the matter weighing it down, it becomes lighter than ordinary objects and floats to the top of the universe, where it remains forever in inactive bliss.

Mahavira's followers pursued such liberation by living ascetic lives and avoiding evil thoughts and actions. The Jains considered all life sacred and tried to live without

● **Jain Ascetic** The most extreme of Jain ascetics not only endured the elements without the help of clothes but were also generally indifferent to bodily comfort. The Jain saint depicted in this eighth-century cave temple has maintained his yogic posture for so long that vines have grown up around him. *(Courtesy, Robert Fisher)*

destroying other life. Some early Jains went to the extreme of starving themselves to death, since it is impossible to eat without destroying at least plants, but most took the less extreme step of distinguishing between different levels of life. The most sacred life forms were human beings, followed by animals, plants, and inanimate objects. A Jain who wished to avoid violence to life became a vegetarian and took pains not to kill any creature, even tiny insects in the air and soil. Farming was impossible for Jains, who tended instead to take up trade. Among the most conservative, priests practiced nudity, for clinging to clothes, even a loincloth, was a form of attachment. Lay Jains could pursue Jain teachings by practicing nonviolence and not eating meat. The Jains' radical nonviolence was motivated by a desire to escape the karmic consequences of causing harm to a life. In other words, violence had to be avoided above all because it harms the person who commits it.

For the first century after Mahavira's death, the Jains were a comparatively small and unimportant sect. Jainism began to flourish under the Mauryan dynasty (ca. 322–185 B.C.E.; see pages 44–46), and Jain tradition claims the Mauryan Empire's founder, Chandragupta, as a major patron. About 300 B.C.E. the Jain scriptures were recorded, and the religion split into two sects, one maintaining the tradition of total nudity, the other choosing to wear white robes on the grounds that clothes were an insignificant external sign, unrelated to true liberation. Over the next few centuries, Jain monks were particularly important in spreading northern culture into the Deccan and Tamil regions of south India.

Although Jainism never took hold as widely as Hinduism and Buddhism, it has been an influential strand in Indian thought and has several million adherents in India today. Fasting and nonviolence as spiritual practices in India owe much to Jain teachings. Mahatma Gandhi was influenced by these ideas through his mother, and Dr. Martin Luther King, Jr., was influenced by Gandhi.

Siddhartha Gautama and Buddhism

Siddhartha Gautama (fl. ca. 500 B.C.E.), also called Shakyamuni ("sage of the Shakya tribe"), is best known as the Buddha ("enlightened one"). He was a contemporary of Mahavira and came from the same social class (that is, warrior, not Brahman). He was born the son of a chief of one of the tribes in the Himalayan foothills in what is now Nepal. At age twenty-nine, unsatisfied with his life of comfort and troubled by the suffering he saw around him, he left home to become a wandering ascetic. He traveled south to the kingdom of Magadha, where he studied with yoga masters but later took up extreme asceticism. According to tradition, while meditating under a bo tree at Bodh Gaya, he reached enlightenment—that is, he gained perfect insight into the processes of the universe. After several weeks of meditation, he preached his first sermon, urging a "middle way" between asceticism and worldly life. For the next forty-five years, the Buddha traveled through the Ganges Valley, propounding his ideas, refuting his adversaries, and attracting followers. To reach as wide an audience as possible, the Buddha preached in the local language, Magadhi, rather than in Sanskrit, which was already becoming a priestly language. Probably because he refused to recognize the divine authority of the Vedas and dismissed sacrifices, he attracted followers mostly from among merchants, artisans, and farmers, rather than Brahmans.

In his first sermon, the Buddha outlined his main message, summed up in the **Four Noble Truths** and the **Eightfold Path**. The truths are as follows: (1) pain and suffering, frustration and anxiety, are ugly but inescapable parts of human life; (2) suffering and anxiety are caused by human desires and attachments; (3) people can understand these weaknesses and triumph over them; and (4) this triumph is made possible by following a simple code of conduct, the Eightfold Path. The basic insight of Buddhism is thus psychological. The deepest human longings can never be satisfied, and even those things that seem to give pleasure cause anxiety because we are afraid of losing them. Attachment to people and things causes sorrow at their loss.

Primary Source: Setting in Motion the Wheel of Law *Siddhartha's first sermon contains the core teaching of Buddhism: to escape, by following the Middle Path, the suffering caused by desire.*

Four Noble Truths *The Buddha's message that pain and suffering are inescapable parts of life; suffering and anxiety are caused by human desires and attachments; people can understand and triumph over these weaknesses; and the triumph is made possible by following a simple code of conduct.*

Eightfold Path *The code of conduct, set forth by the Buddha in his first sermon, which began with "right conduct" and eventually reached "right contemplation."*

Individuals IN SOCIETY

Gosala

The Jain founder in seated meditation.
(Philadelphia Museum of Art: Acquired from the National Museum, New Delhi, India [by exchange] with funds contributed by Mr. and Mrs. Roland L. Taylor [1969-30-1])

Texts that survive from early India are rich in religious and philosophical speculation and in tales of gods and heroes but not in history of the sort written by the early Chinese and Greeks. Because Indian writers and thinkers of antiquity had little interest in recording the actions of rulers or accounting for the rise and decline of different states, few people's lives are known in any detail.

Religious literature, however, does sometimes include details of the lives of followers and adversaries. The life of Gosala, for instance, is known primarily from early Buddhist and Jain scriptures. He was a contemporary of both Mahavira, the founder of the Jains, and Gautama, the Buddha, and both of them saw him as one of their most pernicious rivals.

According to the Jain account, Gosala was born in the north Indian kingdom of Magadha, the son of a professional mendicant. The name Gosala, which means "cowshed," alluded to the fact that he was born in a cowshed where his parents had taken refuge during the rainy season. The Buddhist account adds that he became a naked wandering ascetic when he fled from his enraged master after breaking an oil jar. As a mendicant, he soon fell in with Mahavira, who had recently commenced his life as an ascetic. After accompanying Mahavira on his travels for at least six years, Gosala came to feel that he was spiritually more advanced than his master and left to undertake the practice of austerities on his own. After he gained magical powers, he challenged his master and gathered his own disciples.

Both Jain and Buddhist sources agree that Gosala taught a form of fatalism that they saw as dangerously wrong. A Buddhist source says that he taught that people are good or bad not because of their own efforts but because of fate. "Just as a ball of string, when it is cast forth, will spread out just as far and no farther than it can unwind, so both fools and wise alike, wandering in transmigration exactly for the allotted term, shall then, and only then, make an end of pain."* Some people reach perfection, but not by their own efforts; rather they are individuals who through the course of numerous rebirths over hundreds of thousands of years have rid themselves of bad karma.

The Jains claimed that Gosala lived with a potter woman, violating the celibacy expected of ascetics and moreover teaching that sexual relations were not sinful. The followers of Gosala, a Buddhist source stated, wore no clothing and were very particular about the food they accepted, refusing food specially prepared for them, food in a cooking pan, and food from couples or women with children. Like other ascetics, Gosala's followers owned no property, carrying the principle further than the Jains, who allowed the possession of a food bowl. They made a bowl from the palms of their hands, giving them the name "hand lickers."

Jain sources report that after sixteen years of separation, Mahavira happened to come to the town where Gosala lived. When Gosala heard that Mahavira spoke contemptuously of him, he and his followers went to Mahavira's lodgings, and the two sides came to blows. Soon thereafter Gosala became unhinged, gave up all ascetic restraint and, after six months of singing, dancing, drinking, and other riotous living, died, though not before telling his disciples, the Jains report, that Mahavira was right. Doubt is cast on this version of his end by the fact that for centuries to come, Gosala's followers, called the Ajivikas, were an important sect in several parts of India. Ashoka honored them among other sects and dedicated some caves to them.

Questions for Analysis

1. How would Gosala's own followers have described his life? What sorts of distortions are likely in a life known primarily from the writings of rivals?

2. How would the early Indian economy have been affected by the presence of ascetic mendicants?

*A.F.R. Hoernle, "Ajivikas," in *Encyclopedia of Religion and Ethics,* vol. 1, ed. James Hastings (Edinburgh: T. & T. Clark, 1908), p. 262.

● **Gandharan Frieze**   This carved stone (ca. 200 C.E.) portrays scenes from the life of the Buddha. The Buddha is seated below the Bodhi tree, where he was first enlightened. The soldiers and animals surrounding him are trying to distract him. Note the camel, elephant, horse, and monkey. *(Freer Gallery of Art, Smithsonian Institution, Washington, D.C., Purchase, F1949.9b)*

nirvana   *A state of blissful nothingness and freedom from reincarnation.*

The Buddha offered an optimistic message, however, because all people can set out on the Eightfold Path toward liberation. All they have to do is take steps such as recognizing the universality of suffering, deciding to free themselves from it, and choosing "right conduct," "right speech," "right livelihood," and "right endeavor." For instance, they should abstain from taking life. The seventh step is "right awareness," constant contemplation of one's deeds and words, giving full thought to their importance and whether they lead to enlightenment. "Right contemplation," the last step, entails deep meditation on the impermanence of everything in the world. Those who achieve liberation are freed from the cycle of birth and death and enter the state called **nirvana,** a kind of blissful nothingness and freedom from reincarnation.

Although he accepted the Indian idea of reincarnation, the Buddha denied the integrity of the individual self or soul. He saw human beings as a collection of parts, physical and mental. As long as the parts remain combined, that combination can be called "I." When that combination changes, as at death, the various parts remain in existence, ready to become the building blocks of different combinations. According to Buddhist teaching, life is passed from person to person as a flame is passed from candle to candle.

Buddhism differed from Brahmanism and later Hinduism in that it ignored the caste system. Everyone, noble and peasant, educated and ignorant, male and female, could follow the Eightfold Path. Moreover, the Buddha was extraordinarily undogmatic. Convinced that each person must achieve enlightenment on his or her own, he emphasized that the path was important only because it led the traveler to enlightenment, not for its own sake. He compared it to a raft, essential to cross a river but useless once the traveler reached the far shore. There was no harm in honoring local gods or observing traditional ceremonies, as long as one remembered the goal of enlightenment and did not let sacrifices become snares or attachments.

Like Mahavira, the Buddha formed a circle of disciples, primarily men but including some women as well. He continually reminded them that each person must reach ultimate fulfillment by individual effort, but he also recognized the value of a group of people striving together for the same goal.

sutras   *The written teachings of the Buddha, first transcribed in the second or first century B.C.E.*

The Buddha's followers transmitted his teachings orally until they were written down in the second or first century B.C.E. These scriptures are called **sutras.** The form of monasticism that developed among the Buddhists was less strict than that of the Jains. Buddhist monks moved about for eight months of the year (except the rainy season), consuming only one meal a day obtained by begging, but they could bathe and wear clothes. Within a few centuries, Buddhist monks began to overlook the rule that they should travel. They set up permanent monasteries, generally on land donated by kings or other patrons. Orders of nuns also appeared, giving women the opportunity to seek truth in ways men had traditionally used. The main ritual that monks and nuns performed in their monastic establishments was the communal recitation of the sutras. Lay Buddhists could aid the spread of the Buddhist teachings by providing food for monks and support for their monasteries, and they could pursue their own spiritual progress by adopting practices such as abstaining from meat and alcohol.

Because there was no ecclesiastical authority like that developed by early Christian communities, early Buddhist communities developed several divergent traditions and came to stress different sutras. One of the most important of these, associated with the monk-philosopher Nagarjuna (fl. ca. 100 C.E.), is called **Mahayana,** or "Great Vehicle," because it is a more inclusive form of the religion. It drew on a set of discourses allegedly given by the Buddha and kept hidden by his followers for centuries. One branch of Mahayana taught that reality is empty (that is, nothing exists independently, of itself). Another branch held that ultimate reality is consciousness, that everything is produced by the mind.

> **Mahayana** *The "Great Vehicle," a tradition of Buddhism that aspires to be more inclusive.*

Just as important as the metaphysical literature of Mahayana Buddhism was its devotional side, influenced by the religions then prevalent in Central Asia. The Buddha became deified and placed at the head of an expanding pantheon of other Buddhas and **bodhisattvas.** Bodhisattvas were Buddhas-to-be who had stayed in the world after enlightenment to help others on the path to salvation. These Buddhas and bodhisattvas became objects of veneration, especially the Buddha Amitabha and the bodhisattva Avalokitesvara. With the growth of Mahayana, Buddhism attracted more and more laypeople.

> **bodhisattvas** *Buddhas-to-be who stayed in the world after enlightenment to help others on the path to salvation.*

Buddhism remained an important religion in India until about 1200 C.E. By that time, it had spread widely through East, Central, and Southeast Asia. After 1200 Buddhism declined in India, and the number of Buddhists in India today is small. In Sri Lanka and Nepal, however, Buddhism never lost its hold, and today it is also a major religion in Southeast Asia, Tibet, China, Korea, and Japan.

Hinduism

Both Buddhism and Jainism were direct challenges to the old Brahmanic religion. Both rejected animal sacrifice, which by then was a central element in Brahmanic power. Even more important, both religions tacitly rejected the caste system, accepting people of any caste into their ranks. In response to this challenge, over the next several centuries (ca. 400 B.C.E.–200 C.E.) the Brahmanic religion evolved in a more devotional direction, today commonly called Hinduism. In Hinduism Brahmans retained their high social status, but it became possible for individual worshipers to have more direct contact with the gods, showing their devotion to them without the aid of priests as intermediaries.

The bedrock of Hinduism is the belief that the Vedas are sacred revelations and that a specific caste system is implicitly prescribed in them. Hinduism is a guide to life, the goal of which is to reach union with brahman, the ground of all being. There are four steps in this search, progressing from study of the Vedas in youth to complete asceticism in old age. In their

● **Shiva** One of the three most important Vedic gods, Shiva represented both destruction and procreation. Here Shiva, mounted on a bull and carrying a spear, attacks the demon Andhaka. Shiva is seen as a fierce and bloodthirsty warrior. *(C. M. Dixon/Ancient Art & Architecture Collection)*

dharma *The moral law that Hindus observe in their quest for brahman.*

quest for brahman, people are to observe **dharma,** the moral law. Dharma stipulates the legitimate pursuits of Hindus: material gain, as long as it is honestly and honorably achieved; pleasure and love, for the perpetuation of the family; and moksha, release from the wheel of life and unity with brahman. Because it recognizes the need for material gain and pleasure, Hinduism allows a joyful embracing of life.

Hinduism assumes that there are innumerable legitimate ways of worshiping the supreme principle of life. Consequently, it readily incorporates new sects, doctrines, beliefs, rites, and deities. After the third century B.C.E., Hinduism began to emphasize the roles and personalities of thousands of powerful gods. Brahma, the creator; Shiva, the cosmic dancer who both creates and destroys; and Vishnu, the preserver and sustainer of creation, are three main male deities. Female deities included Lakshmi, goddess of wealth, and Saraswati, goddess of learning and music. People could reach brahman by devotion to personal gods, usually represented by images. A worshiper's devotion to one god did not entail denial of other deities; ultimately all were manifestations of the divine force that pervades the universe.

A central ethical text of Hinduism is the *Bhagavad Gita,* a part of the world's longest ancient epic, the *Mahabharata.* The *Bhagavad Gita* offers guidance on the most serious problem facing a Hindu—how to live in the world and yet honor dharma and thus achieve release. The heart of the *Bhagavad Gita* is the spiritual conflict confronting Arjuna, a human hero about to ride into battle against his kinsmen. As he surveys the battlefield, struggling with the grim notion of killing his relatives, Arjuna voices his doubts to his charioteer, none other than the god Krishna. When at last Arjuna refuses to spill his family's blood, Krishna instructs him on the true meaning of Hinduism:

You grieve for those beyond grief,
and you speak words of insight;
but learned men do not grieve
for the dead or the living.

Never have I not existed,
nor you, nor these kings;
and never in the future
shall we cease to exist.

Just as the embodied self
enters childhood, youth, and old age,
so does it enter another body;
this does not confound a steadfast man.

Contacts with matter make us feel
heat and cold, pleasure and pain.
Arjuna, you must learn to endure
fleeting things—they come and go!

When these cannot torment a man,
when suffering and joy are equal
for him and he has courage,
he is fit for immortality.

Nothing of nonbeing comes to be,
nor does being cease to exist;
the boundary between these two
is seen by men who see reality.

Indestructible is the presence
that pervades all this;
no one can destroy
this unchanging reality.

Our bodies are known to end,
but the embodied self is enduring,
indestructible, and immeasurable;
therefore, Arjuna, fight the battle!

He who thinks this self a killer
and he who thinks it killed,
both fail to understand;
it does not kill, nor is it killed.

It is not born,
it does not die;
having been,
it will never not be;
unborn, enduring,
constant, and primordial,
it is not killed
when the body is killed.[1]

Krishna then clarifies the relationship between human reality and the eternal spirit. He explains compassionately to Arjuna the duty to act—to live in the world and carry out his duties as a warrior. Indeed, the *Bhagavad Gita* emphasizes the necessity of action, which is essential for the welfare of the world. Arjuna makes it the warrior's duty to wage war in compliance with his dharma. Only those who live within the divine law without complaint will be released from rebirth. One person's dharma may be different from another's, but both individuals must follow their own dharmas.

Besides providing a religion of enormous emotional appeal, Hinduism also inspired the preservation, in Sanskrit and the major regional languages of India, of literary masterpieces. Among these are the *Puranas,* which are stories of the gods and great warrior clans, and the *Mahabharata* and *Ramayana,* which are verse epics of India's early kings. Hinduism also validated the caste system, adding to the stability of everyday village life, since people all knew where they stood in society.

● ● ● ● ● ● ● ● ● ● ● ● ● ● ● ● ● ● ● ●

INDIA AND THE WEST
(CA. 513–298 B.C.E.)

How did India respond to the expansion of the Persian and Greek empires?

In the late sixth century B.C.E., west India was swept up in events that were changing the face of the ancient Middle East. During this period the Persians were creating an empire that stretched from the west coast of Anatolia to the Indus River (see pages 20–22). India became involved in these events when the Persian emperor Darius conquered the Indus Valley and Kashmir about 513 B.C.E.

Persian control did not reach eastward beyond the Punjab. Even so, it fostered increased contact between India and the Middle East and led to the introduction of new ideas, techniques, and materials into India. From Persian administrators Indians learned more about how to rule large tracts of land and huge numbers of people. They also learned the technique of minting silver coins, and they adopted the Persian monetary standard to facilitate trade with other parts of the empire. Even states in the Ganges Valley, which were never part of the Persian Empire, adopted the use of coinage.

Another result of contact with Persia was introduction of the Aramaic script, used to write the official language of the Persian Empire. To keep records and publish proclamations just as the Persians did, Indians in northwest India adapted the Aramaic script for writing several local languages (elsewhere, Indians developed the Brahmi script, the ancestor of the script used for modern Hindi). In time the sacred texts of the Buddhists and the Jains, as well as the epics and other literary works, all came to be recorded.

The Persian Empire in turn succumbed to Alexander the Great, and in 326 B.C.E. Alexander led his Macedonian and Greek troops through the Khyber Pass into the Indus Valley (see page 89). The India that Alexander encountered was composed of many rival states. He defeated some of these states in the northwest and heard reports of others. Porus, king of west Punjab, fought Alexander with a battalion of two thousand war elephants. After being defeated, he agreed to become a subordinate king under Alexander.

Alexander had heard of the sophistication of Indian philosophers and summoned some to instruct him or debate with him. The Greeks were impressed with Taxila, a major center of trade in the Punjab (see Map 2.1), and described it as "a city great and prosperous, the biggest of those between the Indus River and the Hydaspes [the modern Jhelum River]—a region not inferior to Egypt in size, with especially good pastures and rich in fine fruits."[2] From Taxila, Alexander followed the Indus River south, hoping to find the end of the world. His men, however, mutinied and refused to continue. When Alexander turned back, he left his general Seleucus in charge of his easternmost region.

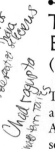

THE MAURYAN EMPIRE (CA. 322–185 B.C.E.)

What were the consequences of the unification of much of India by Chandragupta and Ashoka?

The one to benefit most from Alexander's invasion was Chandragupta the ruler of a growing state in the Ganges Valley. He took advantage of the crisis caused by Alexander's invasion to expand his territories, and by 322 B.C.E. he had made himself sole master of north India. In 304 B.C.E. he defeated the forces of Seleucus.

With stunning effectiveness, Chandragupta applied the lessons learned from Persian rule. He adopted the Persian practice of dividing the area into provinces. Each province was assigned a governor, usually drawn from Chandragupta's own family. He established a complex bureaucracy to see to the operation of the state and a bureaucratic taxation system that financed public services through taxes on agriculture. He also built a regular army, complete with departments for everything from naval matters to the collection of supplies.

From his capital at Pataliputra in the Ganges Valley (now Patna in Bihar), Chandragupta sent agents to the provinces to oversee the workings of government and to keep him informed of conditions in his realm. For the first time in Indian history, one man governed most of the subcontinent, exercising control through delegated power. In designing his bureaucratic system, Chandragupta enjoyed the able assistance of his great minister Kautilya, who wrote a treatise on how a king should seize, hold, and manipulate power, rather like the Legalist treatises produced in China later that century (see pages 70–71). Kautilya urged the king to use propaganda to gain support—for instance, to disguise secret agents to look like gods so that people would be awed when they saw him in their company. The king was also alerted to the fact that all his immediate neighbors were his enemies but the princes directly beyond them were his natural friends. When a neighboring prince was in trouble, that was the perfect time to attack him. Interstate relations were likened to the law of the fish: the large swallow the small.

Megasthenes, a Greek ambassador sent by Seleucus to Chandragupta's court, left a lively description of life there. He described the city as square and surrounded by wooden walls, twenty-two miles on each side, with 570 towers and 64 gates. It had a university, a library, and magnificent palaces, temples, gardens, and parks. The king personally presided over court sessions where legal cases were heard and petitions received. The king claimed for the state all mines and forests, and there were large state farms, granaries, shipyards, and spinning and weaving factories. Even prostitution was controlled by the state.

Megasthenes described Chandragupta as afraid of treachery and attempts at assassination:

Attendance on the king's person is the duty of women, who indeed are bought from their fathers. Outside the gates of the palace stand the bodyguards and the rest of the soldiers. . . . Nor does the king sleep during the day, and at night he is forced at various hours to change his bed because of those plotting against him. Of his non-military departures from the palace one is to the courts, in which he passes the day hearing cases to the end, even if the hour arrives for attendance on his person. . . . When he leaves to hunt, he is thickly surrounded by a circle of women, and on the outside by spear-carrying bodyguards. The road is fenced off with ropes, and to anyone who passes within the ropes as far as the women death is the penalty.[3]

Those measures apparently worked, as Chandragupta lived a long life. According to Jain tradition, Chandragupta became a Jain ascetic and died a peaceful death in 298 B.C.E. Although he personally adopted a nonviolent philosophy, he left behind a kingdom with the military might to maintain order and defend India from invasion.

The Reign of Ashoka (ca. 269–232 B.C.E.)

The years after Chandragupta's death were an epoch of political greatness, thanks largely to his grandson Ashoka, one of India's most remarkable figures. The era of Ashoka was enormously important in the religious history of the world, because Ashoka embraced Buddhism and promoted its spread beyond India.

As a young prince, Ashoka served as governor of two prosperous provinces where Buddhism flourished. At the death of his father about 274 B.C.E., Ashoka rebelled against his older brother, who had succeeded to the throne, and after four years of fighting won his bid for the throne. Crowned king, Ashoka ruled intelligently and energetically. He was equally serious about his pleasures, especially those of the banquet hall and harem.

In the ninth year of his reign, 261 B.C.E., Ashoka conquered Kalinga, on the east coast of India. In a grim and savage campaign, Ashoka reduced Kalinga by wholesale slaughter. As Ashoka himself admitted, "One hundred and fifty thousand were forcibly abducted from their homes, 100,000 were killed in battle, and many more died later on."[4] Instead of exulting like a conqueror, however, Ashoka was consumed with remorse and revulsion at the horror of war. He embraced Buddhism and used the machinery of his empire to spread Buddhist teachings throughout India. He supported the doctrine of not hurting humans or animals, then spreading among religious people of all sects. He banned animal sacrifices, and in place of hunting expeditions, he took pilgrimages. Two years after his conversion, he undertook a 256-day pilgrimage to all the holy sites of Buddhism, and on his return he sent missionaries to all known countries. Buddhist tradition also credits him with erecting eighty-four thousand stupas (Buddhist reliquary mounds) throughout India, among which the ashes or other bodily remains of the Buddha were distributed, beginning the association of Buddhism with monumental art and architecture.

Ashoka's remarkable crisis of conscience, like the later conversion to Christianity of the Roman emperor Constantine (see pages 126–127), affected the way he ruled. He emphasized compassion, nonviolence, and adherence to dharma. He appointed officials to oversee the moral welfare of the realm and required local officials to govern humanely. He may have perceived dharma as a kind of civic virtue, a universal ethical model capable of uniting the diverse peoples of his extensive empire. Ashoka erected stone pillars, on the Persian model, with inscriptions to inform the people of his policies. He also had long inscriptions carved into large rock surfaces near trade routes. In one inscription he spoke to his people like a father:

Whatever good I have done has indeed been accomplished for the progress and welfare of the world. By these shall grow virtues namely: proper support of mother and father, regard for preceptors and elders, proper treatment of Brahmans and ascetics, of the poor and the destitute, slaves and servants.[5]

These inscriptions are the earliest fully dated Indian texts. (Until the script in which they were written was deciphered in 1837, nothing was known of Ashoka's achievements.) The pillars on which they are inscribed are also the first examples of Indian art to survive since the end of the Indus civilization.

Ashoka felt the need to protect his new religion and to keep it pure. He warned Buddhist monks that he would not tolerate schism—divisions based on differences of opinion about doctrine or ritual. According to Buddhist tradition, a great council of Buddhist monks was held at Pataliputra, where the earliest canon of Buddhist texts was codified. At the same time, Ashoka honored India's other religions, even building

● **Ashokan Pillar** The best preserved of the pillars that King Ashoka erected in about 240 B.C.E. is this one in the Bihar region, near Nepal. The solid shaft of polished sandstone rises 32 feet in the air. It weighs about 50 tons, making its erection a remarkable feat of engineering. Like other Ashokan pillars, it is inscribed with accounts of Ashoka's political achievements and instructions to his subjects on proper behavior. These pillars are the earliest extant examples of Indian writing and a major historical source for the Mauryan period. *(Borromeo/ Art Resource, NY)*

shrines for Hindu and Jain worshipers. In one edict he banned rowdy popular fairs, allowing only religious gatherings.

Despite his devotion to Buddhism, Ashoka never neglected his duties as emperor. He tightened the central government of the empire and kept a close check on local officials. He also built roads and rest spots to improve communication within the realm. Ashoka himself described this work: "On the highways Banyan trees have been planted so that they may afford shade to men and animals; mango-groves have been planted; watering-places have been established for the benefit of animals and men."[6] These measures also facilitated the march of armies and the armed enforcement of Ashoka's authority.

Ashoka's inscriptions indirectly tell us much about the Mauryan Empire. He directly administered the central part of the empire, focusing on Magadha. Beyond it were four large provinces, under princes who served as viceroys, each with its own sets of smaller districts and officials. The interior of south India was described as inhabited by undefeated forest tribes. Farther south, along the coasts, were peoples that Ashoka maintained friendly relations with but did not rule, such as the Cholas and Pandyas. Relations with Sri Lanka were especially close under Ashoka, and the king sent a branch of the tree under which the Buddha gained enlightenment to the Sri Lankan king. According to Buddhist legend, Ashoka's son Mahinda traveled to Sri Lanka to convert the people there.

Ashoka ruled for thirty-seven years. After he died in about 232 B.C.E., the Mauryan dynasty went into decline, and India broke up into smaller units, much like those in existence before Alexander's invasion. Even though Chandragupta had instituted bureaucratic methods of centralized political control and Ashoka had vigorously pursued the political and cultural integration of the empire, the institutions they created were not entrenched enough to survive periods with weaker kings.

● ● ● ● ● ● ● ● ● ● ● ● ● ● ● ● ● ●

SMALL STATES AND TRADING NETWORKS (200 B.C.E.–300 C.E.)

How was India shaped by political disunity and contacts with other cultures?

After the Mauryan dynasty collapsed in 185 B.C.E., and for much of subsequent Indian history, political unity would be the exception rather than the rule. By this time, however, key elements of Indian culture—the caste system; the religious traditions of Hinduism, Buddhism, and Jainism; and the great epics and legends—had given India a cultural unity strong enough to endure even without political unity.

In the years after the fall of the Mauryan dynasty, a series of foreign powers dominated the Indus Valley and adjoining regions. The first were hybrid Indo-Greek states ruled by the inheritors of Alexander's defunct empire stationed in what is now Afghanistan. The city of Taxila became a major center of trade, culture, and education, fusing elements of Greek and Indian culture.

The great, slow movement of nomadic peoples out of East Asia that brought the Scythians to the Middle East brought the Shakas to northwest India. They controlled the region from about 94 to 20 B.C.E., when they were displaced by a new nomadic invader, the Kushans, who ruled the region of today's Afghanistan, Pakistan, and west India as far south as Gujarat. Their king Kanishka (r. ca. 78–ca. 103 C.E.) is known from Buddhist sources. The famous silk trade from China to Rome (see pages 140–141) passed through his territory.

During the Kushan period, Greek culture had a considerable impact on Indian art. Indo-Greek artists and sculptors working in India adorned Buddhist shrines, modeling the earliest representation of the Buddha on Hellenistic statues of Apollo.

Another contribution from the Indo-Greek states was coins cast with images of the king, which came to be widely adopted by Indian rulers, aiding commerce and adding evidence to the historical record. Cultural exchange also went in the other direction. Old Indian animal folktales were translated into Syriac and Greek and from that source eventually made their way to Europe. South India in this period was also the center of active seaborne trade, with networks reaching all the way to Rome. Indian sailing technology was highly advanced, and much of this trade was in the hands of Indian merchants. Roman traders based in Egypt followed the routes already used by Arab traders, sailing with the monsoon from the Red Sea to the west coast of India in about two weeks, returning about six months later when the direction of the winds reversed. In the first century C.E. a Greek merchant involved in this trade reported that the traders sold coins, topaz, coral, crude glass, copper, tin, and lead and bought pearls, ivory, silk (probably originally from China), jewels of many sorts (probably many from Southeast Asia), and above all cinnamon and pepper. More Roman gold coins of the first and second centuries C.E. have been found near the southern tip of India than in any other area. The local rulers had slits made across the image of the Roman emperor to show that his sovereignty was not recognized, but they had no objection to the coins' circulating. (By contrast, the Kushan rulers in the north had Roman coins melted down to use to make coins with their own images on them.)

Even after the fall of Rome, many of the traders on the southwest coast of India remained. These diasporic communities of Christians and Jews lived in the coastal cities into modern times. When Vasco da Gama, the Portuguese explorer, reached Calicut in 1498, he found a local Jewish merchant who was able to interpret for him.

During these centuries there were significant advances in science, mathematics, and philosophy. This was also the period when Indian law was codified. The **Code of Manu,** which lays down family, caste, and commercial law, was compiled in the second or third century C.E.

Regional cultures tend to flourish when there is no dominant unifying state. In south India the third century B.C.E. to the third century C.E. is considered the classical period of Tamil culture, when many great works of literature were written under the patronage of the regional kings. Some of the poems take a hard look at war:

Harvest of War

Great king
you shield your men from ruin,
so your victories, your greatness
are bywords.

Loose chariot wheels
lie about the battleground
with the long white tusks
of bull-elephants.

Flocks of male eagles
eat carrion
with their mates.

Headless bodies
dance about
before they fall
to the ground.

Blood glows,
like the sky before nightfall,
in the red center
of the battlefield.

Demons dance there.
And your kingdom
is an unfailing harvest
of victorious wars.[7]

● **Kushan Gold Coin**
Kanishka I had coins made depicting a standing Buddha with his right hand raised in a gesture of renunciation. The reverse side shows the king performing a sacrifice, the legend reading "Kanishka the Kushan, king of kings." *(Courtesy of the Trustees of the British Museum)*

Code of Manu *The codification of Indian law from the second or third century C.E.; it lays down family, caste, and commercial law.*

**Primary Source:
The Laws of Manu**
See how the principle of dharma justifies the traditional roles of men and women, and of priests, warriors, merchants, and servants in Hindu society.

Chapter Summary

To assess your mastery of this chapter, go to
bedfordstmartins.com/mckayworld

Key Terms

Harappan
Aryans
Rigveda
raja
Brahmans
caste system
varna
outcastes
samsara
karma
moksha
brahman
Four Noble Truths
Eightfold Path
nirvana
sutras
Mahayana
bodhisattvas
dharma
Code of Manu

• *What does archaeology tell us about the earliest civilization in India?*

From archaeology, we know that the Harappan civilization emerged in the Indus River valley in the third millennium B.C.E. The large cities that have been excavated were made of kiln-dried brick and were carefully planned, with straight streets and sewers. Although many intriguing artifacts have been excavated, many questions remain about this civilization, and its script has not been deciphered. Scholars can only speculate why Harappan cities were largely abandoned by 1800 B.C.E.

• *What kind of society and culture did the Indo-European Aryans create?*

From originally oral texts like the *Rigveda*, we know much about the values and social practices of the Aryans, speakers of an early form of Sanskrit (which is an Indo-European language). In the period 1500–500 B.C.E. Aryan warrior tribes fought using chariots and bronze swords and spears, gradually expanding into the Ganges River valley. The first stages of the Indian caste system date to this period, when warriors and priests were ranked above merchants, artisans, and farmers. Key religious ideas that date to this period are the notions of karma and rebirth and the importance of sacrifice.

• *What ideas and practices were taught by the founders of Jainism, Buddhism, and Hinduism?*

Beginning around 500 B.C.E. three of India's major religions emerged. Mahavira was the founder of the Jain religion. He taught his followers to live ascetic lives, avoid doing harm to any living thing, and renounce evil thoughts and actions. The founder of Buddhism, Siddhartha Gautama or the Buddha, similarly taught his followers a path to liberation that involved avoiding violence and freeing themselves from desires. The Buddha, however, did not think extreme asceticism was the best path and put more emphasis on mental detachment. In response to the popularity of Jainism and Buddhism, both of which rejected animal sacrifice and ignored the caste system, the traditional Brahmanic religion evolved in a devotional direction that has been called Hinduism. Hindu traditions validated sacrifice and caste but stressed the individual's relationship to the gods he or she worshiped.

• *How did India respond to the expansion of the Persian and Greek empires?*

In the sixth century B.C.E. the Persian empire expanded into the Indus River valley, and in the fourth century Alexander the Great's troops took the same region. From contact with the Persians and Greeks, new political techniques, ideas, and art styles entered the Indian repertoire.

• *What were the consequences of the unification of much of India by Chandragupta and Ashoka?*

Shortly after the arrival of the Greeks, much of north India was politically unified by the Mauryan Empire. Its greatest ruler was Ashoka, who converted to Buddhism and promoted its spread outside India. The inscriptions he had carved on stones and erected many places in his empire provide some of the best-dated sources on early Indian history.

• How was India shaped by political disunity and contacts with other cultures?

After the decline of the Mauryan empire, India was politically fragmented. Indian cultural identity remained strong, however, because of shared religious ideas and shared literature, including the great early epics. Trade and other contact with the outside world brought new elements into Indian civilization. And just as India came to absorb some Persian bureaucratic techniques and Greek artistic styles, other regions borrowed crops, textiles, inventions, and religious ideas from India.

Suggested Reading

Basham, A. L. *The Wonder That Was India,* 3d rev. ed. 1968. Classic, appreciative account of early Indian civilization by a scholar deeply immersed in Indian literature.

Embree, Ainslee, ed. *Sources of Indian Tradition,* 2d ed. 1988. An excellent introduction to Indian religion, philosophy, and intellectual history through translations of major sources.

Koller, John M. *The Indian Way,* 2d ed. 2004. An accessible introduction to the variety of Indian religions and philosophies.

Kulke, Hermann, and Dietmar Rothermund. *A History of India,* 3d ed. 1998. A good, balanced introduction to Indian history.

Lopez, Donald S., Jr. *The Story of the Buddha: A Concise Guide to Its History and Teachings.* 2001. Puts emphasis on Buddhist practice, drawing examples from many different countries and time periods.

Miller, Barbara, trans. *The Bhagavad-Gita: Krishna's Counsel in Time of War.* 1986. One of several excellent translations of India's classical literature.

Possehl, Gregory L. *The Indus Civilization.* 2002. Recent overview of Harappan civilization.

Renfew, Colin. *Archaeology and Language: The Puzzle of Indo-European Origins.* 1987. Analyzes the question of the origins of the Aryans in depth.

Scharff, Harmut. *The State in Indian Tradition.* 1989. A scholarly analysis of the period from the Aryans to the Muslims.

Thapar, Romilia. *Early India to 1300.* A freshly revised overview by a leading Indian historian.

Notes

1. Excerpt from Barbara Stoler Miller, trans., *The Bhagavad-gita: Krishna's Counsel in Time of War* (New York: Columbia University Press, 1986), pp. 31–32. Translation copyright © 1986 by Barbara Stoler Miller. Used by permission of Bantam Books, a division of Random House, Inc.

2. Arrian, *Anabasis* 5.8.2; Plutarch, *Alexander* 59.1. Translated by John Buckler.

3. *Strabo,* 15.1.55. Translated by John Buckler.

4. Quoted in H. Kulke and D. Rothermund, *A History of India,* 3d ed. (London: Routledge, 1998), p. 62.

5. Quoted in B. G. Gokhale, *Asoka Maurya* (New York: Twayne Publishers, 1966), p. 169.

6. Quoted ibid., pp. 168–169.

7. A. K. Ramanujan, ed. and trans., *Poems of Love and War: From the Eight Anthologies and the Ten Long Poems of Classical Tamil* (New York: Columbia University Press, 1985), p. 115. Copyright 1985 by Columbia University Press. Reproduced with permission of Columbia University Press in the format Textbook via Copyright Clearance Center.

Listening to the PAST

Rama and Sita

The Ramayana, *an epic poem of about fifty thousand verses, is attributed to the third-century* B.C.E. *poet Valmiki. Its main character, Rama, the oldest son of a king, is an incarnation of the great god Vishnu. As a young man, he wins the princess Sita as his wife when he alone among her suitors proves strong enough to bend a huge bow. Rama and Sita love each other deeply, but court intrigue disturbs their happy life. After the king announces that he will retire and consecrate Rama as his heir, the king's beautiful junior wife, wishing to advance her own son, reminds the king that he has promised her a favor of her choice. She then asks to have him appoint her son heir and to have Rama sent into the wilderness for fourteen years. The king is forced to consent, and Rama obeys his father.*

The passage below gives the conversations between Rama and Sita after Rama learns he must leave. In subsequent parts of the very long epic, the lovers undergo many other tribulations, including Sita's abduction by the lord of the demons, the ten-headed Ravana, and her eventual recovery by Rama with the aid of monkeys.

The Ramayana *eventually appeared in numerous versions in all the major languages of India. Hearing it recited was said to bring religious merit. Sita, passionate in her devotion to her husband, has remained the favorite Indian heroine. Rama, Sita, and the monkey Hanuman are cult figures in Hinduism, with temples devoted to their worship.*

"For fourteen years I must live in Dandaka, while my father will appoint Bharata prince regent. I have come to see you before I leave for the desolate forest. You are never to boast of me in the presence of Bharata. Men in power cannot bear to hear others praised, and so you must never boast of my virtues in front of Bharata. . . . When I have gone to the forest where sages make their home, my precious, blameless wife, you must earnestly undertake vows and fasts. You must rise early and worship the gods according to custom and then pay homage to my father Dasaratha, lord of men. And my aged mother Kausalya, who is tormented by misery, deserves your respect as well, for she has subordinated all to righteousness. The rest of my mothers, too, must always receive your homage. . . . My beloved, I am going to the great forest, and you must stay here. You must do as I tell you, my lovely, and not give offense to anyone."

So Rama spoke, and Sita, who always spoke kindly to her husband and deserved kindness from him, grew angry just because she loved him, and said, "My lord, a man's father, his mother, brother, son, or daughter-in-law all experience the effects of their own past deeds and suffer an individual fate. But a wife, and she alone, bull among men, must share her husband's fate. Therefore I, too, have been ordered to live in the forest. It is not her father or mother, not her son or friends or herself, but her husband, and he alone, who gives a woman permanent refuge in this world and after death. If you must leave this very day for the trackless forest, Rama, I will go in front of you, softening the thorns and sharp *kusa* grass. Cast out your anger and resentment, like so much water left after drinking one's fill. Do not be reluctant to take me, my mighty husband. There is no evil in me. The shadow of a husband's feet in any circumstances surpasses the finest mansions, an aerial chariot, or even flying through the sky. . . . O Rama, bestower of honor, you have the power to protect any other person in the forest. Why then not me? . . .

"If I were to be offered a place to live in heaven itself, Rama, tiger among men, I would refuse it if you were not there. I will go to the trackless forest teeming with deer, monkeys, and elephants, and live there as in my father's house, clinging to your feet alone, in strict self-discipline. I love no one else; my heart is so attached to you that were we to be parted I am resolved to die. Take me, oh please grant my request. I shall not be a burden to you." . . .

When Sita finished speaking, the righteous prince, who knew what was right and cherished it, attempted to dissuade her. . . .

"Sita, give up this notion of living in the forest. The name 'forest' is given only to wild regions where hardships abound. . . . There are lions that live in mountain caves; their roars are redoubled by mountain torrents and are a painful thing to hear—the forest is

Rama and Sita in the forest, from a set of miniature paintings done in about 1600. (National Museum, New Delhi)

a place of pain. At night worn with fatigue, one must sleep upon the ground on a bed of leaves, broken off of themselves—the forest is a place of utter pain. And one has to fast, Sita, to the limit of one's endurance, wear clothes of barkcloth and bear the burden of matted hair. . . . There are many creeping creatures, of every size and shape, my lovely, ranging aggressively over the ground. . . . Moths, scorpions, worms, gnats, and flies continually harass one, my frail Sita—the forest is wholly a place of pain. . . ."

Sita was overcome with sorrow when she heard what Rama said. With tears trickling down her face, she answered him in a faint voice. . . . "If from feelings of love I follow you, my pure-hearted husband, I shall have no sin to answer for, because my husband is my deity. My union with you is sacred and shall last even beyond death. . . . If you refuse to take me to the forest despite the sorrow that I feel, I shall have no recourse but to end my life by poison, fire, or water."

Though she pleaded with him in this and every other way to be allowed to go, great-armed Rama would not consent to taking her to the desolate forest. And when he told her as much, Sita fell to brooding, and drenched the ground, it seemed, with the hot tears that fell from her eyes. . . . She was nearly insensible with sorrow when Rama took her in his arms and comforted her. . . . "Without knowing your true feelings, my lovely, I could not consent to your living in the wilderness, though I am perfectly capable of protecting you. Since you are determined to live with me in the forest, Sita, I could no sooner abandon you than a self-respecting man his reputation. . . . My father keeps to the path of righteousness and truth, and I wish to act just as he instructs me. That is the eternal way of righteousness. Follow me, my timid one, be my companion in righteousness. Go now and bestow precious objects on the brahmans, give food to the mendicants and all who ask for it. Hurry, there is no time to waste."

Finding that her husband had acquiesced in her going, the lady was elated and set out at once to make the donations.

Questions for Analysis

1. What can you infer about early Indian family life and social relations from this story?

2. What do Sita's words and actions indicate about women's roles in Indian society of the time?

3. What do you think accounts for the continuing popularity of the story of Rama throughout Indian history?

Source: *The Ramayana of Valmiki: An Epic of India, vol. 2: Ayodhyakanda,* trans. Sheldon I. Pollock, ed. Robert P. Goldman (Princeton, N.J.: Princeton University Press, 1986), pp. 134–142, modified slightly. Copyright © 1986 by Princeton University Press. Reprinted by permission of Princeton University Press.

Bronze Vessel (twelfth century B.C.E.). About 10 inches tall, this bronze is covered with symmetrical animal imagery, including stylized *taotie* masks. *(The Metropolitan Museum of Art. Purchase, Arthur M. Sackler Gift, 1974 [1974.268.2ab]. Photograph © 1979 The Metropolitan Museum of Art)*

chapter

3 CHINA'S CLASSICAL AGE, TO 256 B.C.E.

The early development of China's civilization occurred with little contact with the other early civilizations of Eurasia. The reason for China's relative isolation was geographic: communication with West and South Asia was very difficult, impeded by high mountains and vast deserts. Thus, in comparison to India and the ancient Middle East, there was less cross-fertilization through trade and other contact with other comparably advanced civilizations. Moreover, there were no cultural breaks comparable to the rise of the Aryans in India or the Assyrians in Mesopotamia; there were no new peoples bringing new languages.

The impact of early China's relative isolation is found in many distinctive or unique features of its culture. Perhaps the most important is its writing system. Unlike the other major societies of Eurasia, China retained a logographic writing system with a separate symbol for each word. This writing system shaped not only Chinese literature and thought but also key social and political processes, such as the nature of the ruling class and the way Chinese interacted with non-Chinese.

Chinese history is commonly discussed in terms of a succession of dynasties. The Shang Dynasty (ca. 1500–ca. 1050 B.C.E.) was the first to have writing, metalworking, cities, and chariots. The Shang kings played priestly roles, serving as intermediaries with both their royal ancestors and the high god Di. The Shang were overthrown by one of their vassal states, which founded the Zhou Dynasty (ca. 1050–256 B.C.E.). The Zhou rulers set up a decentralized feudal governmental structure. After several centuries, this structure evolved into a multistate system. As warfare between the states intensified from the sixth century B.C.E. on, social and cultural change also quickened. Aristocratic privileges declined, and China entered one of its most creative periods, when the philosophies of Confucianism, Daoism, and Legalism were developed.

THE EMERGENCE OF CIVILIZATION IN CHINA

When, where, and how did writing, bronze technology, and other elements of civilization develop in China?

The term *China,* like the term *India,* does not refer to the same geographical entity at all points in history. The historical China, also called China proper, was smaller than present-day China, not larger like the historical India. The contemporary People's Republic of China includes Tibet, Inner Mongolia, Turkestan, Manchuria, and other territories that in premodern times were not inhabited by Chinese or ruled directly by Chinese states (see Map 3.1).

China proper, about a thousand miles north to south and east to west, occupies much of the temperate zone of East Asia. The northern part, drained by the Huang (Yellow) River, is colder, flatter, and more arid than the south. Rainfall in many areas is less than twenty inches a year, making the land well suited to crops like wheat and millet. The dominant soil is **loess**—fine wind-driven earth that is fertile and easy to work even with primitive tools. Because so much of the loess ends up as silt in the Huang River, the riverbed rises and easily floods unless diked. Drought is another perennial problem for farmers in the north. The Yangzi River is the dominant feature of the warmer, wetter, and more lush south, a region well suited to rice cultivation and double cropping. The Yangzi and its many tributaries are navigable, so boats were traditionally the preferred means of transportation in the south.

Mountains, deserts, and grasslands separated China proper from other early civilizations. Between China and India lay Tibet, with its vast mountain ranges and high plateaus. North of Tibet are great expanses of desert where nothing grows except in rare oases, and north of the desert stretch grasslands from the Ukraine to eastern Siberia. Chinese civilization did not spread into any of these Inner Asian regions, above all because they were not suited to crop agriculture. Inner Asia, where raising animals is a more productive use of land than planting crops, became the heartland of China's traditional enemies, such as the Xiongnu and Mongols.

loess *Soil deposited by wind. It is fertile and easy to work.*

● **Neolithic Jade Plaque** This small plaque (2.5 inches by 3.25 inches), dating from about 2000 B.C.E., is similar to others of the Liangzhu area near modern Shanghai. It is incised to depict a human figure who merges into a monster mask. The lower part could be interpreted as his arms and legs but at the same time resembles a monster mask with bulging eyes, prominent nostrils, and a large mouth. *(Zheijiang Provincial Institute of Archaeology/Cultural Relics Publishing House)*

The Neolithic Age

From about 10,000 B.C.E. agriculture was practiced in China, apparently originating independently of somewhat earlier developments in Egypt and Mesopotamia, but perhaps influenced by developments in Southeast Asia, where rice was also cultivated very early. By 5000 B.C.E. there were Neolithic village settlements in several regions of China. The primary Neolithic crops were drought-resistant millet, grown in the loess soils of the north, and rice, grown in the wetlands of the lower reaches of the Yangzi River, where it was supplemented by fish. In both areas pigs, dogs, and cattle were domesticated, and by 3000 B.C.E. sheep had become important in the north and water buffalo in the south.

Over the course of the fifth to third millennia B.C.E., many distinct regional Neolithic cultures emerged. For instance, in the northwest during the fourth and third millennia B.C.E., people made fine red pottery vessels decorated in black pigment with bold designs, including spirals, sawtooth lines, and zoomorphic stick figures. At the same time in the east, pottery was rarely painted but was made into distinctive shapes, including three-legged, deep-bodied tripods. Jade ornaments, blades, and ritual objects, sometimes of extraordinary craftsmanship, have been found in several eastern sites but are rare in western ones.

Over time Neolithic cultures came to share more by way of material culture and social and cultural practices. Many practices related to treatment of the dead spread out of their original area, including use of coffins, ramped chambers, large numbers of grave goods, and divination based on interpreting cracks in cattle bones. Fortified walls, made of rammed earth, came to be built around settlements in many areas, suggesting not only increased contact but also increased conflict.

The Shang Dynasty
(ca. 1500–ca. 1050 B.C.E.)

After 2000 B.C.E. a Bronze Age civilization appeared in north China with the traits found in Bronze Age civilizations elsewhere, such as writing, metalworking, domestication of the horse, class stratification, and cult centers. These findings can be linked to the Shang Dynasty, long known from early texts.

Shang civilization was not as densely urban as Mesopotamia, but Shang kings ruled from large settlements. The best excavated is **Anyang,** from which the Shang kings ruled for more than two centuries. At the center of Anyang were large palaces, temples, and altars. These buildings were constructed on rammed-earth foundations (a feature of Chinese building practice that would last for centuries). Outside the central core were industrial areas where bronzeworkers, potters, stone carvers, and other artisans lived and worked. Many homes were built partly below ground level, probably as a way to conserve heat. Beyond these urban settlements were farming areas and large forests. Deer, bears, tigers, wild boars, elephants, and rhinoceros were still plentiful in north China in this era.

The divinatory texts found in the royal tombs at Anyang show that Shang kings were military chieftains. The king regularly sent out armies of three thousand to five thousand men on campaigns, and when not at war they would go on hunts lasting for months. They fought rebellious vassals and foreign tribes, but the situation constantly changed as vassals became enemies and enemies accepted offers of alliance. War booty was an important source of the king's revenue, especially the war captives who could be made into slaves. Captives not needed as slaves might end up as sacrificial victims—or perhaps the demands of the gods and ancestors for sacrifices were a motive for going to war.

Bronze-tipped spears and halberds were widely used by Shang warriors. Bronze was also used for the fittings of the chariots that came into use around 1200 B.C.E., probably as a result of diffusion across Asia. The chariot provided commanders with a mobile station from which they could supervise their troops; it also gave archers and soldiers armed with long halberds increased mobility.

Shang power did not rest solely on military supremacy. The Shang king was also the high priest, the one best qualified to offer sacrifices to the royal ancestors and the high god Di. Royal ancestors were viewed as able to intervene with Di, send curses, produce dreams, assist the king in battle, and so on. The king divined his ancestors' wishes by interpreting the cracks made in heated cattle bones or tortoise shells prepared for him by professional diviners.

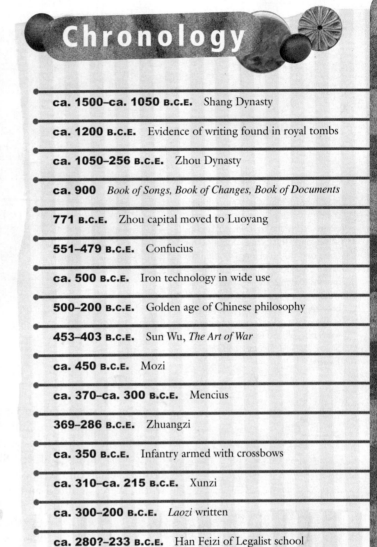

Chronology

ca. 1500–ca. 1050 B.C.E.	Shang Dynasty
ca. 1200 B.C.E.	Evidence of writing found in royal tombs
ca. 1050–256 B.C.E.	Zhou Dynasty
ca. 900	*Book of Songs, Book of Changes, Book of Documents*
771 B.C.E.	Zhou capital moved to Luoyang
551–479 B.C.E.	Confucius
ca. 500 B.C.E.	Iron technology in wide use
500–200 B.C.E.	Golden age of Chinese philosophy
453–403 B.C.E.	Sun Wu, *The Art of War*
ca. 450 B.C.E.	Mozi
ca. 370–ca. 300 B.C.E.	Mencius
369–286 B.C.E.	Zhuangzi
ca. 350 B.C.E.	Infantry armed with crossbows
ca. 310–ca. 215 B.C.E.	Xunzi
ca. 300–200 B.C.E.	*Laozi* written
ca. 280?–233 B.C.E.	Han Feizi of Legalist school

Anyang   *One of the Shang Dynasty capitals.*

● **Royal Tomb at Anyang**
Eleven large tombs and more than a thousand small graves have been excavated at the royal burial ground at Anyang. This grave, about 60 feet deep and 300 feet long, would have taken thousands of laborers many months to complete. But even more wealth was expended to fill it with bronze, stone, pottery, jade, and textile grave goods. Human victims were also placed in it. (*Academia Sinica, Institute of History and Philology, Taiwan*)

Shang palaces were undoubtedly splendid but were constructed of perishable material like wood, and nothing of them remains today, unlike the stone buildings and monuments so characteristic of the ancient West. What has survived are the lavish underground tombs built for Shang kings and their consorts. They were filled with bronze vessels and weapons, jade and ivory ornaments, and often people, some of whom were sacrificed and others who chose to follow their lord in death. Human sacrifice did not occur only at funerals. Inscribed bones report sacrifices of war captives in the dozens and hundreds.

Shang society was marked by sharp status distinctions. The Shang royal family and aristocracy lived in large houses built on huge platforms of rammed earth. The king and other noble families had family and clan names transmitted along patrilineal lines, from father to son. Kingship similarly passed along patrilines, from elder to younger brother and father to son, but never to or through sisters or daughters. The kings and the aristocracy owned slaves, many of whom had been captured in war. In the urban centers there were substantial numbers of craftsmen who worked in stone, bone, and bronze.

Shang farmers were essentially serfs of the aristocrats. Their life was not that different from that of their Neolithic ancestors, and they worked the fields with similar stone tools. They usually lived in small, compact villages surrounded by fields. Some new crops became common in Shang times, most notably wheat, which had spread from West Asia.

● **Jade Figure**   Among the valuables placed in royal Shang tombs were many jade objects, such as this figure, 2¾ inches tall. Since Neolithic times, jade has had the place in China occupied by gold in many other cultures: it is valued for its beauty, rarity, and endurance. This figure was one of seven hundred jade pieces in the tomb of Lady Hao. (*Institute of Archaeology, Beijing/DNP Archives*)

Writing   The survival of divination texts inscribed on bones from Shang tombs demonstrates that writing was already a major element in Chinese culture by 1200 B.C.E. Writing must have been developed earlier, but the early stages cannot be traced, probably because writing was done on wood, bamboo, silk, or other perishable materials.

Once writing was invented, it had profound effects on China's culture and government. A written language made possible a bureaucracy capable of keeping records and conducting correspondence with commanders and governors far from the palace. Hence literacy became the ally of royal rule, facilitating communication with and effective control over the realm. Literacy also preserved the learning, lore, and experience of early Chinese society and facilitated the development of abstract thought.

Like ancient Egyptian and Sumerian, the Chinese script was **logographic:** each word was represented by a single symbol. In the Chinese case, some of these symbols were pictures, but for the names of abstract concepts other methods were adopted. Sometimes the symbol for a different word was borrowed because the two words were pronounced alike. Sometimes two different symbols were combined; for instance, to represent different types of trees, the symbol for *tree* could be combined with another symbol borrowed for its pronunciation (see Figure 3.1).

In western Eurasia logographic scripts were eventually modified or replaced by phonetic scripts, but that never happened in China (although, because of changes in the spoken language, today many words are represented by two or three characters rather than a single one). Because China retained its logographic writing system, many years were required to gain full mastery of reading and writing, which added to the prestige of education.

Why did China retain a logographic writing system even after encounters with phonetic ones? Although phonetic systems have many real advantages, especially with

logographic *A language in which each word is represented by a single symbol, such as the Chinese script.*

MAP 3.1   **China Under the Shang and Zhou Dynasties**   Chinese civilization developed in the temperate regions drained by the Huang (Yellow) and Yangzi Rivers. The early Zhou government controlled larger areas than the Shang did, but the independent states of the Warring States Period were more aggressive about pushing out their frontiers, greatly extending the geographical boundaries of Chinese civilization.

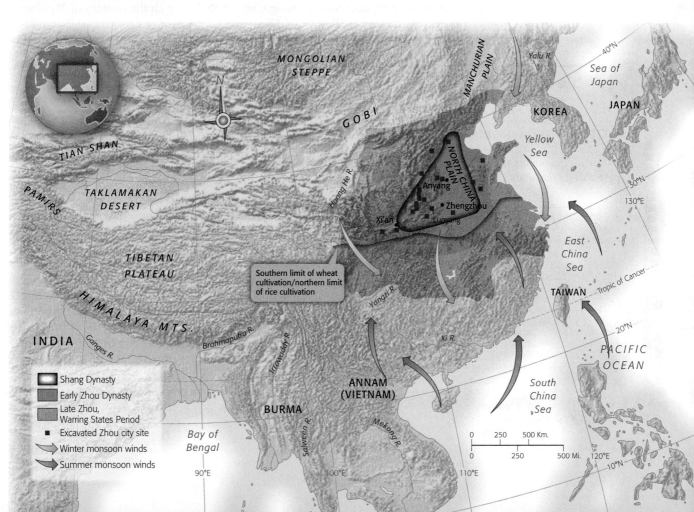

WORD	ox	goat, sheep	tree	moon	earth	water	to show, declare	then (men and bowl)	heaven	to pray
SHANG SYMBOL	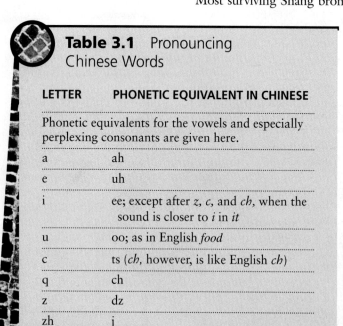									
MODERN CHARACTER	牛	羊	木	月	土	水	示	就	天	祝

● FIGURE 3.1 **The Origins of Chinese Writing** The modern Chinese writing system (bottom row) evolved from the script employed by diviners in the Shang period (upper row). *(Source: Adapted from Patricia Buckley Ebrey, The Cambridge Illustrated History of China [Cambridge: Cambridge University Press, 1996], p. 26. Reprinted by permission of Cambridge University Press.)*

respect to ease of learning to read, there are some costs to dropping a logographic system. Those who learned to read Chinese could communicate with a wider range of people than those who read scripts based on speech. Since characters did not change when the pronunciation changed, educated Chinese could read texts written centuries earlier without the need for them to be translated. Moreover, as the Chinese language developed regional variants, readers of Chinese could read books and letters by contemporaries whose oral language they could not comprehend. Thus the Chinese script played a large role in holding China together and fostering a sense of connection with the past. In addition, many of China's neighbors (Japan, Korea, and Vietnam, in particular) adopted the Chinese script, allowing communication through writing between people whose languages were totally unrelated. In this regard, the Chinese language was like Arabic numerals, which have the same meaning however they are pronounced.

Bronzes As in Egypt, Mesopotamia, and India, the development of more complex forms of social organization in Shang China coincided with the mastery of metalworking, specifically bronze. Bronze, in Shang times, was used more for ritual than for war. Most surviving Shang bronze objects are vessels such as cups, goblets, steamers, and cauldrons that would have originally been used during sacrificial ceremonies. They were beautifully formed in a great variety of shapes and sizes. Complex designs were achieved through mold casting and prefabrication of parts. For instance, legs, handles, and other protruding members were cast first, before the body was cast onto them.

The decoration on Shang bronzes seems to say something interesting about Shang culture, but scholars do not agree about what it says. In the art of ancient Egypt, Assyria, and Babylonia, representations of agriculture (domesticated plants and animals) and of social hierarchy (kings, priests, scribes, and slaves) are very common, matching our understandings of the social, political, and economic development of those societies. In Shang China, by contrast, images of wild animals predominate. Some animal images readily suggest possible meanings. Jade cicadas were sometimes found in the mouths of the dead, and images of cicadas on bronzes are easy to interpret as images evocative of rebirth in the realm of ancestral spirits, as cicadas spend years underground before emerging. Birds, similarly, suggest to many the idea of messengers that can communicate with other realms,

Table 3.1 Pronouncing Chinese Words

LETTER	PHONETIC EQUIVALENT IN CHINESE
Phonetic equivalents for the vowels and especially perplexing consonants are given here.	
a	ah
e	uh
i	ee; except after *z*, *c*, and *ch*, when the sound is closer to *i* in *it*
u	oo; as in English *food*
c	ts (*ch*, however, is like English *ch*)
q	ch
z	dz
zh	j
x	sh

especially realms in the sky. More problematic is the most common image, the stylized animal face called the **taotie**. To some it is a monster—a fearsome image that would scare away evil forces. Others imagine a dragon—an animal whose vast powers had more positive associations. Some hypothesize that it reflects masks used in rituals. Others associate it with animal sacrifices, totemism, or shamanism. Still others see these images as hardly more than designs. Without new evidence, scholars can only speculate.

Bronze technology spread beyond Shang territories into areas the Shang would have considered enemy lands. In 1986, in the western province of Sichuan, discovery was made of a bronze-producing culture contemporaneous with the late Shang but very different from it. This culture did not practice human sacrifice, but two sacrificial pits contained the burned remains of elephant tusks and a wide range of gold, bronze, jade, and stone objects. Among them were a life-size statue and many life-size bronze heads, all with angular facial features and enormous eyes. No human sacrifices were found, leading some scholars to speculate that the masks were used to top wood or clay statues buried in place of humans in a sacrificial ceremony. Archaeologists are continuing to excavate in this region, and new discoveries may provide fuller understanding of the religion of the people who lived there.

● **Inscribed Pan** This bronze vessel, dating to before 900 B.C.E., was one of 103 vessels discovered in 1975 by farmers clearing a field. The inscription tells the story of the first six Zhou kings and of the family of scribes who served them. It was cast by Scribe Qiang. *(Zhou Yuan Administrative Office of Cultural Relics, Fufeng, Shaanxi Province)*

taotie *A common image in Chinese bronzes; it is a stylized animal face.*

- - - - - - - - - - - - - - - - - -

THE EARLY ZHOU DYNASTY (CA. 1050–500 B.C.E.)

How was China governed in the period looked back on as its golden age?

The Shang campaigned constantly against enemies. To the west were the fierce Qiang, considered barbarian tribesmen by the Shang and perhaps speaking an early form of Tibetan. Between the Shang capital and the Qiang was a frontier state called Zhou, which seems to have both inherited cultural traditions from the Neolithic cultures of the northwest and absorbed most of the material culture of the Shang. In about 1050 B.C.E., the Zhou rose against the Shang and defeated them in battle.

Zhou Politics

The early Zhou period is the first one for which transmitted texts exist in some abundance. The **Book of Documents** describes the Zhou conquest of the Shang as the victory of just and noble warriors over decadent courtiers who were led by a dissolute, sadistic king. At the same time, these documents show that the Zhou recognized the Shang as occupying the center of the world, were eager to succeed to that role themselves, and saw history as a major way to legitimate power. The three early Zhou rulers who are given the most praise are King Wen (the "cultured" or "literate" king), who expanded the Zhou domain; his son King Wu (the "martial" king), who conquered the Shang; and Wu's brother, the Duke of Zhou, who consolidated the conquest and served as loyal regent for Wu's heir.

Primary Source: The Book of Documents *Discover how rulers gain or lose the right to rule, an authority known as the* Mandate of Heaven.

Book of Documents *One of the earliest of the "Confucian" classics, containing documents, speeches, and historical accounts.*

Like the Shang kings, the Zhou kings sacrificed to their ancestors, but they also sacrificed to Heaven. The *Book of Documents* assumes a close relationship between Heaven and the king, who was called the Son of Heaven. Heaven gives the king a mandate to rule only as long as he rules in the interests of the people. Thus it was because the last king of the Shang had been decadent and cruel that Heaven took the mandate away from him and entrusted it to the virtuous Zhou kings. Because this theory of the **Mandate of Heaven** does not seem to have had any place in Shang cosmology, it may have been elaborated by the early Zhou rulers as a kind of propaganda to win over the conquered subjects of the Shang. Whatever its origins, it remained a central feature of Chinese political ideology from the early Zhou period on.

Rather than attempt to rule all their territories directly, the early Zhou rulers set up a decentralized feudal system. They sent out relatives and trusted subordinates with troops to establish walled garrisons in the conquered territories. Such a vassal was generally able to pass his position on to a son, so that in time the domains became hereditary fiefs. By 800 B.C.E. there were about two hundred lords with domains large and small. Each lord appointed officers to serve him in ritual, administrative, or military capacities. These posts and their associated titles tended to become hereditary as well.

The decentralized rule of the early Zhou period had from the beginning carried within it the danger that the regional lords would become so powerful that they would no longer obey the commands of the king. As generations passed and ties of loyalty and kinship grew more distant, this indeed happened. In 771 B.C.E. the Zhou king was killed by an alliance of Rong tribesmen and Zhou vassals. One of his sons was put on the throne, and then for safety's sake the capital was moved east out of the Wei River valley to modern Luoyang, just south of the Huang River in the heart of the central plains (see Map 3.1).

The revived Zhou Dynasty never fully regained control over its vassals, and China entered a prolonged period without a strong central authority. For a couple of centuries a code of chivalrous or sportsmanlike conduct still regulated warfare between the states: one state would not attack another while it was in mourning for its ruler; during battles one side would not attack before the other side had time to line up; ruling houses were not wiped out, so that successors could continue to sacrifice to their ancestors; and so on. Thereafter, however, such niceties were abandoned, and China entered a period of nearly constant conflict.

Zhou Society

During the Zhou Dynasty, Chinese society underwent radical changes. Early Zhou rule was highly aristocratic. Inherited ranks placed people in a hierarchy ranging downward from the king to the rulers of states with titles like duke and marquis, the hereditary great officials of the states, the lower ranks of the aristocracy (men who could serve in either military or civil capacities, known as **shi**), and finally to the ordinary people (farmers, craftsmen, and traders). Patrilineal family ties were very important in this society, and at the upper reaches, at least, sacrifices to ancestors were one of the key rituals used to forge social ties.

Glimpses of what life was like at various social levels in the early Zhou Dynasty can be found in the **Book of Songs,** which contains the earliest Chinese poetry. Some of the songs are hymns used in court religious ceremonies, such as offerings to ancestors. Others clearly had their origins in folk songs. Some of these folk songs depict farmers at work clearing fields, plowing and planting, gathering mulberry leaves for silkworms, and spinning and weaving. Farming life involved not merely the cultivation of crops like millet, hemp (for cloth), beans, and vegetables, but also hunting small animals and collecting grasses and rushes to make rope and baskets.

Many of the folk songs are love songs that depict a more informal pattern of courtship than prevailed in later China. One stanza reads:

Mandate of Heaven *The theory that Heaven gives the king a mandate to rule only as long as he rules in the interests of the people.*

shi *The lower ranks of Chinese aristocracy; these men could serve in either military or civil capacities.*

Book of Songs *The earliest collection of Chinese poetry; it provides glimpses of what life was like in the early Zhou Dynasty.*

Please, Zhongzi,
Do not leap over our wall,
Do not break our mulberry trees.
It's not that I begrudge the mulberries,
But I fear my brothers.
You I would embrace,
But my brothers' words—those I dread.[1]

There were also songs of complaint, such as this one in which the ancestors are rebuked for failing to aid their descendants:

The drought has become so severe
That it cannot be stopped.
Glowing and burning,
We have no place.
The great mandate is about at an end.
Nothing to look forward to or back upon.
The host of dukes and past rulers
Does not help us.
As for father and mother and the ancestors,
How can they bear to treat us so?[2]

Other songs in this collection are court odes that reveal attitudes of the aristocrats. One such ode expresses a deep distrust of women's involvement in politics:

Clever men build cities,
Clever women topple them.
Beautiful, these clever women may be
But they are owls and kites.
Women have long tongues
That lead to ruin.
Disorder does not come down from heaven;
It is produced by women.[3]

● **Bronze Relief of Hunters** Hunting provided an important source of food in the Zhou period, and hunters were often depicted on inlaid bronzes of the period. *(The Avery Brundage Collection/Laurie Platt Winfrey, Inc.)*

Part of the reason for distrust of women in politics was the practice of concubinage. Rulers regularly demonstrated their power and wealth by accumulating large numbers of concubines and thus would have children by several women. In theory, succession went to the eldest son of the wife, then to younger sons by her, and only in their absence to sons of concubines; but in actual practice, the ruler of a state or the head of a powerful ministerial family could select a son of a concubine to be his heir if he wished. This led to much scheming for favor among the various sons and their mothers and the common perception that women were incapable of taking a disinterested view of the larger good.

THE WARRING STATES PERIOD (500–221 B.C.E.)

What were the consequences of the breakup of Zhou unity and the rise of independent states?

> **Warring States Period** *The period of Chinese history between 403 and 221 B.C.E. when states fought each other and one after another was destroyed until only one remained.*

> **crossbow** *A powerful, mechanical bow developed during the Warring States Period.*

Social and economic change quickened after 500 B.C.E. Cities began appearing all over north China. Thick earthen walls were built around the palaces and ancestral temples of the ruler and other aristocrats, and often an outer wall was added to protect the artisans, merchants, and farmers who lived outside the inner wall. Accounts of sieges launched against these walled citadels, with scenes of the scaling of walls and the storming of gates, are central to descriptions of military confrontations in this period.

The old aristocratic social structure of the Zhou was being undermined by advances in military technology. Large, well-drilled infantry armies became a potent military force in the **Warring States Period,** able to withstand and defeat chariot-led forces. By 300 B.C.E. states were sending out armies of a couple hundred thousand drafted foot soldiers, usually accompanied by horsemen. Adding to the effectiveness of armies of drafted foot soldiers was the development of the **crossbow** around 350 B.C.E. The trigger of a crossbow was an intricate bronze mechanism that allowed a foot soldier to shoot farther than could a horseman carrying a light bow. One text of the period reports that a skilled soldier with a powerful crossbow and a sharp sword was the match of a hundred ordinary men. To defend against crossbows, soldiers began wearing armor and helmets. Most of the armor was made of leader strips tied with cords. Helmets were sometimes made of iron.

The introduction of cavalry in this period also reduced the need for a chariot-riding aristocracy. Shooting bows and arrows from horseback was first perfected by non-Chinese peoples to the north of China proper, who at that time were making the transition to a nomadic pastoral economy. The northern state of Jin, to defend itself from the attacks of these horsemen, developed its own cavalry armies. Once it started using cavalry against other Chinese states, they too had to master the new technology. From this time on, acquiring and pasturing horses was a key component of military preparedness.

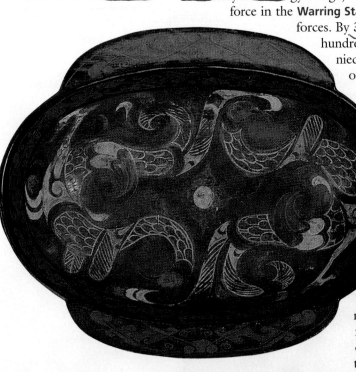

● **Lacquer Cup** This 6-inch-long lacquer cup, decorated with images of two intertwined birds, was one of many lacquered eating vessels found in a third-century B.C.E. tomb. Lacquer is made from the sap of a tree native to China. It is remarkably light, strong, smooth, and waterproof. Lacquered dishes, cups, boxes, musical instruments, and sculptures became highly sought-after luxury items. *(Jingzhou Prefecture Museum/© Cultural Relics Publishing House)*

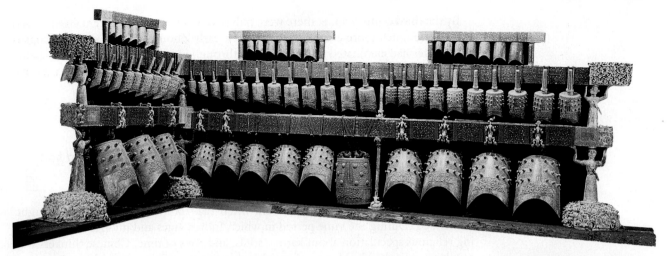

● **Bells of the Marquis of Zeng** Music played a central role in court life in ancient China. The tomb of a minor ruler who died about 400 B.C.E. contained 124 musical instruments, including drums, flutes, mouth organs, pan pipes, zithers, a set of 32 chime stones, and this 64-piece bell set. The bells bear inscriptions that name the two tones each bell could make, depending on where it was struck. Five men, using poles and mallets and standing on either side of the set of bells, would have played the bells by hitting them from outside. (© Cultural Relics Publishing House)

Because these developments made commoners and craftsmen central to military success, rulers tried to find ways to increase their populations. To increase agricultural output, they brought new land into cultivation, drained marshes, and dug irrigation channels. Rulers began surveying their land and taxing farmers. They wanted to undermine the power of lords over their subjects in order to get direct access to the peasants' labor power. Serfdom thus gradually declined. Registering populations led to the extension of family names to commoners at an earlier date than anywhere else in the world.

To encourage trade, rulers began casting coins. The development of iron technology in the early Zhou Dynasty also promoted economic expansion. By the fifth century B.C.E. iron was being widely used for both farm tools and weapons. By the third century B.C.E. the largest smelters employed two hundred or more workmen. A new powerful group also emerged in society—the rich who had acquired their wealth through trade or industry rather than inheritance or political favor. Late Zhou texts frequently mention cross-regional trade in objects such as furs, copper, dyes, hemp, salt, and horses.

Social mobility increased in this period. Rulers more often sent out their own officials rather than delegate authority to hereditary lesser lords. This trend toward centralized bureaucratic control created opportunities for social advancement for the shi on the lower end of the old aristocracy. Competition among such men guaranteed rulers a ready supply of able and willing subordinates, and competition among rulers for talent meant that ambitious men could be selective in deciding where to offer their services. (See the feature "Individuals in Society: Guan Zhong.")

The development of infantry armies also created the need for a new type of general, and rulers became less willing to let men lead troops merely because of aristocratic birth. Treatises on the art of war described the ideal general as a master of maneuver, illusion, and deception. In *The Art of War,* Master Sun argued that heroism is a useless virtue that leads to needless deaths. But discipline is essential, and he insisted that the entire army had to be trained to follow the orders of its commanders without questioning them.

States on the periphery that had been considered barbarian or semibarbarian during the early Zhou were gradually brought into the cultural sphere of the Central States, as the core region of China was called. For instance, the southern state of Chu expanded rapidly in the Yangzi Valley, defeating and absorbing fifty or more small states as it extended its reach north to the heartland of Zhou and east to absorb the old states of Wu and Yue. By the late Zhou period, Chu was on the forefront of cultural innovation and produced the greatest literary masterpiece of the era, the *Songs of Chu,* a collection of fantastical poems full of images of elusive deities and shamans who can fly through the spirit world.

By the third century B.C.E. there were only seven important states remaining. These states were much more centralized than their early Zhou predecessors. The kings of these states had eliminated indirect control through vassals and in its place dispatched royal officials to remote cities, controlling them from a distance through the transmission of documents and dismissing them at will.

CONFUCIUS AND HIS FOLLOWERS

What ideas did Confucius teach, and how were they a response to his times?

The Warring States Period was the era when the "Hundred Schools of Thought" contended. During the same period in which Indian sages and mystics were developing religious speculation about karma, souls, and eons of time, Chinese thinkers were arguing about the ideal forms of social and political organization and man's connections to nature.

Confucius (traditional dates: 551–479 B.C.E.) was one of the first men of ideas. As a young man, Confucius served in the court of his home state of Lu without gaining much influence. After leaving Lu, he set out with a small band of students and wandered through neighboring states in search of a ruler who would take his advice.

Confucius's ideas are known to us primarily through the sayings recorded by his disciples in the *Analects*. The thrust of his thought was ethical rather than theoretical or metaphysical. He talked repeatedly of an ideal age in the early Zhou Dynasty when everyone was devoted to fulfilling his or her role: superiors looked after those dependent on them; inferiors devoted themselves to the service of their superiors; parents and children, husbands and wives, all wholeheartedly embraced what was expected of them.

Confucius considered the family the basic unit of society. He extolled **filial piety**, which to him meant more than just reverent obedience of children to their parents:

> **filial piety**   *Reverent attitude of children to their parents; it was extolled by Confucius.*

The Master said, "You can be of service to your father and mother by remonstrating with them tactfully. If you perceive that they do not wish to follow your advice, then continue to be reverent toward them without offending or disobeying them; work hard and do not murmur against them."[4]

The relationship between father and son was one of the five cardinal relationships stressed by Confucius. The others were between ruler and subject, husband and wife, elder and younger brother, and friend and friend. Mutual obligations of a hierarchical sort underlay the first four of these relationships: the senior leads and protects; the junior supports and obeys. The exception was the relationship between friends, which was conceived in terms of mutual obligations between equals.

A man of moderation, Confucius was an earnest advocate of gentlemanly conduct. He redefined the term *gentleman* (*junzi*) to mean a man of moral cultivation rather than a man of noble birth. He repeatedly urged his followers to aspire to be gentlemen rather than petty men intent on personal gain. The gentleman, he said, "feels bad when his capabilities fall short of the task. He does not feel bad when people fail to recognize him."[5] Confucius did not advocate social equality, but his teachings minimized the importance of class distinctions and opened the way for intelligent and talented people to rise in the social scale. The Confucian gentleman found his calling in service to the ruler. Loyal advisers should encourage their rulers to govern through ritual, virtue, and concern for the welfare of their subjects, and much of the *Analects* concerns the way to govern well.

To Confucius the ultimate virtue was humanity (**ren**). A person of humanity cares about others and acts accordingly:

> **ren**   *The ultimate Confucian virtue; it is translated as perfect goodness, benevolence, humanity, human-heartedness, and nobility.*

Zhonggong asked about humanity. The Master said, "When you go out, treat everyone as if you were welcoming a great guest. Employ people as though you were conducting a great

Guan Zhong

By the time of Confucius, the success of states was often credited more to the lord's astute advisers than to the lord himself. To Confucius, the most praiseworthy political adviser was Guan Zhong (ca. 720–645 B.C.E.), the genius behind the rise of the state of Qi, in eastern China.

The earliest historical sources to recount Guan Zhong's accomplishments are the "commentaries" compiled in the Warring States Period to elaborate on the dry chronicle known as the *Spring and Autumn Annals.* The *Zuo Commentary,* for instance, tells us that in the year 660 B.C.E. Guan Zhong advised Duke Huan to aid the small state of Xing, then under attack by the non-Chinese Rong tribes: "The Rong and the Di are wolves who cannot be satiated. The Xia (Chinese) states are kin who should not be abandoned." In 652 B.C.E., it tells us, Guan Zhong urged the duke to maintain the respect of the other states by refusing the offer of the son of a recently defeated state's ruler to ally himself with Qi if Qi would help him depose his father. Because the duke regularly listened to Guan Zhong's sound advice, Qi brought the other states under its sway, and the duke came to be recognized as the first *hegemon,* or leader of the alliance of states.

Guan Zhong was also credited with strengthening the duke's internal administration. He encouraged the employment of officials on the basis of their moral character and ability rather than their birth. He introduced a system of drafting commoners for military service. In the history of China written by Sima Qian in about 100 B.C.E., Guan Zhong is also given credit for enriching Qi by promoting trade, issuing coins, and standardizing merchants' scales. He was credited with the statement "When the granaries are full, the people will understand ritual and moderation. When they have enough food and clothing, they will understand honor and disgrace."

Sima Qian's biography of Guan Zhong emphasizes his early poverty and the key role played by a friend, Bao Shuya, who recognized his worth. As young men, both Bao and Guan Zhong served brothers of the duke of Qi. When this duke was killed and a messy succession struggle followed, Bao's patron won out and became the next duke, while Guan Zhong's patron had to flee and in the end was killed. Bao, however, recommended Guan Zhong to the new duke, Duke Huan, and Guan Zhong took up a post under him.

The inlaid decoration on bronze vessels of the Warring States Period often shows people engaged in warfare, hunting, preparing food, performing rituals, and making music. *(From E. Consten,* Das alte China*)*

In the *Analects,* one of Confucius's disciples thought that Guan Zhong's lack of loyalty to his first lord made him a man unworthy of respect: "When Duke Huan killed his brother Jiu, Guan Zhong was unable to die with Jiu but rather became prime minister to Duke Huan." Confucius disagreed: "Guan Zhong became prime minister to Duke Huan and made him hegemon among the lords, uniting and reforming all under Heaven. The people, down to the present, continued to receive benefits from this. Were it not for Guan Zhong our hair would hang unbound and we would fold our robes on the left [that is, live as barbarians]."*

A book of the teachings associated with Guan Zhong, the *Guanzi,* was in circulation by the late Warring States Period. Although it is today not thought to reflect the teachings of the historical Guan Zhong, the fact that later statecraft thinkers would borrow his name is an indication of his fame as a great statesman.

Questions for Analysis

1. How did the form of government promoted by Guan Zhong differ from the early Zhou political system?

2. What can one infer about Chinese notions of loyalty from the story of Guan Zhong and his friend Bao Shuya?

3. Did Guan Zhong and Confucius share similar understandings of the differences between Chinese and barbarians?

Analects, 14.18. Translated by Patricia Ebrey.

● **Serving Parents with Filial Piety** This illustration of a passage in the *Classic of Filial Piety* shows how commoners should serve their parents: by working hard at productive jobs such as farming and tending to their parents' daily needs. The married son and daughter-in-law bring food or drink to offer the older couple as their own children look on, thus learning how they should treat their own parents after they become aged themselves. *(National Palace Museum, Taipei, Taiwan)*

sacrifice. Do not do unto others what you would not have them do unto you. Then neither in your country nor in your family will there be complaints against you."[6]

Confucius encouraged the men who came to study with him to master the poetry, rituals, and historical traditions that we know today as Confucian classics. Many passages in the *Analects* reveal Confucius's confidence in the power of study:

The Master said, "I am not someone who was born wise. I am someone who loves the ancients and tries to learn from them."

The Master said, "I once spent a whole day without eating and a whole night without sleeping in order to think. It was of no use. It is better to study."[7]

The eventual success of Confucian ideas owes much to Confucius's followers in the three centuries following his death. The most important of them were Mencius (ca. 370–ca. 300 B.C.E.) and Xunzi (ca. 310–ca. 215 B.C.E.).

Mencius, like Confucius, traveled around offering advice to rulers of various states. (See the feature "Listening to the Past: The Book of Mencius" on pages 74–75.) Over and over he tried to convert them to the view that the ruler able to win over the people through benevolent government would succeed in unifying "all under Heaven." Mencius proposed concrete political and financial measures for easing tax burdens and otherwise improving the people's lot. Men willing to serve an unworthy ruler earned his contempt, especially when they worked hard to fill the ruler's coffers or expand his territory. With his disciples and fellow philosophers, Mencius also discussed other issues in moral philosophy, arguing strongly, for instance, that human nature is fundamentally good, as everyone is born with the capacity to recognize what is right and act on it.

Xunzi, a half century later, took the opposite view of human nature, arguing that people are born selfish and that it is only through education and ritual that they learn to put moral principle above their own interest. Much of what is desirable is not inborn but must be taught:

When a son yields to his father, or a younger brother yields to his elder brother, or when a son takes on the work for his father or a younger brother for his elder brother, their actions go against their natures and run counter to their feelings. And yet these are the way of the filial son and the principles of ritual and morality.[8]

Neither Confucius nor Mencius had had much actual political or administrative experience, but Xunzi had worked for many years in the court of his home state. Not surprisingly, he showed more consideration than either Confucius or Mencius for the difficulties a ruler might face in trying to rule through ritual and virtue. Xunzi was also a more rigorous thinker than his predecessors and developed the philosophical foundations of many ideas merely outlined by Confucius or Mencius. Confucius, for instance, had declined to discuss gods, portents, and anomalies and had spoken of sacrificing as if the spirits were present. Xunzi went farther and explicitly argued that Heaven does not intervene in human affairs. Praying to Heaven or to gods, he asserted, does not induce them to act. "Why does it rain after a prayer for rain? In my opinion, for no reason. It is the same as raining when you had not prayed."[9]

Even though he did not think praying could bring rain or other benefits from Heaven, Xunzi did not propose abandoning traditional rituals. In contrast to Daoists and Mohists (discussed below), who saw rituals as unnatural or extravagant, Xunzi saw them as an efficient way to attain order in society. Rulers and educated men should continue traditional ritual practices such as complex funeral protocols because the rites themselves have positive effects on performers and observers. Not only do they let people express feelings and satisfy desires in an orderly way, but because they specify graduated ways to perform the rites according to social rank, ritual traditions sustain the social hierarchy. Xunzi compared and contrasted ritual and music: music shapes people's emotions and creates feelings of solidarity, while ritual shapes people's sense of duty and creates social differentiation.

The Confucian vision of personal ethics and public service found a small but ardent following in the Warring States Period. In later centuries, rulers came to see men educated in Confucian virtues as ideal advisers and officials. Neither revolutionaries nor toadies, Confucian scholar-officials opposed bad government and upheld the best ideals of statecraft. Confucian political ideals shaped Chinese society into the twentieth century.

The Confucian vision also provided the moral basis for the Chinese family into modern times. Repaying parents and ancestors came to be seen as a sacred duty. Because people owe their very existence to their parents, they should reciprocate by respecting them, making efforts to please them, honoring their memories, and placing the interests of the family line above personal preferences. Since this family line is a patrilineal line from father to son to grandson, placing great importance on it has had the effect of devaluing women.

DAOISM, LEGALISM, AND OTHER SCHOOLS OF THOUGHT

What did those who opposed Confucianism argue?

During the Warring States Period, rulers took advantage of the destruction of states to recruit newly unemployed men to serve as their advisers and court assistants. Lively debate often resulted as these strategists proposed policies and defended their ideas against challengers. Followers took to recording their teachers' ideas, and the circulation of these "books" (rolls of silk, or strips of wood or bamboo tied together) served further to stimulate debate.

Many of these schools of thought directly opposed the ideas of Confucius and his followers. Mozi proposed that every idea should be tested on the basis of utility: does it benefit the people and the state? He objected to Confucian emphasis on ritual because it interrupts work and is wasteful. Mozi did not approve of Confucian emphasis on treating only one's family with special concern, saying that the principle should be concern for everyone equally. The Daoists and Legalists opposed other Confucian principles.

Daoism

Confucius and his followers believed in moral effort and statecraft. They thought men of virtue should devote themselves to making the government work to the benefit of the people. Those who came to be labeled Daoists disagreed. They thought striving to make things better generally makes them worse. Daoists defended private life and wanted the rulers to leave the people alone. They sought to go beyond everyday concerns and to let their minds wander freely. Rather than making human beings and human actions the center of concern, they focused on the larger scheme of things, the whole natural order identified as **the Way,** or Dao.

Early Daoist teachings are known from two surviving books, the *Laozi* and the *Zhuangzi,* both dating to the third century B.C.E. Laozi, the putative author of the *Laozi,* may not be a historical figure, but the text ascribed to him has been of enduring importance. A recurrent theme in this brief, aphoristic text is the mystical superiority of yielding over assertion and silence over words: "The Way that can be discussed is not the constant Way."[10] The highest good is like water: "Water benefits all creatures but does not compete. It occupies the places people disdain and thus comes near to the Way."[11]

Because purposeful action is counterproductive, the ruler should let people return to a natural state of ignorance and contentment:

Do not honor the worthy,
And the people will not compete.
Do not value rare treasures,
And the people will not steal.
Do not display what others want,
And the people will not have their hearts confused.
A sage governs this way:
He empties people's minds and fills their bellies.
He weakens their wills and strengthens their bones.
Keep the people always without knowledge and without desires,
For then the clever will not dare act.
Engage in no action and order will prevail.[12]

In the philosophy of the *Laozi,* the people would be better off if they knew less, gave up tools, renounced writing, stopped envying their neighbors, and lost their desire to travel or engage in war.

Zhuangzi (369–286 B.C.E.), the author of the book of the same name, was a historical figure who shared many of the central ideas of the *Laozi.* He was proud of his disinterest in politics. In one of his many anecdotes, he reported that the king of Chu once sent an envoy to invite him to take over the government of his realm. In response Zhuangzi asked the envoy whether a tortoise that had been held as sacred for three thousand years would prefer to be dead with its bones venerated or alive with its

the Way *The Dao, the whole natural order.*

● **Inscribed Bamboo Slips**
In 1993 Chinese archaeologists discovered a late-fourth-century B.C.E. tomb in Hubei province that contained 804 bamboo slips, bearing some 12,000 Chinese characters. Scholars have been able to reconstruct more than a dozen books from them, some of which match transmitted texts fairly closely, but others are books previously unknown. *(Courtesy, Jingmen City Museum, Hubei)*

tail dragging in the mud. When the envoy agreed that life was preferable, Zhuangzi told the envoy to leave. He preferred to drag his tail in the mud.

The *Zhuangzi* is filled with parables, flights of fancy, and fictional encounters between historical figures, including Confucius and his disciples. A more serious strain of Zhuangzi's thought concerned death. He questioned whether we can be sure life is better than death. People fear what they do not know, the same way a captive girl will be terrified when she learns she is to become the king's concubine. Perhaps people will discover that death has as many delights as life in the palace.

When a friend expressed shock that Zhuangzi was not weeping at his wife's death but rather singing, Zhuangzi explained:

When she first died, how could I have escaped feeling the loss? Then I looked back to the beginning before she had life. Not only before she had life, but before she had form. Not only before she had form, but before she had vital energy. In this confused amorphous realm, something changed and vital energy appeared; when the vital energy was changed, form appeared; with changes in form, life began. Now there is another change bringing death. This is like the progression of the four seasons of spring and fall, winter and summer. Here she was lying down to sleep in a huge room and I followed her, sobbing and wailing. When I realized my actions showed I hadn't understood destiny, I stopped.[13]

● **Embroidered Silk** From ancient times, silk was one of China's most famous products. Women traditionally did most of the work involved in making silk, from feeding mulberry leaves to the silkworms, to reeling and twisting the fibers, to weaving and embroidering. The embroidered silk depicted here is from a robe found in a fourth-century B.C.E. tomb in central China. The flowing, curvilinear design incorporates dragons, phoenixes, and tigers. *(Jingzhou Museum)*

Zhuangzi was similarly iconoclastic in his political ideas. In one parable a wheelwright insolently tells a duke that books are useless since all they contain are the dregs of men long dead. The duke, insulted, threatens to execute him if he cannot give an adequate explanation of his remark. The wheelwright replies:

I see things in terms of my own work. When I chisel at a wheel, if I go slow, the chisel slides and does not stay put; if I hurry, it jams and doesn't move properly. When it is neither too slow nor too fast, I can feel it in my hand and respond to it from my heart. My mouth cannot describe it in words, but there is something there. I cannot teach it to my son, and my son cannot learn it from me. So I have gone on for seventy years, growing old chiseling wheels. The men of old died in possession of what they could not transmit. So it follows that what you are reading are their dregs.[14]

To put this another way, truly skilled craftsmen respond to situations spontaneously; they do not analyze or reason or even keep in mind the rules they have mastered. This strain of Daoist thought denies the validity of verbal reasoning and the sorts of knowledge conveyed through words.

Daoism can be seen as a response to Confucianism, a rejection of many of its basic premises. Nevertheless, over the course of Chinese history, many people felt the pull of both Confucian and Daoist ideas and studied the writings of both schools. Even Confucian scholars who had devoted much of their lives to public service might find that the teachings of the *Laozi* or *Zhuangzi* helped to put their frustrations in perspective. Whereas Confucianism often seems sternly masculine, Daoism is more accepting of feminine principles and even celebrates passivity and yielding. Those drawn to the arts were also often drawn to Daoism, with its validation of spontaneity and freedom. Rulers, too, were drawn to the Daoist notion of the ruler who can have great power simply by being himself without instituting anything.

Legalism

Legalists *Political theorists who emphasized the need for rigorous laws and laid the basis for China's later bureaucratic government.*

As one small state after another was conquered, the number of surviving states dwindled. Rulers fearful that their states might be next were ready to listen to political theorists who claimed expertise in the accumulation of power. These theorists, labeled **Legalists** because of their emphasis on the need for rigorous laws, argued that strong government depended not on the moral qualities of the ruler and his officials, as Confucians claimed, but on establishing effective laws and procedures. Legalism, though eventually discredited, laid the basis for China's later bureaucratic government.

In the fourth century B.C.E. the state of Qin, under the leadership of its chief minister, Lord Shang (d. 338 B.C.E.), adopted many Legalist policies. It abolished the aristocracy. Social distinctions were to be based on military ranks determined by the objective criterion of the number of enemy heads cut off in battle. In place of the old fiefs, Qin divided the country into counties and appointed officials to govern them according to the laws decreed at court. To increase the population, migrants were recruited from other states with offers of land and houses. To encourage farmers to work hard and improve their land, they were allowed to buy and sell it. Ordinary farmers were thus freed from serf-like obligations to the local nobility, but direct control by the state could be even more onerous. Taxes and labor service obligations were heavy. Travel required a permit, and vagrants could be forced into penal labor service. All families were grouped into mutual responsibility groups of five and ten families; whenever anyone in the group committed a crime, all the others were equally liable unless they reported it.

In the century after Lord Shang, Legalism found its greatest exponent in Han Feizi (ca. 280?–233 B.C.E.). Han Feizi had studied with the Confucian master Xunzi but had little interest in Confucian values of goodness or ritual. In his writings he warned rulers of the political pitfalls awaiting them. They had to be careful where they placed their trust, for "when the ruler trusts someone, he falls under that person's control."[15] This is true even of wives and concubines, who think of the interests of their sons. Given subordinates' propensities to pursue their own selfish interests, the ruler should keep them ignorant of his intentions and control them by manipulating competition among them. Warmth, affection, or candor should have no place in his relationships with others.

Han Feizi saw the Confucian notion that government could be based on virtue as naive:

Think of parents' relations to their children. They congratulate each other when a son is born, but complain to each other when a daughter is born. Why do parents have these divergent responses when both are equally their offspring? It is because they calculate their long-term advantage. Since even parents deal with their children in this calculating way, what can one expect where there is no parent-child bond? When present-day scholars counsel rulers, they all tell them to rid themselves of thoughts of profit and follow the path of mutual love. This is expecting rulers to go further than parents.[16]

If rulers would make the laws and prohibitions clear and the rewards and punishments automatic, then the officials and common people would be easy to govern. Uniform laws get people to do things they would not otherwise be inclined to do, such as work hard and fight wars, essential to the goal of establishing hegemony over all the other states.

The laws of the Legalists were designed as much to constrain officials as to regulate the common people. The third-century B.C.E. tomb of a Qin official has yielded statutes detailing the rules for keeping accounts, supervising subordinates, managing penal labor, conducting investigations, and many other responsibilities of officials. Infractions were generally punishable through the imposition of fines.

Legalism saw no value in intellectual debate or private opinion. Divergent views of right and wrong lead to weakness and disorder. The ruler should not allow others to undermine his laws by questioning them. In Legalism, there were no laws above or independent of the wishes of the rulers, no laws that might set limits on rulers' actions in the way that natural or divine laws did in Greek thought. Indeed, a ruler's right to exercise the law as he saw fit was demonstrated in the violent deaths of the two leading Legalist thinkers: Lord Shang was drawn and quartered by chariots in 338 B.C.E., and Han Feizi was imprisoned and forced to drink poison in 233 B.C.E.

Rulers of several states adopted some Legalist ideas, but only the state of Qin systematically followed them. The extraordinary but brief success Qin had with these policies is discussed in Chapter 6.

Yin and Yang

Cosmological speculation formed another important strain of early Chinese thought. The concepts of **yin and yang** are found in early form in the divination manual the *Book of Changes,* but late Zhou theorists developed much more elaborate theories based on them. Yin is the feminine, dark, receptive, yielding, negative, and weak; yang is the masculine, bright, assertive, creative, positive, and strong. Yin and yang are complementary poles rather than distinct entities or opposing forces. The movement of yin and yang accounts for the transition from day to night and from summer to winter. These models based on observation of nature were extended to explain not

yin and yang *A concept of complementary poles, one of which represents the feminine, dark, and receptive, and the other the masculine, bright, and assertive.*

only phenomena we might classify as natural, such as illness, storms, and earthquakes, but also social phenomena, such as the rise and fall of states and conflict in families. In all these realms, unwanted things happen when the balance between yin and yang gets disturbed.

In recent decades archaeologists have further complicated our understanding of early Chinese thought by unearthing records of the popular religion of the time—astrological manuals, handbooks of lucky and unlucky days, medical prescriptions, exercises, and ghost stories. The tomb of an official who died in 316 B.C.E. has records of divinations showing that illness was seen as the result of unsatisfied spirits or malevolent demons, best dealt with through exorcisms or offering sacrifices to the astral god Taiyi (Grand One).

● **Dagger Depicting Taiyi** Recent archaeological excavations of manuscripts from the Warring States Period have given us a much clearer understanding of religious beliefs and practices in early China. The deity Taiyi ("Grand One"), depicted on this late-fourth-century B.C.E. drawing of a dagger, was the god of the pole star. Sacrifices were made to Taiyi to avert evil or gain his protection in battle. *(From Michael Loewe and Edward Shaughnessy, eds.,* Cambridge History of Ancient China *[New York: Cambridge University Press, 1999]. Reprinted with permission of Cambridge University Press)*

Chapter Summary

To assess your mastery of this chapter, go to
bedfordstmartins.com/mckayworld

Key Terms

loess
Anyang
logographic
taotie
Book of Documents
Mandate of Heaven
shi
Book of Songs
Warring States Period
crossbow
filial piety
ren
the Way
Legalists
yin and yang

• *When, where, and how did writing, bronze technology, and other elements of civilization develop in China?*

After a long Neolithic period, China entered the Bronze Age with the Shang Dynasty. In Shang times, the kings served also as priests, and great wealth was invested in extraordinarily complex bronze ritual vessels. From Shang times on, the Chinese language has been written in a logographic script, which shaped the ways people have become educated and the value assigned to education.

• *How was China governed in the period looked back on as its golden age?*

The Zhou Dynasty, which overthrew the Shang in about 1050 B.C.E., parceled out its territory to lords, whose titles gradually became hereditary. The texts transmitted from this period present Heaven as the high god. Kings were called Sons of Heaven because they had to have Heaven's approval to gain the throne. If they did not rule in the interests of the people, Heaven could take the Mandate away from them and confer it on a worthier person.

• *What were the consequences of the breakup of Zhou unity and the rise of independent states?*

The ties between the Zhou king and his lords gradually weakened, and the domains over time came to act like independent states. After 500 B.C.E. China is best thought of as a multistate realm. Social and cultural change was particularly rapid under these conditions of intense competition. Changes in military technology included the introduction of cavalry, infantry armies, and the crossbow. Iron utensils came into use, as did metal coinage.

• *What ideas did Confucius teach, and how were they a response to his times?*

This Warring States Period was the golden age of Chinese philosophy. Confucius and his followers advocated a deeply moral view of the way to achieve order through the cultivation of virtues by everyone from the ruler on down. Key virtues were sincerity, loyalty, benevolence, and filial piety. Over the next two centuries Confucius's message was elaborated by important followers, including Mencius, who urged rulers to rule through goodness and argued that human nature is good, and Xunzi, who stressed the power of ritual and argued that human nature is selfish and must be curbed through education.

• *What did those who opposed Confucianism argue?*

In the contentious spirit of the age, many thinkers countered Confucian principles. Daoists like Laozi and Zhuangzi looked beyond the human realm to the entire cosmos and spoke of the relativity of concepts such as good and bad and life and death. The Legalists were hardheaded men who heaped ridicule on the idea that a ruler could get his people to be good by being good himself and proposed instead clear laws with strict rewards and punishments. Natural philosophers explored issues Confucius had neglected, such as the forces that bring about the changes in the seasons and health and illness.

Suggested Reading

Blunden, Caroline, and Mark Elvin. *Cultural Atlas of China.* 1983. Valuable both for its historical maps and its well-illustrated topical essays.

Chang, Kwang-chih. *Archeology of Ancient China,* 4th ed. 1986. An overview by a leading archaeologist.

de Bary, Wm. Theodore, and Irene Bloom. *Sources of Chinese Tradition.* 1999. Large collection of primary sources for Chinese intellectual history, with lengthy introductions.

Ebrey, Patricia Buckley. *Cambridge Illustrated History of China.* 1996. Well-illustrated brief overview of Chinese history.

Graham, A. C. *Disputers of the Tao: Philosophical Argument in Ancient China.* 1989. A philosophically rich overview of the intellectual flowering of the Warring States Period.

Ledderose, Lothar. *Ten Thousand Things: Module and Mass Production in Chinese Art.* 2000. A new interpretation of Chinese culture in terms of modules; offers fresh perspectives on the Chinese script and the production of bronzes.

Loewe, Michael, and Edward Shaughnessy, eds. *The Cambridge History of Ancient China: From the Origins of Civilization to 221 B.C.* 1999. An authoritative collection of chapters, half by historians, half by archaeologists.

Mote, F. W. *Intellectual Foundations of China.* 1989. Brief but stimulating introduction to early Chinese thought.

Thorp, Robert, and Richard Vinograd. *Chinese Art and Culture.* 2001. Broad coverage of all of China's visual arts.

Yang, Xin, ed. *The Golden Age of Chinese Archaeology.* 1999. The well-illustrated catalogue of a major show of Chinese archaeological finds.

Notes

1. *Chinese Civilization: A Sourcebook,* 2d ed., revised and expanded by Patricia Buckley Ebrey (New York: Free Press/Macmillan, 1993), p. 11. All quotations from this work reprinted and edited with the permission of The Free Press, a Division of Simon & Schuster Adult Publishing Group. Copyright © 1993 by Patricia Buckley Ebrey. All rights reserved.

2. Edward Shaughnessy, "Western Zhou History," in M. Loewe and E. Shaughnessy, eds., *The Cambridge History of Ancient China* (New York: Cambridge University Press, 1999), p. 336. Reprinted with the permission of Cambridge University Press and Edward L. Shaughnessy.

3. Patricia Buckley Ebrey, *The Cambridge Illustrated History of China* (Cambridge: Cambridge University Press, 1996), p. 34.

4. Ebrey, *Chinese Civilization,* p. 21.
5. Ibid., p. 19.
6. Ibid.
7. *Analects* 7.19, 15.30. Translated by Patricia Ebrey.
8. Ebrey, *Chinese Civilization,* p. 26.
9. Ibid., p. 24, modified.
10. Ibid., p. 27.
11. Ibid., p. 28, modified.
12. Ibid., p. 28.
13. Ibid., p. 31.
14. Ibid.
15. Ibid., p. 33.
16. Ibid., p. 35.

Listening to the PAST

The Book of Mencius

The book that records the teachings of Mencius (ca. 370–ca. 300 B.C.E.) was modeled on the Analects of Confucius. It presents, in no particular order, conversations between Mencius and several rulers, philosophers, and disciples. Unlike the Analects, however, the Book of Mencius includes extended discussions of particular points, suggesting that Mencius had a hand in recording the conversations.

Mencius had an audience with King Hui of Liang. The king said, "Sir, you did not consider a thousand *li* too far to come. You must have some ideas about how to benefit my state."

Mencius replied, "Why must Your Majesty use the word 'benefit'? All I am concerned with are the benevolent and the right. If Your Majesty says, 'How can I benefit my state?' your officials will say, 'How can I benefit my family,' and officers and common people will say, 'How can I benefit myself?' Once superiors and inferiors are competing for benefit, the state will be in danger.

"When the head of a state of ten thousand chariots is murdered, the assassin is invariably a noble with a fief of a thousand chariots. When the head of a fief of a thousand chariots is murdered, the assassin is invariably head of a subfief of a hundred chariots. Those with a thousand out of ten thousand, or a hundred out of a thousand, had quite a bit. But when benefit is put before what is right, they are not satisfied without snatching it all. By contrast, there has never been a benevolent person who neglected his parents or a righteous person who put his lord last. Your Majesty perhaps will now also say, 'All I am concerned with are the benevolent and the right.' Why mention 'benefit'?"

After seeing King Xiang of Liang, Mencius said to someone, "When I saw him from a distance, he did not look like a ruler, and when I got closer, I saw nothing to command respect. But he asked, 'How can the realm be settled?'

"I answered, 'It can be settled through unity.'

"'Who can unify it?' he asked.

"I answered, 'Someone not fond of killing people.'

"'Who could give it to him?'

"I answered, 'Everyone in the world will give it to him. Your Majesty knows what rice plants are? If there is a drought in the seventh and eighth months, the plants wither, but if moisture collects in the sky and forms clouds and rain falls in torrents, the plants suddenly revive. This is the way it is; no one can stop the process. In the world today there are no rulers disinclined toward killing. If there were a ruler who did not like to kill people, everyone in the world would crane their necks to catch sight of him. This is really true. The people would flow toward him the way water flows down. No one would be able to repress them.'"

After an incident between Zou and Lu, Duke Mu asked, "Thirty-three of my officials died but no common people died. I could punish them, but I could not punish them all. I could refrain from punishing them, but they did angrily watch their superiors die without saving them. What would be the best course for me to follow?"

Mencius answered, "When the harvest failed, even though your granaries were full, nearly a thousand of your subjects were lost—the old and weak among them dying in the gutters, the able-bodied scattering in all directions. Your officials never reported the situation, a case of superiors callously inflicting suffering on their subordinates. Zengzi said, 'Watch out, watch out! What you do will be done to you.' This was the first chance the people had to pay them back. You should not resent them. If Your Highness practices benevolent government, the common people will love their superiors and die for those in charge of them."

King Xuan of Qi asked, "Is it true that Tang banished Jie and King Wu took up arms against Zhou?"

Mencius replied, "That is what the records say."

"Then is it permissible for a subject to assassinate his lord?"

Mencius said, "Someone who does violence to the good we call a villain; someone who does violence to the right we call a criminal. A person who is both a villain and a criminal we call a scoundrel. I have heard that the scoundrel Zhou was killed, but have not heard that a lord was killed."

King Xuan of Qi asked about ministers.

Mencius said, "What sort of ministers does Your Majesty mean?"

The king said, "Are there different kinds of ministers?"

"There are. There are noble ministers related to the ruler and ministers of other surnames."

The king said, "I'd like to hear about noble ministers."

Mencius replied, "When the ruler makes a major error, they point it out. If he does not listen to their repeated remonstrations, then they put someone else on the throne."

The king blanched. Mencius continued, "Your Majesty should not be surprised at this. Since you asked me, I had to tell you truthfully."

After the king regained his composure, he asked about unrelated ministers. Mencius said, "When the king makes an error, they point it out. If he does not heed their repeated remonstrations, they quit their posts."

Bo Gui said, "I'd like a tax of one part in twenty. What do you think?"

Mencius said, "Your way is that of the northern tribes. Is one potter enough for a state with ten thousand households?"

"No, there would not be enough wares."

"The northern tribes do not grow all the five grains, only millet. They have no cities or houses, no ritual sacrifices. They do not provide gifts or banquets for feudal lords, and do not have a full array of officials. Therefore, for them, one part in twenty is enough. But we live in the central states. How could we abolish social roles and do without gentlemen? If a state cannot do without potters, how much less can it do without gentlemen.

"Those who want to make government lighter than it was under Yao and Shun are to some degree barbarians. Those who wish to make government heavier than it was under Yao and Shun are to some degree [tyrants like] Jie."

Gaozi said, "Human nature is like whirling water. When an outlet is opened to the east, it flows east; when an outlet is opened to the west, it flows west. Human nature is no more inclined to good or bad than water is inclined to east or west."

Mencius responded, "Water, it is true, is not inclined to either east or west, but does it have no preference for high or low? Goodness is to human nature like flowing downward is to water. There are no people who are not good and no water that does not flow down. Still, water, if splashed, can go higher than your head; if forced, it can be brought up a hill. This isn't the nature of water; it is the specific circumstances. Although people can be made to be bad, their natures are not changed."

Opening page of a 1617 edition of the Book of Mencius. *(Rare Books Collections, Harvard-Yenching Library, Harvard University)*

Questions for Analysis

1. Does Mencius give consistent advice to the kings he talks to?

2. Do you see a link between Mencius's views on human nature and his views on the true king?

3. What role does Mencius see for ministers?

Source: Reprinted and edited with the permission of The Free Press, a Division of Simon & Schuster Adult Publishing Group, from *Chinese Civilization: A Sourcebook,* Second Edition, revised and expanded by Patricia Buckley Ebrey. Copyright © 1993 by Patricia Buckley Ebrey. All rights reserved.

Tetrapylon of Aphrodisias. This monumental gate celebrates the beautiful and rich city of Aphrodisias in modern Turkey. *(John Buckler)*

chapter 4

THE GREEK EXPERIENCE (CA. 3500–146 B.C.E.)

The people of ancient Greece developed a culture that fundamentally shaped the civilization of the western part of Eurasia much as the Chinese did for the eastern part. The Greeks were the first in the Mediterranean and neighboring areas to explore most of the questions that still concern thinkers today. Going beyond mythmaking, the Greeks strove to understand the world in logical, rational terms. The result was the birth of philosophy and science, subjects as important to many of them as religion. From daily life they developed the concept of politics. Their contributions to the arts and literature still fertilize intellectual life today.

The history of the Greeks is divided into two broad periods: the Hellenic, roughly the time between the arrival of the Greeks and the triumph of Macedonia in 338 B.C.E.; and the Hellenistic, the years from Alexander the Great (336–323 B.C.E.) to the Roman conquest (200–146 B.C.E.).

HELLAS: THE LAND AND THE POLIS (CA. 3500–CA. 800 B.C.E.)

How did the geography of Greece divide the land so that small communities naturally developed?

Hellas, as the Greeks call their land, encompasses the Greek peninsula and the islands surrounding it, the area known as the Aegean basin. This basin in turn included the Greek settlements in Ionia in Asia Minor, the western coast of modern Turkey. Geography acts as an enormously divisive force in Greek life because the rugged terrain led to political fragmentation. Consequently, no strong central state became permanently dominant.

● **Mycenaean Lion Hunt** *The Mycenaeans were a robust, warlike people who enjoyed the thrill and the danger of hunting. This scene on the blade of a dagger depicts hunters armed with spears and protected by shields defending themselves against charging lions. (National Archaeological Museum/ Archaeological Receipts Fund)*

The Earliest Settlers

At the faint dawn of history, small farming communities worked much of the land. They prospered and expanded in a gradual process still little understood. Historians can, however, describe two well-documented early civilizations. The Minoan culture, the earlier of the two, arose about 3500 B.C.E. on the island of Crete. Its modern discoverers named it after the mythical king Minos. The second society, the Mycenaean, flourished between about 1575 and 1000 B.C.E. Its name, too, is modern, derived from the small Greek town where its remains were first discovered. Because both the Minoans and Mycenaeans used bronze instruments, modern scholars name this the Bronze Age.

At the head of Minoan society stood a king and his nobles governing a society of farmers and maritime merchants. Besides spreading throughout Crete, the Minoans traded with Egypt and the coastal cities of the ancient Near East. Their trading ventures also brought them into contact with the Mycenaeans on the Greek peninsula. The Mycenaeans founded numerous kingdoms from Thessaly in the north to the southern Peloponnesos. The kingdom was the basic Mycenaean political unit, headed by a king and his warrior aristocracy. Owners of most of the land, they relied on non-noble artisans, traders, and farmers to run the economy. Slaves, at the bottom of the social scale, were owned by the king and aristocrats. Mycenaean commerce quickly spread throughout the eastern Mediterranean, reaching Asia Minor, Cyprus, and Egypt. Prosperity, however, did not bring peace, and between 1300 and 1000 B.C.E. various kingdoms ravaged one another in a savage series of wars that destroyed both the Minoan and Mycenaean civilizations.

The fall of these first kingdoms ushered in a period of poverty and disruption usually called Greece's "Dark Age" (ca. 1100–800 B.C.E.). Despite daunting challenges, Greece actually became even more Greek during these years. Some Greeks entered the peninsula for the first time, the most important being the Dorians, who became the historical Spartans, Argives, and Messenians. Others migrated eastward to Asia Minor. By the end of the Dark Age Greeks and their culture had spread throughout the Aegean basin (see Map 4.1).

The Polis (ca. 800 B.C.E.)

polis *Generally translated as "city-state," it was the basic political and institutional unit of Greece.*

During the Dark Age, the Greeks developed the **polis,** which is generally translated as "city-state." More than a political institution, the polis was a community of citizens with their own customs and laws. Even though the physical, religious, and political form of the polis varied from place to place, it was the very badge of Greekness.

acropolis *An elevated point within a city on which stood temples, altars, public monuments, and various dedications to the gods of the polis.*

The polis included the town and its surrounding countryside. The people of the polis typically lived in a compact group of houses within a city, which by the fifth century B.C.E. was generally surrounded by a wall. The city contained a point, usually elevated, called the **acropolis,** and a public square or marketplace, the *agora.* On the acropolis stood the temples, altars, public monuments, and various dedications to the gods of the polis. The agora was originally the place where the warrior assembly met, and it became the political center of the polis. In the agora were porticoes, shops, public buildings, and courts.

The *chora,* which included the arable land, pastureland, and wasteland of the polis, was typically its source of wealth. Farmers left the city each morning to work their fields or tend their flocks of sheep and goats, and they returned at night. On the wasteland people often quarried stone or mined for precious metals. Thus the polis was the scene of both urban and agrarian life.

The size of the polis varied according to geographical circumstances. But regardless of its size or wealth, the polis was fundamental to Greek life. The very smallness of the polis enabled Greeks to see how the individual fit into the overall system—how the human parts made up the social whole. The Greeks were their own magistrates, administrators, and soldiers.

The polis could be governed in several ways. In a **monarchy,** a term derived from the Greek for "the rule of one man," a king represented the community, reigning according to law and respecting the rights of the citizens. The aristocracy could govern the state. A literal political translation of the term *aristocracy* means "power in the hands of the best." Or the running of the polis could be the prerogative of an **oligarchy,** which literally means "the rule of a few"—in this case a small group of wealthy citizens not necessarily of aristocratic birth. Still another form of government was **tyranny,** rule by a man who had seized power by extralegal means. Or the polis could be governed as a **democracy,** through the rule of the people, a concept that in Greece meant that all citizens, regardless of birth or wealth, administered the workings of government.

Because the bonds that held the polis together were so intimate, Greeks were extremely reluctant to allow foreigners to share fully in its life. Nor could women play political roles. Women participated in some religious ceremonies, and served as priestesses, but the polis had no room for them in state affairs. In Greek democracy, citizenship was extended to many but not all males whose families had long lived in the polis.

Although each polis was jealous of its independence, some Greeks banded together to create leagues of city-states. Here was the birth of Greek federalism, a political system in which several states formed a central government while remaining independent in their internal affairs. United in a league, a confederation of city-states was far stronger than any of the individual members and better able to withstand external attack.

The passionate individualism of the polis proved to be another serious weakness. The citizens of each polis were determined to remain free and autonomous. Since the Greeks were rarely willing to unite in larger political bodies, the political result was almost constant warfare. A polis could dominate, but unlike Rome it could not incorporate other cities.

Chronology

ca. 3500–338 B.C.E.	Hellenic period
ca. 3500–ca. 1000 B.C.E.	Minoan and Mycenaean civilizations
ca. 1100–800 B.C.E.	Evolution of the polis; Greece's "Dark Age"
ca. 800–500 B.C.E.	Rise of Sparta and Athens
776 B.C.E.	Foundation of the Olympic games
ca. 750–550 B.C.E.	Greek colonization of the Mediterranean
525–322 B.C.E.	Birth and development of tragedy, historical writing, and philosophy
499–404 B.C.E.	Persian and Peloponnesian Wars
ca. 470–322 B.C.E.	Philosophies of Socrates, Plato, and Aristotle
367–100 B.C.E.	Growth of mystery religions
340–262 B.C.E.	Rise of Epicurean and Stoic philosophies
336–100 B.C.E.	Hellenistic period
336–323 B.C.E.	Reign of Alexander the Great
326–146 B.C.E.	Spread of commerce from the Mediterranean Sea to India
310–212 B.C.E.	Period of scientific advancements

monarchy *Derived from the Greek for "the rule of one man," it was a type of Greek government in which a king represented the community.*

oligarchy *"The rule of a few," a type of Greek government in which a small group of wealthy citizens, not necessarily of aristocratic birth, ruled.*

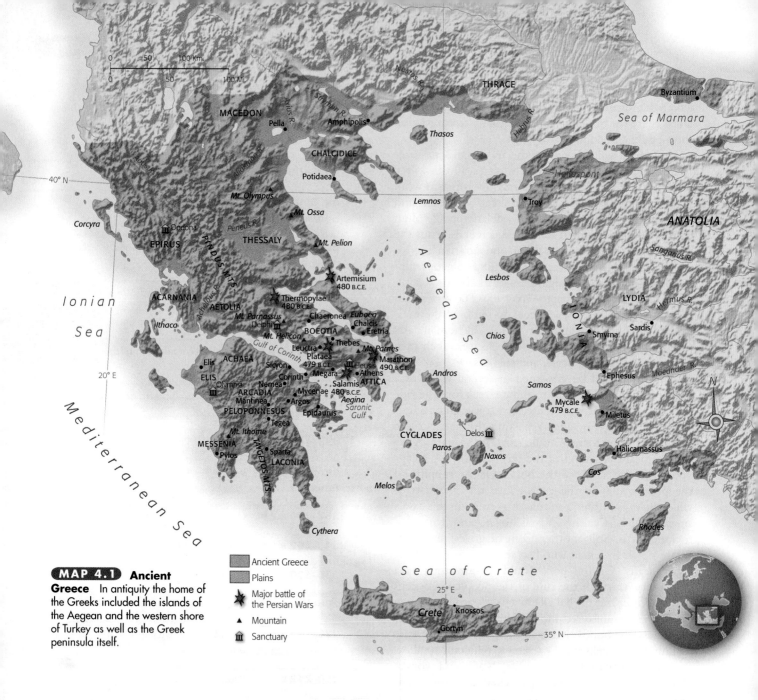

MAP 4.1 **Ancient Greece** In antiquity the home of the Greeks included the islands of the Aegean and the western shore of Turkey as well as the Greek peninsula itself.

Ancient Greece
Plains
Major battle of the Persian Wars
Mountain
Sanctuary

(see Map 4.2).

THE ARCHAIC AGE (CA. 800–500 B.C.E.)

What were the major accomplishments of the Archaic age, and why were they important?

The maturation of the polis coincided with an era that gave rise to two developments of lasting importance. The first was another geographical expansion of Greeks, who now ventured as far east as the Black Sea and as far west as the Atlantic Ocean. The next saw Sparta and Athens, the two poles of the Greek experience, rise to prominence.

Overseas Expansion

With stability and prosperity, the Greek world grew in wealth and numbers, which brought new problems. Given the infertility of Greece, the increase in population led to land hunger. The resulting social and political tensions drove many Greeks to seek new homes outside Greece (see Map 4.2).

tyranny *Rule by a tyrant, a man who used his wealth to gain a political following that could take over the existing government.*

democracy *A type of Greek government in which all citizens, without regard to birth or wealth, administered the workings of government. It is translated as "the power of the people."*

From about 750 to 550 B.C.E. Greeks poured onto the coasts of the northern Aegean and the Black Sea, westward along the north Africa coast, Sicily, southern Italy, and beyond to Spain and the Atlantic. In all these places the Greeks established flourishing cities that turned the Mediterranean into a Greek lake. A later wave of colonization spread Greeks throughout the northern coast of the Black Sea as far east as southern Russia. Colonization on this scale meant that the future culture of this entire area would be Greek, and to this heritage Rome would later fall heir.

The Growth of Sparta

During the Archaic period the Spartans also faced problems of overpopulation and land hunger. They solved both by conquering the rich region of Messene in 715 B.C.E. They made the Messenians *helots*, state slaves, who soon rose in a revolt that took the Spartans thirty years to crush. Afterwards, non-nobles who had shared in the fighting demanded rights equal to those of the nobility. Under intense pressure the aristocrats agreed to remodel the state in a system called the Lycurgan regimen after Lycurgus, a legendary lawgiver. All Spartans were given equal political rights. Two kings ruled, assisted by a council of nobles. Executive power lay in the hands of five *ephors*, overseers, elected by the people. Economically, the helots did all the work, while Spartan citizens devoted their time to military training.

In the Lycurgan system every citizen owed primary allegiance to Sparta. Suppression of the individual together with emphasis on military prowess led to a barracks state. Family life itself was sacrificed to the polis. After long, hard military training that began at age seven, citizen men became lifelong soldiers, the best in Greece. Family life remained important to Spartan society, but it was second to the needs of military

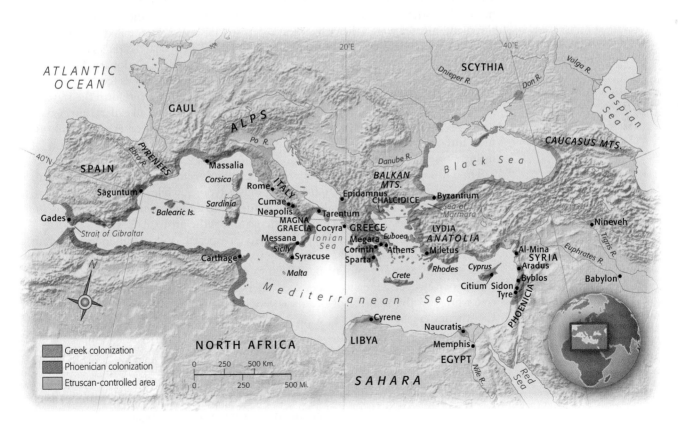

MAP 4.2 **Colonization of the Mediterranean** Though the Greeks and Phoenicians colonized the Mediterranean basin at about the same time, the Greeks spread much farther.

hoplite *The heavily armed infantry man who was the backbone of the Greek army.*

defense. In battle Spartans were supposed to stand and die rather than retreat. **Hoplites,** heavily armed infantrymen, were urged to come back with their shields or be carried dead on them. In the Lycurgan regimen Spartans were expected to train vigorously, do with little, and like it.

In this martial atmosphere women were remarkably free. The Spartans viewed maternal health as crucial for the bearing of healthy children and thus encouraged women to participate in athletics and to eat well. With men in military service much of their lives, citizen women ran the estates and owned land in their own right. They were not physically restricted or secluded. Spartans expected them to be good wives and strict mothers of future soldiers. Not only in time of war but also in peace men often did not see their wives for long periods. Men's most meaningful relations were same-sex ones. The Spartan military leaders viewed such relationships as militarily advantageous because they felt that men would fight even more fiercely for lovers and comrades. Close links among men thus contributed to Spartan civic life, which was admired throughout the Greek world.

The Evolution of Athens

Like Sparta, Athens faced pressing social and economic problems during the Archaic period, but the Athenians eventually extended to all citizens the right and duty of governing the polis. The late seventh century B.C.E. was for Athens a time of turmoil because aristocrats had begun to seize the holdings of smaller landowners. In 621 B.C.E. the aristocrat Draco, under pressure from the peasants and with the consent of the nobles, published the first law code of the Athenian polis. Though harsh, his code nonetheless embodied the ideal that the law belonged to all citizens. Yet the aristocracy still governed Athens oppressively, and by the early sixth century B.C.E. the social and economic situation remained dire, as noble landholders forced small farmers into economic dependence. Many families were sold into slavery, while others were exiled and their land mortgaged to the rich. Solon, an aristocrat and a poet, railed against these injustices in his poems, which he recited in the agora for all to hear. Solon's sincerity and good sense convinced other aristocrats that he was no crazed revolutionary. Moreover, the common people trusted him. Around 594 B.C.E. the nobles elected him *archon,* chief magistrate of the polis, and gave him extraordinary power to reform the state.

Solon immediately freed all people enslaved for debt, recalled all exiles, canceled all debts on land, and made enslavement for debt illegal. He allowed even the poorest men into the old aristocratic assembly, where they could vote in the election of magistrates.

Though solving some immediate problems, Solon's reforms did not bring peace to Athens. Some aristocrats tried to make themselves tyrants, while others opposed them. In 546 B.C.E. Pisistratus, an exiled noble, returned to Athens, defeated his opponent, and became tyrant. Pisistratus reduced the power of the aristocracy while supporting the common people. Under his rule Athens prospered, and his building program made Athens into a splendid city. His reign as tyrant promoted the growth of democratic ideas by arousing rudimentary feelings of equality among many Athenians.

Democracy became reality under the leadership of Cleisthenes, a prominent aristocrat who won the support of ordinary people to emerge triumphant in 508 B.C.E. Cleisthenes created the **deme,** a local unit that kept the roll of citizens within its jurisdiction.

deme *A local unit that served as the basic element of Cleisthenes's political system.*

The democracy functioned on the ideal that all full citizens were sovereign. Yet not all citizens could take time from work to participate in government. They therefore delegated their power to other citizens by creating various offices to run the democracy. The most prestigious of them was the board of ten archons, elected for one year, who handled legal and military affairs. After leaving office, they entered the *Areopagos,* a select council of ex-archons who handled cases involving homicide, wounding, and arson.

Legislation was in the hands of two bodies, the *boule,* or council, composed of five hundred members, and the *ecclesia,* the assembly of all citizens. The boule, separate from the Areopagos, was perhaps the major institution of the democracy. By supervising the various committees of government and proposing bills to the assembly, it guided Athenian political life. It received foreign envoys and forwarded treaties to the assembly for ratification. The ecclesia by a simple majority vote, however, had the final word.

Athenian democracy demonstrated that a large group of people, not just a few, could efficiently run the affairs of state. Because citizens could speak their minds, they were not forced to rebellion or conspiracy to express their views. Like all democracies in ancient Greece, however, the Athenian was limited. Women, slaves, and outsiders could not be citizens. Their opinions were neither recorded nor legally binding.

THE CLASSICAL PERIOD (500–338 B.C.E.)

Although the classical period saw tremendous upheavals, what were its lasting achievements?

In the years between 500 and 338 B.C.E. Greek civilization reached its highest peak in politics, thought, and art. In this period the Greeks beat back the armies of the Persian Empire. Then, turning their spears against one another, they destroyed their own political system in a century of warfare. Some thoughtful Greeks recorded these momentous events. Herodotus (ca. 485–425 B.C.E.), "the father of history," described the Persian War of 490–479 B.C.E., followed by Thucydides (ca. 460–ca. 399 B.C.E.), whose account of the Peloponnesian War remains a literary classic. This era also saw the flowering of philosophy, as thinkers like Socrates (ca. 470–399 B.C.E.), Plato (427–347 B.C.E.), and Aristotle (384–322 B.C.E.) pondered the meaning of the universe and human nature. The Greeks invented drama, and Greek architects reached the zenith of their art. Because of these various intellectual and artistic achievements, this age is called the classical period.

Delian League *A grand naval alliance, created by the Athenians and aimed at liberating Ionia from Persian rule.*

The Deadly Conflicts (499–404 B.C.E.)

Warfare marked the entire classical period. In 499 B.C.E. the Ionian Greeks with feeble Athenian help unsuccessfully rebelled against the Persian Empire. In retaliation the Persians struck at Athens, only to be defeated at Marathon (see Map 4.1). In 480 B.C.E. the Persian king Xerxes invaded Greece on a massive scale. Under the leadership of Sparta by land and Athens by sea, many Greeks united to defeat the Persians in hard-fought battles at the pass of Thermopylae and in the waters off Artemsium in 480 B.C.E. In 479 B.C.E., after the loss of Athens, the Greeks defeated the Persians at the decisive battle of Salamis and finally again at Plataea later that year.

In 478 B.C.E. the victorious Athenians and their allies formed the **Delian League,** a grand naval alliance intended to liberate Ionia from Persian rule. While driving the Persians out of Asia Minor, the Athenians also turned the league into an Athenian empire. Under their great leader Pericles (ca. 494–429 B.C.E.) the Athenians grew so powerful and aggressive that they alarmed Sparta and its allies. In 431 B.C.E. Athenian imperialism finally drove Sparta into the conflict known as the Peloponnesian War. At its outbreak a Spartan ambassador warned the Athenians: "This day will be the beginning of great evils

● **Leonidas at Thermopylae** This heroic statue symbolizes the sacrifice of King Leonidas at the battle. Together with his Spartans, the Thespians, and the Thebans, he heroically died to stop the Persians at the pass of Thermopylae. *(Professor Paul Cartledge)*

for the Greeks."[1] Few have ever spoken more prophetically. The Peloponnesian War lasted a generation (431–404 B.C.E.) and brought widespread destruction and huge loss of life. In 404 B.C.E. the Athenians finally surrendered, but not before Greek civilization had been struck a serious blow.

Athenian Arts in the Age of Pericles

In the last half of the fifth century B.C.E. Pericles turned Athens into the showplace of Greece by making the Acropolis a wonder for all time. He appropriated allied money to pay for a huge building program that erected temples and other buildings to honor Athena, the patron goddess of the city, and to show the Greek world the glory of Athens. The Propylaea is a magnificent gateway to a living cultural museum. The nearby temple of Athena Nike (Athena the Victorious) is a small gem. Above all, the Parthenon stands splendidly as a monumental gift to Athena. In many ways the Athenian Acropolis is the epitome of Greek art and its spirit. Although the buildings were dedicated to the gods and most of the sculptures portray gods, they all nonetheless express the Greek fascination with the human form. The Acropolis also exhibits the rational side of Greek art. Greek artists portrayed action in a balanced and restrained fashion, capturing the noblest aspects of human beings: their reason and dignity.

Other aspects of Athenian cultural life were also rooted in the life of the polis. The development of drama was tied to the religious festivals of the city. The polis sponsored the production of plays and required wealthy citizens to pay the expenses of their production. Although many plays were highly controversial, they were neither suppressed nor censored.

Aeschylus (525–456 B.C.E.) was the first dramatist to explore such basic questions as the rights of the individual, the conflict between society and the individual, and the nature of good and evil. In his trilogy of plays, *The Oresteia,* he treats the themes of betrayal, murder, and reconciliation, urging that reason and justice be applied to reconcile fundamental conflicts. The final play concludes with a prayer that civil dissension never be allowed to destroy the city.

Sophocles (496–406 B.C.E.) also deals with matters personal, political, and divine. In *Antigone* he emphasizes the precedence of divine law over political law and family custom. In *Oedipus the King* he tells the story of a good man doomed by the gods to kill his father and marry his mother. When Oedipus fails to avoid his fate, in despair he blinds himself and flees into exile. In *Oedipus at Colonus* Sophocles treats the last days of the broken man, whose patient suffering and uncomplaining piety ultimately win the blessings and honor of the gods. Sophocles urges people to obey the will of the gods even without fully understanding it, for the gods stand for justice and order.

Euripides (ca. 480–406 B.C.E.), the last of the three great tragic dramatists, likewise explored the theme of personal conflict within the polis and sounded the depths of the individual. With Euripides drama entered a new and more personal phase. To him the gods mattered far less than people. The essence of his tragedy is the flaws of people who bring disaster on themselves because their passions overwhelm reason.

Writers of Athenian comedy treated the affairs of the polis bawdily and often coarsely. Even so, their plays too were performed at religious festivals. They used humor as political commentary in an effort to suggest and support the proper policies of the polis. Best known of the comedians is Aristophanes (ca. 445–386 B.C.E.), a merciless critic of cranks, quacks, and fools. He used his art of sarcasm to dramatize his ideas on the right conduct of the citizen and his leaders for the good of the polis.

Despite the undeniable achievements of the Athenians, many modern historians have exaggerated their importance. This Athenocentrism fails to do justice to the other Greeks who also shaped society, culture, and history.

Aspects of Social Life in Athens

The Athenians, like other Greeks, lived comparatively simple lives with few material possessions. The Athenian house was rather simple. It consisted of a series of rooms opening onto a central courtyard that contained a well, an altar, and a washbasin. Larger houses often had a room at the front, where the men of the family ate and entertained guests, and women's quarters at the back. If the family lived in the country, stalls for animals faced the courtyard. Farmers kept oxen for plowing, various animals for food, and donkeys for transportation. Even in the city chickens and perhaps a goat or two roamed the courtyard with dogs and cats.

In the city a man might support himself as a craftsman, potter, bronzesmith, or tanner, or he could contract with the polis to work on public buildings. Certain crafts, including spinning and weaving, were generally done by women. Men and women without skills worked as paid laborers, but competed with slaves, who were usually foreigners or prisoners of war. Citizens and slaves were paid the same amount for their work.

The social conditions of Athenian women have been the subject of much debate and little agreement, in part because the sources are fragmentary. Women rarely played notable roles in public affairs, and we know the names of no female poets, artists, or philosophers from classical Athens. Women did manage the household and attend religious festivals. The status of a free woman was strictly protected by law. Only her children could be citizens. Only she was in charge of the household and the family's possessions, yet the law protected her primarily to protect her husband's interests. Women in Athens and elsewhere in Greece, like those in Mesopotamia, brought dowries to their husbands upon marriage, which legally remained their property.

● **Woman Grinding Grain** Here a woman takes the grain raised on the family farm and grinds it by hand in a mill. She needed few tools to turn the grain into flour. *(National Archaeological Museum, Athens/Archaeological Receipts Fund)*

● **Sacrificial Scene** Much of Greek religion was simple and festive, as this scene demonstrates. The participants include women and boys dressed in their finest clothes and crowned with garlands. Musicians add to the festivities. Only the sheep will not enjoy the ceremony. *(National Archaeological Museum, Athens/ Archaeological Receipts Fund)*

A citizen woman's main functions were to bear and raise children. Respectable citizen women ideally lived secluded lives in which the only men they usually saw were relatives and tradesmen. How far this ideal was actually a reality is impossible to say, but prosperous women probably spent much of their time at home. There they oversaw domestic slaves and hired labor, and together with servants and friends worked wool into cloth. In a sense, poor and noncitizen women lived freer lives than did wealthier women. They performed manual labor in the fields or sold goods in the agora, going about their affairs much as men did. Prostitution was legal in Athens, and some prostitutes added intellectual accomplishments to physical beauty. These *hetairai* accompanied men in public settings where their wives would not have been welcome, serving men as social as well as sexual partners.

In classical Athens, part of a male adolescent citizen's training in adulthood was supposed to entail a hierarchical sexual and tutorial relationship with an older man, who most likely was married and may have had other female sexual partners as well. These relationships between adolescents and men were often celebrated in literature and art, in part because Athenians regarded perfection as possible only in the male. Women were generally seen as inferior to men, dominated by their bodies rather than their minds.

Same-sex relations did not mean that people did not marry, for Athenians saw the continuation of the family line as essential. Sexual desire and procreation were both important aspects of life, but they were not necessarily linked for ancient Greeks.

Greek Religion

It is extremely difficult to understand Greek religion, since, unlike modern peoples, the ancient Greeks had no uniform faith or creed. Although the Greeks usually worshiped the same deities—Zeus, Hera, Apollo, Athena, and others—the cults of these divinities varied from polis to polis. The Greeks had no sacred books such as the Bible, and Greek religion was often a matter more of ritual than belief. Nor did cults impose an ethical code of conduct. Unlike the Egyptians and Hebrews, the Greeks lacked a priesthood as the modern world understands the term. In Greece priests and priestesses existed to care for temples and sacred property and to conduct the proper rituals, but not to make religious rules or doctrines, much less to enforce them. In short, there existed in Greece no central ecclesiastical authority and no organized creed.

The most important members of the Greek pantheon were Zeus, the king of the gods, and his consort, Hera. Although they were the mightiest and most honored of the deities who lived on Mount Olympus, their divine children were closer to ordinary people. Apollo was especially popular. He represented the epitome of youth, beauty, benevolence, and athletic skill. He was also the god of music and culture, in many ways symbolizing the best of Greek culture. His sister Athena, who patronized women's crafts such as weaving, was also a warrior-goddess who had been born from the head of Zeus without a mother. Best known for her cult at Athens, to which she gave her name, she was highly revered throughout Greece. Besides these Olympian gods, each polis had its own minor deities, each with his or her own local cult. Much religion was local and domestic. Each village possessed its own cults and rituals, and individual families honored various deities in their homes.

Though Greek religion in general was individual or related to the polis, the Greeks also shared some Pan-Hellenic festivals, the chief of which were held at Olympia to honor Zeus and at Delphi to honor Apollo. The festivities at Olympia included the famous athletic contests that have inspired the modern Olympic games. Held every four years, they attracted visitors from all over the Greek world and lasted well into Christian times. The Pythian games at Delphi were also held every four years, but these contests included musical and literary competitions. Both the Olympic and Pythian games were unifying factors in Greek life.

The Flowering of Philosophy

The Greeks, like peoples before them, originally spun myths and epics to explain the origin of the universe. Yet going further, they created philosophy to understand the cosmos in purely physical terms. Some Greeks in Ionia began an intellectual revolution that still flourishes today. These thinkers are called the Pre-Socratics because their rational efforts preceded those of Socrates. Taking individual facts, they wove them into general theories. Despite appearances, they concluded, the universe is actually simple and subject to natural laws. Drawing on their observations, they speculated about the basic building blocks of the universe.

The first of these Pre-Socratic thinkers, Thales (ca. 600 B.C.E.) sought to determine the basic element of the universe from which all else sprang. He surmised that it was water. Although he was wrong, it was the beginning of the scientific method. Another Pre-Socratic, Anaximander (d. 547 B.C.E.) was the first to use general concepts, which are essential to abstract thought. Heraclitus (ca. 500 B.C.E.) declared the primal element to be fire, which is ever changing and eternal. Democritus (ca. 460 B.C.E.) created the atomic theory that the universe is made up of invisible, indestructible particles. The culmination of Pre-Socratic thought was the theory that four simple substances make up the universe: fire, air, earth, and water.

This stream of thought also branched into other directions. Hippocrates (ca. 470–400 B.C.E.), the father of medicine, sought natural explanations for diseases and natural means to treat them. He relied on empirical knowledge rather than religion or magic to further his work. The Sophists took the direction of making a distinction between science and philosophy. While differing on particulars, they all agreed that human beings were the proper subject of study. They also believed that excellence could be taught. They held that nothing is absolute; everything is relative.

Socrates (ca. 470–399 B.C.E.) shared the Sophists' belief that people are the essential subjects of philosophical inquiry. He started with a general topic and narrowed it

Primary Source:
Apologia
Learn why Socrates was condemned to death, and why he refused to stop questioning the wisdom of his countrymen.

to its essentials by posing questions, then sought answers. This is the Socratic method. He felt that through knowledge people could approach the supreme good and thus find happiness. Yet in 399 B.C.E. the Athenians executed him for corrupting the youth and for impiety.

Socrates' student Plato (427–347 B.C.E.) founded the Academy, a school dedicated to philosophy. Plato developed the theory that all tangible things are unreal and temporary, copies of "forms" or "ideas" that are constant and indestructible. The highest form is the idea of good, which he equated with god.

Aristotle (384–322 B.C.E.) went beyond his teacher Plato by using observation and analysis of natural phenomena to explain the cosmos. He argued that the universe was finite, spherical, and eternal. He postulated four principles: matter, form, movement, and goal. His theory of cosmology added ether as one of the building blocks of the universe. He wrongly concluded that the earth is the center of the universe and that the stars and planets revolve around it.

The philosophies of Plato and Aristotle both viewed women as inferior beings. Plato associated women with the body and emotions and men with superior faculties of mind and reason. Aristotle thought that women's primary purpose was to bear children. Even though Athenian philosophers pushed beyond the limited thinking of previous generations, they still reflected the accepted values and concepts of their times.

> **Primary Source:**
> **Aristotle on Politics**
> *Discover the strengths and weaknesses, as Aristotle saw them, of kingdoms, aristocracies, and democracies.*

From Polis to Monarchy (404–323 B.C.E.)

MAP 4.3 **Alexander's Conquests** This map shows the course of Alexander's invasion of the Persian Empire and the speed of his progress. More important than the great success of his military campaigns was his founding of Hellenistic cities in the East.

Immediately after the Peloponnesian War, Sparta began striving for empire over the Greeks. Yet even with Persian help, Sparta could not maintain its hold on Greece. In 371 B.C.E. at Leuctra in Boeotia, a Theban army under Epaminondas destroyed the flower of the Spartans. But the Thebans were unable to bring peace to Greece. In 362 B.C.E. Epaminondas was killed in battle, and a period of stalemate followed. Philip II,

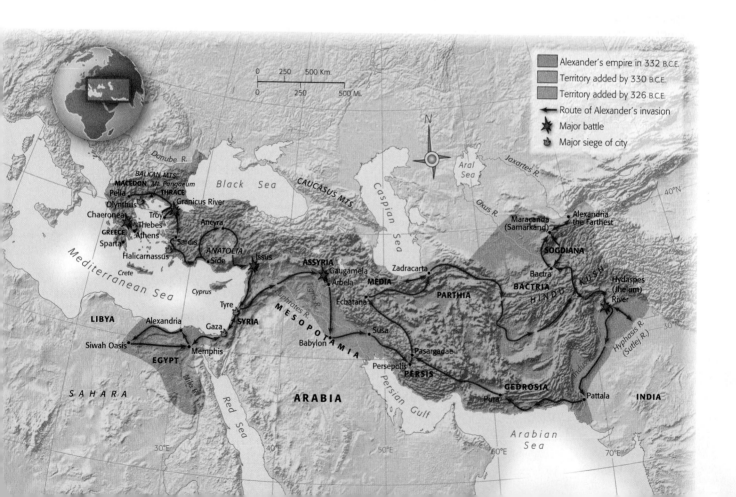

● **Alexander at the Battle of Issus**   At left, Alexander the Great, bareheaded and wearing a breastplate, charges King Darius, who is standing in a chariot. The moment marks the turning point of the battle, as Darius turns to flee from the attack. *(National Museum, Naples/Alinari/Art Resource, NY)*

king of Macedonia (r. 359–336 B.C.E.), turned the situation to his advantage. By clever use of his wealth and superb army, Philip won control of the northern Aegean, awakening fear in Athens. Finally, in 338 B.C.E. he defeated a combined Theban-Athenian army at Chaeronea. He had conquered Greece and become its arbiter. Because the Greeks could not put aside their quarrels, they fell to an invader.

Philip used his victory to unite the Greek states with his Macedonian kingdom to proclaim a crusade to liberate the Ionian Greeks from Persian rule. Before he could launch his crusade, Philip fell to an assassin's dagger in 336 B.C.E. His young son Alexander, soon to be known as "the Great," vowed to carry on Philip's mission. In 334 B.C.E. Alexander led an army of Macedonians and Greeks into western Asia. In the next three years he won three major battles—at the Granicus River, at Issus, and at Gaugamela—on his march to the east (see Map 4.3). Having overthrown the Persian Empire, in 326 B.C.E. he entered India. Finally, at the Hyphasis River his troops refused to go farther. Alexander reluctantly turned south to the Arabian Sea and then back west. In 324 B.C.E. Alexander returned to Susa, and died the next year Babylon.

The political consequence of Alexander's premature death was chaos. Since several of the chief Macedonian officers aspired to Alexander's position as emperor while others opposed them, civil war lasting forty-three years tore Alexander's empire apart. By the end of this conflict, the most successful generals had carved out their own smaller and generally stable monarchies.

Ptolemy immediately seized Egypt and transformed the native system into a Greco-Macedonian kingdom. Seleucus meanwhile won the bulk of Alexander's empire, his monarchy extending from western Asia to India. In the third century B.C.E., however, the eastern parts of Seleucus's monarchy gained their independence. The Parthians, a native people, came to power in Iran, and the Greeks created a monarchy of their own in Bactria. Antigonus maintained control of the Macedonian kingdom in Europe. Until the arrival of the Romans in the eastern Mediterranean in the second century B.C.E., the great monarchies waged frequent wars that brought no lasting results. The Hellenistic monarchy was no improvement on the Greek polis.

THE SPREAD OF HELLENISM (336–100 B.C.E.)

After Alexander the Great's conquest of the Persian Empire, how did Greek immigrants and the native peoples there create a new society?

When the Greeks and Macedonians entered Asia and Egypt, they encountered civilization older than their own. In some ways the Eastern cultures were more advanced than theirs, in others less so. Thus this third great tide of Greek migration differed from preceding waves that had spread over land inhabited by less-developed peoples. In this process both Greeks and native peoples confronted a new cultural reality. The Greeks saw themselves as "the West," while the peoples of the ancient Near East made up "the East." "East" as yet had no wider meaning for the Greeks, who had only just learned of India and knew nothing of China and lands beyond. Since the Eastern civilization was older and in some ways more sophisticated than the Greek, the newcomers had a great deal to learn from it. Yet the Greeks also proved surprisingly successful in spreading their own vibrant culture among the easterners. The result was the blending of Hellenism and Near Eastern cultures that is now called "Hellenistic." No comparable spread and sharing of cultures had occurred in this area since the days of the Mesopotamians.

Cities and Kingdoms

A major development in this new world was the supremacy of monarchy that for the Greeks replaced the polis as the chief political unit of society. Furthermore, these new kingdoms consisted of numerous different peoples who at first had little in common. Although the native populations found kingdoms traditional and familiar, to the Greeks monarchy was new and somewhat alien. To them civilized life without the polis was unthinkable. Hellenistic kings solved the problem by combining the concepts of monarchy and polis to embrace all their subjects. The kingdom became dominant in political affairs, and the polis, now only a city, served as the administrative and cultural unit. The Greek city thereby became the linchpin of the Hellenistic monarchy.

A problem, however, remained with this solution. The Greek polis had been **sovereign,** and in a monarchy only the king held sovereignty. Unwilling to create a real polis, Hellenistic kings gave their cities all the external trappings of a polis but none of the political power. Consequently, the Hellenistic city resembled a modern city. It was a cultural center with theaters, temples, and libraries—a seat of learning and a place for amusement. The Hellenistic city was also an economic center—a marketplace, a scene of trade and manufacturing. On these terms Hellenistic cities proved remarkably effective.

sovereign *An independent, autonomous state run by its citizens, free of any outside power or restraint.*

Building a Shared Society

Despite difficulties, Hellenistic monarchies successfully spread Greek culture. If the Hellenistic component was sometimes largely a veneer, it at least touched nearly every life. At the same time the Greeks became increasingly influenced by the societies they conquered. These two tendencies produced a mutually recognized common Hellenistic culture, remarkably widespread and healthy. Even so, Hellenistic kingdoms were never entirely unified in language, customs, and thought. Greek culture took firmest hold along the shores of the Mediterranean, where it thrived until the coming of the Arabs. It also prospered farther inland. In Bactria Greek and Iranian settlements led to an independent society that was soundly founded and well integrated. Bactria itself became an outpost of Hellenism, from which the Han Dynasty learned of civilized societies other than the Chinese (see page 137). Greco-Bactrians prospered until invaders from Central Asia overwhelmed their settlements in the first century B.C.E. Nonetheless, its cultural influence lasted another century.

The Seleucid kings most successfully built a shared society by their extensive colonization. Their military settlements spread from western Asia Minor along the banks of the Tigris and Euphrates and father east to India. Although the Seleucids had no elaborate plan for Hellenizing the native population, they nevertheless introduced a large and vigorous Greek population to these lands. Their presence alone had an impact. Seleucid military colonies were generally founded near native villages, thus exposing each to the other's culture. Farther east Greek kings won their independence from the Seleucids and extended their influence into India.

By contrast, the Ptolemies in Egypt at first made no effort to spread their culture, and unlike other Hellenistic kings they were not city builders. Indeed, they founded only the city of Ptolemais near Thebes. The native Egyptian population, the descendants of the pharaoh's people, originally kept their traditional language, religion, and way of life. They also continued to be the foundation of the state. They fed it by their labor in the fields and financed it with their taxes. In the second century B.C.E., however, Greeks and native Egyptians began to intermarry and mingle their cultures and languages. Some natives adopted Greek customs and language and began to play a role in the administration of the kingdom and even to serve in the army. Although more slowly than elsewhere, the overall result was the evolution of a widespread Greco-Egyptian culture.

For natives the prime advantage of Hellenistic culture was its very pervasiveness. The Greek language became the common speech of the entire eastern Mediterranean. A new Greek dialect called the **koine,** which means common, became the speech of the royal court, bureaucracy, and army. Everyone, Greek or easterner, who wanted to find an official position or compete in business had to learn it. As early as the third century B.C.E. some Greek cities granted citizenship to Hellenized natives.

koine *A common dialect of the Greek language that influenced the speech of all Greeks.*

Though Greeks and easterners adapted to each other's ways, there was never a true fusion of cultures. Nonetheless, each found many useful things in the civilization of the other, and they fertilized each other. This mingling of Greek and eastern elements made Hellenistic culture energetic and successful.

The Economic Scope of the Hellenistic World

Alexander's conquest not only changed the political face of the ancient world but also merged it into one broad economic sphere. Yet the period did not see a revolution in the way people lived and worked. The material demands of Hellenistic society remained as simple as before. Yet the spread of Greeks eastward created new markets and stimulated trade. The economic unity of the Hellenistic world, like its cultural bonds, later proved valuable to the Romans.

When Alexander conquered the Persian Empire, he found the royal treasury filled with vast sums of gold, silver, and other treasure. The victors used this wealth to finance the building of roads, the development of harbors, and most especially the founding of new cities. Whole new markets opened to all merchants, who eagerly took advantage of the unforeseen opportunities. In this fresh economic environment Greeks and local residents learned of each other's customs and traditions while forging new contacts. In the process they also spread immediate knowledge of their own cultures.

The Seleucid and Ptolemaic dynasties traded as far afield as India, Arabia, and sub-Saharan Africa. Overland trade with India and Arabia was conducted by caravan that was largely in the hands of easterners. The caravan trade never dealt in bulk goods or essential commodities. Once goods reached the Hellenistic monarchies, Greek merchants took a hand in the trade. Essential to this trade from the Mediterranean to Afghanistan and India was the southern route through Arabia. The desert of Arabia lies west of the Iranian plateau, from which trade routes stretched to the south and farther east to China. Commerce from the east arrived at Egypt and the harbors of Palestine, Phoenicia, and Syria. From these ports goods flowed to Greece, Italy, and Spain.

Over these routes traveled luxury goods that were light, rare, and expensive. In time these luxury items became necessities. This whole development was in part the result of an increased volume of trade. In the prosperity of the period, more people could afford to buy gold, silver, precious stones, and many other easily transportable goods. The most prominent goods in terms of volume were tea and silk. Indeed, the trade in silk gave the major route the name the **Great Silk Road.** In return the peoples of the eastern Mediterranean sent east manufactured items, especially metal weapons, cloth, wine, and olive oil. Although these caravan routes can trace their origins to earlier times, they became far more prominent in the Hellenistic period. Business customs developed and became standardized so that merchants of different nationalities, aided especially by koine, communicated in a way understandable to them all.

> **Great Silk Road** *The name of the major route for the silk trade.*

More economically important than this exotic trade were commercial dealings in essential commodities like raw materials, grain, and industrial products. The Hellenistic monarchies usually raised enough grain for their own needs as well as a surplus for export. For the cities of the Aegean the trade in grain was essential, because many of them could not grow enough. Fortunately for them, abundant wheat supplies were available nearby in Egypt and in the Crimea in southern Russia.

The Greek cities paid for their grain by exporting olive oil and wine. Another significant commodity was fish, which for export was either salted, pickled, or dried. This trade was doubly important because fish provided poor people with an essential element of their diet. Important also was the trade in honey, dried fruit, nuts, and vegetables. Of raw materials wood was high in demand.

Throughout the Hellenistic world slaves almost always found a ready market. Only the Ptolemies discouraged both the trade and slavery itself, but they did so only for economic reasons. Their system had no room for slaves, who only would have competed with inexpensive free labor. Otherwise slave labor could be found in cities and temples, in factories and fields, and in the homes of wealthier people.

Most trade in bulk commodities was seaborne, and the Hellenistic merchant ship was the workhorse of the day. The merchant ship had a broad beam and relied on sails for propulsion. It was far more seaworthy than the Hellenistic warship, which was long, narrow, and built for speed. A small crew of experienced sailors easily handled the merchant vessel. Maritime trade also provided opportunities for workers in many other industries and trades, particularly shipbuilders, dockworkers, teamsters, and pirates. Piracy was a constant factor in the Hellenistic world and remained so until Rome cleared it from the seas.

While demand for goods increased during the period, few new techniques of production appeared. Manual labor far more than machinery continued to turn out agricultural produce, raw materials, and the few manufactured goods the Hellenistic world used. Typical was mining, where slaves, criminals, or forced laborers dug the ore under frightful conditions. The Ptolemies ran their gold mines along harsh lines. One historian gives a grim picture of the miners' lives:

The kings of Egypt condemn [to the mines] those found guilty of wrong-doing and those taken prisoner in war, those who were victims of false accusations and were put into jail because of royal anger. . . . The condemned—and they are very many—all of them are put in chains, and they work persistently and continually, both by day and throughout the night, getting no rest and carefully cut off from escape.[2]

The Ptolemies even condemned women and children to work in the mines. Besides gold and silver, used primarily for coins and jewelry, iron was the most important metal and saw the most varied use. Even so, the method of production never became very sophisticated. Despite these shortcomings, the volume of goods produced increased in this period. Small manufacturing establishments existed nearly everywhere.

All Hellenistic kings paid special attention to agriculture. Much of their revenue came from the produce of royal lands, rents paid by the tenants of royal lands, and taxation of them. The Ptolemies, who made the greatest strides in agriculture, sponsored experiments to improve seed grain. These efforts apart, most people supported themselves in the traditional ways that supplied their basic needs.

HELLENISTIC INTELLECTUAL ADVANCES

How did the intellectual meeting of two vibrant cultures lead to a very fertile intellectual development?

The peoples of the Hellenistic era advanced the ideas and ideals of the classical Greeks to new heights. Their achievements created the religious and intellectual atmosphere that deeply influenced Roman thinking and that of Judaism and early Christianity. Far from being stagnant, this was instead a period of vigorous growth, especially in the areas of philosophy, science, and medicine.

Religion in the Hellenistic World

In religion the most significant new ideas arose outside of Greece. The Hellenistic period saw at first the spread of Greek cults throughout the Near East. When Hellenistic kings founded cities, they also built temples with new cults and priesthoods for the old Olympian gods. Greek cults, as before, sponsored literary, musical, and athletic contests, which were staged in beautiful surroundings among splendid Greek buildings. On the whole, however, the civic cults were primarily concerned with ritual and neither appealed to religious emotions nor embraced matters such as sin and redemption. While lavish in pomp and display, the new cults could not satisfy deep religious feelings or spiritual yearnings.

Greek increasingly sought solace from other sources. Some relied on philosophy as a guide to life, while others turned to superstition, magic, or astrology. Still others shrugged and spoke of **Tyche,** which means "fate," "chance," or "doom"—a capricious and sometimes malevolent force.

Beginning in the second century B.C.E. some individuals were increasingly attracted to new **mystery religions,** so called because they featured a body of ritual and beliefs not divulged to anyone not initiated into the cult. These new mystery cults incorporated aspects of both Greek and Eastern religions and held broad appeal for people who yearned for personal immortality. Already familiar with old mystery cults such as the Eleusinian mysteries in Attica, the new cults did not strike the Greeks as alien. Familiar, too, was the concept of preparation for an initiation. Devotees of the Eleusinian mysteries and other such cults had to prepare themselves mentally, physically, and spiritually before entering the gods' presence. The mystery cults thus fit well with Greek practice.

The new religions enjoyed one tremendous advantage over the old Greek mystery cults. Whereas old Greek cults were tried to particular places, such as Eleusis, the new religions spread

Tyche *The Greek goddess of fate and luck, eventually identified with the Roman goddess Fortuna.*

mystery religions *Any of several religious systems in the Greco-Roman world characterized by secret doctrines and rituals of initiation.*

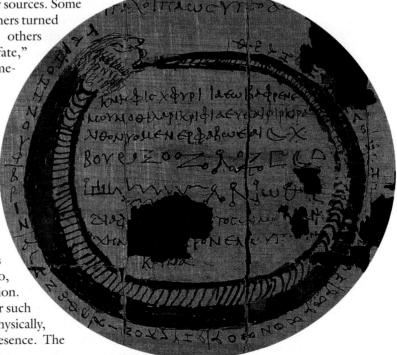

● **Hellenistic Magic** This magical text, written in Greek and Egyptian, displays a snake surrounding the magical incantation. The text is intentionally obscure. *(British Library)*

● **Hellenistic Mystery Cult** The scene depicts part of the ritual of initiation into the cult of Dionysus. The young woman here has just completed the ritual. She now dances in joy as the official with the sacred staff looks on. *(Scala/Art Resource, NY)*

throughout the Hellenistic world. People did not have to undertake long and expensive pilgrimages just to become members of the religion. In that sense the mystery religions came to the people, for temples of the new deities sprang up wherever Greeks lived.

The mystery religions all claimed to save their adherents from the worst that fate could do and promised life for the soul after death. They all had a single concept in common: the belief that by the rites of initiation devotees became united with a deity who had also died and risen from the dead. The sacrifice of the god and his victory over death saved the devotee from eternal death. Similarly, all mystery religions demanded a period of preparation in which the converts strove to become holy, that is, to live by the religion's precepts. Once aspirants had prepared themselves, they went through an initiation in which they learned the secrets of the religion. The initiation was usually a ritual of great emotional intensity, symbolizing the entry into a new life.

Among the mystery religions the Egyptian cults of Serapis and Isis took the Hellenistic world by storm. Serapis, who was invented by King Ptolemy, was believed to be the judge of souls who rewarded virtuous and righteous people with eternal life. The cult of Isis enjoyed even wider appeal than that of Serapis. Isis, wife of Osiris, was believed to have conquered Tyche and promised to save any mortal who came to her. She became the most important goddess of the Hellenistic world, especially among women. Her priests claimed that she had bestowed on humanity the gift of civilization and founded law and literature. She was the goddess of marriage, conception, and childbirth. Like Serapis, she promised to save the souls of her believers.

Mystery religions took care of the big things in life, but many people resorted to ordinary magic for daily matters. When a cat walked across their path, they threw three rocks across the road. People often purified their houses to protect them from Hecate, a sinister goddess associated with witchcraft. Many people had dreams that only seers and augurs could interpret. Some of these superstitions are familiar today because some old fears still live.

Epicureanism *A Greek system of philosophy founded on the teachings of Epicurus, which emphasized that a life of contentment, free from fear and suffering, was the greatest good.*

Philosophy and the People

During the Hellenistic period philosophy touched more people than ever before. Two significant philosophies caught the minds and hearts of many Greeks and easterners, as well as many later Romans. The first was **Epicureanism,** a practical philosophy of serenity in an often tumultuous world. Epicurus (340–270 B.C.E.) taught that the principal good of life is pleasure, which he defined as the absence of pain. He concluded that any violent emotion is undesirable. He advocated instead mild self-discipline and even considered poverty good so long as people had enough food, clothing, and shelter. Epicurus also taught that people can most easily attain peace and serenity by ignoring the outside world and looking instead into their personal feelings. His followers ignored politics, for it led to tumult, which would disturb the soul.

Opposed to the passivity of the Epicureans, Zeno (335–262 B.C.E.) came to Athens, where he formed his own school, **Stoicism,** named after the Stoa, the building where he taught. To the Stoics the important matter was not whether they achieved anything, but whether they lived virtuous lives. In that way they could triumph over Tyche, which could destroy their achievements but not the nobility of their lives. Stoicism became the most popular Hellenistic philosophy and the one that later captured the mind of Rome.

Zeno and his fellow Stoics considered nature an expression of divine will. In their view, people could be happy only when living in accordance with nature. They stressed "the brotherhood of man," the concept that all people were kindred who were obliged to help one another. The Stoics' most lasting practical achievement was the creation of the concept of natural law. The Stoics concluded that as all people were brothers, partook of divine reason, and were in harmony with the universe, one **natural law** governed them all.

Hellenistic Science

Hellenistic culture achieved its greatest triumphs in science. The most notable of the Hellenistic astronomers was Aristarchus of Samos (ca. 310–230 B.C.E.), who was educated at Aristotle's school. Aristarchus concluded that the sun is far larger than the earth and that the stars are enormously distant from the earth. He argued against Aristotle's view that the earth is the center of the universe. Aristarchus instead propounded the **heliocentric theory**—that the earth and planets revolve around the sun. His work is all the more impressive because he lacked even a rudimentary telescope. Aristarchus's theories, however, did not persuade the ancient world. His heliocentric theory lay dormant until resurrected in the sixteenth century by the brilliant astronomer Nicolaus Copernicus.

In geometry Euclid (ca. 300 B.C.E.), a mathematician living in Alexandria, compiled a valuable textbook of existing knowledge. His book *The Elements of Geometry* became the standard introduction to the subject. Generations of students from antiquity to the present have learned the essentials of geometry from it.

Stoicism *The most popular of Hellenistic philosophies; it considers nature an expression of divine will and holds that people can be happy only when living in accordance with nature.*

natural law *The belief that the laws governing ethical behavior are written into nature itself and therefore possess universal validity.*

heliocentric theory *The belief that the earth revolves around the sun.*

● **Tyche**   The statue depicts Tyche as the bringer of bounty to people. Some Hellenistic Greeks worshiped Tyche in the hope that she would be kind to them. Philosophers tried to free people from her whimsies. Others tried to placate her. *(Fatih Cimok, Turkey)*

● **Catapult** This model shows a catapult as its crew would have seen it in action. The arrow was loaded on the long horizontal beam, its point fitting into the housing. There the torsion spring under great pressure released the arrow at the target, which could be some 400 yards away. *(Courtesy, Noel Kavan)*

The greatest thinker of the period was Archimedes (ca. 287–212 B.C.E.). A clever inventor, he devised new artillery for military purposes. In peacetime he created the Archimedian screw to draw water from a lower to a higher level. (See the feature "Individuals in Society: Archimedes and the Practical Application of Science.") He invented the compound pully to lift heavy weights. His chief interest, however, lay in pure mathematics. He founded the science of hydrostatics and discovered the principle that the weight of a solid floating in a liquid is equal to the weight of the liquid displaced by the solid.

Archimedes willingly shared his work with others, among them Eratosthenes (285–ca. 204 B.C.E.), who was the librarian of the vast royal library in Alexandria. Eratosthenes used mathematics to further the geographical studies for which he is most famous. He calculated the circumference of the earth geometrically, estimating it as about 24,675 miles. He was not wrong by much: the earth is actually 24,860 miles in circumference. Eratosthenes further concluded that the earth is a spherical globe and that the ocean surrounds the land mass.

Besides these tools for peace, Hellenistic science applied theories of mechanics to build machines that revolutionized warfare. The catapult shot large arrows and small stones against enemy targets. Engineers also built wooden siege towers as artillery platforms. Generals added battering rams to bring down large portions of walls. If these new engines made warfare more efficient, they also added to the misery of the people. War came to embrace the whole population.

Hellenistic Medicine

The study of medicine flourished during the Hellenistic period, and Hellenistic physicians carried the work of Hippocrates into new areas. Herophilus, who lived in the first half of the third century B.C.E., approached the study of medicine in a systematic, scientific fashion. He dissected corpses and measured what he observed. He discovered the nervous system and concluded that two types of nerves, motor and sensory, existed. Herophilus also studied the brain, which he considered the center of intelligence. In the process he discerned the cerebrum and cerebellum. His other work dealt with the liver, lungs, and uterus.

In about 280 B.C.E. Philinus and Serapion, pupils of Herophilus, concentrated on the observation and cure of illnesses rather than focusing on dissection. They also laid heavier stress on the use of drugs and medicines to treat illnesses. Heraclides of Tarentum (perhaps first century B.C.E.) carried on this tradition by discovering the benefits of opium and other drugs that relieved pain.

The Hellenistic world was also plagued by people who claimed to cure illnesses through incantations and magic. Quacks tried to heal and alleviate pain by administering weird potions and bogus concoctions. The medical abuses that arose during the period were so flagrant that many people developed an intense distrust of physicians. Nevertheless, the work of men like Herophilus and Serapion made valuable contributions to the knowledge of medicine, and the fruits of their work were handed on to posterity.

Archimedes and the Practical Application of Science

Archimedes' mill. A slave turns a large cylinder fitted with blades to form a screw that draws water from a well. *(Courtesy, Soprintendenza Archeologica di Pompei. Photograph by Penelope M. Allison)*

Throughout the ages generals have besieged cities to force them to surrender. Sieges were particularly hard and violent, bringing misery to soldiers and civilians alike. Between 213 and 211 B.C.E. the Roman general Marcellus laid close siege to the strongly walled city of Syracuse, the home of Archimedes. Not a soldier, Archimedes was the greatest scientist of his age. He towered above all others in abstract thought. The Roman siege challenged him to a practical response. Hiero, king of Syracuse and friend of Archimedes, turned to him for help.

The king persuaded Archimedes to prepare for him offensive and defensive engines to be used in every kind of warfare. These he had never used himself, because he spent the greater part of his life in freedom from war and amid the festal rites of peace. But at the present time his apparatus stood the Syracusans in good stead, and, with the apparatus, its fabricator. When, therefore, the Romans assaulted them by sea and land, the Syracusans were stricken dumb with terror. They thought that nothing could withstand so furious an onset by such forces.

Archimedes, however, began to ply his engines, and shot against the land forces of the attackers all sorts of missiles and immense masses of stones, which came down with incredible din and speed. Nothing whatever could ward off their weight, but they knocked down in heaps those who stood in their way, and threw their ranks into confusion. At the same time huge beams were suddenly projected over the ships from the walls, which sank some of them with great weights plunging down from on high. Others were seized at the prow by iron claws, or beaks like the beaks of cranes, drawn straight up into the air, and then plunged stern first into the depths, or were turned round and round by means of enginery within the city, and dashed upon the steep cliffs that jutted out beneath the wall of the city, with great destruction of the fighting men on board, who perished in the wrecks. Frequently, too, a ship would be lifted out of the water into mid-air, whirled here and there as it hung there, a dreadful spectacle, until its crew had been thrown out and hurled in all directions. Then it would fall empty upon the walls, or slip away from the clutch that had held it. As for the engine that Marcellus was bringing up on the bridge of ships, and which was called "sambuca" [large mechanically operated scaling ladders carried on ships].

While it was still some distance off in its approach to the wall, a stone of 500 pounds' weight was discharged at it, then a second and a third. Some of them, falling upon it with great noise and surge of wave, crushed the foundation of the engine, shattered its framework, and dislodged it from the platform, so that Marcellus, in perplexity, ordered his ships to sail back as fast as they could and his land forces to retire. . . .

Many of their ships, too, were dashed together, and they could not retaliate in any way upon their foes. For Archimedes had built most of his engines close behind the wall, and the Romans seemed to be fighting against the gods, now that countless mischiefs were poured out upon them from an invisible source.

At last the Romans became so fearful that whenever they saw a bit of rope or a stick of timber projecting a little over the wall. "There it is," they shouted, "Archimedes is training some engine upon us." They then turned their backs and fled. Seeing this, Marcellus desisted from all the fighting and assault, and thenceforth depended on a long siege.

For all his genius, Archimedes did not survive the siege. His deeds of war done, he returned to his thinking and his mathematical problems, even with the siege still in the background. When Syracuse was betrayed to the Romans, soldiers streamed in, spreading slaughter and destruction throughout the city. A Roman soldier came upon Archimedes in his study and killed him outright, thus ending the life of one of the world's greatest thinkers.

Questions for Analysis

1. How did Archimedes' engines repulse the Roman attacks?

2. What effect did his weapons have on the Roman attackers?

3. What is the irony of Archimedes' death?

Source: Reprinted by permission of the publishers and the Trustees of the Loeb Classical Library™ from *Plutarch: Volume V,* Loeb Classical Library™ Volume 87, trans. Bernadotte Perrin (Cambridge, Mass.: Harvard University Press), 1917. The Loeb Classical Library™ is a registered trademark of the President and Fellows of Harvard College.

Chapter Summary

Key Terms

polis
acropolis
monarchy
oligarchy
tyranny
democracy
hoplite
deme
Delian League
sovereign
koine
Great Silk Road
Tyche
mystery religions
Epicureanism
Stoicism
natural law
heliocentric theory

To assess your mastery of this chapter, go to
bedfordstmartins.com/mckayworld

• How did the geography of Greece divide the land so that small communities naturally developed?

Terrain divided the land of Greece and the Aegean into small parcels that nurtured small communities. Some groups of people joined together in kingdoms, notably the Minoan kingdom in Crete and the Mycenaean on the mainland. The fall of these kingdoms led to a period known as the Greek Dark Age (ca. 1100–ca. 800 B.C.E.). Greek culture survived the collapse and developed the polis in which individuals governed themselves without elaborate political machinery. They created two prominent forms of governing—oligarchy, rule by a few citizens, and democracy, rule by all citizens. The success of the polis made it the ideal Greek government.

• What were the major accomplishments of the Archaic age, and why were they important?

In the Archaic period (ca. 800–500 B.C.E.), Greece prospered until it produced a burgeoning population that colonized the Mediterranean from the Atlantic Ocean to the Black Sea. Sparta created the most successful military polis, while the Athenian polis became democratic.

• Although the classical period saw tremendous upheavals, what were its lasting achievements?

The Greeks of the classical period (500–338 B.C.E.) successfully defended themselves from Persian invasions but nearly destroyed themselves in the Peloponnesian War. Yet they built comfortable cities decorated with architectural monuments and fine sculpture. They invented drama to explain individuals and their place in society. They refined their religious beliefs and evolved philosophy the better to understand life.

• After Alexander the Great's conquest of the Persian Empire, how did Greek immigrants and the native peoples there create a new society?

When Alexander the Great defeated the Persians, he opened western and central Asia to Greek expansion, resulting in the blending of these civilizations. In the Hellenistic period (336–146 B.C.E.) kingdoms and their cities sponsored a common culture linked by a common Greek dialect, the koine. Hellenistic society promoted commerce, and trade routes connected distant places as never before. Larger populations produced more goods, grew wealthier, and enjoyed broader outlooks. These developments led to greater advances in religion, which was marked by new mystery cults that promised eternal life.

• *How did the intellectual meeting of two vibrant cultures lead to a very fertile intellectual development?*

The new philosophies of Epicureanism and Stoicism helped people cope successfully with Tyche and the new demands of life. Hellenistic thinkers furthered knowledge of the earth and the entire universe. Advances in medicine made the Hellenistic world a healthier place. All these advances resulted in a large, generally satisfied, and worldly society.

Suggested Reading

Archibald, Z. H., et al. *Hellenistic Economics*. 2001. A very informative treatment of the subject.

Boardman, J. *The Greeks Overseas*. 2001. Very valuable coverage of Greek colonization.

Bosworth, A. B. *Conquest and Empire*. 1988. The most balanced discussion of Alexander the Great.

Buckler, J. *Aegean Greece in the Fourth Century BC*. 2003. The only modern study of this period.

Hansen, M. H. *Polis*. 2006. Already the classic treatment of the subject.

Hodkinson, S. *Property and Wealth in Classical Sparta*. 2000. Discusses many vital aspects of Spartan life.

Kingsley, P. *Ancient Philosophy*. 1996. A balanced survey of the entire field.

Patterson, C. B. *The Family in Greek History*. 2001. Treats public and private family relations.

Price, S. *Religions of the Ancient Greeks*. 1999. Covers all religions from ca. 800 B.C.E. to 500 C.E.

Thomas, C. G., and C. Conant. *Citadel to City-State*. 2003. An excellent treatment of early Greece and modern ideas about it.

Notes

1. Thucydides 2.12, translated by J. Buckler.
2. Diodoros 3.12.2–3, translated by J. Buckler.

Alexander and the Brotherhood of Man

One historical problem challenged historians throughout the twentieth century and has yet to be solved to everyone's satisfaction. After returning to Opis, north of Babylon in modern Iraq, Alexander found himself confronted with a huge and unexpected mutiny by his Macedonian veterans. He held a banquet to pacify them, and he included in the festivities some Persians and other Asian followers, some nine thousand in all. During the festivities he offered a public prayer for harmony and partnership in rule between the Macedonians and Persians. Many modern scholars have interpreted this prayer as an expression of his desire to establish a "brotherhood of man." The following passage provides the evidence for this view. From it all readers can determine for themselves whether Alexander attempted to introduce a new philosophical ideal or whether he harbored his own political motives for political cooperation.

8. When [Alexander] arrived at Opis, he collected the Macedonians and announced that he intended to discharge from the army those who were useless for military service either from age or from being maimed in the limbs; and he said he would send them back to their own abodes. He also promised to give those who went back as much extra reward as would make them special objects of envy to those at home and arouse in the other Macedonians the wish to share similar dangers and labours. Alexander said this, no doubt, for the purpose of pleasing the Macedonians; but on the contrary they were, not without reason, offended by the speech which he delivered, thinking that now they were despised by him and deemed to be quite useless for military service. Indeed, throughout the whole of this expedition they had been offended at many other things; for his adoption of the Persian dress, thereby exhibiting his contempt for their opinion often caused them grief, as did also his accoutring the foreign soldiers called Epigoni in the Macedonian style, and the mixing of the alien horsemen among the ranks of the Companions. Therefore they could not remain silent and control themselves, but urged him to dismiss all of them from his army; and they advised him to prosecute the war in company with his father, deriding Ammon by

this remark. When Alexander heard this . . . , he ordered the most conspicuous of the men who had tried to stir up the multitude to sedition to be arrested. He himself pointed out with his hand to the shield-bearing guards those whom they were to arrest, to the number of thirteen; and he ordered these to be led away to execution. When the rest, stricken with terror, became silent, he mounted the platform again, and spoke as follows:

9. "The speech which I am about to deliver will not be for the purpose of checking your start homeward, for, so far as I am concerned, you may depart wherever you wish; but for the purpose of making you understand when you take yourselves off, what kind of men you have been to us who have conferred such benefits upon you. . . .

10. . . . Most of you have golden crowns, the eternal memorials of your valour and of the honour you receive from me. Whoever has been killed has met with a glorious end and has been honoured with a splendid burial. Brazen statues of most of the slain have been erected at home, and their parents are held in honour, being released from all public service and from taxation. But no one of you has ever been killed in flight under my leadership. And now I was intending to send back those of you who are unfit for service, objects of envy to those at home; but since you all wish to depart, depart all of you! Go back and report at home that your king Alexander, the conqueror of the Persians, Medes, Bactrians, and Sacians; the man who has subjugated the Uxians, Arachotians, and Drangians; who has also acquired the rule of the Parthians, Chorasmians, and Hyrcanians, as far as the Caspian Sea . . . —report that when you returned to Susa you deserted him and went away, handing him over to the protection of conquered foreigners. Perhaps this report of yours will be both glorious to you in the eyes of men and devout I ween in the eyes of the gods. Depart!"

11. Having thus spoken, he leaped down quickly from the platform, and entered the palace, where he paid no attention to the decoration of his person, nor was any of his Companions admitted to see him. Not

even on the morrow was any one of them admitted to an audience; but on the third day he summoned the select Persians within, and among them he distributed the commands of the brigades, and made the rule that only those whom he proclaimed his kinsmen should have the honour of saluting him with a kiss. But the Macedonians who heard the speech were thoroughly astonished at the moment, and remained there in silence near the platform; nor when he retired did any of them accompany the king, except his personal Companions and the confidential body-guards. Though they remained most of them had nothing to do or say; and yet they were unwilling to retire. But when the news was reported to them . . . they were no longer able to restrain themselves; but running in a body to the palace, they cast their weapons there in front of the gates as signs of supplication to the king. Standing in front of the gates, they shouted, beseeching to be allowed to enter, and saying that they were willing to surrender the men who had been the instigators of the disturbance on that occasion, and those who had begun the clamour. They also declared they would not retire from the gates either day or night, unless Alexander would take some pity upon them. When he was informed of this, he came out without delay; and seeing them lying on the ground in humble guise, and hearing most of them lamenting with loud voice, tears began to flow also from his own eyes. He made an effort to say something to them, but they continued their importunate entreaties. At length one of them, Callines by name, a man conspicuous both for his age and because he was a captain of the Companion cavalry, spoke as follows, "O king, what grieves the Macedonians is that you have already made some of the Persians kinsmen to yourself, and that Persians are called Alexander's kinsmen, and have the honour of saluting you with a kiss; whereas none of the Macedonians have as yet enjoyed this honour." Then Alexander, interrupting him, said, "But all of you without exception I consider my kinsmen, and so from this time I shall call you." When he had said this, Callines advanced and saluted him with a kiss, and so did all those who wished to salute him. Then they took up their weapons and returned to the camp, shouting and singing a song of thanksgiving. After this Alexander offered sacrifice to the gods to whom it was his custom to sacrifice, and gave a public banquet, over which he himself presided, with the Macedonians sitting around him; and next to them the Persians; after whom came the men of the other nations, preferred in honour for their personal rank or for some meritorious action. The king and his guests drew wine from the same bowl and poured out the same libations, both the Grecian prophets and the Magians commencing the ceremony. He prayed for other blessings, and especially that harmony and community of rule might exist between the Macedonians and Persians.

Questions for Analysis

1. What was the purpose of the banquet at Opis?

2. Were all of the guests treated equally?

3. What did Alexander gain from bringing together the Macedonians and Persians?

Source: Arrian, *Anabasis of Alexander* 7.8.1–11.9 in F. R. B. Goldophin, ed., *The Greek Historians*, vol. 2. Copyright 1942 and renewed 1970 by Random House, Inc. Used by permission of Random House, Inc.

The Roman Forum. *(Josephine Powell, Photographer, Courtesy of Special Collections, Fine Arts Library, Harvard College Library)*

5 THE WORLD OF ROME (753 B.C.E.–479 C.E.)

Like the Persians under Cyrus and the Macedonians under Alexander, the Romans conquered vast territories in less than a century. Their singular achievement lay in their ability to incorporate conquered peoples into the Roman system. Unlike the Greeks, who refused to share citizenship, the Romans extended theirs first to the Italians and later to the peoples of the provinces. With that citizenship went Roman government and law. Rome created a state that embraced the entire Mediterranean area and extended northward. After a grim period of civil war, in 31 B.C.E. the emperor Augustus restored peace. He extended Roman power and law as far east as the Euphrates River and created the structure that the modern world calls the "Roman Empire."

Roman history is usually divided into two periods: the republic, the age in which Rome grew from a small city-state to ruler of an empire; and the empire, the period when the republican constitution gave way to a constitutional monarchy.

THE ROMANS IN ITALY (CA. 750–290 B.C.E.)

How did the Romans come to dominate Italy, and what political institutions did they create?

While the Greeks pursued their destiny in the eastern Mediterranean, two peoples—the Etruscans and Romans—entered the peninsula of Italy. The Etruscans developed the first cities and a rich cultural life, but the Romans eventually came to dominate the peninsula.

The Etruscans and Rome

The arrival of the Etruscans in the region of Etruria can reasonably be dated to about 750 B.C.E. The Etruscans established permanent settlements that evolved into the first Italian cities, which resembled the

Greek city-states in political organization. They spread their influence over the surrounding countryside, which they farmed and mined for its rich mineral resources. From an early period the Etruscans began to trade natural products, especially iron, with their Greek neighbors in the Mediterranean in exchange for luxury goods. They thereby built a rich cultural life that became the foundation of civilization throughout Italy. In the process they encountered a small collection of villages subsequently called Rome.

The Romans had settled in Italy by the eighth century B.C.E. According to one legend, Romulus and Remus founded the city in 753 B.C.E., Romulus making his home on the Palatine Hill, while Remus chose the Avertine. Under Etruscan influence the Romans prospered, occupying all of Rome's seven hills. Located at an easy crossing point on the Tibur River, Rome stood astride the main avenue of communications between northern and southern Italy. Its seven hills provided safety from attackers and from the floods of the Tibur (see Map 5.1).

From 753 to 509 B.C.E. a line of Etruscan kings ruled the city and introduced numerous customs. The Romans adopted the Etruscan alphabet, which the Etruscans themselves had adoped from the Greeks. The Romans later handed on this alphabet to medieval Europe and thence to the modern Western world. Even the **toga,** the white woolen robe won by citizens, came from the Etruscans. Under the Etruscans Rome enjoyed contacts with the larger Mediterranean world, while the city continued to grow. In the years 753 to 550 B.C.E. temples and public buildings began to grace the city. The **Forum** ceased to be a cemetery and began its history as a public meeting place similar to the Greek agora. Trade in metalwork became common, and wealthier Romans began to import fine Greek vases. The Etruscans had found Rome a collection of villages and made it a city.

The Roman Conquest of Italy (509–290 B.C.E.)

Legend held that the republic was established when the son of the Etruscan king raped Lucretia, a virtuous Roman wife, who committed suicide at the shame, causing the people to rise up in anger. The republic was actually founded in years after 509, when the Romans fought numerous wars with their Italian neighbors. Not until roughly a century after the founding of the republic did the Romans drive the Etruscans entirely out of Latium. The Romans very early learned the value of alliances with

toga *The distinctive garment of Roman men, made of a long sash wrapped around the body. The wearing of the toga was forbidden to noncitizens.*

Forum *A public area in the center of Rome that served as focal point of the political, spiritual, and economic life of the city.*

● **Sarcophagus of Lartie Seianti** The woman portrayed on this lavish sarcophagus is the noble Etruscan Lartie Seianti. Although the sarcophagus is her place of burial, she is portrayed as in life, comfortable and at rest. The influence of Greek art on Etruscan is apparent in almost every feature of the sarcophagus. (*Archaeological Museum, Florence/Nimatallah/ Art Resource, NY*)

the Latin towns around them, which provided them all with security and the Romans with a large reservoir of manpower. These alliances involved the Romans in still other wars that took them farther afield in the Italian peninsula.

Around 390 B.C.E. the Romans suffered a major setback when a new people, the Celts—or Gauls, as the Romans called them—swept aside a Roman army and sacked Rome. More intent on loot than land, they agreed to abandon Rome in return for a thousand pounds of gold. In the century that followed the Romans rebuilt their city and recouped their losses. They brought Latium and their Latin allies fully under their control and conquered the Etruscans. In a series of bitter wars the Romans subdued southern Italy, all the while developing their superior military organization. That and the strength of Roman manpower led them to conquer all of Italy, where they stood unchallenged (see Map 5.1).

All the while, the Romans also spread their religious cults and culture throughout Italy. Although they did not force their beliefs on others, they welcomed their neighbors to religious places of assembly. The Romans and Italians grew closer by the mutual understanding of participation in religious rites.

In politics the Romans shared full Roman citizenship with many of their oldest allies, particularly the Latin cities. In other instances they granted citizenship without the **franchise,** that is, without the right to vote or hold Roman office. These allies were subject to Roman taxes and calls for military service but ran their own local affairs. The Latin allies could acquire full Roman citizenship by moving to Rome. Mundane but vital was Roman road-building. Roman roads, like the Persian Royal Road, facilitated the flow of communication, trade, and armies from the capital to outlying areas. They were the tangible sinews of unity.

The Roman Republic

The Romans summed up their political existence in a single phrase: *senatus populusque Romanus,* "the Roman senate and the people," which they abbreviated "SPQR." This sentiment reflects the republican ideal of shared government rather than power concentrated in a monarchy. It stands for the beliefs, customs, and laws of the republic—its unwritten constitution that evolved over two centuries to meet the demands of the governed.

In the early republic social divisions determined the shape of politics. Political power was in the hands of the aristocracy—the **patricians,** who were wealthy landowners. Patrician families formed clans, as did aristocrats in early Greece. Patricians dominated the affairs of state, provided military leadership in time of war, and monopolized knowledge of law and legal procedure. The common people of Rome, the **plebeians,** were free citizens with a voice in politics, but they could not hold high office or marry into patrician families. While some plebeian merchants rivaled the patricians in wealth, most plebeians were poor artisans, small farmers, and landless urban dwellers.

Chronology

735 B.C.E.	Traditional founding of Rome
ca. 750–509 B.C.E.	Etruscan rule of an evolving Rome
509–290 B.C.E.	Roman conquest of Italy
ca. 494–287 B.C.E.	Struggle of the Orders
264–45 B.C.E.	Punic Wars and conquest of the Mediterranean
88–31 B.C.E.	Civil war
44 B.C.E.	Assassination of Julius Caesar
31 B.C.E.	Triumph of Augustus
27 B.C.E.–68 C.E.	Julio-Claudian emperors, expansion in Europe, prosperity in the empire
ca. 3 B.C.E.–29 C.E.	Life of Jesus
30–312 C.E.	Spread of Christianity
96–180 C.E.	"Golden age" of peace and prosperity, reigns of the five good emperors
193–284 C.E.	Military monarchy, military conflict, and commercial contact with central and eastern Asia
284–337 C.E.	Diocletian and Constantine reconstruct the empire, dividing it into western and eastern halves, construction of Constantinople
380 C.E.	Christianity the official religion of the empire

franchise *The rights, privileges, and protections of citizenship.*

patricians *The aristocracy; wealthy landowners who held political power.*

plebeians *The common people of Rome, who had few of the patricians' advantages.*

praetors *A new office created in 366 B.C.E.; these people acted in place of consuls when the consuls were away, although they primarily dealt with the administration of justice.*

MAP 5.1 **Roman Italy, ca. 265 B.C.E.** The geographical configuration of the Italian peninsula shows how Rome stood astride north-south communication routes and how the state that united Italy stood poised to move into Sicily and northern Africa.

The chief magistrates of the republic were the two consuls, elected for one-year terms. At first the consulship was open only to patrician men. The consuls commanded the army in battle, administered state business, and supervised financial affairs. When the consuls were away from Rome, **praetors** acted in their place. Otherwise, the praetors dealt primarily with the administration of justice. After the age of overseas conquest, the Romans divided the Mediterranean into provinces governed by ex-consuls and ex-praetors. Because of their experience in Roman politics, they were all suited to administer the affairs of the provincials and to fit Roman law and custom into new contexts.

Other officials included *quaestors,* who took charge of the public treasury and prosecuted criminals in the popular courts. *Censors* held many responsibilities including the supervision of public morals, the power to determine who could lawfully sit in the

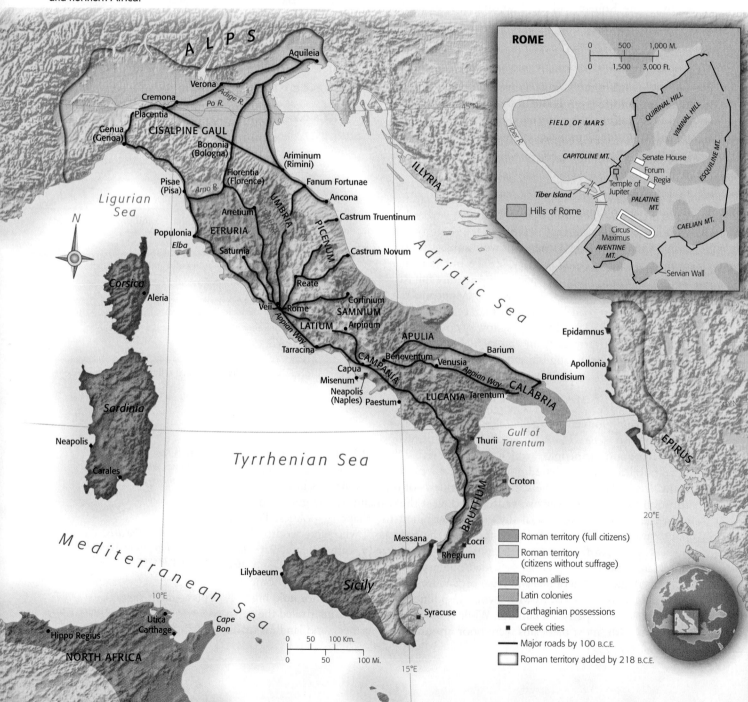

● **Guard Dog**   The doorway of the house opened directly onto the street. This entrance is protected by a dog who is always on guard. The notice warns "CAVE CANEM" (beware of the dog). *(Robert Frerck/Odyssey/Chicago)*

senate, the registration of citizens, and the leasing of public contracts. Lastly, the aediles supervised the streets and markets and presided over public festivals.

Perhaps the greatest institution of the republic was the senate, which had originated under the Etruscans as a council of noble elders who advised the king. During the republic the senate advised the consuls and other magistrates. Because the senate sat year after year, while magistrates changed annually, it provided stability. The senate could not technically pass legislation. It could only offer its advice. Yet increasingly, because of the senate's prestige, its advice came to have the force of law.

A lasting achievement of the Romans was their development of law. Roman civil law, the *ius civile,* consisted of statutes, customs, and forms of procedure that regulated the lives of citizens. As the Romans came into more frequent contact with foreigners, the praetors resorted to the law of equity, the *ius gentium,* the "law of the peoples," which they thought just to all parties. It led to a universal conception of law. By the late republic Roman jurists reached the concept of *ius naturale,* "natural law," based in part on Stoic beliefs, that applied to all societies.

Social Conflict in Rome

Inequality between plebeians and patricians led to a conflict known as the **Struggle of the Orders.** To solve their differences the plebeians nonviolently used the boycott to apply their power as a group. The patricians in turn generally responded peacefully by resorting to practical compromise.

The first showdown between the plebeians and patricians came, according to tradition, in 494 B.C.E. To force the patricians to grant concessions, the plebeians literally walked out of Rome and refused to serve in the army. The plebeians' general strike worked, and the patricians made important concessions. They allowed patricians and plebeians to marry one another. They recognized the right of plebeians to elect their own officials, the tribunes, who could bring plebeian grievances to the senate for resolution. Surrendering their legal monopoly, the patricians codified and published the Law of the

Struggle of the Orders
A great social conflict that developed between patricians and plebeians; the plebeians wanted real political representation and safeguards against patrician domination.

Twelve Tables, so called because they were inscribed on twelve bronze plaques. They also made public legal procedures so that plebeians could argue cases in court.

After a ten-year battle, the plebeians gained the Licinian-Sextian Rogations (or laws) that allowed wealthy plebeians access to all the magistracies of Rome. Once plebeians could hold the consulship, they could also sit in the senate and advise on policy. They also won the right to hold one of the two consulships. Though decisive, this victory did not automatically end the Struggle of the Orders. That happened only in 287 B.C.E. with the passage of the *lex Hortensia* that gave the resolutions of the *concilium plebis,* the Assembly of the People, the force of law for patricians and plebeians alike. This compromise established a new nobility of wealthy plebeians and patricians. Yet the Struggle of the Orders had made all citizens equal before the law, resulting in a Rome stronger and better united than before.

ROMAN EXPANSION AND ITS REPERCUSSIONS

How did Rome expand its power beyond Italy, and what were the effects of success on Rome?

With their internal affairs settled, the Romans turned their attention abroad. In a series of wars they conquered the Mediterranean, creating an overseas empire that brought them unheard of power and wealth. The new situation made many of them more cosmopolitan and comfortable. Yet it also caused social unrest at home and opened unprecedented opportunities for ambitious generals who wanted to rule Rome like an empire. Hard civil war ensued, which Julius Caesar quelled for a moment. Only his grandnephew Octavius, better known to history as Augustus, finally restored peace and order to Rome.

The Age of Overseas Conquest (264–45 B.C.E.)

In 282 B.C.E., when the Romans had reached southern Italy, they embarked upon a series of wars that left them the rulers of the Mediterranean world. Although they sometimes declared war reluctantly, they nonetheless felt the need to dominate, to eliminate any state that could endanger them. Yet they did not map out grandiose strategies to conquer the world. Rather they responded to situations as they arose.

Their presence in southern Italy brought the Romans to Sicily, next door. There they collided with the Carthaginians, Phoenician colonists living in North Africa (see Map 5.2). Conflicting ambitions in Sicily led to the First Punic War, which lasted from 264 to 241 B.C.E. Roman victory led to the island's becoming its first province. Still a formidable enemy, Carthage sent its brilliant general Hannibal (ca. 247–183 B.C.E.) against Rome. During the Second Punic War (218–201 B.C.E.) Hannibal won three major victories, including the devastating blow at Cannae in 216 B.C.E. Carrying the fighting to the very gates of Rome, he spread devastation farther across the Italian countryside. The Roman general Scipio Africanus (ca. 236–ca. 183 B.C.E.) led the counterattack to Carthage itself. In 202 B.C.E., near the town of Zama, Scipio defeated Hannibal in one of history's truly decisive battles. Scipio's victory meant that Rome's heritage would be passed on to posterity.

After defeating Carthage a last time in 146 B.C.E., the Romans turned east. After provocation from the king of Macedonia, Roman legions quickly conquered Macedonia and Greece and defeated the Seleucid monarchy. In 133 B.C.E. the king of Pergamum in Asia Minor willed his kingdom to Rome when he died. The Ptolemies of Egypt meekly obeyed Roman wishes. The Mediterranean had become *mare nostrum,* "our sea."

Old Values and Greek Culture

Rome had conquered the Mediterranean world, but some Romans considered that victory a misfortune. The historian Sallust (86–34 B.C.E.), writing from hindsight, complained that the acquisition of an empire was the beginning of Rome's troubles:

But when through labor and justice our Republic grew powerful . . . then fortune began to be harsh and to throw everything into confusion. The Romans had easily borne labor, danger, and hardship. To them leisure, riches—otherwise desirable—proved to be burdens and torments. So at first money, then desire for power, grew great. These things were a sort of cause of all evils.[1]

Instead, in the second century B.C.E. the Romans learned that they could not return to a simple life. Having become world rulers, they began to build a huge imperial system. They had to change their institutions, social patterns, and way of thinking to shape a new era. In the end Rome triumphed here just as on the battlefield, for out of turmoil came the *pax Romana*—"Roman peace" (see page 112).

Two attitudes represent the major ways in which the Romans met these challenges. One longed for the good old days and an idealized agrarian way of life. The other embraced the new urban culture.

In Roman society, whether traditional or new-fashioned, the head of the family was the **paterfamilias,** the oldest dominant male of the family. He held nearly absolute power over the lives of his wife and children as long as he lived. Until he died, his sons could not legally own property. To deal with important matters, he usually called a council of the adult males. In these councils the women of the family had no formal part, but they could inherit and own property. Romans viewed the family as important and thought that children should be raised by their mothers. Women who fulfilled these ideals were accorded respect. They handled the early education of the children. After the age of seven, sons and often daughters began their formal education.

An influx of slaves came from Rome's conquests. To the Romans slavery was a misfortune that befell some people, but it did not entail any racial theories. Not even later Christians questioned the institution of slavery. For loyal slaves the Romans always held out the possibility of freedom. **Manumission,** the freeing of individual slaves by their masters, became common.

For most Romans religion played an important role in life. Jupiter, the sky-god, and his wife, Juno, became equivalent to the Greek Zeus and Hera. Mars was the god of war but also guaranteed the welfare of the farm. In addition to the great gods, the Romans believed in spirits who haunted fields and even the home itself. Some of the deities were hostile, and only magic could ward them off. Some spirits were ghosts who haunted places where they had lived.

The new feeling of wealth and leisure is most readily seen in Rome, now a great city, where the spoils of war financed the building of baths, theaters, and other places of amusement. Romans developed new tastes and especially a liking for Greek culture. During this period the Greek custom of bathing became a Roman passion. Now large buildings containing pools and exercise rooms became essential parts of the Roman city. The baths were prominent places where men and women went to see and be seen. Despite the objections of the conservatives, these new social customs did not corrupt the Romans. They still continued efficiently to rule their empire.

The Late Republic (133–31 B.C.E.)

The wars of conquest created serious political problems for the Romans. When the legionaries returned home, they found their farms

paterfamilias *A term that means far more than merely "father"; it indicates the oldest dominant male of the family who holds nearly absolute power over the lives of family members as long as he lives.*

manumission *The freeing of individual slaves by their masters.*

● **African Acrobat** Conquest and prosperity brought exotic pleasure to Rome. Every feature of this sculpture is exotic. The young African woman and her daring gymnastic pose would catch anyone's attention. To add to the spice of her act, she performs using a live crocodile as her platform. Americans would have loved it. *(Courtesy of the Trustees of the British Museum)*

MAP 5.2 **Roman Expansion During the Republic** The main spurt of Roman expansion occurred between 264 and 133 B.C.E., when most of the Mediterranean fell to Rome, followed by the conquest
of Gaul and the eastern Mediterranean by 44 B.C.E.

Roman territory in 264 B.C.E.

Roman territory added by 133 B.C.E.

Roman territory added by 44 B.C.E.

Parthian Empire in 44 B.C.E.

★ Major battle

● Roman Table Manners
This mosaic is a floor that can never be swept clean. It whimsically suggests what a dining room floor looked like after a lavish dinner and also tells something about the menu: a chicken head, a wishbone, and remains of various seafood, vegetables, and fruit are easily recognizable. *(Museo Gregoriano Profano, Vatican Museums/Scala/Art Resource, NY)*

looking like those of the people they had conquered. Many were forced to sell their land, and they found ready buyers in those who had grown rich from the wars. These wealthy men created huge estates called **latifundia**. Landless veterans moved to the cities, especially Rome, but could not find work. These developments threatened Rome's army because landless men were forbidden to serve.

latifundia *Huge Roman estates created by buying up several small farms.*

The landless veterans were willing to follow any leader who promised help. Tiberius Gracchus (163–133 B.C.E.), an aristocrat who was appalled by the situation, was elected tribune in 133 B.C.E. Tiberius proposed dividing public land among the poor, but a group of wealthy senators murdered him, launching a long era of political violence that would destroy the republic. Still, Tiberius's brother Gaius Gracchus (153–121 B.C.E.) passed a law providing the urban poor with cheap grain and urged practical reforms. Once again senators tried to stem the tide of reform by murdering him.

The next reformer, Gaius Marius (ca. 157–86 B.C.E.) recruited landless men into the army to put down a rebel king in Africa. He promised them land for their service. But after his victory, the senate refused to honor his promise. From then on, Roman soldiers looked to their commanders, not to the senate or the state, to protect their interests. The turmoil continued until 88 B.C.E., when the Roman general Sulla made himself dictator. Although he voluntarily stepped down nine years later, it was too late to restore the republican constitution. The senate and other institutions of the Roman state had failed to meet the needs of empire. They had lost control of their generals and army. The soldiers put their faith in generals rather than the state, and that doomed the republic.

The history of the late republic is the story of power struggles among many famous Roman figures. Pompey used military success in Spain to force the senate to allow him to run for consul. In 59 B.C.E. he was joined in a political alliance called the **First Triumvirate** by Crassus and Julius Caesar (100–44 B.C.E.). Born of a noble family, Caesar, an able general, was also a brilliant politician with unbridled ambition. Recognizing that military success led to power, he led his troops to victory in Spain and Gaul, modern France. Having later defeated his Roman opponents, he made himself

First Triumvirate *A political alliance between Caesar, Crassus, and Pompey in which they agreed to advance one another's interests.*

**Primary Source:
A Man of Unlimited
Ambition: Julius Caesar**
*Find out how Roman attitudes
toward kingship led to the
assassination of Julius Caesar.*

dictator. Using his victory wisely, he enacted basic reforms. He extended citizenship to many provincials outside Italy who had supported him. To relieve the pressure of Rome's huge population, he sent eighty thousand poor people to plant colonies in Gaul, Spain, and North Africa. These new communities—formed of Roman citizens, not subjects—helped spread Roman culture.

In 44 B.C.E. a group of conspirators assassinated Caesar and set off another round of civil war. His grandnephew and heir, the eighteen-year-old Octavian, better known as Augustus, joined with two of Caesar's followers, Marc Antony and Lepidus, in the Second Triumvirate. After defeating Caesar's murderers, they had a falling-out. Octavian forced Lepidus out of office and waged war against Antony, who had become allied with Cleopatra, queen of Egypt. In 31 B.C.E., with the might of Rome at his back, Octavian defeated the combined forces of Antony and Cleopatra at the Battle of Actium in Greece. His victory ended the age of civil war. For his success the senate in 27 B.C.E. voted Octavian the name *Augustus*.

pax Romana *A period during the first and second centuries C.E. of security, order, harmony, flourishing culture, and expanding economy.*

The Pax Romana

When Augustus ended the civil wars, he faced the monumental problems of reconstruction. From 29–23 B.C.E. Augustus toiled to heal Rome's wounds. He first had to rebuild the constitution and the organs of government. He next had to demobilize much of the army and care for the welfare of the provinces. Then he had to meet the danger of barbarians on Rome's European frontiers. Augustus was highly successful in meeting these challenges. The world came to know this era as the **pax Romana,** the Roman peace. His gift of peace to a war-torn world sowed the seeds of the empire's golden age.

Augustus claimed that in restoring constitutional government he was also restoring the republic. Yet he had to modify republican forms and offices to meet the new circumstances. While expecting the senate to shoulder heavy administrative burdens, he failed to give it enough actual power to do the job. Many of the senate's prerogatives thus shifted by default to Augustus and his successors.

Augustus also had to fit his own position into the republican constitution. He became **princeps civitatis,** "First Citizen of the State," a prestigious title without power. His real power resided in the multiple magistracies he held and in the powers granted him by the senate. He held the consulship annually. The senate voted him the full power of the tribunes, giving him the right to call the senate into session, present legislation to the people, and defend their rights. He held control of the army, which he made a permanent, standing organization. He kept all this power in the background. Failing to restore the republic, he actually created a constitutional monarchy. Without saying so, he also created the office of emperor. Yet he failed to find a way to institutionalize his position with the army, which remained personal. Although the Augustan principate worked well at first, by the third century C.E. the army would make and break emperors at will.

Augustus put provincial administration on an orderly basis and improved its functioning. He encouraged local self-government and urbanism. As a spiritual bond between the provinces and Rome, Augustus encouraged the

● **Augustus as Imperator** Here Augustus, dressed in breastplate and uniform, emphasizes the imperial majesty of Rome and his role as imperator. The figures on his breastplate represent the restoration of peace, one of Augustus's greatest accomplishments and certainly one that he frequently stressed. *(Erich Lessing/Art Resource, NY)*

cult of *Roma et Augustus,* "Rome and Augustus," as the guardians of the state. The cult spread rapidly and became a symbol of Roman unity.

One of the most momentous aspects of Augustus's reign was Roman expansion into northern and western Europe (see Map 5.3). Augustus completed the conquest of Spain. In Gaul he founded twelve new towns, and the Roman road system linked new settlements with one another and with Italy. After hard fighting, he made the Rhine River and the Roman frontier in Germany. Meanwhile, generals extended the Roman standards as far as the Danube. Roman legions penetrated the areas of modern Austria, southern Bavaria, and western Hungary. The regions of modern Serbia, Bulgaria, and Romania fell. Within this area the legionaries built fortified camps. Roads linked these camps with one another, and settlements grew up around the camps.

Amid the vast expanse of forests, Roman towns, trade, language, and law began to exert a civilizing influence on the barbarians. Many military camps became towns, and many modern European cities owe their origins to the forts of the Roman army. For the first time, the barbarian north came into direct and continuous contact with Mediterranean culture. The Romans maintained peaceful relations with the barbarians whenever possible, but Roman legions remained on the frontier to repel hostile barbarians.

• • • • • • • • • • • • •

THE COMING OF CHRISTIANITY

What was Christianity, and how did it affect life in the empire?

During the reign of the emperor Tiberius (14–37 C.E.), in the Roman province of Judaea, created out of the Jewish kingdom of Judah, Jesus of Nazareth preached, attracting a following, and was executed on the order of the Roman prefect Pontius Pilate. Much contemporary scholarship has attempted to understand who Jesus was and what he meant by his teachings. Views vary widely. Some see him as a visionary and a teacher, others as a magician and a prophet, and still others as a rebel and a revolutionary. A great many people believe that he was the son of God. The search for the historical Jesus is complicated by many factors. One is the difference between history and faith. History relies on evidence and proof for its conclusions; faith depends on belief. Thus, whether Jesus is divine is not an issue to be decided by historians. Their role is to understand his religious, cultural, social, and historical context.

Unrest in Judaea

The civil wars that destroyed the Roman republic left their mark on Judaea, where Jewish leaders had taken sides in the conflict. The turmoil created a climate of violence throughout the area. Among the Jews two movements spread. First was the rise of the Zealots, who fought to rid Judaea of the Romans. The second movement was the growth of militant apocalypticism, the belief that the coming of the Messiah was near. The Messiah would destroy the Roman legions and then inaugurate a period of happiness and plenty for Jews.

The pagan world played its part in the story of early Christianity. The term **pagan** refers to all those who believed in the Greco-Roman gods. Paganism at the time of Jesus' birth can be broadly divided into three spheres: the official state religion of Rome, the traditional Roman cults of hearth and countryside, and the new mystery religions that arose in the Hellenistic world (see pages 93–94). The mystery religions gave their adherents what neither the official religion nor traditional cults could, but they were exclusive. None of these religious sentiments met many people's spiritual needs.

princeps civitatis   *A Latin term meaning "first citizen" used as an official title by the early Roman emperors, from Augustus through Diocletian, followed by a Latin term meaning a city under Roman imperial authority possessing some limited degree of autonomy.*

pagan   *From a Latin term meaning "of the country," used to describe followers of a folk religion.*

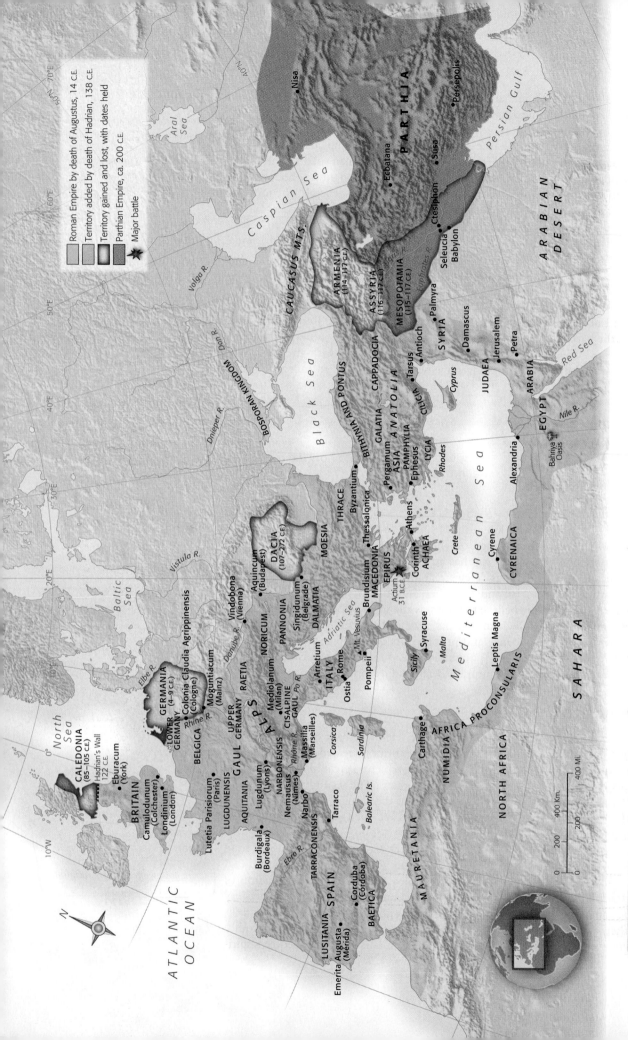

MAP 5.3 Roman Expansion Under the Empire Following Roman expansion during the republic, Augustus added vast tracts of Europe to the Roman Empire, which the emperor Hadrian later enlarged by assuming control over parts of central Europe, the Near East, and North Africa.

Roman Empire by death of Augustus, 14 C.E.

Territory added by death of Hadrian, 138 C.E.

Territory gained and lost, with dates held

Parthian Empire, ca. 200 C.E.

Major battle

ATLANTIC OCEAN

North Sea

CALEDONIA (85–105 C.E.)

BRITAIN

Camulodunum (Colchester)
Londinium (London)
Eburacum (York)
Hadrian's Wall 122 C.E.

Baltic Sea

Vistula R.

GERMANIA (4–9 C.E.)

LOWER GERMANY
Colonia Claudia Agrippinensis (Cologne)
UPPER GERMANY
Moguntiacum (Mainz)
BELGICA
Rhine R.
RAETIA
ALPS
GAUL
LUGDUNENSIS
AQUITANIA
Lutetia Parisiorum (Paris)
Lugdunum (Lyons)
NARBONENSIS
Nemausus (Nimes)
Narbo
Massilia (Marseilles)
Burdigala (Bordeaux)

Vindobona (Vienna)
Aquincum (Budapest)
NORICUM
PANNONIA
Singidunum (Belgrade)
DALMATIA
Danube R.
CISALPINE GAUL
Mediolanum (Milan)
Po R.
Arretium
ITALY
Rome
Ostia
Pompeii
Mt. Vesuvius

DACIA (107–272 C.E.)
MOESIA
THRACE
Byzantium
BITHYNIA AND PONTUS

Black Sea

Dnieper R.
Don R.
BOSPORAN KINGDOM

Volga R.

Aral Sea

Caspian Sea

CAUCASUS MTS.

ARMENIA (114–117 C.E.)
ASSYRIA (116–117 C.E.)
MESOPOTAMIA (115–117 C.E.)
CAPPADOCIA
GALATIA
ASIA ANATOLIA
Pergamum
Ephesus
PAMPHYLIA
LYCIA
CILICIA
Tarsus
Rhodes
Antioch
SYRIA
Damascus
Palmyra

PARTHIA

Nisa

Ecbatana
Susa
Ctesiphon
Seleucia
Babylon
Persepolis

Persian Gulf

ARABIAN DESERT

Red Sea

Nile R.

EGYPT
Bahriya Oasis
Alexandria

JUDAEA
Jerusalem
Petra
ARABIA

Adriatic Sea
Brundisium
EPIRUS
Actium 31 B.C.E.
MACEDONIA
Thessalonica
ACHAEA
Corinth
Athens
Crete

Vesuvius
Syracuse
Sicily
Malta

Mediterranean Sea

Cyprus

Cyrene
CYRENAICA
Leptis Magna

Carthage
AFRICA PROCONSULARIS
NUMIDIA
NORTH AFRICA
MAURETANIA

SAHARA

TARRACONENSIS
Tarraco
Balearic Is.
Corsica
Sardinia
Ebro R.
SPAIN
LUSITANIA
Emerita Augusta (Mérida)
Corduba (Cordoba)
BAETICA

Rhone R.

Elbe R.

0°   10°E   20°E   30°E   40°E   50°E   60°E   70°E

50°N
40°N

10°W

N

0   200   400 Km.
0   200   400 Mi.

The Life and Teachings of Jesus

Into this climate of Messianic hope and Roman religious yearning came Jesus of Nazareth (ca. 3 B.C.E.–29 C.E.). He was raised in Galilee, stronghold of the Zealots. The principal evidence for his life and deeds are the four Gospels of the New Testament. These Gospels—their name means "good news"—are records of his teachings and religious doctrines with certain details of his life. They are neither biographies of Jesus nor histories of his life. The earliest Gospels were written some seventy-five years after his death, and there are discrepancies among the four accounts. These differences indicate that early Christians had a diversity of beliefs about Jesus' nature and purpose. Only slowly, as the Christian church became an institution, were lines drawn more clearly between what was considered correct teaching and what was considered incorrect, or **heresy.**

Despite this diversity, there were certain things about Jesus' teachings that almost all the sources agree on: Jesus preached of a heavenly kingdom, one of eternal happiness in a life after death. His teachings were essentially Jewish. His orthodoxy enabled him to preach in the synagogue and the temple. His major deviation from orthodoxy was his insistence that he taught in his own name, not in the name of Yahweh. Was he then the Messiah? A small band of followers thought so, and Jesus claimed that he was. Yet Jesus had his own conception of the Messiah. He would establish a spiritual kingdom, not an earthly one.

● **Pontius Pilate and Jesus** This Byzantine mosaic from Ravenna illustrates a dramatic moment in Jesus' trial and crucifixion. Jesus stands accused before Pilate, but Pilate symbolically washes his hands of the whole affair. *(Scala/Art Resource, NY)*

heresy *A non-orthodox religious practice or belief.*

The prefect Pontius Pilate knew little about Jesus' teachings. He was concerned with maintaining peace and order. The crowds following Jesus at the time of Passover, a highly emotional time in the Jewish year, alarmed Pilate, who faced a volatile situation. Some Jews believed that Jesus was the long-awaited Messiah. Others hated and feared Jesus because they thought him religiously dangerous. To avert riot and bloodshed, Pilate condemned Jesus to death, and his soldiers carried out the sentence. On the third day after Jesus' crucifixion, some of his followers claimed that he had risen from the dead. For the earliest Christians and for generations to come, the resurrection of Jesus became a central element of faith: he had triumphed over death, and his resurrection promised all Christians immortality.

The Spread of Christianity

The memory of Jesus and his teachings survived and flourished. Believers in his divinity met in small assemblies or congregations, often in one another's homes, to discuss the meaning of Jesus' message. These earliest Christians defined their faith to fit the life of Jesus into an orthodox Jewish context. Only later did these congregations evolve into what can be called a church with a formal organization and set of beliefs.

The catalyst in the spread of Jesus' teachings and the formation of the Christian church was Paul of Tarsus, a Hellenized Jew who was comfortable in both the Roman and Jewish worlds. He had begun by persecuting the new sect, but on the road to Damascus he was converted to belief in Jesus. He was the single most important figure responsible for changing Christianity from a Jewish sect into a separate religion. He urged the Jews to include Gentiles, non-Jews, in the faith. His was the first universal message of Christianity.

Many early Christian converts were Gentile women, especially from the wealthier classes, and women were active in spreading Christianity. Paul greeted male and female converts by name in his letters and noted that women often provided financial support for his activities. Missionaries and others spreading the Christian message worked through families and friendship networks. The growing Christian communities differed in their ideas about the proper gender order; some favored giving women a larger role in church affairs, while others were more restrictive.

universalism *The belief that all human beings will ultimately be reconciled to God and achieve salvation.*

● **The Catacombs of Rome** The early Christians used underground crypts and rock chambers to bury their dead. The bodies were placed in these galleries and then sealed up. The catacombs became places of pilgrimage, and in this way the dead continued to be united with the living. *(Catacombe di Priscilla, Rome/Scala/Art Resource, NY)*

Christianity might have remained just another local sect had it not reached Rome, the capital of a far-flung empire. Rome proved to be a dramatic feature in the spread of Christianity for different reasons. First, Jesus had told his followers to spread his word throughout the world, thus making his teachings universal. The pagan Romans also considered their secular empire universal, and the early Christians combined the two concepts of **universalism.** Secular Rome provided another advantage to Christianity. If all roads led to Rome, they also led outward to the provinces. The very stability and extent of the Roman Empire enabled early Christians easily to spread their faith throughout the known world.

The Appeal of Christianity

Christianity offered its adherents the promise of salvation. Christians believed that Jesus had defeated evil and that he would reward his followers with eternal life after death. Christianity also offered the possibility of forgiveness. Human nature was weak, and even the best Christians would fall into sin. But Jesus loved sinners and forgave those who repented. Christianity was also attractive to many because it gave the Roman world a cause. Instead of passivity, Christians stressed the ideal of striving for a goal. By spreading the word of Christ, Christians played their part in God's plan for the triumph of Christianity on earth. They were not discouraged by temporary setbacks, believing Christianity to be invincible. Christianity likewise gave its devotees a sense of community. Believers met regularly to celebrate the **eucharist,** the Lord's Supper. Each individual community was in turn a member of a greater community. And that community, according to Christian Scripture, was indestructible, for Jesus had promised that "the gates of hell shall not prevail against it."[2]

> **eucharist** *A Christian sacrament in which the death of Christ is communally remembered through a meal of bread and wine.*

THE "GOLDEN AGE"

How did efficient Roman rule lead to a "golden age" for the empire?

Augustus's success in creating solid political institutions was tested by the dynasty he created, but later in the first century Rome entered a period of political stability. This era later became known as the "golden age," a time of growing cities and economic well-being.

Politics in the Empire

For fifty years after Augustus's death the dynasty that he established—known as the Julio-Claudians because they were all members of the Julian and Claudian clans—provided the emperors of Rome. Some of the Julio-Claudians, such as Tiberius and Claudius, were sound rulers and able administrators. Others, including Caligula and Nero, were weak and frivolous men. Nonetheless, the Julio-Claudians for the most part gave the empire peace and prosperity.

In 68 C.E. Nero's inept rule led to military rebellion and widespread disruption. Yet only two years later Vespasian (9–79 C.E.), who established the Flavian dynasty, restored order. He also turned Augustus's principate into a monarchy. The Flavians (69–96 C.E.) repaired the damage of civil war to give the Roman world peace, and paved the way for the **five good emperors,** the golden age of the empire (96–180 C.E.). The era of the five good emperors was a period of almost unparalleled prosperity for the empire (see the feature "Individuals in Society: Plutarch of Chaeronea"). Wars generally ended victoriously and were confined to the frontiers. The five good emperors—Nerva, Trajan, Hadrian, Antoninus Pius, and Marcus Aurelius—were among the most dedicated and ablest men in Roman history.

In addition to the full-blown monarchy of the Flavians, other significant changes had occurred in Roman government since Augustus's day. Claudius had created an imperial bureaucracy, which Hadrian, who became emperor in 117 C.E., put on an organized, official basis. He established imperial administrative departments and separated civil from military service. His bureaucracy demanded professionalism from its members. These innovations made for more efficient running of the empire while increasing the authority of the emperor, who was now the ruling power of the bureaucracy.

In these years the Roman army changed from a mobile unit to a defensive force. The frontiers became firmly fixed and defended by a system of forts. Behind them

> **five good emperors** *Five consecutive Roman emperors (Nerva, Trajan, Hadrian, Antoninus Pius, and Marcus Aurelius) distinguished by their benevolence and moderation.*

● **Canopus, Hadrian's Villa**   This view of Hadrian's villa embodies sublime and serene beauty. The columns and statues lend dignity, and the pond suggests rest. In the background a spacious house offers a retreat from the cares of imperial duties. *(Mark Edward Smith/TIPS Images)*

roads were increased and improved both to supply the forts and to reinforce them in times of trouble. The army had evolved into a garrison force, with legions guarding specific areas for long periods.

Life in the Golden Age

This era of peace gave the empire unparalleled prosperity both in Rome and in the provinces. Rome was truly an extraordinary city. It was enormous, with a population somewhere between 500,000 and 750,000. Although it could boast of stately palaces, noble buildings, and beautiful residential areas, most people lived in jerrybuilt houses. Fire and crime were perennial problems even in Augustus's day. Sanitation was a serious problem. Under the five emperors, urban planning and new construction greatly improved the situation. By comparison with later European cities, Rome became a very attractive place to live.

Rome grew so large that it became ever more difficult to feed. The emperor solved the problem by providing citizens with free bread, oil, and wine. By doing so, he also kept their favor. He likewise entertained the people with gladiatorial contests and chariot races. Many gladiators were criminals, some the slaves of gladiatorial schools, others prisoners of war. A few free people, men and women, volunteered for the arena. The Romans actually preferred chariot racing to gladiatorial contests. Two-horse and four-horse chariots ran a course of seven laps, about five miles. Four permanent teams, each with its own color, competed against each other.

In the province and on the frontiers, the era of the five good emperors was one of extensive prosperity. Peace and security opened Britain, Gaul, Germany, and the lands of the Danube to immigration (see Map 5.4). Agriculture flourished in the hands of free tenant farmers. The holders of small parcels of land thrived as never before. Consequently, the small tenant farmer became the backbone of Roman agriculture.

In continental Europe the army was largely responsible for the new burst of expansion. The areas where legions were stationed became Romanized. Upon retirement, legionaries often settled where they had served. Having learned a trade in the army, they brought essential skills to areas that badly needed trained men. These veterans used their retirement pay to set themselves up in business.

Plutarch of Chaeronea

During the era of the five good emperors (96–180 C.E.) people throughout the Roman Empire enjoyed nearly unparalleled peace and prosperity. The five good emperors encouraged Romans and non-Romans alike to embrace concepts and ideas beyond narrow, local boundaries. Plutarch (ca. 50–ca. 120 C.E.) provides an excellent example of this attitude and policy. Born in the small but lovely city of Chaeronea in Greece, he came from a prominent family, but one with only local prestige. He received a typical education in writing, literature, and mathematics. His exploration of the countryside in his spare hours inspired an interest in history. As a youth and later in his life he especially sought out small temples and abandoned battlefields.

When Plutarch reached young manhood, his family sent him to Athens, no longer a mighty military power but instead a center of philosophy and rhetoric. In Athens he polished his innate talents and took advantage of the opportunity to learn about and enjoy the cultural treasures of the city, all the while becoming acquainted with many wealthy and influential young men from elsewhere in the Roman Empire. In the era of the five good emperors, prominent Romans often sent their sons to Athens, not simply to learn but also to become culturally refined. These young men befriended Plutarch and widened his social horizon.

When Plutarch finished his studies, he began a tour of the Roman Empire beyond Athens. With enthusiasm he traveled abroad, forged new friendships, and became acquainted with new-to-him regions and their history. He also avidly read books previously unavailable to him.

Plutarch journeyed to the Peloponnesus, Asia Minor, Crete, and northern Egypt. All along the way he took notes describing what he saw and learned. Like tourists everywhere, he saw the sights; and from his articulate and well-educated friends he encountered information and lore not readily found elsewhere.

At Rome, the political and social center of the empire, Plutarch met leading figures and made many useful social connections. He learned enough Latin to read literary works but never became fluent enough to speak it easily. Consequently he gave public lectures in Greek, which his educated audiences had no difficulty understanding. His good nature opened many doors, and he took advantage of every opportunity to examine official records and other documents to gain information about the early years of the Roman republic and the first Roman emperors. His personal popularity

This Renaissance popularization of Plutarch depicts one of the favorite writers of that time period and today. *(Courtesy, Antiquity Project/Visual Connection Archive)*

afforded him an intimate glimpse of life among the Roman elite.

Plutarch returned to Chaeronea where he spent his days writing many influential and compelling biographies of eminent Greeks and Romans, including Themistocles, Pericles, Caesar, and Antony. Both a biographer and a literary artist, he used the careers of his subjects to explore their characters. He made these historical figures human beings. He had also mastered philosophy and wrote extensively on Plato and his teachings. His writings included treatises on moral philosophy as a guide to everyday life. Plutarch was the ideal type of the refined and learned man of his day, a genteel product of Greco-Roman culture. Very popular in his own day, his works hugely influenced the Renaissance and remain popular today.

In the tranquil surroundings of Chaeronea he spent his life. Even now, people visiting the museum at Delphi can see the inscription with which his fellow citizens honored him. Though remaining a lifelong citizen of Chaeronea, Plutarch also symbolizes the urbanity of the Roman Empire in the era of the five good emperors.

Questions for Analysis

1. What factors helped to propel Plutarch to prominence?

2. What does Plutarch's career indicate about social mobility in the Roman world?

3. Since Plutarch wrote biographies of both Greeks and Romans, does that indicate that he saw a basic unity in classical civilization?

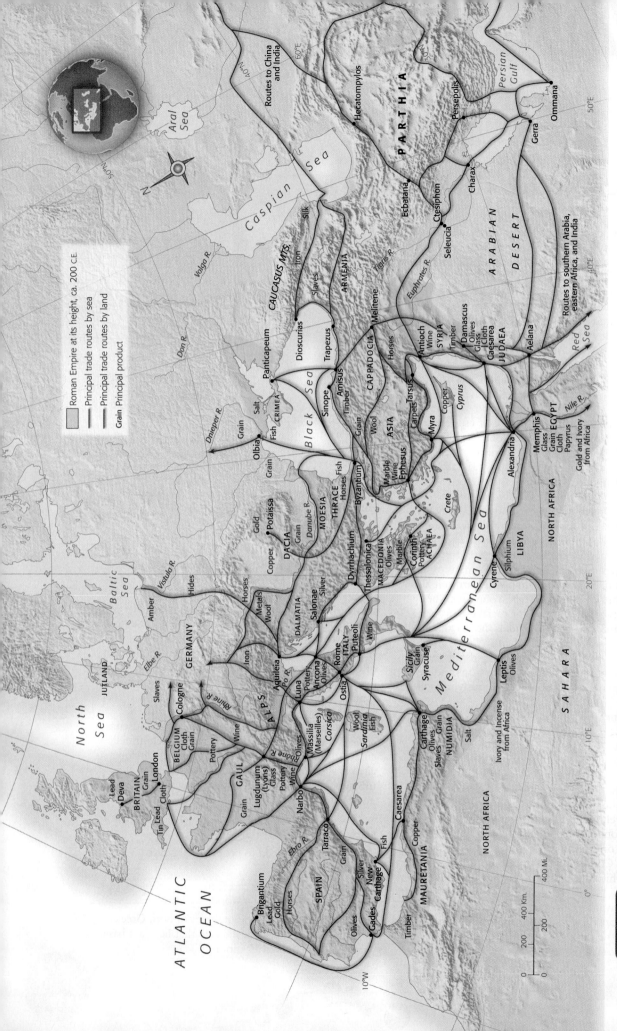

MAP 5.4 **The Economic Aspect of the Pax Romana** The Roman Empire was not merely a political and military organization but also an intricate economic network through which goods from Armenia and Syria were traded for Western products from as far away as Spain and Britain.

The Roman Provinces

The eastern part of the empire shared in the boom in part by trading with other areas and in part because of local industries. The cities of the east built extensively, beautifying themselves with new amphitheaters, temples, and other public buildings. Especially in the eastern empire this was the heyday of the city.

Trade among the provinces increased dramatically. Britain and Belgium became prime grain producers, much of their harvests going to the armies of the Rhine. Britain's wool industry probably got its start under the Romans. Italy and southern Gaul produced wine in huge quantities. Roman colonists introduced the olive to southern Spain and northern Africa, which soon produced most of the oil consumed in the western empire. In the east the oil production of Syrian farmers reached an all-time high. Egypt produced tons of wheat that fed the Roman populace. The Roman army in Mesopotamia consumed a high percentage of the raw materials and manufactured products of Syria and Asia Minor. During the time of the five good emperors the empire had become an economic as well as a political reality (see Map 5.4).

The growth of industry in the provinces was a striking feature of this period. Cities in Gaul and Germany eclipsed the old Mediterranean manufacturing centers. In the second century C.E. Gaul and Germany took over the pottery market. Lyons in Gaul and later Cologne in Germany became the new centers of the glassmaking industry. The cities of Gaul were nearly unrivaled in the manufacture of bronze and brass. Europe and western Asia had entered fully into a united economic, political, and cultural world.

● **Gladiatorial Games**
Though hardly games, the contests were vastly popular among the Romans. Gladiators were usually slaves, but successful ones could gain their freedom. The fighting was hard but fair, and the gladiators shown here look equally matched. *(Interfoto Pressebildagentur/Alamy)*

Eastward Expansion

Their expansion took the Romans into Central Asia, which had two immediate effects. The first was a long military confrontation between the Romans and their Iranian neighbors. Second, Roman military movement eastward coincided with Chinese expansion to the west, resulting in a period when the major ancient civilizations of the world came into contact with each other (see page 144).

When their expansion took the Romans farther eastward, they encountered the Parthians, who had established a kingdom in Iran in the Hellenistic period (see page 89). The Romans tried unsuccessfully to drive the Parthians out of Armenia and Mesopotamia until the Parthians fell to the Sasanids, a people indigenous to southern Iran, in 226 C.E. When the Romans continued their attacks against this new enemy, the Sasanid king Shapur defeated the Roman legions of the emperor Valerius, whom he took prisoner. Not until the reign of Diocletian and Constantine was Roman rule again firmly established in western Asia.

Although warfare disrupted parts of Asia, it did not stop trade that had prospered from Hellenistic times (see pages 91–93). Rarely did a merchant travel the entire distance from China to Mesopotamia. Protecting their own profits, the Parthians acted as middlemen to prevent the Chinese and Romans from making direct contact. Chinese merchants sold their wares to the Parthians at the Stone Tower, located in modern Tashkughan in Afghanistan. The Parthians then carried the goods overland to Mesopotamia or Egypt, where they were shipped throughout the Roman Empire. Silk was still a major commodity from east to west, along with other luxury goods. In return the Romans traded glassware, precious gems, and slaves. The Parthians added exotic fruits, rare birds, and other products desired by the Chinese (see the feature "Global Trade: Pottery" on pages 124–125).

Contacts Between Rome and China

This was also an era of exciting maritime exploration. Roman ships sailed from Egyptian ports to the mouth of the Indus River, where they traded local merchandise and wares imported by the Parthians. Merchants who made the voyage contended with wind, shoal waters, and pirates. Despite such dangers and discomforts, hardy mariners pushed into the Indian Ocean and beyond, reaching Malaya, Sumatra, and Java, when they traded with equally hardy local sailors.

Maritime trade between Chinese and Roman ports began in the second century C.E., though no merchant traveled the entire distance. The period of this contact coincided with the era of Han greatness in China (see pages 135–144). The Han emperor Wu Ti encouraged trade by land as well as sea, and Chinese merchants traded in the Parthian Empire along what came to be known as the "Great Silk Road." Indeed, a later Han emperor sent an ambassador directly to the Roman Empire by sea. The ambassador, Kan Ying, sailed to the Roman province of Syria during the reign of the emperor Nerva (96–98 C.E.), the first Chinese official to see for himself the Greco-Roman world. Although he left a fascinating report of his travels to his emperor, the Romans paid no attention to the contact. For the Romans China remained more of a mythical than a real place, and they never bothered to learn more about it.

• • • • • • • • • • • • •

TURMOIL AND REFORM (284–337 C.E.)

How did barbarian invasions and political turmoil shape the Roman Empire in the third and fourth centuries?

The era of the five good emperors gave way to a period of chaos and stress. During the third century C.E. the Roman Empire was stunned by civil war and barbarian invasions. By the time peace was restored, the economy was shattered, cities had shrunk in size, and agriculture was becoming manorial. In the disruption of the third century and the reconstruction of the fourth, the transition from the classical to the medieval world began.

Reconstruction Under Diocletian and Constantine

At the close of the third century C.E. the emperor Diocletian (r. 284–305 C.E.) ended the period of chaos. Repairing the damage done in the third century was the major work of the emperor Constantine (r. 306–337 C.E.) in the fourth. But if the price was high, so was the prize.

Under Diocletian the princeps became *dominus,* "lord." The emperor claimed that he was "the elect of god," that he ruled because of divine favor. To underline the emperor's exalted position, Diocletian and Constantine adopted the court ceremonies and trappings of the Persian Empire.

Diocletian recognized that the empire had become too great for one man to handle and so divided it into a western and an eastern half (see Map 5.5). Diocletian assumed direct control of the eastern part, while giving the rule of the western part to a colleague along with the title *augustus,* which had become synonymous with emperor. Diocletian and his fellow augustus further delegated power by appointing two men to assist them. Each man was given the title of *caesar* to indicate his exalted rank. Although this system is known as the *Tetrarchy* because four men ruled the empire, Diocletian was clearly the senior partner and final source of authority.

MAP 5.5 **The Roman World Divided** Under Diocletian, the Roman Empire was first divided into a western and an eastern half, a development that foreshadowed the medieval division between the Latin West and the Byzantine East.

Diocletian's political reforms were a momentous step. The Tetrarchy soon failed, but Diocletian's division of the empire into two parts became permanent. Throughout the fourth century C.E. the eastern and western sections drifted apart. In later centuries the western part witnessed the decline of Roman government and the rise of barbarian kingdoms, while the eastern half evolved into the Byzantine Empire.

Economic Hardship and Consequences

Major economic, social, and religious problems also confronted Diocletian and Constantine. They needed additional revenues to support the army and the imperial court. Yet the wars and invasions had struck a serious blow to Roman agriculture. Christianity had become too strong either to ignore or to crush. The way Diocletian, Constantine, and their successors responded to these problems left a permanent impression on future developments.

The empire itself was less capable of recovery than in earlier times. Wars and invasions had disrupted normal commerce and the means of production. Mines were exhausted in the attempt to supply much-needed ores, especially gold and silver. In the

POTTERY

Today we often consider pottery in utilitarian and decorative terms, but it served a surprisingly large number of purposes in the ancient world. Families used earthen pottery for cooking and tableware, for storing grains and liquids, and for lamps. On a larger scale pottery was used for the transportation and protection of goods traded overseas.

The creation of pottery dates back to the Neolithic period. Pottery required few resources to make, as potters needed only abundant sources of good clay and wheels upon which to throw their vessels. Once made, the pots were baked in specially constructed kilns. Although the whole process was relatively simple, skilled potters formed groups that made utensils for entire communities. Later innovations occurred when the artisans learned to glaze their pots by applying a varnish before baking them in a kiln.

The earliest potters focused on coarse ware: plain plates, cups, and cooking pots that remained virtually unchanged throughout antiquity. Increasingly, however, potters began to decorate these pieces with simple designs. In this way pottery became both functional and decorative. One of the most popular pieces was the amphora, a large two-handled jar with a wide mouth, a round belly, and a base. It became the workhorse of maritime shipping because it protected contents from water and rodents, was easy and cheap to produce, and could be reused. Amphoras contained goods as different as wine and oil, spices and unguents, dried fish and

The Pottery Trade

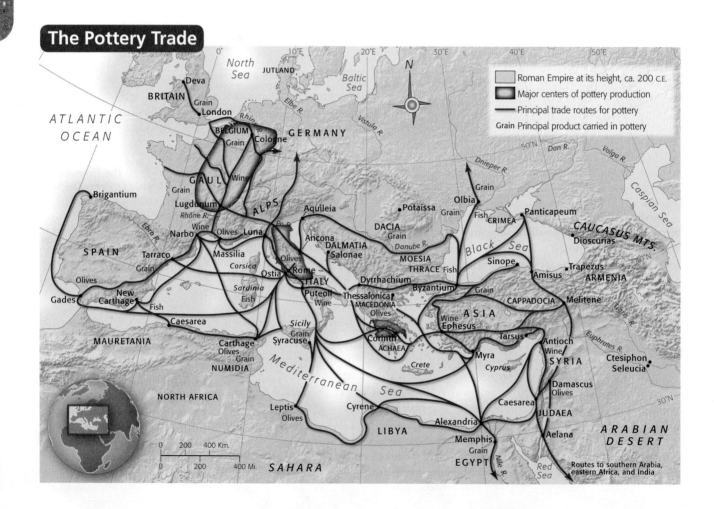

Roman Empire at its height, ca. 200 C.E.

Major centers of pottery production

Principal trade routes for pottery

Grain Principal product carried in pottery

*The Greeks captured Troy by concealing themselves in a wooden horse, which the
Trojans pulled into the city. On this piece from a pot found in Mykonos, probably dating
to the seventh century B.C.E., Greeks have just launched their attack from inside the
horse.* (Archaeological Receipts Fund, Athens)

pitch. The amphora's dependability and versatility kept
it in use from the fourth century B.C.E. to the beginning
of the Middle Ages.

In classical Greece individual potters sold their wares
directly to local customers or traders; manufacturer and
buyer alone determined the quantity of goods for sale
and their price. In the Hellenistic and Roman periods
amphoras became common throughout the Mediterranean and carried goods eastward to the Black Sea,
Persian Gulf, and Red Sea. The Ptolemies of Egypt sent
amphoras and their contents even farther, to Arabia,
eastern Africa, and India. Thus merchants and mariners
who had never seen the Mediterranean depended on
these containers.

Other pots proved as useful as the amphora, and all
became a medium of decorative art. By the eighth century B.C.E. Greek potters and artists began to decorate
their wares by painting them with patterns and scenes
from mythology, legend, and daily life. They portrayed
episodes such as the chariot race at Patroclus's funeral
or battles from the *Iliad*. Some portrayed the gods,
such as Dionysos at sea. These images widely spread
knowledge of Greek religion and culture. In the West,
especially the Etruscans in Italy and the Carthaginians in
North Africa eagerly welcomed the pots, their decora-

tion, and their ideas. The Hellenistic kings shipped
these pots as far east as China. Pottery thus served as a
cultural exchange among people scattered across huge
portions of the globe.

The Romans took the manufacture of pottery to an
advanced stage by introducing a wider range of vessels
for new purposes. The Roman ceramic trade spread
from Italy throughout the Mediterranean. The Roman
army provides the best example of how this ordinary
industry affected the broader culture. Especially on the
European frontiers the army used its soldiers to produce
the pottery it needed. These soldiers made their own
Italian *terra sigallata,* which was noted for its smooth
red glaze. Native potters immediately copied this style,
thus giving rise to local industries. Indeed, terra sigallata remained the dominant pottery style in northern
Europe until the seventh century C.E. When Roman
soldiers retired, they often settled where they had
served, especially if they could continue their trades.
Such ordinary Romans added local ideas to their craft.
This exchange resulted in a culture that was becoming European, rather than just Roman, and extended
into Britain, France, the Low Countries, and southern
Germany.

cities markets, trade, and industry were disrupted, and travel became dangerous. The devastation of the countryside increased the difficulty of feeding and supplying the cities. Merchant and artisan families rapidly left devastated regions. Economic hardship had been met by cutting the silver content of coins until money was virtually worthless. The immediate result was crippling inflation throughout the empire.

Diocletian's attempt to curb inflation illustrates the methods of absolute monarchy. In a move unprecedented in Roman history, Diocletian issued an edict that fixed maximum prices and wages throughout the empire. The emperors dealt with the tax system just as strictly and inflexibly. Taxes became payable in kind, that is, in goods and services instead of money. All those involved in the growing, preparation, and transportation of food and other essentials were locked into their professions. A baker or shipper could not go into any other business, and his son took up the trade at his death. In this period of severe depression, many localities could not pay their taxes. In such cases local tax collectors, who were themselves locked into service, had to make up the difference from their own funds. This system soon wiped out a whole class of moderately wealthy people.

Because of worsening conditions during the third century C.E., many free tenant farmers and their families were killed, fled the land to escape the barbarians or brigands, or abandoned farms ravaged in the fighting. Large tracts of land consequently lay deserted. Great landlords with ample resources began at once to reclaim as much of this land as they could. The huge estates that resulted, called villas, were self-sufficient. Since they produced more than they consumed, they successfully competed with the declining cities by selling their surplus in the countryside. They became islands of stability in an unsettled world.

The rural residents who remained on the land were exposed to the raids of barbarians and brigands and to the tyranny of imperial officials. In return for the protection and security landlords could offer, the small landholders gave over their lands and their freedom. They could no longer decide to move elsewhere. Henceforth, they and their families worked their patrons' land, not their own. Free people were becoming what would later be called serfs.

The Acceptance of Christianity

The Roman attitude toward Christianity evolved as well during this period of empire. At first many pagans genuinely misunderstood Christian practices and rites. They thought that such secret rites as the Lord's Supper, at which Christians said that they ate and drank the body and blood of Jesus, were acts of cannibalism. Pagans thought that Christianity was one of the worst of the mystery cults with immoral and indecent rituals. They also feared that the gods would withdraw their favor from the Roman Empire because of the Christian insistence that the pagan gods either did not exist or were evil spirits.

The Christians also exaggerated the degree of pagan hostility to them, and most of the gory stories about the martyrs are fictitious. There were indeed some cases of pagan persecution of the Christians, but with few exceptions they were local and sporadic in nature. Even Nero's notorious persecution was temporary and limited to Rome. No constant persecution of Christians occurred. As time went on, pagan hostility and suspicion decreased. Pagans realized that Christians were not working to overthrow the state and that Jesus was no rival of Caesar. The emperor Trajan forbade his governors to hunt down Christians. Though admitting that he considered Christianity an abomination, he preferred to leave Christians in peace.

The stress of the third century C.E., however, seemed to some emperors the punishment of the gods. Although the Christians depicted Diocletian as a fiend, he persecuted them in the hope that the gods would restore their blessing on Rome. Yet even his persecutions were never very widespread or long-lived. By the late third century C.E. pagans had become used to Christianity, and Constantine recognized Christianity as a legitimate religion. He himself died a Christian in 337 c.e. In time the Christian triumph would be complete. In 380 c.e. the emperor Theodosius made Christianity the official religion of the Roman Empire. At that point Christians began to persecute the pagans for their religion. History had come full circle.

The Construction of Constantinople

The triumph of Christianity was not the only event that made Constantine's reign a turning point in Roman history. Constantine took the bold step of building a new capital for the empire. Constantinople, the New Rome, was constructed on the site of Byzantium, the old Greek city on the Bosporus. Throughout the third century c.e. emperors had found Rome and western Europe hard to defend. The eastern part of the empire was more easily defensible and so escaped the worst of the barbarian devastation. It was wealthy and its urban life still vibrant. Moreover, Christianity was more widespread in the east than in the west, and the city of Constantinople was intended to be a Christian center.

● **Arch of Constantine**   Though standing in stately surroundings, Constantine's arch in Rome is decorated with art plundered from the arches of Trajan and Marcus Aurelius. He robbed them rather than decorate his own with the inferior work of his own day. *(Michael Reed, photographer/www.mike-reed.com)*

From the Classical World to Late Antiquity

Although Constantine had restored order, he could not undo the past. Too much had changed forever. The two-faced Roman god Janus, who looked both ways, in this case looked both to the past and the future and well symbolizes this period. A great deal of the past remained through these years of change. People still lived under the authority of the emperors and the guidance of Roman law. They still communicated with one another as usual, in Latin throughout the west and Greek in the east. Grecoroman art, architecture, and literature surrounded them as part of daily life.

Yet changes were also underway. Government had evolved from the pagan republic of the past to the Christian monarchy of the new age. The empire itself was split into east and west. The east remained the world of urbanism and empire, while the west became the home of independent barbarian kingdoms built on classical foundations.

Paganism faded into the background as Christianity prevailed. Greek philosophy was replaced by Christian theology, as thinkers tried earnestly to understand Jesus' message. Through all these changes the lives of ordinary people did not change dramatically. They farmed, worked in cities, and nurtured their families. They took new ideas, blended them with the old, and created new cultural forms. The classical world gradually gave way to a new intellectual, spiritual, and political life that forever changed the face of western Eurasia.

Chapter Summary

Key Terms

toga
Forum
franchise
patricians
plebeians
praetors
Struggle of the Orders
paterfamilias
manumission
latifundia
First Triumvirate
pax Romana
princeps civitatis
pagan
heresy
universalism
eucharist
five good emperors

To assess your mastery of this chapter, go to
bedfordstmartins.com/mckayworld

• How did the Romans come to dominate Italy, and what political institutions did they create?

The Etruscans and Romans both settled in Italy and the Etruscans developed the first cities and a rich cultural life. Ruling as kings, the Etruscans introduced Romans to urbanism, industry, trade, and the alphabet. The Romans fought numerous wars with the Etruscans, and in 509 B.C.E. the Romans won their independence and created the republic. The republic functioned through a shared government of the people directed by the senate, summarized by the expression SPQR—*senatus populusque Romanus,* the Roman senate and people. In resolving a social conflict known as the "Struggle of the Orders," Roman nobles and ordinary people created a state administered by magistrates elected from the entire population and a legal code common to all.

• How did Rome expand its power beyond Italy, and what were the effects of success on Rome?

Once united, the Romans launched a series of wars that took them from Spain in the west to Pergamum in Asia Minor. Their empire brought wealth, which led to a grand building program and a rich life for very many Romans. Increased power brought political problems, and during the late republic many poor people sought political and social reforms. Ambitious generals fought for power until Julius Caesar restored order. His adopted son Augustus transformed the republic into the empire by creating a constitutional monarchy in which he was the sole executive of the state. He directed the organs of government and the army, while encouraging local government.

• What was Christianity, and how did it affect life in the empire?

Christians developed as an offshoot of Judaism, when Jesus of Nazareth proclaimed himself the son of God. He taught that belief in his divinity led to eternal life. His followers spread their belief across the empire, transforming it from a Jewish sect into a new religion.

• How did efficient Roman rule lead to a "golden age" for the empire?

Augustus was followed by a series of efficient emperors who created an official bureaucracy to administer the empire. The five good emperors divided civil from military service, and made the army a garrison force to guard the frontiers. During this golden period Rome became the magnificent capital of the empire, increasingly adorned with beautiful buildings and improved urban housing, and harboring a well-fed populace. Rome also became a city of fun, marked by gladiatorial games and chariot racing. This was also a period of thriving agriculture and commercial expansion throughout the empire.

• How did barbarian invasions and political turmoil shape the Roman Empire in the third and fourth centuries?

When Rome expanded eastward from Europe, it met opposition, yet even during the fighting, commerce among the Romans, the Iranians, and the Chinese empire thrived through a series of trade routes, the most famous being the Great Silk Road. After the five good emperors, the empire fell prey to civil war and foreign invasion, both of which devastated the land and caused political chaos. Two gifted emperors, Diocletian and Constantine, restored order and then permanently divided the empire into western and eastern halves. Their rigid control of the economy was not successful. Rich landowners reclaimed land and created villas worked by tenants instead of free farmers. Meanwhile, the emperors legalized Christianity. The symbol of change became the new capital of the empire, Constantinople, the New Rome. The classical world gave way to the medieval.

Suggested Reading

Bruun, C., ed. *The Roman Middle Republic, ca. 400–133 B.C.* 2000. Treats the central issues of the period.

Burn, T. S. *Rome and the Barbarians, 100 B.C.–A.D. 400.* 2003. Analyzes the mutual impact of Romans and barbarians.

D'Ambra, E. *Roman Women.* 2007. A comprehensive and learned treatment of all aspects of women's life, private and public.

Esler, P. *The Early Christian World.* 2004. A collection of studies that cover all aspects of the topic.

Goldsworthy, A. *Roman Warfare.* 2000. A concise treatment of warfare from republican to imperial times.

Goodman, M. *The Roman World, 44 B.C.–A.D. 180.* 1997. A solid general treatment of the empire.

Kamm, A. *Julius Caesar.* 2006. An excellent brief biography that deals with all important aspects of his life.

MacMullen, R. *Roman Social Relations, 50 B.C.–A.D. 284.* 1981. Still an excellent discussion of the topic by a leading scholar.

Scullard, H. H. *A History of the Roman World,* 4th ed. 1993. Still the best single account of Roman history.

Turcam, R. *The Gods of Ancient Rome.* 2000. Provides a concise survey of the Roman pantheon.

Notes

1. Sallust, *War with Cataline* 10.1–3, translated by J. Buckler.
2. Matthew 16:18.

Listening to the
PAST

Titus Flamininus and the Liberty of the Greeks

After his arrival in Greece in 197 B.C.E., Titus Flamininus defeated the Macedonians in Thessaly. He next sent his recommendations on the terms of the peace agreement to the Roman senate. The following year the senate sent him ten commissioners, who agreed with his ideas. The year 196 B.C.E. was also the occasion when the great Pan-Hellenic Isthmian games were regularly celebrated near Corinth. Many of the dignitaries and the most prominent people of the Hellenistic world were present. Among them was Flamininus, who came neither as a participant in the games nor solely as a spectator of them. Instead, he took the occasion to make a formal announcement about Roman policy. There in Isthmia he officially announced that Rome granted freedom to the Greeks. He assured his audience that Rome had not come as a conqueror. The eminent Greek biographer Plutarch has left a vivid account of the general response to this pronouncement.

Accordingly, at the Isthmian games, where a great throng of people were sitting in the stadium and watching the athletic contests (since, indeed, after many years Greece had at last ceased from wars waged in hopes of freedom, and was now holding festival in time of assured peace), the trumpet signalled a general silence, and the herald, coming forward into the midst of the spectators, made proclamation that the Roman senate and Titus Quinctius Flamininus proconsular general, having conquered King Philip and the Macedonians, restored to freedom, without garrisons and without imposts, and to the enjoyment of their ancient laws, the Corinthians, the Locrians, the Phocians, the Euboeans, the Achaeans of Phthiotis, the Magnesians, the Thessalians, and the Perrhaebians. At first, then, the proclamation was by no means generally or distinctly heard, but there was a confused and tumultuous movement in the stadium of people who wondered what had been said, and asked one another questions about it, and called out to have the proclamation made again; but when silence had been restored, and the herald in tones that were louder

than before and reached the ears of all, had recited the proclamation, a shout of joy arose, so incredibly loud that it reached the sea. The whole audience rose to their feet, and no heed was paid to the contending athletes, but all were eager to spring forward and greet and hail the saviour and champion of Greece.

And that which is often said of the volume and power of the human voice was then apparent to the eye. For ravens which chanced to be flying overhead fell down into the stadium. The cause of this was the rupture of the air; for when the voice is borne aloft loud and strong, the air is rent asunder by it and will not support flying creatures, but lets them fall, as if they were over a vacuum, unless, indeed, they are transfixed by a sort of blow, as of a weapon, and fall down dead. It is possible, too, that in such cases there is a whirling motion of the air, which becomes like a waterspout at sea with a refluent flow of the surges caused by their very volume.

Be that as it may, had not Titus, now that the spectacle was given up, at once foreseen the rush and press of the throng and taken himself away, it would seem that he could hardly have survived the concourse of so many people about him at once and from all sides. But when they were tired of shouting about his tent, and night was already come, then, with greetings and embraces for any friends and fellow citizens whom they saw, they betook themselves to banqueting and carousing with one another. And here, their pleasure naturally increasing, they moved to reason and discourse about Greece, saying that although she had waged many wars for the sake of her freedom, she had not yet obtained a more secure or more delightful exercise of it than now, when others had striven in her behalf, and she herself, almost without a drop of blood or a pang of grief, had borne away the fairest and most enviable of prizes. Verily, they would say, valour and wisdom are rare things among men, but the rarest of all blessings is the just man. For men like Agesilaüs, or Lysander, or Nicias, or Alcibiades could indeed conduct wars well, and understood how to be victorious commanders in battles by land and sea, but they would

This coin provides a contemporary profile of Titus Flamininus, which also illustrates Roman realism in portraiture. *(Courtesy of the Trustees of the British Museum)*

not use their successes so as to win legitimate favour and promote the right. Indeed, if one excepts the action at Marathon, the sea-fight at Salamis, Plataea, Thermopylae, and the achievements of Cimon at the Eurymedon and about Cyprus, Greece has fought all her battles to bring servitude upon herself, and every one of her trophies stands as a memorial of her own calamity and disgrace, since she owed her overthrow chiefly to the baseness and contentiousness of her leaders. Whereas men of another race, who were thought to have only slight sparks and insignificant traces of a common remote ancestry, from whom it was astonishing that any helpful word or purpose should be vouchsafed to Greece—these men underwent the greatest perils and hardships in order to rescue Greece and set her free from cruel despots and tyrants.

So ran the thoughts of the Greeks; and the acts of Titus were consonant with his proclamations. For at once he sent Lentulus to Asia to set Bargylia free, and Stertinius to Thrace to deliver the cities and islands there from Philip's garrisons. Moreover, Publius Villius sailed to have a conference with Antiochus concerning the freedom of the Greeks who were under his sway. Titus himself also paid a visit to Chalcis, and then sailed from there to Magnesia, removing their garrisons and restoring to the peoples their constitutions. He was also appointed master of ceremonies for the Nemeian games at Argos, where he conducted the festival in the best possible manner, and once more

publicly proclaimed freedom to the Greeks. Then he visited the different cities, establishing among them law and order, abundant justice, concord, and mutual friendliness. He quieted their factions and restored their exiles, and plumed himself on his persuading and reconciling the Greeks more than on his conquest of the Macedonians, so that their freedom presently seemed to them the least of his benefactions. . . .

. . . In the case of Titus and the Romans, . . . gratitude for their benefactions to the Greeks brought them, not merely praises, but also confidence among all men and power, and justly too. For men not only received the officers appointed by them, but actually sent for them and invited them and put themselves in their hands. And this was true not only of peoples and cities, nay, even kings who had been wronged by other kings fled for refuge into the hands of Roman officials, so that in a short time—and perhaps there was also divine guidance in this—everything became subject to them. But Titus himself took most pride in his liberation of Greece.

Questions for Analysis

1. Did Titus Flamininus really want peace for the Greeks, or was this a cynical propaganda gesture?

2. What caused Greek political difficulties in the first place?

3. Was the Greek response to Titus Flamininus's proclamation genuine and realistic?

Source: Reprinted by permission of the publishers and the Trustees of the Loeb Classical Library from *Plutarch: Volume X—Parallel Lives.* Loeb Classical Library Volume L 102, trans. B. Perrin (Cambridge, Mass.: Harvard University Press, 1921). The Loeb Classical Library® is a registered trademark of the President and Fellows of Harvard College.

The Chinese Buddhist Monk Ganjin (688–763 c.e.).
Ganjin was blind by the time he finally reached Japan on
the sixth attempt in 754 and began his missionary work.
(Suzanne Perrin/Japan Interlink)

6 EAST ASIA AND THE SPREAD OF BUDDHISM, 256 B.C.E.–800 C.E.

Chapter Preview

The Age of Empire in China
• *What were the social, cultural, and political consequences of the unification of China under a strong centralized government?*

The Spread of Buddhism Out of India
• *How were both Buddhism and China changed by the spread of Buddhism across Asia?*

The Chinese Empire Re-created: Sui (581–618) and Tang (618–907)
• *In what ways was China's second empire different from its first?*

The East Asian Cultural Sphere
• *What elements of Chinese culture were adopted by Koreans, Vietnamese, and Japanese, and how did they adapt them to their own circumstances?*

East Asia was transformed over the millennium from 200 B.C.E. to 800 C.E. In 200 B.C.E. only one of the societies in the region had writing, iron technology, large cities, and complex state organizations. Over the course of the next several centuries, this situation changed dramatically as war, trade, diplomacy, missionary activity, and pursuit of learning brought increased contact among the peoples of the region. Buddhism came to provide a common set of ideas and visual images for the entire area. Chinese was widely used as an international language outside its native area.

Increased communication stimulated state formation in Central Asia, Tibet, Korea, Manchuria, and Japan. The new states usually adopted political models from China. Nevertheless, by 800 each of these regions was well on its way to developing a distinct political and cultural identity. Ancient China is treated in Chapter 3; this is the first chapter to treat Korea and Japan.

THE AGE OF EMPIRE IN CHINA

What were the social, cultural, and political consequences of the unification of China under a strong centralized government?

In much the same period in which Rome created a huge empire, the Qin and Han rulers in China created an empire on a similar scale. Like the Roman Empire, the Chinese empire was put together through force of arms and held in place by sophisticated centralized administrative machinery.

The Qin Unification (221–206 B.C.E.)

In 221 B.C.E., after decades of constant warfare, the state of Qin, the state that had adopted Legalist policies (see pages 70–71), succeeded in defeating the last of its rivals. China was unified for the first time in many centuries. The king of Qin decided that the title

● **Army of the First Emperor** The thousands of life-size ceramic soldiers buried in pits about a half mile from the First Emperor's tomb help us imagine the Qin military machine. It was the Qin emperor's concern with the afterlife that led him to construct such a lifelike guard. The soldiers were originally painted in bright colors, and they held real bronze weapons. *(Robert Harding World Imagery)*

"king" was not grand enough and invented the title "emperor" (*huangdi*). He called himself the First Emperor (Shihuangdi) in anticipation of a long line of successors.

Once Qin ruled all of China, the First Emperor and his shrewd Legalist minister Li Si embarked on a sweeping program of centralization that touched the lives of nearly everyone in China. To cripple the nobility of the defunct states, the First Emperor ordered the nobles to leave their lands and move to the capital. To administer the territory that had been seized, he dispatched officials, then controlled them through a long list of regulations, reporting requirements, and penalties for inadequate performance. These officials owed their power and positions entirely to the favor of the emperor and had no hereditary rights to their offices.

To harness the enormous human resources of his people, the First Emperor ordered a census of the population. Census information helped the imperial bureaucracy to plan its activities—to estimate the costs of public works, the tax revenues needed to pay for them, and the labor force available for military service and building projects. To make it easier to administer all regions uniformly, the script was standardized, along with weights, measures, coinage, even the axle lengths of carts. Private possession of arms was outlawed to make it more difficult for subjects to rebel. To make it easier for Qin armies to move rapidly, thousands of miles of roads were built. Most of the labor on these projects came from farmers performing required corvée labor or convicts working their sentences.

Some twentieth-century Chinese historians glorified the First Emperor as a bold conqueror who let no obstacle stop him, but the traditional evaluation of him was almost entirely negative. For centuries Chinese historians castigated him as a cruel, arbitrary, impetuous, suspicious, and superstitious megalomaniac. Hundreds of thousands of subjects were drafted to build the **Great Wall**, a rammed-earth fortification along the northern border between the Qin realm and the land controlled by the

Great Wall *A rammed-earth fortification built along the northern border of China during the reign of the First Emperor.*

nomadic Xiongnu. After Li Si complained that scholars used records of the past to denigrate the emperor's achievements and undermine popular support, the emperor had all writings other than useful manuals on topics such as agriculture, medicine, and divination collected and burned. As a result of this massive book burning, many ancient texts were lost.

Three times assassins tried to kill the First Emperor, and perhaps as a consequence he became obsessed with discovering the secrets of immortality. He spent lavishly on a tomb designed to protect him in the afterlife. Although the central chambers have not yet been excavated, in nearby pits archaeologists have unearthed thousands of life-size terra-cotta figures of armed soldiers and horses lined up to protect him.

After the First Emperor died in 210 B.C.E., the Qin state unraveled. The Legalist institutions designed to concentrate power in the hands of the ruler made the stability of the government dependent on his strength and character. The First Emperor's heir was murdered by his younger brother, and uprisings soon followed.

The Han Dynasty (206 B.C.E.–220 C.E.)

The eventual victor in the struggle for power that ensued was Liu Bang, known in history as Emperor Gaozu (r. 202–195 B.C.E.). The First Emperor of Qin was from the Zhou aristocracy. Gaozu was, by contrast, from a modest family of commoners, so his elevation to emperor is evidence of how thoroughly the Qin Dynasty had destroyed the old order.

Gaozu did not disband the centralized government created by the Qin, but he did remove its most unpopular features. Harsh laws were canceled, taxes were sharply reduced, and a policy of laissez faire was adopted in an effort to promote economic recovery. With policies of this sort, relative peace, and the extension of China's frontiers, the Chinese population grew rapidly in the first two centuries of the Han Dynasty. The census of 2 C.E. recorded a population of 58 million, the earliest indication of the large size of China's population.

In contrast to the Qin promotion of Legalism, the Han came to promote Confucianism and recruit officials on the basis of their Confucian learning or Confucian moral qualities. Under the most activist of the Han emperors, Emperor Wu, the "Martial Emperor" (r. 141–87 B.C.E.), Confucian scholars were given a privileged position. The Han government's efforts to recruit men trained in the Confucian classics marked the beginning of the Confucian scholar-official system, one of the most distinctive features of imperial China. Chinese officials, imbued with Confucian values, did not comply automatically with the policies of the ruler, above all because they saw criticism of the government as one of their duties. Their willingness to stand up to the ruler also reflected the fact that most of the Confucian scholars selected to serve

Chronology

ca. 230–208 B.C.E.	Construction of Great Wall to protect against Xiongnu
221 B.C.E.	China unified under Qin Dynasty
206 B.C.E.–220 C.E.	Han Dynasty
145–ca. 85 B.C.E.	Sima Qian, Chinese historian
111 B.C.E.	Emperor Wu conquers Nam Viet
108 B.C.E.	Han government establishes colonies in Korea
105 C.E.	Chinese invention of paper
ca. 200 C.E.	Buddhism begins rapid growth in China
220–589 C.E.	Age of Division in China
313–668 C.E.	Three Kingdoms Period in Korea
372 C.E.	Buddhism introduced in Korea
538 C.E.	Buddhism introduced in Japan
581–618 C.E.	Sui Dynasty
604 C.E.	Prince Shōtoku's "Seventeen Principles" in Japan
618–907 C.E.	Tang Dynasty
668 C.E.	Silla unifies Korea
690 C.E.	Empress Wu declares herself emperor, becoming the only Chinese woman emperor
710 C.E.	Japan's capital moved to Nara
735–737 C.E.	Smallpox epidemic in Japan
845 C.E.	Tang emperor begins persecution of Buddhism

as officials came from landholding families, much like those who staffed the Roman government, which gave them some economic independence.

The Han government was supported largely by the taxes and labor service demanded of farmers, but this revenue regularly fell short of the government's needs. To pay for his military campaigns, Emperor Wu took over the minting of coins, confiscated the land of nobles, sold offices and titles, and increased taxes on private businesses. A widespread suspicion of commerce as an unproductive exploitation of the true producers made it easy to levy especially heavy assessments on merchants. The worst blow to businessmen, however, was the government's decision to enter into market competition with them by selling the commodities that had been collected as taxes. In 119 B.C.E. government monopolies were established in the production of iron, salt, and liquor. These enterprises had previously been sources of great profit for private entrepreneurs. Large-scale grain dealing also had been a profitable business, which the government now took over. Grain was to be bought where it was plentiful and its price low and to be either stored in granaries or transported to areas of scarcity. This procedure was supposed to eliminate speculation in grain, provide more constant prices, and bring profit to the government.

Inner Asia and the Silk Road

The difficulty of defending against the nomadic pastoral peoples to the north is a major reason China came to favor a centralized bureaucratic form of government. Resources from the entire subcontinent were needed to maintain control of the northern border.

Beginning long before the Han Dynasty, China's contacts with its northern neighbors had involved both trade and military conflict. China's neighbors sought Chinese products such as silk and lacquer ware. When they did not have goods to trade or when trading relations were disrupted, raiding was considered an acceptable alternative in the tribal cultures of the region. Chinese sources speak of defending against raids of "barbarians" from Shang times (ca. 1500–ca. 1050 B.C.E.) on, but not until the rise of nomadism in the mid-Zhou period (fifth–fourth centuries B.C.E.) did the horsemen of the north become China's main military threat.

The economy of these nomads was based on raising sheep, goats, camels, and horses. Families lived in tents that could be taken down and moved north in summer and south in winter as groups of families moved in search of pasture. Herds were tended on horseback, and everyone learned to ride from a young age. Especially awesome from the Chinese perspective was the ability of nomad horsemen to shoot arrows while riding horseback. The typical social structure of the steppe nomads was fluid, with family and clan units linked through loyalty to tribal chiefs selected for their military prowess. Charismatic tribal leaders could form large coalitions and mobilize the entire society for war.

Chinese farmers and Inner Asian herders had such different modes of life that it is not surprising that they had little respect for each other. For most of the imperial period, Chinese farmers looked on the northern non-Chinese horsemen as gangs of bullies who thought robbing was easier than working for a living. The nomads identified glory with military might and viewed farmers as contemptible weaklings.

● **Xiongnu Metalwork** The metal ornaments of the Xiongnu provide convincing evidence that they were in contact with nomadic pastoralists farther west in Asia, such as the Scythians, who also fashioned metal plaques and buckles in animal designs. This buckle or ornament is made of gold and is about 3 inches tall. *(The Metropolitan Museum of Art, Gift of J. Pierpont Morgan, 1917 [17.190.1672]. Photograph © 1981 The Metropolitan Museum of Art)*

In the late third century B.C.E. the Xiongnu (known in the West as the Huns) formed the first great confederation of nomadic tribes (see Map 6.1). The Qin's Great Wall was built to defend against them, and the Qin sent out huge armies against them. The early Han emperors tried to make peace with them, offering generous gifts of silk, rice, cash, and even imperial princesses as brides. But these policies were controversial, since critics thought they merely strengthened the enemy. Certainly Xiongnu power did not decline, and in 166 B.C.E. 140,000 Xiongnu raided to within a hundred miles of the Chinese capital.

Emperor Wu decided that China had to push the Xiongnu back. He sent several armies of one hundred thousand to three hundred thousand troops deep into Xiongnu territory. These costly campaigns were of limited value since the Xiongnu were a moving target: fighting nomads was not like attacking walled cities. If the Xiongnu did not want to fight the Chinese troops, they simply moved their camps. To try to find allies and horses, Emperor Wu turned his attention west, toward Central Asia. From the envoy he sent into Bactria, Parthia, and Ferghana in 139 B.C.E., the Chinese learned for the first time of other civilized states comparable to China (see Map 6.1). The envoy described Ferghana as an urban society ten thousand *li* (about three thousand miles) west of China, where grapes were grown for wine and the horses were particularly fine. In Parthia, he was impressed by the use of silver coins stamped with the image of the king's face. These regions, he reported, were familiar with Chinese products, especially silk, and did a brisk trade in them.

MAP 6.1 **The Han Empire** The Han Dynasty asserted sovereignty over vast regions from Korea in the east to Central Asia in the west and Vietnam in the south. Once garrisons were established, traders were quick to follow, leading to considerable spread of Chinese material culture in East Asia. Chinese goods, especially silk, were in demand far beyond East Asia, promoting long-distance trade across Eurasia.

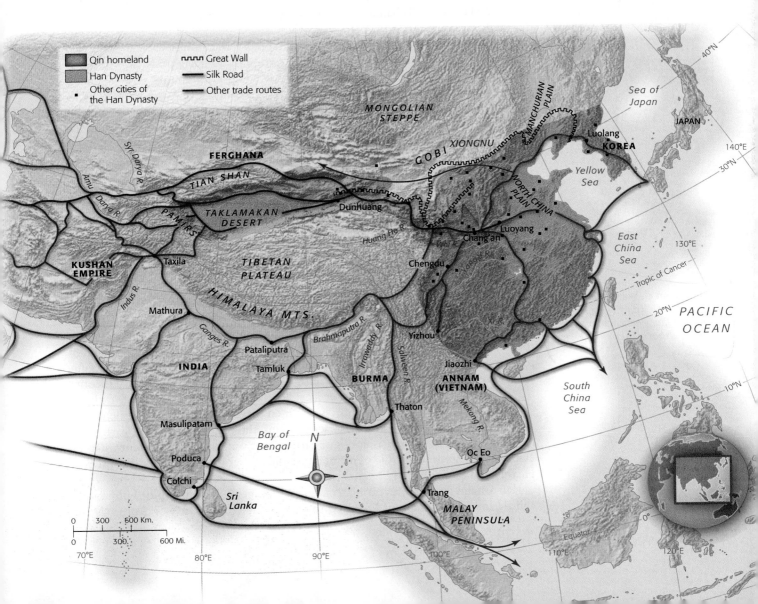

Silk Road *The trade routes across Central Asia through which Chinese silk and other items were traded.*

tributary system *A system used by China to regulate contact with foreign powers. States and tribes beyond its borders sent envoys bearing gifts and received gifts in return.*

Emperor Wu sent an army into Ferghana and gained recognition of Chinese overlordship in the area, thus obtaining control over the trade routes across Central Asia commonly called the **Silk Road.** The city-states along this route did not resist the Chinese presence. They could carry out the trade on which they depended more conveniently with Chinese garrisons to protect them than with rival tribes raiding them.

At the same time, Emperor Wu sent troops into northern Korea to establish military districts that would flank the Xiongnu on their eastern border. By 111 B.C.E. the Han government also had extended its rule south into what is now northern Vietnam. Thus during Emperor Wu's reign, the territorial reach of the Han state was vastly extended.

During the Han Dynasty, China developed a **tributary system** to regulate contact with foreign powers. States and tribes beyond its borders sent envoys bearing gifts and received gifts in return. Over the course of the dynasty the Han government's outlay on these gifts was huge, perhaps as much as 10 percent of state revenue. In 25 B.C.E., for instance, the government gave tributary states twenty thousand rolls of silk cloth and about twenty thousand pounds of silk floss. Although the tribute system was a financial burden to the Chinese, it reduced the cost of defense and offered China confirmation that it was the center of the civilized world.

The silk given to the Xiongnu and other northern tributaries often entered the trading networks of Sogdian, Parthian, and Indian merchants, who carried it by caravans across Asia. There was a market both for skeins of silk thread and for silk cloth woven in Chinese or Syrian workshops. Caravans returning to China carried gold, horses, and occasionally handicrafts of West Asian origin, such as glass beads and cups. Through the trade along the Silk Road, the Chinese learned of new foodstuffs, including walnuts, pomegranates, sesame, and coriander, all of which came to be grown in China. This trade was largely carried by the two-humped Bactrian camel, which had been bred in Central Asia since the first century B.C.E. With a heavy coat of hair to withstand the bitter cold of winter, each camel could carry about five hundred pounds of cargo. (See the feature "Global Trade: Silk" on pages 140–141.)

Maintaining a military presence so far from the center of China was expensive. To cut costs, the government set up self-supporting military colonies, recruited Xiongnu tribes to serve as auxiliary forces, and established vast government horse farms. Still, military expenses threatened to bankrupt the Han government.

Han Intellectual and Cultural Life

Confucian classics *The ancient texts recovered during the Han Dynasty that Confucian scholars treated as sacred scriptures.*

Confucianism made a comeback during the Han Dynasty, but it was a changed Confucianism. Although Confucian texts had fed the First Emperor's bonfires, some dedicated scholars had hidden their books, and others had memorized whole works: one ninety-year-old man was able to recite two long books almost in their entirety. The ancient books recovered in this way (called the **Confucian classics**) were revered as repositories of the wisdom of the past. Scholars studied them with piety and attempted to make them more useful as sources of moral guidance by writing commentaries on them. Many Confucian scholars specialized in a single classic, and teachers passed on to their disciples their understanding of each sentence in the work. Other Han Confucians went to the opposite extreme, developing comprehensive cosmological theories that explained the world in terms of cyclical flows of yin and yang and the five phases (fire, water, earth, metal, and wood). Some used these theories to elevate the role of the emperor, who alone had the capacity to link the realms of Heaven, earth, and man. Natural disasters such as floods or earthquakes were viewed as portents that the emperor had failed in his role of maintaining the proper balance among the forces of Heaven and earth.

Han art and literature reveal a fascination with omens, portents, spirits, immortals, and occult forces. Emperor Wu tried to make contact with the world of gods and immortals through elaborate sacrifices, and he welcomed astrologers, alchemists, seers, and shamans to his court. He marveled at stories of the paradise of the Queen Mother of the West and the exploits of the Yellow Emperor, who had taken his entire court with him when he ascended to the realm of the immortals. Much of this interest in immortality and communicating with the spirit world was absorbed into the emerging religion of Daoism, which also drew on the philosophical ideas of Laozi and Zhuangzi.

A major intellectual accomplishment of the Han Dynasty was history writing. Sima Qian (145–ca. 85 B.C.E.) wrote a comprehensive history of China from the time of the mythical sage-kings of high antiquity to his own day, dividing his account into a chronology recounting political events, biographies of key individuals, and treatises on subjects such as geography, taxation, and court rituals. As an official of the emperor, he had access to important people and documents and to the imperial library. Like the Greeks Herodotus and Thucydides (see page 83), Sima Qian believed fervently in visiting the sites where history was made, examining artifacts, and questioning people about events. He was also interested in China's geography and local history. The result of his research, ten years in the making, was **Records of the Grand Historian,** a massive work of literary and historical genius. In the chapter devoted to "moneymakers," he described how the Ping family made its fortune:

Lu people are customarily cautious and miserly, but the Ping family of Cao were particularly so. They started out by smelting iron and in time accumulated a fortune of a hundred million cash. All the members of the family from the father and elder brothers down to the sons and grandsons, however, made a promise that they would "Never look down without picking up something useful; never look up without grabbing something of value." They traveled about to all the provinces and kingdoms, selling goods on credit, lending money and trading. It was because of their influence that so many people in Zou and Lu abandoned scholarship and turned to the pursuit of profit.[1]

From examples like these Sima Qian concluded that wealth has no permanent master: "It finds its way to the man of ability like the spokes of a wheel converging upon the hub, and from the hands of the worthless it falls like shattered tiles."[2] For centuries to come, Sima Qian's work set the standard for Chinese historical writing, although most of the histories modeled after it covered only a single dynasty. The first of these was the work of three members of the Ban family in the first century C.E. (See the feature "Individuals in Society: The Ban Family.")

The circulation of books like Sima Qian's was made easier by the invention of paper, which the Chinese traditionally date to 105 C.E. Scribes had previously written on strips of bamboo and wood or rolls of silk. Cai Lun, to whom the Chinese attribute the invention of paper, worked the fibers of rags, hemp, bark, and other scraps into sheets of paper. Paper, thus, was somewhat similar to the papyrus made from pounded reeds in ancient Egypt. Though much less durable than wood, paper was far cheaper than silk and became a convenient means of conveying the written word. Compared to papyrus, it depended less on a specific source of plant fiber and so could be produced many places.

Records of the Grand Historian *A comprehensive history of China written by Sima Qian.*

Economy and Society in Han China

How were ordinary people's lives affected by the creation of a huge bureaucratic empire? The lucky ones who lived in Chang'an or Luoyang, the great cities of the empire, got to enjoy the material benefits of increased long-distance trade and a boom in the production of luxury goods.

The government did not promote trade per se. The Confucian elite, like ancient Hebrew wise men, considered trade necessary but lowly. Agriculture and crafts were more honorable because they produced something, but merchants merely took

SILK

Silk was one of the earliest commodities to stimulate international trade. By 2500 B.C.E. Chinese farmers had domesticated *Bombyx mori,* the Chinese silkworm, and by 1000 B.C.E. they were making fine fabrics with complex designs. Sericulture (silk making) is labor-intensive. In order for silkworms to spin their cocoons, they have to be fed leaves from mulberry trees. The leaves have to be picked and chopped, then fed to the worms every few hours, day and night, during the month between hatching and spinning. The cocoons consist of a single filament several thousand feet long but a minuscule 0.025 millimeter thick. More than two thousand cocoons are needed to make a pound of silk. After the cocoons are boiled to loosen the natural gum that binds the filament, several strands of filament are twisted together to make yarns.

What made silk the most valued of all textiles was its beauty and versatility. It could be made into sheer gauzes, shiny satins, multicolored brocades, and plush velvets. Fine Han silks have been found in Xiongnu tombs in northern Mongolia. Korea and Japan not only imported silk but also began silk production themselves, and silk came to be used in both places in much the way it was used in China—for the clothes of the elite,

The Silk Trade

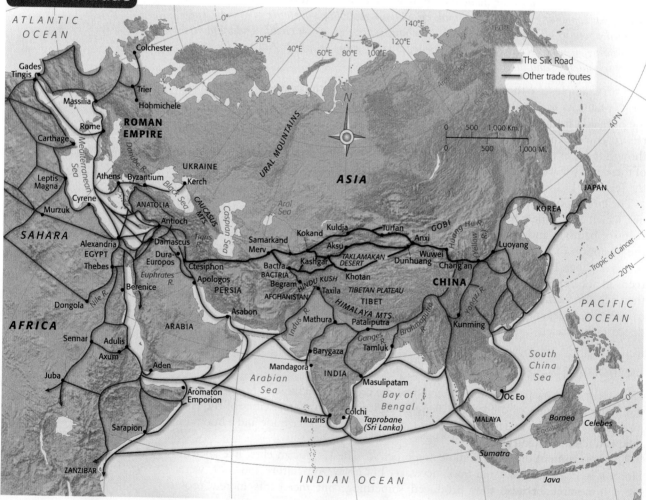

This fragment of a silk damask, about a foot square, was woven in China in the eleventh or twelfth century C.E., then transported by sea to Persia, where it was excavated along with southern Chinese porcelains of similar date. The design on the damask shows baby boys among pomegranates and flowers. Pomegranates have many seeds, making them symbols for ample progeny, a message conveyed even more concretely by the boys. (The Metropolitan Museum of Art. Purchase, Rogers Fund, 1952 [52.8]. Photograph © 1997 The Metropolitan Museum of Art)

for temple banners, and as a surface for writing and painting. Central Asia, Persia, India, and Southeast Asia also became producers of silk in distinctive local styles. Lacking suitable climates to produce silk, Mongolia and Tibet remained major importers of Chinese silks into modern times.

What makes the silk trade famous, however, is not the trade within Asia but the trade across Asia to Europe. In Roman times, silk carried by caravans across Asia or by ships across the Indian Ocean became a high-status luxury item, said to cost its weight in gold. To satisfy Roman taste, imported silk fabrics were unraveled and rewoven in Syrian workshops. Although the techniques of sericulture gradually spread through Asia, they remained a mystery in the West until the Byzantine emperor Justinian in the sixth century had two monks bring back silkworms from China along with knowledge of how to care for them and process their cocoons.

In medieval times, most of the silk imported into Europe came from Persia, the Byzantine Empire, or the Arab world. Venetian merchants handled much of the trade. Some of this fabric still survives in ancient churches, where it was used for vestments and altar clothes and to wrap relics. In the eleventh century, Roger I, king of Sicily, captured groups of silk-workers from Athens and Corinth and moved them to Sicily, initiating the production of silk in western Europe. Over the next couple of centuries, Italy became a major silk producer, joined by France in the fifteenth century.

When Marco Polo traveled across Asia in the late thirteenth century, he found local silk for sale in Baghdad, Georgia, Persia, and elsewhere, but China remained the largest producer. He claimed that more than a thousand cartloads of silk were brought into the capital of China every day.

With the development of the sea route between western Europe and China from the sixteenth century on, Europe began importing large quantities of Chinese silk, much of it as silk floss—raw silk—to supply Italian, French, and English silk weavers. In 1750 almost 70,000 kilograms (77.2 tons) of raw silk and nearly 20,000 lengths of silk cloth were carried from China to Europe. By this period the aristocracy of Europe regularly wore silk clothes, including silk stockings.

Mechanization of silk making began in Europe in the seventeenth century. The Italians developed machines to "throw" the silk—doubling and twisting raw silk into threads having the required strength and thickness. In the early nineteenth century, the introduction of Jacquard looms using punched cards made complex patterns easier to weave.

In the 1920s the silk industry was hit hard by the introduction of synthetic fibers, especially rayon and nylon. In the 1940s women in the United States and Europe switched from silk stockings to the much less expensive nylon stockings. European production of silk almost entirely collapsed.

In the 1980s silk made a comeback as China in the post-Mao era rapidly expanded its silk production. By 2003 there were more than two thousand silk enterprises in China, employing a million workers and supplying 80 percent of the total world trade in silk.

advantage of others' shortages to make profits as middlemen. This attitude justified the government's takeover of the grain, iron, and salt businesses. Still, the government indirectly promoted commerce by building cities and roads.

Markets were the liveliest places in the cities. Besides stalls selling goods of all kinds, markets offered fortunetellers and entertainers. People flocked to puppet shows and performances of jugglers and acrobats. The markets also were used for the execution of criminals, to serve as a warning to onlookers.

Government patronage helped maintain the quality of craftsmanship in the cities. By the beginning of the first century C.E., China had about fifty state-run ironworking factories. Chinese metalworking was the most advanced in the world at the time. In contrast to Roman blacksmiths, who hammered heated iron to make wrought iron tools, the Chinese knew how to liquefy iron and pour it into molds, producing tools with a higher carbon content that were harder and more durable. Han workmen turned out iron plowshares, agricultural tools with wooden handles, and weapons and armor.

Iron was replacing bronze in tools, but bronzeworkers still turned out a host of goods. Bronze was prized for jewelry, mirrors, and dishes. Bronze was also used for minting coins and for precision tools such as carpenters' rules and adjustable wrenches. Surviving bronze gear-and-cog wheels bear eloquent testimony to the sophistication of Han machinery. Han metal-smiths were mass-producing superb crossbows long before the crossbow was dreamed of in Europe.

The bulk of the population in Han times and even into the twentieth century consisted of peasants living in villages of a few hundred households. Since the Han empire, much like the contemporaneous Roman Empire, drew its strength from a large population of free peasants who contributed both taxes and labor services to the state, the government had to try to keep peasants independent and productive. The economic insecurity of small holders was described by one official in 178 B.C.E. in terms that could well have been repeated in most later dynasties:

They labor at plowing in the spring and hoeing in the summer, harvesting in the autumn and storing foodstuff in winter, cutting wood, performing labour service for the local government, all the while exposed to the dust of spring, the heat of summer, the storms of autumn, and the chill of winter. Through all four seasons they never get a day off. They need funds to cover such obligations as entertaining guests, burying the dead, visiting the sick, caring for orphans, and bringing up the young. No matter how hard they work they can be ruined by floods or droughts, or cruel and arbitrary officials who impose taxes at the wrong times or keep changing their orders. When taxes fall due, those with produce have to sell it at half price [to raise the needed cash], and those without [anything to sell] have to borrow [at such high rates] they will have to pay back twice what they borrowed. Some as a consequence sell their lands and houses, even their children and grandchildren.[3]

To fight peasant poverty, the government kept land taxes low (one-thirtieth of the harvest), provided relief in time of famine, and promoted up-to-date agricultural methods. Still, many hard-pressed peasants were left to choose between migration to areas where new lands could be opened and quasi-servile status as the dependents of a magnate. Throughout the Han period, Chinese farmers in search of land to till pushed into frontier areas, expanding Chinese domination at the expense of other ethnic groups, especially in central and south China.

The Chinese family in Han times was much like the Roman (see page 109) and the Indian (see pages 315–316) family. In all three societies, senior males had great authority, marriages were arranged by parents, and brides normally joined their husbands' families. Other practices were more distinctive to China, such as the universality of patrilineal family names, the practice of dividing land equally among the sons in a family, and the great emphasis placed on the virtue of filial piety. The brief *Classic of Filial Piety,* which claimed that filial piety was the root of all virtue, gained wide

The Ban Family

Ban Biao (3–54 C.E.), a successful official from a family with an envied library, had three highly accomplished children: his twin sons, the general Ban Chao (32–102) and the historian Ban Gu (32–92); and his daughter, Ban Zhao (ca. 45–120).

After distinguishing himself as a junior officer in campaigns against the Xiongnu, Ban Chao was sent in 73 C.E. to the Western Regions to see about the possibility of restoring Chinese overlordship there, lost since Wang Mang's time (early first century C.E.). Ban Chao spent most of the next three decades in Central Asia. Through patient diplomacy and a show of force, he reestablished Chinese control over the oasis cities of Central Asia, and in 92 he was appointed protector general of the area.

His twin brother Ban Gu was one of the most accomplished writers of his age, excelling in a distinctive literary form known as the rhapsody (*fu*). His "Rhapsody on the Two Capitals" is in the form of a dialogue between a guest from Chang'an and his host in Luoyang. It describes the palaces, spectacles, scenic spots, local products, and customs of the two great cities. Emperor Zhang (r. 76–88) was fond of literature and often had Ban Gu accompany him on hunts or travels. He also had him edit a record of the court debates he held on issues concerning the Confucian classics.

Ban Biao was working on a history of the Western Han Dynasty when he died in 54. Ban Gu took over this project, modeling it on Sima Qian's *Records of the Grand Historian.* He added treatises on law, geography, and bibliography, the last a classified list of books in the imperial library.

Because of his connection to a general out of favor, Ban Gu was sent to prison in 92, where he soon died. At that time the *History of the Former Han Dynasty* was still incomplete. The emperor called on Ban Gu's widowed sister, Ban Zhao, to finish it. She came to the palace, where she not only worked on the history but also became a teacher of the women of the palace. According to the *History of the Later Han,* she taught them the classics, history, astronomy, and mathematics. In 106 an infant succeeded to the throne, and the widow of an earlier emperor became regent. This empress frequently turned to Ban Zhao for advice on government policies.

Ban Zhao credited her own education to her learned father and cultured mother and became an advocate of the education of girls. In her *Admonitions for*

Ban Zhao continued to be considered the ideal woman teacher into the eighteenth century, when this imaginary portrait depicted her taking up her brush among women and children. *(National Palace Museum, Taipei, Taiwan)*

Women, Ban Zhao objected that many families taught their sons to read but not their daughters. She did not claim girls should have the same education as boys; after all, "just as yin and yang differ, men and women have different characteristics." Women, she wrote, will do well if they cultivate the womanly virtues such as humility. "Humility means yielding and acting respectful, putting others first and oneself last, never mentioning one's own good deeds or denying one's own faults, enduring insults and bearing with mistreatment, all with due trepidation."* In subsequent centuries, Ban Zhao's *Admonitions* became one of the most commonly used texts for the education of girls.

Questions for Analysis

1. What inferences would you draw from the fact that a leading general had a brother who was a literary man?

2. What does Ban Zhao's life tell us about women in her society? How do you reconcile her personal accomplishments with the advice she gave for women's education?

*Patricia Buckley Ebrey, ed., *Chinese Civilization: A Sourcebook,* rev. ed. (New York: Free Press, 1993), p. 75.

Primary Source:
Lessons for Women
Discover what Ban Zhao, the foremost female writer in Han China, had to say about the proper behavior of women.

circulation in Han times. The virtues of loyal wives and devoted mothers were extolled in the *Biographies of Exemplary Women*, which told the stories of women from China's past who were notable for giving their husbands good advice, knowing how to educate their sons, and sacrificing themselves when forced to choose between their fathers and husbands. The book also contained a few cautionary tales of scheming, jealous, manipulative women who brought destruction to all around them.

China and Rome

The empires of China and Rome have often been compared. Both were large, complex states governed by monarchs, bureaucracies, and standing armies. Both reached directly to the people through taxation and conscription policies. Both invested in infrastructure such as roads and waterworks. Both had to work hard to keep land from becoming too concentrated in the hands of hard-to-tax wealthy magnates. In both empires people in neighboring areas that came under political domination were attracted to the conquerors' material goods, productive techniques, and other cultural products, resulting in gradual cultural assimilation. Both China and Rome had similar frontier problems and tried similar solutions, such as using "barbarian" auxiliaries and settling soldier-colonists.

Nevertheless, the differences between Rome and Han China are worth as much notice as the similarities. The Roman Empire was linguistically and culturally more diverse than China. In China there was only one written language; but in the Roman Empire people still wrote in Greek and several other languages, and people from the East could claim more ancient civilizations. Politically, the dynastic principle was stronger in China than in Rome. Han emperors were never chosen by the army or by any institution comparable to the Roman senate, nor were there any republican ideals in China. In contrast to the graduated forms of citizenship in Rome, Han China drew no distinctions between original and added territories. The social and economic structures also differed in the two empires. Slavery was much more important in Rome than in China, and merchants were more favored. Over time these differences put Chinese and Roman social and political development on rather different trajectories.

The Fall of the Han and the Age of Division

In the second century C.E. the Han government suffered a series of blows. A succession of child emperors allowed their mothers' relatives to dominate the court. Emperors turned to **eunuchs** (castrated palace servants) for help in ousting the consort families (families of empresses), only to find that they were just as difficult to control. In 166 and 169 scholars who had denounced the eunuchs were arrested, killed, or banished from the capital and official life. Then in 184 a millenarian religious sect rose in massive revolt. The armies raised to suppress the rebels soon took to fighting among themselves. In 189 one general slaughtered two thousand eunuchs in the palace and took the Han emperor captive. After years of fighting, a stalemate was reached, with three warlords each controlling distinct territories in the north, the southeast, and the southwest. In 220 one of them forced the last of the Han emperors to abdicate, formally ending the Han Dynasty.

The period after the fall of the Han Dynasty is often referred to as the **Age of Division** (220–589). A brief reunification from 280 to 316 came to an end when non-Chinese who had been settling in north China since Han times seized the opportunity afforded by the political turmoil to take power. For the next two and a half centuries north China was ruled by one or more non-Chinese dynasty (the Northern Dynasties), and the south was ruled by a sequence of four short-lived Chinese dynasties (the Southern Dynasties) centered in the area of the present-day city of Nanjing.

In the south a hereditary aristocracy entrenched itself in the higher reaches of

eunuchs *Castrated males who played an important role as palace servants.*

Age of Division *The period after the fall of the Han Dynasty, during which time China was politically divided.*

officialdom. These families intermarried only with families of equivalent pedigree and compiled lists and genealogies of the most eminent families. They saw themselves as maintaining the high culture of the Han and looked on the emperors of the successive dynasties as upstarts—as military men rather than men of culture. In this aristocratic culture, the arts of poetry and calligraphy flourished, and people began collecting writings by famous calligraphers.

Establishing the capital at Nanjing, south of the Yangzi River, had a beneficial effect on the economic development of the south. To pay for an army and to support the imperial court and aristocracy in a style that matched their pretensions, the government had to expand the area of taxable agricultural land, whether through settling migrants or converting the local inhabitants into taxpayers. The south, with its temperate climate and ample supply of water, offered nearly unlimited possibilities for such development.

The Northern Dynasties are interesting as the first case of alien rule in China. Ethnic tensions flared from time to time. In the late fifth century the Northern Wei Dynasty (386–534) moved the capital from near the Great Wall to the ancient city of Luoyang, adopted Chinese-style clothing, and made Chinese the official language. The Xianbei tribesmen, who still formed the main military force, saw themselves as marginalized by these policies and rebelled in 524. For the next fifty years north China was torn apart by struggles for power. It had long been the custom of the northern pastoral tribes to enslave those they captured; sometimes the residents of entire cities were enslaved. In 554, when the city of Jiangling was taken, one hundred thousand civilians were enslaved and distributed to generals and officials.

THE SPREAD OF BUDDHISM OUT OF INDIA

How were both Buddhism and China changed by the spread of Buddhism across Asia?

In much the same period that Christianity was spreading out of its original home in ancient Israel, Buddhism was spreading beyond India. Like Christianity, Buddhism was shaped by its contact with cultures in the different areas into which it spread, leading to several distinct forms. The Mahayana form of Buddhism (see page 41) that spread via Central Asia to China, Korea, and Japan is distinct from the Theravada form that spread from India to Sri Lanka and Southeast Asia and the Tantric form that spread to Tibet.

Central Asia is a loose term used to refer to the vast area between the ancient civilizations of Persia, India, and China. Modern political borders are a product of competition among the British, Russians, and Chinese for empire in the mid-nineteenth century and have relatively little to do with the earlier history of the region. Through most of recorded history, the region was ethnically and culturally diverse; it was home to urban centers, especially at the oases along the Silk Road, and to pastoralists in the mountains and grasslands.

Under Ashoka (see pages 45–46) Buddhism began to spread to Central Asia. This continued under the Kushan empire (ca. 50–250 C.E.), especially under the greatest Kushan king, Kanishka I (ca. 100 C.E.). In this region, where the influence of Greek art was strong, artists began to depict the Buddha in human form. Over the next several centuries most of the city-states of Central Asia became centers of Buddhism, from Bamiyan, northwest of Kabul, to Kucha, Khotan, Loulan, Turfan, and Dunhuang (see Map 6.2). Because the remarkable Buddhist civilization of Central Asia was later supplanted by Islam, it was not until early in the twentieth century that European archaeologists discovered its traces. The main sites yielded not only numerous

Buddhist paintings but also thousands of texts in a variety of languages. In Khotan, for instance, an Indian language was used for administrative purposes long after the fall of the Kushan empire. Other texts were in various Persian languages, showing the cultural mix of the region.

The first translators of Buddhist texts into Chinese were not Indians but Parthians, Sogdians, and Kushans from Central Asia. One of the most important interpreters of Buddhism in China was the eminent Central Asian monk Kumarajiva (350–413) from Kucha, who settled in Chang'an and directed several thousand monks in the translation of Buddhist texts.

Why did Buddhism find so many adherents in China during the three centuries after the fall of the Han Dynasty in 220? There were no forced conversions, but still the religion spread rapidly. In the unstable political environment, many people were open to new ideas. To Chinese scholars the Buddhist concepts of the transmigration of souls, karma, and nirvana posed a stimulating intellectual challenge. To rulers the Buddhist religion offered a source of magical power and a political tool to unite

MAP 6.2 **The Spread of Buddhism** Buddhism spread throughout India in Ashoka's time and beyond India in later centuries. The different forms of Buddhism found in Asia today reflect this history. The Mahayana Buddhism of Japan came via Central Asia, China, and Korea, with a secondary later route through Tibet. The Theravada Buddhism of Southeast Asia came directly from India and indirectly through Sri Lanka.

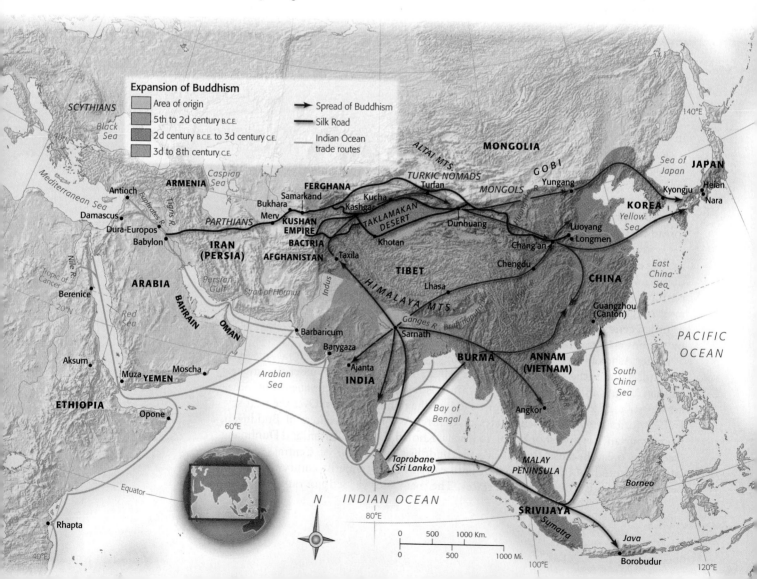

Chinese and non-Chinese. In a rough and tumultuous age Buddhism's emphasis on kindness, charity, and eternal bliss was deeply comforting. As in India, Buddhism posed no threat to the social order, and the elite who were drawn to Buddhism encouraged its spread to people of all classes. (See the feature "Listening to the Past: Copying Buddhist Sutras" on pages 160–161.)

The monastic establishment grew rapidly in China. Like their Christian counterparts in medieval Europe, Buddhist monasteries played an active role in social, economic, and political life. By 477 there were said to be 6,478 Buddhist temples and 77,258 monks and nuns in the north. Some decades later south China had 2,846 temples and 82,700 clerics. Given the importance of family lines in China, becoming a monk was a major decision, since a man had to give up his surname and take a vow of celibacy, thus cutting himself off from the ancestral cult. Those not ready to become monks or nuns could pursue Buddhist goals as pious laypeople by performing devotional acts and making contributions to monasteries. Among the most generous patrons were rulers in both the north and south.

In China women turned to Buddhism as readily as men. Although incarnation as a female was considered lower than incarnation as a male, it was also viewed as temporary, and women were encouraged to pursue salvation on terms nearly equal to men. Joining a nunnery became an alternative for a woman who did not want to marry or did not want to stay with her husband's family in widowhood.

● **Meditating Monk**   This monk, wearing the traditional patchwork robe, sits in the crossed-legged meditation position. His small niche is to the left of the main image of the Buddha in cave 285 at Dunhuang, a cave completed in 539 under the patronage of a prince of the Northern Wei imperial house who was then the local governor. *(Photo: Lois Conner. Courtesy, Dunhuang Academy)*

Buddhism had an enormous impact on the visual arts in China, especially sculpture and painting. Before Buddhism, Chinese had not set up statues of gods in temples, but now they decorated temples with a profusion of images. Inspired by the cave-temples of India and Central Asia, in China, too, caves were carved into rock faces to make temples.

Buddhist temples were just as splendid in the cities. One author described the ceremony held each year on the seventh day of the fourth month at the largest monastery in the northern capital, Luoyang. All the Buddhist statues in the city, more than a thousand altogether, would be brought to the monastery, and the emperor would come in person to scatter flowers as part of the Great Blessing ceremony:

The gold and the flowers dazzled in the sun, and the jewelled canopies floated like clouds; there were forests of banners and a fog of incense, and the Buddhist music of India shook heaven and earth. All kinds of entertainers and trick riders performed shoulder to shoulder. Virtuous hosts of famous monks came, carrying their staves; there were crowds of the Buddhist faithful, holding flowers; horsemen and carriages were packed beside each other in an endless mass.[4]

● **Yungang Colossal Buddha** Beginning about 460 C.E. the Northern Wei rulers constructed a series of caves at Yungang, not far from their capital. The large Buddha shown here in a lotus meditation posture is 45 feet (13.7 meters) tall. Notice the long ears and the robe across the Buddha's shoulders, both features associated with the Buddha. *(Dean Conger/Corbis)*

Not everyone was won over by Buddhist teachings. Critics of Buddhism labeled it immoral, unsuited to China, and a threat to the state since monastery land was not taxed and monks did not perform labor service. Twice in the north orders were issued to close monasteries and force monks and nuns to return to lay life, but these suppressions did not last long, and no attempt was made to suppress belief in Buddhism.

THE CHINESE EMPIRE RE-CREATED: SUI (581–618) AND TANG (618–907)

In what ways was China's second empire different from its first?

In the 570s and 580s, the long period of division in China was brought to an end under the leadership of the Sui Dynasty. Yang Jian, who both founded the Sui Dynasty and oversaw the reunification of China, was from a Chinese family that had intermarried with the non-Chinese elite of the north. His conquest of the south involved naval as well as land battles, with thousands of ships on both sides contending for control of the Yangzi River. The Sui reasserted Chinese control over northern Vietnam and campaigned into Korea and against the new force on the steppe, the Turks. The Sui strengthened central control of the government by curtailing the power of local officials to appoint their own subordinates and by instituting competitive written examinations for the selection of officials.

The crowning achievement of the Sui Dynasty was the **Grand Canal,** which connected the Huang (Yellow) and Yangzi River regions. The canal facilitated the shipping of tax grain from the prosperous Yangzi Valley to the centers of political and military power in north China. Henceforth the rice-growing Yangzi Valley and south China played an ever more influential role in the country's economic and political life, strengthening China's internal cohesion.

Despite these accomplishments, the Sui Dynasty lasted for only two reigns. The ambitious projects of the two Sui emperors led to exhaustion and unrest, and in the ensuing warfare Li Yuan, a Chinese from the same northwest aristocratic circles as the founder of the Sui, seized the throne.

Grand Canal *A canal, built during the Sui Dynasty, that connected the Huang (Yellow) and Yangzi Rivers.*

The Tang Dynasty (618–907)

The dynasty founded by Li Yuan, the Tang, was one of the high points of traditional Chinese civilization. Especially during this dynasty's first century, its capital, Chang'an, was the cultural center of East Asia, drawing in merchants, pilgrims, missionaries, and students to a degree never matched before or after. This position of strength gave the Chinese the confidence to be open to what they could learn from the outside world, leading to a more cosmopolitan culture than in any other period before the twentieth century.

The first two Tang rulers, Gaozu (r. 618–626) and Taizong (r. 626–649), were able monarchs. Adding to their armies auxiliary troops composed of Turks, Tanguts, Khitans, and other non-Chinese led by their own chieftains, they campaigned into Korea, Vietnam, and Central Asia. In 630 the Chinese turned against their former allies, the Turks, gaining territory from them and winning for Taizong the title of Great Khan, so that he was for a short period simultaneously head of both the Chinese and the Turkish empires.

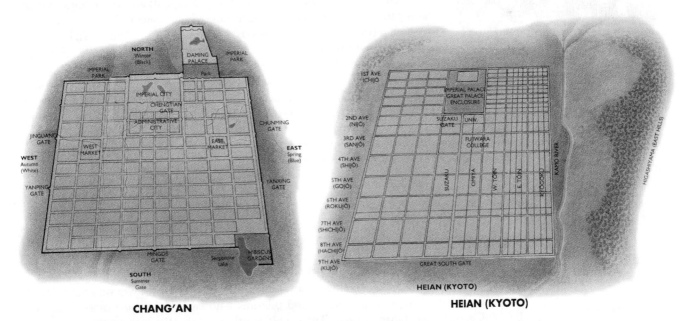

CHANG'AN

HEIAN (KYOTO)

● **Urban Planning** Chang'an in Tang times attracted merchants, pilgrims, and students from all over East Asia. The city was laid out on a square grid (*left*) and divided into walled wards, the gates to which were closed at night. Temples were found throughout the city, but trade was limited to two government-supervised markets. In the eighth and ninth centuries the Japanese copied the general plan of Chang'an in designing their capitals—first at Nara, then at Heian, shown on the right. *(From Cradles of Civilization: China [Weldon Owen Pty Limited, Australia])*

● **Five-Stringed Pipa/Biwa** This musical instrument, decorated with fine wood marquetry, was probably presented by the Tang court to a Japanese envoy. It was among the objects placed in a royal storage house (Shōsōin) in 756. *(Courtesy, Nara National Museum)*

Primary Source:
The Christian Monument
An eighth-century inscription tells a remarkable tale: how a Christian sect from Syria was supported by the Chinese emperor.

In the civil sphere Tang accomplishments far outstripped anything known in Europe until the growth of national states in the seventeenth century. Tang emperors subdivided the administration of the empire into departments, much like the numerous agencies of modern governments. They built on the Sui precedent of using written examinations to select officials. Although only about thirty men were recruited this way each year, the prestige of passing the examinations became so great that more and more men attempted them. Candidates had to master the Confucian classics and the rules of poetry, and they had to be able to analyze practical administrative and political matters. Government schools were founded to prepare the sons of officials and other young men for service as officials.

The mid-Tang Dynasty saw two women—Empress Wu and Consort Yang Guifei—rise to positions of great political power. Empress Wu was the consort of the weak and sickly Emperor Gaozong. After Gaozong suffered a stroke in 660, she took full charge. She continued to rule after Gaozong's death, summarily deposing her own two sons and dealing harshly with all opponents. In 690 she proclaimed herself emperor, the only woman who took that title in Chinese history. To gain support, she circulated a Buddhist sutra that predicted the imminent reincarnation of the Buddha Maitreya as a female monarch, during whose reign the world would be free of illness, worry, and disaster. Although despised by later historians as an evil usurper, Empress Wu was an effective leader. It was not until she was over eighty that members of the court were able to force her out in favor of her son.

Her grandson, the emperor Xuanzong (r. 713–756), in his early years presided over a brilliant court and patronized leading poets, painters, and calligraphers. In his later years, however, after he became enamored of his consort Yang Guifei, he let things slide. This was a period when ample and rounded proportions were much admired in women, and Yang was said to be such a full-figured beauty. The emperor allowed her to place friends and relatives in important positions in the government. One of her favorites was the general An Lushan, who, after getting into a quarrel with Yang's brother over control of the government, rebelled in 755. Xuanzong had to flee the capital, and the troops that accompanied him forced him to have Yang Guifei executed.

The rebellion of An Lushan was devastating to the Tang Dynasty. Peace was restored only by calling on the Uighurs, a Turkish people allied with the Tang, who looted the capital after taking it from the rebels. After the rebellion was finally suppressed in 763, the central government had to keep meeting the extortionate demands of the Uighurs. Many military governors came to treat their provinces as hereditary kingdoms and withheld tax returns from the central government. In addition, eunuchs gained increasing power at court and were able to prevent both the emperors and Confucian officials from doing much about them.

Tang Culture

The reunification of north and south led to cultural flowering. The Tang capital cities of Chang'an and Luoyang became great metropolises; Chang'an and its suburbs grew to more than 2 million inhabitants. The cities were laid out in rectangular grids and contained a hundred-odd walled "blocks" inside their walls.

In these cosmopolitan cities, knowledge of the outside world was stimulated by the presence of envoys, merchants, and pilgrims who came from neighboring states in Central Asia, Japan, Korea, Tibet, and Southeast Asia. Because of the presence of foreign merchants, many religions were practiced, including Nestorian Christianity, Manichaeism, Zoroastrianism, Judaism, and Islam, although none of them spread into the Chinese population the way Buddhism had a few centuries earlier. Foreign fashions in hair and clothing were often copied, and foreign amusements such as polo found followings among the well-to-do. The introduction of new musical instruments

● **Woman Playing Polo**   Notions of what makes women attractive have changed over the course of Chinese history. The figurines found in Tang tombs reveal that active women, even women playing polo on horseback like the one shown here, were viewed as appealing. In earlier and later periods, female beauty was identified with slender waists and delicate faces, but in Tang times women were admired for their plump bodies and full faces. *(Chinese. Equestrienne [tomb figure], buff earthenware with traces of polychromy, first half 8th cent., 56.2 x 48.2 cm. Gift of Mrs. Pauline Palmer Wood, 1970.1073. Photograph © 1998, The Art Institute of Chicago)*

and tunes from India, Iran, and Central Asia brought about a major transformation in Chinese music.

The Tang Dynasty was the great age of Chinese poetry. Skill in composing poetry was tested in the civil service examinations, and educated men had to be able to compose poems at social gatherings. The pain of parting, the joys of nature, and the pleasures of wine and friendship were all common poetic topics. One of Li Bo's (701–762) most famous poems describes an evening of drinking with only the moon and his shadow for company:

A cup of wine, under the flowering trees;
I drink alone, for no friend is near.
Raising my cup I beckon the bright moon,
For he, with my shadow, will make three men.
The moon, alas, is no drinker of wine;
Listless, my shadow creeps about at my side.

. . .

Now we are drunk, each goes his way.
May we long share our odd, inanimate feast,
And we meet at last on the cloudy River of the sky.[5]

Primary Source:
Memorial on Buddhism
Read how Han Yu, upset at the growing influence of Buddhism, denigrated that religion as "un-Chinese" in a text addressed to the Tang emperor.

The poet Bo Juyi (772–846) often wrote of more serious subjects. At times he worried about whether he was doing his job justly and well:

From these high walls I look at the town below
Where the natives of Pa cluster like a swarm of flies.
How can I govern these people and lead them aright?
I cannot even understand what they say.
But at least I am glad, now that the taxes are in,
To learn that in my province there is no discontent.[6]

In Tang times Buddhism fully penetrated Chinese daily life. Stories of Buddhist origin became widely known, and Buddhist festivals, such as the festival for feeding hungry ghosts in the summer, became among the most popular holidays. Buddhist monasteries became an important part of everyday life. They ran schools for children. In remote areas they provided lodging for travelers. Merchants entrusted their money and wares to monasteries for safekeeping, in effect transforming the monasteries into banks and warehouses. The wealthy often donated money or land to support temples and monasteries, making monasteries among the largest landlords.

At the intellectual and religious level, Buddhism was developing in distinctly Chinese directions. Two schools that thrived were Pure Land and Chan. **Pure Land** appealed to laypeople. The simple act of calling on the Buddha Amitabha and his chief helper, the compassionate bodhisattva Guanyin, could lead to rebirth in Amitabha's paradise, the Pure Land. Among the educated elite the **Chan** school (known in Japan as Zen) also gained popularity. Chan teachings rejected the authority of the scriptures and claimed the superiority of mind-to-mind transmission of Buddhist truths. The "northern" tradition emphasized meditation and monastic discipline. The "southern" tradition was even more iconoclastic, holding that enlightenment could be achieved suddenly through insight into one's own true nature, even without prolonged meditation.

In the late Tang period, opposition to Buddhism reemerged. In addition to concerns about the fiscal impact of removing so much land from the tax rolls and so many men from the labor service force, there were concerns about Buddhism's foreign origins. As China's international position weakened, xenophobia emerged. During the persecution of 845, more than 4,600 monasteries and 40,000 temples and shrines were destroyed, and more than 260,000 Buddhist monks and nuns were forced to return to secular life. Although this ban was lifted after a few years, the monastic establishment never fully recovered. Among laypeople Buddhism retained a strong hold, and basic Buddhist ideas like karma and reincarnation had become fully incorporated into everyday Chinese thinking. But Buddhism was never again as central to Chinese life.

Pure Land *A school of Buddhism that taught that by paying homage to the Buddha Amitabha and his chief helper, one could achieve rebirth in Amitabha's paradise.*

Chan *A school of Buddhism (known in Japan as Zen) that rejected the authority of the sutras and claimed the superiority of mind-to-mind transmission of Buddhist truths.*

THE EAST ASIAN CULTURAL SPHERE

What elements of Chinese culture were adopted by Koreans, Vietnamese, and Japanese, and how did they adapt them to their own circumstances?

During the millennium from 200 B.C.E. to 800 C.E. China exerted a powerful influence on its immediate neighbors, who began forming states of their own. By Tang times China was surrounded by independent states in Korea, Manchuria, Tibet, the area that is now Yunnan province, Vietnam, and Japan. All of these states were much smaller than China in area and population, making China by far the dominant force politically and culturally until the nineteenth century. Nevertheless, each of these separate states developed a strong sense of uniqueness and independent identity.

The earliest information about each of these countries is found in Chinese sources. Han armies brought Chinese culture to Korea and Vietnam, but even in those cases much cultural borrowing was entirely voluntary as the elite, merchants, and craftsmen adopted the techniques, ideas, and practices they found appealing. In Japan much of the process of absorbing elements of Chinese culture was mediated via Korea. In Korea, Japan, and Vietnam the fine arts—painting, architecture, and ceramics in particular— were all strongly influenced by Chinese models. Tibet, though a thorn in the side of Tang China, was as much in the Indian sphere of influence as in the Chinese and thus followed a somewhat different trajectory. Most significant, it never adopted Chinese characters as its written language, nor was it as influenced by Chinese artistic styles as other areas. Moreover the form of Buddhism that became dominant in Tibet came directly from India, not through Central Asia and China.

In each area, literate Chinese-style culture was at first an upper-level overlay over an indigenous cultural base, but in time many products and ideas adopted from China became incorporated into everyday life, ranging from written language to chopsticks and soy sauce. By the eighth century the Chinese language was a written lingua franca among educated people throughout East Asia. Educated Vietnamese, Koreans, and Japanese could communicate in writing when they could not understand each other's spoken languages, and envoys to Chang'an could carry out "brush conversations" with each other. The books that educated people read included the Chinese classics, histories, and poetry, as well as Buddhist sutras translated into Chinese. The great appeal of Buddhism known primarily through Chinese translation was a powerful force promoting cultural borrowing.

Vietnam

Vietnam is today classed with the countries to its west as part of Southeast Asia, but its ties are at least as strong to China. The Vietnamese first appear in Chinese sources as a people of south China called the Yue, who gradually migrated farther south as the Chinese state expanded. The people of the Red River valley in northern Vietnam had achieved a relatively advanced level of Bronze Age civilization by the first century B.C.E. The bronze heads of their arrows often were dipped in poison to facilitate killing large animals such as elephants, whose tusks were traded to China for iron. Power was held by hereditary tribal chiefs who served as civil, religious, and military leaders, with the king as the most powerful chief.

The collapse of the Qin Dynasty in 206 B.C.E. had an impact on this area because a former Qin general, Zhao Tuo (Trieu Da in Vietnamese), finding himself in the far south, set up his own kingdom of Nam Viet (Nan Yue in Chinese). This kingdom covered much of south China and was ruled by Trieu Da from his capital near the present site of Guangzhou. Its population consisted chiefly of the Viet people. After killing all officials loyal to the Chinese emperor, Trieu Da adopted the customs of the Viet and made himself the ruler of a vast state that extended as far south as modern-day Da Nang.

After almost a hundred years of diplomatic and military duels between the Han Dynasty and Trieu Da and his successors, Nam Viet was conquered in 111 B.C.E. by Chinese armies. Chinese administrators were assigned to replace the local nobility. Chinese

● **Bronze Drum** By 300 B.C.E. large bronze drums were being cast in what is now northern Vietnam. They were regularly decorated with scenes of daily life, war, and rituals. This drum, called the Ngoc Lu Drum, has depictions of boats carrying warriors on its sides. The three concentric rings on top show birds, deer, houses, and pairs of people pounding rice. *(From A. J. Bernet Kempers,* The Kettledrums of South Asia: A Bronze Age World and Its Aftermath *[Leiden, The Netherlands: A. A. Balkema, 1988, Tozzer Library, Harvard College Library])*

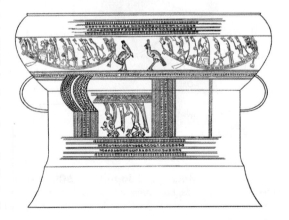

political institutions were imposed, and Confucianism became the official ideology. The Chinese language was introduced as the medium of official and literary expression, and Chinese ideographs were adopted as the written form for the Vietnamese spoken language. The Chinese built roads, waterways, and harbors to facilitate communication within the region and to ensure that they maintained administrative and military control over it. Chinese art, architecture, and music had a powerful impact on their Vietnamese counterparts.

Chinese innovations that were beneficial to the Vietnamese were readily integrated into the indigenous culture, but the local elite were not reconciled to Chinese political domination. The most famous early revolt took place in 39 C.E., when two widows of local aristocrats, the Trung sisters, led an uprising against foreign rule. After overwhelming Chinese strongholds, they declared themselves queens of an independent Vietnamese kingdom. Three years later a powerful army sent by the Han emperor reestablished Chinese rule.

China retained at least nominal control over northern Vietnam through the Tang Dynasty, and there were no real borders between China proper and Vietnam during this time. The local elite became culturally dual, serving as brokers between the Chinese governors and the native people.

Korea

Korea is a mountainous peninsula some 600 miles long extending south from Manchuria and Siberia. At its tip it is about 120 miles from Japan (see Map 6.3). Archaeological, linguistic, and anthropological evidence indicates that the Korean people share a common ethnic origin with other peoples of North Asia, including those of Manchuria, Siberia, and Japan. Linguistically, Korean is not related to Chinese.

Bronze and iron technology spread from China and North Asia in the Zhou period. In about 194 B.C.E. Wiman, an unsuccessful rebel against the Han Dynasty, fled to Korea and set up a state called Chosŏn in what is now northwest Korea and southern Manchuria. In 108 B.C.E. this state was overthrown by the armies of the Han emperor Wu. Four commanderies were established there, and Chinese officials were dispatched to govern them.

The impact of the Chinese commanderies in Korea was similar to that of the contemporaneous Roman colonies in Britain in encouraging the spread of culture and political forms. The commanderies survived not only through the Han Dynasty, but also for nearly a century after the fall of the dynasty, to 313 C.E. The Chinese never controlled the entire Korean peninsula, however. The Han commanderies coexisted with the native Korean kingdom of Koguryŏ, founded in the first century B.C.E. Chinese sources describe this kingdom as a society of aristocratic tribal warriors who had under them a mass of serfs and slaves, mostly from conquered tribes. After the Chinese colonies were finally overthrown, the kingdoms of Paekche and Silla emerged farther south on the peninsula in the third and fourth centuries C.E., leading to what is called the Three Kingdoms Period (313–668 C.E.). In all three Korean kingdoms Chinese was used as the language of government and learning. Each of the three kingdoms had hereditary kings, but their power

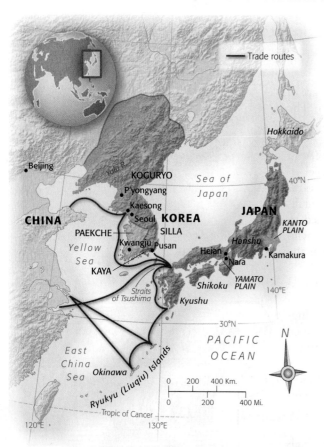

MAP 6.3 **Korea and Japan, ca. 600** Korea and Japan are of similar latitude, but Korea's climate is more continental, with harsher winters. Of Japan's four islands, Kyushu is closest to Korea and mainland Asia.

was curbed by the existence of very strong hereditary elites.

Buddhism was officially introduced in Koguryŏ from China in 372 and in the other states not long after. Buddhism placed Korea in a pan-Asian cultural context. Buddhist monks went back and forth between China and Korea. One even made the journey to India and back, and others traveled on to Japan to aid in the spread of Buddhism there.

When the Sui Dynasty finally reunified China in 589, it tried to establish control of at least a part of Korea. But the Korean kingdoms were much stronger than their predecessors in Han times, and they repeatedly repulsed Chinese attacks. The Tang government then tried allying itself with one state to fight another. Silla and Tang jointly destroyed Paekche in 660 and Koguryŏ in 668. The unification under Silla marks the first political unification of Korea.

Although Silla quickly forced the Tang to withdraw, for the next century Silla embarked on a policy of wholesale borrowing of Chinese culture and institutions. Annual embassies were sent to Chang'an, and large numbers of students studied in China. The Silla government was modeled on the Tang, although modifications were made to accommodate Korea's more aristocratic social structure.

Japan

Japan does not touch China as do Korea, Tibet, and Vietnam. The heart of Japan is four mountainous islands off the coast of Korea (see Map 6.3). Japan's early development was closely tied to that of the mainland, especially to Korea. Physical anthropologists have discerned several major waves of immigrants into Japan. People of the Jōmon culture, established by about 10,000 B.C.E. after an influx of people from Southeast Asia, practiced hunting and fishing and fashioned clay pots. New arrivals from northeast Asia brought agriculture and a distinct culture called Yayoi (ca. 300 B.C.E.–300 C.E.). Later Yayoi communities

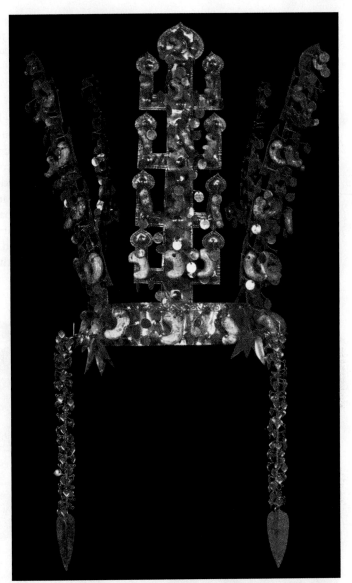

● **Gold Crown**   Excavated from a fifth- to sixth-century royal Silla tomb, this magnificent crown reflects metalwork traditions found in scattered places across the Eurasian steppe. The crown is decorated with dangling gold disks and comma-shaped beads of jadeite. The upright bars at the top are thought to represent deer antlers. *(Kyongju National Museum, Kyongju)*

were marked by complex social organization with rulers, soldiers, artisans, and priests. Objects of Chinese and Korean manufacture found their way into Japan, an indication that people were traveling back and forth as well. In the third century C.E. Chinese histories begin to report on the land called Wa made up of mountainous islands. It had numerous communities, markets, granaries, tax collection, and class distinctions. The people ate with their fingers, used body paint, purified themselves by bathing after a funeral, and liked liquor. Of their rulers the Chinese historian wrote:

The country formerly had a man as ruler. For some seventy or eighty years after that there were disturbances and warfare. Thereupon the people agreed upon a woman for their ruler. Her name was Himiko. She occupied herself with magic and sorcery, bewitching the people. Though mature in age, she remained unmarried. She had a younger brother who assisted her in ruling the country. After she became the ruler, there were few who saw her. She had one thousand women as attendants, but only one man. He served her food and drink and acted as a medium of communication. . . .

When Himiko passed away, a great mound was raised, more than a hundred paces in diameter. Over a hundred male and female attendants followed her to the grave. Then a king was placed on the throne, but the people would not obey him. Assassination and murder followed; more than one thousand were thus slain.

A relative of Himiko named Iyo, a girl of thirteen, was then made queen and order was restored.[7]

During the fourth through sixth centuries, new waves of migrants from Korea brought with them the language that evolved into Japanese. They also brought sericulture (silk making), bronze swords, crossbows, iron plows, and the Chinese written language. In this period, a social order similar to Korea's emerged, dominated by a warrior aristocracy organized into clans. Clad in helmet and armor, these warriors wielded swords, battle-axes, and often bows. Some of them rode into battle on horseback. Those vanquished in battle were made slaves. Each clan had its own chieftain, who marshaled clansmen for battle and served as chief priest. Over time the clans fought with each other, and their numbers were gradually reduced through conquest and alliance. By the fifth century the chief of the clan that claimed descent from

● **Hōryūji Temple** Japanese Buddhist temples, like those in China and Korea, consisted of several buildings within a walled compound. The buildings of the Hōryūji Temple (built 670–711; Prince Shōtoku's original temple burned down) include the oldest wooden structures in the world and house some of the best early Buddhist sculpture in Japan. The three main buildings depicted here are the pagoda, housing relics; the main hall, with the temple's principal images; and the lecture hall, for sermons. The five-story pagoda could be seen from far away, much like the steeples of cathedrals in medieval Europe. *(The Orion Press)*

the sun-goddess, located in the Yamato plain around modern Osaka, had come to occupy the position of Great King—or Queen, as female rulers were not uncommon in this period.

The Yamato rulers used their religion to subordinate the gods of their rivals, much as Hammurabi had used Marduk in Babylonia (see page 7). They established the chief shrine of the sun-goddess near the seacoast, where she could catch the first rays of the rising sun. Cults to other gods also were supported as long as they were viewed as subordinate to the sun-goddess. This native religion was later termed **Shinto**, the Way of the Gods.

In the sixth century Prince Shōtoku (574–622) undertook a sweeping reform of the state designed to strengthen Yamato rule by adopting Chinese-style bureaucratic practices. His "Seventeen Principles" of 604 drew from both Confucian and Buddhist teachings. In it he likened the ruler to Heaven and instructed officials to put their duty to the ruler above the interest of their families. He instituted a ladder of official ranks similar to China's, admonished the nobility to avoid strife and opposition, and urged adherence to Buddhist precepts. Near his seat of government, Prince Shōtoku built the magnificent Hōryūji Temple and staffed it with monks from Korea. He also opened direct relations with China, sending four missions during the brief Sui Dynasty.

State-building efforts continued through the seventh century and culminated in the establishment in 710 of Japan's first permanent capital at **Nara**, north of modern Osaka. Nara, which was modeled on the Tang capital of Chang'an, gave its name to an era that lasted until 794 and that was characterized by the avid importation of Chinese ideas and methods. Seven times missions with five hundred to six hundred men were sent on the difficult journey to Chang'an. Chinese and Korean craftsmen were often brought back to Japan, especially to help with the decoration of the many Buddhist temples then under construction. Musical instruments and tunes were imported as well, many originally from Central Asia. Chinese practices were instituted, such as the compilation of histories and law codes, the creation of provinces, and the appointment of governors to collect taxes from them. By 750 some seven thousand men staffed the central government.

Increased contact with the mainland had unwanted effects as well, such as the great smallpox epidemic of 735–737, which is thought to have reduced the population of about 5 million by 30 percent. (Smallpox did not become an endemic childhood disease in Japan until the tenth or eleventh century.)

The Buddhist monasteries that ringed Nara were both religious centers and wealthy landlords, and the monks were active in the political life of the capital. Copying the policy of the Tang Dynasty in China, the government ordered that every province establish a Buddhist temple with twenty monks and ten nuns to chant sutras and perform other ceremonies on behalf of the emperor and the state. When an emperor abdicated in 749 in favor of his daughter, he became a Buddhist priest, a practice many of his successors would later follow.

Many of the temples built during the Nara period still stand, the wood, clay, and bronze statues in them exceptionally well preserved. The largest of these temples was the Tōdaiji, with its huge bronze statue of the Buddha, which stood fifty-three feet tall and was made from more than a million pounds of metal. When the temple and statue were completed in 752, an Indian monk painted the eyes, and the ten thousand monks present for the celebration had a magnificent vegetarian feast. Objects from the dedication ceremony were placed in a special storehouse, the Shōsōin, and about ten thousand of them are still there, including books, weapons, mirrors, screens, and objects of gold, lacquer, and glass, most made in China but some coming from Central Asia and Persia via the Silk Road.

Shinto *The "Way of the Gods," it was the native religion espoused by the Yamato rulers.*

Nara *Japan's first true city; it was established in 710 north of modern Osaka.*

Primary Source: Chronicles of Japan
These guidelines for imperial officials show how the Soga clan welcomed Chinese influence in an attempt to increase the authority of the Japanese imperial family.

Chapter Summary

Key Terms

Great Wall
Silk Road
tributary system
Confucian classics
Records of the Grand Historian
eunuchs
Age of Division
Grand Canal
Pure Land
Chan
Shinto
Nara

To assess your mastery of this chapter, go to
bedfordstmartins.com/mckayworld

• What were the social, cultural, and political consequences of the unification of China under a strong centralized government?

The unification of China in 221 B.C.E. by the Qin Dynasty had momentous consequences. During the four centuries of the subsequent Han Dynasty, unified government provided internal peace and promoted Confucian principles. It aided economic development by building roads and providing relief in cases of floods, droughts, and famines. It could draw on its vast resources to send huge armies against the nomadic Xiongnu, who regularly raided settlements in the north. These armies made possible a major expansion of Chinese territory both to the south and into Central Asia. Overlordship in Central Asia allowed trade along the Silk Road to flourish. The Han was so successful that its memory inspired many efforts to reunify China during the four centuries of division that followed.

• How were both Buddhism and China changed by the spread of Buddhism across Asia?

In the final years of the Han Dynasty, Buddhism reached China. Conquest had little to do with the spread of Buddhism in East Asia (in contrast with the spread of Christianity and Islam, which often followed a change of rulers). Rather it was merchants and missionaries who brought Buddhism across the Silk Road. By the time it reached China, Buddhism was a religion with a huge body of scriptures, celibate monks and nuns, traditions of depicting Buddhas and bodhisattvas in statues and paintings, and a strong proselytizing tradition, all of which distinguished it from China's indigenous religious traditions. Buddhism brought to China new philosophical concepts, new artistic styles, and the new social roles of celibate monks and nuns.

• In what ways was China's second empire different from its first?

After centuries of division, China was reunified in 589 by the Sui and Tang Dynasties. China regained overlordship along the Silk Road into Central Asia and once again had to deal with powerful northern neighbors, this time the Turks and Uighurs. But there was also much that was different between the Han and Tang empires. The south had become a much more major part of the economy, settled by many more Chinese. Perhaps in part because of the enormous popularity of Buddhism, Chinese culture in Tang times was highly receptive to influences from outside during this period, especially from Persia and India. Poetry played a much larger part in intellectual life, and the examination system was becoming steadily more important as well.

• What elements of Chinese culture were adopted by Koreans, Vietnamese, and Japanese, and how did they adapt them to their own circumstances?

In this era, China's neighbors, especially Korea, Japan, and Vietnam, began to adopt elements of China's material, political, and religious culture, including the

Chinese writing system. Force of arms helped bring Chinese culture to both Korea and Vietnam. But military might was not the primary means by which culture spread in this period. Particularly in Korea and Japan, ambitious rulers sought out Chinese expertise and Chinese products, believing the adoption of the most advanced ideas and technologies to be to their advantage. They could pick and choose, adopting those elements of the more advanced cultures that suited them while retaining features of their earlier cultures, in the process developing distinctive national styles.

Suggested Reading

Barfield, Thomas. *Perilous Frontier: Nomadic Empires and China, 221 B.C.–A.D. 1757.* 1989. A bold interpretation of the relationship between the rise and fall of dynasties in China and the rise and fall of nomadic confederations that derived resources from them.

Elvin, Mark. *The Pattern of the Chinese Past.* 1973. Analyzes the military dimensions of China's unification.

Farris, Wayne. *Population, Disease, and Land in Early Japan, 645–900.* 1985. Shows the impact of the introduction of smallpox to Japan in the eighth century on the government and rural power structure.

Hardy, Grant. *Worlds of Bronze and Bamboo: Sima Qian's Conquest of History.* 1999. An excellent introduction to the methods of China's earliest historian. Although Sima Qian seems to present just the facts, Hardy shows how he brings out different perspectives and interpretations in different chapters.

Holcomb, Charles. *The Genesis of East Asia, 221 B.C.–A.D. 907.* 2001. A thought-provoking analysis of the connections between China and Korea, Japan, and Vietnam, which emphasizes the use of the Chinese script.

Schafer, Edward. *The Golden Peaches of Samarkand.* 1963. Draws on Tang literature to show the place of the western regions in Tang life and imagination.

Seth, Michael J. *A Concise History of Korea: From the Neolithic Period Through the Nineteenth Century.* 2006. An up-to-date and well-balanced introduction to Korean history.

Totman, Conrad. *A History of Japan.* 1999. A broad and up-to-date history of Japan.

Waley, Arthur. *The Life and Times of Po Chu-i, 772–846 A.D.* 1949. A lively biography of a Tang official, which draws heavily on his poetry.

Wright, Arthur. *Buddhism in Chinese History.* 1959. This short book remains a good introduction to China's encounter with Buddhism and the ways Buddhism was adapted to China.

Notes

1. Burton Watson, trans. *Records of the Grand Historian of China,* vol. 2 (New York: Columbia University Press, 1961), p. 496.
2. Ibid., p. 499.
3. Patricia Buckley Ebrey, *The Cambridge Illustrated History of China* (Cambridge: Cambridge University Press, 1996), p. 74.
4. W. F. Jenner, *Memories of Loyang: Yang Hsüan-chih and the Lost Capital (493–534)* (Oxford: Clarendon Press, 1981), p. 208.
5. Arthur Waley, trans., *More Translations from the Chinese* (New York: Knopf, 1919), p. 27. Reprinted by permission of the Arthur Waley Estate.
6. Ibid., p. 71.
7. *Sources of Japanese Tradition,* by de Bary, Keene, Tanabe, and Varley, eds. Copyright © 2001 by Columbia University Press. Reproduced with permission of COLUMBIA UNIVERSITY PRESS in the format Textbook via Copyright Clearance Center.

Listening to the PAST

Copying Buddhist Sutras

Buddhism was not merely a set of ideas but also a set of practices. In Chinese, Japanese, and Korean monasteries, as in Western ones, monks and nuns, under the direction of an abbot or abbess, would read and copy scriptures as an act of devotion. Pious laypeople might pay to have sutras copied as a means of earning religious merit. Sometimes at the end of a sutra a copyist attached a statement explaining the circumstances that had surrounded the act of copying. Here are two such statements, one from a sutra found in Dunhuang, on the northwest fringe of China proper, dated 550, and the other from Korea, dated 755.

1.

Happiness is not fortuitous: pray for it and it will be found. Results are not born of thin air: pay heed to causes and results will follow. This explains how the Buddhist disciple and nun Daorong—because her conduct in her previous life was not correct—came to be born in her present form, a woman, vile and unclean.

Now if she does not honor the awesome decree of Buddha, how can future consequences be favorable for her? Therefore, having cut down her expenditures on food and clothing, she reverently has had the *Nirvana sutra* copied once. She prays that those who read it carefully will be exalted in mind to the highest realms and that those who communicate its meaning will cause others to be so enlightened.

She also prays that in her present existence she will have no further sickness or suffering, that her parents in seven other incarnations (who have already died or will die in the future) and her present family and close relatives may experience joy in the four elements [earth, water, fire, and air], and that whatever they seek may indeed come to pass. Finally, she prays that all those endowed with knowledge may be included within this prayer. Dated the 29th day of the fourth month of 550.

2.

The copying began on the first day of the eighth month of 754, and was completed on the fourteenth day of the second month of the following year.

One who made a vow to copy the scripture is Dharma master Yongi of Hwangnyong Monastery. His purposes were to repay the love of his parents and to pray for all living beings in the dharma realm to attain the path of the Buddha.

The scripture is made as follows: First scented water is sprinkled around the roots of a paperbark mulberry tree to quicken its growth; the bark is then peeled and pounded to make paper with a clean surface. The copyists, the artisans who make the centerpiece of the scroll, and the painters who draw the images of buddhas and bodhisattvas all receive the bodhisattva ordination and observe abstinence. After relieving themselves, sleeping, eating, or drinking, they take a bath in scented water before returning to the work. Copyists are adorned with new pure garments, loose trousers, a coarse crown, and a deva crown. Two azure-clad boys sprinkle water on their heads and . . . azure-clad boys and musicians perform music. The processions to the copying site are headed by one who sprinkles scented water on their path, another who scatters flowers, a dharma master who carries a censer, and another dharma master who chants Buddhist verses. Each of the copyists carries incense and flowers and invokes the name of the Buddha as he progresses.

This gilt bronze image of Maitreya, not quite 3 feet tall, was made in Korea in about 600. It depicts the Buddha Maitreya, the Future Buddha who presides over Tushita Heaven. The rounded face, slender body, and gracefully draped robe help convey the idea that the Buddha is neither male nor female but beyond such distinctions. *(Courtesy, Yushin Yoo)*

Upon reaching the site, all take refuge in the three Jewels (the Buddha, the Dharma, and the Order), make three bows, and offer the *Flower Garland Scripture* and others to buddhas and bodhisattvas. Then they sit down and copy the scripture, make the centerpiece of the scroll, and paint the buddhas and bodhisattvas. Thus, azure-clad boys and musicians cleanse everything before a piece of relic is placed in the center.

Now I make a vow that the copied scripture will not break till the end of the future—even when a major chilicosm [millions of universes] is destroyed by the three calamities, this scripture shall be intact as the void. If all living things rely on this scripture, they shall witness the Buddha, listen to his dharma, worship the relic, aspire to enlightenment without backsliding, cultivate the

vows of the Universally Worthy Bodhisattva, and achieve Buddhahood.

Questions for Analysis

1. How does the nun who wrote the first note explain her birth as a woman? Whom does she hope to benefit by the act of copying the sutra?

2. What do you make of the emphasis on rituals surrounding copying the sutra in the second statement?

Sources: Patricia Buckley Ebrey, ed., *Chinese Civilization: A Sourcebook* (New York: Free Press, 1993), pp. 102–103; Peter H. Lee, ed., *Sourcebook of Korean Civilization* (New York: Columbia University Press, 1993), pp. 201–202, modified.

Hagia Sophia ("Holy Wisdom"), built by the emperor Justinian in the sixth century, was the largest Christian cathedral in the world for a thousand years. After Constantinople was conquered by the Ottoman Turks in 1453, it became a mosque, and today it is a museum. *(Courtesy, Editore Sadea Sansoni, Florence)*

7 EUROPE AND WESTERN ASIA, CA. 350–850

Chapter Preview

The Byzantine Empire
• *How was the Byzantine Empire able to survive for so long, and what were its most important achievements?*

The Growth of the Christian Church
• *What factors enabled the Christian church to expand and thrive?*

Christian Ideas and Practices
• *How did Christian thinkers and missionaries adapt Greco-Roman ideas to Christian theology and develop effective techniques to convert barbarian peoples to Christianity?*

Migrating Peoples
• *How did the barbarians shape social, economic, and political structures in Europe and western Asia?*

From the third century onward, the Western Roman Empire slowly disintegrated. The last Roman emperor in the West, Romulus Augustus, was deposed by the Ostrogothic chieftain Odoacer in 476, but much of the empire had already come under the rule of various barbarian tribes well before this. Scholars have long seen this era as one of the great turning points in Western history, but during the last several decades, focus has shifted to continuities as well as changes. What is now usually termed "late antiquity" has been recognized as a period of creativity and adaptation in Europe and western Asia, not simply of decline and fall.

The two main agents of continuity were the Eastern Roman (or Byzantine) Empire and the Christian church. The Byzantine Empire lasted until 1453, a thousand years longer than the Western Roman Empire, and preserved and transmitted much of ancient law, philosophy, and institutions. Missionaries and church officials spread Christianity within and far beyond the borders of what had been the Roman Empire, transforming a small sect into the most important and wealthiest institution in Europe. The main agents of change in late antiquity were the barbarian groups migrating throughout much of Europe and western Asia. They brought different social, political, and economic structures with them, but as they encountered Roman and Byzantine culture and became Christian, their own ways of doing things were also transformed.

THE BYZANTINE EMPIRE

How was the Byzantine Empire able to survive for so long, and what were its most important achievements?

The Emperor Constantine (see page 122) had tried to maintain the unity of the Roman Empire, but during the fifth and sixth centuries the Western and Eastern halves drifted apart. From Constantinople, Eastern Roman emperors worked to hold the empire together and to reconquer at least some of the West from barbarian

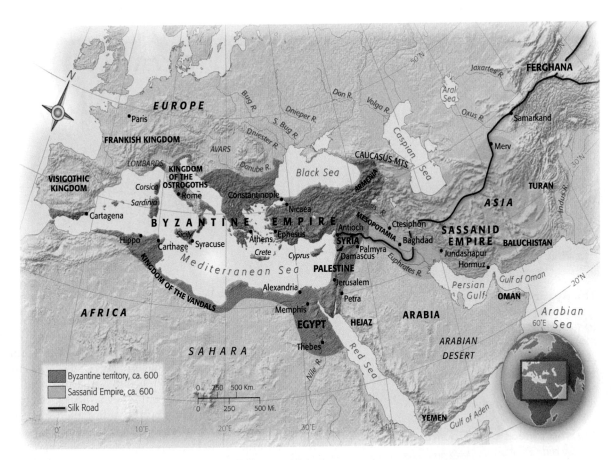

MAP 7.1 **The Byzantine and Sassanid Empires** Both the Byzantine and Sassanid Empires included territory that had earlier been part of the Roman Empire. The Sassanid Persians fought Roman armies before the founding of the Byzantine Empire. Later Byzantium and the Sassanids engaged in a series of wars that weakened both and brought neither lasting territorial acquisitions.

tribes. Justinian (r. 527–565) waged long wars against the Ostrogoths and temporarily regained Italy and North Africa, but the costs were high. Justinian's wars exhausted the resources of the state, destroyed Italy's economy, and killed a large part of Italy's population. Weakened, Italy fell easily to another Germanic tribe, the Lombards, shortly after Justinian's death. In the late sixth century, the territory of the Western Roman Empire came once again under Germanic sway.

However, the Roman Empire continued in the East. The Eastern Roman or Byzantine Empire (see Map 7.1) preserved the forms, institutions, and traditions of the old Roman Empire, and its people even called themselves Romans. Byzantium passed the intellectual heritage of Greco-Roman civilization on to later cultures and also developed its own distinctive characteristics.

Sources of Byzantine Strength

While the Western parts of the Roman Empire gradually succumbed to Germanic invaders, the Eastern Roman or Byzantine Empire survived. (The Byzantines themselves called their state the "Roman Empire," and only in the sixteenth century did people begin to use the term "Byzantine Empire.") Byzantine emperors traced their lines back past Constantine to Augustus (see page 112). While evolving into a Christian and Greek-speaking state with a multiethnic population centered in the eastern Mediterranean and the Balkans, the Byzantines retained the legal and administrative system of the empire centered at Rome. Thus, the senate that sat in Constantinople

carried on the traditions and preserved the glory of the old Roman senate. The army that defended the empire was the direct descendant of the old Roman legions.

That army was kept very busy, for the Byzantine Empire survived waves of attacks. In 559 a force of Huns and Slavs reached the gates of Constantinople. In 583 the Avars, a mounted Mongol people who had swept across Russia and southeastern Europe, seized Byzantine forts along the Danube and also reached the walls of Constantinople. Between 572 and 630 the Greeks were repeatedly at war with the Sassanid Persians (see below). Beginning in 632 the Arabs pressured the Greek empire. Why didn't one or a combination of these enemies capture Constantinople, as the Germans had taken Rome? The answer lies, first, in the strong military leadership the Greeks possessed. General Priskos (d. 612) skillfully led Byzantine armies to a decisive victory over the Avars in 601. Then, after a long war, the well-organized emperor Heraclius I (r. 610–641) crushed the Persians at Nineveh in Iraq.

Second, the city's location and excellent fortifications proved crucial. The site of Constantinople was not absolutely impregnable, but it was almost so. Constantinople had the most powerful defenses in the ancient world. Massive triple walls protected the city from sea invasion. Within the walls huge cisterns provided water, and vast gardens and grazing areas supplied vegetables and meat. Such strong fortifications and provisions meant that if attacked by sea, a defending people could hold out far longer than a besieging army. The site chosen for the imperial capital in the fourth century enabled Constantinople to survive in the eighth century. Because the city survived, the empire, though reduced in territory, endured.

Chronology

226–651	Sassanid dynasty
312	Constantine legalizes Christianity in Roman Empire
340–419	Life of Saint Jerome; creation of the Vulgate
354–430	Life of Saint Augustine
380	Theodosius makes Christianity official religion of Roman Empire
385–461	Life of Saint Patrick
481–511	Reign of Clovis
527–565	Reign of Justinian
529	*The Rule of Saint Benedict*
541–543	"Justinian plague"
730–843	Iconoclastic controversy
768–814	Reign of Charlemagne; Carolingian Renaissance
1054	Schism between Roman Catholic and Greek Orthodox churches

The Sassanid Empire of Persia and Byzantium

For several centuries the Sassanid Empire of Persia was Byzantium's most regular foe. In 226, Ardashir I (r. 226–243) founded the Sassanid dynasty, which lasted until 651, when it was overthrown by the Muslims. Ardashir expanded his territory and absorbed the Roman province of Mesopotamia.

Centered in the fertile Tigris-Euphrates Valley, but with access to the Persian Gulf and extending south to Meshan (modern Kuwait), the Sassanid Empire's economic prosperity rested on agriculture; its location also proved well suited for commerce. A lucrative caravan trade from Ctesiphon north to Merv and then east to Samarkand linked the Sassanid Empire to the Silk Road and China (see page 138). Persian metalwork, textiles, and glass were exchanged for Chinese silks, and these goods brought about considerable cultural contact between the Sassanids and the Chinese.

Whereas the Parthians had tolerated many religions, the Sassanid Persians made Zoroastrianism the official state religion. Religion and the state were inextricably tied together. The king's power rested on the support of nobles and Zoroastrian priests, who monopolized positions in the court and in the imperial bureaucracy. A highly elaborate court ceremonial and ritual exalted the status of the king and emphasized his semidivine pre-eminence over his subjects. (The Byzantine monarchy, the Roman papacy, and the Muslim caliphate subsequently copied aspects of this Persian

● **Sassanid Silver and Gold Plate** This exquisitely wrought Sassanid plate shows a king hunting from horseback. Hunting was a favorite aristocratic pastime, and fine horses were exported from Persia to many parts of the world, as were Sassanid plates and drinking cups. *(Erich Lessing/Art Resource, NY)*

diaspora *The dispersion of the Jews from Jerusalem between 132 and 135.*

corpus juris civilis *The "body of civil law," it is composed of the* Code, *the* Digest, *and the* Institutes.

ceremonial.) Zoroastrianism promoted hostility toward Christians because of what was perceived as their connections to Rome and Constantinople, and the sizable Jewish population in Mesopotamia after the **diaspora** (dispersion of the Jews from Jerusalem between 132 and 135) suffered intermittent persecution.

An expansionist foreign policy brought Persia into frequent conflict with Byzantium, and neither side was able to achieve a clear-cut victory. The long wars financed by higher taxation, on top of the arrival of the bubonic plague (see page 168), compounded discontent in both Byzantine and Persian societies. Internal political instability weakened the Sassanid dynasty, and in the seventh century Persian territories were absorbed into the Islamic caliphate (see page 194).

The Law Code of Justinian

Byzantine emperors organized and preserved Roman law, making a lasting contribution to the medieval and modern worlds. Roman law had developed from many sources—decisions by judges, edicts of the emperors, legislation passed by the senate, and the opinions of jurists expert in the theory and practice of law. By the fourth century, Roman law had become a huge, bewildering mass. Its sheer bulk made it almost unusable.

The emperor Justinian appointed a committee of eminent jurists to sort through and organize the laws. The result was the *Code,* which distilled the legal genius of the Romans into a coherent whole, eliminated outmoded laws and contradictions, and clarified the law itself.

Justinian next set about bringing order to the equally huge body of Roman *jurisprudence,* the science or philosophy of law. To harmonize the often differing opinions of Roman jurists, Justinian directed his jurists to clear up disputed points and to issue definitive rulings. Accordingly, in 533 his lawyers published the *Digest,* which codified Roman legal thought. Then Justinian's lawyers compiled a handbook of civil law, the *Institutes.* These three works—the *Code,* the *Digest,* and the *Institutes*—are the backbone of the **corpus juris civilis,** the "body of civil law," which is the foundation of law for nearly every modern European nation.

Byzantine Intellectual Life

The Byzantines prized education, and because of them many masterpieces of ancient Greek literature survived to influence the intellectual life of the modern world. The literature of the Byzantine Empire was predominately Greek, although Latin was long spoken by top politicians, scholars, and lawyers. Among members of the large reading public, history was a favorite subject.

The most remarkable Byzantine historian was Procopius (ca. 500–ca. 562), who left a rousing account of Justinian's reconquest of North Africa and Italy. Procopius's *Secret History,* however, is a vicious and uproarious attack on Justinian and his wife, the empress Theodora, which continued the wit and venom of earlier Greek and Roman writers. (See the feature "Individuals in Society: Theodora of Constantinople.")

Theodora of Constantinople

The empress Theodora shown with the halo symbolic of power in Eastern art. *(Scala/Art Resource, NY)*

The most powerful woman in Byzantine history was the daughter of a bear trainer for the circus. Theodora (ca. 497–548) grew up in what her contemporaries regarded as an undignified and morally suspect atmosphere, and she worked as a dancer and burlesque actress, both dishonorable occupations in the Roman world. Despite her background, she caught the eye of Justinian, who was then a military leader and whose uncle (and adoptive father) Justin had himself risen from obscurity to become the emperor of the Byzantine Empire. Under Justinian's influence, Justin changed the law to allow an actress who had left her disreputable life to marry whom she liked, and Justinian and Theodora married in 525. When Justinian was proclaimed co-emperor with his uncle Justin on April 1, 527, Theodora received the rare title of *augusta,* empress. Thereafter her name was linked with Justinian's in the exercise of imperial power.

Most of our knowledge of Theodora's early life comes from the *Secret History,* a tell-all description of the vices of Justinian and his court, written by Procopius (ca. 550), who was the official court historian and thus spent his days praising those same people. In the *Secret History,* he portrays Theodora and Justinian as demonic, greedy, and vicious, killing courtiers to steal their property. In scene after detailed scene, Procopius portrays Theodora as particularly evil, sexually insatiable, depraved, and cruel, a temptress who used sorcery to attract men, including the hapless Justinian.

In one of his official histories, *The History of the Wars of Justinian,* Procopius presents a very different Theodora. Riots between the supporters of two teams in chariot races—who formed associations somewhat like street gangs and somewhat like political parties—had turned deadly, and Justinian wavered in his handling of the perpetrators. Both sides turned against the emperor, besieging the palace while Justinian was inside it. Shouting N-I-K-A (Victory), the rioters swept through the city, burning and looting, and destroyed half of Constantinople. Justinian's counselors urged flight, but, according to Procopius, Theodora rose and declared:

For one who has reigned, it is intolerable to be an exile. . . . If you wish, O Emperor, to save yourself, there is no difficulty: we have ample funds and there are the ships. Yet reflect whether, when you have once escaped to a place of security, you will not prefer death to safety. I agree with an old saying that the purple [that is, the color worn only by emperors] is a fair winding sheet [to be buried in].

Justinian rallied, had the rioters driven into the hippodrome, and ordered between thirty and thirty-five thousand men and women executed. The revolt was crushed and Justinian's authority restored, an outcome approved by Procopius.

Other sources describe or suggest Theodora's influence on imperial policy. Justinian passed a number of laws that improved the legal status of women, such as allowing women to own property the same way that men could and to be guardians over their own children. He forbade the exposure of unwanted infants, which happened more often to girls than to boys, since boys were valued more highly. Theodora presided at imperial receptions for Arab sheiks, Persian ambassadors, Germanic princesses from the West, and barbarian chieftains from southern Russia. When Justinian fell ill from the bubonic plague in 542, Theodora took over his duties, banning those who discussed his possible successor. Justinian is reputed to have consulted her every day about all aspects of state policy, including religious policy regarding the doctrinal disputes that continued throughout his reign. Theodora's favored interpretation of Christian doctrine about the nature of Christ was not accepted by the main body of theologians in Constantinople—nor by Justinian—but she urged protection of her fellow believers and in one case hid an aged scholar in the women's quarters of the palace.

Theodora's influence over her husband and her power in the Byzantine state continued until she died, perhaps of cancer, twenty years before Justinian. Her influence may have even continued after death, for Justinian continued to pass reforms favoring women and, at the end of his life, accepted her interpretation of Christian doctrine. Institutions that she established, including hospitals, orphanages, houses for the rehabilitation of prostitutes, and churches, continued to be reminders of her charity and piety.

Theodora has been viewed as a symbol of the manipulation of beauty and cleverness to attain position and power, and also as a strong and capable co-ruler who held the empire together during riots, revolts, and deadly epidemics. Just as Procopius expressed both views, the debate has continued to today among writers of science fiction and fantasy as well as biographers and historians.

Questions for Analysis

1. How would you assess the complex legacy of Theodora?
2. Since the public and private views of Procopius are so different regarding the empress, should he be trusted at all as a historical source?

In mathematics and science, the Byzantines discovered little that was new, though they passed Greco-Roman learning on to the Arabs. The best-known Byzantine scientific discovery was an explosive compound known as "Greek fire" made of crude oil mixed with resin and sulfur, which was heated and propelled by a pump through a bronze tube. As the liquid jet left the tube, it was ignited, somewhat like a modern flamethrower. Greek fire saved Constantinople from Arab assault in 678.

The Byzantines devoted a great deal of attention to medicine, and the general level of medical competence was far higher in the Byzantine Empire than it was in western Europe. Yet their physicians could not cope with the terrible disease, often called "the Justinian plague," that swept through the Byzantine Empire and parts of western Europe between 541 and 543. Probably originating in northwestern India and carried to the Mediterranean region by ships, the disease was similar to modern forms of bubonic plague. Characterized by high fevers, chills, delirium, and enlarged lymph nodes, or by inflammation of the lungs that caused hemorrhages of black blood, the plague carried off tens of thousands of people. The epidemic had profound political as well as social consequences. It weakened Justinian's military resources, thus hampering his efforts to restore unity to the Mediterranean world. Losses from the plague also further weakened Byzantine and Persian forces that had badly damaged each other, contributing to their inability to offer more than token opposition to the Muslim armies (see pages 194–195).

● **Justinian and His Attendants**   This mosaic detail is composed of thousands of tiny cubes of colored glass or stone called *tessarae*, which are set in plaster against a blazing golden background. Some attempt has been made at naturalistic portraiture. *(Scala/Art Resource, NY)*

Constantinople: The Second Rome

In the tenth century Constantinople was the greatest city in the Christian world: the seat of the imperial court and administration, a large population center, and the pivot of a large volume of international trade. As a natural geographical entrepôt between East and West, the city's markets offered goods from many parts of the world. Furs and timber flowed across the Black Sea from the Rus (Russia) to the capital, as did slaves across the Mediterranean from northern Europe and the Balkans via Venice. Spices, silks, jewelry, and luxury goods came to Constantinople from India and China by way of Arabia, the Red Sea, and the Indian Ocean. By the eleventh century, only Baghdad exceeded Constantinople in the quantity and value of goods exchanged there.

Jewish, Muslim, and Italian merchants controlled most foreign trade. Among the Greeks, aristocrats and monasteries usually invested their wealth in real estate, which involved little risk but brought little gain. As in western Europe and China, the landed aristocracy always held the dominant social position. Merchants and craftsmen, even when they acquired considerable wealth, never won social prominence.

Constantinople did not enjoy constant political stability. Between the accession of Heraclius in 610 and the fall of the city to Western Crusaders in 1204 (see page 364), four separate dynasties ruled at Constantinople. Imperial government involved such intricate court intrigue, assassinations, and military revolts that the word *byzantine* is sometimes used in English to mean extremely entangled and complicated politics.

What do we know about private life in Constantinople? Research has revealed a fair amount about the Byzantine *oikos,* or household. The Greek household included family members and servants, some of whom were slaves. Artisans lived and worked in their shops. Clerks, civil servants, minor officials, business people—those who today would be called middle class—commonly dwelt in multistory buildings perhaps comparable to the apartment complexes of modern American cities. Wealthy aristocrats resided in freestanding mansions that frequently included interior courts, galleries, large reception halls, small sleeping rooms, reading and writing rooms, baths, and chapels.

In the homes of the upper classes, the segregation of women seems to have been the first principle of interior design. As in ancient Athens, private houses contained a *gynaceum,* or women's apartment, where women were kept strictly separated from the outside world. The fundamental reason for this segregation was the family's honor: "An unchaste daughter is guilty of harming not only herself but also her parents and relatives. That is why you should keep your daughters under lock and key, as if proven guilty or imprudent, in order to avoid venomous bites," as an eleventh-century Byzantine writer put it.[1]

Marriage served as part of a family's strategy for social advancement. The family and the entire kinship group participated in the selection of brides and grooms, choosing spouses that might enhance the family's wealth or prestige.

• • • • • • • • • • • • •

THE GROWTH OF THE CHRISTIAN CHURCH

What factors enabled the Christian church to expand and thrive?

As the Western Roman Empire disintegrated in the fourth and fifth centuries, the Christian church survived and grew, becoming the most important institution in Europe. The able administrators and creative thinkers of the church gradually established an orthodox set of beliefs and adopted a system of organization based on that of the Roman state.

The Church and Its Leaders

In early Christian communities believers elected their leaders, but as the centuries passed appointment by existing church leaders or secular rulers became the common pattern. During the reign of Diocletian (284–305), the empire had been divided for administrative purposes into geographical units called **dioceses,** and Christianity adopted this pattern. Each diocese was headed by a bishop who was responsible for organizing preaching, overseeing the community's goods, and maintaining orthodox (established or correct) doctrine. The center of a bishop's authority was his cathedral, a word deriving from the Latin *cathedra,* meaning "chair."

dioceses *Geographic administrative districts of the Church, each under the authority of a bishop and centered around a cathedral.*

The early Christian church benefited from the brilliant administrative abilities of some bishops. Bishop Ambrose, for example, the son of the Roman prefect of Gaul, was a trained lawyer and the governor of a province. He is typical of the Roman aristocrats who held high public office, were converted to Christianity, and subsequently became bishops. The church received support from the emperors, and in return the emperors expected the support of the Christian church in maintaining order and unity.

In the fourth century, theological disputes frequently and sharply divided the Christian community. Some disagreements had to do with the nature of Christ. For example, **Arianism,** which originated with Arius (ca. 250–336), a priest of Alexandria, held that Jesus was created by the will of God the Father and thus was not co-eternal with him. Arius also reasoned that Jesus the Son must be inferior to God the Father, because the Father is incapable of suffering and did not die. Orthodox theologians branded Arius's position a *heresy*—denial of a basic doctrine of faith.

Arianism *A theological belief, originating with Arius, a priest of Alexandria, that denied that Christ was divine and co-eternal with God the Father.*

Arianism enjoyed such popularity and provoked such controversy that Constantine, to whom religious disagreement meant civil disorder, interceded. In 325 he summoned a council of church leaders to Nicaea in Asia Minor and presided over it personally. The council produced the Nicene Creed, which defined the orthodox position that Christ is "eternally begotten of the Father" and of the same substance as the Father. Arius and those who refused to accept the creed were banished, the first case of civil punishment for heresy. This participation of the emperor in a theological dispute within the church paved the way for later emperors to claim that they could do the same.

In 380 the emperor Theodosius went further than Constantine and made Christianity the official religion of the empire. Theodosius stripped Roman pagan temples of statues, made the practice of the old Roman state religion a treasonable offense, and persecuted Christians who dissented from orthodox doctrine. Most significant, he allowed the church to establish its own courts. Church courts began to develop their own body of law, called **canon law.** These courts, not the Roman government, had jurisdiction over the clergy and ecclesiastical disputes. The foundation for later growth in church power had been laid.

canon law *The body of internal law that governs the church.*

The Western Church and the Eastern Church

The position of the church differed considerably in the Byzantine East and the Germanic West. The fourth-century emperors Constantine and Theodosius had wanted the church to act as a unifying force within the empire, but the Germanic invasions made that impossible. The bishops of Rome repeatedly called on the emperors at Constantinople for military support against the invaders, but rarely could the emperors send it. The church in the West became less dependent on the emperors' power, and gradually took over political authority, charging taxes, sending troops, and enforcing laws.

After the removal of the imperial capital and the emperor to Constantinople, the bishop of Rome exercised considerable influence in the West, in part because he had no real competitor there. In addition, successive bishops of Rome stressed their special role. According to tradition, Peter, the chief of Christ's first twelve followers, had lived and been executed in Rome. The popes claimed to be successors to Peter and heirs to his authority, based on Jesus' words: "You are Peter, and on this rock I will build my church. . . . Whatever you declare bound on earth shall be bound in heaven." Theologians call this statement the **Petrine Doctrine.** The bishops of Rome came to be known as popes—from the Latin *papa,* for "father"—and in the fifth century began to stress their supremacy over other Christian communities.

In the East, the bishops of Antioch, Alexandria, Jerusalem, and Constantinople had more power than other bishops, but the emperor's jurisdiction over the church was also fully acknowledged. The emperor in Constantinople nominated the *patriarch,* as the highest prelate of the Eastern church was called. The Eastern emperors looked on religion as a branch of the state. They considered it their duty to protect the faith not only against heathen enemies but also against heretics within the empire. Following the pattern set by Constantine, the emperors summoned councils of bishops and theologians to settle doctrinal disputes.

Petrine Doctrine *The statement used by popes, bishops of Rome, based on Jesus' words, to substantiate their claim of being the successors of Saint Peter and heirs to his authority as chief of the apostles.*

The Iconoclastic Controversy

Several theological disputes split the Eastern Christian Church (also called the Orthodox Church) in the centuries after Constantine. The most serious was a controversy over *icons*—images or representations of God the Father, Jesus, the Virgin, or the saints in a painting, bas-relief, or mosaic. Since the third century the church had allowed people to venerate icons. Although all prayer had to be directed to God the Father, Christian teaching held that icons representing the saints fostered reverence and that Jesus and the saints could most effectively plead a cause to God the Father. *Iconoclasts,* those who favored the destruction of icons, argued that people were worshiping the image itself rather than what it signified. This, they claimed, constituted *idolatry,* a violation of the prohibition of images in the Ten Commandments.

The result of the controversy over icons was a terrible theological conflict that split the Byzantine world for a century. In 730 the emperor Leo III (r. 717–741) ordered the destruction of the images. The removal of icons from Byzantine churches provoked a violent reaction: entire provinces revolted, and the empire and Roman papacy severed relations. Since Eastern monasteries were the fiercest defenders of icons, Leo's son Constantine V (r. 741–775), nicknamed "Copronymous" ("Dung-name") by his enemies, took the war to the monasteries. He seized their property, executed some of the monks, and forced others into the army. Theological disputes and civil disorder over the icons continued intermittently until 843, when the icons were restored.

The implications of the **iconoclastic controversy** extended far beyond strictly theological issues. Iconoclasm raised the question of the right of the emperor to intervene in religious disputes—a central problem in the relations of church and state. Iconoclasm antagonized the pope and served to encourage him in his quest for an alliance with the Frankish monarchy (see page 182). This further divided the two parts of Christendom, and in 1054 a theological disagreement led the bishop of Rome and the patriarch of Constantinople to excommunicate each other. The outcome was a continuing **schism,** or split, between the Roman Catholic and the Greek Orthodox churches. Finally, the acceptance of icons profoundly influenced subsequent religious art within Christianity. That art rejected the Judaic and Islamic prohibition of figural representation and continued in the Greco-Roman tradition of human representation.

Primary Source:
A Report on the Embassy to Constantinople
Read how a Catholic bishop was insulted by his Byzantine hosts—and how he insulted them back—after delivering a marriage proposal from emperor Otto I.

iconoclastic controversy *The conflict that resulted from the destruction of Christian images in Byzantine churches in 730.*

schism *A division, or split, in church leadership; there were several major schisms in Christianity.*

Christian Monasticism

Like the great East Asian religions of Jainism and Buddhism (see pages 37–41), Christianity soon developed an ascetic component: monasticism. Christianity began and spread as a city religion. As early as the first century, however, some especially pious Christians felt that the only alternative to the decadence of urban life was complete separation from the world. This desire to withdraw from ordinary life led to the

eremitical *A form of monasticism that began in Egypt in the third century in which individuals and small groups withdrew from cities and organized society to seek God through prayer.*

coenobitic *Communal living in monasteries, encouraged by Saint Basil and the church because it provided an environment for training the aspirant in the virtues of charity, poverty, and freedom from self-deception.*

development of the monastic life, which took two forms: **eremitical** (isolated) and **coenobitic** (communal). The people who lived in caves and sought shelter in the desert and mountains were called *hermits,* from the Greek word *eremos.*

Monasticism began in Egypt in the third century. At first individuals and small groups withdrew from cities and organized society to seek God through prayer in caves and shelters in the desert or mountains. Gradually large colonies of monks emerged in the deserts of Upper Egypt. Many devout women also were attracted to this eremitical life. Although monks and nuns led isolated lives, ordinary people soon recognized them as holy people and sought them as spiritual guides.

Church leaders did not really approve of eremitical life. Hermits sometimes claimed to have mystical experiences—direct communications with God. If hermits could communicate directly with the Lord, what need had they for the priest and the institutional church? The church hierarchy encouraged coenobitic monasticism, communal living in monasteries, which provided an environment for training the aspirant in the virtues of charity, poverty, and freedom from self-deception. In the fourth, fifth, and sixth centuries, many different kinds of communal monasticism developed in Gaul, Italy, Spain, Anglo-Saxon England, and Ireland.

In 529 Benedict of Nursia (480–543), who had experimented with both the eremitical and the communal forms of monastic life, wrote a brief set of regulations for the monks who had gathered around him at Monte Cassino between Rome and Naples. Benedict's guide for monastic life, known as the *Rule,* slowly replaced all others. *The Rule of Saint Benedict* has influenced all forms of organized religious life in the Roman church.

Men and women who lived in monastic houses all followed sets of rules, first those of Benedict and later those written by other individuals, and because of this came to be called **regular clergy,** from the Latin word *regulus* (rule). Priests and bishops who staffed churches in which people worshiped and who were not cut off from the world were called **secular clergy.** (According to official church doctrine, women are not members of the clergy, but this distinction was not clear to most medieval people.)

regular clergy *Clergy who live under the rule (Latin: regulus) of a monastic house; monks and nuns.*

secular clergy *Clergy who staffed the churches where people worshiped and were therefore not separated from the world (Latin: saeculum); priests and bishops.*

The Rule of Saint Benedict offered a simple code for ordinary men. It outlined a monastic life of regularity, discipline, and moderation in an atmosphere of silence. Each monk had ample food and adequate sleep. The monk spent part of each day in formal prayer, chanting psalms and other prayers from the Bible. The rest of the day was passed in manual labor, study, and private prayer.

Why did the Benedictine form of monasticism eventually replace other forms of Western monasticism? The monastic life as conceived by Saint Benedict struck a balance between asceticism and activity. It thus provided opportunities for men of entirely different abilities and talents—from mechanics to gardeners to literary scholars. The Benedictine form of religious life also proved congenial to women. Five miles from Monte Cassino at Plombariola, Benedict's twin sister Scholastica (480–543) adapted the *Rule* for the use of her community of nuns.

Benedictine monasticism also succeeded partly because it was so materially successful. In the seventh and eighth centuries, monasteries pushed back forest and wasteland, drained swamps, and experimented with crop rotation. Such Benedictine houses made a significant contribution to the agricultural development of Europe, earning immense wealth in the process. The communal nature of their organization, whereby property was held in common and profits were pooled and reinvested, made this contribution possible.

Finally, monasteries conducted schools for local young people. Some learned about prescriptions and herbal remedies and went on to provide medical treatment for their localities. A few copied manuscripts and wrote books. Local and royal governments drew on the services of the literate men and able administrators the monasteries produced.

Monasticism in the Greek Orthodox world differed in fundamental ways from the monasticism that evolved in western Europe. First, while *The Rule of Saint Benedict* gradually became the universal guide for all western European monasteries, each individual house in the Byzantine world developed its own set of rules for organization and behavior. Second, education never became a central feature of the Greek houses. Monks and nuns had to be literate to perform the services of the choir, and children destined for the monastic life were taught to read and write, but no monastery assumed responsibility for the general training of the local young. Since bishops and patriarchs of the Greek church were recruited only from the monasteries, Greek houses did, however, exercise a cultural influence.

CHRISTIAN IDEAS AND PRACTICES

How did Christian thinkers and missionaries adapt Greco-Roman ideas to Christian theology and develop effective techniques to convert barbarian peoples to Christianity?

The evolution of Christianity was not simply a matter of institutions such as the papacy and monasteries, but also of ideas. Initially, Christians had believed that the end of the world was near and that they should dissociate themselves from the "filth" of Roman culture. Gradually, however, Christians developed a culture of ideas that drew on classical influences. At the same time, missionaries sponsored by bishops and monasteries spread Christian ideas and institutions far beyond the borders of the Roman Empire, often adapting them to existing notions as they assimilated pagan peoples to Christianity.

● **The Marys at Jesus' Tomb** This late-fourth-century ivory panel tells the story of Mary Magdalene and another Mary who went to Jesus' tomb to anoint the body (Matthew 28:1–7). At the top guards collapse when an angel descends from Heaven, and at the bottom the Marys listen to the angel telling them that Jesus had risen. Immediately after this, in Matthew's Gospel, Jesus appears to the women. Here the artist uses Roman artistic styles to convey Christian subject matter, an example of the assimilation of classical form and Christian teaching. *(Castello Sforzesco/Scala/Art Resource, NY)*

Adjustment to Classical Culture

Christians in the first and second centuries believed that Christ would soon fulfill his promise to return and that the end of the world was near. Thus they considered knowledge useless and learning a waste of time, and they preached the duty of Christians to prepare for the Second Coming of the Lord. The church father Tertullian (ca. 160–220) claimed: "We have no need for curiosity since Jesus Christ, nor for inquiry since the gospel."

On the other hand, Christianity encouraged adjustment to the ideas and institutions of the Roman world. Some biblical texts urged Christians to accept the existing social, economic, and political establishment. Christians really had little choice. Jewish and Roman cultures were the only cultures early Christians knew; they had to adapt their Roman education to their Christian beliefs. The result was compromise, as evidenced by the distinguished theologian Saint Jerome (340–419). He thought that Christians should study the best of ancient thought because it would direct their minds to God, and he translated the Old and New Testaments from Hebrew and Greek into vernacular Latin; his edition is known as the Vulgate.

Christian attitudes toward gender and sexuality provide a good example of the ways early Christians both adopted and adapted the views of their contemporary world. In his plan of salvation, Jesus considered women the equal of men. He attributed no disreputable qualities to women and did not refer to them as inferior creatures. On the contrary, women were among his earliest and most faithful converts.

Women took an active role in the spread of Christianity, preaching, acting as missionaries, being martyred alongside men, and perhaps even baptizing believers. Because early Christians believed that the Second Coming of Christ was imminent, they devoted their energies to their new spiritual family of co-believers. Early Christians often met in people's homes and called one another brother and sister, a metaphorical use of family terms that was new to the Roman Empire. Some women embraced the ideal of virginity and either singly or in monastic communities declared themselves "virgins in the service of Christ." All this made Christianity seem dangerous to many Romans, especially when becoming Christian actually led some young people to avoid marriage, which was viewed by Romans as the foundation of society and the proper patriarchal order.

Not all Christian teachings about gender were radical, however. In the first century C.E. male church leaders began to place restrictions on female believers. Paul and later writers forbade women to preach, and women were gradually excluded from holding official positions in Christianity other than in women's monasteries. In so limiting the activities of female believers Christianity was following classical Mediterranean culture, just as it patterned its official hierarchy after that of the Roman Empire.

Christian teachings about sexuality also built on classical culture. Many early church leaders, who are often called the church fathers, renounced marriage and sought to live chaste lives not only because they expected the Second Coming imminently, but also because they accepted the hostility toward the body that derived from certain strains of Hellenistic philosophy. Just as spirit was superior to matter, the mind was superior to the body. Though God had clearly sanctioned marriage, celibacy was the highest good. This emphasis on self-denial led to a strong streak of misogyny (hatred of women) in their writings, for they saw women and female sexuality as the chief obstacles to their preferred existence. They also saw intercourse as little more than animal lust, the triumph of the inferior body over the superior mind. Same-sex relations—which were generally acceptable in the Greco-Roman world, especially if they were between socially unequal individuals—were evil. The church fathers' misogyny and hostility toward sexuality had a greater influence on the formation of later attitudes than did the relatively egalitarian actions and words of Jesus.

Saint Augustine

The most influential church father in the West was Saint Augustine of Hippo (354–430). Saint Augustine was born into an urban family in what is now Algeria in North Africa. His father, a minor civil servant, was a pagan; his mother, Monica, a devout Christian. It was not until adulthood that he converted to his mother's religion. As bishop of the city of Hippo Regius, he was a renowned preacher, a vigorous defender of orthodox Christianity, and the author of more than ninety-three books and treatises.

Augustine's autobiography, *The Confessions,* is a literary masterpiece. Written in the rhetorical style and language of late Roman antiquity, it marks the synthesis of Greco-Roman forms and Christian thought. *The Confessions* describes Augustine's moral struggle, the conflict between his spiritual aspirations and his sensual self. Many Greek and Roman philosophers had taught that knowledge and virtue are the same: a person who knows what is right will do what is right. Augustine rejected this idea, arguing that people do not always act on the basis of rational knowledge. Instead the basic or dynamic force in any individual is the will. When Adam ate the fruit forbidden by God in the Garden of Eden (Genesis 3:6), he committed the "original sin" and corrupted the will, wrote Augustine. Adam's sin was not simply his own, but was passed on to all later humans through sexual intercourse; even infants were tainted. Augustine viewed sexual desire as the result of Adam and Eve's disobedience, linking sexuality even more clearly with sin than had earlier church fathers. Because Adam disobeyed God, all human beings have an innate tendency to sin: their will is weak. But according to Augustine, God restores the strength of the will through grace, which is transmitted in certain rituals that the church defined as **sacraments.** Augustine's ideas on sin, grace, and redemption became the foundation of all subsequent Western Christian theology, Protestant as well as Catholic.

Missionary Activity

The word *catholic* derives from a Greek word meaning "general," "universal," or "worldwide." Christ had said that his teaching was for all peoples, and Christians sought to make their faith catholic—that is, worldwide or believed everywhere. The Mediterranean served as the highway over which Christianity spread to the cities of the empire (see Map 7.2). From there missionaries took Christian teachings to the countryside, and then to areas beyond the borders of the empire.

Religion was not a private or individual matter. It was a social affair, and the religion of the chieftain or king determined the religion of the people. Thus missionaries

> **Primary Source:**
> **Saint Augustine Denounces Paganism and Urges Romans to Enter the City of God**
> *In* The City of God, *Augustine uses sarcasm to condemn the rituals of Rome's pre-Christian religion.*

sacraments *Certain rituals of the church believed to act as a conduit of God's grace. The Eucharist and baptism were among the sacraments.*

concentrated their initial efforts not on the people, but on kings or tribal chieftains. According to custom, kings negotiated with all foreign powers, including the gods. Because the Christian missionaries represented a "foreign" power (the Christian God), the king dealt with them. Barbarian kings accepted Christianity because they believed the Christian God was more powerful than pagan gods and the Christian God would deliver victory in battle; or because Christianity taught obedience to (kingly) authority; or because Christian priests possessed knowledge and a charisma that could be associated with kingly power. Kings who converted, such as Ethelbert of Kent and the Frankish chieftain Clovis, sometimes had wives who had converted first and influenced their husbands. Tradition identifies the conversion of Ireland with Saint Patrick (ca. 385–461). After a vision urged him to Christianize Ireland, Patrick studied in Gaul and in 432 was consecrated a bishop. He returned to Ireland, where he converted the Irish tribe by tribe, first baptizing the king.

The Christianization of the English really began in 597, when Pope Gregory I sent a delegation of monks to England. The conversion of the English had far-reaching consequences because Britain later served as a base for the Christianization of the European continent (see Map 7.2). Between the fifth and tenth centuries, the great

MAP 7.2 **The Spread of Christianity and Islam** Originating in the area near Jerusalem, Christianity spread throughout the cities of the Roman world along sea-lanes and roads, then into more rural areas. Islam spread from the Arabian peninsula into the Mediterranean, first by land and then by sea.

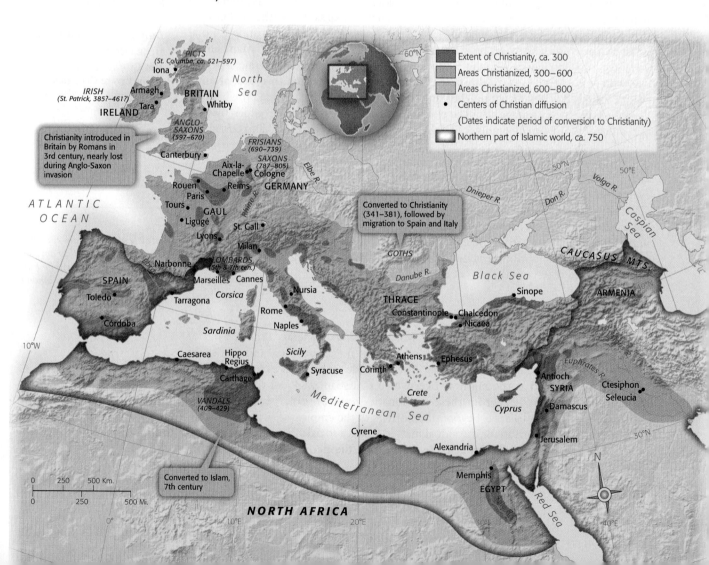

majority of peoples living on the European continent and the nearby islands accepted the Christian religion—that is, they received baptism, though baptism in itself did not automatically transform people into Christians.

In eastern Europe, missionaries traveled far beyond the boundaries of the Byzantine Empire. In 863 the emperor Michael III sent the brothers Cyril (826–869) and Methodius (815–885) to preach Christianity in Moravia (the region of modern central Czech Republic). Other missionaries succeeded in converting the Russians in the tenth century. Cyril invented a Slavic alphabet using Greek characters, and this script (called the "Cyrillic alphabet") is still in use today. Cyrillic script made possible the birth of Russian literature. Similarly, Byzantine art and architecture became the basis of and inspiration for Russian forms. The Byzantines were so successful that the Russians claimed to be the successors of the Byzantine Empire. For a time Moscow was even known as the "Third Rome" (the second Rome being Constantinople).

Conversion and Assimilation

Most of the peoples living in northern and eastern Europe idealized the military virtues of physical strength, ferocity in battle, and loyalty to the leader. Thus they had trouble accepting the Christian precepts of "love your enemies" and "turn the other cheek," and they found the Christian notions of sin and repentance virtually incomprehensible. How did missionaries and priests get masses of pagan and illiterate peoples to understand Christian ideals and teachings? They did it through preaching, through assimilation, and through the penitential system.

Preaching aimed at presenting the basic teachings of Christianity and strengthening the newly baptized in their faith through stories about the lives of Christ and the saints. Deeply ingrained pagan customs and practices, however, could not be stamped out by words alone or even by imperial edicts. Christian missionaries often pursued a policy of assimilation, easing the conversion of pagan men and women by stressing similarities between their customs and beliefs and those of Christianity. In the same way that classically trained scholars such as Jerome and Augustine blended Greco-Roman and Christian ideas, missionaries and converts mixed pagan ideas and practices with Christian ones. Bogs and lakes sacred to Germanic gods became associated with saints, as did various aspects of ordinary life, such as traveling, planting crops, and worrying about a sick child. Aspects of existing midwinter celebrations, which often centered on the return of the sun as the days became longer, were incorporated into celebrations of Christmas. Spring rituals involving eggs and rabbits (both symbols of fertility) were added to Easter.

Also instrumental in converting pagans was the rite of reconciliation in which the sinner was able to receive God's forgiveness. The penitent knelt individually before the priest, who asked about the sins the penitent might have committed. A penance such as fasting on bread and water for a period of time or saying specific prayers was imposed as medicine for the soul. The priest and penitent were guided by manuals known as **penitentials,** which included lists of sins and the appropriate penance. Penitentials gave pagans a sense of the behavior expected of Christians. The penitential system also encouraged the private examination of conscience and offered relief from the burden of sinful deeds.

penitentials *Manuals for the examination of conscience.*

Most religious observances continued to be community matters, however, as they had been in the ancient world. People joined with family members, friends, and neighbors to celebrate baptisms and funerals, presided over by a priest. They prayed to saints or to the Virgin Mary to intercede with God, or they simply asked the saints for protection and blessing. The entire village participated in processions marking saints' days or points in the agricultural year, often carrying images of saints or their **relics**—bones, articles of clothing, or other objects associated with the life of a saint—around the houses and fields.

relics *Bones, articles of clothing, or other material objects associated with the life of a saint, used as an expedient to worship or to invoke the blessing and protection of that particular saint.*

● **Procession to a New Church** In this sixth-century ivory carving, two men in a wagon, accompanied by a procession of people holding candles, carry a relic casket to a church under construction. Workers are putting tiles on the church roof. New churches often received holy items when they were dedicated, and processions were common ways in which people expressed community devotion. *(Cathedral Treasury, Trier/Photo: Ann Muenchow)*

MIGRATING PEOPLES

How did the barbarians shape social, economic, and political structures in Europe and western Asia?

The migration of peoples from one area to another has been a continuing feature of world history. The causes of early migrations varied and are not thoroughly understood by scholars. But there is no question that they profoundly affected both the regions to which peoples moved and the regions they left behind.

Celts, Huns, and Germans

In surveying the world around them, the ancient Greeks often conceptualized things in dichotomies, or sets of opposites: light and dark, hot and cold, wet and dry, mind and body, male and female, and so on. One of their key dichotomies was Greek and non-Greek, and the Greeks coined the word *barbaros* for those whose native language was not Greek, because they seemed to the Greeks to be speaking nonsense syllables—bar, bar, bar. ("Bar-bar" is the Greek equivalent to "blah-blah" or "yada-yada.") *Barbaros* originally meant simply someone who did not speak Greek, but gradually it also implied unruly, savage, and more primitive than the advanced civilization of Greece. The word brought this meaning with it when it came into Latin and other European languages, with the Romans referring to those who lived beyond the northeastern boundary of Roman territory as **"barbarians."**

barbarians *A name given by the Romans to all peoples living outside the frontiers of the Roman Empire (except the Persians).*

Migrating groups that the Romans labeled barbarians had pressed along the Rhine-Danube frontier of the Roman Empire since about 150 C.E. (see page 122). In the third and fourth centuries, increasing pressures on the frontiers from the east and north placed greater demands on Roman military manpower, which plague and a declining birthrate had reduced. Therefore, Roman generals recruited refugees and tribes allied with the Romans to serve in the Roman army, and some rose to the highest ranks.

Why did the barbarians migrate? In part, they were searching for more regular supplies of food, better farmland, and a warmer climate. Conflicts within and among barbarian groups also led to war and disruption, which motivated groups to move. Franks fought Alemanni in Gaul, while Visigoths fought Vandals in the Iberian peninsula and across North Africa. Pressure from Germanic-speaking groups caused Celtic-speaking peoples to move westward, settling in Brittany (modern northwestern France) and throughout the British Isles (England, Wales, Scotland, and Ireland). The Picts of Scotland as well as the Welsh, Britons, and Irish were peoples of Celtic descent (see Map 7.3).

A very significant factor in barbarian migration was pressure from nomadic steppe peoples from central Asia. This included the Alans, Avars, Bulghars, Khazars, and most prominently the Huns, who attacked the Black Sea area and the Eastern Roman Empire beginning in the fourth century. Under the leadership of their warrior-king Attila, the Huns swept into central Europe in 451, attacking Roman settlements in the Balkans and Germanic settlements along the Danube and Rhine Rivers. After Attila turned his army southward and crossed the Alps into Italy, a papal delegation,

● **Vandal Landowner** In this mosaic, a Vandal landowner rides out from his Roman-style house. His clothing—Roman short tunic, cloak, and sandals—reflects the way some Celtic and Germanic tribes accepted Roman lifestyles, though his beard is more typical of barbarian men's fashion. *(Courtesy of the Trustees of the British Museum)*

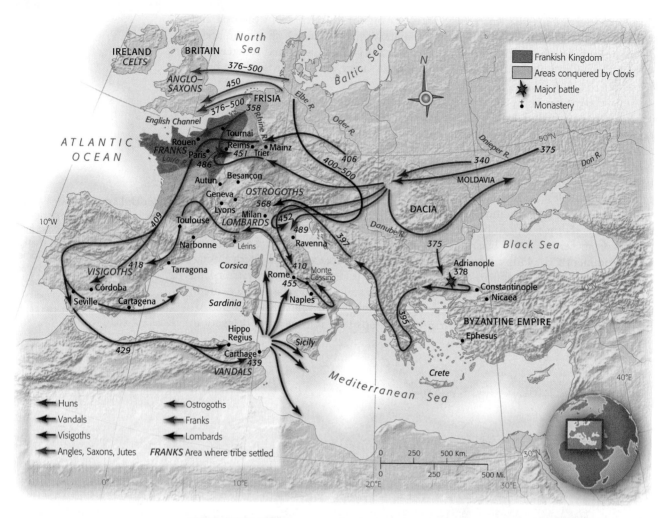

MAP 7.3 **The Barbarian Migrations** Various barbarian groups migrated throughout Europe and western Asia in late antiquity, pushed and pulled by a number of factors. Many of them formed loosely structured states, of which the Frankish Kingdom would become the most significant.

including Pope Leo I himself, asked him not to attack Rome. Though papal diplomacy was later credited with stopping the advance of the Huns, a plague that spread among Hunnic troops and their dwindling food supplies were probably much more important. The Huns retreated from Italy, and within a year Attila was dead. Later leaders were not as effective, and the Huns were never again an important factor in European history. Their conquests had slowed down the movements of various other groups, however, allowing barbarian peoples to absorb more of Roman culture as they picked the Western Roman Empire apart.

The largest group of barbarians were people who spoke Germanic languages. Many modern scholars have tried to explain who the Germans were. The present consensus, based on the study of linguistic and archaeological evidence, is that there were not one but rather many Germanic peoples with somewhat different cultural traditions.

Barbarian Society

Germanic and Celtic society had originated in the northern parts of central and western Europe and the southern regions of Scandinavia during the Iron Age (800–

500 B.C.E.). After the end of the Western Roman Empire, barbarian customs and traditions formed the basis of European society for centuries.

Barbarians generally had no notion of the state as we use the term today; they thought in social, not political, terms. The basic social unit was the tribe, a group whose members believed that they were all descended from a common ancestor. Blood united them; kinship protected them. Law was custom—unwritten, preserved in the minds of the elders of the tribe, and handed down by word of mouth from generation to generation.

Barbarian tribes were led by tribal chieftains, who are often called kings, though this implies broader power than they actually had. The chief was the member recognized as the strongest and bravest in battle and was elected from among the male members of the strongest family. He led the tribe in war, settled disputes among its members, conducted negotiations with outside powers, and offered sacrifices to the gods. The period of migrations and conquests of the Western Roman Empire witnessed the strengthening of kingship among tribes.

Early barbarian tribes had no written laws, but beginning in the late sixth century some tribal chieftains began to collect, write, and publish lists of their customs at the urging of Christian missionaries. The churchmen wanted to understand barbarian ways in order to assimilate the tribes to Christianity. Moreover, by the sixth century many barbarian kings needed regulations for the Romans under their jurisdiction as well as for their own people.

Today, if a person holds up a bank, American law maintains that the robber attacks both the bank and the state in which it exists—a sophisticated notion involving the abstract idea of the state. In early Germanic law, all crimes were regarded as crimes against a person.

According to the code of one Germanic tribe, the Salian Franks, every person had a particular monetary value to the tribe. This value was called the **wergeld,** which literally means "man-money" or "money to buy off the spear." Men of fighting age had the highest wergeld, then women of childbearing age, children, and finally the aged. Everyone's value reflected his or her potential military worthiness. If a person accused of a crime agreed to pay the wergeld and if the victim and his or her family accepted the payment, there was peace. If the accused refused to pay the wergeld or if the victim's family refused to accept it, a blood feud ensued.

wergeld *"Man-money" or "money to buy off the spear"; according to the code of the Salian Franks, this is the particular monetary value of each member of the tribe.*

Social and Economic Structures

Barbarian groups usually resided in small villages, and climate and geography determined the basic patterns of agricultural and pastoral life. Many tribes lived in small settlements on the edges of clearings where they raised barley, wheat, oats, peas, and beans. Men and women tilled their fields with simple wooden scratch plows and harvested their grains with small iron sickles. The kernels of grain were eaten as porridge, ground up for flour, or fermented into strong, thick beer. The vast majority of people's caloric intake came from grain in some form.

Within the small villages, there were great differences in wealth and status. Free men and their families constituted the largest class. The number of cattle a man possessed indicated his wealth and determined his social status. Free men also shared in tribal warfare. Slaves (prisoners of war) worked as farm laborers, herdsmen, and household servants.

Barbarian tribes were understood as made up of kin groups, and those kin groups were made up of families, the basic social unit in barbarian society. Families were responsible for the debts and actions of their members and for keeping the peace in general. Germanic society was patriarchal: within each household the father had authority over his wife, children, and slaves. Some wealthy and powerful men had more than one wife, a pattern that continued even after they became Christian, but polygamy was not widespread among ordinary people. A woman was considered to be under the legal guardianship of a man, and she had fewer rights to own property than did Roman women in the late empire. However, once they were widowed (and there must have been many widows in such a violent, warring society), women sometimes assumed their husbands' rights over family property and held the guardianship of their children.

The Frankish Kingdom

Between 450 and 565, Germanic tribes established a number of kingdoms, but none other than the Frankish kingdom lasted very long. The Germanic kingdoms did not have definite geographical boundaries, and their locations are approximate. The Vandals, whose destructive ways are commemorated in the word *vandal,* settled in North Africa. In northern and western Europe in the sixth century, the Burgundians ruled over part of what is now France and the Ostrogoths much of what is now Italy.

The most enduring Germanic kingdom was established by the Frankish chieftain Clovis (r. 481–511). Originally only a petty chieftain in northwestern Gaul (modern Belgium), Clovis began to expand his territories in 486. His Catholic wife Clothild worked to convert her husband and supported the founding of churches and monasteries. Clothild typifies the role women played in the Christianization and Romanization of the Germanic kingdoms. Clovis's conversion to Orthodox Christianity in 496 won him the crucial support of the papacy and the bishops of Gaul. (See the feature "Listening to the Past: The Conversion of Clovis" on pages 188–189.) As the defender of Roman Catholicism against heretical Germanic tribes, Clovis went on to conquer the Visigoths, extending his domain to include much of what is now France and southwestern Germany. Because he was descended from the half-legendary chieftain Merovech, the dynasty that Clovis founded has been called **Merovingian.**

Merovingian *A dynasty founded in 481 by the Frankish chieftain Clovis in what is now France, so called because Clovis claimed descent from the semi-legendary leader Merovech.*

When Clovis died, following Frankish custom, his kingdom was divided among his four sons. For the next two centuries, the land was often wracked by civil war. So brutal were these wars that historians used to use the term *Dark Ages* to apply to the entire Merovingian period. Yet recent research has presented a more complex picture.

Merovingian kings based their administration on the *civitas,* the city and the surrounding territory over which a *count* presided. The count raised troops, collected royal revenues, and provided justice on the basis of local, not royal, law. At the king's court—that is, wherever the king was present—an official called the *mayor of the palace* supervised legal, financial, and household officials; the mayor of the palace also governed in the king's absence. In the seventh century, that position was held by members of an increasingly powerful family, the **Carolingians,** who further increased their power through advantageous marriages, a well-earned reputation for military strength, and the help of the church.

Carolingians *A Frankish family that increased its power through selective marriage, political acumen, and military victory to the point that it was able to replace the Merovingians as the rulers of the Frankish kingdom during the seventh century.*

The Carolingians replaced the Merovingians as rulers of the Frankish kingdom, cementing their authority when the Carolingian Charles Martel defeated Muslim invaders in 732 at the Battle of Poitiers in central France. Muslims and Christians have interpreted the battle differently. Muslims considered it a minor skirmish and attributed the Frankish victory to Muslim difficulties in maintaining supply lines over long distances and to ethnic conflicts and unrest in Islamic Spain. Charles Martel and later Carolingians used it to portray themselves as defenders of Christendom against the Muslims.

The battle of Poitiers helped the Carolingians acquire the support of the church, perhaps their most important asset. They further strengthened their ties to the church by supporting the work of missionaries who preached Christianity to pagan peoples, along with the Christian duty to obey secular authorities.

North
Sea

Baltic
Sea

ATLANTIC
OCEAN

NORWAY

SWEDEN

DENMARK

DANISH MARCH

Iona
SCOTLAND

Armagh
Limerick
IRELAND
Dublin

Jarrow

NORTHUMBRIA
York

WALES
MERCIA
EAST
ANGLIA
DEVON
CORNWALL
WESSEX
ESSEX
Canterbury
SUSSEX
KENT
Utrecht

SAXONY
804

FLANDERS
Aachen
Rouen
BRITTANY
Echternach
Mainz
Fulda
AUSTRASIA
NEUSTRIA
Paris
Orléans

Elbe R.

Oder R.

TRIBUTARY

PEOPLES

Danube R.

Tours
Poitiers

ALEMANNIA
St.
Gall
BAVARIA
788

AQUITAINE
BURGUNDY
Bordeaux
Lyons
GASCONY

VENETIA
Milan
Venice
Pavia
ISTRIA
Genoa
LOMBARDY
DALMATIA

Oviedo
ASTURIAS
Roncesvalles
Aniane

SPANISH
MARCH 811
Marseilles
Lérins
PAPAL
STATES
Ravenna

CALIPHATE OF
CÓRDOBA
Toledo
Barcelona

Corsica

Spoleto
DUCHY OF
SPOLETO
Rome
Monte Cassino
DUCHY OF
BENEVENTO
Naples
Salerno

Córdoba

Balearic Is.
Sardinia

Mediterranean
Sea

BYZANTINE EMPIRE

Sicily

| 0 | 200 | 400 Km. |
| 0 | 200 | 400 Mi. |

Frankish Kingdom, 768
Areas conquered by Charlemagne
Tributary peoples
Byzantine territory
Viking settlement
Early Viking raids, trade, and
colonization routes

TREATY OF VERDUN, 843

Aachen
Paris
Verdun
KINGDOM
OF LOUIS
THE GERMAN
Strasbourg
KINGDOM OF
CHARLES
THE BALD

TRIBUTARY
PEOPLES

KINGDOM
OF LOTHAIR
PAPAL
STATES

Rome

Charles the Bald
Lothair
Louis the German
Tributary peoples

| 0 | 200 | 400 Km. |
| 0 | 200 | 400 Mi. |

MAP 7.4 **The Carolingian World and Viking Expansion** Charlemagne added large amounts of territory to the Frankish Kingdom, although his actual power in these areas was often quite limited. His grandsons weakened the kingdom by dividing it into three parts. Viking invasions and migrations, which began in the eighth century, also diminished Frankish holdings and power.

Charlemagne

The most powerful of the Carolingians was Charles the Great (r. 768–814), generally known as Charlemagne. In the autumn of the year 800, Charlemagne visited Rome, where on Christmas Day Pope Leo III crowned him Holy Roman Emperor. The event had momentous consequences. In taking as his motto *Renovatio romani imperi* (Revival of the Roman Empire), Charlemagne was deliberately perpetuating old Roman imperial ideas while identifying with the new Rome of the Christian church. From Baghdad, Harun al Rashid, caliph of the Abbasid Empire (786–809), congratulated Charlemagne on his coronation with the gift of an elephant. But although the Muslim caliph recognized Charlemagne as a fellow sovereign, the Greeks regarded the papal acts as rebellious and Charlemagne as a usurper. The imperial coronation thus marks a decisive break between Rome and Constantinople.

Charlemagne built on the military and diplomatic foundations of his ancestors. His most striking characteristic was his phenomenal energy, which helps explain his great military achievements. Continuing the expansionist policies of his ancestors, Charlemagne fought more than fifty campaigns, and by around 805 the Frankish kingdom included all of continental Europe except Spain, Scandinavia, southern Italy, and the Slavic fringes of the East (see Map 7.4).

For administrative purposes, Charlemagne divided his entire kingdom into counties. Each of the approximately six hundred counties was governed by a count, who had full military and judicial power and held his office for life but could be removed by the emperor for misconduct. As a link between local authorities and the central government, Charlemagne appointed officials called *missi dominici,* "agents of the lord king." Each year beginning in 802, two missi, usually a count and a bishop or abbot, visited assigned districts. They checked up on the counts and their districts' judicial, financial, and clerical activities.

It is ironic that Charlemagne's most enduring legacy was the stimulus he gave to scholarship and learning. Barely literate, preoccupied with the control of vast territories, much more a warrior than a thinker, Charlemagne nevertheless set in motion a cultural revival that later historians called the "Carolingian Renaissance." The Carolingian Renaissance was a rebirth of interest in, study of, and preservation of the language, ideas, and achievements of classical Greece and Rome. Scholars at Charlemagne's capital of Aachen copied books and manuscripts and built up libraries.

Charlemagne left his vast empire to his sole surviving son, Louis the Pious (r. 814–840), who attempted to keep the empire intact. This proved to be impossible. Members of the nobility engaged in plots and open warfare against the emperor, often allying themselves with one of Louis's three sons. In 843, shortly after Louis's death, those sons agreed to the **Treaty of Verdun,** which divided the empire into three parts: Charles the Bald received the western part, Lothar the middle and the title of emperor, and Louis the eastern part, from which he acquired the title "the German." Though of course no one knew it at the time, this treaty set the pattern for political bound-

● **Germanic Bracteate (Gold Leaf) Pendant** This late-fifth-century piece, with the head of Rome above a wolf suckling Romulus and Remus, reflects Germanic assimilation of Roman legend and artistic design. *(Courtesy of the Trustees of the British Museum)*

aries in Europe that has been maintained until today. Other than brief periods under Napoleon and Hitler, Europe would never again see as large a unified state as it had under Charlemagne, which is one reason he has become a symbol of European unity in the twenty-first century.

The weakening of central power was hastened by invasions and migrations from the north, south, and east. Thus Charlemagne's empire ended in much the same way that the Roman Empire had earlier, a combination of internal weakness and external pressure.

Treaty of Verdun *A treaty, ratified in 843, that divided the territories of Charlemagne between his three surviving grandsons and formed the precursor states of modern Germany, France, and Italy.*

Chapter Summary

To assess your mastery of this chapter, go to
bedfordstmartins.com/mckayworld

• How was the Byzantine Empire able to survive for so long, and what were its most important achievements?

Late antiquity was a period of rupture and transformation in Europe and western Asia, but also of continuities and assimilation. In the east, the Byzantine Empire withstood attacks from Germanic tribes and steppe peoples and remained a state until 1453, a thousand years longer than the Western Roman Empire. Byzantium preserved the philosophical and scientific texts of the ancient world—which later formed the basis for study in science and medicine in both Europe and the Arabic world—and produced a great synthesis of Roman law, the Justinian *Code,* which shapes legal structures in much of Europe and former European colonies to this day.

• What factors enabled the Christian church to expand and thrive?

Christianity gained the support of the fourth-century emperors and gradually adopted the Roman system of hierarchical organization. The church possessed able administrators and leaders whose skills were tested in the chaotic environment of the end of the Roman Empire in the West. Bishops expanded their activities, and in the fifth century the bishops of Rome began to stress their supremacy over other Christian communities. Monasteries offered opportunities for individuals to develop deeper spiritual devotion and also provided a model of Christian living, a pattern of agricultural development, and a place for education and learning.

• How did Christian thinkers and missionaries adapt Greco-Roman ideas to Christian theology and develop effective techniques to convert barbarian peoples to Christianity?

Christian thinkers reinterpreted the classics in a Christian sense, incorporating elements of Greek and Roman philosophy and of various pagan religious groups into Christian teachings. Of these early thinkers, Augustine of Hippo was the most influential. His ideas about sin, free will, sexuality, and the role

Key Terms

- diaspora
- corpus juris civilis
- dioceses
- Arianism
- canon law
- Petrine Doctrine
- iconoclastic controversy
- schism
- eremitical
- coenobitic
- regular clergy
- secular clergy
- sacraments
- penitentials
- relics
- barbarians
- wergeld
- Merovingian
- Carolingians
- Treaty of Verdun

of government shaped western European thought from the fifth century on. Christianity had a dynamic missionary policy, and the church slowly succeeded in assimilating—that is, adapting—Germanic, Celtic, and Slavic peoples to Christian teaching. Christianity refashioned the Germanic and classical legacies, creating new rituals and practices that were meaningful to people.

• How did the barbarians shape social, economic, and political structures in Europe and western Asia?

The migration of barbarian groups into Europe from the east, caused by many factors, affected both the regions to which peoples moved and the ones they left behind. Barbarian customs and traditions formed the basis of European society for centuries. Most people lived in family groups in villages, where men, women, and children shared in the agricultural labor that sustained society. Barbarians are often divided into large linguistic groups, such as the Celtic and Germanic tribes, with ties to other tribes based on kinship and military alliances, not on loyalty to a particular government. Most barbarian states were weak and short-lived, though that of the Franks was relatively more unified and powerful. First rulers in the Merovingian dynasty, and then in the Carolingian, used military victories and strategic marriage alliances to enhance their authority. Carolingian government reached the peak of its development under Charlemagne, who built on the military and diplomatic foundations of his ancestors to build a state that controlled most of central and western continental Europe except for Muslim Spain.

Suggested Reading

Barbero, Allesandro. *Charlemagne: Father of a Continent.* 2004. A wonderful new biography of Charlemagne and a study of the times in which he lived that argues for the complexity of his legacy.

Brown, Peter. *Augustine of Hippo,* rev. ed. 2000. The best biography of Saint Augustine, which treats him as a symbol of change.

Brown, Peter. *The Body and Society: Men, Women, and Sexual Renunciation in Early Christianity.* 1988. Explores early Christian attitudes on sexuality and how they replaced Roman attitudes.

Brown, Peter. *The World of Late Antiquity,* A.D. 150–750, rev. ed. 1989. A lavishly illustrated survey that stresses social and cultural change and has clearly written introductions to the entire period.

Burns, Thomas S. *Rome and the Barbarians, 100 B.C.–400 A.D.* 2003. Argues that Germanic and Roman culture assimilated more than they conflicted.

Cameron, Averil. *The Mediterranean World in Late Antiquity,* A.D. 395–600. 1993. Focuses especially on political and economic changes.

Clark, Gilian. *Women in Late Antiquity: Pagan and Christian Lifestyles.* 1994. Explores law, marriage, and religious life.

Dunn, Marilyn. *The Emergence of Monasticism: From the Desert Fathers to the Early Middle Ages.* 2003. Focuses on the beginnings of monasticism.

Evans, James Allan. *The Empress Theodora: Partner of Justinian.* 2003. Provides a brief, yet balanced and thorough, treatment of the empress's life.

Fletcher, Richard. *The Barbarian Conversion: From Paganism to Christianity.* 1998. A superbly written analysis of conversion to Christianity.

Herrin, Judith. *The Formation of Christendom.* 1987. The best synthesis of the development of the Christian church from the third to the ninth centuries.

Macmullen, Ramsey. *Christianity and Paganism in the Fourth to Eighth Centuries.* 1998. Explores the influences of Christianity and paganism on each other.

Norwich, John Julius. *Byzantium: The Early Centuries.* 1989. An elegantly written brief survey.

Pelikan, Jaroslav. *The Excellent Empire: The Fall of Rome and the Triumph of the Church.* 1987. Describes how interpretations of the fall of Rome have influenced our understanding of Western culture.

Riche, Pierre. *Daily Life in the World of Charlemagne,* trans. JoAnn McNamara. 1978. A detailed study of many facets of Carolingian society.

Todd, Malcolm. *The Early Germans,* 2d ed. 2004. Uses archaeological and literary sources to analyze Germanic social structure, customs, and religion and to suggest implications for an understanding of migration and ethnicity.

Wells, Peter S. *The Barbarians Speak: How the Conquered Peoples Shaped Roman Europe.* 1999. Presents extensive evidence of Celtic and Germanic social and technical development.

Wood, Ian. *The Merovingian Kingdoms, 450–751.* 1994. The best general treatment of the Merovingians.

Notes

1. Quoted in E. Patlagean, "Byzantium in the Tenth and Eleventh Centuries," in *A History of Private Life.* Vol. 1: *From Pagan Rome to Byzantium,* ed. P. Ariès and G. Duby (Cambridge, Mass.: Harvard University Press, 1987), p. 573.

The Conversion of Clovis

Modern Christian doctrine holds that conversion is a process, the gradual turning toward Jesus and the teachings of the Christian Gospels. But in the early medieval world, conversion was perceived more as a one-time event determined by the tribal chieftain. If he accepted baptism, the mass conversion of his people followed. The selection here about the Frankish king Clovis is from The History of the Franks *by Gregory, bishop of Tours (ca. 504–594), written about a century after the events it describes.*

The first child which Clotild bore for Clovis was a son. She wanted to have her baby baptized, and she kept urging her husband to agree to this. "The gods whom you worship are no good," she would say. "They haven't even been able to help themselves, let alone others. . . . Take your Saturn, for example, who ran away from his own son to avoid being exiled from his kingdom, or so they say; and Jupiter, that obscene perpetrator of all sorts of mucky deeds, who couldn't keep his hands off other men, who had his fun with all his female relatives and couldn't even refrain from intercourse with his own sister. . . .

"You ought instead to worship Him who created at a word and out of nothing heaven, and earth, the sea and all that therein is, who made the sun to shine, who lit the sky with stars, who peopled the water with fish, the earth with beasts, the sky with flying creatures, by whose hand the race of man was made, by whose gift all creation is constrained to serve in deference and devotion the man He made." However often the Queen said this, the King came no nearer to belief. . . .

The Queen, who was true to her faith, brought her son to be baptized. . . . The child was baptized; he was given the name Ingomer; but no sooner had he received baptism than he died in his white robes. Clovis was extremely angry. He began immediately to reproach his Queen. "If he had been dedicated in the name of my gods," he said, "he would have lived without question; but now that he has been baptized in the name of your God he has not been able to live a single day!"

"I give thanks to Almighty God," replied Clotild, "the Creator of all things who has not found me completely unworthy, for He has deigned to welcome into his Kingdom a child conceived in my womb. . . ."

Some time later Clotild bore a second son. He was baptized Chlodomer. He began to ail and Clovis said, "What else do you expect? It will happen to him as it happened to his brother: no sooner is he baptized in the name of your Christ than he will die!" Clotild prayed to the Lord and at His commands the baby recovered.

Queen Clotild continued to pray that her husband might recognize the true God and give up his idol-worship. Nothing could persuade him to accept Christianity. Finally war broke out against the Alamanni and in this conflict he was forced by necessity to accept what he had refused of his own free will. It so turned out that when the two armies met on the battlefield there was a great slaughter and the troops of Clovis were rapidly being annihilated. He raised his eyes to heaven when he saw this, felt compunction in his heart and was moved to tears. "Jesus Christ," he said, "you who Clotild maintains to be the Son of the living God, you who deign to give help to those in travail and victory to those who trust in you, in faith I beg the glory of your help. If you will give me victory over my enemies, and if I may have evidence to that miraculous power which the people dedicated to your name say that they have experienced, then I will believe in you and I will be baptized in your name. I have called upon my own gods, but, as I see only too clearly, they have no intention of helping me. I therefore cannot believe that they possess any power for they do not come to the assistance of those who trust them. I now call upon you. I want to believe in you, but I must first be saved from my enemies." Even as he said this the Alamanni turned their backs and began to run away. As soon as they saw that their King was killed, they submitted to Clovis. "We beg you," they said, "to put an end to this slaughter. We are prepared to obey you." Clovis stopped the war. He made a speech in which he called for peace. Then he went home. He

Ninth-century ivory carving showing Clovis being baptized by Saint Remi. (Musée Condé, Chantilly/Laurie Platt Winfrey, Inc.)

told the Queen how he had won a victory by calling on the name of Christ. This happened in the fifteenth year of his reign (496).

The Queen then ordered Saint Remigius, Bishop of the town of Rheims, to be summoned in secret. She begged him to impart the word of salvation to the King. The Bishop asked Clovis to meet him in private and began to urge him to believe in the true God, Maker of heaven and earth, and to forsake his idols, which were powerless to help him or anyone else. The King replied: "I have listened to you willingly, holy father. There remains one obstacle. The people under my command will not agree to forsake their gods. I will go and put to them what you have just said to me." He arranged a meeting with his people, but God in his power had preceded him, and before he could say a word all those present shouted in unison: "We will give up worshipping our mortal gods, pious King, and we are prepared to follow the immortal God about whom Remigius preaches." This news was reported to the Bishop. He was greatly pleased and he ordered the baptismal pool to be made ready. . . . The baptistry was prepared, sticks of incense gave off clouds of perfume, sweet-smelling candles gleamed bright and the holy place of baptism was filled with divine fragrance. God filled the hearts of all present with such grace that they imagined themselves to have been transported to some perfumed paradise. King Clovis asked that he might be baptized first by the Bishop.

Like some new Constantine he stepped forward to the baptismal pool, ready to wash away the sores of his old leprosy and to be cleansed in flowing water from the sordid stains which he had borne so long.

King Clovis confessed his belief in God Almighty, three in one. He was baptized in the name of the Father, the Son and the Holy Ghost, and marked in holy chrism [an anointing oil] with the sign of the Cross of Christ. More than three thousand of his army were baptized at the same time.

Questions for Analysis

1. Who took the initiative in urging Clovis's conversion? What can we deduce from that?

2. According to this account, why did Clovis ultimately accept Christianity?

3. For the Salian Franks, what was the best proof of divine power?

4. On the basis of this selection, do you consider *The History of the Franks* reliable history? Why?

Sources: L. Thorpe, trans., *The History of the Franks by Gregory of Tours* (Harmondsworth, England: Penguin, 1974), p. 159; P. J. Geary, ed., *Readings in Medieval History* (Peterborough, Ontario: Broadview Press, 1991), pp. 165–166.

The Patio of the Lions (fourteenth century), the Alhambra, Granada, Spain. *(George Holton/Photo Researchers, Inc.)*

chapter 8

THE ISLAMIC WORLD, CA. 600–1400

Chapter Preview

The Origins of Islam
• *Who was Muhammad, and what did he teach?*

Islamic States and Their Expansion
• *What forms of government did Islam establish, and how did they contribute to the rapid spread of Islam?*

Fragmentation and Military Challenges (900–1400)
• *How were the Muslim lands governed from 900 to 1400, and what new challenges did they face?*

Muslim Society: The Life of the People
• *What social distinctions were important in Muslim society?*

Trade and Commerce
• *Did Islamic teachings contribute to the thriving trade that passed through Muslim lands?*

Cultural Developments
• *What advances were made in the arts, sciences, and education?*

Around 610 in the city of Mecca in what is now Saudi Arabia, a merchant called Muhammad began to have religious experiences. By the time he died in 632, most of Arabia had accepted his teachings. A century later his followers controlled Syria, Palestine, Egypt, what is now Iraq, Persia (present-day Iran), northern India, North Africa, Spain, and part of France. Within another century Muhammad's beliefs had been carried across Central Asia to the borders of China and India. In the ninth, tenth, and eleventh centuries, the Muslims created a brilliant civilization centered at Baghdad in Iraq, a culture that profoundly influenced the development of both Eastern and Western civilizations.

THE ORIGINS OF ISLAM
Who was Muhammad, and what did he teach?

The Arabian peninsula, about a third of the size of Europe or the United States, covers about a million square miles, much but not all of it desert. By the sixth century C.E., farming prevailed in the southwestern mountain valleys with their ample rainfall. In other areas scattered throughout the peninsula, oasis towns sustained sizable populations including artisans, merchants, and religious leaders. In Mecca the presence of the Ka'ba, a temple containing a black stone thought to be a god's dwelling place, attracted pilgrims and enabled Mecca to become the economic and cultural center of western Arabia.

Thinly spread over the entire peninsula were nomadic Bedouins who migrated from place to place, grazing their sheep, goats, and camels. Though always small in number, Bedouins were the most important political and military force in the region because of their toughness, solidarity, fighting traditions, possession of horses, and ability to control trade and lines of communication.

● **Qur'an with Kufic
Script** Kufic takes its name from
the town of Kufa, south of Baghdad
in Iraq, at one time a major center of
Muslim learning. Kufic scripts were
angular and derived from inscriptions on stone monuments. *(Mashed
Shrine Library, Iran/Robert Harding
World Imagery)*

Ka'ba *The temple in Mecca
containing a black stone thought
to be God's dwelling place.*

Qur'an *The sacred book of
Islam.*

caliph *The successor to
Muhammad; the representative or
deputy of God.*

For all Arabs, the basic social unit was the *tribe*—a group
of blood relations connected through the male line. The tribe
provided protection and support and in turn expected members' total loyalty. Like the Germanic peoples in the age of
their migrations (see pages 178–180), Arab tribes were not
static entities but continually evolving groups. A particular
tribe might include both nomadic and sedentary members.

Strong economic links joined all Arab peoples. Nomads
and seminomads depended on the agriculturally productive
communities for food they could not produce, cloth, metal
products, and weapons. Nomads paid for these goods with
livestock, milk and milk products, hides, and hair, items in
demand in oasis towns. Nomads acquired income by serving
as desert guides and as guards for caravans. Plundering caravans and extorting protection money also yielded income.

In northern and central Arabia in the early seventh century,
tribal confederations with their warrior elite were dominant.
In the southern parts of the peninsula, religious aristocracies
tended to hold political power. Many oasis or market towns
contained members of one holy family who served the deity
who resided in the town and acted as guardians of the deity's
shrine. At the shrine, a *mansib,* or cultic leader, adjudicated
disputes and tried to get agreements among warrior tribes. All
Arabs respected the shrines because they served as neutral
places for arbitration among warring tribes.

The power of the northern warrior class rested on its fighting skills. The southern religious aristocracy, by contrast, depended on its cultic and economic power. Located in
agricultural areas that were also commercial centers, the reli-
gious aristocracy had a stronger economic base than the warrior-aristocrats. The political genius of Muhammad was to bind together these different tribal groups into a
strong unified state.

Muhammad

Much like the earliest sources for Jesus, the earliest account of the life of Muhammad
(ca. 570–632) comes from oral traditions passed down among followers and not recorded for several decades or generations. According to these traditions, Muhammad
was orphaned at the age of six and brought up by his paternal uncle. As a young man,
he became a merchant in the caravan trade. Later he entered the service of a wealthy
widow, Khadija, and their subsequent marriage brought him financial security while
she lived. Muhammad was extremely pious and devoted to contemplation. At about
age forty, in a cave in the hills near Mecca where he was accustomed to pray, Muhammad had a vision of an angelic being who commanded him to preach the revelations
that God would be sending him. Muhammad began to preach to the people of Mecca,
urging them to give up their idols and submit to the one indivisible God. During his
lifetime, Muhammad's followers jotted down his revelations haphazardly. After his
death, scribes organized the revelations into chapters. In 651 they published the version of them that Muslims consider authoritative, the **Qur'an.** Muslims revere the
Qur'an for its sacred message and for the beauty of its Arabic language.

After the death of Muhammad, two or three centuries passed before the emergence
of a distinct Muslim identity, a period some writers call the Age of Arab Monotheism.
Theological issues, such as the oneness of God, the role of angels, the prophets, the
Scriptures, and Judgment Day, as well as political issues, such as the authority of
Muhammad and that of the **caliph** (successor to Muhammad, representative or deputy

of God), all had to be worked out. Likewise, legal issues relating to the **hadith**, collections of the sayings of or anecdotes about Muhammad, required investigation. Muhammad's example as revealed in the hadith became the legal basis for the conduct or behavior of every Muslim. The life of Muhammad, who is also known as the Prophet, provides the "normative example," or **Sunna**, for the Muslim believer. Once Islamic theology and law had evolved into a religious system, Muhammad was revealed as the perfect man, the embodiment of the will of God. The Muslim way of life rests on Muhammad's example.

The Islamic Faith

Islam, the strict monotheistic faith that is based on the teachings of Muhammad, rests on the principle of the absolute unity and omnipotence of God (Allah). The word *Islam* means "submission to God," and *Muslim* means "a person who submits." Muslims believe that Muhammad was the last of the prophets, completing the work begun by Abraham, Moses, and Jesus. According to the Qur'an, both Jewish and Christian authorities acknowledged the coming of a final prophet. The Qur'an asserts that the Prophet Muhammad descended from Adam, the first man, and that the Prophet Abraham built the Ka'ba. The Qur'an holds that the holy writings of both Jews and Christians represent divine revelation, but it claims that both Jews and Christians tampered with the books of God.

Muslims believe that they worship the same God as Jews and Christians. Monotheism had flourished in Middle Eastern Semitic and Persian cultures for centuries before Muhammad. Islam accepts much of the Old and New Testaments; it obeys the Mosaic law about circumcision, ritual bathing, and restrictions on eating pork and shellfish; and the Qur'an calls Christians "nearest in love" to Muslims. Muhammad insisted that he was not preaching a new message; rather, he was calling people back to the one true God, urging his contemporaries to reform their lives, to return to the faith of Abraham, the first monotheist.

Muhammad displayed genius as both a political strategist and a religious teacher. He gave Arabs the idea of a unique and unified **umma**, or community, which consisted of all those whose primary identity and bond was a common religious faith and commitment, not a tribal tie. The umma was to be a religious and political community led by Muhammad for the achievement of God's will on earth. In the early seventh century, the southern Arab tribal confederations lacked cohesiveness and unity and were constantly warring. The Islamic notion of an absolute higher authority transcended the boundaries of individual tribal units and fostered the political consolidation of the tribal confederations. All authority came from God through Muhammad. Within the umma, the law of God was discerned and applied through Muhammad.

The Qur'an prescribes a strict code of moral behavior. A Muslim must recite the profession of faith in God and in Muhammad as his prophet: "There is no God but

Chronology

622	Muhammad and followers emigrate from Mecca to Medina
632	Abu Bakr becomes first caliph
642	Muslim defeat of Persians marks end of Sassanid empire
650–1000	Evolution of core Muslim doctrines and beliefs
651	Publication of Qur'an
661	Ali assassinated; split between Shi'ites and Sunnis
711	Muslims defeat Visigothic kingdom in Spain
750–1258	Abbasid caliphate
762	Baghdad founded by Abbasids
869–883	Zanj (slave) revolts
900–1300	Height of Muslim learning and creativity
950–1100	Entry on a large scale of Turks into the Middle East
1000–1350	Foundation of many madrasas
1055	Baghdad falls to Seljuk Turks
1099–1187	Christian Crusaders hold Jerusalem
ca. 1100–1300	Progressive loss of most of Spain to the reconquista
1126–1198	Averroës writes on the works of Aristotle
1258	Mongols capture Baghdad and kill last Abbasid caliph

hadith *Collections of the sayings of and anecdotes about Muhammad.*

Sunna *An Arabic term meaning "trodden path." The term refers to the deeds and sayings of Muhammad, which constitute the obligatory example for Muslim life.*

umma *A community of those who share a religious faith and commitment rather than a tribal tie.*

God, and Muhammad is his Prophet." A believer must also pray five times a day, fast and pray during the sacred month of Ramadan, make a pilgrimage to the holy city of Mecca once during his or her lifetime, and give alms to the Muslim poor. These fundamental obligations are known as the **Five Pillars of Islam.**

Islam forbids alcoholic beverages and gambling. It condemns usury in business—that is, lending money and charging the borrower interest—and taking advantage of market demand for products by charging high prices. Most scholars hold that compared with earlier Arab standards, the Qur'an set forth an austere sexual code. Muslim jurisprudence condemned licentious behavior by both men and women and specified the same punishments for both. (By contrast, contemporary Frankish law punished prostitutes, but not their clients.)

Islam warns about Judgment Day and the importance of the life to come. Like the Christian Judgment Day, on that day God will separate the saved and the damned. The Qur'an describes in detail the frightful tortures with which God will punish the damned and the heavenly rewards of the saved and the blessed. The Muslim vision of Heaven features lush green gardens surrounded by refreshing streams. There the saved, clothed in rich silks, lounge on brocade couches, nibbling ripe fruits, sipping delicious beverages, and enjoying the companionship of physically attractive people.

Five Pillars of Islam *The basic tenets of the Islamic faith; they include reciting a profession of faith in God and in Muhammad as God's prophet, prayer five times daily, fasting and prayer during the month of Ramadan, a pilgrimage to Mecca once in one's lifetime, and contribution of alms to the poor.*

Primary Source:
The Qur'an
These selections contain a number of the tenets of Islam, and shed light on the connections among Islam, Judaism, and Christianity.

ISLAMIC STATES AND THEIR EXPANSION

What forms of government did Islam establish, and how did they contribute to the rapid spread of Islam?

According to Muslim tradition, Muhammad's preaching at first did not appeal to many people. Legend has it that for the first three years he attracted only fourteen believers. Muhammad preached a transformation of the social order and called for the destruction of the idols in the Ka'ba. The townspeople of Mecca turned against him, and he and his followers were forced to flee to Medina. This *hijra*, or emigration, occurred in 622, and Muslims later dated the beginning of their era from that event.

At Medina, Muhammad attracted increasing numbers of believers, and his teachings began to have an impact. By the time he died in 632, he had welded together all the Bedouin tribes. After the Prophet's death, Islam eventually emerged not only as a religious faith but also as a gradually expanding culture of worldwide significance (see Map 8.1).

In the sixth century, two powerful empires divided the Middle East: the Greek-Byzantine empire centered at Constantinople and the Persian-Sassanid empire concentrated at Ctesiphon (near Baghdad in present-day Iraq). The Byzantine Empire stood for Hellenistic culture and championed Christianity. The Sassanid empire espoused Persian cultural traditions and favored the religious faith known as Zoroastrianism. Although each empire maintained an official state religion, neither possessed religious unity. Both had sizable Jewish populations, and within Byzantium sects whom Orthodox Greeks considered heretical—Monophysites and Nestorians—served as a politically divisive force. Between the fourth and sixth centuries, these two empires had fought each other fiercely to expand their territories and to control and tax the rich trade coming from Arabia and the Indian Ocean region.

The second and third successors of Muhammad, Umar (r. 634–644) and Uthman (r. 644–656; see page 197), launched a two-pronged attack. One force moved north from Arabia against the Byzantine provinces of Syria and Palestine. The Greek armies there could not halt them (see page 165). From Syria, the Muslims conquered the rich province of Egypt, taking the commercial and intellectual hub of Alexandria in 642. Simultaneously, Arab armies swept into the Sassanid empire. The Muslim defeat of the Persians at Nihawand in 642 signaled the collapse of the Sassanid empire.[1]

● **Dome of the Rock, Jerusalem** Completed in 691 and revered by Muslims as the site where Muhammad ascended to Heaven, the Dome of the Rock is the oldest surviving Islamic sanctuary and, after Mecca and Medina, the holiest place in Islam. Although influenced by Byzantine and Persian architecture, the 700 feet of carefully selected Qur'anic inscriptions and vegetal motifs, however, represent distinctly Arabic features. *(Sonia Halliday Photographs)*

The Muslims continued their drive eastward. In the mid-seventh century, they occupied the province of Khurasan, where the city of Merv became the center of Muslim control over eastern Persia and the base for campaigns farther east. By 700 the Muslims had crossed the Oxus River and swept toward Kabul, today the capital of Afghanistan. They penetrated Kazakhstan and then seized Tashkent, one of the oldest cities in Central Asia. The clash of Muslim horsemen with a Chinese army at the Talas River in 751 marked the farthest Islamic penetration into Central Asia. From southern Persia, a Muslim force marched into the Indus Valley in northern India and in 713 founded an Islamic community there. Beginning in the eleventh century, Muslim dynasties from Ghazni in Afghanistan carried Islam deeper into the Indian subcontinent.

Likewise to the west, Arab forces moved across North Africa, crossed the Strait of Gibraltar, and in 711 at the Guadalete River easily defeated the Visigothic kingdom of Spain. A few Christian princes supported by Merovingian rulers held out in the Cantabrian Mountains, but the Muslims controlled most of Spain until the thirteenth century.

Reasons for the Spread of Islam

By the beginning of the eleventh century, the crescent of Islam flew from the Iberian heartlands to northern India. How can this rapid and remarkable expansion be explained? Muslim historians attribute Islamic victories to God's support for the Islamic faith. True, the Arabs possessed a religious fervor that their enemies could not equal. Perhaps they were convinced of the necessity of the **jihad,** or holy war. The Qur'an does not precisely explain the concept. Thus modern Islamicists, as well as early Muslims, have debated the meaning of jihad, sometimes called the sixth pillar of Islam. Some students hold that it signifies the individual struggle against sin and toward perfection on "the straight path" of Islam. Other scholars claim that jihad has a social and communal implication—a militancy as part of a holy war against unbelievers living in territories outside the control of the Muslim community. The Qur'an states, "Fight those in the way of God who fight you. . . . Fight those wheresoever you find them, and expel them from the place they had turned you out from. . . . Fight until

jihad *"Holy War," an Arabic term that some scholars interpret as the individual struggle against sin and others interpret as having a social and communal implication.*

MAP 8.1 **The Islamic World, ca. 900** The rapid expansion of Islam in a relatively short span of time testifies to the Arabs' superior fighting skills, religious zeal, and economic ambition as well as to their enemies' weakness. Plague, famine, and political troubles in Sassanid Persia contributed to Muslim victory there.

sedition comes to an end and the law of God [prevails]" (Qur'an 4:74–76).[2] Since the Qur'an suggests that God sent the Prophet to establish justice on earth, it would follow that justice will take effect only where Islam triumphs. Just as Christians have a missionary duty to spread their faith, so Muslims have the obligation, as individuals and as a community, to extend the power of Islam. For some Islam came to mean the struggle to expand Islam, and those involved in that struggle were assured happiness in the world to come.

The Muslim practice of establishing garrison cities or camps facilitated expansion. Rather than scattering as landlords of peasant farmers over conquered lands, Arab soldiers remained together in garrison cities, where their Arab ethnicity, tribal organization, religion, and military success set them apart.

diwān *Unit of government.*

All soldiers were registered in the **diwān,** an administrative organ adopted from the Persians or Byzantines. Soldiers received a monthly ration of food for themselves and their families and an annual cash stipend. In return, they had to be available for military service. Fixed salaries, regular pay, and the lure of battlefield booty attracted rugged tribesmen from Arabia. Except for the Berbers of North Africa, whom the Arabs could not pacify, Muslim armies initially did not seek to convert or recruit warriors from conquered peoples. Instead, conquered peoples became slaves. In later campaigns to the east, many recruits were recent converts to Islam from Christian, Persian, and Berber backgrounds. The assurance of army wages secured the loyalty of these very diverse men. Still, in the first two centuries of Muslim expansion, Arab military victories probably resulted as much from the weaknesses of their enemies (the Sassanid Persians and the Byzantines) as from Arab strength.

The Muslim conquest of Syria offers an example of the mixed motives that propelled early Muslim expansion. Syria had been under Byzantine Christian or Roman rule for centuries. Arab caravans knew the market towns of southern Syria and the rich commercial centers of the north, such as Edessa, Aleppo, and Damascus. Syria's economic prosperity probably attracted the Muslims, and perhaps Muhammad saw the land as a potential means of support for the poor who flooded Medina. Syria also contained sites important to the faith: Jerusalem, where Jesus and other prophets mentioned in the Qur'an had lived and preached, and Hebron, the traditional burial place of Abraham, the father of monotheism.

How did the conquered peoples make sense of their new subordinate situations? Defeated peoples almost never commented on the actions and motives of the Arabs. Jews and Christians both tried to minimize the damage done to their former status and played down the gains of their new masters. Christians regarded the conquering Arabs as God's punishment for their sins, while Jews saw the Arabs as instruments for their deliverance from Greek and Sassanid persecution.[3]

> **Primary Source:**
> **The Constitution of Medina: Muslims and Jews at the Dawn of Islam**
> *Learn how Muhammad, whose teaching was at first rejected in Mecca, met with success in Medina—in part by allying himself with the local Jewish community.*

The Caliphate

When Muhammad died in 632, he left a large Muslim umma, but this community stood in danger of disintegrating into separate tribal groups. How was the vast empire that came into existence within one hundred years of his death to be governed? Neither the Qur'an nor the Sunna offered guidance for the succession.

In this crisis, according to tradition, a group of Muhammad's ablest followers elected Abu Bakr (573–634), a close supporter of the Prophet and his father-in-law, and hailed him as caliph, a term combining the ideas of leader, successor, and deputy (of the Prophet). This election marked the victory of the concept of a universal community of Muslim believers.

Because the law of the Qur'an was to guide the community, there had to be an authority to enforce the law. Muslim teaching held that the law was paramount. God is the sole source of the law, and the ruler is bound to obey the law. Government exists not to make law but to enforce it. Muslim teaching also maintained that there is no distinction between the temporal and spiritual domains: social law is a basic strand in the fabric of comprehensive religious law. Thus religious belief and political power are inextricably intertwined: the first sanctifies the second, and the second sustains the first. The creation of Islamic law in an institutional sense took three or four centuries and is one of the great achievements of medieval Islam.

In the two years of his rule (632–634), Abu Bakr governed on the basis of his personal prestige within the Muslim umma. He sent out military expeditions, collected taxes, dealt with tribes on behalf of the entire community, and led the community in prayer. Gradually, under Abu Bakr's first three successors, Umar (r. 634–644), Uthman (r. 644–656), and Ali (r. 656–661), the caliphate emerged as an institution. Umar succeeded in exerting his authority over the Bedouin tribes involved in ongoing conquests. Uthman asserted the right of the caliph to protect the economic interests of the entire umma. Uthman's publication of the definitive text of the Qur'an showed his concern for the unity of the umma. But Uthman's enemies accused him of nepotism—of using his position to put his family in powerful and lucrative jobs—and of unnecessary cruelty. Opposition coalesced around Ali, and when Uthman was assassinated in 656, Ali was chosen to succeed him.

The issue of responsibility for Uthman's murder raised the question of whether Ali's accession was legitimate. Uthman's cousin Mu'awiya, a member of the Umayyad family who had built a power base as governor of Syria, refused to recognize Ali as caliph. In the ensuing civil war, Ali was assassinated, and Mu'awiya (r. 661–680) assumed the caliphate. Mu'awiya founded the Umayyad Dynasty and shifted the capital of the Islamic state from Medina in Arabia to Damascus in Syria. When the Umayyad family assumed the leadership of Islam, there was no Muslim state, no formal impersonal institutions of government exercising jurisdiction over a very wide area. The first four caliphs were elected by their peers, and the theory of an elected caliphate remained the Islamic legal ideal. Three of the four "patriarchs," as they were called, were murdered, however, and civil war ended the elective caliphate. Beginning with Mu'awiya, the office of caliph was in fact, but never in theory, dynastic. Two successive dynasties, the Umayyad (661–750) and the Abbasid (750–1258), held the caliphate.

From its inception the caliphate rested on the theoretical principle that Muslim political and religious unity transcended tribalism. Mu'awiya sought to enhance the power of the caliphate by making the tribal leaders dependent on him for concessions and special benefits. At the same time, his control of a loyal and well-disciplined army enabled him to develop the caliphate in an authoritarian direction. Through intimidation he forced the tribal leaders to accept his son Yazid as his heir, thereby establishing the dynastic principle of succession. By distancing himself from a simple life within the umma and withdrawing into the palace that he built at Damascus, and by surrounding himself with symbols and ceremony, Mu'awiya laid the foundations for an elaborate caliphal court. Many of Mu'awiya's innovations were designed to protect him from assassination. A new official, the *hajib,* or chamberlain, restricted access to the caliph, who received visitors seated on a throne surrounded by bodyguards.

The assassination of Ali and the assumption of the caliphate by Mu'awiya had another profound consequence. It gave rise to a fundamental division in the umma and in Muslim theology. Ali had claimed the caliphate on the basis of family ties—he was Muhammad's cousin and son-in-law. When Ali was murdered, his followers argued—partly because of the blood tie, partly because Muhammad had designated Ali **imam,** or leader in community prayer—that Ali had been the Prophet's designated successor.

imam *The leader in community prayer.*

Shi'ites *Arabic term meaning "supporters of Ali"; they make up one of the two main divisions of Islam.*

Sunnis *Members of the larger of the two main sects of Islam; the division between Sunnis and Shi'ites began in a dispute about succession to Muhammad, but over time many differences in theology developed.*

ulama *A group of religious scholars whom Sunnis trust to interpret the Qur'an and the Sunna.*

● **Qibla Compass** Religious precepts inspired Muslims to considerable scientific knowledge. For example, the Second Pillar of Islam requires them to pray five times a day facing the Ka'ba in Mecca. To determine the direction of Mecca, called the *qibla,* Muslims adapted the compass, first invented in China. Modern worshipers still use the qibla compass. *(Robert Selkowitz)*

These supporters of Ali were called **Shi'ites,** or *Shi'at Ali,* or simply *Shi'a*—Arabic terms all meaning "supporters" or "partisans" of Ali. In succeeding generations, opponents of the Umayyad Dynasty emphasized their blood descent from Ali and claimed to possess divine knowledge that Muhammad had given them as his heirs.

Other Muslims adhered to the practice and beliefs of the umma based on the precedents of the Prophet. They were called **Sunnis,** which derived from Sunna (examples from Muhammad's life). When a situation arose for which the Qur'an offered no solution, Sunni scholars searched for a precedent in the Sunna, which gained an authority comparable to the Qur'an itself.

Both Sunnis and Shi'ites maintain that authority within Islam lies first in the Qur'an and then in the Sunna. Who interprets these sources? Shi'ites claim that the imam does, for he is invested with divine grace and insight. Sunnis insist that interpretation comes from the consensus of the **ulama,** the group of religious scholars.

The Umayyad caliphs were Sunnis, and throughout the Umayyad period the Shi'ites constituted a major source of discontent. Shi'ite rebellions expressed religious opposition in political terms. The Shi'ites condemned the Umayyads as worldly and sensual rulers, in contrast to the pious true successors of Muhammad. The Abbasid clan, which based its claim to the caliphate on the descent of Abbas, Muhammad's uncle, exploited the situation. The Abbasids agitated the Shi'ites, encouraged dissension among tribal factions, and contrasted Abbasid piety with the pleasure-loving style of the Umayyads.

The Abbasid Caliphate

In 747 Abu' al-Abbas led a rebellion against the Umayyads, and in 750 he won general recognition as caliph. Damascus had served as the headquarters of Umayyad rule. Abu' al-Abbas's successor, al-Mansur (r. 754–775), founded the city of Baghdad in 762 and made it his capital. Thus the geographical center of the caliphate shifted eastward to former Sassanid territories. The first three Abbasid caliphs crushed their opponents, eliminated their Shi'ite supporters, and created a new ruling elite drawn from newly converted Persian families that had traditionally served the ruler. The Abbasid revolution established a basis for rule and citizenship more cosmopolitan and Islamic than the narrow, elitist, and Arab basis that had characterized Umayyad government.

The Abbasids worked to identify their rule with Islam. They patronized the ulama, built mosques, and supported the development of Islamic scholarship. Moreover, under the Umayyads the Muslim state had been a federation of regional and tribal armies; during the Abbasid caliphate, provincial governors gradually won semi-independent power. Although at first Muslims represented only a small minority of the conquered peoples, Abbasid rule provided the religious-political milieu in which Islam gained, over time, the allegiance of the vast majority of the populations from Spain to Afghanistan.

The Abbasids also borrowed heavily from Persian culture. Following Persian tradition, the Abbasid caliphs claimed to rule by divine right, as reflected in the change of their title from "successor of the Prophet" to "deputy of God." A magnificent palace with hundreds of attendants and elaborate court ceremonial deliberately isolated the caliph from the people he ruled. Subjects had to bow before the caliph, kissing the ground, a symbol of his absolute power.

Under the third caliph, Harun al-Rashid (r. 786–809), Baghdad emerged as a flourishing commercial, artistic, and scientific center—the greatest city in Islam and one of the most cosmopolitan cities in the world. Its population of about 1 million people—an astoundingly large size in preindustrial times—represented a huge demand for goods and services. Baghdad served as an entrepôt for textiles, slaves, and foodstuffs coming from Oman, East Africa, and India. Harun al-Rashid established a library that translated Greek medical and philosophical texts. The scholar Hunayn ib Ishaq al-Ibadi (808–873) translated Galen's medical works into Arabic and made Baghdad a center for the study and practice of medicine. Likewise, impetus was given to the study of astronomy, and through a program of astronomical observations, Muslim astronomers sought to correct and complement Ptolemaic astronomy. Above all, studies in Qur'anic textual analysis, history, poetry, law, and philosophy—all in Arabic—reflected the development of a distinctly Islamic literary and scientific culture.

> **Primary Source:**
> **Book of Travels**
> *Read how the caliph of Baghdad appointed a Jew named Daniel as "Head of the Captivity of all Israel."*

The early Abbasid caliphal court was magnificent. In the caliph's palace complexes, maintained by staffs numbering in the tens of thousands, an important visitor would be conducted through elaborate rituals and confronted with indications of the caliph's majesty and power: rank upon rank of lavishly appointed guards, pages, servants, slaves, and other retainers; lush parks full of exotic wild beasts; and fantastic arrays of gold and silver objects, ornamented furniture, precious carpets and tapestries, pools of mercury, and ingenious mechanical devices. The most famous of the mechanical devices was a gold and silver tree with leaves that rustled, branches that swayed, and mechanical birds that sang as the breezes blew.

An important innovation of the Abbasids was the use of slaves as soldiers. The caliph al-Mu'taşim (r. 833–842) acquired several thousand Turkish slaves who were converted to Islam and employed in military service. Scholars have offered varied explanations for this practice: that the use of slave soldiers was a response to a manpower shortage; that as heavy cavalry with expertise as horse archers, the Turks had military skills superior to those of the Arabs and other peoples; and that al-Mu'taşim felt he could trust the Turks more than the Arabs, Persians, Khurasans, and other recruits. In any case, slave soldiers—later including Slavs, Indians, and sub-Saharan blacks—became a standard feature of Muslim armies in the Middle East down to the twentieth century.

Administration of the Islamic Territories

The Islamic conquests brought into being a new imperial system. The Muslims adopted the patterns of administration used by the Byzantines in Egypt and Syria and by the Sassanids in Persia. Arab **emirs,** or governors, were appointed and given overall responsibility for good order, maintenance of the armed forces, and tax collection. Below them, experienced native officials—Greeks, Syrians, Copts (Egyptian Christians)—remained in office. Thus there was continuity with previous administrations.

The Umayyad caliphate witnessed the further development of the imperial administration. At the head stood the caliph, who led the holy war against unbelievers. Theoretically, he had the ultimate responsibility for the interpretation of the sacred law. In practice, the ulama interpreted the law as revealed in the Qur'an and the Sunna. In the course of time, the ulama's interpretations constituted a rich body of law, the **shari'a,** which covered social, criminal, political, commercial, and ritual matters. The ulama enjoyed great prestige in the Muslim community and was consulted by the caliph on difficult legal and spiritual matters. The **qadis,** or judges, who were well versed in the sacred law, carried out the judicial functions of the state. Nevertheless, Muslim law prescribed that all people have access to the caliph, and he set aside special times for hearing petitions and for the direct redress of grievances.

The central administrative organ was the diwān, which collected the taxes that paid soldiers' salaries (see page 196) and financed charitable and public works that the caliph undertook, such as aid to the poor and the construction of mosques, irrigation works, and public baths. As Arab conquests extended into Spain, Central Asia, and Afghanistan, lines of communication had to be kept open. Emirs and other officials, remote from the capital at Damascus and later Baghdad, might revolt. Thus a relay network was established to convey letters and intelligence reports between the capital and the various outposts.

The early Abbasid period witnessed considerable economic expansion and population growth, so the work of government became more complicated. New and specialized departments emerged, each with a hierarchy of officials. The most important new official was the **vizier,** a position that the Abbasids adopted from the Persians. The vizier was the caliph's chief assistant, advising the caliph on matters of general policy, supervising the bureaucratic administration, and, under the caliph, overseeing the army, the provincial governors, and relations with foreign governments. As the caliphs withdrew from leading Friday prayers and other routine functions, the viziers gradually assumed power. But the authority and power of the vizier usually depended on the caliph's personality and direct involvement in state affairs. Many viziers used their offices for personal gain and wealth. Although some careers ended with the vizier's execution, there were always candidates seeking the job.

emirs *Arab governors who were given overall responsibility for good order, maintenance of the armed forces, and tax collection.*

shari'a *Muslim law, which covers social, criminal, political, commercial, and religious matters.*

qadis *Muslim judges who carried out the judicial functions of the state.*

vizier *The caliph's chief assistant.*

FRAGMENTATION AND MILITARY CHALLENGES (900–1400)

How were the Muslim lands governed from 900 to 1400, and what new challenges did they face?

In theory, the caliph and his central administration governed the whole empire. In practice, the many parts of the empire enjoyed considerable local independence. As long as public order was maintained and taxes were forwarded, the central government rarely interfered. The enormous distance separating many provinces from the imperial capital, and the long time it took to travel between them by horse or camel,

● **Ivory Chest of Pamplona, Spain**   The court of the Spanish Umayyads prized small, intricately carved ivory chests, often made in a royal workshop and used to store precious perfumes. This exquisite side panel depicts an eleventh-century caliph flanked by two attendants. An inscription on the front translates as "In the Name of God. Blessings from God, goodwill, and happiness." *(Museo Navarra, Pamplona/Institut Amatller d'Art Hispanic)*

made it difficult for the caliph to prevent provinces from breaking away. Particularism and ethnic or tribal loyalties, combined with strength and fierce ambition, led to the creation of local dynasties in much of the Islamic world, including Spain, Iran, Central Asia, northern India, and Egypt. None of these states repudiated Islam, but they did stop sending tax revenues to Baghdad. Moreover, most states became involved with costly wars against their neighbors in their attempts to expand. Sometimes these conflicts were worsened by Sunni-Shi'ite antagonisms.

One of the first to break away from the Baghdad-centered caliphate was Spain. In 755 an Umayyad prince who had escaped death at the hands of the triumphant Abbasids and fled to Spain set up an independent regime at Córdoba (see Map 8.1). Others soon followed. In 800 the emir in Tunisia in North Africa set himself up as an independent ruler and refused to place the caliph's name on the local coinage. In 820 Tahir, the son of a slave, was rewarded with the governorship of Khurasan because he had supported the caliphate. Once there, Tahir ruled independently of Baghdad, not even mentioning the caliph's name in the traditional Friday prayers in recognition of caliphal authority.

In 969 the Fatimids, a Shi'ite dynasty who claimed descent from Muhammad's daughter Fatima, conquered the Abbasid province of Egypt. The Fatimids founded the city of Cairo as their capital. They extended their rule over North Africa, with the result that for a century or so, Shi'ites were in ascendancy in much of the western parts of the Islamic world.

In 946 a Shi'ite Iranian clan overran Iraq and occupied Baghdad. The caliph was forced to recognize the leader as commander-in-chief and to allow the celebration of Shi'ite festivals—though the caliph and most of the people were Sunnis. A year later, the caliph was accused of plotting against his new masters, snatched from his throne, dragged through the streets, and blinded. Blinding was a practice adopted from the Byzantines as a way of rendering a ruler incapable of carrying out his duties. This incident marks the practical collapse of the Abbasid caliphate. Abbasid caliphs, however, remained as puppets of a series of military commanders and symbols of Muslim unity until the Mongols killed the last Abbasid caliph in 1258.

Egypt, too, saw successive overlords. The Ayyubids were able to take over Egypt from the Fatimids, and in 1250 the Mamluks replaced the Ayyubids and ruled Egypt until the Ottoman conquest in 1517. The Mamluks were originally slave soldiers, and they continued to staff their armies with slaves, mostly unconverted Turks or Christians, acquired from the northern fringes of Muslim lands.

The Ascendancy of the Turks

In the mid-tenth century, the Turks began to enter the Islamic world in large numbers. First appearing in Mongolia in the sixth century, groups of Turks gradually appeared across the grasslands of Eurasia (see Chapter 11). Skilled horsemen, they became prime targets for slave raids, as they made good slave soldiers. Once they understood that Muslims could not be captured for slaves, more and more of them

● **Great Mosque at Isfahan in Persia** Begun in the late eighth century and added to over the centuries, the Great Mosque in Isfahan is one of the masterpieces of Islamic architecture. The huge dome and the vaulted niches around the courtyard are covered with blue, turquoise, white, and yellow tile. *(© Roger Wood/Corbis)*

converted to Islam (and often became *ghazi,* holy warriors, who raided unconverted Turks to capture slaves). The first to convert accepted Sunni Islam near Bukhara (then a great Persian commercial and intellectual center).

Seljuk Turks overran Persia in the 1020s and 1030s, then pushed into Iraq and Syria. Baghdad fell to them on December 18, 1055, and the caliph became a puppet of the Turkish *sultan*—literally, "he with authority." The Turks rapidly gave up pastoralism and took up the sedentary style of life of the people they governed.

The Turks brought to the Islamic world badly needed military strength. They played a major part in recovering Jerusalem after it was held by the European Crusaders for nearly a century between 1099 and 1187. They also were important in preventing the later Crusades from accomplishing much. Turks also became staunch Sunnis and led a campaign against Shi'ites.

The influx of Turks from 950 on also helped provide a new expansive dynamic. At the battle of Manzikert in 1071, Seljuk Turks broke through Byzantine border defenses, opening Anatolia to Turkish migration. Over the next couple of centuries, perhaps a million Turks entered the area—including bands of ghazis (holy warriors) and dervishes (Sufi brotherhoods). Seljuk Turks set up the Sultanate of Rum, which lasted until the Mongols invaded in 1243. With the Turks came many learned men from the Persian-speaking east. Over time, many of the Christians in Anatolia converted to Islam and became fluent in Turkish.

The Mongol Invasions

In the early thirteenth century the Mongols arrived in the Middle East. Originally from the grasslands of Mongolia (see pages 296–298), in 1206 they had elected Chinggis Khan (1162–1227) as their leader, and he welded Mongol, Tatar, and Turkish tribes into a strong confederation that rapidly subdued neighboring settled societies. After conquering much of north China, they swept westward, leaving a trail of blood and destruction. The Mongols used terror as a weapon, and out of fear many cities surrendered without a fight.

In 1219–1221, the years the Mongols first reached the Islamic lands, the areas from Iran through the central Asian cities of Herat and Samarkand were part of the kingdom of Khwarizm. The ruler—the son of a Turkish slave who had risen to governor of a province—was a conqueror himself, having conquered much of Persia. He had the audacity to execute Chinggis's envoy who demanded his surrender. Chinggis retaliated with a force of a hundred thousand soldiers that sacked city after city, often slaughtering the residents or enslaving them and sending them to Mongolia. Millions are said to have died. The irrigation systems that were needed for agriculture in this dry region were destroyed as well.

Not many Mongol forces were left in Persia after the campaign of 1219–1221, and another campaign was sent in 1237, which captured Isfahan. In 1251 the decision was taken to push farther west. Chinggis Khan's grandson Hülegü (1217–1265) led the attack on the Abbasids. His armies sacked and burned Baghdad and killed the last Abbasid caliph in 1258. Baghdad and the Abbasid caliphate fell in 1258, Damascus in 1260. Mamluk soldiers from Egypt, however, were able to withstand the Mongols and win a major victory at Ayn Jalut in Syria, which has been credited with saving Egypt and the Muslim lands in North Africa and perhaps Spain. It should be pointed out, however, that in 1260 the Great Khan died, and the top Mongol generals withdrew to Mongolia for the selection of the next Great Khan.

Hülegü and his descendants ruled the central Muslim lands (referred to as the Il-Khanate) for eighty years. In 1295 his descendant Ghazan embraced Islam and worked for the revival of Muslim culture. As the Turks had done earlier, the Mongols, once converted, injected new vigor into the faith and spirit of Islam. In the Il-Khanate, the Mongols governed through Persian viziers and native financial officials.

● **Jonah and the Whale** When the Mongol ruler Ghazan asked his chief minister, the remarkable Persian polymath Rashid al-Din—a Jew by birth who converted to Islam and a physician by training—to write a history of the Mongols in Persia, he responded with the *Collection of Histories,* which treats China, India, the Jews, Muhammad and the caliphs, pre- and post-Islamic Persia, even the Franks (Europeans). To explain the section on the Jews, a Chinese artist inserted this illustration of the Old Testament prophet Jonah. The Chinese artist had never seen a whale, but he possessed imagination and mastery of movement. *(Courtesy of Edinburgh University Library, Or Ms 20, fol 23N)*

MUSLIM SOCIETY: THE LIFE OF THE PEOPLE

What social distinctions were important in Muslim society?

When the Prophet appeared, Arab society consisted of independent Bedouin tribal groups loosely held together by loyalty to a strong leader and by the belief that all members of a tribe were descended from a common ancestor. Heads of families elected the *sheik,* or tribal chief. He was usually chosen from among elite warrior families who believed their birth made them superior. According to the Qur'an, however, birth counted for nothing; zeal for Islam was the only criterion for honor: "O ye folk, verily we have created you male and female. . . . Verily the most honourable of you in the sight of God is the most pious of you."[4] The idea of social equality was a basic Muslim doctrine.

When Muhammad defined social equality, he was thinking about equality among Muslims alone. But even among Muslims, a sense of pride in ancestry could not be destroyed by a stroke of the pen. Claims of birth remained strong among the first Muslims, and after Islam spread outside of Arabia, full-blooded Arab tribesmen regarded themselves as superior to foreign converts.

The Classes of Society

In the Umayyad period, Muslim society consisted of several classes. At the top were the caliph's household and the ruling Arab Muslims. Descended from Bedouin tribespeople and composed of warriors, veterans, governing officials, and town settlers, this class constituted the ruling elite. Because birth continued to determine membership, it was more a caste than a class. It was also a relatively small group, greatly outnumbered by Muslim villagers and country people.

Converts constituted the second class in Islamic society. Converts to Islam had to attach themselves to one of the Arab tribes as clients. They greatly resented having to do this, since they believed they represented a culture superior to the culture of the Arab tribespeople. From the Muslim converts eventually came the members of the commercial and learned professions—merchants, traders, teachers, doctors, artists, and interpreters of the shari'a. Second-class citizenship led some Muslim converts to adopt Shi'ism (see page 198) and other unorthodox doctrines inimical to the caliphate. Over the centuries, Berber, Copt, Persian, Aramaean, and other converts to Islam intermarried with their Muslim conquerors. Gradually, assimilation united peoples of various ethnic and "national" backgrounds.

Dhimmis, or "protected peoples"—Jews, Christians, and Zoroastrians—formed the third class. They were allowed to practice their religions, maintain their houses of worship, and conduct their business affairs as long as they gave unequivocal recognition to Muslim political supremacy and paid a small tax. Because many Jews and Christians were found to be well educated, they were often appointed to high positions in provincial capitals as well as in Damascus and Baghdad. Restrictions placed on Christians and Jews were not severe, and both groups seem to have thrived under Muslim rule. Outbursts of violence against Christians and Jews were rare. The social position of the "protected peoples" deteriorated during the Crusades (see pages 362–365) and the Mongol invasions, when there was a general rise of religious loyalties. At those times, Muslims suspected the dhimmis, often rightly, of collaborating with the enemies of Islam.

What was the fate of Jews living under Islam? How does their experience compare with that of Jews living in Christian Europe? Recent scholarship shows that in Europe, Jews were first marginalized in the Christian social order, then completely expelled from it. In Islam, though marginalized, Jews participated fully in commercial and professional activities, some attaining economic equality with their Muslim counterparts. The seventeenth Sura (chapter) of the Qur'an, titled Bani Isra'il, "The Children of Israel," accords to the Jews a special respect because they were "the people of the Book." Also, Islamic culture was an urban and commercial culture that gave the merchant considerable respect; medieval Christian culture was basically rural and agricultural and did not revere the business person.

> **dhimmis** *A term meaning "protected peoples"; they included Jews, Christians, and Zoroastrians.*

Slavery

At the bottom of the social scale were slaves. Slavery had long existed in the ancient Middle East, and the Qur'an accepted slavery much the way the Old and New Testaments did. But the Qur'an prescribes just and humane treatment of slaves. A master should feed and clothe his slaves adequately; give them moderate, not excessive, work; and not punish them severely. The Qur'an also explicitly encourages the freeing of slaves and urges owners whose slaves ask for their freedom to give them the opportunity to buy it.

Muslim expansion ensured a steady flow of slaves captured in war. The great Muslim commander Musa ibn Nusayr, himself the son of a Christian enslaved in Iraq, is reputed to have taken three hundred thousand prisoners of war in his North African campaigns (708–818) and thirty thousand virgins from the Visigothic nobility of Spain. (These numbers are surely greatly inflated, as most medieval numbers are.) Every soldier, from general to private, had a share of slaves from captured prisoners.

Women slaves worked as cooks, cleaners, laundresses, and nursemaids. A few performed as singers, musicians, dancers, and reciters of poetry. Many women also served as concubines. Not only rulers but also high officials and rich merchants owned many

● **Slaves Dancing** A few women slaves performed as dancers, singers, and musicians, usually before an elite audience of rulers, officials, and wealthy merchants. This reconstructed wall-painting adorned a harem in a royal palace in Samarra. *(Bildarchiv Preussischer Kulturbesitz/Art Resource, NY)*

concubines. Down the economic ladder, artisans and tradesmen often had a few concubines who assumed domestic as well as sexual tasks.

According to tradition, the seclusion of women in the harem protected their virtue (see page 209), and when men had the means the harem was secured by eunuch guards. The use of eunuch guards seems to have been a practice Muslims adopted from the Byzantines and Persians. Early Muslim law forbade castration, so in the early Islamic period Muslims secured eunuchs from European, African, and Central Asian slave markets. In the tenth century the caliph of Baghdad had seven thousand black eunuchs and four thousand white ones in his palace. In contrast to China, where only the emperor could have eunuch servants, in the Muslim world, the well-to-do could purchase them to guard their harems. Because of the insatiable demand for eunuch guards, the cost of eunuchs was very high, perhaps seven times that of uncastrated male slaves.

Muslims also employed eunuchs as secretaries, tutors, and commercial agents, possibly because unlike men with ordinary desires, eunuchs were said to be more tractable and dependable. Besides administrative, business, or domestic services, male slaves, eunuchs or not, were also set to work as longshoremen on the docks, as oarsmen on ships, in construction crews, in factories, and in gold and silver mines.

Male slaves also fought as soldiers. Any free person could buy a slave, but only a ruler could own military slaves. In the ninth century, the rulers of Tunisia formed a special corps of black military slaves, and at the end of that century the Tulunid rulers of Egypt built an army of twenty-four thousand white and forty-five thousand black slaves. The Fatimid rulers of Egypt (969–1171) raised large black battalions, and a Persian visitor to Cairo between 1046 and 1049 estimated an army of a hundred thousand slaves, of whom thirty thousand were black soldiers.

Slavery in the Islamic world differed in at least two fundamental ways from the slavery later practiced in South and North America. First, Muslims did not identify slavery with blackness as Europeans did in the Americas. The general and widespread use of Caucasian slaves in Islamic societies made that connection impossible. Second, slavery in the Islamic world was not the virtual equivalent of commercial plantation agriculture as practiced in the southern United States, the Caribbean, and Brazil in the eighteenth and nineteenth centuries. True, in the tenth century, large numbers of black slaves worked on the date plantations in northeastern Arabia. But massive revolts of black slaves called Zanj from East Africa, provoked by mercilessly harsh labor conditions in the salt flats and on the sugar and cotton plantations of southwestern Persia, erupted in 869. Gathering momentum, the Zanj captured the rich cities of Ahwaz, Basra, and Wasit and threatened Baghdad. Only the strenuous efforts of the commander of the caliph's armies, which were composed of Turkish slaves and included naval as well as land forces, halted and gradually crushed the Zanj in 883. The long and destructive Zanj revolt ended the Muslim experiment with plantation agriculture.[5]

Women in Classical Islamic Society

Arab tribal law gave women virtually no legal status. At birth girls could be buried alive by their fathers. They were sold into marriage by their guardians. Their husbands could terminate the union at will. And women had virtually no property or succession rights. The Qur'an sought to improve the social position of women.

The hadith—records of what Muhammad said and did, and what believers in the first two centuries after his death believed he said and did (see page 193)—also provide information about his wives. Some hadith portray the Prophet's wives as subject to common human frailties, such as jealousy; other hadith report miraculous events in their lives. Most hadith describe the wives as "mothers of the believers"—models of piety and righteousness whose every act illustrates their commitment to promoting God's order on earth by personal example.

Although the hadith usually depict women in terms of moral virtue, domesticity, and saintly ideals, the hadith also show some prominent women in "public" and political roles. For example, Aisha, daughter of the first caliph and probably Muhammad's favorite wife, played a "leading role" in rallying support for the movement opposing Ali, who succeeded Uthman in 656 (see page 197). Likewise, Umm Salama, a member of a wealthy and prominent clan in Mecca, at first supported Ali, then switched sides and supported the Umayyads.[6] (See the feature "Listening to the Past: The Etiquette of Marriage" on pages 226–227.)

The Qur'an, like the religious writings of all traditions, represents moral precept rather than social practice, and the texts are open to different interpretations. Yet modern scholars tend to agree that the Islamic sacred book intended women to be the spiritual and sexual equals of men and gave them considerable economic rights. In the early Umayyad period, moreover, women played an active role in the religious, economic, and political life of the community. They owned property. They had freedom of movement and traveled widely. Women participated with men in the public religious rituals and observances. But this Islamic ideal of women and men of equal value to the community did not last.[7] As Islamic society changed, the precepts of the Qur'an were interpreted to meet different circumstances.

In the later Umayyad period, the status of women declined. The rapid conquest of vast territories led to the influx of large numbers of slave women. As wealth replaced birth as the criterion of social status, scholars speculate, men more and more viewed women as possessions, as a form of wealth. The increasingly inferior status of women is revealed in three ways: in the relationship of women to their husbands, in the practice of veiling women, and in the seclusion of women in harems (see page 209).

On the rights and duties of a husband to his wife, the Qur'an states that "men are in charge of women because Allah hath made the one to excel the other, and because they (men) spend of their property (for the support of women). So good women are obedient, guarding in secret that which Allah hath guarded."[8] A tenth-century interpreter, Abu Ja'far Muhammad ibn-Jarir al-Tabari, commented on that passage in this way:

Men are in charge of their women with respect to disciplining (or chastising) them, and to providing them with restrictive guidance concerning their duties toward God and themselves (i.e., the men), by virtue of that by which God has given excellence (or preference) to the men over their wives: i.e., the payment of their dowers to them, spending of their wealth on them, and providing for them in full.[9]

A thirteenth-century commentator on the same Qur'anic passage goes into more detail and argues that women are incapable of and unfit for any public duties, such as participating in religious rites, giving evidence in the law courts, or being involved in any public political decisions.[10] Muslim society fully accepted this view, and later interpreters further categorized the ways in which men were superior to women.

The Sunni aphorism "There shall be no monkery Islam" captures the importance of marriage in Muslim culture and the Muslim belief that a sexually frustrated person is dangerous to the community. Islam vehemently discourages sexual abstinence. Islam expects that every man and woman, unless physically incapable or financially unable, will marry: marriage is a safeguard of chastity, essential to the stability both of the family and of society.

As in medieval Europe and traditional India and China, marriage in Muslim society was considered too important an undertaking to be left to the romantic emotions of the young. Families or guardians, not the prospective bride and groom, identified suitable partners and finalized the contract. The official wedding ceremony consisted of an offer and its acceptance by representatives of the bride's and groom's parents at a meeting before witnesses. A wedding banquet at which men and women feasted separately followed; the quality of the celebration, of the gifts, and of the food depended on the relative wealth of the two families. Because it was absolutely essential that the bride be a virgin, marriages were arranged shortly after the onset of the girl's menarche at age twelve or thirteen. Husbands were perhaps ten to fifteen years older. Youthful marriages ensured a long period of fertility.

A wife's responsibilities depended on the financial status of her husband. A farmer's wife helped in the fields, ground the corn, carried water, prepared food, and did the myriad tasks necessary in rural life. Shopkeepers' wives in the cities sometimes helped in business. In an upper-class household, the lady supervised servants, looked after all domestic arrangements, and did whatever was needed for her husband's comfort.

In every case, children were the wife's special domain. A mother exercised authority over her children and enjoyed their respect. A Muslim tradition asserts that "Paradise is at the mother's feet." Thus, as in Chinese culture, the prestige of the young wife depended on the production of children—especially sons—as rapidly as possible. A wife's failure to have children was one of the main reasons for a man to take a second wife or to divorce his wife entirely.

Like the Jewish tradition, Muslim law permits divorce. The law prescribes that if a man intends to divorce his wife, he should avoid hasty action and not have intercourse with her for three months; hopefully, they will reconcile. If the woman becomes pregnant during that period, the father can be identified. Divorce was not, however, encouraged. The commentator Ibn Urnan reported the Prophet as saying, "The lawful thing which God hates most is divorce."

Interpretations of the Qur'an's statements on polygamy give an example of the declining status of women in Muslim society. The Qur'an permits a man to have four wives, provided "that all are treated justly. . . . Marry of the women who seem good to you, two or three or four; and if ye fear that you cannot do justice (to so many) then one (only) or the captives that your right hand possess."[11] Muslim jurists interpreted the statement as having legal force. The Prophet's emphasis on justice to the several wives, however, was understood as a mere recommendation.[12] Although the Qur'an allows polygamy, only very wealthy men could afford several wives. The vast majority of Muslim males were monogamous because women could not earn money and men had difficulty enough supporting one wife.

In contrast to the Christian view of sexual activity as something inherently shameful and even within marriage only a cure for concupiscence, Islam maintains a healthy acceptance of sexual pleasure for both males and females. Islam holds that sexual satisfaction for both partners in marriage is necessary to prevent extramarital activity. Men, however, are entitled to as many as four legal partners. Women have to be content with one.

In many present-day Muslim cultures, few issues are more sensitive than those of the veiling and the seclusion of women. These practices have their roots in pre-Islamic times, and they took firm hold in classical Islamic society. The head veil seems to have been the mark of freeborn urban women; wearing the veil distinguished free women from slave women. Country and desert women did not wear veils because they interfered with work. Probably of Byzantine or Persian origin, the veil indicated respectability and modesty. As the Arab conquerors subjugated various peoples, they adopted some of the vanquished peoples' customs, one of which was veiling. The Qur'an contains no specific rule about the veil, but its few vague references have been interpreted as sanctioning the practice. Gradually, all parts of a woman's body were considered *pudendal* (shameful because they are capable of arousing sexual desire) and were not allowed to be seen in public.

Even more restrictive of the freedom of women than veiling was the practice of *purdah*, literally, seclusion behind a screen or curtain—the **harem** system. The English word *harem* comes from the Arabic *haram*, meaning "forbidden" or "sacrosanct," which the women's quarters of a house or palace were considered to be. The practice of secluding women in a harem also derives from Arabic contacts with other Eastern cultures. Scholars do not know precisely when the harem system began, but by 800 women in more prosperous households stayed out of sight. The harem became another symbol of male prestige and prosperity, as well as a way to distinguish upper-class women from peasants.

harem *The separate quarters of a house or palace where women live and men are excluded.*

TRADE AND COMMERCE

Did Islamic teachings contribute to the thriving trade that passed through Muslim lands?

Islam had a highly positive disposition toward profit-making enterprises. In the period from 1000 to 1500, there was less ideological resistance to the striving for profit in trade and commerce in the Muslim world than there was in the Christian West or the Confucian East. Again in contrast to the social values of the medieval West and the Confucian East, Muslims tended to look with disdain on agricultural labor. Muhammad had earned his living in business as a representative of the city of Mecca, which carried on a brisk trade from southern Palestine to southwestern Arabia. According to the sayings of the Prophet:

The honest, truthful Muslim merchant will stand with the martyrs on the Day of Judgment. I commend the merchants to you, for they are the couriers of the horizons and God's trusted servants on earth.[13]

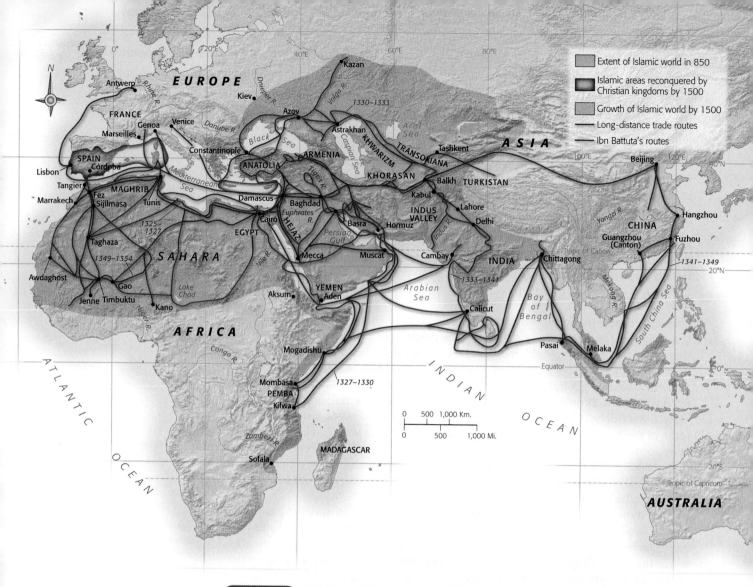

MAP 8.2 **The Expansion of Islam and Its Trading Networks in the Thirteenth and Fourteenth Centuries** By 1500 Islam had spread extensively in north and east Africa, into the Balkans, the Caucuses, Central Asia, India, and island Southeast Asia. Muslim merchants played a major role in bringing their religion as they extended their trade networks. They were active in the Indian Ocean long before the arrival of Europeans.

The Qur'an, moreover, has no prohibition against trade with Christians or other unbelievers.

Waterways served as the main commercial routes of the Islamic world (see Map 8.2). They ranged from the Mediterranean to the Black Sea; the Caspian Sea and the Volga River, which gave access deep into Russia; the Aral Sea, from which caravans departed for China; the Gulf of Aden; and the Arabian Sea and the Indian Ocean, which linked the Arabian gulf region with eastern Africa, the Indian subcontinent, and eventually Indonesia and the Philippines.

Cairo was a major Mediterranean entrepôt for intercontinental trade. An Egyptian official served as the legal representative of foreign merchants from Central Asia, Persia, Iraq, northern Europe (especially Venice), the Byzantine Empire, and Spain. They or their agents sailed up the Nile to the Aswan region, traveled east from Aswan by caravan to the Red Sea, and sailed down the Red Sea to Aden, whence they crossed the Indian Ocean to India. They exchanged textiles, glass, gold, silver, and copper for Asian spices, dyes, and drugs and for Chinese silks and porcelains. Muslim and Jewish merchants dominated the trade with India; both spoke and wrote Arabic. Their commercial practices included the *sakk,* an Arabic word that is the root of the English *check,* an order to a banker to pay money held on account to a third party; the practice can be traced to Roman Palestine. Muslims developed other business devices, such as the bill of exchange, a written order from one person to another to pay a specified sum of money to a designated person or party, and the idea of the joint stock company, an arrangement that lets a group of people invest in a venture and share its profits (and losses) in proportion to the amount each has invested.

Between 1250 and 1500, Islamic trade changed markedly. In maritime technology, the adoption from the Chinese of the magnetic compass, an instrument for determining directions at sea by means of a magnetic needle turning on a pivot, allowed greater reconnaissance of the Arabian Sea and the Indian Ocean. The construction of larger ships led to a shift in long-distance cargoes from luxury goods such as pepper, spices, and drugs to bulk goods such as sugar, rice, and timber. Venetian galleys sailing the Mediterranean came to carry up to 250 tons of cargo, but the *dhows* plying the Indian Ocean were built to carry even more, up to 400 tons. The teak forests of western India supplied the wood for Arab ships.

Commercial routes also shifted. The Mongol invasions, culminating in the capture of Baghdad and the fall of the Abbasid caliphate (see page 203), led to the decline of Iraq and the rise of Egypt as the center of Muslim trade. Beginning in the late twelfth century, Persian and Arab seamen sailed down the east coast of Africa and established trading towns between Somalia and Sofala (see page 249). These thirty to fifty urban centers— each merchant-controlled, fortified, and independent—linked Zimbabwe in southern Africa (see page 252) with the Indian Ocean trade and the Middle Eastern trade.

A private ninth-century list mentions a great variety of commodities transported into and through the Islamic world by land and by sea:

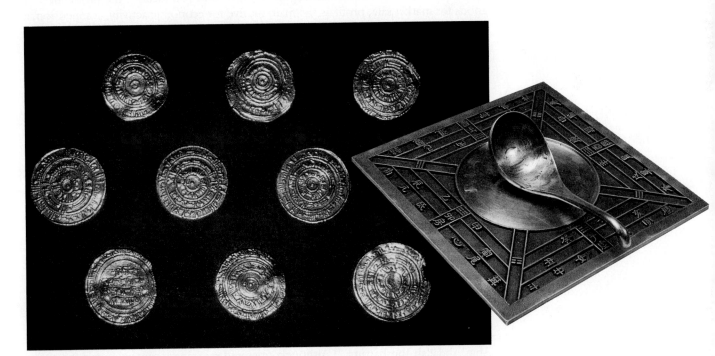

● **Arab Trade and Commerce** A mariner's compass determines direction at sea. Arab traders brought this Chinese south-pointing compass (*right*) to the West, probably in the twelfth century. In 1984, archaeologists unearthed these coins (*left*) on the island of Pemba, off the coast of modern Kenya. Deriving from Tunisian, Egyptian, and Syrian mints and bearing Arabic scripts, the coins testify to Muslim trade with the Swahili city-states. (*right: Ontario Science Center, Toronto; left: Ashmolean Museum, Oxford*)

Imported from India: tigers, leopards, elephants, leopard skins, red rubies, white sandalwood, ebony, and coconuts

From China: aromatics, silk, porcelain, paper, ink, peacocks, fiery horses, saddles, felts, cinnamon

From the Byzantines: silver and gold vessels, embroidered cloths, fiery horses, slave girls, rare articles in red copper, strong locks, lyres, water engineers, specialists in plowing and cultivation, marble workers, and eunuchs

From Arabia: Arab horses, ostriches, thoroughbred she-camels, and tanned hides

From Barbary and Maghrib (the Arabic name for northwest Africa, an area that included Morocco, Algeria, and Tunisia): leopards, acacia, felts, and black falcons

From Egypt: ambling donkeys, fine cloths, papyrus, balsam oil, and, from its mines, high-quality topaz

From the Khazars (a people living on the northern shore of the Black Sea): slaves, slave women, armor, helmets, and hoods of mail

From Samarkand: paper

From Ahwaz (a city in southwestern Persia): sugar, silk brocades, castanet players and dancing girls, kinds of dates, grape molasses, and candy.[14]

Camels made long-distance land transportation possible. Stubborn and vicious, camels nevertheless proved more efficient for desert transportation than did horses or oxen. The use of the camel to carry heavy and bulky freight facilitated the development of overland commerce.

Did Muslim economic activity amount to a kind of capitalism? If by capitalism is meant private (not state) ownership of the means of production, the production of goods for market sale, profit as the main motive for economic activity, competition, a money economy, and the lending of money at interest, then, unquestionably, the medieval Muslim economy had capitalistic features. Students of Muslim economic life have not made a systematic and thorough investigation of Muslims' industries, businesses, and seaports, but the impressionistic evidence is overwhelming: "Not only did the Muslim world know a capitalist sector, but this sector was apparently the most extensive in history before the establishment of the world market created by the Western European bourgeoisie, and this did not outstrip it in importance until the sixteenth century."[15] Its only real competition was Song China (see pages 333–334).

One byproduct of the extensive trade through Muslim lands was the spread of useful plants. Cotton, sugar cane, and sugar spread from India to other places with suitable climates. A tenth-century geographer reported that cotton and rice were being planted in Iraq. Citrus fruits made their way to Muslim Spain from Southeast Asia and India.

• • • • • • • • • • • •

CULTURAL DEVELOPMENTS

What advances were made in the arts, sciences, and education?

Long-distance trade provided the wealth that made possible a gracious and sophisticated culture in the cities of the Muslim world. (See the feature "Individuals in Society: Abu 'Abdallah Ibn Battuta.") Although cities and mercantile centers dotted the entire Islamic world, the cities of Baghdad and Córdoba at their peak in the tenth century stand out as the finest examples of cosmopolitan Muslim civilization. On Baghdad's streets thronged a kaleidoscope of races, creeds, costumes, and cultures, an almost infinite variety of peoples: returning travelers, administrative officials, slaves, visitors, and

Abu 'Abdallah Ibn Battuta

A traveler, perhaps Ibn Battuta, as depicted on a 1375 European map. *(Bibliothèque nationale de France)*

In 1354 the sultan of Morocco appointed a scribe to write an account of the travels of Ibn Battuta (1304–1368), who between 1325 and 1354 had traveled through most of the Islamic world. The two men collaborated. The result was a travel book written in Arabic and later hailed as the richest eyewitness account of fourteenth-century Islamic culture. It has often been compared to the slightly earlier *Travels* of the Venetian Marco Polo (see page 306).

Ibn Battuta was born in Tangiers to a family of legal scholars. As a youth, he studied Muslim law, gained fluency in Arabic, and acquired the qualities considered essential for a civilized Muslim gentleman: courtesy, manners, the social polish that eases relations among people.

At age twenty-one, he left Tangiers to make the *hajj* (pilgrimage) to Mecca. He crossed North Africa and visited Alexandria, Cairo, Damascus, and Medina. Reaching Mecca in October 1326, he immediately praised God for his safe journey, kissed the Holy Stone at the Ka'ba, and recited the ritual prayers. There he decided to see more of the world.

In the next four years, Ibn Battuta traveled to Iraq and to Basra and Baghdad in Persia, then returned to Mecca before sailing down the coast of Africa as far as modern Tanzania. On the return voyage, he visited Oman and the Persian Gulf region, then traveled by land across central Arabia to Mecca. Strengthened by his stay in the holy city, he decided to go to India by way of Egypt, Syria, and Anatolia; across the Black Sea to the plains of western Central Asia, detouring to see Constantinople; back to the Asian steppe; east to Khurasan and Afghanistan; and down to Delhi in northern India.

For eight years, Ibn Battuta served as a judge in the service of the sultan of Delhi. In 1341 the sultan chose him to lead a diplomatic mission to China. When the expedition was shipwrecked off the southeastern coast of India, Ibn Battuta used the disaster to travel through southern India, Sri Lanka, and the Maldive Islands. Thence he went on his own to China, stopping in Bengal and Sumatra before reaching the southern coast of China, then under Mongol rule. Returning to Mecca in 1346, he set off for home, getting to Morocco in 1349. After a brief trip across the Strait of Gibraltar to Granada, he undertook his last journey, by camel caravan across the Sahara to Mali in the West African Sudan (see page 236), returning home in 1354. Scholars estimate that he had traveled about seventy-five thousand miles.

Ibn Battuta had a driving intellectual curiosity to see and understand the world. At every stop, he sought out the learned jurists and pious men at the mosques and madrasas. He marveled at the Lighthouse of Alexandria, eighteen hundred years old in his day; at the vast harbor at Kaffa (in southern Ukraine on the Black Sea) whose two hundred Genoese ships were loaded with silks and slaves for the markets at Venice, Cairo, and Damascus; and at the elephants in the sultan's procession in Delhi, which carried machines that tossed gold and silver coins to the crowds.

Ibn Battuta must have had an iron constitution. Besides walking long distances on his land trips, he endured fevers, dysentery, malaria, the scorching heat of the Sahara, and the freezing cold of the steppe. His thirst for adventure was stronger than his fear of nomadic warriors and bandits on land and the dangers of storms and pirates at sea.

Questions for Analysis

1. Trace the routes of Ibn Battuta's travels on a map.

2. How did a common Muslim culture facilitate his travels?

Source: R. E. Dunn, *The Adventures of Ibn Battuta: A Muslim Traveler of the Fourteenth Century* (Berkeley: University of California Press, 1986).

merchants from Asia, Africa, and Europe. Shops and marketplaces offered the rich and extravagant a dazzling and exotic array of goods from all over the world.

The caliph Harun al-Rashid (r. 786–809) presided over a glamorous court. He invited writers, dancers, musicians, poets, and artists to live in Baghdad, and he is reputed to have rewarded one singer with a hundred thousand silver pieces for a single song. This brilliant era provided the background for the tales that appear in *The Thousand and One Nights.*

The central plot of the fictional tales involves the efforts of Scheherazade to keep her husband, Schariar, legendary king of Samarkand, from killing her. She entertains him with one tale a night for 1,001 nights. The best-known tales are "Aladdin and His Lamp," "Sinbad the Sailor," and "Ali Baba and the Forty Thieves." Also known as *The Arabian Nights,* this book offers a sumptuous collection of caliphs, viziers, and genies, varieties of sexual experiences, and fabulous happenings. *The Arabian Nights,* though folklore, has provided many of the images that Europeans have used since the eighteenth century to describe the Islamic world.

Córdoba in southern Spain competed with Baghdad for the cultural leadership of the Islamic world. In the tenth century, no city in Asia or Europe could equal dazzling Córdoba. Its streets were well paved and lighted, and the city had an abundant supply of fresh water. With a population of about 1 million, Córdoba contained 1,600 mosques, 900 public baths, 213,177 houses for ordinary people, and 60,000 mansions for generals, officials, and the wealthy. In its 80,455 shops, 13,000 weavers produced silks, woolens, and brocades that were internationally famous. Córdoba utilized the Syrian process of manufacturing crystal. It was a great educational center with 27 free schools and a library containing 400,000 volumes. (By contrast, the great Benedictine abbey of Saint-Gall in Switzerland had about 600 books.) Through Iran and Córdoba, the Indian game of chess entered western Europe. Córdoba's scholars made contributions in chemistry, medicine and surgery, music, philosophy, and mathematics. Its fame was so great it is no wonder that the contemporary Saxon nun Hrosthwita of Gandersheim (d. 1000) described the city as the "ornament of the world."[16]

Education and Intellectual Life

Urban and sophisticated Muslim culture possessed a strong educational foundation. Muslim culture placed extraordinary emphasis on knowledge, especially religious knowledge. Knowledge provided the guidelines by which men and women should live.

Conquering Arabs took enormous pride in their Arabic language, and they feared their sons would adopt a corrupted Arabic by contact with subject peoples speaking other languages. Thus parents established elementary schools for the training of their sons. After the caliph Uthman (see page 197) ordered the preparation of an approved codex of the Qur'an, and after copies of it were made, the Qur'an became the basic text. From the eighth century onward, formal education for male children and youths involved reading, writing, and the study of the Qur'an, believed essential for its religious message and for its training in proper grammar and syntax.

Of great aid to learning was the Muslim transmission and improvement of papermaking techniques. The Chinese had been making paper for centuries from rags and woody fibers from such plants as hemp, jute, and bamboo. After their techniques spread westward, Muslim papermakers improved on Chinese techniques by adding starch to fill the pores in the surfaces of the sheets. Muslims carried this new method to Baghdad in Iraq, Damascus in Syria, Cairo in Egypt, and the Maghrib (North Africa), from which it entered Spain. Papermaking, even before the invention of printing, had a revolutionary impact on the collection and diffusion of knowledge and thus on the transformation of society.

madrasa *A school for the study of Muslim law and religious science.*

Islam is a religion of the law, and the institution for instruction in Muslim jurisprudence was the **madrasa,** the school for the study of Muslim law and religious science.

● **Teachers Disputing in a Madrasa** Although Islamic education relied heavily on memorization of the Qur'an, religious scholars frequently debated the correct interpretation of a particular text. Listening to this lively disputation, students in the audience are learning to think critically and creatively. *(Bibliothèque nationale de France, Ms. Arabe 6094, fol. 16)*

By 1193 thirty madrasas existed in Damascus; between 1200 and 1250, sixty more were established there. Aleppo, Jerusalem, Alexandria, and above all Cairo also witnessed the foundation of madrasas.

Schools were urban phenomena. Wealthy merchants endowed them, providing salaries for the teachers, stipends for students, and living accommodations for both. The teacher served as a guide to the correct path of living. All Islamic higher education rested on a close relationship between teacher and students, so in selecting a teacher, the student (or his father) considered the character and intellectual reputation of the teacher, not that of any institution. Students built their subsequent careers on the reputation of their teachers.

Learning depended heavily on memorization. In primary school, which was often attached to an institution of higher learning, a boy began his education by memorizing the entire Qur'an. Normally, he achieved this feat by the time he was seven or eight! In adolescence a student learned by heart an introductory work in one of the branches of knowledge, such as jurisprudence or grammar. Later he analyzed the texts in detail. Memorizing four hundred to five hundred lines a day was considered outstanding. Every class day, the teacher examined the student on the previous day's learning and determined whether the student fully understood what he had memorized. Students, of course, learned to write, for they had to write down the teacher's commentary on a particular text. But the overwhelming emphasis was on the oral transmission of knowledge.

Because Islamic education focused on particular books, when the student had mastered a text to his teacher's satisfaction, the teacher issued the student a certificate stating that he had studied the book or collection of traditions with his teacher. The certificate allowed the student to transmit a text to the next generation on the authority of his teacher.

Apart from the fundamental goal of preparing men to live wisely and in accordance with God's law, Muslim higher education aimed at preparing men to perform religious and legal functions as Qur'an—or hadith—readers; as preachers in the mosques; as professors, educators, copyists; and especially as judges. Judges issued *fatwas,* or legal opinions, in the public courts; their training was in the Qur'an, hadith, or some text forming part of the shari'a. Islam did not know the division between religious and secular knowledge characteristic of the modern Western world.

What educational opportunities were available to women? Although tradition holds that Muhammad said, "The seeking of knowledge is a duty of every Muslim," Islamic culture was ambivalent on the issue of female education. Because of the basic Islamic principle that "Men are the guardians of women, because God has set the one over the other," the law excluded women from participation in the legal, religious, or civic occupations for which the madrasa prepared young men. Moreover, educational theorists insisted that men should study in a sexually isolated environment because feminine allure would distract male students. Nevertheless, many young women received substantial educations from their parents or family members; the initiative invariably rested with their fathers or older brothers. The daughter of Ali ibn Muhammad al-Diruti al Mahalli, for example, memorized the Qur'an, learned to write, and received instruction in several sacred works. One biographical dictionary containing the lives of 1,075 women reveals that 411 had memorized the Qur'an, studied with a particular teacher, and received a certificate. After marriage, responsibility for a woman's education belonged to her husband.[17]

How does Islamic higher education compare with that available in Europe or China at the time (see pages 371–372, 334–336)? There are some striking similarities and some major differences. The church operated schools and universities in Europe. In China the government, local villages, and lineages all ran schools, and private tutoring was very common. In the Islamic world, as in China, the personal relationship of teacher and student was seen as key to education. In Europe the reward for satisfactory completion of a course of study was a degree granted by the university. In China, at the very highest levels, the imperial civil service examination tested candidates' knowledge and rewarded achievement with appoint-

● **Mechanical Hand Washer** Building on the work of the Greek engineer and inventor Archimedes (see page 97), the Arab scientist ibn al-Razzaz al-Raziri (ca. 1200) designed practical devices to serve general social needs and illustrated them in a mechanical engineering handbook. In this diagram, a device in the form of a servant pours water with his right hand and offers a towel with his left. The device resembles a modern faucet that releases water when hands are held under it. *(Courtesy of the Freer Gallery of Art, Smithsonian Institution, Washington, D.C. Purchase, F1930.75a)*

● **Pharmacist Preparing Drugs** The translation of Greek scientific treatises into Arabic, combined with considerable botanical experimentation, gave Muslims virtually unrivaled medical knowledge.
Treatment for many ailments was by prescription drugs. In this thirteenth-century illustration, a pharmacist
prepares a drug in a cauldron over a brazier. It has been said that the pharmacy as an institution is an
Islamic invention. *(The Metropolitan Museum of Art, Bequest of Cora Timken Burnett Collection of Persian Minia-
tures and Other Persian Art Objects, Bequest of Cora Timken Burnett, 1957 [57.51.21]. Photograph © 1991 The
Metropolitan Museum of Art)*

ments in the state bureaucracy. In Muslim culture it was not the school or the state
but the individual teacher whose evaluation mattered and who granted certificates.

In all three cultures education rested heavily on the study of basic religious, legal,
or philosophical texts: the Old and New Testaments or the Justinian *Code* in Europe;
the Confucian classics and commentaries in China; the Qur'an, hadith, and legal texts
deriving from these in the Muslim world. Also in all three cultures memorization
played a large role in the acquisition and transmission of information. In all three
teachers lectured on particular passages, and sometimes leading teachers disagreed
fiercely about the correct interpretations of a particular text, forcing students to question, to think critically, and to choose between divergent opinions. Finally, educated
people in each culture shared the same broad literary and religious or ethical culture,
giving that culture cohesion and stability. Just as a man who took a degree at Cambridge University in England shared the Latin language and general philosophical
outlook of someone with a degree from Montpellier in France or Naples in Italy, so a
Muslim gentleman from Cairo spoke and read the same Arabic and knew the same

hadith as a man from Baghdad or Samarkand. In China those who had studied the Chinese classics from distant parts of China and even Korea, Japan, and Vietnam were less likely to be able to talk about them together, but they could have "brush conversations," the classical Chinese language serving as a lingua franca of the educated in East Asia the way Arabic did in the Muslim world and Latin did in Europe.

In the Muslim world the spread of the Arabic language, not only among the educated classes but also among all people, was the decisive element in the creation of a common means of communication and a universal culture. Recent scholarship demonstrates that after the establishment of the Islamic empire, the major influence in the cultural transformation of the Byzantine–Sassanid–North African and the Central Asian worlds was language. The Arabic language proved more important than religion in this regard. Whereas conversion to Islam was gradual, linguistic conversion went much faster. Arabic became the official language of the state and its bureaucracies in former Byzantine and Sassanid territories. Muslim conquerors forbade Persian-speaking people to use their native language. Islamic rulers required tribute from monotheistic peoples—the Persians and Greeks—but they did not force them to change their religions. Conquered peoples were, however, compelled to submit to a linguistic conversion—to adopt the Arabic language.[18] In time Arabic produced a cohesive and "international" culture over a large part of the Eurasian world.

As a result of Muslim creativity and vitality, modern scholars consider about 900 to 1300 one of the most brilliant periods in the world's history. The Persian scholar al-Khwarizmi (d. ca. 850) harmonized Greek and Indian findings to produce astronomical tables that formed the basis for later Eastern and Western research. Al-Khwarizmi also studied mathematics, and his textbook on algebra (from the Arabic *al-Jabr*) was the first work in which the word *algebra* is used to mean the "transposing of negative terms in an equation to the opposite side."

Muslim medical knowledge far surpassed that of the West. The Baghdad physician al-Razi (865–925) produced an encyclopedic treatise on medicine that was translated into Latin and circulated widely in the West. Al-Razi was the first physician to make the clinical distinction between measles and smallpox. The great surgeon of Córdoba, al-Zahrawi (d. 1013), produced an important work in which he discussed the cauterization of wounds (searing with a branding iron) and the crushing of stones in the bladder. In Ibn Sina of Bukhara (980–1037), known in the West as Avicenna, Muslim science reached its peak. His *al-Qanun* codified all Greco-Arabic medical thought, described the contagious nature of tuberculosis and the spreading of diseases, and listed 760 pharmaceutical drugs. Muslim scholars also wrote works on geography and jurisprudence. Al-Kindi (d. ca. 870) was the first Muslim thinker to try to harmonize Greek philosophy and the religious precepts of the Qur'an. He sought to integrate Islamic concepts of human beings and their relations to God and the universe with the principles of ethical and social conduct discussed by Plato and Aristotle.

Inspired by Plato's *Republic* and Aristotle's *Politics,* the distinguished philosopher al-Farabi (d. 950) wrote a political treatise describing an ideal city whose ruler is morally and intellectually perfect and who has as his goal the citizens' complete happiness. Avicenna maintained that the truths found by human reason cannot conflict with the truths of revelation as given in the Qur'an. Ibn Rushid, or Averroës (1126–1198), of Córdoba, a judge in Seville and later royal court physician, paraphrased and commented on the works of Aristotle. He insisted on the right to subject all knowledge, except the dogmas of faith, to the test of reason and on the essential harmony between religion and philosophy.

Sufism

Like the world's other major religions—Buddhism, Hinduism, Judaism, and Christianity—Islam also developed a mystical tradition. It arose in the ninth and tenth

● **Sufi Collective Ritual** Collective or group rituals, in which Sufis tried through ecstatic experiences to come closer to God, have always fascinated outsiders, including non-Sufi Muslims. Here the sixteenth-century Persian painter Sultan Muhammad illustrates the writing of the fourteenth-century lyric poet Hafiz. Just as Hafiz's poetry moved back and forth between profane and mystical themes, so it is difficult to determine whether the ecstasy achieved here is alcoholic or spiritual. Notice the various musical instruments and the delicate floral patterns so characteristic of Persian art. *(Courtesy of the Arthur M. Sackler Museum, Harvard University Art Museums. Promised gift of Mr. and Mrs. Stuart Cary Welch, Jr. Partially owned by the Metropolitan Museum of Art and the Arthur M. Sackler Museum, Harvard University, 1988. In honor of the students of Harvard University and Radcliffe College, 1988.460.3. Photo: Imaging Department, © President and Fellows of Harvard College)*

centuries as a popular reaction to the materialism of the Umayyad regime. *Sufis* were ascetics. They wanted a personal union with God—divine love and knowledge through intuition rather than through rational deduction and study of the shari'a. They followed an ascetic routine (denial of physical desires to gain a spiritual goal), dedicating themselves to fasting, prayer, meditation on the Qur'an, and the avoidance of sin.

The woman mystic Rabi'a (717–801) epitomized this combination of renunciation and devotion. An attractive woman who refused marriage so that nothing would distract her from a total commitment to God, Rabi'a attracted followers, whom she served as a spiritual guide. Her poem captures her deep devotion: "O my lord, if I worship thee from fear of hell, and if I worship thee in hope of paradise, exclude me thence, but if I worship thee for thine own sake, then withhold not from me thine eternal beauty."[19]

In the twelfth century groups of Sufis gathered around teachers. A member of a Sufi order was called a *dervish*. The ritual of Sufi brotherhoods directed the dervish to a hypnotic or ecstatic trance, either through the constant repetition of certain prayers or through physical exertions such as whirling or dancing (hence the English phrase "whirling dervish" for one who dances with abandonment). Some Sufis acquired reputations as charismatic holy men to whom ordinary Muslims came seeking spiritual consolation, healing, charity, or political mediation between tribal and factional rivals.

Probably the most famous medieval Sufi was the Spanish mystic-philosopher Ibn al-'Arabi (1165–1240). He traveled widely in Spain, North Africa, and Arabia seeking masters of Sufism. He visited Mecca, where he received a "divine commandment" to begin his major work, *The Meccan Revelation,* which evolved into a personal encyclopedia of 560 chapters. At Mecca the wisdom of a beautiful young girl inspired him to write a collection of love poems, *The Interpreter of Desires,* for which he composed a mystical commentary. In 1223, after visits to Egypt, Anatolia, Baghdad, and Aleppo, Ibn al-'Arabi concluded his pilgrimage through the Islamic world at Damascus, where he produced *The Bezels [Edges] of Wisdom,* considered one of the greatest works of Sufism.

Muslim-Christian Encounters

During the early centuries of the development of Islam, it came into contact with the other major religions of Eurasia—Hinduism in India, Buddhism in Central Asia, Zoroastrianism in Persia, and Judaism and Christianity both at home in Western Asia and to the west in Europe. As Islam developed, the relationship that did the most to define Muslim identity was its relationship with Christianity. To put this another way, the most significant "other" to Muslims in the heartland of Islam was Christendom. The close physical proximity and the long history of military encounters undoubtedly contributed to making the Christian-Muslim encounter so important to both sides.

In the classical period of Islam, Muslims learned about Christianity from the Christians they met in conquered territories; from biblical texts, the Old and New Testaments; from Jews; and from Jews and Christians who converted to Islam. Before 1500 a wide spectrum of Muslim opinion about Jesus and Christians existed. At the time of the Crusades (see pages 362–365) and of the Christian reconquest of Muslim Spain (see page 362), polemical anti-Christian writings understandably appeared. In other periods, Muslim views were more positive.

In the medieval period Christians and Muslims met frequently in business and trade. Commercial contacts, especially when European merchants resided for a long time in the Muslim East, gave Europeans, notably the Venetians, familiarity with Muslim art and architecture. Likewise, when in the fifteenth century Muslim artists in the Ottoman Empire and in Persia became acquainted with Western artists, such as Gentile Bellini, they admired and imitated them. We have already seen the striking parallels

**Primary Source:
"Frank-land": An Islamic View of the West**
A twelfth-century Islamic scholar saw western Europeans as courageous—and dirty!

between aspects of Western and Muslim higher education; Christians had very probably borrowed from Islam.

Christian Europeans and Middle Eastern Muslims were geographical neighbors. They shared a common cultural heritage from the Judeo-Christian past. In the Christian West, Islam had the greatest cultural impact in Andalusia in southern Spain. Between roughly the eighth and twelfth centuries, Muslims, Christians, and Jews lived in close proximity in Andalusia, and some scholars believe the period represents a remarkable era of interfaith harmony. Many Christians adopted Arabic patterns of speech and dress, gave up the practice of eating pork, and developed a special appreciation for Arabic music and poetry. Some Christian women of elite status chose the Muslim practice of going out in public with their faces veiled. Records describe Muslim and Christian youths joining in celebrations and merrymaking. These assimilated Christians, called **Mozarabs,** did not attach much importance to the doctrinal differences between the two religions.

Mozarabs soon faced the strong criticism of both Muslim scholars and Christian clerics. Muslim teachers feared that close contact between the two peoples would lead to Muslim contamination and become a threat to the Islamic faith. Christian bishops worried that a knowledge of Islam would lead to ignorance of essential Christian doctrines. Both Muslim scholars and Christian theologians argued that assimilation led to sensuality and that sensuality was ruining their particular cultures.

Thus, beginning in the late tenth century, Muslim regulations closely defined what Christians and Muslims could do. A Christian, however much assimilated, remained an **infidel.** An infidel was an unbeliever, and the word carried a pejorative or disparaging connotation. Mozarabs had to live in special sections of cities; could not learn the Qur'an, employ Muslim workers or servants, or build new churches; and had to be buried in their own cemeteries. A Muslim who converted to Christianity immediately incurred a sentence of death. By about 1250 the Christian reconquest of Muslim Spain had brought most of the Iberian Peninsula under Christian control. Christian kings set up schools that taught both Arabic and Latin, but these schools were intended to produce missionaries.

Beyond Andalusian Spain, mutual animosity restricted contact between the two peoples. The Muslim assault on Christian Europe in the eighth and ninth centuries—with villages burned, monasteries sacked, and Christians sold into slavery—left a legacy of bitter hostility. Christians felt threatened by a faith that acknowledged God as creator of the universe but denied the doctrine of the Trinity; that accepted Jesus as a prophet but denied his divinity; that believed in the Last Judgment but seemed to make sensuality Heaven's greatest reward. Europeans' perception of Islam as a menace helped inspire the Crusades of the eleventh through thirteenth centuries.

Muslim scholars often wrote sympathetically about Jesus. For example, the great historian al Tabari (d. 923), relying on Arabic sources, wrote positively of Jesus' life, focusing on his birth and crucifixion; at the same time, al Tabari used Old Testament

● **Lusterware Bowl from Egypt** An outstanding example of brightly glazed pottery with sharply etched figures, this bowl by a Muslim potter named Sa'ad shows a Christian priest swinging a censer with burning incense to purify a religious space. After the Islamic conquest, most of Egypt's Coptic Christians held on to their faith, but the Crusades bred Muslim suspicions and led to the forced conversion of many Egyptian Copts. *(Courtesy of the Trustees of the Victoria & Albert Museum)*

Mozarabs *Christians who adopted some Arabic customs but did not convert.*

infidel *An unbeliever; the Muslim term for a Christian, no matter how assimilated.*

books to prove Muhammad's prophethood and stressed the truth of Islam over Christianity. Ikhwan al-Safa, an eleventh-century Islamic brotherhood, held that in his preaching Jesus deliberately rejected the harsh punishments reflected in the Jewish Torah and tried to be the healing physician teaching by parables and trying to touch people's hearts by peace and love. The prominent theologian and qadi (judge) of Teheran, Abd al-Jabbar (d. 1024), though not critical of Jesus, argued that Christians had rejected Jesus' teachings: they failed to observe ritual purity of prayer, substituting poems by Christian scholars for scriptural prayers; they gave up circumcision, the sign of their covenant with God and Abraham; they replaced the Sabbath with Sunday; they allowed the eating of pork and shellfish; and they adopted a Greek idea, the Trinity, defending it by quoting Aristotle. Thus, al-Jabbar maintained—and he was followed later by many other Muslim theologians and scholars—that Christians failed to observe the laws of Moses and Jesus and distorted Jesus' message.

By the thirteenth century Western literature sometimes displayed a sympathetic view of Islam. The Bavarian knight Wolfram von Eschenbach's *Parzival* and the Englishman William Langland's *Piers the Plowman*—two poems that survive in scores of manuscripts, suggesting that they circulated widely—reveal broad-mindedness and tolerance toward Muslims. Some travelers in the Middle East were impressed by the kindness and generosity of Muslims and with the strictness and devotion with which Muslims observed their faith.[20] Frequently, however, Christian literature portrayed Muslims as the most dreadful of Europe's enemies, guilty of every kind of crime. In his *Inferno,* the great Florentine poet Dante (1265–1321) placed the Muslim philosophers Avicenna and Averroës with other virtuous "heathens," among them Socrates and Aristotle, in the first circle of Hell, where they endured only moderate punishment. Muhammad, however, Dante consigned to the ninth circle, near Satan himself, where he was condemned as a spreader of discord and scandal. His punishment was to be continually torn apart from his chin to his anus.

The Christian and Muslim worlds had an impact on each other even when they rejected each other most forcefully. Art styles, technology, and even institutional practices were frequently adopted or adapted. During the Crusades, Muslims adopted Frankish weapons and methods of fortification. Christians in contact with Muslim scholars recovered ancient Greek philosophical texts that survived only in Arabic translation.

Chapter Summary

To assess your mastery of this chapter, go to
bedfordstmartins.com/mckayworld

Key Terms

Ka'ba
Qur'an
caliph
hadith
Sunna
umma
Five Pillars of Islam
jihad
diwān
imam
Shi'ites
Sunnis
ulama
emirs
shari'a
qadis
vizier
dhimmis
harem
madrasa
Mozarabs
infidel

• Who was Muhammad, and what did he teach?

Muhammad was born in the Arabian peninsula among the traders, farmers, and nomadic pastoralists of the region. He taught strict monotheism—there is one and only one God, and believers must submit to God's will. This God is the same God of the Christians and Jews, and Muhammad was familiar with the Old and New Testaments. A few decades after his death, his followers recorded both his revealed teachings—the Qur'an—and traditions about his words and actions.

• What forms of government did Islam establish, and how did they contribute to the rapid spread of Islam?

The spread of Islam was one of the most momentous developments in world history. Driven by the religious zeal of the jihad, Muslims carried their faith from the Arabian peninsula through the Middle East to North Africa, Spain, and southern France in the west and to the borders of China and northern India in the east—all within the short span of a century. Successors to Muhammad established the caliphate, which coordinated rule of all Muslim lands until about 900 under two successive dynasties—the Umayyad, centered at Damascus in Syria, and the Abbasid, with its capital at Baghdad in Iraq.

• How were the Muslim lands governed from 900 to 1400, and what new challenges did they face?

As provincial governors acquired independent power, which the caliphs could not check, centralized authority within the Islamic state disintegrated, and after 900 the Islamic lands are more accurately viewed as composed of many local dynasties, often in competition with each other. Turks played more and more important roles in the armies and came to be the effective rulers in many places. In the mid-thirteenth century the central Muslim lands from Damascus to Afghanistan and Central Asia fell to the Mongols, who ruled the region for about eighty years.

• What social distinctions were important in Muslim society?

Even in periods of political division, the Muslim lands shared much of their culture. Muhammad had insisted that birth was unimportant; what mattered was religious piety. Still, as in virtually every other society, social distinctions made a large difference in how people lived. At the top were the Arabs, descended from the original followers of the Prophet. Next were converts, such as the Copts, Berbers, and Persians who adopted Islam in subsequent centuries. Below them were Jews, Christians, and Zoroastrians, recognized as "protected people" because they recognized only one God; they were allowed to continue their religions. Below them were a substantial number of slaves, many of whom had been enslaved as war captives. Slaves normally were converted to Islam and might come to hold important positions, especially in the army. Distinctions between men and women in Islamic society were strict. In the Qur'an men were said to be in charge of women because they excel them, and women were enjoined to be obedient. In time, seclusion and veiling of women became common practices, especially among the well-to-do.

• *Did Islamic teachings contribute to the thriving trade that passed through Muslim lands?*

Islam developed and flourished in a mercantile milieu. By land and sea Muslim merchants transported a rich variety of goods across Asia, the Middle East, Africa, and western Europe. Muslim business procedures and terminology greatly influenced the West.

• *What advances were made in the arts, sciences, and education?*

On the basis of the wealth that trade generated, a gracious, sophisticated, and cosmopolitan culture developed with centers at Baghdad and Córdoba. In the tenth and eleventh centuries the Islamic world witnessed enormous intellectual vitality and creativity. Muslim scholars produced important work in many disciplines, especially mathematics, medicine, and philosophy. Muslim civilization in the Middle Ages was far in advance of that of Christian Europe, and Muslims, with some justification, looked on Europeans as ignorant barbarians. By 1400 Islamic learning as revealed in astronomy, mathematics, medicine, architecture, and philosophical investigation was highly advanced, perhaps the most creative in the world. In the development and transmission of ancient Egyptian, Persian, and Greek wisdom, Muslims played a vital role, as they did in the transmission of innovations from China and India.

Suggested Reading

Berkey, Jonathan *The Transmission of Knowledge in Medieval Cairo.* 1992. A study of religious education and its social context.

Cohen, Mark R. *Under Crescent and Cross: The Jews in the Medieval Ages.* 1994. Argues that Jews were less marginalized and persecuted under Islamic states than under Christian states.

Constable, Olivia Remie. *Trade and Traders in Muslim Spain: The Commercial Realignment of the Iberian Peninsula, 900–1500.* 1994. An excellent study of Muslim trade and commerce, drawing on a wide range of both Western and Arabic sources.

Ettinghausen, Richard, Oleg Grabar, and Marilyn Jenkins-Madina. *The Art and Architecture of Islam, 650–1250.* 2001. A stunningly illustrated overview of Islamic art.

Fletcher, Richard. *The Cross and the Crescent.* 2003. A balanced, fascinating, and lucidly written short account of the earliest contacts between Christians and Muslims.

Hourani, Albert, and Malise Ruthven. *A History of the Arab Peoples,* 2d ed. 2003. An important synthesis.

Lewis, Bernard. *Race and Slavery in the Middle East.* 1990. Explores the culture of slavery beginning from before Islam, with particular attention to slaves from Africa.

Long, Pamela O. *Technology and Society in the Medieval Centuries: Byzantium, Islam, and the West, 500–1300.* 2003. A useful survey of Arab scientific and military developments.

Peters, F. E. *The Hajj: The Muslim Pilgrimage to Mecca and the Holy Places.* 1994. Covers the social, commercial, and political significance of the obligatory Muslim pilgrimage to Mecca.

Stowasser, Barbara Freyer. *Women in the Qur'an: Traditions and Interpretation.* 1994. A fine analysis of the Qur'an's statement on women.

Notes

1. See F. M. Donner, "Muhammad and the Caliphate," in *The Oxford History of Islam,* ed. J. L. Esposito (New York: Oxford University Press, 1999), pp. 3–13.

2. F. E. Peters, *A Reader on Classical Islam* (Princeton: Princeton University Press, 1994), pp. 154–155.

3. R. G. Hoyland, ed., *Seeing Islam as Others Saw It: A Survey and Evaluation of Christian, Jewish and Zoroastrian Writings on Early Islam* (Princeton, N.J.: Darwin Press, 1997), pp. 524–525.

4. Quoted in R. Levy, *The Social Structure of Islam,* 2d ed. (Cambridge: Cambridge University Press, 1957), p. 56.

5. R. Segal, *Islam's Black Slaves* (New York: Farrar, Straus, and Giroux, 2001), p. 44.

6. See B. F. Stowasser, *Women in the Qur'an, Tradition, and Interpretation* (New York: Oxford University Press, 1994), pp. 94–118.

7. N. Coulson and D. Hinchcliffe, "Women and Law Reform in Contemporary Islam," in *Women in the Muslim World,* ed. L. Beck and N. Keddie (Cambridge, Mass.: Harvard University Press, 1982), p. 37.

8. Quoted in B. F. Stowasser, "The Status of Women in Early Islam," in *Muslim Women,* ed. F. Hussain (New York: St. Martin's Press, 1984), p. 25.

9. Quoted ibid., pp. 25–26.

10. Ibid., p. 26.

11. Ibid., p. 16.

12. G. Nashat, "Women in Pre-Revolutionary Iran: A Historical Overview," in *Women and Revolution in Iran,* ed. G. Nashat (Boulder, Colo.: Westview Press, 1983), pp. 47–48.

13. Quoted in B. Lewis, ed. and trans., *Islam: From the Prophet Muhammad to the Capture of Constantinople,* vol. 2: *Religion and Society* (New York: Harper & Row, 1975), p. 126.

14. Adapted from ibid, pp. 154–157.

15. M. Rodinson, *Islam and Capitalism,* trans. Brian Pearce (Austin: University of Texas Press, 1981), p. 56.

16. R. Hillenbrand, "Cordoba," in *Dictionary of the Middle Ages,* vol. 3, ed. J. R. Strayer (New York: Scribner's, 1983), pp. 597–601.

17. I have leaned here on the important study of J. Berkey, *The Transmission of Knowledge in Medieval Cairo: A Social History of Islamic Education* (Princeton, N.J.: Princeton University Press, 1992), pp. 22–43, 161–181; the quotations are on p. 161.

18. A. Dallal, "Science, Medicine, and Technology: The Making of a Scientific Culture," in *The Oxford History of Islam,* ed. J. L. Esposito (New York: Oxford University Press, 1999), pp. 158–159.

19. Margaret Smith, *Readings from the Mystics of Islam* (London; Luzac and Co., 1950), p. 11.

20. JoAnn Hoeppner Moran Cruz, "Western Views of Islam in Medieval Europe," in *Perceptions of Islam,* ed. D. Blanks and M. Frassetto (New York: St. Martin's Press, 1999), pp. 55–81.

The Etiquette of Marriage

Abu Hamid Al-Ghazali (1058–1111) was a Persian philosopher, theologian, jurist, Sufi, and prolific author of more than seventy books. His magnum opus, The Revival of the Religious Sciences, *is divided into four parts:* Acts of Worship, Norms of Daily Life, The Ways to Perdition, *and* The Ways of Salvation. *His lengthy discussion of marriage falls under the* Norms of Daily Life. *The passages selected here are only a small part of this lengthy treatise, full of quotations from the Qur'an and the traditions about the words and actions of Muhammad.*

There are five advantages to marriage: procreation, satisfying sexual desire, ordering the household, providing companionship, and disciplining the self in striving to sustain them. The first advantage—that is, procreation—is the prime cause, and on its account marriage was instituted. The aim is to sustain lineage so that the world would not want for humankind. . . .

It was for the purpose of freeing the heart that marriage with the bondmaid was permitted when there was fear of hardship, even though it results in enslaving the son, which is a kind of attrition; such marriage is forbidden to anyone who can obtain a free woman. However, the enslaving of a son is preferable to destroying the faith, for enslavement affects temporarily the life of the child, while committing an abomination results in losing the hereafter; in comparison to one of its days the longest life is insignificant. . . .

It is preferable for a person with temperament so overcome by desire that one woman cannot curb it to have more than one woman, up to four. For God will grant him love and mercy, and will appease his heart by them; if not, replacing them is recommended. Seven nights after the death of Fatimah, Ali got married. It is said that al-Hasan, the son of Ali, was a great lover having married more than two hundred women. Perhaps he would marry four at a time, and perhaps he would divorce four at a time replacing them with others. . . .

The fourth advantage [of marriage]: being free from the concerns of household duties, as well as of preoccupation with cooking, sweeping, making beds, cleaning utensils, and means for obtaining support. . . .

Ali used to say, "The worst characteristics of men constitute the best characteristics of women; namely, stinginess, pride, and cowardice. For if the woman is stingy, she will preserve her own and her husband's possessions; if she is proud, she will refrain from addressing loose and improper words to everyone; and if she is cowardly, she will dread everything and will therefore not go out of her house and will avoid compromising situations for fear of her husband. . . ."

Some God-fearing men as a precaution against delusion would not marry off their daughters until they are seen. Al-Amash said, "Every marriage occurring without looking ends in worry and sadness." It is obvious that looking does not reveal character, religion, or wealth; rather, it distinguishes beauty from ugliness. . . .

The Messenger of God declared that "The best women are those whose faces are the most beautiful and whose dowries are the smallest." He enjoined against excessiveness in dowries. The Messenger of God married one of his wives for a dowry of ten dirhams and household furnishings that consisted of a hand mill, a jug, a pillow made of skin stuffed with palm fibers, and a stone; in the case of another, he feasted with two measures of barley; and for another, with two measures of dates and two of mush. . . .

It is incumbent upon the guardian also to examine the qualities of the husband and to look after his daughter so as not to give her in marriage to one who is ugly, ill-mannered, weak in faith, negligent in upholding her rights, or unequal to her in descent. The Prophet has said, "Marriage is enslavement; let one, therefore, be careful in whose hands he places his daughter." . . .

The Prophet asked his daughter Fatimah, "What is best for a woman?" She replied, "That she should see no man, and that no man should see her." So he hugged her and said they were "descendants one of another" [Qur'an 3:33]. Thus he was pleased with her answer. . . .

The Prophet permitted women to go to the mosques; the appropriate thing now, however, is to prevent them [from doing so], except for the old [ones]. Indeed such [prevention] was deemed proper during the days of the companions; A'ishah declared, "If the Prophet only knew of the misdeeds that women would bring about after his time, he would have prevented them from going out." . . .

If [a man] has several wives, then he should deal equitably with them and not favor one over the other; should he go on a journey and desire to have one [of his wives] accompany him, he should cast lots among them, for such was the practice of the Messenger. If he cheats a woman of her night, he should make up for it, for making up for it is a duty upon him. . . .

Let [a man] proceed with gentle words and kisses. The Prophet said, "Let none of you come upon his wife like an animal, and let there be an emissary between them." He was asked, "What is this emissary, O Messenger of God?" He said, "The kiss and [sweet] words."

One should not be overjoyed with the birth of a male child, nor should he be excessively dejected over the birth of a female child, for he does not know in which of the two his blessings lie. Many a man who has a son wishes he did not have him, or wishes that he were a girl. The girls give more tranquility and [divine] remuneration, which are greater.

Concerning divorce, let it be known that it is permissible; but of all permissible things, it is the most detestable to Almighty God. . . .

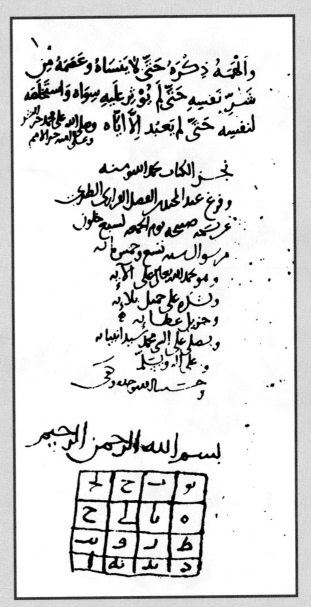

Last page of the manuscript of the *Munquidh min al Dalah*, contained in no. 1712 of the Sehid Ali Pasa of Istanbul. *(From Richard Joseph McCarthy, S.J., Deliverance from Error [Louisville, Ky.: Fons Vitae])*

Questions for Analysis

1. In what ways are the views toward marriage and gender expressed by Al-Ghazali similar to those seen in other traditions?

2. Did the author think it was always appropriate to do what Muhammad and his early followers did?

Source: Madelain Farah, *Marriage and Sexuality in Islam: A Translation of Al-Ghazali's Book on the Etiquette of Marriage from the Ihyā'* (Salt Lake City: University of Utah Press, 1984), pp. 53, 63, 64, 66, 85–86, 88–89, 91, 95–96, 100, 103, 106, 113, 116, slightly modified.

Oni of Ife. Bronze striated head (marked with stripes, grooves, or ridges in parallel lines) showing an Oni of Ife, thirteenth to fourteenth century. *(© Jerry Thompson)*

9 AFRICAN SOCIETIES AND KINGDOMS, CA. 400–1450

Chapter Preview

The Land and Peoples of Africa
• *What patterns of social and political organization prevailed among the peoples of Africa, and what types of agriculture and commerce did Africans engage in?*

African Kingdoms and Empires (ca. 800–1450)
• *What values do Africans' art, architecture, and religions express?*

U ntil fairly recently, ethnocentrism and racism limited what the outside world knew about Africa. But as recent scholarship has allowed us to learn more about early African civilizations, we can now appreciate the richness, diversity, and dynamism of those cultures. We know now that between about 400 and 1500, some highly centralized, bureaucratized, and socially stratified civilizations developed in Africa alongside communities that had a looser form of social organization and functioned as lineage or descent groups.

THE LAND AND PEOPLES OF AFRICA

What patterns of social and political organization prevailed among the peoples of Africa, and what types of agriculture and commerce did Africans engage in?

Africa is immense. The world's second largest continent (after Asia), it covers 20 percent of the earth's land surface. Five climatic zones roughly divide the continent (see Map 9.1). Fertile land with unpredictable rainfall borders parts of the Mediterranean coast in the north and the southwestern coast of the Cape of Good Hope in the south. Inland from these areas lies dry steppe country with little plant life. The steppe gradually gives way to Africa's great deserts: the Sahara in the north and the Namib and Kalahari in the south. The vast Sahara—3.5 million square miles—takes its name from the Arabic word for "tan," the color of the desert. (Folk etymology ascribes the word *Sahara* to an ancient Arabic word that sounds like a parched man's gasp for water.) The Sahara's southern fringe is called the Sahel. The Savanna—flat grassland—extends in a swath across the widest part of the continent, across parts of south-central Africa and along the eastern coast. It is one of the richest habitats in the world, accounting for perhaps 55 percent of the African continent. Dense, humid tropical rain forests stretch along coastal West Africa and on both sides of the equator in central Africa. Africa's climate is mostly tropical, with subtropical climates limited to the northern and southern coasts and to regions of high elevation. Rainfall is seasonal on most of the continent and is very sparse in desert and semidesert areas.

Geography and climate have significantly shaped African economic development. In the eastern African plains, the earliest humans hunted wild animals. The drier steppe regions favored herding. Wetter Savanna regions, like the Nile Valley, encouraged grain-based agriculture. Tropical forests favored hunting and gathering and, later, root-based agriculture. Rivers and lakes supported economies based on fishing.

Africa's peoples are as diverse as the continent's topography. In North Africa, contacts with Asian and European civilizations date back to the ancient Phoenicians, Greeks, and Romans. The native Berbers, living along the Mediterranean, have intermingled with many different peoples—with Muslim Arabs, who first conquered North Africa in the seventh and eighth centuries C.E.; with Spanish Muslims and Jews, many of whom settled in North Africa after their expulsion from Spain in 1492 (see page 402); and with sub-Saharan blacks.[1] The peoples living along the east, or Swahili, coast developed a maritime civilization and had rich commercial contacts with southern Arabia, the Persian Gulf, India, China, and the Malay Archipelago.

Black Africans inhabited the region south of the Sahara, an area of savanna and rain forest. The ancient Greeks called them *Ethiopians,* which means "people with burnt faces." The Berbers coined the term *Akal-n-Iquinawen,* which survives today as *Guinea.* The Arabs introduced another term, *Bilad al-Sudan,* which survives as *Sudan.* The Berber and Arab terms both mean "land of the blacks." Short-statured peoples, sometimes inaccurately referred to as Pygmies, inhabited the equatorial rain forests. South of those forests, in the continent's southern third, lived the Khoisan, a small people of yellow-brown skin color who primarily were hunters but also had domesticated livestock.

Egypt, Africa, and Race

Popular usage of the term *race* has often been imprecise and inaccurate. Unfortunately, the application of general characteristics and patterns of behavior to peoples based on perceptions of physical differences is one of the legacies of imperialism and colonialism. Anthropologists insist that when applied to geographical, national, religious, linguistic, or cultural groups, the concept of race is inappropriate and has been refuted by the scientific data. But the issue of race continues to engender fierce debate, as the example of Egypt shows.

Geographically, Egypt is obviously a part of the African continent. But from the days of the ancient Greek historian Herodotus of Halicarnassus, who visited Egypt (see page 8), down to the present, scholars have vigorously, even violently, debated whether racially and culturally Egypt is part of the Mediterranean world or part of the African world. Were Egyptians of the first century B.C.E.—who made enormous contributions to the Western world in architecture (the pyramids), mathematics, philosophy (the ideas of Socrates), science, and religion (the idea of divine kingship)—black people? The late Senegalese scholar Cheikh Anta Diop argued that much Western historical writing since the eighteenth century has been a "European racist plot" to destroy evidence showing that the people of the pharaohs were black. Diop and his followers in Africa and the United States have amassed architectural and linguistic evidence, as well as a small mountain of quotations from Greek and Roman writers and from the Bible, to insist that the ancient Egyptians belonged to the black race. Diop claimed to have examined the skin of ancient Egyptian mummies and said that on the basis of "infallible scientific techniques . . . the epidermis of those mummies was pigmented in the same way as that of all other (sub-Saharan) African negroes."[2]

Against this view, another group of scholars holds that the ancient Egyptians were Caucasians. They believe that Phoenician, Berber, Libyan, Hebrew, and Greek peoples populated Egypt and created its civilization. These scholars claim that Diop badly misunderstood the evidence. For example, whereas Diop relied on the book of Genesis to support his thesis, his detractors argue that the Hebrew Scriptures are not an anthropological treatise but a collection of Hebrew, Mesopotamian, and Egyptian legends concerned with the origins of all human peoples—by which the Hebrew writers meant ethnic groups, not racial groups in the twentieth-century sense. They point out that the pharaohs of the first century B.C.E. descended from the Macedonian generals whom Alexander the Great had placed over Egypt. They were white. A few scholars presenting a "white thesis" assert that Egypt exercised a "civilizing mission" in sub-Saharan Africa. Genetic theories, perhaps inevitably, have been challenged on many fronts, notably an archaeological one that proves no direct Egyptian influence in tropical Africa. Rather, the evidence suggests that indigenous cultures south of the Sahara developed independently, without any Egyptian influence. Both the "black thesis" and the "white thesis" are extremist.

A third proposition, perhaps the most plausible, holds that ancient Egypt, at the crossroads of three continents, was a melting pot of different cultures and peoples. To attribute Egyptian civilization to any one group is blatant racism. Many diverse peoples contributed to the great achievements of Egyptian culture. Moderate scholars believe that black Africans resided in ancient Egypt, primarily in Upper Egypt (south of what is now Cairo), but that other racial groups constituted the majority of the population.[3] On this complex issue, the jury is still out.

In the seventh and early eighth centuries, the Arabs conquered all of North Africa, taking control of Egypt between 639 and 642 (see page 194); ever since, Egypt has been an integral part of the Muslim world. Egypt's strategic location and commercial importance made it a logical target for Crusaders in the Middle Ages. In 1250 the Mamluks, a military warrior caste that originated in Anatolia, took over Egypt. With their slave soldiers, the Mamluks ruled until they were overthrown by the Ottoman Turks in 1517.

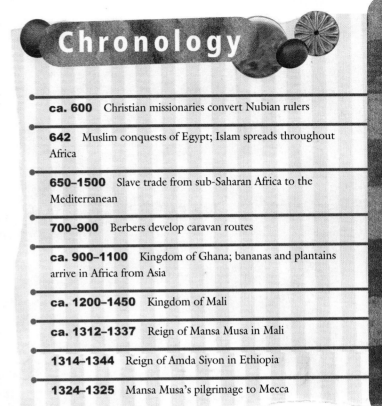

Chronology

ca. 600 Christian missionaries convert Nubian rulers

642 Muslim conquests of Egypt; Islam spreads throughout Africa

650–1500 Slave trade from sub-Saharan Africa to the Mediterranean

700–900 Berbers develop caravan routes

ca. 900–1100 Kingdom of Ghana; bananas and plantains arrive in Africa from Asia

ca. 1200–1450 Kingdom of Mali

ca. 1312–1337 Reign of Mansa Musa in Mali

1314–1344 Reign of Amda Siyon in Ethiopia

1324–1325 Mansa Musa's pilgrimage to Mecca

Early African Societies

Agriculture began very early in Africa. Archaeologists suggest that knowledge of plant cultivation moved west from ancient Judaea (southern Palestine), arriving in the Nile Delta in Egypt about the fifth millennium B.C.E. Settled agriculture then traveled down the Nile Valley and moved west across the Sahel to the central and western Sudan. By the first century B.C.E., settled agriculture existed in West Africa. From there it spread to the equatorial forests. African farmers learned to domesticate plants, including millet, sorghum, and yams. Cereal-growing people probably taught forest people to plant regular fields. Gradually African farmers also learned to clear land by burning. They evolved a sedentary way of life: living in villages, clearing fields, relying on root crops, and fishing.

● **Tassili Rock Painting**
This scene of cattle grazing near the group of huts (represented on the left by stylized white ovals) reflects the domestication of animals and the development of settled pastoral agriculture. Women and children seem to perform most of the domestic chores. Tassili is a mountainous region in the Sahara. *(Henri Lhote, Montrichard, France)*

Between 1500 and 1000 B.C.E., settled agriculture also spread southward from Ethiopia along the Rift Valley of present-day Kenya and Tanzania. Archaeological evidence reveals that the peoples of this region grew cereals, raised cattle, and used wooden and stone tools. Cattle raising spread more quickly than did planting. Early African peoples prized cattle highly. Many trading agreements, marriage alliances, political compacts, and treaties were negotiated in terms of cattle.

Cereals such as millet and sorghum are indigenous to Africa. Scholars speculate that traders brought bananas, taros (a type of yam), sugar cane, and coconut palms to Africa from Southeast Asia. Because tropical forest conditions were ideal for banana trees, their cultivation spread rapidly; they were easier to raise than cereal grains. Africans also domesticated donkeys, pigs, chickens, geese, and ducks.

The evolution to a settled life had profound effects. In contrast to nomadic conditions, settled societies made shared or common needs more apparent, and those needs strengthened ties among extended families. Population also increased:

The change from a hunter-gatherer economy to a settled farming economy affected population numbers. . . . What remains uncertain is whether in the agricultural economy there were more people, better fed, or more people, less well fed. . . . In precolonial Africa agricultural and pastoral populations may not have increased steadily over time, but fluctuated cyclically, growing and declining, though overall slowly growing.[4]

Scholars dispute the route by which ironworking spread to sub-Saharan Africa. Some believe the Phoenicians brought the iron-smelting technique to northwestern Africa, from where it spread southward. Others insist it spread from the Meroë region on the Nile westward. Most of West Africa had acquired knowledge of ironworking by 250 B.C.E., however, and archaeologists believe Meroë achieved pre-eminence as an iron-smelting center only in the first century B.C.E. Thus a stronger case can probably be made for the Phoenicians. The great trans-Saharan trade routes may have carried ironworking south from the Mediterranean coast. In any case, ancient iron tools found at the village of Nok on the Jos Plateau in present-day Nigeria seem to prove a

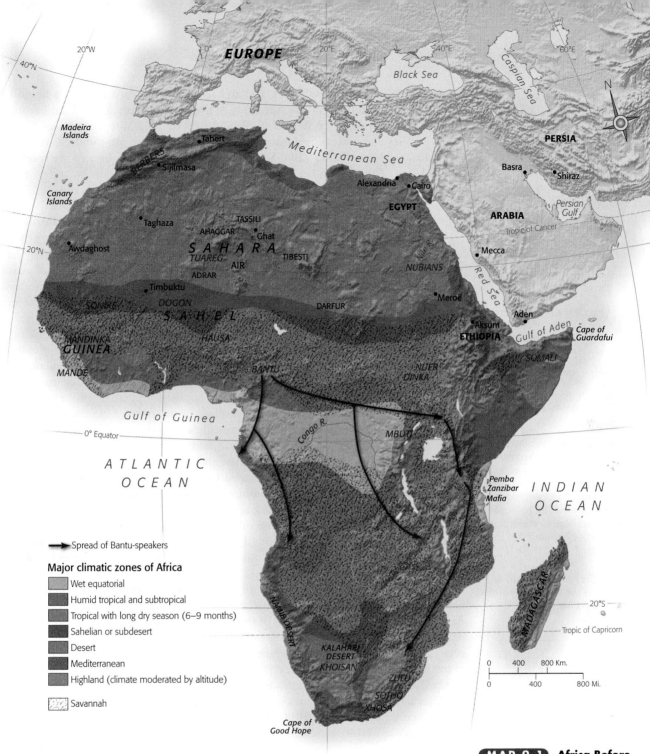

Map labels (partial):
EUROPE · Black Sea · Caspian Sea · PERSIA · Madeira Islands · Tahert · Sijilmasa · BERBERS · Mediterranean Sea · Alexandria · Cairo · EGYPT · Basra · Shiraz · Persian Gulf · ARABIA · Tropic of Cancer · Canary Islands · Taghaza · TASSILI · AHAGGAR · Ghat · Mecca · SAHARA · Awdaghost · TUAREG · AIR · TIBESTI · NUBIANS · Red Sea · ADRAR · Timbuktu · SONINKE · DOGON · DARFUR · Meroë · SAHEL · Aden · HAUSA · Aksum · MANDINKA · GUINEA · ETHIOPIA · Gulf of Aden · Cape of Guardafui · MANDE · BANTU · SOMALI · NUER · DINKA · Gulf of Guinea · Congo R. · MBUTI · 0° Equator · ATLANTIC OCEAN · Pemba · Zanzibar · Mafia · INDIAN OCEAN · NAMIB DESERT · MADAGASCAR · 20°S · Tropic of Capricorn · KALAHARI DESERT · KHOISAN · ZULU · SOTHO · XHOSA · Cape of Good Hope

→ Spread of Bantu-speakers

Major climatic zones of Africa

- Wet equatorial
- Humid tropical and subtropical
- Tropical with long dry season (6–9 months)
- Sahelian or subdesert
- Desert
- Mediterranean
- Highland (climate moderated by altitude)
- Savannah

MAP 9.1 **Africa Before 1500** Africa's climate zones have always played a critical role in the history of the continent and its peoples. These zones mirror each other north and south of the equator: tropical forest, savannah, subdesert, desert, and Mediterranean climate. Note also how the Bantu-speakers left the savannah of central West Africa, moved through the tropical forest at the equator, and reached the savannah of eastern and southern Africa.

knowledge of ironworking in West Africa. The Nok culture, which enjoys enduring fame for its fine terra-cotta (baked clay) sculptures, flourished from about 800 B.C.E. to 200 C.E.

Bantu Migrations

The spread of ironworking is linked to the migrations of Bantu-speaking peoples. Today the overwhelming majority of the 70 million people living south of the Congo River speak a **Bantu** language. Because very few Muslims or Europeans penetrated into the interior, very few written sources for the early history of central and southern Africa survive. Lacking written sources, modern scholars have tried to reconstruct the history of the Bantu-speakers on the basis of linguistics, oral traditions (rarely reliable

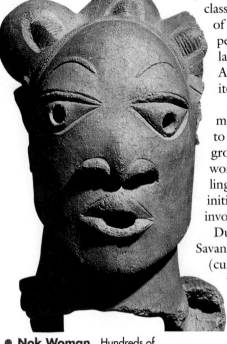

● **Nok Woman** Hundreds of terra-cotta sculptures such as the head of this woman survive from the Nok culture, which originated in the central plateau of northern Nigeria in the first millennium B.C.E. *(National Museum, Lagos, Nigeria/Werner Forman Archive/Art Resource, NY)*

Bantu *The people living in Africa south of the Congo River who speak a Bantu language.*

Sudan *The African region surrounded by the Sahara, the Gulf of Guinea, the Atlantic Ocean, and the mountains of Ethiopia.*

beyond three hundred years back), and archaeology. The word *Bantu* is a linguistic classification, and linguistics (the study of the nature, structure, and modification of human speech) has helped scholars explain the migratory patterns of African peoples east and south of the equatorial forest. There are hundreds of Bantu languages, including Zulu, Sotho, and Xhosa, which are part of the southern African linguistic and cultural nexus. Swahili is spoken in eastern, and to a limited extent central, Africa.

Bantu-speaking peoples originated in the Benue region, the borderlands of modern Cameroon and Nigeria. In the second millennium B.C.E., they began to spread south and east into the forest zone of equatorial Africa. From there, groups moved onto the Savanna along the lower Congo River. Since they had words for fishing, fishhooks, fish traps, dugout canoes, paddles, yams, and goats, linguists assume that they were fishermen and that they cultivated roots. Because initially they lacked words for grains and cattle herding, they probably were not involved in those activities.

During the next fifteen hundred years, Bantu-speakers migrated throughout the Savanna, adopted mixed agriculture, and learned ironworking. Mixed agriculture (cultivating cereals and raising livestock) and ironworking were practiced in western East Africa (the region of modern Burundi) in the first century B.C.E. In the first millennium C.E., Bantu-speakers migrated into eastern and southern Africa. They did not displace earlier peoples but assimilated with them. The earlier inhabitants gradually adopted a Bantu language.

The settled cultivation of cereals and the keeping of livestock, together with intermarriage with indigenous peoples, apparently led over a long time to considerable population increases and the need to migrate further. The so-called Bantu migrations should not be seen as a single movement of cultivating, ironworking, Bantu-speaking black people sweeping across Africa from west to east and displacing all peoples in their path. Rather, those migrations were "a series of interrelated diffusions and syntheses, as small groups of Bantu-speakers interacted with preexisting peoples and new technical developments to produce a range of distinct cultural syntheses across the southern half of Africa."[5]

The Bantu-speakers' expansion and subsequent land settlement that dominated the first millennium and a half C.E. of eastern and southern African history was uneven. Enormous differences in the quality of the environment conditioned settlement. Some regions were well watered; others were very arid. This situation resulted in very uneven population distribution. The largest concentration of people seems to have been in the region bounded on the west by the Congo River and on the north, south, and east by Lakes Edward and Victoria and Mount Kilimanjaro, comprising parts of modern Uganda, Rwanda, and Tanzania. There the agricultural system rested on sorghum and yam cultivation. Between 900 and 1100, bananas and plantains (a starchy form of the banana) arrived from Asia. Because little effort was needed for their cultivation and the yield was much higher than for yams, bananas soon became the staple crop. The rapidly growing Bantu-speaking population led to further migration southward and eastward.[6] By the eighth century Bantu-speaking people had reached the region of present-day Zimbabwe, and by the fifteenth century Africa's southeastern coast.

Kingdoms of the Western Sudan (ca. 1000 B.C.E.–1500 C.E.)

The **Sudan** is that region bounded by the Sahara to the north, the Gulf of Guinea to the south, the Atlantic Ocean to the west, and the mountains of Ethiopia to the east. In the Savanna of the western Sudan—where the Bantu migrations originated—a series of dynamic kingdoms emerged in the millennium before European intrusion.

Between 1000 B.C.E. and 200 C.E., the peoples of the western Sudan made the momentous shift from nomadic hunting to settled agriculture. The rich Savanna proved ideally suited to the production of cereals, especially rice, millet, and sorghum. People situated near the Senegal River and Lake Chad supplemented their diet with fish. Food supply affects population, and the peoples of the region—known as the Mande-speakers and the Chadic-speakers, or Sao—increased dramatically in number. By 400 C.E. the entire Savanna, particularly the areas around Lake Chad, the Niger River bend, and present-day central Nigeria (see Map 9.1), had a large population.

Families and clans affiliated by blood kinship lived together in villages or small city-states. The basic social unit was the extended family. A chief, in consultation with a council of elders, governed a village. Some villages seem to have formed kingdoms. Village chiefs were responsible to regional heads, who answered to provincial governors, who in turn were responsible to a king. The chiefs and their families formed an aristocracy.

Kingship in the Sudan may have emerged from the priesthood, whose members were believed to make rain and to have contact with spirit powers. African kings always had religious sanction or support for their authority and were often considered divine. In this respect, early African kingship bears a strong resemblance to Germanic kingship of the same period: the king's authority rested in part on the ruler's ability to negotiate with outside powers, such as the gods.

African religions were animistic and polytheistic. Most people believed that a supreme being had created the universe and was the source of all life. The supreme being breathed spirit into all living things, and the *anima,* or spirit, residing in such things as trees, water, and earth had to be appeased. During the annual agricultural cycle, for example, all the spirits had to be propitiated from the time of clearing the land through sowing the seed to the final harvest. Because special ceremonies were necessary to satisfy the spirits, special priests with the knowledge and power to communicate with them through sacred rituals were needed. Thus the heads of families and villages were likely to be priests. Each family head was responsible for maintaining the family ritual cults—ceremonies honoring the dead and living members of the family.[7]

In sum, the most prominent feature of early African society was a strong sense of community based on blood relationship and on religion. Extended families made up the villages that collectively formed small kingdoms. What spurred the expansion of these small kingdoms into formidable powers controlling sizable territory was the development of long-distance trade. And what made long-distance or trans-Saharan trade possible was the camel.

The Trans-Saharan Trade

The expression "trans-Saharan trade" refers to the north-south trade across the Sahara (see Map 9.2). The camel had an impact on this trade comparable to the very important impact of the horse on European agriculture. Although scholars dispute exactly when the camel was introduced from Central Asia—first into North Africa, then into the Sahara and the Sudan—they agree that it was before 200 C.E. Camels can carry about five hundred pounds as far as twenty-five miles a day and can go for days without drinking, living on the water stored in their stomachs. Sometimes stupid and vicious, camels had to be loaded on a daily, sometimes twice-daily, basis. And much of the cargo for a long trip was provisions for the journey itself. Nevertheless, camels proved more efficient for desert transportation than horses or oxen, and the use of this beast to carry heavy and bulky freight not only brought economic and social change to Africa but also affected the development of world commerce.

Sometime in the fifth century, the North African **Berbers** fashioned a saddle for use on the camel. This saddle had no direct effect on commercial operations, for a merchant usually walked and guided the camel on foot. But the saddle gave the Berbers and later the region's Arabian inhabitants maneuverability on the animal and thus a powerful political and military advantage: they came to dominate the desert and to create lucrative routes across it. The Berbers determined who could enter the desert,

Berbers *North African peoples who were the first to develop saddles for use on the camel.*

and they extracted large sums of protection money from merchant caravans in ex-change for a safe trip.

Between 700 and 900 C.E., the Berbers developed a network of caravan routes be-tween the Mediterranean coast and the Sudan (see Map 9.1). The Morocco-Niger route ran from Fez to Sijilmassa on the desert's edge and then south by way of Tag-haza and Walata and back to Fez. Another route originated at Sijilmassa and extended due south to Timbuktu with a stop at Taghaza. A third route ran south from Tripoli to Lake Chad. A fourth ran from Egypt to Gao by way of the Saharan oases of Ghat and Agades and then on to Takedda.

The long expedition across the Sahara testifies to the spirit of the traders and to their passion for wealth. Because of the blistering sun and daytime temperatures reaching 110 degrees, caravan drivers preferred night travel, when temperatures might drop to the low 20s. Ibn Battuta, an Arab traveler in the fourteenth century when the trade was at its height, left us one of the best descriptions of the trans-Saharan traffic (see page 213).

Nomadic raiders, the Tuareg Berbers, posed a serious threat. The Tuaregs lived in the desert uplands and preyed on the caravans as a way of life. Thus merchants made safe-conduct agreements with them and selected guides from among them. Caravans of twelve thousand camels were reported in the fourteenth century. Large numbers of merchants crossed the desert together to discourage attack. Blinding sandstorms of-ten isolated part of a line of camels and on at least one occasion buried alive some camels and drivers. Water was the biggest problem. The Tuaregs sometimes poisoned wells to wipe out caravans and steal their goods. To satisfy normal thirst and to com-pensate for constant sweating, each person required a gallon of water per day. Desper-ate thirst sometimes forced the traders to kill camels and drink the foul, brackish water in their stomachs. It took Ibn Battuta twenty-five days to travel from Sijilmassa to the oasis of Taghaza and another sixty-five days to travel from Taghaza to the important market town of Walata.

The Arab-Berber merchants from North Africa who controlled the caravan trade carried manufactured goods—silk and cotton cloth, beads, mirrors—as well as dates and salt (essential in tropical climates to replace the loss from perspiration) from the Saharan oases and mines to the Sudan. These products were exchanged for the much-coveted commodities of the West African savanna—gold, ivory, gum, kola nuts (eaten as a stimulant), and captive slaves.

The steady growth of trans-Saharan trade had three important effects on West Af-rican society. The trade stimulated gold mining and the search for slaves. Parts of modern-day Senegal, Nigeria, and Ghana contained rich veins of gold. Both sexes shared in mining it. Men sank the shafts, hacked out gold-bearing rocks, and crushed them, separating the gold from the soil. Women washed the gold in gourds. Alluvial gold (mixed with soil, sand, or gravel) was separated from the soil by panning. Scholars estimate that by the eleventh century nine tons were exported to Europe annually—a prodigious amount for the time, since even with modern machinery and sophisticated techniques, the total gold exports from the same region in 1937 amounted to only twenty-one tons. A large percentage of this metal went to Egypt. From there it was transported down the Red Sea and eventually to India (see Map 8.2 on page 210) to pay for the spices and silks demanded by Mediterranean commerce. West African gold proved "absolutely vital for the monetization of the medieval Mediterranean economy and for the maintenance of its balance of payments with South Asia."[8] African gold linked the entire world, exclusive of the Western Hemisphere.

Slaves were West Africa's second most valuable export (after gold). African slaves, like their early European and Asian counterparts, seem to have been peoples captured in war. In the Muslim cities of North Africa, southern Europe, and southwestern Asia, there was a high demand for household slaves among the elite. Slaves also worked the gold and salt mines. Recent research suggests, moreover, that large numbers of black slaves were recruited through the trans-Saharan trade for Muslim military service.

Table 9.1 Estimated Magnitude of Trans-Saharan Slave Trade, 650–1500

YEARS	ANNUAL AVERAGE OF SLAVES TRADED	TOTAL
650–800	1,000	150,000
800–900	3,000	300,000
900–1100	8,700	1,740,000
1100–1400	5,500	1,650,000
1400–1500	4,300	430,000

Source: From R. A. Austen, "The Trans-Saharan Slave Trade: A Tentative Census," in *The Uncommon Market: Essays in the Economic History of the Atlantic Slave Trade,* ed. H. A. Gemery and J. S. Hogendorn (New York: Academic Press, 1979). Used with permission.

High death rates from disease, manumission, and the assimilation of some blacks into Muslim society meant that the demand for slaves remained high for centuries. Table 9.1 shows one scholar's tentative conclusions, based on many kinds of evidence, about the scope of the trans-Saharan slave trade. The total number of blacks enslaved over an 850-year period may be tentatively estimated at more than 4 million.[9]

Slavery in Muslim societies, as in European and Asian countries before the fifteenth century, was not based on skin color. Muslims also enslaved Caucasians who had been purchased, seized in war, or kidnapped from Europe. Wealthy Muslim households in Córdoba, Alexandria, and Tunis often included slaves of a number of races, all of whom had been completely cut off from their cultural roots. Likewise, West African kings who sold blacks to northern traders also bought a few white slaves—Slavic, British, and Turkish—for their domestic needs. Race had little to do with the phenomenon of slavery.[10]

The trans-Saharan trade also stimulated the development of vigorous urban centers in West Africa. Scholars date the growth of African cities from around the early ninth century. Families that had profited from trade tended to congregate in the border zones between the Savanna and the Sahara. They acted as middlemen between the miners to the south and Muslim merchants from the north. By the early thirteenth century, these families had become powerful black merchant dynasties. Muslim traders from the Mediterranean settled permanently in the trading depots, from which they organized the trans-Saharan caravans. The concentration of people stimulated agriculture and the craft industries. Gradually cities of sizable population emerged. Jenne, Gao, and Timbuktu, which enjoyed commanding positions on the Niger River bend, became centers of the export-import trade. Sijilmassa grew into a thriving market center. Kumbi, with between fifteen thousand and twenty thousand inhabitants, was probably the largest city in the western Sudan in the twelfth century. (By European standards, Kumbi was a metropolis; London and Paris achieved its size only in the late thirteenth century.) Between 1100 and 1400, these cities played a dynamic role in the commercial life of West Africa and Europe and became centers of intellectual creativity.

Perhaps the most influential consequence of the trans-Saharan trade was the introduction of Islam to West African society. In the eighth century, Arab invaders overran all of coastal North Africa. The Berbers living there gradually became Muslims. As traders, these Berbers carried Islam to sub-Saharan West Africa, the region known in Arabic as Bilad al-Sudan, "Land of the Blacks." From the eleventh century onward,

Primary Source:
The Book of Routes and Realms
This account by an Islamic geographer tells how a guest of the king of Ghana averted a drought, and thereby led the king to accept Islam.

militant Almoravids, a coalition of fundamentalist western Saharan Berbers, preached Islam to the rulers of Ghana, Mali, Songhai, and Kanem-Bornu, who, admiring Muslim administrative techniques and wanting to protect their kingdoms from Muslim attacks, accepted Islamic conversion. Some merchants also sought to preserve their elite mercantile status by adopting Islam. By the tenth century, Muslim Berbers controlled the north-south trade routes to the Savanna. By the eleventh century, African rulers of Gao and Timbuktu had accepted Islam. The king of Ghana was also influenced by Islam. Muslims quickly became integral to West African government and society. Hence in the period from roughly 1000 to 1400, Islam in West Africa was a class-based religion with conversion inspired by political or economic motives. Rural people retained their traditional animism.

Conversion to Islam introduced West Africans to a rich and sophisticated culture. By the late eleventh century, Muslims were guiding the ruler of Ghana in the operation of his administrative machinery. The king of Ghana adopted the Muslim dīwān, the agency for keeping financial records (see page 196). Because efficient government depends on the preservation of records, the arrival of Islam in West Africa marked the advent of written documents there. Arab Muslims also taught the rulers of Ghana how to manufacture bricks, and royal palaces and mosques began to be built of brick. African rulers corresponded with Muslim architects, theologians, and other intellectuals, who advised them on statecraft and religion. Islam accelerated the development of the West African empires of the ninth through fifteenth centuries.

After the Muslim conquest of Egypt in 642 (see page 194), Islam spread southward from Egypt up the Nile Valley and west to Darfur and Wadai. This Muslim penetration came not by military force but, as in the trans-Saharan trade routes in West Africa, by gradual commercial passage.

Muslim expansion from the Arabian peninsula across the Red Sea to the Horn of Africa, then southward along the coast of East Africa, represents a third direction of Islam's growth in Africa. From ports on the Red Sea and the Gulf of Aden, maritime trade carried the Prophet's teachings to East Africa and the Indian Ocean. Muslims founded the port city of **Mogadishu,** today Somalia's capital. In the twelfth century, Mogadishu developed into a Muslim sultanate, a monarchy that employed a slave military corps against foreign and domestic enemies. Archaeological evidence, confirmed by Arabic sources, reveals a rapid Islamic expansion along Africa's east coast in the thirteenth century. Many settlers came from Yemen in the southern Arabian peninsula, and one family set up the Abul-Mawahib dynasty in Kilwa.[11] Ibn Battuta discovered a center for Islamic law when he visited Kilwa in 1331.

Mogadishu *A Muslim port city founded between the eighth and tenth centuries; today it is the capital of Somalia.*

AFRICAN KINGDOMS AND EMPIRES (CA. 800–1450)

What values do Africans' art, architecture, and religions express?

All African societies shared one basic feature: a close relationship between political and social organization. Ethnic or blood ties bound clan members together. What scholars call **stateless societies** were culturally homogeneous ethnic societies. The smallest ones numbered fewer than a hundred people and were nomadic hunting groups. Larger stateless societies of perhaps several thousand people lived a settled and often agricultural or herding life.

The period from about 800 to 1450 witnessed the flowering of several powerful African states. In the western Sudan, the large empires of Ghana and Mali developed, complete with large royal bureaucracies. On the east coast emerged powerful city-states based on sophisticated mercantile activities and, like Sudan, very much influenced by Islam. In Ethiopia, in central East Africa, kings relied on the Christian faith

stateless societies *African societies bound together by ethnic or blood ties rather than being political states.*

of their people to strengthen political authority. In South Africa, the empire of Great Zimbabwe, built on the gold trade with the east coast, flourished.

The Kingdom of Ghana (ca. 900–1100)

So remarkable was the kingdom of **Ghana** during the age of Africa's great empires that writers throughout the medieval world, such as the fourteenth-century Muslim historian Ibn Khaldun, praised it as a model for other rulers. Medieval Ghana also holds a central place in the historical consciousness of the modern state of Ghana. Since this former British colony attained independence in 1957, its political leaders have hailed the medieval period as a glorious heritage. The name of the modern republic of Ghana—which in fact lies far from the site of the old kingdom—was selected to signify the rebirth of an age of gold in black Africa.

Ghana *The name of a great African kingdom inhabited by the Soninke people.*

The nucleus of the territory that became the kingdom of Ghana was inhabited by Soninke people who called their ruler **ghana**, or war chief. By the late eighth century, Muslim traders and other foreigners applied the word to the region where the Soninke lived, the black kingdom south of the Sahara. The Soninke themselves called their land "Aoukar" or "Awkar," by which they meant the region north of the Senegal and Niger Rivers. Only the southern part of Aoukar received enough rainfall to be agriculturally productive, and it was in this area that the civilization of Ghana developed. Skillful farming and an efficient system of irrigation led to the production of abundant crops, which eventually supported a population of as many as two hundred thousand.

ghana *The name used by the Soninke people for their ruler.*

The Soninke name for their king—war chief—aptly describes the king's major preoccupation in the tenth century. In 992 Ghana captured the Berber town of Awdaghost, strategically situated on the trans-Saharan trade route (see Map 9.1). Thereafter Ghana controlled the southern portion of a major caravan route. Before the year 1000, the rulers of Ghana had extended their influence almost to the Atlantic coast and had captured a number of small kingdoms in the south and east. By the early eleventh century, the king exercised sway over a territory approximately the size of Texas. No other power in the West African region could successfully challenge him.

Throughout this vast West African area, all authority sprang from the king. Religious ceremonies and court rituals emphasized the king's sacredness and were intended to strengthen his authority. The king's position was hereditary in the matrilineal line—that is, the ruling king's heir was one of the king's sister's sons (presumably the eldest or fittest for battle). According to the eleventh-century Spanish Muslim geographer al-Bakri (1040?–1094), "This is their custom . . . the kingdom is inherited only by the son of the king's sister. He the king has no doubt that his successor is a son of his sister, while he is not certain that his son is in fact his own."[12]

A council of ministers assisted the king in the work of government, and from the ninth century on most of these ministers were Muslims. Detailed evidence about the early Ghanaian bureaucracy has not survived, but scholars suspect that separate agencies were responsible for taxation, royal property, foreigners, forests, and the army. The royal administration was well served by Muslim ideas, skills, and especially literacy. The king and his people, however, clung to their ancestral religion and basic cultural institutions.

The king of Ghana held his court in **Kumbi**. Al-Bakri provides a valuable picture of the city in the eleventh century:

Kumbi *The city where the king of Ghana held his court.*

The city of Ghana consists of two towns lying on a plain, one of which is inhabited by Muslims and is large, possessing twelve mosques—one of which is a congregational mosque for Friday prayer; each has its imam, its muezzin and paid reciters of the Quran. The town possesses a large number of jurisconsults and learned men.[13]

Either for their own protection or to preserve their special identity, the Muslims lived separate from the African artisans and tradespeople. The Muslim community in Ghana must have been large and prosperous to have supported twelve mosques. The *imam* was the religious leader who conducted the ritual worship, especially the main prayer service on Fridays (see page 198). The *muezzin* led the prayer responses after the imam; he needed a strong voice so that those at a distance and the women in the harems, or enclosures, could hear (see page 209). Muslim religious leaders exercised civil authority over their coreligionists. Their presence and that of other learned Muslims also suggests vigorous intellectual activity.

Al-Bakri describes the town where the king lived and the royal court:

The town inhabited by the king is six miles from the Muslim one and is called Al Ghana. . . . The residence of the king consists of a palace and a number of dome-shaped dwellings, all of them surrounded by a strong enclosure, like a city wall. In the town . . . is a mosque, where Muslims who come on diplomatic missions to the king pray. The town where the king lives is surrounded by domed huts, woods, and copses where priest-magicians live; in these woods also are the religious idols and tombs of the kings. Special guards protect this area and prevent anyone from entering it so that no foreigners know what is inside. Here also are the king's prisons, and if anyone is imprisoned there, nothing more is heard of him.[14]

The king adorns himself, as do the women here, with necklaces and bracelets; on their heads they wear caps decorated with gold, sewn on material of fine cotton stuffing. When he holds court in order to hear the people's complaints and to do justice, he sits in a pavilion around which stand ten horses wearing golden trappings; behind him ten pages stand, holding shields and swords decorated with gold; at his right are the sons of the chiefs of the country, splendidly dressed and with their hair sprinkled with gold. The governor of the city sits on the ground in front of the king with other officials likewise sitting around him. Excellently pedigreed dogs guard the door of the pavilion. . . . The noise of a sort-of drum, called a daba, and made from a long hollow log, announces the start of the royal audience. When the king's coreligionists appear before him, they fall on their knees and toss dust on their heads—this is their way of greeting their sovereign. Muslims show respect by clapping their hands.[15]

What sort of juridical system did Ghana have? How was the guilt or innocence of an accused person determined? Justice derived from the king, who heard cases at court or on his travels throughout his kingdom. As al-Bakri recounts:

When a man is accused of denying a debt or of having shed blood or some other crime, a headman (village chief) takes a thin piece of wood, which is sour and bitter to taste, and pours upon it some water which he then gives to the defendant to drink. If the man vomits, his innocence is recognized and he is congratulated. If he does not vomit and the drink remains in his stomach, the accusation is accepted as justified.[16]

This appeal to the supernatural for judgment was very similar to the justice by ordeal that prevailed among the Germanic peoples of western Europe at the same time. Complicated cases in Ghana seem to have been appealed to the king, who often relied on the advice of Muslim legal experts.

The king's elaborate court, the administrative machinery he built, and the extensive territories he governed were all expensive. Ghana's king needed a lot of money, and he apparently had four main sources of support. The royal estates—some hereditary, others conquered in war—produced annual revenue, mostly in the form of foodstuffs for the royal household. The king also received tribute annually from subordinate chieftains (lack of evidence prevents an estimate of the value of this tax). Customs duties on goods entering and leaving the country generated revenues. Salt was the largest import. Berber merchants paid a tax to the king on the cloth, metalwork, weapons, and other goods that they brought into the country from North Africa; in return these traders received royal protection from bandits. African traders bringing gold into Ghana from the south also paid the customs duty.

Finally, the royal treasury held a monopoly on the export of gold. The gold industry was undoubtedly the king's largest source of income. It was on gold that the fame of medieval Ghana rested. The ninth-century geographer al-Ya-qubi wrote, "Its king

is mighty, and in his lands are gold mines. Under his authority are various other king-doms—and in all this region there is gold."[17]

The governing aristocracy—the king, his court, and Muslim administrators—occupied the highest rung on the Ghanaian social ladder. On the next rung stood the merchant class. Considerably below the merchants stood the farmers, cattle breeders, gold mine supervisors, and skilled craftsmen and weavers—what today might be called the middle class. Some merchants and miners must have enjoyed great wealth, but, as in all aristocratic societies, money alone did not suffice. High status was based on blood and royal service. On the social ladder's lowest rung were slaves, who worked in households, on farms, and in the mines. As in Asian and European societies of the time, slaves accounted for only a small percentage of the population.

Apart from these social classes stood the army. According to al-Bakri, "the king of Ghana can put 200,000 warriors in the field, more than 40,000 being armed with bow and arrow." Like most medieval estimates, this is probably a gross exaggeration. Even a modern industrialized state with sophisticated means of transportation, com-munication, and supply lines would have enormous difficulty mobilizing so many men for battle. The king of Ghana, however, was not called "war chief" for nothing. He maintained at his palace a crack standing force of a thousand men, comparable to the Roman Praetorian Guard. These thoroughly disciplined, well-armed, totally loyal troops protected the king and the royal court. They lived in special compounds, en-joyed the king's favor, and sometimes acted as his personal ambassadors to subordi-nate rulers. In wartime, this regular army was augmented by levies of soldiers from conquered peoples and by the use of slaves and free reserves. The force that the king could field was sizable, if not as huge as al-Bakri estimated.

The Kingdom of Mali (ca. 1200–1450)

During the century after the collapse of Kumbi, a cloud of obscurity hung over the western Sudan. The kingdom of Ghana split into several small kingdoms that feuded among themselves. One people, the Mandinke, lived in the kingdom of Kangaba on the upper Niger River. The Mandinke had long been part of the Ghanaian empire, and the Mandinke and Soninke belonged to the same language group. Kangaba formed the core of the new empire of Mali. Building on Ghanaian foundations, Mali developed into a better-organized and more powerful state than Ghana.

● **The Great Friday Mosque, Jenne** The mosque at Jenne was built in the form of a parallelogram. Inside, nine long rows of adobe columns run along a north-south axis and support a flat roof of palm logs. A pointed arch links each column to the next in its row, forming nine east-west archways facing the *mihrab,* the niche indicating the direction of Mecca and from which the *imam* (prayer leader) speaks. This mosque (rebuilt in 1907 on a thirteenth-century model) testifies to the considerable wealth, geometrical knowledge, and manpower of the region. *(Copyright Carollee Pelos. From Spectacular Vernacular: The Adobe Tradition, Chapter 11, "Histories of the Great Mosques of Djenné" [New York: Aperture, 1996])*

● **Dogon Couple** This seated couple, made of wood and metal, tells us a great deal about the culture of the people living in the Dogon region at the Niger River bend in West Africa, in what is now Mali. The man's right arm circles the woman's shoulder and rests on her breast; his left hand points toward his genitals. He carries a quiver on his back; she bears an infant on hers. The mutually dependent figures indicate that the man is progenitor, protector, and provider; the woman is child-bearer and nurturer. Dogon society was strongly patrilineal and famous for its artwork. This piece was done between the sixteenth and twentieth centuries. (*The Metropolitan Museum of Art, Gift of Lester Wunderman, 1977 [1977.394.15]. Photograph © 1993 The Metropolitan Museum of Art*)

The kingdom of Mali (see Map 9.2) owed its greatness to two fundamental assets. First, its strong agricultural and commercial base provided for a large population and enormous wealth. Second, Mali had two rulers, Sundiata and Mansa Musa, who combined military success with exceptionally creative personalities.

The earliest surviving evidence about the Mandinke, dating from the early eleventh century, indicates that they were extremely successful at agriculture. Consistently large harvests throughout the twelfth and thirteenth centuries meant a plentiful supply of food, which encouraged steady population growth. The geographical location of Kangaba also placed the Mandinke in an ideal position in West African trade. Earlier, during the period of Ghanaian hegemony, the Mandinke had acted as middlemen in the gold and salt traffic flowing north and south. In the thirteenth century Mandinke traders formed companies, traveled widely, and gradually became a major force in the entire West African trade.

Sundiata (r. ca. 1230–1255) set up his capital at Niani, transforming the city into an important financial and trading center. He then embarked on a policy of imperial expansion. Through a series of military victories, Sundiata and his successors absorbed into Mali other territories of the former kingdom of Ghana and established hegemony over the trading cities of Gao, Jenne, and Walata.

These expansionist policies were continued in the fourteenth century by Sundiata's descendant Mansa Musa (r. ca. 1312–1337), early Africa's most famous ruler. In the language of the Mandinke, *mansa* means "emperor." Mansa Musa fought many campaigns and checked every attempt at rebellion. Ultimately his influence extended northward to several Berber cities in the Sahara, eastward to Timbuktu and Gao, and westward as far as the Atlantic Ocean. Throughout his territories, he maintained strict royal control over the rich trans-Saharan trade. Thus this empire, roughly twice the size of the Ghanaian kingdom and containing perhaps 8 million people, brought Mansa Musa fabulous wealth.

Mansa Musa built on the foundations of his predecessors. The stratified aristocratic structure of Malian society perpetuated the pattern set in Ghana, as did the system of provincial administration and annual tribute. The emperor took responsibility for the territories that formed the heart of the empire and appointed governors to rule the outlying provinces or dependent kingdoms. But Mansa Musa made a significant innovation: in a practice strikingly similar to a system used in both China and France at that time, he appointed members of the royal family as provincial governors. He could count on their loyalty, and they received valuable experience in the work of government.

In another aspect of administration, Mansa Musa also differed from his predecessors. He became a devout Muslim. Although most of the Mandinke clung to their ancestral animism, Islamic practices and influences in Mali multiplied.

The most celebrated event of Mansa Musa's reign was his pilgrimage to Mecca in 1324–1325, during which he paid a state visit to the sultan of Egypt. Mansa Musa's entrance into Cairo was magnificent. Preceded by five hundred slaves, each carrying a six-pound staff of gold, he followed with a huge host of retainers, including one hundred elephants each bearing one hundred pounds of gold. The emperor lavished his wealth on the citizens of the Egyptian capital. Writing twelve years later, al-Omari, one of the sultan's officials, recounts:

This man Mansa Musa spread upon Cairo the flood of his generosity: there was no person, officer of the court, or holder of any office of the Sultanate who did not receive a sum of gold from him. The people of Cairo earned incalculable sums from him, whether by buying and selling or by gifts. So much gold was current in Cairo that it ruined the value of money.[18]

Mansa Musa's gold brought about terrible inflation throughout Egypt. For the first time, the Mediterranean world gained concrete knowledge of Mali's wealth and power, and the black kingdom began to be known as one of the world's great empires. Mali retained this international reputation into the fifteenth century.

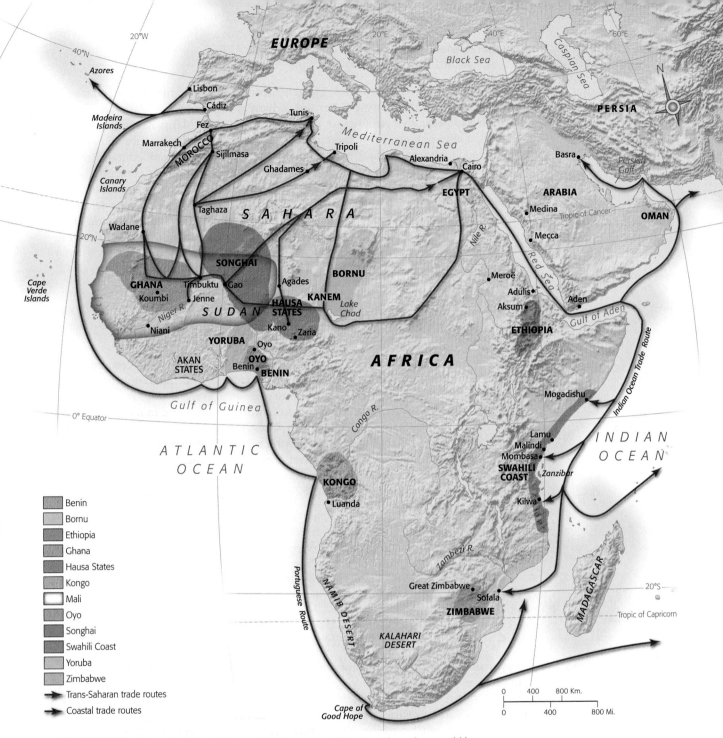

MAP 9.2 **Sub-Saharan African Kingdoms and Trade** Throughout world history powerful kingdoms have generally been closely connected to far-flung trade networks. Here we can see how the large empires in western, central, and southern Africa were linked either to the great trans-Saharan trade network, the Indian Ocean trade network, or, in the case of the Congo, to the massive interior trade network of central Africa and the Congo River basin. Although not a kingdom, the large and wealthy Swahili city-states along the East African coast owed their existence to the trade reaching across the Indian Ocean to India, Southeast Asia, and China.

Musa's pilgrimage also had significant consequences within Mali. He gained some understanding of the Mediterranean countries and opened diplomatic relations with the Muslim rulers of Morocco and Egypt. His zeal for the Muslim faith and Islamic culture increased. Musa brought back from Arabia the distinguished architect al-Saheli, whom he commissioned to build new mosques at Timbuktu and other cities. These mosques served as centers for the conversion of Africans. Musa employed

Muslim engineers to build in brick. He also encouraged Malian merchants and traders to wear the distinctive flowing robes and turbans of Muslim males.

Timbuktu began as a campsite for desert nomads. Under Mansa Musa, it grew into a thriving entrepôt, attracting merchants and traders from North Africa and all parts of the Mediterranean world. These people brought with them cosmopolitan attitudes and ideas. In the fifteenth century, Timbuktu developed into a great center for scholarship and learning. Architects, astronomers, poets, lawyers, mathematicians, and theologians flocked there. One hundred fifty schools were devoted to Qur'anic studies. The school of Islamic law enjoyed a distinction in Africa comparable to the prestige of the school at Cairo (see page 215). A vigorous trade in books flourished in Timbuktu. Leo Africanus, a sixteenth-century Muslim traveler and writer who later converted to Christianity, recounts that around 1500 Timbuktu had a

> *great store of doctors, judges, priests, and other learned men that are bountifully maintained at the king's cost and charges. And hitherto are brought diverse manuscripts or written books out of Barbarie the north African states, from Egypt to the Atlantic Ocean which are sold for more money than any other merchandise.*

It is easy to understand why the university at Timbuktu was called by a contemporary writer "the Queen of the Sudan." Timbuktu's tradition and reputation for African scholarship lasted until the eighteenth century.

Moreover, in the fourteenth and fifteenth centuries, many Muslim intellectuals and Arab traders married native African women. These unions brought into being a group of racially mixed people. The necessity of living together harmoniously, the traditional awareness of diverse cultures, and the cosmopolitan atmosphere of Timbuktu all contributed to a rare degree of racial toleration and understanding. After visiting the court of Mansa Musa's successor in 1352–1353, Ibn Battuta observed that

> *the Negroes possess some admirable qualities. They are seldom unjust, and have a greater abhorrence of injustice than any other people. Their sultan shows no mercy to anyone who is guilty of the least act of it. There is complete security in their country. Neither traveler nor inhabitant in it has anything to fear from robbers. . . . They do not confiscate the property of any white man who dies in their country, even if it be uncounted wealth. On the contrary, they give it into the charge of some trustworthy person among the whites.*[19]

Ethiopia: The Christian Kingdom of Aksum

Egyptian culture exerted a profound influence on the sub-Saharan kingdom of Nubia in northeastern Africa. Nubia's capital was at Meroë (see Map 9.2); thus the country is often referred to as the Nubian kingdom of Meroë. As part of the Roman Empire, Egypt was naturally subject to Hellenistic and Roman cultural forces, and it became an early center of Christianity. Nubia, however, was never part of the Roman Empire; its people clung to ancient Egyptian religious ideas. Christian missionaries went to the Upper Nile region and succeeded in converting the Nubian rulers around 600 C.E. By that time, there were three separate Nubian states, of which the kingdom of Nobatia, centered at Dongola, was the strongest. The Christian rulers of Nobatia had close ties with **Ethiopia.**

Two-thirds of the country consists of the Ethiopian highlands, the rugged plateau region of East Africa. The Great Rift Valley divides this territory into two massifs (mountain masses), of which the Ethiopian Plateau is the larger. Sloping away from each side of the Great Rift Valley are a series of mountains and valleys. Together with this mountainous environment, the three Middle Eastern religions—Judaism, Christianity, and Islam—have conditioned Ethiopian society, bringing symbols of its cultural identity.

In the first century C.E., the author of the *Periplus of the Erythraean Sea* (see page 248) described the kingdom of **Aksum** in northwestern Ethiopia as a sizable trading

---

Timbuktu   *Originally a campsite for desert nomads, it grew into a thriving city under Mansa Musa.*

Ethiopia   *The first black African society that can be studied from written records; it was the site of the kingdom of Aksum.*

Aksum   *A kingdom in northwestern Ethiopia that was a sizable trading state and the center of Christian culture.*

state. Merchants at Adulis, its main port on the Red Sea, sold ivory, gold, emeralds, rhinoceros horns, shells, and slaves to the Sudan, Arabia, Yemen, and various cities across the Indian Ocean in exchange for glass, ceramics, fabrics, sugar, oil, spices, and precious gems. Adulis contained temples, stone-built houses, and irrigated agriculture. Between the first and eighth centuries, Aksum served as the capital of an empire extending over much of what is now northern Ethiopia. The empire's prosperity rested on trade. Aksum even minted specie (coins) modeled on the Roman *solidus;* at that time, only the Roman Empire, Persia, and some Indian states issued coins that circulated in Middle Eastern trade.

The expansion of Islam into northern Ethiopia in the eighth century (see page 237) weakened Aksum's commercial prosperity. The Arabs first imposed a religious test on Byzantine merchants who traded on the Dahklak Islands (in the southern Red Sea), thereby ousting the Greeks. Then, Muslims attacked and destroyed Adulis. Some Aksumites converted to Islam; many others found refuge in the rugged mountains north of Lasta and Tigray, where they were isolated from outside contacts. Thus began the insularity that characterized later Ethiopian society.

Tradition ascribes to Frumentius (ca. 300–380 C.E.), a Syrian Christian trader, the introduction of Christianity into Ethiopia. Kidnapped en route from India to Tyre (now a town in southern Lebanon), Frumentius was taken to Aksum and appointed tutor to the future king, Ezana. Later, Frumentius went to Alexandria in Egypt, where he was consecrated the first bishop of Aksum. Thus Christianity came to Ethiopia from Egypt in the Monophysite form. Shortly after members of the royal court accepted Christianity, it became the Ethiopian state religion. Ethiopia's future was to be inextricably tied up with Christianity, a unique situation in black Africa.

Ethiopia's acceptance of Christianity led to the production of ecclesiastical documents and royal chronicles, making Ethiopia the first black African society that can be studied from written records. The Scriptures were translated into Ge'ez, the language of Aksum; pagan temples were dedicated to Christian saints; and, as in early medieval Ireland and in the Orthodox Church of the Byzantine world, the monasteries were the main cultural institutions of the Christian faith in Ethiopia. From the monasteries, monks went out to preach and convert the people, who resorted to the monasteries in times of need. As the Ethiopian state expanded, vibrant monasteries provided inspiration for the establishment of convents for nuns, as in medieval Europe (see page 172).

Monastic records provide fascinating information about early Ethiopian society. Settlements were made on the warm and moist plateau lands, not in the arid lowlands or the river valleys. Farmers used a scratch plow (unique in sub-Saharan Africa) to cultivate wheat and barley and to rotate those cereals. Plentiful rainfall seems to have helped produce abundant crops, which in turn led to population growth. In contrast to most of sub-Saharan Africa, both sexes probably married

● **Christianity and Islam in Ethiopia** The prolonged contest between the two religions in Ethiopia was periodically taken to the battlefield. This drawing by an Ethiopian artist shows his countrymen advancing victoriously (*from left to right*) and celebrates national military success. (© British Library Board. All rights reserved. OR 533 f50v)

● **The Queen of Sheba and King Solomon** The queen often figured prominently in European, as well as Ethiopian, art. Here, sitting enthroned in Jerusalem, Solomon receives gifts from Sheba's servants. Both are dressed in late medieval European garb, and in his left hand he holds a scepter (staff), symbol of his royal and Christian authority. Aside from the anachronistic costumes and scepter (what Jewish king would carry a Christian cross?), the inscription surrounding the scene—"Solomon joins himself to the Queen of Sheba and introduces her to his faith"—combines a number of myths. *(Erich Lessing/Art Resource, NY)*

young. Because of ecclesiastical opposition to polygyny, monogamy was the norm, except for kings and the very rich. The abundance of land meant that young couples could establish independent households. Widely scattered farms, with the parish church as the central social unit, seem to have been the usual pattern of existence.

Above the broad class of peasant farmers stood warrior-nobles. Their wealth and status derived from their fighting skills, which kings rewarded with grants of estates and with the right to collect tribute from the peasants. To acquire lands and to hold warriors' loyalty, Ethiopian kings had to pursue a policy of constant territorial expansion. (See the feature "Individuals in Society: Amda Siyon.") Nobles maintained order in their regions, supplied kings with fighting men, and displayed their superior status by the size of their households and their generosity to the poor.

Sometime in the fourteenth century, six scribes in the Tigrayan highlands, combining oral tradition, apocryphal texts, Jewish and Islamic commentaries, and Christian patristic writings, produced the *Kebre Negast* (*The Glory of Kings*). This history served the authors' goals: it became an Ethiopian national epic, glorifying a line of rulers descended from the Hebrew king Solomon (see page 17), arousing patriotic feelings, and linking Ethiopia's identity to the Judeo-Christian tradition. The book mostly deals with the origins of Emperor Menilek I in the tenth century B.C.E.

The *Kebre Negast* asserts that Queen Makeda of Ethiopia (called Sheba in the Jewish tradition) had little governmental experience when she came to the throne. So she sought the advice and wise counsel of King Solomon (r. 961–922 B.C.E.) in Jerusalem. Makeda learned Jewish statecraft, converted to Judaism, and expressed her gratitude to Solomon with rich gifts of spices, gems, and gold. Desiring something more precious, Solomon prepared a lavish banquet for his attractive pupil. Satiated with spicy food and rich wines, Makeda fell asleep. Solomon placed jugs of water near her couch. When she woke up, she gulped down some water, and Solomon satisfied his lust. Their son, Menilek, was born some months later. When Menilek reached maturity, he visited Solomon in Jerusalem. There Solomon anointed him crown prince of Ethiopia and sent a retinue of young Jewish nobles to accompany him home as courtiers. They, however, unable to face life without the Hebrews' Ark of the Covenant, stole the cherished wooden chest, which the Hebrews believed contained the Ten Commandments. God apparently approved the theft, for he lifted the youths, pursued by Solomon's army, across the Red Sea and into Ethiopia. Thus, according to the *Kebre Negast*, Menilek avenged his mother's shame, and God gave his legal covenant to Ethiopia, Israel's successor.[20] Although much of this narrative is myth and legend, it effectively served the purpose of building nationalistic fervor.

Consuming a spiked drink may not be the most dignified or auspicious way to found an imperial dynasty, but from the tenth to the sixteenth century, and even in the Ethiopian constitution of 1955, rulers of Ethiopia claimed that they belonged to the Solomonic line of succession. Church and state in Ethiopia were inextricably linked.

Ethiopia's high mountains encouraged an inward concentration of attention and hindered access from the outside. Twelfth-century Crusaders returning from the

Amda Siyon

Scholars consider Amda Siyon (r. 1314–1344) the greatest ruler of Ethiopia's Solomonic dynasty. Yet we have no image or representation of him. We know nothing of his personal life, though if he followed the practice of most Ethiopian kings, he had many wives and children. Nor do we know anything of his youth and education. The evidence of what he did, however, suggests a tough military man who personified the heroic endurance and physical pain expected of warriors. Once, surrounded by enemies, his face set hard as stone, he

clove the ranks of the rebels and struck so hard that he transfixed two men as one with the blow of his spear, through the strength of God. Thereupon the rebels scattered and took to flight, being unable to hold their ground in his presence.

Amda Siyon reinforced control over his kingdom's Christian areas. He then expanded into neighboring regions of Shewa, Gojam, and Damot. Victorious there, he gradually absorbed the Muslim states of Ifat and Hedya to the east and southeast. These successes gave him effective control over the central highlands and also over the Indian Ocean trade routes to the Red Sea (see Map 9.2). He governed in a quasi-feudal fashion (see page 352). Theoretically the owner of all land, he assigned *gults,* or fiefs, to his ablest warriors. In return for nearly complete authority in their regions, these warrior-nobles conscripted soldiers for the king's army, required agricultural services from the farmers working on their land, and collected taxes in kind.

Ethiopian rulers received imperial coronation at Aksum, but their kingdom had no permanent capital. Rather, the ruler and court were peripatetic. They constantly traveled around the country to check up on the warrior-nobles' management of the gults, to crush revolts, and to impress ordinary people with royal dignity.

Territorial expansion had important economic and religious consequences. Amda Siyon concluded trade agreements with Muslims by which Muslims were allowed to trade with his country in return for Muslim recognition of his authority, and their promise to accept his administration and to pay taxes. Economic growth followed. As a result of these agreements, the flow of Ethiopian gold, ivory, and slaves to Red Sea ports for export to the Islamic heartlands and to South Asia accelerated. Profits from commercial exchange improved people's lives, or at least the lives of the upper classes. Monk-missionaries from traditional Christian areas flooded newly conquered regions,

A monk entering the Holy of Holies in the Urai Kidane Miharet church, one of the many monasteries established by Amda Siyon. *(Kazuyoshi Nomachi/Pacific Press Service)*

stressing that Ethiopia was a new Zion, a second Israel, a Judeo-Christian nation defined by religion. Ethiopian Christianity focused on the divinity of the Old Testament Jehovah, rather than on the humanity of the New Testament Jesus. Jewish dietary restrictions, such as the avoidance of pork and shellfish, shaped behavior, and the holy Ark of the Covenant had a prominent place in the liturgy. But the monks also taught New Testament values, especially the importance of charity and spiritual reform. Following the Byzantine pattern, the Ethiopian priest-king claimed the right to summon church councils and to issue doctrinal degrees. Christianity's stress on monogamous marriage, however, proved hard to enforce. As in other parts of Africa (and in Islamic lands, China, and South Asia), polygyny remained common, at least among the upper classes.

Questions for Analysis

1. What features mark Ethiopian culture as unique and distinctive among early African societies?

2. Referring to Solomonic Ethiopia, assess the role of legend in history.

3. The German ruler Charles (r. 768–814) was also called "the Great"—or "Charlemagne" (see pages 184–185). Compare and contrast him with Amda Siyon of Ethiopia with respect to territorial expansion, relations with the church, and methods of governing.

Sources: H. G. Marcus, *A History of Ethiopia,* updated ed. (Berkeley: University of California Press, 2002); J. Iliffe, *Africans: The History of a Continent,* 2d ed. (New York: Cambridge University Press, 2007).

Middle East told of a powerful Christian ruler, Prester John, whose lands lay behind Muslim lines and who was eager to help restore the Holy Land to Christian control. Europeans identified that kingdom with Ethiopia. In the later thirteenth century, the dynasty of the Solomonic kings witnessed a literary and artistic renaissance particularly notable for works of hagiography (biographies of saints), biblical exegesis, and manuscript illumination. The most striking feature of Ethiopian society in the period from 500 to 1500 was the close relationship between the church and the state. Christianity inspired fierce devotion and tended to equate doctrinal heresy with political rebellion, thus reinforcing central monarchical power.

The East African City-States

In the first century C.E., a merchant seaman from Alexandria in Egypt sailed down the Red Sea and out into the Indian Ocean. Along the coasts of East Africa and India, he found seaports. He took careful notes on all he observed, and the result, *Periplus of the Erythraean Sea* (as the Greeks called the Indian Ocean), is the earliest surviving literary evidence of the city-states of the East African coast. Although primarily preoccupied with geography and navigation, the *Periplus* includes accounts of the local peoples and their commercial activities. Even in the days of the Roman emperors, the *Periplus* testifies, the East African coast had strong commercial links with India and the Mediterranean.

Greco-Roman ships traveled from Adulis on the Red Sea around the tip of the Gulf of Aden and down the African coast that the Greeks called "Azania" in modern-day Kenya and Tanzania (see Map 9.2). These ships carried manufactured goods—cotton cloth, copper and brass, iron tools, and gold and silver plate. At the African coastal emporiums, Mediterranean merchants exchanged these goods for cinnamon, myrrh and frankincense, captive slaves, and animal byproducts such as ivory, rhinoceros horns, and tortoise shells. Somewhere around Cape Guardafui on the Horn of Africa, the ships caught the monsoon winds eastward to India (see page 425), where ivory was in great demand.

An omission in the *Periplus* has created a debate over the racial characteristics of the native peoples in East Africa and the dates of Bantu migrations into the area. The author, writing in the first century, did not describe the natives; apparently he did not find their skin color striking enough to comment on. Yet in the fifth century, there are references to these peoples as "Ethiopians." Could this mean that migrating black Bantu-speakers reached the east coast between the first and fifth centuries? Possibly. The distinguished archaeologist Neville Chittick, however, thinks not: "The writer of the *Periplus* made few comments on the physical nature of the inhabitants of the countries which he described . . . therefore nothing can be based on the mere omission of any mention of skin color."[21]

In the early centuries of the Christian era, many merchants and seamen from the Mediterranean settled in East African coastal towns. Succeeding centuries saw the arrival of more traders. The great emigration from Arabia after the death of Muhammad accelerated Muslim penetration of the area, which the Arabs called the *Zanj*, "land of the blacks." Along the coast, Arabic Muslims established small trading colonies whose local peoples were ruled by kings and practiced various animistic religions. Eventually—whether through Muslim political hegemony or gradual assimilation—the coastal peoples slowly converted to Islam. Indigenous African religions, however, remained strong in the continent's interior. (See the feature "Listening to the Past: A Tenth-Century Muslim Traveler Describes Parts of the East African Coast" on pages 254–255.)

Beginning in the late twelfth century, fresh waves of Arabs and of Persians from Shiraz poured down the coast, first settling at Mogadishu, then pressing southward to Kilwa (see Map 9.2). Everywhere they landed, they introduced Islamic culture to the indigenous population. Similarly, from the earliest Christian centuries through the Middle Ages, Indonesians crossed the Indian Ocean and settled on the African coast and on the large island of Madagascar, or Malagasy, an Indonesian name. All these immigrants intermarried with Africans, and the resulting society combined Asian, African, and especially Islamic traits. The East African coastal culture was called **Swahili**, after a Bantu language whose vocabulary and poetic forms exhibit a strong Arabic influence. The thirteenth-century Muslim mosque at Mogadishu and the fiercely Muslim populations of Mombasa and Kilwa in the fourteenth century attest to strong Muslim influence.

By the late thirteenth century, **Kilwa** had become the most powerful city on the coast, exercising political hegemony as far north as Pemba and as far south as Sofala

Swahili *The East African coastal culture, named after a Bantu language whose vocabulary and poetic forms exhibit strong Arabic influences.*

Kilwa *The most powerful city on the coast of Africa by the late thirteenth century.*

● **Great Mosque at Kilwa** Built between the thirteenth and fifteenth centuries to serve the Muslim commercial aristocracy of Kilwa on the Indian Ocean, the mosque attests to the wealth and power of the East African city-states. *(Karen Samson Photography)*

(see Map 9.2). In the fourteenth and fifteenth centuries, the coastal cities were great commercial empires comparable to Venice (see page 370). Like Venice, Kilwa, Mombasa, and Mafia were situated on offshore islands. The tidal currents that isolated them from the mainland also protected them from landside attack.

Much current knowledge about life in the East African trading societies rests on the account of Ibn Battuta. When he arrived at Kilwa, he found, in the words of a modern historian,

the city large and elegant, its buildings, as was typical along the coast, constructed of stone and coral rag [roofing slate]. Houses were generally single storied, consisting of a number of small rooms separated by thick walls supporting heavy stone roofing slabs laid across mangrove poles. Some of the more formidable structures contained second and third stories, and many were embellished with cut stone decorative borders framing the entrance-ways. Tapestries and ornamental niches covered the walls and the floors were carpeted. Of course, such appointments were only for the wealthy; the poorer classes occupied the time-less mud and straw huts of Africa, their robes a simple loincloth, their dinner a millet porridge.[22]

On the mainland were fields and orchards of rice, millet, oranges, mangoes, and bananas and pastures and yards for cattle, sheep, and poultry. Yields were apparently high; Ibn Battuta noted that the rich enjoyed three enormous meals a day and were very fat.

From among the rich mercantile families that controlled the coastal cities arose a ruler who by the fourteenth century had taken the Arabic title *sheik*. The sheik governed both the island city and the nearby mainland. Farther inland, tribal chiefs ruled with the advice of councils of elders.

● **Copper Coin from Mogadishu, Twelfth Century** Islamic proscriptions against representation of the human form, combined with a deep veneration for writing, prevented the use of rulers' portraits on coinage, unlike the practice of the Romans, Byzantines, and Sassanids. Instead, Islamic coins since the Umayyad period were decorated exclusively with writing. Sultan Haran ibn Sulayman of Kilwa on the East African coast minted this coin, a symbol of the region's Muslim culture and of its rich maritime trade. *(Courtesy of the Trustees of the British Museum)*

The Portuguese, approaching the East African coastal cities in the late fifteenth century, were astounded at their enormous wealth and prosperity. This wealth rested on monopolistic control of all trade in the area. Some coastal cities manufactured goods for export: Mogadishu produced cloth for the Egyptian market; Mombasa and Malindi processed iron tools; and Sofala made cottons for the interior trade. The bulk of the cities' exports, however, consisted of animal products—leopard skins, tortoise shell, ambergris, ivory—and gold. The gold originated in the Mutapa region south of the Zambezi River, where the Bantu mined it. As in tenth-century Ghana, gold was a royal monopoly in the fourteenth-century coastal city-states. The Mutapa kings received it as annual tribute, prohibited outsiders from entering the mines or participating in the trade, and controlled shipments down the Zambezi to the coastal markets. Kilwa's prosperity rested on its traffic in gold.

African goods satisfied the widespread aristocratic demand for luxury goods. In Arabia leopard skins were made into saddles, shells were made into combs, and ambergris was used in the manufacture of perfumes. Because African elephants' tusks were larger and more durable than the tusks of Indian elephants, African ivory was in great demand in India for sword and dagger handles, carved decorative objects, and the ceremonial bangles used in Hindu marriage rituals. Wealthy Chinese valued African ivory for use in the construction of sedan chairs.

In exchange for these natural products, the Swahili cities bought pottery, glassware and beads, and many varieties of cloth. Swahili kings imposed enormous duties on imports, perhaps more than 80 percent of the value of the goods themselves. Even so, traders who came to Africa made fabulous profits.

Slaves were another export from the East African coast. Reports of slave trading began with the *Periplus*. The trade accelerated with the establishment of Muslim settlements in the eighth century and continued down to the arrival of the Portuguese in the late fifteenth century. In fact, the East African coastal slave trade persisted at least to the beginning of the twentieth century.

As in West Africa, traders obtained slaves primarily through raids and kidnapping. As early as the tenth century, Arabs from Oman enticed hungry children with dates. When the children accepted the sweet fruits, they were abducted and enslaved. Profit was the traders' motive.

The Arabs called the northern Somalia coast *Ras Assir* (Cape of Slaves). From there, Arab traders transported slaves northward up the Red Sea to the markets of Arabia and Persia. Muslim dealers also shipped blacks from the region of Zanzibar across the Indian Ocean to markets in India. Rulers of the Deccan Plateau in central India used large numbers of black slave soldiers in their military campaigns. Slaves also worked on the docks and *dhows* (typical Arab lateen-rigged ships) in the Muslim-controlled Indian Ocean and as domestic servants and concubines throughout South and East Asia.

As early as the tenth century, sources mention persons with "lacquer-black bodies" in the possession of wealthy families in Song China.[23] In 1178 a Chinese official noted in a memorial to the emperor that Arab traders were shipping thousands of blacks from East Africa to the Chinese port of Guangzhou (Canton) by way of the Malay Archipelago. The Chinese employed these slaves as household servants, as musicians, and, because East Africans were often expert swimmers, as divers to caulk the leaky seams of ships below the water line.

By the thirteenth century, Africans living in many parts of South and East Asia had made significant economic and cultural contributions to their societies. Neither Asian nor Western scholars have adequately explored this subject. It appears, however, that in Indian, Chinese, and East African markets, slaves were never as valuable a commodity as ivory. Thus the volume of the Eastern slave trade did not approach that of the trans-Saharan slave trade.[24]

Southern Africa

Southern Africa, bordered on the northwest by the Kalahari Desert and on the northeast by the Zambezi River (see Map 9.2), enjoys a mild and temperate climate. Desert conditions prevail along the Atlantic coast, which gets less than five inches of annual rainfall. Eastward, rainfall increases, though some areas receive less than twenty inches a year. Although the Limpopo Valley in the east is very dry, temperate grasslands characterize the highlands in the interior. Considerable variations in climate occur throughout much of southern Africa from year to year.

Located at the southern extremity of the Afro-Eurasian landmass, southern Africa has a history that is very different from the histories of West Africa, the Nile Valley, and the east coast. Over the centuries, North and West Africa felt the influences of Phoenician, Greek, Roman, and Muslim cultures; the Nile Valley experienced the impact of major Egyptian, Assyrian, Persian, and Muslim civilizations; and the coast of East Africa had important contacts across the Indian Ocean with southern and eastern Asia and across the Red Sea with Arabia and Persia. Southern Africa, however,

● **Ruins of Great Zimbabwe** Considered the most impressive monument in the African interior south of the Ethiopian highlands, these ruins of Great Zimbabwe consist of two complexes of dry-stone buildings, some surrounded by a massive serpentine wall 32 feet high and 17 feet thick at its maximum. Great Zimbabwe was the center of a state whose wealth rested on gold. Towers were probably used for defensive purposes. *(Werner Forman Archive/Art Resource, NY)*

● **Bird at Top of Monolith, Great Zimbabwe, ca. 1200–1400 C.E.** The walls and buildings at Great Zimbabwe seem intended to reflect the ruler's wealth and power. Among the archaeological finds there are monoliths crowned by soapstone birds. This monolith (14½ inches high) also appears to have an alligator-like creature on its side. Scholars debate the significance of these birds: Were they symbols of royal power? eagles? messengers from the spiritual world to the terrestrial? And what does the alligator mean? *(Courtesy of the National Archives of Zimbabwe)*

Great Zimbabwe *A ruined African city discovered by a German explorer in 1871; it is considered the most powerful monument south of the Nile Valley and Ethiopian highlands.*

remained far removed from the outside world until the Portuguese arrived in the late fifteenth century—with one important exception. Bantu-speaking people reached southern Africa in the eighth century. They brought with them skills in ironworking and mixed farming (settled crop production plus cattle and sheep raising) and immunity to the kinds of diseases that later decimated the Amerindians of South America (see page 445).

Southern Africa has enormous mineral resources: gold, copper, diamonds, platinum, and uranium. Preindustrial peoples mined some of these deposits in open excavations down several feet, but fuller exploitation required modern technology. Today, gold mining operations can penetrate two miles below the surface.

The earliest residents of southern Africa were hunters and gatherers. In the first millennium C.E., new farming techniques from the north arrived. Lack of water and of timber (both needed to produce the charcoal used in iron smelting) slowed the spread of iron technology and tools and thus of crop production in southwestern Africa. These advances, however, reached the western coastal region by 1500. By that date, Khoisan-speakers were farming in the arid western regions. The area teemed with wild game—elephants, buffalo, lions, hippopotami, leopards, zebras, and many varieties of antelope. To the east, descendants of Bantu-speaking immigrants grew sorghum, raised cattle and sheep, and fought with iron-headed spears. Disease-bearing insects, such as the tsetse fly, which causes sleeping sickness, however, attacked these animals and retarded their domestication.

The nuclear family was the basic social unit among early southern African peoples, who practiced polygyny and traced descent in the male line. Several families numbering between twenty and eighty people formed bands. Such bands were not closed entities; people in neighboring territories identified with bands speaking the same language. As in most preindustrial societies, a division of labor existed whereby men hunted and women cared for children and raised edible plants. People lived in caves or in camps made of portable material, and they moved from one watering or hunting region to another as seasonal or environmental needs required.

In 1871 a German explorer came upon the ruined city of **Great Zimbabwe** southeast of what is now Nyanda in Zimbabwe. Archaeologists consider Great Zimbabwe the most impressive monument in Africa south of the Nile Valley and the Ethiopian highlands. The ruins consist of two vast complexes of dry-stone buildings, a fortress, and an elliptically shaped enclosure commonly called the Temple. Stone carvings, gold and copper ornaments, and Asian ceramics once decorated the buildings. The ruins extend over sixty acres and are encircled by a massive wall. The entire city was built from local granite between the eleventh and fifteenth centuries without any outside influence.

These ruins tell a remarkable story. Great Zimbabwe was the political and religious capital of a vast empire. During the first millennium C.E., settled crop cultivation, cattle raising, and work in metal led to a steady buildup in population in the Zambezi-Limpopo region. The area also contained a rich gold-bearing belt. Gold ore lay near the surface; alluvial gold lay in the Zambezi River tributaries. In the tenth century, the inhabitants collected the alluvial gold by panning and washing; after the year 1000, the gold was worked in open mines with iron picks. Traders shipped the gold eastward to Sofala (see Map 9.2). Great Zimbabwe's wealth and power rested on this gold trade.[25]

Great Zimbabwe declined in the fifteenth century, perhaps because the area had become agriculturally exhausted and could no longer support the large population. Some people migrated northward and settled in the Mazoe River valley, a tributary of the Zambezi. This region also contained gold, and there the settlers built a new empire in the tradition of Great Zimbabwe. This empire's rulers were called "Mwene Mutapa," and their power too was based on the gold trade down the Zambezi River to Indian Ocean ports. It was this gold that the Portuguese sought when they arrived on the East African coast in the late fifteenth century.

Chapter Summary

To assess your mastery of this chapter, go to
bedfordstmartins.com/mckayworld

• *What patterns of social and political organization prevailed among the peoples of Africa, and what types of agriculture and commerce did Africans engage in?*

In the fifteenth century, the African continent contained a number of very different societies and civilizations and many diverse ethnic groups. All of North Africa, from Morocco in the west to Egypt in the east, was part of the Muslim world. In West Africa, Mali continued the brisk trade in salt, gold, and slaves that had originated many centuries earlier. Islam, which had spread to sub-Saharan Africa through the caravan trade, had a tremendous influence on the peoples of the western Sudan, their governmental bureaucracies, and their vibrant urban centers. Between the first and eighth centuries, Christianity had penetrated the mountainous kingdom of Aksum (Ethiopia), beginning an enduring identification of the Ethiopian kingdom with the Judeo-Christian tradition. By virtue of their claim to Solomonic blood and by force of arms, kings of Ethiopia ruled a uniquely Christian state. Flourishing trade with Egypt, Arabia, and the East African city-states gave Aksum cultural access to much of southwestern Asia. The impact of the Islamic faith was also felt in East Africa, whose bustling port cities were in touch with the cultures of the Indian Ocean and the Mediterranean Sea. While the city-states along the eastern coast— Kilwa, Mombasa, and Mogadishu—conducted complicated mercantile activities with foreign societies, the mountain-protected kingdom of Ethiopia increasingly led an isolated, inward-looking existence. In southern Africa, the vast empire of Great Zimbabwe was yielding to yet another kingdom whose power was based on precious gold.

• *What values do Africans' art, architecture, and religions express?*

The student beginning the study of African history should bear in mind the enormous diversity of African peoples and cultures, a diversity both within and across regions. It is, therefore, difficult and often dangerous to make broad generalizations about African life. Statements such as "African culture is . . . " or "African peoples are . . . " are virtually meaningless. African peoples are not now and never have been homogeneous. This rich diversity helps explain why the study of African history is so exciting and challenging.

Suggested Reading

Allen, J. de Vere. *Swahili Origins.* 1993. A study of the problem of Swahili identity.

Austen, Ralph. *African Economic History.* 1987. Classic study of Africa's economic history.

Beck, Roger B. *The History of South Africa.* 2000. Introduction to this large and important country.

Bouvill, E.W., and Robin Hallett. *The Golden Trade of the Moors: West African Kingdoms in the Fourteenth Century.* 1995. Classic description of the trans-Saharan trade.

Bulliet, R. W. *The Camel and the Wheel.* 1995. The importance of the camel to African trade.

(continued on page 256)

Listening to the PAST

A Tenth-Century Muslim Traveler Describes Parts of the East African Coast

Except for Ethiopia, early African societies left no written accounts of their institutions and cultures. So modern scholars rely for information on the chronicles of travelers and merchants. Outsiders, however, come with their own preconceptions, attitudes, and biases. They tend to measure what they visit and see by the conditions and experiences with which they are familiar.

Sometime in the early tenth century, the Muslim merchant-traveler Al Mas'udi (d. 945 C.E.), in search of African ivory, visited Oman, the southeast coast of Africa, and Zanzibar. He referred to all the peoples he encountered as Zanj, a term that earlier had meant all the black slaves seized in the East Africa coastal region and that later was applied to the maritime Swahili culture of the area's towns. What does Al Mas'udi's report, excerpted here, tell us about these peoples?

The pilots of Oman pass by the channel [of Berbera] to reach the island of Kanbalu, which is in the Zanj sea. It has a mixed population of Muslims and Zanj idolaters. . . . The aforesaid Kanbalu is the furthest point of their voyages on the Zanj sea, and the land of Sofala and the Waqwaq, on the edge of the Zanj mainland and at the end of this branch of the sea. . . . I have sailed much on the seas, those of China, Rum, the Khazar, Qulzum and Yemen, but I do not know of one more dangerous than that of the Zanj, of which I have just spoken. There the whale is found. . . . There are also many other kinds of fish, with all sorts of shapes. . . . Amber* is found in great quantities on the Zanj coast and also near Shihr in Arabia. . . . The best amber is that found in the islands and on the shores of the Zanj sea: it is round and pale blue, sometimes as big as an ostrich egg, sometimes slightly less. The fish called the whale, which I have already mentioned, swallows it: when the sea is very rough it vomits up pieces of amber as large as rocks, and this fish swallows them. It is asphyxiated by them and then swims up to the surface. Then the Zanj, or men from other

lands, who have been biding their time in their boats, seize the fish with harpoons and tackle, cut its stomach open, and take the amber out. The pieces found near the bowels have a nauseating smell, and are called *nedd* by the Iraqi and Persian chemists: but the pieces found near the back are purer than those which have been a long time in the inner part of the body. . . .

The land of Zanj produces wild leopard skins. The people wear them as clothes, or export them to Muslim countries. They are the largest leopard skins and the most beautiful for making saddles. The sea of Zanj and that of Abyssinia lie on the right of the sea of India, and join up. They also export tortoise-shell for making combs, for which ivory is likewise used. The most common animal in these countries is the giraffe. . . . They [the Zanj] settled in that area, which stretches as far as Sofala, which is the furthest limit of the land and the end of the voyages made from Oman and Siraf on the sea of Zanj. In the same way that the sea of China ends with the land of Japan, the sea of Zanj ends with the land of Sofala and the Waqwaq, which produces gold and many other wonderful things. It has a warm climate and is fertile. The Zanj capital is there and they have a king called the *Mfalme*. This is the ancient name of their kings, and all the other Zanj kings are subject to him: he has 300,000 horsemen. The Zanj use the ox as a beast of burden, for they have no horses, mules or camels in their land, and do not know of their existence. . . . The land of Zanj begins with the branch which leaves the upper Nile and continues to the land of Sofala and the Waqwaq. The villages stretch for 700 parasangs and the same distance inland: the country is cut up into valleys, mountains and stony deserts. There are many wild elephants but no tame ones. The Zanj do not use them for war or anything else, but only hunt and kill them. When they want to catch them, they throw down the leaves, bark and branches of a certain tree which grows in their country: then they wait in ambush until the elephants come to drink. The water burns them and makes them drunk. They fall down and cannot get up: their limbs will not articulate. The Zanj rush upon them armed with very long spears,

*A fossil resin used in the manufacture of ornamental objects such as beads and women's combs.

254

An ancient mosque near Ras Mkumbuu in Pemba, which Al Mas'udi called Kanbalu. *(Visual Connection Archives)*

and kill them for their ivory. It is from this country that come tusks weighing fifty pounds and more. They usually go to Oman, and from there are sent to China and India. This is the chief trade route, and if it were not so, ivory would be common in Muslim lands.

In China the kings and military and civil officers use ivory palanquins†: no officer or notable dares to come into the royal presence in an iron palanquin, and ivory alone can be used. Thus they seek after straight tusks in preference to the curved, to make the things we have spoken of. They also burn ivory before their idols and cense their altars with it, just as Christians use the Mary incense and other perfumes. The Chinese make no other use of the elephant, and consider it unlucky to use it for domestic purposes or war. This fear has its origin in a tradition about one of their most ancient military expeditions. In India ivory is much sought after. It is used for the handles of daggers called *harari* or *harri* in the singular: and also for the curved sword-scabbards called *kartal,* in the plural *karatil.* But the chief use of ivory is making chessmen and backgammon pieces. . . .

The Zanj, although always busied hunting the elephant and collecting its ivory, make no use of it for domestic purposes. They use iron instead of gold and silver, just as they use oxen, as we said before, both for beasts of burden and for war. These oxen are harnessed like a horse. . . .

To go back to the Zanj and their kings, these are known as *Wafalme,* which means son of the Great Lord, since he is chosen to govern them justly. If he is tyrannical or strays from the truth, they kill him and exclude his seed from the throne; for they consider that in acting wrongfully he forfeits his position as the son of the Lord, the King of Heaven and Earth. They call God *Maliknajlu,* which means Great Lord.

The Zanj have an elegant language and men who preach in it. One of their holy men will often gather a crowd and exhort his hearers to please God in their lives and to be obedient to him. He explains the punishments that follow upon disobedience, and reminds them of their ancestors and kings of old. These people have no religious law: their kings rule by custom and by political expediency.

The Zanj eat bananas, which are as common among them as they are in India; but their staple food is millet and a plant called *kalari* which is pulled out of the earth like truffles. It is plentiful in Aden and the neighbouring part of Yemen near to the town. It is like the cucumber of Egypt and Syria. They also eat honey and meat. Every man worships what he pleases, be it a plant, an animal or a mineral.‡ They have many islands where the coconut grows: its nuts are used as fruit by all the Zanj peoples. One of these islands, which is one or two days' sail from the coast, has a Muslim population and a royal family. This is the island of Kanbalu of which we have already spoken.

Questions for Analysis

1. Identify on a map the places that Al Mas'udi mentions.

2. What commodities were most sought after by Muslim traders? Why? Where were they sold?

3. How would you describe Al Mas'udi's attitude toward the Zanj peoples and their customs?

Source: "10th Century Muslim Traveler Describes Part of the East African Coast," from Al Mas'udi, as appeared in G. S. P. Freeman-Grenville, *The East African Coast,* 1962, 14–17.

†An enclosed litter attached to poles that servants supported on their shoulders.

‡These are forms of animism.

Ehret, Christopher. *An African Classical Age: Eastern and Southern Africa in World History, 1000 B.C. to 400 A.D.* 2001. Solid introduction by a renowned African scholar.

Ehret, Christopher. *The Civilizations of Africa: A History to 1800.* 2002. The best study of pre-1800 African history.

Gilbert, Erik, and Jonathan Reynolds. *Africa in World History.* 2007. Best study of Africa's place in world history.

Iliffe, John. *Africans: The History of a Continent.* 2d ed. 2007. Thoughtful introduction to African history.

Levtzion, Nehemia, and Randall L. Pouwels. *History of Islam in Africa.* 2000. Comprehensive survey of Islam's presence in Africa.

Marcus, H. G. *A History of Ethiopia.* 2002. Standard introduction to Ethiopian history.

Mitchell, Peter. *African Connections: Archaeological Perspectives on Africa and the Wider World.* 2005. Places ancient Africa and its history in a global context.

Newman, J. L. *The Peopling of Africa: A Geographic Interpretation.* 1995. Explores population distribution and technological change down to the late nineteenth century.

Reader, J. *Africa: A Biography of a Continent.* 1997. Well-researched, popular account.

Schmidt, Peter R. *Historical Archaeology in Africa: Representation, Social Memory, and Oral Traditions.* 2006. An excellent introduction to archaeology and the reconstruction of Africa's history.

Notes

1. J. Hiernaux, *The People of Africa* (New York: Scribner's, 1975), pp. 46–48.

2. C. A. Diop, "The African Origins of Western Civilization," and R. Mauny, "A Review of Diop," in *Problems in African History: The Precolonial Centuries,* ed. R. O. Collins et al. (New York: Markus Weiner Publishing, 1994), pp. 32–40, 41–49; the quotations are on p. 42.

3. Mauny, "A Review of Diop." For contrasting views of Afrocentrism in American higher education, see T. Martin, *The Jewish Onslaught: Dispatches from the Wellesley Battlefront* (Dover, Mass.: The Majority Press, 1993), and M. Lefkowitz, *Not Out of Africa: How Afrocentrism Became an Excuse to Teach Myth as History* (New York: Basic Books, 1996).

4. "African Historical Demography," in *Proceedings of a Seminar Held in the Centre of African Studies,* University of Edinburgh, April 29–30, 1977, p. 3.

5. T. Spear, "Bantu Migrations," in *Problems in African History: The Precolonial Centuries,* p. 98.

6. J. Iliffe, *Africans: The History of a Continent,* 2d ed. (Cambridge: Cambridge University Press, 2007), pp. 100–110; J. L. Newman, *The Peopling of Africa: A Geographic Interpretation* (New Haven, Conn.: Yale University Press, 1995), pp. 140–147.

7. J. S. Trimingham, *Islam in West Africa* (Oxford: Oxford University Press, 1959), pp. 6–9.

8. R. A. Austen, *African Economic History* (London: James Currey/Heinemann, 1987), p. 36.

9. R. A. Austen, "The Trans-Saharan Slave Trade: A Tentative Census," in *The Uncommon Market: Essays in the Economic History of the Atlantic Slave Trade,* ed. H. A. Gemery and J. S. Hogendorn (New York: Academic Press, 1979), pp. 1–71, esp. p. 66.

10. R. N. July, *Precolonial African Economic and Social History* (New York: Scribner's, 1975), pp. 124–129.

11. See N. Levtzion, "Islam in Africa to 1800: Merchants, Chiefs, and Saints," in *The Oxford History of Islam,* ed. J. L. Esposito (New York: Oxford University Press, 1999), pp. 502–504.

12. Quoted in J. O. Hunwick, "Islam in West Africa, A.D. 1000–1800," in *A Thousand Years of West African History,* ed. J. F. Ade Ajayi and I. Espie (New York: Humanities Press, 1972), pp. 244–245.

13. Quoted in A. A. Boahen, "Kingdoms of West Africa, c. A.D. 500–1600," in *The Horizon History of Africa* (New York: American Heritage, 1971), p. 183.

14. Al-Bakri, *Kitab al-mughrib fdhikr bilad Ifriqiya wa'l-Maghrib (Description de l'Afrique Septentrionale),* trans. De Shane (Paris: Adrien-Maisonneuve, 1965), pp. 328–329.

15. Quoted in R. Oliver and C. Oliver, eds., *Africa in the Days of Exploration* (Englewood Cliffs, N.J.: Prentice-Hall, 1965), p. 10.

16. Quoted in Boahen, "Kingdoms of West Africa, c. A.D. 500–1600," p. 184.

17. This quotation and the next appear in E. J. Murphy, *History of African Civilization* (New York: Delta, 1972), pp. 109, 111.

18. Quoted ibid., p. 120.

19. Quoted in Oliver and Oliver, *Africa in the Days of Exploration,* p. 18.

20. See H. G. Marcus, *A History of Ethiopia,* updated ed. (Berkeley: University of California Press, 2002), pp. 17–20.

21. H. N. Chittick, "The Peopling of the East African Coast," in *East Africa and the Orient: Cultural Syntheses in Pre-Colonial Times,* ed. H. N. Chittick and R. I. Rotberg (New York: Africana Publishing, 1975), p. 19.

22. July, *Precolonial Africa,* p. 209.

23. Austen, "The Trans-Saharan Slave Trade," p. 65; J. H. Harris, *The African Presence in Asia* (Evanston, Ill.: Northwestern University Press, 1971), pp. 3–6, 27–30; and P. Wheatley, "Analecta Sino-Africana Recensa," in Chittick and Rotberg, *East Africa and the Orient,* p. 109.

24. I. Hrbek, ed., *General History of Africa,* vol. 3, *Africa from the Seventh to the Eleventh Century* (Berkeley: University of California Press; New York: UNESCO, 1991), pp. 294–295, 346–347.

25. P. Curtin et al., *African History,* rev. ed. (New York: Longman, 1984), pp. 284–287.

Engraved Mississippian Copper Plate. This ornamental copper plate was excavated in Etowah Mound, Georgia, a Mississippian site first settled in about 1000 C.E. The copper may have been mined along the shore of Lake Superior in what is now northern Michigan, the largest source of copper in North America. *(National Museum of American History, Smithsonian Institution, Washington, D.C.)*

10 CIVILIZATIONS OF THE AMERICAS, 2500 B.C.E.–1500 C.E.

Chapter Preview

The Early Peoples of the Americas
• How did early peoples in the Americas adapt to their environment as they created economic and political systems?

Early Civilizations
• What physical, social, and intellectual features characterized early civilizations in the Americas?

Classical Era Mesoamerica and North America
• How did Mesoamerican and North American peoples develop prosperous and stable societies in the classical era?

The Aztecs
• How did the Aztecs both build on the achievements of earlier Mesoamerican cultures and develop new traditions to create their large empire?

The Incas
• What were the sources of strength and prosperity, and of problems, for the Incas as they created their enormous empire?

From the beginning of recorded history—that is, from the earliest invention of writing systems—the Eastern and Western Hemispheres developed in isolation from one another. In both areas people initially gathered and hunted their food, and then some groups began to plant crops, adapting plants that were native to the areas they settled. Techniques of plant domestication spread, allowing for greater density of population because harvested crops provided a more regular food supply than did gathered food. In certain parts of both hemispheres, efficient production and transportation of food supplies allowed for the development of cities, with monumental buildings constructed to honor divine and human power, specialized production of a wide array of products, and marketplaces where those products were exchanged. New products included improved military equipment, which leaders used to enhance their power and build up the large political entities we call "kingdoms" and "empires." The power of those leaders also often rested on religious ideas, in which providing service to a king was viewed as a way to honor divine power. These large political units did not develop everywhere in either hemisphere, however, nor was settled agriculture the only economic system. In many places, particularly where the climate or environment made growing crops difficult or impossible, gathering and hunting, sometimes combined with raising animals for food, continued to provide for human sustenance.

The separate but parallel paths of the two hemispheres were radically changed by Columbus's voyage and the events that followed. The greater availability of metals, especially iron, in the Eastern Hemisphere meant that the military technology of the Europeans who came to the Western Hemisphere was more deadly than anything indigenous peoples had developed. Even more deadly, however, were the germs Europeans brought with them: measles, mumps, bubonic plague, influenza, and smallpox. Because the two hemispheres had been out of contact for so long, indigenous people had no resistance, and they died in astounding numbers. Population estimates of the Western Hemisphere in the 1400s vary,

ATLANTIC
OCEAN

Gulf of Mexico

Tropic of Cancer

Caribbean Sea

Equator

PACIFIC
OCEAN

Tropic of Capricorn

PIRO People

0   500   1000 Km.

0   500   1000 Mi.

60°W

MAP 10.1 **The Peoples of Mesoamerica and South America** The major indigenous peoples of Mesoamerica and South America represented a great variety of languages and cultures adapted to a wide range of environments. *(Source: Adapted from* The Times Atlas of World History, 3d ed., *p. 149. Reprinted by permission of HarperCollins Publishers Ltd.)*

but many demographers place the total population at about 70 million people. They also estimate that in many parts of the Western Hemisphere, 90 percent of the population died within the first decades of European contact.

Disease often spread ahead of actual groups of conquerors or settlers, when a few or even one native person came into contact with a European landing party and then returned to the village. Germs spread to other people as they did normal things like preparing food, carrying children, or talking about what they had seen. People became sick and died quickly, so that when Europeans got to an area several weeks or months later, they found people who were already weak and fewer in number.

The history of the Western Hemisphere *after* Columbus shapes all the words we use to describe it. About a decade after Columbus's first voyage, another Italian explorer and adventurer, Amerigo Vespucci, wrote a letter to his old employers, the Medici rulers in Italy, trumpeting the wonders of the "new world" he had seen. He claimed to have been the first to see what is now Venezuela on a voyage in 1497, a year before Columbus got there. This letter was published many times in many different languages, and the phrase "New World" began to show up on world maps around 1505. Shortly after that the word *America,* meaning "the land of Amerigo," also appeared, because mapmakers read and believed Vespucci's letter. By just a few years later, mapmakers and others knew that Columbus had been the first to this new world. They wanted to omit the label "America" from future maps, but the name had already stuck.

Our use of the word *Indian* for the indigenous peoples of the Americas stems from another mistake. Columbus was trying to reach Asia by sailing west and thought he was somewhere in the East Indies when he landed, which is why he called the people he met "Indians." They apparently called themselves "Tainos," and people who lived on nearby islands called themselves other things. In many cases people died so fast that we have no idea now what they actually called themselves, so the words we use for various indigenous groups come from other indigenous groups or from European languages and were sometimes originally insulting or derogatory nicknames. Many indigenous groups today are returning to designations from their own languages, and scholars are attempting to use terminology that is historically accurate, so certain groups are known by multiple names. The use of the word *Indian* is itself highly controversial, and various other terms are often used, including Native Americans, Amerindians, and (in Canada) First Peoples. Each of these substitutes has supporters and opponents, including people who are themselves of indigenous background. There is no term for all the inhabitants of the Western Hemisphere that is universally accepted, though in the United States "American Indians" is now preferred. The many peoples of the Americas did not think of themselves as belonging to a single group, any more than the peoples living in sixteenth-century Europe thought of themselves as Europeans (see Map 10.1).

All these issues were in the future in 1492, of course. Columbus's voyage resulted in a devastating chain of events for the inhabitants of the Western Hemisphere and determined the language we use to talk about them. In fact, even Western Hemisphere is a post-Columbus concept, as it requires setting an arbitrary line that divides the two halves of the world. Many different points were proposed over the centuries, and only in the nineteenth century was the current prime meridian at Greenwich—a suburb of London—agreed on.

This huge area had a highly complex history for millennia before Columbus, however, and a great diversity of peoples, cultures, and linguistic groups. New information about these cultures is emerging every year, provoking vigorous debates among scholars. In no other chapter of this book are the basic outlines of what most people agree happened changing as fast as they are for this chapter.

Chronology

40,000–15,000 B.C.E.   Initial human migration to the Americas (date disputed)

ca. 8000 B.C.E.   Beginnings of agriculture

ca. 2500 B.C.E.   First cities in Norte Chico; earliest mound building in North America

ca. 1500–300 B.C.E.   Olmec civilization

ca. 1200 B.C.E.   Emergence of Chavin culture

ca. 200 B.C.E.– 600 C.E.   Hopewell culture

ca. 100 B.C.E.–750 C.E.   Height of Teotihuacán civilization

ca. 600–900 C.E.   Peak of Maya civilization

ca. 1050–1250   Construction of mounds at Cahokia

1325   Construction of Aztec city of Tenochtitlán begins

mid-1400s   Height of Aztec culture

ca. 1500   Inca Empire reaches its largest extent

• • • • • • • • • • • •
THE EARLY PEOPLES OF THE AMERICAS

How did early peoples in the Americas adapt to their environment as they created economic and political systems?

Mesoamerica *The term used by scholars to designate the area of present-day Mexico and Central America.*

As in the development of early human cultures in Afroeurasia (Chapter 1), the environment shaped the formation of human settlements in the Americas. North America includes arctic tundra, dry plains, coastal wetlands, woodlands, deserts, and temperate rain forests. **Mesoamerica,** a term scholars use to designate the area of present-day Mexico and Central America, is dominated by high plateaus with a temperate climate and good agricultural land bounded by coastal plains. The Caribbean coast of Central America—modern Belize, Guatemala, Honduras, Nicaragua, El Salvador, Costa Rica, and Panama—is characterized by thick jungle lowlands, heavy rainfall, and torrid heat. South America is a continent of extremely varied terrain. The entire western coast is edged by the Andes, the highest mountain range in the Western Hemisphere. Three-fourths of South America—almost the entire interior of the continent—is lowland plains. The Amazon River, at four thousand miles the second-longest river in the world, is bordered by tropical lowland rain forests with dense growth and annual rainfall in excess of eighty inches. All these environments have supported extensive human settlement at various times, though it is easier to learn about those in dryer areas because artifacts survive longer there.

Settling the Americas

The traditions of many American Indian peoples teach that the group originated independently, often through the actions of a divine figure. Many creation accounts, including that of the book of Genesis in the Bible, begin with people who are created out of earth and receive assistance from supernatural beings—who set out certain ways people are supposed to behave. Both Native American and biblical creation accounts continue to have deep spiritual importance for many people.

Archaeological and DNA evidence indicates that the earliest humans came to the Americas from Siberia and East Asia, but exactly when and how this happened is currently being hotly debated. The traditional account is that people crossed the Bering Strait from what is now Russian Siberia to what is now Alaska about fifteen thousand years ago, mostly by walking. This was the end of the last Ice Age, so that more of the world's water was frozen and ocean levels were much lower than they are today. (This situation is the opposite of what is occurring today; global warming is melting polar ice, which will raise water levels around the world.) The people migrated southward through North America between two large ice sheets that were slowly melting and retreating, and relatively quickly they spread through the entire hemisphere. They lived by gathering and hunting, using spears with stone tips that archaeologists term *Clovis points* after the town in New Mexico where they were first discovered.

Clovis points have been found widely throughout the Americas, and many archaeologists see the Clovis people as the ancestors of most indigenous people in the Western Hemisphere. There is some difference of opinion about exactly when the Clovis culture flourished, for various methods of carbon-14 dating produce slightly different results, with some scholars accepting 11,000 B.C.E. as the height of Clovis technology and others 9000 B.C.E. (Carbon-14 dating uses the rate at which the radioactive isotope of carbon—present in all living things—breaks down into a nonradioactive form to determine how old things are.)

Disagreements regarding the age of the Clovis culture are significant because they are part of a much broader debate about the traditional account of migration to the Americas. Archaeologists working at Monte Verde along the coast of Chile have excavated a site that they date to about 9000 B.C.E., and perhaps much earlier. This site is ten thousand miles from the Bering Land bridge, which would have meant a very fast walk. Monte Verde and a few other sites are leading increasing numbers of archaeologists to conclude that migrants over the land bridge were preceded by people who traveled along the coast in skin boats, perhaps as early as forty thousand years ago. They lived by fishing and gathering rather than hunting big game, and they slowly worked their way southward. The coasts that they traveled along are today far under water, so archaeological evidence is difficult to obtain, but DNA and other genetic evidence has lent support to this idea. (DNA evidence has generally not supported various other theories of early migrations from Europe or Australia.)

However and whenever people got to the Western Hemisphere—and a consensus about this may emerge in the next decade—they lived by gathering, fishing, and hunting, as did everyone throughout the world at that point. Some groups were nomadic and followed migrating game, while others did not have to travel to be assured of a regular food supply. Coastal settlements from the Pacific Northwest to the southern end of South America relied on fish and shellfish, and some also hunted seals and other large marine mammals.

The Development of Agriculture

About 8000 B.C.E., people in some parts of the Americas began raising crops as well as gathering wild produce. As in the development of agriculture in Afroeurasia, people initially planted the seeds of native plants. Pumpkins and other members of the gourd family were one of the earliest crops, as were chilies, beans, and avocados. At some point, people living in what is now southern Mexico also began raising what would become the most important crop in the Americas—maize, which we generally call "corn." Exactly how this happened is not clear. In contrast to other grain crops such as wheat and rice, the kernels of maize—which are the seeds as well as the part that is eaten for food—are wrapped in a husk, so that the plant cannot propagate itself easily. In addition, no wild ancestor of maize has been found. What many biologists now think happened is that a related grass called *teosinte* developed mutant forms with large kernels enclosed in husks, and people living in the area quickly realized its benefits. They began to intentionally plant these kernels and crossbred the results to get a better crop each year.

People bred various types of maize for different purposes and for different climates, making it the staple food throughout the highlands of Mesoamerica. They often planted maize along with squash, beans, and other crops in a field called a **milpa;** the beans use the maize stalks for support as they both grow and also fix nitrogen in the soil, acting as a natural fertilizer. Crops can be grown in milpas year after year, in contrast to single-crop planting in which rotation is needed so as not to exhaust the soil. Maize came to have a symbolic and religious meaning; it was viewed as the source of human life and was a prominent feature in sculptures of kings and gods.

In central Mexico, along with milpas, people also built *chinampas,* floating gardens. They dredged soil from the bottom of a lake or pond, placed the soil on mats of woven twigs, and then planted crops in the soil. Chinampas were enormously productive, yielding up to three harvests a year.

Knowledge of maize cultivation, and maize seeds themselves, spread out from Mesoamerica into both North and South America. By 3000 B.C.E. farmers in what is now Peru and Uruguay were planting maize, and by 2000 B.C.E. farmers in southwest North America were as well. The crop then spread into the Mississippi Valley and to northeastern North America, where farmers bred slightly different variants for the different growing conditions. After 1500 C.E. maize cultivation spread to Europe, Africa, and Asia as well, becoming an essential food crop there. (In the twentieth century maize became even more successful; about one-quarter of the nearly fifty thousand items in the average American supermarket now contain corn.)

milpa *A system of effective agriculture used throughout Mesoamerica that relies on crop rotation and the planting of multiple crops in a single field. The term is derived from a Nahuatl word meaning "field."*

The expansion of maize was the result of contacts between different groups that can be traced through trade goods as well. Copper from the Great Lakes was a particularly valuable item and was traded throughout North America, reaching Mexico by 3000 B.C.E. Obsidian from the Rocky Mountains, used for blades, was traded widely, as were shells and later pottery.

Different cultivars of maize could be developed for many different climates, but maize was difficult to grow in high altitudes. Thus in the high Andes, people relied on potatoes, terracing the slopes with stone retaining walls to keep the hillsides from sliding. High-altitude valleys were connected to mountain life and vegetation to form a single interdependent agricultural system called "vertical archipelagoes" capable of supporting large communities. Such vertical archipelagoes often extended more than thirty-seven miles from top to bottom. The terraces were shored up with earthen walls to retain moisture, enabling the production of bumper crops of many different types of potatoes. Potatoes ordinarily cannot be stored for long periods, but Andean

● **Inca Terraces** In order to create more land for farming and limit soil erosion, Andean peoples built terraces up steep slopes. Later the Incas built systems of aqueducts and canals to bring water to terraced fields. *(Wolfgang Kaehler/Corbis)*

peoples developed a product called *chuñu,* freeze-dried potatoes made by subjecting potatoes alternately to nightly frosts and daily sun. Chuñu will keep unspoiled for several years. Coca (the dried leaves of a plant native to the Andes from which cocaine is derived), chewed in moderation as a dietary supplement, enhanced people's stamina and their ability to withstand the cold.

Maize will also not grow in hot, wet climates very well. In Amazonia, manioc, a tuber that can be cooked in many ways, became the staple food. It was planted along with other crops, including fruits, nuts, and various types of palm trees. People domesticated peach palms, for example, which produce fruit, pulp that is made into flour, heart of palm that is eaten raw, and juice that can be fermented into beer. Just how many people Amazonian agriculture supported before the introduction of European diseases is an issue hotly debated by anthropologists, but increasing numbers see the original tropical rain forest not as a pristine wilderness, but as an ecosystem managed effectively by humans for thousands of years. The oldest known pottery in the Americas has been found along the Amazon River, as well as in the Andes.

Farming in the Americas was not limited to foodstuffs. Beginning about 2500 B.C.E., people living along the coast of Peru used irrigation to raise cotton, and textiles became an important part of Peruvian culture. Agriculture in the Americas was extensive, though it was limited by the lack of an animal that could be harnessed to pull a plow. People throughout the Americas domesticated dogs, and in the Andes they domesticated llamas and alpacas to carry loads through the mountains. But no native species allowed itself to be harnessed as horses, oxen, and water buffalo did in Asia and Europe, which meant that all agricultural labor was human-powered.

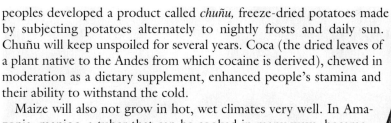

● **Colombian Lime Container**   The use of coca in rituals and to withstand bodily discomfort is an ancient tradition in South America. Pieces of coca leaves were placed in the mouth with small amounts of powdered lime made from seashells. The lime helped release the hallucinogens in the coca. This 9-inch gold bottle for holding lime shows a seated figure with rings in the ears and beads across the forehead and at the neck, wrists, knees, and ankles. A tiny spatula would be used to secure the lime through the bottle's narrow neck. *(The Metropolitan Museum of Art, Jan Mitchell and Sons Collection, Gift of Jan Mitchell, 1991 [1991.419.22]. Photograph © 1992 The Metropolitan Museum of Art)*

EARLY CIVILIZATIONS

What physical, social, and intellectual features characterized early civilizations in the Americas?

Agricultural advancement had definitive social and political consequences. Careful cultivation of the land brought a reliable and steady food supply, which contributed to a relatively high fertility rate and in turn to a population boom. Population in the Americas grew steadily and may have been about 15 million people by the first century B.C.E. This growth in population allowed for greater concentrations of people and the creation of the first urban societies.

Mounds, Towns, and Trade in North and South America

In North America by 2500 B.C.E., some groups began to build massive earthworks, mounds of earth and stone. The mounds differed in shape, size, and purpose: some were conical, others elongated or wall-like, others pyramidical, and still others, called effigy mounds, in serpentine, bird, or animal form. The Ohio and Mississippi Valleys

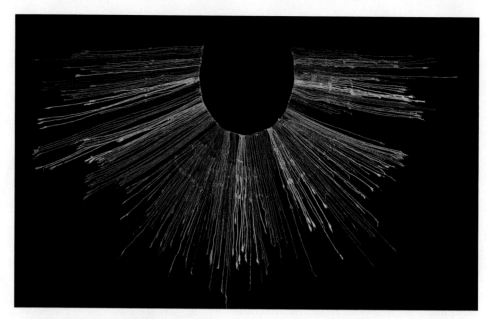

● **Inca Khipu, ca. 1400 C.E.** This khipu, a collection of colored, knotted strings, recorded numeric information and allowed Inca administrators to keep track of the flow of money, goods, and people in their large empire. Every aspect of the khipu—the form and position of the knots, the colors and spin of the string—may have provided information. Administrators read them visually and by running their hands through them, as Braille text is read today. *(Museo Arqueologico Rafael Larco Herrera, Lima, Peru)*

Norte Chico *A region along the coast of Peru that possessed a highly developed urban culture characterized by massive stepped pyramids and extensive use of cotton as early as 2500 B.C.E.*

khipu *A intricate system of knotted and colored strings used by early Peruvian cultures to store information such as census and tax records.*

contain the richest concentration of mounds, but they have been found from the Great Lakes down to the Gulf of Mexico (see Map 10.3 on page 273). One early large mound at Poverty Point, Louisiana, on the banks of the Mississippi, dates from about 1300 B.C.E. and consists of six octagonal ramparts, one within the other, that measure 6 feet high and more than 400 yards across. The area was home to perhaps five thousand people and was inhabited for hundreds of years, with trade goods brought in by canoe and carved stone beads exported.

Large structures for political and religious purposes began to be built earlier in South America than in North America. By about 2500 B.C.E. cities grew along river valleys on the coast of Peru in the region called **Norte Chico.** Stepped pyramids, some more than ten stories high, dominated these settlements, which were built at about the same time the pyramids were being constructed in Egypt. Cities in Norte Chico often used irrigation to produce crops of squash, beans, cotton, and other crops. Those along the coast relied extensively on fish and shellfish, which they traded with inland cities for the cotton needed to make nets. The largest city, Caral, had many plazas, houses, and temples, built with quarried stone using woven cotton and grass bags filled with smaller stones for support. Cotton was used in Norte Chico for many things, including the earliest example yet discovered of a **khipu** (also spelled *quipu*), a collection of knotted strings that was used to record information. Later Peruvian cultures, including the Incas, developed ever more complex khipu, using the colors of the string and the style and position of the knots to represent tax obligations, census records, and other numeric data.

Along with khipu, Norte Chico culture also developed religious ideas that may have been adopted by later Andean cultures. The oldest religious image yet found in the Americas, a piece of gourd with a drawing of a fanged god holding a staff, comes from Norte Chico, dating about 2250 B.C.E. This Staff God became a major deity in many Andean cultures, one of a complex pantheon of deities. Religious ceremonies, as well as other festivities, in Norte Chico involved music, as a large number of bone flutes have been discovered.

The earliest cities in the Andes were built by the **Chavin** people beginning about 1200 B.C.E. They built pyramids and other types of monumental architecture, quarrying and trimming huge blocks of stone and assembling them without mortar. They worked gold and silver into human and animal figurines, trading these and other goods to coastal peoples.

Chavin *A culture that developed in the Andes Mountains of Peru around 1200 B.C.E. and was responsible for the earliest cities in the region.*

The Olmecs

The **Olmecs** created the first society with cities in Mesoamerica. The word *Olmec* comes from an Aztec term for the peoples living in southern Veracruz and western Tabasco, Mexico, between about 1500 and 300 B.C.E. They did not call themselves Olmecs or consider themselves a unified group, but their culture penetrated and influenced all parts of Mesoamerica. Until 1993 knowledge of the Olmecs rested on archaeological evidence—pyramids, jade objects, axes, figurines, and stone monuments—but that year two linguists deciphered Olmec writing. Since then, understanding of Olmec and other contemporary Mesoamerican cultures such as the Zapotecs also comes from the written records they left.

Olmecs *The oldest of the early advanced Amerindian civilizations.*

The Olmecs cultivated maize, squash, beans, and other plants and supplemented that diet with wild game and fish. Originally they lived in egalitarian societies that had no distinctions based on status or wealth. After 1500 B.C.E. more complex, hierarchical societies evolved. Most peoples continued to live in small villages along the rivers of the region, while the leaders of the societies resided in the large cities today known as San Lorenzo, La Venta, Tres Zapotes, and Laguna de los Cerros. These cities contained palaces (large private houses) for the elite, large plazas, temples (ritual centers), ball courts, water reservoirs, and carved stone drains for the disposal of wastes. Like the Chavin (with whom they had no contact), the Olmecs created large pyramid-shaped buildings. They also carved huge stone heads of rulers or gods, beginning a tradition of monumental stone sculptures adopted by later Mesoamerican civilizations. In order to trace celestial phenomena—which they believed influenced human life—they developed a complex calendar involving three different ways of counting time. The need to record time led to the development of a writing system. Whereas the earliest written records from Mesopotamia are tax records for payments to the temple (see page 4), the earliest written records from Mesoamerica, dating from about 700 B.C.E., are dates. Many early records also record the deeds of kings, so that the political history of Mesoamerica is becoming more detailed as scholars learn to read various writing systems.

The Olmecs had sacred ceremonial sites where they sometimes practiced human sacrifice, another tradition adopted by later Mesoamerican cultures. They erected special courts on which men played a game with a hard rubber ball that was both religious ritual and sport. Finally, the Olmecs engaged in long-distance trade, exchanging rubber, cacao (from which chocolate is made), pottery, figurines, jaguar pelts, and the services of painters and sculptors for obsidian (a hard, black volcanic glass from which paddle-shaped weapons were made), basalt, iron ore, shells, and various perishable goods. Commercial networks extended as far away as central and western Mexico and the Pacific coast.

Around 900 B.C.E. San Lorenzo, the center of early Olmec culture, was destroyed, probably by migrating peoples from the north, and power passed to La Venta in Tabasco. Archaeological excavation at La Venta has uncovered a huge volcano-shaped pyramid. Standing 110 feet high at an inaccessible site on an island in the Tonala River, the so-called Great Pyramid was the center of the Olmec religion. The upward thrust of this monument, like ziggurats in Mesopotamia or cathedrals of medieval Europe, may have represented the human effort to get closer to the gods. Built of huge stone slabs, the Great Pyramid required, scholars estimated, some eight hundred thousand man-hours of labor. It testifies to the region's bumper harvests, which were able to support a labor force large enough to build such a monument.

CLASSICAL ERA MESOAMERICA AND NORTH AMERICA

How did Mesoamerican and North American peoples develop prosperous and stable societies in the classical era?

Maya *A highly developed Mesoamerican culture centered in the Yucatán peninsula of Mexico. The Maya created the most intricate writing system in the Western Hemisphere.*

The urban culture of the Olmecs and other Mesoamerican peoples influenced subsequent Mesoamerican societies. Especially in what became known as the classical era (300–900 C.E.), various groups developed large states centered on cities, with high levels of technological and intellectual achievement. Of these, the **Maya** were the most long-lasting, but other city-states were significant as well. Peoples living in North America built communities that were smaller than those in Mesoamerica, but many also used irrigation techniques to enhance agricultural production and built earthwork mounds for religious purposes.

● Palace Doorway Lintel at Yaxchilan, Mexico
Lady Xoc, principal wife of King Shield-Jaguar, who holds a torch over her, pulls a thorn-lined rope through her tongue to sanctify with her blood the birth of a younger wife's child—reflecting the importance of blood sacrifice in Maya culture. The elaborate headdresses and clothes of the couple show their royal status. (© *Justin Kerr 1985*)

Maya Technology and Trade

The word *Maya* seems to derive from *Zamna,* the name of a Maya god. Linguistic evidence leads scholars to believe that the first Maya were a small North American Indian group that emigrated from the area that is now southern Oregon and northern California to the western highlands of Guatemala. Between the third and second millennia B.C.E., various groups, including the Cholans and Tzeltalans, broke away from the parent group and moved north and east into the Yucatán peninsula. The Cholan-speaking Maya, who occupied the area during the time of great cultural achievement, apparently created the culture.

Maya culture rested on agriculture. The staple crop in Mesoamerica was maize, often raised in multiple-crop milpas with other foodstuffs, including beans, squash, chili peppers, some root crops, and fruit trees. The Maya also practiced intensive agriculture in raised, narrow, rectangular plots that they built above the low-lying, seasonally flooded land bordering rivers.

The raised-field and milpa systems of intensive agriculture yielded food sufficient to support large population centers. The entire Maya region could have had as many as 14 million inhabitants. At Uxmal, Uaxactún, Copán, Piedras Negras, Tikal, Palenque, and Chichén Itzá (see Map 10.2), archaeologists have uncovered the palaces of nobles, elaborate pyramids where nobles were buried, engraved *steles* (stone-slab monuments), masonry temples, altars, sophisticated polychrome pottery, and courts for games played with a rubber ball. The largest site, Tikal, may have had forty thousand people and served as a religious and ceremonial center.

Public fairs for trading merchandise accompanied important religious festivals. Jade, obsidian, beads of red spiny oyster shell, lengths of cloth, and cacao beans—all in high demand in the

Mesoamerican world—served as media of exchange. The extensive trade among Maya communities, plus a common language, promoted the union of the peoples of the region and gave them a common sense of identity. Merchants trading beyond Maya regions, such as with the Zapotecs of the Valley of Oaxaca and the Teotihuacános of the central valley of Mexico, were considered state ambassadors bearing "gifts" to royal neighbors, who reciprocated with their own "gifts." Since this long-distance trade played an important part in international relations, the merchants conducting it were high nobles or even members of the royal family.

The extensive networks of rivers and swamps in the area ruled by the Maya were the main arteries of transportation; over them large canoes carved out of hardwood trees carried cargoes of cloth and maize. Wide roads also linked Maya centers; on the roads merchants and lords were borne in litters, goods and produce on human backs. Trade produced considerable wealth that seems to have been concentrated in a noble class, for the Maya had no distinctly mercantile class. They did have a sharply defined hierarchical society. A hereditary elite owned private land, defended society, carried on commercial activities, exercised political power, and directed religious rituals. Artisans and scribes made up the next social level. The rest of the people were workers, farmers, and slaves, the latter including prisoners of war.

Wars were fought in Maya society for a variety of reasons. Long periods without rain caused crop failure, which led to famine and then war with other centers for food. Certain cities, such as Tikal, extended their authority over larger areas through warfare with neighboring cities. Within the same communities, domestic strife between factions over the succession to the kingship or property led to violence.

MAP 10.2 **The Maya World, 300–900 c.e.** The Maya built dozens of cities, linked together in trading networks of roads and rivers. Only the largest of them are shown here. They developed a complex writing system, using it to record political events, astronomical calculations, and religious ideas.

Maya Science and Religion

The Maya developed the most complex writing system in the Americas, a script with nearly a thousand characters that represent concepts and sounds. They used it to record chronology, religion, and astronomy in books made of bark paper and deerskin, on stone pillars archaeologists term "steles," on pottery, and on the walls of temples and other buildings. The deciphering of this writing over the last fifty years has demonstrated that inscriptions on steles are historical documents recording the births, accessions, marriages, wars, and deaths of Maya kings. The writing and pictorial imagery often represent the same events and have allowed for a fuller understanding of Maya dynastic history.

Learning about Maya religion through written records is more difficult. In the sixteenth century Spanish religious authorities ordered all books of Maya writing to be destroyed, viewing them as demonic. Only three (and part of a fourth) survived, because they were already in Europe. These texts do provide information about religious rituals and practices, as well as astronomical calculations. Further information comes from the **Popul Vuh,** or Book of Council, a book of mythological narratives and dynastic history written in the Maya language but in Roman script in the middle of the sixteenth century. Like the Bible in Judeo-Christian tradition, the *Popul Vuh* gives

Popul Vuh *The Book of Council, a collection of mythological narratives and dynastic histories that constitutes the primary record of the Maya civilization.*

● **Maya Ballplayers** Two teams of two players each face off in this lively scene on a painted ceramic vessel. Note that the ballplayers are wearing deer and vulture headdresses, Maya symbols of hunting and war. War was sometimes called the "hunting of men." *(Chrysler Museum of Art, Norfolk, Va., © Justin Kerr)*

the Maya view of the creation of the world, concepts of good and evil, and the entire nature and purpose of the living experience. Because almost all religious texts from Mesoamerica—not just Maya texts, but those from other cultures as well—were destroyed by Spanish Christian authorities, its significance is enormous.

Maya religious practice emphasized performing rituals at specific times, which served as an impetus for further refinements of the calendar. From careful observation of the earth's movements around the sun, the Maya devised a calendar of eighteen 20-day months and one 5-day month, for a total of 365 days. Their religious calendar, like that of the Olmecs, was a cycle of 260 days based perhaps on the movement of the planet Venus. When these two calendars coincided, which happened once every fifty-two years, the Maya celebrated a period of feasting, ballgame competitions, and religious observance. These observances—and those at other times as well—included human sacrifice to honor the gods and demonstrate the power of earthly kings.

Using a system of bars (— = 5) and dots (○ = 1), the Maya devised a form of mathematics based on the vigesimal (20) rather than the decimal (10) system. More unusual was their use of the number zero, which allows for more complex calculations than are possible in number systems without it. The zero may have actually been "discovered" by the Olmecs, who used it in figuring their calendar, but the Maya used it mathematically as well. (At about the same time, mathematicians in India also began using zero.) They proved themselves masters of abstract knowledge—notably in astronomy, mathematics, calendric development, and the recording of history.

Maya civilization lasted about a thousand years, reaching its peak between approximately 600 and 900 C.E., the period when the Tang Dynasty was flourishing in China, Islam was spreading in the Middle East, and Carolingian rulers were extending their sway in Europe. Between the eighth and tenth centuries, the Maya abandoned their cultural and ceremonial centers, and Maya civilization collapsed. Archaeologists and historians attribute the decline to a combination of agricultural failures due to land exhaustion and drought; overpopulation; disease; and constant wars fought as an extension of economic and political goals. These wars brought widespread destruction, which aggravated agrarian problems. Maya royal ideology also played a role in their decline: just as in good times kings attributed moral authority and prosperity to themselves, so in bad times, when military, economic, and social conditions deteriorated, they became the objects of blame.

Teotihuacán and the Toltecs

The Maya were not alone in creating a complex culture in Mesoamerica during the classic period. In the isolated valley of Oaxaca at modern-day Monte Albán in southern Mexico, Zapotecan-speaking peoples established a great religious center whose temples and elaborately decorated tombs testify to the wealth of the nobility. To the north of Monte Albán, **Teotihuacán** in central Mexico witnessed the flowering of a remarkable civilization built by a new people from regions east and south of the Valley of Mexico. The city of Teotihuacán had a population of over two hundred thousand—larger than any European city at the time. The inhabitants were stratified into distinct social classes. The rich and powerful resided in houses of palatial splendor in a special precinct. Ordinary working people, tradespeople, artisans, and obsidian craftsmen lived in apartment compounds, or *barrios,* on the edge of the city. Agricultural laborers lived outside the city. Teotihuacán was a great commercial center, the entrepôt for trade and culture for all of Mesoamerica. It was also the ceremonial center, a capital filled with artworks, a mecca that attracted thousands of pilgrims a year.

In the center of the city stood the Pyramids of the Sun and the Moon. The Pyramid of the Sun is built of sun-dried bricks and faced with stone. Each of its sides is seven hundred feet long and two hundred feet high. The smaller Pyramid of the Moon is similar in construction. In lesser temples, natives and outlanders worshiped the rain-god and the feathered serpent later called Quetzalcoatl. These gods were associated with the production of corn, the staple of the people's diet.

Around 750 C.E. less-developed peoples from the southwest burned Teotihuacán, and the city-state fell apart. This collapse, plus that of the Maya, marks the end of the classical period in Mesoamerica for most scholars, just as the end of the Roman Empire in the west marks the end of the classical era in Europe. As in Europe, a period characterized by disorder, militarism, and domination by smaller states followed.

Whereas nature gods and their priests seem to have governed the great cities of the earlier period, militant gods and warriors dominated the petty states that now arose. Among these states, the most powerful heir to Teotihuacán was the Toltec confederation, a weak union of strong states. The **Toltecs** admired the culture of their predecessors and sought to absorb and preserve it. Through intermarriage, they assimilated with the Teotihuacán people. In fact, every new Mesoamerican confederation became the cultural successor of earlier confederations.

Under Topiltzin (r. ca. 980–1000), the Toltecs extended their hegemony over most of central Mexico. Topiltzin established his capital at Tula. Its splendor and power became legendary during his reign. After the reign of Topiltzin, troubles beset the Toltec state. Drought led to crop failure. Northern peoples, the Chichimecas, attacked the borders in waves. Weak, incompetent rulers could not quell domestic uprisings. When the last Toltec king committed suicide in 1174, the Toltec state collapsed.

Teotihuacán *A city in central Mexico that became a great commercial center during the classic period.*

Toltecs *An heir to Teotihuacán, this confederation extended its hegemony over most of central Mexico under the reign of Topiltzin.*

● **Maya Burial Urn** After tightly wrapping the bodies of royal and noble persons in cloth, the K'iché Maya people of Guatemala placed them in urns and buried them in pyramids or sacred caves. The lid represents a divine being through whose mouth gifts may have been offered to the deceased. The figure with corncobs on top of the lid is the maize-god, a sacred figure to all Mesoamerican peoples. *(Museum of Fine Arts, Boston, Gift of Landon T. Clay [1988.1290]. © 2008 Museum of Fine Arts, Boston)*

● **Zapotec Deity** This Zapotec image of a god was found at Monte Albán, the primary Zapotec religious center. Made to be worn as a breast ornament, it was created through lost-wax casting, in which a mold is made from a wax model, and molten gold poured in to replace the wax. *(Giraudon/The Bridgeman Art Library)*

Hohokam *A Native American culture that emerged around 300 B.C.E. and was centered around the Gila River in Arizona. The Hohokam practiced a system of agriculture that relied on irrigation trenches, dams, and terraces to cultivate their arid land.*

Anasazi *A Native American culture that dominated the Four Corners region of the southwestern United States; remarkable for their construction of numerous cliff-dwellings in the region.*

Hopewell *An important mound-building Native American culture that thrived between 200 B.C.E. and 600 C.E. The culture was centered near the town of Hopewell, Ohio, and was noted for extensive canals and a trade network that extended from the Caribbean to Illinois.*

Hohokam, Hopewell, and Mississippian

Mesoamerican trading networks extended into southwestern North America, where by 300 B.C.E. the **Hohokam** people and other groups were using irrigation canals, dams, and terraces to enhance their farming of the arid land (see Map 10.3). The Hohokam built platforms for ceremonial purposes and played ballgames with rubber balls similar to those of the Olmecs and other Mesoamerican people. The rubber balls themselves were imported, for rubber trees do not grow in the desert, with turquoise and other precious stones exported in return. Religious ideas came along with trade goods, as the feathered serpent god became important to desert peoples. Other groups, including the **Anasazi,** Yuma, and later Pueblo, also built settlements in this area, using large sandstone blocks and masonry to construct thick-walled houses that offered protection from the heat. Mesa Verde, the largest Anasazi town, had a population of about twenty-five hundred living in houses built into and on cliff walls. Roads connected Mesa Verde to other Anasazi towns, allowing timber and other construction materials to be brought in more easily. Drought, deforestation, and soil erosion led to decline in both the Hohokam and Anasazi cultures, increasing warfare between towns.

To the east, the mound building that had first been developed at settlements along the Mississippi around 2000 B.C.E. spread more widely along many river basins. The most important mound-building culture in the first several centuries B.C.E. was the **Hopewell** culture, named for a town in Ohio near where the most extensive mounds were built. Some mounds were burial chambers for priests, leaders, and other high-status individuals, or for thousands of more average people. Others were platforms for the larger houses of important people. Still others were simply huge mounds of earth shaped like animals or geometric figures. Mound building thus had many purposes: it was a way to honor the gods, to remember the dead, and to make distinctions between leaders and common folk

Hopewell earthwork construction also included canals that enabled trading networks to expand, bringing products from the Caribbean far into the interior. Those

MAP 10.3 **Major North American Agricultural Societies, 600–1500 C.E.** Many North American groups used agriculture to increase the available food supply and allow for greater population density and the development of urban centers. Shown here are three of these cultures: the Mississippian, Anasazi, and Hohokam. Most mound-building cultures raised crops, and many were connected in an extensive trading network.

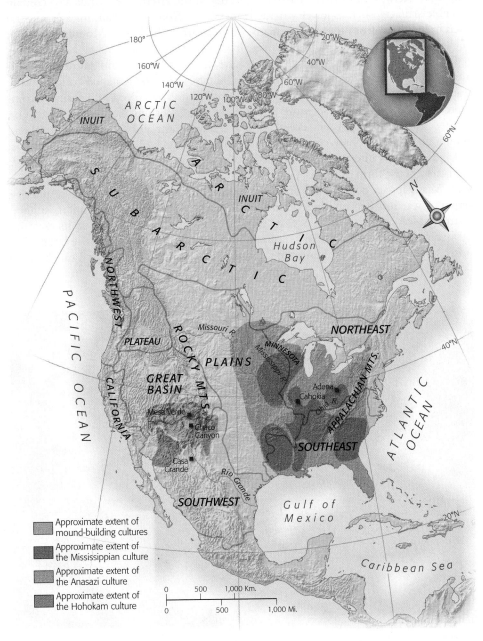

Approximate extent of mound-building cultures

Approximate extent of the Mississippian culture

Approximate extent of the Anasazi culture

Approximate extent of the Hohokam culture

trading networks also carried maize, allowing more intensive agriculture to spread throughout the eastern woodlands of North America.

At Cahokia, near the confluence of the Mississippi and Missouri Rivers in Illinois, archaeologists have uncovered the largest mound of all. Begun about 1050 C.E. and completed about 1250 C.E., the complex at Cahokia covered five and a half square miles and was the ceremonial center for perhaps thirty-eight thousand people. A fence of wooden posts surrounded the core. More than five hundred rectangular mounds or houses, inside and outside the fence, served as tombs and as the bases for temples and palaces. Within the fence, the largest mound rose in four stages to a height of one hundred feet and was more than one thousand feet long, larger than the largest Egyptian pyramid. At its top, a small conical platform supported a wooden fence and a rectangular temple. The mounds at Cahokia represent the culture of the **Mississippian** mound builders.

Mississippian *An important mound-building culture that thrived between 800 and 1500 C.E. in a territory that extended from the Mississippi River to the Appalachian Mountains. The largest mound produced by this culture is found at Cahokia, Illinois.*

What do the mounds tell us about Mississippian societies? The largest mounds served as burial chambers for leaders and, in many cases, the women and retainers who were sacrificed in order to assist the leader in the afterlife. Mounds also contain valuable artifacts, such as jewelry made from copper from Michigan, mica (a mineral used in building) from the Appalachians, obsidian from the Rocky Mountains, conch shells from the Caribbean, and pipestone from Minnesota.

From these burial items, archaeologists have deduced that mound culture was hierarchical. The leader had religious responsibilities and also managed long-distance trade and gift-giving. The exchange of goods was not perceived as a form of commerce, but as a means of showing respect and of establishing bonds among diverse groups. Large towns housed several thousand inhabitants and served as political and ceremonial centers. They controlled surrounding villages of a few hundred people, but did not grow into politically unified city-states the way Tikal or Teotihuacán did.

Pottery in the form of bowls, jars, bottles, and effigy pipes in various shapes best reveals Mississippian peoples' art and religious ideas. Designs showing eagles, plumed serpents, warriors decapitating victims, and ceremonially ornamented priests suggest a strong Mesoamerican influence. At its peak, about 1150, Cahokia and its environs probably housed between thirty thousand and fifty thousand people, the largest city north of Mesoamerica. Building the interior wooden fence had denuded much of the

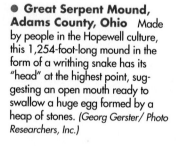

● **Great Serpent Mound, Adams County, Ohio** Made by people in the Hopewell culture, this 1,254-foot-long mound in the form of a writhing snake has its "head" at the highest point, suggesting an open mouth ready to swallow a huge egg formed by a heap of stones. *(Georg Gerster/ Photo Researchers, Inc.)*

MAP 10.4 **The Aztec (Mexica) Empire** The Mexica migrated into the central valley of what is now Mexico from the north, conquering other groups and establishing an empire, later called the Aztec Empire. The capital of the Aztec Empire was Tenochtitlán, built on islands in Lake Texcoco.

surrounding countryside of trees, however, which made spring floods worse and destroyed much of the city. An earthquake at the beginning of the thirteenth century knocked down more, and the city never recovered. Thus ecological crises appear to have played a part in bringing an end to various North American cultures, though their technologies and religious ideas were often maintained by those that developed later in the same areas.

Mississippian mound builders relied on agriculture to support their complex cultures, and by the time Cahokia was built, maize agriculture had spread to the Atlantic coast. Particularly along riverbanks and the coastline, fields of maize, beans, and squash surrounded large, permanent villages. Hunting provided meat protein, but the bulk of people's foodstuffs came from farming. The earliest European reports from Virginia and New England describe these villages and sometimes show illustrations of rows of houses within walls. By several decades after contact, disease had destroyed village life.

THE AZTECS

How did the Aztecs both build on the achievements of earlier Mesoamerican cultures and develop new traditions to create their large empire?

The **Aztecs** provide a spectacular example of a culture that adopted many things from earlier peoples and also adapted them to create an even more powerful state. Around 1300, a group of **Nahuatl**-speaking people are believed to have migrated southward from what is now northern Mexico, settling on the shores and islands in Lake Texcoco in the central valley of Mexico (see Map 10.4). Here they built the twin cities of Tenochtitlán and Tlatelolco, which by 1500 were probably larger than any city in Europe except Istanbul. As they migrated, these people conquered many neighboring city-states and established an empire. This empire was later termed the "Aztec" Empire and the people called the "Aztecs." This was not a word used at the time,

Aztec *A term coined by nineteenth-century historians to describe the Mexica people.*

Nahuatl *The language of both the Toltecs and the Aztecs.*

Mexica *Another term for Aztec; it is a pre-Columbian term designating the dominant ethnic people of the island capital of Tenochtitlán-Tlatelolco.*

however, and now most scholars prefer the term **Mexica** to refer to the empire and its people; we use both terms here.

Religion and War in Aztec Society

In Mexica society, religion was the dynamic factor that transformed other aspects of the culture: economic security, social mobility, education, and especially war. War was an article of religious faith. The state religion of the Aztecs initially gave them powerful advantages over other groups in central Mexico; it inspired them to conquer vast territories in a remarkably short time. War came to be seen as a religious duty to the Mexicas, through which nobles, and occasionally commoners, honored the gods, gained prestige, and often acquired wealth.

The Mexicas worshiped a number of gods and goddesses as well as some deities that had dual natures as both male and female. The basic conflict in the world was understood as one between order and disorder, though the proper life balances these two, as disorder could never be completely avoided. Disorder was linked to dirt and uncleanness, so temples, shrines, and altars were kept very clean; rituals of purification often involved sweeping or bathing. Like many polytheists, Mexicas took the deities of people they encountered into their own pantheon, or mixed their attributes with those of existing gods. Quetzalcoatl, for example, the feathered serpent god found among many Mesoamerican groups, was generally revered by the Mexicas as a creator deity and source of knowledge.

Huitzilopochtli *The chief among the Aztecs' many gods, who symbolized the sun blazing at high noon.*

Among the deities venerated by Mexica and other Mesoamerican groups was **Huitzilopochtli,** a young warrior god whose name translates fully as "Blue Hummingbird of the South" (or "on the Left") and who symbolized the sun blazing at high noon. The sun, the source of all life, had to be kept moving in its orbit if darkness was not to overtake the world. To keep it moving, Aztecs believed, the sun had to be frequently fed precious fluids—that is, human blood. Human sacrifice was a sacred duty, essential for the preservation and prosperity of humankind. (See the feature "Individuals in Society: Tlacaélel.")

Most victims were war captives, for the Aztecs controlled their growing empire by sacrificing prisoners seized in battle, by taking hostages from among defeated peoples as ransom against future revolt, and by demanding from subject states an annual tribute of people to be sacrificed to Huitzilopochtli. Unsuccessful generals, corrupt judges, and careless public officials, even people who accidentally entered forbidden precincts of the royal palaces, were routinely sacrificed. In some years it was difficult to provide enough war captives, so other types of people, including criminals, slaves, and people supplied as tribute, were sacrificed as well. Such victims did not have the same status as captives, however, and Mexicas engaged in special wars simply to provide victims for sacrifices, termed "flower (or flowery) wars." Flowers were frequently associated metaphorically with warfare in Mexica culture, with blood described as a flower of warfare, swords and banners as blooming like flowers, and a warrior's life as fleeting like a flower's blooming. The objective of flower wars was capturing warriors from the other side, not killing them.

The Mexica state religion required constant warfare for two basic reasons. One was to meet the gods' needs for human sacrifice; the other was to acquire warriors for the next phase of imperial expansion. The sacred campaigns of Huitzilopochtli were synchronized with the political and economic needs of the Mexica nation as a whole. Moreover, defeated peoples had to pay tribute in foodstuffs to support rulers, nobles, warriors, and the imperial bureaucracy. The vanquished supplied laborers for agriculture, the economic basis of Mexica society. Likewise, conquered peoples had to produce workers for the construction and maintenance of the entire Aztec infrastructure—roads, dike systems, aqueducts, causeways, and the royal palaces. Finally, merchants also benefited, for war opened new markets for traders' goods in subject territories.

Tlacaélel

Tlacaélel emphasized human sacrifice as one of the Aztecs' religious duties. *(Scala/Art Resource, NY)*

The hummingbird god Huitzilopochtli was originally a somewhat ordinary god of war and of young men, but in the fifteenth century he was elevated in status among the Mexica. He became increasingly associated with the sun and gradually became the Mexicas' most important deity. This change was primarily the work of Tlacaélel, the very long-lived chief adviser to the emperors Itzcóatl (r. 1427–1440), Montezuma I (r. 1440–1469), and Axayacatl (r. 1469–1481). Tlacaélel first gained influence during wars in the 1420s in which the Mexicas defeated the rival Tepanecs, after which he established new systems of dividing military spoils and enemy lands. At the same time, he advised the emperor that new histories were needed in which the destiny of the Mexica people was made clearer. Older historical texts were destroyed, and in these new chronicles the fate of the Mexicas was directly connected to Huitzilopochtli. Mexica writing was primarily pictographic, drawn and then read by specially trained scribes, who used written records as an aid to oral presentation, especially for legal issues, historical chronicles, religious and devotional poetry, and astronomical calculations.

According to these new texts, the Mexicas had been guided to Lake Texcoco by Huitzilopochtli; there they saw an eagle perched on a cactus, which a prophecy had told would mark the site of their new city. Huitzilopochtli kept the world alive by bringing the sun's warmth, but to do this he required the Mexicas, who increasingly saw themselves as the "people of the sun," to provide a steady offering of human blood.

The worship of Huitzilopochtli became linked to cosmic forces as well as daily survival. In Nahua tradition, the universe was understood to exist in a series of five suns, or five cosmic ages. Four ages had already passed, and their suns had been destroyed; the fifth sun, the age in which the Mexicas were now living, would also be destroyed unless the Mexicas fortified the sun with the energy found in blood. Warfare thus not only brought new territory under Mexica control, but also provided sacrificial victims for their collaboration with divine forces. With these ideas, Tlacaélel created what Miguel León-Portilla, a leading contemporary scholar of Nahuatl religion and philosophy, has termed a "mystico-militaristic" conception of Aztec destiny.

Human sacrifice was practiced in many cultures of Mesoamerica, including the Olmec and the Maya as well as the Mexica, before the changes introduced by Tlacaélel, but the number of victims is believed to have increased dramatically during the last period of Mexica rule. A huge pyramid-shaped temple in the center of Tenochtitlán, dedicated to Huitzilopochtli and the water god Tlaloc, was renovated and expanded many times, the last in 1487. Each expansion was dedicated by priests sacrificing war captives. Similar ceremonies were held regularly throughout the year on days dedicated to Huitzilopochtli and were attended by many observers, including representatives from neighboring states as well as masses of Mexicas. According to many accounts, victims were placed on a stone slab and their hearts cut out with an obsidian knife; the officiating priest then held the heart up as an offering to the sun. Sacrifices were also made to other gods at temples elsewhere in Tenochtitlán, and perhaps in other cities controlled by the Mexicas.

Estimates about the number of people sacrificed to Huitzilopochtli and other Mexica gods vary enormously and are impossible to verify. Both Mexica and later Spanish accounts clearly exaggerated the numbers, but most historians today assume that between several hundred and several thousand people were killed each year.

Questions for Analysis

1. How did the worship of Huitzilopochtli contribute to Aztec expansion? To hostility toward the Aztecs?

2. Why might Tlacaélel have seen it as important to destroy older texts as he created this new Aztec mythology?

Sources: León-Portilla, Miguel. *Pre-Columbian Literatures of Mexico* (Norman: University of Oklahoma Press, 1969); Clendinnen, Inga. *Mexicas: An Interpretation* (Cambridge: Cambridge University Press, 1991).

● **The Goddess Tlazolteotl** The Aztecs believed that cleanliness was a way to honor the gods, and that Tlazolteotl (sometimes called "Mother of the Gods") consumed the sins of humankind by eating refuse. She was also the goddess of childbirth. Notice the squatting position for childbirth, then common all over the world. *(Dumbarton Oaks, Pre-Columbian Collection, Washington, D.C.)*

tecuhtli *Provincial governors who exercised full political, judicial, and military authority on the Aztec emperor's behalf.*

The Life of the People

A wealth of information has survived about fifteenth- and sixteenth-century Mexico. The Aztecs wrote many books recounting their history, geography, and religious practices. They loved making speeches, which scribes wrote down. The Aztecs also preserved records of their legal disputes, which alone amounted to vast files. The Spanish conquerors subsequently destroyed much of this material. But enough documents remain to construct a picture of the Mexica people at the time of the Spanish intrusion.

No sharp social distinctions existed among the Aztecs during their early migrations. All were equally poor. The head of a family was both provider and warrior, and a sort of tribal democracy prevailed in which all adult males participated in important decision making. By the early sixteenth century, however, Aztec society had changed. A stratified social structure had come into being, and the warrior aristocracy exercised great authority.

Scholars do not yet understand precisely how this change occurred. According to Aztec legend, the Mexica admired the Toltecs and chose their first king, Acamapichti, from among them. The many children he fathered with Mexica women formed the nucleus of the noble class. At the time of the Spanish intrusion into Mexico, men who had distinguished themselves in war occupied the highest military and social positions in the state. Generals, judges, and governors of provinces were appointed by the emperor from among his servants who had earned reputations as war heroes. These great lords, or **tecuhtli,** dressed luxuriously and lived in palaces. The provincial governors exercised full political, judicial, and military authority on the emperor's behalf. In their territories they maintained order, settled disputes, and judged legal cases; oversaw the cultivation of land; and made sure that tribute—in food or gold—was paid. The governors also led troops in wartime. These functions resembled those of feudal lords in western Europe during the Middle Ages (see pages 367–368). Just as only nobles in France and England could wear fur and carry swords, just as gold jewelry and elaborate hairstyles for women distinguished royal and noble classes in African kingdoms, so in Mexica societies only the tecuhtli could wear jewelry and embroidered cloaks. The growth of a strong mercantile class as the empire expanded led to an influx of tropical wares and luxury goods: cotton, feathers, cocoa, skins, turquoise jewelry, and gold. The upper classes enjoyed an elegant and extravagant lifestyle.

Beneath the great nobility of soldiers and imperial officials was the class of warriors. Theoretically every free man could be a warrior, and parents dedicated their male children to war, burying a male child's umbilical cord with some arrows and a shield on the day of his birth. In actuality the sons of nobles enjoyed advantages deriving from their fathers' position and influence in the state. At the age of six, boys entered a school that trained them for war. Future warriors were taught to fight with a *macana,* a paddle-shaped wooden club edged with bits of obsidian. Youths were also trained in the use of spears, bows and arrows, and lances fitted with obsidian points. They learned to live on little food and sleep and to accept pain without complaint. At about age eighteen, a warrior fought his first campaign. If he captured a prisoner for ritual sacrifice, he acquired the title *iyac,* or warrior. If in later campaigns he succeeded in killing or capturing four of the enemy, he became a *tequiua*—one who shared in the booty and thus was a member of the nobility. If a young man failed in several campaigns to capture the required four prisoners, he joined the **maceualtin,** the plebeian or working class.

The maceualtin were the ordinary citizens—the backbone of Aztec society and the vast majority of the population. The word *maceualti* means "worker" and implies boorish speech and vulgar behavior. Members of this class performed all sorts of agricultural, military, and domestic services and carried heavy public burdens not required of noble warriors. Government officials assigned the maceualtin work on the temples, roads, and bridges. Army officers called them up for military duty, but Mexica considered this an honor and a religious rite, not a burden. Unlike nobles, priests, orphans, and slaves, maceualtin paid taxes. Maceualtin in the capital, however, possessed certain rights: they held their plots of land for life, and they received a small share of the tribute paid by the provinces to the emperor.

Beneath the maceualtin were the *tlalmaitl,* the landless workers or serfs. Some social historians speculate that this class originated during the period of migrations and upheavals following the end of the classical period (see page 271), when weak and defenseless people placed themselves under the protection of strong warriors, just as European peasants had become serfs after the end of the Roman Empire (see page 126). The tlalmaitl provided agricultural labor, paid rents in kind, and were bound to the soil—they could not move off the land. The tlalmaitl resembled in many ways the serfs of western Europe, but unlike serfs they performed military service when called on to do so. They enjoyed some rights as citizens and generally were accorded more respect than slaves.

Slaves were the lowest social class. Like Asian, European, and African slaves, most were prisoners captured in war or kidnapped from enemy tribes. But Aztecs who stole from a temple or private house or plotted against the emperor could also be enslaved, and people in serious debt sometimes voluntarily sold themselves into slavery. Female

● **Aztec Youth** As shown in this codex, Aztec society had basic learning requirements for each age (indicated by dots) of childhood and youth. In the upper panel, boys of age thirteen gather firewood and collect reeds and herbs in a boat, while girls learn to make tortillas on a terra-cotta grill. At fourteen (lower panel), boys learn to fish from a boat, and girls are taught to weave. *(The Bodleian Library, University of Oxford, MS Arch. Selden. A.1, fol. 60r)*

slaves often became their masters' concubines. Mexica slaves, however, differed fundamentally from European ones, for they could possess goods, save money, buy land and houses and even slaves for their own service, and purchase their freedom. If a male slave married a free woman, their offspring were free, and a slave who escaped and managed to enter the emperor's palace was automatically free. Most slaves eventually gained their freedom. Mexica slavery, therefore, had some humane qualities and resembled slavery in Islamic societies (see pages 205–207).

Women of all social classes played important roles in Mexica society, but those roles were restricted entirely to the domestic sphere. As the little hands of the newborn male child were closed around a tiny bow and arrow indicating his warrior destiny, so the infant female's hands were wrapped around miniature weaving instruments and a small broom: weaving was a sacred and exclusively female art; the broom signaled a female's responsibility for the household shrines and for keeping the household swept and free of contamination. Almost all of the Mexica people married, a man at about twenty when he had secured one or two captives, a woman a couple of years earlier. As in premodern Asian and European societies, parents selected their children's spouses, using neighborhood women as go-betweens. Save for the few women vowed to the service of the temple, marriage and the household were a woman's fate; marriage represented social maturity for both sexes. Pregnancy became the occasion for family and neighborhood feasts, and a successful birth launched celebrations lasting from ten to twenty days.

Women were expected to pray for their husbands' success in battle while they were gone. As one prayer to Huitzilopochtli went:

O great Lord of All Things, remember your servant
Who has gone to exalt your honor and the greatness of your name.
He will offer blood in that sacrifice that is war.
Behold, Lord, that he did not go out to work for me
Or for his children . . . He went for your sake,
In your name, to obtain glory for you . . .
Give him victory in this war so that he may return
To rest in his home and so that my children and I may see
His countenance again and feel his presence."[1]

Alongside the secular social classes stood the temple priests. Huitzilopochtli and each of the numerous lesser gods had many priests to oversee the upkeep of the temple, assist at religious ceremonies, and perform ritual sacrifices. The priests also did a brisk business in foretelling the future from signs and omens. Aztecs consulted priests on the selection of wives and husbands, on the future careers of newborn babies, and before leaving on journeys or for war. Temples possessed enormous wealth in gold and silver ceremonial vessels, statues, buildings, and land. From the temple revenues and resources, the priests supported schools, aided the poor, and maintained hospitals. The chief priests had the ear of the emperor and often exercised great power and influence.

At the peak of the social pyramid stood the emperor. The various Aztec historians contradict one another about the origin of the imperial dynasty, but modern scholars tend to accept the verdict of one sixteenth-century authority that the "custom has always been preserved among the Mexicans (that) the sons of kings have not ruled by right of inheritance, but by election."[2] A small oligarchy of the chief priests, warriors, and state officials made the selection. If none of the sons proved satisfactory, a brother or nephew of the emperor was chosen, but election was always restricted to the royal family.

The Aztec emperor was expected to be a great warrior who had led Mexica and allied armies into battle. All his other duties pertained to the welfare of his people. It was up to the emperor to see that justice was done—he was the final court of appeal. He also held ultimate responsibility for ensuring an adequate food supply. The emperor Montezuma I (r. 1440–1467) distributed twenty thousand loads of stock-piled grain when a flood hit Tenochtitlán. The records show that the Aztec emperors took their public duties seriously.

The Cities of the Aztecs

When the Spanish entered **Tenochtitlán** (which they called Mexico City) in November 1519, they could not believe their eyes. According to Bernal Díaz, one of Cortés's companions:

when we saw all those cities and villages built in the water, and other great towns on dry land, and that straight and level causeway leading to Mexico, we were astounded. These great towns and cues (temples) and buildings rising from the water, all made of stone, seemed like an enchanted vision. . . . Indeed, some of our soldiers asked whether it was not all a dream.[3]

Tenochtitlán had about sixty thousand households. The upper class practiced polygamy and had many children, and many households included servants and slaves. The total population probably numbered around 250,000. At the time, no European city and few Asian ones could boast a population even half that size. The total Aztec Empire has been estimated at around 5 million inhabitants, with the total population of Mesoamerica estimated at between 20 and 30 million.

Originally built on salt marshes, Tenochtitlán was approached by four great highways that connected it with the mainland. Bridges stood at intervals (comparable to modern Paris). Stone and adobe walls surrounded the city itself, making it (somewhat like medieval Constantinople; see page 169) highly defensible and capable of resisting

Tenochtitlán *A large and prosperous Aztec city that was admired by the Spanish when they entered in 1519.*

● **Tenochtitlán**   The great Mexican archaeologist Ignacio Marquina designed this reconstruction of the central plaza of the Mexica city as it looked in 1519. The temple precinct, an area about 500 square yards, contained more than eighty structures, pyramids, pools, and homes of gods and of the men and women who served them. Accustomed to the clutter and filth of Spanish cities, the Spaniards were amazed by the elegance and cleanliness of Tenochtitlán. *(Enrique Franco-Torrijos)*

a prolonged siege. Wide, straight streets and canals crisscrossed the city. Boats and canoes plied the canals. Lining the roads and canals stood thousands of rectangular one-story houses of mortar faced with stucco. Although space was limited, many small gardens and parks were alive with the colors and scents of flowers.

A large aqueduct whose sophisticated engineering astounded Cortés carried pure water from distant springs and supplied fountains in the parks. Streets and canals opened onto public squares and marketplaces. Tradespeople offered every kind of merchandise. Butchers hawked turkeys, ducks, chickens, rabbits, and deer; grocers sold kidney beans, squash, avocados, corn, and all kinds of peppers. Artisans sold intricately designed gold, silver, and feathered jewelry. Seamstresses offered sandals, loincloths and cloaks for men, and blouses and long skirts for women—the clothing customarily worn by ordinary people—and embroidered robes and cloaks for the rich. Slaves for domestic service, wood for building, herbs for seasoning and medicine, honey and sweets, knives, jars, smoking tobacco, even human excrement used to cure animal skins—all these wares made a dazzling spectacle.

At one side of the central square of Tenochtitlán stood the great temple of Huitzilopochtli. Built as a pyramid and approached by three flights of 120 steps each, the temple was about one hundred feet high and dominated the city's skyline. According to Cortés, it was "so large that within the precincts, which are surrounded by a very high wall, a town of some five hundred inhabitants could easily be built. All round inside this wall there are very elegant quarters with very large rooms and corridors where their priests live."[4]

Travelers, perhaps inevitably, compare what they see abroad with what is familiar to them at home. Tenochtitlán thoroughly astounded Cortés, and in his letter to the emperor Charles V, he describes the city in comparison to his homeland: "the market square," where sixty thousand people a day came to buy and sell, "was twice as big as Salamanca"; the beautifully constructed "towers," as the Spaniards called the pyramids, rose higher "than the cathedral at Seville"; Montezuma's palace was "so marvelous that it seems to me to be impossible to describe its excellence and grandeur[;] . . . in Spain there is nothing to compare with it." Accustomed to the squalor and filth of Spanish cities, the cleanliness of Tenochtitlán dumbfounded the Spaniards, as did all the evidence of its ordered and elegant planning.[5]

- - - - - -

THE INCAS

What were the sources of strength and prosperity, and of problems, for the Incas as they created their enormous empire?

In the center of Peru rise the cold highlands of the Andes. Six valleys of fertile and wooded land at altitudes ranging from eight thousand to eleven thousand feet punctuate highland Peru. The largest of these valleys are the Huaylas, Cuzco, and Titicaca. It was there that Inca civilization developed and flourished. Like the Aztecs, the **Incas** were a small militaristic group that came to power, conquered surrounding groups, and established one of the most extraordinary empires in the world. Gradually, Inca culture spread throughout Peru.

Incas *The Peruvian empire that was at its peak from 1438 until 1532.*

Earlier Peruvian Cultures

Inca achievements built on those of cultures that preceded them in the Andes and the Peruvian coast. These included the Chavin and the **Moche** civilization, which flourished along a 250-mile stretch of Peru's northern coast between 100 and 800 C.E. Rivers that flowed out of the Andes into the valleys allowed the Moche people to develop complex irrigation systems for agricultural development. Each Moche valley contained a large ceremonial center with palaces and pyramids surrounded by settlements of up to ten thousand people. The dazzling gold and silver artifacts, elaborate

Moche *A Native American culture that thrived along Peru's northern coast between 100 and 800 C.E. The culture existed as a series of city-states rather than a single empire and is distinguished by an extraordinarily rich and diverse pottery industry.*

headdresses, and ceramic vessels display a remarkable skill in metalwork and pottery.

Politically, Moche culture was a series of small city-states rather than one unified state, which increased warfare. As in Aztec culture, war provided victims for human sacrifice, frequently portrayed on Moche pottery. Beginning about 500, the Moche suffered several severe *El Niños,* the change in ocean current patterns in the Pacific that brings both searing drought and flooding. Their leaders were not able to respond effectively, and the cities lost population.

In the Andes, various states developed after Chavin that were each able to carve out a slightly larger empire. They built cities around large public plazas, with temples, palaces, and elaborate stonework. Using terraces and other means to increase the amount of arable soil, they grew potatoes and other crops, even at very high altitudes. Enough food was harvested to feed not only the farmers themselves but also massive armies and administrative bureaucracies and thousands of industrial workers. These cultures were skilled at using fibers for a variety of purposes, including building boats to use on Lake Titicaca and bridges for humans and pack llamas to cross steep valleys.

Inca Imperialism

Who were the Incas? *Inca* was originally the name of the governing family of an Amerindian group that settled in the basin of Cuzco (see Map 10.5). From that family, the name was gradually extended to all peoples living in the Andes valleys. The Incas themselves used the word to identify their ruler or emperor. Here the term is used for both the ruler and the people. As with the Aztecs, so with the Incas: religious ideology was the force that transformed the culture. Religious concepts created pressure for imperialist expansion.

The Incas believed their ruler descended from the sun-god and that the health and prosperity of the state depended on him. Dead rulers were thought to link the people to the sun-god. When the ruler died, his corpse was preserved as a mummy in elaborate clothing and housed in a sacred and magnificent chamber. His royal descendants as a group managed his lands and sources of income for him and used the revenues to care for his mummy, maintain his cult, and support themselves. New rulers did not inherit these riches, so they had to win their own possessions by means of war and imperial expansion.

Around 1000 C.E. the Incas were one of many small groups fighting among themselves for land and water. The cult of royal mummies provided the impetus for expansion. The desire for conquest provided incentives for courageous (or ambitious) nobles: those who were victorious in battle and gained new territories for the state could expect lands, additional wives, servants, herds of llamas, gold, silver, fine clothes, and other symbols of high status. Even common soldiers who distinguished themselves in battle could be rewarded with booty and raised to noble status. The imperial interests of the emperor paralleled those of other social groups. Under Pachacuti Inca (1438–1471) and his successors, Inca domination was gradually extended by warfare to the frontier of present-day Ecuador and Colombia in the north and to the Maule River in present-day Chile in the south (see Map 10.5), an area of about 350,000 square miles. Eighty provinces, scores of ethnic groups, and 16 million people came under Inca control. A remarkable system of roads held the empire together.

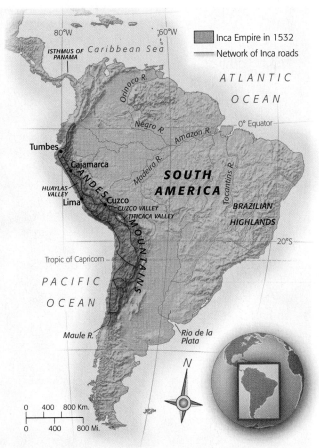

MAP 10.5 The Inca Empire, 1532 Beginning in the fifteenth century, the Incas expanded their holdings through warfare. They built an extensive network of roads to hold their ethnically diverse empire together.

● **Portrait Vessel of a Ruler** Artisans of the Moche culture on the northern coast of Peru produced objects representing many aspects of their world, including this flat-bottomed stirrup-spout jar with a ruler's face. The commanding expression conveys a strong sense of power, as does the elaborate headdress with the geometric designs of Moche textiles worn only by elite persons. (*South America, Peru, North Coast, Moche Culture, Portrait Vessel of a Ruler, earthenware with pigmented clay slip, 300–700, 35.6 x 24.1, Kate S. Buckingham Endowment, 1955.2338, 3/4 view. Photograph by Robert Hashimoto. Photograph © 1999, The Art Institute of Chicago*)

Quechua *First deemed the official language of the Incas under Pachacuti, it is still spoken by most Peruvians today.*

Primary Source: Chronicles
Learn how the Incas used the elaborate knotted ropes called khipus as record-keeping devices that helped them govern a vast and prosperous empire.

Before Inca civilization, each group that entered the Andes valleys had its own distinct language. These languages were not written and have become extinct. Scholars will probably never understand the linguistic condition of Peru before the fifteenth century when Pachacuti made the Inca language, which the Spanish called **Quechua** (pronounced "keshwa"), the official language of his people and administration. Conquered peoples were forced to adopt the language, and Quechua spread the Inca way of life throughout the Andes. Though not written until the Spanish in Peru adopted it as a second official language, Quechua had replaced local languages by the seventeenth and eighteenth centuries and is still spoken by most Peruvians today.

Both the Aztecs and the Incas ruled very ethnically diverse peoples. Whereas the Aztecs tended to control their subject peoples through terror, the Incas governed by means of imperial unification. They imposed not only their language but also their entire panoply of gods. Magnificent temples scattered throughout the expanding empire housed images of these gods. Priests led prayers and elaborate rituals, and on such occasions as a terrible natural disaster or a great military victory, they sacrificed human beings to the gods. Subject peoples were required to worship the state gods.

Imperial unification was also achieved through the forced participation of local chieftains in the central bureaucracy and through a policy of colonization. To prevent rebellion in newly conquered territories, Pachacuti Inca and subsequent rulers transferred all their inhabitants to other parts of the empire, replacing them with workers who had lived longer under Inca rule. They drafted local men for distant wars, breaking up kin groups that had existed in Andean society for centuries.

An excellent system of roads—averaging three feet in width, some paved and others not—facilitated the transportation of armies and the rapid communication of royal orders by runners. The roads followed straight lines wherever possible but also crossed pontoon bridges and tunneled through hills. This great feat of Inca engineering bears striking comparison with Roman roads, which also linked an empire.

Ruling an empire requires a bureaucracy as well as an army, and Inca officials, tax collectors, and accountants traveled throughout the empire. They made increasingly elaborate khipus (see page 266) to record financial and labor obligations, the output of fields, population levels, land transfers, and other numerical records. Scholars have deciphered the way numbers were recorded on khipus, finding a base-ten system. Khipus may also have been used to record narrative history, but this is more speculative, as knowledge of how to read them died out after the Spanish conquest. Just as the Spanish destroyed books in Mesoamerica, they destroyed khipus in the Andes because they thought they might contain religious messages and encourage people to resist Spanish authority. About 750 Inca khipus survive today, more than half in museums in Europe.

Rapid Inca expansion, however, produced stresses. Although the pressure for growth remained unabated, open lands began to be scarce. Attempts to penetrate the tropical Amazon forest east of the Andes led to repeated military disasters. The Incas waged wars with highly trained armies drawn up in massed formation and fought pitched battles on level ground, often engaging in hand-to-hand combat. But in dense jungles, the troops could not maneuver or maintain order against enemies using guerrilla tactics and sniping at them with deadly blowguns. Another source of stress was revolts among subject peoples in conquered territories. Even the system of roads and trained runners eventually caused administrative problems. The average runner could cover about 50 leagues, or 175 miles, per day—a remarkable feat of physical endurance, especially at high altitude—but the larger the empire became, the greater the distances to be covered. The roundtrip from the capital at Cuzco to Quito in Ecuador, for example, took from ten to twelve days, so that an emperor might have to base urgent decisions on incomplete or out-of-date information. The empire was overextended.

When the Inca Huayna Capac died in 1525, his throne was bitterly contested by two of his sons, Huascar and Atauhualpa. Huascar's threat to do away with the cult of royal mummies led the nobles—who often benefited from managing land and wealth for a deceased ruler—to throw their support behind Atauhualpa. In the civil war that began in 1532, Atauhualpa's veteran warriors easily defeated Huascar's green recruits, but the conflict weakened the Incas. On his way to his coronation at Cuzco, Atauhualpa encountered Pizarro and 168 Spaniards who had recently entered the kingdom. The Spaniards quickly became the real victors in the Inca kingdom (see pages 442–443).

● **Machu Picchu** The Inca city of Machu Picchu, surrounded by mountains in the clouds, clings to a spectacular crag in upland Peru. It was built around 1450, at the point that the Inca Empire was at its height, and abandoned about a century later. *(Will McIntyre/Photo Researchers, Inc.)*

● **An Inca Cape** Inca artisans could produce gorgeous textiles, and on ceremonial occasions nobles proudly paraded in brightly colored feathers or in garments made of luxurious alpaca wool. This exquisite cape is fashioned from the feathers of a blue and yellow macaw; the pattern, befitting aristocratic tastes, features lordly pelicans carried on litters by less exalted birds. *(The Textile Museum, Washington, D.C., 91.395. Acquired by George Hewitt Myers in 1941)*

Inca Society

ayllu *A clan; it served as the fundamental social unit of Inca society.*

curacas *The headman of the Inca clan; he was responsible for conducting relations with outsiders.*

mita *A draft rotary system that determined when men of a particular hamlet performed public works.*

The **ayllu,** or clan, served as the fundamental social unit of Inca society. All members of the ayllu owed allegiance to the **curacas,** or headman, who conducted relations with outsiders. The ayllu held specific lands, granted it by village or provincial authorities on a long-term basis, and individual families tended to work the same plots for generations. Cooperation in the cultivation of the land and intermarriage among members of the ayllu wove people there into a tight web of connections.

In return for the land, all men had to perform public duties and pay tribute to the authorities. Their duties included building and maintaining palaces, temples, roads, and irrigation systems. Tribute consisted of potatoes, corn, and other vegetables paid to the village head, who in turn paid them to the provincial governor. A draft rotary system called **mita** (turn) determined when men of a particular village performed public works. As the Inca Empire expanded, this pattern of social and labor organization was imposed on other, newly conquered indigenous peoples. After the conquest, the Spaniards adopted and utilized the Incas' ways of organizing their economy and administration, just as the Incas (and, in Mesoamerica, the Aztecs) had built on earlier cultures.

The Incas had well-established mechanisms for public labor drafts and tribute collection. The emperors sometimes gave newly acquired lands to victorious generals, distinguished civil servants, and favorite nobles. These lords subsequently exercised authority previously held by the native curacas. Whether long-time residents or new colonists, common people had the status of peasant farmers, which entailed heavy agricultural or other obligations. Just as in medieval Europe peasants worked several days each week on their lord's lands, so the Inca people had to work on state lands (that is, the emperor's lands) or on lands assigned to the temple. Peasants also labored on roads and bridges; terraced and irrigated new arable land; served on construction crews for royal palaces, temples, and public buildings such as fortresses; acted as runners on the post roads; and excavated in the imperial gold, silver, and copper mines. The imperial government annually determined the number of laborers needed for these various undertakings, and each district had to supply an assigned quota. The government also made an ayllu responsible for the state-owned granaries and for the production of cloth for army uniforms.

The state required everyone to marry and even decided when and sometimes whom a person should marry. Men married around the age of twenty, women a little younger. The Incas did not especially prize virginity; premarital sex was common. The marriage ceremony consisted of the joining of hands and the exchange of a pair of sandals. This ritual was followed by a large wedding feast at which the state presented the bride and groom with two sets of clothing, one for everyday wear and one for festive occasions. If a man or woman did not find a satisfactory mate, the provincial governor selected one for him or her. Travel was forbidden, so couples necessarily came from the same region. Like most warring societies with high male death rates, the Incas practiced polygamy, though the cost of supporting many wives restricted it largely to the upper classes.

The Incas relied heavily on local authorities and cultural norms for day-to-day matters. In some ways, however, the common people were denied choice and initiative and led regimented lives. The Incas did, however, take care of the poor and aged, distribute grain in times of shortage and famine, and supply assistance in natural disasters. Scholars have debated whether Inca society was socialistic, totalitarian, or a forerunner of the welfare state; it may be merely a matter of definition. Although the Inca economy was strictly regulated, there certainly was not an equal distribution of wealth. Everything above and beyond the masses' basic needs went to the emperor and the nobility.

The backbreaking labor of ordinary people in the fields and mines made possible the luxurious lifestyle of the great Inca nobility. The nobles—called *oregones,* or "big ears," by the Spanish because they pierced their ears and distended the lobes with heavy jewelry—were the ruling Inca's kinsmen. Lesser nobles included the curacas, royal household servants, public officials, and entertainers.

In the fifteenth century Inca rulers superimposed imperial institutions on those of kinship. They ordered allegiance to be paid to the ruler at Cuzco rather than to the curacas and relocated the entire populations of certain regions. Entirely new ayllus were formed, based on residence rather than kinship. As the empire expanded, there arose a noble class of warriors, governors, and local officials whose support the ruling Inca secured with gifts of land, precious metals, and llamas and alpacas (llamas were used as beasts of burden; alpacas were raised for their long fine wool). The nobility was exempt from agricultural work and from other kinds of public service.

Chapter Summary

Key Terms

Mesoamerica
milpa
Norte Chico
khipu
Chavin
Olmecs
Maya
Popul Vuh
Teotihuacán
Toltecs
Hohokam
Anasazi
Hopewell
Mississippian
Aztec
Nahuatl
Mexica
Huitzilopochtli
tecuhtli
maceualtin
Tenochtitlán
Incas
Moche
Quechua
ayllu
curacas
mita

To assess your mastery of this chapter, go to **bedfordstmartins.com/mckayworld**

• *How did early peoples in the Americas adapt to their environment as they created economic and political systems?*

The environment shaped the formation of human settlements in the Americas, which began when people crossed into the Western Hemisphere from Asia. All the highly varied environments, from polar tundra to tropical rain forests, came to support human settlement. About 8000 B.C.E., people in some parts of the Americas began raising crops as well as gathering wild produce. Maize became the most important crop, with knowledge about its cultivation spreading out from Mesoamerica into North and South America.

• *What physical, social, and intellectual features characterized early civilizations in the Americas?*

Agricultural advancement led to an increase in population, which allowed for greater concentrations of people and the creation of the first urban societies. In certain parts of North and South America, towns dependent on agriculture flourished, especially in coastal areas and river valleys. Some in North America began to build large earthwork mounds, while those in South America practiced irrigation. The Olmecs created the first society with cities in Mesoamerica, with large ceremonial buildings, an elaborate and accurate calendar, and a system of writing.

• *How did Mesoamerican and North American peoples develop prosperous and stable societies in the classical era?*

The urban culture of the Olmecs and other Mesoamerican peoples influenced subsequent societies. Especially in what became known as the classical era (300–900 C.E.), various groups developed large states centered on cities, with high levels of technological and intellectual achievement. Of these, the Maya were the most long-lasting, creating a complex written language and elegant art. Peoples living in North America built communities that were smaller than those in Mesoamerica, but many also used irrigation techniques to enhance agricultural production and continued to build earthwork mounds for religious purposes.

• *How did the Aztecs both build on the achievements of earlier Mesoamerican cultures and develop new traditions to create their large empire?*

The Aztecs, also known as the Mexica, built a unified culture based heavily on the heritage of earlier Mesoamerican societies and distinguished by achievements in engineering, sculpture, and architecture. In Mexica society, religion was the dynamic factor that transformed other aspects of the culture: economic security, social mobility, education, and especially war. War was an article of religious faith, providing riches and land, and also sacrificial victims for ceremonies honoring the Aztec gods. Aztec society was hierarchical, with nobles and priests having special privileges. The Aztec empire centered on Tenochtitlán, the most spectacular and one of the largest cities in the world in 1500.

• **What were the sources of strength and prosperity, and of problems, for the Incas as they created their enormous empire?**

The Peruvian coast and Andean highlands were home to a series of cultures that cultivated cotton as well as food crops. Of these, the largest empire was created by the Incas, who began as a small militaristic group and conquered surrounding groups. The Incas established a far-flung empire that stretched along the Andes, keeping this together through a system of roads, along which moved armies and administrators. Andean society was dominated by clan groups, and Inca measures to disrupt these and move people great distances created resentment.

Suggested Reading

Clendinnen, I. *Aztecs: An Interpretation.* 1992. Pays particular attention to the role that rituals and human sacrifice played in Aztec culture.

Coe, M. *The Mayas.* 2005. A new edition of a classic survey that incorporates the most recent scholarship.

Conrad, G. W., and A. A. Demarest. *Religion and Empire: The Dynamics of Aztec and Inca Expansionism.* 1993. Compares the two largest American empires.

D'Altroy, T. *The Incas.* 2003. Examines the ways in which the Incas drew on earlier traditions to create their empire; by a leading scholar.

Freidel, D. *A Forest of Kings: The Untold Story of the Ancient Maya.* 1990. A splendidly illustrated work providing expert treatment of the Maya world.

Kehoe, Alice Beck. *America Before the European Invasion.* 2002. An excellent survey of North America before the coming of the Europeans, by an eminent anthropologist.

Knight, A. *Mexico: From the Beginnings to the Spanish Conquest.* 2002. Provides information on many Mesoamerican societies.

León-Portilla, M. *The Aztec Image of Self and Society: An Introduction to Nahua Culture.* 1992. The best appreciation of Aztec religious ritual and symbolism.

Mann, Charles C. *1491: New Revelations of the Americas Before Columbus.* 2005. A thoroughly researched overview of all the newest scholarship, written for a general audience.

Milner, G. *The Moundbuilders: Ancient Peoples of Eastern North America.* 2005. Beautifully illustrated book that discusses the mounds and the societies that built them; could also be used as a tourist guide.

Wright, R. *Time Among the Mayas.* 1989. A highly readable account of Maya agricultural and religious calendars.

Notes

1. Fray Diego Durán, *Mexicas: The History of the Indies of New Spain,* translated, with notes, by Doris Heyden and Fernand Horcasitas (New York: Orion Press, 1964), p. 203.

2. Quoted in J. Soustelle, *Daily Life of the Aztecs on the Eve of the Spanish Conquest,* trans. P. O'Brian (Stanford, Calif.: Stanford University Press, 1970), p. 89.

3. B. Díaz, *The Conquest of New Spain,* trans. J. M. Cohen (New York: Penguin Books, 1978), p. 214.

4. Quoted in J. H. Perry, *The Discovery of South America* (New York: Taplinger, 1979), pp. 161–163.

5. Quoted in I. Clendinnen, *Aztecs: An Interpretation* (New York: Cambridge University Press, 1992), pp. 16–17.

Listening to the PAST

The Death of Inca Yupanque (Pachacuti Inca) in 1471

In 1551 the Spaniard Juan de Betanzos began to write Narrative of the Incas. *Although Betanzos had only the Spanish equivalent of a grade school education when he arrived in Peru, and although he lacked dictionaries and grammar books, he had two powerful assets. First, he learned Quechua and earned a reputation for being the best interpreter and translator in postconquest Peru. Second, Betanzos had married Angelina Yupanque, an Inca noblewoman (her Inca name was Cuxirimay Ocllo) who was the widow of Atahualpa. Through her, Betanzos gained immediate and firsthand access to the Inca oral tradition. When he finished his book six years later, modern scholars believe he had produced "the most authentic chronicle that we have."*

Narrative of the Incas *provides a gold mine of information about Inca customs and social history. There is so much description of marriage, childbirth, and raising children—activities that were seen as the realm of women in both Inca and Spanish society—that scholars suspect Angelina Yupanque provided her husband with much of his information. Here is his account of the death of Inca Yupanque (Pachacuti Inca) in 1471.*

Since there were instructions for the idolatries and activities that you have heard about, Inca Yupanque ordered that immediately after he died these activities and sacrifices should be done. In addition, as soon as this was done, word should be sent to all the land, and from all the provinces and towns they should bring again all that was necessary for the service of the new lord, including gold, silver, livestock, clothing, and the rest of the things needed to replenish all the storehouses that, because of his death, had been emptied for the sacrifices and things he ordered to be done, and it should be so abundant because he realized that the state of the one who was thus Inca was growing greater.

While Inca Yupanque was talking and ordering what was to be done after he died, he raised his voice in a song that is still sung today in his memory by those of his generation. This song went as follows: "Since I bloomed like the flower of the garden, up to now I

have given order and justice in this life and world as long as my strength lasted. Now I have turned into earth." Saying these words of his song, Inca Yupanque Pachacuti expired, leaving in all the land justice and order, as already stated. And his people were well supplied with idols, idolatries, and activities. After he was dead, he was taken to a town named Patallacta, where he had ordered some houses built in which his body was to be entombed. He was buried by putting his body in the earth in a large new clay urn, with him very well dressed. Inca Yupanque ordered that a golden image made to resemble him be placed on top of his tomb. And it was to be worshiped in place of him by the people who went there. Soon it was placed there. He ordered that a statue be made of his fingernails and hair that had been cut in his lifetime. It was made in that town where his body was kept. They very ceremoniously brought this statue on a litter to the city of Cuzco for the fiestas in the city. This statue was placed in the houses of Topa Inca Yupanque. When there were fiestas in the city, they brought it out for them with the rest of the statues. What is more laughable about this lord Inca Yupanque is that, when he wanted to make some idol, he entered the house of the Sun [the temple to the sun in Cuzco] and acted as though the Sun spoke to him, and he himself answered the Sun to make his people believe that the Sun ordered him to make those idols and *guacas** and so that they would worship them as such.

When the statue was in the city, Topa Inca Yupanque ordered those of his own lineage to bring this statue out for the feasts that were held in Cuzco. When they brought it out like this, they sang about the things that the Inca did in his life, both in the wars and in his city. Thus they served and revered him, changing its garments as he used to do, and serving it as he was served when he was alive. All of which was done thus.

This statue, along with the gold image that was on top of his tomb, was taken by Manco Inca from

*Any object, place, or person worshiped as a deity.

EL NOVENO INGA
PACHACVTI INGA
IVPANQVI

Reynohas — ta chile y se to — dasucor selleta
pachaqui

Revered as a great conqueror and lawgiver, Pachacuti Inca here wears the sacred fringed headband symbolizing his royal authority and the large earrings of the *oregones*, the nobility. *(Pachacuti Inca, from* Nueva Coronica & Buen Gobierno, *by Guaman Poma de Ayala. Courtesy, Musée du Quai Branly/ Scala Picture Library)*

the city when he revolted. On the advice that Doña Angelina Yupanque gave to the Marquis Don Francisco Pizarro, he got it and the rest of the wealth with it. Only the body is in Patallacta at this time, and judging by it, in his lifetime he seems to have been a tall man. They say that he died at the age of one hundred twenty years. After his father's death, Topa Inca Yupanque ordered that none of the descendants of his father, Inca Yupanque, were to settle the area beyond the rivers of Cuzco. From that time until today the descendants of Inca Yupanque were called *Capacaillo Ynga Yupanque haguaynin,* which means "lineage of kings," "descendants and grandchildren of Inca Yupanque." These are the most highly regarded of all the lineages of Cuzco. These are the ones who were ordered to wear two feathers on their heads.

As time passed, this generation of *orejones* [*oregones*]† multiplied. There were and are today many who became heads of families and renowned as firstborn. Because they married women who were not of their lineage, they took a variety of family names. Seeing this, those of Inca Yupanque ordered that those who had mixed with other people's blood should take

†Nobles.

new family names and extra names so that [only] those of his lineage could clearly be called *Capacaillo* and descendants of Inca Yupanque.

Questions for Analysis

1. Juan de Betanzos clearly shows his disapproval of the cult of the royal mummies through his choice of words, but he also includes details that help explain its power. Judging by his description, why did people honor deceased rulers? Why did rulers (or at least Inca Yupanque) think they deserved such honors?

2. In the last paragraph, Inca Yupanque's descendants seek to limit their special title of *Capacaillo.* Why might they have done this? What effect might this have on marriage patterns among the descendants of an Inca king?

Source: Narrative of the Incas by Juan de Betanzos, trans. and ed. Roland Hamilton and Dana Buchanan from the Palma de Mallorca manuscript (Austin: University of Texas Press, 1996), pp. 138–139. Copyright © 1996. Used by permission of the University of Texas Press.

Mongol Army Attacking a Walled City, from a
Persian manuscript. Note the use of catapults on both
sides. *(Bildarchiv Preussischer Kulturbesitz/Art Resource, NY)*

11 CENTRAL AND SOUTHERN ASIA, TO 1400

Chapter Preview

Central Asian Nomads
• *What gave the nomadic pastoralists of Central Asia military advantages over nearby settled civilizations?*

Chinggis Khan and the Mongol Empire
• *How was the world changed by the Mongol conquests of much of Eurasia?*

East-West Communication During the Mongol Era
• *How did the Mongol conquests facilitate the spread of ideas, religions, inventions, and diseases?*

India, 300–1400
• *How did India respond to its encounters with Turks, Mongols, and Islam?*

Southeast Asia, to 1400
• *How did states develop along the maritime trade routes of Southeast Asia?*

The large chunks of Asia treated in this chapter underwent profound changes during the centuries examined here. The Central Asian grasslands gave birth to nomadic confederations capable of dominating major states—first the Turks, then later, even more spectacularly, the Mongols. In the Indian subcontinent regional cultures flourished and the area had its first encounter with Islam. Southeast Asia developed several distinct cultures, most of them adopting Buddhism and other ideas and techniques from India.

Ancient India is covered in Chapter 2. This is the first chapter to treat Southeast Asia and to look at Central Asia on its own terms rather than as a problem for nearby agricultural societies.

CENTRAL ASIAN NOMADS

What gave the nomadic pastoralists of Central Asia military advantages over nearby settled civilizations?

One experience Rome, Persia, India, and China all shared was conflict with **nomads** who came from the very broad region referred to as Central Asia. This broad region was dominated by the arid **grasslands** (also called the **steppe**) that stretched from Hungary, through southern Russia and across Central Asia (today's Tajikistan, Turkmenistan, Kazakhstan, Kyrgyzstan, and Uzbekistan) and adjacent parts of China, to Mongolia and parts of north China. Easily crossed by horses but too dry for crop agriculture, the grasslands could support only a thin population of nomadic herders who lived off their flocks of sheep, goats, camels, horses, or other animals. At least twice a year they would break camp and move their animals to new pastures, in the spring moving north, in the fall south.

In their search for water and good pastures, nomadic groups often came into conflict with other nomadic groups pursuing the same resources,

nomads *Groups of people who move from place to place in search of food, water, and pasture for their animals, usually following the seasons.*

grasslands *Also called the steppe, these lands are too dry for crops but support pasturing animals.*

steppe *Another name for the grasslands that are common across much of the center of Eurasia.*

which the two would then fight over, as there was normally no higher political authority able to settle disputes. Groups on the losing end, especially if they were small, faced the threat of extermination or slavery, which prompted them to make alliances with other groups or move far away. Thus, over the centuries, the ethnic groups living in particular sections of the grasslands would change. Groups on the winning end of intertribal conflicts could exact tribute from those they defeated, sometimes so much that they could devote themselves entirely to war, leaving to their slaves and vassals the work of tending herds.

To get the products of nearby agricultural societies, especially grain, woven textiles, iron, tea, and wood, nomadic herders would trade their own products, such as horses and furs. When trade was difficult, they would turn to raiding to seize what they needed. Much of the time nomadic herders raided other nomads, but nearby agricultural settlements were common targets as well. The nomads' skill as horsemen and archers made it difficult for farmers and townsmen to defend against them. It was largely to defend against the raids of the Xiongnu nomads, for example, that the Chinese built the Great Wall (see page 134).

Political organization among nomadic herders was generally very simple. Clans had chiefs, as did tribes (which were coalitions of clans, often related to each other). Leadership within a group was based on military prowess and was often settled by fighting. Occasionally a charismatic leader would emerge who was able to extend alliances to form confederations of tribes. From the point of view of the settled societies, which have left most of the records about these nomadic groups, large confederations were much more of a threat, since they could plan coordinated attacks on cities and towns. Large confederations rarely lasted more than a century or so, however, and when they broke up, tribes again spent much of their time fighting with each other, relieving some of the pressure on their settled neighbors.

The three most wide-ranging and successful confederations were those of the Xiongnu/Huns, who emerged in the third century B.C.E. in the area near China; the Turks, who had their origins in the same area in the fourth and fifth centuries C.E.; and the Mongols, who did not become important until the late twelfth century. In all three cases, the entire steppe region was eventually swept up in the movement of peoples and armies.

The Turks

The Turks are the first of the Inner Asian peoples to have left a written record in their own language; the earliest Turkish documents date from the eighth century. Turkic languages may have already been spoken in dispersed areas of the Eurasian steppe when the Turks first appeared; today these languages are spoken by the Uighurs in western China, the Uzbeks, Kazakhs, Kyrghiz, and Turkmens of Central Asia, and the Turks of modern Turkey. The original religion of the Turks was shamanistic and involved worship of Heaven, making it similar to the religions of many other groups in the steppe region.

In 552 a group called Turks who specialized in metalworking rebelled against their overlords, the Rouruan, whose empire then dominated the region from the eastern Silk Road cities of Central Asia through Mongolia. The Turks quickly supplanted the Rouruan as overlords. When the first Turkish khagan (ruler) died a few years later, the Turkish Empire was divided between his younger brother, who took the western part (modern Central Asia), and his son, who took the eastern part (modern Mongolia). Sogdians working for the Western Turks convinced them to send embassies to both the Persian and the Byzantine courts. Repeat embassies in both directions did not prevent hostilities, however, and in 576 the Western Turks captured the Byzantine city of Bosporus in the Crimea.

The Eastern Turks frequently raided into China and just as often fought among themselves. The Chinese history of the Sui Dynasty records that "The Turks prefer to destroy each other rather than to live side-by-side. They have a thousand, nay ten thousand clans who are hostile to and kill one another. They mourn their dead with much grief and swear vengeance."[1] In the early seventh century the empire of the Eastern Turks ran up against the growing military might of the Tang Dynasty in China and soon broke apart. In the eighth century a Turkic people called the Uighurs formed a new empire based in Mongolia that survived about a century. It had close ties to Tang China, providing military aid but also extracting large payments in silk. During this period many Uighurs adopted religions then current along the Silk Road, notably Buddhism, Nestorian Christianity, and Manichaeism. In the ninth century this Uighur empire was destroyed by another Turkic people from north of Mongolia called the Kyrgyz. Some fled to what is now western China (Kansu and Xinjiang provinces). Setting up their capital city in Kucha, these Uighurs created a remarkably stable and prosperous kingdom that lasted four centuries (ca. 850–1250). Because of the dry climate of the region, many buildings, wall paintings, and manuscripts written in a variety of languages have been preserved from this era. They reveal a complex, urban civilization in which Buddhism, Manichaeism, and Christianity existed side by side, practiced by Turks as well as by Tokharians, Sogdians, and other Iranian peoples.

Farther west in Central Asia other groups of Turks, such as the Karakhanids, Ghaznavids, and Seljuks, rose to prominence. Often local Muslim forces would try to capture them, convert them, and employ them as slave soldiers (see pages 206–207). By the mid- to late tenth century many were serving in the Abbasid armies. It was also in the tenth century that Central Asian Turks began converting to Islam (which protected them from being abducted as slaves). Then they took to raiding unconverted Turks.

In the mid-eleventh century the Turks had gained the upper hand in the caliphate, and the caliphs became little more than figureheads. From there Turkish power was extended into Syria, Palestine, and other parts of the realm. (Asia Minor is now called Turkey because Turks migrated there by the thousands over several centuries.) In 1071 Seljuk Turks inflicted a devastating defeat on the Byzantine army in eastern Anatolia and even took the Byzantine emperor captive. Other Turkish confederations established themselves in Afghanistan and extended their control into north India (see page 312).

In India, Persia, and Anatolia, the formidable military skills of nomadic Turkish warriors made it possible for them to become overlords of settled societies. By the end of the thirteenth century nomad power prevailed through much of Eurasia. Just as the Uighurs developed a hybrid urban culture along the eastern end of the Silk Road, adopting many elements from the mercantile Sogdians, the Turks of Central and Western Asia created an Islamic culture that drew from both Turkish and Iranian sources. Often Persian was used as the administrative language of the states they formed. Nevertheless, despite the presence of Turkish overlords all along the southern fringe of the steppe, no one group of Turks was able to unite them all into a single

Chronology

ca. 320–480 Gupta Empire in India

ca. 380–450 Life of India's greatest poet, Kalidasa

ca. 450 White Huns invade India

ca. 500–1400 India's medieval age; caste system reaches its mature form

552 Turks rebel against Rouruan and rise to power

ca. 780 Borobudur temple complex begun in Srivijaya (modern Java)

802–1432 Khmer Empire of Cambodia

ca. 850–1250 Kingdom of the Uighurs

870–1030 Turks raid north India

939 Vietnamese gain independence from China

12th century Buddhism declines in India

1206 Chinggis proclaimed Great Khan; Mongol language recorded

ca. 1240 *The Secret History of the Mongols*

1276 Mongol conquest of China

ca. 1300 Plague spreads throughout Mongol Empire

1405 Death of Tamerlane

political unit. That feat had to wait for the next major power on the grasslands, the Mongols.

The Mongols

In Mongolia in the twelfth century ambitious Mongols did not aspire to match the Turks or other groups that had migrated west, but rather the groups that had stayed in the east and mastered ways to extract resources from China, the largest and richest country in the region. In the tenth and eleventh centuries the Khitans had accomplished this; in the twelfth century the Jurchens had overthrown the Khitans and extended their reach even deeper into China. The Khitans and Jurchens formed hybrid nomadic-urban states, with northern sections where tribesmen continued to live in the traditional way and southern sections politically controlled by the non-Chinese rulers but settled largely by tax-paying Chinese. The Khitans and Jurchens had scripts created to record their languages and adopted many Chinese governing practices. They built cities in pastoral areas as centers of consumption and trade. In both cases, their elite became culturally dual, adept in Chinese ways as well as in their own traditions.

The Mongols lived north of these hybrid nomadic-settled societies and maintained their traditional ways. Chinese, Persian, and European observers have all left descriptions of the daily life of the Mongols, which they found strikingly different from their own. The daily life of the peasants of China, India, Vietnam, and Japan had much more in common with each other than with the Mongol pastoralists. Before considering the military conquests of the Mongols, it is useful to look more closely at their way of life.

Daily Life

Before their great conquests the Mongols did not have cities, towns, or villages. Rather, they moved with their animals between winter and summer pastures. They had to keep their belongings to a minimum because they had to be able to pack up and move everything they owned when it was time to move.

yurts *Tents in which the pastoral nomads lived; they could be quickly dismantled and loaded onto animals or carts.*

To make their settlements portable, the Mongols lived in tents called **yurts** rather than in houses. The yurts, about twelve to fifteen feet in diameter, were constructed of light wooden frames covered by layers of wool felt, greased to make them waterproof. The yurts were always round, since this shape held up better against the strong winds that blew across the treeless grasslands. They could be dismantled and loaded onto pack animals or carts in a short time. The floor of the yurt would be covered with dried grass or straw, then felt, skins, or rugs. In the center would be the hearth, directly under the smoke hole. Usually the yurt was set up with the entrance facing south. The master's bed would be on the north. Goat horns would be attached to the frame of the yurt and used as hooks to hang joints of meat, cooking utensils, bows, quivers of arrows, and the like. A group of families traveling together would set up their yurts in a circle open to the south and draw up their wagons in a circle around the yurts for protection.

For food the Mongols ate mostly animal products. Without granaries to store food for years of famine, the Mongols' survival was endangered whenever weather or diseases of their animals threatened their food supply. The most common meat was mutton, supplemented with wild game. When grain or vegetables could be obtained through trade, they were added to the diet. Wood was scarce, so the common fuel for the cook fires was dried animal dung or grasses.

The Mongols milked sheep, goats, cows, and horses and made cheese and fermented alcoholic drinks from the milk. A European visitor to Mongolia in the 1250s described how they milked mares, a practice unfamiliar to Europeans:

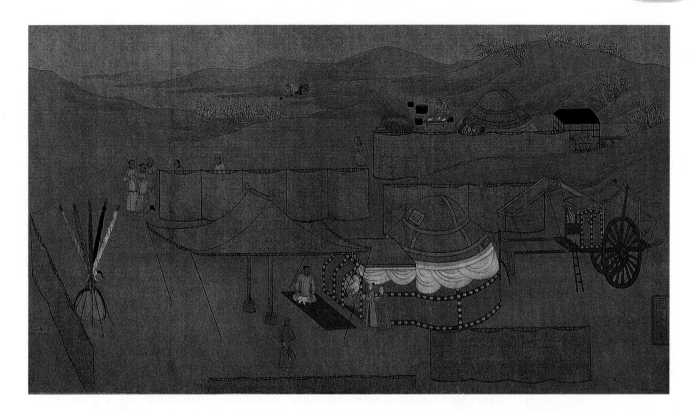

They fasten a long line to two posts standing firmly in the ground, and to the line they tie the young colts of the mares which they mean to milk. Then come the mothers who stand by their foals, and allow themselves to be milked. And if any of them be too unruly, then one takes her colt and puts it under her, letting it suck a while, and presently taking it away again, and the milker takes its place.[2]

He also described how they made the alcoholic drink kumiss from the milk, a drink that "goes down very pleasantly, intoxicating weak brains."[3]

Because of the intense cold of the grasslands in the winter, the Mongols made much use of furs and skins for clothing. Both men and women usually wore silk trousers and tunics (the silk obtained from China). Over these they wore robes of fur, for the very coldest times in two layers—an inner layer with the hair on the inside and an outer layer with the hair on the outside. Hats were of felt or fur, boots of felt or leather. Men wore leather belts to which their bows and quivers could be attached. Women of high rank wore elaborate headdresses decorated with feathers.

Mongol women had to work very hard and had to be able to care for the animals when the men were away hunting or fighting. They normally drove the carts and set up and dismantled the yurts. They were also the ones who milked the sheep, goats, and cows and made the butter and cheese. In addition, they made the felt, prepared the skins, and sewed the clothes. Because water was scarce, clothes were not washed with water, nor were dishes. Women, like men, had to be expert riders, and many also learned to shoot. Women participated actively in family decisions, especially as wives and mothers. In *The Secret History of the Mongols,* a work written in Mongolian in the mid-thirteenth century, Chinggis Khan's mother and wife frequently make impassioned speeches on the importance of family loyalty. (See the feature "Listening to the Past: The Abduction of Women in *The Secret History of the Mongols*" on pages 324–325.)

Mongol men kept as busy as the women. They made carts and wagons and the frames for the yurts. They also made harnesses for the horses and oxen, leather saddles, and the equipment needed for hunting and war, such as bows and arrows. Men

● **Mongol Yurt** A Chinese artist captured the essential features of a Mongol yurt to illustrate the story of a Chinese woman who married a nomad. *(The Metropolitan Museum of Art, Ex coll.: C. C. Wang Family, Gift of The Dillon Fund, 1973 [1973.120.3]. Photograph © 1994 The Metropolitan Museum of Art)*

also had charge of the horses, and they milked the mares. Young horses were allowed to run wild until it was time to break them in. Catching them took great skill in the use of a long springy pole with a noose at the end. One specialist among the nomads was the blacksmith, who made stirrups, knives, and other metal tools.

Kinship underlay most social relationships among the Mongols. Normally each family occupied a yurt, and groups of families camping together were usually related along the male line (brothers, uncles, nephews, and so on). More distant patrilineal relatives were recognized as members of the same clan and could call on each other for aid. People from the same clan could not marry each other, so men had to get wives from other clans. When a woman's husband died, she would be inherited by another male in the family, such as her husband's brother or his son by another woman. Tribes were groups of clans, often distantly related. Both clans and tribes had recognized chiefs who would make decisions on where to graze and when to retaliate against another tribe that had stolen animals or people. Women were sometimes abducted for brides. When tribes stole men from each other, they normally made them into slaves, and slaves were forced to do much of the heavy work. They would not necessarily remain slaves their entire lives, however, as their original tribes might be able to recapture them or make exchanges for them, or their masters might free them.

Even though population was sparse in the regions where the Mongols lived, conflict over resources was endemic, and each camp had to be on the alert for attacks. Defending against attacks and retaliating against raids was as much a part of the Mongols' daily life as caring for their herds and trading with nearby settlements.

Mongol children learned to ride at a young age, first riding on goats. The horses they later rode were short and stocky, almost like ponies, but nimble and able to endure long journeys and bitter cold. Even in the winter they survived by grazing, foraging beneath the snow. The prime weapon boys had to learn to use was the compound bow, which had a pull of about 160 pounds and a range of more than 200 yards. Other commonly used weapons were small battle-axes and lances fitted with hooks to pull enemies off their saddles.

From their teenage years Mongol men participated in battles, and among the Mongols courage in battle was essential to male self-esteem. Hunting was a common form of military training. Each year there would be one big hunt when mounted hunters would form a vast ring perhaps ten or more miles in circumference, then gradually shrink it down, trapping all the animals before killing them. On military campaigns a Mongol soldier had to be able to ride for days without stopping to cook food; he had to carry a supply of dried milk curd and cured meat, which could be supplemented by blood let from the neck of his horse. When time permitted, the soldiers would pause to hunt, adding to their food dogs, wolves, foxes, mice, and rats.

A common specialist among the Mongols was the shaman, a religious expert able to communicate with the gods. The high god of the Mongols was Heaven, but they recognized many other gods as well. Some groups of Mongols, especially those closer to settled communities, converted to Buddhism, Nestorian Christianity, or Manichaeism.

CHINGGIS KHAN AND THE MONGOL EMPIRE

How was the world changed by the Mongol conquests of much of Eurasia?

In the mid-twelfth century the Mongols were just one of many peoples in the eastern grasslands, neither particularly numerous nor especially advanced. Why did the Mongols suddenly emerge on the historical stage? One explanation is ecological. A drop in the mean annual temperature created a subsistence crisis. As pastures shrank, the Mongols and other nomads had to get more of their food from the agricultural world.

But the Mongols ended up getting much more than enough to eat. A second reason for their sudden rise is the appearance of a single individual, the brilliant but utterly ruthless Temujin (ca. 1162–1227), later called Chinggis.

Chinggis's early career was recorded in *The Secret History of the Mongols*, written within a few decades of his death. In Chinggis's youth his father had built up a modest following. When Chinggis's father was poisoned by a rival, his followers, not ready to follow a boy of twelve, drifted away, leaving Chinggis and his mother and brothers in a vulnerable position. In 1182 Chinggis was captured and carried in a cage to a rival's camp. After a daring midnight escape, he led his followers to join a stronger chieftain whom his father had once aided. With the chieftain's help, Chinggis began avenging the insults he had received.

As Chinggis subdued the Tartars, Kereyids, Naimans, Merkids, and other Mongol and Turkish tribes, he built up an army of loyal followers. He mastered the art of winning allies through displays of personal courage in battle and generosity to his followers. He also was willing to turn against former allies who proved troublesome. To those who opposed him, he could be merciless. He once asserted that nothing gave more pleasure than massacring one's enemies, seizing their horses and cattle, and ravishing their women. Sometimes Chinggis would kill all the men in a defeated tribe to prevent any later vendettas. At other times he would take them on as soldiers in his own armies. Courage impressed him. One of his leading generals, Jebe, first attracted his attention when he held his ground against overwhelming opposition and shot Chinggis's horse out from under him. Another prominent general, Mukhali, became Chinggis's personal slave at age twenty-seven after his tribe was defeated by Chinggis in 1197. Within a few years he was leading a corps of a thousand men from his own former tribe.

In 1206, at a great gathering of tribal leaders, Chinggis was proclaimed the **Great Khan**. He decreed that Mongol, until then an unwritten language, be written down in the script used by the Uighur Turks. With this script a record was made of the Mongol laws and customs, ranging from the rules for the annual hunt to punishments of death for robbery and adultery. Another measure adopted at this assembly was a postal relay system to send messages rapidly by mounted courier.

Great Khan *The title given to the Mongol ruler Chinggis in 1206 and later to his successors.*

With the tribes of Mongolia united, the energies previously devoted to infighting and vendettas were redirected to exacting tribute from the settled populations nearby, starting with the Jurchen (Jin) state that extended into north China (see Map 12.2 on page 334). In this Chinggis was following the precedent of the Jurchens, who had defeated the Khitans to get access to China's wealth a century earlier.

After Chinggis subjugated a city, he would send envoys to cities farther out to demand submission and threaten destruction. Those who opened their city gates and submitted without fighting could become allies and retain local power, but those who resisted faced the prospect of mass slaughter. He despised city dwellers and would sometimes use them as living shields in the next battle. After the Mongol armies swept across north China in 1212–1213, ninety-odd cities lay in rubble. Beijing, captured in 1215, burned for more than a month. Not surprisingly many governors of cities and rulers of small states hastened to offer submission.

Chinggis preferred conquest to administration and did not stay in north China to set up an administrative structure. He left that to subordinates and turned his attention westward, to Central Asia and Persia, then dominated by different groups of Turks. In 1218 Chinggis proposed to the Khwarizm shah of Persia that he accept Mongol overlordship and establish trade relations. The shah, to show his determination to resist, ordered the envoy and the merchants who had accompanied him killed. The next year Chinggis led an army of one hundred thousand soldiers west to retaliate. Mongol forces destroyed the shah's army and sacked one Persian city after another, demolishing buildings and massacring hundreds of thousands of people.

After returning from Central Asia, Chinggis died in 1227 during the siege of a city in northwest China. Before he died, he instructed his sons not to fall out among themselves but instead to divide the spoils.

Chinggis's Successors

khanates *The states ruled by a khan; the four units into which Chinggis divided the Mongol Empire.*

Although Mongol tribal leaders traditionally had had to win their positions, after Chinggis died the empire was divided into four **khanates,** with one of the lines of his descendants taking charge of each one. Chinggis's third son, Ögödei, became Great Khan, and he directed the next round of invasions.

In 1237 representatives of all four lines led 150,000 Mongol, Turkish, and Persian troops into Europe. During the next five years they gained control of Moscow and Kievan Russia and looted cities in Poland and Hungary. They were poised to attack deeper into Europe when they learned of the death of Ögödei in 1241. To participate in the election of a new khan, the army returned to the Mongols' new capital city, Karakorum.

Once Ögödei's son was certified as his successor, the Mongols turned their attention to Persia and the Middle East. In 1256 a Mongol army took northwest Iran, then pushed on to the Abbasid capital of Baghdad. When it fell in 1258, the last Abbasid caliph was murdered, and the population was put to the sword. The Mongol onslaught was successfully resisted, however, by both the Delhi sultanate (see page 312) and the Mamluk rulers in Egypt (see page 203).

Under Chinggis's grandson Khubilai (r. 1260–1294) the Mongols completed their conquest of China. South China had never been captured by non-Chinese, in large part because horses were of no strategic advantage in a land of rivers and canals. Perhaps because they were entering a very different type of terrain, the Mongols proceeded deliberately. First they surrounded the Song empire by taking its westernmost province in 1252, destroying the Nanzhao kingdom in modern Yunnan in 1254, and then continuing south and taking Annam (northern Vietnam) in 1257. A surrendered Song commander advised them to build a navy to attack the great Song cities located on rivers. During the five-year siege of a central Chinese river port, both sides used thousands of boats and tens of thousands of troops. The Mongols employed experts in naval and siege warfare from all over their empire—Chinese, Korean, Jurchen, Uighur, and Persian. Catapults designed by Muslim engineers launched a barrage of rocks weighing up to a hundred pounds each. During their advance toward the Chinese capital of Hangzhou, the Mongols ordered the total slaughter of the people of the major city of Changzhou, and in 1276 the Chinese empress dowager surrendered in hopes of sparing the people of the capital a similar fate.

Having overrun China and Korea, Khubilai turned his eyes toward Japan. In 1274 a force of 30,000 soldiers and support personnel sailed from Korea to Japan. In 1281 a combined Mongol and Chinese fleet of about 150,000 made a second attempt to conquer Japan. On both occasions the Mongols managed to land but were beaten back by Japanese samurai armies. Each time fierce storms destroyed the Mongol fleets. The Japanese claimed that they had been saved by the *kamikaze,* the "divine wind" (which later lent its name to the thousands of Japanese aviators who crashed their airplanes into American warships during World War II). A decade later, in 1293, Khubilai tried sending a fleet to the islands of Southeast Asia, including Java, but it met with no more success than the fleets sent to Japan.

Why were the Mongols so successful against so many different types of enemies? Even though their population was tiny compared to the populations of the large agricultural societies they conquered, their tactics, their weapons, and their organization all gave them advantages. Like other nomads before them, they were superb horsemen and excellent archers. Their horses were extremely nimble, able to change direction quickly, thus allowing the Mongols to maneuver easily and ride through infantry forces armed with swords, lances, and javelins. Usually the only armies that could stand up well against the Mongols were other nomadic ones like the Turks.

Marco Polo left a vivid description of the Mongol soldiers' endurance and military skill:

Mongol Conquests

1206	Chinggis made Great Khan
1215	Fall of Beijing (Jurchens)
1219–1220	Fall of Bukhara and Samarkand in Central Asia
1227	Death of Chinggis
1237–1241	Raids into eastern Europe
1257	Conquest of Annam (northern Vietnam)
1258	Conquest of Abbasid capital of Baghdad Conquest of Korea
1260	Accession of Khubilai
1274	First attempt at invading Japan
1276	Surrender of Song Dynasty (China)
1281	Second attempt at invading Japan
1293	Expedition to Java
mid-14th century	Decline of Mongol power; ouster or absorption

They are brave in battle, almost to desperation, setting little value upon their lives, and exposing themselves without hesitation to all manner of danger. Their disposition is cruel. They are capable of supporting every kind of privation, and when there is a necessity for it, can live for a month on the milk of their mares, and upon such wild animals as they may chance to catch. The men are habituated to remain on horseback during two days and two nights, without dismounting, sleeping in that situation whilst their horses graze. No people on earth can surpass them in fortitude under difficulties, nor show greater patience under wants of every kind.[4]

The Mongols were also open to new military technologies and did not insist on fighting in their traditional ways. To attack walled cities, they learned how to use catapults and other engines of war. At first they employed Chinese catapults, but when they later learned that those used by the Turks in Afghanistan were half again as powerful, they quickly adopted the better model. The Mongols also used exploding arrows and gunpowder projectiles developed by the Chinese.

Because of his early experiences with intertribal feuding, Chinggis mistrusted traditional Mongol tribal loyalties, and as he fashioned a new army, he gave it a new, nontribal structure. Chinggis also created an elite bodyguard of ten thousand sons and brothers of commanders, which served directly under him. Chinggis allowed commanders to pass their posts to their sons, but he could remove them at will. Marco Polo explained the decimal hierarchy of his armies this way:

When one of the great Tartar chiefs proceeds on an expedition, he puts himself at the head of an army of a hundred thousand horses, and organizes them in the following manner. He appoints an officer to the command of every ten men, and others to command a hundred, a thousand, and ten thousand men, respectively. Thus ten of the officers commanding ten men take their orders from him who commands a hundred; of these, each ten, from him who

> **Primary Source:**
> **Description of the World**
> *Follow Marco Polo, and hear him relate the natural—and sometimes supernatural—wonders he encountered on his journey to Khubilai Khan.*

commands a thousand; and each ten of these latter, from him who commands ten thousand. By this arrangement each officer has only to attend to the management of ten men or ten bodies of men.[5]

The Mongols also made good use of intelligence and tried to exploit internal divisions in the countries they attacked. Thus, in north China they appealed to the Khitans, who had been defeated by the Jurchens a century earlier, to join them in attacking the Jurchens. In Syria they exploited the resentment of Christians against their Muslim rulers.

The Mongols as Rulers

The success of the Mongols in ruling vast territories was due in large part to their willingness to incorporate other ethnic groups into their armies and governments. Whatever their original country or religion, those who served the Mongols loyally were rewarded and given important posts. Uighurs, Tibetans, Persians, Chinese, and Russians came to hold powerful positions in the Mongol government. Chinese helped breach the walls of Baghdad in the 1250s, and Muslims operated the catapults that helped reduce Chinese cities in the 1270s. Mongol armies incorporated the armies they vanquished and in time had large numbers of Turkish troops.

Since, in Mongol eyes, the purpose of fighting was to gain riches, they regularly would loot the settlements they conquered, taking whatever they wanted, including the residents. Land would be granted to military commanders, nobles, and army units, to be governed and exploited as the recipients wished. Those who had worked on the land would be given to them as serfs. The Mongols built a capital city called Karakorum in modern Mongolia, and to bring it up to the level of the cities they

● **Gold-Decorated Saddle** The Mongols, like earlier nomads, prized fine metalwork. The gold panels that decorate this saddle were found in the tomb of a Mongol girl of about eighteen. The central motif of the front arch is a reclining deer; surrounding it are peonies. *(Collection of Inner Mongolia Autonomous Region Museum, Hohhot City, China)*

conquered, they transported skilled workers from those cities. For instance, after Bukhara and Samarkand were captured in 1219–1220, some thirty thousand artisans were seized and transported to Mongolia (see Map 11.1). Sometimes these slaves gradually improved their status. A French goldsmith working in Budapest named Guillaume Boucher was captured by the Mongols in 1242 and taken to Karakorum, where he lived for at least the next fifteen years. He gradually won favor and was put in charge of fifty workers to make gold and silver vessels for the Mongol court.

The traditional nomad disdain for farmers led some commanders to suggest turning north China into a gigantic pasture after it was conquered. In time, though, the Mongols came to realize that simply appropriating the wealth and human resources of the settled lands was not as good as extracting regular revenue from them. A Sinified Khitan who had been working for the Jurchens in China explained to the Mongols that collecting taxes from farmers would be highly profitable: they could extract a revenue of 500,000 ounces of silver, 80,000 bolts of silk, and more than 20,000 tons of grain from the region by taxing it. The Mongols gave this a try, but soon political rivals convinced the khan that he would gain even more by letting Central Asian Muslim merchants bid against each other for licenses to collect taxes any way they could, a system called **tax-farming**. Ordinary Chinese found this method of tax collecting much more oppressive than traditional Chinese methods, since there was little to keep the tax collectors from seizing everything they could.

tax-farming *Assigning the collection of taxes to whoever bids the most for the privilege.*

By the second half of the thirteenth century there was no longer a genuine pan-Asian Mongol Empire. Much of Asia was in the hands of Mongol successor states, but these were generally hostile to each other. Khubilai was often at war with the khanate of Central Asia, then held by his cousin Khaidu, and he had little contact with the khanate of the Golden Horde in south Russia. The Mongols adapted their methods of government to the existing traditions of each place they ruled, and the regions now went their separate ways.

In China the Mongols resisted assimilation and purposely avoided many Chinese social and political practices. The rulers conducted their business in the Mongol language and spent their summers in Mongolia. Khubilai discouraged Mongols from marrying Chinese and took only Mongol women into the palace. Some Mongol princes preferred to live in yurts erected on the palace grounds rather than in the grand palaces constructed at Beijing. Chinese were treated as legally inferior not only to the Mongols but also to all other non-Chinese.

In Central Asia, Persia, and Russia the Mongols tended to merge with the Turkish groups already there and like them converted to Islam. Russia in the thirteenth century was not a strongly centralized state, and the Mongols were satisfied to see Russian princes and lords continue to rule their territories as long as they turned over adequate tribute (which, of course, added to the burden on peasants). The city of Moscow became the center of Mongol tribute collection and grew in importance at the expense of Kiev. In the Middle East the Mongol Il-khans were more active as rulers, again continuing the traditions of the caliphate. In Mongolia itself, however, Mongol traditions were maintained.

Mongol control in each of the khanates lasted about a century. In the mid-fourteenth century the Mongol dynasty in China deteriorated into civil war, and in the 1360s the Mongols withdrew back to Mongolia. There was a similar loss of Mongol power in Persia and Central Asia. Only on the south Russian steppe was the Golden Horde able to maintain its hold for another century. As Mongol rule in Central Asia declined, a new conqueror emerged, known as Tamerlane (Timur the Lame). Not a nomad but a highly civilized Turkish noble, Tamerlane in the 1360s struck out from his base in Samarkand into Persia, north India, southern Russia, and beyond. His armies used the terror tactics that the Mongols had perfected, massacring the citizens of cities that resisted. With his death in 1405, however, Tamerlane's empire fell apart.

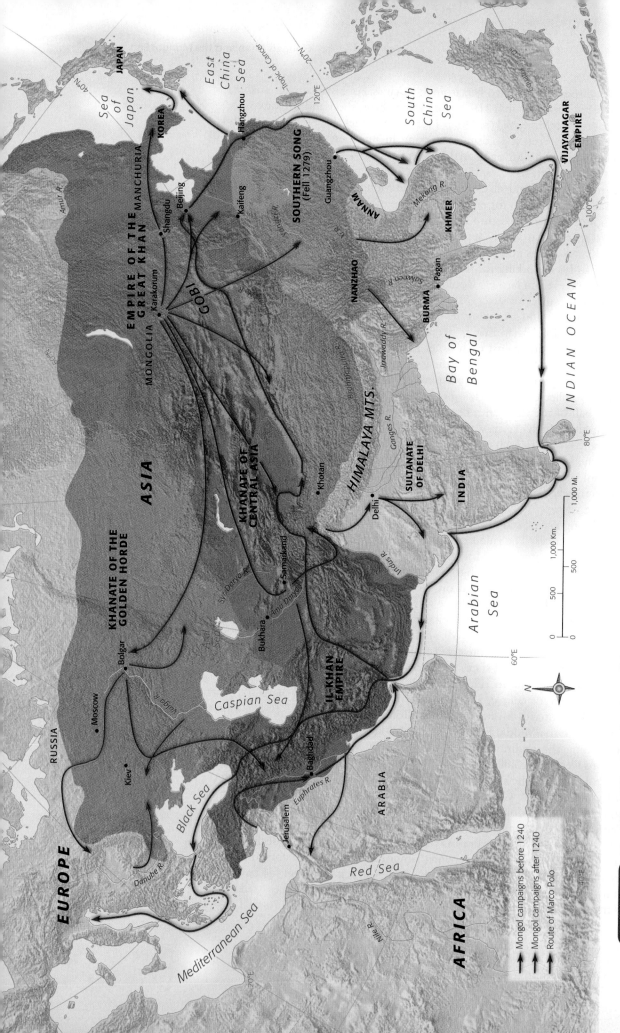

MAP 11.1 The Mongol Empire The creation of the vast Mongol Empire facilitated communication across Eurasia and led to both the spread of deadly plagues and the transfer of technical and scientific knowledge. After the death of Chinggis in 1227, the empire was divided into four khanates, ruled by different lines of his successors. In the 1270s the Mongols conquered southern China, but most of their subsequent campaigns did not lead to further territorial gains.

Mongol campaigns before 1240
Mongol campaigns after 1240
Route of Marco Polo

EAST-WEST COMMUNICATION DURING THE MONGOL ERA

How did the Mongol conquests facilitate the spread of ideas, religions, inventions, and diseases?

The Mongol governments did more than any earlier political entities to encourage the movement of people and goods across Eurasia. The Mongols had never looked down on merchants the way the elites of many traditional states did, and they welcomed the arrival of merchants from distant lands. Even when different groups of Mongols were fighting among themselves, they usually allowed caravans to pass unharassed.

The Mongol practice of transporting skilled people from the lands they conquered also brought people into contact with each other in new ways. Besides those forced to move, the Mongols recruited administrators from all over. Chinese, Persians, and Arabs served the Mongols, and the Mongols often sent them far from home. Especially prominent were the Uighur Turks of Chinese Central Asia, whose familiarity with Chinese civilization and fluency in Turkish were extremely valuable in facilitating communication. Literate Uighurs were many of the clerks and administrators running the Mongol administration.

One of the most interesting of those who served the Mongols was Rashid al-Din (ca. 1247–1318). A Jew from Persia and the son of an apothecary, Rashid al-Din converted to Islam at the age of thirty and entered the service of the Mongol Il-khan of Persia as a physician. He rose in government service, traveled widely, and eventually became prime minister. Rashid al-Din became friends with the ambassador from China, and together they arranged for translations of Chinese works on medicine, agronomy, and statecraft. He had ideas on economic management that he communicated to Mongol officials in Central Asia and China. Aware of the great differences between cultures, he believed that the Mongols should try to rule in accord with the moral principles of the majority in each land. On that basis he convinced the Mongol khan of Persia to convert to Islam. Rashid al-Din undertook to explain the great variety of cultures by writing a history of the world that was much more comprehensive than any previously written.

The Mongols were remarkably open to religious experts from all the lands they encountered. More Europeans made their way as far as Mongolia and China in the Mongol period than ever before. Popes and kings sent envoys to the Mongol court in the hope of enlisting the Mongols on their side in their long-standing conflict with Muslim forces over the Holy Land. These and other European visitors were especially interested in finding Christians who had been cut off from the West by the

● **Depictions of Europeans**   The Mongol Empire, by facilitating travel across Asia, increased knowledge of faraway lands. Rashid al-Din's *History of the World* included a history of the Franks, illustrated here with images of Western popes (*left*) conferring with Byzantine emperors (*right*). (*Topkapi Saray Museum, Ms. H.1654, fol. 303a*)

spread of Islam, and in fact there were considerable numbers of Nestorian Christians in Central Asia. In 1245 Pope Innocent IV wrote two letters to the "King and people of the Tartars" that were delivered to a Mongol general in Armenia. The next year another envoy, Giovanni di Pian de Carpine, reached the Volga River and the camp of Batu, the khan of the Golden Horde. Batu sent him on to the new Great Khan in Karakorum with two Mongol guides, riding so fast that they had to change horses five to seven times a day. Their full journey of more than three thousand miles took five and a half months. Carpine spent four months at the Great Khan's court but never succeeded in convincing the Great Khan to embrace Christianity or drop his demand that the pope appear in person to tender his submission. When Carpine returned, he wrote a report that urged preparation for a renewed Mongol attack on Europe. The Mongols had to be resisted "because of the harsh, indeed intolerable, and hitherto unheard-of slavery seen with our own eyes, to which they reduce all peoples who have submitted to them."[6]

A few years later, in 1253, Flemish friar William of Rubruck set out with the permission of King Louis IX of France as a missionary to convert the Mongols. He too made his way to Karakorum, where he found many Europeans. At Easter, Hungarians, Russians, Georgians, Armenians, and Alans all took communion in a Nestorian church. Rubruck also gathered some information about China while in Mongolia, such as the Chinese use of paper money and practice of writing with a brush.

The most famous European visitor to the Mongol lands was the Venetian Marco Polo. In his famous *Travels,* Marco Polo described all the places he visited or learned about during his seventeen years away from home. He reported being warmly received by Khubilai, who impressed him enormously. He was also awed by the wealth and splendor of Chinese cities and spread the notion of Asia as a land of riches. Even in Marco Polo's lifetime, some skeptics did not believe his tale, and today some scholars speculate that he may have learned about China from Persian merchants he met in the Middle East without actually going to China. But Marco Polo also has staunch

● **Horse and Groom** Zhao Mengfu (1254–1322), the artist of this painting and a member of the Song imperial family, took up service under the Mongol emperor Khubilai. The Mongol rulers, great horsemen themselves, would likely have appreciated this depiction of a horse buffeted by the wind. *(National Palace Museum, Taipei, Taiwan)*

defenders, even though they admit that he stretched the truth in more than one place to make himself look good. One leading Mongol scholar titled his review of the controversy "Marco Polo Went to China."[7] Regardless of the final verdict on Marco Polo's veracity, there is no doubt that the great popularity of his book contributed to European interest in finding new routes to Asia.

The more rapid transfer of people and goods across Central Asia spread more than ideas and inventions. It also spread diseases, the most deadly of which was the plague known in Europe as the Black Death. Scholars once thought that this plague was the bubonic plague, transmitted through rats and fleas, but some scholars now question that supposition. What is known is that it spread from Central Asia into West Asia, the Mediterranean, and western Europe. When the Mongols were assaulting the city of Kaffa in the Crimea in 1346, they themselves were infected by the plague and had to withdraw. They purposely spread the disease to their enemy by catapulting the bodies of victims into the city. Soon the disease was carried from port to port throughout the Mediterranean by ship. The confusion of the mid-fourteenth century that led to the loss of Mongol power in China, Iran, and Central Asia undoubtedly owes something to the effect of the spread of the plague and other diseases.

Traditionally, the historians of each of the countries conquered by the Mongols portrayed them as a scourge. Russian historians, for instance, saw this as a period of bondage that set Russia back and cut it off from western Europe. Today it is more common to celebrate the genius of the Mongol military machine and treat the spread of ideas and inventions as an obvious good, probably because we see global communication as a good in our own world. There is no reason to assume, however, that every person or every society benefited equally from the improved communications and the new political institutions of the Mongol era. Merchants involved in long-distance trade prospered, but those enslaved and transported hundreds or thousands of miles from home would have seen themselves not as the beneficiaries of opportunities to encounter cultures different from their own, but rather as the most pitiable of victims.

The places that were ruled by Mongol governments for a century or more—China, Central Asia, Persia, and Russia—do not seem to have advanced at a more rapid rate during that century than they did in earlier centuries, either economically or culturally. By Chinese standards Mongol imposition of hereditary status distinctions was a step backward from a much more mobile and open society, and placing Persians, Arabs, or Tibetans over Chinese did not arouse interest in foreign cultures. Much more foreign music and foreign styles in clothing, art, and furnishings were integrated into Chinese civilization in Tang times than in Mongol times.

In terms of the spread of technological and scientific ideas, Europe seems to have been by far the main beneficiary of increased communication, largely because in 1200 it lagged farther behind than the other areas. Chinese inventions such as printing, gunpowder, and the compass spread westward. Persian and Indian expertise in astronomy and mathematics also spread. In terms of the spread of religions, Islam

● **Kalyan Minaret**   The Silk Road city of Bukhara (in today's Uzbekistan) is still graced by a 48-meter-tall minaret completed in 1127. Made of baked bricks laid in ornamental patterns, it is topped by a rotunda with sixteen arched windows, from which local Muslims were called to prayer five times a day. In times of war, the minaret could also serve as a watchtower. *(C. Rennie/Robert Harding World Imagery)*

probably gained the most. It spread into Chinese Central Asia, which had previously been Buddhist.

Perhaps because it was not invaded itself, Europe also seems to have been energized by the Mongol-imposed peace in ways that the other major civilizations were not. The goods from China and elsewhere in the East brought by merchants like Marco Polo to Europe whetted the appetites of Europeans for increased contacts with the East, and the demand for Asian goods eventually culminated in the great age of European exploration and expansion (see Chapter 15). By comparison, in areas the Mongols had directly attacked, protecting their own civilization became a higher priority than drawing from the outside to enrich or enlarge it.

INDIA (300–1400)

How did India respond to its encounters with Turks, Mongols, and Islam?

South Asia, far from the heartland of the steppe, still felt the impact of developments there. Over the course of many centuries, the Shakas, Huns, Turks, and Mongols all sent armies south to raid or invade north India.

Chapter 2 traces the early development of Indian civilization, including the emergence of the principal religious traditions of Hinduism, Buddhism, and Jainism; the impact of the Persian and Greek invasions; and the Mauryan Empire, with its great pro-Buddhist king, Ashoka. As discussed at the end of that chapter, after the Mauryan Empire broke apart in 184 B.C.E., India was politically divided into small kingdoms for several centuries.

The Gupta Empire (ca. 320–480)

In the early fourth century a state emerged in the Ganges plain that was able to bring large parts of north India under its control. The rulers of this Indian empire, the Guptas, consciously modeled their rule after that of the Mauryan Empire, and the founder took the name of the founder of that dynasty, Chandragupta. Although the Guptas never controlled as much territory as the Mauryans had, they united north India and received tribute from states in Nepal and the Indus Valley, thus giving large parts of India a period of peace and political unity.

The Guptas' administrative system was not as centralized as that of the Mauryans. In the central regions they drew their revenue from a tax on agriculture of one-quarter of the harvest and maintained monopolies on key products such as metals and salt (reminiscent of Chinese practice). They also exacted labor service for the construction and upkeep of roads, wells, and irrigation systems. More distant areas were assigned to governors who were allowed considerable leeway, and governorships often became hereditary. Areas still farther away were encouraged to become vassal states, able to participate in the splendor of the capital and royal court in subordinate roles and to engage in profitable trade, but not required to turn over much in the way of revenue.

The Gupta kings were patrons of the arts. Poets composed epics for the courts of the Gupta kings, and other writers experimented with prose romances and popular tales. India's greatest poet, Kalidasa (ca. 380–450), like Shakespeare, wrote poems as well as plays in verse. His most highly esteemed play, *Shakuntala*, concerns a daughter of a hermit who enthralls a king out hunting. The king sets up house with her, then returns to his court and owing to a curse forgets her. Only much later does he acknowledge their child as his true heir. Equally loved is Kalidasa's one-hundred-verse poem "The Cloud Messenger," about a demigod who asks a passing cloud to carry a message to his wife, from whom he has long been separated. At one point he instructs the cloud to tell her:

● **Wall Painting at Ajanta** Many of the best surviving examples of Gupta period painting are found at the twenty-nine Buddhist cave temples at Ajanta in central India. The walls of these caves were decorated in the fifth and sixth centuries with scenes from the former lives of the Buddha. These two scenes, showing a royal couple on the right and a princess and her attendants on the left, offer us glimpses of what the royal courts of the period must have looked like. (Benoy K. Behl)

I see your body in the sinuous creeper, your gaze in the startled eyes of deer,
your cheek in the moon, your hair in the plumage of peacocks,
and in the tiny ripples of the river I see your sidelong glances,
but alas, my dearest, nowhere do I see your whole likeness.[8]

In mathematics, too, the Gupta period could boast of impressive intellectual achievements. The so-called Arabic numerals were actually of Indian origin. Indian mathematicians developed the place-value notation system, with separate columns for ones, tens, and hundreds, as well as a zero sign to indicate the absence of units in a given column. This system greatly facilitated calculation and spread as far as Europe by the seventh century.

The Gupta rulers were Hindus but tolerated all faiths. Buddhist pilgrims from other areas of Asia reported that Buddhist monasteries with hundreds or even thousands of monks and nuns flourished in the cities.

The great crisis of the Gupta Empire was the invasion of the Huns. The migration of these nomads from Central Asia shook much of Eurasia. Around 450 a group of them known as the White Huns thundered into India. Mustering his full might, the ruler Skandagupta (r. ca. 455–467) threw back the invaders. Although the Huns failed to uproot the Gupta Empire, they dealt the dynasty a fatal blow.

India's Medieval Age (ca. 500–1400) and the First Encounter with Islam

After the decline of the Gupta Empire, India once again broke into separate kingdoms that were frequently at war with each other. Most of the dynasties were short-lived, but a balance of power was maintained between the four major regions of India, with none gaining enough of an advantage to conquer the others. Particularly notable are

MAP 11.2 **South and Southeast Asia in the Thirteenth Century** The extensive coastlines of South and Southeast Asia and the predictable monsoon winds aided seafaring in this region. Note the Strait of Malacca, through which most east-west sea trade passed.

the Cholas, who dominated the southern tip of the peninsula, Sri Lanka, and much of the eastern Indian Ocean to the twelfth century (see Map 11.2).

Political division fostered the development of regional cultures. Literature came to be written in regional languages, among them Marathi, Bengali, and Assamese. Commerce continued as before, and the coasts of India remained important in the sea trade of the Indian Ocean.

The first encounters with Islam occurred in this period. In 711, after pirates had plundered a richly laden Arab ship near the mouth of the Indus, the Umayyad governor of Iraq sent a force with six thousand horses and six thousand camels to seize the Sind area. The western part of India remained a part of the caliphate for centuries, but Islam did not spread much beyond this foothold. During the ninth and tenth centuries Turks from Central Asia moved into the region of today's northeastern Iran and western Afghanistan, then known as Khurasan. Converts to Islam, they first served as military forces for the caliphate in Baghdad, but as its authority weakened (see pages 200–203), they made themselves rulers of an effectively independent Khurasan and frequently sent raiding parties into north India. Beginning in 997, Mahmud of Ghazni (r. 997–1030) led seventeen annual forays into India from his base in modern Afghanistan. His goal was plunder to finance his wars against other Turkish rulers in

Central Asia. Toward this end, he systematically looted Indian palaces and temples, viewing religious statues as infidels' idols. Eventually even the Arab conquerors of the Sind fell to the Turks. By 1030 the Indus Valley, the Punjab, and the rest of northwest India were in the grip of the Turks.

The new rulers encouraged the spread of Islam, but the Indian caste system made it difficult to convert higher-caste Indians. Al-Biruni (d. 1048), a Persian scholar who spent much of his later life at the court of Mahmud and learned Sanskrit, gave some thought to the obstacles to Hindu-Muslim communication. The most basic barrier, he wrote, was language, but the religious gulf was also fundamental:

They totally differ from us in religion, as we believe in nothing in which they believe, and vice versa. On the whole, there is very little disputing about theological topics among them; at the utmost they fight with words, but they will never stake their soul or body or property on religious controversy. . . . They call foreigners impure and forbid having any connection with them, be it by intermarriage or any kind of relationship, or by sitting, eating, and drinking with them, because thereby, they think, they would be polluted.[9]

After the initial period of raids and destruction of temples, the Muslim Turks came to an accommodation with the Hindus, who were classed as a **protected people**, like the Christians and Jews, and allowed to follow their religion. They had to pay a special tax but did not have to perform military service. Local chiefs and rajas were often allowed to remain in control of their domains as long as they paid tribute. Most Indians looked on the Muslim conquerors as a new ruling caste, capable of governing and taxing them but otherwise peripheral to their lives. The myriad castes largely governed themselves, isolating the newcomers. Nevertheless, over the course of several centuries Islam gained a strong hold on north India, especially in the Indus Valley (modern Pakistan) and in Bengal at the mouth of the Ganges River (modern Bangladesh). Moreover, the sultanate seems to have had a positive effect on the economy. Much of the wealth confiscated from temples was put to more productive use, and India's first truly large cities emerged. The Turks also were eager to employ skilled workers, giving new opportunities to low-caste manual and artisan labor.

The Muslim rulers were much more hostile to Buddhism than to Hinduism, seeing Buddhism as a competitive proselytizing religion. In 1193 a Turkish raiding party destroyed the great Buddhist university at Nalanda in Bihar. Buddhist monks were killed or forced to flee to Buddhist centers in Southeast Asia, Nepal, and Tibet. Buddhism, which had thrived for so long in peaceful and friendly competition with Hinduism, was forced out of its native land.

Hinduism, however, remained as strong as ever. South India was largely unaffected by these invasions, and traditional Hindu culture flourished

protected people *The Muslim classification used for Hindus, Christians, and Jews; they were allowed to follow their religions but had to pay a special tax.*

● **Hindu Temple** Medieval Hindu temples were frequently decorated with scenes of sexual passion. Here Vishnu caresses Lakshami at the Parshvinath Temple. *(Richard Ashworth/Robert Harding World Imagery)*

there under native kings ruling small kingdoms (see the feature "Individuals in Society: Bhaskara the Teacher"). Temple-centered Hinduism flourished, as did devotional cults and mystical movements. This was a great age of religious art and architecture in India. Extraordinary temples covered with elaborate bas-relief were built in many areas. Sexual passion and the union of men and women were frequently depicted, symbolically representing passion for and union with the temple god.

In the twelfth century a new line of Turkish rulers arose in Afghanistan, led by Muhammad of Ghur (d. 1206). Muhammad captured Delhi and extended his control nearly throughout north India. When Muhammad of Ghur fell to an assassin in 1206, one of his generals, the former slave Qutb-ud-din, seized the reins of power and established a government at Delhi, separate from the government in Afghanistan. This sultanate of Delhi lasted for three centuries, even though dynasties changed several times.

The North African Muslim world traveler Ibn Battuta (1304–1368) (see page 213), who journeyed through Africa and Asia from 1325 to 1354, served for several years as a judge at the court of one of the Delhi sultans. He praised the sultan for his insistence on the observance of ritual prayers and many acts of generosity to those in need, but he also considered the sultan overly violent. Here is just one of many examples he offered of how quick the sultan was to execute:

During the years of the famine, the Sultan had given orders to dig wells outside the capital, and have grain crops sown in those parts. He provided the cultivators with the seed, as well as with all that was necessary for cultivation in the way of money and supplies, and required them to cultivate these crops for the [royal] grain-store. When the jurist 'Afif al-Din heard of this, he said, "This crop will not produce what is hoped for." Some informer told the Sultan what he had said, so the Sultan jailed him, and said to him, "What reason have you to meddle with the government's business?" Some time later he released him, and as 'Afif al-Din went to his house he was met on the way by two friends of his, also jurists, who said to him, "Praise be to God for your release," to which our jurist replied, "Praise be to God who has delivered us from the evildoers." They then separated, but they had not reached their houses before this was reported to the Sultan, and he commanded all three to be fetched and brought before him. "Take out this fellow," he said, referring to 'Afif al-Din, "and cut off his head baldrickwise," that is, the head is cut off along with an arm and part of the chest, "and behead the other two." They said to him, "He deserves punishment, to be sure, for what he said, but in our case for what crime are you killing us?" He replied, "You heard what he said and did not disavow it, so you as good as agreed with it." So they were all put to death, God Most High have mercy on them.[10]

A major accomplishment of the Delhi sultanate was holding off the Mongols. Chinggis Khan and his troops entered the Indus Valley in 1221 in pursuit of the shah of Khurasan. The sultan wisely kept out of the way, and when Chinggis left some troops in the area, the sultan made no attempt to challenge them. Two generations later, in 1299, a Mongol khan launched a campaign into India with two hundred thousand men, but the sultan of the time was able to defeat them. Two years later the Mongols returned and camped at Delhi for two months, but they eventually left without taking the sultan's fort. Another Mongol raid in 1306–1307 also was successfully repulsed.

Although the Turks by this time were highly cosmopolitan, they had retained their martial skills and understanding of steppe warfare. They were expert horsemen, and horses thrived in northwest India. The south and east of India, like the south of China, were less hospitable to raising horses and generally had to import them. In India's case, though, the climate of the south and east was well suited to elephants, which had been used as weapons of war in India since early times. Rulers in the northwest imported elephants from more tropical regions. The Delhi sultanate is said to have had as many as one thousand war elephants at its height.

During the fourteenth century, however, the Delhi sultanate was in decline and proved unable to ward off the armies of Tamerlane (see page 303), who took Delhi in

Bhaskara the Teacher

The observatory where Bhaskara worked in Ujjain today stands in ruins. (Dinodia Picture Agency)

In India, as in many other societies, astronomy and mathematics were closely linked, and many of the most important mathematicians served their rulers as astronomers. Bhaskara (1114–ca. 1185) was such an astronomer-mathematician. For generations his Brahman family had been astronomers at the Ujjain astronomical observatory in north-central India, and his father had written a popular book on astrology.

Bhaskara was a highly erudite man. A disciple wrote that he had thoroughly mastered eight books on grammar, six on medicine, six on philosophy, five on mathematics, and the four Vedas. Bhaskara eventually wrote six books on mathematics and mathematical astronomy. They deal with solutions to simple and quadratic equations and show his knowledge of trigonometry, including the sine table and relationships between different trigonometric functions, and even some of the basic elements of calculus. Earlier Indian mathematicians had explored the use of zero and negative numbers. Bhaskara developed these ideas further, in particular improving on the understanding of division by zero.

A court poet who centuries later translated Bhaskara's book titled *The Beautiful* explained its title by saying Bhaskara wrote it for his daughter named Beautiful (Lilavati) as consolation when his divination of the best time for her to marry went awry. Whether or not Bhaskara wrote this book for his daughter, many of the problems he provides in it have a certain charm:

On an expedition to seize his enemy's elephants, a king marched two yojanas the first day. Say, intelligent calculator, with what increasing rate of daily march did he proceed, since he reached his foe's city, a distance of eighty yojanas, in a week?*

Out of a heap of pure lotus flower, a third part, a fifth, and a sixth were offered respectively to the gods Siva, Vishnu, and the Sun; and a quarter was presented to Bhavani. The remaining six lotuses were given to the venerable preceptor. Tell quickly the whole number of lotus.†

If eight best variegated silk scarfs, measuring three cubits in breadth and eight in length, cost a hundred nishkas, say quickly, merchant, if thou understand trade, what a like scarf, three and a half cubits long and half a cubit wide will cost.‡

In the conclusion to *The Beautiful,* Bhaskara wrote:

Joy and happiness is indeed ever increasing in this world for those who have The Beautiful *clasped to their throats, decorated as the members are with neat reduction of fractions, multiplication, and involution, pure and perfect as are the solutions, and tasteful as is the speech which is exemplified.*

Bhaskara had a long career. His first book on mathematical astronomy, written in 1150 when he was thirty-six, dealt with such topics as the calculation of solar and lunar eclipses or planetary conjunctions. Thirty-three years later he was still writing on the subject, this time providing simpler ways to solve problems encountered before. Bhaskara wrote his books in Sanskrit, already a literary language rather than a vernacular language, but even in his own day some of them were translated into other Indian languages.

Within a couple of decades of his death, a local ruler endowed an educational institution to study Bhaskara's works, beginning with his work on mathematical astronomy. In the text he had inscribed at the site, the ruler gave the names of Bhaskara's ancestors for six generations, as well as of his son and grandson, who had continued in his profession.

Questions for Analysis

1. What are the advantages of making occupations like astronomer hereditary?

2. Do you think there are connections between Bhaskara's broad erudition and his accomplishments as a mathematician?

*Quotations from Haran Chandra Banerji, *Colebrooke's Translation of the Lilanvanti,* 2d ed. (Calcutta: The Book Co., 1927), pp. 80–81, 30, 51, 200. The answer is that each day he must travel 22/7 yojanas farther than the day before.
†The answer is 120.
‡The answer, from the formula $x = (1 \times 7 \times 1 \times 100) / (8 \times 3 \times 8 \times 2 \times 2)$, is given in currencies smaller than the nishka: 14 drammas, 9 panas, 1 kakini, and $6\frac{2}{3}$ cowry shells. (20 cowry shells = 1 kakini, 4 kakini = 1 pana, 16 panas = 1 dramma, and 16 drammas = 1 nishka.)

● **The God Ganesha** Known as the Destroyer of Obstacles, the elephant-headed Ganesha is one of the best-loved gods in the Hindu pantheon, invoked by those in need of a solution to a difficult situation. This stone sculpture was carved in southern India in the thirteenth century and is 37 inches tall. *(Gift of the de Young Museum Society Auxiliary, B68S4. © Asian Art Museum of San Fransisco. Used by permisson)*

1398. Tamerlane's chronicler reported that when the troops drew up for battle outside Delhi, the sultanate had 10,000 horsemen, 20,000 foot soldiers, and 120 war elephants with archers riding on them. Though alarmed at the sight of the elephants, Tamerlane's men dug trenches to trap them and also shot at their drivers. The sultan fled, leaving the city to surrender. Tamerlane took as booty all the elephants, loading them with treasures seized from the city. Ruy Gonzalez de Clavijo, an ambassador from the king of Castile who arrived in Samarkand in 1403, was greatly impressed by these well-trained elephants. "When all the elephants together charged abreast, it seemed as though the solid earth itself shook at their onrush," he observed, noting that he thought each elephant was worth a thousand foot soldiers in battle.[11]

Daily Life in Medieval India

To the overwhelming majority of people in medieval India, the size of the territory controlled by their king did not matter much. Local institutions played a much larger role in their lives than did the state. Guilds oversaw conditions of work and trade; local councils handled law and order at the town or village level; local castes gave members a sense of belonging and identity.

Like peasant societies elsewhere, including in China, Japan, and Southeast Asia, agricultural life in India ordinarily meant village life. The average farmer worked a small plot of land outside the village. All the family members pooled their resources—human, animal, and material—under the direction of the head of the family. Joint struggles strengthened family solidarity.

The agricultural year began with spring plowing. The ancient plow, drawn by two oxen wearing yokes and collars, had an iron-tipped share and a handle with which the farmer guided it. Rice, the most important and popular grain, was sown at the beginning of the long rainy season. Beans, lentils, and peas were the farmer's friends, for they grew during the cold season and were harvested in the spring when fresh food was scarce. Cereal crops such as wheat, barley, and millet provided carbohydrates and other nutrients. Sugar cane was another important crop. Some families cultivated vegetables, spices, fruit trees, and flowers in their gardens.

Cattle were raised for plowing and milk, hides, and horns, but Hindus did not slaughter them for meat. Like the Islamic and Jewish prohibition on the consumption of pork, the eating of beef was forbidden among Hindus.

Local craftsmen and tradesmen lived and worked in specific parts of a town or village. They were frequently organized into guilds, with guild heads and guild rules. The textile industries were particularly well developed. Silk (which had entered India from China), linen, wool, and cotton fabrics were produced in large quantities and traded throughout India and beyond. The cutting and polishing of precious stones was another industry associated closely with foreign trade.

In the cities shops were open to the street; families lived on the floors above. The busiest tradesmen dealt in milk and cheese, oil, spices, and perfumes. Equally prominent but disreputable were tavern keepers. Indian taverns were haunts of criminals and con artists, and in the worst of them fighting was as common as drinking. In addition to these tradesmen and merchants, a host of peddlers shuffled through towns and villages selling everything from needles to freshly cut flowers.

The Chinese Buddhist pilgrim Faxian, during his six years in Gupta India, described India as a peaceful land where people could move about freely without needing passports and where the upper castes were vegetarians. He was the first to make explicit reference to "untouchables," remarking that they hovered around the margins of Indian society, carrying gongs to warn upper-caste people of their polluting presence.

Villages were often walled, as in north China and the Middle East. The streets were unpaved, and the rainy season turned them into a muddy soup. Cattle and sheep roamed as freely as people. Some families kept pets, such as cats or parrots. Half-wild mongooses served as effective protection against snakes. The pond outside the village was its main source of water and also a spawning ground for fish, birds, and mosquitoes. Women drawing water frequently encountered water buffalo wallowing in the shallows. After the farmers returned from the fields in the evening, the village gates were closed until morning.

In this period the caste system reached its mature form. Within the broad division into the four *varna* (strata) of Brahman, Kshatriya, Vaishya, and Shudra, the population was subdivided into numerous castes, or **jati**. Each caste had a proper occupation. In addition, its members married only within the caste and ate only with other members. Members of high-status castes feared pollution from contact with lower-caste individuals and had to undertake rituals of purification to remove the taint. Eventually Indian society comprised perhaps as many as three thousand castes. Each caste had its own governing body, which enforced the rules of the caste. Those incapable of living up to the rules were expelled, becoming outcastes. These unfortunates lived hard lives, performing tasks that others considered unclean or lowly.

jati *Indian castes.*

The life of the well-to-do is described in the *Kamasutra* (Book on the Art of Love). Comfortable surroundings provided a place for men to enjoy poetry, painting, and music in the company of like-minded friends. Well-trained courtesans added to the pleasures of the wealthy. A man who had more than one wife was advised not to let one speak ill of the other and to try to keep each of them happy by taking them to gardens, giving them presents, telling them secrets, and loving them well.

For all members of Indian society, regardless of caste, marriage and the family were the focus of life. As in China, the joint family was under the authority of the eldest male, who might take several wives. The family affirmed its solidarity by the religious ritual of honoring its dead ancestors—a ritual that linked the living and the dead, much like ancestor worship in China. People commonly lived in extended families: grandparents, uncles and aunts, cousins, and nieces and nephews all lived together in the same house or compound.

Children were viewed as a great source of happiness. The poet Kalidasa depicts children as the greatest joy of their father's life:

With their teeth half-shown in causeless laughter,
and their efforts at talking so sweetly uncertain,
when children ask to sit on his lap
a man is blessed, even by the dirt on their bodies.[12]

Children in poor households worked as soon as they were able. Children in wealthier households faced the age-old irritations of reading, writing, and arithmetic. Less attention was paid to daughters, though in more prosperous families they were often literate. Because girls who had lost their virginity could seldom hope to find good husbands and thus would become financial burdens and social disgraces to their families, daughters were customarily married as children, with consummation delayed until they reached puberty.

Wives' bonds with their husbands were so strong that it was felt a wife should have no life apart from her husband. A widow was expected to lead the hard life of the ascetic, sleeping on the ground; eating only one simple meal a day, without meat, wine, salt, or honey; wearing plain undyed clothes without jewelry; and shaving her head. She was viewed as inauspicious to everyone but her children, and she did not attend family festivals. Among high-caste Hindus, a widow would be praised for throwing herself on her husband's funeral pyre. Buddhist sects objected to this practice, called **sati,** but some writers declared that by self-immolation a widow could expunge both her own and her husband's sins, so that both would enjoy eternal bliss in Heaven.

Within the home the position of a wife often depended chiefly on her own intelligence and strength of character. Wives were traditionally supposed to be humble, cheerful, and diligent even toward worthless husbands. As in other patriarchal societies, however, occasionally a woman ruled the roost. For women who did not want to accept the strictures of married life, the main way out was to join a Buddhist or Jain religious community.

sati *A practice whereby a high-caste Hindu woman would throw herself on her husband's funeral pyre.*

• • • • • • • • • • • • •

SOUTHEAST ASIA, TO 1400

How did states develop along the maritime trade routes of Southeast Asia?

Much as Roman culture spread to northern Europe and Chinese culture spread to Korea, Japan, and Vietnam, in the first millennium C.E. Indian learning, technology, and material culture spread to Southeast Asia, both mainland and insular.

Southeast Asia is a tropical region that is more like India than China, with temperatures hovering around 80°F and rain falling dependably throughout the year. The topography of mainland Southeast Asia is marked by north-south mountain ranges separated by river valleys. It was easy for people to migrate south along these rivers but harder for them to cross the heavily forested mountains that divided the region into areas that had limited contact with each other. The indigenous population was originally mostly Malay, but migrations over the centuries brought many other peoples, including speakers of Austro-Asiatic, Austronesian, and Sino-Tibetan-Burmese languages, some of whom moved on to the islands offshore.

● **Bayan Relief, Angkor Wat** Among the many relief sculptures at the amazing complex of Angkor Wat are depictions of royal processions, armies at war, trade, cooking, cockfighting, and other scenes of everyday life. In the relief shown here, the boats and fish convey something of the significance of the sea to life in Southeast Asia. *(Robert Wilson, photographer)*

The northern part of modern Vietnam was under Chinese political control off and on from the second century B.C.E. to the tenth century C.E. (see pages 153–154), but for the rest of Southeast Asia, Indian influence was of much greater significance. The first state to appear in Southeast Asia, called Funan by Chinese visitors, had its capital in southern Vietnam. In the first to sixth centuries C.E. Funan extended its control over much of Indochina and the Malay Peninsula. Merchants from northwest India would offload their goods and carry them across the narrowest part of the Malay Peninsula. The ports of Funan offered food and lodging to the merchants as they waited for the winds to shift to continue their voyages. Brahman priests and Buddhist monks from India settled along with the traders, serving the Indian population and attracting local converts. Rulers often invited Indian priests and monks to serve under them, using them as foreign experts knowledgeable about law, government, architecture, and other fields.

Sixth-century Chinese sources report that the Funan king lived in a multistory palace and the common people lived in houses built on piles with roofs of bamboo leaves. The king rode about on an elephant, but narrow boats measuring up to ninety feet long were a more important means of transportation. The people enjoyed both cockfighting and pig fighting. Instead of drawing water from wells, as the Chinese did, they made pools, from which dozens of nearby families would draw water.

After the decline of Funan, maritime trade continued to grow, and petty kingdoms appeared in many places. Indian traders frequently established small settlements, generally located on the coast. Contact with the local populations led to intermarriage and the creation of hybrid cultures. Local rulers often adopted Indian customs and values, embraced Hinduism and Buddhism, and learned **Sanskrit,** India's classical

Sanskrit *India's classical literary language.*

GLOBAL TRADE

SPICES

From ancient times on, for both Europeans and Chinese, a major reason to trade with South and Southeast Asia was to acquire spices, especially pepper, nutmeg, cloves, and cinnamon. These and other spices were in high demand not only because they could be used to flavor food but also because they were thought to have positive pharmacological properties. Unlike other highly desired products of India and farther east—such as sugar, cotton, rice, and silk—no way was found to produce the spices close to where they were in demand. Because of the location where

these spices were produced, this trade was from earliest times largely a maritime trade conducted through a series of middlemen. The spices were transported from where they were grown to nearby ports, and from there to major entrepôts, where merchants would take them in many different directions.

Two types of pepper grew in India and Southeast Asia. Black pepper is identical to our familiar pepper corns. "Long pepper," from a related plant, was hotter. The Mediterranean world imported its pepper from India; China imported it from Southeast Asia. After the discovery of the New World the importation of long pepper declined, as the chili pepper found in

The Spice Trade

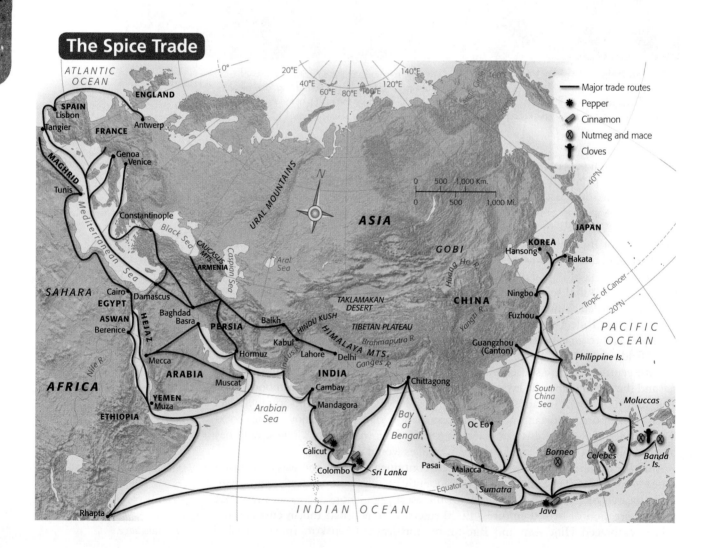

Major trade routes
Pepper
Cinnamon
Nutmeg and mace
Cloves

Mexico was at least as spicy and grew well in Europe and China.

Already in Greek and Roman times trade in pepper was substantial. According to the Greek geographer Strabo (64 B.C.E.–24 C.E.), 120 ships a year made the trip to India to acquire pepper, the round trip taking a year because they had to wait for the monsoon winds to be blowing in the right direction. Pliny in about 77 C.E. complained that the Roman Empire wasted fifty million sesterces per year on long pepper and white and black pepper combined.

Cloves and nutmeg entered the repertoire of spices somewhat later than pepper. They are interesting because they could be grown in only a handful of small islands in the eastern part of the Indonesian archipelago. Merchants in China, India, Arab lands, and Europe got them through intermediaries and did not know where they were grown. An Arab source from about 1000 C.E. reported that cloves came from an island near India that had a Valley of Cloves, and that they were acquired by a silent barter. The sailors would lay out on the beach the items they were willing to trade, and the next morning they would find cloves in their place.

The demand for these spices in time encouraged Chinese, Indian, and Arab seamen to make the trip to the Straits of Malacca or east Java. Malay seamen in small craft such as outrigger canoes would bring the spices the thousand or more miles to the major ports where foreign merchants would purchase them. This trade was important to the prosperity of the Srivijaya kingdom. The trade was so profitable, however, that it also attracted pirates.

In the Mongol era travelers like Marco Polo, Ibn Battuta, and Odoric of Pordenone reported on the cultivation and marketing of spices in the various places they visited. Ibn Battuta described pepper plants as vines planted to grow up coconut palms. He also reported seeing the trunks of cinnamon trees floated down rivers in India. Odoric reported that pepper was picked like grapes from groves so huge it would take eighteen days to walk around them. Marco Polo referred to the 7,459 islands in the China Sea that local mariners could navigate and that produced a great variety of spices as well as aromatic wood. He also reported that spices could be acquired at the great island of Java, including pepper, nutmeg, and cloves, perhaps not understanding that these had often been shipped from the innumerable small islands to Java.

Gaining direct access to the spices of the East was one of the motivations behind Christopher Columbus's voyages. Not long after, Portuguese sailors did reach India by sailing around Africa, and soon the Dutch were competing with them for control of the spice trade and setting up rival trading posts. Pepper was soon successively planted in other tropical places, including Brazil. India, however, has remained the largest exporter of spices to this day.

literary language. Sanskrit gave different peoples a common mode of written expression, much as Chinese did in East Asia and Latin did in Europe.

When the Indians entered mainland Southeast Asia, they encountered both long-settled peoples and migrants moving southward from the frontiers of China. As in other such extensive migrations, the newcomers fought one another as often as they fought the native populations. In 939 the Vietnamese finally became independent of China and extended their power southward along the coast of present-day Vietnam. The Thais had long lived in what is today southwest China and north Burma. In the eighth century the Thai tribes united in a confederacy and even expanded northward against Tang China. Like China, however, the Thai confederacy fell to the Mongols in 1253. Still farther west another tribal people, the Burmese, migrated to the area of modern Burma in the eighth century. They also established a state, which they ruled from their capital, Pagan, and came into contact with India and Sri Lanka.

The most important mainland state was the Khmer Empire of Cambodia (802–1432), which controlled the heart of the region. The Khmers were indigenous to the area. Their empire, founded in 802, eventually extended south to the sea and the northeast Malay Peninsula. Indian influence was pervasive; the impressive temple complex at Angkor Wat was dedicated to the Hindu god Vishnu. Social organization, however, was modeled not on the Indian caste system but on indigenous traditions. A large part of the population was of servile status, many descended from non-Khmer mountain tribes defeated by the Khmers. Generally successful in a long series of wars with the Vietnamese, the Khmers reached the peak of their power in 1219 and then gradually declined.

Srivijaya *A maritime empire that held the Strait of Malacca and the waters around Sumatra, Borneo, and Java.*

Far different from these land-based states was the maritime empire of **Srivijaya,** based on the island of Sumatra. From the sixth century on, it held the important Strait of Malacca, through which most of the sea traffic between China and India passed. (See the feature "Global Trade: Spices" on pages 318–319.) This state, held together as much by alliances as by direct rule, was in many ways like the Gupta state in India, securing its prominence and binding its vassals and allies through its splendor and the promise of riches through trade.

Much as the Korean and Japanese rulers adapted Chinese models (see page 157), the Srivijayan rulers drew on Indian traditions to justify their rule and organize their state. The Sanskrit writing system was used for government documents, and Indians were often employed as priests, scribes, and administrators. Using Sanskrit overcame the barriers raised by the many different native languages of the region. Indian mythology took hold, as did Indian architecture and sculpture. Kings and their courts, the first to embrace Indian culture, consciously spread it to their subjects. The Chinese Buddhist monk Yixing (d. 727) stopped at Srivijaya for six months in 671 on his way to India and for four years on his return journey. He found a thousand monks there, some of whom helped him translate Sanskrit texts.

Borobudur, the magnificent Buddhist temple complex, was begun around 780. This stone monument depicts the ten tiers of Buddhist cosmology. When pilgrims made the three-mile-long winding ascent, they passed numerous sculpted reliefs depicting the journey from ignorance to enlightenment.

After several centuries of prosperity, Srivijaya suffered a stunning blow in 1025. The Chola state in south India launched a large naval raid and captured the Srivijayan king and capital. Unable to hold their gains, the Indians retreated, but the Srivijaya Empire never regained its vigor.

Buddhism became progressively more dominant in Southeast Asia after 800. Mahayana Buddhism became important in Srivijaya and Vietnam, but Theravada Buddhism, closer to the original Buddhism of early India, became the dominant form in the rest of mainland Southeast Asia. Buddhist missionaries from India and Sri Lanka played a prominent role in these developments. Local converts continued the process by making pilgrimages to India and Sri Lanka to worship and to observe Indian life for themselves.

The Spread of Indian Culture in Comparative Perspective

The social, cultural, and political systems developed in India, China, and Rome all had enormous impact on neighboring peoples whose cultures were originally not as advanced. Some of the mechanisms for cultural spread were similar in all three cases, but differences were important as well.

In the case of Rome and both Han and Tang China, strong states directly ruled outlying regions, bringing their civilizations with them. India's states, even its largest empires, such as the Mauryan and Gupta, did not have comparable bureaucratic reach. Outlying areas tended to be in the hands of local lords who had consented to recognize the overlordship of the stronger state. Moreover, most of the time India was politically divided.

The expansion of Indian culture into Southeast Asia thus came not from conquest and extending direct political control, but from the extension of trading networks, with missionaries following along. This made it closer to the way Japan adopted features of Chinese culture, often through the intermediary of Korea. In both cases, the cultural exchange was largely voluntary, as the Japanese or Southeast Asians sought to adopt more up-to-date technologies (such as writing) or were persuaded of the truth of religious ideas they learned from foreigners.

Chapter Summary

To assess your mastery of this chapter, go to bedfordstmartins.com/mckayworld

Key Terms

- nomads
- grasslands
- steppe
- yurts
- Great Khan
- khanates
- tax-farming
- protected people
- jati
- sati
- Sanskrit
- Srivijaya

• What gave the nomadic pastoralists of Central Asia military advantages over nearby settled civilizations?

The nomadic pastoral societies that stretched across Eurasia had the great military advantage of being able to raise horses in large numbers and support themselves from their flocks. Their mastery of the horse and mounted archery allowed them repeatedly to overawe or conquer their neighbors. Nomadic pastoralists generally were organized on the basis of clans and tribes that selected chiefs for their military talent. Much of the time these tribes fought with each other, but several times in history leaders rose who formed larger confederations capable of coordinated attacks on cities and towns. From the fifth to the twelfth centuries, the most successful nomadic groups on the Eurasian grasslands were Turks of one sort or another.

• How was the world changed by the Mongol conquests of much of Eurasia?

The greatest of the nomadic military leaders was the Mongol Chinggis Khan. In the early thirteenth century, through his charismatic leadership and military genius, he was able to lead victorious armies from one side of Eurasia to another. The initial conquests were quite destructive, with the inhabitants of many cities enslaved or killed. After the empire was divided into four khanates ruled by different lines of Chinggis's descendants, more stable forms of government were developed. The Mongols rewarded loyalty and gave important positions to those willing to serve them faithfully. The Mongols did not try to change the cultures or religions of the countries they conquered. In Mongolia and China the Mongol rulers welcomed those learned in all religions. In Central Asia and Persia the Mongol khans converted to Islam and gave it the support earlier rulers there had done.

• How did the Mongol conquests facilitate the spread of ideas, religions, inventions, and diseases?

For a century Mongol hegemony fostered unprecedented East-West trade and contact. The Mongols encouraged trade and often moved craftsmen and other specialists from one place to another. More Europeans made their way east than ever before, and Chinese inventions such as printing and the compass made their way west. Because Europe was further behind in 1200, it benefited most from the spread of technical and scientific ideas. Diseases also spread, including, it seems, the plague referred to as the Black Death in Europe.

• How did India respond to its encounters with Turks, Mongols, and Islam?

India was invaded by the Mongols, but not conquered. After the fall of the Gupta Empire in about 480, India was for the next millennium ruled by small kingdoms, which allowed regional cultures to flourish. The north and northwest were frequently raided by Turks from Afghanistan or Central Asia, and for several centuries Muslim Turks ruled a state in north India called the Delhi Sultanate. Over time Islam gained adherents throughout South Asia. Hinduism continued to flourish, but Buddhism went into decline.

• How did states develop along the maritime trade routes of Southeast Asia?

Throughout the medieval period India continued to be the center of a very active seaborne trade, and this trade helped carry Indian ideas and practices to Southeast Asia. Local rulers used experts from India to establish strong states, such as the Khmer kingdom in Cambodia and the Srivijaya kingdom in Malaysia and Indonesia. Buddhism became the dominant religion throughout the region, though Hinduism also played an important role.

Suggested Reading

Abu-Lughod, Janet L. *Before European Hegemony: The World System A.D. 1250–1350*. 1989. Examines the period of Mongol domination from a global perspective.

Ali, Daud. *Courtly Culture and Political Life in Early Medieval India*. 2004. Explores the growth of royal households and the development of a courtly worldview in India from 350 to 1200.

Chaudhuri, K. N. *Asia Before Europe*. 1990. Discusses the economy and civilization of cultures within the basin of the Indian Ocean.

Findley, Carter Vaughn. *The Turks in World History*. 2005. Covers both the early Turks and the connections between the Turks and the Mongols.

Franke, Herbert, and Denis Twitchett, eds. *The Cambridge History of China*, vol. 6, *Alien Regimes and Border States*. 1994. Clear and thoughtful accounts of the Mongols and their predecessors in East Asia.

Jackson, Peter. *The Delhi Sultanate*. 2003. Provides a close examination of north India in the thirteenth and fourteenth centuries.

Jackson, Peter. *The Mongols and the West, 1221–1410*. 2005. A close examination of many different types of connections between the Mongols and both Europe and the Islamic lands.

Ratchnevsky, Paul. *Genghis Khan: His Life and Legacy*. 1992. A reliable account by a major Mongolist.

Rossabi, Morris. *Khubilai Khan: His Life and Times*. 1988. Provides a lively account of the life of one of the most important Mongol rulers.

Shaffer, Lynda. *Maritime Southeast Asia to 1500*. 1996. A short account of early Southeast Asia from a world history perspective.

Notes

1. Trans. in Denis Sinor, "The Establishment and Dissolution of the Türk Empire," in *The Cambridge History of Early Inner Asia,* ed. Denis Sinor (Cambridge: Cambridge University Press, 1990), p. 307.
2. Manuel Komroff, ed., *Contemporaries of Marco Polo* (New York: Dorset Press, 1989), p. 65.
3. Ibid.
4. *The Travels of Marco Polo, the Venetian,* ed. Manuel Komroff (New York: Boni and Liveright, 1926), p. 93.
5. Ibid., pp. 93–94.
6. Cited in John Larner, *Marco Polo and the Discovery of the World* (New Haven, Conn.: Yale University Press, 1999), p. 22.
7. Igor de Rachewiltz, "Marco Polo Went to China," *Zentralasiatische Studien* 27(1997): 34–92. See also Larner, *Marco Polo and the Discovery of the World.*

8. Quoted in A. L. Basham, *The Wonder That Was India,* 2d ed. (New York: Grove Press, 1959), p. 420. All quotations from this work are reprinted by permission of Pan Macmillan, London.
9. Edward C. Sachau, *Alberuni's India,* vol. 1 (London: Kegan Paul, 1910), pp. 19–20, slightly modified.
10. H. A. R. Gibb, *The Travels of Ibn Battuta* (Cambridge: Cambridge University Press for the Hukluyt Society, 1971), pp. 700–701.
11. Guy le Strang, trans., *Clavijo, Embassy to Tamerlane, 1403–1406* (London: Routledge, 1928), pp. 265–266.
12. Quoted in Basham, *The Wonder That Was India,* p. 161.

Listening to the PAST

The Abduction of Women in *The Secret History of the Mongols*

Within a few decades of Chinggis Khan's death, oral traditions concerning his rise were written down in the Mongolian language. They begin with the cycles of revenge among the tribes in Mongolia, many of which began when women were abducted for wives. These passages relate how Temujin's (Chinggis's) father Yesugei seized Hogelun, Temujin's future mother, from a passing Merkid; how twenty years later three Merkids in return seized women from Temujin; and Temujin's revenge.

That year Yesugei the Brave was out hunting with his falcon on the Onan. Yeke Chiledu, a nobleman of the Merkid tribe, had gone to the Olkhunugud people to find himself a wife, and he was returning to the Merkid with the girl he'd found when he passed Yesugei hunting by the river. When he saw them riding along Yesugei leaned forward on his horse. He saw it was a beautiful girl. Quickly he rode back to his tent and just as quick returned with his two brothers, Nekun Taisi and Daritai Odchigin. When Chiledu saw the three Mongols coming he whipped his dun-colored horse and rode off around a nearby hill with the three men behind him. He cut back around the far side of the hill and rode to Lady Hogelun, the girl he'd just married, who stood waiting for him at the front of their cart. "Did you see the look on the faces of those three men?" she asked him. "From their faces it looks like they mean to kill you. As long as you've got your life there'll always be girls for you to choose from. There'll always be women to ride in your cart. As long as you've got your life you'll be able to find some girl to marry. When you find her, just name her Hogelun for me, but go now and save your own life!" Then she pulled off her shirt and held it out to him, saying: "And take this to remember me, to remember my scent." Chiledu reached out from his saddle and took the shirt in his hands. With the three Mongols close behind him he struck his dun-colored horse with his whip and took off down the Onan River at full speed.

The three Mongols chased him across seven hills before turning around and returning to Hogelun's cart. Then Yesugei the Brave grasped the reins of the cart, his elder brother Nekun Taisi rode in front to guide them, and the younger brother Daritai Odchigin rode along by the wheels. As they rode her back toward their camp, Hogelun began to cry, . . . and she cried till she stirred up the waters of the Onan River, till she shook the trees in the forest and the grass in the valleys. But as the party approached their camp Daritai, riding beside her, warned her to stop: "This fellow who held you in his arms, he's already ridden over the mountains. This man who's lost you, he's crossed many rivers by now. You can call out his name, but he can't see you now even if he looks back. If you tried to find him now you won't even find his tracks. So be still now," he told her. Then Yesugei took Lady Hogelun to his tent as his wife. . . .

[Some twenty years later] one morning just before dawn Old Woman Khogaghchin, Mother Hogelun's servant, woke with a start, crying: "Mother! Mother! Get up! The ground is shaking, I hear it rumble. The Tayichigud must be riding back to attack us. Get up!"

Mother Hogelun jumped from her bed, saying: "Quick, wake my sons!" They woke Temujin and the others and all ran for the horses. Temujin, Mother Hogelun, and Khasar each took a horse. Khachigun, Temuge Odchigin, and Belgutei each took a horse. Bogorchu took one horse and Jelme another. Mother Hogelun lifted the baby Temulun onto her saddle. They saddled the last horse as a lead and there was no horse left for [Temujin's wife] Lady Borte. . . .

Old Woman Khogaghchin, who'd been left in the camp, said: "I'll hide Lady Borte." She made her get into a black covered cart. Then she harnessed the cart to a speckled ox. Whipping the ox, she drove the cart away from the camp down the Tungelig. As the first light of day hit them, soldiers rode up and told them to stop. "Who are you?" they asked her, and Old Woman Khogaghchin answered: "I'm a servant of Temujin's. I've just come from shearing his sheep. I'm on my way back to my own tent to make felt

This portrait of Chinggis's wife, Borte, is found in a shrine to her in Mongolia. *(Courtesy of Genghis Khan Shrine, Yijinhuoluo Banner)*

from the wool." Then they asked her: "Is Temujin at his tent? How far is it from here?" Old Woman Khogaghchin said: "As for the tent, it's not far. As for Temujin, I couldn't see whether he was there or not. I was just shearing his sheep out back." The soldiers rode off toward the camp, and Old Woman Khogaghchin whipped the ox. But as the cart moved faster its axletree snapped. "Now we'll have to run for the woods on foot," she thought, but before she could start the soldiers returned. They'd made [Temujin's half brother] Belgutei's mother their captive, and had her slung over one of their horses with her feet swinging down. They rode up to the old woman shouting: "What have you got in that cart!" "I'm just carrying wool," Khogaghchin replied, but an old soldier turned to the younger ones and said, "Get off your horses and see what's in there." When they opened the door of the cart they found Borte inside. Pulling her out, they forced Borte and Khogaghchin to ride on their horses, then they all set out after Temujin. . . .

The men who pursued Temujin were the chiefs of the three Merkid clans, Toghtoga, Dayin Usun, and Khagatai Darmala. These three had come to get their revenge, saying: "Long ago Mother Hogelun was stolen from our brother, Chiledu." When they couldn't catch Temujin they said to each other: "We've got our revenge. We've taken their wives from them," and they rode down from Mount Burkhan Khaldun back to their homes. . . .

Having finished his prayer Temujin rose and rode off with Khasar and Belgutei. They rode to [his father's sworn brother] Toghoril Ong Khan of the Kereyid camped in the Black Forest on the Tula River. Temujin spoke to Ong Khan, saying: "I was attacked by surprise by the three Merkid chiefs. They've stolen

my wife from me. We've come to you now to say, 'Let my father the Khan save my wife and return her.'" . . .

[Temujin and his allies] moved their forces from Botoghan Bogorjin to the Kilgho River where they built rafts to cross over to the Bugura Steppe, into [the Merkid] Chief Toghtoga's land. They came down on him as if through the smoke-hole of his tent, beating down the frame of his tent and leaving it flat, capturing and killing his wives and his sons. They struck at his door-frame where his guardian spirit lived and broke it to pieces. They completely destroyed all his people until in their place there was nothing but emptiness. . . .

As the Merkid people tried to flee from our army running down the Selenge with what they could gather in the darkness, as our soldiers rode out of the night capturing and killing the Merkid, Temujin rode through the retreating camp shouting out: "Borte! Borte!"

Lady Borte was among the Merkid who ran in the darkness and when she heard his voice, when she recognized Temujin's voice, Borte leaped from her cart. Lady Borte and Old Woman Khogaghchin saw Temujin charge through the crowd and they ran to him, finally seizing the reins of his horse. All about them was moonlight. As Temujin looked down to see who had stopped him he recognized Lady Borte. In a moment he was down from his horse and they were in each other's arms, embracing. . . .

Questions for Analysis

1. What do you learn from these stories about the Mongol way of life?

2. "Marriage by capture" has been practiced in many parts of the world. Can you infer from these stories why such a system would persist? What was the impact of such practices on kinship relations?

3. Can you recognize traces of the oral origins of these stories?

Source: Paul Kahn, trans., *The Secret History of the Mongols: The Origin of Chinghis Khan,* © Paul Kahn (Boston: Cheng & Tsui Company, 1998) Permission granted by Cheng & Tsui Company.

City Life. A well-developed system of river and canal transport kept the Song capital well supplied with goods from across China. *(The Palace Museum, Beijing)*

12 EAST ASIA, CA. 800–1400

Chapter Preview

The Medieval Chinese Economic Revolution (800–1100)
• What allowed China to become a world leader economically and intellectually in this period?

China During the Song Dynasty (960–1279)
• How did the civil service examinations and the scholar-official class shape Chinese society and culture?

Japan's Heian Period (794–1185)
• How did the Heian form of government contribute to the cultural flowering of the period?

The Samurai and the Kamakura Shogunate (1185–1333)
• What were the causes and consequences of military rule in Japan?

D uring the six centuries between 800 and 1400, East Asia was the most advanced region of the world. For several centuries the Chinese economy had grown spectacularly, and in fields as diverse as rice cultivation, the production of iron and steel, and the printing of books, China's methods of production were highly advanced. Its system of government was also advanced for its time. In the Song period the principle that the government should be in the hands of highly educated scholar-officials, selected through competitive written civil service examinations, became well established.

During the previous millennium basic elements of Chinese culture had spread beyond China's borders, creating a large cultural sphere centered on the use of Chinese as the language of civilization. Beginning around 800, however, the pendulum shifted toward cultural differentiation in East Asia, as Japan, Korea, and Vietnam developed in distinctive ways. This is particularly evident in the case of Japan, which in the samurai developed a military elite that was radically different from the Chinese scholar-official class.

THE MEDIEVAL CHINESE ECONOMIC REVOLUTION (800–1100)

What allowed China to become a world leader economically and intellectually in this period?

Chinese historians traditionally viewed dynasties as following a standard pattern. Founders were vigorous men able to recruit able followers to serve as officials and generals. Externally they would extend China's borders; internally they would bring peace. They would collect low but fairly assessed taxes. Over time, however, emperors born in the palace would get used to luxury and lack the founders' strength and wisdom. Entrenched interests would find ways to avoid taxes, forcing the government to impose heavier taxes on the poor. Impoverished peasants would flee; the morale of those in the government and armies would decline; and the dynasty would find itself able neither to maintain internal peace nor to defend its borders.

Viewed in terms of this theory of the **dynastic cycle,** by 800 the Tang Dynasty was in decline. It had ruled China for nearly two centuries, and its high point was in the past. A massive rebellion had wracked it in the mid-eighth century, and the Uighur Turks and Tibetans were menacing its borders. Many of the centralizing features of the government had been abandoned, with power falling more and more to regional military governors.

Chinese political theorists always made the assumption that a strong, centralized government was better than a weak one or political division, but if anything the late Tang period seems to have been both intellectually and economically more vibrant than the early Tang. Less control from the central government seems to have stimulated trade and economic growth.

In 742 China's population was still approximately 50 million, very close to what it had been in 2 C.E. Over the next three centuries, with the expansion of rice cultivation in central and south China, the country's food supply steadily increased, and so did its population, which reached 100 million by 1100. China was certainly the largest country in the world at the time; its population probably exceeded that of all of Europe (as it has ever since).

Agricultural prosperity and denser settlement patterns aided commercialization of the economy. Peasants in Song China did not aim at self-sufficiency. They had found that producing for the market made possible a better life. Peasants sold their surpluses and bought charcoal, tea, oil, and wine. In many places, farmers specialized in commercial crops, such as sugar, oranges, cotton, silk, and tea. (See the feature "Global Trade: Tea" on pages 330–331.) The need to transport the products of inter-regional trade stimulated the inland and coastal shipping industries, providing employment for shipbuilders and sailors and business opportunities for enterprising families with enough capital to purchase a boat. Marco Polo, the Venetian merchant who wrote of his visit to China in the late thirteenth century, was astounded at the boat traffic on the Yangzi River. He claimed to have seen no fewer than fifteen thousand vessels at one city on the river, "and yet there are other towns where the number is still greater."[1]

As marketing increased, demand for money grew enormously, leading eventually to the creation of the world's first **paper money.** The late Tang government's decision to abandon the use of bolts of silk as supplementary currency had increased the demand for copper coins. By 1085 the output of coins had increased tenfold to more than 6 billion coins a year. To avoid the weight and bulk of coins for large transactions, local merchants in late Tang times started trading receipts from deposit shops where they had left money or goods. The early Song authorities awarded a small set of shops a monopoly on the issuing of these certificates of deposit, and in the 1120s the government took over the system, producing the world's first government-issued paper money. Marco Polo was amazed:

The coinage of this paper money is authenticated with as much form and ceremony as if it were actually of pure gold or silver; for to each note a number of officers, specially appointed, not only subscribe their names, but affix their signets also; and when this

dynastic cycle *The theory that Chinese dynasties go through a predictable cycle, from early vigor and growth to subsequent decline as administrators become lax and the well-off find ways to avoid paying taxes, cutting state revenues.*

Primary Source:
The Craft of Farming
Look inside a twelfth-century Chinese treatise on farming, with advice on when to plow, which crops to plant, and how to use compost as fertilizer.

paper money *Legal currency issued on paper; it developed in China as a convenient alternative to metal coins.*

● **Chinese Paper Money** Chinese paper currency indicated the unit of currency and the date and place of issue. The Mongols continued the use of paper money; this note dates from the Mongol period. *(DNP Archives)*

has been regularly done by the whole of them, the principal officer . . . having dipped into vermilion the royal seal committed to his custody, stamps with it the piece of paper, so that the form of the seal tinged with the vermilion remains impressed upon it.[2]

With the intensification of trade, merchants became progressively more specialized and organized. They set up partnerships and joint stock companies, with a separation of owners (shareholders) and managers. In the large cities merchants were organized into guilds according to the type of product sold, and they arranged sales from wholesalers to shop owners and periodically set prices. When government officials wanted to requisition supplies or assess taxes, they dealt with the guild heads.

Foreign trade also flourished in the Song period. In 1225 the superintendent of customs at the coastal city of Quanzhou wrote an account of the foreign places Chinese merchants visited. It includes sketches of major trading cities from Srivijaya to Malabar, Cairo, and Baghdad. Pearls were said to come from the Persian Gulf, ivory from Aden, pepper from Java and Sumatra, and cotton from the various kingdoms of India. In this period Chinese ships began to displace Indian and Arab merchants in the South Seas. Ship design was improved in several ways. Watertight bulkheads improved buoyancy and protected cargo. Stern-mounted rudders improved steering. Some of the ships were powered by both oars and sails and were large enough to hold several hundred men.

Also important to oceangoing travel was the perfection of the **compass**. The way a magnetic needle would point north had been known for some time, but in Song times the needle was reduced in size and attached to a fixed stem (rather than floated in water). In some cases it was put in a small protective case with a glass top, making it suitable for sea travel. The first reports of a compass used in this way date to 1119.

Chronology

794–1185	Heian period in Japan
804	Two Japanese Buddhist monks, Saichō and Kūkai, travel to China
960–1279	Song Dynasty in China; emergence of scholar-official class; invention of movable type
995–1027	Fujiwara Michinaga is dominant at Heian court
ca. 1010	*The Tale of Gengi,* world's first novel
1069	Wang Anshi introduces sweeping political and economic reforms
1100–1400	Zen Buddhism flourishes in Japan
1119	First reported use of compass
1120s	First government-issued paper money introduced by Song
1126	Loss of north China to the Jurchens; capital relocated to Hangzhou
1130–1200	Zhu Xi, Neo-Confucian philosopher
1185–1333	Kamakura Shogunate in Japan
ca. 1275–1292	Marco Polo travels in China

The Song also witnessed many advances in industrial techniques. Heavy industry, especially iron, grew astoundingly. With advances in metallurgy, iron production reached around 125,000 tons per year in 1078, a sixfold increase over the output in 800. At first charcoal was used in the production process, leading to deforestation of parts of north China. By the end of the eleventh century, however, bituminous coke had largely taken the place of charcoal. Much of this iron was put to military purposes. Mass-production methods were used to make iron armor in small, medium, and large sizes. High-quality steel for swords was made through high-temperature metallurgy. Huge bellows, often driven by water wheels, were used to superheat the molten ore. The needs of the army also brought Chinese engineers to experiment with the use of gunpowder. In the wars against the Jurchens, those defending a besieged city used gunpowder to propel projectiles at the enemy.

The quickening of the economy fueled the growth of cities. Dozens of cities had fifty thousand or more residents, and quite a few had more than a hundred thousand. Both the capitals, Kaifeng and Hangzhou, are estimated to have had in the vicinity of

compass *A tool developed in Song times to aid in navigation at sea; it consisted of a magnetic needle that would point north in a small protective case.*

TEA

Tea is made from the young leaves and leaf buds of *Camellia sinensis,* a plant native to the hills of southwest China. As an item of trade, tea has a very long history. Already by Han times (206 B.C.E.–220 C.E.), tea was being grown and drunk in southwest China, and for several centuries thereafter it was looked on as a local product of the region with useful pharmacologic properties, such as countering the effects of wine. By Tang times (608–907) it was being widely cultivated in the Yangzi River valley and was a major item of interregional trade. Tea was common enough in Tang life that poets often mentioned it in their poems. In the eighth century Lu Yu wrote an entire treatise on the wonders of tea.

During the Tang Dynasty tea was a major commercial crop, especially in the southeast. The most intensive time for tea production was the harvest season, since young leaves were of much more value than mature ones. Mobilized for about a month each year, women would come out to help pick the tea. Not only were tea merchants among the wealthiest merchants, but from the late eighth century on, taxes on tea became a major source of government revenue.

Tea circulated in several forms, loose and compressed (brick), powder and leaf. The cost of tea varied both by form and by region of origin. In Song times (960–1279), the cheapest tea could cost as little as 18 cash per catty, the most expensive 275. In Kaifeng in the 1070s the most popular type was loose tea

The Tea Trade

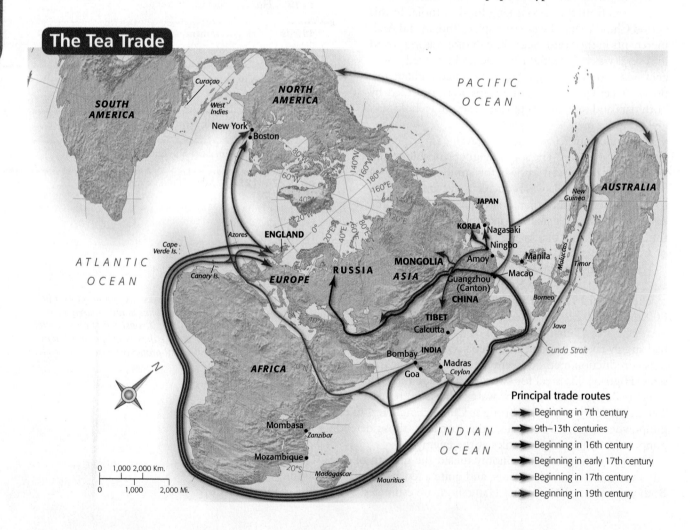

Principal trade routes
- Beginning in 7th century
- 9th–13th centuries
- Beginning in 16th century
- Beginning in early 17th century
- Beginning in 17th century
- Beginning in 19th century

Tea-leaf jar, fourteenth century, south China. This 42-centimeter-tall jar (about 16½ inches) was imported to Japan, where it was treasured as an art object and used by tea masters. In the sixteenth century it came into the possession of the first Tokugawa shogun, Ieyasu. (Tokugawa Art Museum, Nagoya)

powdered at water mills. The tea exported from Sichuan to Tibet, however, was formed into solid bricks.

The Song Dynasty established a government monopoly on tea. Only those who purchased government licenses could legally trade in tea. The dynasty also used its control of tea to ensure a supply of horses, needed for military purposes. The government could do this because the countries on its borders that produced the best horses—Tibet, Central Asia, Mongolia, and so on—were not suitable for growing tea. Thus the Song government insisted on horses for tea.

Tea reached Korea and Japan as a part of Buddhist culture. Buddhist monks drank it to help them stay awake during long hours of recitation or meditation. The priest Saichō, patriarch of Tendai Buddhism, visited China in 804–805 and reportedly brought back tea seeds. Tea drinking did not become widespread in Japan, however, until the twelfth century, when Zen monasteries popularized its use. By the fourteenth century tea imported from China was still prized, but the Japanese had already begun to appreciate the distinctive flavors of teas from different regions of Japan. With the development of the tea ceremony, tea drinking became an art in Japan, with much attention to the selection and handling of tea utensils. In both Japan and Korea, offerings of tea became a regular part of offerings to ancestors.

Tea did not become important in Europe until the seventeenth century. Tea first reached Russia in 1618, when a Chinese embassy presented some to the tsar. Under agreements between the Chinese and Russian governments, camel trains would arrive in China laden with furs and would return carrying tea, taking about a year for the round trip.

By 1700 Russia was receiving more than 600 camel loads of tea annually. By 1800 it was receiving more than 6,000 loads, amounting to more than 3.5 million pounds. Tea reached western Europe in the sixteenth century, both via Arabs and via Jesuit priests traveling on Portuguese ships.

In Britain, where tea drinking would become a national institution, tea was first drunk in coffeehouses. In his famous diary Samuel Pepys recorded having his first cup of tea in 1660. By the end of the seventeenth century tea made up more than 90 percent of China's exports to England. In the eighteenth century tea drinking spread to homes and tea gardens. Queen Anne (r. 1702–1714) was credited with starting the custom of drinking tea instead of ale for breakfast. In the nineteenth century afternoon tea became a central feature of British social life.

Already by the end of the eighteenth century Britain imported so much tea from China that it worried about the outflow of silver to pay for it. Efforts to balance trade with China involved promoting the sale of Indian opium to China and efforts to grow tea in British colonies. Using tea seeds collected in China and a tea plant indigenous to India's Assam province, both India and Sri Lanka eventually grew tea successfully. By the end of the nineteenth century huge tea plantations had been established in India, and India surpassed China as an exporter of tea.

The spread of the popularity of drinking tea also stimulated the desire for fine cups to drink it from. Importation of Chinese ceramics, therefore, often accompanied adoption of China's tea customs.

331

**Primary Source:
A Description of
Foreign Peoples**
*Discover the rich commodities
and exotic customs of Arabia
and southern Spain, as seen by a
thirteenth-century Chinese trade
official.*

a million residents. Marco Polo described Hangzhou as the finest and most splendid city in the world. He reported that it had ten marketplaces, each half a mile long, where forty thousand to fifty thousand people would go to shop on any given day. There were also bathhouses; permanent shops selling things such as spices, drugs, and pearls; and innumerable courtesans—"adorned in much finery, highly perfumed, occupying well-furnished houses, and attended by many female domestics."[3]

The medieval economic revolution shifted the economic center of China south to the Yangzi River drainage area. This area had many advantages over the north China plain. Rice, which grew in the south, provides more calories per unit of land and therefore allows denser settlement. The milder temperatures often allowed two crops to be grown on the same plot of land, a summer and then a winter crop. The abundance of rivers and streams facilitated shipping, which reduced the cost of transportation and thus made regional specialization economically more feasible. In the first half of the Song Dynasty, the capital was still in the north, but on the Grand Canal, which linked it to the rich south.

The economic revolution of Song times cannot be attributed to intellectual change, as Confucian scholars did not reinterpret the classics to defend the morality of commerce. But neither did scholar-officials take a unified stand against economic development. As officials they had to work to produce revenue to cover government expenses such as defense, and this was much easier to do when commerce was thriving.

Ordinary people benefited from the Song economic revolution in many ways. There were more opportunities for the sons of farmers to leave agriculture and find work in cities. Those who stayed in agriculture had a better chance to improve their situations by taking up sideline production of wine, charcoal, paper, or textiles. Energetic farmers who grew cash crops such as sugar, tea, mulberry leaves (for silk), and cotton (recently introduced from India) could grow rich. Greater interregional trade led to the availability of more goods at the rural markets held every five or ten days.

Of course, not everyone grew rich. Poor farmers who fell into debt had to sell their

● **City Life** In Song times many cities in China grew to fifty thousand or more people, and the capital, Kaifeng, reached over a million. The bustle of a commercial city is shown here in a detail from a 17-foot-long handscroll painted in the twelfth century. *(The Palace Museum, Beijing)*

● **Transplanting Rice** To get the maximum yield per plot and to make it possible to grow two crops in the same field, Chinese farmers grew rice seedlings in a seed bed and then, when a field was free, transplanted the seedlings into the flooded field. Because the Song government wanted to promote up-to-date agricultural technology, in the twelfth century it commissioned a set of twelve illustrations of the steps to be followed. This painting comes from a later version of those illustrations. *(Courtesy of the Freer Gallery of Art, Smithsonian Institution, Washington, D.C. [54.21])*

land, and if they still owed money, they could be forced to sell their daughters as maids, concubines, or prostitutes. The prosperity of the cities created a huge demand for women to serve the rich in these ways, and Song sources mention that criminals would kidnap girls and women to sell in distant cities at huge profits.

CHINA DURING THE SONG DYNASTY (960–1279)

How did the civil service examinations and the scholar-official class shape Chinese society and culture?

In the tenth century Tang China broke up into separate contending states, some of which had non-Chinese rulers. The two states that proved to be long lasting were the Song, which came to control almost all of China proper south of the Great Wall, and the Liao, whose ruling house was Khitan and who held the territory of modern Beijing and areas north (see Map 12.1). Although the Song Dynasty had a much larger population, the Liao was militarily the stronger of the two.

The founder of the Song Dynasty, Taizu (r. 960–976), was a general whose troops elevated him to emperor (somewhat reminiscent of Roman practice). Taizu worked to make sure that such an act could not happen in the future by placing the armies under central government control. He retired or rotated his own generals and assigned civil officials to supervise them. In time civil bureaucrats came to dominate every aspect of Song government and society. The civil service examination system was greatly expanded to provide the dynasty with a constant flow of men trained in the Confucian classics.

Curbing the generals ended warlordism but did not solve the military problem of defending against the Khitans to the north. After several attempts to push them back beyond the Great Wall, the Song concluded a peace treaty with them. The Song agreed to make huge annual payments of gold and silk to the Khitans, in a sense paying them

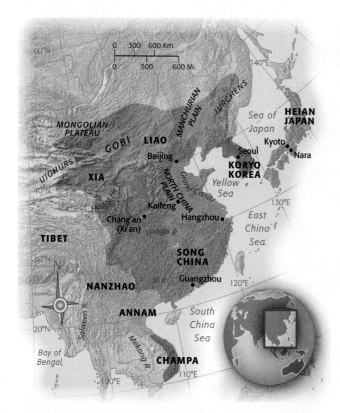

MAP 12.1 **East Asia in 1000** The Song Empire did not extend as far as its predecessor, the Tang, and faced powerful rivals to the north—the Liao Dynasty of the Khitans and the Xia Dynasty of the Tanguts. Korea under the Koryo Dynasty maintained regular contact with Song China, but Japan, by the late Heian period, was no longer deeply involved with the mainland.

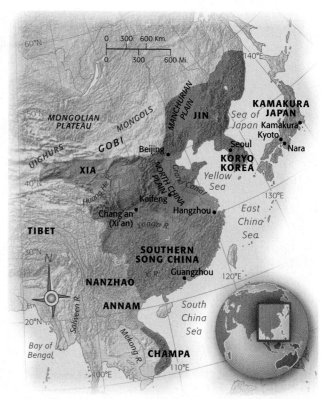

MAP 12.2 **East Asia in 1200** By 1200 military families dominated both Korea and Japan, but their borders were little changed. On the mainland, the Liao Dynasty had been overthrown by the Jurchens' Jin Dynasty, which also seized the northern third of the Song Empire. Because the Song relocated its capital to Hangzhou in the south, this period is called the Southern Song period.

not to invade. Even so, the Song rulers had to maintain a standing army of more than a million men. By the middle of the eleventh century military expenses consumed half the government's revenues. Song had the industrial base to produce swords, armor, and arrowheads in huge quantities, but had difficulty maintaining enough horses and well-trained horsemen. Even though China was the economic powerhouse of the region with by far the largest population, in this period, when the horse was a major weapon of war, it was not easy to convert wealth to military advantage.

In the early twelfth century the military situation rapidly worsened when the Khitan state was destroyed by another tribal confederation led by the Jurchens. Although the Song allied with the Jurchens, the Jurchens quickly realized how easy it would be to defeat the Song. When they marched into the Song capital in 1126, they captured the emperor and took him and his entire court hostage. Song forces rallied around a prince who reestablished a Song court in the south at Hangzhou (see Map 12.2). This Southern Song Dynasty controlled only about two-thirds of the former Song territories, but the social, cultural, and intellectual life there remained vibrant until the Song fell to the Mongols in 1279.

The Scholar-Officials and Neo-Confucianism

The Song period saw the full flowering of one of the most distinctive features of Chinese civilization, the scholar-official class certified through highly competitive civil service examinations. This elite was both broader and better educated than the elites of earlier periods in Chinese history. Once the **examination system** was fully developed, aristocratic habits and prejudices largely disappeared.

The invention of printing should be given some credit for this development. Tang craftsmen developed the art of carving words and pictures into wooden blocks, inking the blocks, and then pressing paper onto them. Each block held an entire page of text and illustrations. Such whole-page blocks were used for printing as early as the middle of the ninth century, and in the eleventh century **movable type** (one piece of type for each character) was invented. Movable type was never widely used in China because whole-block printing was cheaper. In China as in Europe, the introduction of printing dramatically lowered the price of books, thus aiding the spread of literacy.

Among the upper class the availability of cheaper books enabled scholars to amass their own libraries. Song publishers printed the classics of Chinese literature in huge editions to satisfy scholarly appetites. Works on philosophy, science, and medicine also were avidly consumed, as were Buddhist texts. Han and Tang poetry and historical works became the models for Song writers. One popular literary innovation was the encyclopedia, which first appeared in the Song period, at least five centuries before publication of a European encyclopedia.

The examination system came to carry such prestige that the number of scholars entering each competition escalated rapidly, from fewer than 30,000 early in the eleventh century, to nearly 80,000 by the end of that century, to about 400,000 by the dynasty's end. To prepare for the examinations, men had to memorize the classics in order to be able to recognize even the most obscure passages. They also had to master specific forms of composition, including poetry, and be ready to discuss policy issues, citing appropriate historical examples. Those who became officials this way had usually tried the exams several times and were on average a little over thirty years of age when they succeeded. The great majority of those who devoted years to preparing for the exams, however, never became officials.

The life of the educated man involved more than study for the civil service examinations. Many took to refined pursuits such as collecting antiques or old books and

examination system   *A system of selecting officials based on competitive written examinations.*

movable type   *A system of printing in which one piece of type was used for each unique character.*

● **On a Mountain Path in Spring**   With spare, sketchy strokes, the court painter Ma Yuan (ca. 1190–1225) depicts a scholar on an outing accompanied by his boy servant carrying a lute. The scholar gazes into the mist, his eyes attracted by a bird in flight. The poetic couplet was inscribed by Emperor Ningzong (r. 1194–1124), at whose court Ma Yuan served. *(National Palace Museum, Taipei, Taiwan)*

practicing the arts—especially poetry writing, calligraphy, and painting. For many individuals these cultural interests overshadowed any philosophical, political, or economic concerns; others found in them occasional outlets for creative activity and aesthetic pleasure. In the Song period the engagement of the elite with the arts led to extraordinary achievement in calligraphy and painting, especially landscape painting. A large share of the informal social life of upper-class men was centered on these refined pastimes, as they gathered to compose or criticize poetry, to view each other's treasures, and to patronize young talents.

The new scholar-official elite produced some extraordinary men, able to hold high court offices while pursuing diverse intellectual interests. (See the feature "Individuals in Society: Shen Gua.") Ouyang Xiu spared time in his busy official career to write love songs, histories, and the first analytical catalogue of rubbings of ancient stone and bronze inscriptions. Sima Guang, besides serving as prime minister, wrote a narrative history of China from the Warring States Period (403–221 B.C.E.) to the founding of the Song Dynasty. Su Shi wrote more than twenty-seven hundred poems and eight hundred letters while active in opposition politics. He was also an esteemed painter, calligrapher, and theorist of the arts. Su Song, another high official, constructed an eighty-foot-tall mechanical clock. He adapted the water-powered clock invented in the Tang period by adding a chain-driven mechanism. The clock told not only the time of day but also the day of the month, the phase of the moon, and the position of certain stars and planets in the sky. At the top was a mechanically rotated armillary sphere.

These highly educated men accepted the Confucian responsibility to aid the ruler in the governing of the country. In this period, however, this commitment tended to embroil them in unpleasant factional politics. In 1069 the chancellor Wang Anshi proposed a series of sweeping reforms designed to raise revenues and help small farmers. Many well-respected scholars and officials thought that Wang's policies would do more harm than good and resisted enforcing them. Animosities grew as critics were assigned far from the capital. Those sent away later got the chance to retaliate, escalating the conflict.

Besides politics, scholars also debated issues in ethics and metaphysics. For several centuries Buddhism had been more vital than Confucianism. Beginning in the late Tang period Confucian teachers began claiming that the teachings of the Confucian sages contained all the wisdom one needed and a true Confucian would reject Buddhist teachings. During the eleventh century many Confucian teachers gathered around them students whom they urged to set their sights not on exam success but on the higher goals of attaining the wisdom of the sages. Metaphysical theories about the workings of the cosmos in terms of *li* (principle) and *qi* (vital energy) were developed in response to the challenge of the sophisticated metaphysics of Buddhism.

Neo-Confucianism *The revival of Confucian thinking that began in the eleventh century.*

Neo-Confucianism, as this movement is generally termed, was more fully developed in the twelfth century by the immensely learned Zhu Xi (1130–1200). Besides serving in office, he wrote, compiled, or edited almost a hundred books; corresponded with dozens of other scholars; and still regularly taught groups of disciples, many of whom stayed with him for years at a time. Although he was treated as a political threat during his lifetime, within decades of his death his writings came to be considered orthodox, and in subsequent centuries candidates for the examinations had to be familiar with his commentaries on the classics.

Women's Lives

With the spread of printing, more books and more types of books survive from the Song period than from earlier periods, letting us catch more glimpses of women's lives. Song stories, documents, and legal cases show us widows who ran inns, maids sent out by their mistresses to do errands, midwives who delivered babies, pious women who spent their days chanting Buddhist sutras, nuns who called on such

Shen Gua

In the eleventh century it was not rare for Chinese men of letters to have broad interests, but few could compare to Shen Gua (1031–1095), a man who tried his hand at everything from mathematics, geography, economics, engineering, medicine, divination, and archaeology to military strategy and diplomacy.

In his youth Shen Gua traveled widely with his father, who served as a provincial official. His own career as an official, which started when he was only twenty, also took him to many places, adding to his knowledge of geography. He received a post in the capital in 1066, just before Wang Anshi's rise to power, and he generally sided with Wang in the political disputes of the day. He eventually held high astronomical, ritual, and financial posts and became involved in waterworks and the construction of defense walls. He was sent as an envoy to the Khitans in 1075 to try to settle a boundary dispute. When a military campaign that he advised failed in 1082, he was demoted and later retired to write.

It is from his book of notes that we know the breadth of his interests. In one note Shen describes how, on assignment to inspect the frontier, he made a relief map of wood and glue-soaked sawdust to show the mountains, roads, rivers, and passes. The emperor was so impressed when he saw it that he ordered all the border prefectures to make relief maps. Elsewhere Shen describes the use of petroleum and explains how to make movable type from clay. Shen Gua often applied a mathematical approach to issues that his contemporaries did not think of in those terms. He once computed the total number of possible situations on a go board, and another time he calculated the longest possible military campaign given the limits of human carriers, who had to carry their own food as well as food for the soldiers.

Shen Gua is especially known for what might be called scientific explanations. In one place, he explains the deflection of the compass from due south. In another, he identifies petrified bamboo and from its existence argues that the region where it was found must have been much warmer and more humid in ancient times. He argued against the theory that tides are caused by the rising and setting of the sun, demonstrating that they correlate rather with the cycles of the moon. He proposed switching from a lunar calendar to a solar one of 365 days, saying that even though his contemporaries would reject his idea, "surely in the fu-

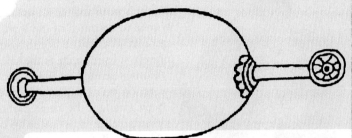

Among the advances of the Song period was the development of gunpowder. An eleventh-century manual on military technology illustrated this "thunderbolt ball," filled with gunpowder and iron scraps and hurled at the enemy with a catapult. (Zeng Gongliang and Ding Du, Wujing zongyao [Zhong-guo bingshu jicheng, 1988 ed.], 12:59, p. 640)

ture some will adopt my idea." To convince his readers that the sun and the moon were spherical, not flat, he suggested that they cover a ball with fine powder on one side and then look at it obliquely. The powder was the part of the moon illuminated by the sun, and as the viewer looked at it obliquely, the white part would be crescent shaped, like a waxing moon. Shen Gua, however, did not realize that the sun and moon had entirely different orbits, and he explained why they did not collide by positing that both were composed of *qi* (vital energy) and had form but not substance.

Shen Gua also wrote on medicine and criticized his contemporaries for paying more attention to old treatises than to clinical experience. Yet he, too, was sometimes stronger on theory than on observation. In one note he argues that longevity pills could be made from cinnabar. He reasoned that if cinnabar could be transformed in one direction, it ought to be susceptible to transformation in the opposite direction as well. Therefore, since melted cinnabar causes death, solid cinnabar should prevent death.

Questions for Analysis

1. Do you think Shen Gua's wide travels added to his curiosity about the material world?

2. In what ways could Shen Gua have used his scientific interests in his work as an official?

3. How does Shen Gua's understanding of the natural world compare to that of the early Greeks?

women to explain Buddhist doctrine, girls who learned to read with their brothers, farmers' daughters who made money by weaving mats, childless widows who accused their nephews of stealing their property, wives who were jealous of the concubines their husbands brought home, and women who used part of their own large dowries to help their husbands' sisters marry well.

Families who could afford it usually tried to keep their wives and daughters at home, where there was plenty for them to do. Not only was there the work of tending children and preparing meals, but spinning, weaving, and sewing also were considered women's work and took a great deal of time. Families that raised silkworms also needed women to do much of the work of coddling the worms and getting them to spin their cocoons. Within the home women generally had considerable say and took an active interest in issues such as the selection of marriage partners for their children.

Women tended to marry between the ages of sixteen and twenty. The husbands were, on average, a couple of years older than they were. The marriage would have been arranged by their parents, who would have either called on a professional matchmaker (most often an older woman) or turned to a friend or relative for suggestions. Before the wedding took place, written agreements would be exchanged, which would list the prospective bride's and groom's birth dates, parents, and grandparents; the gifts that would be exchanged; and the dowry the bride would bring. The goal was to match families of approximately equal status, but a young man who had just passed the civil service exams would be considered a good prospect even if his family had little wealth.

A few days before the wedding the bride's family would send to the groom's family her dowry, which at a minimum would contain boxes full of clothes and bedding. In better-off families, the dowry also would include items of substantial value, such as gold jewelry or deeds to land. On the day of the wedding the groom and some of his friends and relatives would go to the bride's home to get her. She would be elaborately dressed and would tearfully bid farewell to everyone in her family. She would be carried to her new home in a fancy sedan chair to the sound of music, alerting everyone on the street that a wedding was taking place. Meanwhile the groom's family's friends and relatives would have gathered at his home, and when the bridal party arrived, they would be there to greet them. The bride would have to kneel and bow to her new parents-in-law and later also to the tablets representing her husband's ancestors. A classical ritual still practiced was for the new couple to drink wine from the same cup. A ritual that had become popular in Song times was to attach a string to both of them, literally tying them together. Later they would be shown to their new bedroom, where the bride's dowry had already been placed, and people would toss beans or rice on the bed, symbolizing the desired fertility. After teasing them, the guests would leave them alone and go out to the courtyard for a wedding feast.

The young bride's first priority was to try to win over her mother-in-law, since everyone knew that mothers-in-law were hard to please. One way to do this was to quickly bear a son for the family. Within the patrilineal system, a woman fully secured her position in the family by becoming the mother of one of the men. Every community had older women skilled in midwifery who could be called to help when a woman went into labor. If the family was well-to-do, arrangements might be made for a wet nurse to help her take care of the newborn.

Women frequently had four, five, or six children, but likely one or more would die in infancy. If a son reached adulthood and married before the woman herself was widowed, she would be considered fortunate, for she would have always had an adult man who could take care of business for her—first her husband, then her grown son. But in the days when infectious diseases took many

● **Woman Attendant** The Song emperors were patrons of a still-extant temple in northern China that enshrined a statue of the "holy mother," the mother of the founder of the ancient Zhou Dynasty. The forty-two maids who attend her, one of whom is shown here, seem to have been modeled on the palace ladies who attended Song emperors. *(© Cultural Relics Press)*

people in their twenties and thirties, it was not uncommon for a woman to be widowed while in her twenties, when her children were still very young.

A woman with a healthy and prosperous husband faced another challenge in middle age: her husband could bring home a **concubine** (more than one if he could afford it). Moralists insisted that it was wrong for a wife to be jealous of her husband's concubines, but everyone agreed that jealousy was very common. Wives outranked concubines and could give them orders in the house, but a concubine had her own ways of getting back through her hold on the husband. The children born to a concubine were considered just as much children of the family as the wife's children, and if the wife had had only daughters and the concubine had a son, the wife would find herself dependent on the concubine's son in her old age.

As a woman's children grew up, she would start thinking of suitable marriage partners. Many women liked the idea of bringing a woman from her natal family—perhaps her brother's daughter—to be her daughter-in-law. No matter who was selected, her life became easier once she had a daughter-in-law to do the cooking and cleaning. Many found more time for religious devotions at this stage of their lives. Their sons, still living with them, could be expected to look after them and do their best to make their late years comfortable.

Neo-Confucianism is sometimes blamed for a decline in the status of women in Song times, largely because one of the best known of the Neo-Confucian teachers, Cheng Yi, once told a follower that it would be better for a widow to die of starvation than to lose her virtue by remarrying. In later centuries this saying was often quoted to justify pressuring widows, even very young ones, to stay with their husbands' families and not remarry. In Song times, however, widows frequently remarried.

It is true that **foot binding** began during the Song Dynasty, but it was not recommended by Neo-Confucian teachers; rather it was associated with the pleasure quarters and with women's efforts to beautify themselves. Mothers bound the feet of girls aged five to eight with long strips of cloth to keep them from growing and to bend the four smaller toes under to make the foot narrow and arched. The hope was that the girl would be judged more beautiful. Foot binding spread gradually during Song times but was probably still largely an elite practice. In later centuries it became extremely common in north and central China, eventually spreading to all classes. Women with bound feet were less mobile than women with natural feet, but only those who could afford servants bound their feet so tightly that walking was difficult.

concubine   *A woman contracted to a man as a secondary spouse; although subordinate to the wife, her sons were considered legitimate heirs.*

foot binding   *The practice of binding the feet of girls with long strips of cloth to keep them from growing large.*

JAPAN'S HEIAN PERIOD (794–1185)

How did the Heian form of government contribute to the cultural flowering of the period?

As discussed in Chapter 6, during the seventh and eighth centuries the Japanese ruling house pursued a vigorous policy of adopting useful ideas, techniques, and policies from the more advanced civilization of China. The rulers built a splendid capital along Chinese lines in Nara and fostered the growth of Buddhism. Monasteries grew so powerful in Nara, however, that in less than a century the court decided to move away from them and encourage other sects of Buddhism.

The new capital was built not far away at Heian (modern Kyoto). Heian was, like Nara, modeled on the Tang capital of Chang'an (although neither of the Japanese capitals had walls, a major feature of Chinese cities), and for the first century at Heian the government continued to follow Chinese models. With the decline of the Tang Dynasty in the late ninth century, the Japanese turned away from dependence on Chinese models. The last official embassy to China made the trip in 894.

Fujiwara Rule

Only the first two Heian emperors were activists. Thereafter political management was taken over by a series of regents from the Fujiwara family, who supplied most of the empresses in this period. The emperors continued to be honored, even venerated, because of their presumed divine descent, but it was the Fujiwaras who ruled. Fujiwara dominance represented the privatization of political power and a reversion to clan politics. Political history thus took a very different course in Japan than in China, where political contenders sought the throne and successful contenders deposed the old emperor and founded new dynasties. In Japan for the next thousand years, political contenders sought to manipulate the emperors rather than supplant them.

The Fujiwaras reached the apogee of their glory under Fujiwara Michinaga (966–1027). Like many aristocrats of the period, he was learned in Buddhism, music, poetry, and Chinese literature and history. He dominated the court for more than thirty years as the father of four empresses, the uncle of two emperors, and the grandfather of three emperors. He acquired great landholdings and built fine palaces for himself and his family. After ensuring that his sons could continue to rule, he retired to a Buddhist monastery, all the while continuing to maintain control himself.

By the end of the eleventh century several emperors who did not have Fujiwara mothers found a device to counter Fujiwara control: they abdicated but continued to exercise power by controlling their young sons on the throne. This system of rule has been called **cloistered government** because the retired emperors took Buddhist orders. Thus for a time the imperial house was a contender for political power along with other aristocratic groups.

cloistered government
A system in which an emperor retired to a Buddhist monastery, but continued to exercise power by controlling his young son on the throne.

Aristocratic Culture

A brilliant aristocratic culture developed in the Heian period. It was strongly focused on the capital, where nobles, palace ladies, and imperial family members lived a highly refined and leisured life. Their society was one in which niceties of birth, rank, and breeding counted for everything. From their diaries we know of the pains aristocratic women took in selecting the color combinations of the kimonos they wore, layer upon layer. Even among men, knowing how to dress tastefully was more important than skill with a horse or sword. The elegance of one's calligraphy and the allusions in one's poems were matters of intense concern to both men and women at court. Courtiers did not like to leave the capital, and some like the court lady Sei Shonagon shuddered at the sight of ordinary working people. In her *Pillow Book*, she wrote of encountering a group of commoners on a pilgrimage: "They looked like so many basket-worms as they crowded together in their hideous clothes, leaving hardly an inch of space between themselves and me. I really felt like pushing them all over sideways."[4] (See the feature "Listening to the Past: *The Pillow Book* of Sei Shonagon" on pages 348–349.)

In this period a new script was developed for writing Japanese phonetically. Each symbol, based on a simplified Chinese character, represented one of the syllables used in Japanese (such as *ka, ki, ku, ke, ko*). Although "serious" essays, histories, and government documents continued to be written in Chinese, less formal works such as poetry and memoirs were written in Japanese. Mastering the new writing system took much less time than mastering writing in Chinese and aided the spread of literacy, especially among women in court society.

In Heian, women played important roles at all levels of society. Women educated in the arts and letters could advance at court as attendants to the rulers' consorts. Women could inherit property from their parents, and they would compete with their brothers for shares of the family property. In political life, marrying a daughter to an emperor or shogun was one of the best ways to gain power, and women often became major players in power struggles.

The literary masterpiece of this period is *The Tale of Genji,* written in Japanese by Lady Murasaki over several years (ca. 1000–1010). This long narrative depicts a cast of characters enmeshed in court life, with close attention to dialogue and personality. Murasaki also wrote a diary that is similarly revealing of aristocratic culture. In one passage she tells of an occasion when word got out that she had read the Chinese classics:

Worried what people would think if they heard such rumors, I pretended to be unable to read even the inscriptions on the screens. Then Her Majesty asked me to read to her here and there from the collected works of [the Tang Chinese poet] Bo Juyi, and, because she evinced a desire to know much more about such things, we carefully chose a time when other women would not be present and, amateur that I was, I read with her the two books of Bo Juyi's New Ballads *in secret; we started the summer before last.*[5]

Despite the reluctance of Murasaki and the lady she served to let others know of their learning, there were, in fact, quite a few women writers in this period. The wife of a high-ranking court official wrote a poetic memoir of her unhappy twenty-year marriage to him and his rare visits. One woman wrote both an autobiography that related her father's efforts to find favor at court and a love story of a hero who travels to China. Another woman even wrote a history that concludes with a triumphal biography of Fujiwara Michinaga.

Buddhism remained very strong throughout the Heian period. A mission sent to China in 804 included two monks in search of new texts. Saichō spent time at Mount Tiantai and brought back Tendai teachings. Tendai's basic message is that all living beings share the Buddha nature and can be brought to salvation. Tendai practices include strict monastic discipline, prayer, textual study, and meditation. Once back in Japan, Saichō established a monastery on Mount Hiei, outside Kyoto, which grew to be one of the most important monasteries in Japan. By the twelfth century this monastery and its many branch temples had vast lands and a powerful army of monk-soldiers to protect its interests. Whenever the monastery felt that its interests were at risk, it sent the monk-soldiers into the capital to parade its sacred symbols in an attempt to intimidate the civil authorities.

Kūkai, the other monk on the 804 mission to China, came back with texts from another school of Buddhism—Shingon, "True Word," a form of **Esoteric Buddhism.** Esoteric Buddhism is based on the idea that teachings containing the secrets of enlightenment had been secretly transmitted from the Buddha. An adept can gain access to these mysteries through initiation into the mandalas (cosmic diagrams), mudras (gestures), and mantras (verbal formulas). On his return to Japan, Kūkai attracted many followers and was allowed to establish a monastery at Mount Kōya, south of Osaka. The popularity of Esoteric Buddhism proved a great stimulus to art.

The Tale of Genji *A Japanese literary masterpiece written by Lady Murasaki about court life.*

Esoteric Buddhism *A sect of Buddhism that maintains that the secrets of enlightenment have been secretly transmitted from the Buddha and can be accessed through initiation into the mandalas, mudras, and mantras.*

THE SAMURAI AND THE KAMAKURA SHOGUNATE (1185–1333)

What were the causes and consequences of military rule in Japan?

The rise of a warrior elite finally brought an end to the domination of the Fujiwaras and other Heian aristocratic families. In 1156 civil war broke out between the Taira and Minamoto clans, warrior clans with bases in western and eastern Japan, respectively. Both clans relied on skilled warriors, later called samurai, who were rapidly becoming a new social class. A samurai and his lord had a double bond: in return for the samurai's loyalty and service, the lord granted him land or income. From 1159 to 1181 a Taira named Kiyomori dominated the court, taking the position of prime minister and marrying his daughter to the emperor. His relatives became governors of more than thirty provinces, managed some five hundred tax-exempt estates, and amassed a fortune in the trade with Song China and Koryŏ Korea. Still, the Minamoto clan managed to defeat them, and the Minamoto leader, Yoritomo, became shogun, or general-in-chief. With him began the Kamakura Shogunate (1185–1333). This period is often referred to as Japan's feudal period because it was dominated by a military class whose members were tied to their superiors by bonds of loyalty and supported by landed estates rather than salaries.

Military Rule

The similarities between military rule in Japan and feudalism in medieval Europe have fascinated scholars, as have the very significant differences. In Europe feudalism emerged out of the fusion of Germanic and Roman social institutions and flowered under the impact of Muslim and Viking invasions. In Japan military rule evolved from a combination of the native warrior tradition and Confucian ethical principles of duty to superiors.

The emergence of the samurai was made possible by the development of private landholding. The government land allotment system, copied from Tang China, began breaking down in the eighth century (much as it did in China). By the ninth century local lords began escaping imperial taxes and control by formally giving (commending) their land to tax-exempt entities such as monasteries, the imperial family, and certain high-ranking officials. The local lord then received his land back as a tenant and paid his protector a small rent. The monastery or privileged individual received a steady income from the land, and the local lord escaped imperial taxes and control. By the end of the thirteenth century most land seems to have been taken off the tax rolls this way. Each plot of land could thus have several people with rights to shares of its produce, ranging from the cultivator, to a local lord, to an estate manager working for him, to a regional strongman, to a noble or temple in the capital. Unlike peasants in medieval Europe, where similar practices of commendation occurred, the cultivators in Japan never became serfs. Moreover, Japanese lords rarely lived on the lands they had rights in, unlike English or French lords who lived on their manors.

Samurai resembled European knights in several ways. Both were armed with expensive weapons, and both fought on horseback. Just as the knight was supposed to live according to the chivalric code, so Japanese samurai were expected to live according to Bushido, or "Way of the Warrior," a code that stressed military honor, courage, stoic acceptance of hardship, and, above all, loyalty. Physical hardship was accepted as routine, and soft living was despised as weak and unworthy. Disloyalty brought social disgrace, which the samurai could avoid only through *seppuku*, ritual suicide by slashing his belly.

The Kamakura Shogunate derives its name from Kamakura, a city near modern Tokyo that was the seat of the Minamoto clan. The founder, Yoritomo, ruled the country much the way he ran his own estates, appointing his retainers to newly created offices. To cope with the emergence of hard-to-tax estates, he put **military land stewards** in charge of seeing to the estates' proper operation. To bring order to the lawless countryside, he appointed **military governors** to oversee the military and enforce the law in the provinces. They supervised the conduct of the land stewards in peacetime and commanded the provincial samurai in war.

Bushido   *Literally, the "Way of the Warrior," this was the code of conduct by which samurai were expected to live.*

military land stewards   *Officials placed in charge of overseeing estates.*

military governors   *Officials appointed to enforce the law in the provinces and oversee the samurai there.*

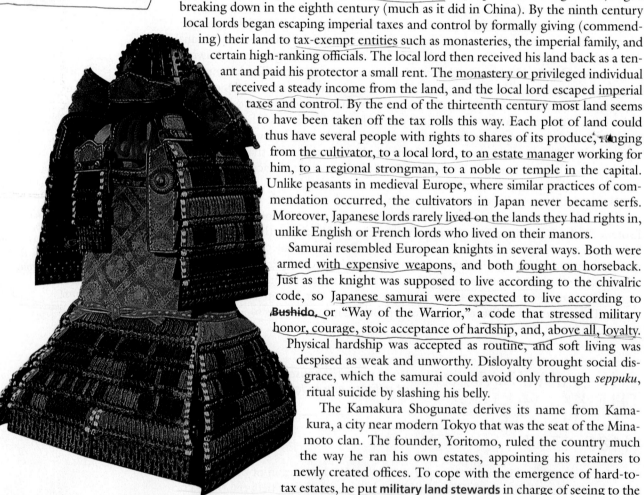

● **Samurai Armor**   A member of the Taira clan once wore this twelfth-century set of armor. Armor had to serve the practical purpose of defense, but as in medieval Europe and medieval Islam, it was often embellished, turning armor into works of art. *(Suzanne Perrin/Japan Interlink)*

Yoritomo's wife Masako protected the interests of her own family, the Hōjōs, especially after Yoritomo died. She went so far as to force her first son to abdicate when he showed signs of preferring the family of his wife to the family of his mother. She later helped her brother take power away from her father. Thus the process of reducing power holders to figureheads went one step further in 1219 when the Hōjō family reduced the shogun to a figurehead. The Hōjō family held the reins of power until 1333.

The Mongols' two massive seaborne invasions in 1274 and 1281 (see page 300) were a huge shock to the shogunate. The Kamakura government was hard-pressed to gather adequate resources for its defense. Temples were squeezed, farmers taken away from their fields to build walls, and warriors promised generous rewards. Although the Hōjō regents, with the help of a "divine wind" (*kamikaze*), repelled the Mongols, they were unable to reward their vassals in the traditional way because little booty was found among the wreckage of the Mongol fleets. Discontent grew among the samurai, and by the fourteenth century the entire political system was breaking down. Both the imperial and the shogunate families were fighting among themselves. As land grants were divided, samurai became impoverished and took to plunder and piracy, or shifted their loyalty to local officials who could offer them a better living.

The factional disputes among Japan's leading families remained explosive until 1331, when the emperor Go-Daigo tried to recapture real power. His attempt sparked an uprising by the great families, local lords, samurai, and even Buddhist monasteries, which had thousands of samurai retainers. Go-Daigo destroyed the Kamakura Shogunate in 1333 but soon lost the loyalty of his followers. By 1338 one of his most important military supporters, Ashikaga Takauji, had turned on him and established the Ashikaga Shogunate, which lasted until 1573. Takauji's victory was also a victory for the samurai, who took over civil authority throughout Japan.

Cultural Trends

The cultural distance between the elites and the commoners narrowed a little during the Kamakura period. In this period Buddhism was vigorously spread to ordinary Japanese by energetic preachers. Hōnen propagated the Pure Land teaching (see page 152), preaching that paradise could be reached through simple faith in the Buddha and repeating the name of the Buddha Amitabha. Neither philosophical understanding of Buddhist scriptures nor devotion to rituals was essential. His follower Shinran taught that monks should not shut themselves off in monasteries but should marry and have children. Nichiren, a fiery and intolerant preacher, proclaimed that to be saved people had only to invoke sincerely the Lotus Sutra. These lay versions of Buddhism found a receptive audience among ordinary people in the countryside.

It was also during the Kamakura period that **Zen** (Chan) came to flourish in Japan. As mentioned in Chapter 6, Zen teachings originated in Tang China. Rejecting the authority of the sutras, Zen teachers claimed the superiority of mind-to-mind transmission of Buddhist truth. When Japanese monks went to

Zen *A school of Buddhism that emphasized meditation and truths that could not be conveyed in words.*

● **The Shogun Minamoto Yoritomo in Court Dress** This wooden sculpture, 27.8 inches tall (70.6 cm), was made about a half century after Yoritomo's death for use in a shrine dedicated to his memory. The bold shapes convey Yoritomo's dignity and power. (*Tokyo National Museum/image: TNM Image Archives; http://TnmArchives.jp/*)

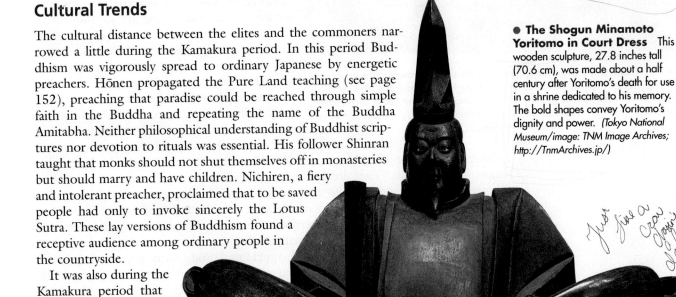

● **The Itinerant Preacher Ippen** The monk Ippen traveled through Japan urging people to call on the Amida Buddha through song and dance. This detail from a set of twelve paintings done in 1299, a decade after his death, shows him with his belongings on his back as he approaches a village. *(Tokyo National Museum/ image: TNM Image Archives; http://TnmArchives.jp/)*

China in the twelfth century looking for ways to revitalize Japanese Buddhism, they were impressed by the rigorous monastic life of the Chan/Zen monasteries. One school of Zen held that enlightenment could be achieved suddenly through insight into one's own true nature. This school taught rigorous meditation and the use of kōan riddles to unseat logic and free the mind for enlightenment. This teaching found eager patrons among the samurai, who were attracted to its discipline and strong master-disciple bonds.

Buddhism remained central to the visual arts. Many temples in Japan still house fine sculptures done in this period. In painting, narrative handscrolls brought to life the miracles that faith could bring and the torments of Hell awaiting unbelievers. All forms of literature could be depicted in these scrolls, including *The Tale of Genji,* war stories, and humorous anecdotes.

During the Kamakura period the tradition of long narrative prose works was continued with the war tale. *The Tale of the Heike,* written by a courtier in the early thirteenth century, tells the story of the fall of the Taira family and the rise of the Minamoto clan. The tale reached a large audience because blind minstrels would chant sections of the tale to the accompaniment of the lute. The story is suffused with the Buddhist idea of the transience of life and the illusory nature of glory. Yet it also celebrates strength, courage, loyalty, and pride. The Minamoto warriors from the east are portrayed as the toughest. In one scene one of them dismisses his own prowess with the bow, claiming that other warriors from his region could pierce three sets of armor with their arrows. He then brags about the martial spirit of warriors from the east: "They are bold horsemen who never fall, nor do they let their horses stumble on the roughest road. When they fight they do not care if even their parents or children are killed; they ride over their bodies and continue the battle."[6] In this they stood in contrast to the warriors of the west who in good Confucian fashion would retire from battle to mourn their parents.

After stagnating in the Heian period, agricultural productivity began to improve in the Kamakura period, and the population grew, reaching perhaps 8.2 million by 1333. Much like farmers in contemporary Song China, Japanese farmers in this period adopted new strains of rice, often double-cropped in warmer regions, made increased use of fertilizers, and improved irrigation for paddy rice. Besides farming, ordinary people could make their livings as artisans, traders, fishermen, and entertainers. Although trade in human beings was banned, those who fell into debt might sell themselves or their children, and professional slave traders kidnapped women and children. A vague category of outcastes occupied the fringes of society. Buddhist strictures against killing and Shinto ideas of pollution probably account for the exclusion of butchers, leatherworkers, morticians, and lepers, but other groups, such as bamboo whisk makers, were also traditionally excluded for no obvious reason.

● **Zen Rock Garden** Rock gardens, such as this one at Ryoanji in Kyoto, capture the austere aesthetic of Zen Buddhism. *(Ryoanji Temple/DNP Archives)*

Chapter Summary

To assess your mastery of this chapter, go to **bedfordstmartins.com/mckayworld**

• What allowed China to become a world leader economically and intellectually in this period?

In the period from 800 to 1100, China's population doubled to 100 million, and its economy became increasingly commercialized. There was a huge increase in the use of money and even the introduction of paper money. Cities grew, and the economic center of China shifted from the north China plain to the south, the region drained by the Yangzi River.

• How did the civil service examinations and the scholar-official class shape Chinese society and culture?

China's great wealth could not be easily converted to military supremacy, and Song had to pay tribute to its northern neighbors. The booming economy and the invention of printing did allow a great expansion in the size of the educated class in the Song period, which came to dominate the government. The

Key Terms

dynastic cycle
paper money
compass
examination system
movable type
Neo-Confucianism
concubine
foot binding
cloistered government
The Tale of Genji
Esoteric Buddhism
Bushido
military land stewards
military governors
Zen

life of the educated class in Song times was strongly shaped by the civil service examinations, which most educated men spent a decade or more studying for, often unsuccessfully. Their high levels of education fostered interests in literature, antiquities, philosophy, and art, but may well have been a disadvantage when the times called for military leadership. Because there were more educated men, more books were written, and because of the spread of printing, a much greater share of them have survived to the present, making it possible to see dimensions of life poorly documented for earlier periods, such as the lives of women.

• How did the Heian form of government contribute to the cultural flowering of the period?

In marked contrast to Song China, in Heian Japan a tiny aristocracy dominated government and society. More important than the emperors were a series of regents, most of them from the Fujiwara family and fathers-in-law of the emperors. The aristocratic court society put great emphasis on taste and refinement. Women were influential at the court and wrote much of the best literature of the period. The Heian aristocrats had little interest in life in the provinces, which gradually came under the control of military clans.

• What were the causes and consequences of military rule in Japan?

After a civil war between the two leading military clans, a military government, called the shogunate, was established in the east. Emperors were still placed on the throne, but they had little power. During this period of military rule, culture was no longer so capital-centered, and Buddhism was vigorously spread to ordinary people. Arts that appealed to the samurai, such as war stories and Zen Buddhism, all flourished.

Suggested Reading

Bol, Peter K. *"This Culture of Ours": Intellectual Transitions in T'ang and Sung China.* 1992. A challenging inquiry into how intellectuals evaluated learning and culture.

Chaffee, John W. *The Thorny Gates of Learning in Sung China: A Social History of Examinations.* 1985. Documents the wide-ranging impact of the examination system and the ways men could improve their chances.

Ebrey, Patricia Buckley. *The Inner Quarters: Marriage and the Lives of Chinese Women in the Sung Period.* 1993. Overview of the many facets of women's lives, from engagements to dowries, childrearing, and widowhood.

Egan, Ronald. *Word, Image, and Deed in the Life of Su Shi.* 1994. A sympathetic portrait of one of the most talented men of the age.

Farris, Wayne W. *Heavenly Warriors.* 1992. Argues against Western analogies in explaining the dominance of the samurai.

Friday, Karl F. *Hired Swords.* 1992. Treats the evolution of state military development in connection with the emergence of the samurai.

Gernet, Jacques. *Daily Life in China on the Eve of the Mongol Invasion, 1250–76.* 1962. An accessible, lively introduction to the Song period.

Hansen, Valerie. *Changing the Gods in Medieval China, 1127–1276.* 1990. A portrait of the religious beliefs and practices of ordinary people in Song times.

Morris, Ivan. *The World of the Shining Prince: Court Life in Ancient Japan.* 1964. An engaging portrait of Heian culture based on both fiction and nonfiction sources.

Souyri, Pierre François. *The World Turned Upside Down: Medieval Japanese Society.* 2001. A thought-provoking analysis of both the social system and the mentalities of Japan's Middle Ages.

Notes

1. *The Travels of Marco Polo, the Venetian,* ed. Manuel Komroff (New York: Boni and Liveright, 1926), p. 227.
2. Ibid., p. 159.
3. Ibid., p. 235.
4. Ivan Morris, trans., *The Pillow Book of Sei Shonagon* (New York: Penguin Books, 1970), p. 258.
5. Quoted in M. Collcott, M. Jansen, and I. Kumakura, *Cultural Atlas of Japan* (New York: Facts on File, 1988), p. 82, slightly modified.
6. Ibid., p. 101.

Listening to the PAST

The Pillow Book of Sei Shonagon

Beginning in the late tenth century, Japan produced a series of great women writers. At the time women were much freer than men to write in vernacular Japanese, giving them a large advantage. Lady Murasaki, author of the novel The Tale of Genji, *is the most famous of the women writers of the period, but her contemporary Sei Shonagon is equally noteworthy. Sei Shonagon served as a lady in waiting to Empress Sadako during the last decade of the tenth century (990–1000). Her only known work is* The Pillow Book, *a collection of notes, character sketches, anecdotes, descriptions of nature, and eccentric lists such as boring things, awkward things, hateful things, and things that have lost their power.*

The Pillow Book portrays the lovemaking/marriage system among the aristocracy more or less as it is depicted in The Tale of Genji. *Marriages were arranged for family interests, and men could have more than one wife. Wives and their children commonly stayed in their own homes, where their husbands and fathers would visit them. But once a man had an heir by his wife, there was nothing to prevent him from establishing relations with other women. Some relationships were long-term, but many were brief, and men often had several lovers at the same time. Some women became known for their amorous conquests, others as abandoned women whose husbands ignored them. The following passage from* The Pillow Book *looks on this lovemaking system with amused detachment.*

It is so stiflingly hot in the Seventh Month that even at night one keeps all the doors and lattices open. At such times it is delightful to wake up when the moon is shining and to look outside. I enjoy it even when there is no moon. But to wake up at dawn and see a pale sliver of a moon in the sky—well, I need hardly say how perfect that is.

I like to see a bright new straw mat that has just been spread out on a well-polished floor. The best place for one's three-foot curtain of state is in the front of the room near the veranda. It is pointless to put it in the rear of the room, as it is most unlikely that anyone will peer in from that direction.

It is dawn and a woman is lying in bed after her lover has taken his leave. She is covered up to her head with a light mauve robe that has a lining of dark violet; the colour of both the outside and the lining is fresh and glossy. The woman, who appears to be asleep, wears an unlined orange robe and a dark crimson skirt of stiff silk whose cords hang loosely by her side, as if they have been left untied. Her thick tresses tumble over each other in cascades, and one can imagine how long her hair must be when it falls freely down her back.

Nearby another woman's lover is making his way home in the misty dawn. He is wearing loose violet trousers, an orange hunting costume, so lightly coloured that one can hardly tell whether it has been dyed or not, a white robe of still silk, and a scarlet robe of glossy, beaten silk. His clothes, which are damp from the mist, hang loosely about him. From the dishevelment of his side locks one can tell how negligently he must have tucked his hair into the black lacquered headdress when he got up. He wants to return and write his next-morning letter before the dew on the morning glories has had time to vanish; but the path seems endless, and to divert himself he hums "the sprouts in the flax fields."

As he walks along, he passes a house with an open lattice. He is on his way to report for official duty, but cannot help stopping to lift up the blind and peep into the room. It amuses him to think that a man has probably been spending the night here and has only recently got up to leave, just as happened to himself. Perhaps that man too had felt the charm of the dew.

Looking around the room, he notices near the woman's pillow an open fan with a magnolia frame and purple paper; and at the foot of her curtain of state he sees some narrow strips of Michinoku paper and also some other paper of a faded colour, either orange-red or maple.

The woman senses that someone is watching her and, looking up from under her bedclothes, sees a gentleman leaning against the wall by the threshold, a smile on his face. She can tell at once that he is the

During the Heian period, noblewomen were fashion-conscious. Wearing numerous layers of clothing gave women the opportunity to choose different designs and colors for their robes. The layers also kept them warm in drafty homes. *(The Museum Yamato Bunkakan)*

sort of man with whom she need feel no reserve. All the same, she does not want to enter into any familiar relations with him, and she is annoyed that he should have seen her asleep.

"Well, well, Madam," says the man, leaning forward so that the upper part of his body comes behind her curtains, "what a long nap you're having after your morning adieu! You really are a lie-abed!"

"You call me that, Sir," she replied, "only because you're annoyed at having had to get up before the dew had time to settle."

Their conversation may be commonplace, yet I find there is something delightful about the scene.

Now the gentleman leans further forward and, using his own fan, tries to get hold of the fan by the woman's pillow. Fearing his closeness, she moves further back into her curtain enclosure, her heart pounding. The gentleman picks up the magnolia fan and, while examining it, says in a slightly bitter tone, "How standoffish you are!"

But now it is growing light; there is a sound of people's voices, and it looks as if the sun will soon be up. Only a short while ago this same man was hurrying home to write his next-morning letter before the mists had time to clear. Alas, how easily his intentions have been forgotten!

While all this is afoot, the woman's original lover has been busy with his own next-morning letter, and now, quite unexpectedly, the messenger arrives at her house. The letter is attached to a spray of bush-clover, still damp with dew, and the paper gives off a delicious aroma of incense. Because of the new visitor, however, the woman's servants cannot deliver it to her.

Finally it becomes unseemly for the gentleman to stay any longer. As he goes, he is amused to think that a similar scene may be taking place in the house he left earlier that morning.

Questions for Analysis

1. What sorts of images does Sei Shonagon evoke to convey an impression of a scene?

2. What can you learn from this passage about the material culture of Japan in this period?

3. Why do you think Sei Shonagon was highly esteemed as a writer?

Source: Ivan Morris, trans., *The Pillow Book of Sei Shonagon* (New York: Penguin Books, 1970), pp. 60–62. Copyright © 1970. Reprinted by permission of Oxford University Press.

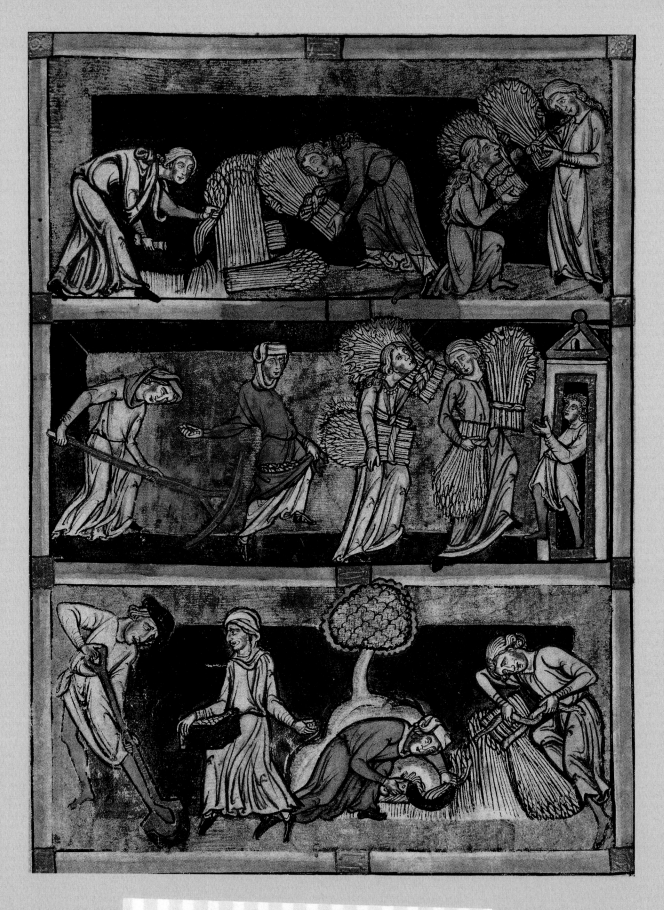

Scenes of Agricultural Work, ca. 1190, from a German manuscript, *Speculum Virginum*. The artist shows many tasks and portrays the way these were shared by men, women, and children. *(Landschaftsverband Rheinland/Rheinisches Landesmuseum, Bonn)*

chapter

13

EUROPE IN THE MIDDLE AGES, 850–1400

Chapter Preview

Political Developments
• *How did medieval rulers overcome internal divisions and external threats, and work to create larger and more stable territories?*

Revival and Reform in the Christian Church
• *How did the Christian church enhance its power and create new institutions and religious practices?*

The Crusades
• *What were the motives, course, and consequences of the Crusades?*

The Changing Life of the People
• *What was life like for the common people of medieval Europe, and how were the lives of nobles and townspeople different?*

The Culture of the Middle Ages
• *What were the primary new cultural institutions and forms developed in medieval Europe?*

Crises of the Later Middle Ages
• *Why has the late Middle Ages been seen as a time of calamity and crisis?*

The Italian Renaissance humanist Francesco Petrarch (1304–1374) coined the term *Middle Ages* to describe the period in European history from the end of the Roman Empire until his own time. Petrarch believed that his own age was a golden age marked by intellectual and cultural brilliance that recaptured the cultural splendor of ancient Roman civilization. Between the Roman world and the Renaissance, Petrarch believed, were the "Middle Ages," a time of Gothic barbarism and intellectual stagnation. Petrarch's terminology and time divisions have been widely adapted, but he had it wrong about barbarism and stagnation. Europeans developed new political and economic structures in the medieval period and displayed enormous intellectual energy and creative vitality.

One of the concepts that became more widely used was, in fact, the notion of "Europe." Classical geographers used the term *Europe* to distinguish this landmass from Africa and Asia, but in the medieval period the idea that there was a distinctive European culture began to take shape. While the peoples living there did not define themselves as European for centuries, a European identity began to be forged in the medieval period. That identity was shaped by interactions with other parts of the world and by Europeans' own expansion in this era.

POLITICAL DEVELOPMENTS

How did medieval rulers overcome internal divisions and external threats, and work to create larger and more stable territories?

Petrarch dated the beginning of the Middle Ages to the fifth century, the time of the fall of the Roman Empire in the West. The growth of Germanic kingdoms such as those of the Merovingians and Carolingians (see page 182) are thus generally viewed as the beginning of "medieval" politics in Europe. After a period of disruption in the ninth and tenth centuries, rulers built on Carolingian models to restore order and create new systems of law and justice.

Feudalism and Manorialism

vassal *A knight who has sworn loyalty to a particular lord. Vassal is derived from a Celtic word meaning "servant."*

fief *A portion of land, the use of which was given by a lord to a vassal in exchange for the latter's oath of loyalty.*

feudalism *A medieval European political system that defines the military obligations and relations between a lord and his vassals and involves the granting of fiefs.*

manorialism *The economic system that governed rural life in medieval Europe, in which the landed estates of a lord were worked by the peasants under his jurisdiction in exchange for his protection.*

serf *A peasant who lost his freedom and became permanently bound to the landed estate of a lord.*

The large-scale division of Charlemagne's empire was accompanied by a decentralization of power at the local level. Civil wars weakened the power and prestige of kings who could do little about domestic violence. Likewise, the great invasions of the ninth century, especially the Viking invasions (see page 353), weakened royal authority. The Frankish kings could do little to halt the invaders, and the local aristocracy had to assume responsibility for defense. Common people turned for protection to the strongest power, the local counts, whom they considered their rightful rulers. Thus, in the ninth and tenth centuries great aristocratic families increased their authority.

The most powerful nobles were those able to gain the allegiance of warriors, often symbolized in an oath-swearing ceremony of homage and fealty that grew out of earlier Germanic oaths of loyalty. In this ceremony, a warrior (knight) swore his loyalty as a **vassal**—from a Celtic term meaning "servant"—to the more powerful individual, who became his lord. In return for the vassal's loyalty, aid, and military assistance, the lord promised him protection and material support. This support might be a place in the lord's household but was more likely land of the vassal's own, called a **fief** (*feudum* in Latin). The fief might contain forests, churches, and towns. The fief theoretically still belonged to the lord, and the vassal only had the use of it. Peasants living on a fief produced the food and other goods necessary to maintain the knight.

Though historians debate this, fiefs appear to have been granted extensively first by Charles Martel and then by his successors, including Charlemagne and his grandsons. These fiefs went to their most powerful nobles, who often took the title of count. As the Carolingians' control of their territories weakened, the practice of granting fiefs moved to the local level, with lay lords, bishops, and abbots as well as kings granting fiefs. This system, later named **feudalism,** was based on personal ties of loyalty cemented by grants of land rather than on allegiance to an abstract state or governmental system.

Feudalism concerned the rights, powers, and lifestyles of the military elite. **Manorialism** involved the services of the peasant class. The two were linked. The economic power of the warrior class rested on landed estates, which were worked by peasants. Peasants needed protection, and lords demanded something in return for that protection. Free farmers surrendered themselves and their land to the lord's jurisdiction. The land was given back to them to farm, but they were tied to the land by various payments and services. Those obligations varied from place to place, but certain practices became common everywhere. The peasant had to give the lord a percentage of the annual harvest, pay a fine to marry someone from outside the lord's estate, and pay a fine—usually the best sheep or cow owned—to inherit property. Most significant, the peasant lost his freedom and became a **serf,** part of the lord's permanent labor force, bound to the land and unable to leave it without the lord's permission. With large tracts of land and a small pool of labor, the most profitable form of capital was not land but laborers.

● **Homage and Fealty** Although the rite of entering a feudal relationship varied widely across Europe and sometimes was entirely verbal, we have a few illustrations of it. Here the vassal kneels before the lord, places his clasped hands between those of the lord, and declares, "I become your man." Sometimes the lord handed over a clump of earth, representing the fief, and the ceremony concluded with a kiss, symbolizing peace between them. *(Osterreichische Nationalbibliothek)*

The transition from freedom to serfdom was slow, depending on the degree of political order in a given region. By the year 800, though, perhaps 60 percent of the population of western Europe had been reduced to serfdom. While there were many economic levels within this serf class, from the highly prosperous to the desperately poor, all had lost their freedom.

Invasions and Migrations

From the moors of Scotland to the mountains of Sicily, there arose in the ninth century the prayer, "Save us, O God, from the violence of the Northmen." The Northmen, also known as Normans or Vikings, were pagan Germanic peoples from Norway, Sweden, and Denmark who had remained beyond the sway of the Christianizing and civilizing influences of the Carolingian Empire. Some scholars believe that the name *Viking* derives from the Old Norse word *vik,* meaning "creek." A Viking, then, was a pirate who waited in a creek or bay to attack passing vessels.

Viking assaults began around 800, and by the midtenth century the Vikings had brought large sections of continental Europe and Britain under their sway. In the east, they pierced the rivers of Russia as far as the Black Sea. In the west, they established permanent settlements on Iceland and short-lived ones in Greenland and Newfoundland in Canada (see Map 13.1).

The Vikings were superb seamen with advanced methods of boatbuilding. Propelled either by oars or by sails, deckless, and about sixty-five-feet long, a Viking ship could carry between forty and sixty men—quite enough to harass an isolated monastery or village. Against these ships navigated by thoroughly experienced and utterly fearless sailors, the Carolingian Empire, with no navy, was helpless. At first the Vikings attacked and sailed off laden with booty. Later, on returning, they settled down and colonized the areas they had conquered.

Along with the Vikings, groups of central European steppe peoples known as Magyars also raided villages in the late ninth century, taking plunder and captives and forcing leaders to pay tribute in an effort to prevent further looting and destruction. Moving westward, small bands of Magyars on horseback reached as far as Spain and the Atlantic coast. They subdued northern Italy, compelled Bavaria and Saxony to pay tribute, and penetrated even into the Rhineland and Burgundy. People thought of them as returning Huns, so the Magyars came to be known as Hungarians. They settled in the area that is now Hungary, became Christian, and in the eleventh century allied with the papacy.

From the south, the Muslims also began new encroachments, concentrating on the two southern peninsulas, Italy and Spain. In Italy the Muslims held Sicily, then drove northward and sacked Rome in 846. Most of Spain had remained under their domination since the eighth century. Expert seamen, they sailed around the Iberian Peninsula and braved the dangerous shoals and winds of the Atlantic coast. They also attacked Mediterranean settlements along the coast of Provence.

Chronology

ca. 800–950   Viking, Magyar, and Muslim attacks on Europe

1066–1087   Reign of William the Conqueror

1075–1122   Investiture controversy

1085–1248   Reconquista, the Christian reconquest of Spain from Muslims

1086   *Domesday Book*

1095–1270   Crusades

1180–1270   Height of construction of cathedrals in France

1215   Magna Carta

1225–1274   Life of Saint Thomas Aquinas, author of *Summa Theologica*

1309–1376   Papacy in Avignon

1315–1322   Famine in northern Europe

ca. 1337–1453   Hundred Years' War

1347   Black Death arrives in Europe

1358   Jacquerie peasant uprising in France

1378–1417   Great Schism

1431   Joan of Arc declared a heretic and burned at the stake

Viking, Magyar, and Muslim attacks accelerated the development of feudalism. Lords capable of rallying fighting men, supporting them, and putting up resistance to the invaders did so. They also assumed political power in their territories. Weak and defenseless people sought the protection of local strongmen. From the perspective of a person in what had been Charlemagne's empire, this was a period of chaos.

People in other parts of Europe might have had a different opinion, however. In Muslim Spain scholars worked in thriving cities, and new crops such as cotton and sugar enhanced ordinary people's lives. In eastern Europe states such as Moravia and Hungary became strong kingdoms. A Viking point of view might be the most positive, for by 1100 descendants of the Vikings not only ruled their homelands in Denmark, Norway, and Sweden, but also ruled northern France (a province known as Normandy), England, Sicily, Iceland, and Kievan Rus, with an outpost in Greenland and occasional voyages to North America.

MAP 13.1   **Invasions and Migrations of the Ninth Century**   Vikings, Magyars, and Muslims all moved into central and western Europe in the ninth century, and Viking ships also sailed the rivers of Russia and the northern Atlantic ocean

DEDERVNT:HAROLDO: hIC RE   SIDET:HAROLD   ISTI MIRANT
CORO   NA: REGIS   REX:AN   GLORVM:
STIGANT
ARCHIEPS

● **The Bayeux Tapestry**   William's conquest of England was recorded in thread on a narrative embroidery panel measuring 231 feet by 19 inches. In this scene, two nobles and a bishop acclaim Harold Godwinson, William's rival, as king of England. The nobles hold a sword, symbol of military power, and the bishop holds a stole, symbol of clerical power. Harold himself holds a scepter and an orb, both symbols of royal power. The embroidery provides an important historical source for the clothing, armor, and lifestyles of the Norman and Anglo-Saxon warrior class. It eventually ended up in Bayeux in northern France, where it is displayed in a museum today, and is incorrectly called a "tapestry," which is a different kind of needlework. *(Tapisserie de Bayeux et avec autorisation spéciale de la Ville de Bayeux)*

The Restoration of Order

The eleventh century witnessed the beginnings of political stability in western Europe. Foreign invasions gradually declined, and in some parts of Europe rulers began to strengthen and extend their authority, creating more unified states out of the feudal system. Medieval rulers had common goals. To increase public order, they wanted to establish an effective means of communication with all peoples. They also wanted more revenue and efficient bureaucracies. The solutions they found to these problems laid the foundations for modern national states.

Political developments in England, France, and Germany provide good examples of the beginnings of the national state in the central Middle Ages. Under the pressure of Viking invasions in the ninth and tenth centuries, the seven kingdoms of Anglo-Saxon England united under one king. At the same time, England was divided into local shires, or counties, each under the jurisdiction of a sheriff appointed by the king. The kingdom of England, therefore, had a political head start on the rest of Europe.

When Edward the Confessor (r. 1042–1066) died, his cousin, Duke William of Normandy, claimed the English throne and won it by defeating his Anglo-Saxon rival at the Battle of Hastings. As William the Conqueror (r. 1066–1087) subdued the rest of the country, he distributed land to his Norman followers and required all feudal lords to swear an oath of allegiance to him as king. He retained the Anglo-Saxon institution of sheriff. The sheriff had the responsibility of catching criminals, collecting taxes, and raising soldiers for the king when ordered.

In 1085 William decided to conduct a systematic survey of the entire country to determine how much wealth there was and who had it. Groups of royal officials or judges were sent to every part of England. A priest and six local people swore an oath to answer truthfully. Because they swore (Latin, *juror*), they were called **jurors,** and from this small body of local people, the jury system in English-speaking countries gradually evolved. The records collected from the entire country, called *Domesday*

jurors   *In William the Conqueror's reign, a priest and six local people who swore an oath to answer truthfully all questions about their wealth.*

Book, provided William and his descendants with vital information for governing the country.

In 1128 William's granddaughter Matilda married Geoffrey of Anjou. Their son, who became Henry II of England, inherited the French provinces of Normandy, Anjou, and Touraine in northwestern France. When Henry married the great heiress Eleanor of Aquitaine in 1152, he claimed lordship over Aquitaine, Poitou, and Gascony in southwestern France as well. The histories of England and France were thus closely intertwined in the central Middle Ages.

In the early twelfth century France consisted of a number of nearly independent provinces, each governed by its local ruler. The work of unifying France began under Philip II (r. 1180–1223), called "Augustus" because he vastly enlarged the territory of the kingdom. By the end of his reign, Philip was effectively master of northern France. His descendants acquired important holdings in southern France, and by 1300 most of the provinces of modern France had been added to the royal domain through diplomacy, marriage, war, and inheritance.

In central Europe, the German king Otto I (r. 936–973) defeated many other lords to build up his power. The basis of Otto's power was an alliance with and control of the church. Otto asserted the right to control church appointments. Bishops and abbots had to perform feudal homage for the lands that accompanied the church office. This practice, later called **lay investiture,** led to a grave crisis in the eleventh century (see page 360). German rulers were not able to build up centralized power. Under Otto I and his successors, a sort of confederacy (a weak union of strong principalities), later called the Holy Roman Empire, developed in which the emperor shared power with princes, dukes, counts, archbishops, and bishops.

Frederick Barbarossa (r. 1152–1190) of the house of Hohenstaufen tried valiantly to make the Holy Roman Empire a united state. He made alliances with the great lay princes and even compelled the great churchmen to become his vassals. Unfortunately, Frederick did not concentrate his efforts and resources in one area. He became embroiled in the affairs of Italy, hoping to cash in on the wealth Italian cities had gained through trade. He led six expeditions into Italy, but his brutal methods provoked revolts, and the cities, allied with the papacy, defeated him in 1176. Frederick was forced to recognize the autonomy of the cities. Meanwhile, back in Germany, Frederick's absence allowed the princes and other rulers of independent provinces to consolidate their power.

Law and Justice

Throughout Europe in the twelfth and thirteenth centuries, the law was a hodgepodge of customs, feudal rights, and provincial practices. Kings wanted to blend these elements into a uniform system of rules acceptable and applicable to all their peoples. In France and England, kings successfully contributed to the development of national states through the administration of their laws.

The French king Louis IX (r. 1226–1270) was famous in his time for his concern for justice. Each French province, even after being made part of the kingdom of France, retained its unique laws and procedures, but Louis IX created a royal judicial system. He established the Parlement of Paris, a kind of supreme court that welcomed appeals from local administrators and from the courts of feudal lords throughout France.

Under Henry II (r. 1154–1189), England developed and extended a **common law**—a law common to and accepted by the entire country. No other country in medieval Europe did so. Each year Henry sent out *circuit judges* (royal officials who traveled in a given circuit or district) to hear civil and criminal cases. Wherever the king's judges sat, there sat the king's court. Slowly, the king's court gained jurisdiction over all property disputes and criminal actions.

lay investiture *The selection and appointment of church officials by secular authorities.*

common law *A law that originated in, and was applied by, the king's court.*

Proving guilt or innocence in criminal cases could pose a problem. Where there was no specific accuser, the court sought witnesses, then looked for written evidence. If the judges found neither and the suspect had a bad reputation in the community, the person went to trial by ordeal. He or she was bound hand and foot and dropped into a lake or river. Because water was supposed to be a pure substance, it would reject anything foul or unclean. Thus the innocent person would sink and the guilty person float. Because God determined guilt or innocence, a priest had to be present to bless the water. Henry disliked the system because the clergy controlled the procedure and because many suspicious people seemed to beat the system and escape punishment, but he had no alternative. Then in 1215 the church's Fourth Lateran Council forbade priests' participation in such trials, effectively ending them. Royal justice was desacralized. In the course of the thirteenth century, the king's judges adopted the practice of calling on twelve people to decide the accused's guilt or innocence. Trial by jury was only gradually accepted; medieval Europeans had more confidence in the judgment of God than in that of ordinary people.

Henry's son John (r. 1199–1216) met with serious disappointment. He lost the French province of Normandy to Philip Augustus in 1204 and spent the rest of his reign trying to win it back. Saddled with heavy debt from his father and brother Richard (r. 1189–1199), John tried to squeeze more money from nobles and town-dwellers, which created an atmosphere of resentment.

When John's military campaign failed in 1214, it was clear that the French lands that had once belonged to the English king were lost for good. His ineptitude as a soldier in a culture that idealized military glory turned the people against him. The barons revolted and in 1215 forced him to attach his seal to Magna Carta—the "Great Charter," which became the cornerstone of English justice and law.

Magna Carta signifies the principle that the king and the government shall be under the law and that everyone, including the king, must obey the law. If a government is to be legitimate, the theory emerged, then government must operate according to the *rule of law*. Some clauses of Magna Carta contain the germ of the ideas of *due process of law* and the right to a fair and speedy trial. A person may not be arbitrarily arrested and held indefinitely in prison without being accused of crime and brought to trial. Every English king in the Middle Ages reissued Magna Carta as evidence of his promise to observe the law. Centuries later, ideas of the rule of law and due process had global consequences.

Primary Source: Magna Carta: The Great Charter of Liberties
Learn what rights and liberties the English nobility, on behalf of all free Englishmen, forced King John to grant them in 1215.

REVIVAL AND REFORM IN THE CHRISTIAN CHURCH

How did the Christian church enhance its power and create new institutions and religious practices?

The eleventh century witnessed the beginnings of a remarkable religious revival. Monasteries remodeled themselves, and new religious orders were founded. After a century of corruption and decadence, the papacy reformed itself. The popes worked to clarify church doctrine and codify church law. Religion structured people's daily lives and the yearly calendar. Christianity expanded into Europe's northern and eastern regions, and Christian rulers expanded their holdings in Muslim Spain.

Monastic Reforms

The Viking, Magyar, and Muslim invaders attacked and ransacked many monasteries across Europe. Some religious communities fled and dispersed. In the period of political disorder that followed the disintegration of the Carolingian Empire, many religious houses fell under the control and domination of local feudal lords. Powerful laymen appointed themselves as abbots but kept their wives or mistresses. They took for themselves the lands and goods of monasteries, spending monastic revenues and selling monastic offices. The level of spiritual observance and intellectual activity declined.

An opportunity for reform came in 909, when William the Pious, duke of Aquitaine, established the abbey of Cluny in Burgundy. Duke William declared that the monastery was to be free from any feudal responsibilities to him or any other lord, its members subordinate only to the pope. The first two abbots of Cluny set very high standards of religious behavior and stressed strict observance of *The Rule of Saint Benedict.* Cluny gradually came to stand for clerical celibacy and the suppression of *simony* (the sale of church offices). In a disorderly world, Cluny represented religious and political stability. Laypersons placed lands under Cluny's custody and monastic houses under its jurisdiction for reform.

Deeply impressed laypeople showered gifts on monasteries with good reputations, but with this wealth came lay influence. And as the monasteries became richer, the lifestyle of the monks grew increasingly luxurious. Monastic observance and spiritual fervor declined. Soon fresh demands for reform were heard. The result was the founding of new religious orders in the late eleventh and early twelfth centuries.

The best representative of the new reforming spirit was the Cistercian order. The Cistercians combined a very simple liturgical life, a radical rejection of the traditional feudal sources of income (such as the possession of mills and serfs), and many innovative economic practices. The Cistercians' dynamic growth and rapid expansion had a profound impact on European society.

Throughout the Middle Ages, social class defined the kinds of religious life open to women and men in Europe. Kings and nobles often established convents for their daughters, sisters, aunts, or aging mothers. Entrance was restricted to women of the founder's class. (See the feature "Individuals in Society: Hildegard of Bingen.") Monks and nuns came into the convent or monastery as children.

The pattern of life within individual monasteries varied widely from house to house and from region to region. One central activity, however, was performed everywhere. Daily life centered on the *liturgy* or *Divine Office,* psalms, and other prayers, which monks and nuns prayed seven times a day and once during the night. Prayers were offered for peace, rain, good harvests, the civil authorities, the monks' and nuns' families, and their benefactors. Monastic patrons in turn lavished gifts on the monasteries, which often became very wealthy, controlling large tracts of land and the peasants who farmed them.

In the thirteenth century the growth of cities provided a new challenge for the church. Many urban people thought that the church did not fulfil their spiritual needs. They turned instead to heresies, many of which, somewhat ironically, denied the value of material wealth. Combating heresy became a principal task of new types of religious orders, most prominently the Dominicans and Franciscans, who preached, ministered to city dwellers, and also staffed the papal Inquisition, a special court designed to root out heresy. Dominicans and Franciscans also acted as missionaries in border areas of Europe, and beginning in the sixteenth century would be important agents of the spread of Christianity into European colonies around the world.

Papal Reforms

Serious efforts at papal reform began under Pope Leo IX (r. 1049–1054). He traveled widely, holding councils that issued decrees against violence, simony, and clerical marriage. Although celibacy had technically been an obligation for ordination since the fourth century, in the tenth and eleventh centuries probably a majority of European priests were married or living with a woman.

A church council produced another reform—removing the influence of Roman aristocratic factions in papal elections. Since the eighth century the priests of the

Hildegard of Bingen

The tenth child of a lesser noble family, Hildegard (1098–1179) was given when eight years old as an oblate to an abbey in the Rhineland, where she learned Latin and received a good education. She spent most of her life in various women's religious communities, two of which she founded herself. When she was a child, she began having mystical visions, often of light in the sky, but told few people about them. In middle age, however, her visions became more dramatic: "And it came to pass . . . when I was 42 years and 7 months old, that the heavens were opened and a blinding light of exceptional brilliance flowed through my entire brain. And so it kindled my whole heart and breast like a flame, not burning but warming . . . and suddenly I understood of the meaning of expositions of the books."* She wanted the church to approve of her visions and wrote first to St. Bernard of Clairvaux, who answered her briefly and dismissively, and then to Pope Eugenius, who encouraged her to write them down. Her first work was *Scivias* (Know the Ways of the Lord), a record of her mystical visions that incorporates vast theological learning (see the illustration).

Obviously possessed of leadership and administrative talents, Hildegard left her abbey in 1147 to found the convent of Rupertsberg near Bingen. There she produced *Physica* (On the Physical Elements) and *Causa et Curae* (Causes and Cures), scientific works on the curative properties of natural elements; poems; a mystery play; and several more works of mysticism. She carried on a huge correspondence with scholars, prelates, and ordinary people. When she was over fifty, she left her community to preach to audiences of clergy and laity, and she was the only woman of her time whose opinions on religious matters were considered authoritative by the church.

Hildegard's visions have been explored by theologians and also by neurologists, who judge that they may have originated in migraine headaches, as she reports many of the same phenomena that migraine sufferers do: auras of light around objects, areas of blindness, feelings of intense doubt and intense euphoria. The interpretations that she develops come from her theological insight and learning, however, not her illness. That same insight also emerges in her music, which is what she is best known for today. Eighty of her compositions survive—a huge number for a medieval composer—most of them written to be sung by the nuns in her convent, so they have strong lines for female voices. Many of her songs and chants

In one of her visions, Hildegard saw the Synagogue (the building where Jews worship) metaphorically as a very tall woman who holds in her arms Moses with the stone tablets of the Ten Commandments. *(Rheinisches Bildarchiv, Koln)*

have been recorded recently by various artists and are available on compact disk, as downloads, and on several websites.

Questions for Analysis

1. Why do you think Hildegard might have kept her visions secret? Why do you think she sought church approval for them?

2. In what ways might Hildegard's vision of Synagogue have been shaped by her own experiences? How does this vision compare with other ideas about the Jews that you have read about in this chapter?

*From *Scivias*, trans. Mother Columba Hart and Jane Bishop, *The Classics of Western Spirituallity* (New York/Mahwah: Paulist Press, 1990).

major churches around Rome had constituted a special group, called a "college," that advised the pope. They were called "cardinals," from the Latin *cardo,* or "hinge." They were the hinges on which the church turned. The Lateran Synod of 1059 decreed that these cardinals had the sole authority and power to elect the pope and that they would govern the church when the office was vacant.

By 1073 the reform movement was well advanced. That year, Cardinal Hildebrand was elected as Pope Gregory VII, and reform took on a political character. Gregory believed that the pope, as the successor of Saint Peter, was the vicar of God on earth and that papal orders were the orders of God. He insisted that the church should be completely free of lay control, and in 1075 he ordered clerics who accepted investiture from laymen to be deposed, and laymen who invested clerics to be *excommunicated*—cut off from the sacraments and the Christian community. The rulers of Europe immediately protested this restriction of their power.

The strongest reaction came from Henry IV of the Holy Roman Empire. Gregory excommunicated church officials who supported Henry, and suspended him from the emperorship. In January 1077 Henry arrived at the pope's residence in Canossa in northern Italy and, according to legend, stood outside in the snow for three days seeking forgiveness. As a priest, Gregory was obliged to grant absolution and readmit the emperor into the Christian community. Although the emperor, the most powerful ruler in Europe, bowed before the pope, Henry actually won a victory—albeit a temporary one. He regained the emperorship and authority over his subjects, but the controversy encouraged German nobles to resist any expansion in the emperor's power. The nobles gained power, subordinating knights and reducing free men and serfs to servile status. When the investiture issue was finally settled in 1122 by a compromise, the nobility held the balance of power in Germany.

Popular Religion

Religion was not simply a matter of institutions and officials in medieval Europe, but of everyday practice. Apart from the land, the weather, and local legal and social conditions, religion had the greatest impact on the daily lives of ordinary people. Religious practices varied widely from country to country and even from province to province. But nowhere was religion a one-hour-a-week affair. Most people in medieval Europe were Christian, but there were small Jewish communities scattered in many parts of Europe, as well as Muslims in the Iberian peninsula, Sicily, other Mediterranean islands, and southeastern Europe.

For Christians, the village church was the center of community life—social, political, and economic as well as religious—with the parish priest in charge of a host of activities. Every Sunday and on holy days, the villagers stood at Mass or squatted on the floor (there were no chairs), breaking the painful routine of work. The feasts that accompanied baptisms, weddings, funerals, and other celebrations were commonly held in the churchyard. Popular religion consisted largely of rituals heavy with symbolism. Before slicing a loaf of bread, the pious woman tapped the sign of the cross on it with her knife. Before planting, the village priest customarily went out and sprinkled the fields with water, symbolizing refreshment and life. Everyone participated in village processions. The entire calendar was designed with reference to Christmas, Easter, and Pentecost, events in the life of Jesus and his disciples.

Along with days marking events in the life of Jesus, the Christian calendar was filled with saints' days. **Saints** were individuals who had lived particularly holy lives and were honored locally or more widely for their connection with the divine. The cult of the saints, which developed in a rural and uneducated environment, represents a central feature of popular culture in the Middle Ages. People believed that the saints possessed supernatural powers that enabled them to perform miracles, and the saint became the special property of the locality in which his or her relics rested. Relics such as bones, articles of clothing, the saint's tears, saliva, and even the dust from the

saints *Individuals who had lived particularly holy lives and were consequently accorded great honor by medieval Christians. Saints were believed to possess the power to work miracles and were frequently invoked for healing and protection.*

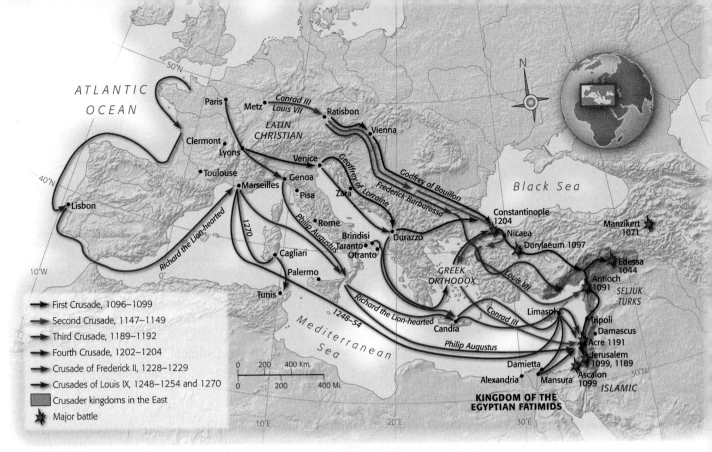

MAP 13.2 **The Routes of the Crusades** The Crusaders took many different sea and land routes on their way to Jerusalem, often crossing the lands of the Byzantine Empire, which led to conflict with eastern Christians. The Crusader kingdoms in the East lasted only briefly.

Map legend:
- First Crusade, 1096–1099
- Second Crusade, 1147–1149
- Third Crusade, 1189–1192
- Fourth Crusade, 1202–1204
- Crusade of Frederick II, 1228–1229
- Crusades of Louis IX, 1248–1254 and 1270
- Crusader kingdoms in the East
- Major battle

---

literally "taking the cross," from the cross that soldiers sewed on their garments as a Christian symbol. At the time people going off to fight simply said they were taking "the way of the cross" or "the road to Jerusalem." Although people of all ages and classes participated in the Crusades, so many knights did so that crusading became a distinctive feature of the upper-class lifestyle. In an aristocratic, military society, men coveted reputations as Crusaders; the Christian knight who had been to the Holy Land enjoyed great prestige.

Background of the Crusades

In the eleventh century the papacy had strong reasons for wanting to launch an expedition against Muslims in the East. It had been involved in the bitter struggle over church reform and lay investiture. If the pope could muster a large army against the enemies of Christianity, his claim to be leader of Christian society in the West would be strengthened. Moreover, in 1054 a serious theological disagreement had split the Greek church of Byzantium and the Roman church of the West. The pope believed that a crusade would lead to strong Roman influence in Greek territories and eventually the reunion of the two churches.

In 1071 at Manzikert in eastern Anatolia, Turkish soldiers defeated a Greek army and occupied much of Asia Minor. The emperor at Constantinople appealed to the West for support. Shortly afterward, the holy city of Jerusalem fell to the Turks. Pilgrimages to holy places in the Middle East became very dangerous, and the papacy claimed to be outraged that the holy city was in the hands of unbelievers. Since the Muslims had held Palestine since the eighth century, the papacy actually feared that the Seljuk Turks would be less accommodating to Christian pilgrims than the previous Muslim rulers had been.

In 1095 Pope Urban II called for a great Christian holy war against the infidels. He urged Christian knights who had been fighting one another to direct their energies against the true enemies of God, the Muslims. At the same time Crusaders could acquire spiritual merit and earn themselves a place in paradise. Ideas about pilgrimage, holy warfare, and the threat to Christendom were not new; Urban tied them all together.

The Course of the Crusades

Thousands of people of all classes joined the crusade. Although most of the Crusaders were French, pilgrims from many regions streamed southward from the Rhineland, through Germany and the Balkans. Of all of the developments of the High Middle Ages, none better reveals Europeans' religious and emotional fervor and the influence of the reformed papacy than the extraordinary outpouring of support for the First Crusade.

The First Crusade was successful, mostly because of the dynamic enthusiasm of the participants. The Crusaders had little more than religious zeal. They knew little of the geography or climate of the Middle East. Although there were several counts with military experience, the Crusaders could never agree on a leader. Lines of supply were never set up. Starvation and disease wracked the army, and the Turks slaughtered hundreds of noncombatants. Nevertheless, convinced that "God wills it," the war cry of the Crusaders, the army pressed on and in 1099 captured Jerusalem. Although the Crusaders fought bravely, Arab disunity was a chief reason for their victory. At Jerusalem, Edessa, Tripoli, and Antioch, Crusader kingdoms were founded on the Western feudal model (see Map 13.2).

Between 1096 and 1270, the crusading ideal was expressed in eight papally approved expeditions to the East. Despite the success of the First Crusade, none of the later ones accomplished very much. During the Fourth Crusade (1202–1204), careless preparation and inadequate financing had disastrous consequences for Latin-Byzantine relations. In April 1204 the Crusaders and Venetians stormed Constantinople; sacked the city, destroying its magnificent library; and grabbed thousands of relics, which were later sold in Europe. The Byzantine Empire, as a political unit, never recovered from this destruction. The empire splintered into three parts and soon consisted of little more than the city of Constantinople. Moreover, the assault of one Christian people on another—when one of the goals of the crusade was reunion of the Greek and Latin churches—made the split between the churches permanent and discredited the entire crusading movement.

Much of medieval warfare consisted of the besieging of towns and castles. Help could not enter nor could anyone leave; the larger the number of besiegers, the greater was the chance the fortification would fall. Women swelled the numbers of besiegers. Women assisted in filling with earth the moats surrounding fortified places so that ladders and war engines could be brought close. In war zones some women concealed their sex by donning chain mail and helmets and fought with the knights.

In the late thirteenth century Turkish armies gradually conquered all other Muslim rulers and then turned against the Crusader states. In 1291 their last stronghold, the port of Acre, fell in a battle that was just as bloody as the first battle for Jerusalem two centuries earlier. Knights then needed a new battlefield for military actions, which some found in Spain, where the rulers of Aragon and Castile continued fighting Muslims until 1492.

Consequences of the Crusades

The Crusades provided an outlet for nobles' dreams of glory. Wars of foreign conquest had occurred before the Crusades, as the Norman Conquest of England in 1066 illustrates (see page 377), but for many knights migration began with the taking

Primary Source: Annals
Read a harrowing, firsthand account of the pillage of Constantinople by Western Crusaders on April 13, 1204.

of the cross. The Crusades introduced some Europeans to Eastern luxury goods, but their immediate cultural impact on the West remains debatable. By the late eleventh century strong economic and intellectual ties with the East had already been made. The Crusades were a boon to Italian merchants, however, who profited from outfitting military expeditions as well as from the opening of new trade routes and the establishment of trading communities in the Crusader states.

The Crusades proved to be a disaster for Jewish-Christian relations. In the eleventh century Jews played a major role in the international trade between the Muslim Middle East and the West. Jews also lent money to peasants, townspeople, and nobles. When the First Crusade was launched, many poor knights had to borrow from Jews to equip themselves for the expedition. Debt bred resentment. Hostility to Jews was further enhanced by Christian beliefs that they engaged in the ritual murder of Christians to use their blood in religious rituals. Such accusations led to the killing of Jewish families and sometimes entire Jewish communities, sometimes by burning people alive in the synagogue or Jewish section of town.

Legal restrictions on Jews gradually increased. Jews were forbidden to have Christian servants or employees, to hold public office, to appear in public on Christian holy days, or to enter Christian parts of town without a badge marking them as Jews.

The Crusades also left an inheritance of deep bitterness in Christian-Muslim relations. Each side dehumanized the other, viewing those who followed the other religion as unbelievers. (See the feature "Listening to the Past: An Arab View of the Crusades" on pages 384–385.) Whereas Europeans perceived the Crusades as sacred religious movements, Muslims saw them as expansionist and imperialistic. The ideal of a sacred mission to conquer or convert Muslim peoples entered Europeans' consciousness and became a continuing goal. When in 1492 Christopher Columbus sailed west, hoping to reach India, he used the language of the Crusades in his diaries, which show that he was preoccupied with the conquest of Jerusalem (see Chapter 15). Columbus wanted to establish a Christian base in India from which a new crusade against Islam could be launched.

THE CHANGING LIFE OF THE PEOPLE

What was life like for the common people of medieval Europe, and how were the lives of nobles and townspeople different?

In the late ninth century medieval intellectuals described Christian society as composed of those who pray (the monks), those who fight (the nobles), and those who work (the peasants). This image of society became popular in the Middle Ages, especially among people who were worried about the changes they saw around them. They asserted that the three orders had been established by God and that every person had been assigned a fixed place in the social order.

The tripartite model does not fully describe medieval society, however. There were degrees of wealth and status within each group. The model does not take townspeople and the emerging commercial classes into consideration. It completely excludes those who were not Christian, such as Jews, Muslims, and pagans. Those who used the model, generally bishops and other church officials, ignored the fact that each of these groups was made up of both women and men; they spoke only of warriors, monks, and farmers. Despite—or perhaps because of—these limitations, the model of the three orders was a powerful mental construct. We can use it to organize our investigation of life in the Middle Ages, though we can broaden our categories to include groups and issues that medieval authors did not. (See page 358 for discussion of the life of monks—"those who pray.")

Those Who Work

The men and women who worked the land in the twelfth and thirteenth centuries made up the overwhelming majority of the population, probably more than 90 percent. The evolution of localized feudal systems into more centralized states had relatively little impact on the daily lives of peasants except when it involved warfare. While only nobles fought, their battles often destroyed the houses, barns, and fields of ordinary people, who might also be killed either directly or as a result of the famine and disease that often accompanied war. People might seek protection in the local castle during times of warfare, but typically they worked and lived without paying much attention to the political developments underway there.

This lack of attention went in the other direction as well. Since villagers did not perform what were considered "noble" deeds, the aristocratic monks and clerics who wrote the records that serve as historical sources did not spend time or precious writing materials on them. So it is more difficult to find information on the vast majority of Europeans who were peasants than on the small group at the top of society.

Medieval theologians lumped everyone who worked the land into the category of "those who work," but in fact there were many levels of peasants, ranging from complete slaves to free and very rich farmers. Slaves were found in western Europe in the central Middle Ages, but in steadily declining numbers. That the word *slave* derives from *Slav* attests to the widespread trade in men and women from the Slavic areas. Legal language differed considerably from place to place, and the distinction between slave and serf was not always clear. Both lacked freedom—the power to do as they wished—and both were subject to the arbitrary will of one person, the lord. A serf, however, could not be bought and sold like an animal or an inanimate object, as a slave could.

The serf was required to perform labor services on the lord's land. The number of workdays varied, but it was usually three days a week except in the planting or harvest seasons, when it increased. Serfs frequently had to pay arbitrary levies, as for marriage or inheritance. The precise amounts of tax paid to the lord depended on local custom and tradition. A free person had to do none of these things. For his or her landholding, rent had to be paid to the lord, and that was often the sole obligation. A free person could move and live as he or she wished.

Serfdom was a hereditary condition. A person born a serf was likely to die a serf, though many serfs did secure their freedom. More than anything else, the economic revival that began in the eleventh century (see pages 368–371) advanced the cause of freedom for serfs. The revival saw the rise of towns, increased land productivity, the growth of long-distance trade, and the development of a money economy. With the advent of a money economy, serfs could save money and, through a third-person intermediary, use it to buy their freedom. Many energetic and hard-working serfs acquired their freedom through this method of manumission in the High Middle Ages.

The thirteenth century witnessed enormous immigration to many parts of Europe that previously had been sparsely settled. Immigration and colonization provided the opportunity for freedom and social mobility.

Another opportunity for increased personal freedom, or at least for a reduction in traditional manorial obligations and dues, was provided by the reclamation of wasteland and forestland in the eleventh and twelfth centuries. Marshes and fens were drained and slowly made arable. This type of agricultural advancement frequently improved the peasants' social and legal condition.

In the Middle Ages most European peasants, free and unfree, lived on a manor, the estate of a lord (see page 352). The manor was the basic unit of medieval rural organization and the center of rural life. The arable land of the manor was divided into two sections. The *demesne,* or home farm, was cultivated by the peasants for the lord. The other, usually larger, section was held by the peasantry. All the arable land, both the lord's and the peasants', was divided into strips, and the strips belonging to any

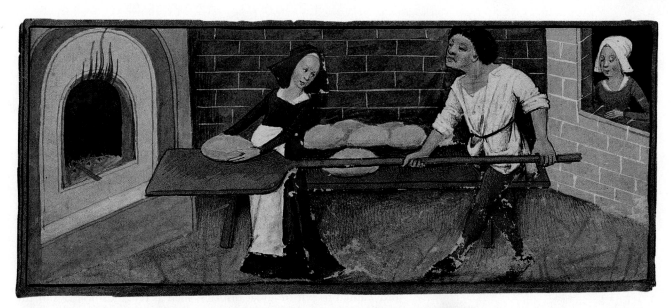

● **Baking Bread** Bread and beer or ale were the main manorial products for local consumption. While women dominated the making of ale and beer, men and women cooperated in the making and baking of bread—the staple of the diet. Most people did not have ovens in their own homes because of the danger of fire, but used the communal manorial oven, which, like a modern pizza oven, could bake several loaves at once. (Bibliothèque nationale de France)

given individual were scattered throughout the manor. All peasants cooperated in the cultivation of the land, working it as a group. All shared in any disaster as well as in any large harvest.

The peasants' work was typically divided according to gender. Men were responsible for clearing new land, plowing, and caring for large animals, and women were responsible for the care of small animals, spinning, and food preparation. Both sexes harvested and planted, though often there were gender-specific tasks within each of these major undertakings. Women and men worked in the vineyards and in the harvest and preparation of crops needed by the textile industry—flax and plants used for dyeing cloth.

Scholars have recently spent much energy investigating the structure of medieval peasant households. It appears that in western and central Europe a peasant household consisted of a simple nuclear family: a married couple alone or with a couple of children, or a widow or widower with children. The typical household numbered about five people, and blended households with half-siblings and step-parents were common, as death frequently took a first spouse and the survivor remarried.

The mainstay of the diet for peasants everywhere—and for all other classes—was bread. The diet of those living in an area with access to a river, lake, or stream was supplemented with fish, which could be preserved by salting. In many places, severe laws against hunting and trapping in the forests restricted deer and other game to the king and nobility. Except for the rare chicken or illegally caught wild game, meat appeared on the table only on the great feast days of the Christian year: Christmas, Easter, and Pentecost. Some scholars believe that by the mid-thirteenth century, there was a great increase in the consumption of meat generally. If so, this improvement in diet is evidence of an improved standard of living.

Those Who Fight

The nobility, though a small fraction of the total population, strongly influenced all aspects of medieval culture—political, economic, religious, educational, and artistic.

● **Saint Maurice** Certain individuals were held up to young men as models of ideal chivalry. One of these was Saint Maurice (d. 287), a soldier apparently executed by the Romans for refusing to renounce his Christian faith. He first emerges in the Carolingian period, and later he was held up as a model knight and declared a patron of the Holy Roman Empire and protector of the imperial (German) army in wars against the pagan Slavs. Until 1240 he was portrayed as a white man, but after that he was usually represented as a black man, as in this sandstone statue from Magdeburg Cathedral (ca. 1250). We have no idea why this change happened. Who commissioned this statue? Who carved it? Did an actual person serve as the model, and if so what was he doing in Magdeburg? *(Image of the Black Project, Harvard University/ Hickey-Robertson, Houston)*

chivalry *A code of conduct that governed the conduct of a knight, characterized by the virtues of bravery, generosity, honor, graciousness, mercy, and gallantry toward women.*

Despite political, scientific, and industrial revolutions, the nobility continued to hold real political and social power in Europe down to the nineteenth century.

Members of the nobility enjoyed a special legal status. A nobleman was free personally and in his possessions. He was limited only by his military obligation to king, duke, or prince. As the result of his liberty, he had certain rights and responsibilities. He raised troops and commanded them in the field. He held courts that dispensed a sort of justice. Sometimes he coined money for use within his territories. As lord of the people who settled on his lands, he made political decisions affecting them, resolved disputes among them, and protected them in time of attack. The liberty and privileges of the noble were inheritable, perpetuated by blood and not by wealth alone.

As a vassal a noble was required to fight for his lord or for the king when called on to do so. By the mid-twelfth century, this service was limited in most parts of western Europe to forty days a year. The noble was obliged to attend his lord's court on important occasions when the lord wanted to put on great displays, such as religious holidays or the marriage of a son or daughter.

Originally, most knights focused solely on military skills, but gradually a different ideal of knighthood emerged, usually termed **chivalry.** Chivalry was a code of conduct originally devised by the clergy to transform the crude and brutal behavior of the knightly class. It may have originated in oaths administered to Crusaders in which fighting was declared to have a sacred purpose and knights vowed loyalty to the church as well as to their lords. Other qualities gradually became part of chivalry: bravery, generosity, honor, graciousness, mercy, and eventually gallantry toward women. The chivalric ideal—and it was an ideal, not a standard pattern of behavior—created a new standard of masculinity for nobles, in which loyalty and honor remained the most important qualities, but graceful dancing and intelligent conversation were not considered unmanly.

Until the late thirteenth century, when royal authority intervened, a noble in France or England had great power over the knights and peasants on his estates. He maintained order among them and dispensed justice to them. The quality of life on the manor and its productivity were related in no small way to the temperament and decency of the lord—and his lady.

Women played a large and important role in the functioning of the estate. They were responsible for the practical management of the household's "inner economy"—cooking, brewing, spinning, weaving, caring for yard animals. When the lord was away for long periods, his wife became the sole manager of the family properties. Often the responsibilities of the estate fell permanently to her when she became a widow.

Towns and Cities

The rise of towns and the growth of a new business and commercial class was a central part of Europe's recovery after the disorders of the tenth century. The growth of towns was made possible by several factors: a rise in population; increased agricultural output, which provided an adequate food supply for new town dwellers; and a minimum of peace and political stability, which allowed merchants to transport and sell goods. The development of towns was to lay the foundations for Europe's transformation, centuries later, from a rural agricultural society into an urban industrial society—a change with global implications. In their backgrounds and abilities, townspeople represented diversity and change. Their occupations and their preoccupations were different from those of the feudal nobility and the laboring peasantry. Medieval towns had a few characteristics in common. Walls enclosed the town. (The terms *burgher* and *bourgeois* derive from the Old English and Old German words *burg, burgh, borg,* and *borough* for "a walled or fortified place.") The town had a marketplace. It was likely to have a mint for the coining of money and a court to settle disputes. In each town, many people inhabited a small, cramped area. As population increased, towns rebuilt their walls, expanding the living space to accommodate growing numbers.

The history of towns in the eleventh through thirteenth centuries consists largely of merchants' efforts to acquire liberties. In the Middle Ages *liberties* meant special privileges. For the town dweller, liberties included the privilege of living and trading on the lord's land. The most important privilege a medieval townsperson could gain was personal freedom. It gradually developed that an individual who lived in a town for a year and a day, and was accepted by the townspeople, was free of servile obligations and servile status. More than anything else, perhaps, the personal freedom that came with residence in a town contributed to the emancipation of many serfs in the central Middle Ages. Liberty meant citizenship, and, unlike foreigners and outsiders of any kind, a full citizen of a town did not have to pay taxes and tolls in the market. Obviously, this exemption increased profits.

In the acquisition of full rights of self-government, the **merchant guilds** played a large role. Medieval people were long accustomed to communal enterprises. In the late tenth and early eleventh centuries, those who were engaged in foreign trade joined together in merchant guilds; united enterprise provided them greater security and less risk of losses than did individual action. At about the same time, the artisans and craftsmen of particular trades formed their own guilds. These were the butchers, bakers, and candlestick makers. Members of the **craft guilds** determined the quality, quantity, and price of the goods produced and the number of apprentices and journeymen affiliated with the guild. Formal membership in guilds was generally limited to men, but women worked less formally in guild shops.

By the late eleventh century, especially in the towns of the Low Countries (modern Netherlands, Belgium, and Luxembourg) and northern Italy, the leaders of the merchant guilds were rich and powerful. They constituted an oligarchy in their towns, controlling economic life and bargaining with kings and lords for political independence and full rights of self-government.

Medieval cities served, above all else, as markets. In some respects the entire city was a marketplace. The place where a product was made and sold was typically the merchant's residence. Usually the ground floor was the scene of production. A window or

merchant guilds *Associations of merchants and traders organized to provide greater security and minimize loss in commercial ventures.*

craft guilds *Associations of artisans and craftsmen organized to regulate the quality, quantity, and price of the goods produced as well as the number of affiliated apprentices and journeymen.*

● **Medieval City Street** This illumination shows a street scene of a medieval town with a barber, cloth merchants, and an apothecary all offering their wares and services on the ground floor of their household-workshops. *(Bibliothèque nationale de France)*

door opened from the main workroom directly onto the street, and passersby could look in and see the goods being produced. The merchant's family lived above the business on the second or third floor. As the business and the family expanded, the merchant built additional stories on top of the house.

Most medieval cities developed haphazardly. There was little town planning. Air and water pollution presented serious problems. Many families raised pigs for household consumption in sties next to their houses. Horses and oxen, the chief means of transportation and power, dropped tons of dung on the streets every year. It was universal practice in the early towns to dump household waste, both animal and human, into the road in front of one's house. The stench must have been abominable. Lack of space, air pollution, and sanitation problems bedeviled urban people in medieval times, as they do today. Still, people wanted to get into medieval cities because they represented opportunities for economic advancement, social mobility, and improvement in legal status.

The Expansion of Long-Distance Trade

The growth of towns went hand-in-hand with a remarkable expansion of trade, as artisans and craftsmen manufactured goods for local and foreign consumption. Most trade centered in towns and was controlled by professional traders. The transportation of goods involved serious risks. Shipwrecks were common. Pirates infested the sea-lanes, and robbers and thieves roamed almost all of the land routes. Since the risks were so great, merchants preferred to share them. A group of people would thus pool some of their capital to finance an expedition to a distant place. When the ship or caravan returned and the goods brought back were sold, the investors would share the profits. If disaster struck the caravan, an investor's loss was limited to the amount of that individual's investment.

The Italian cities, especially Venice, led the West in trade in general and completely dominated the Asian market. In 1082 Venice made an important commercial treaty with the Byzantine Empire, gaining significant trading privileges in Constantinople. The sacking of that city during the Fourth Crusade (see page 364) brought Venice vast trading rights. Venice was ideally located at the northwestern end of the Adriatic Sea, with easy access to the transalpine land routes as well as the Adriatic and Mediterranean sea-lanes. The markets of North Africa, Byzantium, and Russia and the great fairs of Ghent in Flanders and Champagne in France provided commercial opportunities that Venice quickly seized. Venetian ships carried salt from the Venetian lagoon, pepper and other spices from North Africa, and slaves, silk, and purple textiles from the East to northern and western Europe. Wealthy European consumers had greater access to foreign luxuries, and their tastes became more sophisticated.

Merchants from other cities in northern Italy such as Florence and Milan were also important traders, and they developed new business procedures that facilitated the movement of goods and money. The towns of Bruges, Ghent, and Ypres in Flanders were also leaders in long-distance trade and built up a vast industry in the manufacture of cloth. This was made easier by Flanders' geographical situation. Just across the Channel from England, Flanders had easy access to English wool.

Wool was the cornerstone of the English medieval economy. Population growth in the twelfth century and the success of the Flemish and Italian textile industries created foreign demand for English wool. The production of English wool stimulated Flemish manufacturing, and the expansion of the Flemish cloth industry in turn spurred the production of English wool. The availability of raw wool also encouraged the development of domestic cloth manufacture within England, and commercial families in these towns grew fabulously rich.

In much of northern Europe, the **Hanseatic League** (known as the Hansa for short), a mercantile association of towns formed to achieve mutual security and exclusive trading rights, controlled trade. During the thirteenth century perhaps two hundred

Hanseatic League *A mercantile association of towns that allowed for mutual protection and security.*

cities from Holland to Poland joined the league, but Lübeck always remained the dominant member. The ships of the Hansa cities carried furs, wax, copper, fish, grain, timber, and wine. These goods were exchanged for finished products, mainly cloth and salt, from western cities. At cities such as Bruges and London, Hanseatic merchants secured special trading concessions exempting them from all tolls and allowing them to trade at local fairs. Hanseatic merchants established foreign trading centers, which they called "factories." The term *factory* was subsequently used in the seventeenth and eighteenth centuries to mean business offices and places in Asia and Africa where goods were stored and slaves held before being shipped to Europe or the Americas. (See Table 9.1 on page 237 for the size of the trans-Saharan slave trade.)

These developments added up to what is often called the **commercial revolution.** In giving the transformation this name, historians point not only to an increase in the sheer volume of trade and in the complexity and sophistication of business procedures, but also to the new attitude toward business and making money. Some even detect a "capitalist spirit" in which making a profit is regarded as a good thing in itself, regardless of the uses to which that profit is put.

The commercial revolution created a great deal of new wealth, which did not escape the attention of kings and other rulers. Wealth could be taxed, and through taxation kings could create strong and centralized states. In the years to come, alliances with the middle classes were to enable kings to defeat feudal powers and aristocratic interests and to build the states that came to be called "modern."

The commercial revolution also provided the opportunity for thousands of serfs to improve their social position. The slow but steady transformation of European society from almost completely rural and isolated to relatively more sophisticated constituted the greatest effect of the commercial revolution that began in the eleventh century.

commercial revolution *The transformation of the economic structure of Europe, beginning in the eleventh century, from a rural, manorial society to a more complex mercantile society.*

THE CULTURE OF THE MIDDLE AGES

What were the primary new cultural institutions and forms developed in medieval Europe?

Just as the first strong secular states emerged in the thirteenth century, so did the first universities. This was no coincidence. The new bureaucratic states and the church needed educated administrators, and universities were a response to this need. This period also gave rise to new styles of architecture and literature.

Universities and Scholasticism

Since the time of the Carolingian Empire, monasteries and cathedral schools had offered the only formal instruction available. Monasteries were located in rural environments and geared to religious concerns. In contrast, schools attached to cathedrals and run by the bishop and his clergy were frequently situated in bustling cities, and in the eleventh century in Bologna and other Italian cities wealthy businessmen established municipal schools. Inhabited by people of many backgrounds and "nationalities," cities stimulated the growth and exchange of ideas. In the course of the twelfth century, cathedral schools in France and municipal schools in Italy developed into universities.

The beginnings of the universities in Europe owe at least one central idea to the Islamic world. As we have seen, features in the structure of Muslim higher education bear striking parallels to later European ones (see page 214). The most significant of these developments was the **college,** which appeared in Europe about a century after its Muslim counterpart, the madrasa, in the Islamic world. First at Paris, then at Oxford in England, universities began as collections of colleges, privately endowed residences for the lodging of poor students. A medieval university was a corporation, an abstract juristic or legal entity with rights and personality. Islamic law accepted only

college *A university was made up of a collection of these privately endowed residences for the lodging of poor students.*

an actual physical person as having a legal personality. Europeans adapted their legal principles to Muslim ideas of the college, and the notion of the university emerged in the West.

The growth of the University of Bologna coincided with a revival of interest in Roman law. The study of Roman law as embodied in Justinian's *Code* had never completely died out in the West, but this sudden burst of interest seems to have been inspired by Irnerius (d. 1125), a great teacher at Bologna. Irnerius not only explained the Roman law of Justinian's *Code* but also applied it to difficult practical situations.

At Salerno, interest in medicine had persisted for centuries. Greek and Muslim physicians there had studied the use of herbs as cures and experimented with surgery. The twelfth century ushered in a new interest in Greek medical texts and in the work of Arab and Greek doctors.

In the first decades of the twelfth century, students converged on Paris. These young men crowded into the cathedral school of Notre Dame and spilled over into the area later called the Latin Quarter—whose name probably reflects the Italian origin of many of the students. The cathedral school's international reputation had already drawn to Paris scholars from all over Europe. One of the most famous of them was Peter Abélard (1079–1142). Fascinated by logic, which he believed could be used to solve most problems, Abélard used a method of systematic doubting in his writing and teaching. As he put it, "By doubting we come to questioning, and by questioning we perceive the truth." Other scholars merely asserted theological principles; Abélard discussed and analyzed them.

In northern Europe—at Paris and later at Oxford and Cambridge in England—associations or guilds of professors organized universities. University faculties grouped themselves according to academic disciplines, or schools—law, medicine, arts, and theology. The professors, known as schoolmen or **Scholastics,** developed a method of thinking, reasoning, and writing in which questions were raised and authorities cited on both sides of a question. The goal of the Scholastic method was to arrive at definitive answers and to provide a rational explanation for what was believed on faith.

Thirteenth-century Scholastics devoted an enormous amount of time to collecting and organizing knowledge on all topics. These collections were published as *summa,* or reference books. There were summa on law, philosophy, vegetation, animal life, and theology. Saint Thomas Aquinas (1225–1274), a professor at Paris, produced the most famous collection, the *Summa Theologica,* which deals with a vast number of theological questions.

At all universities, the standard method of teaching was the *lecture*—that is, a reading. The professor read a passage from the Bible, Justinian's *Code,* or one of Aristotle's treatises. He then explained and interpreted the passage; his interpretation was called a *gloss.* Students wrote down everything. Because books had to be copied by hand, they were extremely expensive, and few students could afford them. Examinations were given after three, four, or five years of study, when the student applied for a degree. Examinations were oral and very difficult. If the candidate passed, he was awarded the first, or bachelor's, degree. Further study, about as long, arduous, and expensive as it is today, enabled the graduate to try for the master's and doctor's degrees. Degrees were technically licenses to teach. Most students, however, did not become teachers. They staffed the expanding royal and papal administrations.

> **Scholastics** *Medieval professors who developed a method of thinking, reasoning, and writing in which questions were raised and authorities cited on both sides of a question.*

> **Primary Source:**
> *Summa Theologica*: On Free Will
> *This selection from Thomas Aquinas, on the question of free will, shows a synthesis of Aristotelian logic and Christian theology.*

Cathedrals

As we have seen, religious devotion was expressed through daily rituals, holiday ceremonies, and the creation of new institutions such as universities and religious orders. People also wanted permanent visible representations of their piety, and both church and city leaders wanted physical symbols of their wealth and power. These aims found their outlet in the building of tens of thousands of churches, chapels, abbeys, and, most spectacularly, **cathedrals** in the twelfth and thirteenth centuries. A cathedral is the church of a bishop and the administrative headquarters of a diocese, a church district headed by a bishop. The word comes from the Greek word *kathedra*, meaning seat, because the bishop's throne, a symbol of the office, is located in the cathedral.

Between 1180 and 1270 in France alone, eighty cathedrals, about five hundred abbey churches, and tens of thousands of parish churches were constructed. All these churches displayed a new architectural style. Fifteenth-century critics called the new style **Gothic** because they mistakenly believed that the fifth-century Goths invented it. It actually developed partly in reaction to the earlier Romanesque style, which resembled ancient Roman architecture. Cathedrals, abbeys, and village churches testify to the deep religious faith and piety of medieval people.

The inspiration for the Gothic style originated in the brain of Suger, abbot of Saint-Denis, who had decided to reconstruct the old Carolingian church at his monastery. The basic features of Gothic architecture—the pointed arch, the ribbed vault, and the flying buttress—allowed unprecedented interior lightness. From Muslim Spain, Islamic methods of ribbed vaulting seem to have heavily influenced the building of Gothic churches. Since the ceiling of a Gothic church weighed less than that of a

cathedral *A church, headed by a bishop, which forms the administrative center of a diocese. From the Greek term* kathedra, *meaning "seat," since the cathedral housed the throne of the bishop.*

Gothic *The term for the architectural and artistic style that prevailed in Europe from the mid-twelfth to the sixteenth century.*

● **Notre Dame Cathedral, Paris (begun 1163), View from the South** This view offers a fine example of the twin towers (*left*), the spire, the great rose window over the south portal, and the flying buttresses that support the walls and the vaults. Like hundreds of other churches in medieval Europe, it was dedicated to the Virgin. With a nave rising 226 feet, Notre Dame was the tallest building in Europe. (*David R. Frazier/Photo Researchers, Inc.*)

Romanesque church, the walls could be thinner. Stained-glass windows were cut into the stone, so that the interior, Suger exulted, "would shine with the wonderful and uninterrupted light of most sacred windows, pervading the interior beauty."[1]

Cathedrals served secular as well as religious purposes. The sanctuary containing the altar and the bishop's chair belonged to the clergy, but the rest of the church belonged to the people. In addition to marriages, baptisms, and funerals, there were scores of feast days on which the entire town gathered in the cathedral for festivities. Local guilds met in the cathedrals to arrange business deals and to plan recreational events and the support of disabled members. Magistrates and municipal officials held political meetings there. Pilgrims slept there, lovers courted there, and traveling actors staged plays there. First and foremost, however, the cathedral was intended to teach the people the doctrines of Christian faith through visual images. Architecture became the servant of theology.

Troubadour Poetry

troubadours *Medieval poets in southern Europe who wrote and sang lyrical verses devoted to the themes of love, desire, beauty, and gallantry.*

While amateur musicians played for peasant festivities, professional musicians and poets performed and composed at the courts of nobles and rulers in medieval Europe. In southern Europe, especially in the area of southern France known as Provence, poets who called themselves **troubadours** wrote and sang lyric verses celebrating love, desire, beauty, and gallantry. The word *troubadour* comes from the Provençal word *trobar*, which in turn derives from the Arabic *taraba*, meaning "to sing" or "to sing poetry." Troubadour songs had a variety of themes. Men sang about "courtly love," the pure love a knight felt for his lady, whom he sought to win by military prowess and patience; about the love a knight felt for the wife of his feudal lord; or about carnal desires seeking satisfaction. Some poems exalted the married state, and others idealized adulterous relationships; some were earthy and bawdy, and others advised young girls to remain chaste in preparation for marriage.

Troubadours certainly felt Hispano-Arabic influences. In the eleventh century Christians of southern France were in intimate contact with the Arabized world of Andalusia, where reverence for the lady in a "courtly" tradition had long existed. Troubadour poetry represents another facet of the strong Muslim influence on European culture and life.

● ● ● ● ● ● ● ● ● ● ● ●

CRISES OF THE LATER MIDDLE AGES

Why has the late Middle Ages been seen as a time of calamity and crisis?

During the later Middle Ages, the last book of the New Testament, the book of Revelation, inspired thousands of sermons and hundreds of religious tracts. The book of Revelation deals with visions of the end of the world, with disease, war, famine, and death. It is no wonder this part of the Bible was so popular. Between 1300 and 1450 Europeans experienced a frightful series of shocks: climate change, economic dislocation, plague, war, social upheaval, and increased crime and violence. Death and preoccupation with death make the fourteenth century one of the most wrenching periods of history in Europe.

The Great Famine and the Black Death

Economic difficulties originating in the later thirteenth century were fully manifest by the start of the fourteenth. In the first decade, the countries of northern Europe experienced considerable price inflation. The costs of grain, livestock, and dairy products rose sharply. Severe weather, which historical geographers label the Little Ice Age, made a serious situation frightful. An unusual number of storms brought torrential rains, ruining the wheat, oat, and hay crops on which people and animals almost everywhere depended. Population had steadily increased in the twelfth and thirteenth centuries. The amount of food yielded, however, did not match the level of population growth. Bad weather had disastrous results. Poor harvests—one in four was likely to be poor—led to scarcity and starvation. Almost all of northern Europe suffered a terrible famine in the years 1315 to 1322. Famine had dire social consequences: peasants were forced to sell or mortgage their lands for money to buy food; the number of vagabonds, or homeless people, greatly increased, as did petty crime. An undernourished population was ripe for the Grim Reaper, who appeared in 1347 in the form of the **Black Death** (see Map 13.3).

Plague symptoms were first described in 1331 in southwestern China, part of the Mongol Empire. Plague-infested rats accompanied Mongol armies and merchant caravans carrying silk, spices, and gold across central Asia in the 1330s. Then they stowed away on ships, carrying the disease to the ports of the Black Sea by the 1340s. In October 1347 Genoese ships traveling from the Crimea in southern Russia brought the bubonic plague to Messina, from which it spread across Sicily and up into Italy. By late spring of 1348 southern Germany was attacked. Frightened French authorities chased a galley bearing the disease from the port of Marseilles, but not before plague had

Black Death *The bubonic plague that first struck Europe in 1347. It spread either in the bubonic form by flea bites or in the pneumonic form directly from the breath of one person to another. In less virulent forms, the disease reappeared many times until the early eighteenth century.*

MAP 13.3 **The Course of the Black Death in Fourteenth-Century Europe** The bubonic plague followed trade routes as it spread into and across Europe, carried by rats on board ship and in merchants' bags and parcels. A few cities that took strict quarantine measures were spared.

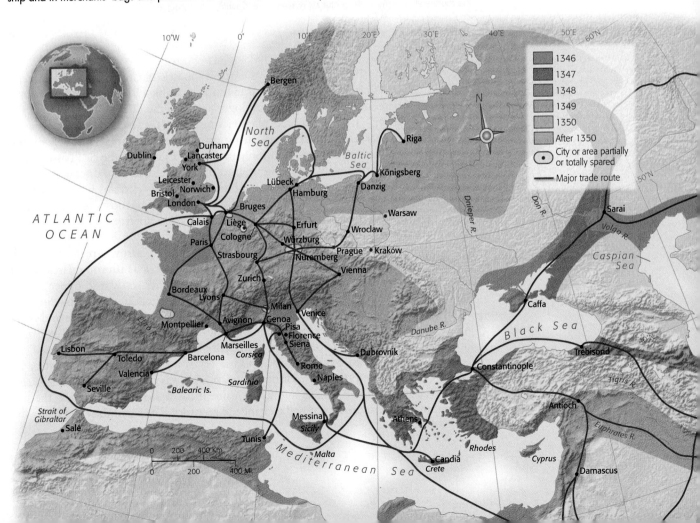

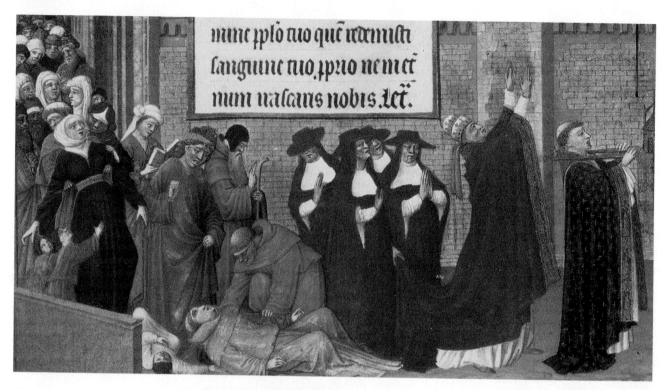

● **Procession of Saint Gregory** According to the *Golden Legend*, a thirteenth-century collection of saints' lives, the bubonic plague ravaged Rome when Gregory I was elected pope (r. 590–604). He immediately ordered special prayers and processions around the city. Here, as people circle the walls, new victims fall (center). The architecture, the cardinals, and the friars all indicate that this painting dates from the fourteenth, not the sixth, century. *(Musée Condé, Chantilly/Art Resource, NY)*

infected the city. In June 1348 two ships entered the Bristol Channel and introduced it into England. All Europe felt the scourge of this horrible disease.

Most historians and almost all microbiologists identify the disease that spread in the fourteenth century as the bubonic plague, caused by the bacillus *Yersinia pestis.* The disease normally afflicts rats. Fleas living on the infected rats drink their blood; the bacteria that cause the plague multiply in the flea's gut; and the flea passes them on to the next rat it bites by throwing up into the bite. Usually the disease is limited to rats and other rodents, but at certain points in history—perhaps when most rats have been killed off—the fleas have jumped from their rodent hosts to humans and other animals. The bacillus could also be transmitted directly from person to person through coughing.

Urban conditions were ideal for the spread of disease. Narrow streets filled with mud, refuse, and human excrement were as much cesspools as thoroughfares. Dead animals and sore-covered beggars greeted the traveler. Houses whose upper stories projected over the lower ones eliminated light and air. And extreme overcrowding was commonplace. Standards of personal hygiene remained frightfully low. Fleas and body lice were universal afflictions: one more bite did not cause much alarm. But if that nibble came from a bacillus-bearing flea, an entire household or area was doomed.

The classic symptom of the bubonic plague was a growth the size of a nut or an apple in the armpit, in the groin, or on the neck. This was the boil, or *bubo,* that gave the disease its name and caused agonizing pain. If the bubo was lanced and the pus thoroughly drained, the victim had a chance of recovery. The secondary stage was the appearance of black spots or blotches caused by bleeding under the skin. Finally, the victim began to cough violently and spit blood. This stage, indicating the presence of thousands of bacilli in the bloodstream, signaled the end, and death followed in two or three days.

Physicians could sometimes ease the pain but had no cure. Most people—lay, scholarly, and medical—believed that the Black Death was caused by some "vicious property in the air" that carried the disease from place to place. When ignorance was joined to fear and ancient bigotry, savage cruelty sometimes resulted. Many people believed that the Jews had poisoned the wells of Christian communities and thereby infected the drinking water. This charge led to the murder of thousands of Jews across Europe.

Because population figures for the period before the arrival of the plague do not exist for most countries and cities, only educated guesses can be made about mortality rates. Of a total English population of perhaps 4.2 million, probably 1.4 million died of the Black Death in its several visits. Densely populated Italian cities endured incredible losses. Florence lost between one-half and two-thirds of its population when the plague visited in 1348. The disease recurred intermittently in the 1360s and 1370s and reappeared many times down to the early 1700s.

Economic historians and demographers sharply dispute the impact of the plague on the economy in the late fourteenth century. The traditional view that the plague had a disastrous effect has been greatly modified. Many parts of Europe suffered from overpopulation in the early fourteenth century. Population decline brought increased demand for labor, which meant greater mobility among peasant and working classes. Wages rose, providing better distribution of income. Per capita wealth among those who survived increased, and some areas experienced economic prosperity as a long-term consequence of the plague.

The psychological consequences of the plague were profound. It is not surprising that some people sought release in orgies and gross sensuality, while others turned to the severest forms of asceticism and frenzied religious fervor. Groups of *flagellants,* men and women who whipped and scourged themselves as penance for their and society's sins, believed that the Black Death was God's punishment for humanity's wickedness.

The Hundred Years' War

The plague ravaged populations in Asia, North Africa, and Europe; in western Europe a long international war added further death and destruction. England and France had engaged in sporadic military hostilities from the time of the Norman Conquest in 1066, and in the middle of the fourteenth century these became more intense. From 1337 to 1453, the two countries intermittently fought one another in what was the longest war in European history, ultimately dubbed the Hundred Years' War though it actually lasted 116 years.

The Hundred Years' War had both distant and immediate causes. The immediate cause of the war was a dispute over who would inherit the French throne. The English claimed Aquitaine as an ancient feudal inheritance. In 1329 England's King Edward III (r. 1327–1377) paid homage to Philip VI (r. 1328–1350) for Aquitaine. French policy, however, was strongly expansionist, and in 1337 Philip, determined to exercise full jurisdiction there, confiscated the duchy. Edward III maintained that the only way he could exercise his rightful sovereignty over Aquitaine was by assuming the title of king of France. As the grandson and eldest surviving male descendant of Philip the Fair, he believed he could rightfully make this claim.

More distant causes included economic factors involving the wool trade and the control of Flemish towns. The wool trade between England and Flanders was the cornerstone of both countries' economies; they were closely interdependent. Flanders was a fief of the French crown, and the Flemish aristocracy was highly sympathetic to

● **Siege of the Castle of Mortagne near Bordeaux (1377)** Medieval warfare usually consisted of small skirmishes and attacks on castles. This miniature of a battle in the Hundred Years' War shows the French besieging an English-held castle, which held out for six months. Most of the soldiers use longbows, although at the left two men shoot primitive muskets above a pair of cannon. Painted in the late fifteenth century, the scene reflects military technology available at the time it was painted, not the time of the actual siege. (© British Library Board. All Rights Reserved. MS royal 14e. iv f.23)

the monarchy in Paris. But the wealth of Flemish merchants and cloth manufacturers depended on English wool, and Flemish burghers strongly supported the claims of Edward III.

The Hundred Years' War was popular because it presented unusual opportunities for wealth and advancement. Poor and unemployed knights were promised regular wages. Great nobles expected to be rewarded with estates. Royal exhortations to the troops before battles repeatedly stressed that, if victorious, the men might keep whatever they seized. The war, fought almost entirely in France and the Low Countries, consisted mainly of a series of random sieges and cavalry raids. During the war's early stages, England was highly successful, using longbows fired by foot soldiers and early cannons against French mounted knights. By 1419 the English had advanced to the walls of Paris. But the French cause was not lost. Though England scored the initial victories, France won the war.

The ultimate French success rests heavily on the actions of an obscure French peasant girl, Joan of Arc, whose vision and work revived French fortunes and led to victory. Born in 1412 to well-to-do peasants, Joan of Arc grew up in a pious household. During adolescence she began to hear voices, which she later said belonged to Saint

Michael, Saint Catherine, and Saint Margaret. In 1428 these voices told her that the dauphin (the uncrowned King Charles VII) had to be crowned and the English expelled from France. Joan went to the French court and secured the support of the dauphin for her relief of the besieged city of Orléans.

Joan arrived before Orléans on April 28, 1429. Seventeen years old, she knew little of warfare and believed that if she could keep the French troops from swearing and frequenting brothels, victory would be theirs. On May 8 the English, weakened by disease and lack of supplies, withdrew from Orléans. Ten days later, Charles VII was crowned king at Reims. These two events marked the turning point in the war.

In 1430 England's allies, the Burgundians, captured Joan and sold her to the English. The French did not intervene. The English wanted Joan eliminated for obvious political reasons, but sorcery (witchcraft) was the charge at her trial. Witch persecution was increasing in the fifteenth century, and Joan's wearing of men's clothes appeared not only aberrant but indicative of contact with the Devil. In 1431 the court condemned her as a heretic, and she was burned at the stake in the marketplace at Rouen. A new trial in 1456 rehabilitated her name. In 1920 she was canonized, and today she is revered as the second patron saint of France.

The relief of Orléans stimulated French pride and rallied French resources. As the war dragged on, loss of life mounted, and money appeared to be flowing into a bottomless pit, demands for an end increased in England. Slowly the French reconquered Normandy and finally ejected the English from Aquitaine. At the war's end in 1453, only the town of Calais remained in English hands.

The long war had a profound impact on the political and cultural lives of the two countries. Most notably, it stimulated the development of the English Parliament. Between 1250 and 1450, representative assemblies from several classes of society flourished in many European countries, but only the English Parliament became a powerful national body. Edward III's constant need for money to pay for the war compelled him to summon it many times, and its representatives slowly built up their powers.

In England and France the war promoted *nationalism*—the feeling of unity and identity that binds together a people who speak the same language, have a common ancestry and customs, and live in the same area. In the fourteenth century nationalism largely took the form of hostility toward foreigners. Both Philip VI and Edward III drummed up support for the war by portraying the enemy as an alien, evil people. Perhaps no one expressed this national consciousness better than Joan of Arc when she exulted that the enemy had been "driven out of *France.*"

Challenges to the Church

In times of crisis or disaster, people of all faiths have sought the consolation of religion. While local clergy eased the suffering of many, a dispute over who was the legitimate pope weakened the church as an institution. In 1309, pressure by the French monarchy led the popes to move their court to Avignon in southern France, the location of the papal summer palace. Not surprisingly, all the Avignon popes were French, and they concentrated on bureaucratic and financial matters to the exclusion of spiritual objectives.

In 1376, one of the French popes returned to Rome, and when he died there several years later Roman citizens demanded an Italian pope who would remain in Rome. The cardinals elected Urban VI, but his tactless, arrogant, and bullheaded manner caused them to regret their decision. The cardinals slipped away from Rome and declared Urban's election invalid because it had come about under threats from the Roman mob. They elected a French cardinal, who took the name Clement VII (r. 1378–1394) and set himself up at Avignon in opposition to Urban. There were thus two popes, a situation that was later termed the **Great Schism.**

Great Schism *The period from 1378 to 1417 during which the Western Christian church had two popes, one in Rome and one in Avignon.*

The powers of Europe aligned themselves with Urban or Clement along strictly political lines. France recognized the Frenchman, Clement; England, France's historic enemy, recognized Urban. The scandal provoked horror and vigorous cries for reform. The common people—hard-pressed by inflation, wars, and plague—were thoroughly confused about which pope was legitimate. The schism weakened the religious faith of many Christians.

A first attempt to heal the schism led to a threefold schism, but finally, because of the pressure of the Holy Roman emperor Sigismund, a great council met at Constance (1414–1418). The council eventually deposed the three schismatic popes and elected a new leader, who took the name Martin V (1417–1431). Martin dissolved the council, and the schism was over. Nothing was done about reform, however, though many people hoped the council would address this. In the later fifteenth century the papacy concentrated on Italian problems to the exclusion of universal Christian interests.

Peasant and Urban Revolts

In 1358, when French taxation for the Hundred Years' War fell heavily on the poor, the frustrations of the French peasantry exploded in a massive uprising called the **Jacquerie,** after a supposedly happy agricultural laborer, Jacques Bonhomme (Good Fellow). Recently hit by plague and experiencing famine in some areas, peasants erupted in anger and frustration. Crowds swept through the countryside, slashing the throats of nobles, burning their castles, raping their wives and daughters, and killing or maiming their horses and cattle. Artisans, small merchants, and parish priests joined the peasants. Urban and rural groups committed terrible destruction, and for several weeks the nobles were on the defensive. Then the upper class united to repress the revolt with merciless ferocity. Thousands of the "Jacques," innocent as well as guilty, were cut down.

The Peasants' Revolt in England in 1381, involving perhaps a hundred thousand people, was probably the largest single uprising of the entire Middle Ages. The causes of the rebellion were complex and varied from place to place. In general, though, the thirteenth century had witnessed the steady commutation of labor services for cash rents, and the Black Death had drastically cut the labor supply. As a result, peasants demanded higher wages and fewer manorial obligations. Their lords countered with a law freezing wages and binding workers to their manors. Unable to climb higher, the peasants found release for their economic frustrations in revolt. But economic grievances combined with other factors. The south of England, where the revolt broke out, had been subjected to frequent and destructive French raids. The English government did little to protect the south, and villages grew increasingly scared and insecure. Moreover, decades of aristocratic violence, much of it perpetrated against the weak peasantry, had bred hostility and bitterness.

The straw that broke the camel's back in England was the reimposition of a head tax on all adult males. Beginning with assaults on the tax collectors, the uprising in England followed much the same course as had the Jacquerie in France. Castles and manors were sacked; manorial records were destroyed. Many nobles, including the archbishop of Canterbury, who had ordered the collection of the tax, were murdered. Urban discontent merged with rural violence. Apprentices and journeymen, frustrated because the highest positions in the guilds were closed to them, rioted.

The boy-king Richard II (r. 1377–1399) met the leaders of the revolt, agreed to charters ensuring the peasants' freedom, tricked them with false promises, and then proceeded to crush the uprising with terrible ferocity. Although the nobility tried to restore ancient duties of serfdom, virtually a century of freedom had elapsed, and the commutation of manorial services continued. Rural serfdom had disappeared in England by 1550.

Jacquerie *A massive uprising by French peasants in 1358 protesting heavy taxation.*

Conditions in England and France were not unique. In Florence in 1378 the *ciompi*, or poor propertyless workers, revolted. Serious social trouble occurred in Lübeck, Brunswick, and other German cities. In Spain in 1391 massive uprisings in Seville and Barcelona took the form of vicious attacks on Jewish communities. Rebellions and uprisings everywhere revealed deep peasant and working-class frustration and the general socioeconomic crisis of the time.

Chapter Summary

To assess your mastery of this chapter, go to
bedfordstmartins.com/mckayworld

Key Terms

- vassal
- fief
- feudalism
- manorialism
- serf
- jurors
- lay investiture
- common law
- saints
- reconquista
- Crusades
- chivalry
- merchant guilds
- craft guilds
- Hanseatic League
- commercial revolution
- college
- Scholastics
- cathedral
- Gothic
- troubadours
- Black Death
- Great Schism
- Jacquerie

• *How did medieval rulers overcome internal divisions and external threats, and work to create larger and more stable territories?*

As Charlemagne's empire broke down, a new form of decentralized government, later known as feudalism, emerged. Local strongmen provided what little security existed. No European political power was strong enough to put up effective resistance to external attack, which came from many directions. Vikings from Scandinavia carried out raids for plunder along the coasts and rivers of Europe and traveled as far as Iceland, Greenland, North America, and Russia. In many places they set up permanent states, as did the Magyars, who came into Europe from the east. The end of the great invasions signaled the beginning of profound changes in European society. As domestic disorder slowly subsided, rulers began to develop new institutions of government and legal codes that enabled them to assert their power over lesser lords and the general population.

• *How did the Christian church enhance its power and create new institutions and religious practices?*

The eleventh century witnessed the beginnings of a religious revival. Monasteries remodeled themselves, and new religious orders were founded. After a century of corruption and decadence, the papacy reformed itself. The popes worked to clarify church doctrine and codify church law. Religion structured people's daily lives and the yearly calendar. Christianity expanded into Europe's northern and eastern regions, and Christian rulers expanded their holdings in Muslim Spain.

• *What were the motives, course, and consequences of the Crusades?*

A papal call to retake the holy city of Jerusalem led to the Crusades, nearly two centuries of warfare between Christians and Muslims. The enormous popular response to papal calls for crusading reveals the influence of the reformed papacy and a new sense that war against the church's enemies was a duty of nobles. The Crusades were initially successful, and small Christian states were established in the Middle East. These did not last very long, however, and other effects of the Crusades were disastrous. Jewish communities in Europe were regularly attacked; relations between the Western and Eastern Christian churches were poisoned by the Crusaders' attack on Constantinople; and Christian-Muslim relations became more uniformly hostile than they had been earlier.

• *What was life like for the common people of medieval Europe, and how were the lives of nobles and townspeople different?*

The performance of agricultural services and the payment of rents preoccupied peasants throughout the Middle Ages. Though peasants led hard lives, the reclamation of wasteland and forestlands, migration to frontier territory, or flight to a town offered a means of social mobility. Nobles were a tiny fraction of the total population, but they exerted great power over all aspects of life. Aristocratic values and attitudes, often described as chivalry, shaded all aspects of medieval culture. Medieval cities recruited people from the countryside with the promise of greater freedom and new possibilities. Cities provided economic opportunity, which, together with the revival of long-distance trade and a new capitalistic spirit, led to greater wealth, a higher standard of living, and upward social mobility for many people. Merchants and artisans formed guilds to protect their means of livelihood. Not everyone in medieval cities shared in the prosperity, however, for many residents lived hand-to-mouth on low wages.

• *What were the primary new cultural institutions and forms developed in medieval Europe?*

The towns that became centers of trade and production in the High Middle Ages developed into cultural and intellectual centers. Trade brought in new ideas as well as merchandise, and in many cities a new type of educational institution—the university—emerged from cathedral and municipal schools. Universities developed theological, legal, and medical courses of study based on classical models and provided trained officials for the new government bureaucracies. Economic growth meant that merchants, nobles, and guild masters had disposable income they could spend on artistic products and more elaborate consumer goods. They supported the building of churches and cathedrals as visible symbols of their Christian faith and their civic pride; cathedrals in particular grew larger and more sumptuous, with high towers, stained-glass windows, and multiple altars. University education was in Latin and limited to men, but the High Middle Ages also saw the creation of new types of vernacular literature. Poems, songs, and stories were written down in local dialects and celebrated things of concern to ordinary people. In this, the troubadours of southern France led the way, using Arabic models to create romantic stories of heterosexual love.

• *Why has the late Middle Ages been seen as a time of calamity and crisis?*

In the fourteenth and fifteenth centuries bad weather brought poor harvests, which contributed to the international economic depression and fostered disease. The Black Death caused enormous population losses, with social, psychological, and economic consequences. The Hundred Years' War devastated much of the French countryside and bankrupted England. When peasant frustrations exploded in uprisings, the frightened nobility crushed the revolts. But events had heightened social consciousness among the poor.

Suggested Reading

Bartlett, Robert. *The Making of Europe: Conquest, Colonization and Cultural Change, 950–1350.* 1993. A broad survey of many of the developments traced in this chapter.

Bennett, Judith M. *A Medieval Life: Cecelia Penifader of Brigstock, c. 1297–1344.* 1998. An excellent brief introduction to all aspects of medieval village life from the perspective of one woman, designed for students.

Brooke, Rosalind, and Christopher Brooke. *Popular Religion in the Middle Ages.* 1984. A readable synthesis of material on the beliefs and practices of ordinary Christians.

Glick, Leonard B. *Abraham's Heirs: Jews and Christians in Medieval Europe.* 1999. Provides information on many aspects of Jewish life and Jewish-Christian relations.

Herlihy, David. *The Black Death and the Transformation of the West,* 2d ed. 1997. A fine treatment of the causes and cultural consequences of the disease that remains the best starting point for study of the great epidemic.

Koch, H. W. *Medieval Warfare.* 1978. A beautifully illustrated book covering strategy, tactics, armaments, and costumes of war.

Lawrence, C. H. *Medieval Monasticism: Forms of Religious Life in Western Europe in the Middle Ages.* 1988. Provides a solid introduction to monastic life as it was practiced.

Madden, Thomas. *The New Concise History of the Crusades.* 2005. A highly readable brief survey by the preeminent American scholar of the Crusades.

Sawyer, Peter, ed. *The Oxford Illustrated History of the Vikings.* 1997. Provides a sound account of the Vikings by an international team of scholars.

Shahar, Shulamit. *The Fourth Estate: A History of Women in the Middle Ages,* 2d ed. 2003. Analyzes attitudes toward women and provides information on the lives of women in many situations, including nuns, peasants, noblewomen, and townswomen, in Western Europe between the twelfth and the fifteenth centuries.

Tellenbach, Gerd. *The Church in Western Europe from the Tenth to the Twelfth Century.* 1993. A very good survey by an expert on the investiture controversy.

Tuchman, Barbara. *A Distant Mirror: The Calamitous Fourteenth Century.* 1978. Written for a general audience, the book remains a vivid description of this tumultuous time.

Notes

1. E. Panofsky, trans. and ed., *Abbot Suger on the Abbey Church of St.-Denis and Its Art Treasures* (Princeton, N.J.: Princeton University Press, 1946), p. 101.

Listening to the PAST

An Arab View of the Crusades

*T*he Crusades helped shape the understanding that Arabs and Europeans had of each other and all subsequent relations between the Christian West and the Arab world. To medieval Christians, the Crusades were papally approved military expeditions for the recovery of holy places in Palestine; to the Arabs, these campaigns were "Frankish wars" or "Frankish invasions" for the acquisition of territory.

Early in the thirteenth century, Ibn Al-Athir (1160–1223), a native of Mosul, an important economic and cultural center in northern Mesopotamia (modern Iraq), wrote a history of the First Crusade. He relied on Arab sources for the events he described. Here is his account of the Crusaders' capture of Antioch.

The power of the Franks first became apparent when in the year 478/1085–86* they invaded the territories of Islam and took Toledo and other parts of Andalusia [in Spain]. Then in 484/1091 they attacked and conquered the island of Sicily and turned their attention to the African coast. Certain of their conquests there were won back again but they had other successes, as you will see.

In 490/1097 the Franks attacked Syria. This is how it all began: Baldwin, their King, a kinsman of Roger the Frank who had conquered Sicily, assembled a great army and sent word to Roger saying: "I have assembled a great army and now I am on my way to you, to use your bases for my conquest of the African coast. Thus you and I shall become neighbors."

Roger called together his companions and consulted them about these proposals. "This will be a fine thing for them and for us!" they declared, "for by this means these lands will be converted to the Faith!" At this Roger raised one leg and farted loudly, and swore that it was of more use than their advice. "Why?" "Because if this army comes here it will need quantities of provisions and fleets of ships to transport it to Africa, as well as reinforcements from my own troops. Then,

if the Franks succeed in conquering this territory they will take it over and will need provisioning from Sicily. This will cost me my annual profit from the harvest. If they fail they will return here and be an embarrassment to me here in my own domain." . . .

He summoned Baldwin's messenger and said to him: "If you have decided to make war on the Muslims your best course will be to free Jerusalem from their rule and thereby win great honor. I am bound by certain promises and treaties of allegiance with the ruler of Africa." So the Franks made ready to set out to attack Syria.

Another story is that the Fatimids of Egypt were afraid when they saw the Seljuqids extending their empire through Syria as far as Gaza, until they reached the Egyptian border and Atsiz invaded Egypt itself. They therefore sent to invite the Franks to invade Syria and so protect Egypt from the Muslims.[†] But God knows best.

When the Franks decided to attack Syria they marched east to Constantinople, so that they could cross the straits and advance into Muslim territory by the easier, land route. When they reached Constantinople, the Emperor of the East refused them permission to pass through his domains. He said: "Unless you first promise me Antioch, I shall not allow you to cross into the Muslim empire." His real intention was to incite them to attack the Muslims, for he was convinced that the Turks, whose invincible control over Asia Minor he had observed, would exterminate every one of them. They accepted his conditions and in 490/1097 they crossed the Bosphorus at Constantinople. . . . They . . . reached Antioch, which they besieged.

When Yaghi Siyan, the ruler of Antioch, heard of their approach, he was not sure how the Christian people of the city would react, so he made the Muslims go outside the city on their own to dig trenches, and the next day sent the Christians out alone to continue the task. When they were ready to return

---

*Muslims traditionally date events from Muhammad's hegira, or emigration, to Medina, which occurred in 622 according to the Christian calendar.

[†]Although Muslims, Fatimids were related doctrinally to the Shi'ites, but the dominant Sunni Muslims considered the Fatimids heretics.

Miniature showing heavily armored knights fighting Muslims.
(Bibliothèque nationale de France)

home at the end of the day he refused to allow them. "Antioch is yours," he said, "but you will have to leave it to me until I see what happens between us and the Franks." "Who will protect our children and our wives?" they said. "I shall look after them for you." So they resigned themselves to their fate, and lived in the Frankish camp for nine months, while the city was under siege.

Yaghi Siyan showed unparalleled courage and wisdom, strength and judgment. If all the Franks who died had survived they would have overrun all the lands of Islam. He protected the families of the Christians in Antioch and would not allow a hair of their heads to be touched.

After the siege had been going on for a long time the Franks made a deal with . . . a cuirass-maker called Ruzbih whom they bribed with a fortune in money and lands. He worked in the tower that stood over the riverbed, where the river flowed out of the city into the valley. The Franks sealed their pact with the cuirass-maker, God damn him! and made their way to the water-gate. They opened it and entered the city. Another gang of them climbed the tower with their ropes. At dawn, when more than 500 of them were in the city and the defenders were worn out after the night watch, they sounded their trumpets. . . . Panic seized Yaghi Siyan and he opened the city gates and fled in terror, with an escort of thirty pages. His army commander arrived, but when he discovered on

enquiry that Yaghi Siyan had fled, he made his escape by another gate. This was of great help to the Franks, for if he had stood firm for an hour, they would have been wiped out. They entered the city by the gates and sacked it, slaughtering all the Muslims they found there. This happened in jumada I (491/April/May 1098). . . .

It was the discord between the Muslim princes . . . that enabled the Franks to overrun the country.

Questions for Analysis

1. From the Arab perspective, when did the crusade begin?

2. How did Ibn Al-Athir explain the Crusaders' expedition to Syria?

3. Why did Antioch fall to the Crusaders?

4. The use of dialogue in historical narrative is a very old device dating from the Greek historian Thucydides (fifth century B.C.E.). Assess the value of Ibn Al-Athir's dialogues for the modern historian.

Sources: P. J. Geary, ed., *Readings in Medieval History* (Peterborough, Ontario: Broadview Press, 1991), pp. 443–444; E. J. Costello, trans., *Arab Historians of the Crusades* (Berkeley and Los Angeles: University of California Press, 1969).

The Sistine Chapel. Michelangelo's frescoes in the Sistine Chapel in the Vatican were commissioned by the pope. The huge ceiling includes biblical scenes, and the far wall shows a dramatic and violent Last Judgment. *(Vatican Museum)*

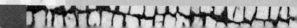

14

EUROPE IN THE RENAISSANCE AND REFORMATION, 1350–1600

While the Four Horsemen of the Apocalypse seemed to be carrying war, plague, famine, and death across northern Europe, a new culture was emerging in southern Europe. The fourteenth century witnessed the beginnings of remarkable changes in many aspects of Italian intellectual, artistic, and cultural life. Artists and writers thought that they were living in a new golden age, but not until the sixteenth century was this change given the label we use today—the **Renaissance,** from the French version of a word meaning rebirth. That word was first used by the artist and art historian Giorgio Vasari (1511–1574) to describe the art of "rare men of genius" such as his contemporary Michelangelo. Through their works, Vasari judged, the glory of the classical past had been reborn—or perhaps even surpassed—after centuries of darkness. The word *Renaissance* came to be used not just for art, but for many aspects of life of the period. The new attitude had a slow diffusion out of Italy, with the result that the Renaissance "happened" at different times in different parts of Europe: Italian art of the fourteenth through the early sixteenth century is described as "Renaissance," and so is English literature of the late sixteenth century, including Shakespeare's plays and poetry.

At the same time that Vasari was describing a break with the past in art, religious reformers were carrying out an even more dramatic change. In 1500 there was one Christian church in western Europe to which all Christians at least nominally belonged. Fifty years later there were many, as a result of a religious reform movement that gained wide acceptance and caused Christianity to break into many divisions. This movement, termed the **Protestant Reformation,** looked back to the early Christian church for its inspiration, and many of its reforming ideas had been advocated for centuries. There were thus strong elements of continuity, but it was still a radical change. Along with the Renaissance, the Reformation is often seen as a key element in the creation of the "modern" world.

Renaissance *A French word, translated from the Italian* rinascita, *first used by art historian and critic Giorgio Vasari (1511–1574), meaning rebirth of the culture of classical antiquity. English-speaking students adopted the French term.*

Protestant Reformation *A reform movement that began in the early sixteenth century that rejected the institutionalization of Christianity that characterized the Roman Catholic Church and emphasized individual salvation by grace through faith alone.*

Primary Source:
The Practice of Commerce
Get advice from an experienced Florentine merchant before planning your next overland business trip to Cathay!

signori *An Italian word used to describe the rulers of city-states and the states ruled by these men.*

patrons *Wealthy individuals who provide financial support to scholars, painters, sculptors, poets, and/or architects.*

RENAISSANCE CULTURE

What were the major cultural developments of the Renaissance?

The Renaissance was characterized by self-conscious awareness among fourteenth- and fifteenth-century Italians, particularly scholars and writers known as humanists, that they were living in a new era. Their ideas influenced education and were spread through the new technology of the printing press. Interest in the classical past and in the individual also shaped Renaissance art in terms of style and subject matter.

Economic and Political Context

The cultural achievements of the Renaissance rest on the economic and political developments of earlier centuries. Economic growth laid the material basis for the Italian Renaissance, and ambitious merchants gained political power to match their economic power. They then used their money and power to buy luxuries and hire talent.

The first artistic and literary manifestations of the Italian Renaissance appeared in Florence, which possessed enormous wealth because Florentine merchants and bankers had acquired control of papal banking toward the end of the thirteenth century. From their position as tax collectors for the papacy, Florentine mercantile families began to dominate European banking on both sides of the Alps, setting up offices in major European and North African cities. The profits from loans, investments, and money exchanges that poured back to Florence were pumped into urban industries. Such profits contributed to the city's economic vitality and allowed banking families to control the city's politics and culture.

In the twelfth century many Italian cities, including Florence, won their independence from local feudal nobles. The nobles frequently moved into the cities, marrying into rich commercial families and starting their own businesses. This merger of the northern Italian feudal nobility and the commercial elite created a powerful oligarchy that ruled the city and surrounding countryside. In the thirteenth century the common people in many cities revolted against oligarchic rule, but these revolts generally resulted in a greater concentration of power rather than a more broadly based government.

Many cities in Italy became **signori,** in which one man ruled and handed down the right to rule to his son. In the fifteenth century the signori in many cities and the most powerful merchant oligarchs in others transformed their households into courts. They built magnificent palaces in the centers of cities and required all political business be done there. They became **patrons** of the arts, hiring architects to design and build these palaces, artists to fill them with paintings and sculptures, and musicians and composers to fill them with music. The Medici rulers of Florence, for example, who made their money in banking and trade, supported an academy for scholars and a host of painters, sculptors, poets, and architects. Courtly culture afforded signori and oligarchs the opportunity to display and assert their wealth and power.

In the fifteenth century five powers dominated the Italian peninsula: Venice, Milan, Florence, the Papal States, and the kingdom of Naples (see Map 14.1 on page 404). The major Italian powers competed furiously among themselves for territory and tried to extend their power over smaller city-states. The large cities used diplomacy, spies, paid informers, and any other available means to get information that could be used to advance their ambitions. While the states of northern Europe were moving toward centralization and consolidation, the world of Italian politics resembled a jungle where the powerful dominated the weak.

In one significant respect, however, the Italian city-states anticipated future relations among competing European states after 1500. Whenever one Italian state appeared to gain a predominant position within the peninsula, other states combined to establish a *balance of power* against the major threat. In the formation of these alliances, Renaissance Italians invented the machinery of modern diplomacy: permanent embassies with resident ambassadors in capitals where political relations and commercial ties needed continual monitoring.

The resident ambassador was one of the great political achievements of the Italian Renaissance, but diplomacy did not prevent invasions of Italy, which began in 1494. Italy became the focus of international ambitions and the battleground of foreign armies, and the Italian cities suffered severely from continual warfare. Thus the failure of the city-states to form some type of federal system, to consolidate, or at least to establish a common foreign policy led to centuries of subjugation by outside invaders. Italy was not to achieve unification until 1870.

Intellectual Change

The Renaissance was a self-conscious intellectual movement. The realization that something new and unique was happening first came to writers in the fourteenth century, especially to the poet and humanist Francesco Petrarch (1304–1374). For Petrarch, the Germanic migrations had caused a sharp cultural break with the glories of Rome and inaugurated what he called the "Dark Ages." Along with many of his contemporaries, Petrarch believed that he was witnessing a new golden age of intellectual achievement.

Petrarch and other poets, writers, and artists showed a deep interest in the ancient past, in both the physical remains of the Roman Empire and classical Latin texts. The study of Latin classics became known as the *studia humanitates,* usually translated as "liberal studies" or the "liberal arts." All programs of study contain an implicit philosophy, which in the case of the liberal arts is generally known as **humanism.** Humanism emphasized human beings, their achievements, interests, and capabilities. Whereas medieval writers looked to the classics to reveal God, Renaissance humanists studied the classics to understand human nature.

Renaissance humanists retained a Christian perspective, however: men (and women, though to a lesser degree) were made in the image and likeness of God. Humanists generally rejected classical ideas that were opposed to Christianity, or they sought through reinterpretation an underlying harmony between the pagan and secular and the Christian faith.

Interest in human achievement led humanists to emphasize the importance of the individual. Groups such as families, guilds, and religious organizations continued to provide strong support for the individual and to exercise great social influence. Yet in the Renaissance, artists and intellectuals, unlike their counterparts in the Middle Ages, prized their own uniqueness. This attitude of **individualism** stressed the full development of one's special capabilities and talents. (See the feature "Individuals in Society: Leonardo da Vinci.")

Chronology

1434–1494	Medici family in power in Florence
1450s	Invention of movable metal type in Germany
1469	Marriage of Isabella of Castile and Ferdinand of Aragon
1513	Niccolò Machiavelli, *The Prince*
1521	Diet of Worms
1521–1555	Charles V's wars against Valois kings
1525	Peasant revolts in Germany
1527	Henry VIII of England asks Pope Clement VII to annul his marriage to Catherine of Aragon
1536	John Calvin, *The Institutes of the Christian Religion*
1540	Founding of the Society of Jesus (Jesuits)
1545–1563	Council of Trent
1555	Peace of Augsburg
1558–1603	Reign of Elizabeth in England
1560–1660	Height of European witch-hunt
1568–1578	Civil war in the Netherlands
1572	Saint Bartholomew's Day massacre
1598	Edict of Nantes

humanism   *A term first used by Florentine rhetorician Leonard Bruni as a general word for "the new learning"; the critical study of Latin and Greek literature with the goal of realizing human potential.*

individualism   *A basic feature of the Italian Renaissance stressing personality, uniqueness, genius, and self-consciousness.*

● **Bennozzo Gozzoli: Procession of the Magi, 1461** This segment of a huge fresco covering three walls of a chapel in the Medici palace in Florence shows members of the Medici family and other contemporary individuals in a procession accompanying the biblical three wise men as they brought gifts to the infant Jesus. Reflecting the self-confidence of his patrons, Gozzoli places several members of the Medici family at the head of the procession, accompanied by their grooms. *(Scala/Art Resource, NY)*

One of the central preoccupations of the humanists was education and moral behavior. Humanists taught that a life active in the world should be the aim of all educated individuals and that education was not simply for private or religious purposes, but to benefit the public good.

Humanists put their ideas into practice. They opened schools and academies in Italian cities and courts in which pupils began with Latin grammar and rhetoric, went on to study Roman history and political philosophy, and then learned Greek in order to study Greek literature and philosophy. These classics, humanists taught, would provide models of how to write clearly, argue effectively, and speak persuasively, important skills for future diplomats, lawyers, military leaders, businessmen, and politicians. Gradually humanist education became the basis for intermediate and advanced education for a large share of middle- and upper-class men.

Humanists were ambivalent about education for women. While they saw the value of exposing women to classical models of moral behavior and reasoning, they also thought that a program of study that emphasized eloquence and action was not proper for women, whose sphere was private and domestic. Humanists never established schools for girls, though a few women of very high social status did gain a humanist education from private tutors. The ideal Renaissance woman looked a great deal more like her medieval counterpart than did the Renaissance man.

Secularism

No Renaissance book on any topic has been more widely read than the short political treatise *The Prince* by Niccolò Machiavelli (1469–1527). The subject of *The Prince* (1513) is political power: how the ruler should gain, maintain, and increase it. The prince should combine the cunning of a fox with the ferocity of a lion to achieve his goals. Asking rhetorically whether it is better for a ruler to be loved or feared, Machiavelli writes, "It will naturally be answered that it would be desirable to be both the one and the other; but as it is difficult to be both at the same

The Prince *A 1513 treatise by Machiavelli on ways to gain, keep, and expand power; because of its subsequent impact, probably the most important literary work of the Renaissance.*

time, it is much more safe to be feared than to be loved, when you have to choose between the two."[1]

Unlike medieval political theorists, Machiavelli maintained that the ruler should be concerned with the way things actually are rather than aiming for an ethical ideal. The sole test of a good government is whether it is effective—whether the ruler increases his power. Machiavelli did not advocate amoral behavior, but he believed that political action cannot be restricted by moral considerations. Nevertheless, on the basis of a crude interpretation of *The Prince,* the word *Machiavellian* entered the language as a synonym for the politically devious, corrupt, and crafty, indicating actions in which the end justifies the means.

Leonardo da Vinci

Leonardo da Vinci, *Lady with an Ermine*. The enigmatic smile and smoky quality of this portrait can be found in many of Leonardo's works. *(Czartoryski Museum, Krakow/The Bridgeman Art Library)*

What makes a genius? An infinite capacity for taking pains? A deep curiosity about an extensive variety of subjects? A divine spark as manifested by talents that far exceed the norm? Or is it just "one percent inspiration and ninety-nine percent perspiration," as Thomas Edison said? To most observers, Leonardo da Vinci was one of the greatest geniuses in the history of the Western world. In fact, Leonardo was one of the individuals that the Renaissance label "genius" was designed to describe: a special kind of human being with exceptional creative powers.

Leonardo (who, despite the title of a recent best-seller, is always called by his first name) was born in Vinci, near Florence, the illegitimate son of Caterina, a local peasant girl, and Ser Piero da Vinci, a notary public. Caterina later married another native of Vinci. When Ser Piero's marriage to Donna Albrussia produced no children, he and his wife took in Leonardo. Ser Piero secured Leonardo's apprenticeship with the painter and sculptor Andrea del Verrocchio in Florence. In 1472, when Leonardo was just twenty years old, he was listed as a master in Florence's "Company of Artists."

Leonardo's most famous portrait, *Mona Lisa*, shows a woman with an enigmatic smile that Giorgio Vasari described as "so pleasing that it seemed divine rather than human." The portrait, probably of the young wife of a rich Florentine merchant (her exact identity is hotly debated), may actually be the best-known painting in the history of art. One of its competitors in that designation would be another work of Leonardo's, *The Last Supper*, which has been called "the most revered painting in the world."

Leonardo's reputation as a genius does not rest simply on his paintings, however, which are actually few in number, but rather on the breadth of his abilities and interests. In these, he is often understood to be the first "Renaissance man," a phrase we still use for a multi-talented individual. He wanted to reproduce what the eye can see, and he drew everything he saw around him, including executed criminals hanging on gallows as well as the beauties of nature. Trying to understand how the human body worked, Leonardo studied live and dead bodies, doing autopsies and dissections to investigate muscles and circulation. He carefully analyzed the effects of light, using his analysis to paint strong contrasts of light and shadow, and he experimented with perspective.

Leonardo used his drawings as the basis for his paintings and also as a tool of scientific investigation. He drew plans for hundreds of inventions, many of which would become reality centuries later, such as the helicopter, tank, machine gun, and parachute. He was hired by one of the powerful new rulers in Italy, Duke Ludovico Sforza of Milan, to design practical things that the duke needed, including weapons, fortresses, and water systems, as well as to produce works of art. Leonardo left Milan when Sforza was overthrown in war and spent the last years of his life painting, drawing, and designing for the pope and the French king.

Leonardo experimented with new materials for painting and sculpture, some of which worked and some of which did not. The experimental method he used to paint *The Last Supper* caused the picture to deteriorate rapidly, and it began to flake off the wall as soon as it was finished. Leonardo actually regarded it as never quite completed, for he could not find a model for the face of Christ that would evoke the spiritual depth he felt it deserved. His gigantic equestrian statue in honor of Ludovico's father, Duke Francesco Sforza, was never made. The clay model collapsed, and only notes survived. He planned to write books on many subjects but never finished any of them, leaving only notebooks. Leonardo once said that "a painter is not admirable unless he is universal." The patrons who supported him—and he was supported very well—perhaps wished that his inspirations would have been a bit less universal in scope, or at least accompanied by more perspiration.

Questions for Analysis

1. In what ways do the notion of a genius and the notion of a Renaissance man support one another? In what ways do they contradict one another? Which seems a better description of Leonardo?

2. Has the idea of artistic genius changed since the Renaissance? If so, how?

Sources: Giorgio Vasari, *Lives of the Artists,* vol. 1, trans. G. Bull (London: Penguin Books, 1965); S. B. Nuland, *Leonardo da Vinci* (New York: Lipper/Viking, 2000).

Primary Source:

The Prince: Power Politics During the Italian Renaissance

Learn from the man himself what it means to be "Machiavellian."

Machiavelli's *The Prince* is often seen as a prime example of another aspect of the Renaissance, secularism. **Secularism** involves a basic concern with the material world instead of with the eternal world of spirit. A secular way of thinking tends to find the ultimate explanation of everything and the final end of human beings within the limits of what the senses can discover. Even though medieval business people ruthlessly pursued profits and medieval monks fought fiercely over property, the dominant ideals focused on the otherworldly, on life after death. Renaissance people often had strong and deep spiritual interests, but in their increasingly secular society, attention was concentrated on the here and now. The rich, social-climbing residents of Venice, Florence, and Rome came to see life more as an opportunity to be enjoyed than as a painful pilgrimage to the City of God.

Church leaders did little to combat the new secular spirit. In the fifteenth and early sixteenth centuries, the papal court and the households of the cardinals were just as worldly as those of great urban patricians. Renaissance popes beautified the city of Rome, patronized artists and men of letters, and expended enormous enthusiasm and huge sums of money. Pope Julius II (1503–1513) tore down the old Saint Peter's Basilica and began work on the present structure in 1506. Michelangelo's dome for Saint Peter's is still considered his greatest architectural work.

Despite their interest in secular matters, however, few people (including Machiavelli) questioned the basic tenets of the Christian religion. The thousands of pious paintings, sculptures, processions, and pilgrimages of the Renaissance period prove that strong religious feeling persisted.

Christian Humanism

secularism *An attitude that tends to find the ultimate explanation of everything and the final end of human beings in what reason and the senses can discover, rather than in any spiritual or transcendental belief.*

In the last quarter of the fifteenth century, students from the Low Countries, France, Germany, and England flocked to Italy, imbibed the "new learning," and carried it back to their countries. Northern humanists, often called **Christian humanists,** interpreted Italian ideas about and attitudes toward classical antiquity, individualism, and humanism in terms of their own traditions. Christian humanists had profound faith in the power of the human intellect and thought that human nature was capable of improvement through education. They developed a program for broad social reform based on Christian ideals.

Christian humanists *Scholars from northern Europe who, in the later years of the fifteenth century, developed programs for broad social reform based on concepts set forth in the Renaissance and on the ideals of the Christian faith.*

The Englishman Thomas More (1478–1535) envisioned a society that would bring out this inherent goodness in his revolutionary book *Utopia* (1516). *Utopia,* whose title means both "a good place" and "nowhere," describes an ideal community on an island somewhere off the mainland of the New World. All children receive a good education, primarily in the Greco-Roman classics, and learning does not cease with maturity, for the goal of all education is to develop rational faculties. Adults divide their days between manual labor or business pursuits and intellectual activities. Because profits from business and property are held in common, there is absolute social equality. Citizens of Utopia lead an ideal, nearly perfect existence because they live by reason; their institutions are perfect.

Contrary to the long-prevailing view that vice and violence existed because people themselves were basically corrupt, More maintained that society's flawed institutions, especially private property, were responsible for corruption and war. According to More, the key to improvement and reform of the individual was reform of the social institutions that molded the individual. His ideas were profoundly original in the sixteenth century.

Better known by contemporaries than Thomas More was the Dutch humanist Desiderius Erasmus (1466?–1536) of Rotterdam. His fame rested largely on his exceptional knowledge of Greek and the Bible. Erasmus's long list of publications includes *The Education of a Christian Prince* (1504), a book combining idealistic and practical suggestions for the formation of a ruler's character through the careful study

● **The Print Shop** This sixteenth-century engraving captures the busy world of a print shop: On the left, men set pieces of type, and an individual wearing glasses checks a copy. At the rear, another applies ink to the type, while a man carries in fresh paper on his head. At the right, the master printer operates the press, while a boy removes the printed pages and sets them to dry. The well-dressed figure in the right foreground may be the patron checking to see whether his job is done. *(Giraudon/Art Resource, NY)*

of Plutarch, Aristotle, Cicero, and Plato; *The Praise of Folly* (1509), a satire of worldly wisdom and a plea for the simple and spontaneous Christian faith of children; and, most important, a critical edition of the Greek New Testament (1516). For Erasmus, education was the key to moral and intellectual improvement, and true Christianity is an inner attitude of the spirit, not outward actions.

The Printed Word

The fourteenth-century humanist Petrarch and the sixteenth-century humanist Erasmus had similar ideas about many things, but the immediate impact of their ideas was very different because of one thing: the printing press with movable metal type. The ideas of Petrarch were spread slowly from person to person by hand copying. The ideas of Erasmus were spread quickly through print, in which hundreds or thousands of identical copies could be made in a short time. Print shops were gathering places for those interested in new ideas.

Printing with movable metal type developed in Germany in the middle of the fifteenth century as a combination of existing technologies. (While printing with movable type was invented in China [see page 335], movable *metal* type was actually developed in the thirteenth century in Korea, though it was tightly controlled by the monarchy and did not have the broad impact that printing did in Europe. Historians have speculated whether German printers somehow learned of the Korean invention, but there is no evidence that they did.) Several metal-smiths, most prominently Johan Gutenberg, transformed the metal stamps used to mark signs on jewelry into type that could be covered with ink and used to mark symbols onto a surface. This type could be rearranged for every page and so used over and over. The printing revolution was also enabled by the ready availability of paper, which was made using techniques that had originated in China and spread into Europe from Muslim Spain.

The effects of the invention of movable-type printing were not felt overnight. Nevertheless, within a half century of the publication of Gutenberg's Bible of 1456, movable type had brought about radical changes. Historians estimate that somewhere between 8 million and 20 million books were printed in Europe before 1500, many more than the number of books produced in all of Western history up to that point. Printing transformed both the private and the public lives of Europeans. It gave hundreds or even thousands of people identical books, so that they could more easily discuss the ideas that the books contained with one another in person or through letters.

Government and church leaders both used and worried about printing. They printed laws, declarations of war, battle accounts, and propaganda, and they also attempted to censor or ban books and authors whose ideas they thought were wrong, though these efforts were rarely effective.

Printing also stimulated the literacy of laypeople and eventually came to have a deep effect on their private lives. Although most of the earliest books and pamphlets dealt with religious subjects, printers produced anything that would sell: professional reference sets, historical romances, biographies, and how-to manuals for the general public. They discovered that illustrations increased a book's sales, so they published both history and pornography full of woodcuts and engravings. Single-page broadsides and flysheets allowed great public events and "wonders" such as comets and two-headed calves to be experienced vicariously by the stay-at-home. Since books and other printed materials were read aloud to illiterate listeners, print bridged the gap between the written and oral cultures.

Art and the Artist

No feature of the Renaissance evokes greater admiration than its artistic masterpieces. In Renaissance Italy powerful urban groups and individuals commissioned works of art. Wealthy merchants and bankers and popes and princes spent vast sums on the arts as a means of glorifying themselves and their families. Patrons varied in their level of involvement as a work progressed; some simply ordered a specific subject or scene, while others oversaw the work of the artist or architect very closely, suggesting themes and styles and demanding changes while the work was in progress.

The content and style of Renaissance art were often different from those of the Middle Ages. The individual portrait emerged as a distinct artistic genre. Rather than reflecting a spiritual ideal, as medieval painting and sculpture tended to do, Renaissance portraits showed human ideals, often portrayed in a more realistic style. The sculptor Donatello (1386–1466) revived the classical figure, with its balance and self-awareness. In architecture, Filippo Brunelleschi (1377–1446) looked to the classical past for inspiration, designing a dome for the cathedral in Florence and a hospital for orphans and foundlings in which all proportions were carefully thought out to achieve a sense of balance and harmony.

As the fifteenth century advanced, classical themes and motifs, such as the lives and loves of pagan gods and goddesses, figured increasingly in painting and sculpture. Religious topics, such as the Annunciation of the Virgin and the Nativity, remained popular among both patrons and artists, but frequently the patron had himself and his family portrayed in the scene.

In the fifteenth century the center of the new art shifted from Florence to Rome, where wealthy cardinals and popes wanted visual expression of the church's and their own families' power and piety. Michelangelo went to Rome about 1500 and began the series of statues, paintings, and architectural projects from which he gained an international reputation: the Pietà, Moses, the redesigning of the Capitoline Hill in central Rome, and, most famously, the ceiling and altar wall of the Sistine Chapel. Pope Julius II, who commissioned the Sistine Chapel, demanded that Michelangelo work as fast as he could and frequently visited the artist at his work with suggestions and criticisms. Michelangelo complained in person and by letter about the pope's meddling, but his reputation did not match the power of the pope, and he kept working. Raphael Sanzio (1483–1520), another Florentine, got the commission for

● **Sandro Botticelli: Primavera, or Spring (ca. 1482)** Venus, the Roman goddess of love, is flanked on her left by Flora, goddess of flowers and fertility, and on her right by the Three Graces, goddesses of banquets, dance, and social occasions. Above, Venus's son Cupid, the god of love, shoots darts of desire, while at the far right the wind god Zephyrus chases the nymph Chloris. Botticelli captured the ideal for female beauty in the Renaissance: slender, with pale skin, a high forehead, red-blond hair, and sloping shoulders. *(Digital image © The Museum of Modern Art/Licensed by Scala/Art Resource, NY)*

frescoes in the papal apartments, and in his relatively short life he painted hundreds of portraits and devotional images, becoming the most sought-after artist in Europe.

Praising their talents, Vasari described both Michelangelo and Raphael as "divine" and "rare men of genius." This adulation of the artist had led many historians to view the Renaissance as the beginning of the concept of the artist as genius. In the Middle Ages, people believed that only God created, albeit through individuals; the medieval conception recognized no particular value in artistic originality. Renaissance artists and humanists came to think that a work of art was the deliberate creation of a unique personality, of an individual who transcended traditions, rules, and theories. A genius had a peculiar gift, which ordinary laws should not inhibit.

Whether in Italy or northern Europe, most Renaissance artists trained in the workshops of older artists. Though they might be "men of genius," artists were still expected to be well-trained in proper artistic techniques and stylistic conventions, for the notion that artistic genius could show up in the work of an untrained artist did not emerge until the twentieth century. By the later sixteenth century formal artistic "academies" were also established to train artists. Like universities, artistic workshops and academies were male-only settings in which men of different ages came together for training and created bonds of friendship, influence, patronage, and sometimes intimacy. Several women did become well-known as painters during the Renaissance, but they were trained by their painter fathers and often quit painting when they married.

● **Artemisia Gentileschi: Esther Before Ahaseurus (ca. 1630)**   In this oil painting, Gentileschi shows an Old Testament scene of the Jewish woman Esther who saved her people from being killed by her husband, King Ahaseurus. This deliverance is celebrated in the Jewish holiday of Purim. Both figures are in the elaborate dress worn in Renaissance courts. Typical of a female painter, Artemisia Gentileschi was trained by her father. She mastered the dramatic style favored in the early seventeenth century and became known especially for her portraits of strong biblical and mythological heroines. *(Image copyright © The Metropolitan Museum of Art/Art Resource, NY)*

Women were not alone in being excluded from the institutions of Renaissance culture. Though a few "rare men of genius" such as Leonardo or Michelangelo emerged from artisanal backgrounds, most scholars and artists came from families with at least some money. Renaissance culture did not influence the lives of most people in cities and did not affect life in the villages at all. A small, highly educated minority of literary humanists and artists created the culture of and for an exclusive elite. The Renaissance maintained, or indeed enhanced, a gulf between the learned minority and the uneducated multitude that has survived for many centuries.

SOCIAL HIERARCHIES

What were the key social hierarchies in Renaissance Europe, and how did ideas about hierarchy shape people's lives?

The division between educated and uneducated people was only one of many social hierarchies evident in the Renaissance. Every society has social hierarchies; in ancient Rome, for example, there were patricians and plebians (see page 105). Such hierarchies are to some degree descriptions of social reality, but they are also idealizations—

that is, they describe how people *imagine* their society to be, without all the messy reality of social-climbing merchants or groups that do not fit the standard categories. Social hierarchies in the Renaissance built on those of the Middle Ages but also developed new features that contributed to modern social hierarchies.

Race

Renaissance people did not use the word *race* the way we do, but often used *race, people,* and *nation* interchangeably for ethnic, national, and religious groups—the French race, the Jewish nation, the Irish people, and so on. They did make distinctions based on skin color that provide some of the background for later conceptualizations of race, but these distinctions were interwoven with other characteristics when people thought about human differences.

Ever since the time of the Roman republic, a few black Africans had lived in western Europe. They had come, along with white slaves, as the spoils of war. Even after the collapse of the Roman Empire, Muslim and Christian merchants continued to import them. Unstable political conditions in many parts of Africa enabled enterprising merchants to seize people and sell them into slavery. Local authorities afforded them no protection. Long tradition, moreover, sanctioned the practice of slavery. The evidence of medieval art attests to the continued presence of Africans in Europe throughout the Middle Ages and to Europeans' awareness of them.

Beginning in the fifteenth century sizable numbers of black slaves entered Europe. By the mid-sixteenth century blacks, slave and free, constituted roughly 3 percent of the Portuguese population. In the Iberian Peninsula African slaves intermingled with the people they lived among and sometimes intermarried. Cities such as Lisbon had significant numbers of people of mixed African and European descent.

Although blacks were concentrated in the Iberian Peninsula, there were some Africans in other parts of Europe as well. Black servants were much sought after; aristocrats had their portraits painted with their black pageboys to indicate their wealth and, in the case of noblewomen, to highlight their fair skin (see Gozzoli's *Procession of the Magi* on page 390, in which the Medici rulers of Florence are shown with a black groom). In Renaissance Spain and Italy, blacks performed as dancers, as actors and actresses in courtly dramas, and as musicians, sometimes making up full orchestras.

Africans were not simply amusements at court. In Portugal, Spain, and Italy, slaves supplemented the labor force in virtually all occupations—as servants, agricultural laborers, craftsmen, and seamen on ships. Agriculture in Europe did not involve large plantations, so large-scale agricultural slavery did not develop there; African slaves formed the primary work force on the sugar plantations set up by Europeans on the Atlantic islands in the late fifteenth century, however (see page 446).

Until the voyages down the African coast in the late fifteenth century, Europeans had little concrete knowledge of Africans and their cultures. They perceived Africa as a remote place, the home of strange people isolated by heresy and Islam from superior European civilization. Africans' contact, even as slaves, with Christian Europeans could only "improve" the blacks, they believed. The expanding slave trade only reinforced negative preconceptions about the inferiority of black Africans.

Class

The notion of class—working class, middle class, upper class—did not exist in the Renaissance. By the thirteenth century, however, and even more so by the fifteenth, the idea of a changeable hierarchy based on wealth, what would later come to be termed "social class," was emerging alongside the medieval concept of orders (see page 365). This was particularly true in towns. Most residents of towns were technically members of the "third estate," that is "those who work" rather than "those who fight" and "those who pray." However, this group now included wealthy merchants

● **Vittore Carpaccio: Black Laborers on the Venetian Docks (detail)** Enslaved and free blacks, besides working as gondoliers on the Venetian canals, served on the docks. Here, seven black men careen—clean, caulk, and repair—a ship. Carpaccio's reputation as one of Venice's outstanding painters rests on his eye for details of everyday life. *(Gallerie dell'Accademia, Venice/Scala/Art Resource, NY)*

who oversaw vast trading empires, held positions of political power, and lived in splendor that rivaled the richest nobles.

The development of a hierarchy of wealth did not mean an end to the hierarchy of orders, however, and even poorer nobles still had higher status than merchants. If this had not been the case, wealthy Italian merchants would not have bothered to buy noble titles and country villas, nor would wealthy English and Spanish merchants have been eager to marry their daughters and sons into often impoverished noble families. The nobility maintained its status in most parts of Europe not by maintaining rigid boundaries, but by taking in and integrating the new social elite of wealth.

Gender

debate about women *A discussion, which began in the later years of the fourteenth century, that attempted to answer fundamental questions of gender and define the role of women in society.*

Renaissance people would not have understood the word *gender* to refer to categories of people, but they would have easily grasped the concept. Toward the end of the fourteenth century learned men (and a few women) began what was termed the **"debate about women"** (*querelle des femmes*), a debate about women's character and nature that would last for centuries. Misogynist critiques of women from both clerical and secular authors denounced females as devious, domineering, and demanding. In answer, several authors compiled long lists of famous and praiseworthy women exemplary for their loyalty, bravery, and morality. Some writers, including a few women who had gained a humanist education, were not only interested in defending women, but also in exploring the reasons behind women's secondary status—that is, why the great philosophers, statesmen, and poets had generally been men. In this they were anticipating recent discussions about the "social construction of gender" by six hundred years.

Beginning in the sixteenth century, the debate about women also became one about female rulers, sparked primarily by dynastic accidents in many countries, including Spain, England, France, and Scotland, which led to women serving as advisers to child kings or ruling in their own right. There were no successful rebellions against female rulers simply because they were women, but in part this was because female rulers, especially Queen Elizabeth I of England, emphasized qualities regarded as masculine—physical bravery, stamina, wisdom, duty—whenever they appeared in public.

Ideas about women's and men's proper roles determined the actions of ordinary men and women even more forcefully. The dominant notion of the "true" man was that of the married head of household, so men whose class and age would have normally conferred political power but who remained unmarried were sometimes excluded from ruling positions. Actual marriage patterns in Europe left many women unmarried until quite late in life, but this did not lead to greater equality. If they worked for wages, and many women did, women earned about half to two-thirds of what men did even for the same work. Of all the ways in which Renaissance society was hierarchically arranged—class, age, level of education, rank, race, occupation—gender was regarded as the most "natural" and therefore the most important to defend.

● **Italian City Scene**   In this detail from a fresco, the Italian painter Lorenzo Lotto captures the mixing of social groups in a Renaissance Italian city. The crowd of men in the right foreground includes wealthy merchants in elaborate hats and colorful coats. Two mercenary soldiers (carrying a sword and a pike) wear short doublets and tight hose stylishly slit to reveal colored undergarments, while boys play with toy weapons at their feet. Clothing like that of the soldiers, which emphasized the masculine form, was frequently criticized for its expense and its "indecency." At the left, women sell vegetables and bread, which would have been a common sight at any city marketplace. *(Scala/Art Resource, NY)*

POLITICS AND THE STATE IN THE RENAISSANCE (CA. 1450–1521)

How did the nation-states of western Europe evolve in this period?

The High Middle Ages had witnessed the origins of many of the basic institutions of the modern state. Sheriffs, inquests, juries, circuit judges, professional bureaucracies, and representative assemblies all trace their origins to the twelfth and thirteenth centuries. The linchpin for the development of states, however, was strong monarchy. Beginning in the fifteenth century rulers utilized aggressive methods to build up their governments. They began the work of reducing violence, curbing unruly nobles, and establishing domestic order. They emphasized royal majesty and royal sovereignty and insisted on the respect and loyalty of all subjects.

France

The Hundred Years' War left France drastically depopulated, commercially ruined, and agriculturally weak (see page 379). Nonetheless, the ruler whom Joan of Arc had seen crowned at Reims, Charles VII (r. 1422–1461), revived the monarchy and France. He reorganized the royal council, giving increased influence to middle-class men, and strengthened royal finances through such taxes as the *gabelle* (on salt) and the *taille* (land tax). These taxes remained the Crown's chief sources of income until the Revolution of 1789. By establishing regular companies of cavalry and archers—recruited, paid, and inspected by the state—Charles created the first permanent royal army. By 1453 French armies had expelled the English from French soil except in Calais. His son Louis XI (r. 1461–1483), called the "Spider King" because of his treacherous character, improved upon Charles's army and used it to stop aristocratic brigandage, curb urban independence, and conquer the largest remaining noble holding on France's borders.

Two further developments strengthened the French monarchy. The marriage of Louis XII (r. 1498–1515) and Anne of Brittany added the large western duchy of Brittany to the state. Then the French king Francis I and Pope Leo X reached a mutually satisfactory agreement about church and state powers in 1516. The new treaty, the Concordat of Bologna, approved the pope's right to receive the first year's income of new bishops and abbots. In return, Leo X recognized the French ruler's right to select French bishops and abbots. French kings thereafter effectively controlled the appointment and thus the policies of church officials in the kingdom.

England

English society suffered severely in the fourteenth and fifteenth centuries. Population, decimated by the Black Death, continued to decline. Between 1455 and 1471 adherents of the ducal houses of York and Lancaster waged civil war, commonly called the **Wars of the Roses** because the symbol of the Yorkists was a white rose and that of the Lancastrians a red one. The chronic disorder hurt trade, agriculture, and domestic industry, and the authority of the monarchy sank lower than it had been in centuries.

The Yorkist Edward IV (r. 1461–1483) began establishing domestic tranquility. He succeeded in defeating the Lancastrian forces and after 1471 began to reconstruct the monarchy and consolidate royal power. Henry VII (r. 1485–1509) of the Welsh house of Tudor worked to restore royal prestige, to crush the power of the nobility, and to establish order and law at the local level. Because the government halted the long period of anarchy, it won the key support of the merchant and agricultural upper middle

Wars of the Roses *An exhausting conflict in fifteenth-century England between the ducal houses of York (represented by a white rose) and Lancaster (represented by a red rose). The war lasted from 1455 until 1471 and ended with a victory of the Yorkist forces led by Edward IV.*

class. Edward IV and subsequently the Tudors, excepting Henry VIII, conducted foreign policy on the basis of diplomacy, avoiding expensive wars. Thus the English monarchy did not depend on Parliament for money, and the Crown undercut that source of aristocratic influence.

Henry VII did summon several meetings of Parliament in the early years of his reign, primarily to confirm laws, but the center of royal authority was the royal council, which governed at the national level. There Henry VII revealed his distrust of the nobility: very few great lords were among the king's closest advisers, who instead were lesser landowners and lawyers. They were, in a sense, middle class. The royal council handled any business the king put before it—executive, legislative, and judicial. For example, the council conducted negotiations with foreign governments and secured international recognition of the Tudor dynasty through the marriage in 1501 of Henry VII's eldest son Arthur to Catherine of Aragon, the daughter of Ferdinand and Isabella of Spain.

Secretive, cautious, and thrifty, Henry VII rebuilt the monarchy. He encouraged the cloth industry and built up the English merchant marine. English exports of wool and the royal export tax on that wool steadily increased. Henry crushed an invasion from Ireland and secured peace with Scotland through the marriage of his daughter Margaret to the Scottish king. When Henry VII died in 1509, he left a country at peace both domestically and internationally, a substantially augmented treasury, and the dignity and role of the royal majesty much enhanced.

Spain

While England and France laid the foundations of unified nation-states during the Renaissance, Spain remained a conglomerate of independent kingdoms. Even the wedding in 1469 of the dynamic and aggressive Isabella of Castile and the crafty and persistent Ferdinand of Aragon did not bring about administrative unity. Rather, their marriage constituted a dynastic union of two royal houses, not the political union of two peoples, though they did pursue a common foreign policy.

Ferdinand and Isabella were able to exert their authority in ways similar to the rulers of France and England, however. They curbed aristocratic power by excluding aristocrats and great territorial magnates from the royal council, and instead appointed only men of middle-class background. The council and various government boards recruited men trained in Roman law, which exalted the power of the Crown. They also secured from the Spanish pope Alexander VI the right to appoint bishops in Spain and in the Hispanic territories in America, enabling them to establish the equivalent of a national church. In 1492 their armies conquered Granada, the last territory held by Arabs in southern Spain.

There still remained a sizable and, in the view of the majority of the Spanish people, potentially dangerous minority, the Jews. When the kings of France and England had expelled the Jews from their kingdoms, many had sought refuge in Spain. During the long centuries of the reconquista, Christian kings had renewed Jewish rights and privileges; in fact, Jewish industry, intelligence, and money had supported royal power. While Christians of all classes borrowed from Jewish moneylenders and while all who could afford them sought Jewish physicians, a strong undercurrent of resentment of Jewish influence and wealth festered.

In the fourteenth century anti-Semitism in Spain was aggravated by fiery anti-Jewish preaching, by economic dislocation, and by the search for a scapegoat during the Black Death. Anti-Semitic pogroms swept the towns of Spain; one scholar estimates that 40 percent of the Jewish population was killed or forced to convert.[2] Those converted were called *conversos* or **New Christians**. Conversos were often well-educated and held prominent positions in government, the church, medicine, law, and business.

New Christians *The translation of the Spanish word* conversos, *referring to Spanish Jews who converted to Christianity in the fourteenth century in order to avoid persecution.*

● **Felipe Bigarny: Ferdinand and Isabella** In these wooden sculptures, the Burgundian artist Felipe Bigarny portrays Ferdinand and Isabella as paragons of Christian piety, kneeling at prayer. Ferdinand is shown in armor, a symbol of his military accomplishments and masculinity. Isabella wears a simple white head covering rather than something more elaborate to indicate her modesty, a key virtue for women, though her actions and writings indicate that she was more determined and forceful than Ferdinand. *(Capilla Real, Granada/Laurie Platt Winfrey, Inc.)*

Such successes bred resentment. Aristocratic grandees resented their financial dependence; the poor hated the converso tax collectors; and churchmen doubted the sincerity of their conversions. Queen Isabella shared these suspicions, and she and Ferdinand received permission from Pope Sixtus IV to establish an Inquisition to "search out and punish converts from Judaism who had transgressed against Christianity by secretly adhering to Jewish beliefs and performing rites of the Jews."[3] Investigations and trials began immediately, as officials of the Inquisition looked for conversos who showed any sign of incomplete conversion, such as not eating pork.

Recent scholarship has carefully analyzed documents of the Inquisition. Most conversos identified themselves as sincere Christians; many came from families that had received baptism generations before. In response, officials of the Inquisition developed a new type of anti-Semitism. A person's status as a Jew, they argued, could not be changed by religious conversion, but was in their blood and was heritable, so Jews could never be true Christians. In what were known as "purity of the blood" laws, having pure Christian blood became a requirement for noble status. Ideas about Jews developed in Spain were important components in European concepts of race, and discussions of "Jewish blood" later expanded into notions of the "Jewish race."

Shortly after the conquest of Granada, Isabella and Ferdinand issued an edict expelling all practicing Jews from Spain. Of the community of perhaps 200,000 Jews, 150,000 fled. Absolute religious orthodoxy and "purity of blood" served as the theoretical foundation of the Spanish national state.

The Habsburgs

War and diplomacy were important ways that states increased their power in sixteenth-century Europe, but so was marriage. Because almost all of Europe was ruled by hereditary dynasties—the papal states and a few cities being the exceptions—claiming and holding resources involved shrewd marital strategies, for it was far cheaper to gain land by inheritance than by war. Royal and noble sons and daughters were important tools of state policy.

The benefits of an advantageous marriage stretched across generations, a process that can be seen most dramatically with the Habsburgs. The Holy Roman emperor Frederick III, a Habsburg who was the ruler of most of Austria, acquired only a small amount of territory—but a great deal of money—with his marriage to Princess Eleonore of Portugal in 1452. He arranged for his son Maximilian to marry Europe's most prominent heiress, Mary of Burgundy, in 1477; she inherited the Netherlands, Luxembourg, and the county of Burgundy in what is now eastern France. Through this union with the rich and powerful duchy of Burgundy, the Austrian house of Habsburg, already the strongest ruling family in the empire, became an international power. The marriage of Maximilian and Mary angered the French, however, who considered Burgundy French territory, and inaugurated centuries of conflict between the Austrian house of Habsburg and the kings of France. Within the empire, German principalities that resented Austria's pre-eminence began to see that they shared interests with France.

Maximilian learned the lesson of marital politics well, marrying his son and daughter to the children of Ferdinand and Isabella, the rulers of Spain, much of southern Italy, and eventually the Spanish New World empire. His grandson Charles V (1500–1558) fell heir to a vast and incredibly diverse collection of states and peoples, each governed in a different manner and held together only by the person of the emperor (see Map 14.1 and page 410). Charles was convinced that it was his duty to maintain the political and religious unity of Western Christendom. This conviction would be challenged far more than Charles ever anticipated.

• • • • • • • • • • • • • • •

THE PROTESTANT REFORMATION

What were the central ideas of Protestant reformers, and why were they appealing to various groups across Europe?

Calls for reform in the church came from many quarters in early-sixteenth-century Europe—from educated laypeople such as Christian humanists and urban residents, from villagers and artisans, and from church officials themselves. This dissatisfaction helps explain why the ideas of Martin Luther, an obscure professor from a new and not very prestigious German university, found a ready audience. Within a decade of his first publishing his ideas (using the new technology of the printing press), much of central Europe and Scandinavia had broken with the Catholic Church, and even more radical concepts of the Christian message were being developed and linked to calls for social change.

Criticism of the Church

Sixteenth-century Europeans were deeply pious. Despite—or perhaps because of—the depth of their piety, many people were also highly critical of the Roman Catholic Church and its clergy. Papal conflicts with rulers and the Great Schism badly damaged the prestige of church leaders. Humanists denounced corruption in the church, the superstitions of the parish clergy, and the excessive rituals of the monks. Many ordinary

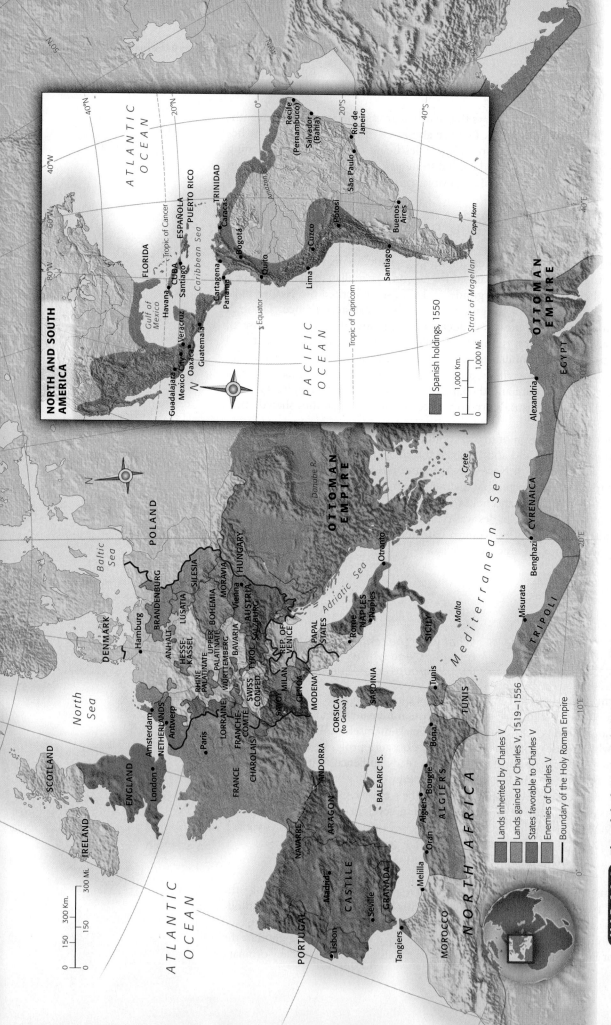

MAP 14.1 **The Global Empire of Charles V** Charles V exercised theoretical jurisdiction over more European territory than anyone since Charlemagne. He also claimed authority over large parts of North and South America, though actual Spanish control was weak in much of this area.

NORTH AND SOUTH AMERICA

ATLANTIC OCEAN

PACIFIC OCEAN

Spanish holdings, 1550

FLORIDA
CUBA
Havana
Mexico City
Guadalajara
Veracruz
Oaxaca
Guatemala
ESPAÑOLA
PUERTO RICO
TRINIDAD
Caribbean Sea
Gulf of Mexico
Santiago
Cartagena
Panamá
Bogotá
Caracas
Quito
Lima
Cuzco
Potosí
Recife (Pernambuco)
Salvador (Bahia)
Rio de Janeiro
São Paulo
Buenos Aires
Santiago
Amazon
Equator
Tropic of Cancer
Tropic of Capricorn
Strait of Magellan
Cape Horn

0 1,000 Km.
0 1,000 Mi.

ATLANTIC OCEAN
North Sea
Baltic Sea
Mediterranean Sea
Adriatic Sea
Danube R
Crete
Malta

SCOTLAND
IRELAND
ENGLAND
London
NETHERLANDS
Amsterdam
Antwerp
DENMARK
Hamburg
POLAND
BRANDENBURG
LUSATIA
SILESIA
ANHALT
HESSE KASSEL
RHINE PALATINATE
WÜRTEMBERG
UPPER PALATINATE
BOHEMIA
MORAVIA
BAVARIA
AUSTRIA
HUNGARY
TYROL SALZBURG
Vienna
SWISS CONFED.
FRANCE
Paris
LORRAINE
FRANCHE-COMTE
CHAROLAIS
SAVOY
MILAN
GENOA
MODENA
REP. OF VENICE
PAPAL STATES
Rome
NAPLES
Naples
Otranto
CORSICA (to Genoa)
SARDINIA
SICILY
PORTUGAL
Lisbon
CASTILE
Madrid
Seville
GRANADA
ARAGON
NAVARRE
ANDORRA
BALEARIC IS.
Melilla
Oran
Algiers
Bougie
Bona
Tunis
MOROCCO
Tangiers
NORTH AFRICA
MOROCCO
ALGIERS
TUNIS
TRIPOLI
Misurata
Benghazi
CYRENAICA
OTTOMAN EMPIRE
EGYPT
Alexandria

0 150 300 Mi.
0 150 300 Km.

Lands inherited by Charles V
Lands gained by Charles V, 1519–1556
States favorable to Charles V
Enemies of Charles V
Boundary of the Holy Roman Empire

people agreed. Court records, bishops' visitations of parishes, and even popular songs and printed images show widespread **anticlericalism,** or opposition to the clergy.

In the early sixteenth century critics of the church concentrated their attacks on three disorders—clerical immorality, clerical ignorance, and clerical absenteeism. Charges of clerical immorality were aimed at a number of priests who were drunkards, neglected the rule of celibacy, gambled, or indulged in fancy dress. Charges of clerical ignorance applied to barely literate priests who delivered poor quality sermons and who were obviously ignorant of the Latin words of the Mass.

In regard to absenteeism, many clerics, especially higher ecclesiastics, held several *benefices* (or offices) simultaneously—a practice termed *pluralism*—but seldom visited the benefices, let alone performed the spiritual responsibilities those offices entailed. Instead, they collected revenues from all of them and hired a poor priest, paying him just a fraction of the income to fulfill the spiritual duties of a particular local church.

There was also local resentment of clerical privileges and immunities. Priests, monks, and nuns were exempt from civic responsibilities, such as defending the city and paying taxes. Yet religious orders frequently held large amounts of urban property, in some cities as much as one-third. City governments were increasingly determined to integrate the clergy into civic life. This brought city leaders into opposition with bishops and the papacy, which for centuries had stressed the independence of the church from lay control and the distinction between members of the clergy and laypeople.

anticlericalism *A widespread sentiment in the early sixteenth century characterized by resentment of clerical immorality, ignorance, and absenteeism. An important cause of the Protestant Reformation.*

Martin Luther

By itself, widespread criticism of the church did not lead to the dramatic changes of the sixteenth century. Those resulted from the personal religious struggle of a German university professor, Martin Luther (1483–1546). Luther's middle-class father wanted him to be a lawyer, but a sense of religious calling led him to join the Augustinian friars, an order whose members often preached, taught, and assisted the poor. Luther was ordained a priest in 1507 and after additional study earned a doctorate of theology. From 1512 until his death in 1546, he served as professor of the Scriptures at the new University of Wittenberg.

Martin Luther was a very conscientious friar. His scrupulous observance of the religious routine, frequent confessions, and fasting, however, gave him only temporary relief from anxieties about sin and his ability to meet God's demands. Through his study of Saint Paul's letters in the New Testament, he gradually arrived at a new understanding of Christian doctrine. His understanding is often summarized as "faith alone, grace alone, Scripture alone." He believed that salvation and justification come through faith. Faith is a free gift of God, not the result of human effort. God's word is revealed only in Scripture, not in the traditions of the church.

At the same time Luther was engaged in scholarly reflections and professorial lecturing, Pope Leo X authorized a special St. Peter's indulgence to finance his building plans in Rome. An **indulgence** was a document, signed by the pope or another church official, that substituted for penance. The archbishop who controlled the area in which Wittenberg was located, Albert of Mainz, was an enthusiastic promoter of this indulgence sale. He received a share of the profits in order to pay off a debt from a wealthy banking family, a debt he had incurred in order to purchase a papal dispensation allowing him to become the bishop of several other territories as well. Albert's indulgence sale, run by a Dominican friar who mounted an advertising blitz, promised that the purchase of indulgences would bring full forgiveness for one's own sins or release from purgatory for a loved one. One of the slogans—"As soon as coin in coffer rings, the soul from purgatory springs"—brought phenomenal success.

Luther was severely troubled that many people believed that they had no further need for repentance once they had purchased indulgences. He wrote a letter to Archbishop Albert on the subject and enclosed in Latin "Ninety-five Theses on the Power

Primary Source: Table Talk *Read Martin Luther in his own words, speaking out forcefully and candidly—and sometimes with humor—against Catholic institutions.*

indulgence *A papal statement granting remission of a priest-imposed penalty for sin (no one knew what penalty God would impose after death).*

● **The Folly of Indulgences** In this woodcut from the early Reformation, the church's sale of indulgences is viciously satirized. With one claw in holy water, another resting on the coins paid for indulgences, and a third stretched out for offerings, the church, in the form of a rapacious bird, writes out an indulgence with excrement. The creature's head and gaping mouth represent Hell, with foolish Christians inside, others being cooked in a pot above, and a demon delivering the pope in a three-tiered crown and holding the keys to Heaven, a symbol of papal authority. Illustrations such as this, often printed as single-sheet broadsides and sold very cheaply, clearly conveyed criticism of the church to people who could not read. *(Kunstsammlungen der Veste Coburg)*

Diet of Worms *An assembly of the Estates of the Holy Roman Empire convened by Charles V in the German city of Worms. It was here that Martin Luther refused to recant his writings.*

Protestant *Originally meaning "a follower of Luther," this term came to be generally applied to all non-Catholic Christians.*

of Indulgences." His argument was that indulgences undermined the seriousness of the sacrament of penance and competed with the preaching of the Gospel. After Luther's death, biographies reported that the theses were also posted on the door of the church at Wittenberg Castle on October 31, 1517. Such an act would have been very strange—they were in Latin and written for those learned in theology, not for normal churchgoers—but it has become a standard part of Luther lore. In any case, Luther intended the theses for academic debate, but by December 1517 they had been translated into German and were read throughout the Holy Roman Empire.

Luther was ordered to come to Rome, which he was able to avoid because of the political situation in the Holy Roman Empire. The pope ordered him to recant many of his ideas, and Luther publicly burned the papal letter. In this highly charged atmosphere, the twenty-one-year-old emperor Charles V held his first diet (assembly of the Estates of the empire) in the German city of Worms. Charles summoned Luther to appear before the **Diet of Worms.** When ordered to recant, Luther replied in language that rang all over Europe:

Unless I am convinced by the evidence of Scripture or by plain reason—for I do not accept the authority of the Pope or the councils alone, since it is established that they have often erred and contradicted themselves—I am bound by the Scriptures I have cited and my conscience is captive to the Word of God. I cannot and will not recant anything, for it is neither safe nor right to go against conscience. God help me. Amen.[4]

Protestant Thought and Its Appeal

As he developed his ideas, Luther gathered followers, who came to be called Protestants. The word **Protestant** derives from a "protest" drawn up by a small group of reforming German princes in 1529. At first *Protestant* meant "a follower of Luther" but with the appearance of many protesting sects, it became a general term applied to all non-Catholic western European Christians.

Protestants agreed on many things. First, how is a person to be saved? Traditional Catholic teaching held that salvation is achieved by both faith and good works. Protestants held that salvation comes by faith alone, irrespective of good works or the sacraments. God, not people, initiates salvation. (See the feature "Listening to the Past: Martin Luther, *On Christian Liberty*" on pages 422–423.) Second, where does religious authority reside? Christian doctrine had long maintained that authority rests both in the Bible and in the traditional teaching of the church. For Protestants, authority rests in the Bible alone. For a doctrine or issue to be valid, it had to have a scriptural basis. Third, what is the church? Protestants held that the church is a spiritual *priesthood of all believers,* an invisible fellowship not fixed in any place or person, which differed markedly from the Roman Catholic practice of a clerical, hierarchical institution headed by the pope in Rome. Fourth, what is the highest form of Christian life? The medieval church had stressed the superiority of the monastic and religious life over the secular. Luther disagreed and argued that every person should serve God in his or her individual calling.

Pulpits and printing presses spread Luther's message all over Germany. By the time of his death, people of all social classes had become Lutheran. What was the immense appeal of Luther's religious ideas and those of other Protestants?

Educated people and humanists were much attracted by Luther's ideas. He advocated a simpler personal religion based on faith, a return to the spirit of the early church, the centrality of the Scriptures in the liturgy and in Christian life, and the abolition of elaborate ceremonies—precisely the reforms the Christian humanists had been calling for. His insistence that everyone should read and reflect on the Scriptures attracted the literate and thoughtful middle classes partly because Luther appealed to their intelligence. This included many priests and monks, who became clergy in the new Protestant churches. Luther's ideas also appealed to townspeople who envied the church's wealth and resented paying for it. After cities became Protestant, the city council taxed the clergy and placed them under the jurisdiction of civil courts.

Scholars in many disciplines have attributed Luther's fame and success to the invention of the printing press, which rapidly reproduced and made known his ideas. Many printed works included woodcuts and other illustrations, so that even those who could not read could grasp the main ideas. Hymns such as "A Mighty Fortress Is Our God" (which Luther wrote) were also important means of conveying central points of doctrine. Equally important was Luther's incredible skill with language; his linguistic skill, together with his translation of the New Testament into German in 1523, led to the acceptance of his dialect of German as the standard version of German.

Luther lived in a territory ruled by a noble—the Elector of Saxony—and he also worked closely with political authorities, viewing them as fully justified in reforming the church in their territories. He instructed all Christians to obey their secular rulers, whom he saw as divinely ordained to maintain order. Individuals may have been convinced of the truth of Protestant teachings by hearing sermons, listening to hymns, or reading pamphlets, but a territory became Protestant when its ruler, whether a noble or a city council, brought in a reformer or two to reeducate the territory's clergy, sponsored public sermons, and confiscated church property. This happened in many of the states of the empire during the 1520s and then moved beyond the empire to Denmark-Norway and Sweden.

In the sixteenth century the practice of religion remained a public matter. The ruler determined the official form of religious practice in his (or occasionally her) jurisdiction. Almost everyone believed that the presence of a faith different from that of the majority represented a political threat to the security of the state. Few believed in religious liberty; those with different ideas had to convert or leave.

The Radical Reformation and the German Peasants' War

Some individuals and groups rejected the idea that church and state needed to be united, and sought to create a voluntary community of believers as they understood it to have existed in New Testament times. In terms of theology and spiritual practices, these individuals and groups varied widely, though they are generally termed "radicals" for their insistence on a more extensive break with the past. Some adopted the baptism of believers—for which they were given the title of "Anabaptists" or rebaptizers by their enemies—while others saw all outward sacraments or rituals as misguided. Some groups attempted communal ownership of property, living very simply and rejecting anything they thought unbiblical. Some reacted harshly to members who deviated, but others argued for complete religious toleration and individualism.

Religious radicals were met with fanatical hatred and bitter persecution. Protestants and Catholics all saw—quite correctly—that the radicals' call for the separation of church and state would lead ultimately to the secularization of society. Radicals were either banished or cruelly executed by burning, beating, or drowning. Their community spirit and the edifying example of their lives, however, contributed to the survival of radical ideas. Later, the Quakers, with their gentle pacifism; the Baptists, with their emphasis on inner spiritual light; the Congregationalists, with their democratic church organization; and in 1787 the authors of the U.S. Constitution, with their opposition to the "establishment of religion" (state churches), would all trace their origins, in part, to the radicals of the sixteenth century.

In the early sixteenth century the economic condition of the peasantry varied from place to place but was generally worse than it had been in the fifteenth century and was deteriorating. Peasants demanded limitations on the new taxes and services their noble landlords were imposing. They peasants believed that their demands conformed to the Scriptures and cited Luther as a theologian who could prove that they did.

Luther wanted to prevent rebellion. Initially he sided with the peasants, blasting the lords for robbing their subjects. But when rebellion broke out, the peasants who expected Luther's support were soon disillusioned. Freedom for Luther meant independence from the authority of the Roman church; it did *not* mean opposition to legally established secular powers. Firmly convinced that rebellion would hasten the end of civilized society, he wrote the tract *Against the Murderous, Thieving Hordes of the Peasants:* "Let everyone who can smite, slay, and stab [the peasants], secretly and openly, remembering that nothing can be more poisonous, hurtful or devilish than a rebel."[5] The nobility ferociously crushed the revolt. Historians estimate that more than seventy-five thousand peasants were killed in 1525.

The German Peasants' War of 1525 greatly strengthened the authority of lay rulers. Not surprisingly, the Reformation lost much of its popular appeal after 1525, though peasants and urban rebels sometimes found a place for their social and religious ideas in radical groups. Peasants' economic conditions did moderately improve, however. For example, in many parts of Germany, enclosed fields, meadows, and forests were returned to common use.

The Reformation and Marriage

Luther and other Protestants believed that a priest's or nun's vows of celibacy went against human nature and God's commandments. Luther married a former nun, Katharina von Bora (1499–1532), who quickly had several children. Most other Protestant reformers also married, and their wives had to create a new and respectable role for themselves—pastor's wife—to overcome being viewed as simply a new type of priest's concubine. They were living demonstrations of their husband's convictions about the superiority of marriage to celibacy, and they were expected to be models of wifely obedience and Christian charity.

Protestants did not break with medieval Scholastic theologians in their idea that women were to be subject to men. Women were advised to be cheerful rather than grudging in their obedience, for in doing so they demonstrated their willingness to follow God's plan. Men were urged to treat their wives kindly and considerately, but also to enforce their authority, through physical coercion if necessary. Both continental and English marriage manuals use the metaphor of breaking a horse for teaching a wife obedience, though laws did set limits on the husband's power to do so. A few women took Luther's idea about the priesthood of all believers to heart and wrote religious pamphlets and hymns, but no sixteenth-century Protestants officially allowed women to hold positions of religious authority. Monarchs such as Elizabeth I of England and female territorial rulers of the states of the Holy Roman Empire did determine religious policies, however.

Catholics viewed marriage as a sacramental union that, if validly entered into, could not be dissolved. Protestants saw marriage as a contract in which each partner promised the other support, companionship, and the sharing of mutual goods. Marriages in which spouses did not comfort or support one another endangered their own souls

● **Lucas Cranach the Elder: Martin Luther and Katharina von Bora** Cranach painted this double marriage portrait to celebrate Luther's wedding in 1525 to Katharina von Bora, a former nun. The couple quickly became a model of the ideal marriage, and many churches wanted their portraits. More than sixty similar paintings, with slight variations, were produced by Cranach's workshop and hung in churches and wealthy homes. *(Uffizi, Florence/Scala/Art Resource, NY)*

and the surrounding community, and most Protestants came to allow divorce. Divorce remained rare, however, as marriage was such an important social and economic institution.

The Reformation generally brought the closing of monasteries and convents, and marriage became virtually the only occupation for upper-class Protestant women. Women in some convents recognized this and fought the Reformation, or argued that they could still be pious Protestants within convent walls. Most nuns left, however, and we do not know what happened to them. The Protestant emphasis on marriage made unmarried women (and men) suspect, for they did not belong to the type of household regarded as the cornerstone of a proper, godly society.

The Reformation and German Politics

Criticism of the church was widespread in Europe in the early sixteenth century, and calls for reform came from many areas. Yet such movements could be more easily squelched by the strong central governments of Spain, France, and England. The Holy Roman Empire, in contrast, included hundreds of largely independent states. The authority of the emperor was far less than that of the monarchs of western Europe, and local rulers continued to exercise great power.

Luther's ideas appealed to German rulers for a variety of reasons. Though Germany was not a nation, people did have an understanding of being German because of their language and traditions. Luther frequently used the phrase "we Germans" in his attacks on the papacy. Luther's appeal to national feeling influenced many rulers. Some German rulers were sincerely attracted to Lutheran ideas, but material considerations swayed many others to embrace the new faith. The rejection of Roman Catholicism and adoption of Protestantism would mean the legal confiscation of lush farmlands, rich monasteries, and wealthy shrines. Thus many political authorities in the empire used the religious issue to extend their financial and political power and to enhance their independence from the emperor.

Charles V, elected as emperor in 1521, must share blame with the German princes for the disintegration of imperial authority in the empire. He neither understood nor took an interest in the constitutional problems of Germany, and he lacked the material resources to oppose Protestantism effectively there. Throughout his reign, he was preoccupied with his Flemish, Spanish, Italian, and American territories. Moreover, the expansion of the Ottoman Empire prevented him from acting effectively against the Protestants; the Ottoman Turks threatened Habsburg lands in southeastern Europe at just the point that the Reformation began, and in 1529 were even besieging Vienna.

Five times between 1521 and 1555, Charles V went to war with the Valois kings of France. The cornerstone of French foreign policy in the sixteenth and seventeenth centuries was the desire to keep the German states divided. Thus Europe witnessed the paradox of the Catholic king of France supporting the Lutheran princes in their challenge to his fellow Catholic, Charles V. The Habsburg-Valois Wars advanced the cause of Protestantism and promoted the political fragmentation of the German Empire.

Finally, in 1555, Charles agreed to the Peace of Augsburg, which officially recognized Lutheranism. Each prince was permitted to determine the religion of his territory. Most of northern and central Germany became Lutheran; the south remained Roman Catholic. The Peace of Augsburg ended religious war in Germany for many decades. His hope of uniting his empire under a single church dashed, Charles V abdicated in 1556, transferring power over his Spanish and Netherlandish holdings to his son Philip and his imperial power to his brother Ferdinand.

The Spread of the Protestant Reformation

States within the Holy Roman Empire and the kingdom of Denmark-Norway were the earliest territories to accept the Protestant Reformation, but by the later 1520s religious change came to England, France, and eastern Europe. In all these areas, a second generation of reformers built on earlier ideas to develop their own theology and plans for institutional change.

As on the continent, the Reformation in England had economic as well as religious causes. As elsewhere, too, Christian humanists had for decades been calling for the purification of the church. However, the impetus for England's break with Rome was the ruler's desire for a new wife. When the personal matter of the divorce of King Henry VIII (r. 1509–1547) became enmeshed with political issues, a complete break with Rome resulted.

In 1527, after eighteen years of marriage, Henry's wife, Catherine of Aragon, had failed to produce a male child, and Henry claimed that only a male child could prevent a disputed succession. Henry had also fallen in love with a lady at court, Anne Boleyn. So Henry petitioned Pope Clement VII for an annulment of his marriage to Catherine. When the pope procrastinated in granting the annulment, Henry decided to remove the English church from papal authority.

Henry used Parliament to legalize the Reformation in England and to make himself the supreme head of the Church of England. Some opposed the king and were

● **Allegory of the Tudor Dynasty** The unknown creator of this work intended to glorify the virtues of the Protestant succession; the painting has no historical reality. Enthroned Henry VIII (r. 1509–1547) hands the sword of justice to his Protestant son Edward VI (r. 1547–1553). At left the Catholic Queen Mary (r. 1553–1558) and her husband Philip of Spain are followed by Mars, god of war, signifying violence and civil disorder. At right the figures of Peace and Plenty accompany the Protestant Elizabeth I (r. 1558–1603), symbolizing England's happy fate under her rule. *(Yale Center for British Art, Paul Mellon Collection/The Bridgeman Art Library)*

beheaded, among them Thomas More, the king's chancellor and author of *Utopia* (see page 392). When Anne Boleyn failed twice to produce a male child, Henry VIII charged her with adulterous incest and in 1536 had her beheaded. His third wife, Jane Seymour, gave Henry the desired son, Edward, but she died in childbirth. Henry went on to three more wives.

Between 1535 and 1539, under the influence of his chief minister Thomas Cromwell, Henry decided to dissolve the English monasteries because he wanted their wealth. Hundreds of properties were sold to the middle and upper classes, strengthening the upper classes and tying them to the Tudor dynasty. Henry's motives combined personal, political, social, and economic elements. What about everyday English people? Recent scholarship points out that people rarely "converted" from Catholicism to Protestantism overnight. People responded to an action of the Crown that was played out in their own neighborhood—the closing of a monastery, the ending of masses for the dead—with a combination of resistance, acceptance, and collaboration.

Loyalty to the Catholic Church was particularly strong in Ireland. Ireland had been claimed by English kings since the twelfth century, but in reality the English had firm control of only the area around Dublin known as the Pale. In 1536, on orders from London, the Irish parliament, which represented only the English landlords and the people of the Pale, approved the English laws severing the church from Rome. The (English) ruling class adopted the new reformed faith, but most of the Irish people remained Roman Catholic. Irish armed opposition to the Reformation led to harsh repression by the English, thus adding religious antagonism to the ethnic hostility that had been a feature of English policy toward Ireland for centuries (see page 362).

In the short reign of Henry's sickly son, Edward VI (r. 1547–1553), strongly Protestant ideas exerted a significant influence on the religious life of the country. The equally brief reign of Mary Tudor (r. 1553–1558) witnessed a sharp move back to Catholicism. The devoutly Catholic daughter of Catherine of Aragon, Mary rescinded the Reformation legislation of her father's reign and restored Roman Catholicism. Mary's marriage to her cousin Philip of Spain, son of the emperor Charles V, proved highly unpopular in England, and her execution of several hundred Protestants further alienated her subjects. During her reign, many Protestants fled to the continent. Mary's death raised to the throne her sister Elizabeth (r. 1558–1603) and inaugurated the beginning of religious stability.

Elizabeth, Henry's daughter with Anne Boleyn, had been raised a Protestant, but at the start of her reign sharp differences existed in England. On the one hand, Catholics wanted a Roman Catholic ruler. On the other hand, a vocal number of returning exiles wanted all Catholic elements in the Church of England eliminated. The latter, because they wanted to "purify" the church, were called "Puritans." Shrewdly, Elizabeth chose a middle course between Catholic and Puritan extremes. She referred to herself as the "supreme governor of the Church of England," which allowed Catholics to remain loyal to her without denying the pope. She required her subjects to attend church or risk a fine, but did not interfere with their privately held beliefs. The Anglican Church, as the Church of England was called, moved in a moderately Protestant direction.

Calvinism

In 1509, while Luther was preparing for a doctorate at Wittenberg, John Calvin (1509–1564) was born in Noyon in northwestern France. As a young man he studied law, which had a decisive impact on his mind and later thought. In 1533 he experienced a religious crisis, as a result of which he converted to Protestantism. Calvin believed that God had specifically selected him to reform the church. Accordingly, he accepted an invitation to assist in the reformation of the city of Geneva. There, beginning in 1541, Calvin worked assiduously to establish a Christian society ruled by God through civil magistrates and reformed ministers. Geneva, "a city that was a church," became the model of a Christian community for sixteenth-century Protestant reformers.

To understand Calvin's Geneva, it is necessary to understand Calvin's ideas. These he embodied in *The Institutes of the Christian Religion,* first published in 1536 and definitively issued in 1559. The cornerstone of Calvin's theology was his belief in the absolute sovereignty and omnipotence of God and the total weakness of humanity. Before the infinite power of God, he asserted, men and women are as insignificant as grains of sand.

Calvin did not ascribe free will to human beings because that would detract from the sovereignty of God. Men and women cannot actively work to achieve salvation; rather, God in his infinite wisdom decided at the beginning of time who would be saved and who damned. This viewpoint constitutes the theological principle called **predestination.** Many people consider the doctrine of predestination, which dates back to Saint Augustine and Saint Paul, to be a pessimistic view of the nature of God. But "this terrible decree," as even Calvin called it, did not lead to pessimism or fatalism. Rather, predestination served as an energizing dynamic, convincing people that hardships were part of the constant struggle against evil.

predestination *Calvin's teaching that, by God's decree, some persons are guided to salvation and others to damnation; that God has called us not according to our works but according to his purpose and grace.*

Calvin aroused Genevans to a high standard of morality. In the reformation of the city, the Genevan Consistory also exercised a powerful role. This body of laymen and pastors was assembled "to keep watch over every man's life [and] to admonish amiably those whom they see leading a disorderly life."[6] Although all municipal governments in early modern Europe regulated citizens' conduct, none did so with the severity of Geneva's Consistory under Calvin's leadership. Absence from sermons, criticism of ministers, dancing, card playing, family quarrels, and heavy drinking were all investigated and punished by the Consistory.

Religious refugees from France, England, Spain, Scotland, and Italy visited Calvin's Geneva. Subsequently, the Reformed church of Calvin served as the model for the Presbyterian church in Scotland, the Huguenot church in France, and the Puritan churches in England and New England.

The Calvinist ethic of the "calling" dignified all work with a religious aspect. Hard work, well done, was pleasing to God. This doctrine encouraged an aggressive, vigorous activism. These factors, together with the social and economic applications of Calvin's theology, made Calvinism the most dynamic force in sixteenth- and seventeenth-century Protestantism.

• • • • • • • • • • • • • • •

THE CATHOLIC REFORMATION

How did the Catholic Church respond to the new religious situation?

Between 1517 and 1547 Protestantism made remarkable advances. Nevertheless, the Roman Catholic Church made a significant comeback. After about 1540 no new large areas of Europe, other than the Netherlands, accepted Protestant beliefs (see Map 14.2). Many historians see the developments within the Catholic Church after the Protestant Reformation as two interrelated movements, one a drive for internal reform linked to earlier reform efforts, and the other a Counter-Reformation that opposed Protestants intellectually, politically, militarily, and institutionally. In both movements, the papacy, new religious orders, and the Council of Trent that met from 1545 to 1563 were important agents.

The Reformed Papacy and the Council of Trent

Renaissance popes and advisers were not blind to the need for church reforms, but they resisted calls for a general council representing the entire church, fearing loss of power, revenue, and prestige. This changed beginning with Pope Paul III (1534–1549), and the papal court became the center of the reform movement rather than its chief opponent. The lives of the pope and his reform-minded cardinals, abbots, and bishops were models of decorum and piety.

In 1542 Pope Paul III established the Sacred Congregation of the **Holy Office**, with jurisdiction over the Roman Inquisition, a powerful instrument of the Catholic Reformation. The Inquisition was a committee of six cardinals with judicial authority over all Catholics and the power to arrest, imprison, and execute. Within the Papal States, the Inquisition effectively destroyed heresy (and some heretics).

Pope Paul III also called an ecumenical council, which met intermittently from 1545 to 1563 at Trent, an imperial city close to Italy. It was called not only to reform the church but also to secure reconciliation with the Protestants. Lutherans and Calvinists were invited to participate, but their insistence that the Scriptures be the sole basis for discussion made reconciliation impossible.

Nonetheless, the decrees of the Council of Trent laid a solid basis for the spiritual renewal of the Catholic Church. It gave equal validity to the Scriptures and to tradition

Holy Office *An official Roman Catholic agency founded in 1542 to combat international doctrinal heresy and to promote sound doctrine on faith and morals.*

Predominant religion in 1555

- Lutheran
- Calvinist (Reformed)
- Church of England
- Roman Catholic
- Orthodox
- Muslim
- ➤ Spread of Calvinism
- ▲ Huguenot center
- ◯ Ottoman Empire, 1566

400 Mi.
0 200 400 Km.

N

ATLANTIC OCEAN

IRELAND
Dublin

SCOTLAND 1560
Edinburgh
John Knox, 1505–1572
Penetration of Calvinism to England after 1558

ENGLAND 1536
Oxford
John Wyclif, 1320–1384
London
Plymouth

North Sea

NORWAY 1536/1607
Bergen

SWEDEN
Stockholm

DENMARK
Copenhagen

Baltic Sea

Helsinki

Riga

LITHUANIA

PRUSSIA

Warsaw

POLAND

BRANDENBURG
Hamburg
Wittenberg
Birthplace of Martin Luther, 1483–1546

SAXONY
Eisleben
Erfurt
Leipzig

NETHERLANDS
Amsterdam
Antwerp
Brussels
Münster

HOLY ROMAN EMPIRE

Marburg
Worms
Speyer
Edict of Worms, 1521
Strasbourg
Nuremberg
Stuttgart
Augsburg
Munich

Prague
Jan Hus, 1369–1415

BOHEMIA

MORAVIA

AUSTRIA
Vienna

Birthplace of Martin Luther, Wittenberg

FRANCE
Noyon
Birthplace of John Calvin, 1509–1564
Paris
Rennes
Orléans
Nantes
Edict of Nantes, 1598
La Rochelle
Bordeaux
Toulouse
Marseilles
Avignon

Basel
Zurich
Ulrich Zwingli, 1484–1531
Geneva
John Calvin
Milan
Pavia
Genoa
Pisa
Florence

Council of Trent, 1545–1563
Trent
Venice

ITALY

Rome
Roman Inquisition established, 1542
Naples
Bari

Corsica
Sardinia
Sicily

Adriatic Sea

Mediterranean Sea

HUNGARY
Buda
Pest
Belgrade
SERBIA

TRANSYLVANIA
MOLDAVIA
WALLACHIA
Danube R.
BESSARABIA

BULGARIA

OTTOMAN EMPIRE

GREECE

Black Sea

SPAIN
Madrid
Toledo
Seville
Granada
Valencia
Barcelona
Balearic Is.
Loyola
Birthplace of Ignatius Loyola, 1491–1556

PORTUGAL
Lisbon

MOROCCO

ALGIERS
OTTOMAN EMPIRE

TUNIS

60°N
50°N
40°N
30°N

10°W
0°
10°E
20°E
30°E

MAP 14.2 **Religious Divisions in Europe** The Reformation shattered the religious unity of Western Christendom. The situation was even more complicated than a map of this scale can show. Many cities within the Holy Roman Empire, for example, accepted a different faith than did the surrounding countryside; Augsburg, Basel, and Strasbourg were all Protestant, though surrounded by territory ruled by Catholic nobles.

as sources of religious truth and authority. It reaffirmed the seven sacraments and the traditional Catholic teaching on transubstantiation. It tackled the disciplinary matters that had disillusioned the faithful, requiring bishops to reside in their own dioceses, suppressing pluralism and simony, and forbidding the sale of indulgences. Clerics who kept concubines were to give them up. In a highly original decree, the council required every diocese to establish a seminary for the education and training of the clergy. Seminary professors were to determine whether candidates for ordination had *vocations,* genuine callings to the priesthood. This was a novel idea, since from the time of the early church, parents had determined their sons' (and daughters') religious careers. Finally, great emphasis was laid on preaching and instructing the laity, especially the uneducated. One decision had especially important social consequences for laypeople. The Council of Trent stipulated that for a marriage to be valid, consent (the essence of marriage) as given in the vows had to be made publicly before witnesses, one of whom had to be the parish priest. Trent thereby ended the widespread practice of secret marriages in Catholic countries. The decrees of the Council of Trent laid a solid basis for the spiritual renewal of the church. For four centuries the doctrinal and disciplinary legislation of Trent served as the basis for Roman Catholic faith, organization, and practice.

New Religious Orders

The establishment of new religious orders within the church reveals a central feature of the Catholic Reformation. Most of these new orders developed in response to one crying need: to raise the moral and intellectual level of the clergy and people. Education was a major goal of the two most famous orders.

The Ursuline order of nuns, founded by Angela Merici (1474–1540), attained enormous prestige for the education of women. The daughter of a country gentleman, Angela Merici worked for many years among the poor, sick, and uneducated around her native Brescia in northern Italy. In 1535 she established the first women's religious order concentrating exclusively on teaching young girls, with the goal of re-Christianizing society by training future wives and mothers. After receiving papal approval in 1565, the Ursulines rapidly spread to France and the New World.

The Society of Jesus, or **Jesuits,** founded by Ignatius Loyola (1491–1556), played a powerful international role in strengthening Catholicism in Europe and spreading the faith around the world. While recuperating from a severe battle wound in his legs, Loyola studied a life of Christ and other religious books and decided to give up his military career and become a soldier of Christ. The first Jesuits, whom Loyola recruited primarily from the wealthy merchant and professional classes, saw the Reformation as a pastoral problem, its causes and cures related not to doctrinal issues but to people's spiritual condition. Reform of the church, as Luther and Calvin understood that term, played no role in the future the Jesuits planned for themselves. Their goal was "to help souls." The Society of Jesus developed into a highly centralized, tightly knit organization. In addition to the traditional vows of poverty, chastity, and obedience, professed members vowed to go anywhere the pope said they were needed. They attracted many recruits and achieved phenomenal success for the papacy and the reformed Catholic Church, carrying Christianity to India and Japan before 1550 and to Brazil, North America, and the Congo in the seventeenth century. Within Europe the Jesuits brought southern Germany and much of eastern Europe back to Catholicism. Jesuit schools adopted the modern humanist curricula and methods, educating the sons of the nobility as well as the poor. As confessors and spiritual directors to kings, Jesuits exerted great political influence.

● **Teresa of Ávila.** Teresa of Ávila (1515–1582) was a Spanish nun who began to experience mystical visions that led her to reform convents, making them stricter and less hierarchical. This seventeenth-century enamelwork shows one of her visions, of an angel piercing her heart. Teresa founded new religious houses, seeing these as answers to the Protestant takeover of Catholic churches. She became a saint and in 1970 was the first woman declared a Doctor of the Church, a title given to a theologian of outstanding merit. (By gracious permission of Catherine Hamilton Kappauf)

Jesuits *Members of the Society of Jesus, founded by Ignatius Loyola and approved by the papacy in 1540, whose goal was the spread of the Roman Catholic faith through humanistic schools and missionary activity.*

• • • • • • • • • •

RELIGIOUS VIOLENCE

What were the causes and consequences of religious violence, including riots, wars, and witch-hunts?

In 1559 France and Spain signed the Treaty of Cateau-Cambrésis, which ended the long conflict known as the Habsburg-Valois Wars. However, over the next century religious differences led to riots, civil wars, and international conflicts. Especially in France and the Netherlands, Protestants and Catholics used violent actions as well as preaching and teaching against other, for each side regarded the other as a poison in the community that would provoke the wrath of God. Catholics and Protestants alike feared people of other faiths, whom they often saw as agents of Satan. Even more, they feared those who were explicitly identified with Satan: witches living in their midst. This era was the time of the most virulent witch persecutions in European history, as both Protestants and Catholics tried to make their cities and states more godly.

French Religious Wars

The costs of the Habsburg-Valois Wars, waged intermittently through the first half of the sixteenth century, forced the French to increase taxes and borrow heavily. King Francis I's treaty with the pope (see page 400) gave the French crown a rich supplement of money and offices, and also a vested financial interest in Catholicism. Significant numbers of French people, however, were attracted to the "reformed religion," as Calvinism was called. Initially, Calvinism drew converts from among reform-minded members of the Catholic clergy, the industrious middle classes, and artisan groups. Many French Calvinists (called **"Huguenots"**) lived in major cities such as Paris, Lyons, and Rouen. When Henry II died in 1559, perhaps one-tenth of the population had become Calvinist.

Huguenots *French Calvinists, many of whom lived in the major cities of Paris, Lyons, and Rouen.*

The feebleness of the French monarchy was the seed from which the weeds of civil violence sprang. The three weak sons of Henry II who occupied the throne could not provide the necessary leadership, and they were often dominated by their mother, Catherine de' Medici. The French nobility took advantage of this monarchical weakness. Just as German princes in the Holy Roman Empire had adopted Lutheranism as a means of opposition to Emperor Charles V, so French nobles frequently adopted the reformed religion as a religious cloak for their independence. Armed clashes between Catholic royalist lords and Calvinist antimonarchical lords occurred in many parts of France. Both Calvinists and Catholics believed that the others' books, services, and ministers polluted the community. Preachers incited violence, and religious ceremonies such as baptisms, marriages, and funerals triggered it.

iconoclasm *The destruction of a religious symbol or monument. During the Reformation, images of the saints, stained-glass windows, and paintings were destroyed by Protestants on the ground that they violated the biblical command against "graven images."*

Calvinist teachings called the power of sacred images into question, and mobs in many cities took down and smashed statues, stained-glass windows, and paintings. Though it was often inspired by fiery Protestant sermons, this **iconoclasm** is an example of men and women carrying out the Reformation themselves, rethinking the church's system of meaning and the relationship between the unseen and the seen. Catholic mobs responded by defending images, and crowds on both sides killed their opponents, often in gruesome ways.

Saint Bartholomew's Day massacre *A savage 1572 Catholic attack on Calvinists in Paris that led to a long civil war.*

A savage Catholic attack on Calvinists in Paris on August 24, 1572 (Saint Bartholomew's Day), followed the usual pattern. The occasion was the marriage ceremony of the king's sister Margaret of Valois to the Protestant Henry of Navarre, which was intended to help reconcile Catholics and Huguenots. Instead Huguenot wedding guests in Paris were massacred, and other Protestants were slaughtered by mobs. Religious violence spread to the provinces, where thousands were killed. This **Saint Bartholomew's Day massacre** led to a civil war that dragged on for fifteen years. Agriculture in many areas was destroyed; commercial life declined severely; and starvation and death haunted the land.

What ultimately saved France was a small group of moderates of both faiths called **politiques** who believed that only the restoration of a strong monarchy could reverse the trend toward collapse. The politiques also favored accepting the Huguenots as an officially recognized and organized pressure group. The death of Catherine de' Medici, followed by the assassination of King Henry III, paved the way for the accession of Henry of Navarre (the unfortunate bridegroom of the St. Bartholomew's Day massacre), a politique who became Henry IV (r. 1589–1610).

Henry's willingness to sacrifice religious principles to political necessity saved France. He converted to Catholicism but also issued the **Edict of Nantes,** which granted liberty of conscience and liberty of public worship to Huguenots in 150 fortified towns. The reign of Henry IV and the Edict of Nantes prepared the way for French absolutism in the seventeenth century by helping restore internal peace in France.

The Netherlands Under Charles V

In the Netherlands, what began as a movement for the reformation of the church developed into a struggle for Dutch independence. Emperor Charles V had inherited the seventeen provinces that compose present-day Belgium and the Netherlands (see page 403). In the Netherlands as elsewhere, corruption in the Roman church and the critical spirit of the Renaissance provoked pressure for reform, and Lutheran ideas took root. Charles V had grown up in the Netherlands, however, and he was able to limit their impact. But Charles V abdicated in 1556 and transferred power over the Netherlands to his son Philip, who had grown up in Spain. Protestant ideas spread.

By the 1560s Protestants in the Netherlands were primarily Calvinists. Calvinism's intellectual seriousness, moral gravity, and emphasis on any form of labor well done appealed to middle-class merchants and financiers and working-class people. Whereas Lutherans taught respect for the powers that be, Calvinism tended to encourage opposition to "illegal" civil authorities.

In the 1560s Spanish authorities attempted to suppress Calvinist worship and raised taxes, which sparked riots and a wave of iconoclasm. Philip II sent twenty thousand Spanish troops under the duke of Alva to pacify the Low Countries. Alva interpreted "pacification" to mean the ruthless extermination of religious and political dissidents. On top of the Inquisition, he opened his own tribunal, soon called the "Council of Blood." On March 3, 1568, fifteen hundred men were executed.

For ten years, civil war raged in the Netherlands between Catholics and Protestants and between the seventeen provinces and Spain. Eventually the ten southern provinces—the Spanish Netherlands (the future Belgium)—came under the control of the Spanish

● **Giorgio Vasari: Massacre of Coligny and the Huguenots (1573)** The Italian artist Vasari depicts the Saint Bartholomew's Day massacre in Paris, one of many bloody events in the religious wars that accompanied the Reformation. Here Admiral Coligny, a leader of the French Protestants (called Huguenots) is hurled from a window while his followers are slaughtered. This fresco was commissioned by Pope Gregory XIII to decorate a hall in the Vatican Palace in Rome. Both sides used visual images to win followers and celebrate their victories. *(Vatican Palace/Scala/Art Resource, NY)*

politiques *A group of moderate Catholics and Huguenots who sought to end the religious violence in France by restoring a strong monarchy and granting official recognition to the Huguenots.*

Edict of Nantes *A declaration issued in 1598 by Henry IV which granted liberty of conscience and liberty of public worship to Huguenots in 150 fortified French towns.*

Union of Utrecht *A treaty signed in 1579 that united the seven northern provinces of the Netherlands (all of which were Protestant) into a single political unity. This led to their declaration of independence from Catholic Spain in 1581.*

Habsburg forces. The seven northern provinces, led by Holland, formed the **Union of Utrecht** and in 1581 declared their independence from Spain. The north was Protestant; the south remained Catholic. Philip did not accept this, and war continued. England was even drawn into the conflict, supplying money and troops to the United Provinces. (Spain launched the Spanish Armada, an unsuccessful invasion of England in response.) Hostilities ended in 1609 when Spain agreed to a truce that recognized the independence of the United Provinces.

The Great European Witch-Hunt

The relationship between the Reformation and the upsurge in trials for witchcraft that occurred at roughly the same time is complex. Increasing persecution for witchcraft actually began before the Reformation in the 1480s, but it became especially common about 1560. Religious reformers' extreme notions of the Devil's powers and the insecurity created by the religious wars contributed to this increase. Both Protestants and Catholics tried and executed witches, with church officials and secular authorities acting together.

The heightened sense of God's power and divine wrath in the Reformation era was an important factor in the witch-hunts, but other factors were also significant. In the later Middle Ages, many educated Christian theologians, canon lawyers, and officials added a demonological component to existing ideas about witches. For them, the essence of witchcraft was making a pact with the Devil that required the witch to do the Devil's bidding. Witches were no longer simply people who used magical power to do harm and get what they wanted, but rather people used by the Devil to do what *he* wanted. Some demonological theorists also claimed that witches were organized in an international conspiracy to overthrow Christianity.

Trials involving this new notion of witchcraft as diabolical heresy began in Switzerland and southern Germany in the late fifteenth century, became less numerous in the early decades of the Reformation when Protestants and Catholics were busy fighting each other, and then picked up again about 1560, spreading to much of western Europe and to European colonies in the Americas. Scholars estimate that during the sixteenth and seventeenth centuries somewhere between 100,000 and 200,000 people were officially tried for witchcraft, and between 40,000 and 60,000 were executed. While the trials were secret, executions were not, and the list of charges were read out for all to hear.

Though the gender balance varied widely in different parts of Europe, between 75 and 85 percent of those tried and executed were women. Ideas about women, and the roles women actually played in society, were thus important factors shaping the

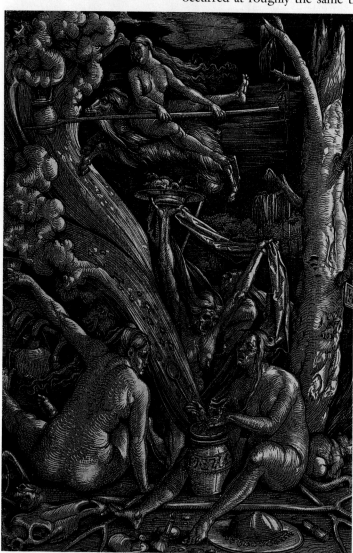

● **Hans Baldung Grien: Witches' Sabbat (1510)** In this woodcut, Grien combines learned and popular beliefs about witches: they traveled at night, met at sabbats (or assemblies), feasted on infants (in dish held high), concocted strange potions, and had animal "familiars" that were really demons (here a cat). Grien also highlights the sexual nature of witchcraft by portraying the women naked and showing them with goats, which were common symbols of sexuality. *(Germanisches Nationalmuseum Nürnberg)*

witch-hunts. Some demonologists expressed virulent **misogyny,** or hatred of women, viewing women as weaker and so more likely to give in to the Devil.

Most witch trials began with a single accusation in a village or town. Individuals accused someone they knew of using magic to spoil food, make children ill, kill animals, raise a hailstorm, or do other types of harm. Tensions within families, households, and neighborhoods often played a role in these accusations. Suspects were questioned and tortured by legal authorities, and often implicated others. The circle of the accused grew, sometimes into a much larger hunt that historians have called a "witch panic." Panics were most common in the part of Europe that saw the most witch accusations in general—the Holy Roman Empire, Switzerland, and parts of France. Most of this area consisted of very small governmental units that were jealous of each other and, after the Reformation, were divided by religion. The rulers of these small territories often felt more threatened than did the monarchs of western Europe, and they saw persecuting witches as a way to demonstrate their piety and concern for order.

Panics often occurred after some type of climatic disaster, such as an unusually cold and wet summer, and they came in waves. In large-scale panics a wider variety of suspects were taken in—wealthier people, children, a greater proportion of men. Mass panics tended to end when it became clear to legal authorities, or to the community itself, that the people being questioned or executed were not what they understood witches to be, or that the scope of accusations was beyond belief. Some from their community might be in league with Satan, they thought, but not this type of person and not as many as this.

Similar skepticism led to the gradual end of witch-hunts in Europe. Even in the sixteenth century a few individuals questioned whether witches could ever do harm, make a pact with the Devil, or engage in the wild activities attributed to them. Doubts about whether secret denunciations were valid or torture would ever yield a truthful confession gradually spread among the same type of religious and legal authorities who had so vigorously persecuted witches. Prosecutions for witchcraft became less common and were gradually outlawed. The last official execution for witchcraft in England was in 1682, though the last one in the Holy Roman Empire was not until 1775.

misogyny *A negative attitude toward women as a group. The fact that between 75 and 85 percent of the victims in the witchcraft trials of the sixteenth and seventeenth centuries were women is indicative of the misogynistic attitude that characterized European society.*

Chapter Summary

To assess your mastery of this chapter, go to
bedfordstmartins.com/mckayworld

Key Terms

Renaissance
Protestant Reformation
signori
patrons
humanism
individualism
The Prince
secularism
Christian humanists
debate about women
Wars of the Roses
New Christians
anticlericalism
indulgence
Diet of Worms
Protestant
predestination
Holy Office
Jesuits
Huguenots
iconoclasm
Saint Bartholomew's Day
  massacre
politiques
Edict of Nantes
Union of Utrecht
misogyny

• What were the major cultural developments of the Renaissance?

The Italian Renaissance rested on the phenomenal economic growth of Italian city-states, such as Florence, in which merchant oligarchs held political power. The Renaissance was characterized by self-conscious awareness among fourteenth- and fifteenth-century Italians, particularly scholars and writers known as humanists, that they were living in a new era. Key to this attitude was a serious interest in the Latin classics, a belief in individual potential, and a more secular attitude toward life. Humanists opened schools for boys and young men to train them for an active life of public service, but they had doubts about whether humanist education was appropriate for women. As humanism spread to northern Europe, religious concerns became more pronounced, and Christian humanists set out plans for the reform of church and society. Their ideas were spread to a much wider audience than those of early humanists because of the development of the printing press with movable metal type, which revolutionized communication. Interest in the classical past and in the individual also shaped Renaissance art in terms of style and subject matter.

• What were the key social hierarchies in Renaissance Europe, and how did ideas about hierarchy shape people's lives?

Social hierarchies in the Renaissance built on those of the Middle Ages, but also developed new features that contributed to the modern social hierarchies of race, class, and gender. Black Africans entered Europe in sizable numbers for the first time since the collapse of the Roman Empire, and Europeans fit them into changing understandings of ethnicity and race. The medieval hierarchy of orders based on function in society intermingled with a new hierarchy based on wealth, with new types of elites becoming more powerful. The Renaissance debate about women led many to discuss women's nature and proper role in society, a discussion sharpened by the presence of a number of ruling queens in this era.

• How did the nation-states of western Europe evolve in this period?

With taxes provided by business people, kings in western Europe established greater peace and order, both essential for trade. Feudal monarchies gradually evolved in the direction of nation-states. In Spain, France, and England, rulers also emphasized royal dignity and authority, and they utilized Machiavellian ideas to ensure the preservation and continuation of their governments. Like the merchant oligarchs and signori of Italian city-states, Renaissance monarchs manipulated culture to enhance their power.

• What were the central ideas of Protestant reformers, and why were they appealing to various groups across Europe?

The Catholic Church in the early sixteenth century had serious problems, and many individuals and groups had long called for reform. This background of discontent helps explain why Martin Luther's ideas found such a ready audience. Luther and other Protestants developed a new understanding of Christian doctrine that emphasized faith, the power of God's grace, and the centrality of the Bible. Protestant ideas were attractive to educated people and urban residents, and they spread rapidly through preaching, hymns, and the printing press. Some reformers developed more radical ideas about infant baptism, the ownership of property, and the separation between church and state. Both Protestants and Catholics regarded these as dangerous, and radicals were banished or executed. The German Peasants' War, in which Luther's ideas were linked to calls for social and economic reform, was similarly put down harshly. The Protestant reformers did not break with medieval ideas about the proper gender hierarchy, though they did elevate the status of marriage and viewed orderly households as the key building blocks of society. The progress of the Reformation was shaped by the political situation in the Holy Roman Empire, in which decentralization allowed the Reformation to spread. In England the political issue of the royal succession triggered the break with Rome, and a Protestant church was established. Protestant ideas also spread into France and eastern Europe. In all these areas, a second generation of reformers, the most important of whom was John Calvin, developed their own theology and plans for institutional change.

• How did the Catholic Church respond to the new religious situation?

The Roman Catholic Church responded slowly to the Protestant challenge, but by the 1530s the papacy was leading a movement for reform within the church instead of blocking it. Catholic doctrine was reaffirmed at the Council of Trent, and reform measures such as the opening of seminaries for priests and a ban on holding multiple church offices were introduced. New religious orders such as the Jesuits and the Ursulines spread Catholic ideas through teaching, and in the case of the Jesuits through missionary work.

• What were the causes and consequences of religious violence, including riots, wars, and witch-hunts?

Religious differences led to riots, civil wars, and international conflicts in the later sixteenth century. In France and the Netherlands, Calvinist Protestants and Catholics used violent actions against one another, and religious differences mixed with political and economic grievances. Long civil wars resulted, which in the case of the Netherlands became an international conflict. War ended in France with the Edict of Nantes in which Protestants were given some civil rights, and in the Netherlands with a division of the country into a Protestant north and Catholic south. The era of religious wars was also the time of the most extensive witch persecutions in European history, as both Protestants and Catholics tried to rid their cities and states of people they regarded as linked to the Devil.

(continued on page 424)

Listening to the PAST

Martin Luther, *On Christian Liberty*

The idea of liberty or freedom has played a powerful role in the history of human society and culture, but the meaning and understanding of liberty has undergone continual change and interpretation. In the Roman world, where slavery was a basic institution, liberty meant the condition of being a free man, independent of obligations to a master. In the Middle Ages, possessing liberty meant having special privileges or rights that other persons or institutions did not have. A lord or a monastery, for example, might speak of his or its liberties, and citizens in London were said to possess the "freedom of the city," which allowed them to practice trades and own property without interference. Likewise, the first chapter of Magna Carta (1215), often called the "Charter of Liberties," states: "Holy Church shall be free and have its rights entire and its liberties inviolate," meaning that the English church was independent of the authority of the king.

The idea of liberty also has a religious dimension, and the reformer Martin Luther formulated a classic interpretation of liberty in his treatise *On Christian Liberty* (sometimes translated as *On the Freedom of a Christian*), arguably his finest piece. Written in Latin for the pope but translated immediately into German and published widely, it contains the main themes of Luther's theology: the importance of faith, the relationship of Christian faith and good works, the dual nature of human beings, and the fundamental importance of Scripture. Luther writes that Christians were freed through Christ, not by their own actions, from sin and death.

Christian faith has appeared to many an easy thing; nay, not a few even reckon it among the social virtues, as it were; and this they do because they have not made proof of it experimentally, and have never tasted of what efficacy it is. For it is not possible for any man to write well about it, or to understand well what is rightly written, who has not at some time tasted of its spirit, under the pressure of tribulation; while he who has tasted of it, even to a very small extent, can never write, speak, think, or hear about it sufficiently. . . .

I hope that . . . I have attained some little drop of faith, and that I can speak of this matter, if not with more elegance, certainly with more solidity. . . .

A Christian man is the most free lord of all, and subject to none; a Christian man is the most dutiful servant of all, and subject to everyone.

Although these statements appear contradictory, yet, when they are found to agree together, they will do excellently for my purpose. They are both the statements of Paul himself, who says, "Though I be free from all men, yet have I made myself a servant unto all" (I Cor. 9:19), and "Owe no man anything but to love one another" (Rom. 13:8). Now love is by its own nature dutiful and obedient to the beloved object. Thus even Christ, though Lord of all things, was yet made of a woman; made under the law; at once free and a servant; at once in the form of God and in the form of a servant.

Let us examine the subject on a deeper and less simple principle. Man is composed of a twofold nature, a spiritual and a bodily. As regards the spiritual nature, which they name the soul, he is called the spiritual, inward, new man; as regards the bodily nature, which they name the flesh, he is called the fleshly, outward, old man. The Apostle speaks of this: "Though our outward man perish, yet the inward man is renewed day by day" (II Cor. 4:16). The result of this diversity is that in the Scriptures opposing statements are made concerning the same man, the fact being that in the same man these two men are opposed to one another; the flesh lusting against the spirit, and the spirit against the flesh (Gal. 5:17).

We first approach the subject of the inward man, that we may see by what means a man becomes justified, free, and a true Christian; that is, a spiritual, new, and inward man. It is certain that absolutely none among outward things, under whatever name they may be reckoned, has any influence in producing Christian righteousness or liberty, nor, on the other hand, unrighteousness or slavery. This can be shown by an easy argument.

What can it profit to the soul that the body should be in good condition, free, and full of life, that it should eat, drink, and act according to its pleasure, when even the most impious slaves of every kind of vice are prosperous in these matters? Again, what harm

On effective preaching, especially to the uneducated, Luther urged the minister "to keep it simple for the simple." *(Church of St. Marien, Wittenberg/The Bridgeman Art Library)*

can ill health, bondage, hunger, thirst, or any other outward evil, do to the soul, when even the most pious of men, and the freest in the purity of their conscience, are harassed by these things? Neither of these states of things has to do with the liberty or the slavery of the soul.

And so it will profit nothing that the body should be adorned with sacred vestment, or dwell in holy places, or be occupied in sacred offices, or pray, fast, and abstain from certain meats, or do whatever works can be done through the body and in the body. Something widely different will be necessary for the justification and liberty of the soul, since the things I have spoken of can be done by an impious person, and only hypocrites are produced by devotion to these things. On the other hand, it will not at all injure the soul that the body should be clothed in profane raiment, should dwell in profane places, should eat and drink in the ordinary fashion, should not pray aloud, and should leave undone all the things above mentioned, which may be done by hypocrites.

. . . One thing, and one alone, is necessary for life, justification, and Christian liberty; and that is the most Holy Word of God, the Gospel of Christ, as He says, "I am the resurrection and the life; he that believeth in me shall not die eternally" (John 9:25), and also, "If the Son shall make you free, ye shall be free indeed" (John 8:36), and "Man shall not live by bread alone, but by every word that proceedeth out of the mouth of God" (Matt. 4:4).

Let us therefore hold it for certain and firmly established that the soul can do without everything except the Word of God, without which none at all of its wants is provided for. But, having the Word, it is rich and wants for nothing, since that is the Word of life, of truth, of light, of peace, of justification, of salvation, of joy, of liberty, of wisdom, of virtue, of grace, of glory, and of every good thing. . . .

But you will ask, "What is this Word, and by what means is it to be used, since there are so many words of God?" I answer, "The Apostle Paul (Rom. 1) explains what it is, namely the Gospel of God, concerning His Son, incarnate, suffering, risen, and glorified

through the Spirit, the Sanctifier." To preach Christ is to feed the soul, to justify it, to set it free, and to save it, if it believes the preaching. For faith alone, and the efficacious use of the Word of God, bring salvation. "If thou shalt confess with thy mouth the Lord Jesus, and shalt believe in thine heart that God hath raised Him from the dead, thou shalt be saved" (Rom. 9:9); . . . and "The just shall live by faith" (Rom. 1:17). . . .

But this faith cannot consist of all with works; that is, if you imagine that you can be justified by those works, whatever they are, along with it. . . . Therefore, when you begin to believe, you learn at the same time that all that is in you is utterly guilty, sinful, and damnable, according to that saying, "All have sinned, and come short of the glory of God" (Rom. 3:23). . . . When you have learned this, you will know that Christ is necessary for you, since He has suffered and risen again for you, that, believing on Him, you might by this faith become another man, all your sins being remitted, and you being justified by the merits of another, namely Christ alone.

. . . [A]nd since it [faith] alone justifies, it is evident that by no outward work or labour can the inward man be at all justified, made free, and saved; and that no works whatever have any relation to him. . . . Therefore the first care of every Christian ought to be to lay aside all reliance on works, and strengthen his faith alone more and more, and by it grow in knowledge, not of works, but of Christ Jesus, who has suffered and risen again for him, as Peter teaches (I Peter 5).

Questions for Analysis

1. What did Luther mean by liberty?

2. Why, for Luther, was Scripture basic to Christian life?

Source: Luther's Primary Works, ed. H. Wace and C. A. Buchheim (London: Holder and Stoughton, 1896). Reprinted in *The Portable Renaissance Reader,* ed. James Bruce Ross and Mary Martin McLaughlin (New York: Penguin Books, 1981), pp. 721–726.

Suggested Reading

Bossy, John. *Christianity in the West, 1500–1700.* 1985. A lively, brief overview.

Earle, T. F., and K. J. P. Lowe, eds. *Black Africans in Renaissance Europe.* 2005. Includes essays discussing many aspects of ideas about race and the experience of Africans in Europe.

Ertman, Thomas. *The Birth of Leviathan: Building States and Regimes in Medieval and Early Modern Europe.* 1997. A good introduction to the creation of nation-states.

Grafton, Anthony, and Lisa Jardine. *From Humanism to the Humanities: Education and the Liberal Arts in Fifteenth and Sixteenth Century Europe.* 1986. Discusses humanist education and other developments in Renaissance learning.

Hale, J. R. *The Civilization of Europe in the Renaissance.* 1994. Provides a comprehensive treatment of the period, arranged thematically.

Holmes, George, ed. *Art and Politics in Renaissance Italy.* 1993. Treats the art of Florence and Rome against a political background.

Hsia, R. Po-Chia. *The World of Catholic Renewal, 1540–1770.* 1998. Situates the Catholic Reformation in a global context and provides coverage of colonial Catholicism.

Levack, Brian. *The Witchhunt in Early Modern Europe,* 3d ed. 2007. Provides a good introduction and helpful bibliographies to the vast literature on witchcraft.

Lindbergh, Carter. *The European Reformations.* 1996. Provides a thorough discussion of the Protestant Reformation and some discussion of Catholic issues.

Man, John. *Gutenberg Revolution: The Story of a Genius and an Invention That Changed the World.* 2002. Presents a rather idealized view of Gutenberg, but has good discussions of his milieu and excellent illustrations.

Nauert, Charles. *Humanism and the Culture of Renaissance Europe.* 1995. Provides a thorough introduction to humanism throughout Europe.

Oberman, Heiko. *Luther: Man Between God and the Devil.* 1989. Provides a thorough grounding in Luther's thought.

Wiesner-Hanks, Merry E. *Women and Gender in Early Modern Europe,* 3d ed. 2008. Discusses all aspects of women's lives and ideas about gender.

Notes

1. C. E. Detmold, trans., *The Historical, Political, and Diplomatic Writings of Niccolò Machiavelli* (Boston: J. R. Osgood, 1882), pp. 54–55.

2. See B. F. Reilly, *The Medieval Spains* (New York: Cambridge University Press, 1993), pp. 198–203.

3. B. Netanyahu, *The Origins of the Inquisition in Fifteenth Century Spain* (New York: Random House, 1995), p. 921.

4. Quoted in E. H. Harbison, *The Age of Reformation* (Ithaca, N.Y.: Cornell University Press, 1963), p. 52.

5. Quoted ibid., p. 284.

6. Ibid., p. 137.

Porcelain from a Seventeenth-Century Chinese Ship's Cargo, recovered from the sea, which was intended for European markets. *(Christie's Images)*

15 THE ACCELERATION OF GLOBAL CONTACT

Chapter Preview

The Indian Ocean: Hub of an Afro-Eurasian Trading World
• *What were the distinctive features of Southeast Asian cultures and trade, and what was the impact of Islam and Christianity on Southeast Asian peoples?*

European Discovery, Reconnaissance, and Expansion
• *How and why did Europeans undertake ambitious voyages of expansion that would usher in a new era of global contact?*

The Impact of Contact
• *What was the impact of European conquest on the peoples and ecologies of the New World?*

New Global Economies, Forced Migrations, and Encounters
• *How was the era of global contact shaped by new commercial empires, cultural encounters, and forced migrations?*

Prior to 1500 Europeans were relatively marginal players in a centuries-old trading system that linked Africa, Asia, and Europe. Elite classes everywhere prized Chinese porcelains and silks, while wealthy members of the Celestial Kingdom, as China called itself, wanted ivory and black slaves from East Africa and exotic goods and peacocks from India. African people wanted textiles from India and cowrie shells from the Maldive Islands. Europeans craved spices and silks, but they had few desirable goods to offer their trading partners.

The locus of these desires and commercial exchanges was the Indian Ocean. Arab, Persian, Turkish, Indian, black African, Chinese, and European merchants and adventurers fought each other for the trade that brought great wealth. They also jostled with Muslim scholars, Buddhist teachers, and Christian missionaries, who competed for the religious adherence of the peoples of the Malay Archipelago, Sumatra, Java, Borneo, and the Philippine Islands. The ancient civilizations of Africa, the Americas, Asia, and Southeast Asia confronted each other, and those confrontations sometimes led to conquest, exploitation, and profound social change.

The European search for better access to Southeast Asian spices led to a new overseas empire in the Indian Ocean and the accidental discovery of the Western Hemisphere. Within a short time, South and North America had joined a worldwide web. Europeans came to dominate trading networks and political empires of truly global proportions. The era of "globalization" had begun. Global contacts created new forms of cultural exchange, assimilation, conversion, and resistance. Europeans sought to impose their cultural values on the people they encountered and struggled to comprehend the peoples and societies they found. The Age of Discovery laid the foundations for the modern world as we know it today.

THE INDIAN OCEAN: HUB OF AN AFRO-EURASIAN TRADING WORLD

What were the distinctive features of Southeast Asian cultures and trade, and what was the impact of Islam and Christianity on Southeast Asian peoples?

Covering 20 percent of the earth's total ocean area, the Indian Ocean is the globe's third-largest waterway (after the Atlantic and Pacific). The Chinese called this vast region the Southern Ocean. Arabs, Indians, and Persians described it as "the lands below the winds," meaning the seasonal monsoons that carried ships across the ocean. Moderate and predictable, the monsoon winds blow from the west or south between April and August and from the northwest or northeast between December and March. Only in the eastern periphery, near the Philippine Islands, is there a dangerous typhoon belt—whirlwinds bringing tremendous rains and possible tornadoes.

High temperatures and abundant rainfall all year round contribute to a heavily forested environment. Throughout Southeast Asia, forests offer "an abundance and diversity of forms (of trees) . . . without parallel anywhere else in the world."[1] The abundance of bamboo, teak, mahogany, and other woods close to the waterways made the area especially favorable for maritime activity.

Peoples and Cultures

From at least the first millennium B.C.E., the peoples of Southeast Asia have been open to waterborne commerce. With trade came settlers from the Malay Peninsula (the southern extremity of the Asian continent), India, China, and East Africa, resulting in

● **Agricultural Work in Southeast Asia** Using a water buffalo (a common draft animal in Southeast Asia), a man plows a rice field, while a woman husks rice in this Filipino scene from the early eighteenth century. Their house is on stilts as protection against floods. *(Bibliothèque nationale de France)*

an enormous variety of languages, cultures, and religions. In spite of this diversity, certain sociocultural similarities connected the region.

First, by the fifteenth century, the peoples of what we call Indonesia, Malaysia, the Philippines, and the many islands in between all spoke languages of the Austronesian family, reflecting continuing interactions among the peoples speaking them. Second, a common environment led to a diet based on rice, fish, palms, and palm wine. Rice, harvested by women, is probably indigenous to the region, and it formed the staple of the diet from Luzon in the Philippines westward to Java, Sumatra, Siam (Thailand), and Vietnam. The seas provided many varieties of fish, crabs, and shrimp. Everywhere fishing, called "the secondary industry" (after commerce), served as the chief male occupation, well ahead of agriculture. Lacking grasslands, Southeast Asia has no pastoral tradition, no cattle or sheep, and thus meat and milk products from these animals played a small role in the diet. Animal protein came mostly from chickens and from pigs, which were raised almost everywhere and were the center of feasting. Cucumbers, onions, and gourds supplemented the diet, and fruits—coconuts, bananas, mangoes, limes, and pineapples (after they were introduced from the Americas)—substituted for vegetables. Sugar cane grew in profusion. It was chewed as a confectionery and used as a sweetener.[2]

In comparison to India, China, or even Europe (after the Black Death), Southeast Asia was sparsely populated. People were concentrated in port cities and in areas of intense rice cultivation. The seventeenth and eighteenth centuries witnessed slow but steady population growth, while the nineteenth century, under European colonial rule, witnessed very rapid expansion. Almost all Southeast Asian people married at a young age (about twenty). Marriage practices varied greatly from Indian, Chinese, and European ones, reflecting marked differences in the status of women.

The important role played by women in planting and harvesting rice gave them authority and economic power. Because of women's reproductive role, daughters had a high value. In contrast to India, China, the Middle East, and Europe, in Southeast Asia the more daughters a man had, the richer he was. At marriage the groom paid the bride (or sometimes her family) a sum of money called **bride wealth,** which remained under her control. This practice was in sharp contrast to the Chinese, Indian, and European dowry, which came under the husband's control. Unlike the Chinese practice, a married couple usually resided in the wife's village. Property was administered jointly, in contrast to the Chinese principle and Indian practice that wives had no say in the disposal of family property. All children, regardless of gender, inherited equally, and when Islam arrived in the region, the rule that sons receive double the inheritance of daughters was never implemented.

Although rulers commonly had multiple wives or concubines, the vast majority of ordinary people were monogamous. In contrast to most parts of the world except Africa, Southeast Asian peoples regarded premarital sexual activity with indulgence, and no premium was placed on virginity at marriage. Divorce was easy if a pair proved incompatible; common property and children were divided. Divorce carried no social stigma, and either the woman or the man could initiate it.[3]

Chronology

1450–1650	Age of Discovery
1492	Columbus lands on San Salvador
1511	Portuguese capture Malacca from Muslims
1518	Atlantic slave trade begins
1520	Spaniards defeat Aztec army
1532	Pizarro arrives in Peru and defeats Inca Empire
1542	First Jesuit, Saint Francis Xavier, arrives in Malacca
1547	Oviedo, *General History of the Indies*
1550–1700	Disease leads to 80 percent population decline in American Southeast
1570–1630	Worldwide commercial boom
1571	Spanish missionaries arrive in Southeast Asia
1602	Dutch East India Company established
1635	Tokugawa Shogunate closes Japan to trade; Japanese expel Spanish and Portuguese missionaries

bride wealth *A Southeast Asian custom whereby at marriage the groom paid the bride or her family a sum of money that remained under her control.*

Religious Revolutions

Diversity—by district, community, village, and even individual—characterized religious practice in Southeast Asia. People practiced a kind of animism, believing that spiritual powers inhabited natural objects. To survive and prosper, a person had to know how to please, appease, and manipulate those forces. To ensure human fertility, cure sickness, produce a good harvest, safeguard the living, and help the dead attain a contented afterlife, the individual propitiated the forces by providing sacrificial offerings or feasts. For example, in the Philippines and eastern Indonesia, certain activities were forbidden during the period of mourning following death, but great feasting then followed. Exquisite clothing, pottery, and jewelry were buried with the corpse to ensure his or her status in the afterlife. In Borneo, Cambodia, Burma, and the Philippines, slaves were sometimes killed to serve their deceased owners. Death rituals, like life rituals, had enormous variation in Southeast Asia.

Throughout the first millennium C.E., Hindu and Buddhist cults, Confucianists, and Jewish, Christian, and Muslim traders and travelers carried their beliefs to Southeast Asia. Beginning in the late thirteenth century, Muslim merchants established sizable trading colonies in the ports of northern Sumatra, eastern Java, Champa, and the east coast of the Malay Peninsula (see Map 15.1). Once the ruler of Malacca, the largest port city in Indonesia, accepted Islam, Muslim businessmen controlled commercial transactions there; the saying went that these transactions were "sealed with a handshake and a glance at heaven." The very name *Malacca* derives from the Arabic *malakat,* meaning "market," an apt description for this center of Indian Ocean trade. Islamic success continued from 1400 to 1650. Rulers of the port states on the spice route to northern Java and the Moluccas (Maluku), and those on the trading route to Brunei in Borneo and Manila in the Philippines, adhered to the faith of Allah.

With the arrival of the Portuguese (see page 439) and their capture of Malacca in 1511, fierce competition ensued between Muslims and Christians. The mid-sixteenth century witnessed the galvanized energy of the Counter-Reformation in Europe and the expansion of the Ottoman Empire through southwestern Asia and southeastern Europe. From Rome the first Jesuit, Saint Francis Xavier (1506–1552), reached Malacca in 1542. Likewise, Suleiman the Magnificent and his successors sent proselytizers. After the Spanish occupation of Manila in the Philippines in 1571, the Spanish crown flooded Southeast Asia with missionaries. Unlike Southeast Asian animism, Islam and Christianity insisted on an exclusive path to salvation: the renunciation of paganism and some outward sign of membership in the new faith.

What was the reaction of Southeast Asian peoples to these religions? How did adherents of the Middle Eastern religions spread their faith? Southeast Asians saw Muslims and Christians as wealthy, powerful traders and warriors. Thus native peoples believed that the foreigners must possess some secret ability to manipulate the spirit world. A contemporary Spaniard wrote that Southeast Asians believed

● **Woman Offering Betel** In Southeast Asia, betel served as the basic social lubricant. A combination of the betel nut, leaf, and lime, betel sweetened the breath and relaxed the mind; it was central to the rituals of lovemaking; and it was offered on all important social occasions, such as birth, marriage, and death. (Leiden University Library, ms. Or. 8655)

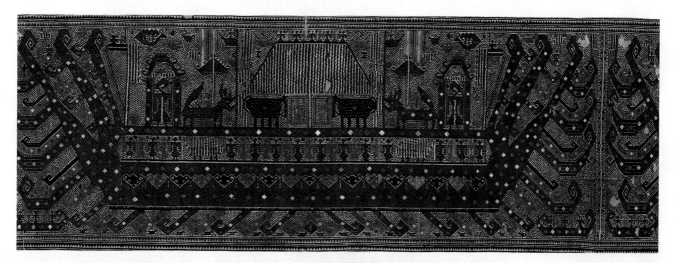

● **Palepai, or Ship Cloth (woven cotton textile, Sumatra, nineteenth century)**   In Southeast Asian society, where the sea permeated so many aspects of life and culture, it is natural that it would influence art. Produced for millennia, ship cloths—depicting fabulous sailing vessels with multiple decks, birds, and animals—signified the transition from one social or spiritual state to another. They were displayed by the aristocracy only on important occasions, such as weddings or the presentation of a first grandchild to maternal grandparents. *(Museum of Fine Arts, Boston, The William E. Nickerson Fund No. 2 [1980.172]. Indonesian, Dutch colonial rule, mid-19th century, cotton plain weave, discontinuous supplementary weft patterning, 73.7 x 382.3 cm. © 2008 Museum of Fine Arts, Boston)*

"that paradise and successful (business) enterprises are reserved for those who submit to the religion of the Moros (Muslims) of Brunei[;] . . . they are the richer people." Southeast Asians also were impressed by Muslim and European ships and firearms. The foreigners seemed to have a more ruthless view of war than the natives (perhaps because they had no place to retreat to). As the Muslims and Christians fought for commercial superiority throughout the sixteenth century, indigenous peoples watched closely, "partly for reasons of self-preservation, partly that they might adopt the spiritual and practical techniques of the winners."[4]

Christian priests and Muslim teachers quickly learned the locals' languages and translated their Scriptures into those languages. The instruction of rulers and the educated into either faith was by memorization of the catechism, or sacred texts; teaching the masses was oral—they were expected to learn the basic prayers and customs of the new faiths. The Muslims and Christians differed in one fundamental strategy: whereas the Christians relied on a celibate clergy who defined the new community through baptism, the Muslims often married locally and accepted Southeast Asian cultures. No Asian was ordained a priest or served as catechist before 1700. By contrast, the Muslims showed little of the iconoclastic zeal for the destruction of pagan idols, statues, and temples that the Christians did. The Muslims did face a major obstacle, however: the indigenous peoples' attachment to pork, the main meat source and the central dish in all feasting.

Acceptance of one of the prophetic religions varied with time and place. Coastal port cities on major trade routes had "substantial" numbers of Muslims, and rulers of the port states of Sumatra, the Malay Peninsula, northern Java, and the Moluccas identified themselves as Muslims. By 1700 most rural and urban people had abandoned pork and pagan practices, adopted Islamic dress, submitted to circumcision, and considered themselves part of the international Muslim community. In the Philippines Islam achieved some success, especially in the south. But Magellan's military conquest, the enormous enthusiasm of the Jesuit missionaries, and the vigorous support of the Spanish crown led to the Christianization of most of the islands. As elsewhere, whether individuals conformed to Muslim or Christian standards was another

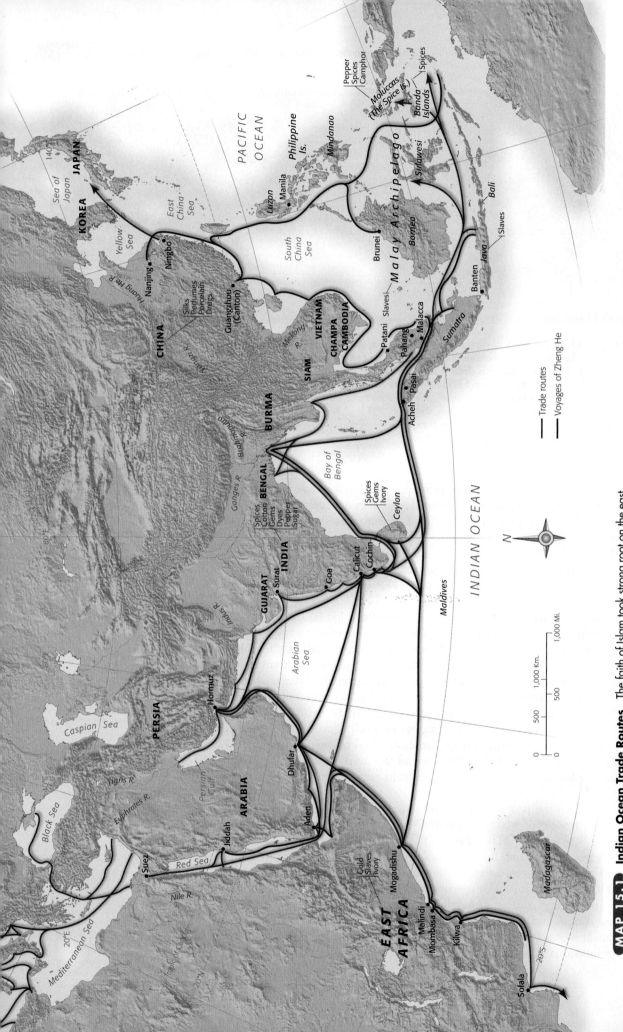

MAP 15.1 Indian Ocean Trade Routes The faith of Islam took strong root on the east coast of Africa and in northern India, Sumatra, the Malay Archipelago, and the southern Philippines. In the sixteenth and seventeenth centuries, Christianity competed with Islam for the adherence of peoples on all the Indian Ocean islands. (*Source: Some data from The Times Atlas of World History, 3d ed., page 146.*)

matter. Recent scholars speak of the "adherence" of peoples in the sixteenth century to Islam, rather than their "conversion." Still, the official acceptance of one of the two Scripture-based religions by more than half the people of Southeast Asia has had lasting importance. Today Indonesia has the largest Muslim population in the world.

Trade and Commerce

Since Han and Roman times, seaborne trade between China (always the biggest market for Southeast Asian goods), India, the Middle East, and Europe had flowed across the Indian Ocean. From the seventh through the thirteenth centuries, the volume of this trade steadily increased. In the late fourteenth century, with the European and West Asian populations recovering from the Black Death, demand for Southeast Asian goods accelerated.

Other developments stimulated the market for Southeast Asian goods. The collapse of the Central Asian overland caravan route, the famous Silk Road, gave a boost to traffic originating in the Indian Ocean and flowing up the Red Sea to Mediterranean ports. Chinese expansion into Vietnam and Burma increased the population of the Celestial Kingdom and the demand for exotic goods. Above all, the seven voyages of the Chinese admiral Zheng He in 1405 launched for Southeast Asia the "age of commerce." (See the feature "Individuals in Society: Zheng He.")

In the fifteenth century Malacca became the great commercial entrepôt on the Indian Ocean. To Malacca came Chinese porcelains, silks, and camphor (used in the manufacture of many medications, including those to reduce fevers); pepper, cloves, nutmeg, and raw materials such as sappanwood and sandalwood from the Moluccas; sugar from the Philippines; and Indian printed cotton and woven tapestries, copper weapons, incense, dyes, and opium (which already had a sizable market in China). Muslim merchants in other port cities, such as Patani on the Malay Peninsula, Pasai in Sumatra, and Demak in Java, shared in this trade. They also exchanged cowrie shells from the Maldive Islands. These shells were in enormous demand throughout Africa as symbols of wealth and status, as decoration, and as a medium of currency in African trade. Muslim businessmen in Southeast Asia thus had dealings with their coreligionists in the East African ports of Mogadishu, Kilwa, and Sofala.

Merchants at Malacca stockpiled goods in fortified warehouses while waiting for the next monsoon. Whereas the wealth of cities in Mughal India rested mainly on agriculture, that of Malacca and other Southeast Asian cities depended on commerce. In all of Asia, Malacca, with its many mosques and elegant homes, enjoyed the reputation of being a sophisticated city, full of "music, ballads, and poetry."[5]

EUROPEAN DISCOVERY, RECONNAISSANCE, AND EXPANSION

How and why did Europeans undertake ambitious voyages of expansion that would usher in a new era of global contact?

Europe was by no means isolated before the voyages of exploration and the "discovery" of the New World; Europeans were aware of and in contact with the riches of the Indian Ocean trading world. From the time of the Crusades, Italian merchants brought the products of the East to luxury markets in Europe eager for silks, spices, porcelain, and other fine goods. But because they did not produce many products desired by Eastern elites, Europeans were relatively modest players in trade beyond its borders. Their limited role was reduced even further in the mid-fourteenth century, when the Black Death, combined with the ravages of the Mongol warlord Tamerlane, led to a collapse in trade routes and commercial markets.

From these lows, however, Europeans would soon undertake new and unprecedented expansion. As population and trade recovered, new European players entered the scene, eager to spread Christianity and to undo Italian dominance of trade with the East. A century after the plague, Iberian explorers began the overseas voyages that helped create the modern world, with staggering consequences for their own continent and the rest of the planet.

Causes of European Expansion

European expansion had multiple causes. The European market was eager for luxury goods from the East and for spices in particular. The spices not only added flavor to the monotonous European diet, but they also served as perfumes, medicines, and dyes. Apart from a desire for trade goods, religious fervor was another important catalyst for expansion. The passion and energy ignited by the Iberian reconquista encouraged the Portuguese and Spanish to continue the Christian crusade. Since organized Muslim polities such as the Ottoman Empire were too strong to defeat, Iberians turned their attention to non-Christian peoples elsewhere.

Individual explorers combined these motivations in unique ways. Christopher Columbus was a devout Christian who was increasingly haunted by messianic obsessions in the last years of his life. As Bartholomew Diaz put it, his own motives were "to serve God and His Majesty, to give light to those who were in darkness and to grow rich as all men desire to do." When Vasco da Gama reached the port of Calicut, India, in 1498 and a native asked what the Portuguese wanted, he replied, "Christians and spices."[6] The bluntest of the Spanish conquistadors, Hernando Cortés, announced as he prepared to conquer Mexico, "I have come to win gold, not to plow the fields like a peasant."[7]

Eagerness for exploration could be heightened by a lack of opportunity at home. After the reconquista, young men of the Spanish upper classes found their economic and political opportunities greatly limited. The ambitious turned to overseas trade to seek their fortunes.[8] A desire for glory and the urge to explore motivated many as well.

Whatever the reasons, the voyages were made possible by the growth of government power. Individuals did not possess the massive sums needed to explore vast oceans and control remote continents. The Spanish monarchy was stronger than before and in a position to support foreign ventures. In Portugal explorers looked to Prince Henry the Navigator (1394–1460) for financial support and encouragement. Like voyagers, monarchs shared a mix of motivations, from desire to please God to desire to win glory and profit from trade.

For ordinary sailors, life at sea was dangerous, overcrowded, unbearably stench-ridden, filled with hunger, and ill-paid. For months at a time, 100 to 120 people lived and worked in a space of between 150 and 180 square meters. Horses, cows, pigs, chickens, rats, and lice accompanied them on the voyages. As one scholar concluded, "traveling on a ship must have been one of the most uncomfortable and oppressive experiences in the world."[9]

Why did men choose to join these miserable crews? They did so to escape poverty at home, to continue a family trade, to win a few crumbs of the great riches of empire, or to find a better life as illegal immigrants in the colonies. Moreover, many orphans and poor boys were placed on board as young pages and had little say in the decision. Women also paid a price for the voyages of exploration. Left alone for months or years at a time and frequently widowed, sailors' wives struggled to feed their families. The widow of a sailor lost on Magellan's 1519 voyage had to wait until 1547 to collect her husband's salary from the Crown.[10]

The people who stayed at home had a powerful impact on the process. Court coteries and factions influenced a monarch's decisions and could lavishly reward individuals or cut them out of the spoils of empire. Then there was the public: the small

**Primary Source:
The Agreement with Columbus of April 17 and 30, 1492**
Read the contract signed by Columbus and his royal patrons, and see what riches he hoped to gain from his expedition.

Individuals IN SOCIETY

Zheng He

In 1403 the Chinese emperor Yongle ordered his coastal provinces to build a vast fleet of ships, with construction centered at Longjiang near Nanjing; the inland provinces were to provide wood and float it down the Yangzi River. Thirty thousand shipwrights, carpenters, sailmakers, ropers, and caulkers worked in a frenzy. As work progressed, Yongle selected a commander for the fleet. The emperor chose Zheng He (1371–1433), despite fearing that he was too old (thirty-five) for so politically important an expedition. The decision rested on Zheng He's unquestioned loyalty, strength of character, energy, ability, and eloquence. These qualities apparently were expected to compensate for Zheng He's lack of seamanship.

The southwestern province of Yunnan had a large Muslim population, and Zheng He was born into that group. When the then prince Zhi Di defeated the Mongols in Yunnan, Zheng He's father was killed in the related disorder. The young boy was taken prisoner and, as was the custom, castrated. Raised in Zhi Di's household, he learned to read and write, studied Confucian writings, and accompanied the prince on all military expeditions. By age twenty, Zheng He was not the soft, effeminate stereotype of the eunuch; rather he was "seven feet tall and had a waist five feet in circumference. His cheeks and forehead were high . . . [and] he had glaring eyes . . . [and] a voice loud as a bell. . . . He was accustomed to battle." Zheng He must have made an imposing impression. A devout Muslim, he persuaded the emperor to place mosques under imperial protection after a period of persecution. On his travels, he prayed at mosques at Malacca and Hormuz. Unable to sire sons, he adopted a nephew. In Chinese history, he was the first eunuch to hold such an important command.

The first fleet, composed of 317 ships, including junks, supply ships, water tankers, warships, transports for horses, and patrol boats, and carrying twenty-eight thousand sailors and soldiers, represents the largest naval force in world history before World War I. Because it bore tons of beautiful porcelains, elegant silks, lacquer ware, and exquisite artifacts to be exchanged for goods abroad, it was called the "treasure fleet."

Between 1405 and 1433, Zheng He led seven voyages, which combined the emperor's diplomatic, political, geographical, and commercial goals (see Map 15.1). Yongle wanted to secure China's hegemony over tributary states and collect pledges of loyalty

Zheng He, voyager to India, Persia, Arabia, and Africa. *(From Lo Monteng, The Western Sea Cruises of Eunuch San Pao, 1597)*

from them. To gain information on winds, tides, distant lands, and rare plants and animals, Zheng He sailed as far west as Egypt. Smallpox epidemics had recently hit China, and one purpose of his voyages was to gather pharmacological products; an Arab text on drugs and therapies was secured and translated into Chinese. He also brought back a giraffe and mahogany, a wood ideal for ships' rudders because of its hardness.

Just before his death, Zheng He recorded his accomplishments on stone tablets. The expeditions had unified "seas and continents . . . the countries beyond the horizon from the ends of the earth have all become subjects . . . and the distances and routes between distant lands may be calculated," implying that China had accumulated considerable geographical information. From around the Indian Ocean, official tribute flowed to the Ming court. A vast immigration of Chinese people into Southeast Asia, sometimes called the Chinese diaspora, followed the expeditions. Immigrants carried with them Chinese culture, including social customs, diet, and practical objects of Chinese technology—calendars, books, scales for weights and measures, and musical instruments. With legends collected about him and monuments erected to him, Zheng He became a great cult hero.

Questions for Analysis

1. What do the voyages of the treasure fleet tell us about China in the fifteenth century?

2. What was Zheng He's legacy?

Source: Louise Levathes, *When China Ruled the Seas: The Treasure Fleet of the Dragon Throne, 1405–1433* (New York: Oxford University Press, 1996).

number of people who could read were a rapt audience for tales of fantastic places and unknown peoples. Scholars have frequently described the European discoveries as a manifestation of Renaissance curiosity about the physical universe—the desire to know more about the geography and peoples of the world. Fernández de Oviedo's *General History of the Indies* (1547), a detailed eyewitness account of plants, animals, and peoples, was widely read. Indeed, the elite's desire for the exotic goods brought by overseas trade helped stimulate the whole process of expansion.

Technological Stimuli to Exploration

Technological developments in shipbuilding, weaponry, and navigation provided another impetus for European expansion. Since ancient times, most seagoing vessels had been narrow, open boats called *galleys* propelled largely by slaves or convicts manning the oars. Though well suited to the placid waters of the Mediterranean, galleys could not withstand the rough winds and uncharted shoals of the Atlantic. The need for sturdier craft, as well as population losses caused by the Black Death, forced the development of a new style of ship that would not require much manpower to sail.

In the course of the fifteenth century, the Portuguese developed the **caravel,** a small, light, three-masted sailing ship. Though somewhat slower than the galley, the caravel held more cargo. Its triangular lateen sails and sternpost rudder also made the caravel a much more maneuverable vessel. When fitted with cannon, it could dominate larger vessels.

Great strides in cartography and navigational aids were also made in this period. The magnetic compass enabled sailors to determine their direction and position at sea. Around 1410 Arab scholars reintroduced Europeans to **Ptolemy's Geography.** Written in the second century C.E. by a Hellenized Egyptian, the work synthesized the geographical knowledge of the classical world. It also treated the idea of latitude and longitude. The astrolabe, an instrument invented by the ancient Greeks and perfected by Muslim navigators, was used to determine the altitude of the sun and other celestial bodies. It permitted mariners to plot their latitude, or position north or south of the equator.

Although it showed the world as round, Ptolemy's work also contained crucial errors. Unaware of the Americas, he showed the world as much smaller than it is, so that Asia appeared not very distant from Europe to the west. Based on this work, cartographers fashioned new maps that combined classical knowledge with the latest information from mariners. First the Genoese and Venetians, and then the Portuguese and Spanish, took the lead in these advances.[11]

Much of the new technology that Europeans used in their voyages was borrowed from the East. For example, gunpowder, the compass, and the sternpost rudder were all Chinese inventions. The lateen sail, which allowed European ships to tack against the wind, was a product of the Indian Ocean trade world and was brought to the Mediterranean on Arab ships. Navigational aids, such as the astrolabe, were also acquired from others, and advances in cartography drew on the rich tradition of Judeo-Arabic mathematical and astronomical learning in Iberia.

The Portuguese Overseas Empire

At the end of the fourteenth century Portugal was a small and poor nation on the margins of European life whose principal activities were fishing and subsistence farming. It would have been hard to predict Portugal's phenomenal success overseas in the next two centuries. Yet Portugal had a long history of seafaring and navigation. Blocked from access to western Europe by Spain, the Portuguese turned to the Atlantic and North Africa, whose waters they knew better than other Europeans. Nature also favored the Portuguese: winds blowing along their coast offered passage to Africa, its Atlantic islands, and, ultimately, Brazil.

General History of the Indies *A fifty-volume firsthand description of the natural plants, animals, and peoples of Spanish America. Oviedo was a former colonial administrator who was named Historian of the Indies by the King of Spain in 1532.*

caravel *A small, maneuverable, three-mast sailing ship developed by the Portuguese in the fifteenth century. The caravel gave the Portuguese a distinct advantage in exploration and trade.*

Ptolemy's Geography *A second century C.E. work that synthesized the classical knowledge of geography and treated the concepts of longitude and latitude. The work was reintroduced to Europeans in 1410 by Arab scholars and provided a template for later geographical scholarship.*

In the early phases of Portuguese exploration, Prince Henry, a younger son of the king, played a leading role. A nineteenth-century scholar dubbed Henry "the Navigator" because of his support for the study of geography and navigation and for the annual expeditions he sponsored down the western coast of Africa. Although he never personally participated in voyages of exploration, Henry's involvement ensured that Portugal did not abandon the effort despite early disappointments.

The objectives of Portuguese policy included aristocratic desires for martial glory, the historic Iberian crusade to Christianize Muslims, and the quest to find gold, slaves, an overseas route to the spice markets of India, and the mythical king Prester John. Portugal's conquest of Ceuta, an Arab city in northern Morocco, in 1415 marked the beginning of European exploration and control of overseas territory. In the 1420s, under Henry's direction, the Portuguese began to settle the Atlantic islands of Madeira (ca. 1420) and the Azores (1427). In 1443 the Portuguese founded their first African commercial settlement at Arguim in present-day Mauritania. By the time of Henry's death in 1460, his support for exploration was vindicated by thriving sugar plantations on the Atlantic islands and new access to gold.

● **Nocturnal** An instrument for determining the hour of night at sea by finding the progress of certain stars around the polestar (center aperture). *(National Maritime Museum, London)*

In the fifteenth century most of the gold that reached Europe came from the Sudan in West Africa and from the Akan peoples living near the area of present-day Ghana. Muslim caravans brought the gold north across the Sahara to Mediterranean ports. Then the Portuguese muscled in on this commerce in gold. Under King John II (r. 1481–1495) the Portuguese established trading posts and forts on the gold-rich Guinea coast and penetrated into the African continent all the way to Timbuktu (see Map 15.2). By 1500 Portugal controlled the flow of African gold to Europe. The golden century of Portuguese prosperity had begun.

Still the Portuguese pushed farther south down the west coast of Africa. In 1487 Bartholomew Diaz rounded the Cape of Good Hope at the southern tip, but storms and a threatened mutiny forced him to turn back. On a later expedition in 1497 Vasco da Gama commanded a fleet of four ships in search of a sea route to the Indian Ocean trade. Da Gama's ships rounded the Cape and sailed up the east coast of Africa. With the help of an Indian guide, da Gama sailed across the Arabian Sea to the port of Calicut in India. Overcoming local hostility, he returned to Lisbon with spices and samples of Indian cloth. He had failed to forge any trading alliances with local powers, but he had proved the possibility of lucrative trade with the East via the Cape route.

King Manuel (r. 1495–1521) promptly dispatched thirteen ships under the command of Pedro Alvares Cabral, assisted by Diaz, to set up trading posts in India. Half the fleet was lost on the return voyage, but the six spice-laden vessels that dropped anchor in Lisbon harbor in July 1501 more than paid for the entire expedition. Thereafter, a Portuguese convoy set out for passage around the Cape every March. Lisbon became the entrance port for Asian goods into Europe—but this was not accomplished without a fight.

Muslims (of Middle Eastern, Indian, Southeast Asian, and Chinese ethnic backgrounds) had controlled the Indian Ocean trade for centuries. With the Portuguese

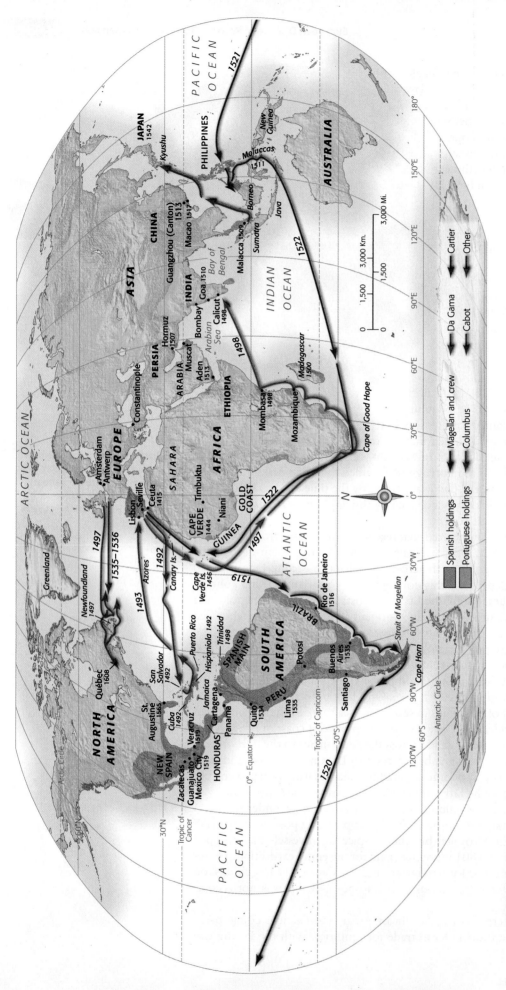

MAP 15.2 **European Exploration and Conquest, Fifteenth and Sixteenth Centuries**
The voyages of discovery marked another phase in the centuries-old migrations of European peoples. Consider the major contemporary significance of each of the voyages depicted on the map.

● **Pepper Harvest**   To break the monotony of their bland diet, Europeans had a passion for pepper, which—along with cinnamon, cloves, nutmeg, and ginger—was the main object of the Asian trade. Since one kilo of pepper cost 2 grams of silver at the place of production in the East Indies and from 10 to 14 grams of silver in Alexandria, Egypt, 14 to 18 grams in Venice, and 20 to 30 grams at the markets of northern Europe, we can appreciate the fifteenth-century expression "as dear as pepper." Here natives fill vats, and the dealer tastes a peppercorn for pungency. *(Bibliothèque nationale de France)*

entry into the region, the brisk Muslim trade was violently disrupted as the Portuguese sank or plundered every Muslim spice ship they met. In 1511 Afonso de Albuquerque, whom the Portuguese crown had named governor of India (1509–1515), captured Malacca, the great Indian Ocean trading entrepôt. Thereafter Portuguese commercial wealth gradually increased, and the Portuguese dominated the European spice market. Albuquerque's bombardment of Goa, Calicut, and Malacca laid the foundations for Portuguese imperialism in the sixteenth and seventeenth centuries.

In March 1493, between the voyages of Diaz and da Gama, Spanish ships under a triumphant Genoese mariner named Christopher Columbus (1451–1506), in the service of the Spanish crown, entered Lisbon harbor. Spain also had begun the quest for an empire.

The Problem of Christopher Columbus

Christopher Columbus is a controversial figure in history—glorified by some as the brave discoverer of America, vilified by others as a cruel exploiter of Native Americans. It is important to put him into the context of his own time. First, what kind of man was Columbus, and what forces or influences shaped him? Second, in sailing westward from Europe, what were his goals? Third, did he achieve his goals, and what did he make of his discoveries?

In his dream of a westward passage to the Indies, the Genoese Columbus embodied centuries-old Italian traditions of involvement with Eastern trade. Columbus was also very knowledgeable about the sea. He had worked as a mapmaker, and he was familiar with such fifteenth-century Portuguese navigational developments as *portolans*—written

● **Intercontinental Exchange**
In 1515 an Indian prince sent the king of Portugal a splendid gift—the first Indian rhinoceros to reach Europe since the fall of the Roman Empire. The subject of a famous engraving by the painter Albrecht Dürer and reproduced repeatedly by minor artists for the next two centuries, a drawing of the exotic rhinoceros must have made an excellent conversation piece for European hosts and their guests. *(Luisa Ricciarini)*

descriptions of the courses along which ships sailed, showing bays, coves, capes, ports, and the distances between these places—and the use of the compass as a nautical instrument. As he implied in his *Journal,* he had acquired not only theoretical but also practical experience: "I have spent twenty-three years at sea and have not left it for any length of time worth mentioning, and I have seen everything from east to west [meaning he had been to England] and I have been to Guinea [north and west Africa]."[12] Although some of Columbus's geographical information, such as his measurement of the distance from Portugal west to Japan as 2,760 miles when it is actually 12,000, proved inaccurate, his successful thirty-three-day voyage to the Caribbean owed a great deal to his seamanship.

Columbus was also a deeply religious man. He had witnessed the Spanish reconquest of Granada and shared fully in the religious and nationalistic fervor surrounding that event. Like the Spanish rulers and most Europeans of his age, Columbus understood Christianity as a missionary religion that should be carried to places where it did not exist. He viewed himself as a divine agent: "God made me the messenger of the new heaven and the new earth of which he spoke in the Apocalypse of St. John . . . and he showed me the post where to find it."[13]

What was the object of this first voyage? Columbus wanted to find a direct ocean trading route to Asia. Rejected by the Portuguese in 1483 and by Ferdinand and Isabella of Spain in 1486, the project finally won the backing of the Spanish monarchy in 1492. Inspired by the stories of Marco Polo, Columbus dreamed of reaching the court of the Great Khan (not realizing that the Ming Dynasty had overthrown the Mongols in 1368). Based on Ptolemy's *Geography* and other texts, he expected to pass the islands of Japan and then land on the east coast of China.

How did Columbus interpret what he had found, and in his mind did he achieve what he had set out to do? On October 12 he landed in the Bahamas, which he christened San Salvador. Columbus believed he had found some small islands off the east coast of Cipangu (Japan). On encountering natives of the islands, he gave them some beads and "many other trifles of small value," pronouncing them delighted with these gifts and eager to trade. In a letter he wrote to Ferdinand and Isabella on his return to Spain, Columbus described the natives as handsome, peaceful, and primitive people whose body painting reminded him of the Canary Islands natives. He concluded that they would make good slaves and could quickly be converted to Christianity. (See the feature "Listening to the Past: Columbus Describes His First Voyage" on pages 458–459.)

Columbus received reassuring reports—via hand gestures and mime—of the presence of gold and of a great king in the vicinity. From San Salvador, Columbus sailed southwest, believing that this course would take him to Japan or the coast of China. He landed on Cuba on October 28. Deciding that he must be on the mainland near the coastal city of Quinsay (Hangzhou), he sent a small embassy inland with letters from Ferdinand and Isabella and instructions to locate the grand city. The expedition included an Arabic-speaker to serve as interpreter with the khan.

The landing party, however, found only small villages with simple peoples. Confronted with this disappointment, Columbus apparently gave up on his aim to meet the Great Khan. Instead, he focused on trying to find gold or other valuables among the peoples he had discovered. In January, confident that gold would later be found, he headed back to Spain. News of his voyage spread rapidly across Europe.[14]

Over the next decades, the Spanish confirmed Columbus's change of course by adopting the model of conquest and colonization they had already introduced in the Canary Islands rather than one of exchange with equals (as envisaged for the Mongol khan). On his second voyage, Columbus forcibly subjugated the island of Hispaniola, enslaved its indigenous peoples, and laid the basis for a system of land grants tied to their labor service. Columbus himself, however, had little interest in or capacity for governing. Revolt soon broke out against him and his brother on Hispaniola. A royal expedition sent to investigate returned the brothers to Spain in chains. Columbus was quickly cleared of wrongdoing, but he did not recover his authority over the territories. Instead, they came under royal control.

Columbus was very much a man of his times. To the end of his life in 1506, he believed that he had found small islands off the coast of Asia. He never realized the scope of his achievement: to have found a vast continent unknown to Europeans, except for a fleeting Viking presence centuries earlier. He could not know that the scale of his discoveries would revolutionize world power, raising issues of trade, settlement, government bureaucracy, and the rights of native and African peoples.

New World Conquest

In 1519, the year Magellan departed on his worldwide expedition, a brash and determined Spanish **conquistadore** ("conqueror") named Hernando Cortés (1485–1547) crossed from Hispaniola in the West Indies to mainland Mexico in search of gold. Accompanied by six hundred men, seventeen horses, and ten cannon, Cortés was to launch the conquest of Aztec Mexico.

Cortés landed at Veracruz in February 1519. From there he led a march to Tenochtitlán (now Mexico City), capital of the sophisticated **Aztec Empire** ruled by Montezuma II (r. 1502–1520). Larger than any European city of the time, the capital was the heart of a civilization with advanced mathematics, astronomy, and engineering, with a complex social system, and with oral poetry and historical traditions.

The Spaniards arrived in the capital when the Aztecs were preoccupied with harvesting their crops. According to a later Spanish account, the timing was ideal. A series of natural phenomena, signs, and portents seemed to augur disaster for the Aztecs. A comet was seen in daytime, and two temples were suddenly destroyed, one by lightning unaccompanied by thunder. These and other apparently inexplicable events had an unnerving and demoralizing effect on Montezuma.

Even more important was the empire's internal weakness. The Aztec state religion, the sacred cult of Huitzilopochtli, necessitated constant warfare against neighboring peoples to secure captives for religious sacrifice and laborers for agricultural and infrastructural work. When Cortés landed, recently defeated tribes were not yet fully integrated into the empire. Increases in tribute provoked revolt, which led to reconquest, retribution, and demands for higher tribute, which in turn sparked greater resentment

conquistadore *Spanish for "conqueror," the term refers to Spanish soldier-explorers, such as Hernando Cortés and Francisco Pizarro, who sought to conquer the New World for the Spanish crown.*

Aztec Empire *A Native American civilization that possessed advanced mathematical, astronomical, and engineering technology. Its capital, Tenochtitlán (now the site of Mexico City), was larger than any contemporary European city. Conquered by Cortés in 1520.*

● **Doña Marina Translating for Hernando Cortés During His Meeting with Montezuma** In April 1519 Doña Marina (or La Malinche as she is known in Mexico) was among twenty women given to the Spanish as slaves. Fluent in Nahuatl and Yucatec Mayan (spoken by a Spanish priest accompanying Cortés), she acted as an interpreter and diplomatic guide for the Spanish. She had a close personal relationship with Cortés and bore his son in 1522. Doña Marina has been seen variously as a traitor to her people, as a victim of Spanish conquest, and as the founder of the Mexican people. She highlights the complex interaction between native peoples and the Spanish and the role women often played as cultural mediators between the two sides. (The Granger Collection, New York)

and fresh revolt. When the Spaniards appeared, the Totonacs greeted them as liberators, and other subject peoples joined them against the Aztecs.[15]

Montezuma himself refrained from attacking the Spaniards as they advanced toward his capital and welcomed Cortés and his men into Tenochtitlán. Historians have often condemned the Aztec ruler for vacillation and weakness. But he relied on the advice of his state council, itself divided, and on the dubious loyalty of tributary communities. When Cortés—with incredible boldness—took Montezuma hostage, the emperor's influence over his people crumbled.

Later, in retaliation for a revolt by the entire population of Tenochtitlán that killed many Spaniards, Montezuma was executed. Afterwards, the Spaniards escaped from the city and inflicted a crushing defeat on the Aztec army at Otumba near Lake Texcoco on July 7, 1520. After this victory Cortés began the systematic conquest of Mexico.

Inca Empire *The Peruvian empire that was at its peak from 1438 until 1532.*

More amazing than the defeat of the Aztecs was the fall of the remote **Inca Empire** perched at 9,800 to 13,000 feet above sea level. (The word *Inca* refers both to the people who lived in the valleys of the Andes Mountains in present-day Peru and to their ruler.) The borders of this vast and sophisticated empire were well fortified, but the Inca neither expected foreign invaders nor knew of the fate of the Aztec Empire to the north. The imperial government, based in the capital city of Cuzco, commanded loyalty from the people, but at the time of the Spanish invasion it had been embroiled in a civil war over succession. The Inca Huascar had been fighting his half-brother Atauhualpa for five years over the crown.

Francisco Pizarro (ca. 1475–1541), a conquistador of modest Spanish origins, landed on the northern coast of Peru on May 13, 1532, the very day Atauhualpa won the decisive battle. The Spaniard soon learned about the war and its outcome. As

Pizarro advanced across the steep Andes toward Cuzco, Atauhualpa was proceeding to the capital for his coronation. Like Montezuma in Mexico, Atauhualpa was kept fully informed of the Spaniards' movements and accepted Pizarro's invitation to meet in the provincial town of Cajamarca. Intending to extend a peaceful welcome to the newcomers, Atauhualpa and his followers were unarmed. The Spaniards captured him and collected an enormous ransom in gold. Instead of freeing the new emperor, however, they executed him on trumped-up charges.

Decades of violence ensued, marked by Incan resistance and internal struggles among Spanish forces for the spoils of empire. By the 1570s the Spanish crown had succeeded in imposing control. With Spanish conquest, a new chapter opened in European relations with the New World.

• • • • • • • • • • • •

THE IMPACT OF CONTACT

What was the impact of European conquest on the peoples and ecologies of the New World?

In the sixteenth and seventeenth centuries, following Columbus's voyages, substantial numbers of Spaniards crossed the Atlantic for ports in the Caribbean, the Spanish Main, and present-day Argentina. Thousands of Portuguese sailed for Brazil. The ships on which they traveled were not as large as the so-called Indiamen going to the Indian Ocean; the latter had larger carrying capacities and were expected to return with tons of spices, pepper, sugar, and gold. Only half the migrants, merchants, missionaries, royal officials, soldiers, wives, concubines, and slaves reached American (or Indian Ocean) ports. Poor health, poor shipboard hygiene, climatic extremes, rancid food, and putrid water killed the other half.[16] Those who reached America, however, eventually had an enormous impact not only there but also on the whole world.

Colonial Administration

Having seized the great Amerindian and Andean ceremonial centers in Mexico and Peru, the Spanish conquistadors proceeded to subdue the main areas of Native American civilization in the New World. Columbus, Cortés, and Pizarro claimed the lands they had "discovered" for the Spanish crown. How were these lands to be governed?

According to the Spanish theory of absolutism, the Crown was entitled to exercise full authority over all imperial lands. In the sixteenth century the Crown divided Spain's New World territories into four **viceroyalties,** or administrative divisions. New Spain, with its capital at Mexico City, consisted of Mexico, Central America, and present-day California, Arizona, New Mexico, and Texas. Peru, with its viceregal seat at Lima, originally consisted of all the lands in continental South America but later was reduced to the territory of modern Peru, Chile, Bolivia, and Ecuador. New Granada, with Bogotá as its administrative center, included present-day Venezuela, Colombia, Panama, and, after 1739, Ecuador. La Plata, with Buenos Aires as its capital, consisted of Argentina, Uruguay, and Paraguay. Within each territory a *viceroy,* or imperial governor, had broad military and civil authority as the Spanish sovereign's direct representative. The viceroy presided over the **audiencia,** twelve to fifteen judges who served as an advisory council and as the highest judicial body.

From the early sixteenth century to the beginning of the nineteenth, the Spanish monarchy acted on the mercantilist principle that the colonies existed for the financial benefit of the mother country. The mining of gold and silver was always the most important industry in the colonies. The Crown claimed the **quinto,** one-fifth of all precious metals mined in the Americas. Gold and silver yielded the Spanish monarchy 25 percent of its total income. In return, Spain shipped manufactured goods to the New World and discouraged the development of native industries.

viceroyalties *The name for the four administrative units of Spanish possessions in the Americas: New Spain, Peru, New Granada, and La Plata.*

audiencia *Presided over by the viceroy, the twelve to fifteen judges who served as an advisory council and as the highest judicial body.*

quinto *One-fifth of all precious metals mined in the Americas that the Crown claimed as its own.*

The Portuguese governed their colony of Brazil in a similar manner. After the union of the Portuguese and Spanish crowns in 1580, Spanish administrative forms were introduced. Local officials called *corregidores* held judicial and military powers. Mercantilist policies placed severe restrictions on Brazilian industries that might compete with those of Portugal. In the seventeenth century the use of black slave labor made possible the cultivation of coffee, cotton, and sugar. In the eighteenth century Brazil produced one tenth of the world's sugar.

The Columbian Exchange

Columbian Exchange *The exchange of animals, plants, and diseases between the Old and the New Worlds.*

The Age of Discovery led to the migration of peoples, which in turn led to an exchange of fauna and flora—of animals, plants, and diseases, a complex process known as the **Columbian Exchange.** Spanish and Portuguese immigrants to the Americas wanted the diet with which they were familiar, so they searched for climatic zones favorable to those crops. Everywhere they settled they brought and raised wheat—in the highlands of Mexico, the Rio de la Plata, New Granada (in northern South America), and Chile. By 1535 Mexico was exporting wheat. Grapes did well in parts of Peru and Chile. It took the Spanish longer to discover areas where suitable soil and adequate rainfall would nourish olive trees, but by the 1560s the coastal valleys of Peru and Chile were dotted with olive groves. Columbus had brought sugar plants on his second voyage; Spaniards also introduced rice and bananas from the Canary Islands, and the Portuguese carried these items to Brazil. All plants and trees had to be brought from Europe, but not all plants arrived intentionally. In clumps of mud on shoes and in the folds of textiles came the seeds of immigrant grasses.

Apart from wild turkeys and game, Native Americans had no animals for food; apart from alpacas and llamas, they had no animals for travel or to use as beasts of burden. On his second voyage in 1493 Columbus introduced horses, cattle, sheep, dogs, pigs, chickens, and goats. The multiplication of these animals proved spectacular. The horse enabled the Spanish conquerors and the Amerindians to travel faster and farther and to transport heavy loads.

The Spanish and Portuguese returned to Europe with maize (corn), white potatoes, and many varieties of beans, squash, pumpkins, avocados, and tomatoes. Because maize grows in climates too dry for rice and too wet for wheat, gives a high yield per unit of land, and has a short growing season, it proved an especially important crop for Europeans. So too did the nutritious white potato, which slowly spread from west to east—to Ireland, England, and France in the seventeenth century; and to Germany, Poland, Hungary, and Russia in the eighteenth. Ironically, the white potato reached New England from old England in 1718.

Spanish Settlement and Indigenous Population Decline

In the sixteenth century perhaps two hundred thousand Spaniards immigrated to the New World. Mostly soldiers and adventurers unable to find employment in Spain, they came for profits. After assisting in the conquest of the Aztecs and the subjugation of the Incas, these men carved out vast estates in temperate grazing areas and imported Spanish sheep, cattle, and horses for the kinds of ranching with which they were familiar. In coastal tropic areas unsuited for grazing the Spanish erected huge plantations to supply sugar for the European market. Around 1550 silver was discovered in present-day Bolivia and Mexico. How were the cattle ranches, sugar plantations, and silver mines to be worked? The conquistadors first turned to the Amerindians.

encomienda system *The Spanish system whereby the Crown granted the conquerors the right to employ groups of Amerindians in a town or area as agricultural or mining laborers or as tribute payers; it was a disguised form of slavery.*

The Spanish quickly established the **encomienda system,** in which the Crown granted the conquerors the right to employ groups of Amerindians as agricultural or mining laborers or as tribute payers. Laboring in the blistering heat of tropical cane fields or in the dark, dank, and dangerous mines, the Amerindians died in staggering numbers.

Students of the history of medicine have suggested another crucial explanation for indigenous population losses: disease. Having little or no resistance to diseases brought from the Old World, the inhabitants of the highlands of Mexico and Peru, especially, fell victim to smallpox, typhus, influenza, and other diseases. According to one expert, small-pox caused "in all likelihood the most severe single loss of aboriginal population that ever occurred."[17] (The old belief that syphilis was a New World disease imported to Europe by Columbus's sailors has been discredited by the discovery of pre-Columbian skeletons in Europe bearing signs of the disease.)

Although disease was a leading cause of death, there were many others, including malnutrition and starvation as people were forced to neglect their own fields. Many indigenous peoples also died through outright violence.[18] According to the Franciscan missionary Bartolomé de Las Casas (1474–1566), the Spanish maliciously murdered thousands:

To these quiet Lambs . . . came the Spaniards like most c(r)uel Tygres, Wolves and Lions, enrag'd with a sharp and tedious hunger; for these forty years past, minding nothing else but the slaughter of these unfortunate wretches, whom with divers kinds of torments neither seen nor heard of before, they have so cruelly and inhumanely butchered, that of three millions of people which Hispaniola itself did contain, there are left remaining alive scarce three hundred persons.[19]

Las Casas's remarks concentrate on the Caribbean islands, but the death rate elsewhere was also overwhelming.

The Franciscan, Dominican, and Jesuit missionaries who accompanied the conquistadors and settlers played an important role in converting the Amerindians to Christianity, teaching them European methods of agriculture, and inculcating loyalty to the Spanish crown. In terms of numbers of people baptized, missionaries enjoyed phenomenal success, though the depth of the Amerindians' understanding of Christianity remains debatable. Missionaries, especially Las Casas, asserted that the Amerindians had human rights, and through Las Casas's and others' persistent pressure the emperor Charles V abolished the worst abuses of the encomienda system in 1531.

For colonial administrators the main problem posed by the astronomically high death rate was the loss of a subjugated labor force. As early as 1511 King Ferdinand of Spain observed that the Amerindians seemed to be "very frail" and that "one black could do the work of four Indians."[20] Thus was born an absurd myth and the new tragedy of the Atlantic slave trade.

> **Primary Source:**
> **General History of the Things of New Spain**
> *Read an account of the Spanish conquest of the Aztec Empire, compiled from eyewitness testimony by the Aztecs themselves.*

• • • • • • • • • • • • • • • • • • • •

NEW GLOBAL ECONOMIES, FORCED MIGRATIONS, AND ENCOUNTERS

How was the era of global contact shaped by new commercial empires, cultural encounters, and forced migrations?

The centuries-old Afro-Eurasian trade world was forever changed by the European voyages of discovery and their aftermath. For the first time, a truly global economy emerged in the sixteenth and seventeenth centuries, and it forged new links among far-flung peoples, cultures, and societies. The ancient civilizations of Europe, Africa, the Americas, Asia, and Southeast Asia confronted each other in new and rapidly evolving ways, and those confrontations sometimes led to conquest, exploitation, and profound social and cultural change.

Sugar and Slavery

Throughout the Middle Ages slavery was deeply entrenched in the Mediterranean. The bubonic plague, famines, and other epidemics created severe shortages of agricultural and domestic workers throughout Europe, encouraging Italian merchants to buy slaves from the Black Sea region and the Balkans. Renaissance merchants continued the slave trade despite papal threats of excommunication. The Genoese set up colonial stations in the Crimea and along the Black Sea; according to an international authority on slavery, these outposts were "virtual laboratories" for the development of slave plantation agriculture in the New World.[21] This form of slavery had nothing to do with race; almost all slaves were white. Black African slavery entered the European picture and took root in South and then North America after the 1453 Ottoman capture of Constantinople halted the flow of white slaves. Mediterranean Europe, cut off from its traditional source of slaves, then turned to sub-Saharan Africa, which had a long history of slave trading.

sugar *Originally from the South Pacific, sugar quickly became a demanded luxury in Europe. Sugar plants were brought to the New World by Columbus and became the primary crop for export. The desire for workers on sugar plantations, particularly in Brazil, led to a tremendous increase in the African slave trade.*

Native to the South Pacific, **sugar** was taken in ancient times to India, where farmers learned to preserve cane juice as granules that could be stored and shipped. From there, sugar traveled to China and the Mediterranean, where islands like Crete, Sicily, and Cyprus had the necessary warm and wet climate. When Genoese and other Italians colonized the Canary Islands and the Portuguese settled on the Madeira Islands, sugar plantations came to the Atlantic. In this stage of European expansion, "the history of slavery became inextricably tied up with the history of sugar."[22] Originally sugar was an expensive luxury that only the very affluent could afford, but population increases and monetary expansion in the fifteenth century led to an increasing demand for it.

Resourceful Italians provided the capital, cane, and technology for sugar cultivation on plantations in southern Portugal, Madeira, and the Canary Islands. Meanwhile, in

● **A New World Sugar Refinery, Brazil** Sugar, a luxury in great demand in Europe, was the most important and most profitable plantation crop in the New World. This image shows the processing and refinement of sugar on a Brazilian plantation. Sugar cane was grown, harvested, and processed by African slaves who labored under brutal and ruthless conditions to generate enormous profits for plantation owners. *(The Bridgeman Art Library/Getty Images)*

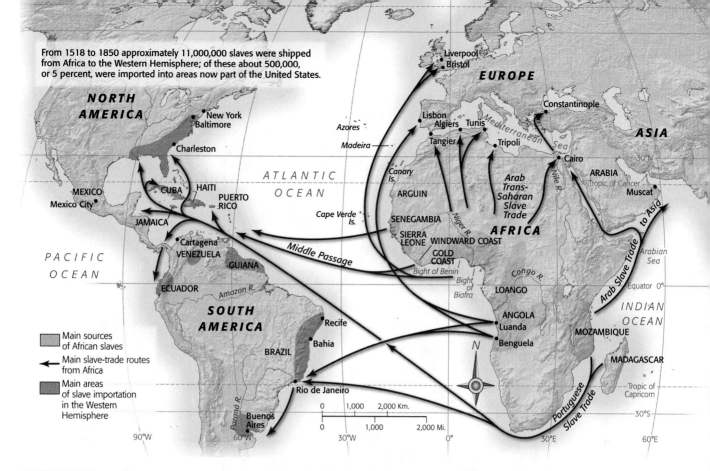

From 1518 to 1850 approximately 11,000,000 slaves were shipped from Africa to the Western Hemisphere; of these about 500,000, or 5 percent, were imported into areas now part of the United States.

MAP 15.3 **The African Slave Trade** Decades before the discovery of America, Greek, Russian, Bulgarian, Armenian, and then black slaves worked the plantation economies of southern Italy, Sicily, Portugal, and Mediterranean Spain—thereby serving as models for the American form of slavery.

the period 1490 to 1530, Portuguese traders brought between three hundred and two thousand black slaves to Lisbon each year (see Map 15.3), where they performed most of the manual labor and constituted 10 percent of the city's population. From there slaves were transported to the sugar plantations of Madeira, the Azores, and the Cape Verde Islands. Sugar and the small Atlantic islands gave New World slavery its distinctive shape. Columbus himself, who spent a decade in Madeira, brought sugar plants on his voyages to "the Indies."

In Africa, where slavery was entrenched (as it was in the Islamic world, southern Europe, and China), African kings and dealers sold black slaves to European merchants who participated in the transatlantic trade. The Portuguese brought the first slaves to Brazil; by 1600 four thousand were being imported annually. After its founding in 1621, the Dutch West India Company, with the full support of the government of the United Provinces, transported thousands of Africans to Brazil and the Caribbean. In the late seventeenth century, with the chartering of the Royal African Company, the English got involved. Altogether, traders from all these countries brought around twelve million African slaves to the West Indies and North America.

European sailors found the Atlantic passage cramped and uncomfortable, but conditions for African slaves were lethal. Before 1700, when slavers decided it was better business to improve conditions, some 20 percent of slaves died on the voyage.[23] The most common cause of death was from dysentery induced by poor-quality food and water, intense crowding, and lack of sanitation. Men were often kept in irons during the passage, while women and girls were fair game for sailors. To increase profits, slave traders packed several hundred captives on each ship. One slaver explained that he removed his boots before entering the slave hold because he had to crawl over their packed bodies.[24]

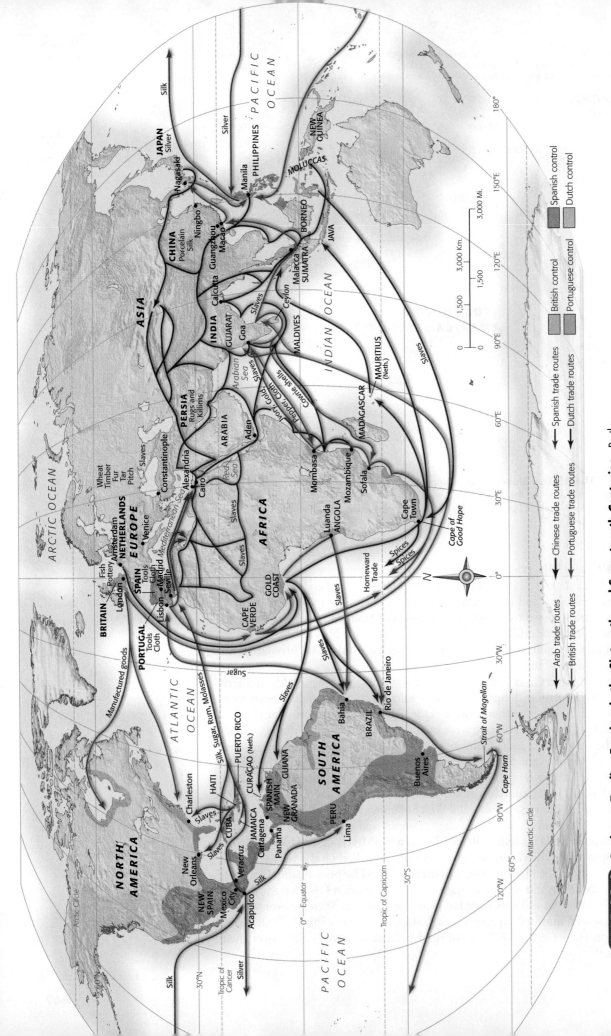

MAP 15.4 **Seaborne Trading Empires in the Sixteenth and Seventeenth Centuries** By the mid-seventeenth century, trade linked all parts of the world except for Australia. Notice that trade in slaves was not confined to the Atlantic but involved almost all parts of the world.

The eighteenth century witnessed the peak of the Atlantic slave trade. In 1790 there were 757,181 blacks in a total U.S. population of 3,929,625. In Brazil during the same decade, blacks numbered about 2 million in a total population of 3.25 million.

Global Trade Networks

The Europeans' discovery of the Americas and their exploration of the Pacific for the first time linked the entire world by intercontinental seaborne trade. That trade brought into being three successive European commercial empires: the Portuguese, the Spanish, and the Dutch.

In the sixteenth century, naval power and shipborne artillery gave Portugal hegemony over the sea route to India. To Lisbon the Portuguese fleet brought spices, which the Portuguese paid for with textiles produced at Gujarat and Coromandel in India and with gold and ivory from East Africa (see Map 15.4). From their fortified bases at Goa on the Arabian Sea and at Malacca on the Malay Peninsula, ships of Malabar teak carried goods to the Portuguese settlement at Macao in the South China Sea. From Macao, loaded with Chinese silks and porcelains, Portuguese ships sailed to the Japanese port of Nagasaki and to the Philippine port of Manila, where Chinese goods were exchanged for Spanish (that is, Latin American) silver. Throughout Asia, the Portuguese traded in slaves—black Africans, Chinese, and Japanese. To India the Portuguese exported horses from Mesopotamia and copper from Arabia; from India they exported hawks and peacocks for the Chinese and Japanese markets.

Across the Atlantic, Portuguese Brazil provided most of the sugar consumed in Europe in the sixteenth and early seventeenth centuries. African slave labor produced sugar on Brazilian plantations, and Portuguese merchants controlled both the slave trade between West Africa and Brazil and the commerce in sugar between Brazil and Portugal. The Portuguese were the first worldwide traders, and Portuguese was the language of the Asian maritime trade.

Spanish possessions in the New World constituted basically a land empire, and in the sixteenth century the Spaniards devised a method of governing that empire (see page 443). But across the Pacific, the Spaniards also built a seaborne empire, centered at Manila in the Philippines, which had been "discovered" by Ferdinand Magellan in 1521. Between 1564 and 1571, the Spanish navigator Miguel Lopez de Legazpi sailed from Mexico and through a swift and almost bloodless conquest took over the Philippine Islands. Legazpi founded Manila, which served as the transpacific bridge between Spanish America and the extreme Eastern trade.

Chinese silk, sold by the Portuguese in Manila for American silver, was transported to Acapulco in Mexico, from which it was carried overland to Veracruz for re-export to Spain. Because hostile Pacific winds prohibited direct passage from the Philippines to Peru, large shipments of silk also arrived at Acapulco for transport to Peru (see Map 15.4). Spanish merchants could never satisfy the European demand for silk, so huge amounts of bullion went from Acapulco to Manila. For example, in 1597, 12 million pesos of silver, almost the total value of the transatlantic trade, crossed the Pacific. After about 1640, the Spanish silk trade declined because it could not compete with Dutch imports.

Stimulated by a large demand for goods in Europe, India, China, and Japan, a worldwide commercial boom occurred from about 1570 to 1630. In Japan the gradual decline of violence, unification, and the development of marketing networks led to a leap in orders for foreign products: textiles from India, silks and porcelains from China, raw materials and spices from Southeast Asia; enslaved humans from Africa. The Japanese navy expanded, and Japanese mines poured out vast quantities of silver that paid for those wares. Then, in 1635, maritime trade stopped when the Tokugawa Shogunate closed the islands to trade and forbade merchants to travel abroad under penalty of death.

● **The Port of Banten in Western Java** Influenced by Muslim traders and emerging in the early sixteenth century as a Muslim kingdom, Banten evolved into a thriving entrepôt. The city stood on the trade route to China; as this Dutch engraving suggests, in the seventeenth century the Dutch East India Company used Banten as an important collection point for spices purchased for sale in Europe. *(Archives Charmet/The Bridgeman Art Library)*

age of commerce *A period of heavy trading from 1570 to 1630 in which Southeast Asia exchanged its spices and other raw materials for textiles from India, silver from the Americas and Japan, and silk, ceramics, and manufactures from China.*

China, with a population increase, urban growth, and a rare period of government-approved foreign trade, also underwent international commercial expansion. China wanted raw materials, sugar, and spices from Southeast Asia; ivory and slaves from Africa; and cotton cloth from India. Merchants in Mughal India conducted a huge long-distance trade extending as far north as Poland and Russia. India also sought spices from the Moluccas, sugar from Vietnam and the Philippines, and rice and raw materials from Southeast Asia. In this early modern **age of commerce,** Southeast Asia exchanged its pepper, spices, woods, resin, pearls, and sugar for textiles from India; silver from the Americas and Japan; and silk, ceramics, and manufactures from China. The Southeast Asian merchant marine also expanded. The European demand for Indian pepper, Southeast Asian nutmeg and cloves, and Chinese silks and porcelains was virtually insatiable. But Europeans offered nothing that Asian peoples wanted. Therefore, Europeans had to pay for their purchases with silver or gold—hence the steady flow of specie from Mexico and South America to Asia.

In the latter half of the seventeenth century, the worldwide Dutch seaborne trade predominated. The Dutch Empire was built on spices. In 1599 a Dutch fleet returned to Amsterdam carrying 600,000 pounds of pepper and 250,000 pounds of cloves and nutmeg. Those who had invested in the expedition received a profit of 100 percent. The voyage led to the establishment in 1602 of the Dutch East India Company, founded with the stated intention of capturing the spice trade from the Portuguese.

The Dutch fleet, sailing from the Cape of Good Hope and avoiding the Portuguese forts in India, steered directly for the Sunda Strait in Indonesia (see Map 15.4). The Dutch wanted direct access to and control of the Indonesian sources of spices. In return for assisting Indonesian princes in local squabbles and disputes with the

Portuguese, the Dutch won broad commercial concessions. Through agreements, seizures, and outright war, they gained control of the western access to the Indonesian archipelago. Gradually, they acquired political domination over the archipelago itself. Exchanging European manufactured goods—armor, firearms, linens, and toys—the Dutch soon had a monopoly on the very lucrative spice trade.[25] The seaborne empires of Portugal, Spain, and Holland paved the way for the eighteenth-century mercantilist empires of France and Great Britain.

The Chinese and Japanese Discovery of the West

Why did Europeans, rather than Chinese, take the lead in exploring parts of the globe distant from their native countries? In the fifteenth century China was obviously the largest geographical power in Asia. Chinese sailors had both the theoretical maritime knowledge and the practical experience of long-distance ocean travel (see page 435). In 1435 the Chinese knew some of the Pacific Ocean, all of the Indian Ocean, the Arabian Sea, and the Red Sea. Europeans knew little more than the Mediterranean Sea and the Atlantic Ocean along the northwestern coast of Africa. About 1500 China had a population between 65 million and 80 million, whereas the population of Spain was only about 6.5 million, barely one-tenth of China's. The emperors' wealth was more than double that of the kings of Spain and France combined.

Europeans, as we have seen, sailed to the Americas and Asia seeking spices, gold, and trade. Was Chinese culture hostile to trade and foreign commerce? According to traditional scholarship, Chinese Confucian teaching disparaged commerce and merchants. In the orthodox Confucian ordering of social classes—scholars, farmers, artisans, and merchants—merchants ranked lowest. Moreover, Confucian belief held that trade encouraged competition, competition led to social mobility and change, and change promoted disorder in society. But whatever theoretical ideas the Chinese literati may have had about merchants, Western observers took a different view. One later expert on China wrote that the Chinese had "a singular penchant for trade"[26]; another writer commented that the Chinese were "a race of traders than whom there has not been in the world a shrewder and a keener." Following Zheng He's voyages (see page 435), tens of thousands of Chinese emigrated to the Philippines, where they acquired commercial dominance of Luzon by 1600. Thus hostility to trade and commerce does not explain China's failure to expand.

Rather, internal and domestic difficulties offer better explanations. In the fifteenth century Mongol pressures on China's northern border forced the emperors to focus on domestic security rather than foreign exploration. The emperor Zhengtong (r. 1436–1449 and 1457–1464) held that overseas expeditions brought little visible return. At a time when he was forced to conserve resources for the army, he stopped maritime expeditions, closed China's borders, and forbade foreign travel (the last law was widely flouted). Administrative disorder also aggravated imperial financial difficulties. At the time when the "new monarchs" of Europe (see page 400) were reducing disorderly elements in their societies and centralizing their administrations, Chinese emperors were losing domestic control and threatened by strong foreign invaders. The failure to utilize rich maritime knowledge opened China's vast coastline first to Japanese pirates and then to persistent and aggressive European traders.

The desire to Christianize pagan peoples was a major motive in Europeans' overseas expansion. In 1582 the Jesuit Matteo Ricci (1552–1610) settled at Macao on the mouth of the Canton River. Like the Christian monks who had converted the Germanic tribes of early medieval Europe, Ricci sought first to convert the emperor and elite groups and then, through gradual assimilation, to win the throngs of Chinese. He tried to present Christianity to the Chinese in Chinese terms. He understood the Chinese respect for learning and worked to win converts among the scholarly class. When Ricci was admitted to the Imperial City at Beijing (Peking), he addressed the emperor Wanli:

Primary Source: Journals: Matteo Ricci
This story about Jesuit missionaries in China provides an interesting look at the nexus of religion and politics in the early seventeenth century.

Li Ma-tou [Ricci's name transliterated into Chinese], your Majesty's servant, comes from the Far West, addresses himself to Your Majesty with respect, in order to offer gifts from his country. Despite the distance, fame told me of the remarkable teaching and fine institutions with which the imperial court has endowed all its peoples. I desired to share these advantages and live out my life as one of Your Majesty's subjects, hoping in return to be of some small use.[27]

Ricci presented the emperor with two clocks, one of them decorated with dragons and eagles in the Chinese style. The emperor's growing fascination with clocks gave Ricci the opportunity to display other examples of Western technology. He instructed court scholars about astronomical equipment and the manufacture of cannon and drew for them a map of the world—with China at its center. These inventions greatly impressed the Chinese intelligentsia. Over a century later, a Jesuit wrote, "The Imperial Palace is stuffed with clocks, . . . watches, carillons, repeaters, organs, spheres, and astronomical clocks of all kinds—there are more than four thousand pieces from the best masters of Paris and London."[28] The Chinese first learned about Europe from the Jesuits.

But the Christians and the Chinese did not understand one another. Because the Jesuits served the imperial court as mathematicians, astronomers, and cartographers, the Chinese emperors allowed them to remain in Beijing. The Jesuits, however, were primarily interested in converting the Chinese to Christianity. The missionaries thought that by showing the pre-eminence of Western science, they were demonstrating the superiority of Western religion. This was a relationship that the Chinese did not acknowledge. They could not accept a religion that required total commitment and taught the existence of an absolute. Only a small number among intellectual elites became Christians. Most Chinese were hostile to the Western faith. They accused Christians of corrupting Chinese morals because they forbade people to honor their ancestors—and corruption of morals translated into disturbing the public order. They

● **Kangnido Map (1684)** Diplomatic relations between Korea and the Ming Chinese court brought Korean scholars in touch with Chinese thought. This Korean map of the world is probably based on a Chinese model. (© British Library Board. All rights reserved. From Lee Chan, Hanguk ui ko chido/Yi Chan cho [Old Maps of Korea], 1997)

also accused Christians of destroying Chinese sanctuaries, of revering a man (Christ) who had been executed as a public criminal, and of spying on behalf of the Japanese. In the mid-eighteenth century the emperor forbade Christianity and expelled the missionaries.

The Christian West and the Chinese world learned a great deal from each other. The Jesuits probably were "responsible for the rebirth of Chinese mathematics in the seventeenth and eighteenth centuries," and Western contributions stimulated the Chinese development of other sciences.[29] From the Chinese, Europeans got the idea of building bridges suspended by chains. The first Western experiments in electrostatics and magnetism in the seventeenth century derived from Chinese models. Travel accounts about Chinese society and customs had a profound impact on Europeans, making them more sensitive to the beautiful diversity of peoples and manners.

Initial Japanese contacts with Europeans paralleled those of the Chinese. In 1542 Portuguese merchants arrived in Japan. They vigorously supported Christian missionary activity, and in 1547 the Jesuit missionary Saint Francis Xavier landed at Kagoshima, preached widely, and in two years won many converts. From the beginning, however, the Japanese government feared that native converts might have conflicting political loyalties. Divided allegiance could encourage Euro-

pean invasion of the islands—the Japanese authorities had the example of the Philippines, where Spanish conquest followed missionary activity.

Convinced that European merchants and missionaries had contributed to the civil disorder that the regime was trying to eradicate, the Japanese government decided to expel the Spanish and Portuguese and to close Japan to all foreign influence. A decree of 1635 was directed at the commissioners of the port of Nagasaki, a center of Japanese Christianity:

If there is any place where the teachings of the padres (Catholic priests) is practiced, the two of you must order a thorough investigation. . . . If there are any Southern Barbarians (Westerners) who propagate the teachings of the padres, or otherwise commit crimes, they may be incarcerated in the prison.[30]

In 1639 an imperial memorandum decreed, "Hereafter entry by the Portuguese galeota [galleon or large oceangoing warship] is forbidden. If they insist on coming [to Japan], the ships must be destroyed and anyone aboard those ships must be beheaded."[31]

When tens of thousands of Japanese Christians made a stand on the peninsula of Shimabara, the Dutch lent the Japanese government cannon. The Protestant Dutch hated Catholicism, and as businessmen they hated the Portuguese, their great commercial rivals. Convinced that the Dutch had come only for trade and did not want to proselytize, the imperial government allowed them to remain. But Japanese authorities ordered them to remove their factory-station from Hirado on the western tip of Kyushu to the tiny island of Deshima, which covered just 2,100 square feet. The government limited Dutch trade to one ship a year, watched the Dutch very closely, and required Dutch officials to pay an annual visit to the capital to renew their loyalty. The

● **Arrival of the Nanbanjin or "Southern Barbarians"**   Just as wealthy eighteenth-century Europeans craved Chinese silken wallpaper because of its "exotic" quality, so rich Japanese decorated their homes with screens depicting the "strange" Westerners; the gold leaf suggests the screen's great value. In the central panel, a Portuguese ship captain (shaded by a parasol carried by a black servant) arrives in the port of Nagasaki. Black porters carry boxes of goods and rare animals as gifts "to sweeten up" Japanese merchants. They are received by tall, black-robed Jesuits. Europeans were called "barbarians" because of what the Japanese perceived as their terrible manners and the stench they emitted from a meat-based diet and lack of bathing. *(Michael Holford)*

Japanese also compelled the Dutch merchants to perform servile acts that other Europeans considered humiliating.

Long after Christianity ceased to be a possible threat to the Japanese government, the fear of Christianity sustained a policy of banning Western books on science and religion. Until well into the eighteenth century, Japanese intellectuals were effectively cut off from Western development, and Japanese opinions of Westerners were not high.

The Worldwide Economic Effects of Spanish Silver

The economic effects of exchange between Spain and China were perhaps even more important than the cultural ones. Silver mined in the Americas played a major role in both European and Asian economic development in the sixteenth and seventeenth centuries. In 1545, at an altitude of fifteen thousand feet, the Spanish discovered an incredible source of silver at Potosí (in present-day Bolivia) in territory conquered from the Inca Empire. The frigid place where nothing grew had not been settled. A half-century later, 160,000 people lived there, making it about the size of the city of London. In the second half of the sixteenth century Potosí yielded perhaps 60 percent of all the silver mined in the world. From Potosí and the mines at Zacatecas and Guanajuato in Mexico, huge quantities of precious metals poured forth, destined for the port of Seville in Spain.

The mining of gold and silver became the most important industry in the colonies. The Crown claimed the quinto, one-fifth of all precious metals mined in South America. Gold and silver yielded the Spanish monarchy 25 percent of its total income. Spanish predominance, however, proved temporary.

In the sixteenth century Spain experienced a steady population increase, creating a sharp rise in the demand for food and goods. Spanish colonies in the Americas also represented a demand for products. Since Spain had expelled some of the best farmers and businessmen—the Muslims and Jews—in the fifteenth century, the Spanish economy was suffering and could not meet the new demands. Prices rose. Because the cost of manufacturing cloth and other goods increased, Spanish products could not compete in the international market with cheaper products made elsewhere. The textile industry was badly hurt. Prices spiraled upward faster than the government could levy taxes to dampen the economy. (Higher taxes would have cut the public's buying power; with fewer goods sold, prices would have come down.)

Did the flood of silver bullion from America cause the inflation? Prices rose most steeply before 1565, but bullion imports reached their peak between 1580 and 1620. Thus there is no direct correlation between silver imports and the inflation rate. Did the substantial population growth accelerate the inflation rate? It may have done so. After 1600, when the population pressure declined, prices gradually stabilized. One fact is certain: the price revolution severely strained government budgets. Several times between 1557 and 1647, Spain's King Philip II and his successors repudiated the state debt, thereby undermining confidence in the government and leading the economy into a shambles.

As Philip II paid his armies and foreign debts with silver bullion, Spanish inflation was transmitted to the rest of Europe. Between 1560 and 1600, much of Europe experienced large price increases. Prices doubled and in some cases quadrupled. Spain suffered most severely, but all European countries were affected. People who lived on fixed incomes, such as the continental nobles, were badly hurt because their money bought less. Those who owed fixed sums of money, such as the middle class, prospered: in a time of rising prices, debts had less value each year. Food costs rose most sharply, and the poor fared worst of all.

And what of Asia? What economic impact did the Spanish and Portuguese discoveries have on Asian societies and on world trade? Some recent scholars argue that the key to understanding world trade in the sixteenth and early seventeenth centuries is not Europe, where hitherto most research has focused, but China. Within China the overissue of paper money had by 1450 reduced the value of that medium of currency to virtually nothing. Gold was too valuable for ordinary transactions. So the Ming government shifted to a silver-based currency. The result was that China was the main buyer of world silver—that is, China exchanged its silks and porcelains for silver.

While the mines of South America and Mexico poured out silver, so too did Japanese mines, shipping to Manila and Macao perhaps two hundred tons a year. American and Japanese silver had a profound impact on China. On the one hand, it contributed to the rise of a merchant class that converted to a silver zone. On the other hand, the Ming Dynasty, by allowing the payment of taxes in silver instead of the traditional rice, weakened its financial basis. As the purchasing power of silver declined in China, so did the value of silver taxes. This development led to a fiscal crisis that helped bring down the Ming Dynasty and contributed to the rise of the Qing.

Beyond China itself, Chinese imports of silver had crucial global ramifications: "When silver from Mexico and Japan entered the Ming Empire in great quantity, the value of silver began to decline and inflation set in, for as the metal became more abundant its buying power diminished."[32] This inflationary trend affected the values of commodities across the world. From a global perspective, the economic impact of China on the West was thus greater than any European influence on China or the rest of Asia.[33]

At the heart of world trade was not Europe, but China. The silver market drove world trade, with the Americas and Japan being the mainstays on the supply side and China dominating the demand side. Europeans were only the middlemen in the trade among Europe, the New World, and China.

Chapter Summary

To assess your mastery of this chapter, go to
bedfordstmartins.com/mckayworld

• *What were the distinctive features of Southeast Asian cultures and trade, and what was the impact of Islam and Christianity on Southeast Asian peoples?*

Prior to Columbus's voyages, well-developed trade routes linked the peoples and products of Africa, Asia, and Europe. The Indian Ocean was the center of the Afro-Eurasian trade world, ringed by cosmopolitan commercial cities such as Mombasa, Malacca, and Macao. Rice and seafood were staples of the diet, and women gained prestige from their role in rice cultivation. Southeast Asia's traditional animist beliefs were challenged in the sixteenth and seventeenth centuries by the arrival of Christian missionaries and Muslim teachers. Eventually, more than half the area's population accepted one of these two religions.

• *How and why did Europeans undertake ambitious voyages of expansion that would usher in a new era of global contact?*

Originally, Europeans played a minor role in the Afro-Eurasian trading world, since they did not produce many products desired by Eastern elites. In the sixteenth and seventeenth centuries, Europeans for the first time gained access to large parts of the globe. European peoples had the intellectual curiosity, driving ambition, and material incentive to challenge their marginal role in

Key Terms

bride wealth
General History of the Indies
caravel
Ptolemy's *Geography*
conquistadore
Aztec Empire
Inca Empire
viceroyalties
audiencia
quinto
Columbian Exchange
encomienda system
sugar
age of commerce

the pre-existing trade world. The revived monarchies of the sixteenth century now possessed sufficient resources to back ambitious seafarers like Christopher Columbus and Vasco da Gama.

• *What was the impact of European conquest on the peoples and ecologies of the New World?*

In the New World, Europeans discovered territories wholly unknown to them and forcibly established new colonies. European intrusion into the Americas led to the subjugation of native peoples for use in American silver and gold mines, along with the establishment of political and ecclesiastical administrations to govern the new territories. The resulting Columbian Exchange decimated native populations and fostered exchange of myriad plant, animal, and viral species. The spread of American plants, especially maize and potatoes, improved the diets of Asian, African, and European peoples and contributed to an almost worldwide population boom beginning in the mid-seventeenth century. Europeans carried smallpox and other diseases to the Americas, along with new weapons of war and economic exploitation, causing a massive population decline among Native American peoples.

• *How was the era of global contact shaped by new commercial empires, cultural encounters, and forced migrations?*

Exploration and exploitation contributed to a more sophisticated standard of living in Europe, in the form of spices and Asian luxury goods, and to terrible inflation resulting from the influx of South American silver and gold. Governments, the upper classes, and the peasantry were badly hurt by the resulting inflation. Meanwhile, the middle class of bankers, shippers, financiers, and manufacturers prospered for much of the seventeenth century.

Other consequences of European expansion had global proportions. Indian Ocean trade, long dominated by Muslim merchants operating from autonomous city-ports, increasingly fell under the control of Portuguese, and later Dutch, merchants. In China the lure of international trade encouraged the development of the porcelain and silk industries, as well as the immigration of thousands of Chinese people to Southeast Asia. In Japan the Indian Ocean trade in spices, silks, and Indian cotton prompted the greater exploitation of Japanese silver mines to yield the ore with which to pay for foreign goods. Both Chinese and Japanese leaders rebuffed efforts by Christian missionaries to spread their faith. Most tragically, the slave trade took on new proportions of scale and intensity as many millions of Africans were transported to labor in horrific conditions in the mines and plantations of the New World.

Suggested Reading

Crosby, Alfred W. *The Columbian Exchange: Biological and Cultural Consequences of 1492,* 30th anniversary ed. 2003. An innovative and highly influential account of the environmental impact of Columbus's voyages.

Davis, David B. *Slavery and Human Progress.* 1984. A moving and authoritative account of New World slavery.

Fernández-Armesto, Felip. *Columbus.* 1992. An excellent biography of Christopher Columbus.

Frederickson, George M. *The Arrogance of Race: Historical Perspectives on Slavery, Racism, and Social Inequality.*

1988. Analyzes the social and economic circumstances associated with the rise of plantation slavery.

Greenblatt, Stephen. *Marvelous Possessions: The Wonder of the New World.* 1991. Describes the cultural impact of New World discoveries on Europeans.

Northrup, David, ed. *The Atlantic Slave Trade.* 1994. Collected essays by leading scholars on many different aspects of the slave trade.

Pérez-Mallaína, Pablo E. *Spain's Men of the Sea: Daily Life on the Indies Fleet in the Sixteenth Century.* 1998. A description of recruitment, daily life, and career paths for ordinary sailors and officers in the Spanish fleet.

Pomeranz, Kenneth, and Steven Topik. *The World That Trade Created: Society, Culture and the World Economy, 1400 to the Present.* 1999. The creation of a world market presented through rich and vivid stories of merchants, miners, slaves, and farmers.

Restall, Matthew. *Seven Myths of Spanish Conquest.* 2003. A re-examination of common ideas about why and how the Spanish conquered native civilizations in the New World.

Scammell, Geoffrey V. *The World Encompassed: The First European Maritime Empires, c. 800–1650.* 1981. A detailed overview of the first European empires, including the Italian city-states, Portugal, and Spain.

Subrahamanyam, Sanjay. *The Career and Legend of Vasco da Gama.* 1998. A probing biography that places Vasco da Gama in the context of Portuguese politics and society.

Notes

1. A. Reid, *Southeast Asia in the Age of Commerce, 1450–1680.* Vol. 1: *The Land Under the Winds* (New Haven, Conn.: Yale University Press, 1988), p. 2.
2. Ibid., pp. 3–20.
3. Ibid., pp. 146–155.
4. A. Reid, *Southeast Asia in the Age of Commerce, 1450–1680.* Vol. 2: *Expansion and Crisis* (New Haven, Conn.: Yale University Press, 1993), pp. 133–192; the quotation is on p. 151.
5. Ibid., Chaps. 1 and 2, pp. 1–131.
6. Quoted in C. M. Cipolla, *Guns, Sails, and Empires: Technological Innovation and the Early Phases of European Expansion, 1400–1700* (New York: Minerva Press, 1965), p. 132.
7. Quoted in F. H. Littell, *The Macmillan Atlas: History of Christianity* (New York: Macmillan, 1976), p. 75.
8. See C. R. Phillips, *Ciudad Real, 1500–1750: Growth, Crisis, and Readjustment in the Spanish Economy* (Cambridge, Mass.: Harvard University Press, 1979), pp. 103–104, 115.
9. Ibid., p. 134.
10. Ibid., p. 19.
11. Scammell, *The World Encompassed: The First European Trade Empires, c. 800–1650* (London: Methuen, 1981), p. 207.
12. Quoted in F. Maddison, "Tradition and Innovation: Columbus' First Voyage and Portuguese Navigation in the Fifteenth Century," in *Circa 1492: Art in the Age of Exploration,* ed. J. A. Levenson (Washington, D.C.: National Gallery of Art, 1991), p. 69.
13. Quoted in R. L. Kagan, "The Spain of Ferdinand and Isabella," in *Circa 1492: Art in the Age of Exploration,* ed. J. A. Levenson (Washington, D.C.: National Gallery of Art, 1991), p. 60.
14. Peter Hulme, *Colonial Encounters: Europe and the Native Caribbean, 1492–1797* (London and New York: Methuan, 1986), pp. 22–31.
15. G. W. Conrad and A. A. Demarest, *Religion and Empire: The Dynamics of Aztec and Inca Expansionism* (New York: Cambridge University Press, 1993), pp. 67–69.
16. A. J. R. Russell-Wood, *The Portuguese Empire, 1415–1808: A World on the Move* (Baltimore: Johns Hopkins University Press, 1998), pp. 58–59.
17. Quoted in A. W. Crosby, *The Columbian Exchange: Biological and Cultural Consequences of 1492* (Westport, Conn.: Greenwood, 1972), p. 39.
18. Ibid., pp. 35–59.
19. Quoted in C. Gibson, ed., *The Black Legend: Anti-Spanish Attitudes in the Old World and the New* (New York: Knopf, 1971), pp. 74–75.
20. Quoted in L. B. Rout, Jr., *The African Experience in Spanish America* (New York: Cambridge University Press, 1976), p. 23.
21. C. Verlinden, *The Beginnings of Modern Colonization,* trans. Y. Freccero (Ithaca, N.Y.: Cornell University Press, 1970), pp. 5–6, 80–97.
22. This section leans heavily on D. B. Davis, *Slavery and Human Progress* (New York: Oxford University Press, 1984), pp. 54–62; the quotation is on p. 58.
23. Herbert S. Klein, "Profits and the Causes of Mortality," in David Northrup, ed., *The Atlantic Slave Trade* (Lexington, Mass.: D. C. Heath and Co., 1994), p. 116.
24. Malcolm Cowley and Daniel P. Mannix, "The Middle Passage," in David Northrup, ed., *The Atlantic Slave Trade* (Lexington, Mass.: D. C. Heath and Co., 1994), p. 101.
25. Parry, *The Age of Reconnaissance* (Berkeley: University of California Press, 1981), Chaps. 12, 14, and 15.
26. Arthur Henderson Smith, *Village Life in China: A Study in Sociology* (New York: F.H. Revell Co., 1899), p. 49.
27. Quoted in S. Neill, *A History of Christian Missions* (New York: Penguin Books, 1977), p. 163.
28. Quoted in C. M. Cipolla, *Clocks and Culture: 1300–1700* (New York: W. W. Norton, 1978), p. 86.
29. J. Gernet, *A History of Chinese Civilization* (New York: Cambridge University Press, 1982), p. 458.
30. Quoted in A. J. Andrea and J. H. Overfield, *The Human Record,* vol. 1 (Boston: Houghton Mifflin, 1990), pp. 406–407.
31. Quoted ibid., p. 408.
32. Quoted in D. O. Flynn and A. Giráldez, "Born with a 'Silver Spoon': The Origin of World Trade in 1571," *Journal of World History* 6 (Fall 1985): 203.
33. Ibid., pp. 217–218.

Listening to the PAST

Columbus Describes His First Voyage

On his return voyage to Spain in January 1493, Christopher Columbus composed a letter intended for wide circulation and had copies of it sent ahead to Isabella and Ferdinand and others when the ship docked at Lisbon. Because the letter sums up Columbus's understanding of his achievements, it is considered the most important document of his first voyage.

Since I know that you will be pleased at the great success with which the Lord has crowned my voyage, I write to inform you how in thirty-three days I crossed from the Canary Islands to the Indies, with the fleet which our most illustrious sovereigns gave me. I found very many islands with large populations and took possession of them all for their Highnesses; this I did by proclamation and unfurled the royal standard. No opposition was offered.

I named the first island that I found "San Salvador," in honour of our Lord and Saviour who has granted me this miracle. . . . When I reached Cuba, I followed its north coast westwards, and found it so extensive that I thought this must be the mainland, the province of Cathay.* . . . From there I saw another island eighteen leagues eastwards which I then named "Hispaniola."† . . .

Hispaniola is a wonder. The mountains and hills, the plains and meadow lands are both fertile and beautiful. They are most suitable for planting crops and for raising cattle of all kinds, and there are good sites for building towns and villages. The harbours are incredibly fine and there are many great rivers with broad

channels and the majority contain gold.‡ The trees, fruits and plants are very different from those of Cuba. In Hispaniola there are many spices and large mines of gold and other metals.§ . . .

The inhabitants of this island, and all the rest that I discovered or heard of, go naked, as their mothers bore them, men and women alike. A few of the women, however, cover a single place with a leaf of a plant or piece of cotton which they weave for the purpose. They have no iron or steel or arms and are not capable of using them, not because they are not strong and well built but because they are amazingly timid. All the weapons they have are canes cut at seeding time, at the end of which they fix a sharpened stick, but they have not the courage to make use of these, for very often when I have sent two or three men to a village to have conversation with them a great number of them have come out. But as soon as they saw my men all fled immediately, a father not even waiting for his son. And this is not because we have harmed any of them; on the contrary, wherever I have gone and been able to have conversation with them, I have given them some of the various things I had, a cloth and other articles, and received nothing in exchange. But they have still remained incurably timid. True, when they have been reassured and lost their fear, they are so ingenuous and so liberal with all their possessions that no one who has not seen them would believe it. If one asks for anything they have they never say no. On the contrary, they offer a share to anyone with demonstrations of heartfelt affection, and they are immediately content with any small thing, valuable or valueless, that is given them. I forbade the men to give them bits of broken crockery, fragments of glass or tags of laces, though if they could get them they fancied them the finest jewels in the world.

I hoped to win them to the love and service of their Highnesses and of the whole Spanish nation and to

---

*Cathay is the old name for China. In the log-book and later in this letter Columbus accepts the native story that Cuba is an island that they can circumnavigate in something more than twenty-one days, yet he insists here and later, during the second voyage, that it is in fact part of the Asiatic mainland.

†Hispaniola is the second largest island of the West Indies; Haiti occupies the western third of the island, the Dominican Republic the rest.

‡This did not prove to be true.

§These statements are also inaccurate.

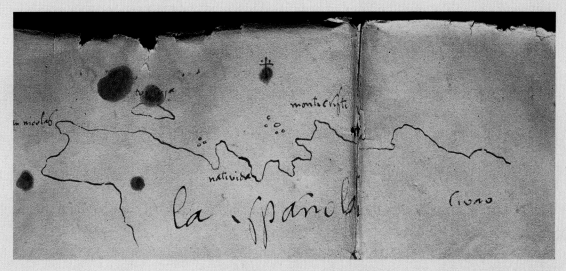

Columbus's map of Hispaniola. Would this small, vague sketch of Hispaniola (now Haiti and the Dominican Republic) have been of much use to explorers after Columbus? *(Col. Duke of Alba, Madrid/Institut Amatller d'Art Hispanic)*

persuade them to collect and give us of the things which they possessed in abundance and which we needed. They have no religion and are not idolaters; but all believe that power and goodness dwell in the sky and they are firmly convinced that I have come from the sky with these ships and people. In this belief they gave me a good reception everywhere, once they had overcome their fear; and this is not because they are stupid—far from it, they are men of great intelligence, for they navigate all those seas, and give a marvellously good account of everything—but because they have never before seen men clothed or ships like these. . . .

In all these islands the men are seemingly content with one woman, but their chief or king is allowed more than twenty. The women appear to work more than the men and I have not been able to find out if they have private property. As far as I could see whatever a man had was shared among all the rest and this particularly applies to food. . . . In another island, which I am told is larger than Hispaniola, the people have no hair. Here there is a vast quantity of gold, and from here and the other islands I bring Indians as evidence.

In conclusion, to speak only of the results of this very hasty voyage, their Highnesses can see that I will give them as much gold as they require, if they will render me some very slight assistance; also I will give them all the spices and cotton they want. . . . I will also bring them as much aloes as they ask and as many slaves, who will be taken from the idolaters. I believe also that I have found rhubarb and cinnamon and there will be countless other things in addition. . . .

So all Christendom will be delighted that our Redeemer has given victory to our most illustrious King and Queen and their renowned kingdoms, in this great matter. They should hold great celebrations and render solemn thanks to the Holy Trinity with many solemn prayers, for the great triumph which they will have, by the conversion of so many peoples to our holy faith and for the temporal benefits which will follow, for not only Spain, but all Christendom will receive encouragement and profit.

This is a brief account of the facts.
Written in the caravel off the Canary Islands.‖
15 February 1493

At your orders
THE ADMIRAL

Questions for Analysis

1. How did Columbus explain the success of his voyage?

2. What was Columbus's view of the Native Americans he met?

3. Evaluate his statements that the Caribbean islands possessed gold, cotton, and spices.

4. Why did Columbus cling to the idea that he had reached Asia?

Source: J. M. Cohen, ed. and trans., *The Four Voyages of Christopher Columbus* (Penguin Classics, 1958), pp. 115–123. Copyright © J. M. Cohen, 1958. Reproduced by permission of Penguin Books, Ltd.

‖Actually, Columbus was off Santa Maria in the Azores.

Hyacinthe Rigaud: Louis XIV, King of France and Navarre (1701). Louis XIV is surrounded by the symbols of his power: the sword of justice, the scepter of power, and the crown. The vigor and strength of the king's stocking-covered legs contrast with the age and wisdom of his lined face. *(Scala/Art Resource, NY)*

chapter

16 ABSOLUTISM AND CONSTITUTIONALISM IN EUROPE, CA. 1589–1725

Chapter Preview

Seventeenth-Century Crisis and Rebuilding

• What were the common crises and achievements of seventeenth-century European states?

Absolutism in France and Spain

• How and why did Louis XIV of France lead the way in forging the absolute state, and why did Spain experience decline in the same period?

Absolutism in Eastern Europe: Austria, Prussia, and Russia

• How did Austrian, Prussian, and Russian rulers in eastern Europe build absolute monarchies—monarchies that proved even more durable than that of Louis XIV?

Constitutionalism

• How and why did the constitutional state triumph in Holland and England?

The seventeenth century was a period of crisis and transformation in Europe. Agricultural and manufacturing slumps meant that many people struggled to feed themselves and their families. After a long period of growth, population rates stagnated or even fell. Religious and dynastic conflicts led to almost constant war, visiting violence and destruction on ordinary people.

The demands of war reshaped European states. Armies grew larger than they had been since the time of the Roman Empire. To pay for these armies, governments greatly increased taxes. They also created new bureaucracies to collect the taxes and to foster economic activity that might increase state revenue. Despite numerous obstacles, European states succeeded in gathering more power during this period. What one historian described as the long European "struggle for stability" that originated with the Reformation in the early sixteenth century was largely resolved by 1680.[1] Thus at the same time that powerful governments were emerging and evolving in Asia—such as the Qing Dynasty in China, the Tokugawa Shogunate in Japan, and the Mughal Empire in India—European rulers also increased the power of the central state.

Important differences existed, however, in terms of which authority within the state possessed sovereignty—the Crown or privileged groups. Between roughly 1589 and 1715 two basic patterns of government emerged in Europe: absolute monarchy and the constitutional state. Almost all subsequent European governments have been modeled on one of these patterns, which have also influenced greatly the rest of the world in the past three centuries.

SEVENTEENTH-CENTURY CRISIS AND REBUILDING

What were the common crises and achievements of seventeenth-century European states?

Historians often refer to the seventeenth century as an "age of crisis." After the economic and demographic growth of the sixteenth century, Europe faltered into stagnation and retrenchment. This was partially due to climate changes beyond anyone's control, but it also resulted from bitter religious divides, increased governmental pressures, and war. Overburdened peasants and city-dwellers took action to defend themselves, sometimes profiting from elite conflicts to obtain relief. In the long run, however, governments proved increasingly able to impose their will on the populace. This period witnessed a spectacular growth in army size as well as new forms of taxation, government bureaucracies, and increased state sovereignty.

moral economy *A historian's term for an economic perspective in which the needs of a community take precedence over competition and profit.*

Economic and Demographic Crisis

European rural society lived on the edge of subsistence. Because of the crude technology and low crop yield, peasants were constantly threatened by scarcity and famine.

In the seventeenth century a period of colder and wetter climate, dubbed by historians as a "little ice age," meant a shorter farming season. A bad harvest created dearth; a series of bad harvests could lead to famine. Recurrent famines significantly reduced the population of early modern Europe. Most people did not die of outright starvation, but rather of diseases brought on by malnutrition and exhaustion. Facilitated by the weakened population, outbreaks of bubonic plague continued in Europe until the 1720s.

Industry also suffered. While the evidence does not permit broad generalizations, it appears that the output of woolen textiles, one of the most important European manufactures, declined sharply in the first half of the seventeenth century. Food prices were high, wages stagnated, and unemployment soared. This economic crisis was not universal: it struck various regions at different times and to different degrees. In the middle decades of the century, Spain, France, Germany, and England all experienced great economic difficulties.

The urban poor and peasants were the hardest hit. When the price of bread rose beyond their capacity to pay, they frequently took action. In towns they invaded bakers' shops to seize bread and resell it at a "just price." In rural areas they attacked convoys taking grain away to the cities. Women often led these actions, since their role as mothers gave them some impunity in authorities' eyes. Historians have labeled this vision of a world in which community needs predominate over competition and profit a **moral economy.**

● **Estonia in the 1660s** The Estonians were conquered by German military nobility in the Middle Ages and reduced to serfdom. The German-speaking nobles ruled the Estonian peasants with an iron hand, and Peter the Great reaffirmed their domination when Russia annexed Estonia (see Map 16.4 on page 476). *(Time Life Pictures/Getty Images)*

The Return of Serfdom in the East

While economic and social hardship were common across Europe, important differences existed between east and west. In the west the demographic losses of the Black Death allowed peasants to escape from serfdom, and a small number of peasants in each village owned both enough land to feed themselves and the livestock and ploughs necessary to work their land. In eastern Europe seventeenth-century peasants had largely lost their ability to own land independently. Unlike those in the west, eastern European peasants had unsuccessfully countered efforts by noble lords to increase their exploitation in the labor shortages following the Black Death. Eastern lords triumphed because they made their kings and princes issue laws that restricted the right of their peasants to move to take advantage of better opportunities elsewhere. In Prussian territories by 1500, the law required that runaway peasants be hunted down and returned to their lords. Moreover, lords steadily took more and more of their peasants' land and arbitrarily imposed heavier and heavier labor obligations. By the early 1500s lords in many territories could command their peasants to work for them without pay for as many as six days a week.

The gradual erosion of the peasantry's economic position was bound up with manipulation of the legal system. The local lord was also the local prosecutor, judge, and jailer. There were no independent royal officials to provide justice or uphold the common law.

Between 1500 and 1650 the consolidation of serfdom in eastern Europe was accompanied by the growth of estate agriculture, particularly in Poland and eastern Germany. As economic expansion and population growth resumed after 1500, eastern lords had powerful economic incentives to increase the production of their estates, and they succeeded in squeezing sizable surpluses out of the impoverished peasants. These surpluses were sold to foreign merchants, who exported them to the growing cities of wealthier western Europe.

Finally, with the approval of weak kings, the landlords systematically undermined the medieval privileges of the towns and the power of the urban classes. For example, eastern towns also lost their medieval right of refuge and were compelled to return runaways to their lords. The population of the towns and the urban middle classes declined greatly. This development both reflected and promoted the supremacy of noble landlords in most of eastern Europe in the sixteenth century.

The Thirty Years' War

In the first half of the seventeenth century, the fragile balance of life was violently upturned by the ravages of the Thirty Years' War (1618–1648). The Holy Roman Empire was a confederation of hundreds of principalities, independent cities, duchies, and other polities loosely united under an elected emperor. The uneasy truce between Catholics and Protestants created by the Peace of Augsburg of 1555 deteriorated as the faiths of various

Chronology

ca. 1400–1650	Re-emergence of serfdom in eastern Europe
1533–1584	Reign of Ivan the Terrible in Russia
1589–1610	Reign of Henry IV in France
1598–1613	"Time of Troubles" in Russia
1602	Dutch East India Company founded
1620–1740	Growth of absolutism in Austria and Prussia
1642–1649	English civil war, which ends with execution of Charles I
1643–1715	Reign of Louis XIV in France
1652	Nikon reforms Russian Orthodox Church
1653–1658	Military rule in England under Oliver Cromwell
1660	Restoration of English monarchy under Charles II
1665–1683	Jean-Baptiste Colbert applies mercantilism to France
1670	Charles II agrees to re-Catholicize England in secret agreement with Louis XIV
1670–1671	Cossack revolt led by Stenka Razin
ca. 1680–1750	Construction of baroque palaces
1682–1725	Reign of Peter the Great in Russia
1683–1718	Habsburgs defend Vienna; win war with Ottoman Turks
1685	Edict of Nantes revoked
1688–1689	Glorious Revolution in England
1701–1713	War of the Spanish Succession

Legend:
- Austrian Habsburg lands
- Spanish Habsburg lands
- Other German states
- Swedish lands by 1648
- Ottoman Empire and tributary states
- ▬▬ Boundary of the Holy Roman Empire

MAP 16.1 **Europe After the Thirty Years' War** Which country emerged from the Thirty Years' War as the strongest European power? What dynastic house was that country's major rival in the early modern period?

areas shifted. Lutheran princes felt compelled to form the **Protestant Union** (1608), and Catholics retaliated with the Catholic League (1609). Each alliance was determined that the other should make no religious or territorial advance. Dynastic interests were also involved; the Spanish Habsburgs strongly supported the goals of their Austrian relatives—the unity of the empire and the preservation of Catholicism within it.

The war is traditionally divided into four phases. The first, or Bohemian, phase (1618–1625) was characterized by civil war in Bohemia between the Catholic League and the Protestant Union. In 1620 Catholic forces defeated Protestants at the Battle of the White Mountain. The second, or Danish, phase of the war (1625–1629)—so called because of the leadership of the Protestant king Christian IV of Denmark (r. 1588–1648)—witnessed additional Catholic victories. The Catholic imperial army led by Albert of Wallenstein swept through Silesia, north to the Baltic, and east into Pomerania, scoring smashing victories. Habsburg power peaked in 1629. The emperor issued the Edict of Restitution, whereby all Catholic properties lost to Protestantism since 1552 were restored, and only Catholics and Lutherans were allowed to practice their faiths.

The third, or Swedish, phase of the war (1630–1635) began with the arrival in Germany of the Swedish king Gustavus Adolphus (r. 1594–1632). The ablest administrator of his day and a devout Lutheran, he intervened to support the empire's Protestants. The French chief minister, Cardinal Richelieu, subsidized the Swedes, hoping to weaken Habsburg power in Europe. Gustavus Adolphus won two important battles but was fatally wounded in combat. The final, or French, phase of the war (1635–1648) was prompted by Richelieu's concern that the Habsburgs would rebound after the death of Gustavus Adolphus. Richelieu declared war on Spain and sent military as well as financial assistance. Finally, in October 1648 peace was achieved.

The 1648 **Peace of Westphalia** that ended the Thirty Years' War marked a turning point in European history. Conflicts fought over religious faith ended. The treaties recognized the independent authority of more than three hundred German princes (see Map 16.1), reconfirming the emperor's severely limited authority. The Augsburg agreement of 1555 became permanent, adding Calvinism to Catholicism and Lutheranism as legally permissible creeds. The north German states remained Protestant; the south German states, Catholic.

The Thirty Years' War was probably the most destructive event for the central European economy and society prior to the twentieth century. Perhaps one-third of urban residents and two-fifths of the rural population died, leaving entire areas depopulated. Trade in southern German cities, such as Augsburg, was virtually destroyed. Agricultural areas suffered catastrophically. Many small farmers lost their land, allowing nobles to enlarge their estates and consolidate their control.[2]

Seventeenth-Century State-Building: Common Obstacles and Achievements

In this context of economic and demographic depression, monarchs began to make new demands on their people. Traditionally, historians have distinguished sharply between the "absolutist" governments of France, Spain, Central Europe, and Russia and the constitutional monarchies of England and the Dutch Republic. Whereas absolutist monarchs gathered all power under their personal control, constitutional monarchs were obliged to respect laws passed by representative institutions. More recently, historians have emphasized commonalities among these powers. Despite their political differences, absolutist and constitutional states shared common projects of protecting and expanding their frontiers, raising new taxes, and consolidating central control.

Rulers who wished to increase their authority encountered formidable obstacles. Some were purely material. Without paved roads, telephones, or other modern

Protestant Union *An alliance formed by Lutheran princes in the Holy Roman Empire that eventually led to the Thirty Years' War.*

Peace of Westphalia *The name of a series of treaties that concluded the Thirty Years' War in 1648.*

technology, it took weeks to convey orders from the central government to the provinces. Rulers also suffered from a lack of information about their realms, making it impossible to police and tax the population effectively. Local power structures presented another serious obstacle. Nobles, the church, the legislative corps, town councils, guilds, and other bodies held legal privileges, which could not easily be rescinded. In some kingdoms, many people spoke a language different from the Crown's, further diminishing their willingness to obey its commands.

Nonetheless, over the course of the seventeenth century both absolutist and constitutional governments achieved new levels of central control. This increased authority focused in four areas in particular: greater taxation, growth in armed forces, larger and more efficient bureaucracies, and the increased ability to compel obedience from their subjects. Over time, centralized power added up to something close to **sovereignty**. A state may be termed sovereign when it possesses a monopoly over the instruments of justice and the use of force within clearly defined boundaries. In a sovereign state, no system of courts, such as ecclesiastical tribunals, competes with state courts in the dispensation of justice; and private armies, such as those of feudal lords, present no threat to central authority. While seventeenth-century states did not acquire total sovereignty, they made important strides toward that goal.

sovereignty *The exercise of complete and autonomous authority over a political body. The rulers of early modern states strove to achieve sovereignty, in competition with traditional power-holders like noble estates, the church, and town councils.*

ABSOLUTISM IN FRANCE AND SPAIN

How and why did Louis XIV of France lead the way in forging the absolute state, and why did Spain experience decline in the same period?

In the Middle Ages jurists held that as a consequence of monarchs' coronation and anointment with sacred oil, they ruled "by the grace of God." Law was given by God; kings discovered or "found" the law and acknowledged that they must respect and obey it. In the absolutist state, kings amplified these claims, asserting that, as they were chosen by God, they were responsible to God alone. They claimed exclusive power to make and enforce laws, denying any other institution or group the authority to check their power. Historians have been debating since his reign how successfully Louis XIV and other absolutist monarchs realized these claims.

The Foundations of Absolutism: Henry IV, Sully, and Richelieu

Louis XIV's absolutism had long roots. In 1589 his grandfather Henry IV (r. 1589–1610), the founder of the Bourbon dynasty, acquired a devastated country. Civil wars between Protestants and Catholics had wracked France since 1561. Poor harvests had reduced peasants to starvation, and commercial activity had declined drastically. "Henri le Grand" (Henry the Great), as the king was called, promised "a chicken in every pot" and inaugurated a remarkable recovery.

He did so by keeping France at peace during most of his reign. Although he had converted to Catholicism, he issued the Edict of Nantes, allowing Protestants the right to worship in 150 traditionally Protestant towns throughout France. He sharply lowered taxes and instead charged royal officials an annual fee to guarantee heredity in their offices. He also improved the infrastructure of the country, building new roads and canals and repairing the ravages of years of civil war. Yet despite his efforts at peace, Henry was murdered in 1610 by François Ravaillac, a Catholic zealot, setting off a national crisis.

After the death of Henry IV his wife, the queen-regent Marie de' Medici, headed the government for the child-king Louis XIII (r. 1610–1643). In 1628 Armand Jean du Plessis—Cardinal Richelieu (1585–1642)—became first minister of the French

crown. Richelieu's maneuvers allowed the monarchy to maintain power within Europe and within its own borders despite the turmoil of the Thirty Years' War.

Cardinal Richelieu's political genius is best reflected in the administrative system he established to strengthen royal control. He extended the use of **intendants,** commissioners for each of France's thirty-two districts who were appointed directly by the monarch, to whom they were solely responsible. They recruited men for the army, supervised the collection of taxes, presided over the administration of local law, checked up on the local nobility, and regulated economic activities in their districts. As the intendants' power increased under Richelieu, so did the power of the centralized French state.

Under Richelieu, the French monarchy also acted to repress Protestantism. Louis personally supervised the siege of La Rochelle, fourth largest of the French Atlantic ports and a major commercial center with strong ties to Protestant Holland and England. After the city fell in October 1628, its municipal government was suppressed. Protestants retained the right of public worship, but the Catholic liturgy was restored. The fall of La Rochelle was one step in the removal of Protestantism as a strong force in French life.

Richelieu did not aim to wipe out Protestantism in the rest of Europe, however. His main foreign policy goal was to destroy the Catholic Habsburgs' grip on territories that surrounded France. Consequently, Richelieu supported Habsburg enemies, including Protestants. In 1631 he signed a treaty with the Lutheran king Gustavus Adolphus promising French support against the Habsburgs in the Thirty Years' War. For the French cardinal, interests of state outweighed religious considerations.

Richelieu's successor as chief minister for the next boy-king, Louis XIV, was Cardinal Jules Mazarin (1602–1661). Along with the regent, Queen Mother Anne of Austria, Mazarin continued Richelieu's centralizing policies. His struggle to increase royal revenues to meet the costs of war led to the uprisings of 1648–1653 known as the **Fronde.** A *frondeur* was originally a street urchin who threw mud at the passing carriages of the rich, but the word came to be applied to the many individuals and groups who opposed the policies of the government. The most influential of these groups were the robe nobility—court judges—and the sword nobility—the aristocracy. During the first of several riots, the queen mother fled Paris with Louis XIV. As the rebellion continued, civil order broke down completely. In 1651 Anne's regency ended with the declaration of Louis as king in his own right. Much of the rebellion died away, and its leaders came to terms with the government.

The conflicts of the Fronde had significant results for the future. The twin evils of noble factionalism and popular riots left the French wishing for peace and for a strong monarch to reimpose order. This was the legacy that Louis XIV inherited when he assumed personal rule in 1661. Humiliated by his flight from Paris, he was determined to avoid any recurrence of rebellion.

Louis XIV and Absolutism

In the reign of Louis XIV (r. 1643–1715), the longest in European history, the French monarchy reached the peak of absolutist development. In the magnificence of his court and the brilliance of the culture that he presided over, the "Sun King" dominated his age. Religion, Anne, and Mazarin all taught Louis the doctrine of the **divine right of kings:** God had established kings as his rulers on earth, and they were answerable ultimately to God alone. Kings were divinely anointed and shared in the sacred nature of divinity; however, they could not simply do as they pleased. They had to obey God's laws and rule for the good of the people.

Louis worked very hard at the business of governing. He ruled his realm through several councils of state and insisted on taking a personal role in many of the councils' decisions. He selected councilors from the recently ennobled or the upper middle

intendants *Commissioners for each of France's thirty-two administrative districts. Appointed by and answering directly to the monarch, they were key elements in Richelieu's plan to centralize the French state.*

Fronde *A series of violent uprisings during the minority of Louis XIV triggered by oppressive taxation and growing royal authority; the last attempt of the French nobility to resist the king by arms.*

divine right of kings *The doctrine that kings were established in their rule by God and were accountable only to God. In such a system, the will of God and that of the king become inseparable. Characteristic of absolute monarchies.*

class because he wanted "people to know by the rank of the men who served him that he had no intention of sharing power with them."[3]

Despite increasing financial problems, Louis never called a meeting of the Estates General. The nobility therefore had no means of united expression or action. Nor did Louis have a first minister; he kept himself free from worry about the inordinate power of a Richelieu.

In 1682 Louis moved his court to the newly renovated palace at Versailles, requiring all great nobles to spend part of the year in attendance on him there. Since the king controlled the distribution of offices, pensions, and other benefits, nobles vied to win his favor through elaborate rituals of court etiquette. (See the feature "Listening to the Past: The Court at Versailles" on pages 490–491.) The grandeur of the palace and its gardens broadcast the king's glory to visiting dignitaries, and Versailles was soon copied by would-be absolutist monarchs across Europe.

Although personally tolerant, Louis hated division within the realm and insisted that religious unity was essential to his royal dignity and to the security of the state. He thus pursued the policy of Protestant repression launched by Richelieu. In 1685 Louis revoked the Edict of Nantes, by which his grandfather Henry IV had granted liberty of conscience to French Huguenots. The new law ordered the destruction of Huguenot churches, the closing of schools, the Catholic baptism of Huguenots, and the exile of Huguenot pastors who refused to renounce their faith. The result was the departure of some of his most loyal and industrially skilled subjects.

Despite his claims to absolute authority, there were multiple constraints on Louis's power. In practice he governed through collaboration with nobles, who maintained tremendous prestige and authority in their ancestral lands. He achieved new centralized authority by reaffirming the traditional privileges of the nobility, while largely excluding them from active involvement in government.

Financial and Economic Management Under Louis XIV: Colbert

France's ability to build armies and fight wars depended on a strong economy. Fortunately for Louis, his controller general, Jean-Baptiste Colbert (1619–1683), proved himself a financial genius. His central principle was that the wealth and the economy of France should serve the state. To this end he rigorously applied mercantilist policies to France.

mercantilism *A system of economic regulations aimed at increasing the power of the state.*

Mercantilism is a collection of governmental policies for the regulation of economic activities by and for the state. In seventeenth- and eighteenth-century economic theory, a nation's international power was thought to be based on its wealth, specifically its gold supply. To accumulate gold, a country always had to sell more goods abroad than it bought. Colbert thus insisted that France should be self-sufficient, able to produce within its borders everything French subjects needed.

Colbert supported old industries and created new ones, focusing especially on textiles, the most important sector of the economy. Colbert enacted new production regulations, created guilds to boost quality standards, and encouraged foreign craftsmen to immigrate to France. To encourage the purchase of French goods, he abolished many domestic tariffs and raised tariffs on foreign products. In 1664 Colbert founded the Company of the East Indies with (unfulfilled) hopes of competing with the Dutch for Asian trade.

Colbert also hoped to make Canada—rich in untapped minerals and some of the best agricultural land in the world—part of a vast French empire. He sent four thousand peasants from western France to Quebec, whose capital was founded in 1608 under Henry IV. Subsequently, the Jesuit Jacques Marquette and the merchant Louis Joliet sailed down the Mississippi River and claimed possession of the land on both sides as far south as present-day Arkansas. In 1684 French explorers continued

● **Rubens: The Death of Henri IV and the Proclamation of the Regency (1622–1625)** In 1622 the regent Marie de' Medici commissioned Peter Paul Rubens to paint a cycle of paintings depicting her life. This one portrays two distinct moments: the assassination of Henry IV (shown on the left ascending to Heaven), and Marie's subsequent proclamation as regent. The other twenty-three canvasses in the cycle similarly glorify Marie, a tricky undertaking given her unhappy marriage to Henry IV and her tumultuous relationship with her son Louis XIII, who removed her from the regency in 1617. As in this image, Rubens frequently resorted to allegory and classical imagery to elevate the events of Marie's life. *(Réunion des Musées Nationaux/Art Resource, NY)*

down the Mississippi to its mouth and claimed vast territories and the rich delta for Louis XIV. The area was called, naturally, "Louisiana."

During Colbert's tenure as controller general, Louis was able to pursue his goals without massive tax increases and without creating a stream of new offices. The constant pressure of warfare after Colbert's death, however, undid many of his economic achievements.

Louis XIV's Wars

Louis XIV wrote that "the character of a conqueror is regarded as the noblest and highest of titles." In pursuit of the title of conqueror, he kept France at war for thirty-three of the fifty-four years of his personal rule. François le Tellier (later, marquis de Louvois), Louis's secretary of state for war, equaled Colbert's achievements in the economic realm. Louvois created a professional army in which the French state, rather than private nobles, employed the soldiers. The French army grew in size from roughly 125,000 men in the Thirty Years' War (1630–1648) to 250,000 during the Dutch War (1672–1678) and 340,000 during the War of the League of Augsburg (1688–1697).[4] Uniforms and weapons were standardized and a rational system of training and promotion devised. Many historians believe that the new loyalty, professionalism, and size of the French army is the best case for the success of absolutism under Louis XIV. Whatever his compromises elsewhere, the French monarch had firm control of his armed forces. As in so many other matters, Louis's model was followed across Europe.

Louis's goal was to expand France to what he considered its "natural" borders and to secure those lands from any threat of outside invasion. His armies managed to expand French borders to include important commercial centers in the Spanish Netherlands and Flanders, as well as all of Franche-Comté between 1667 and 1678. In 1681 Louis seized the city of Strasbourg, and three years later he sent his armies into the province of Lorraine. At that moment the king seemed invincible. In fact, Louis had reached the limit of his expansion. The wars of the 1680s and 1690s brought no additional territories but placed unbearable strains on French resources. Colbert's successors resorted to desperate measures to finance these wars, including devaluation of the currency and new taxes.

Louis's last war was endured by a French people suffering high taxes, crop failure, and widespread malnutrition and death. In 1700 the childless Spanish king Charles II (r. 1665–1700) died, opening a struggle for control of Spain and its colonies. His will bequeathed the Spanish crown and its empire to Philip of Anjou, Louis XIV's grandson (Louis's wife, Maria-Theresa, had been Charles's sister). This testament violated a prior treaty by which the European powers had agreed to divide the Spanish possessions between the king of France and the Holy Roman emperor, both brothers-in-law of Charles II. Claiming that he was following both Spanish and French interests, Louis broke with the treaty and accepted the will.

In 1701 the English, Dutch, Austrians, and Prussians formed the Grand Alliance against Louis XIV. War dragged on until 1713. The **Peace of Utrecht,** which ended the war, applied the principle of partition. Louis's grandson Philip remained the first Bourbon king of Spain on the understanding that the French and Spanish crowns would never be united. France surrendered Newfoundland, Nova Scotia, and the Hudson Bay territory to England, which also acquired Gibraltar, Minorca, and control of the African slave trade from Spain (see Map 16.2).

The Peace of Utrecht represented the balance-of-power principle in operation, setting limits on the extent to which any one power—in this case, France—could expand. It also marked the end of French expansion. Thirty-five years of war had brought rights to all of Alsace and some commercial centers in the north. But at what price? In 1714 an exhausted France hovered on the brink of bankruptcy. It is no wonder that when Louis XIV died on September 1, 1715, many subjects felt as much relief as they did sorrow.

Peace of Utrecht *A series of treaties, from 1713 to 1715, that ended the War of the Spanish Succession, ended French expansion in Europe, and marked the rise of the British Empire.*

The Decline of Absolutist Spain in the Seventeenth Century

As French power was growing, Spanish power was diminishing. By the early seventeenth century the seeds of disaster were sprouting. Between 1610 and 1650 Spanish trade with the colonies fell 60 percent, due to competition from local industries in the colonies and from Dutch and English traders. At the same time, the native Indians and African slaves who toiled in the South American silver mines suffered frightful epidemics of disease. Ultimately, the lodes started to run dry, and the quantity of metal produced steadily declined after 1620.

In Madrid, however, royal expenditures constantly exceeded income. To meet mountainous state debt and declining revenues, the Crown repeatedly devalued the coinage and declared bankruptcy. Given the frequency of state bankruptcies, national credit plummeted.

Seventeenth-century Spain was the victim of its past. It could not forget the grandeur of the sixteenth century and respond to changing circumstances. Although Spain lacked the finances to fight expensive wars, the imperial tradition demanded the revival of war with the Dutch at the expiration of a twelve-year truce in 1622 and a long war with France over Mantua (1628–1659). Spain thus became embroiled in the Thirty Years' War. These conflicts, on top of an empty treasury, brought disaster.

In 1640 Spain faced serious revolts in Catalonia and Portugal. The Portuguese succeeded in regaining independence from Habsburg rule under their new king, John IV (r. 1640–1656). In 1643 the French inflicted a crushing defeat on a Spanish army at Rocroi in what is now Belgium. By the Treaty of the Pyrenees of 1659, which ended

● **Peeter Snayers: Spanish Troops (detail)** The long wars that Spain fought over Dutch independence, in support of Habsburg interests in Germany, and against France left the country militarily exhausted and financially drained by the mid-1600s. Here Spanish troops—thin, emaciated, and probably unpaid—straggle away from battle. *(Museo Nacional del Prado, Madrid. Photo: José Baztan y Alberto Otero)*

the French-Spanish conflict, Spain was compelled to surrender extensive territories to France.

Spain's decline can also be traced to a failure to invest in productive enterprises. In contrast to the other countries of western Europe, Spain had only a tiny middle class. Public opinion condemned moneymaking as vulgar and undignified. Thousands entered economically unproductive professions: there were said to be nine thousand monasteries in the province of Castile alone. Some three hundred thousand people who had once been Muslims were expelled by Philip III in 1609, significantly reducing the pool of skilled workers and merchants. Those working in the textile industry were forced out of business when the flood of gold and silver produced severe inflation, pushing their production costs to the point where they could not compete in colonial and international markets.[5]

Spanish aristocrats, attempting to maintain an extravagant lifestyle they could no longer afford, increased the rents on their estates. High rents and heavy taxes in turn drove the peasants from the land. Agricultural production suffered, and peasants departed for the large cities, where they swelled the ranks of unemployed beggars. Spain also ignored new scientific methods because they came from heretical nations, Holland and England.

ABSOLUTISM IN EASTERN EUROPE: AUSTRIA, PRUSSIA, AND RUSSIA

How did Austrian, Prussian, and Russian rulers in eastern Europe build absolute monarchies—monarchies that proved even more durable than that of Louis XIV?

The rulers of eastern Europe also labored to build strong absolutist states in the seventeenth century. But they built on social and economic foundations different from those in western Europe, namely serfdom and the strong nobility who benefited from it.

Despite the strength of the nobility, strong kings did begin to emerge in many eastern European lands in the course of the seventeenth century. There were endless

MAP 16.2 **Europe in 1715** The series of treaties commonly called the Peace of Utrecht (April 1713–November 1715) ended the War of the Spanish Succession and redrew the map of Europe. A French Bourbon king succeeded to the Spanish throne. France surrendered to Austria the Spanish Netherlands (later Belgium), then in French hands, and France recognized the Hohenzollern rulers of Prussia. Spain ceded Gibraltar to Great Britain, for which it has been a strategic naval station ever since. Spain also granted to Britain the *asiento*, the contract for supplying African slaves to America.

Legend:
- French Bourbon lands
- Spanish Bourbon lands
- Austrian Habsburg lands
- Prussian lands
- Great Britain
- Boundary of the Holy Roman Empire
- Russian Empire
- Russian gains, by 1725
- Ottoman Empire, 1722

wars, and in this atmosphere of continuous military emergency monarchs found ways to reduce the political power of the landlord nobility. Cautiously leaving the nobles as unchallenged masters of their peasants, eastern monarchs gradually monopolized political power.

There were important variations on the absolutist theme in eastern Europe. The royal absolutism created in Prussia was stronger and more effective than that established in Austria. As for Russia, it developed its own form of absolutism, which was quite different from that of France or even Prussia.

The Austrian Habsburgs

Like all of central Europe, the Habsburgs emerged from the Thirty Years' War impoverished and exhausted. Their efforts to destroy Protestantism in the German lands and to turn the weak Holy Roman Empire into a real state had failed. Although the Habsburgs remained the hereditary emperors, real power lay in the hands of a bewildering variety of separate political jurisdictions. Defeat in central Europe encouraged the Habsburgs to turn away from a quest for imperial dominance and to focus inward and eastward in an attempt to unify their diverse holdings. If they could not impose Catholicism in the empire, at least they could do so in their own domains.

Habsburg victory over Bohemia during the Thirty Years' War was an important step in this direction. Ferdinand II (r. 1619–1637) drastically reduced the power of the **Bohemian Estates,** the largely Protestant representative assembly. He also confiscated the landholdings of Protestant nobles and gave them to loyal Catholic nobles and to the foreign aristocratic mercenaries who led his armies. After 1650 a large portion of the Bohemian nobility was of recent origin and owed everything to the Habsburgs.

Bohemian Estates *The largely Protestant representative body of the different estates in Bohemia. Significantly reduced in power by Ferdinand II.*

With the help of this new nobility, the Habsburgs established direct rule over Bohemia. The condition of the enserfed peasantry worsened substantially: three days per week of unpaid labor—the *robot*—became the norm. Protestantism was also stamped out. The reorganization of Bohemia was a giant step toward creating absolutist rule.

Ferdinand III (r. 1637–1657) continued to build state power. He centralized the government in the hereditary German-speaking provinces, which formed the core Habsburg holdings. For the first time, a permanent standing army was ready to put down any internal opposition.

The Habsburg monarchy then turned east toward the plains of Hungary, which had been divided between the Ottomans and the Habsburgs in the early sixteenth century. Between 1683 and 1699 the Habsburgs pushed the Ottomans from most of Hungary and Transylvania. The recovery of all the former kingdom of Hungary was completed in 1718.

The Hungarian nobility, despite its reduced strength, effectively thwarted the full development of Habsburg absolutism. Throughout the seventeenth century Hungarian nobles rose in revolt against attempts to impose absolute rule. They never triumphed decisively, but neither were they crushed the way the nobility in Bohemia had been in 1620. In 1703, with the Habsburgs bogged down in the War of the Spanish Succession (see page 470), the Hungarians rose in one last patriotic rebellion under Prince Francis Rákóczy.

Rákóczy and his forces were eventually defeated, but the Habsburgs agreed to restore many of the traditional privileges of the aristocracy in return for Hungarian acceptance of hereditary Habsburg rule. Thus Hungary, unlike Austria and Bohemia, was never fully integrated into a centralized, absolute Habsburg state.

Despite checks on their ambitions in Hungary, the Habsburgs made significant achievements in state-building elsewhere by forging consensus with the church and the nobility. A sense of common identity and loyalty to the monarchy grew among elites in Habsburg lands, even to a certain extent in Hungary. German became the language of the common culture, and zealous Catholicism helped fuse a collective identity. Vienna became the political and cultural center of the empire. By 1700 it was a thriving city with a population of one hundred thousand, with its own version of Versailles, the royal palace of Schönbrunn.

Prussia in the Seventeenth Century

In the fifteenth and sixteenth centuries, the Hohenzollern family had ruled parts of eastern Germany as the imperial electors of Brandenburg and the dukes of Prussia, but they had little real power. Although the **elector of Brandenburg** enjoyed the right to help choose the Holy Roman emperor, nothing would suggest that the Hohenzollern territories would come to play an important role in European affairs.

When he came to power in 1640, the twenty-year-old Frederick William, later known as the "Great Elector," was determined to unify his three provinces and enlarge them by diplomacy and war. These provinces were Brandenburg; Prussia, inherited in 1618; and scattered holdings along the Rhine, inherited in 1614 (see Map 16.3). Each was inhabited by German-speakers, but each had its own estates. Although the estates had not met regularly during the chaotic Thirty Years' War, taxes could not be levied without their consent. The estates of Brandenburg and Prussia were dominated by the nobility and the landowning classes, known as the **Junkers**.

elector of Brandenburg *One of the electors of the Holy Roman Empire, hereditarily held by the Hohenzollern family. Frederick William was able to use and expand the office, ultimately resulting in the consolidation of the Prussian state.*

Junkers *The nobility of Brandenburg and Prussia. Reluctant allies of Frederick William in his consolidation of the Prussian state.*

MAP 16.3 **The Growth of Austria and Brandenburg-Prussia to 1748** Austria expanded to the southwest into Hungary and Transylvania at the expense of the Ottoman Empire. It was unable to hold the rich German province of Silesia, however, which was conquered by Brandenburg-Prussia.

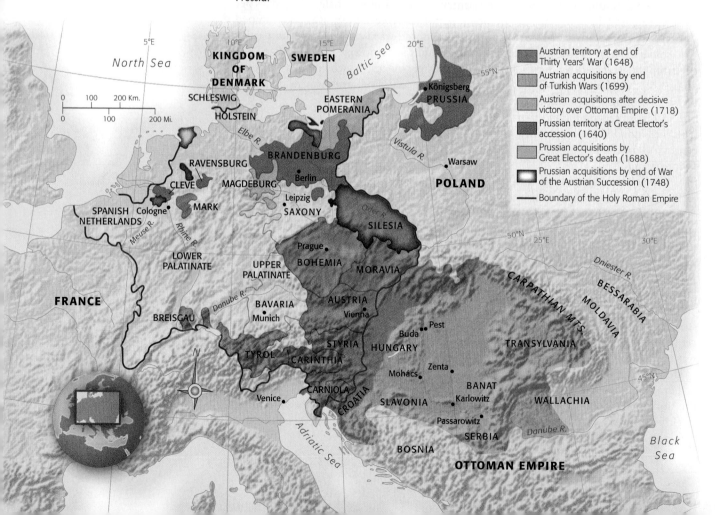

Frederick William profited from ongoing European war and the threat of Tatar invasion to argue for the need for a permanent standing army. In 1660 he persuaded Junkers in the estates to accept taxation without consent in order to fund an army. They agreed to do so in exchange for reconfirmation of their own privileges, including authority over the serfs. Opposition from the towns was crushed ruthlessly.

Thereafter, the estates' power declined rapidly, for the Great Elector had both financial independence and superior force. State revenue tripled during his reign, and the army expanded drastically. In 1688 a population of one million supported a peacetime standing army of thirty thousand. In 1701 the elector's son, Frederick I, received the elevated title of king of Prussia (instead of elector) as a reward for aiding the Holy Roman emperor in the War of the Spanish Succession.

The Consolidation of Prussian Absolutism

Frederick William I, "the Soldiers' King" (r. 1713–1740), completed his grandfather's work, eliminating the last traces of parliamentary estates and local self-government. It was he who truly established Prussian absolutism and transformed Prussia into a military state. Frederick William was intensely attached to military life. He always wore an army uniform, and he lived the highly disciplined life of the professional soldier. Years later he summed up his life's philosophy in his instructions to his son: "A formidable army and a war chest large enough to make this army mobile in times of need can create great respect for you in the world, so that you can speak a word like the other powers."[6]

The king's power grab brought him into considerable conflict with the Junkers; yet, in the end, he successfully enlisted the Prussian nobility to lead his growing army. A new compromise was worked out whereby the proud nobility commanded the peasantry in the army as well as on the estates.

Penny-pinching and hard-working, Frederick William achieved results. Prussia, twelfth in Europe in population, had the fourth largest army by 1740. The Prussian army was the best in Europe, astonishing foreign observers with its precision, skill, and discipline. Frederick William and his ministers also built an exceptionally honest and conscientious bureaucracy to administer the country and foster economic development.

Nevertheless, Prussians paid a heavy and lasting price for the obsessions of their royal drillmaster. Civil society became rigid and highly disciplined. As a Prussian minister later summed up, "To keep quiet is the first civic duty."[7] Thus the policies of Frederick William I combined with harsh peasant bondage and Junker tyranny to lay the foundations for a highly militaristic country.

The Mongol Yoke and the Rise of Moscow

In the thirteenth century the Kievan principality was conquered by the Mongols, a group of nomadic tribes from present-day Mongolia who had come together under Chinggis Khan

● **A Prussian Giant Grenadier** Frederick William I wanted tall, handsome soldiers. He dressed them in tight bright uniforms to distinguish them from the peasant population from which most soldiers came. He also ordered several portraits of his favorites from his court painter, J. C. Merk. Grenadiers wore the miter cap instead of an ordinary hat so that they could hurl their heavy grenades unimpeded by a broad brim. *(The Royal Collection © 2007, Her Majesty Queen Elizabeth II)*

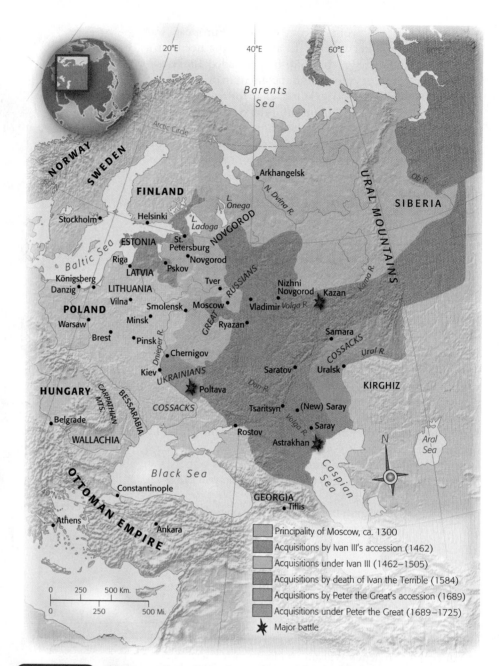

MAP 16.4   **The Expansion of Russia to 1725**   After the disintegration of the Kievan state and the Mongol conquest, the princes of Moscow and their descendants gradually extended their rule over an enormous territory.

Mongol Yoke   *The two-hundred-year rule of the Mongol khan over the former territories of Kievan Rus, a medieval state centered in the city of Kiev and comprising portions of modern-day Ukraine, Russia, and Belarussia. This period is considered a prelude to the rise of absolutist Russia.*

(1162–1227). The two-hundred-year period of rule under the Mongol khan (king), known as the **Mongol Yoke,** set the stage for the rise of absolutist Russia.

The Mongols forced the Slavic princes to submit to their rule and to give them tribute and slaves. Beginning with Alexander Nevsky in 1252, the princes of Moscow became particularly adept at serving the Mongols. They loyally put down popular uprisings and collected the khan's taxes. As reward, the princes of Moscow emerged as hereditary great princes. Eventually the Muscovite princes were able to destroy the other princes who were their rivals for power. Ivan III (r. 1462–1505) consolidated power around Moscow and won Novgorod, almost reaching the Baltic Sea (see Map 16.4).

By about 1480 Ivan III felt strong enough to stop acknowledging the khan as his supreme ruler. To legitimize their new authority, he and his successors declared themselves *autocrats,* meaning that, like the khans, they were the sole source of power. Yet also like the khans, they needed the cooperation of the local elites. The highest ranking nobles or **boyars** enabled them to rule with an extremely limited government apparatus.

Another source of legitimacy lay in Moscow's claim to the political and religious inheritance of the Byzantine Empire. After the fall of Constantinople to the Turks in 1453, the princes of Moscow asserted themselves as the heirs of both the caesars and Orthodox Christianity, the one true faith. (The title **tsar,** first taken by Ivan IV in 1533, is a contraction of *caesar.*) Ivan's marriage to the daughter of the last Byzantine emperor further enhanced the aura of Moscow's imperial inheritance.

boyars *The highest ranking members of the Russian nobility.*

tsar *The Slavic word for* caesar; *Ivan III initiated this title for the absolute ruler of Russia.*

Tsar and People to 1689

Developments in Russia took a chaotic turn with the reign of Ivan IV (r. 1533–1584), the famous "Ivan the Terrible." Ivan's reign was characterized by endless wars and violent purges. He was successful in defeating the remnants of Mongol power, adding

● **Saint Basil's Cathedral, Moscow** With its sloping roofs and colorful onion-shaped domes, Saint Basil's is a striking example of powerful Byzantine influences on Russian culture. According to tradition, an enchanted Ivan the Terrible blinded the cathedral's architects to ensure that they would never duplicate their fantastic achievement, which still dazzles the beholder in today's Red Square. *(George Holton/ Photo Researchers)*

● **Gustaf Cederstrom: The Swedish Victory at Narva** This poignant re-creation focuses on the contrast between the Swedish officers in handsome dress uniforms and the battered Russian soldiers laying down their standards in surrender. Charles XII of Sweden scored brilliant, rapid-fire victories over Denmark, Saxony, and Russia, but he failed to make peace with Peter while he was ahead and eventually lost Sweden's holdings on the Baltic coast. (© The National Museum of Fine Arts, Stockholm)

service nobility *Those upon whom a non-hereditary noble title was bestowed as a result of their military service to Ivan IV.*

Cossacks *Free groups and outlaw armies living on the steppes bordering Russia from the fourteenth century onward. Their numbers were increased by runaway peasants during the time of Ivan the Terrible.*

vast new territories to the realm and laying the foundations for the huge, multiethnic Russian empire. After the sudden death of his beloved wife Anastasia (of the Romanov family), Ivan jailed and executed any he suspected of opposing him. Many victims were from the leading boyar families, and their families, friends, servants, and peasants were also executed. Their large estates were broken up, with some of the land added to the tsar's domain and the rest given to the lower **service nobility,** a group of newly made nobles who served in the tsar's army.

Ivan also took strides toward making all commoners servants of the tsar. As a result, growing numbers fled toward wild, recently conquered territories to the east and south. There they joined the numbers of free peoples and outlaw armies known as **Cossacks.**

Simultaneously, urban traders and artisans were also bound to their towns and jobs so that the tsar could tax them more heavily. Even the wealthiest merchants had no security in their work or property. These restrictions checked the growth of the Russian middle classes and stood in sharp contrast to developments in western Europe.

Following Ivan's death, Russia entered a chaotic period known as the "Time of Troubles" (1598–1613). While Ivan's relatives struggled for power, the Cossacks and peasants rebelled against nobles and officials. This social explosion from below brought the nobility together. They crushed the Cossack rebellion and elected Ivan's sixteen-year-old grandnephew, Michael Romanov, the new hereditary tsar (r. 1613–1645).

Although the new tsar successfully reconsolidated central authority, social and religious uprisings continued.

Despite the turbulence of the period, the Romanov tsars made several important achievements during the second half of the seventeenth century. After a long war, Russia gained a large mass of Ukraine from weak and decentralized Poland in 1667 (see Map 16.4) and completed the conquest of Siberia by the end of the century. Territorial expansion was accompanied by growth of the bureaucracy and the army. The great profits from Siberia's natural resources, especially furs, funded the Romanov's bid for great power status.

The Reforms of Peter the Great

Heir to the first efforts at state-building, Peter the Great (r. 1682–1725) embarked on a tremendous campaign to accelerate and complete these processes. A giant for his time at six feet seven inches, and possessing enormous energy and willpower, Peter was determined to continue the tsarist tradition of territorial expansion. After 1689 Peter ruled independently for thirty-six years, only one of which was peaceful.

Fascinated by foreign technology, the tsar led a group of 250 Russian officials and young nobles on an eighteen-month tour of western Europe. Traveling unofficially to avoid diplomatic ceremonies, Peter worked with his hands at various crafts and met with foreign kings and experts. He was particularly impressed with the growing power of the Dutch and the English, and he considered how Russia could profit from their example.

Suffering initial defeat in war with Sweden in 1701, Peter responded with measures designed to increase state power, strengthen his armies, and gain victory. He required every nobleman to serve in the army or in the civil administration—for life. Since a more modern army and government required skilled technicians and experts, Peter created schools and universities to produce them. Peter established an interlocking military-civilian bureaucracy with fourteen ranks, and he decreed that all had to start at the bottom and work toward the top. Some people of non-noble origins rose to high positions in this embryonic meritocracy. Drawing on his experience abroad,

Primary Source:
Edicts and Decrees
Read a selection of Peter the Great's decrees, and find out how he wished to modernize—and westernize—Russia.

● **Peter the Great in 1723** This compelling portrait by Grigory Musikiysky captures the strength and determination of the warrior tsar after more than three decades of personal rule. In his hand Peter holds the scepter, symbol of royal sovereignty, and across his breastplate is draped an ermine fur, a mark of honor. In the background are the battleships of Russia's new Baltic fleet and the famous St. Peter and St. Paul Fortress that Peter built in St. Petersburg. *(The Bridgeman Art Library)*

Peter searched out talented foreigners and placed them in his service. These measures gradually combined to make the army and government more powerful and efficient.

Peter also greatly increased the service requirements of commoners. He established a regular standing army of more than two hundred thousand peasant-soldiers commanded by noble officers. Taxes on peasants increased threefold during Peter's reign. Serfs were arbitrarily assigned to work in the growing number of factories and mines that serviced the military.

Peter's new war machine was able to crush Sweden's small army in Ukraine at Poltava in 1709, one of the most significant battles in Russian history. Russia's victory was conclusive in 1721, and Estonia and present-day Latvia (see Map 16.4) came under Russian rule for the first time. The cost was high—warfare consumed 80 to 85 percent of all revenues. But Russia became the dominant power in the Baltic and very much a European Great Power.

After his victory at Poltava, Peter channeled enormous resources into building a new western-style capital on the Baltic to rival the great cities of Europe. Originally a desolate and swampy Swedish outpost, the magnificent city of St. Petersburg was designed to reflect modern urban planning with wide, straight avenues, buildings set in a uniform line, and large parks. Each summer, twenty-five to forty thousand peasants were sent to labor in St. Petersburg without pay.

There were other important consequences of Peter's reign. For Peter, modernization meant westernization, and both Westerners and Western ideas flowed into Russia for the first time. He required nobles to shave their heavy beards and wear Western clothing, previously banned in Russia. He required them to attend parties where young men and women would mix together and freely choose their own spouses. From these efforts a new class of Western-oriented Russians began to emerge.

. . . .

CONSTITUTIONALISM
How and why did the constitutional state triumph in Holland and England?

constitutionalism *A form of government in which power is limited by law and balanced between the authority and power of the government on the one hand, and the rights and liberties of the subject or citizen on the other hand.*

While France, Prussia, Russia, and Austria developed the absolutist state, England and Holland evolved toward **constitutionalism,** which is the limitation of government by law. Constitutionalism also implies a balance between the authority and power of the government, on the one hand, and the rights and liberties of the subjects, on the other.

A nation's constitution may be written or unwritten. It may be embodied in one basic document, occasionally revised by amendment, like the Constitution of the United States. Or it may be only partly formalized and include parliamentary statutes, judicial decisions, and a body of traditional procedures and practices, like the English and Dutch constitutions. Whether written or unwritten, a constitution gets its binding force from the government's acknowledgment that it must respect that constitution—that is, that the state must govern according to the laws.

Absolutist Claims in England (1603–1649)

In 1588 Queen Elizabeth I of England exercised very great personal power. A rare female monarch, Elizabeth was able to maintain control over her realm in part by refusing to marry and submit to a husband. She was immensely popular with her people, but left no immediate heir to continue her legacy.

In 1603 Elizabeth's Scottish cousin James Stuart succeeded her as James I (r. 1603–1625). King James was well educated and had thirty-five years' experience as king of Scotland. But he was not as interested in displaying the majesty of monarchy as Elizabeth had been. Urged to wave at the crowds who waited to greet their new ruler, James complained that he was tired and threatened to drop his breeches "so they can cheer at my arse."[8]

James's greatest problem, however, stemmed from his belief that a monarch has a divine (or God-given) right to his authority and is responsible only to God. James went so far as to lecture the House of Commons: "There are no privileges and immunities which can stand against a divinely appointed King." Such a view ran directly counter to the long-standing English idea that a person's property could not be taken away without due process of law. James I and his son Charles I considered such constraints intolerable and a threat to their divine-right prerogative. Consequently, at every Parliament between 1603 and 1640, bitter squabbles erupted between the Crown and the articulate and legally minded Commons. Charles I's attempt to govern without Parliament (1629–1640) and to finance his government by arbitrary nonparliamentary levies brought the country to a crisis.

Religious Divides

Religious issues also embittered relations between the king and the House of Commons. In the early seventeenth century increasing numbers of English people felt dissatisfied with the Church of England established by Henry VIII and reformed by Elizabeth. Many **Puritans** believed that the Reformation had not gone far enough. They wanted to "purify" the Anglican Church of Roman Catholic elements—elaborate vestments and ceremonials, bishops, and even the giving and wearing of wedding rings.

James I responded to such ideas by declaring, "No bishop, no king." For James, bishops were among the chief supporters of the throne. His son and successor, Charles I, further antagonized religious sentiments. Not only did he marry a Catholic princess, but he also supported the heavy-handed policies of the Archbishop of Canterbury William Laud (1573–1645). In 1637 Laud attempted to impose two new elements on church organization in Scotland: a new prayer book, modeled on the Anglican *Book of Common Prayer,* and bishoprics, which the Presbyterian Scots firmly rejected. The Scots therefore revolted. To finance an army to put down the Scots, King Charles was compelled to summon Parliament in November 1640.

Charles had ruled from 1629 to 1640 without Parliament, financing his government through extraordinary stopgap levies considered illegal by most English people. For example, the king revived a medieval law requiring coastal districts to help pay the cost of ships for defense, but he levied the tax, called "ship money," on inland as well as coastal counties. Most members of Parliament believed that such taxation without consent amounted to despotism. Consequently, they were not willing to trust the king with an army. Moreover, many supported the Scots' resistance to Charles's religious innovations and had little wish for military action against them. Accordingly, this Parliament, called the "Long Parliament" because it sat from 1640

Puritans *Members of a sixteenth- and seventeenth-century reform movement within the Church of England that advocated "purifying" it of Roman Catholic elements, such as bishops, elaborate ceremonials, and the wedding ring.*

● **Puritan Occupations**   These twelve engravings depict typical Puritan occupations and show that the Puritans came primarily from the artisan and lower middle classes. The governing classes and peasants adhered to the traditions of the Church of England. *(Visual Connection Archive)*

to 1660, enacted legislation that limited the power of the monarch and made arbitrary government impossible.

In 1641 the Commons passed the Triennial Act, which compelled the king to summon Parliament every three years. The Commons impeached Archbishop Laud and then went further and threatened to abolish bishops. King Charles, fearful of a Scottish invasion—the original reason for summoning Parliament— reluctantly accepted these measures.

The next act in the conflict was precipitated by the outbreak of rebellion in Ireland, where English governors and landlords had long exploited the people. In 1641 the Catholic gentry of Ireland led an uprising in response to a feared invasion by anti-Catholic forces of the British Long Parliament.

Without an army, Charles I could neither come to terms with the Scots nor respond to the Irish rebellion. After a failed attempt to arrest parliamentary leaders, Charles left London for the north of England. There, he recruited an army drawn from the nobility and its cavalry staff, the rural gentry, and mercenaries. The parliamentary army was composed of the militia of the city of London and country squires with business connections.

New Model Army *The parliamentary army, under the command of Oliver Cromwell, that fought the army of Charles I in the English civil war.*

The English civil war (1642–1649) pitted the power of the king against that of the Parliament. After three years of fighting, Parliament's **New Model Army** defeated the king's armies at the battles of Naseby and Langport in the summer of 1645. Charles, though, refused to concede defeat. Both sides jockeyed for position, waiting for a decisive event. This arrived in the form of the army under the leadership of Oliver Cromwell, a member of the House of Commons and a devout Puritan. In 1647 Cromwell's forces captured the king and dismissed members of the Parliament who opposed his actions. In 1649 the remaining representatives, known as the "Rump Parliament," put Charles on trial for high treason. Charles was found guilty and beheaded on January 30, 1649, an act that sent shock waves around Europe.

Puritanical Absolutism in England: Cromwell and the Protectorate

With the execution of Charles, kingship was abolished. A *commonwealth,* or republican government, was proclaimed. Theoretically, legislative power rested in the surviving members of Parliament, and executive power was lodged in a council of state. In fact, the army that had defeated the king controlled the government, and Oliver Cromwell controlled the army. Though called the **Protectorate,** the rule of Cromwell (1653–1658) constituted military dictatorship.

Protectorate *The military dictatorship established by Oliver Cromwell following the execution of Charles I.*

The army prepared a constitution, the Instrument of Government (1653), that invested executive power in a lord protector (Cromwell) and a council of state. The instrument provided for triennial parliaments and gave Parliament the sole power to raise taxes. But after repeated disputes, Cromwell dismissed Parliament in 1655, and the instrument was never formally endorsed. Cromwell continued the standing army and proclaimed quasi-martial law. He divided England into twelve military districts, each governed by a major general. Reflecting Puritan ideas of morality, Cromwell's state forbade sports, kept the theaters closed, and rigorously censored the press.

On the issue of religion, Cromwell favored some degree of toleration, and the Instrument of Government gave all Christians except Roman Catholics the right to practice their faith. Cromwell had long associated Catholicism in Ireland with sedition and heresy. In September of the year that his army came to power, it crushed a rebellion at Drogheda and massacred the garrison. After Cromwell's departure for England, atrocities worsened. The English banned Catholicism in Ireland, executed priests, and confiscated land from Catholics for English and Scottish settlers. These brutal acts left a legacy of Irish hatred for England.

THE ROYALL   OAKE   OF BRITTAYNE

● **Cartoon of 1649: "The Royall Oake of Brittayne"**   Chopping down this tree signifies the end of royal authority, stability, the Magna Carta, and the rule of law. As pigs graze (representing the unconcerned common people) being fattened for slaughter, Oliver Cromwell, with his feet in Hell, quotes Scripture. This is a royalist view of the collapse of Charles I's government and the rule of Cromwell. *(Courtesy of the Trustees of the British Museum)*

Cromwell adopted mercantilist policies similar to those of absolutist France. He enforced a Navigation Act (1651) requiring that English goods be transported on English ships. The navigation act was a great boost to the development of an English merchant marine and brought about a short but successful war with the commercially threatened Dutch. Cromwell also welcomed the immigration of Jews because of their skills, and they began to return to England after four centuries of absence.

The Protectorate collapsed when Cromwell died in 1658 and his ineffectual son succeeded him. Fed up with military rule, the English longed for a return to civilian government and, with it, common law and social stability. By 1660 they were ready to restore the monarchy.

The Restoration of the English Monarchy

The Restoration of 1660 brought to the throne Charles II (r. 1660–1685), eldest son of Charles I, who had been living on the Continent. Both houses of Parliament were also restored, together with the established Anglican church. The Restoration failed to resolve two serious problems, however. What was to be the attitude of the state toward Puritans, Catholics, and dissenters from the established church? And what was to be the relationship between the king and Parliament?

To answer the first question, Parliament enacted the **Test Act** of 1673 against those outside the Church of England, denying them the right to vote, hold public office, preach, teach, attend the universities, or even assemble for meetings. But these restrictions could not be enforced. When the Quaker William Penn held a meeting of his Friends and was arrested, the jury refused to convict him.

Test Act   *Legislation, passed by the English parliament in 1673 designed to secure the position of the Anglican Church. It sought to suppress the influence of Puritans, Catholics, and other dissenters by denying them the right to vote, preach, assemble, hold public office, and attend or teach at the universities.*

In politics Charles II was determined "not to set out in his travels again," which meant that he intended to avoid exile by working well with Parliament. This intention did not last, however. Finding that Parliament did not grant him an adequate income, Charles entered into a secret agreement with his cousin Louis XIV. The French king would give Charles two hundred thousand pounds annually, and in return Charles would relax the laws against Catholics, gradually re-Catholicize England, and convert to Catholicism himself. When the details of this treaty leaked out, a great wave of anti-Catholic sentiment swept England.

When James II (r. 1685–1688) succeeded his brother, the worst English anti-Catholic fears were realized. In violation of the Test Act, James appointed Roman Catholics to positions in the army, the universities, and local government. When these actions were challenged in the courts, the judges, whom James had appointed, decided for the king. The king was suspending the law at will and appeared to be reviving the absolutism of his father and grandfather. He went further. Attempting to broaden his base of support with Protestant dissenters and nonconformists, James issued a declaration of indulgence granting religious freedom to all.

Seeking to prevent the return of Catholic absolutism, a group of eminent persons offered the English throne to James's Protestant daughter Mary and her Dutch husband, Prince William of Orange. In December 1688 James II, his queen, and their infant son fled to France and became pensioners of Louis XIV. Early in 1689 William and Mary were crowned king and queen of England.

The Triumph of England's Parliament: Constitutional Monarchy and Cabinet Government

The English call the events of 1688 and 1689 the "Glorious Revolution" because it replaced one king with another with a minimum of bloodshed. It also represented the destruction, once and for all, of the idea of divine-right monarchy. William and Mary accepted the English throne from Parliament and in so doing explicitly recognized the supremacy of Parliament. The revolution of 1688 established the principle that sovereignty, the ultimate power in the state, was divided between king and Parliament and that the king ruled with the consent of the governed.

The men who brought about the revolution framed their intentions in the Bill of Rights, which was formulated in direct response to Stuart absolutism. Law was to be made in Parliament; once made, it could not be suspended by the Crown. Parliament had to be called at least once every three years. The independence of the judiciary was established, and there was to be no standing army in peacetime. Protestants could possess arms but the Catholic minority could not. Additional legislation granted freedom of worship to Protestant dissenters and required that the English monarch always be Protestant.

Second Treatise of Civil Government *A work of political philosophy published by John Locke in 1690 that argued government's only purpose was to defend the natural rights of life, liberty, and property.*

The Glorious Revolution and the concept of representative government found its best defense in political philosopher John Locke's *Second Treatise of Civil Government* (1690). Locke (1632–1704) maintained that a government that oversteps its proper function—protecting the natural rights of life, liberty, and property—becomes a tyranny. By "natural" rights Locke meant rights basic to all men because all have the ability to reason. (His idea that there are natural or universal rights equally valid for all peoples and societies was especially popular in colonial America.) Under a tyrannical government, the people have the natural right to rebellion. On the basis of this link, he justified limiting the vote to property owners. (American colonists also appreciated his arguments that Native Americans had no property rights since they did not cultivate the land and, by extension, no political rights because they possessed no property.)

The events of 1688 and 1689 did not constitute a democratic revolution. The revolution placed sovereignty in Parliament, and Parliament represented the upper classes.

● **Jan Steen: The Christening Feast** As the mother, surrounded by midwives, rests in bed (*rear left*) and the father proudly displays the swaddled child, thirteen other people, united by gestures and gazes, prepare the celebratory meal. Very prolific, Steen was a master of warm-hearted domestic scenes. In contrast to the order and cleanliness of many seventeenth-century Dutch genre paintings, Steen's more disorderly portrayals gave rise to the epithet "a Jan Steen household," meaning an untidy house. *(Wallace Collection, London/The Bridgeman Art Library)*

The age of aristocratic government lasted at least until 1832 and in many ways until 1928, when women received full voting rights.

The Dutch Republic in the Seventeenth Century

In the late sixteenth century the seven northern provinces of the Netherlands fought for and won their independence from Spain. The independence of the Republic of the United Provinces of the Netherlands was recognized in 1648 in the treaty that ended the Thirty Years' War. In this period, often called the "golden age of the Netherlands," Dutch ideas and attitudes played a profound role in shaping a new and modern worldview. At the same time, the United Provinces was another model of the development of the modern constitutional state.

The government of the United Provinces had none of the standard categories of seventeenth-century political organization. The Dutch were not monarchical but rather fiercely republican. Within each province, an oligarchy of wealthy businessmen called "regents" handled domestic affairs in the local Estates (assemblies). The

States General *The name of the national assembly of the United Provinces of the Netherlands, where the wealthy merchant class held real power; because many issues had to be referred back to the provinces, the United Provinces was a confederation, or weak union of strong states.*

stadholder *The executive officer in each of the United Provinces of the Netherlands; in practice, this position was dominated by the Prince of Orange.*

provincial Estates held virtually all the power. A federal assembly, or **States General,** handled matters of foreign affairs, such as war. But the States General did not possess sovereign authority; all issues had to be referred back to the local Estates for approval. In each province, the estates appointed an executive officer, known as the **stadholder,** who carried out ceremonial functions and was responsible for military defense. Although in theory freely chosen by the Estates and answerable to them, in practice the Princes of Orange were almost always chosen as stadholders. Tensions persisted between supporters of the staunchly republican estates and those of the aristocratic House of Orange. Holland, which had the largest navy and the most wealth, dominated the seven provinces of the republic and the States General.

The political success of the Dutch rested on the phenomenal commercial prosperity of the Netherlands. The moral and ethical bases of that commercial wealth were thrift, frugality, and religious toleration. Although there is scattered evidence of anti-Semitism, Jews enjoyed a level of acceptance and assimilation in Dutch business and general culture unique in early modern Europe. (See the feature "Individuals in Society: Glückel of Hameln.") In the Dutch Republic, toleration paid off: it attracted a great deal of foreign capital and investment.

The Dutch came to dominate the shipping business by putting profits from their original industry—herring fishing—into shipbuilding (see Map 16.5). They boasted the lowest shipping rates and largest merchant marine in Europe, allowing them to undersell foreign competitors. Trade and commerce brought the Dutch the highest standard of living in Europe, perhaps in the world. Salaries were high, and all classes of society ate well. A scholar has described the Netherlands as "an island of plenty in a sea of want." Consequently, the Netherlands experienced very few of the food riots that characterized the rest of Europe.[9]

MAP 16.5 **Seventeenth-Century Dutch Commerce** Dutch wealth rested on commerce, and commerce depended on the huge Dutch merchant marine, manned by perhaps forty-eight thousand sailors. The fleet carried goods from all parts of the globe to the port of Amsterdam.

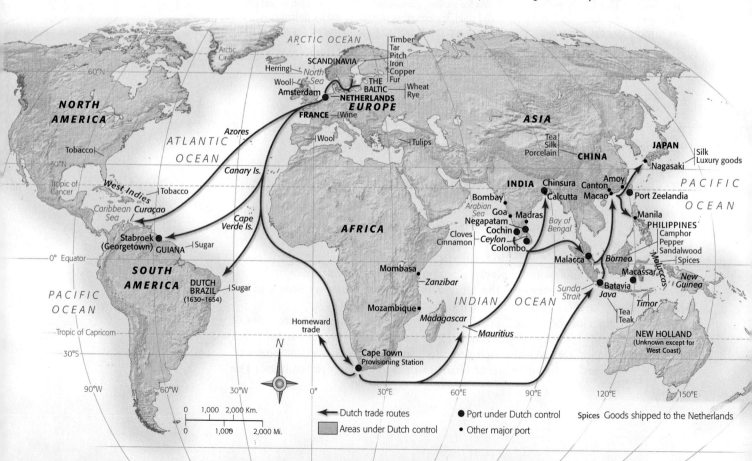

Glückel of Hameln

In 1690 a Jewish widow in the small German town of Hameln* in Lower Saxony sat down to write her autobiography. She wanted to distract her mind from the terrible grief she felt over the death of her husband and to provide her twelve children with a record "so you will know from what sort of people you have sprung, lest today or tomorrow your beloved children or grandchildren came and know naught of their family." Out of her pain and heightened consciousness, Glückel (1646–1724) produced an invaluable source for scholars.

She was born in Hamburg two years before the end of the Thirty Years' War. In 1649 the merchants of Hamburg expelled the Jews, who moved to nearby Altona, then under Danish rule. When the Swedes overran Altona in 1657–1658, the Jews returned to Hamburg "purely at the mercy of the Town Council." Glückel's narrative proceeds against a background of the constant harassment to which Jews were subjected—special papers, permits, bribes—and in Hameln she wrote, "And so it has been to this day and, I fear, will continue in like fashion."

When Glückel was "barely twelve," her father betrothed her to Chayim Hameln. She married at age fourteen. She describes him as "the perfect pattern of the pious Jew," a man who stopped his work every day for study and prayer, fasted, and was scrupulously honest in his business dealings. Only a few years older than Glückel, Chayim earned his living dealing in precious metals and in making small loans on pledges (articles held on security). This work required his constant travel to larger cities, markets, and fairs, often in bad weather, always over dangerous roads. Chayim consulted his wife about all his business dealings. As he lay dying, a friend asked if he had any last wishes. "None," he replied. "My wife knows everything. She shall do as she has always done." For thirty years Glückel had been his friend, full business partner, and wife. They had thirteen children, twelve of whom survived their father, eight then unmarried. As Chayim had foretold, Glückel succeeded in launching the boys in careers and in providing dowries for the girls.

Glückel's world was her family, the Jewish community of Hameln, and the Jewish communities

Gentleness and deep mutual devotion seem to pervade Rembrandt's *The Jewish Bride*. (Rijksmuseum-Stichting Amsterdam)

into which her children married. Social and business activities took her to Amsterdam, Baiersdorf, Bamberg, Berlin, Cleves, Danzig, Metz, and Vienna, so her world was not narrow or provincial. She took great pride that Prince Frederick of Cleves, later king of Prussia, danced at the wedding of her eldest daughter. The rising prosperity of Chayim's businesses allowed the couple to maintain up to six servants.

Glückel was deeply religious, and her culture was steeped in Jewish literature, legends, and mystical and secular works. Above all, she relied on the Bible. Her language, heavily sprinkled with scriptural references, testifies to a rare familiarity with the basic book of Western civilization. The Scriptures were her consolation, the source of her great strength in a hostile world.

Students who would learn about business practices, the importance of the dowry in marriage, childbirth, the ceremony of bris, birthrates, family celebrations, and even the meaning of life can gain a good deal from the memoirs of this extraordinary woman who was, in the words of one of her descendants, the poet Heinrich Heine, "the gift of a world to me."

Questions for Analysis

1. Consider the ways in which Glückel of Hameln was both an ordinary and an extraordinary woman of her times. Would you call her a marginal or a central person in her society?

2. How was Glückel's life affected by the broad events and issues of the seventeenth century?

Source: The Memoirs of Glückel of Hameln (New York: Schocken Books, 1977).

*A town immortalized by the Brothers Grimm. In 1284 the town contracted with the Pied Piper to rid it of rats and mice; he lured them away by playing his flute. When the citizens refused to pay, he charmed away their children in revenge.

Chapter Summary

To assess your mastery of this chapter, go to
bedfordstmartins.com/mckayworld

Key Terms

moral economy
Protestant Union
Peace of Westphalia
sovereignty
intendants
Fronde
divine right of kings
mercantilism
Peace of Utrecht
Bohemian Estates
elector of Brandenburg
Junkers
Mongol Yoke
boyars
tsar
service nobility
Cossacks
constitutionalism
Puritans
New Model Army
Protectorate
Test Act
*Second Treatise of Civil
  Government*
States General
stadholder

• What were the common crises and achievements of seventeenth-century European states?

Most parts of Europe experienced the seventeenth century as a period of severe economic, social, and military crisis. Across the continent, rulers faced popular rebellions from their desperate subjects, who were pushed to the brink by poor harvests, high taxes, and decades of war. Many forces, including powerful noblemen, the church, and regional and local loyalties, constrained the state's authority. Despite these obstacles, most European states emerged from the seventeenth century with increased powers and more centralized control. Whether they ruled through monarchical fiat or parliamentary negotiation, European governments strengthened their bureaucracies, raised more taxes, and significantly expanded their armies.

• How and why did Louis XIV of France lead the way in forging the absolute state, and why did Spain experience decline in the same period?

Under Louis XIV France witnessed the high point of monarchical ambitions in western Europe. The king saw himself as the representative of God on earth, and it has been said that "to the seventeenth century imagination God was a sort of image of Louis XIV."[10] Under Louis's rule, France developed a centralized bureaucracy, a professional army, and a state-directed economy, all of which he personally supervised. Historians now agree that, despite his claims to absolute power, Louis XIV ruled, in practice, by securing the collaboration of high nobles. In exchange for confirmation of their ancient privileges, the nobles were willing to cooperate with the expansion of state power. In Spain, where monarchs made similar claims to absolute power, the seventeenth century witnessed economic catastrophe and a decline in royal capacities.

• How did Austrian, Prussian, and Russian rulers in eastern Europe build absolute monarchies—monarchies that proved even more durable than that of Louis XIV?

Within a framework of resurgent serfdom and entrenched nobility, Austrian and Prussian monarchs also fashioned absolutist states in the seventeenth and early eighteenth centuries. These monarchs won absolutist control over standing armies, permanent taxes, and legislative bodies. But they did not question the underlying social and economic relationships. Indeed, they enhanced the privileges of the nobility, which furnished the leading servitors for enlarged armies and growing government bureaucracies. In Russia social and economic trends were similar to those in Austria and Prussia. Unlike those two states, however, Russia had a long history of powerful princes. Tsar Peter the Great succeeded in tightening up Russia's traditional absolutism and modernizing it by reforming the army, the bureaucracy, and the defense industry. In Russia and throughout eastern Europe war and the needs of the state in times of war weighed heavily in the triumph of absolutism.

• How and why did the constitutional state triumph in Holland and England?

Holland and England defied the general trend toward absolute monarchy. While Holland prospered under a unique republican confederation of separate provinces, England—fortunately shielded from continental armies and military emergencies by its navy and the English Channel—evolved into the first modern constitutional state. After 1688, power was divided between king and Parliament, with Parliament enjoying the greater share. The Bill of Rights marked an important milestone in world history, although the framers left to later generations the task of making constitutional government work.

Suggested Reading

Benedict, Philip, and Myron P. Gutmann, eds. *Early Modern Europe: From Crisis to Stability.* 2005. A helpful introduction to the many facets of the seventeenth-century crisis.

Burke, Peter. *The Fabrication of Louis XIV.* 1992. Explains the use of architecture, art, medals, and other symbols to promote the king's image.

Collins, James B. *The State in Early Modern France.* 1995. A detailed and well-argued survey of French administration from Louis XIII to Louis XVI.

Elliott, John H. *Richelieu and Olivares.* 1984. A comparison of the chief ministers of France and Spain that also reveals differences and similarities in the countries they led.

Gaunt, Peter, ed. *The English Civil War: The Essential Readings.* 2000. A collection showcasing leading historians' interpretations of the civil war.

Hagen, William W. *Ordinary Prussians: Brandenburg Junkers and Villagers, 1500–1840.* 2002. Provides a fascinating encounter with the people of a Prussian estate.

Hughes, Lindsey, ed. *Peter the Great and the West: New Perspectives.* 2001. Essays by leading scholars on the reign of Peter the Great and his opening of Russia to the West.

Ingrao, Charles W. *The Habsburg Monarchy, 1618–1815,* 2d ed. 2000. An excellent synthesis of the political and social development of the Habsburg empire in the early modern period.

Lincoln, W. Bruce. *Sunlight at Midnight: St. Petersburg and the Rise of Modern Russia.* 2001. Captures the spirit of Peter the Great's new northern capital.

McKay, Derek. *The Great Elector: Frederick William of Brandenburg-Prussia.* 2001. Examines the formative years of Prussian power.

Parker, Geoffrey. *The Thirty Years War,* 2d ed. 1997. The standard account of the Thirty Years' War.

Schama, Simon. *The Embarrassment of Riches: An Interpretation of Dutch Culture in the Golden Age.* 1987. A lengthy but vivid and highly readable account of Dutch culture in the seventeenth century, including a chapter on the mania for speculation on the tulip market.

Notes

1. The classic study Theodore K. Rabb, *The Struggle for Stability in Early Modern Europe* (Oxford: Oxford University Press, 1975).

2. H. Kamen, "The Economic and Social Consequences of the Thirty Years' War," *Past and Present* 39 (April 1968): 44–61.

3. Quoted in J. Wolf, *Louis XIV* (New York: W. W. Norton, 1968), p. 146.

4. John A. Lynn, "Recalculating French Army Growth," in *The Military Revolution Debate: Readings on the Military Transformation of Early Modern Europe,* ed. Clifford J. Rogers (Boulder, Colo.: Westview Press, 1995), p. 125.

5. J. H. Elliott, *Imperial Spain, 1469–1716* (New York: Mentor Books, 1963), pp. 306–308.

6. Ibid., p. 43.

7. Quoted in Hans Rosenberg, *Bureaucracy, Aristocracy, and Autocracy* (Cambridge, Mass.: Harvard University Press, 1958), p. 40.

8. For a revisionist interpretation, see J. Wormald, "James VI and I: Two Kings or One?" *History* 62 (June 1983): 187–209.

9. S. Schama, *The Embarrassment of Riches: An Interpretation of Dutch Culture in the Golden Age* (New York: Alfred A. Knopf, 1987), pp. 165–170; quotation is on p. 167.

10. C. J. Friedrich and C. Blitzer, *The Age of Power* (Ithaca, N.Y.: Cornell University Press, 1957), p. 112.

Listening to the PAST

The Court at Versailles

Although the Duc de Saint-Simon (1675–1755) was a soldier, courtier, and diplomat, his enduring reputation rests on The Memoirs (1788), his eyewitness account of the personality and court of Louis XIV. A nobleman of extremely high status, Saint-Simon resented Louis's high-handed treatment of the ancient nobility and his promotion of newer nobles and the bourgeoisie. The Memoirs, excerpted here, remains a monument of French literature and an indispensable historical source, partly for its portrait of the court at Versailles.

Very early in the reign of Louis XIV the Court was removed from Paris, never to return. The troubles of the minority had given him a dislike to that city; his enforced and surreptitious flight from it still rankled in his memory; he did not consider himself safe there, and thought cabals would be more easily detected if the Court was in the country, where the movements and temporary absences of any of its members would be more easily noticed. . . . No doubt that he was also influenced by the feeling that he would be regarded with greater awe and veneration when no longer exposed every day to the gaze of the multitude.

His love-affair with Mademoiselle de la Vallière, which at first was covered as far as possible with a veil of mystery, was the cause of frequent excursions to Versailles. . . . The visits of Louis XIV becoming more frequent, he enlarged the *château* by degrees till its immense buildings afforded better accommodation for the Court than was to be found at St. Germain, where most of the courtiers had to put up with uncomfortable lodgings in the town. The Court was therefore removed to Versailles in 1682, not long before the Queen's death. The new building contained an infinite number of rooms for courtiers, and the King liked the grant of these rooms to be regarded as a coveted privilege.

He availed himself of the frequent festivities at Versailles, and his excursions to other places, as a means of making the courtiers assiduous in their attendance and anxious to please him; for he nominated beforehand those who were to take part in them, and could

thus gratify some and inflict a snub on others. He was conscious that the substantial favours he had to bestow were not nearly sufficient to produce a continual effect; he had therefore to invent imaginary ones, and no one was so clever in devising petty distinctions and preferences which aroused jealousy and emulation. The visits to Marly later on were very useful to him in this way; also those to Trianon [Marly and Trianon were small country houses], where certain ladies, chosen beforehand, were admitted to his table. It was another distinction to hold his candlestick at his *coucher* [preparations for going to bed]; as soon as he had finished his prayers he used to name the courtier to whom it was to be handed, always choosing one of the highest rank among those present. . . .

Not only did he expect all persons of distinction to be in continual attendance at Court, but he was quick to notice the absence of those of inferior degree; at his *lever* [formal rising from bed in the morning], his *coucher*, his meals, in the gardens of Versailles (the only place where the courtiers in general were allowed to follow him), he used to cast his eyes to right and left; nothing escaped him, he saw everybody. If any one habitually living at Court absented himself he insisted on knowing the reason; those who came there only for flying visits had also to give a satisfactory explanation; any one who seldom or never appeared there was certain to incur his displeasure. If asked to bestow a favour on such persons he would reply haughtily: "I do not know him"; of such as rarely presented themselves he would say, "He is a man I never see"; and from these judgements there was no appeal.

He always took great pains to find out what was going on in public places, in society, in private houses, even family secrets, and maintained an immense number of spies and tale-bearers. These were of all sorts; some did not know that their reports were carried to him; others did know it; there were others, again, who used to write to him directly, through channels which he prescribed; others who were admitted by the backstairs and saw him in his private room. Many a man in all ranks of life was ruined by these methods, often very unjustly, without ever being able to discover the

Louis XIV was extremely proud of the gardens at Versailles and personally led ambassadors and other highly ranked visitors on tours of the extensive palace grounds. *(Erich Lessing/Art Resource, NY)*

reason; and when the King had once taken a prejudice against a man, he hardly ever got over it. . . .

No one understood better than Louis XIV the art of enhancing the value of a favour by his manner of bestowing it; he knew how to make the most of a word, a smile, even of a glance. If he addressed any one, were it but to ask a trifling question or make some commonplace remark, all eyes were turned on the person so honored; it was a mark of favour which always gave rise to comment. . . .

He loved splendour, magnificence, and profusion in all things, and encouraged similar tastes in his Court; to spend money freely on equipages [the king's horse carriages] and buildings, on feasting and at cards, was a sure way to gain his favour, perhaps to obtain the honour of a word from him. Motives of policy had something to do with this; by making expensive habits the fashion, and, for people in a certain position, a necessity, he compelled his courtiers to live beyond their income, and gradually reduced them to depend on his bounty for the means of subsistence. This was a plague which, once introduced, became a scourge to the whole country, for it did not take long to spread to Paris, and thence to the armies and the provinces; so that a man of any position is now estimated entirely according to his expenditure on his table and other luxuries. This folly, sustained by pride and ostentation, has already produced widespread confusion; it threatens to end in nothing short of ruin and a general overthrow.

Questions for Analysis

1. What was the role of etiquette and ceremony at the court of Versailles? How could Louis XIV use them in everyday life at court to influence and control nobles?

2. How important do you think Louis's individual character and personality were to his style of governing? What challenges might this present to his successors?

3. Do you think Saint-Simon is an objective and trustworthy recorder of life at court? Why?

Source: F. Arkwright, ed., *The Memoirs of the Duke de Saint Simon,* vol. 5 (New York: Brentano's, n.d.), pp. 271–274, 276–278.

Voltaire, the Renowned Enlightenment Thinker, leans forward on the left to exchange ideas and witty conversation with Frederick the Great, king of Prussia.
(Bildarchiv Preussischer Kulturbesitz/Art Resource, NY)

chapter

17 TOWARD A NEW WORLDVIEW IN THE WEST, 1540–1789

Chapter Preview

The Scientific Revolution
• *What was revolutionary in new attitudes toward the natural world?*

The Enlightenment
• *How did the new worldview affect the way people thought about society and human relations?*

The Enlightenment and Absolutism
• *What impact did this new way of thinking have on political developments and monarchical absolutism?*

The intellectual developments of the seventeenth and eighteenth centuries created the modern worldview that the West continues to hold—and debate—to this day. In the seventeenth century fundamentally new ways of understanding the natural world emerged. In the nineteenth century scholars hailed these achievements as a "scientific revolution" that produced modern science as we know it. The new science created in the seventeenth century entailed the search for precise knowledge of the physical world based on the union of experimental observations with sophisticated mathematics.

In the eighteenth century philosophers extended the use of reason from nature to human society. They sought to bring the light of reason to bear on the darkness of prejudice, outmoded traditions, and ignorance. Self-proclaimed members of an "Enlightenment" movement, they wished to bring the same progress to human affairs as their predecessors had brought to the understanding of the natural world. While the scientific revolution ushered in modern science, the Enlightenment created concepts of human rights, equality, progress, universalism, and tolerance that still guide Western societies today.

While many view the scientific revolution and the Enlightenment as bedrocks of the achievement of Western civilization, others have seen a darker side. For these critics, the mastery over nature permitted by the scientific revolution threatens to overwhelm the earth's fragile equilibrium, and the belief in the universal application of "reason" can lead to arrogance and intolerance, particularly intolerance of other people's spiritual values. Such vivid debates about the legacy of these intellectual and cultural developments testifies to their continuing importance in today's world.

THE SCIENTIFIC REVOLUTION

What was revolutionary in new attitudes toward the natural world?

The emergence of modern science was a development of tremendous long-term significance. A noted historian has said that the scientific revolution was "the real origin both of the modern world and the modern mentality."[1] With the scientific revolution Western society began to acquire its most distinctive traits.

Scientific Thought in 1500

Since developments in astronomy and physics were at the heart of the scientific revolution, one must begin with the traditional European conception of the universe. The practitioners of the scientific revolution did not consider their field *science* but rather **natural philosophy,** and their intention was philosophical: to ask fundamental questions about the nature of the universe, its purpose, and how it functioned. In the early 1500s natural philosophy was still based primarily on the ideas of Aristotle, the great Greek philosopher of the fourth century B.C.E. Medieval theologians such as Thomas Aquinas brought Aristotelian philosophy into harmony with Christian doctrines. According to the revised Aristotelian view, a motionless earth was fixed at the center of the universe. Around it moved ten separate transparent crystal spheres. In the first eight spheres were embedded, in turn, the moon, the sun, the five known planets, and the stars. Then followed two spheres added during the Middle Ages to account for slight changes in the positions of the stars over the centuries. Beyond the tenth sphere was Heaven, with the throne of God and the souls of the saved. Angels kept the spheres moving in perfect circles. Human beings were at the center of the universe, forming the critical link in a "great chain of being" that stretched from the throne of God to the most lowly insect on earth.

Aristotle's views also dominated thinking about physics and motion on earth. Aristotle had distinguished sharply between the celestial spheres and the earth. The celestial spheres consisted of a perfect, incorruptible "quintessence," or fifth essence. The earth was composed of four imperfect, changeable elements. The "light" elements (air and fire) naturally moved upward, while the "heavy" elements (water and earth) naturally moved downward. These natural directions of motion did not always prevail, however, for elements were often mixed together and could be affected by an outside force such as a human being. Aristotle and his followers also believed that a uniform force moved an object at a constant speed and that the object would stop as soon as that force was removed.

natural philosophy *An early modern term for the study of the nature of the universe, its purpose and how it functioned; it encompassed what today we would call science.*

● **The Aristotelian Universe as Imagined in the Sixteenth Century** A round earth is at the center, surrounded by spheres of water, air, and fire. Beyond this small nucleus, the moon, the sun, and the five planets were embedded in their own rotating crystal spheres, with the stars sharing the surface of one enormous sphere. Beyond, the heavens were composed of unchanging ether. *(Image Select/Art Resource, NY)*

The Copernican Hypothesis

The first great departure from the medieval system came from Nicolaus Copernicus (1473–1543). As a young man Copernicus studied church law and astronomy in various European universities. He saw how professional astronomers still depended for their calculations on the second century B.C.E. work of Ptolemy. Copernicus felt that Ptolemy's cumbersome and occasionally inaccurate rules detracted from the majesty of a perfect Creator. He preferred an old Greek idea being discussed in Renaissance Italy: that the sun, rather than the earth, was at the center of the universe. Finishing his studies and returning to a church position in East Prussia, Copernicus worked on his hypothesis from 1506 to 1530. Never questioning the Aristotelian belief in crystal spheres or the idea that circular motion was most perfect and divine, Copernicus theorized that the stars and planets, including the earth, revolved around a fixed sun. Yet fearing ridicule, Copernicus did not publish his *On the Revolutions of the Heavenly Spheres* until 1543, the year of his death.

The **Copernican hypothesis** brought sharp attacks from religious leaders, especially Protestants, who objected to the idea that the earth moved but the sun did not. Martin Luther noted that the theory was counter to the Bible: "as the Holy Scripture tells us, so did Joshua bid the sun stand still and not the earth."[2] John Calvin also condemned Copernicus. Catholic reaction was milder at first. The Catholic Church had never held to literal interpretations of the Bible and did not declare the Copernican hypothesis false until 1616.

This slow reaction also reflected the slow progress of Copernicus's theory. Other events were almost as influential in creating doubts about traditional astronomy. In 1572 a new star appeared and shone very brightly for almost two years. The new star, which was actually a distant exploding star, made an enormous impression. It seemed to contradict the idea that the heavenly spheres were unchanging and therefore perfect. In 1577 a new comet suddenly moved through the sky, cutting a straight path across the supposedly impenetrable crystal spheres. It was time, as a typical scientific writer put it, for "the radical renovation of astronomy."[3]

Chronology

ca. 1540–1690	Scientific revolution
1543	Copernicus, *On the Revolutions of the Heavenly Spheres*
1564–1642	Life of Galileo
1571–1630	Life of Kepler
1662	Royal Society of London founded
1687	Newton, *Principia* and law of universal gravitation
1690	Locke, *Essay Concerning Human Understanding*
ca. 1690–1780	Enlightenment
1694–1778	Life of Voltaire
1700–1789	Growth of book publishing
1720–1780	Rococo style in art and decoration
1740–1786	Reign of Frederick the Great of Prussia
ca. 1750–1790	Enlightened absolutists
1751–1765	Diderot and d'Alembert, *Encyclopedia*
1762	Rousseau, *The Social Contract*
1762–1796	Reign of Catherine the Great of Russia
1780–1790	Reign of Joseph II of Austria

From Brahe to Galileo

One astronomer who agreed was Tycho Brahe (1546–1601). Born into a Danish noble family, Brahe was an imposing man who had lost a piece of his nose in a duel and replaced it with a special bridge of gold and silver alloy. He established himself as Europe's leading astronomer with his detailed observations of the new star of 1572. For twenty years he meticulously observed the stars and planets with the naked eye in the most sophisticated observatory of his day. His limited understanding of mathematics prevented him, however, from making much sense out of his mass of data. Part Ptolemaic, part Copernican, he believed that all the planets except earth revolved around the sun and that the entire group of sun and planets revolved in turn around the earth-moon system.

It was left to Brahe's assistant, Johannes Kepler (1571–1630), to rework Brahe's observations. A brilliant mathematician, Kepler eventually moved beyond his belief that the universe was built on mystical mathematical relationships and a musical harmony of the heavenly bodies.

Copernican hypothesis *The idea that the sun, not the earth, was the center of the universe; this had tremendous scientific and religious implications.*

Primary Source:
Letter to the Grand Duchess Christina
Read Galileo's passionate defense of his scientific research against those who would condemn it as un-Christian.

experimental method *The approach, first developed by Galileo, that the proper way to explore the workings of the universe was through repeatable experiments rather than speculation.*

law of inertia *A law formulated by Galileo that stated that rest was not the natural state of an object. Rather, an object continues in motion forever unless stopped by some external force.*

Kepler formulated three famous laws of planetary motion. First, building on Copernican theory, he demonstrated in 1609 that the orbits of the planets around the sun are elliptical rather than circular. Second, he demonstrated that planets do not move at a uniform speed in their orbits. Third, in 1619 he showed that the time a planet takes to make its complete orbit is precisely related to its distance from the sun. Kepler's contribution was monumental. Whereas Copernicus had speculated, Kepler proved mathematically the precise relations of a sun-centered (solar) system. His work demolished the old system of Aristotle and Ptolemy, and in his third law he came close to formulating the idea of universal gravitation.

While Kepler was unraveling planetary motion, a young Florentine named Galileo Galilei (1564–1642) was challenging the old ideas about motion. Like Kepler and so many early scientists, Galileo was a poor nobleman first marked for a religious career. Instead his fascination with mathematics led to a professorship in which he examined motion and mechanics in a new way. His great achievement was the elaboration of the **experimental method.** That is, rather than speculate about what might or should happen, Galileo conducted controlled experiments to find out what actually *did* happen.

In some of these experiments Galileo measured the movement of a rolling ball across a surface that he constructed, repeating the action again and again to verify his results. In his famous acceleration experiment, he showed that a uniform force—in this case, gravity—produced a uniform acceleration. Through another experiment, he formulated the **law of inertia.** Rest was not the natural state of objects. Rather, an object continues in motion forever unless stopped by some external force. Aristotelian physics was in shambles. In the tradition of Brahe, Galileo also applied the experimental method to astronomy. On hearing details about the invention of the telescope in Holland, Galileo made one for himself. He wrote in 1610 in *Siderus Nuncius*:

By the aid of a telescope anyone may behold [the Milky Way] in a manner which so distinctly appeals to the senses that all the disputes which have tormented philosophers through so many ages are exploded by the irrefutable evidence of our eyes, and we are freed from wordy disputes upon the subject. For the galaxy is nothing else but a mass of innumerable stars planted together in clusters.[4]

Reading these famous lines, one feels a crucial corner in Western civilization being turned. No longer should one rely on established authority. A new method of learning and investigating was being developed, one that proved capable of great extension. A historian investigating documents of the past, for example, is not so different from a Galileo studying stars and rolling balls.

Galileo was employed in Florence by the Medici grand dukes of Tuscany, and his work eventually angered some theologians. In 1624 Pope Urban

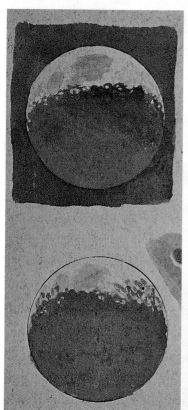
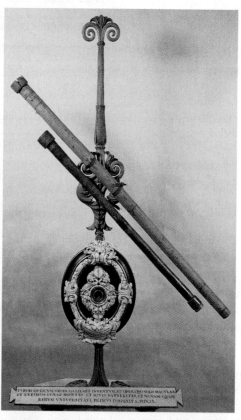

● **Galileo's Paintings of the Moon** When Galileo published the results of his telescopic observations of the moon, he added these paintings to illustrate the marvels he had seen. Galileo made two telescopes, which are shown here. The larger one magnifies fourteen times, the smaller one twenty times. (*Biblioteca Nazionale Centrale, Florence/Art Resource, NY; Museum of Science, Florence/Art Resource, NY*)

VIII ruled that Galileo could write about different possible systems of the world as long as he did not presume to judge which one actually existed. After the publication in Italian of his *Dialogue on the Two Chief Systems of the World* in 1632, which lampooned Aristotle and Ptolemy and defended Copernicus, Galileo was tried for heresy by the papal Inquisition. Imprisoned and threatened with torture, the aging Galileo recanted, "renouncing and cursing" his Copernican errors.

Newton's Synthesis

The accomplishments of Kepler, Galileo, and others had taken effect by about 1640. The old astronomy and physics were in ruins, and several fundamental breakthroughs had been made. But the new findings failed to explain which forces controlled the movement of the planets and objects on earth. That challenge was taken up by the English scientist Isaac Newton (1642–1727). Newton was born into lower English gentry and attended Cambridge University. A genius who spectacularly united the experimental and theoretical-mathematical sides of modern science, Newton was far from being the perfect rationalist eulogized by later centuries. Like many other practitioners of the new science, Newton was both intensely religious and fascinated by alchemy.

He arrived at some of his most basic ideas about physics in 1666 at age twenty-four but was unable to prove them mathematically. In 1684, after years of studying optics, Newton returned to physics for eighteen extraordinarily intensive months. The result was his towering accomplishment, a single explanatory system that could integrate the astronomy of Copernicus, as corrected by Kepler's laws, with the physics of Galileo and his predecessors. Newton did this through a set of mathematical laws that explain motion and mechanics. These laws of dynamics are complex, and it took scientists and engineers two hundred years to work out all their implications. Nevertheless, the key feature of the Newtonian synthesis was the **law of universal gravitation.** According to this law, every body in the universe attracts every other body in the universe in a precise mathematical relationship, whereby the force of attraction is proportional to the quantity of matter of the objects and inversely proportional to the square of the distance between them. The whole universe—from Kepler's elliptical orbits to Galileo's rolling balls—was unified in one majestic system. Newton's synthesis prevailed until the twentieth century.

law of universal gravitation
A law stating that every body in the universe attracts every other body in the universe in a precise mathematical relationship, with the force of attraction being proportional to the quantity of matter of the objects and inversely proportional to the square of the distance between them.

Causes of the Scientific Revolution

The scientific revolution drew on long-term developments in European culture. The first was the development of the medieval university. By the fourteenth and fifteenth centuries leading universities included professorships of mathematics, astronomy, and physics within their faculties of philosophy. Although the prestige of the new fields was low, critical thinking was now applied to scientific problems by a permanent community of scholars. And an outlet existed for the talents of a Galileo or a Newton: all the great pathfinders either studied or taught at universities.

Second, the Renaissance also stimulated scientific progress. The recovery of ancient texts showed that classical mathematicians had their differences; Europeans were forced to try to resolve these ancient controversies by means of their own efforts. Renaissance patrons played a role in funding scientific investigations as well as artistic projects, as the Medicis of Florence did for Galileo.

The navigational problems of long sea voyages in the age of overseas expansion were a third factor in the scientific revolution. As early as 1484 the king of Portugal appointed a commission of mathematicians to perfect tables to help seamen find their latitude. Navigational problems were also critical in the development of many new scientific instruments, such as the telescope, barometer, thermometer, pendulum clock, microscope, and air pump. Better instruments, which permitted more accurate observations, often led to important new knowledge.

The fourth factor in the scientific revolution was the development of better ways of obtaining knowledge about the world. Two important thinkers, Francis Bacon (1561–1626) and René Descartes (1596–1650), were influential in describing and advocating for improved scientific methods based on experimentation and mathematical reasoning.

The English politician and writer Francis Bacon was the greatest early propagandist for the new scientific method. Bacon argued that the researcher who wants to learn more about leaves or rocks should not speculate but rather should collect many specimens and then compare and analyze them. General principles will then emerge. Bacon's contribution was to formalize the empirical method, which had already been used by Brahe and Galileo, into the general theory of inductive reasoning known as **empiricism.**

The French philosopher René Descartes was a genius who made his first great discovery in mathematics. As a twenty-three-year-old soldier serving in the Thirty Years' War, he experienced a life-changing intellectual vision one night in 1619. Descartes saw that there was a perfect correspondence between geometry and algebra and that geometrical, spatial figures could be expressed as algebraic equations and vice versa. A major step forward in the history of mathematics, Descartes's discovery of analytic geometry provided scientists with an important new tool.

Descartes's highest achievement was to develop his initial vision into a whole philosophy of knowledge and science. He decided it was necessary to doubt everything that could reasonably be doubted and then, as in geometry, to use deductive reasoning from self-evident principles to ascertain scientific laws. Descartes's reasoning ultimately reduced all substances to "matter" and "mind"—that is, to the physical and the spiritual. His view of the world as consisting of two fundamental entities is known as **Cartesian dualism.**

Bacon's inductive experimentalism and Descartes's deductive, mathematical reasoning are combined in the modern scientific method, which emerged in the late seventeenth century. Neither man's extreme approach was sufficient by itself. Bacon's inability to appreciate the importance of mathematics and his obsession with practical results revealed the limitations of antitheoretical empiricism. Likewise, some of Descartes's positions—he believed, for example, that it was possible to deduce the whole science of medicine from first principles—demonstrated the inadequacy of dogmatic rationalism. The modern scientific method has joined precise observations and experimentalism with the search for general laws that may be expressed in rigorously logical, mathematical language.

Science and Society

The rise of modern science had many consequences, some of which are still unfolding. First, it created a new social group—the international **scientific community.** Members of this community were linked by common interests and shared values as well as by the journals and learned scientific societies founded in the later seventeenth and the eighteenth centuries. Their success depended on making new discoveries, and science became competitive. Second, as governments intervened to support research, the new scientific community became closely tied to the state and its agendas. National academies of science were created under state sponsorship in London in 1662, Paris in 1666, Berlin in 1700, and later across Europe. At the same time, scientists developed a critical attitude toward established authority that would inspire thinkers to question traditions in other domains as well.

Some things did not change. Scholars have recently analyzed representations of

empiricism *A theory of inductive reasoning that calls for acquiring evidence through observation and experimentation rather than reason and speculation.*

Cartesian dualism *The premise of René Descartes that all of reality could ultimately be reduced to mind and matter.*

scientific community *The new international group of scholars with shared values and professional institutions that emerged in the years following the scientific revolution.*

femininity and masculinity in the scientific revolution and have noted that nature was often depicted as a female whose veil of secrecy needed to be stripped away and penetrated by male experts. (In the same time period, the Americas were similarly depicted as a female terrain whose fertile lands needed to be controlled and impregnated by male colonists.) New "rational" methods for approaching nature did not question traditional inequalities between the sexes. Women were largely excluded from academies and then refused membership into scientific communities because they lacked academic credentials. (This continued for a long time. Marie Curie, the first person to win two Nobel prizes, was rejected by the French Academy of Science in 1911 because she was a woman.[5])

There were, however, some exceptions. In Italy, universities and academies did offer posts to women, attracting some foreigners spurned at home. Other women worked as makers of wax anatomical models and as botanical and zoological illustrators. Women were also very much involved in informal scientific communities, attending salons, participating in scientific experiments, and writing learned treatises. Some female intellectuals were recognized as full-fledged members of the philosophical dialogue. In England, Margaret Cavendish, Anne Conway, and Mary Astell all contributed to debates about Descartes's mind-body dualism, among other issues. Descartes himself conducted an intellectual correspondence with the princess Elizabeth of Bohemia, of whom he stated: "I attach more weight to her judgement than to those messieurs the Doctors, who take for a rule of truth the opinions of Aristotle rather than the evidence of reason."[6]

The scientific revolution had few consequences for economic life and mass living standards until the late eighteenth century. True, improvements in the techniques of navigation facilitated overseas trade, but science had relatively few practical economic applications. Thus the scientific revolution was first and foremost an intellectual revolution. For more than a hundred years its greatest impact was on how people thought and believed.

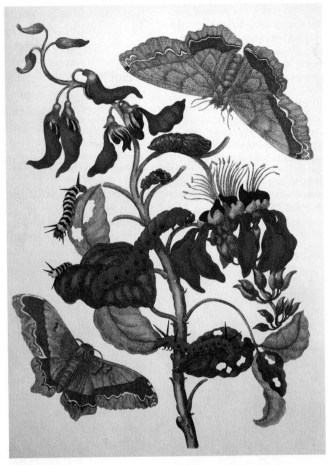

● **Metamorphoses of the Caterpillar and Moth**
Maria Sibylla Merian (1647–1717), the stepdaughter of a Dutch painter, became a celebrated scientific illustrator in her own right. Her finely observed pictures of insects in the South American colony of Surinam introduced many new species, shown in their various stages of development. For Merian, science was intimately tied with art: she not only painted but also bred caterpillars and performed experiments on them. Her two-year stay in Surinam, accompanied by a teenage daughter, was a daring feat for a seventeenth-century woman. *(Bildarchiv Preussischer Kulturbesitz/Art Resource, NY)*

THE ENLIGHTENMENT

How did the new worldview affect the way people thought about society and human relations?

The scientific revolution was the single most important factor in the creation of the new worldview of the eighteenth-century **Enlightenment**. This worldview, which has played a large role in shaping the modern mind, grew out of a rich mix of diverse and often conflicting ideas. Despite the diversity, three central concepts stand at the core of Enlightenment thinking. The most important and original idea was that the methods of natural science could be used to examine and understand all aspects of life. This was what intellectuals meant by *reason,* a favorite word of Enlightenment thinkers.

Enlightenment *An eighteenth-century intellectual movement whose three central concepts were the use of reason, the scientific method, and progress.*

rationalism *The general opinion among Enlightenment thinkers that nothing should be accepted on faith and that everything should be subjected to secular critical examination.*

progress *The goal of Enlightenment thinkers to create better societies and better people by discarding outmoded traditions and embracing rationalism.*

skepticism *The premise, enunciated most clearly by the French Huguenot Pierre Bayle, that nothing could be known beyond all doubt.*

Nothing was to be accepted on faith. Everything was to be submitted to **rationalism,** a secular, critical way of thinking. A second important Enlightenment concept was that the scientific method was capable of discovering the laws of human society as well as those of nature. Thus was social science born. Its birth led to the third key idea, that of **progress.** Armed with the proper method of discovering the laws of human existence, Enlightenment thinkers believed they could help create better societies and better people. Their belief was strengthened by some modest improvements in economic and social life during the eighteenth century.

The Emergence of the Enlightenment

The generation that came of age between the publication of Newton's *Principia* in 1687 and the death of Louis XIV in 1715 tied the knot between the scientific revolution and a new outlook on life. Talented writers of that generation popularized hard-to-understand scientific achievements for the educated elite.

● **Popularizing Science** The frontispiece illustration of *Conversations on the Plurality of Worlds* by Bernard de Fontenelle (1657–1757) invites a nonscientific audience to share the pleasures of astronomy with an elegant lady and an entertaining teacher. The drawing shows the planets revolving around the sun. *(By permission of the Syndics of Cambridge University Library)*

A new generation came to believe that the human mind is capable of making great progress. Medieval and Reformation thinkers had been concerned primarily with sin and salvation. The humanists of the Renaissance had emphasized worldly matters, but their inspiration was the wisdom of the past. Enlightenment thinkers came to believe that, at least in science and mathematics, their era had gone far beyond antiquity. Progress, at least intellectual progress, was very possible.

Some writers of the later seventeenth century came to draw antireligious implications from the scientific revolution. In the wake of the devastation wrought by the Thirty Years' War, some people asked whether ideological conformity in religious matters was really necessary. Others skeptically asked if religious truth could ever be known with absolute certainty and concluded that it could not. This was a new development because many seventeenth-century scientists, like Isaac Newton, believed that their work exalted God and helped explain his creation to fellow believers.

The most famous skeptic was Pierre Bayle (1647–1706), a French Huguenot who found refuge in the Netherlands. Bayle critically examined past religious beliefs and persecutions in his *Historical and Critical Dictionary* (1697). He concluded that nothing can ever be known beyond all doubt, a view known as **skepticism.** His *Dictionary* was reprinted frequently in the Netherlands and in England and was found in more private libraries of eighteenth-century France than any other book.

The rapidly growing travel literature on non-European lands and cultures was another cause of uncertainty. In the wake of the great discoveries, Europeans were learning that the peoples of China, India, Africa, and the Americas all had their own very different beliefs and customs. Europeans shaved their faces and let their hair grow. Turks shaved their heads and let their beards grow. In Europe a man bowed before a woman to show respect. In Siam a man turned his back on a woman when he met her because it was disrespectful to look directly at her. Countless similar examples discussed in the travel accounts helped change the perspective of educated Europeans. They began to look at truth and morality in relative, rather than absolute, terms.

A final cause and manifestation of European intellectual turmoil was John Locke's *Essay Concerning Human Understanding* (1690). Locke's essay brilliantly set forth a new theory about how human beings learn. Rejecting Descartes's view that people are born with certain basic ideas, Locke insisted that all ideas are derived from experience. The human mind at birth is like a blank tablet, or **tabula rasa**, on which the environment writes the individual's understanding and beliefs. Human development is therefore determined by education and social institutions. Along with Newton's *Principia*, Locke's *Essay Concerning Human Understanding* was a key intellectual inspiration of the Enlightenment.

tabula rasa *Literally, a "blank tablet." It is incorporated into Locke's belief that all ideas are derived from experience and that the human mind at birth is like a blank tablet on which the environment writes the individual's understanding and beliefs.*

The Philosophes and the Public

By the time Louis XIV died in 1715, many elements of the new worldview had been assembled. Yet Christian Europe was still strongly attached to its traditional beliefs, as witnessed by the powerful revival of religious orthodoxy in the first half of the eighteenth century. By the outbreak of the American Revolution in 1775, however, a large portion of western Europe's educated elite had embraced the new ideas. This acceptance was the work of the **philosophes**, a group of influential intellectuals who proclaimed that they were bringing knowledge and reason to the world.

Philosophe is the French word for "philosopher," and it was in France that the Enlightenment reached its highest development. There were at least three reasons for this. First, French was the international language of the educated classes, and France was still Europe's wealthiest and most populous country. Second, although censorship existed in France, it was not as thorough as in eastern and east-central Europe. Philosophes like the baron de Montesquieu (1689–1755) used satire and double meanings to spread their message. Third, French philosophes made it their goal to reach a larger audience of elites, many of whom were joined together in the eighteenth-century concept of the "republic of letters"—an imaginary transnational realm of educated critical thinkers.

philosophes *Intellectuals in France who proclaimed that they were bringing the light of knowledge and reason to their fellow creatures in the Age of Enlightenment.*

The influence of writers like Montesquieu on the enlightened public can be seen in the results of his political writing. Disturbed by royal absolutism under Louis XIV and inspired by the example of the physical sciences, Montesquieu set out to apply the critical method to the problem of government. *The Spirit of Laws* (1748) was a complex comparative study of republics, monarchies, and despotisms—a pioneering inquiry in the emerging social sciences. Showing that forms of government were shaped by history, geography, and customs, Montesquieu focused on the conditions that would promote liberty and prevent tyranny. He argued for a **separation of powers**, with political power divided and shared by a variety of classes and estates holding unequal rights and privileges. Admiring greatly the English balance of power among the king, the houses of Parliament, and the independent courts, Montesquieu believed that in France the thirteen high courts—the *parlements*—were frontline defenders of liberty against royal despotism. Apprehensive about the uneducated poor, Montesquieu was no democrat, but his theory of separation of powers had a great impact on the constitutions of the United States in 1789 and of France in 1791.

separation of powers *The belief, developed by a French philosophe that political power in society should be dispersed and shared rather than focused in a single individual or institution.*

The most famous and in many ways most representative philosophe was François Marie Arouet, who was known by the pen name Voltaire (1694–1778). In his long career, this son of a comfortable middle-class family wrote more than seventy witty volumes, hobnobbed with royalty, and made a fortune in shrewd business speculations. His early career, however, was turbulent, and he was twice arrested for insulting noblemen. Voltaire moved to England for three years to escape his enemies and came to share Montesquieu's enthusiasm for English institutions.

> **Primary Source:**
> **Treatise on Toleration**
> *Voltaire makes a powerful argument for cultural and religious tolerance.*

Returning to France, Voltaire had the great fortune of meeting Gabrielle-Emilie Le Tonnelier de Breteuil, marquise du Châtelet (1706–1749), an intellectually gifted woman from the high aristocracy with a passion for science. Inviting Voltaire to live in her country house at Cirey in Lorraine and becoming his long-time companion (under the eyes of her tolerant husband), Madame du Châtelet studied physics and mathematics and published scientific articles and translations. Her translation with an accompanying commentary of Newton's *Principia* into French for the first (and only) time was her greatest work. This female intellectual, who had patiently explained Newton's complex mathematical proofs to Europe's foremost philosophe, had no doubt that women's limited scientific contributions in the past were due to limited and unequal education. She once wrote that if she were a ruler "I would reform an abuse which cuts off, so to speak, half the human race. I would make women participate in all the rights of humankind, and above all in those of the intellect."[7]

While living at Cirey, Voltaire wrote works praising England and popularizing English scientific progress. Newton, he wrote, was history's greatest man, for he had used his genius for the benefit of humanity. "It is," wrote Voltaire, "the man who sways our minds by the prevalence of reason and the native force of truth, not they who reduce mankind to a state of slavery by force and downright violence . . . that claims our reverence and admiration."[8] In the true style of the Enlightenment, Voltaire mixed the glorification of science and reason with an appeal for better individuals and institutions.

Yet like almost all of the philosophes, Voltaire was a reformer, not a revolutionary. He pessimistically concluded that the best one could hope for in government was a good monarch, since human beings "are very rarely worthy to govern themselves." Nor did he believe in social and economic equality. The idea of making servants equal to their masters was "absurd and impossible." The only realizable equality, Voltaire thought, was that "by which the citizen only depends on the laws which protect the freedom of the feeble against the ambitions of the strong."[9]

● **Madame du Châtelet** The marquise du Châtelet was fascinated by the new world system of Isaac Newton. She helped spread Newton's ideas in France by translating his *Principia* and by influencing Voltaire, her companion for fifteen years until her death. *(Giraudon/Art Resource, NY)*

Voltaire's philosophical and religious positions were much more radical. His writings challenged the Catholic Church and Christian theology at almost every point. Voltaire clearly believed in God, but his was a distant, deistic God, the great Clockmaker who built an orderly universe and let it run. Above all, Voltaire and most of the philosophes hated religious intolerance, which they believed led to fanaticism and savage, inhuman action. Simple piety and human kindness—as embodied in Christ's commandments to "love God and your neighbor as yourself"—were religion enough, as may be seen in Voltaire's famous essay on religion.

The ultimate strength of the French philosophes lay in their number, dedication, and organization. The philosophes felt they were engaged in a common undertaking. Their greatest and most representative intellectual achievement was, quite fittingly, a group effort—the seventeen-volume *Encyclopedia: The Rational Dictionary of the Sciences, the Arts, and the Crafts,* edited by Denis Diderot (1713–1784) and Jean le Rond d'Alembert (1717–1783). From different circles and with different interests, the two men enlisted coauthors who would examine the rapidly expanding whole of human knowledge and help them demonstrate how to think critically and objectively about all matters. As Diderot said, he wanted the *Encyclopedia* to "change the general way of thinking."[10]

Not every article was daring or original, but the overall effect was little short of revolutionary. Science and industry were exalted, religion and immortality questioned. Intolerance, injustice, and out-of-date social institutions were openly criticized. The encyclopedists were convinced that greater knowledge would make possible economic, social, and political progress and thus greater human happiness. The *Encyclopedia* was widely read throughout western Europe, especially in less-expensive reprint editions. It summed up the new worldview of the Enlightenment.

Urban Culture and the Public Sphere

Enlightenment ideas did not float on thin air. A series of new institutions and practices emerged in the late seventeenth and eighteenth centuries to facilitate the spread of Enlightenment ideas. First, the production and consumption of books grew dramatically in the eighteenth century. Moreover, the types of books people read changed dramatically. The proportion of religious and devotional books published declined after 1750; history and law held constant; the arts and sciences surged.

Reading more books on many more subjects, Europe's educated public increasingly approached reading in a new way. The result was what some scholars have called

● **Selling Books, Promoting Ideas** This appealing bookshop with its intriguing ads for the latest works offers to put customers "Under the Protection of Minerva," the Roman goddess of wisdom. Large packets of books sit ready for shipment to foreign countries. Book consumption surged in the eighteenth century. *(Musée des Beaux-Arts, Dijon/Art Resource, NY)*

reading revolution *The transition in Europe from a society where literacy consisted of patriarchal and communal reading of religious texts to a society where literacy was commonplace and reading material was broad and diverse.*

a "reading revolution." The old style of reading was centered on a core of sacred texts that inspired reverence and taught earthly duty and obedience to God. Reading was patriarchal and communal, with the father of the family slowly reading the text aloud and the audience savoring each word. Now reading involved a broader field of books that constantly changed. Reading became individual and silent, and texts could be questioned. Subtle but profound, the reading revolution ushered in new ways of relating to the written word.

Conversation and debate also played a critical role in the Enlightenment. Paris set the example, and other European cities followed. In Paris a number of talented wealthy women presided over regular social gatherings in their elegant drawing rooms, or **salons.** There they encouraged the exchange of witty, uncensored observations on literature, science, and philosophy. Talented hostesses, or *salonnières,* mediated the public's freewheeling examination of Enlightenment thought. As one philosophe described his Enlightenment hostess and her salon:

salons *Regular social gatherings held by talented and rich Parisian women in their homes, where philosophes and their followers met to discuss literature, science, and philosophy.*

She could unite the different types, even the most antagonistic, sustaining the conversation by a well-aimed phrase, animating and guiding it at will. . . . Politics, religion, philosophy, news: nothing was excluded. Her circle met daily from five to nine. There one found men of all ranks in the State, the Church, and the Court, soldiers and foreigners, and the leading writers of the day.[11]

As this passage suggests, the salons created a cultural realm free from dogma and censorship. There a diverse but educated public could debate issues and form its own ideas. Through their invitation lists, salon hostesses brought together members of the intellectual, economic, and social elites. In such an atmosphere, the philosophes, the French nobility, and the prosperous middle classes intermingled and influenced one another. Thinking critically about almost any question became fashionable and flourished alongside hopes for human progress.

Admirers of the salonnières, some philosophes championed greater rights and expanded education for women, claiming that the position and treatment of women were the best indicators of a society's level of civilization and decency.[12] To be sure, for these male philosophes greater rights for women did not mean equal rights, and the philosophes were not particularly disturbed by the fact that elite women remained legally subordinate to men in economic and political affairs. Elite women lacked many rights, but so did most men.

While membership at the salons was restricted to the well-born and well-connected, a number of institutions emerged for the rest of society. Lending libraries served an important function for people who could not afford to buy their own books. The coffeehouses that first appeared in the late seventeenth century became meccas of philosophical discussion. In addition, book clubs, Masonic lodges, and journals all played roles in the creation of a new **public sphere** that celebrated open debate informed by critical reason. The public sphere was an idealized space where members of society came together as individuals to discuss issues relevant to the society, economics, and politics of the day.

public sphere *An idealized intellectual environment that emerged in Europe during the Enlightenment, where members of society came together as individuals to discuss issues relevant to the society, economics, and politics of the day.*

What of the common people? Did they participate in the Enlightenment? Philosophes did not direct their message to peasants or urban laborers. They believed that the masses had no time or talent for philosophical speculation and that elevating them would be a long and potentially dangerous process. Deluded by superstitions and driven by violent passions, they thought, the people were like children in need of firm parental guidance. *Encyclopedia* editor d'Alembert characteristically made a sharp distinction between "the truly enlightened public" and "the blind and noisy multitude."[13]

There is some evidence, however, that the people were not immune to the words of the philosophes. At a time of rising literacy, book prices were dropping in cities and towns, and many philosophical ideas were popularized in cheap pamphlets. Moreover,

even illiterate people had access to written material through the practice of public reading. Although they were barred from salons and academies, ordinary people were not wholly isolated from the new ideas in circulation.

Late Enlightenment

After about 1770 a number of thinkers and writers began to attack Enlightenment faith in reason and progress. The most famous of these was the Swiss Jean-Jacques Rousseau (1712–1778), the son of a poor watchmaker who made his way into the world of Paris salons through his brilliant intellect. Appealing but neurotic, Rousseau came to believe that his philosophe friends and the women of the Parisian salons were plotting against him. In the mid-1750s he broke with them, living thereafter as a lonely outsider with his uneducated common-law wife and going in his own highly original direction.

Like other Enlightenment thinkers, Rousseau was passionately committed to individual freedom. Unlike them, however, he attacked rationalism and civilization as destroying, rather than liberating, the individual. Warm, spontaneous feeling had to complement and correct cold intellect. Moreover, the basic goodness of the individual and the unspoiled child had to be protected from the decadent refinements of civilization. Rousseau's ideals greatly influenced the early romantic movement (see pages 682–683), which rebelled against the culture of the Enlightenment.

Rousseau's critique of social mores included an attack on contemporary gender roles. He believed that since nature relegated women to assume a passive role in sexual relations, they should also be passive in social life. Instead, their passion for attending salons and pulling the strings of power had a corrupting effect on both society and politics. Rousseau thus rejected the sophisticated way of life of Parisian elite women, calling on them to abandon their stylish corsets and breast-feed their children.

● **Enlightenment Culture**
Here the seven-year-old Austrian child prodigy Wolfgang Amadeus Mozart (1756–1791) plays his own composition at an "English tea" given by the Princess de Conti near Paris. Mozart's phenomenal creative powers lasted a lifetime, and he produced a vast range of symphonies, operas, and chamber music. *(Réunion des Musées Nationaux/Art Resource, NY)*

Primary Source:
Rousseau Espouses Popular Sovereignty and the General Will
Modern democracies owe much to the political ideas of this French philosopher.

general will *A political concept, first set forth by Jean-Jacques Rousseau, that refers to the collective desires of the citizenry as opposed to individual interests.*

Rousseau's contribution to political theory in *The Social Contract* (1762) would prove enormously influential. His contribution was based on two fundamental concepts: the general will and popular sovereignty. According to Rousseau, the **general will** is sacred and absolute, reflecting the common interests of the people, who have displaced the monarch as the holder of sovereign power. The general will is not necessarily the will of the majority, however. At times the general will may be the authentic, long-term needs of the people as correctly interpreted by a farseeing minority. (The concept has since been used by some dictators who have claimed that they, rather than some momentary majority of the voters, represent the general will.)

As the reading public developed, it joined forces with the philosophes to call for greater freedom of speech. Immanuel Kant (1724–1804), a professor in East Prussia and the greatest German philosopher of his day, posed the question of the age when he published a pamphlet in 1784 entitled *What Is Enlightenment?* Kant answered, "*Sapere Aude!* [dare to know] Have courage to use your own understanding!—that is the motto of enlightenment." He argued that if serious thinkers were allowed to exercise their reason publicly in print, enlightenment would surely follow. Kant was no revolutionary; he also insisted that in their private lives, individuals must obey all laws, no matter how unreasonable, and should be punished for "impertinent" criticism. Kant thus tried to reconcile absolute monarchical authority with a critical public sphere. This balancing act characterized experiments with "enlightened absolutism" in the eighteenth century.

Race and the Enlightenment

In recent years, historians have found in the scientific revolution and the Enlightenment a crucial turning point in European ideas about race. A primary catalyst for new ideas about race was the urge to classify nature unleashed by the scientific revolution's insistence on careful empirical observation. In *The System of Nature* (1735) Swedish botanist Carl von Linné argued that nature was organized into a God-given hierarchy. As scientists developed more elaborate taxonomies of plant and animal species, they also began to classify humans into hierarchically ordered "races" and to investigate the origins of race. The Comte de Buffon argued that humans originated with one species that then developed into distinct races due largely to climactic conditions. According to Immanuel Kant, there were four human races, each of which had derived from an original race of "white brunette" people.

Using the word *race* to designate biologically distinct groups of humans, akin to distinct animal species, was new. Previously, Europeans grouped other peoples into "nations" based on their historical, political, and cultural affiliations, rather than on supposedly innate physical differences. Unsurprisingly, when European thinkers drew up a hierarchical classification of human species, their own "race" was placed at the top. Europeans had long believed they were culturally superior to "barbaric" peoples in Africa and, since 1492, the New World. Emerging ideas about racial difference taught them they were biologically superior as well.

These ideas did not go unchallenged. James Beattie responded directly to claims of white superiority by pointing out that Europeans had started out as savage as non-whites and that many non-European peoples in the Americas, Asia, and Africa had achieved high levels of civilization. (See the feature "Listening to the Past: Diderot Condemns European Colonialism.")

Scholars are only beginning to analyze links between Enlightenment ideas about race and its notions of equality, progress, and reason. There are clear parallels, though, between the use of science to propagate racial hierarchies and its use to defend social inequalities between men and women. As Rousseau used women's "natural" passivity to argue for their passive role in society, so others used non-Europeans' "natural" inferiority to defend slavery and colonial domination. The new powers of science and reason were thus marshaled to imbue traditional stereotypes with the force of natural law.

THE ENLIGHTENMENT AND ABSOLUTISM

What impact did this new way of thinking have on political developments and monarchical absolutism?

How did the Enlightenment influence politics? To this important question there is no easy answer. Most Enlightenment thinkers outside of England and the Netherlands believed that political change should come from above—from the ruler—rather than from below. It was necessary to educate and "enlighten" the monarch, who could then make good laws and promote human happiness.

Many government officials were attracted to philosophical ideas. They were among the best-educated members of society, and their daily involvement in complex affairs of state made them naturally interested in ideas for reforming human society. Encouraged by these officials, some absolutist rulers of the later eighteenth century tried to govern in an enlightened manner. Yet their actual programs and accomplishments varied greatly. One must closely examine the evolution of monarchical absolutism before judging the significance of what historians have often called the **enlightened absolutism** of the later eighteenth century.

Enlightenment teachings inspired European rulers in small as well as large states in the second half of the eighteenth century. Absolutist princes and monarchs in several west German and Italian states, as well as in Scandinavia, Spain, and Portugal, proclaimed themselves more enlightened. A few smaller states were actually the most successful in making reforms, perhaps because their rulers were not overwhelmed by the size and complexity of their realms. Denmark, for example, carried out extensive land reform in the 1780s that practically abolished serfdom and gave Danish peasants secure tenure on their farms. Yet by far the most influential of the new-style monarchs were in Prussia, Russia, and Austria, and they deserve primary attention.

enlightened absolutism
Term coined by historians to describe the rule of eighteenth-century monarchs who, without renouncing their own absolute authority, adopted Enlightenment ideals of rationalism, progress, and tolerance.

Frederick the Great of Prussia

Frederick II (r. 1740–1786), commonly known as Frederick the Great, built masterfully on the work of his father, Frederick William I (see page 475). Although in his youth he embraced culture and literature rather than the crude life of the barracks, by the time he came to the throne Frederick was determined to use the splendid army that his father had left him. Therefore, when Maria Theresa of Austria inherited the Habsburg dominions upon the death of her father Charles VI, Frederick pounced. He invaded her rich, mainly German province of Silesia in violation of an agreement that had guaranteed her succession. In 1742, as other greedy powers were falling on her lands in the general European War of the Austrian Succession (1740–1748), Maria Theresa was forced to cede almost all of Silesia to Prussia. In one stroke Prussia doubled its population to six million people. Now Prussia unquestionably towered above all the other German states and stood as a European Great Power.

Though successful in 1742, Frederick had to spend much of his reign fighting against great odds to save Prussia from total destruction. When the ongoing competition between Britain and France for colonial empire brought another great conflict in 1756, Maria Theresa fashioned an aggressive alliance with the leaders of France and Russia. During the Seven Years' War (1756–1763), the aim of the alliance was to conquer Prussia and divide its territory. Despite invasions from all sides, Frederick fought with stoic courage. In the end he was miraculously saved: Peter III came to the Russian throne in 1762 and called off the attack against Frederick, whom he greatly admired. The terrible struggle of the Seven Years' War tempered Frederick's interest in territorial expansion and brought him to consider how more enlightened policies for his subjects might also strengthen the state. He tolerantly allowed his subjects to believe as they wished in religious and philosophical matters. He promoted the advancement of knowledge, improving his country's schools and permitting scholars to publish their findings. Moreover, Frederick tried to improve the lives of his subjects more directly. As he wrote his friend Voltaire, "I must enlighten my people, cultivate their manners and morals, and make them as happy as human beings can be, or as happy as the means at my disposal permit."

The legal system and the bureaucracy were Frederick's primary tools. Prussia's laws were simplified, torture of prisoners was abolished, and judges decided cases quickly and impartially. Prussian officials became famous for their hard work and honesty. After the Seven Years' War ended in 1763, Frederick's government energetically promoted the reconstruction of agriculture and industry in his war-torn country. Frederick himself set a good example. He worked hard and lived modestly, claiming that he was "only the first servant of the state." Thus Frederick justified monarchy in terms of practical results and said nothing of the divine right of kings.

Frederick's dedication to high-minded government went only so far, however. While he condemned serfdom in the abstract, he accepted it in practice and did not even free the serfs on his own estates. He accepted and extended the privileges of the nobility, who remained the backbone of the army and the entire Prussian state.

Nor did Frederick listen to thinkers like Moses Mendelssohn (1729–1786), who urged that Jews be given freedom and civil rights. (See the feature "Individuals in Society: Moses Mendelssohn and the Jewish Enlightenment.") The vast majority were confined to tiny, overcrowded ghettos; were excluded by law from most business and professional activities; and could be ordered out of the kingdom at a moment's notice.

Catherine the Great of Russia

Catherine the Great of Russia (r. 1762–1796) was one of the most remarkable rulers of her age, and the French philosophes adored her. Catherine was a German princess from Anhalt-Zerbst, an insignificant principality sandwiched between Prussia and Saxony. Her father commanded a regiment of the Prussian army, but her mother was related to the Romanovs of Russia, and that proved to be Catherine's chance.

At the age of fifteen she was married to the heir to the Russian throne. When her husband Peter III came to power in 1762, his decision to withdraw Russian troops from the coalition against Prussia alienated the army. At the end of six months Catherine and her conspirators deposed Peter III in a palace revolution, and the Orlov brothers murdered him. The German princess became empress of Russia.

Catherine had drunk deeply at the Enlightenment well. Never questioning that absolute monarchy was the best form of government, she set out to rule in an enlightened manner. She had three main goals. First, she worked hard to continue Peter the Great's effort to bring the culture of western Europe to Russia. To do so, she imported Western architects, sculptors, musicians, and intellectuals. She bought many masterpieces of Western art and patronized the philosophes. An enthusiastic letter writer, she corresponded extensively with Voltaire and praised him as the "champion of the human race." When the French government banned the *Encyclopedia,* she offered to publish it in St. Petersburg and sent money to Diderot when he needed it. With these actions, Catherine won good press in the West for herself and for her country. Moreover, this intellectual ruler, who wrote plays and loved good talk, set the tone for the Russian nobility. Peter the Great westernized Russian armies, but it was Catherine who westernized the imagination of the Russian elite.

Catherine's second goal was domestic reform, and she began her reign with sincere and ambitious projects. Better laws were a major concern. In 1767 she appointed a special legislative commission to prepare a new law code. No new unified code was ever produced, but Catherine did restrict the practice of torture and allowed limited religious toleration. She also tried to improve education and strengthen local government. The philosophes applauded these measures and hoped more would follow.

Such was not the case. In 1773 a Cossack soldier named Emelian Pugachev sparked a gigantic uprising of serfs. Proclaiming himself the true tsar, Pugachev issued

Moses Mendelssohn and the Jewish Enlightenment

Lavater (*right*) attempts to convert Mendelssohn, in a painting by Moritz Oppenheim of an imaginary encounter. *(Collection of the Judah L. Magnes Museum, Berkeley)*

In 1743 a small, humpbacked Jewish boy with a stammer left his poor parents in Dessau in central Germany and walked eighty miles to Berlin, the capital of Frederick the Great's Prussia. According to one story, when the boy reached the Rosenthaler Gate, the only one through which Jews could pass, he told the inquiring watchman that his name was Moses and that he had come to Berlin "to learn." The watchman laughed and waved him through. "Go Moses, the sea has opened before you."* Embracing the Enlightenment and seeking a revitalization of Jewish religious thought, Moses Mendelssohn did point his people in a new and uncharted direction.

Turning in Berlin to a learned rabbi he had previously known in Dessau, the young Mendelssohn studied Jewish law and eked out a living copying Hebrew manuscripts in a beautiful hand. But he was soon fascinated by an intellectual world that had been closed to him in the Dessau ghetto. There, like most Jews throughout central Europe, he had spoken Yiddish—a mixture of German, Polish, and Hebrew. Now, working mainly on his own, he mastered German; learned Latin, Greek, French, and English; and studied mathematics and Enlightenment philosophy. Word of his exceptional abilities spread in Berlin's Jewish community (1,500 of the city's 100,000 inhabitants). He began tutoring the children of a wealthy Jewish silk merchant, and he soon became the merchant's clerk and later his partner. But his great passion remained the life of the mind and the spirit, which he avidly pursued in his off hours.

Gentle and unassuming in his personal life, Mendelssohn was a bold thinker. Reading eagerly in Western philosophy since antiquity, he was, as a pious Jew, soon convinced that Enlightenment teachings need not be opposed to Jewish thought and religion. Indeed, he concluded that reason could complement and strengthen religion, although each would retain its integrity as a separate sphere.† Developing his idea in his first great work, "On the Immortality of the Soul"

(1767), Mendelssohn used the neutral setting of a philosophical dialogue between Socrates and his followers in ancient Greece to argue that the human soul lived forever. In refusing to bring religion and critical thinking into conflict, he was strongly influenced by contemporary German philosophers who argued similarly on behalf of Christianity. He reflected the way the German Enlightenment generally supported established religion, in contrast to the French Enlightenment, which attacked it. This was the most important difference in Enlightenment thinking between the two countries.

Mendelssohn's treatise on the human soul captivated the educated German public, which marveled that a Jew could have written a philosophical masterpiece. In the excitement, a Christian zealot named Lavater challenged Mendelssohn in a pamphlet to accept Christianity or to demonstrate how the Christian faith was not "reasonable." Replying politely but passionately, the Jewish philosopher affirmed that all his studies had only strengthened him in the faith of his fathers, although he certainly did not seek to convert anyone not born into Judaism. Rather, he urged toleration in religious matters. He spoke up courageously for his fellow Jews and decried the oppression they endured, and he continued to do so for the rest of his life.

Orthodox Jew and German philosophe, Moses Mendelssohn serenely combined two very different worlds. He built a bridge from the ghetto to the dominant culture over which many Jews would pass, including his novelist daughter Dorothea and his famous grandson, the composer Felix Mendelssohn.

Questions for Analysis

1. How did Mendelssohn seek to influence Jewish religious thought in his time?
2. How do Mendelssohn's ideas compare with those of the French Enlightenment?

*H. Kupferberg, *The Mendelssohns: Three Generations of Genius* (New York: Charles Scribner's Sons, 1972), p. 3.

†D. Sorkin, *Moses Mendelssohn and the Religious Enlightenment* (Berkeley: University of California Press, 1996), pp. 8 ff.

MAP 17.1 **The Partition of Poland and Russia's Expansion, 1772–1795** By 1700 Poland had become a weak and decentralized republic with an elected king. All important decisions continued to require the unanimous agreement of all nobles elected to the Polish Diet, which meant that nothing could ever be done to strengthen the state. In 1772 war threatened between Russia and Austria over Russian gains from the Ottoman Empire. To satisfy desires for expansion without fighting, Prussia's Frederick the Great proposed that parts of Poland be divided among Austria, Prussia, and Russia. In 1793 and 1795 the three powers partitioned the remainder, and the ancient republic of Poland vanished from the map.

"decrees" abolishing serfdom, taxes, and army service. Thousands joined his cause, slaughtering landlords and officials over a vast area of southwestern Russia. Pugachev's untrained forces eventually proved no match for Catherine's regular army. Betrayed by his own company, Pugachev was captured and savagely executed.

Pugachev's rebellion put an end to any intentions Catherine might have had about reforming the system. The peasants were clearly dangerous, and her empire rested on noble support. After 1775 Catherine gave the nobles absolute control of their serfs. She extended serfdom into new areas, such as Ukraine. In 1785 she formalized the nobility's privileged position, freeing them from taxes and state service. Under Catherine the Russian nobility attained its most exalted position, and serfdom entered its most oppressive phase.

Catherine's third goal was territorial expansion, and in this respect she was extremely successful. Her armies subjugated the last descendants of the Mongols, the Crimean Tatars, and began conquest of the Caucasus. Her greatest coup by far was the partition

● **Catherine the Great as Equestrian and Miniature of Count Grigory Grigoryevich Orlov** Catherine conspired with her lover, the officer Grigory Orlov, to overthrow her husband Peter III. Grigory and his four officer brothers commanded considerable support among the soldiers stationed in St. Petersburg, who supported the coup. After she became empress, Catherine raised Grigory to the rank of count. Together they had an illegitimate son. (left: Musée des Beaux-Arts, Chartres/The Bridgeman Art Library; right: State Hermitage Museum, St. Petersburg)

of Poland (see Map 17.1). When, between 1768 and 1772, Catherine's armies scored unprecedented victories against the Turks and thereby threatened to disturb the balance of power in eastern Europe, Frederick the Great of Prussia obligingly came forward with a deal. He proposed that Turkey be let off easily and that Prussia, Austria, and Russia each compensate itself by taking a gigantic slice of the weakly ruled Polish territory. Catherine jumped at the chance. The first partition of Poland took place in 1772. Two more partitions, in 1793 and 1795, gave all three powers more Polish territory, and the ancient republic of Poland vanished from the map.

The Austrian Habsburgs

In Austria two talented rulers did manage to introduce major reforms, although traditional power politics was more important than Enlightenment teachings. One was Joseph II (r. 1780–1790), a fascinating individual. For an earlier generation of historians, he was the "revolutionary emperor," a tragic hero whose lofty reforms were undone by the landowning nobility. More recent scholarship has revised this romantic interpretation and has stressed how Joseph II continued the state-building work of his mother, the empress Maria Theresa (1740–1780), a remarkable but old-fashioned absolutist.

Emerging from the long War of the Austrian Succession in 1748 with the serious loss of Silesia, Maria Theresa and her closest ministers were determined to introduce reforms that would make the state stronger and more efficient. Three aspects of these reforms were most important. First, Maria Theresa introduced measures aimed at limiting the papacy's political influence in her realm. Second, a series of administrative reforms strengthened the central bureaucracy, minimized provincial differences, and revamped the tax system, taxing even the lands of some nobles. Third, the government sought to improve the lot of the agricultural population, cautiously reducing the power of lords over their hereditary serfs and their partially free peasant tenants.

Coregent with his mother from 1765 onward and a strong supporter of change, Joseph II moved forward rapidly when he came to the throne in 1780. Most notably, Joseph abolished serfdom in 1781, and in 1789 he decreed that all peasant labor obligations be converted into cash payments. This measure was violently rejected not only by the nobility but also by the peasants it was intended to help since they lacked the necessary cash. When a disillusioned Joseph died prematurely at forty-nine, the entire Habsburg empire was in turmoil. His brother Leopold II (r. 1790–1792) canceled Joseph's radical edicts in order to reestablish order. Peasants once again were required to do forced labor for their lords.

The eastern European absolutists of the later eighteenth century combined old-fashioned state-building with the culture and critical thinking of the Enlightenment. In doing so, they succeeded in expanding the role of the state in the life of society. They perfected bureaucratic machines that were to prove surprisingly adaptive and capable of enduring into the twentieth century. Their failure to implement policies we would recognize as humane and enlightened—such as abolishing serfdom—may reveal inherent failures in Enlightenment thinking about equality and social justice, rather than in their execution of an Enlightenment program. The fact that leading philosophes supported rather than criticized Eastern rulers' policies suggests the blinders of the era.

Chapter Summary

Key Terms

natural philosophy
Copernican hypothesis
experimental method
law of inertia
law of universal gravitation
empiricism
Cartesian dualism
scientific community
Enlightenment
rationalism
progress
skepticism
tabula rasa
philosophes
separation of powers
reading revolution
salons
public sphere
general will
enlightened absolutism

To assess your mastery of this chapter, go to
bedfordstmartins.com/mckayworld

• What was revolutionary in new attitudes toward the natural world?

Decisive breakthroughs in astronomy and physics in the seventeenth century demolished the imposing medieval synthesis of Aristotelian philosophy and Christian theology. These developments had only limited practical consequences at the time, but the impact of new scientific knowledge on intellectual life was enormous. The emergence of modern science was a distinctive characteristic of Western civilization and became a key element of Western identity.

• How did the new worldview affect the way people thought about society and human relations?

Interpreting scientific findings and Newtonian laws in a manner that was both antitradition and antireligion, Enlightenment philosophes extolled the superiority of rational critical thinking. This new method, they believed, promised not just increased knowledge but also the discovery of the fundamental laws of human society. Although they reached differing conclusions when they turned to social and political realities, they did stimulate absolute monarchs to apply reason to statecraft and the search for useful reforms. Above all, the philosophes succeeded in shaping an emerging public opinion and spreading their radically new worldview. During the eighteenth century philosophers drew on scientific principles for new definitions of race, which often justified belief in Western superiority.

• What impact did this new way of thinking have on political developments and monarchical absolutism?

The ideas of the Enlightenment were an inspiration for monarchs, particularly absolutist rulers in central and eastern Europe, who saw in them important tools for reforming and rationalizing their governments. Their primary goal was to strengthen their states and increase the efficiency of their bureaucracies and armies. Enlightened absolutists believed that these reforms would ultimately improve the lot of ordinary people, but this was not their chief concern. With few exceptions, they did not question the institution of serfdom. The fact that leading philosophes supported rather than criticized Eastern rulers' policies suggests some of the limitations of the era.

Suggested Reading

Alexander, John T. *Catherine the Great: Life and Legend.* 1989. The best biography of the famous Russian tsarina.

Beales, Derek. *Joseph II.* 1987. A fine biography of the reforming Habsburg ruler.

Chartier, Roger. *The Cultural Origins of the French Revolution.* 1991. An imaginative analysis of the changing attitudes of the educated public.

Eze, E. Chukwudi, ed. *Race and the Enlightenment: A Reader.* 1997. An invaluable source on the origins of modern racial thinking in the Enlightenment.

Goodman, Dena. *The Republic of Letters: A Cultural History of the Enlightenment.* 1994. An innovative study of the role of salons and salon hostesses in the rise of the Enlightenment.

MacDonagh, Giles. *Frederick the Great.* 2001. An outstanding biography of the Prussian king.

Munck, Thomas. *The Enlightenment: A Comparative History.* 2000. Compares developments in Enlightenment thought in different countries.

Muthu, Sankar. *Enlightenment Against Empire.* 2003. Examines Enlightenment figures' opposition to colonialism.

Outram, Dorinda. *The Enlightenment,* 2d ed. 2006. An outstanding and accessible introduction to Enlightenment debates that emphasizes the Enlightenment's social context and global reach.

Schiebinger, Londa. *The Mind Has No Sex? Women in the Origins of Modern Science.* 1998. Discusses how the new science excluded women.

Shapin, Steven. *The Scientific Revolution.* 2001. A concise and well informed general introduction to the scientific revolution.

Sorkin, David. *Moses Mendelssohn and the Religious Enlightenment.* 1996. A brilliant study of the Jewish philosopher and of the role of religion in the Enlightenment.

Notes

1. H. Butterfield, *The Origins of Modern Science* (New York: Macmillan, 1951), p. viii.
2. Quoted in A. G. R. Smith, *Science and Society in the Sixteenth and Seventeenth Centuries* (New York: Harcourt Brace Jovanovich, 1972), p. 97.
3. Quoted in Butterfield, *The Origins of Modern Science,* p. 47.
4. Ibid., p. 120.
5. L. Schiebinger, *The Mind Has No Sex? Women in the Origins of Modern Science* (Cambridge, Mass.: Harvard University Press, 1989), p. 2.
6. Jacqueline Broad, *Women Philosophers of the Seventeenth Century* (Cambridge: Cambridge University Press, 2003), p. 17.
7. Schiebinger, *The Mind Has No Sex?* p. 64.
8. Quoted in L. M. Marsak, ed., *The Enlightenment* (New York: John Wiley & Sons, 1972), p. 56.
9. Quoted in G. L. Mosse et al., eds., *Europe in Review* (Chicago: Rand McNally, 1964), p. 156.
10. Quoted in P. Gay, "The Unity of the Enlightenment," *History* 3 (1960): 25.
11. Quoted in G. P. Gooch, *Catherine the Great and Other Studies* (Hamden, Conn.: Archon Books, 1966), p. 149.
12. See E. Fox-Genovese, "Women in the Enlightenment," in *Becoming Visible: Women in European History,* 2d ed., ed. R. Bridenthal, C. Koonz, and S. Stuard (Boston: Houghton Mifflin, 1987), esp. pp. 252–259, 263–265.
13. Jean Le Rond d'Alembert, *Eloges lus dans les séances publiques de l'Académie française* (Paris, 1779), p. ix, quoted in Mona Ozouf, "'Public Opinion' at the End of the Old Regime," *The Journal of Modern History* 60, Supplement: Rethinking French Politics in 1788 (September 1988), p. S9.

Listening to the PAST

Diderot Condemns European Colonialism

Europe's global expansion and the travel literature it produced (see Chapter 15) fascinated the philosophes and the reading public. Most travel literature portrayed indigenous peoples as savages, but Enlightenment thinkers often subjected Europeans to unflattering comparisons with indigenous societies in order to criticize European laws and customs.

A small band led by Denis Diderot went further and strongly condemned European conquest and empire building. Diderot wrote many of the unsigned articles in Guillaume Thomas Reynal's History of European Settlements and Commerce in the Two Indies, *a highly critical, banned bestseller. He also reviewed Louis Antoine de Bougainville's* Voyage Around the World *(1771) and in 1772 wrote* Supplement to the Voyage of Bougainville *(published in 1796). In the* Supplement's *second section Diderot uses an imaginary farewell speech by a Tahitian elder to denounce the evils that Bougainville and his companions brought to the island of Tahiti in the South Pacific.*

The Elder's Farewell

. . . You, Bougainville, leader of the ruffians who obey you, pull your ship away swiftly from these shores. We are innocent, we are content, and you can only spoil that happiness. We follow the pure instincts of nature, and you have tried to erase its impression from our hearts. Here, everything belongs to everyone, and you have preached some strange distinction between "yours" and "mine." Our daughters and our wives belong to us all. You shared that privilege with us, and you enflamed them with a frenzy they had never known before. They have become wild in your arms, and you have become deranged in theirs. . . . We are free, but into our earth you have now staked your title to our future servitude. You are neither a god nor a devil. Who are you, then, to make us slaves? Orou, you who understand the language of these men, tell us all, as you have told me, what they have written

on that strip of metal: *This land is ours.* So this land is yours? Why? Because you set foot on it! If a Tahitian should one day land on your shores and engrave on one of your stones or on the bark of one of your trees, *This land belongs to the people of Tahiti,* what would you think then? You are stronger than we are, and what does that mean? When one of the miserable trinkets with which your ship is filled was taken away, what an uproar you made, what revenge you exacted! At that very moment, in the depths of your heart, you were plotting the theft of an entire country! You are not a slave, you would rather die than be one, and yet you wish to make slaves of us. . . . This inhabitant of Tahiti, whom you wish to ensnare like an animal, is your brother. You are both children of Nature. . . .

Leave us to our own customs; they are wiser and more decent than yours. We have no wish to exchange what you call our ignorance for your useless knowledge. Everything that we need and is good for us we already possess. Do we merit contempt because we have not learnt how to acquire superfluous needs? When we are hungry, we have enough to eat. When we are cold, we have enough to wear. You have entered our huts; what do you suppose we lack? Pursue as far as you wish what you call the comforts of life, but let sensible beings stop when they have no more to gain from their labours than imaginary benefits. . . . We have kept our annual and daily labours within the smallest possible limits, because in our eyes nothing is better than leisure. Go back to your own country to agitate and torment yourself as much as you like. But leave us in peace. Do not fill our heads with your false needs and illusory virtues. Look at these men. See how upright, healthy and robust they are. Look at these women. See how they too stand up straight, how healthy, fresh and lovely they are. . . . I can run a league across the plain in less than an hour; your young companions can hardly keep up with me, and yet I'm more than ninety years old.

Woe to this island! Woe to all present Tahitians and to those still to come, from the day of your arrival! We

Painting by Jean-Honoré Fragonard of Denis Diderot, one of the editors of the *Encyclopedia,* the greatest intellectual achievement of the Enlightenment. *(Erich Lessing/Art Resource, NY)*

used to know but one disease, old age, to which men, animals and plants were all equally prey, but you have now brought us a new one [venereal disease]. You have infected our blood. Perhaps we shall be forced to wipe out, with our own hands, some of our daughters, some of our wives and children, those who have lain with your women, and those who have been with your men. . . . A short while ago a young maiden of Tahiti would yield blissfully to the embraces of a Tahitian youth, once she had reached the age of marriage; she would wait impatiently for her mother to lift her veil and expose her breasts; she was proud to stir the desires and attract the amorous glances of a stranger, her relatives, her brother. Without fear or shame, in our presence, in the midst of a circle of innocent Tahitians, to the sound of flutes and between the dances, she welcomed the caresses of the youth whom her young heart and the secret promptings of her senses had selected for her. It was you who first brought the idea of crime and the risk of illness to us.

Our pleasures, once so sweet, are now accompanied with remorse and fear. That man in black [a priest], who stands by your side and listens to me, spoke to our young men; I do not know what he said to our girls, but now they blush and the boys hesitate. If you wish, creep away into the dark forest with the perverse partner of your pleasures, but let the good and simple inhabitants of Tahiti multiply without shame in the light of day under the open sky. What more honest and noble sentiment can you put in the place of the one which we have inspired in them and which nurtures them? When they believe the moment has arrived to enrich the nation and the family with a new citizen, they exalt in it. They eat to live, and to grow; they

grow to multiply, and in that they see neither vice nor shame. Take heed of the effects of your offences. You had hardly arrived among them before they became thieves. You had hardly set foot on our soil before it reeked of blood. The Tahitian who ran to meet you, to greet you, who welcomed you crying, "*taïo,* friend, friend," you killed. And why did you kill him? Because he had been tempted by the glitter of your little serpent's eggs. He offered you his fruits, his wife, his daughter, his hut, and you killed him for a handful of beads which he took without asking. . . .

Go away now, unless your cruel eyes relish the spectacle of death. Go away, leave, and may the guilty seas that spared you on your voyage absolve themselves of their fault and avenge us by swallowing you up before your return.

Questions for Analysis

1. According to the Tahitian elder, in what ways does European expansion and empire building harm Tahitians and other indigenous peoples?

2. What European customs, beliefs, and institutions does Diderot attack through the elder's comparisons of Tahiti and Europe?

Source: Slightly adapted from *Supplement to the Voyage of Bougainville,* in Denis Diderot, *Political Writings,* trans. and ed. John Hope Mason and Robert Wokler (Cambridge: Cambridge University Press, 1992), pp. 41–45. Reprinted with the permission of Cambridge University Press.

Waist Pendant of Benin, Edo Peoples, Nigeria, 16th–19th Centuries. The facial features, the beard, and the ruffled collar are clearly Portuguese, but the braided hair is distinctly African, probably signifying royalty. *(The Metropolitan Museum of Art, Gift of Mr. and Mrs. Klaus G. Perls, 1991 [1991.162.9]. Photograph © 1991 The Metropolitan Museum of Art)*

chapter

18 AFRICA AND THE WORLD, CA. 1400–1800

Chapter Preview

Senegambia and Benin
• *What different types of economic, social, and political structures were found in Senegambia and Benin?*

The Sudan: Songhai, Kanem-Bornu, and Hausaland
• *In what ways was the trans-Saharan trade important to the West African kingdoms of Songhai, Kanem-Bornu, and Hausaland?*

Ethiopia
• *How did the Coptic Christian Church in Ethiopia serve as a unifying force for the society and for the kingdom?*

The Swahili City-States
• *What was the significance of the Indian Ocean to the political and economic organization of the Swahili city-states?*

The African Slave Trade
• *What role did slavery play in African societies before European intrusion?*

African states and societies of the fifteenth through eighteenth centuries comprised hundreds of ethnic groups and a wide variety of languages, cultures, and kinds of economic and political development. Modern European intrusion into Africa beginning in the fifteenth century led to the transatlantic slave trade, one of the greatest forced migrations in world history. Africa made a substantial, though involuntary, contribution to the building of the West's industrial civilization. In the seventeenth century an increasing desire for sugar in Europe resulted in an increasing demand for slave labor in South America and the West Indies. In the eighteenth century Western technological changes created a demand for cotton and other crops that required extensive human labor. As a result, the West's "need" for African slaves increased dramatically.

SENEGAMBIA AND BENIN

What different types of economic, social, and political structures were found in Senegambia and Benin?

In mid-fifteenth century Africa, a number of kingdoms flourished along the two-thousand-mile west coast between Senegambia and the northeastern shore of the Gulf of Guinea. Because much of that coastal region is covered by tropical rain forest, in contrast to the western Sudan, it is called the West African Forest Region (see Map 18.1). The Senegambian states possessed a homogeneous culture and a common history. For centuries Senegambia—named for the Senegal and Gambia Rivers—served as an important entrepôt for desert caravan contact with North African and Middle Eastern Islamic civilizations. Through the transatlantic slave trade, Senegambia came into contact with Europe and the Americas. Thus Senegambia felt the impact of Islamic culture to the north and of European influences from the maritime West.

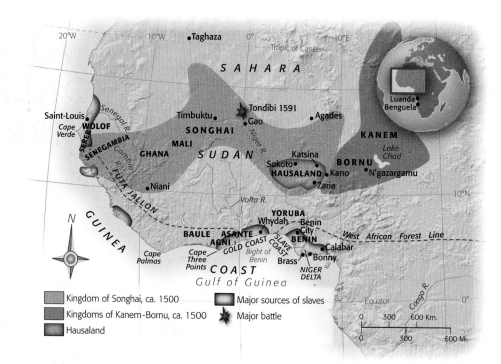

MAP 18.1 **West African Kingdoms and the Slave Trade, ca. 1500–1800** Consider the role that rivers and other geographical factors played in the development of the West African slave trade. Why were Luanda and Benguela the logical Portuguese sources for slaves?

Primary Source:

A Voyage to New Calabar River in the Year 1699
Learn about the slave trade in West Africa, from a Frenchman on an English slave-trading expedition.

age-grade systems *Among the societies of Senegambia, groups of men and women whom the society initiated into adulthood at the same time.*

oba *The name for the king of Benin.*

The Senegambian peoples spoke Wolof, Serer, and Pulaar, which all belong to the West African language group. Both the Wolof-speakers and the Serer-speakers had clearly defined social classes: royalty, nobility, warriors, peasants, low-caste artisans such as blacksmiths and leatherworkers, and slaves. Slaves were individuals who were pawned for debt, house servants who could not be sold, and people who were acquired through war or purchase. Senegambian slavery varied from society to society but generally was not a benign institution. In some places, slaves were treated as harshly as they would be later in the Western Hemisphere. However, many Senegambian slaves were not considered chattel property to be bought and sold, and some served as royal advisers and enjoyed great power and prestige.[1]

Among Senegambia's stateless societies, where kinship and lineage groups tended to fragment communities, **age-grade systems** evolved. Age-grades were groups of teenage males and females whom the society initiated into adulthood at the same time. Age-grades cut across family ties, created community-wide loyalties, and provided a means of local law enforcement, because each age-grade was responsible for the behavior of all its members.

The typical Senegambian community was a small, self-supporting agricultural village of closely related families. Fields were cut from the surrounding forest, and the average six- to eight-acre farm supported a moderate-size family. Millet and sorghum were the staple grains in northern Senegambia; farther south, forest dwellers cultivated yams as a staple. Village markets for produce exchange offered opportunities for receiving outside news and social diversion. As one scholar has put it, "Life was simple, government largely limited to the settlement of disputes by family heads or elders . . . social life centered on the ceremony accompanying birth, death, and family alliance."[2]

The great forest kingdom of Benin (see Map 18.1) emerged in the fifteenth and sixteenth centuries in what is now southern Nigeria. In the later fifteenth century, the **oba** (or king), Ewuare, a great warrior himself, strengthened his army and pushed Benin's borders as far as the Niger River in the east, westward into Yoruba country, and south to the Gulf of Guinea. During the late sixteenth and seventeenth centuries, the office of the oba evolved from a warrior-kingship to a position of spiritual leadership.

At its height in the late sixteenth century, Benin controlled a vast territory, and European visitors described a sophisticated society. The capital, Benin City, "was a stronghold twenty-five miles in circumference, protected by walls and natural defenses, containing an elaborate royal palace and neatly laid-out houses with verandas and balustrades, and divided by broad avenues and smaller intersecting streets."[3] Visitors also noted that Benin City was kept scrupulously clean and had no beggars and that public security was so effective that theft was unknown. The period also witnessed remarkable artistic creativity in ironwork, carved ivory, and especially bronze portrait busts. Over nine hundred brass plaques survive, providing important information about Benin court life, military triumphs, and cosmological ideas.

In 1485 Portuguese and other Europeans began to appear in Benin in pursuit of trade. Europe's impact on Benin was minimal, however. In the early eighteenth century, tributary states and stronger neighbors nibbled at Benin's frontiers, challenging its power. Benin, however, survived as an independent entity until the British conquered and burned Benin City in 1898.

Women, Marriage, and Work

West Africa's population needs (see page 538) profoundly affected marriage patterns and family structure. Wives and children were highly desired because they could clear and cultivate the land and because they brought prestige, social support, and security in old age. The result was intense competition for women, inequality of access to them, an emphasis on male virility and female fertility, and serious tension between male generations. Polygyny was almost universal; as recently as the nineteenth century two-thirds of rural wives were in polygynous marriages.

Men acquired wives in two ways. First, some couples simply eloped and began unions. More commonly, a man's family compensated the bride's family through the payment of bride wealth for the loss of her reproductive abilities: children; food through her labor; and the culture as she raised her children. Because it took time for a young man to acquire the bride wealth, all but the richest men delayed marriage until about age thirty. Women married at about the onset of puberty.

The easy availability of land in Africa reduced the kinds of generational conflict that occurred in western Europe, where land was scarce. Competition for wives between male generations, however, became "one of the most dynamic and enduring forces in African history."[4] On the one hand, myth and folklore stressed respect for the elderly, and the older men in a community imposed their authority over the younger ones by

Chronology

1400–1600s   Salt trade dominates West African economy

ca. 1400–1846   Kanem-Bornu kingdom controls region around Lake Chad

ca. 1440–1550   First Portuguese exploration and settlement along Africa's coasts

ca. 1464–1591   Songhai kingdom dominates the western Sudan

1485   Portuguese and other Europeans first appear in Benin

1492–1528   Muhammad Toure governs and expands kingdom of Songhai

1498   Portuguese explorer Vasco da Gama sails around Africa; Swahili cities' independence begins to decline

ca. 1500–1900   Height of African slave trade

1526   Leo Africanus publishes account of his stay in the Songhai kingdom

1529   Ahmad ibn-Ghazi destroys Ethiopian artistic and literary works and forces conversions to Islam

1541   Portuguese defeat Muslims in Ethiopia

1571–1603   Idris Alooma governs kingdom of Kanem-Bornu

1591   Moroccan army defeats Songhai

1658   Dutch allow importation of slaves into Cape Colony

1680s   Famine from Senegambian coast to Upper Nile

1738–1756   Major famine in West Africa

1788   Olaudah Equiano publishes *Travels*

● **The Oba of Benin** The oba's palace walls were decorated with bronze plaques that date from about the sixteenth to the eighteenth centuries. This plaque vividly conveys the oba's power, majesty, and authority. The necklace (or choker) is his symbol of royalty. His warrior attendants surround and protect him and carry his royal regalia. (*Museum für Wolkerkunde, Kunsthistorisches Museum, Vienna*)

including painful rites of initiation into adulthood, such as circumcision. On the other hand, West African societies were not gerontocracies, as few people lived much beyond forty. Young men possessed the powerful asset of their labor, which could easily be turned into independence where so much land was available.

"Without children you are naked" goes a Yoruba proverb, and children were the primary goal of marriage. Just as a man's virility determined his honor, so barrenness damaged a woman's status. A wife's infidelity was considered a less serious problem than her infertility. A woman might have six widely spaced pregnancies in her fertile years; the universal practice of breast-feeding infants for two, three, or even four years may have inhibited conception. Long intervals between births due to food shortages also may have limited pregnancies and checked population growth. Harsh climate, poor nutrition, and infectious diseases also contributed to a high infant mortality rate.

Both nuclear and extended families were common in West Africa. Nuclear families averaged only five or six members, but the household of a Big Man (a local man of power) included his wives, married and unmarried sons, unmarried daughters, poor relations, dependents, and scores of children. Extended families were common among the Hausa and Malinke peoples. On the Gold Coast in the seventeenth century, a well-to-do man's household might number 150 people, in the Kongo region several hundred. Where one family cultivated extensive land, a large household of young adults, children, and slaves probably proved most efficient.

In agriculture men did the heavy work of felling trees and clearing the land; women then planted, weeded, and harvested. Between 1000 and 1400, cassava (manioc), bananas, and plantains came to West Africa from Asia. Cassava became a staple food, but it had little nutritional value. In the sixteenth century the Portuguese introduced maize (corn), sweet potatoes, and new varieties of yams from the Americas.[5] Fish supplemented the diets of people living near bodies of water. According to Olaudah Equiano, the Ibo people in the mid-eighteenth century ate plantains, yams, beans, and Indian corn, along with stewed poultry, goat, or bullock (castrated steer) seasoned with peppers.[6] Such a protein-rich diet was probably exceptional.

Disease posed perhaps the biggest obstacle to population growth. Malaria, spread by mosquitoes and rampant in West Africa (except in cool, dry Cameroon), was the greatest killer, especially of infants. West Africans developed a relatively high degree of immunity to malaria and other parasitic diseases, including hookworm (which enters the body through shoeless feet and attaches itself to the intestines), yaws (contracted by nonsexual contact and recognized by ulcerating lesions), sleeping sickness (the parasite enters the blood through the bite of the tsetse fly; symptoms are enlarged lymph nodes and, at the end, a comatose state), and a mild nonsexual form of syphilis. Acute strains of smallpox introduced by Europeans certainly did not help population growth, nor did venereal syphilis. As in Chinese and European communities in the early modern period, the sick depended on folk medicine. African medical specialists, such as midwives, bone setters, exorcists using religious methods, and herbalists, administered a variety of treatments including herbal medications like salves, ointments, and purgatives. Still, disease was common where the diet was poor and lacked adequate vitamins. Slaves taken to the Americas grew much taller and broader than their African cousins.

Drought, excessive rain, swarms of locusts, and rural wars that prevented the cultivation of land all meant later food shortages and devastating famines that proved another major check on population growth. In the 1680s famine extended from the Senegambian coast to the Upper Nile, and many people sold themselves into slavery for food. In the eighteenth century "slave exports" (see pages 526–539) "peaked during famines, and one ship obtained a full cargo merely by offering food." [7] The worst disaster occurred from 1738 to 1756, when, according to one chronicler, the poor were reduced to cannibalism, an African metaphor for the complete collapse of civilization.[8]

Trade and Industry

As in all premodern societies, West African economies rested on agriculture. There was some trade and industry, but population shortages encouraged local self-sufficiency, slowed transportation, and hindered exchange. There were very few large markets, and their relative isolation from the outside world and failure to attract large numbers of foreign merchants limited technological innovation.

As elsewhere, water was the cheapest method of transportation, and many small dugout canoes and larger trading canoes plied the Niger and its delta region (see Map 18.1). On land West African peoples used pack animals (camels or donkeys) rather than wheeled vehicles; south of the Sahara, only a narrow belt of land was suitable for animal-drawn carts. When traders reached an area infested with tsetse flies, they transferred each animal's load to human porters. Such difficulties in transport severely restricted long-distance trade, so most people relied on the regional exchange of local specialties.

West African communities had a well-organized market system. At informal markets on riverbanks, fishermen bartered fish for local specialties. More formal markets existed within towns and villages or on neutral ground between them. Markets also rotated among neighboring villages on certain days. People exchanged cotton cloth, thread, palm oil, millet, vegetables, and small articles for daily living. Local sellers were usually women; traders from afar were men.

From time immemorial, salt has been one of the most critical trade items. Salt is essential to human health; the Hausa language has more than fifty words for it. The main salt-mining center was at **Taghaza** (see Map 18.1) in the western Sahara. In the most wretched conditions, slaves dug the salt from desiccated lakes and loaded heavy blocks onto camels' backs. **Tuareg** warriors and later Moors (peoples of Berber and

● **Queen Mother and Attendants**   As in Ottoman, Chinese, and European societies, so the mothers of African rulers sometimes exercised considerable political power because of their influence on their sons. African kings granted the title "Queen Mother" as a badge of honor. In this figure, the long beaded cap, called "chicken's beak," symbolizes the mother's rank, as do her elaborate neck jewelry and attendants. *(Metropolitan Museum of Art. Gift of Mr. and Mrs. Klaus G. Perls, 1991 [1991.17.111]. Photograph © 1991 The Metropolitan Museum of Art)*

Taghaza   *A desolate settlement in the western Sahara; it was the site of the main salt-mining center.*

Tuareg   *Along with the Moors, these warriors controlled the north-south trade in salt.*

Arab descent) traded their salt south for gold, grain, slaves, and kola nuts, which were used by Muslims as stimulants or aphrodisiacs. **Cowrie shells,** imported from the Maldive Islands in the Indian Ocean by way of Gujarat (see page 565) and North Africa, served as the medium of exchange. (Shell money continued as a medium long after European intrusion.)

West African peoples engaged in many crafts, such as basket weaving and pottery making. Ironworking, a specialized skill producing articles useful to hunters, farmers, and warriors, became hereditary in individual families; such expertise was regarded as family property. The textile industry had the greatest level of specialization. The earliest fabric in West Africa was made of vegetable fiber. Muslim traders introduced cotton and its weaving in the ninth century, as the fine-quality fabrics found in Mali reveal. By the fifteenth century the Wolof and Malinke regions had professional weavers producing beautiful cloth, but this cloth was too expensive to compete in the Atlantic and Indian Ocean markets after 1500. Women who spun cotton used only a spindle and not a wheel, which slowed output. Women wove on inefficient broadlooms, men on less clumsy but unproductive narrow looms.[9]

● **Salt Making in the Central Sahara** For centuries camel caravans transported salt south across the Sahara to the great West African kingdoms, where it was exchanged for gold. Here at Teguidda-n-Tessum, Niger, in the central Sahara, salt is still collected by pouring spring water (stored in the larger pools in the background) into the smaller pools dug out of the saline soil. The water leaches out the salt before evaporating in the desert sun, leaving deposits of pure salt behind, which is then shaped into blocks for transport. (Afrique Photo, Cliché Naud, Paris)

Cowrie shells *Imported from the Maldive Islands, these served as the medium of exchange in West Africa.*

THE SUDAN: SONGHAI, KANEM-BORNU, AND HAUSALAND

In what ways was the trans-Saharan trade important to the West African kingdoms of Songhai, Kanem-Bornu, and Hausaland?

The Songhai kingdom, a successor state of Ghana and Mali, dominated the whole Niger region of the western and central Sudan (see Map 18.1). From his capital at Gao, the Songhai king Muhammad Toure (r. 1492–1528) extended his rule as far north as the salt-mining center at Taghaza in the western Sahara and as far east as Agada and Kano. A convert to Islam, Muhammad returned from a pilgrimage to Mecca impressed by what he had seen there. He tried to bring about greater centralization in his own territories by building a strong army, improving taxation procedures, and replacing local Songhai officials with more efficient Arab ones in an effort to substitute royal institutions for ancient kinship ties.

We know little about daily life in Songhai society because of the paucity of written records and surviving artifacts. Some information is provided by Leo Africanus (ca. 1465–1550), a Moroccan captured by pirates and given as a slave to Pope Leo X. Leo Africanus became a Christian, taught Arabic in Rome, and in 1526 published an account of his many travels, including a stay in the Songhai kingdom.

As a scholar, Africanus was naturally impressed by Timbuktu, the second city of the empire, which he visited in 1513. "Here [is] a great store of doctors, judges, priests, and other learned men, that are bountifully maintained at the King's court," he reported.[10] Many of these Islamic scholars had studied in Cairo and other centers of

Muslim learning. They gave Timbuktu a reputation for intellectual sophistication, religious piety, and moral justice.

Songhai under Muhammad Toure seems to have enjoyed economic prosperity. Leo Africanus noted the abundant food supply, which was produced in the southern Savanna and carried to Timbuktu by a large fleet of canoes. The elite had large amounts of money to spend, and expensive North African and European luxuries were much in demand: clothes, copperware, glass and stone beads, perfumes, and horses. The existence of many shops and markets implies the development of an urban culture. At Timbuktu, merchants, scholars, judges, and artisans constituted a distinctive bourgeoisie. The presence of many foreign merchants, including Jews and Italians, gave the city a cosmopolitan atmosphere. Jews largely controlled the working of gold.

Slaves played a very important part in Songhai's economy. On the royal farms scattered throughout the kingdom, slaves produced rice—the staple crop—for the royal granaries. Slaves could possess their own slaves, land, and cattle, but could not bequeath any of this property; the king inherited all of it. Muhammad Toure greatly increased the number of royal slaves. He gave slaves to favorite Muslim scholars, who thus gained a steady source of income. Slaves were also sold at the large market at Gao, where traders from North Africa bought them for resale in Cairo, Constantinople, Lisbon, Naples, Genoa, and Venice.

Despite its considerable economic and cultural strengths, Songhai had serious internal problems. Islam never took root in the countryside, and Muslim officials alienated the king from his people. Muhammad Toure's reforms were a failure. He governed a diverse group of peoples—Tuareg, Malinke, and Fulani, as well as Songhai—who were often hostile to one another, and no cohesive element united them. Finally, the Songhai never developed an effective method of transferring power. Muhammad Toure himself was murdered by one of his sons. His death began a period of political instability that led to the kingdom's slow disintegration.[11]

In 1582 the Moroccan sultanate began to press southward in search of a greater share of the trans-Saharan trade. The Songhai people, lacking effective leadership and believing the desert to be a sure protection against invasion, took no defensive precautions. In 1591 a Moroccan army of three thousand soldiers—many of whom were slaves of European origin equipped with European muskets—crossed the Sahara and inflicted a crushing defeat on the Songhai at Tondibi, spelling the end of the Songhai Empire.

East of Songhai lay the kingdoms of Kanem-Bornu and Hausaland (see Map 18.1). Under the dynamic military leader Idris Alooma (1571–1603), Kanem-Bornu subdued weaker peoples and gained jurisdiction over an extensive area. Well drilled and equipped with firearms, camel-mounted cavalry and a standing army decimated warriors fighting with spears and arrows. Idris Alooma perpetuated a form of feudalism by granting lands to able fighters in return for loyalty and the promise of future military assistance. Meanwhile, agriculture occupied most people, peasants and slaves alike. Kanem-Bornu shared in the trans-Saharan trade, shipping eunuchs and young girls to North Africa in return for horses and firearms. A devout Muslim, Idris Alooma elicited high praise from ibn-Fartura, who wrote a history of his reign called *The Kanem Wars*:

So he made the pilgrimage and visited Medina with delight. . . . Among the benefits which God . . . conferred upon the Sultan Idris Alooma was the acquisition of Turkish musketeers and numerous household slaves who became skilled in firing muskets. . . .

Among the most surprising of his acts was the stand he took against obscenity and adultery, so that no such thing took place openly in his time. Formerly the people had been indifferent to such offences. . . . In fact he was a power among his people and from him came their strength.

The Sultan was intent on the clear path laid down by the Qur'an . . . in all his affairs and actions.[12]

Idris Alooma built mosques at his capital city of N'gazargamu and substituted Muslim courts and Islamic law for African tribunals and ancient customary law. His eighteenth-century successors lacked his vitality and military skills, however, and the empire declined.

Between Songhai and Kanem-Bornu were the lands of the Hausa, an agricultural people who lived in small villages. Hausa merchants, however, carried on a heavy trade in slaves and kola nuts with North African communities across the Sahara, and obscure trading posts evolved into important Hausa city-states like Kano and Katsina, through which Islamic influences entered the region. Kano and Katsina became Muslim intellectual centers and in the fifteenth century attracted scholars from Timbuktu. The Muslim chronicler of the reign of King Muhammad Rimfa of Kano (r. 1463–1499) records that the king introduced the Muslim practices of *purdah,* or seclusion of women; of the *idal-fitr,* or festival after the fast of Ramadan; and of assigning eunuchs to high state offices.[13] As in Songhai and Kanem-Bornu, however, Islam made no strong imprint on the Hausa masses until the nineteenth century.

ETHIOPIA

How did the Coptic Christian Church in Ethiopia serve as a unifying force for the society and for the kingdom?

At the beginning of the sixteenth century, the powerful East African Christian kingdom of Ethiopia extended from Massawa in the north to several tributary states in the south (see Map 18.2). The ruling Solomonic dynasty, however, faced serious troubles. Adal, a Muslim state along the southern base of the Red Sea, began incursions into Ethiopia, and in 1529 the Adal general Ahmad ibn-Ghazi inflicted a disastrous defeat on the Ethiopian emperor Lebna Dengel (r. 1508–1540). Ahmad followed up his victory with systematic devastation of the land, destruction of many Ethiopian artistic and literary works, and the forced conversion of thousands to Islam. Lebna Dengel fled to the mountains and appealed to Portugal for assistance.

In the late twelfth century, tales of Prester John, rumored to be a powerful Christian monarch ruling a vast and wealthy African empire, reached western Europe. The search for Prester John, as well as for gold and spices, spurred the Portuguese to undertake a series of trans-African expeditions. In the 1480s they reached Timbuktu and Mali. Although Prester John was a totally mythical figure, Portuguese emissaries, who by 1508 had reached the Ethiopian capital, triumphantly but mistakenly identified the Ethiopian emperor as Prester John himself.[14] Desirous of converting Ethiopians from Coptic Chris-

● **Saint George in Ethiopian Art** This wall painting of Saint George slaying a dragon resides in the stone-carved Church of St. George at Lalibela, Ethiopia, and attests to the powerful and pervasive Christian influence of Ethiopian culture. *(Galen Frysinger)*

tianity to Roman Catholicism, the Portuguese responded to Lebna Dengel's request for help with a force of musketeers. In 1541 they decisively defeated the Muslims near Lake Tana. No sooner had the Muslim threat ended than Ethiopia encountered three more dangers. The Galla, Cushitic-speaking peoples, moved northward in great numbers, occupying portions of Harar, Shoa, and Amhara. The Ethiopians could not defeat them militarily, and the Galla were not interested in assimilation. For the next two centuries, the two peoples lived together in an uneasy truce. Simultaneous with the Galla migrations was the Ottoman Turks' seizure of Massawa and other coastal cities. Then the Jesuits arrived and attempted to force Roman Catholicism on a proud people whose Coptic form of Christianity long antedated the European version. The overzealous Jesuit missionary Alphonse Mendez tried to revamp the Ethiopian liturgy, rebaptize the people, and replace ancient Ethiopian customs and practices with Roman ones. Since Ethiopian national sentiment was closely tied to Coptic Christianity, violent rebellion and anarchy ensued.

In 1633 the Jesuit missionaries were expelled. For the next two centuries, hostility to foreigners, weak political leadership, and regionalism characterized Ethiopia. Civil conflicts between Galla and Ethiopians erupted continually. The Coptic church, though lacking strong authority, survived as the cornerstone of Ethiopian national identity.

THE SWAHILI CITY-STATES

What was the significance of the Indian Ocean to the political and economic organization of the Swahili city-states?

The word **Swahili,** meaning "People of the Coast," refers to the people living along the East African coast and on the nearby islands. Their history, unlike that of most African peoples, exists in writing. By the eleventh century the Swahili had accepted Islam, and "its acceptance was the factor that marked the acquisition of 'Swahili' identity: Islam gave the society coherent cultural form."[15] Living on the Indian Ocean coast, the Swahili felt the influences of Indians, Indonesians, Persians, and especially Arabs.

Swahili civilization was overwhelmingly maritime. A fertile, well-watered, and intensely cultivated stretch of land no more than ten miles wide extends down the coast: it yielded rice, grains, citrus fruit, and cloves. The region's considerable prosperity, however, rested on trade and commerce. The Swahili acted as middlemen in an Indian Ocean–East African protocapitalism: exchanging ivory, rhinoceros horn, tortoise shells, inlaid ebony chairs, copra (dried coconut meat that yields coconut oil), and inland slaves for Arabian and Persian perfumes, toilet articles, ink, and paper and for Indian textiles, beads, and iron tools. In the fifteenth century the cosmopolitan city-states of Mogadishu, Pate, Lamu, Mombasa, and especially Kilwa enjoyed a worldwide reputation for commercial prosperity and high living standards.[16]

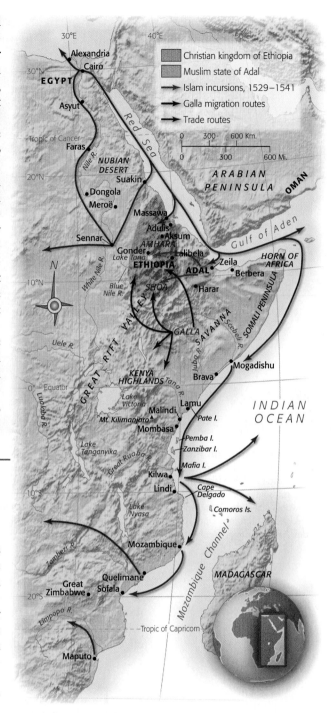

MAP 18.2 **East Africa in the Sixteenth Century** In early modern times, the Christian kingdom of Ethiopia, first isolated and then subjected to Muslim and European pressures, played an insignificant role in world affairs. But the East African city-states, which stretched from Sofala in the south to Mogadishu in the north, had powerfully important commercial relations with Mughal India, China, the Ottoman world, and southern Europe.

Swahili *Meaning "People of the Coast," the term used for the people living along the East African coast and on nearby islands.*

● **Chinese Porcelain Plates** Embedded in an eighteenth-century Kunduchi pillar tomb, these Chinese plates testify to the enormous Asian-African trade that flourished in the fourteenth to sixteenth centuries. Kunduchi, whose ruins lie north of Dar es Salaam in present-day Tanzania, was one of the Swahili city-states. Why would a Muslim African want a Chinese plate embedded in his tomb? Does it indicate that he was involved in the porcelain trade? *(Werner Forman/Art Resource, NY)*

The arrival of the Portuguese explorer Vasco da Gama (see Map 15.2 on page 438) in 1498 spelled the end of the Swahili cities' independence. Lured by the spice trade, da Gama wanted to build a Portuguese maritime empire in the Indian Ocean. Swahili rulers responded in different ways to Portuguese intrusion. The sultan of Malindi quickly agreed to a trading alliance with the Portuguese. The sultan of Mombasa was tricked into commercial agreements. Still other Swahili rulers totally rejected Portuguese overtures, and their cities were subjected to bombardment. To secure alliances made between 1502 and 1507 the Portuguese erected forts at the southern port cities of Kilwa, Zanzibar, and Sofala. These forts—fortified markets and trading posts—served as the foundation of Portuguese commercial power on the Swahili coast.[17] (See the feature "Listening to the Past: Duarte Barbosa on the Swahili City-States" on pages 542–543.) The better-fortified northern cities, such as Mogadishu, survived as important entrepôts for goods to India.

The Portuguese presence in the south proved hollow, however. Rather than accept Portuguese commercial restrictions, the residents deserted the towns, and the town economies crumbled. Large numbers of Kilwa's people, for example, immigrated to northern cities. The gold flow from inland mines to Sofala slowed to a trickle. Swahili noncooperation successfully prevented the Portuguese from gaining control of the local coastal trade.

In 1589 Portugal finally won an administrative stronghold near Mombasa. Called Fort Jesus, it remained a Portuguese base for over a century. In the late seventeenth century, pressures from the northern European maritime powers—the Dutch, French, and English—aided greatly by Omani Arabs, combined with local African rebellions to bring about the collapse of Portuguese influence in Africa. A Portuguese presence remained only at Mozambique in the far south and Angola on the west coast.

The Portuguese had no religious or cultural impact on the Swahili cities. Their sole effect was the cities' economic decline.

THE AFRICAN SLAVE TRADE

What role did slavery play in African societies before European intrusion?

slave *A person who is bound in servitude and often traded as property or as a commodity.*

Long before the European intrusion, the exchange of peoples captured in local and ethnic wars within sub-Saharan Africa, the trans-Saharan **slave** trade with the Mediterranean Islamic world beginning in the seventh century, and the slave traffic across the Indian Ocean all testify to the long tradition and continental dimensions of the African slave trade. "Slavery was . . . fundamental to the social, political, and economic order of parts of the northern savanna, Ethiopia and the East African

● **Fort Jesus, Mombasa**   Designed by the Milanese military architect Joao Batista Cairato in traditional European style, and built between 1593 and 1594, this great fortress still stands as a symbol of Portuguese military and commercial power in East Africa and the Indian Ocean in the sixteenth and seventeenth centuries. *(Wolfgang Kaehler Photography)*

coast. . . . Enslavement was an organized activity, sanctioned by law and custom. Slaves were a principal commodity in trade, including the export sector, and slaves were important in the domestic sphere" as concubines, servants, soldiers, and ordinary laborers.[18]

Islamic practices heavily influenced African slavery. African rulers justified enslavement with the Muslim argument that prisoners of war could be sold and that captured peoples were considered chattel, or personal possessions, to be used in any way the owner saw fit. Between 650 and 1600, black as well as white Muslims transported perhaps as many as 4.82 million black slaves across the trans-Saharan trade route.[19] In the fourteenth and fifteenth centuries the rulers and elites of Mali and Benin imported thousands of white slave women, symbols of wealth and status, from the eastern Mediterranean.[20] In 1444, when Portuguese caravels landed 235 slaves at Algarve in southern Portugal, a contemporary observed that they seemed "a marvelous (extraordinary) sight, for, amongst them, were some white enough, fair enough, and well-proportioned; others were less white, like mulattoes; others again were black as Ethiops."[21]

Meanwhile, the flow of black people to Europe, begun during the Renaissance, continued. In the seventeenth and eighteenth centuries, as many as two hundred thousand Africans entered European societies. Some arrived as slaves, others as servants; the legal distinction was not always clear. Eighteenth-century London, for example, had more than ten thousand blacks, most of whom arrived as sailors on Atlantic crossings or as personal servants brought from the West Indies. In England most were

KITCHIN STUFF.

● **Below Stairs** The prints and cartoons of Thomas Rowlandson (1756–1827) testify to the sizable numbers of blacks in eighteenth-century London, where they worked in naval and military as well as domestic service. Here the household cook, maid, and footman relax before the kitchen fire. Interracial marriages were not uncommon. *(Courtesy of the Trustees of the British Museum)*

free, not slaves. Initially, a handsome black was a fashionable accessory, a rare status symbol. Later, English aristocrats considered black servants too ordinary. The duchess of Devonshire offered her mother an eleven-year-old boy, explaining that the duke did not want a Negro servant because "it was more original to have a Chinese page than to have a black one; everybody had a black one."[22] London's black population constituted a well-organized, self-conscious subculture, with black pubs, black churches, and black social groups assisting the black poor and unemployed. Some black people attained wealth and position, the most famous being Francis Barber, the literary giant Samuel Johnson's servant, who inherited Johnson's sizable fortune.

In 1658 the Dutch East India Company began to allow the importation of slaves into the Cape Colony of southern Africa. Over the next century and a half about 75 percent of the slaves brought into the colony came from Dutch East India Company colonies in India and Southeast Asia or from Madagascar, and the remaining 25 percent from Africa. The Dutch East India Company was the single largest slave owner in the Cape Colony, employing its slaves on public works and company farms. Initially, individual company officials collectively owned the most slaves, working them on their wine and grain estates.[23] By about 1740 urban and rural free burghers owned the majority of the slaves. The slave population at the Cape was never large, although from the early 1700s to the 1820s it outnumbered the European free burgher population. When the British ended slavery in the British Empire in 1834, there were only around thirty-six thousand slaves in the Cape Colony.

Some slaves at the Cape served as domestic servants or as semiskilled artisans, but most worked long and hard as field hands and at any other menial or manual forms of labor needed by their European masters. Slave ownership fostered a strong sense of racial and economic solidarity in the white master class. Although in the seventeenth and eighteenth centuries Holland enjoyed a Europe-wide reputation for religious toleration and intellectual freedom (see page 485), in the Cape Colony the Dutch used a strict racial hierarchy and heavy-handed paternalism to maintain control over native peoples and foreign-born slaves.[24]

The Savanna and Horn regions of East Africa experienced a great expansion of the slave trade in the late eighteenth, and first half of the nineteenth centuries. Slave exports from these areas and from the eastern coast amounted to perhaps thirty thousand a year. Why this demand? Merchants and planters wanted slaves to work the sugar plantations on the Mascarene Islands, located east of Madagascar, the clove plantations on Zanzibar and Pemba, and the food plantations along the Kenyan coast. The eastern coast also exported slaves to the Americas, particularly to Brazil. In the late eighteenth and early nineteenth centuries, precisely when the slave trade to North America and the Caribbean declined, the Eastern and Asian markets expanded. Only with colonial conquest by Great Britain, Germany, and Italy after 1870 did suppression of the trade begin. Slavery, of course, persists even today. (See the feature "Global Trade: Slaves" on pages 530–531.)

● **Charles Davidson Bell (1813–1882): Schoolmaster Reading**   In this watercolor print, a schoolmaster reads and explains the newspaper *Zuid Afrikaan* (The South African) to the (probably illiterate) household, while black servants cook and fan. Chickens peck for crumbs on the floor. *(William Fehr Collection, IZIKO Museums of Cape Town)*

The Atlantic Slave Trade

Although the trade in African people was a worldwide phenomenon, the Atlantic slave trade involved the largest number of enslaved Africans. This forced migration of millions of human beings, extending from the early sixteenth to the late nineteenth centuries, represents one of the most inhumane, unjust, and shameful tragedies in human history. It also immediately provokes a troubling question: why Africa? Why, in the seventeenth and eighteenth centuries, did enslavement in the Americas become exclusively African?

As we have seen (see page 444), Europeans first used indigenous peoples, the Amerindians, to mine Mexican silver and gold. When they proved ill-suited to the harsh rigors of mining, the Spaniards brought in Africans. Although the Dutch had transported Indonesian peoples to the Cape Colony in South Africa, the cost of transporting Chinese or Pacific island peoples to the Americas was far too great.

One scholar has recently argued that across Europe, a pan-European insider-outsider ideology prevailed. This cultural attitude permitted the enslavement of outsiders but made the enslavement of white Europeans taboo. Europeans could not bear the sight of other Europeans doing plantation slave labor. According to this theory, a similar pan-African ideology did not exist, as Africans had no problem with selling Africans to Europeans.[25] Several facts argue against the validity of this theory. English landlords exploited their Irish peasants with merciless severity; French aristocrats often looked on their peasantry with cold contempt; and Russian boyars treated their serfs with casual indifference and harsh brutality. These and other possible examples contradict the existence of a pan-European ideology or culture that opposed the enslavement of white Europeans. Moreover, the flow of white Slavic slaves from the Balkans into the eastern Mediterranean continued unabated during the same period.

Another theory holds that in the Muslim and Arab worlds by the tenth century, an association had developed between blackness and menial slavery. The Arab word *abd,* or

SLAVES

The history of the global slave trade is rife with ironies. The traffic in human persons bought and sold for the profits of their labor cannot decently be compared with that in other commodities; people are not goods. But most societies, with the remarkable exception of the Aborigines in Australia, have treated people as goods and engaged in the slave trade. Those who have been enslaved include captives in war, persons convicted of crimes, persons sold for debt, and persons bought and sold for sex. The ancient Greek philosophers, notably Aristotle, justified slavery as "natural." The Middle Eastern monotheistic faiths—Judaism, Christianity, and Islam—while professing the sacred dignity of each individual, and the Asian religious and sociopolitical ideologies of Buddhism and Confucianism, while stressing an ordered and harmonious society, all tolerated slavery and urged slaves' obedience to established authorities. Until the Enlightenment of the eighteenth century, most people everywhere accepted slavery as a "natural phenomenon." Nor is it without irony that the Thirteenth Amendment to the U.S. Constitution (ratified in 1865), popularly interpreted as abolishing slavery, allows slavery "as a punishment for crime whereof the party shall have been duly convicted."

Between 1500 and 1900, the transatlantic African slave trade accounted for the largest number of people bought and sold. As such, and because of ample documentation, it has attracted much of the attention of scholars, and it also has tended to identify the institution of slavery with African blacks. From a global perspective, however, the trade was far broader.

The Slave Trade

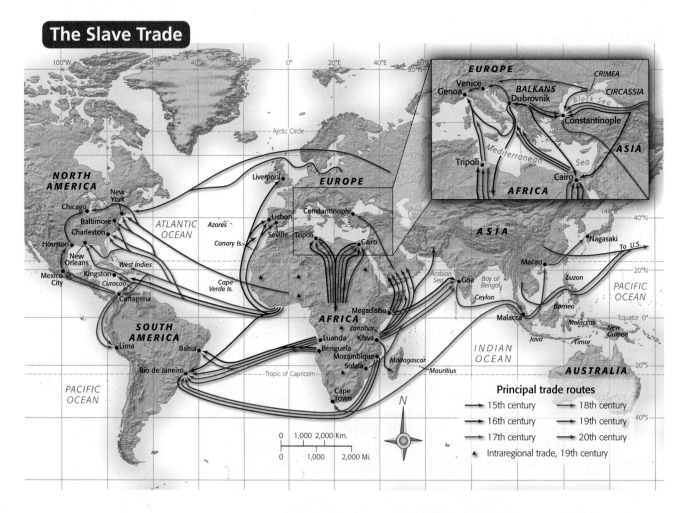

Principal trade routes
- → 15th century
- → 16th century
- → 17th century
- → 18th century
- → 19th century
- → 20th century
- ▲ Intraregional trade, 19th century

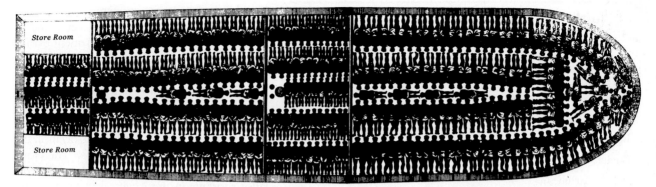

Store Room

Store Room

- The revolting conditions on slave ships sailing to
- Caribbean and North American ports pale in
- barbarity beside conditions on the southern route
- to Brazil, where slaves were literally packed like
- sardines in a can.

Indeed, hundreds of thousands of slaves were white or Asian. The steady flow of women and children from the Crimea, the Caucasus, and the Balkans in the fourteenth to eighteenth centuries for domestic, military, or sexual services in Ottoman lands, Italy, and sub-Saharan Africa; the use of convicts as galley slaves in the Venetian, French, Spanish, and Turkish navies (after the Battle of Lepanto in 1571, ten thousand Christian galley slaves in Turkish service were freed); the enslavement of peoples defeated in war by Aztec, Inca, Sioux, Navajo, and other indigenous peoples of the Americas; the various forms of debt slavery in China and in Russia (where the legal distinction between serf and slave before 1861 was very hazy indeed); the traffic of Indonesian and Pacific Island peoples for slave labor in Dutch South Africa; and the trans-Saharan stream of Africans to Mediterranean ports that continued at medieval rates into the late nineteenth century—all these were different forms of a worldwide practice. Although these forms sometimes had little in common with one another (such as the domestic and military slavery of the Islamic world and the plantation slavery of the Americas), they all involved the buying and selling of human beings who could not move about freely or enjoy the fruits of their labor.

The price of slaves varied widely over time and from market to market, according to age, sex, physical appearance, and buyers' perceptions of the social characteristics of each slave's ethnic background. The Mediterranean and Indian Ocean markets preferred women for domestic service; the Atlantic markets wanted strong young men for mine and plantation work. Changes in supply and demand could lead to great price fluctuations: the arrival of a very large number of slaves in a particular market or the failure of a dealer to appear when expected could drive prices down. We have little solid information on prices for slaves in the Balkans,

Caucasus, or Indian Ocean region. Even in the Atlantic trade, it is difficult to determine, over several centuries, the value of currencies such as the Dutch guilder and the British pound, the cost and insurance on transported slaves, and the cost of goods exchanged for slaves. Yet the grand palazzi of Venice, the gold-encrusted cathedrals of Spain, and the elegant plantation houses of the Southern United States stand as testimony to the vast fortunes made in the slave trade. But how is the human toll measured?

Transformations within societies occurred not only because of local developments but also because of interactions among regions. For example, the virulent racism that in so many ways defines the American experience resulted partly from medieval European habits of dehumanizing the enemy (English versus Irish, German versus Slav, Christian versus Jew and Muslim) and partly from the movement of peoples and ideas all over the globe. American gold prospectors in the 1850s carried the bigotry they had heaped on blacks in the Americas to Australia, where it conditioned attitudes toward Asians and other peoples of color. Racism, like the slave trade, is a global phenomenon.

A final irony exists in the fact that for all the cries for human rights today, the slave trade continues on a broad scale. The ancient Indian Ocean traffic in Indian girls and boys for "service" in the Persian Gulf oil kingdoms and the sale of African children for work in Asia persist. Well-verified British, American, and United Nations reports prove that each year between 1998 and 2000, "criminal elements" brought more than fifty thousand women and children from Latvia, Nigeria, the Philippines, Thailand, China, Russia, and Mexico into the United States to work as sex slaves. They were bought, sold, tricked, and held in captivity, and their labor was exploited for the financial benefit of masters in a global enterprise.

Table 18.1 Estimated Slave Imports by Destination, 1451–1870

DESTINATION	ESTIMATED TOTAL SLAVE IMPORTS
British North America	399,000
Spanish America	1,552,100
British Caribbean	1,665,000
French Caribbean	1,600,200
Dutch Caribbean	500,000
Danish Caribbean	28,000
Brazil	3,646,800
Old World	175,000
	9,566,100

Source: P. D. Curtin, *The Atlantic Slave Trade: A Census* (Madison: University of Wisconsin Press, 1969), p. 268. Used with permission of The University of Wisconsin Press.

"black," had become synonymous with *slave*. Although the great majority of slaves in the Islamic world were white, a racial element existed in Muslim perceptions: not all slaves were black, but blacks were identified with slavery. In Europe, after the arrival of tens of thousands of sub-Saharan Africans in the Iberian Peninsula during the fifteenth century, Christian Europeans also began to make a strong association between slavery and black Africans. Therefore, Africans seemed the "logical" solution to the labor shortage in the Americas.[26] Another important question relating to the African slave trade is this: why were African peoples enslaved in a period when serfdom was declining in western Europe, and when land was so widely available and much of the African continent had a labor shortage? The answer seems to lie in a technical problem related to African agriculture. Partly because of the tsetse fly, which causes sleeping sickness and other diseases, and partly because of easily leached lateritic soils (containing high concentrations of oxides), farmers had great difficulty using draft animals. Tropical soils responded poorly to plowing, and most work had to be done with the hoe. Productivity, therefore, was low. Economists maintain that in most societies, the value of a worker's productivity determines the value of his or her labor. In precolonial Africa, the individual's agricultural productivity was low, so his or her economic value to society was less than the economic value of a European peasant in Europe. Slaves in the Americas were more productive than free producers in Africa. And European slave dealers were very willing to pay a price higher than the value of an African's productivity in Africa.

The incidence of disease in the Americas also helps explain African enslavement. Smallpox took a terrible toll on Native Americans (see page 445), and between 30 and 50 percent of Europeans exposed to malaria succumbed to that sickness. Africans had developed some immunity to both diseases, and in the Americas they experienced the lowest mortality rate of any people, making them, ironically, the most suitable workers for the environment.

The Portuguese "discovered" Brazil in 1500 and founded a sugar colony at Bahia in 1551. Between 1551 and 1575, before the North American traffic began, the Portuguese delivered more African slaves to Brazil than would ever reach British North America (see Table 18.1). Portugal essentially monopolized the slave trade until 1600 and continued to play a large role in the seventeenth century, though the trade was increasingly taken over by the Dutch, French, and English. From 1690 until the House of Commons abolished the slave trade in 1807, England was the leading carrier of African slaves.

Population density and supply conditions along the West African coast and the sailing time to New World markets determined the sources of slaves. As the demand for slaves rose, slavers moved down the West African coast from Senegambia to the more densely populated hinterlands of the Bight of Benin and the Bight of Biafra (see Map 15.3 on page 447). The abundant supply of slaves in Angola, the region south of the Congo River, and the quick passage from Angola to Brazil and the Caribbean established that region as the major coast for Portuguese slavers.

Transatlantic wind patterns partly determined exchange routes. Shippers naturally preferred the swiftest crossing—that is, from the African port nearest the latitude of the intended American destination. Thus Portuguese shippers carried their cargoes

from Angola to Brazil, and British merchants sailed from the Bight of Benin to the Caribbean. The great majority of slaves were intended for the sugar and coffee plantations extending from the Caribbean islands to Brazil.[27] Angola produced 26 percent of all African slaves and 70 percent of all Portuguese slaves. Trading networks extending deep into the interior culminated at two major ports on the Angolan coast, Luanda and Benguela (see Map 18.1). The Portuguese acquired a few slaves through warfare but secured the vast majority through trade with African dealers. Whites did not participate in the inland markets.

Almost all Portuguese shipments went to satisfy the virtually insatiable Brazilian demand for slaves.[28] Here is an excerpt from a Portuguese doctor's 1793 report on conditions in Luanda before the voyage across the Atlantic had begun:

Here takes place the second round of hardships that these unlucky people are forced to suffer . . . their human nature entirely overlooked. The dwelling place of the slave is simply the dirt floor of the compound, and he remains there exposed to harsh conditions and bad weather, and at night there are only a lean-to and some sheds . . . which they are herded into like cattle.

Their food continues scarce as before . . . limited at times to badly cooked beans, at other times to corn. . . .

And when they reach a port . . . , they are branded on the right breast with the coat of arms of the king and nation, of whom they have become vassals. . . . This mark is made with a hot silver instrument in the act of paying the king's duties, and this brand mark is called a carimbo. . . .

In this miserable and deprived condition the terrified slaves remain for weeks and months, and the great number of them who die is unspeakable. With some ten or twelve thousand arriving at Luanda each year, it often happens that only six or seven thousand are finally transported to Brazil.[29]

Olaudah Equiano (see the feature "Individuals in Society: Olaudah Equiano") describes the experience of his voyage from Benin to Barbados in the Caribbean:

● **Queen Njiga (also Nzinga) Mbandi Ana de Sousa** Njiga of Ndongo (r. 1624–1629) is the most important female political figure in the history of early modern Angola. She used military force in her expansionist policy and participated fully in the slave trade, but she fiercely resisted Portuguese attempts to control that trade. Here she sits enthroned, wearing her crown (the cross a sign of her Christian baptism) and bracelets, giving an order. She has become a symbol of African resistance to colonial rule. *(Courtesy, Luigi Araldi, Modena)*

Primary Source:
The Interesting Narrative of Olaudah Equiano: Written by Himself
Read selections from an ex-slave's autobiography, one of the most influential abolitionist books published in England.

At last, when the ship we were in had got in all her cargo [of slaves], they made ready with many fearful noises, and we were all put under deck so that we could not see how they managed the vessel. . . . The stench of the hold while we were on the coast was so intolerably loathsome that it was dangerous to remain there for any time, and some of us had been permitted to stay on the deck for the fresh air; but now that the whole ship's cargo were confined together it became absolutely pestilential. The closeness of the place and the heat of the climate, added to the number in the ship, which was so crowded that each had scarcely room to turn himself, almost suffocated us. This produced copious perspirations, so that the air soon became unfit for respiration from a variety of loathsome smells, and brought on a sickness among the slaves, of which many died, thus falling victims to the improvident avarice, as I may call it, of their purchasers. This wretched situation was again aggravated by the galling of the chains, now become insupportable, and the filth of the necessary tubs [of human waste], into which the children often fell and were almost suffocated. The shrieks of the women and the groans of the dying rendered the whole a scene of horror almost inconceivable. Happily perhaps for myself I was soon reduced so low here that it was thought necessary to keep me almost always on deck, and from my extreme youth I was not put in fetters. . . . Two of my wearied countrymen who were chained together (I was near them at the time), preferring death to such a life of misery, somehow made through the nettings and jumped into the sea: immediately another quite dejected fellow, who on account of his illness was suffered to be out of irons, also followed their example. . . . Two of the wretches were drowned, but they got the other and afterwards flogged him unmercifully. . . . The want of fresh air, . . . and the stench of the necessary tubs carried off many. . . . At last we came in sight of the island of Barbados, at which the whites on board gave a great shout and made many signs of joy to us. . . . We soon anchored amongst them off Bridgetown. Many merchants and planters now came on board, though it was in the evening. They put us in separate parcels and examined us attentively. They also made us jump, and pointed to the land, signifying we were to go there. We thought by this we should be eaten by these ugly men, as they appeared to us. . . . They told us we were not to be eaten but to work, and were soon to go on land where we should see many of our country people. This report eased us much; and sure enough soon after we were landed there came to us Africans of all languages.[30]

Although the demand was great, Portuguese merchants in Angola and Brazil sought to maintain only a steady trickle of slaves from the African interior to Luanda and across the ocean to Bahia and Rio de Janeiro: a flood of slaves would have depressed the American market. Rio, the port capital through which most slaves passed, commanded the Brazilian trade. Planters and mine operators from the provinces traveled to Rio to buy slaves. Between 1795 and 1808, approximately 10,000 Angolans per year stood in the Rio slave market. In 1810 the figure rose to 18,000; in 1828 it reached 32,000.[31]

The English ports of London, Bristol, and particularly Liverpool dominated the British slave trade. In the eighteenth century Liverpool was the world's greatest slave-trading port. In all three cities, small and cohesive merchant classes exercised great public influence. The cities also had huge stores of industrial products for export, growing shipping industries, and large amounts of ready cash for investment abroad. Merchants generally formed partnerships to raise capital and to share the risks; each voyage was a separate enterprise or venture.

Olaudah Equiano

The transatlantic slave trade was a mass movement involving millions of human beings. It was also the sum of individual lives spent partly or entirely in slavery. Most of those lives remain hidden to us. Olaudah Equiano (1745–1797) represents a rare ray of light into the slaves' obscurity; he is probably the best-known African slave.

Equiano was born in Benin (modern Nigeria) of Ibo ethnicity.* His father, one of the village elders (or chieftains), presided over a large household that included "many slaves," prisoners captured in local wars. All people, slave and free, shared in the cultivation of family lands. One day, when all the adults were in the fields, two strange men and a woman broke into the family compound, kidnapped the eleven-year-old Olaudah and his sister, tied them up, and dragged them into the woods. Brother and sister were separated, and Olaudah was sold several times to various dealers before reaching the coast. As it took six months to walk there, his home must have been far inland. The sea, the slave ship, and the strange appearance of the white crew terrified the boy (see page 534). Equiano's master took him to Jamaica, Virginia, and then to England, where he placed him in the custody of a kind family. They gave him the rudiments of an education, and he was baptized a Christian.

Equiano soon went to sea as a captain's boy (servant), serving in the Royal Navy during the Seven Years' War. On shore at Portsmouth, England, after one battle, Equiano was urged by his master to read, study, and learn basic mathematics. This education served him well, for after a voyage to the West Indies, his master sold him to a Philadelphia Quaker, Robert King, who was a rum and sugar merchant. Equiano worked as a clerk in King's warehouse, as a longshoreman loading and unloading cargo ships, and at sea where he developed good navigational skills; for his work, King paid him. Equiano became an entrepreneur himself, buying and selling small goods in the islands and mainland ports. Determined to buy his freedom, Equiano had amassed enough money by 1766, and King signed the deed of manumission. Equiano was twenty-one years old; he had been a slave for ten years.

He returned to London and used his remaining money to hire tutors to teach him hairdressing, mathematics, and how to play the French horn. When money was scarce, he found work as a merchant seaman, traveling to Portugal, Nice, Genoa, Naples, and Turkey. He participated in an Arctic expedition.

Equiano's *Travels* (1788) reveals a complex and sophisticated man. He had a strong constitu-

Olaudah Equiano, 1789, dressed as an elegant Englishman, his Bible open to the book of Acts. *(New York Public Library/Art Resource, NY)*

tion and an equally strong character. His Christian faith undoubtedly sustained him. On the title page of his book, he cited a verse from Isaiah (12:2): "The Lord Jehovah is my strength and my song." The very first thought that came to his mind the day he was freed was a passage from Psalm 126: "I glorified God in my heart, in whom I trusted."

Equiano loathed the brutal slavery he saw in the West Indies and the vicious racism he experienced in the North American colonies. He respected the fairness of Robert King, admired British navigational and industrial technologies, and had many close white friends. He once described himself as "almost an Englishman." He was also involved in the black communities in the West Indies and in London. *Travels* is a well-documented argument for the abolition of slavery and a literary classic that went through nine editions before his death.

Olaudah Equiano spoke to large crowds in the industrial cities of Manchester and Birmingham, arguing that it was in the business interests of manufacturers to support abolition, as Africa was a huge, virtually untapped market for English cloth.

Questions for Analysis

1. How typical was Olaudah Equiano's life as a slave? How atypical?

2. Describe his culture and his sense of himself.

Source: Equiano's Travels: The Interesting Narrative of the Life of Olaudah Equiano, ed. Paul Edwards (Portsmouth, N.H.: Heinemann, 1996).

---

*Recent scholarship has re-examined Equiano's life and raised some questions about his African origins and his experience of the Middle Passage.

● Peddlers, Rio de Janeiro (early nineteenth century) A British army officer sketched this scene of everyday life in Rio de Janeiro, Brazil. The ability to balance large burdens on the head meant that the hands were free for other use. Note the player (*third from right*) of a musical instrument originating in the Congo. We do not know whether the peddlers were free and self-employed or were selling for their owners. *(From "Views and Costumes of the City and Neighborhood of Rio de Janeiro, Brazil," in Drawings Taken by Lieutenant Chamberlain, During the Years 1819 and 1820 [London: Columbian Press, 1822])*

sorting *A collection or batch of British goods that would be traded for a slave or for a quantity of gold, ivory, or dyewood.*

factory-forts *Fortified trading posts that were established on the Gold Coast.*

shore trading *A process for trading goods in which European ships sent boats ashore or invited African dealers to bring traders and slaves out to the ships.*

Slaving ships from Bristol searched the Gold Coast, the Bight of Benin, Bonny, and Calabar. Liverpool's ships drew slaves from Gambia, the Windward Coast, and the Gold Coast. To Africa, British ships carried textiles, gunpowder and flint, beer and spirits, British and Irish linens, and woolen cloth. A collection of goods was grouped together into what was called the **sorting**. An English sorting might include bolts of cloth, firearms, alcohol, tobacco, and hardware; this batch of goods would be traded for an individual slave or a quantity of gold, ivory, or dyewood. Currency was not exchanged; it served as a standard of value and a means of keeping accounts.[32]

European traders had two systems for exchange. First, especially on the Gold Coast, they established **factory-forts**. These fortified trading posts were expensive to maintain but proved useful for fending off European rivals. Second, they used **shore trading**, in which European ships sent boats ashore or invited African dealers to bring traders and slaves out to the ships. The English captain John Adams, who made ten voyages to Africa between 1786 and 1800, described the shore method of trading at Bonny:

This place is the wholesale market for slaves, as not fewer than 20,000 are annually sold here; 16,000 of whom are natives of one nation called Ibo. . . . Fairs where the slaves of the Ibo nation are obtained are held every five or six weeks at several villages, which are situated on the banks of the rivers and creeks in the interior, and to which the African traders of Bonny resort to purchase them.

. . . The traders augment the quantity of their merchandise, by obtaining from their friends, the captains of the slave ships, a considerable quantity of goods on credit. . . . Evening is the period chosen for the time of departure, when they proceed in a body, accompanied by the noise of drums, horns, and gongs. At the expiration of the sixth day, they generally return bringing with them 1,500 or 2,000 slaves, who are sold to Europeans the evening after their arrival, and taken on board the ships. . . .

It is expected that every vessel, on her arrival at Bonny, will fire a salute the instant the anchor is let go, as a compliment to the black monarch who soon afterwards makes his appearance in a large canoe, at which time, all those natives who happen to be alongside the vessel are compelled to proceed in their canoes to a respectful distance, and make way for his Majesty's barge. After a few compliments to the captain, he usually enquires after brother George, meaning the King of England, George III, and hopes he and his family are well. He is not pleased unless he is regaled with the best the ship affords. . . . His power is absolute; and the surrounding country, to a considerable distance, is subject to his dominion.[33]

The shore method of buying slaves allowed the ship to move easily from market to market. The final prices of the slaves depended on their ethnic origin, their availability when the shipper arrived, and their physical health when offered for sale in the West Indies or the North or South American colonies.

Meanwhile, according to one scholar, the northbound trade in slaves across the Sahara "continued without serious disruption until the late nineteenth century, and in a clandestine way and on a much reduced scale it survived well into the twentieth century."[34] The present scholarly consensus is that the trans-Saharan slave trade in the seventeenth and eighteenth centuries was never as important as the transatlantic trade.

Supplying slaves for the foreign market was controlled by a small, wealthy African merchant class, or it was a state monopoly. Gathering a band of raiders and the capital for equipment, guides, tolls, and supplies involved considerable expense. By contemporary standards, slave raiding was a costly operation. Only black African entrepreneurs with sizable capital and labor could afford to finance and direct raiding drives. They exported slaves because the profits on exports were greater than the profits to be made from using labor in the domestic economy:

The export price of slaves never rose to the point where it became cheaper for Europeans to turn to alternative sources of supply, and it never fell to the point where it caused more than a temporary check to the trade. . . . The remarkable expansion of the slave trade in the eighteenth century provides a horrific illustration of the rapid response of producers in an underdeveloped economy to price incentives.[35]

Enslaved African peoples had an enormous impact on the economics of the Portuguese and Spanish colonies of South America and in the Dutch, French, and British colonies of the Caribbean and North America. For example, on the sugar plantations of Mexico and the Caribbean; on the cotton, rice, and tobacco plantations of North America; and in the silver and gold mines of Peru and Mexico, enslaved Africans not only worked in the mines and fields but also filled skilled, supervisory, and administrative positions and performed domestic service. In the United States, African slaves and their descendants influenced many facets of American culture, such as language, music (ragtime and jazz), dance, and diet. Even the U.S. Capitol building, where Congress meets, was built partly by slave labor.[36]

Consequences Within Africa

What economic impact did European trade have on African societies? Africans possessed technology well suited to their environment. Over the centuries, they had cultivated a wide variety of plant foods; developed plant and animal husbandry techniques; and mined, smelted, and otherwise worked a great variety of metals. Apart from firearms, American tobacco and rum, and the cheap brandy brought by the Portuguese, European goods presented no novelty to Africans. They found foreign products desirable because of their low prices. Traders of handwoven Indian cotton textiles, Venetian imitations of African beads, and iron bars from European smelters could undersell African manufacturers. Africans exchanged slaves, ivory, gold, pepper, and animal skins for those goods. Their earnings usually did not remain in Africa. African states eager to expand or to control commerce bought European firearms, although the difficulty of maintaining guns often gave gun owners only marginal superiority over skilled bowmen.[37] The kingdom of Dahomey, however, built its power on the effective use of firearms.

The African merchants who controlled the production of exports gained from foreign trade. Dahomey's king, for example, had a gross income in 1750 of £250,000 from the overseas export of slaves. A portion of his profit was spent on goods that improved his people's living standard. Slave-trading entrepôts, which provided opportunities for traders and for farmers who supplied foodstuffs to towns, caravans, and slave ships, prospered. But such economic returns did not spread very far.[38] International trade did not lead to Africa's economic development. Africa experienced neither technological growth nor the gradual spread of economic benefits in early modern times.

As in the Islamic world (see pages 550–552), women in sub-Saharan Africa also engaged in the slave trade. In Guinea the *signeres,* women slave merchants, acquired considerable riches in the business. One of them, Mae Correia, led a life famous in her region for its wealth and elegance.

The intermarriage of French traders and Wolof women in Senegambia created a *métis,* or mulatto, class. In the emerging urban centers at Saint-Louis, members of this small class adopted the French language, the Roman Catholic faith, and a French manner of life, and they exercised considerable political and economic power. However, European cultural influences did not penetrate West African society beyond the seacoast.

The political consequences of the slave trade varied from place to place. The trade enhanced the power and wealth of some kings and warlords in the short run but promoted conditions of instability and collapse over the long run. In the Congo kingdom, the perpetual Portuguese search for slaves undermined the monarchy, destroyed political unity, and led to constant disorder and warfare; power passed to the village chiefs. Likewise in Angola, which became a Portuguese proprietary colony, the slave trade decimated and scattered the population and destroyed the local economy. By contrast, the military kingdom of Dahomey, which entered into the slave trade in the eighteenth century and made it a royal monopoly, prospered enormously. Dahomey's economic strength rested on the slave trade. The royal army raided deep into the interior, and in the late eighteenth century Dahomey became one of the major West African sources of slaves. When slaving expeditions failed to yield sizable catches and when European demand declined, the resulting depression in the Dahomean economy caused serious political unrest. Iboland, inland from the Niger Delta, from whose great port cities of Bonny and Brass the British drained tens of thousands of slaves, experienced minimal political effects. A high birthrate kept pace with the incursions of the slave trade, and Ibo societies remained demographically and economically strong.

What demographic impact did the slave trade have on Africa? In all, between approximately 1500 and 1900, about 12 million Africans were exported to the Americas, 6 million were exported to Asia, and 8 million were retained within Africa. Table 18.1 and Table 18.2 report the somewhat divergent findings of two careful scholars on the number of slaves shipped to the Americas. Export figures do not include the approximately 10 to 15 percent who died during procurement or in transit.

There is no small irony in the fact that the continent most desperately in need of population, Africa, lost so many millions to the slave trade. Although the British Parliament abolished the slave trade in 1807 and traffic in Africans to Brazil and Cuba gradually declined, *within* Africa the trade continued at the levels of the peak years of the transatlantic trade, 1780–1820. In the later nineteenth century, developing African industries, using slave labor, produced a variety of products for domestic consumption and export. Again, there is irony in the fact that in the eighteenth century, European demand for slaves expanded the trade (and wars) within Africa, yet in the nineteenth century, European imperialists defended territorial aggrandizement by arguing that they were "civilizing" Africans by abolishing slavery. But after 1880, European businessmen (and African governments) did not push abolition; they wanted cheap labor.

● **Sapi-Portuguese Saltcellar** Contact with the Sapi people of present-day Sierra Leone in West Africa led sixteenth-century Portuguese traders to commission this ivory saltcellar, for which they brought Portuguese designs. But the object's basic features—a spherical container and separate lid on a flat base, with men, women, and supporting beams below—are distinctly African. An executioner, holding an ax with which he has beheaded five men, stands on the lid. This piece was probably intended as an example of Sapi artistic virtuosity, rather than for practical table use. *(Courtesy, Museo Nazionale Preistorico ed Etnografico, Rome)*

Western and American markets wanted young male slaves. Asian and African markets preferred young females. Women were sought for their reproductive value, as sex objects, and because their economic productivity was not threatened by the possibility of physical rebellion, as might be the case with young men. Consequently, two-thirds of those exported to the Americas were male, one-third female. The population on the western coast of Africa became predominantly female; the population in the East African Savanna and Horn regions was predominantly male. The slave trade therefore had significant consequences for the institutions of marriage, slavery itself, and the sexual division of labor. Although Africa's overall population may have shown modest growth from roughly 1650 to 1900, that growth was offset by declines in the Horn and on the eastern and western coasts. While Europe and Asia experienced considerable demographic and economic expansion in the eighteenth century, Africa suffered a decline.[39]

Table 18.2   The Transatlantic Slave Trade, 1450–1900

PERIOD	VOLUME	PERCENTAGE
1450–1600	367,000	3.1
1601–1700	1,868,000	16.0
1701–1800	6,133,000	52.4
1801–1900	3,330,000	28.5
Total	11,698,000	100.0

Source: P. E. Lovejoy, *Transformations in Slavery: A History of Slavery in Africa* (Cambridge: Cambridge University Press, 1983), p. 19. Used with permission.

Chapter Summary

To assess your mastery of this chapter, go to
bedfordstmartins.com/mckayworld

• What different types of economic, social, and political structures were found in Senegambia and Benin?

In the early modern world, kingdoms and stateless societies in Africa existed side by side. Stateless, or decentralized, societies oriented around a single village or group of villages without a central capital. The economies of both the kingdoms and the stateless societies were predominantly agricultural and pastoral. The peoples living along the West African coast, in the region known as Senegambia, built their diets around staple grains like millet and sorghum, supplemented by other local foods such as plantains, beans, bananas, and small game like rabbits. Yams were the staple crop in the forest zone to the south, while rice was the principal crop along the Guinea coast. Regional fairs served as sites for the exchange of produce and news and for social interaction. Age-grade systems, which passed on societal norms to successive generations and unified communities, were a common feature of many of these societies. The Wolof-, Serer-, and Pulaar-speaking peoples in Senegambia were also connected to the trans-Saharan caravan trade, which along with goods brought Islamic, and later French, culture to the region.

Key Terms

age-grade systems
oba
Taghaza
Tuareg
cowrie shells
Swahili
slave
sorting
factory-forts
shore trading

• *In what ways was the trans-Saharan trade important to the West African kingdoms of Songhai, Kanem-Bornu, and Hausaland?*

The Sudanic empires immediately south of the Sahara, such as Songhai, Kanem-Bornu, and Hausaland, were heavily involved in commercial activities, controlling the north-south trans-Saharan trade in gold, salt, cloth, leather, and other items, and the Niger River trade that linked markets the length and breadth of that great river. The two major commodities traded across the vast desert were gold and salt. Islam also came south across the desert, and the rulers of the great West African kingdom of Songhai, and its predecessors Ghana and Mali, were all Muslims. Being part of the Islamic world gave these societies not only commercial links to Europe, the Middle East, and beyond, but also access to some of the most advanced centers of scholarship in the world at the time, like Cairo and Baghdad. Timbuktu, in the heart of West Africa, had its own university. Still, although West African societies experienced strong Islamic influences, Muslim culture affected primarily the royal and elite classes and seldom reached the masses. The West African kingdoms of Benin, Kanem-Bornu, and Hausaland maintained their separate existences for centuries.

• *How did the Coptic Christian Church in Ethiopia serve as a unifying force for the society and for the kingdom?*

In eastern Africa, Ethiopia had accepted Christianity long before northern and eastern Europe; Ethiopians practiced Coptic Christianity, which shaped their identity. Europeans came to believe that this Christian kingdom in Africa was ruled over by a fabulously wealthy (but totally mythical) Christian monarch named Prester John. The Prester John fable attracted Europeans to Ethiopia for centuries. The myth partly explains why, when the Ethiopians called for European assistance in fighting off Muslim incursions on their borders in the sixteenth century, the Portuguese came to their aid,

soundly defeating a Muslim force at Lake Tana in 1541. Jesuit missionaries soon followed and tried to convert Ethiopians to Roman Catholicism, but the Ethiopians fiercely resisted, expelling the Jesuits in 1633. Ethiopia then entered a two-hundred-year period of isolation.

• *What was the significance of the Indian Ocean to the political and economic organization of the Swahili city-states?*

The wealthy Swahili city-states on the southeastern coast of Africa possessed a Muslim and mercantile culture. They were also predominantly Islamic and have left a written record of their history. A maritime peoples, they were a mixture of African and Arabic, with close ties as well to Persia (Iran), India, and Indonesia. Cities such as Mogadishu, Kilwa, and Sofala communicated in Arabic and acted independently, and their commercial economies were tied to the Indian Ocean trade. The Swahili acted as middlemen and women for the East African link in the vast Indian Ocean trade network. When the Portuguese arrived in the Indian Ocean in the late fifteenth and early sixteenth centuries, they sought to conquer and control this network. Although the Portuguese had little effect on Swahili culture or religion, their presence caused the economic decline or even death of many Swahili cities.

• *What role did slavery play in African societies before European intrusion?*

Scholars continue to debate the character and extent of African slavery before European intrusion. Many societies had some form of slavery. Generally slaves were obtained as payment for debt, in war, or through simple purchase. Slaves were treated relatively benignly in some societies, serving as wives, house servants, royal guards, or even royal advisers enjoying great prestige. But other slaves suffered under the same harsh and brutal treatment—as field hands, common laborers, sex objects, or miners—as enslaved Africans would experience later in the Western world.

Suggested Reading

Berger, Iris, E. Frances White, and Cathy Skidmore-Heiss. *Women in Sub-Saharan Africa: Restoring Women to History.* 1999. Necessary reading for a complete understanding of African history.

Cooper, Frederick. *Plantation Slavery on the East Coast of Africa.* 1997. Useful study of slavery as practiced in Africa.

Fredrickson, G. M. *Racism: A Short History.* 2002. Contains probably the best recent study of the connection between African slavery and Western racism.

Isichei, Elizabeth. *A History of Christianity in Africa. From Antiquity to the Present.* 1995. Comprehensive survey of Christianity in Africa.

Klein, Martin, and Claire C. Robertson. *Women and Slavery in Africa.* 1997. From perspective that most slaves in Africa were women.

Lovejoy, Paul E. *Transformation in Slavery: A History of Slavery in Africa.* 1983. Essential for an understanding of slavery in an African context.

Manning, P. *Slavery, Colonialism and Economic Growth in Dahomey, 1640–1960.* 1982. An in-depth study of the kingdom of Dahomey, which, after Angola, was the largest exporter of slaves to the Americas.

Middleton, J. *The World of Swahili: An African Mercantile Civilization.* 1992. Introduction to East Africa and the Horn region.

Miers, Suzanne, and Igor Kopytoff. *Slavery in Africa: Historical and Anthropological Perspectives.* 1980. Classic study of slavery in Africa.

Northrup, D. *Africa's Discovery of Europe, 1450–1850.* 2002. Offers a unique perspective on African-European contact.

Pearson, Michael N. *Port Cities and Intruders: The Swahili Coast, India, and Portugal in the Early Modern Era.* 2002. Comprehensive introduction to the Swahili coast and the Indian Ocean trade network.

Powell, Eve Troutt, and John O. Hunwick. *The African Diaspora in the Mediterranean Lands of Islam.* 2002. Important study of Islam and African slave trade.

Robinson, David. *Muslim Societies in African History.* 2004. Valuable introduction to Islam in Africa by a renowned Africanist.

Shell, R. *Children of Bondage: A Social History of the Slave Society at the Cape of Good Hope, 1652–1938.* 1994. A massive study of Cape slave society filled with much valuable statistical data.

Shillington, K. *History of Africa,* 2005. Provides a soundly researched, highly readable, and well-illustrated survey.

Thomas, H. *The Slave Trade.* 1997. Solid, popular account of the transatlantic slave trade.

Thorton, J. *Africa and Africans in the Making of the Atlantic World, 1400–1680.* 1992. Places African developments in an Atlantic context.

Vansina, J. *Kingdoms of the Savanna.* 1966. Classic study of the African Savanna and its peoples.

Notes

1. P. D. Curtin, *Economic Change in Precolonial Africa: Senegambia in the Era of the Slave Trade* (Madison: University of Wisconsin Press, 1975), pp. 34–35; J. A. Rawley, *The Transatlantic Slave Trade: A History*

2. Robert W. July, *Precolonial Africa: An Economic and Social History* (New York: Scribner's, 1975), p. 99.

3. Robert W. July, *A History of the African People* (Prospect Heights, Ill.: Waveland Press, 1998), p. 121.

4. J. Iliffe, *Africans: The History of a Continent* (Cambridge: Cambridge University Press, 2007), pp. 96–97.

5. Ibid., pp. 112–113, 142.

6. *Equiano's Travels: The Interesting Narrative of the Life of Olaudah Equiano,* ed. P. Edwards (Portsmouth, N.H.: Heinemann, 1996), p. 4.

7. Iliffe, *Africans,* p. 137.

8. Ibid., p. 68.

9. Ibid., pp. 86–87.

10. Quoted in R. Hallett, *Africa to 1875* (Ann Arbor: University of Michigan Press, 1970), p. 151.

11. *The Cambridge History of Africa,* vol. 3, *Ca 1050 to 1600,* ed. R. Oliver (Cambridge: Cambridge University Press, 1977), pp. 427–435.

12. A. ibn-Fartura, "The Kanem Wars," in *Nigerian Perspectives,* ed. T. Hodgkin (London: Oxford University Press, 1966), pp. 111–115.

13. "The Kano Chronicle," quoted in *Nigerian Perspectives,* ed. T. Hodgkin (London: Oxford University Press, 1966), pp. 89–90.

14. See A. J. R. Russell-Wood, *The Portuguese Empire: A World on the Move* (Baltimore: Johns Hopkins University Press, 1998), pp. 11–13.

15. J. Middleton, *The World of Swahili: An African Mercantile Civilization* (New Haven, Conn.: Yale University Press, 1992), p. 27.

16. Ibid., pp. 35–38.

17. Russell-Wood, *The Portuguese Empire,* pp. 43–44.

18. P. E. Lovejoy, *Transformations in Slavery: A History of Slavery in Africa* (Cambridge: Cambridge University Press, 1983), p. 19. This section leans heavily on Lovejoy's work.

19. See Table 2.1, "Trans-Saharan Slave Trade, 650–1600," ibid., p. 25.

20. Iliffe, *Africans,* p. 77.

21. Quoted in H. Thomas, *The Slave Trade* (New York: Simon and Schuster, 1997), p. 21.

22. G. Gerzina, *Black London: Life Before Emancipation* (New Brunswick, N.J.: Rutgers University Press, 1995), pp. 29–66, passim; the quotation is on p. 53.

23. C.-H. Shell, *Children of Bondage: A Social History of the Slave Society at the Cape of Good Hope, 1652–1838* (Hanover, N.H.: University Press of New England, 1994), p. 41, fig. 2-1, pp. 149–155, and fig. 5-10.

24. Iliffe, *Africans,* pp. 128–129.

25. See D. Eltis, *The Rise of African Slavery in the Americas* (Cambridge: Cambridge University Press, 2000), Chap. 3; and the review/commentary by J. E. Inikori, *American Historical Review* 106, no. 5 (December 2001): 1751–1753.

26. R. Blackburn, *The Making of New World Slavery: From the Baroque to the Modern, 1492–1800* (New York: Verso, 1998), pp. 79–80.

27. Rawley, *The Transatlantic Slave Trade,* p. 45.

28. Ibid., pp. 41–47.

29. R. E. Conrad, *Children of God's Fire: A Documentary History of Black Slavery in Brazil* (Princeton, N.J.: Princeton University Press, 1983), pp. 20–23.

30. *Equiano's Travels,* pp. 23–26.

31. Rawley, *The Transatlantic Slave Trade,* pp. 45–47.

32. July, *A History of the African People,* p. 171.

33. J. Adams, "Remarks on the Country Extending from Cape Palmas to the River Congo," *Nigerian Perspectives,* ed. T. Hodgkin (London: Oxford University Press, 1966), pp. 178–180.

34. A. G. Hopkins, *An Economic History of West Africa* (New York: Columbia University Press, 1973), p. 83.

35. Ibid., p. 105.

36. J. Thornton, *Africa and Africans in the Making of the Atlantic World* (New York: Cambridge University Press, 1992), pp. 138–142.

37. July, *Precolonial Africa,* pp. 269–270.

38. Hopkins, *An Economic History of West Africa,* p. 119.

39. P. Manning, *Slavery and African Life: Occidental, Oriental, and African Slave Trades* (New York: Cambridge University Press, 1990), pp. 22–23 and Chap. 3, pp. 38–59.

Listening to the PAST

Duarte Barbosa on the Swahili City-States

The Portuguese linguist Duarte Barbosa made two voyages to India. Arriving first in 1500, he acted for five years as interpreter and translator in Cochin and Cananor in Kerala (in southwestern India on the Malabar Coast) and returned to Lisbon in 1506. On his second visit in 1511, he served the Portuguese government as chief scribe in the factory of Cananor (a factory was a warehouse for the storage of goods, not a manufacturing center) and as the liaison with the local Indian rajah (prince). When Afonso de Albuquerque dismissed Barbosa, he went to Calicut. He returned to Cananor about 1520 and died there in 1545.

On the basis of his trips around the Indian Ocean in 1518, Barbosa completed his Libro des Coisas da India, a geographical and ethnographic survey of peoples, lands, and commerce from the Cape of Good Hope to China. It was based largely on his personal observations. First published in Italian, the book won wide acclaim in Europe, and modern scholars consider the geographical information in it very accurate.

Sofala

And the manner of their traffic was this: they came in small vessels named *zambucos* from the kingdoms of Kilwa, Mombasa, and Malindi, bringing many cotton cloths, some spotted and others white and blue, also some of silk, and many small beads, gray, red, and yellow, which things come to the said kingdoms from the great kingdom of Cambay [in Northwest India] in other greater ships. And these wares the said Moors who came from Malindi and Mombasa [purchased from others who bring them hither and] paid for in gold at such a price that those merchants departed well pleased; which gold they gave by weight.

The Moors of Sofala kept these wares and sold them afterwards to the heathen of the Kingdom of Benametapa, who came thither laden with gold which they gave in exchange for the said cloths without weighing it. These Moors collect also great store of ivory which they find hard by Sofala, and this also they sell in the Kingdom of Cambay at five or six cruzados the quintal. They also sell some ambergris, which is brought to them from the Hucicas, and is exceed-

ing good. These Moors are black, and some of them tawny; some of them speak Arabic, but the more part use the language of the country. They clothe themselves from the waist down with cotton and silk cloths, and other cloths they wear over their shoulders like capes, and turbans on their heads. Some of them wear small caps dyed in grain in chequers and other woolen clothes in many tints, also camlets and other silks.

Their food is millet, rice, flesh and fish. In this river as far as the sea are many sea horses, which come out on the land to graze, which horses always move in the sea like fishes; they have tusks like those of small elephants, being whiter and harder, and it never loses color. In the country near Sofala are many wild elephants, exceeding great (which the country-folk know not how to tame), ounces, lions, deer and many other wild beasts. It is a land of plains and hills with many streams of sweet water. . . .

Kilwa

Going along the coast from [the] town of Mozambique, there is an island hard by the mainland which is called Kilwa, in which is a Moorish town with many fair houses of stones and mortar, with many windows after our fashion, very well arranged in streets, with many flat roofs. The doors are of wood, well carved, with excellent joinery. Around it are streams and orchards and fruit-gardens with many channels of sweet water. It has a Moorish king over it. From this place they trade with Sofala, whence they bring back gold, and from here they spread all over . . . the seacoast [which] is well peopled with villages and abodes of Moors.

Before the King our Lord sent out his expedition to discover India the Moors of Sofala, Cuama, Angoya and Mozambique were all subject to the king of Kilwa, who was the most mighty king among them. And in this town was great plenty of gold, as no ships passed towards Sofala without first coming to this island. . . .

This town was taken by force from its king by the Portuguese, as, moved by arrogance, he refused to obey the King our Lord. There they took many prisoners and the king fled from the island, and His

Husuni Kubwa at Kilwa combined a royal palace, a resting place for caravans, and an enclosure for slaves held for later sale. *(From Peter S. Garlake, The Early Islamic Architecture of the East African Coast, Memoir 1 of the British Institute in Eastern Africa, Nairobi, 1966. Original drawing by Peter S. Garlake. Copyright, British Institute in Eastern Africa. Reproduced with permission of BIEA)*

Highness ordered that a fort should be built there, and kept it under his rule and governance. Afterwards he ordered that it should be pulled down, as its maintenance was of no value nor profit to him, and it was destroyed by Antonio de Saldanha. . . .

Malindi

. . . Journeying along the coast towards India, there is a fair town on the mainland lying along a strand, which is named Malindi. It pertains to the Moors and has a Moorish king over it; the which place has many fair stone and mortar houses of many stories, with great plenty of windows and flat roofs, after our fashion. The place is well laid out in streets. The folk are both black and white; they go naked, covering only their private parts with cotton and silk cloths. Others of them wear cloths folded like cloaks and waistbands, and turbans of many rich stuffs on their heads.

They are great barterers, and deal in cloth, gold, ivory, and divers other wares with the Moors and heathen of the great kingdom of Cambay; and to their haven come every year many ships with cargoes of merchandise, from which they get great store of gold, ivory and wax. In this traffic the Cambay merchants make great profits, and thus, on one side and the other, they earn much money. There is great plenty of food in this city, rice, millet, and some wheat which they bring from Cambay, and divers sorts of fruit, inasmuch as there is here abundance of fruit-gardens and

orchards. Here too are plenty of round-tailed sheep, cows and other cattle and great store of oranges, also of hens.

The king and people of this place ever were and are friends of the King of Portugal, and the Portuguese always find in them great comfort and friendship and perfect peace, and there the ships, when they chance to pass that way, obtain supplies in plenty.

Questions for Analysis

1. Locate on a map the city-states that Barbosa discusses.

2. What seems to have impressed Barbosa? What was his attitude toward the various peoples he saw? What Portuguese or Western prejudices do you discern?

3. What was the Portuguese relationship to the Swahili city-states at the time Barbosa saw them?

4. What was the source of Sofala's gold? Of Sofala's and Malindi's ivory? What did Cambay (that is, India) use ivory for?

Source: Basil Davidson, *The African Past: Chronicles from Antiquity to Modern Times* (Boston: Little, Brown, 1964). Copyright © 1964 by Basil Davidson. Reprinted by permission of Curtis Brown, Ltd.

Wedding Procession of Prince Dara-Shikoh, Agra, February 1633. Female musicians ride atop elephants. *(The Royal Collection © 2007, Her Majesty Queen Elizabeth II)*

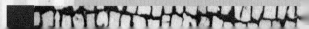

19 THE ISLAMIC WORLD POWERS, CA. 1400–1800

After the breakup of the Mongol Empire, new states emerged in south and west Eurasia. By the sixteenth century the Ottoman Empire centered in Anatolia, the Safavid Empire in Persia, and the Mughal Empire in India controlled vast territories from West Africa to Central Asia, from the Balkans to the Bay of Bengal. Their origins were similar (in Turkish tribal polities), and they similarly had to adjust to ruling large sedentary populations. They all adapted to the decline in the supremacy of the mounted archer that resulted from the introduction of firearms.

Lasting almost five hundred years (1453–1918), the Ottoman Empire was one of the largest, best-organized, and most enduring political entities in world history. In Persia the Safavid Dynasty created a Shi'ite state and presided over a brilliant culture. In India the Mughal leader Babur and his successors gained control of much of the Indian subcontinent. Mughal rule inaugurated a period of radical administrative reorganization in India and the flowering of intellectual and architectural creativity. These three states were not allied to each other—the Safavids and Ottomans were divided on theological grounds between Sunni and Shi'ite and competed for control of Mesopotamia. Still they faced similar challenges and responded in similar ways. Culturally they were strongly linked, with ideas, practices, and styles quickly spreading from one society to another.

THE THREE TURKISH RULING HOUSES: THE OTTOMANS, SAFAVIDS, AND MUGHALS

How were the three Islamic empires established, and what sorts of governments did they set up?

Before the Mongols arrived in Central Asia and Persia, another nomadic Central Asian people, the Turks, had gained overlordship in key territories from Anatolia to Delhi in north India. The Turks had been quick to join the Mongols and formed important elements in the armies and administrations of the Mongol states in Persia and Central Asia. In these regions, Turks far outnumbered ethnic Mongols.

As Mongol strength in Persia and Central Asia deteriorated in the late thirteen and fourteenth centuries, the Turks resumed their expansion. In the late fourteenth century, the Turkish leader Tamerlane (1336–1405) built a Central Asian empire from his base in Samarkand, campaigning into India and through Persia to the Black Sea. Tamerlane campaigned continuously from the 1360s till his death in 1405, trying to repeat the achievements of Chinggis Khan. He did not get involved in administering the new territories, but rather appointed lords and let them make use of existing political structures. Thus, when after his death his sons and grandson fought against each other for succession, his empire quickly fell apart, and power devolved to the local level. Sufi orders thrived, and Islam became the most important force integrating the region. It was from the many small Turkish chiefs that the founders of the three main empires emerged.

The Ottoman Turkish Empire

Ottomans *Ruling house of the Turkish empire that lasted from 1453 to 1918.*

Anatolia *The region of modern Turkey.*

The **Ottomans** took their name from Osman (r. 1280–1324), the chief of a band of seminomadic Turks that had migrated into western **Anatolia** during the era when the Mongol Il-khans still held Persia. The Ottomans gradually expanded at the expense of other Turkish statelets and the Byzantine Empire. The Ottoman ruler called himself "border chief," or leader of the *ghazis,* frontier fighters in the *jihad,* or holy war. The earliest Ottoman historical source, a fourteenth-century saga, describes the ghazis as the "instrument of God's religion . . . God's scourge who cleanses the earth from the filth of polytheism . . . God's pure sword."[1] Although temporarily slowed by defeat at the hands of Tamerlane in 1402, the Ottomans quickly reasserted themselves after Tamerlane's death in 1405.

The holy war was intended to subdue, not destroy. The Ottomans built their empire by absorbing the Muslims of Anatolia and by becoming the protector of the Orthodox church and of the millions of Greek Christians in Anatolia and the Balkans. In 1326 they took Bursa in western Anatolia, and in 1352 they gained a foothold in Europe by seizing Gallipoli. Their victories led more men, including recent converts, to join them as ghazi. In 1389 at Kosovo in the Balkans, the Ottomans defeated a combined force of Serbs and Bosnians. In 1396 on the Danube River in modern Bulgaria, they crushed King Sigismund of Hungary, who was supported by French, German, and English knights. After the victories in the Balkans, the Ottomans added to their military through the creation of slave troops (discussed below). These troops were outfitted with guns and artillery and trained to use them effectively.

The reign of Sultan Mehmet II (r. 1451–1481) saw the Ottoman conquest of Constantinople, capital of the Byzantine Empire, which had lasted a thousand years. The Byzantine emperor Constantine IX Palaeologus (r. 1449–1453), with only about ten thousand men, relied on the magnificent system of circular walls and stone fortifications for his defense. Mehmet II had more than one hundred thousand men and a large fleet, but iron chains spanning the harbor kept him out. Turkish ingenuity and Western technology eventually decided the battle. Mehmet's army carried boats over the steep hills to come in behind the chains blocking the harbor, then bombarded the city from the rear. A Transylvanian cannon founder who deserted the Greeks for the Turks cast huge bronze cannon on the spot (bringing raw materials to the scene of military action was easier than moving guns long distances).[2]

Sultan-i-Rum *The name that the Ottoman sultans took as their title; it means "sultan of Rome."*

With the conquest of Constantinople (renamed Istanbul) as a base, the Ottomans quickly absorbed the rest of the Byzantine Empire. They continued to expand through the Middle East and into North Africa in the sixteenth century. Once Constantinople was theirs, the Ottoman sultans considered themselves successors of both the Byzantine and Seljuk emperors, as their title **Sultan-i-Rum** (sultan of Rome) attests.

To begin the transformation of Istanbul into an imperial Ottoman capital, Mehmet ordered the city cleaned up and the walls repaired. He appointed officials to adapt the city administration to Ottoman ways and ordered wealthy residents to participate in building mosques, markets, water fountains, baths, and other public facilities. The population of Istanbul had declined in the decades before the conquest, and warfare, flight, and the sale of many survivors into slavery had decreased the population further. Therefore, Mehmet transplanted to the city inhabitants of other territories, granting them tax remissions and possession of empty houses. He wanted them to start businesses, make the city prosperous, and transform it into a microcosm of the empire.

Gunpowder, invented by the Chinese and adapted to artillery use by the Europeans, played an influential role in the expansion of the Ottoman state. In the first half of the sixteenth century, the Ottomans gained control of shipping in the eastern Mediterranean, eliminated the Portuguese from the Red Sea and Persian Gulf, and supported Andalusian and North African Muslims in their fight against the Spanish reconquista. Under the superb military leadership of Selim (r. 1512–1520), the Ottomans in 1514 turned the Safavids back from Anatolia. The Ottomans also added Syria and Palestine (1516) and Egypt (1517) to the empire, extending their rule across North Africa to Tunisia and Algeria. Selim's rule marks the beginning of four centuries when most Arabs were under Ottoman rule.

Suleiman (r. 1520–1566) extended Ottoman dominion to its widest geographical extent (see Map 19.1). Suleiman's army crushed the Hungarians at Mohács in 1526, killing the king and thousands of his nobles. Three years later, the Turks besieged the Habsburg capital of Vienna. Only an accident—the army's insistence on returning home before winter—prevented Muslim control of all central Europe. The Ottomans' military discipline, ability to coordinate cavalry and infantry, and capability in logistics were usually superior to those of the Europeans.

From the late fourteenth to the early seventeenth century, the Ottoman Empire was a key player in European politics. In 1525 Francis I of France and Suleiman struck an alliance; both believed that only their collaboration could prevent Habsburg hegemony in Europe. The Habsburg emperor Charles V retaliated by seeking an alliance with Safavid Persia. Suleiman renewed the French agreement with Francis's son, Henry II (r. 1547–1559), and the French entente became the cornerstone of Ottoman policy in western Europe. Suleiman also allied with the German Protestant princes, forcing the Catholic Habsburgs to grant concessions to the Protestants. Ottoman pressure proved an important factor in the official recognition of Lutheran Protestants at the Peace of Augsburg in 1555. In addition to the rising tide of Protestantism, the Ottoman threat strengthened the growth of national monarchy in France.

Chronology

1280–1324	Osman, founder of the Ottoman Dynasty
1336–1405	Life of Tamerlane
ca. mid-1400s	Coffeehouses become center of Islamic male social life
1453	Ottoman conquest of Constantinople
ca. 1498–1805	Mughal Empire
1501–1722	Safavid Empire
1501–1524	Reign of Shah Ismail
1520–1566	Reign of Ottoman emperor Suleiman I; period of artistic flowering in Ottoman Empire
1520–1558	Hürrem wields influence in Ottoman Empire as Suleiman's wife
1521	Piri Reis, *Book of the Sea,* a navigational map book
1548–1557	Pasha Sinan designs and builds Suleimaniye Mosque in Istanbul
1556–1605	Reign of Akbar in Mughal Empire
1570	Turks take control of Cyprus
1571	First major Ottoman defeat by Christians, at Lepanto
1587–1629	Reign of Shah Abbas; height of Safavid power; carpet weaving becomes major Persian industry
1631–1648	Construction of Taj Mahal under Shah Jahan
1658–1707	Reign of Aurangzeb; Mughal power begins to decline
1668	Bombay leased to British East India Company
1763	Treaty of Paris recognizes British control over much of India

In eastern Europe to the north of Ottoman lands stood the Grand Duchy of Moscow. In the fifteenth century, Ottoman rulers did not regard it as a threat; in 1497 they even gave Russian merchants freedom of trade within the empire. But in 1547 Ivan IV (the Terrible) brought under Russian control the entire Volga region (see Map 19.1). In 1557 Ivan's ally, the Cossack chieftain Dimitrash, tried to take Azov, the northernmost Ottoman fortress. Ottoman plans to recapture the area succeeded in uniting Russia, Persia, and the pope against the Turks.

Though usually victorious on land, the Ottomans did not enjoy complete dominion on the seas. Competition with the Habsburgs and pirates for control of the Mediterranean led the Ottomans to conquer Cyprus in 1570 and settle thousands of Turks from Anatolia there. (Thus began the large Turkish presence on Cyprus that continues to the present day.) In response, Pope Pius V organized a Holy League against the Turks, which had a victory in 1571 at Lepanto with a squadron of more than two hundred Spanish, Venetian, and papal galleys. Still, the Turks remained supreme on land and quickly rebuilt their entire fleet.

To the east, war with Persia occupied the sultans' attention throughout the sixteenth century. Several issues lay at the root of the long and exhausting conflicts:

MAP 19.1 **The Ottoman Empire at Its Height, 1566** The Ottomans, like their great rivals the Habsburgs, rose to rule a vast dynastic empire encompassing many different peoples and ethnic groups. The army and the bureaucracy served to unite the disparate territories into a single state.

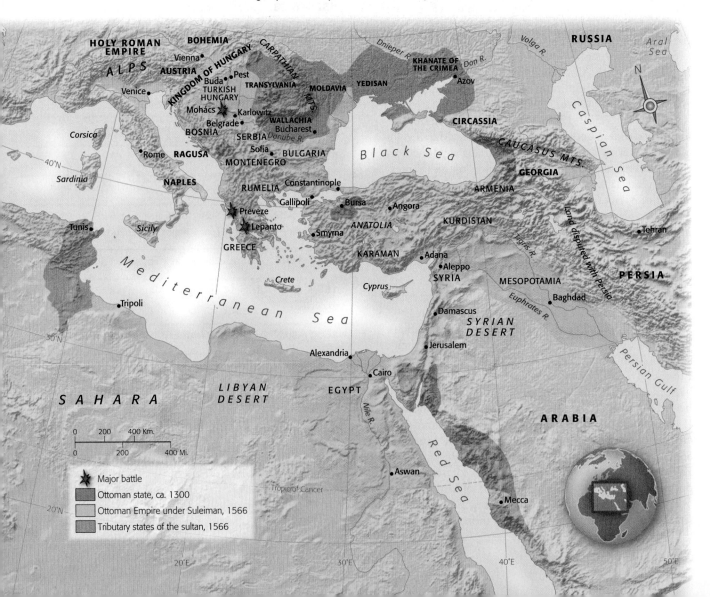

● **Battle of Mohács**   The *Süleymanname* (Book of Suleiman), a biography, contains these wonderful illustrations of the battle that took place in Hungary on August 29, 1526. In the right panel, Suleiman in a white turban sits on a black horse surrounded by his personal guard, while janissaries fire cannon at the enemy. In the left panel, the Europeans are in disarray, in contrast to the Turks' discipline and order. Suleiman inflicted a crushing defeat and absorbed Hungary into the Ottoman Empire. The artist attempted to show the terrain and battle tactics. *(Topkapi Saray Museum, Istanbul)*

religious antagonism between the Sunni Ottomans and the Shi'ite Persians, competition to expand at each other's expense in Mesopotamia, desires to control trade routes, and European alliances. Finally, in 1638, the Ottomans captured Baghdad, and the treaty of Kasr-I-Shirim established a permanent border between the two powers.

The Ottoman political system reached its classic form under Suleiman I. All authority flowed from the **sultan** to his public servants: provincial governors, police officers, military generals, heads of treasuries, viziers. In Turkish history, Suleiman is known as the Lawgiver because of his profound influence on the civil law. He ordered Lütfi Paşa (d. 1562), a poet and juridical scholar of slave origin, to draw up a new general code of laws. This code prescribed penalties for routine criminal acts such as robbery, adultery, and murder. It also sought to reform bureaucratic and financial corruption in areas such as harem intervention in administrative affairs, foreign merchants' payment of bribes to avoid customs duties, imprisonment without trial, and promotion in the provincial administration because of favoritism rather than ability. The legal code also introduced the idea of balanced financial budgets. The head of the religious establishment was given the task of reconciling sultanic law with Islamic law. Suleiman's legal acts influenced many legal codes, including that of the United States. Today, Suleiman's image, along with the images of Solon, Moses, and Thomas Jefferson, appears in the chamber of the U.S. House of Representatives.

sultan   *An Arabic word originally used by the Seljuk Turks to mean authority or dominion; it was used by the Ottomans to connote political and military supremacy.*

devshirme *A process whereby the sultan's agents swept the provinces for Christian youths to become slaves.*

janissaries *Turkish for "recruits"; they formed the elite army corps.*

concubine *A woman who is a recognized spouse but of lower status than a wife.*

Slavery was widespread in the Ottoman empire. Slaves were purchased from Spain, North Africa, and Venice; captured in battle; or drafted through the system known as **devshirme,** by which the sultan's agents compelled Christian families in the Balkans to turn over their boys. As the Ottoman frontier advanced in the fifteenth and sixteenth centuries, Albanian, Bosnian, Wallachian, and Hungarian slave boys filled Ottoman imperial needs. The slave boys were converted to Islam and trained for the imperial civil service and the standing army. The brightest 10 percent entered the palace school, where they learned to read and write Arabic, Ottoman Turkish, and Persian. Other boys were sent to Turkish farms, where they acquired physical toughness in preparation for military service. Known as **janissaries** (Turkish for "recruits"), they formed the elite army corps. Thoroughly indoctrinated and absolutely loyal to the sultan, the janissary slave corps eliminated the influence of old Turkish families and played a central role in Ottoman military affairs in the sixteenth century.

The Ottoman ruling class consisted in part of descendants of Turkish families that had formerly ruled parts of Anatolia and in part of people of varied ethnic origins who rose through the bureaucratic and military ranks, many beginning as the sultan's slaves. All were committed to the Ottoman way: Islamic in faith, loyal to the sultan, and well versed in the Turkish language and the culture of the imperial court. In return for their services to the sultan, they held landed estates for the duration of their lives. The ruling class had the legal right to use and enjoy the profits, but not the ownership, of the land. Since all property belonged to the sultan and reverted to him on the holder's death, Turkish nobles, unlike their European counterparts, did not have a local base independent of the ruler. The absence of a hereditary nobility and private ownership of agricultural land differentiates the Ottoman system from European feudalism.

By the reign of Selim I, the principle was established that the sultan did not contract legal marriage but perpetuated the ruling house through concubinage. A slave **concubine** could have none of the political aspirations or leverage that a native or foreign-born noblewoman had (with a notable exception; see the feature "Individuals in

● **Music in a Garden**
This illustration of a courtly romance depicts several women in a garden, intently listening to a musician, cups of a beverage in their hands. *(Biblioteca Vaticana Apostolica)*

Hürrem

Hürrem (1505?–1558) was born in the western Ukraine (then part of Poland), the daughter of a Ruthenian priest, and was given the Polish name Aleksandra Lisowska. When Tartars raided, they captured and enslaved her. In 1520 she was given as a gift to Suleiman on the occasion of his accession to the throne. The Venetian ambassador (probably relying on secondhand or thirdhand information) described her as "young, graceful, petite, but not beautiful." She was given the Turkish name Hürrem, meaning "joyful."

Hürrem apparently brought joy to Suleiman. Their first child was born in 1521; by 1525 they had four sons and a daughter; sources note that by that year Suleiman visited no other woman. But he waited eight or nine years before breaking Ottoman dynastic tradition by making Hürrem his legal wife, the first slave concubine so honored. For the rest of her life, Hürrem played a highly influential role in the political, diplomatic, and philanthropic life of the Ottoman state. First, great power flowed from her position as mother of the prince, the future sultan Selim II (r. 1566–1574). Then, as the intimate and most trusted adviser of the sultan, she was Suleiman's closest confidant. He was frequently away in the far-flung corners of his multiethnic empire. Hürrem wrote him long letters filled with her love and longing for him, her prayers for his safety in battle, and political information about affairs in Istanbul, the activities of the grand vizier, and the attitudes of the janissaries. At a time when some people believed that the sultan's absence from the capital endangered his hold on the throne, Hürrem acted as his eyes and ears for potential threats.

Hürrem was the sultan's contact with her native Poland, which sent more embassies to Istanbul than any other power. Through her correspondence with King Sigismund I, peace between Poland and the Ottomans was maintained. When Sigismund II succeeded his father in 1548, Hürrem sent congratulations on his accession, along with two pairs of pajamas (originally a Hindu garment, but commonly worn in southwestern Asia) and six handkerchiefs. By sending the shah of Persia gold-embroidered sheets and shirts she had sewn herself, Hürrem sought to display the wealth of the sultanate and to keep peace between the Ottomans and the Safavids.

The enormous stipend that Suleiman gave Hürrem permitted her to participate in his vast building program. In Jerusalem (in the Ottoman province of Palestine), she founded a hospice for fifty-five pilgrims

Hürrem and her ladies in the harem.
(Bibliothèque nationale de France)

that included a soup kitchen that fed four hundred pilgrims a day. In Istanbul Suleiman built and Hürrem endowed the Haseki (meaning "royal favorite concubine") mosque complex and a public bath for women near the Women's Market.

Perhaps Hürrem tried to fulfill two functions hitherto distinct in Ottoman political theory: those of the sultan's favorite and mother of the prince. She also performed the conflicting roles of slave concubine and imperial wife. Turks, however, reviled Hürrem and thought she had bewitched Suleiman.

Questions for Analysis

1. Compare Hürrem to other powerful fifteenth- or sixteenth-century women, such as Isabella of Castile, Catherine de' Medici of France, Elizabeth of England, and Mary Queen of Scots.

2. What was Hürrem's "nationality"? What role did it play in her life?

Source: Leslie P. Pierce, *The Imperial Harem: Women and Sovereignty in the Ottoman Empire* (New York: Oxford University Press, 1993).

MAP 19.2 **The Safavid Empire** In the late sixteenth century, the power of the Safavid kingdom of Persia rested on its strong military force, its Shi'ite Muslim faith, and its extraordinarily rich trade in rugs and pottery. Many of the cities on the map, such as Tabriz, Qum, and Shiraz, were great rug-weaving centers.

Society: Hürrem"). When one of the sultan's concubines became pregnant, her status and her salary increased. If she delivered a boy, she raised him until the age of ten or eleven. Then the child was given a province to govern under his mother's supervision. She accompanied him there, was responsible for his good behavior, and worked through imperial officials and the janissary corps to promote his interests. Since succession to the throne was open to all the sultan's sons, at his death fratricide often resulted, and the losers were blinded or executed.

Slave concubinage paralleled the Ottoman development of slave soldiers and slave viziers. All held positions entirely at the sultan's pleasure, owed loyalty solely to him, and thus were more reliable than a hereditary nobility, as existed in Europe. Great social prestige, as well as the opportunity to acquire power and wealth, was attached to being a slave of the imperial household. Suleiman even made it a practice to marry his daughters to top-ranking slave-officials.

The Safavid Theocracy in Persia

After the collapse of Tamerlane's empire in 1405, Persia was controlled by Turkish lords, no single one dominant until 1501 when fourteen-year-old Ismail led a Turkish army to capture Tabriz and declared himself **shah** (king) and a particular Shi'ia sect the official and compulsory religion of his new empire. In the early twenty-first century, Iran remains the only Muslim state in which Shi'ism is the official religion.

The strength of the early **Safavid** state rested on three crucial features. First, it had the loyalty and military support of Turkish Sufis known as **Qizilbash** (a Turkish word meaning "redheads" that was applied to these people because of the red hats they

**Primary Source:
Letter to Shah Ismail
of Persia**
Ottoman sultan Selim I, a Sunni Muslim, threatens war against the Persian shah, his Shia enemy.

shah *Persian word for "king."*

Safavid *The dynasty that encompassed all of Persia and other regions; its state religion was Shi'ism.*

Qizilbash *Nomadic tribesmen who were Sufis and loyal to and supportive of the early Safavid state.*

wore). The shah secured the loyalty of the Qizilbash by granting them vast grazing lands, especially on the troublesome Ottoman frontier. In return, the Qizilbash supplied him with troops. Second, the Safavid state utilized the skills of urban bureaucrats and made them an essential part of the civil machinery of government. The third source of Safavid strength was the Shi'ite faith. The Shi'ites claimed descent from Ali, Muhammad's cousin and son-in-law, and believed that leadership among Muslims rightfully belonged to them as the Prophet's descendants. Ismail claimed descent from a line of twelve infallible *imams* (leaders) beginning with Ali and was officially regarded as their representative on earth.

Shi'ism gradually shaped the cultural and political identity of Persia (and later Iran). Recent scholarship asserts that Ismail was not "motivated by cynical notions of political manipulation."[3] He imported Shi'ite *ulama* (scholars outstanding in learning and piety) from other Arab lands to instruct and guide his people, and he persecuted and exiled Sunni ulama. With its puritanical emphasis on the holy law and on self-flagellation in penance for any disloyalty to Ali, the Safavid state represented theocracy triumphant throughout the first half century of its existence.

Safavid power reached its height under Shah Abbas (r. 1587–1629), whose military achievements, support for trade and commerce, and endowment of the arts earned him the epithet "the Great." He moved the capital to Isfahan. He adopted the Ottoman practice of building an army of slaves, primarily captives from the Caucuses (especially Armenians and Georgians), who could serve as a counterweight to the Qizilbash. He increased the use of gunpowder weapons and made alliances with European powers against the Ottomans and Portuguese. In his campaigns against the Ottomans, Shah Abbas captured Baghdad, Mosul, and Diarbakr in Mesopotamia (see Map 19.2).

The Mughal Empire in India

Of the three great Islamic empires of the early modern world, the **Mughal** Empire of India was the largest, wealthiest, and most populous. Extending over 1.2 million square miles at the end of the seventeenth century, with a population between 100 million and 150 million, and with fabulous wealth and resources, the Mughal Empire surpassed Safavid Persia and Ottoman Turkey. Among the Mughal ruler's world contemporaries, only the Ming emperor of China could compare with him.

In 1504 Babur (r. 1483–1530), the Turkish ruler of a small territory in Central Asia, captured Kabul and established a kingdom in Afghanistan. An adventurer who claimed descent from Chinggis Khan and Tamerlane, Babur moved southward into India when he could not expand in Afghanistan. In 1526, with a force of only twelve thousand men, Babur defeated the sultan of Delhi at Panipat. Babur's capture of the cities of Agra and Delhi, key fortresses of the north, paved the way for further conquests in northern India. Although many

● **Persian "Ardabil" Carpet from the Safavid Period** The Persians were among the first carpet weavers of ancient times and perfected the art over thousands of years. This carpet, reputably from the Safavid shrine at Ardabil, is one of only three signed and dated (around 1539–1540) carpets from the Safavid period, when Persian carpet making was at its zenith. Hand-knotted and hand-dyed, this wool carpet was royally commissioned with a traditional medallion design, consisting of a central sunburst medallion surrounded by radiating pendants. Mosque lamps project from the top and bottom of the medallion. Inscribed on the carpet is an ode by the fourteenth-century poet Hafiz: "I have no refuge in this world other than thy threshold / My head has no resting place other than this doorway." *(Victoria & Albert Museum/The Art Archive)*

Mughal *A term meaning "Mongol," used to refer to the Muslim empire of India, although its founders were primarily Turks, Afghans, and Persians.*

badshah *Persian word for highest ruler; it was the title that Akbar took at the age of thirteen.*

> **Primary Source:**
> **Akbarnama**
> *These selections from the history of the house of Akbar offer a glimpse inside the policies and religious outlook of the Mughal emperor.*

of his soldiers wished to return north with their spoils, Babur decided to stay in India. A gifted writer, Babur wrote an autobiography in Turkish that recounts his military campaigns, describes places and people he encountered, recounts his difficulties giving up wine, and shows his wide-ranging interests in everything from a Turkish general who excelled at leapfrog to his own love of fruit and swimming. He was not particularly impressed by India, complaining that the country lacked good horses, bread, grapes, and meat, and that people were neither kind, friendly, nor clever.

During the reign of Babur's son Humayun (r. 1530–1540 and 1555–1556), the Mughals lost most of their territories in Afghanistan. Humayun went into temporary exile in Persia, where he developed a deep appreciation for Persian art and literature. The reign of Humayun's son Akbar (r. 1556–1605) may well have been the greatest in the history of India. Under his dynamic leadership, the Mughal state took definite form. A boy of thirteen when he became **badshah,** or imperial ruler, Akbar pursued expansionist policies. The Mughal Empire under Akbar eventually included most of the subcontinent north of the Godavari River (see Map 19.3). No kingdom or coalition of kingdoms could long resist Akbar's armies. The once independent states of northern India were forced into a centralized political system under the sole authority of the Mughal emperor.

Akbar replaced Turkish with Persian as the official language of the Mughal Empire. Persian remained the official language until the British replaced it with English in 1835. To govern this vast region, Akbar developed an administrative bureaucracy centered on four co-equal ministers: for finance and revenue; the army and intelligence; the judiciary and religious patronage; and the imperial household, which included roads, bridges, and infrastructure throughout the empire. Under Akbar's Hindu finance minister, Raja Todar Mal, a uniform system of taxes was put in place. In the provinces, imperial governors, appointed by and responsible solely to the emperor, presided over administrative branches modeled on those of the central government. The government, however, rarely interfered in the life of village communities. Whereas the Ottoman sultans and Safavid shahs made extensive use of slaves acquired from non-Muslim lands for military and administrative positions, Akbar used the services of royal princes, nobles, and warrior-aristocrats. Initially these men were Muslims from Central Asia, but to reduce their influence, Akbar vigorously recruited Persians and Hindus. No single ethnic or religious faction could challenge the emperor.

Akbar's descendants extended the Mughal empire further. His son Jahangir (r. 1605–1628) lacked his father's military abilities and administrative genius, but he did succeed in consolidating Mughal rule in Bengal. Jahangir's son Shah Jahan (r. 1628–1658) launched fresh territorial expansion. Faced with dangerous revolts by the Muslims in Ahmadnagar and the resistance of the newly arrived Portuguese in Bengal, Shah Jahan not only crushed them but also strengthened his northwestern frontier. Shah Jahan's son Aurangzeb (r. 1658–1707) deposed his father and confined him for years in a small cell. A puritanically devout and strictly orthodox Muslim, as well as a skillful general and a clever diplomat, Aurangzeb ruled more of India than did any previous badshah, having extended the realm deeper into south India (see Map 19.3).

• • • • • • • • • • • • •

CULTURAL FLOWERING

What cultural advances occurred under the rule of these three houses?

All three Islamic imperial houses were great patrons and presided over extraordinary artistic flowering. There was much in common across their court cultures, probably because of the common Persian influence on the Turks since the tenth century. In

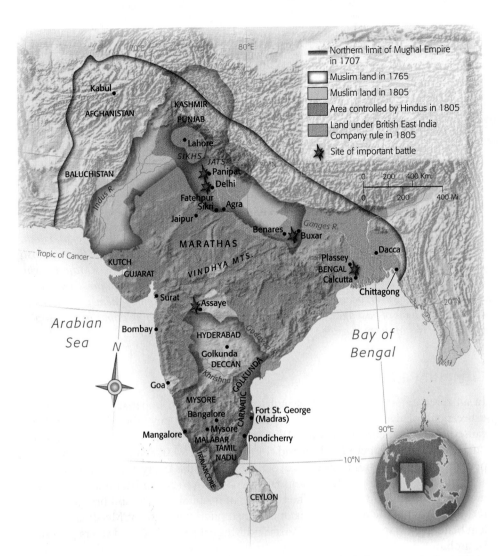

MAP 19.3 **India, 1707–1805**   In the eighteenth century, Mughal power gradually yielded to the Hindu Marathas and to the British East India Company.

addition, artistic styles and intellectual and religious trends would spread from one to the other. This was aided by common languages. Persian was used as the administrative language by the Mughals in India, and Arabic was a lingua franca of the entire region because of its centrality in Islam.

One of the arts all three shared was carpets. Carpet designs and weaving techniques demonstrate both cultural integration and local distinctiveness. Turkic migrants carried their weaving traditions with them as they moved but also readily adopted new motifs, especially from Persia. In Anatolia the town of Usak began its rise as a center of commercial carpet production in the fifteenth century. In Safavid Persia, Shah Abbas was determined to improve his country's export trade and built the small cottage business of carpet weaving into a national industry. In the capital city of Isfahan alone, factories employed more than twenty-five thousand weavers, who produced woolen carpets, brocades, and silks of brilliant color, design, and quality. Because the small hands of women and children can tie tinier knots than the large hands of men, women and children have often been used (and exploited) in the manufacture of expensive rugs.

Another art that spread from Persia to both Ottoman and Mughal lands was miniature painting, especially for book illustration. This tradition had been enriched by the many Chinese artists brought to Persia during the Mongol period. There was also an interplay between carpets and miniature painting. The naturalistic reproduction of lotus blossoms, peonies, chrysanthemums, birds, and even dragons, as well as tulips and carnations, appear in both book illustrations and carpets.

Akbar enthusiastically supported artists who produced magnificent paintings and books in the Indo-Persian style. In Mughal India, as throughout the Muslim world, books were regarded as precious objects. Time, talent, and expensive materials went into their production, and they were highly coveted because they reflected wealth, learning, and power. Akbar reportedly possessed twenty-four thousand books when he died. Abu-l-Fazl describes Akbar's library and love of books:

His Majesty's library is divided into several parts. . . . Prose works, poetical works, Hindi, Persian, Greek, Kashmirian, Arabic, are all separately placed. In this order they are also inspected. Experienced people bring them daily and read them before His Majesty, who hears every book from beginning to end . . . and rewards the readers with presents of cash either in gold or silver, according to the number of leaves read out by them. . . . There are no historical facts of past ages, or curiosities of science, or interesting points of philosophy, with which His Majesty, a leader of impartial sages, is unacquainted.[4]

City and Palace Building

In all three empires, strong rulers built capital cities and imperial palaces as visible expressions of dynastic majesty. Europeans called Suleiman "the Magnificent" because of the grandeur of his court. With annual state revenues of about $80 million (at a time when Elizabeth I of England could expect $150,000 and Francis I of France perhaps $1 million) and thousands of servants, he had a lifestyle no European monarch could begin to rival. He used his fabulous wealth to adorn Istanbul with palaces, mosques, schools, and libraries. The building of hospitals, roads, and bridges and the reconstruction of the water systems of the great pilgrimage sites at Mecca and Jerusalem benefited his subjects. Safavid Persia and Mughal India produced rulers with similar ambitions.

The greatest builder under the Ottomans was Pasha Sinan (1491–1588), a Greek-born devshirme recruit who rose to become imperial architect under Suleiman. A contemporary of Michelangelo, Sinan designed 312 public buildings—mosques, schools, hospitals, public baths, palaces, and burial chapels. His masterpieces, the Shehzade and Suleimaniye mosques in Istanbul, which rivaled the Byzantine church of Hagia Sophia, represented solutions to spatial problems unique to domed buildings and expressed the discipline, power, and devotion to Islam that characterized the Ottoman Empire under Suleiman. Istanbul became a prosperous, bustling city of more than a million people.

Shah Abbas made his capital, Isfahan, the jewel of the Safavid empire. A seventeenth-century English visitor described Isfahan's bazaar as "the surprisingest piece of Greatness in Honour of commerce the world can boast of." Besides splendid rugs, stalls displayed pottery and fine china, metalwork of exceptionally high quality, and silks and velvets of stunning weave and design. A city of perhaps 750,000 people, Isfahan contained 162 mosques, 48 schools where future members of the ulama learned the sacred Muslim sciences, 273 public baths, and the vast imperial palace. Private houses had their own garden courts, and public gardens, pools, and parks adorned the wide streets. Tales of the beauty of Isfahan circulated worldwide, attracting thousands of tourists annually in the seventeenth and eighteenth centuries.

Akbar in India was also a great builder. The birth of a long-awaited son, Jahangir, inspired Akbar to build a new city, Fatehpur-Sikri, to symbolize the regime's Islamic

● **Suleimaniye Mosque**   Designed and built (1548–1557) by Sinan, a janissary who became the greatest architect in Ottoman history, and surrounded by madrasas, a hospital, and shops, this mosque asserts the dynasty's power, religious orthodoxy, and the sultan's position as "God's shadow on earth." Suleiman, who financed it, is buried here. *(Robert Frerck/Odyssey/Chicago)*

foundations. He personally supervised the construction of the city, which combined the Muslim tradition of domes, arches, and spacious courts with the Hindu tradition of flat stone beams, ornate decoration, and solidity. According to the historian Abu-l-Fazl, "His Majesty plans splendid edifices, and dresses the work of his mind and heart in the garment of stone and clay."[5] Completed in 1578, the city included an imperial palace, a mosque, lavish gardens, and a hall of worship, as well as thousands of houses for ordinary people. Unfortunately because of its bad water supply, the city was soon abandoned.

Of Akbar's successors, Shah Jahan had the most sophisticated interest in architecture. Because his capital at Agra was cramped, in 1639 he decided to found a new capital city at Delhi. Hindus considered the area especially sacred, and the site reflects their influence. In the design and layout of the buildings, however, Persian ideas predominated, an indication of the numbers of Persian architects and engineers who had flocked to the subcontinent. The walled palace-fortress alone extended over 125 acres. Built partly of red sandstone, partly of marble, it included private chambers for the emperor; mansions for the wives, widows, and concubines of the imperial household; huge audience rooms for the conduct of public business (treasury, arsenal, and military); baths; and vast gardens filled with flowers, trees, and thirty silver fountains spraying water. In 1650, with living quarters for guards, military officials, merchants, dancing girls, scholars, and hordes of cooks and servants, the palace-fortress housed 57,000 people. It also boasted a covered public bazaar (comparable to a modern

● **Isfahan Tiles** The embellishment of Isfahan under Shah Abbas I created an unprecedented need for tiles—as had the rebuilding of imperial Istanbul after 1453, the vast building program of Suleiman the Magnificent, and a huge European demand. Persian potters learned their skills from the Chinese. By the late sixteenth century, Italian and Austrian potters had imitated the Persian and Ottoman tile makers. *(Courtesy of the Trustees of the Victoria & Albert Museum)*

mall), 270 feet long and 27 feet wide, with arcaded shops. It was probably the first roofed shopping center in India, although such centers were common in western Asia. The sight of the magnificent palace left contemporaries speechless, and the words of an earlier poet were inscribed on the walls:

If there is a paradise on the face of the earth,
It is this, it is this.

Beyond the walls, princes and aristocrats built mansions and mosques on a smaller scale. With a population between 375,000 and 400,000, Delhi gained the reputation of being one of the great cities of the Muslim world.

For his palace, Shah Jahan ordered the construction of the Peacock Throne. (See the feature "Listening to the Past: The Weighing of Shah Jahan on His Forty-Second Lunar Birthday" on pages 572–573.) This famous piece was encrusted with emeralds, diamonds, pearls, and rubies. It took seven years to fashion and cost the equivalent of $5 million. It served as the imperial throne of India until 1739, when the Persian warrior Nadir Shah seized it as plunder and carried it to Persia.

Shah Jahan's most enduring monument is the Taj Mahal. Twenty thousand workers toiled eighteen years to build this memorial in Agra to Shah Jahan's favorite wife, who died giving birth to their fifteenth child. One of the most beautiful structures in the world, the Taj Mahal is both an expression of love and a superb architectural blending of Islamic and Indian culture.

Gardens

Many of the architectural masterpieces of this age had splendid gardens attached to them as well. Gardens represent a distinctive and highly developed feature of Persian culture. From the second century, and with the model of the biblical account of the

Garden of Eden (Genesis 2 and 3), a continuous tradition of gardening had existed in Persia. A garden was a walled area with a pool in the center and geometrically laid-out flowering plants, especially roses. "In Arabic, paradise is simply *al janna,* the garden,"[6] and often as much attention was given to flowers as to food crops. First limited to the ruler's court, gardening soon spread among the wealthy citizens. Gardens served not only as centers of prayer and meditation but also as places of revelry and sensuality. A ruler might lounge near his pool as he watched the ladies of his harem bathe in it.

After the Abbasid conquest of Persia in 636–637, formal gardening spread west and east through the Islamic world, as illustrated by the magnificent gardens of Muslim Spain, southern Italy, and later southeastern Europe. The Mongol followers of Tamerlane took landscape architects from Persia back to Samarkand and adapted their designs to nomad encampments. In 1396 Tamerlane ordered the construction of a garden in a meadow, called House of Flowers. When Tamerlane's descendant Babur established the Mughal Dynasty in India, he adapted the Persian garden to the warmer southern climate. Gardens were laid out near palaces, mosques, shrines, and mausoleums, including the Taj Mahal, which had four water channels symbolizing the four rivers of paradise.

Because it represented paradise, the garden played a large role in Muslim literature. Some scholars hold that to understand Arabic poetry, one must study Arabic gardening. The literary genres of flowers and gardens provided basic themes for Hispano-Arab poets and a model for medieval Christian Europe. The secular literature of Muslim Spain, rife with references such as "a garland of verses," influenced the lyric poetry of southern France, the troubadours, and the courtly love tradition.

Gardens, of course, are seasonal. To remind themselves of "paradise" during the cold winter months, rulers, city people, and nomads ordered Persian carpets, which flower all year. Most Persian carpets of all periods use floral patterns and have a formal garden design.

Intellectual and Religious Trends

During the centuries from 1400 to 1800, there were many advances in mathematics, geographical literature, astronomy, medicine, and the religious sciences in the Islamic empires. Building on the knowledge of earlier Islamic writers and stimulated by Ottoman naval power, the geographer and cartographer Piri Reis produced a map incorporating Islamic and Western knowledge that showed all the known world (1513); another of his maps detailed Columbus's third voyage to the New World. Piri Reis's *Book of the Sea* (1521) contained 129 chapters, each with a map incorporating all Islamic (and Western) knowledge of the seas and navigation and describing harbors, tides, dangerous rocks and shores, and storm

● **Polo** Two teams of four on horseback ride back and forth on a grass field measuring 200 by 400 yards, trying to hit a 4½-ounce wooden ball with a 4-foot mallet through the opponents' goal. Because a typical match involves many high-speed collisions among the horses, each player has to maintain a string of expensive ponies in order to change mounts several times during the game. Students of the history of sports believe the game originated in Persia, as shown in this eighteenth-century miniature, whence it spread to India, China, and Japan. Brought from India to England, where it became very popular among the aristocracy in the nineteenth century, polo is a fine example of cross-cultural influences. *(Private Collection)*

areas. Takiyuddin Mehmet (1521–1585), who served as the sultan's chief astronomer, built an observatory at Istanbul. His *Instruments of the Observatory* catalogued astronomical instruments and described an astronomical clock that fixed the location of heavenly bodies with greater precision than ever before.

There were also advances in medicine. Under Suleiman, however, the imperial palace itself became a center of medical science, and the large number of hospitals established in Istanbul and throughout the empire testifies to his support for medical research and his concern for the sick. Abi Ahmet Celebi (1436–1523), the chief physician of the empire, produced a study on kidney and bladder stones and supported the research of the Jewish doctor Musa Colinus ul-Israil on the application of drugs. Celebi founded the first Ottoman medical school, which served as a training institution for physicians of the empire. The sultans and the imperial court relied on a cadre of elite Jewish physicians.

● Religious Scholar Filling a Wine Cup This seventeenth-century Persian painting on paper illustrates four lines of poetry that make fun of a religious scholar who was persuaded to overcome his usual avoidance of wine. *(Freer Gallery of Art, Smithsonian Institution, Washington, D.C., Gift of Charles Lang Freer, F1907.2)*

Ottoman physicians made less progress on one of the great scourges of the period, recurrent outbreaks of plague. Muhammed had once said not to go to a country where an epidemic existed but also not to leave a place because an epidemic broke out. As a consequence, when European cities began enforcing quarantines to control the spread of plague, Ottoman rulers dismissed their efforts, leading, some scholars believe, to great loss of life from the plague there.[7]

In the realm of religion, the rulers of all three empires were Muslims and drew legitimacy from their support for Islam, at least among their Muslim subjects. The Sunni-Shi'ia split between the Ottomans and Safavids led to efforts to define and enforce religious orthodoxy on both sides. For the Safavids this entailed suppressing Sufi movements and Sunnis, even marginalizing—sometimes massacring—the original Qizilbash warriors.

Sufi fraternities thrived throughout the Muslim world, even when the states tried to limit them. In India, Sufi orders also influenced non-Muslims. The mystical Bhakti movement among Hindus involved dances, poems, and songs reminiscent of Sufi orders. The development of the new religion of the Sikhs also was influenced by Sufis. The Sikhs traced themselves back to a teacher in the sixteenth century who argued that God did not distinguish between Muslims and Hindus but saw everyone as his children. Sikhs rejected the caste system and forbade alcohol and tobacco, and men did not cut their hair (covering it instead with a turban). The Sikh movement was most successful in northwest India, where Sikh men armed themselves to defend their communities.

Despite all the signs of cultural vitality in the three Islamic empires, none of them adopted the printing press or went through the sorts of cultural expansion associated with it in China and Europe. Until 1729, the Ottoman authorities prohibited printing books in Turkish or Arabic (but Jews, Armenians, and

Greeks could establish presses and print in their own languages). Printing was not banned in Mughal India, but neither did the technology spread, even after Jesuit missionaries printed Bibles in Indian languages beginning in the 1550s. The Islamic authorities in each of these empires did not want to see writings circulate that might unsettle society and religious teachings.

Coffeehouses

In the mid-fifteenth century, a new social convention spread throughout the Islamic world—drinking coffee. Arab writers trace the origins of coffee to Yemen, where the mystical Sufis drank coffee in their *dhiks,* or "devotional services." Sufis sought a trancelike concentration on God to the exclusion of everything else, and the use of coffee helped them stay awake. Most Sufis were not professional holy men but were employed as tradesmen and merchants. Therefore, the use of coffee for pious purposes led to its use as a business lubricant—an extension of hospitality to a potential buyer in a shop. Merchants carried the Yemenite practice to Mecca in about 1490. From Mecca, where pilgrims were introduced to it, drinking coffee spread to Egypt and Syria. In 1555 two Syrians opened a coffeehouse in Istanbul.

Coffeehouses provided a place for conversation and male sociability; there a man could entertain his friends cheaply and more informally than at home. But coffeehouses encountered religious and governmental opposition, which are indistinguishable under the shari'a, or holy law. Opponents of coffeehouses rested their arguments on four grounds: (1) because of its chemical composition, coffee is intoxicating and physically harmful; (2) coffee drinking was an innovation, and therefore a violation of Islamic law; (3) the coffeehouse encouraged political discussions that could be dangerous to the sultan; and (4) patrons of coffeehouses tended to be low types who engaged in immoral behavior, such as gambling, using drugs, soliciting prostitutes, and engaging in sodomy. The musical entertainment that coffeehouses provided, critics said, lent an atmosphere of debauchery. Thus coffeehouses drew the attention of government officials, who were also the guardians of public morality.

Although debate over the morality of coffeehouses continued through the sixteenth century, the acceptance of them represented a revolution in Islamic life: socializing was no longer confined to the home. Since the medical profession remained divided on coffee's harmful effects, and since the religious authorities could not prove that coffeehouses violated the shari'a, drinking coffee could not be forbidden. In the seventeenth century, coffee and coffeehouses spread to Europe.

● **Turkish Coffeehouse** This sixteenth-century miniature depicts many activities typical of coffeehouses: patrons enter (*upper left*); some sit drinking coffee in small porcelain cups (*center*); the manager makes fresh coffee (*right*). In the center, on a low sofa, men sit reading and talking. At bottom appear activities considered disreputable: musicians playing instruments, others playing games such as backgammon, a board game where moves are determined by rolls of dice. *(Reproduced by kind permission of the Trustees of the Chester Beatty Library, Dublin, Ms 439, folio 9)*

NON-MUSLIMS UNDER MUSLIM RULE

How did Christians, Jews, Hindus, and other non-Muslims fare under these Islamic states?

Drawing on Qur'anic teachings, Muslims had long practiced a religious toleration unknown in Christian Europe. On the promise of obedience and the payment of a poll tax, the Muslim rulers guaranteed the lives and property of Christians and Jews. In the case of the Ottomans, this included not only the Christians and Jews who had been living under Muslim rule for centuries, but also the Serbs, Bosnians, Croats, and other Orthodox Christians in the newly conquered Balkans. The Ottoman conqueror of Constantinople, Mehmet, nominated the Greek patriarch as official representative of the Greek population. This and other such appointments recognized non-Muslims as functioning parts of Ottoman society and economy. In 1454 one Jewish resident, Isaac Sarfati, sent a circular letter to his coreligionists in the Rhineland, Swabia, Moravia, and Hungary praising the happy conditions of the Jews under the crescent in contrast to the "great torture chamber" under Christian rulers and urging them to come to Turkey.[8] A massive migration to Ottoman lands followed. When Ferdinand and Isabella of Spain expelled the Jews in 1492, many immigrated to the Ottoman Empire.

Babur and his successors acquired even more non-Muslim subjects with their conquests in India, which had not only Hindus, but substantial numbers also of Jains, Zoroastrians, Christians, and Sikhs. Over time, the number of Indians who converted to Islam increased, but the Mughal rulers did not force conversion. The Ganges plain, the geographical area of the subcontinent most intensely exposed to Mughal rule and for the longest span of time, had, when the first reliable census was taken in 1901, a Muslim population of only 10 to 15 percent. In fact, "in the subcontinent as a whole there is an inverse relationship between the degree of Muslim political penetration and the degree of Islamization."[9]

Akbar went the furthest in promoting Muslim-Hindu accommodation. He celebrated important Hindu festivals, such as Diwali, the festival of lights. He wore his uncut hair in a turban "as a concession to Indian usage and to please his Indian subjects."[10] Twice Akbar married Hindu princesses, one of whom became the mother of his heir, Jahangir. He appointed the Spanish Jesuit Antonio Monserrate (1536–1600) as tutor to his second son, Prince Murad. Hindus eventually totaled 30 percent of the

● **Emperor Akbar and Fatehpur-Sikri** In 1569 Akbar founded the city of Fatehpur-Sikri (the City of Victory) to honor the Muslim holy man Shaykh Salim Chishti, who had foretold the birth of Akbar's son and heir Jahangir. Akbar is shown here seated on the cushion in the center overseeing the construction of the city. The image is contained in the *Akbarnama*, a book of illustrations Akbar commissioned to officially chronicle his reign. *(Victoria & Albert Museum/The Bridgeman Art Library)*

imperial bureaucracy. In 1579 Akbar abolished the **jitza,** the tax on non-Muslims. These actions, especially the abolition of the jitza, infuriated the ulama, and serious conflict erupted between them and the emperor. Ultimately, Akbar issued an imperial decree declaring that the Mughal emperor had supreme authority, even above the ulama, in all religious matters. This statement, resting on a policy of benign toleration, represented a severe defeat for the Muslim religious establishment.

Some of Akbar's successors sided more with the ulama. A combination of religious zeal and financial necessity seems to have prompted Aurangzeb to promote stricter forms of Islam. He appointed censors of public morals in important cities to enforce Islamic laws against gambling, prostitution, drinking, and the use of narcotics. He forbade sati—the self-immolation of widows on their husbands' funeral pyres—and the castration of boys to be sold as eunuchs. He also abolished all taxes not authorized by Islamic law. This measure led to a serious loss of state revenues. To replace them, Aurangzeb in 1679 reimposed the jitza, the tax on non-Muslims.

Regulating Indian society according to Islamic law meant modifying the religious toleration and cultural cosmopolitanism instituted by Akbar. Aurangzeb ordered the destruction of some Hindu temples and tried to curb Sikhism. He required Hindus to pay higher customs duties than Muslims. Out of fidelity to Islamic law, he even criticized his mother's tomb, the Taj Mahal: "The lawfulness of a solid construction over a grave is doubtful, and there can be no doubt about the extravagance involved."[11] Aurangzeb employed more Hindus in the imperial administration than had any previous Mughal ruler, but his religious policy proved highly unpopular with the majority of his subjects.

jitza *A tax on non-Muslims.*

SHIFTING TRADE ROUTES AND EUROPEAN PENETRATION

How were the Islamic empires affected by the decline in overland trade and the great growth in maritime commerce, and how were European powers able to use trade to make inroads as this period progressed?

The economic foundation of all three Islamic empires was agriculture, and taxes on farmers supported the government and armies. Some new crops, including coffee, sugar, and tobacco, became important in this period, but new world crops do not seem to have led to population increases that were as rapid as elsewhere in Eurasia. By 1800, the population of India was about 190 million, that of Safavid lands about 8 million, and that of Ottoman lands about 24 million (the three together thus less than China, about 300 million in 1800).

Trade was also a crucial element in the economies of these three empires. In 1450 all the great highways of international trade were in Muslim hands, and the wealth of the Muslim states rested heavily on commerce. In the early seventeen century, world-wide economic depression and silver shortages had a devastating effect on the East-West overland trade, from which it never recovered. By 1750 the Muslims had lost control of the trade, which probably contributed to the political decline of these empires (discussed below).

European colonial expansion and shifting trade patterns isolated the Ottomans and the Safavids from the centers of growth in the Western Hemisphere and the East Indies. European trade with the Americas, Africa, and Asia by means of the Atlantic also meant that the old southwestern Asian trade routes were bypassed. To try to revive trade with Europe, the Ottomans signed a series of agreements known as **capitulations.** A trade compact signed in 1536 and renewed in 1569 virtually exempted French merchants from Ottoman law and allowed them to travel and buy and sell throughout the sultan's dominions and to pay low customs duties on French imports and exports.

capitulations *A series of agreements that basically surrender the rights of one party. The Ottoman government signed these with European powers and gave them a stranglehold on Ottoman trade and commerce.*

● **Kalamkari Textile from Golconda** Golconda, in southeast India, is the site of a great fortress complex and many palaces, mosques, and Hindu temples that were destroyed in 1687 and left in ruins. This textile is called *kalamkari*, meaning pen or brushed work, and represents a style of design and manufacture unique to the region. Containing a rich variety of Persian, Hindu, and Muslim motifs, this superb example of seventeenth-century painted cotton, depicting various scenes of life in the palace and gardens, suggests the beauty and complexity of Indian textile manufacture. *(The Bridgeman Art Library)*

In 1590, in spite of strong French opposition, a group of English merchants gained the right to trade in Ottoman territory in return for supplying the sultan with iron, steel, brass, and tin for his war with Persia. In 1615, as part of a twenty-year peace treaty, the capitulation rights already given to French and English businessmen were extended to the Habsburgs. These capitulations progressively gave European merchants an economic stranglehold on Ottoman trade and commerce.

Whereas trade between Europe and the Ottomans declined as trade routes shifted, direct trade with India expanded greatly. The Mughal period witnessed the growth of a thriving capitalist commercial economy on the Indian subcontinent. Although most people were engaged in agriculture, from which most imperial revenue was derived, a manufacturing industry supported by a money economy and mercantile capitalism expanded.

Block-printed cotton cloth, produced by artisans working at home, was India's chief export. Through an Islamic business device involving advancing payment to artisans, banker-brokers supplied the material for production and the money that the artisans could live on while they worked; the cloth brokers specified the quality, quantity, and design of the finished product. This procedure resembles the later English "domestic" or "putting-out" system (see page 647), for the very good reason that the English took the idea from the Indians. Within India, the demand for cotton cloth, as well as for food crops, was so great that Akbar had to launch a wide-scale road-building campaign. From Gujarat, Indian merchant bankers shipped their cloth worldwide: across the Indian Ocean to Aden and the Muslim-controlled cities on the east coast of Africa; across the Arabian Sea to Muscat and Hormuz and up the Persian Gulf to the cities of Persia; up the Red Sea to the Mediterranean; by sea also to Malacca, Indonesia, China, and Japan; by land across Africa to Ghana on the west coast; and to Astrakhan, Poland, Moscow, and even the Russian cities on the distant Volga River. In many of these places, Indian businessmen had branch offices. All this activity represented enormous trade, which produced fabulous wealth for some Indian merchants. Some scholars have compared India's international trade in the sixteenth century with that of Italian firms, such as the Medici. The Indian trade actually extended over a far wider area. Indian merchants were often devout Hindus, Muslims, Buddhists, or Jains, evidence that undermines the argument of some Western writers, notably Karl Marx (see page 681), that religion retarded Asia's economic development.

European Rivalry for the Indian Trade

Shortly before Babur's invasion of India, the Portuguese under the navigator Pedro Alvares Cabral had opened the subcontinent to Portuguese trade. In 1510 they established the port of Goa on the Arabian Sea as their headquarters and through a policy of piracy and terrorism took control of Muslim shipping in the Indian and Arabian Oceans (see Map 19.3), charging high fees for passage. The Portuguese historian Barrões attempted to justify Portugal's seizure of commercial traffic that the Muslims had long dominated:

It is true that there does exist a common right to all to navigate the seas and in Europe we recognize the rights which others hold against us; but the right does not extend beyond Europe and therefore the Portuguese as Lords of the Sea are justified in confiscating the goods of all those who navigate the seas without their permission.[12]

In short, Western principles of international law should not restrict them in Asia. For almost a century, the Portuguese controlled the spice trade over the Indian Ocean.

In 1602 the Dutch formed the Dutch East India Company with the stated goal of wresting the enormously lucrative spice trade from the Portuguese. The Dutch concentrated their efforts in Indonesia. The scent of fabulous profits also attracted the English. With a charter signed by Queen Elizabeth, eighty London merchants organized the British East India Company. In 1619 Emperor Jahangir granted a British mission important commercial concessions at Surat on the west coast of India. Gifts, medical services, and bribes to Indian rulers enabled the British to set up twenty-seven other coastal forts. Fort St. George on the east coast became the modern city of Madras. In 1668 the city of Bombay—given to England when the Portuguese princess Catherine of Braganza married King Charles II—was leased to the company, marking the virtually total British absorption of Portuguese power in India. In 1690 the company founded a fort that became the city of Calcutta. Thus the three places that later became centers of British economic and political imperialism—Madras, Bombay, and Calcutta (today called Chennai, Mombai, and Kolkata)—date back to before 1700.

Factory-Fort Societies

The British called their trading post at Surat a **factory-fort** and the term was later used for all European settlements in India. The term did not signify manufacturing; it

factory-fort *A term first used by the British for their trading post at Surat, it was later applied to all European walled settlements in India.*

● **English Factory-Fort at Surat** The factory-fort began as a storage place for goods before they were bought and transported abroad; it gradually expanded to include merchants' residences and some sort of fortification. By 1650 the English had twenty-three factory-forts in India. Surat, in the Gujarat region on the Gulf of Cambay, was the busiest factory-fort and port until it was sacked by the Marathas in 1664. *(Mansell Collection)*

designated the walled compound containing the residences, gardens, and offices of British East India Company officials and the warehouses where goods were stored before being shipped to Europe. The company president exercised political authority over all residents.

Factory-forts existed to make profits from the Asian-European trade, and they evolved into flourishing sources of economic profit. The British East India Company sold silver, copper, zinc, lead, and fabrics to the Indians and bought cotton goods, silks, pepper and other spices, sugar, and opium from them. By the late seventeenth century, the company was earning substantial profits. Profitability increased after 1700 when the company began to trade with China. Some Indian merchants in Calcutta and Bombay made gigantic fortunes from trade within Asia.

Because the directors of the British East India Company in London discouraged all unnecessary expenses and financial risks, they opposed any interference in local Indian politics and even missionary activities. Political instability in India in the early eighteenth century caused the company's factories to evolve into defensive installations manned by small garrisons of native troops (**sepoys**) trained in Western military drill and tactics. When warlords appeared or an uprising occurred, people from the

sepoys *The native Indian troops who were trained as infantrymen.*

surrounding countryside flocked into the fort, and the company factory-forts gradually came to exercise political authority over the territories around them.

Indian and Chinese wares enjoyed great popularity in England and on the European continent in the late seventeenth and early eighteenth centuries. The middle classes wanted Indian textiles, which were colorful, durable, cheap, and washable. The upper classes desired Chinese wallpaper and porcelains and Indian silks and brocades. Europeans had to pay for everything they bought from Asia with precious metals because Asians had little interest in European manufactured articles. Thus there was insistent pressure in England, France, and the Netherlands against the importation of Asian goods because of the fear that the drain of gold would hurt their economies.

The Rise of the British East India Company

The French were the last to arrive in India. In the 1670s the French East India Company established factories at Chandernagore in Bengal, Pondicherry, and elsewhere. Joseph Dupleix (1697–1764), who was appointed governor general at Pondicherry in 1742, made allies of Indian princes and built an army of native troops who were trained as infantrymen.

From 1740 to 1763, Britain and France were almost continually engaged in a tremendous global struggle. India, like North America in the Seven Years' War, became a battlefield and a prize. The French won land battles, but English sea power decided the first phase of the war. Then a series of brilliant victories destroyed French power

● **Taj Mahal at Agra**   This tomb is the finest example of Muslim architecture in India. Its white marble exterior is inlaid with semiprecious stones in Arabic inscriptions and floral designs. The oblong pool reflects the building, which asserts the power of the Mughal Dynasty. *(John Elk/Stock, Boston)*

in southern India. By preventing French reinforcements from arriving, British sea power again proved to be the determining factor, and British jurisdiction soon extended over the important northern province of Bengal. The Treaty of Paris of 1763 recognized British control of much of India, and scholars view the treaty as the beginning of the British Empire in India.

How was the vast subcontinent to be governed? Parliament believed that the British East India Company had too much power and considered the company responsible for the political disorders in India, which were bad for business. The Regulating Act of 1773 created the office of governor general, with an advisory council, to exercise political authority over the territory controlled by the company. The India Act of 1784 required that the governor general be chosen from outside the company, and it made company directors subject to parliamentary supervision.

Implementation of these reforms fell to three successive governors, Warren Hastings, (r. 1774–1785), Lord Charles Cornwallis (r. 1786–1794), and the marquess Richard Wellesley (r. 1797–1805). Hastings sought allies among Indian princes, laid the foundations for the first Indian civil service, abolished tolls to facilitate internal trade, placed the salt and opium trades under government control, and planned a codification of Muslim and Hindu laws. Cornwallis introduced the British style of property relations, in effect converting a motley collection of former Mughal officers, tax collectors, and others into English-style landlords. The result was a new system of landholding in which the rents of tenant farmers supported the landlords. Wellesley was victorious over local rulers who resisted British rule and vastly extended British influence in India. Like most nineteenth-century British governors of India, Wellesley believed that British rule strongly benefited the Indians. With supreme condescension, he wrote that British power should be established over the Indian princes in order

to deprive them of the means of prosecuting any measure or of forming any confederacy hazardous to the security of the British empire, and to enable us to preserve the tranquility of India by exercising a general control over the restless spirit of ambition and violence which is characteristic of every Asiatic government.[13]

DYNASTIC DECLINE

Did any common factors lead to the decline of the Islamic empires in the seventeenth and eighteenth centuries?

By the eighteenth century, all three of the major Islamic empires were on the defensive. They faced some common problems—succession difficulties, financial strain, loss of military superiority—but their circumstances differed in significant ways as well.

The first to fall was the Safavid Empire. Shah Abbas was succeeded by inept rulers whose heavy indulgence in wine and the pleasures of the harem weakened the monarchy and fed the slow disintegration of the state. Shi'ite religious institutions grew stronger. Decline in the military strength of the army encouraged increased foreign aggression. In 1722 the Afghans invaded from the east, seized Isfahan, and were able to repulse an Ottoman invasion from the west. In Isfahan thousands of officials and members of the shah's family were executed. In the following centuries some strong men emerged, but no leader was able to reunite all of Persia.

The Ottoman throne also suffered from a series of weak sultans. In the fifteenth and early sixteenth centuries, Turkish practice guaranteed that the sultans would be forceful men. The sultan's sons gained administrative experience as governors of provinces and military experience on the battlefield as part of their education. After the sultan died, any son who wanted to succeed had to contest his brothers to claim the throne, after which the new sultan would have his defeated brothers executed. Although bloody, this system led to the succession of capable, determined men. After Suleiman's reign, however, this tradition was abandoned. To prevent threats of usurpation, sons of the sultan were brought up in the harem and confined there as adults, denied a role in government. After years of indolence and dissipation, not surprisingly, few of these princes turned out to be strong military leaders. Selim II (r. 1566–1574), whom the Turks called "Selim the Drunkard," left the conduct of public affairs to his vizier while he pursued the pleasures of the harem. Turkish sources attribute his death to a fall in his bath caused by dizziness when he tried to stop drinking. A series of rulers who were incompetent or minor children left power in the hands of leading bureaucratic officials and the mothers of the heirs. Political factions formed around viziers, military leaders, and palace women. In the contest for political favor, the devshirme was abandoned, and political and military ranks were filled by Muslims.

As in parts of Europe, rising population without corresponding economic growth caused serious social problems. A long period of peace in the late sixteenth century and again in the mid-eighteenth century and a decline in the frequency of visits of the plague led to a doubling of the population. The land could not sustain so many people, nor could the towns provide jobs for the thousands of agricultural workers who fled to them. The return of demobilized soldiers aggravated the problem. Inflation, famine, and widespread revolts resulted. The economic center of gravity shifted from the capital to the provinces, and politically the empire began to decentralize as well. Local notables and military men, rather than central officials, exercised political power. Provincial autonomy brought more people into political participation, thus laying a foundation for later nationalism.

Ottoman armies began losing wars and territory along their European borders. The army was depending more on mercenaries, and military technology fell behind. The Ottomans did not keep up with the innovations in drill and command and control that were then transforming European armies. By the terms of the peace treaty with Austria signed at Karlowitz (1699), the Ottomans lost the major European provinces of Hungary and Transylvania, along with the tax revenues they had provided.

In Mughal India the old Turkish practice of letting the heirs fight for the throne persisted, leading to frequent struggles over succession, but also to strong rulers. Yet military challenges proved daunting there as well. After defeating his father and brothers, Aurangzeb pushed the conquest of the south. The stiffest opposition came from the Marathas, a militant Hindu group centered in the western Deccan. From 1681 until his death in 1707, Aurangzeb led repeated sorties through the Deccan. He took many forts and won several battles, but total destruction of the Maratha guerrilla bands eluded him. After his death, they played an important role in the collapse of the Mughal Empire.

Aurangzeb's death led to thirteen years of succession struggles, shattering the empire. His eighteenth-century successors were less successful than the Ottomans in making the dynasty the focus of loyalty. Mughal provincial governors began to rule independently, giving only minimal allegiance to the badshah at Delhi. The Marathas, who pressed steadily northward, constituted the gravest threat to Mughal authority. No ruler could defeat them.

In 1739 the Persian adventurer Nadir Shah invaded India, defeated the Mughal army, looted Delhi, and after a savage massacre carried off a huge amount of treasure, including the Peacock Throne. When Nadir Shah withdrew to Afghanistan, he took with him the Mughal government's prestige. Constant skirmishes between the Afghans and the Marathas for control of the Punjab and northern India ended in 1761 at Panipat, where the Marathas were crushed by the Afghans. At that point, India no longer had any power capable of imposing order on the subcontinent or checking the penetration of the rapacious Europeans.

Chapter Summary

To assess your mastery of this chapter, go to
bedfordstmartins.com/mckayworld

Key Terms

Ottomans
Anatolia
Sultan-i-Rum
sultan
devshirme
janissaries
concubine
shah
Safavid
Qizilbash
Mughal
badshah
jitza
capitulations
factory-fort
sepoys

• *How were the three Islamic empires established, and what sorts of governments did they set up?*

After the decline of the Mongols in Central Asia and Persia, many small Turkic-ruled states emerged. Three of them went on to establish large empires: the Ottomans in Anatolia, the Safavids in Persia, and the Mughals in India. In each case, the state steadily expanded for several generations, though it did eventually run up against foes it could not defeat. All three empires responded to the shift in military technology away from the mounted archer toward the use of gunpowder weapons. The Ottomans in particular made effective use of guns and artillery.

• *What cultural advances occurred under the rule of these three houses?*

The wealth of these empires provided the material basis for a great cultural efflorescence. Royal patronage was especially important in the building of palaces and cities. Other major arts of the period included carpets and book illustrations. Intellectually, this was a fertile period for both natural science and religious speculation. Islam received special protection and support from all three governments, but there were key differences: The Ottomans and Mughals supported the Sunni tradition, the Safavids, the Shi'ite tradition.

• *How did Christians, Jews, Hindus, and other non-Muslims fare under these Islamic states?*

All of the Islamic empires had substantial non-Muslim subjects. The Ottomans ruled over the Balkans, where most of the people were Christian. In India, Muslims were outnumbered by Hindus. Following Islamic teachings, Christians and Jews were not persecuted in these empires, and Hindus in India came to be treated as though they too were "protected" people.

• *How were the Islamic empires affected by the decline in overland trade and the great growth in maritime commerce, and how were European powers able to use trade to make inroads as this period progressed?*

The Islamic regions of Eurasia had been the crossroads of East-West and North-South trade for many centuries, but with the great expansion of European maritime trade in the late fifteenth and sixteenth centuries, trade between Europe and India, China, and Southeast Asia shifted decisively to the maritime route. Indian textiles, much desired in Southeast Asia and China, attracted European businessmen. The inability of Indian leaders in the eighteenth century to resolve their domestic differences led first to British intervention and then to British rule of several parts of the Indian subcontinent.

• Did any common factors lead to the decline of the Islamic empires in the seventeenth and eighteenth centuries?

The eighteenth century saw the destruction of the Safavid Empire and the great decline in the reach of the Mughal Empire. The Ottomans, too, suffered major setbacks in the seventeenth and eighteenth centuries (though they would make a comeback in the nineteenth century). Some of the common problems these empires faced were the end of expansion, difficulties with succession, tendencies toward decentralization, and population growth not matched by economic growth. In India, the Mughals faced not only tendencies toward decentralization but also the appearance of new foes, traders from Europe backed by their governments.

Suggested Reading

Atil, Esin. *The Age of Sultan Suleyman the Magnificent.* 1987. A splendidly illustrated celebration of the man and his times.

Dale, Stephen Frederic. *The Garden of the Eight Paradises: Babur and the Culture of Empire in Central Asia, Afghanistan and India, 1483–1750.* 2004. A scholarly biography that draws on and analyzes Babur's autobiography.

Findley, Carter Vaughn. *The Turks in World History.* 2005. Takes a macro look at the three Islamic empires as part of the history of the Turks.

Finkel, Caroline. *Osman's Dream: A History of the Ottoman Empire.* 2006. A new interpretation that views the Ottomans from their own perspective.

Inalcik, Halil, and Renda Günsel. *Ottoman Civilization.* 2002. A huge, beautifully illustrated, government-sponsored overview, with emphasis on the arts and culture.

Jackson, Peter, and Lawrence Lockhart, eds. *The Cambridge History of Iran,* Vol. 6, *The Timurid and Safavid*

Periods. 1986. A set of essays on the social and cultural as well as political and economic history of Iran by leading scholars.

Lapidus, Ira M. *A History of Islamic Societies,* 2nd ed. 2002. A comprehensive yet lucid survey.

Mukhia, Harbans. *The Mughals of India: A Framework for Understanding.* 2004. A short but thoughtful analysis of the Mughal society and state.

Pierce, Leslie. *The Imperial Harem: Women and Sovereignty in the Ottoman Empire.* 1993. A fresh look at the role of elite women under the Ottomans.

Richards, John F. *The Mughal Empire.* 1993. Offers a coherent narrative history of the period 1526–1720.

Ruthven, Malise, and Azim Nanji. *Historical Atlas of Islam.* 2004. Provides numerous maps illustrating the shifting political history of Islamic states.

Notes

1. Quoted in B. Lewis, *The Muslim Discovery of Europe* (New York: W. W. Norton, 1982), p. 29.
2. W. H. McNeill, *The Pursuit of Power: Technology, Armed Force, and Society Since A.D. 1000* (Chicago: University of Chicago Press, 1982), p. 87.
3. D. Morgan, *Medieval Persia, 1040–1797* (New York: Longman, 1988), pp. 112–113.
4. Quoted in M. C. Beach, *The Imperial Image: Paintings for the Mughal Court* (Washington, D.C.: Freer Gallery of Art, Smithsonian Institution, 1981), pp. 9–10.
5. Quoted in V. A. Smith, *The Oxford History of India* (Oxford: Oxford University Press, 1967), p. 398.
6. J. Goody, *The Culture of Flowers* (Cambridge: Cambridge University Press, 1993), p. 103.
7. See William McNeill, *Plagues and Peoples* (New York: Anchor Books, 1998), pp. 198–199.
8. F. Babinger, *Mehmed the Conqueror and His Times,* trans. R. Manheim (Princeton, N.J.: Princeton University Press, 1978), p. 107.
9. R. M. Eaton, *The Rise of Islam and the Bengal Frontier, 1204–1760* (Berkeley: University of California Press, 1993), p. 115.
10. J. F. Richards, *The New Cambridge History of India: The Mughal Empire* (Cambridge: Cambridge University Press, 1995), p. 45.
11. Quoted in S. K. Ikram, *Muslim Civilization in India* (New York: Columbia University Press, 1964), p. 202.
12. Quoted in K. M. Panikkar, *Asia and Western Domination* (London: George Allen & Unwin, 1965), p. 35.
13. Quoted in W. Bingham, H. Conroy, and F. W. Iklé, *A History of Asia,* vol. 2 (Boston: Allyn and Bacon, 1967), p. 74.

Listening to the PAST

The Weighing of Shah Jahan on His Forty-Second Lunar Birthday*

*I*n 1799 the nawab (provincial governor) of Oudh in northern India sent to King George III of Great Britain the Padshahnama, *or official history of the reign of Shah Jahan. A volume composed of 239 folios on very high-quality gold-flecked tan paper with forty-four stunningly beautiful paintings illustrating the text, the* Padshahnama *represents both a major historical chronicle of a Mughal emperor's reign and an extraordinary artistic achievement. One of the great art treasures of the world, it now rests in the Royal Library at Windsor.*

All the Mughal emperors had a strong historical sense and the desire to preserve records of their reigns. They brought to India the traditional Muslim respect for books as sources of secular and religious knowledge and as images of their wealth and power. The Padshahnama, *in stressing Shah Jahan's descent from Tamerlane and his right to the throne, in celebrating his bravery and military prowess, and in magnifying his virtues, is one long glorification of Jahan's rule. The Persian scholar and calligrapher Abdul-Hamid Lahawri wrote the text. Many Persian artists painted the illustrations with detailed precision and an exactitude that art historians consider sensitive and faithful to the original.*

Since alms are beneficial for repelling bodily and psychic harm and for attracting spiritual and corporeal benefits, as all peoples, religions, and nations are agreed, His Majesty Arsh-Ashyani [Akbar] established the custom of weighing and had himself weighed twice [a year], once after the end of the solar year and the other after the end of the lunar year. In the solar weighing he was weighed twelve times, first against gold and then eleven other items, while in the lunar weighing he was weighed eight times, first against silver and then seven other items. . . . The amounts from the weighings were given away in alms.

. . . Inasmuch as it benefited the needy, His Majesty Jahanbani [Shah Jahan] has his perfect self weighed twice, and in his generosity he has ordered that gold and silver be used each time. . . .

The lunar weighing ceremony for the end of the forty-third year of the Emperor's life was held. The Emperor, surrounded by a divine aura, was weighed against gold and the other usual things, and the skirt of the world was held out in expectation of gold and silver. On this auspicious day Muhammad-Ali Beg, the ambassador of Iran, was awarded a gold-embroidered robe of honor, a jeweled belt, an elephant, a female elephant, and four large ashrafis, one weighing 400 tolas [a measure of weight, slightly more than two mithcals], the second 300 tolas, the third 200 tolas, and the fourth 100 tolas, and four rupees also of the weights given above, and he was given leave to depart. From the time he paid homage until the time he set out to return he had been given 316,000 rupees in cash and nearly a lac of rupees in goods.

An earlier weighing ceremony of the Emperor Jahangir, on 1 September 1617, was described by the always observant, and usually skeptical, first English ambassador to the Mughal court, Sir Thomas Roe: "Was the Kings Birthday, and the solemnitie of his weighing, to which I went, and was carryed into a very large and beautifull Garden; the square within all water; on the sides flowres and trees. . . . Here attended the Nobilitie, all sitting about it on Carpets, vntill the King came; who at last appeared clothed, or rather loden with Diamonds, Rubies, Pearles, and other precious vanities, so great, so glorious! . . . Suddenly hee entered into the scales, sate like a woman on his legges, and there was put against him many bagges to fit his weight, which were changed six times, and they say was siluer, and that I vnderstood his weight to be nine thousand *Rupias,* which are almost one thousand pound sterling."

Another official history of Shah Jahan's reign, the 'Amal-i-Salih, *describes the ceremonial weighing that took place another year.*

*A solar year is the time required for the earth to make one complete revolution around the sun (365 days). A lunar year equals 12 lunar months.

The "Weighing of Shah Jahan," who sits cross-legged on one plate of the scales, as bags of gold and silver wait to be placed on the other side. *(The Royal Collection © 2007, Her Majesty Queen Elizabeth II)*

Since it is His Majesty's custom and habit to have beggars sought out, and his generous nature is always looking for a pretext to relieve those who are in need, therefore twice a year he sits, like the orient sun in majesty, in the pan of the scale of auspiciousness in the solar and lunar weighing ceremonies. Twice a year by solar and lunar calculation a magnificent celebration and a large-scale banquet is arranged by order of His Majesty. An amount equal to his weight in gold and silver is distributed among the destitute and the poor according to their deservedness and merits. Although this type of alms is not mentioned in the religious law, nonetheless since scholars of this country are all in agreement that such alms are the most perfect type of alms for repelling corporeal and spiritual catastrophes and calamities, therefore this pleasing method was chosen and established by His Majesty Arsh-Ashyani, whose personality was, like the world-illuminating sun, based upon pure effulgence. By this means the poor attained their wishes, and in truth the custom of *aqiqa*—which is an established custom in the law

of the Prophet and his Companions, and in which on the seventh day after birth the equivalent weight of an infant's shaven hair in silver is given in alms, and a sacrificial animal is divided and distributed among the poor—has opened the way to making this custom permissible.

Questions for Analysis

1. Consider Shah Jahan's motives for the practice of ceremonial weighing. Does it have any theological basis?

2. Compare the Mughal practice to something similar in Ottoman, European, and South American societies.

Source: King of the World. The Padshahnama. An Imperial Mughal Manuscript from the Royal Library, Windsor Castle, ed. Milo Cleveland Beach and Ebba Koch, trans. Wheeler Thackston (Washington, D.C.: Azimuth Editions—Sackler Gallery, 1997, pp. 39–43). Reprinted by permission of W. M. Thackston, translator.

Japanese Society. This detail from a seventeenth-century
six-panel Japanese screen depicts life in the pleasure
quarters, where men and women interacted openly,
playing instruments and enjoying games.
(Hikone Castle Museum)

chapter

20 CONTINUITY AND CHANGE IN EAST ASIA, CA. 1400–1800

The period from 1400 to 1800 witnessed growth and dynamic change throughout East Asia. Although both China and Japan suffered periods of war, each ended up with expanded territories—Japan taking control of the Ryūkyū Islands to the south and pushing back the Ainu in the north, and Qing China taking control of Mongolia and Tibet. The age of exploration brought New World crops to the region, leading to increased agricultural output and population growth. It also brought new opportunities for foreign trade and new religions, to which the countries of East Asia responded in differing ways. Another link between these countries was the massive Japanese invasions of Korea in the late sixteenth century, which led to war between China and Japan.

In China, the native **Ming Dynasty** (1368–1644) replaced the Mongol Yuan Dynasty (1271–1368). Under the Ming, China saw agricultural reconstruction, remarkable maritime expeditions abroad, commercial expansion, and a vibrant urban culture. Even though many of the Ming emperors were incompetent or perverse, educated men continued to compete avidly for places in the government.

In the early seventeenth century, as the Ming Dynasty fell into disorder, the Manchus put together an efficient state beyond Ming's northeastern border. After they were called in to help suppress peasant rebellions, the Manchus took the throne themselves, founding the Qing Dynasty (1644–1911). The Manchus created a multiethnic empire, adding Taiwan, Mongolia, Tibet, and Xinjiang to their realm. The Qing Empire thus was comparable to the other multinational empires of the early modern world, such as the Ottoman, Russian, and Habsburg empires. In China itself the eighteenth century was a time of peace and prosperity.

In the Japanese islands, the fifteenth century saw the start of civil war that lasted a century. At the end of the sixteenth century, the world seemed to have turned upside down when a commoner, Hideyoshi, became the supreme ruler. His ambitions were grand: he sent his armies to Korea as the first step

Ming Dynasty *The Chinese dynasty in power from 1368 to 1644; it marked a period of agricultural reconstruction, foreign expeditions, commercial expansion, and a vibrant urban culture.*

toward conquering the mainland. He did not succeed in passing on his power to an heir, however. Instead, Tokugawa Ieyasu set up a government that lasted into the nineteenth century. Under this Tokugawa Shogunate (1603–1867), Japan restricted contact with the outside world and social mobility among its own people. Yet Japan thrived, as agricultural productivity increased and a lively urban culture developed.

MING CHINA (1368–1644)

What sort of state and society developed in China after the Mongols were ousted?

The founder of the Ming Dynasty, Zhu Yuanzhang (1328–1398), began life in poverty during the last decades of the Mongol Yuan Dynasty. His home region was hit by drought and then plague in the 1340s, and when he was only sixteen years old, his father, oldest brother, and brother's wife all died, leaving two penniless boys with three bodies to bury. With no relatives to turn to, Zhu Yuanzhang asked a monastery to accept him as a novice. The monastery itself was short of funds, and the monks soon sent Zhu out to beg for food. For three or four years he wandered through central China. Only after he returned to the monastery did he learn to read.

A few years later, in 1351, members of a religious sect known as the Red Turbans rose in rebellion against the government. Red Turban teachings drew on Manichaean ideas about the incompatibility of the forces of good and evil as well as on the cult of the Maitreya Buddha, who according to believers would in the future bring his paradise to earth to relieve human suffering. The Red Turbans met with considerable success, even defeating Mongol cavalry. When Zhu Yuanzhang's temple was burned down in the fighting, Zhu joined the rebels and rose rapidly.

Zhu and his followers developed into brilliant generals, and gradually they defeated one rival after another. In 1356 Zhu took the city of Nanjing and made it his base. In 1368 his armies took Beijing, which the Mongol emperor and his closest followers had vacated just days before. Then forty years old, Zhu Yuanzhang declared himself emperor of the Ming ("Bright") Dynasty. As emperor, he is known as Taizu or the Hongwu emperor.

Taizu started his reign wanting to help the poor. To lighten the weight of government exactions, he ordered a full-scale registration of cultivated land and population so that labor service and taxes could be assessed more fairly. He also tried persuasion. He issued instructions to be read aloud to villagers, telling them to be filial to their parents, live in harmony with their neighbors, work contentedly at their occupations, and refrain from evil.

Although in many ways anti-Mongol, Taizu retained some Yuan practices. One was setting up provinces as the administrative layer between the central government and the prefectures. Another was hereditary service obligations for both artisan and military households. Any family classed as a military household had to supply a soldier at all times, replacing those who were injured, who died, or who deserted.

Garrisons were concentrated along the northern border and near the capital. Each garrison was allocated a tract of land that the soldiers took turns cultivating to supply their own food. Although in theory this system should have supplied the Ming with a large but inexpensive army, the reality was less satisfactory. Garrisons were rarely self-sufficient. Men compelled to become soldiers did not necessarily make good fighting men, and desertion was difficult to prevent. Like earlier dynasties, the Ming turned to non-Chinese northerners for much of its armed forces. Many of the best soldiers in the Ming army were Mongols in Mongol units. Taizu did not try to conquer the Mongols, and Ming China did not extend into modern Inner Mongolia.

Taizu had deeply ambivalent feelings about men of education and sometimes brutally humiliated them in open court, even having them beaten. His behavior was so erratic that most likely he suffered from some form of mental illness. As Taizu became more literate, he realized that scholars could criticize him in covert ways, using phrases that had double meanings or that sounded like words for "bandit," "monk," or the like. Even poems in private circulation could be used as evidence of subversive thoughts. When literary men began to avoid official life, Taizu made it illegal to turn down appointments or to resign from office. He began falling into rages that only the empress could stop, and after her death in 1382 no one could calm him. In 1376 Taizu had thousands of officials killed because they were found to have taken a shortcut in their handling of paperwork related to the grain tax. In 1380 Taizu concluded that his chancellor was plotting to assassinate him. Thousands only remotely connected to him were executed. From then on, Taizu acted as his own chancellor, dealing directly with the heads of departments and ministries.

The next important emperor, called Chengzu or the Yongle emperor (r. 1403–1425), was also a military man. One of Taizu's younger sons, he took the throne by force from his nephew and often led troops into battle against the Mongols. Also like his father, Chengzu was willing to use terror to keep government officials in line.

Early in his reign, Chengzu decided to move the capital from Nanjing to Beijing, which had been his own base as a prince and the capital during Mongol times. Beijing was a planned city, like Chang'an in Sui-Tang times (581–907), and like Chang'an was arranged like a set of boxes within boxes built on a north-south axis. The main outer walls were forty feet high and nearly fifteen miles around, pierced by nine gates. Inside was the Imperial City, with government offices, and within that the palace itself, called the Forbidden City, with close to ten thousand rooms. Because the Forbidden City survives today, people can still see the series of audience halls with vast courtyards between them where attending officials would stand or kneel.

The areas surrounding Beijing were not nearly as agriculturally productive as those around Nanjing. To supply Beijing with grain, the Yuan Grand Canal was broadened, deepened, and supplied with more locks and dams. The 15,000 boats and the 160,000 soldiers of the transport army who pulled loaded barges from the towpaths along the canal became the lifeline of the capital.

Chronology

1368–1644	Ming Dynasty in China
1405–1433	Zheng He's naval expeditions
1407–1420	Construction of Beijing as Chinese capital
16th century	Increased availability of books for general audiences in China
1549	Jesuit missionaries land in Japan
1557	Portuguese set up trading base at Macao
1568–1600	Period of national unification in Japan
1575–1620	Silver shortage in China
1603–1867	Tokugawa Shogunate in Japan
1615	Battle of Osaka leads to persecution of Christians in Japan
1629	Tokugawa government bans actresses from the stage
1639	Japan closes its borders
1644–1911	Qing Dynasty in China
1793	Lord Macartney's diplomatic visit to China

Problems with the Imperial Institution

Ming Taizu had decreed that succession should go to the eldest son of the empress or to the son's eldest son if the son predeceased his father, the system generally followed by earlier dynasties. In Ming times, the flaws in this system became apparent as one mediocre, obtuse, or erratic emperor followed another. There were emperors who refused to hold audiences, who fell into irrational fits, and who let themselves be manipulated by palace ladies.

Because Ming Taizu had abolished the position of chancellor, emperors turned to secretaries and eunuchs to manage the paperwork. Eunuchs were essentially slaves.

● **Forbidden City** The palace complex in Beijing, commonly called the Forbidden City, was built in the early fifteenth century when the capital was moved from Nanjing to Beijing. Audience halls and other important state buildings are arranged on a north-south axis with huge courtyards between them, where officials would stand during ceremonies. *(Reproduced by permission of the Commercial Press [Hong Kong] Limited, from* Daily Life in the Forbidden City.*)*

Many boys and young men were acquired by dubious means, often from non-Chinese areas in the south, and after they were castrated, they had no option but to serve the imperial family. Zheng He, for instance (see page 599), was taken from Yunnan as a boy of ten by a Ming general assigned the task of securing boys to be castrated. Society considered eunuchs the basest of servants, and Confucian scholars heaped scorn on them. Yet Ming emperors, like rulers in earlier dynasties, often preferred the always compliant eunuchs to high-minded, moralizing civil service officials.

In Ming times, the eunuch establishment became huge. By the late fifteenth century, the eunuch bureaucracy had grown as large as the civil service, each with roughly twelve thousand positions. After 1500, the eunuch bureaucracy grew even more rapidly, and by the mid-sixteenth century, seventy thousand eunuchs were in service throughout the country, ten thousand in the capital. Tension between the two bureaucracies was high. In 1420 Chengzu set up a eunuch-run secret service to investigate cases of suspected corruption and sedition in the regular bureaucracy. Eunuch control over vital government processes, such as appointments, became a severe problem.

Many Ming officials risked their careers and lives trying to admonish emperors. In 1376, when Taizu asked for criticism, one official criticized harsh punishment of officials for minor lapses. Incensed, Taizu had him brought to the capital in chains and let him starve to death in prison. In 1519 when an emperor announced plans to make a tour of the southern provinces, over a hundred officials staged a protest by kneeling in front of the palace. The emperor ordered the officials to remain kneeling for three days, then had them flogged; eleven died. The Confucian tradition celebrated these acts of political protest as heroic. Rarely, however, did they succeed in moving an emperor to change his mind.

Although the educated public complained about the performance of emperors, no one proposed or even imagined alternatives to imperial rule. High officials were forced to find ways to work around uncooperative emperors but were not able to put in place institutions that would limit the damage an emperor could do. Knowing that strong emperors often acted erratically, they came to prefer weak emperors who let them take care of the government. Probably one reason that so many Ming emperors resisted their officials' efforts to manage them was that the officials were indeed trying to keep the emperors engaged in tasks in which they could do relatively little harm.

The Mongols and the Great Wall

The early Ming emperors held Mongol fighting men in awe and feared they might form another great military machine of the sort Chinggis Khan (ca. 1162–1227) had put together two centuries earlier. In fact, in Ming times the Mongols were never united in a pan-Mongol federation. Still, groups of Mongols could and did raid, and twice they threatened the dynasty: in 1449 the khan of the Western Mongols captured the Chinese emperor, and in 1550 Beijing was surrounded by the forces of the khan of the Mongols in Inner Mongolia. Ming officials were very reluctant to grant any privileges to Mongol leaders, such as trading posts along the borders, and wanted the different groups of Mongols to trade only through the envoy system. When trade was finally liberalized in 1570, friction was reduced.

Two important developments shaped Ming-Mongol relations: the building of the Great Wall and closer relations between Mongolia and Tibet. Much of the Ming Great Wall survives today. It extends about 1,500 miles from northeast of Beijing into Gansu province. In the eastern 500 miles, the wall averages about 35 feet high and 20 feet across, with lookout towers every half mile. Much of the way, the wall is faced with brick, which gives it an imposing appearance that greatly impressed the first Westerners who saw it. It was built as a compromise when Ming officials could agree on no other way to manage the Mongol threat.

While China was building the wall, the Mongols were developing strong ties with Tibet, in this period largely ruled by the major Buddhist monasteries. When Tibetan monasteries needed military assistance, they asked competing Mongol leaders for help, and many struggles were decided by Mongol military intervention. Tsong-kha-pa (1357–1419) founded the Yellow Hat or Gelug-pa sect, whose heads later became known as the Dalai Lamas. In 1577 the third Dalai Lama accepted the invitation of Altan Khan to visit Mongolia, and the khan declared Tibetan Buddhism to be the official religion of all the Mongols. The Dalai Lama gave the khan the title "King of Religion," and the khan swore that the Mongols would renounce blood sacrifice. When the third Dalai Lama's reincarnation was found to be the great-grandson of Altan Khan, the ties between Tibet and Mongolia, not surprisingly, became even stronger.

The Examination Life

In sharp contrast to Europe in this era, Ming China had few social barriers. It had no hereditary aristocracy that could have undermined the emperor's absolute power. Although China had no titled aristocracy, it did have an elite whose status was based on a *combination* of wealth, education, family, and government office. Agricultural land remained the most highly prized form of wealth, but antiques, books, paintings and calligraphies, and urban real estate also brought status. China's merchants did not

**Primary Source:
On Strange Tales and
"On Merchants"**
*Learn how a Ming official
assessed the status of
commerce—and merchants—in
sixteenth-century China.*

● **Civil Service Examinations** The examinations tested candidates' knowledge of the Confucian canon: rituals, history, poetry, cosmology—all believed to provide the basis for a moral life—and calligraphy. By the eighteenth century, the system was under attack because it failed to select the ablest scholars, the number of candidates had not increased in proportion to population, degrees were sold to the rich, and frequently even successful candidates could not find positions. *(Bibliothèque nationale de France)*

civil service examinations
Highly competitive series of tests held at the prefecture, province, and then capital to select men to become officials.

become a politically articulate bourgeoisie. The politically active class was that of the scholars who Confucianism taught should aid the ruler in running the state. With the possible exception of the Jewish people, no people have respected learning as much as the Chinese. Merchants tried to marry into the scholar class in order to rise in the world.

Thus, despite the harsh and arbitrary ways in which the Ming emperors treated their civil servants, educated men were eager to enter the government. Reversing the policies of the Mongol Yuan Dynasty, the Ming government recruited almost all of its officials through **civil service examinations**. Candidates had to study the Confucian classics and the interpretations of them by the twelfth-century Song scholar Zhu Xi, whose teachings were declared orthodox. To become officials, candidates had to pass examinations at the prefecture, the provincial, and the capital levels. To keep the wealthiest areas from dominating the results, quotas were established for the number of candidates that each province could send on to the capital.

Preparation for the examinations required, in essence, learning a new language—the classical written language was quite different from everyday spoken language—and memorizing long texts. Thus education was best started at four or five, because the young are usually better at both memorization and learning languages. Well-off families hired tutors for their boys as in earlier periods, and schools became increasingly available as well.

Families that for generations had pursued other careers, such as physician or merchant, had more opportunities than ever before to become officials through the exams. (See the feature "Individuals in Society: Tan Yunxian, Woman Doctor.") Clans sometimes operated schools for their members because the clan as a whole would enjoy the prestige of a successful member. Most of those who attended school stayed only a few years, but those who seemed most promising moved on to advanced schools where they would practice essay writing and study the essays of men who had succeeded in the exams.

The examinations at the prefecture level lasted a day and drew hundreds if not thousands of candidates. The government compound would be taken over to give all candidates places to sit and write. The provincial and capital examinations had three sessions spread out over a week. In the first session, candidates wrote essays on passages from the classics. In the second and third sessions, candidates had to write essays on practical policy issues and on a passage from the *Classic of Filial Piety*. In addition, they had to show that they could draft state papers such as edicts, decrees, and judicial

Tan Yunxian, Woman Doctor

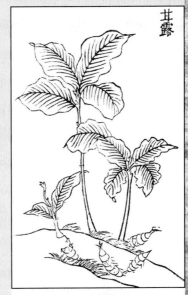

Tan Yunxian would have consulted traditional herbals that included sketches of plants of medicinal value and described their uses. *(Sancai tuhui [Ming Wanli ed.], caomu 10.53a)*

The grandmother of Tan Yunxian (1461–1554) was the daughter of a physician, and her husband had married into her home to learn medicine himself. At least two of their sons—including Tan Yunxian's father—passed the civil service examination and became officials, raising the social standing of the family considerably. The grandparents wanted to pass their medical knowledge down to someone, and because they found Yunxian very bright, they decided to teach it to her.

Tan Yunxian married and raised four children but also practiced medicine, confining her practice to women. At age fifty she wrote an autobiographical account, *Sayings of a Female Doctor.* In the preface she described how, under her grandmother's tutelage, she had first memorized the *Canon of Problems* and *Canon of the Pulse.* Then when her grandmother had time, she asked her granddaughter to explain particular passages in these classic medical treatises.

Yunxian began the practice of medicine by treating her own children, asking her grandmother to check her diagnoses. When her grandmother was old and ill, she gave Yunxian her notebook of prescriptions and her equipment for making medicines, telling her to study them carefully. Later, Yunxian herself became seriously ill and dreamed of her grandmother telling her on what page of which book to find the prescription that would cure her. When she recovered, she began her medical career in earnest.

Tan's book records the cases of thirty-one patients she treated, most of them women with chronic complaints rather than critical illnesses. Many of the women had what the Chinese classed as women's complaints, such as menstrual irregularities, repeated miscarriages, barrenness, and postpartum fatigue. Some had ailments that men too could suffer, such as coughs, nausea, insomnia, diarrhea, rashes, and swellings. Like other literati physicians, Tan regularly prescribed herbal medications. She also practiced moxibustion. It was thought that burning moxa (dried artemisia) at specified points on the body would, like acupuncture, stimulate the circulation of *qi* (life energy). Because the physician applying the moxa had to touch the patient, male physicians could not perform moxibustion on women.

Tan's patients included working women, and Tan seems to have thought that their problems often sprang from overwork. One woman came to her because she had had vaginal bleeding for three years. When questioned, the woman told Tan that she worked all day with her husband at their kiln making bricks and tiles. Tan Yunxian's diagnosis was overwork, and she gave the woman pills to replenish her yin. A boatman's wife came to her complaining of numbness in her hands. When the woman told Tan that she worked in the wind and rain handling the boat, the doctor advised some time off. Tan Yunxian explained to a servant girl that she had gone back to work too soon after suffering a wind damage fever.

By contrast, when patients came from upper-class families, Tan believed negative emotions were the source of their problems, particularly if a woman reported that her mother-in-law had scolded her or that her husband had recently brought a concubine home. Tan told two upper-class women who had miscarried that they lost their babies because they had hidden their anger, causing fire to turn inward and destabilize the fetus.

Tan Yunxian herself lived a long life, dying at age ninety-three.

Questions for Analysis

1. Why do you think Tan Yunxian treated only women? Why might she have been more effective with women patients than a male physician would have been?

2. What do you think of Tan's diagnoses? Do you think she was able to help many of her patients?

Source: Based on Charlotte Furth, *A Flourishing Yin: Gender in China's Medical History, 960–1665* (Berkeley: University of California Press, 1999), pp. 285–295.

rulings. Reading the dynastic histories was a good way to prepare for the policy issue and state paper questions.

The weeklong provincial examinations were major local events. From five thousand to ten thousand candidates descended on the city and filled up its hostels. Candidates would show up a week in advance to present their credentials and gather the paper, ink, brushes, candles, blankets, and food they needed to survive in their small exam cells. No written material could be taken into the cells, and candidates were searched before being admitted. Anyone caught wearing a cheat-sheet (an inner gown covered with the classics in minuscule script) was thrown out of the exams and banned from the next session as well. Clerks used horns and gongs to begin and end each two-day session. Candidates had time to write rough drafts of their essays, correct them, then copy neat final versions. Tension was high. Sometimes rumors that the examiners had been bribed to leak the questions led to riots in the exam quarters, and knocked-over candles occasionally caused fires.

After the papers were handed in, clerks recopied them and assigned them numbers to preserve anonymity. Proofreaders checked the copying before handing the papers on to the assembled examiners, who divided them up to grade. The grading generally took about twenty days. Most candidates stayed in the vicinity to await the results. Those few who passed (around 2 to 10 percent) were invited to the governor's compound for a celebration. By the time they reached home, most of their friends, neighbors, and relatives had already heard their good news. They could not spend long celebrating, however, because they had to begin preparing for the capital exams, less than a year away.

Life of the People

Everyday life in Ming China followed patterns established in earlier periods. The family remained central to most people's lives, and almost everyone married. Marriages were arranged by parents, commonly when children were in their teens. Because getting a bride could be expensive, a poor man might not be able to afford to marry until his mid-twenties or later. Most women were married by age twenty. Sons were highly desired because they were necessary to continue the family line and to make offerings to ancestors.

Beyond the family, people's lives were shaped by the type of work they did and where they lived. Not only did crops differ north and south, but some regions were much more urbanized than others. In place of the paper money that had circulated in Song and Yuan times, silver ingots came into general use as money. Even agricultural taxes came to be paid in silver rather than grain.

Urban Culture   Large towns and cities proliferated in Ming times and became islands of sophistication in the vast sea of rural villages. Small businesses manufactured textiles, paper, and luxury goods such as silks and porcelains. The southeast became a center for the production of cotton and silks; other areas specialized in the grain and salt trades and in silver. Merchants could make fortunes moving these goods across the country.

Printing was invented in Tang times and had a great impact on the life of the educated elite in Song times, but not until Ming times did it transform the culture of the urban middle classes. By the late Ming period, publishing houses were putting out large numbers of books aimed at general audiences. These included fiction, reference books of all sorts, and popular religious tracts, such as ledgers for calculating the moral value of one's good deeds and subtracting the demerits from bad deeds. To make their books attractive in the marketplace, entrepreneurial book publishers commissioned artists to illustrate them. By the sixteenth century, more and more books were being published in the vernacular language (the language people spoke), espe-

● **Romance** Women were among the most avid readers of the scripts for plays, especially romantic ones like *The Western Chamber,* a story of a young scholar who falls in love with a well-educated girl he encounters by chance. In this scene, the young woman looks up at the moon as her maid looks at its reflection in the pond. Meanwhile, her young lover scales the wall. This multicolor woodblock print, made in 1640, was one of twenty-one made to illustrate the play. *(Museum for East Asian Art, Cologne, Inv.-No. R 61,2 [No. 11]. Photo: Rheinisches Bildarchiv, Cologne)*

cially short stories, novels, and plays. Ming vernacular short stories depicted a world much like that of their readers, full of shop clerks and merchants, monks and prostitutes, students and matchmakers.

The full-length novel appeared during the Ming period. The plots of the early novels were heavily indebted to story cycles developed by oral storytellers over the course of several centuries. *Water Margin* is the episodic story of a band of bandits. *The Romance of the Three Kingdoms* is a work of historical fiction based on the exploits of the generals and statesmen contending for power at the end of the Han Dynasty. *The Journey to the West* is a fantastic account of the Tang monk Xuanzang's travels to India; in this book he is accompanied by a pig and a monkey with supernatural powers. *Plum in the Golden Vase* is a novel of manners about a lustful merchant with a wife and five concubines. Competing publishers brought out their own editions of these novels, sometimes adding new illustrations or commentaries.

The Chinese found recreation and relaxation in many ways. The affluent indulged in an alcoholic drink made from fermented and distilled rice. Once tobacco was introduced, both men and women took up pipes. Plays were very popular. The Jesuit missionary Matteo Ricci, who lived in China from 1583 to 1610, described resident troupes in large cities and traveling troupes that "journey everywhere throughout the length and breadth of the country" putting on plays. The leaders of the troupes would purchase young children and train them to sing and perform. Ricci thought too many people were addicted to these performances:

These groups of actors are employed at all imposing banquets, and when they are called they come prepared to enact any of the ordinary plays. The host at the banquet is usually presented with a volume of plays and he selects the one or several he may like. The guests, between eating and drinking, follow the plays with so much satisfaction that the banquet at times may last for ten hours.[1]

People not only enjoyed listening to plays but also avidly read the play scripts. The love stories and social satires of Tang Xianzu, the greatest of the Ming playwrights, were very popular. One play tells the story of a young man who falls asleep while his meal is cooking. In his dream he sees his whole life: he comes in first in the civil service examinations, rises to high office, is unfairly slandered and condemned to death, then is cleared and promoted. At the point of death, he wakes up, sees that his dinner is nearly ready, and realizes that life passes as quickly as a dream.

Life in the Countryside More than bread in Europe, rice supplied most of the calories of the population in central and south China. (In north China, wheat, made into steamed or baked bread or into noodles, served as the staple of the diet.) Terracing and irrigation of mountain slopes, introduced in the eleventh century, had increased rice harvests. Other innovations also brought good results. Farmers began to stock the rice paddies with fish, which continuously fertilized the rice fields, destroyed malaria-bearing mosquitoes, and enriched the diet. Farmers developed commercial cropping in cotton, sugar cane, and indigo. And new methods of crop rotation allowed for continuous cultivation and for more than one harvest per year from a single field.

The Ming rulers promoted the repopulation and colonization of devastated regions through reclamation of land and massive transfers of people (see Table 20.1). Immigrants received large plots of land and exemption from taxation for many years. Reforestation played a dramatic role in the agricultural revolution. In 1391 the Ming government ordered 50 million trees planted in the Nanjing area. Lumber from the trees was intended for the construction of a maritime fleet. In 1392 each family holding colonized land in Anhui province had to plant two hundred mulberry, jujube, and persimmon trees. In 1396 peasants in the present-day provinces of Hunan and Hubei in central China planted 84 million fruit trees. Historians have estimated that 1 billion trees were planted during Taizu's reign.

What were the social consequences of agricultural development? Increased food production led to steady population growth. Population increase led to the multiplication of markets, towns, and small cities. Larger towns had permanent shops; smaller towns had periodic markets—some every five days, some every ten days, some only once a month. They sold essential goods—pins, matches, oil for lamps, candles, paper, incense, tobacco (after it was introduced from the Americas)—to country people from the surrounding hamlets. The market usually included moneylenders, pawnbrokers, a tearoom, and sometimes a wine shop where tea and rice wine were sold and entertainers performed. Tradesmen carrying their wares on their backs and craftsmen—carpenters, barbers, joiners, locksmiths—moved constantly from market to market. Itinerant salesmen depended on the city market for their wares.

Ming Decline

Beginning in the 1590s the Ming government was beset by fiscal, military, and political problems. The government went nearly bankrupt helping defend Korea against a Japanese invasion (see page 600). Then came a series of natural disasters. Failed harvests, floods, droughts, locusts, and epidemics ravaged one region after another. A "little ice age" brought a drop in average temperatures that shortened the growing season and reduced harvests. In areas where food shortages became critical, gangs of army deserters and laid-off soldiers began scouring the countryside in search of food. Once the gangs had stolen all their grain, hard-pressed farmers joined them just to survive. A former shepherd and postal relay worker became the paramount rebel leader in the north. An ex-soldier became the main leader in the central region between the Huang He (Yellow) and Yangzi Rivers. The Ming government had little choice but to try to increase taxes to deal with these threats, but the last thing people needed was heavier taxes.

Adding to the hardship was a sudden drop in the supply of silver. The Ming economy had come to depend on a large influx of silver from Japan and the New World, which was used to pay for the silk and porcelains exported from China (see pages 601–604). Events in Japan and the Philippines led to disruption of trade. The drop in silver imports led to deflation, which caused real rents to rise. Soon there were riots among urban workers and tenant farmers. In 1642 a group of rebels cut the dikes on the Huang He River, causing massive flooding. A smallpox epidemic soon added to the death toll. In 1644 the last Ming emperor, in despair, took his own life when rebels entered Beijing.

Table 20.1 Land Reclamation in Early Ming China

YEAR	RECLAIMED LAND (IN HECTARES; 1 HECTARE = 2.5 ACRES)
1371	576,000
1373	1,912,000
1374	4,974,000
1379	1,486,000

Source: J. Gernet, *A History of Chinese Civilization*, trans. J. R. Foster (Cambridge: Cambridge University Press, 1982), p. 391. Used with permission.

THE MANCHUS AND QING CHINA (1644–1800)

Did the return of alien rule with the Manchus have any positive consequences for China?

The next dynasty, the **Qing Dynasty,** was founded by the Manchus, a non-Chinese people who were descended from the Jurchens who had ruled north China during the Jin Dynasty (1127–1234), when south China was controlled by the Song. Manchu men shaved the front of their heads and wore their hair in a long braid called a queue.

In the Ming period the Manchus had lived in dispersed communities in what is loosely called Manchuria (the northeast of modern-day China). In the more densely populated southern part of Manchuria, the Manchus lived in close contact with Mongols, Koreans, and Chinese (see Map 20.1). They were not nomads but rather hunters, fishermen, and farmers. Like the Mongols, they were excellent horsemen and archers and had a strongly hierarchical social structure, with elites and slaves. Slaves, often Korean or Chinese, were generally acquired through capture. A Korean visitor described many small Manchu settlements, most no larger than twenty households, supported by fishing, hunting for pelts, collecting pine nuts or ginseng, or growing crops such as wheat, millet, and barley. Villages were often at odds with each other over resources, and men did not leave their villages without arming themselves with bows and arrows or swords. Interspersed among these Manchu settlements were groups of nomadic Mongols who lived in yurts.

The Manchus credited their own rise to Nurhaci (1559–1626). Over several decades, he united the Manchus, then expanded their territories. Like Chinggis Khan, who had reorganized the Mongol armies to reduce the importance of tribal affiliations, Nurhaci created a new social basis for his armies in units called **banners.** Each banner was made up of a set of military companies but included the families and slaves of the soldiers as well. Each company had a hereditary captain, often from Nurhaci's own lineage. Over time new companies and new banners were formed, and by 1644 there were eight each of Manchu, Mongol, and Chinese banners. When new groups were defeated, they were distributed among several banners to lessen their potential for subversion.

Qing Dynasty *The dynasty founded by the Manchus that ruled China from 1644 to 1911.*

banners *Units of the Qing army, composed of soldiers, their families, and slaves.*

The distinguished Ming general Wu Sangui, himself a native of southern Manchuria, was near the eastern end of the Great Wall when he heard that the rebels had captured Beijing. The Manchus proposed to Wu that they join forces and liberate Beijing. Wu opened the gates of the Great Wall to let the Manchus in, and within a couple of weeks they occupied Beijing. When the Manchus made clear that they intended to conquer the rest of the country and take the throne themselves, Wu and many other Chinese generals joined forces with them.

In the summer of 1645, the Manchus ordered all Chinese serving in Manchu armies to shave the front of their heads in the Manchu fashion, presumably to make it easier to recognize whose side they were on. Soon this order was extended to all Chinese men. Because so many of those newly conquered by the Qing refused to shave their hair, Manchu commanders felt justified in ordering the slaughter of defiant cities.

After quelling resistance, the Qing put in place policies and institutions that gave China a respite from war and disorder. Most of the political institutions of the Ming Dynasty were taken over relatively unchanged, including the examination system. Between 1700 and 1800, the Chinese population seems to have nearly doubled, from about 150 million to over 300 million (see Table 20.2). Population growth during the course of the eighteenth century has been attributed to many factors: global warming that extended the growing season, expanded use of New World crops, slowing of the spread of new diseases that had accompanied the sixteenth-century

MAP 20.1 **The Qing Empire** The sheer size of the Qing Empire in China almost inevitably led to its profound cultural influence on the rest of Asia. What geographical and political factors limited the extent of the empire?

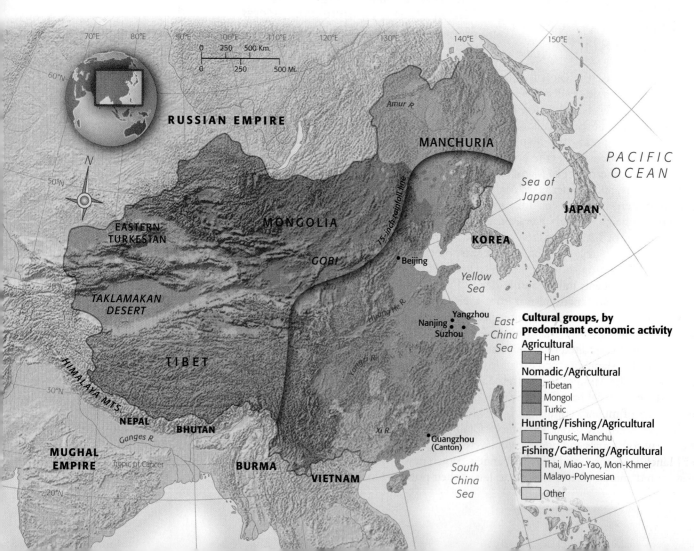

Cultural groups, by predominant economic activity

Agricultural
- Han

Nomadic/Agricultural
- Tibetan
- Mongol
- Turkic

Hunting/Fishing/Agricultural
- Tungusic, Manchu

Fishing/Gathering/Agricultural
- Thai, Miao-Yao, Mon-Khmer
- Malayo-Polynesian
- Other

expansion of global traffic, and the efficiency of the Qing government in providing relief in times of famine.

Some scholars have recently argued that China's overall standard of living in the mid-eighteenth century was comparable to Europe's and that the standards of China's most developed regions, such as the lower Yangzi region, compared favorably to the most developed regions of Europe at the time, such as England and the Netherlands. Life expectancy, food consumption, and even facilities for transportation were at similar levels. The government in this period had the resources to respond to famines and disasters. Indeed, during the eighteenth century, the treasury was so full that the annual land tax was canceled four times.

Competent and Long-Lived Emperors

For more than a century, China was ruled by only three rulers, each of them hard working, talented, and committed to making the Qing Dynasty a success. Two, the Kangxi and Qianlong emperors, had exceptionally long reigns.

Kangxi (r. 1661–1722) proved adept at meeting the expectations of both the Chinese and the Manchu elites. At age fourteen, he announced that he would begin ruling on his own and had his regent imprisoned. Kangxi could speak, read, and write Chinese and appreciated the value of persuading educated Chinese that the Manchus had a legitimate claim to the Mandate of Heaven. He made efforts to attract Ming loyalists who had been unwilling to serve the Qing. He undertook a series of tours of the south, where Ming loyalism had been strongest, and he held a special exam to select men to compile the official history of the Ming Dynasty.

The Qianlong emperor (r. 1736–1795) put much of his energy into impressing his subjects with his magnificence. He understood that the Qing's capacity to hold their multiethnic empire together rested on their ability to appeal to all those they ruled. Besides Manchu and Chinese, Qianlong learned to converse in Mongolian, Uighur, Tibetan, and Tangut, and he addressed envoys in their own languages. He became as much a patron of Tibetan Buddhism as of Chinese Confucianism. He initiated a massive project to translate the Tibetan Buddhist canon into Mongolian and Manchu and had huge multilingual dictionaries compiled.

To demonstrate to the Chinese scholar-official elite that he was a sage emperor, Qianlong worked on affairs of state from dawn until early afternoon, then turned to reading, painting, and calligraphy. He was ostentatious in his devotion to his mother, visiting her daily and tending to her comfort with all the devotion of the most filial Chinese son. He took several tours down the Grand Canal to the southeast, in part to emulate his grandfather, in part to entertain his mother.

Despite these displays of Chinese virtues, the Qianlong emperor was not fully confident that the Chinese supported his rule, and he was quick to act on any suspicion of anti-Manchu thoughts or actions. During a project to catalogue nearly all the books in China, he began to suspect that some governors were holding back books with seditious content. He ordered full searches for books with disparaging references to the Manchus or to previous alien conquerors. Sometimes passages were deleted or rewritten, but when the entire book was offensive, it was destroyed. So thorough was the proscription that no copies survive of more than two thousand titles.

Table 20.2   Registered Population of China, ca. 1390–1790

ca. 1390	50,000,000
ca. 1685	100,000,000*
ca. 1749	177,495,000
1767	209,840,000
1776	268,238,000
1790	301,487,000

*The catastrophic drop in China's registered population from the time of the Ming-Qing transition to the end of Kangxi's wars with three powerful rebels in 1681 was due to civil wars, foreign invasions, bandit actions, natural disasters, virulent epidemics, and the failure of irrigation systems.

Source: J. D. Spence, *The Search for Modern China* (New York: W. W. Norton, 1991), pp. 93–95.

● **Presenting a Horse to the Emperor** This detail from a 1757 handscroll shows the Qianlong emperor, seated, receiving envoys from the Kazakhs. Note how the envoy, presenting a pure white horse, is kneeling to the ground (performing the kowtow). The artist was Guiseppe Castiglione (1688–1768), an Italian who worked as a painter in Qianlong's court. *(Qing, 1757. Handscroll, ink and colors on paper [45 cm x 2.67 m]. Musée Guimet, Paris/Art Resource, NY)*

Through Qianlong's reign, China remained an enormous producer of manufactured goods and led the way in assembly-line production. The government operated huge textile factories, but there were private firms that were even larger. Hangzhou had a textile firm that gave work to four thousand weavers, twenty thousand spinners, and ten thousand dyers and finishers. The porcelain kilns at Jingdezhen employed division of labor on a large scale and were able to supply porcelain to much of the world. The Qing state benefited from the growth of the economy. The treasury was so full that the Qianlong emperor was able to cancel taxes on several occasions, but when he abdicated in 1796, his treasury had 400 million silver dollars in it.

Imperial Expansion

The Qing Dynasty put together a multiethnic empire that was larger than any earlier Chinese dynasty. Taiwan was acquired in 1683 after Qing armies pursued a rebel there. Mongolia was acquired next. In 1696 Kangxi led an army of eighty thousand men into Mongolia, and within a few years Manchu supremacy was accepted there. Cannon and muskets gave Qing forces military superiority over the Mongols, who were armed only with bows and arrows. Thus the Qing could dominate the steppe cheaply, effectively ending two thousand years of Inner Asian military advantage.

In the 1720s, the Qing established a permanent garrison of banner soldiers in Tibet. By this time, the expanding Qing and Russian empires were nearing each other. In 1689 the Manchu and the Russian rulers approved a treaty—written in Russian, Manchu, Chinese, and Latin—defining their borders in Manchuria and regulating trade. Another treaty in 1727 allowed a Russian ecclesiastical mission to reside in Beijing and a caravan to make a trip from Russia to Beijing once every three years.

The last region to be annexed was Chinese Turkestan (the modern province of Xinjiang). Both the Han and the Tang Dynasties had stationed troops in the region, exercising a loose suzerainty, but neither Song nor Ming had tried to control the area. The Qing won the region in the 1750s through a series of campaigns against Uighur and Dzungar Mongol forces.

Both Tibet and Turkestan were ruled lightly. The local populations kept their own religious leaders and did not have to wear the queue.

JAPAN'S MIDDLE AGES (CA. 1400–1600)

How did Japan change during this period of political instability?

In the twelfth century Japan entered an age dominated by military men, an age that can be compared to Europe's feudal age. The Kamakura Shogunate (1185–1333) had its capital in the east, at Kamakura. It was succeeded by the Ashikaga Shogunate

(1336–1573), which returned the government to Kyoto. The fifteenth century was the great age of Zen-influenced Muromachi culture. The sixteenth century brought civil war that led to massive castle building, rulers of obscure origins who unified the realm, and the invasion of Korea.

Muromachi Culture

The headquarters of the Ashikaga shoguns were on Muromachi Street in Kyoto, and the refined and elegant style that they promoted is often called Muromachi culture. The shoguns patronized Zen Buddhism, the school of Buddhism associated with meditation and mind-to-mind transmission of truth. Because Zen monks were able to read and write Chinese, they often assisted the shoguns in handling foreign affairs. Many of the Kyoto Zen temples in this period had rock gardens. In the garden of Ryoanji, for instance, a temple built in the late fifteenth century, raked white sand surrounds fifteen rocks, but only fourteen of them are visible from any one perspective. Rock gardens were seen as aids to Zen meditation.

Zen ideas permeated the arts. The Silver Pavilion built by the shogun Yoshimasa (r. 1449–1473) epitomizes Zen austerity. A white sand cone constructed in the temple garden was designed to reflect moonlight. Yoshimasa was also influential in the development of the tea ceremony, practiced by warriors, aristocrats, and priests but not women. Aesthetes celebrated the beauty of imperfect objects, such as plain or misshapen cups or pots. Spare monochrome paintings fit into this aesthetic, as did simple asymmetrical flower arrangements.

The shoguns were also patrons of the Nō theater. Nō drama originated in popular forms of entertainment, including comical skits and dances directed to the gods. It was transformed into high art by Zeami (1363–1443), an actor and playwright who also wrote on the aesthetic theory of Nō. Nō was performed on a bare stage with a pine tree painted across the backdrop. One or two actors wearing brilliant brocade robes would perform, using stylized gestures and stances. One actor would wear a mask indicating whether the character he was portraying was male or female, old or young, a god, ghost, or demon. The actors would be accompanied by a chorus and a couple of musicians playing drums and flute. Many of the stories concerned ghosts consumed by jealous passions or desire for revenge. Zeami argued that the most meaningful moments came during silence, when the actor's spiritual presence allowed the audience to catch a glimpse of the mysterious and inexpressible.

Civil War

Civil war began in Kyoto in 1467 as a struggle over succession to the shogunate. Rivals used arson as their chief weapon and burned down temples and mansions, destroying much of the city and its treasures. In the early phases defeated opponents were exiled or allowed to retire to monasteries. As the conflict continued, violence escalated; hostages and prisoners were slaughtered and corpses mutilated. Once Kyoto was laid waste, war spread to outlying areas. When the shogun could no longer protect cities, merchants banded together to hire mercenaries. The Lotus League, a commoner-led religious sect united by faith in the saving power of the Lotus Sutra, set up a commoner-run government that collected taxes and settled disputes. In 1536, during eight days of fighting, the monastery Enryakuji attacked the League and its temples, burned much of the city, and killed men, women, and children thought to be believers.

In these confused and violent circumstances, power devolved to the local level, where warlords, called **daimyo,** built their power bases. Unlike earlier power holders, these new lords were not appointed by the court or shogunate and did not send taxes to absentee overlords. Instead they seized what they needed and used it to build up their territories and recruit more samurai. To raise revenues, they surveyed the land

daimyo *Regional lords in Japan; many had built their power by seizing what they needed and promoting irrigation and trade to raise revenues.*

● Matsumoto Castle
Hideyoshi built Matsumoto Castle between 1594 and 1597. Designed to be impregnable, it was surrounded by a moat and had a base constructed of huge stones. In the sixteenth and early seventeenth centuries Spanish and Portuguese missionaries compared Japanese castles favorably to European castles of the period. (Robert Harding World Imagery)

and promoted irrigation and trade. Many of the most successful daimyo were self-made men who rose from obscurity.

This was an age of castle building. The castles were built not on mountaintops but on level plains. A castle was surrounded by moats and walls made from huge stones. Inside was a many-storied keep, usually with white plastered walls and tile roofs. Though relatively safe from incendiary missiles, the keeps were vulnerable to Western-style cannon, introduced in the 1570s. Many of the castles had splendid living quarters for the daimyo; leading painters embellished interior sliding doors and screens.

The Victors: Nobunaga and Hideyoshi

The first daimyo to gain a predominance of power was Oda Nobunaga (1534–1582). A samurai of the lesser daimyo class, he built his retainer band from masterless samurai who had been living by robbery and extortion. After he won control of his native province of Owari in 1559, he immediately set out to extend his power and in 1568 seized Kyoto and became the ruler of central Japan. A key achievement was destroying the military power of the great monasteries. He needed to increase revenues, and toward that end he minted coins, the first government-issued money in Japan since 958. He promoted trade by eliminating customs barriers. He opened the little fishing village of Nagasaki to foreign commerce; it soon became Japan's largest port.

In 1582 Nobunaga was forced by one of his vassals to commit suicide. His general and staunchest adherent, Toyotomi Hideyoshi (1537–1598), avenged him and continued the drive toward unification.

Like the Ming founder, Hideyoshi was a peasant's son who rose to power through military service. Hideyoshi succeeded in bringing northern and western Japan under his control. In 1582 he attacked the great fortress at Takamatsu. When direct assault failed, his troops flooded the castle to force its surrender. A successful siege of the town of Kagoshima then brought the southern island of Kyushu under his domination. Hideyoshi soothed the vanquished daimyo as Nobunaga had done—with lands and military positions—but he also required them to swear allegiance and to obey him down to the smallest particular. For the first time in over two centuries, Japan had a single ruler.

Hideyoshi did his best to ensure that future peasants' sons would not be able to rise as he had. His great sword hunt of 1588 collected weapons from farmers, who were no longer allowed to wear swords. Farmers were to remain farmers; they were forbidden to leave their fields to take up trade in the cities. Restrictions were also placed on samurai; they were prohibited from leaving their lord's service or switching occupations.

To improve tax collection, Hideyoshi ordered a survey of the entire country. His agents collected detailed information about each daimyo's lands and about towns, villages, agricultural produce, and industrial output all over Japan. His surveys tied the peasant population to the land and tightened the collection of the land tax.

With the country pacified, Hideyoshi embarked on an ill-fated attempt to conquer Korea and China that ended only with his death.

THE TOKUGAWA SHOGUNATE (1600–1800)

What was life like in Japan during the Tokugawa peace?

On his deathbed, Hideyoshi set up a council of regents to govern during the minority of his infant son. The strongest regent was Hideyoshi's long-time supporter Tokugawa Ieyasu (1543–1616), who ruled vast territories around Edo (modern-day Tokyo). In 1600 at Sekigahara, Ieyasu smashed a coalition of daimyo defenders of the heir and began building his own government. In 1603 he took the title *shogun*. The **Tokugawa Shogunate** that Ieyasu fashioned lasted until 1867. This era is also called the Edo period because the shogunate was located at Edo, starting Tokyo's history as Japan's most important city (see Map 20.2).

Tokugawa Shogunate *The Japanese government founded by Tokugawa Ieyasu that lasted until 1867; it is also called the Edo period because the shogunate was located at Edo*

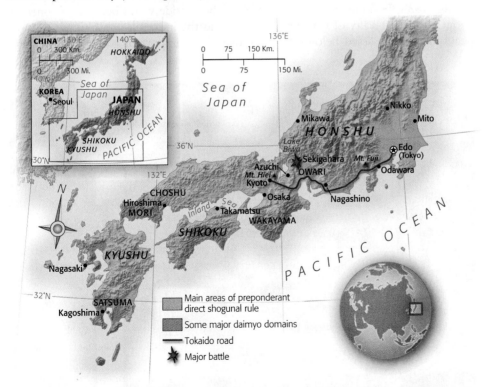

MAP 20.2 **Tokugawa Japan** Consider the cultural and political significance of the fact that Japan is a group of islands. How did the concentration of shogunate lands affect the shogunate's government of Japan?

In the course of the seventeenth century, the Tokugawa shoguns worked to consolidate relations with the daimyo. In a scheme resembling the later residency requirement imposed by Louis XIV in France (see page 467) and Peter the Great in Russia (see page 479), Ieyasu set up the **alternate residence system,** which compelled the lords to live in Edo every other year and to leave their wives and sons there—essentially as hostages. This arrangement had obvious advantages: the shogun could keep tabs on the daimyo, control them through their children, and weaken them financially with the burden of maintaining two residences.

alternate residence system *Arrangement in which lords lived in Edo every other year and left their wives and sons there as hostages.*

The peace that the Tokugawa Shogunate imposed brought a steady rise in population to about 30 million people by 1800 (making Tokugawa Japan about one-tenth the size of Qing China). As demand for goods grew, so did the number of merchants. To maintain stability, the early Tokugawa shoguns froze social status. Laws rigidly prescribed what each class could and could not do. Nobles, for example, were strictly forbidden, whether by day or by night, to go sauntering through the streets or lanes in places where they had no business to be. Daimyo were prohibited from moving troops outside their frontiers, making alliances, and coining money. Designated dress and stiff rules of etiquette distinguished one class from another. As intended, this stratification protected the Tokugawa shoguns from daimyo attack and inaugurated a long era of peace.

The early Tokugawa shoguns also restricted the construction and repair of castles—symbols, in Japan as in medieval Europe, of feudal independence. Continuing Hideyoshi's policy, the Tokugawa regime enforced a policy of complete separation of samurai and peasants. Samurai were defined as those permitted to carry swords. They had to live in castles (which evolved into castle-towns), and they depended on stipends from their lords, the daimyo. Samurai were effectively prevented from establishing ties to the land, so they could not become landholders. Likewise, merchants and artisans had to live in towns and could not own land. Japanese castle-towns evolved into bustling, sophisticated urban centers.

After 1639, Japan limited its contacts with the outside world because of concerns about both the loyalty of Christian converts and the imperialist ambitions of European powers (discussed below). China remained an important trading partner and

● **Interior of Nijo Castle** To assert control over the imperial court and the city of Kyoto, Tokugawa Ieyasu built palace-like Nijo Castle there in 1601–1603. He had the sliding doors painted by leading artists of the period, making the castle as elegant as the imperial palace. *(From Fujioka Michio,* Genshoku Nihon no Bijutsu, *Vol. 12: Shiro to Shoin [Tokyo: Shogakkan, 1968])*

● **Daimyo Procession**   Sankin kōtai, or system of alternate residence, meant that some daimyo were always on the road. Travel with retinues between daimyo residences and Edo, the shogun's residence, stimulated construction of roads, inns, and castle towns. As administrative headquarters, Edo functioned as a major consumer center; other castle towns such as Osaka developed as banking and manufacturing centers. *(Tokugawa Art Museum, Nagoya/Tokugawa Reimeikai Foundation)*

source of ideas—Neo-Confucianism gained a stronger hold among the samurai-turned bureaucrats than it had had earlier. Painting in Chinese styles enjoyed great popularity. The Edo period also saw the development of a school of native learning that rejected Buddhism and Confucianism as alien and tried to identify a distinctly Japanese sensibility.

Commercialization

During the civil war period, warfare seems to have promoted social and economic change, much as it had in China during the Warring States Period (403–221 B.C.E.). Trade grew, and greater use was made of coins imported from Ming China. Markets began appearing at river crossings, at the entrances to temples and shrines, and at other places where people congregated. Towns and cities sprang up all around the country, some of them around the new castles. Traders or artisans dealing in a specific product—such as comb makers, sesame oil producers, or metalworkers—began forming guilds. Money-lending was a very profitable business—annual interest rates reached 300 percent. In Kyoto the powerful monastery Enryakuji licensed the money-lenders, in essence running a lucrative protection racket. Foreign trade also flourished, despite chronic problems with pirates who raided the Japanese, Korean, and Chinese coasts (see page 600).

Recent scholarship demonstrates that the Tokugawa era witnessed the foundations of modern Japanese capitalism: the development of a cash economy, the use of money to make more money, the accumulation of large amounts of capital for investment in factory or technological enterprises, the growth of business ventures operating over a national network of roads, and the expansion of wage labor. That these developments occurred simultaneously with, but entirely independent of, similar changes in Europe fascinates and challenges historians.

In most cities, merchant families with special privileges from the government controlled the urban economy. Frequently, a particular family dominated the trade in a particular product; then that family branched out into other businesses. The family of Kōnoike Shinroku provides a typical example. In 1600 he established a sake brewery in the village of Kōnoike (sake is an alcoholic beverage made from fermented rice). By 1604 he had opened a branch office in Edo, and in 1615 he opened an office in Osaka; that same year, he began shipping tax-rice (taxes paid in rice) from western Japan to Osaka. One of Shinroku's sons, Kōnoike Zen'amon, in 1656 founded a banking or money-changing business in Osaka. Forty years later, the Kōnoike family was doing business in thirty-two daimyo domains. Eventually, the Kōnoike banking house

Primary Source:
Common Sense Teachings for Japanese Children and Greater Learning for Women
A Confucian scholar explains how to raise aristocratic Japanese children.

Primary Source:
Some Observations on Merchants
Why lending money to a daimyo is like gambling, and other business insights from early Tokugawa Japan.

made loans to and handled the tax-rice for 110 daimyo families. The Kōnoike continued to expand their businesses. In 1705, with the interest paid from daimyo loans, the Kōnoike bought a tract of ponds and swampland, turned the land into rice paddies, and settled 480 households on the land. Land reclamation under merchant supervision became a typical feature of Tokugawa business practices. Involved by this time in five or six business enterprises, the "house of Kōnoike" had come a long way from brewing sake.

Japanese merchant families also devised distinct patterns and procedures for their business operations. What today is called "Family Style Management Principles" determined the age of appointment or apprenticeship (between eleven and thirteen); the employee's detachment from past social relations and adherence to the norms of a particular family business; salaries; seniority as the basis of promotion, though job performance at the middle rungs determined who reached the higher ranks; and the time for retirement. All employees in a family business were imbued with the "cardinal tenets" of Tokugawa business law: frugality, resourcefulness, and careful accounting. The successful employee also learned appropriate business behavior and a spirit of self-denial. These values formed the basis of what has been called the Japanese "industrious revolution." They help to explain how, after the Meiji Restoration of 1867 (see page 764), Japan was able to industrialize rapidly and compete successfully with the West.

In the seventeenth century, the surplus rural population, together with underemployed samurai and the ambitious and adventurous, thronged to the cities. All wanted a better way of life than could be found in the dull farming villages. Japan's cities grew tremendously: Kyoto became the center for the manufacture of luxury goods like lacquer, brocade, and fine porcelain. Osaka was the chief market, especially for rice. Edo was a center of consumption by the daimyo, their vassals, and government bureaucrats. Both Osaka and Edo reached about a million residents.

These cities needed to import huge quantities of rice. Osaka came to manage most of this rice trade. Other goods—cotton cloth, oil, sugar, salt, paper, and iron ore—also flowed into Osaka. Granted special privileges by the government and having the facilities necessary for large commodity exchange, Osaka became the commercial center of Japan. Wholesalers and brokers were concentrated there. The city was also closely tied to Kyoto, where the emperor and his court resided, creating a big demand for goods and services.

Two hundred fifty towns came into being. Most ranged in size from 3,000 to 20,000 people, but a few, such as Hiroshima, Kagoshima, and Nagoya, had populations between 65,000 and 100,000. In addition, perhaps two hundred transit towns along the roads and highways emerged to service the needs of men traveling on the alternate residence system. In the eighteenth century, perhaps 4 million people, 15 percent of the Japanese population, resided in cities or towns.

The Life of the People in the Edo Period

The Tokugawa shoguns brought an end to civil war by controlling the military. Stripped of power and required to spend alternate years at Edo, many of the daimyo and samurai passed their lives in idle pursuit of pleasure. They spent frantically on fine silks, paintings, concubines, boys, the theater, and the redecoration of their castles. Around 1700 one scholar observed that the entire military class was living "as in an inn, that is, consuming now and paying later."[2] Eighteenth-century Japanese novels, plays, and histories portray the samurai engrossed in tavern brawls and sexual orgies. These frivolities, plus more sophisticated pleasures and the heavy costs of maintaining an alternate residence at Edo, gradually bankrupted the warrior class.

All major cities contained places of amusement for men—teahouses, theaters, restaurants, and houses of prostitution. Desperately poor parents sometimes sold their daughters to entertainment houses (as they did in China and medieval Europe), and

● **Whaling**   Island peoples often depend on the sea for much of their food. In Japan, where whaling is an old and dangerous pursuit, fishermen first snared the whale in huge nets and then harpooned it. Here the banners tell that a whale has been caught. A Japanese proverb holds that "when one whale is caught, it makes seven villages prosperous." The yellowish oil obtained from whale blubber was used for lighting and for the manufacture of soap and candles. *(National Institute of Japanese Literature)*

the most attractive or talented girls, trained in singing, dancing, and conversational arts, became courtesans, later called *geishas,* or "accomplished persons."

The samurai joined the merchants in patronizing the kabuki theater. An art form created by townspeople, kabuki originated in crude, bawdy skits dealing with love and romance. Performances featured elaborate costumes, song, dance, and poetry. Because actresses were thought to corrupt public morals, the Tokugawa government banned them from the stage in 1629. From that time on, men played all the parts. Male actors in female dress and makeup performed as seductively as possible to entice the burly samurai who thronged the theaters. Homosexuality, long accepted in Japan, was widely practiced among the samurai, who pursued the actors and spent profligately on them. Some moralists and bureaucrats complained from time to time, but the Tokugawa government decided to accept kabuki and prostitution as necessary evils. The practices provided employment, gratified the tastes of samurai and townspeople, and diverted former warriors from potential criminal and political mischief. The samurai paid for their costly pleasures in the way their European counterparts did—by fleecing the peasants and borrowing from the merchants.

Cities were also the center for commercial publishing. The reading public eagerly purchased fiction and the scripts for dramas and puppet plays. Ihara Saikaku (1642–1693) wrote stories of the foibles of townspeople in such books as *Five Women Who Loved Love* and *The Life of an Amorous Man.* One of the puppet plays of Chikamatsu

● **Interior View of a Theater**
Complex kabuki plays, which dealt with heroes, loyalty, and tragedy and which included music and dance, became the most popular form of entertainment in Tokugawa Japan for all classes. Movable scenery and lighting effects made possible the staging of storms, fires, and hurricanes. *(TNM Image Archives. Source: http://TnmArchives.jp/)*

Monzaemon (1653–1724) tells the story of the son of a business owner who, caught between duty to his family and love of a prostitute, decides to resolve the situation by double suicide.

Roads needed for the huge processions of daimyo and their retainers coming and going because of the alternate residence system were built or improved to connect every region to Edo. The shogunate prohibited travel by commoners, but they could get passports to take pilgrimages, visit relatives, or seek the soothing waters of medicinal hot springs. Setting out on foot, groups of villagers would travel to such shrines as Ise, often taking large detours to visit Osaka or Edo to sightsee or attend the theater. Older women with daughters-in-law to run their households were among the most avid pilgrims.

According to Japanese tradition, farmers deserved respect. In practice, peasants were often treated callously. It was government policy to tax them to the level of bare subsistence, and official legislation repeatedly redefined their duties. In 1649 every village in Japan received these regulations:

Peasants are people without sense or forethought. Therefore they must not give rice to their wives and children at harvest time, but must save food for the future. They should eat millet, vegetables, and other coarse food instead of rice. Even the fallen leaves of plants should be saved as food against famine. . . . During the seasons of planting and harvesting, however, when the labor is arduous, the food taken may be a little better. . . .

They must not buy tea or sake to drink nor must their wives.

The husband must work in the fields, the wife must work at the loom. Both must do night work. However good-looking a wife may be, if she neglects her household duties by drinking tea or sightseeing or rambling on the hillsides, she must be divorced.

Peasants must wear only cotton or hemp—no silk. They may not smoke tobacco. It is harmful to health, it takes up time, and costs money. It also creates a risk of fire.[3]

During the seventeenth and eighteenth centuries conspicuous consumption by the upper classes led them to increase taxes from 30 or 40 percent of the rice crop to 50 percent. During the eighteenth century peasant protests were chronic. Oppressive taxation provoked eighty-four thousand farmers in the province of Iwaki to revolt in 1739. After widespread burning and destruction, their demands were met. Natural disasters also added to the peasants' misery. In 1783 Mount Asama erupted, spewing volcanic ash that darkened the skies all summer; crop failures led to famine. When famine recurred again in 1787, commoners rioted for five days in Edo, smashing merchants' stores and pouring sake and rice into the muddy streets. The shogunate responded by trying to control the floating population of day laborers without families in the city. At one point they were rounded up and transported to work the gold mines in an island off the north coast, where most of them died within two or three years.

This picture of peasant hardship tells only part of the story, however. Agricultural productivity increased substantially. Peasants who improved their lands and increased their yields continued to pay the same assessed tax and could pocket the surplus as profit. By the early nineteenth century, there existed a large class of relatively wealthy, educated, and ambitious peasant families. Most villages had a dominant family that monopolized the position of headman, who made decisions for the village after consulting a council of elders.

Women in these better-off families were much more likely to learn to read than women in poor peasant families. Girls from middle-level peasant families might have had from two to five years of formal schooling, but they were thought incapable of learning the difficult Chinese characters, so their education focused on moral instruction intended to instill virtue. Daughters of wealthy peasant families learned penmanship, the Chinese classics, poetry, and the proper forms of correspondence, and they rounded out their education with travel.

By the fifteenth and sixteenth centuries, Japan's family and marriage systems had evolved in the direction of a patrilocal, patriarchal system more like China's, and Japanese women had lost the prominent role in high society that they had occupied during the Heian period (794–1185). It became standard for women to move into their husbands' homes, where they occupied positions subordinate both to their husbands and to their mothers-in-law. Elite families stopped dividing their property among all of their children; instead they retained it for the sons alone or increasingly for a single son who would continue the family line. Marriage, which now had greater consequence, also had a more public character and was marked by greater ceremony. Wedding rituals involved both the exchange of betrothal gifts and the movement of the bride from her natal home to her husband's home. She brought with her a trousseau that provided her with clothes and other items she would need for daily life, but not land, which would have given her economic autonomy. On the other hand, her position within her new family was more secure, for it became more difficult for a husband to divorce his wife. She also gained authority within the family. If her husband was away, she managed family affairs. If her husband fathered children with concubines, she was their legal mother.

A peasant wife shared with her husband responsibility for the family's economic well-being. If of poor or middling status, she worked alongside her husband in the fields, doing the routine work while he did the heavy work. If they were farm hands and worked for wages, the wife invariably earned a third or a half less than her husband. Wives of prosperous farmers never worked in the fields, but they reeled silk, wove cloth, helped in any family business, and supervised the maids. When cotton growing spread to Japan in the sixteenth century, women took on the jobs of spinning and weaving it. Whatever their economic status, Japanese women, like women everywhere in the world, tended the children. Families were growing smaller in this period in response to the spread of single-heir inheritance. From studies of household registers, demographic historians have shown that Japanese families restricted the number of children they had by practicing abortion and infanticide, turning to adoption when no heir survived.

How was divorce initiated, and how frequent was it? Customs among the upper class differed considerably from peasant practices. Divorce in samurai society carried a social stigma; it did not among the peasantry. Widows and divorcées of the samurai elite—where female chastity was the core of fidelity—were not expected to remarry. The husband alone could initiate divorce by ordering his wife to leave or by sending her possessions to her natal home. The wife could not prevent divorce or ensure access to her children.

Among the peasant classes, divorce seems to have been fairly common—at least 15 percent in the villages near Osaka in the eighteenth century. A poor woman wanting a divorce could simply leave her husband's home. It was also possible to secure divorce through a temple. If a married woman entered the temple and performed rites there for three years, her marriage bond was dissolved. Sometimes Buddhist temple priests served as divorce brokers: they went to the village headman and had him force the husband to agree to a divorce. News of the coming of temple officials was usually enough to produce a letter of separation.

The Tokugawa period witnessed a major transformation of agriculture, a great leap in productivity and specialization. The rural population increased, but the agricultural population did not; surplus labor was drawn to other employment and to the cities. In fact, Japan suffered an acute shortage of farm labor from 1720 to 1868. In some villages, industry became almost as important as agriculture. At Hirano near Osaka, for example, 61.7 percent of all arable land was sown in cotton. The peasants had a

● **Cottage Industries** Many of the objects Japanese used in everyday life were made at home or in small workshops. These two screens show stages in the production of textiles. Male and female weavers (*left*) and dyers (*right*) worked in the vicinity of other family members, including children and the elderly. (*left: Werner Forman/Corbis; right: Sakamoto Photo Research/Corbis*)

thriving industry: they ginned the cotton locally before transporting it to wholesalers in Osaka. In many rural places, as many peasants worked in the manufacture of silk, cotton, or vegetable oil as in the production of rice.

As the ruling samurai with their fixed stipends became increasingly poorer, the despised merchants grew steadily wealthier. Merchants had no political power, but they accumulated wealth, sometimes great wealth. They also demonstrated the possibility of social mobility and thus the inherent weakness of the regime's system of strict social stratification. By contemporary standards anywhere in the world, the Japanese mercantile class lived very well. In 1705 the shogunate confiscated the property of a merchant in Osaka "for conduct unbecoming a member of the commercial class." In fact, the confiscation was at the urging of influential daimyo and samurai who owed the merchant gigantic debts. The government seized 50 pairs of gold screens, 360 carpets, several mansions, 48 granaries and warehouses scattered around the country, and hundreds of thousands of gold pieces. This merchant possessed fabulous wealth, but other merchants also lived in luxury.

● ● ● ● ● ● ● ● ● ● ● ● ● ● ● ● ● ●

MARITIME TRADE, PIRACY, AND THE ENTRY OF EUROPE INTO THE ASIAN MARITIME SPHERE

How did the sea link the countries of East Asia, and what happened when Europeans entered this maritime sphere?

In the period 1400–1800, maritime trade and piracy connected China and Japan to each other and also to Korea, Southeast Asia, and Europe. All through the period China and Japan traded extensively with each other as well as with Korea. Both Korea and Japan relied on Chinese coinage, and China relied on silver from Japan. During the fifteenth century, China launched overseas expeditions. Japan in the period was a major source of pirates. In the sixteenth century, European traders appeared, eager for Chinese porcelains and silks. Christian missionaries followed, but despite initial successes, they were later banned by the Japanese and then the Chinese governments. Political changes in Europe changed the international makeup of the European traders, from the Portuguese to the Dutch and then the British. By the eighteenth century Chinese tea had become the product in greatest demand.

Zheng He's Voyages

Early in the Ming period, the Chinese government tried to revive the tribute system of the Han (202–220 C.E.) and Tang Dynasties (618–907), when China had dominated East Asia and envoys had arrived from dozens of distant lands. To invite more countries to send missions, the third Ming emperor (Yongle) authorized an extraordinary series of voyages to the Indian Ocean under the command of the Muslim eunuch Zheng He (1371–1433; see also page 435).

Zheng He's father had made the trip to Mecca, and the seven voyages that Zheng led between 1405 and 1433 followed old Arab trade routes. The first of the seven was made by a fleet of 317 ships, of which 62 were huge, 440 feet long. Each expedition involved from twenty thousand to thirty-two thousand men. Their itineraries included stops in Vietnam, Malaysia, Indonesia, Sri Lanka, India, and, in the later voyages, Hormuz (on the coast of Persia) and East Africa (see Map 15.1 on page 432). At each stop, Zheng He went ashore to visit rulers, transmit messages of China's peaceful intentions, and bestow lavish gifts. Rulers were invited to come to China or send envoys and were offered accommodation on the return voyages. Near the Straits of Malacca, Zheng He's fleet battled Chinese pirates, bringing them under control. Zheng He made other shows of force as well, deposing rulers deemed unacceptable in Java, Sumatra, and Sri Lanka.

On the return of these expeditions, the Ming emperor was delighted by the exotic things the fleet brought back, such as giraffes and lions from Africa, fine cotton cloth from India, and gems and spices from Southeast Asia. Ma Huan, an interpreter who accompanied Zheng He, collected data on the plants, animals, peoples, and geography that they encountered and wrote a book titled *The Overall Survey of the Ocean's Shores*. Still, these expeditions were not voyages of discovery; they followed established routes and pursued diplomatic rather than commercial goals.

Why were these voyages abandoned? Officials complained about their cost and modest return. As a consequence, after 1474, all of the remaining ships with three or more masts were broken up and used for lumber. Chinese did not pull back from trade in the South China Sea and Indian Ocean, but the government no longer promoted trade, leaving the initiative to private merchants and migrants.

Piracy and Japan's Overseas Adventures

One goal of Zheng He's expeditions was to suppress piracy, which had become a problem all along the China coast. Already in the thirteenth century social disorder and banditry in Japan had expanded into seaborne banditry, some of it within the Japanese islands, around the Inland Sea, but also in the straits between Korea and Japan. Japanese "sea bandits" would raid the Korean coast, seizing rice and other goods to take back home. In the sixteenth century, bands several hundred strong would attack and loot Chinese coastal cities or hold them ransom. As maritime trade throughout East Asia grew more lively, "sea bandits" also took to attacking ships to steal their cargo. Although the pirates were called the "Japanese pirates" by both the Koreans and the Chinese, pirate gangs in fact recruited from all countries. The Ryūkyūs and Taiwan became major bases.

Possibly encouraged by the exploits of these bandits, Hideyoshi, after his victories in unifying Japan, decided to extend his territory across the seas. In 1590, after receiving congratulations from Korea on his victories, Hideyoshi sent a letter asking the Koreans to allow his armies to pass through their country, declaring that his real target was China: "Disregarding the distance of the sea and mountain reaches that lie in between, I shall in one fell swoop invade Great Ming. I have in mind to introduce Japanese customs and values to the four hundred and more provinces of that country and bestow upon it the benefits of imperial rule and culture for the coming hundred million years."[4] He also sent demands for submission to countries of Southeast Asia and to the Spanish governor of the Philippines.

In 1592 Hideyoshi mobilized 158,000 soldiers and 9,200 sailors for his invasion, and equipped them with muskets and cannon, which had recently been introduced into Japan. His forces overwhelmed Korean defenders and reached Seoul within three weeks and Pyongyang in two months. A few months later, in the middle of winter, Chinese armies arrived to help defend Korea. Japanese forces were pushed back from Pyongyang. A stalemate lasted till 1597; then Hideyoshi sent new troops. This time the Ming army and the Korean navy were more successful in resisting the Japanese. The Korean navy had for years had to defend against Japanese pirates, and was able to keep the Japanese from being able to supply or reinforce their troops. In 1598, after Hideyoshi's death, the Japanese army withdrew. Korea was left devastated. (See the feature "Listening to the Past: Keinen's Poetic Diary of the Korea Campaign" on pages 606–607.)

● **Transport of Chinese Porcelain** Chinese blue-and-white porcelain, especially the large covered jars shown here, enjoyed enormous popularity in southwestern Asia. This Turkish miniature painting depicts several such pieces, carried for public display in a filigreed cart in a wedding procession; the porcelain was probably part of the bride's dowry. *(Topkapi Saray Museum, Istanbul)*

Europeans Enter the Scene

In the sixteenth century, Portuguese, Spanish, and Dutch merchants and adventurers began to participate in the East Asian maritime world. The trade between Japan, China, and Southeast Asia was very profitable, and the European traders wanted to carry some of it, as well as carry Asian goods to Europe.

The Portuguese and Dutch were not reluctant to use force to gain control of trade, and they seized outposts many places along the trade routes, including Taiwan. Moreover, they made little distinction between trade, smuggling, and piracy. In 1521 the Ming tried to ban the Portuguese from China. Two years later an expeditionary force commissioned by the Portuguese king to negotiate a friendship treaty defeated its mission by firing on Chinese warships near Guangzhou. In 1557, without informing Beijing, local Chinese officials decided that the way to regulate trade was to allow the Portuguese to build a trading post on uninhabited land near the mouth of the Pearl River. The city they built there—Macao—became the first destination for Europeans going to China until the nineteenth century, and it remained a Portuguese possession until 1999.

European products were not in demand in China, but silver was. Japan had supplied much of China's silver, but with the development of silver mines in the New World, European traders began supplying large quantities of silver to China, which had positive effects in allowing the expansion of the economy.

Chinese were quick to take advantage of the new trading ports set up by European powers. In Batavia harbor, Chinese ships outnumbered those from any other country by two or three to one. Manila, under Spanish control, and Taiwan and Batavia, both under Dutch control, all attracted thousands of Chinese colonists. Local people felt the intrusion of Chinese more than Europeans, and there were riots against Chinese that led to massacres on several occasions.

A side benefit of the appearance of European traders was New World crops. Sweet potatoes, maize, peanuts, tomatoes, chili peppers, tobacco, and other crops were quickly introduced. Sweet potatoes and maize in particular facilitated population growth because they could be grown on land previously thought too sandy or too steep to cultivate. Sweet potatoes became a common poor people's food.

Missionaries

The Spanish and Portuguese kings supported missionary activity, and merchant vessels soon brought Catholic missionaries to East Asia. The first to come were Jesuits, from the order founded by Ignatius Loyola in 1534 to promote Catholic scholarship and combat the Protestant Reformation.

The Jesuit priest Francis Xavier had worked in India and the Indies before China and Japan attracted his attention. After many misadventures, in 1549 he landed on Kyushu, Japan's southernmost island (see Map 20.2). After he was expelled by the local lord, he traveled throughout western Japan as far as Kyoto, proselytizing wherever warlords allowed. He soon made many converts among the poor and even some among the daimyo. Xavier then set his sights on China but died on an uninhabited island off the China coast in 1552.

Other missionaries carried on his work. By 1600 there were three hundred thousand baptized Christians in Japan. Most of them lived on Kyushu, where the shogun's power was weakest and the loyalty of the daimyo most doubtful. In 1615 bands of Christian samurai supported Tokugawa Ieyasu's enemies at the fierce Battle of Osaka. A couple of decades later, thirty thousand peasants in the heavily Catholic area of northern Kyushu revolted. The Tokugawa shoguns thus came to associate Christianity with domestic disorder and insurrection. Accordingly, what had been mild persecution of Christians became ruthless repression after 1639. Foreign priests were expelled or tortured, and thousands of Japanese Christians suffered crucifixion.

● **Dutch in Japan** The Japanese were curious about the appearance, dress, and habits of the Dutch who came to Deshima to trade. In this detail from a long handscroll, Dutch traders are shown interacting with a Japanese samurai in a room with tatami mats on the floor. Note also the Western musical instruments. *(Private Collection/The Bridgeman Art Library)*

Meanwhile, in China the Jesuits concentrated on gaining the linguistic and scholarly knowledge they would need to convert the educated class. The Jesuit Matteo Ricci studied for years in Macao before setting himself up in Nanjing and trying to win over members of the educated class. In 1601 he was given permission to reside in Beijing, where he made several high-placed converts. He also interested Chinese educated men in Western-style geography, astronomy, and Euclidean mathematics.

Ricci and his Jesuit successors believed that Confucianism was compatible with Christianity. Both shared similar concerns for morality and virtue. They viewed making offerings to ancestors as an expression of filial reverence rather than a form of worship. The Franciscan and Dominican mendicant orders that arrived in China in the seventeenth century disagreed. In 1715, religious and political quarrels in Europe led the pope to decide that the Jesuit's accommodating approach was heretical. Angry at this insult, the Kangxi emperor forbade all Christian missionary work in China.

Learning from the West

Although both China and Japan ended up prohibiting Christian missionary work, other aspects of Western culture were seen as impressive and worth learning. The "closed country policy" that Japan instituted in 1639 restricted Japanese from leaving the country and kept European merchants in small enclaves. Still, Japanese interest in Europe did not disappear. Through the Dutch enclave on a tiny island in Nagasaki harbor, a stream of Western ideas and inventions trickled into Japan in the eighteenth century. Western writings, architectural illustrations, calendars, watches, medicine, weapons, and paintings deeply impressed the Japanese. Western portraits and other paintings introduced the Japanese to perspective and shading.

In China, too, both individual scholars and rulers showed an interest in Western learning. The Kangxi emperor frequently discussed scientific and philosophical questions with the Jesuits at court. When he got malaria, he accepted the Jesuit's offer of the medicine quinine. He had translations made of a collection of Western works on mathematics and the calendar. The court was impressed with the Jesuits' skill in astronomy and quickly appointed them to the Board of Astronomy. In 1674, the emperor asked them to re-equip the observatory with European instruments. He and his successors employed Italian painters to make imperial portraits. Qianlong had gardens and palaces built in European designs. Firearms and mechanical clocks also were widely admired. The court established its own clock and watch factory, and in 1673 the emperor insisted that the Jesuits manufacture cannons for him and supervise gunnery practice.

There was also, of course, learning that spread in the opposite direction. Although European anatomy was recognized in both China and Japan as more advanced, medicine was not uniformly better in Europe. One Chinese practice that Europeans adopted was "variolation," an early form of smallpox inoculation. In the early eighteenth century, China enjoyed a positive reputation among the educated in Europe. The Manchu emperors were seen as wise and benevolent rulers. Voltaire wrote of the rationalism of Confucianism and saw advantages to the Chinese political system because the rulers did not put up with parasitical aristocrats or hypocritical priests.

● **Gold-Lacquered Stationery Box** The art of lacquer flourished in Japan during the Middle Ages and Tokugawa period. This lacquer box was made to hold everything one needed to write a letter: paper, brushes, an inkstick, and an inkstone (for grinding the ink and mixing it with water). The box is coated in lacquer and decorated with a landscape scene. *(Tokugawa Art Museum, Nagoya/Tokugawa Reimeikai Foundation)*

Primary Source: Edict on Trade with Great Britain *Read how the Chinese emperor dismissed Lord Macartney's mission on behalf of Britain's "barbarian merchants."*

kowtow *The ritual of kneeling on both knees and bowing one's head to the ground, performed by children to their parents and by subjects to the Chinese ruler.*

British Efforts to Expand Trade with China in the Eighteenth Century

The East Asian maritime world underwent many changes from the sixteenth to the eighteenth centuries. The Japanese pulled back their own traders and limited opportunities for Europeans to trade in Japan. The Qing government limited trading contacts with Europe to Guangzhou in the far south in an attempt to curb piracy. Portugal lost many of its bases to the Dutch. And by the eighteenth century, the British had become as active as the Dutch. In the seventeenth century the British and Dutch sought primarily porcelains and silk, but in the eighteenth century, tea became the commodity in most demand. By the end of the century, tea made up 80 percent of Chinese exports to Europe.

By the late eighteenth century, Britain wanted to renegotiate its relations with China. By then Britain was a great power and did not see why China should be able to dictate the terms of trade. British merchants were permitted to trade only in Guangzhou, even though tea, their principal purchase, was grown mostly in the distant Yangzi Valley (see Map 20.1). They also resented other restrictions imposed on them, such as not being allowed to enter the walled city of Guangzhou, learn Chinese, ride in sedan chairs, or bring women or weapons into the part of the city assigned to them. As British purchases of tea escalated, the balance of trade with China became increasingly lopsided. British merchants, however, could find no goods that Chinese merchants were willing to buy from them.

In the 1790s, King George III sent Lord George Macartney on a mission to China. Macartney was instructed to secure a place for British traders to live near the tea-producing areas, negotiate a commercial treaty, create a desire for British products, arrange for diplomatic representation in Beijing, and open Japan and Southeast Asia to British commerce. He traveled with an entourage of eighty-four and six hundred cases packed with British goods that he hoped would impress the Chinese court and attract trade: clocks, telescopes, knives, globes, plate glass, Wedgwood pottery, landscape paintings, woolen cloth, and carpets. The only member of the British party able to speak Chinese, however, was a twelve-year-old boy who had learned a bit of the language by talking with Chinese passengers on the long voyage.

After Lord Macartney arrived in Guangzhou in 1793, he proceeded overland. Because he would not perform the **kowtow** (kneeling on both knees and bowing his head to the ground), he was denied a formal audience in the palace. He was permitted to meet more informally with the Qianlong emperor at his summer retreat, but no negotiations followed this meeting because Qianlong saw no merit in Macartney's requests. As he pointed out in his formal reply, the Qing Empire "possesses all things in prolific abundance and lacks no product within its own borders"; thus trading with Europe was a kindness, not a necessity.[5] The Qing court was as intent on maintaining the existing system of regulated trade as Britain was intent on doing away with it.

Several members of the Macartney mission wrote books about China on their return, updating European understanding of China. These books, often illustrated, contained descriptions of many elements of Chinese culture and social customs—accounts less rosy than the reports written by the Jesuits a century or two earlier. The British writers, for instance, introduced the idea that Chinese women were oppressed, unable even to sit at the same table with their husbands to eat dinner.

● **Porcelain Vase** Among the objects produced in China that were in high demand in Europe in the seventeenth and eighteenth centuries were colorful porcelains. In this period Chinese potters perfected the use of overglaze enamels, which allowed the application of many colors to a single object. Blue, green, yellow, orange, and red all appear on this 18-inch-tall (45.7 cm) vase. *(Image copyright © The Metropolitan Museum/Art Resource, NY)*

Chapter Summary

To assess your mastery of this chapter, go to **bedfordstmartins.com/mckayworld**

Key Terms

Ming Dynasty
civil service examinations
Qing Dynasty
banners
daimyo
Tokugawa Shogunate
alternate residence system
kowtow

• *What sort of state and society developed in China after the Mongols were ousted?*

After the fall of the Mongols, China was ruled by the native Ming Dynasty for three centuries. The dynasty's founder, who knew poverty firsthand, ruled for thirty years, becoming more paranoid and despotic over time. Very few of his successors were particularly good rulers, yet China in the period thrived in many ways. Population grew. Educational levels were high as more and more men prepared for the civil service examinations. Urban culture was very lively. Novels and short stories written in the vernacular found large audiences.

• *Did the return of alien rule with the Manchus have any positive consequences for China?*

The Ming suffered a series of disasters, beginning with a Japanese invasion of Korea at the end of the sixteenth century, and in 1644 fell to a force from beyond the Great Wall, the Manchus. The Manchu rulers proved more competent than the Ming emperors and were able to both maintain peace and extend the empire to its maximum extent, bringing Mongolia, Tibet, and Central Asia within the empire. Population grew steadily, probably reaching 300 million or more.

• *How did Japan change during this period of political instability?*

Japan during the fifteenth and sixteenth centuries was fragmented by civil war. New power holders emerged in the daimyo, who built stone castles to defend their territories. As daimyo attacked and defeated each other, Japan was slowly reunified under Hideyoshi.

• *What was life like in Japan during the Tokugawa peace?*

After Hideyoshi's death, power was seized by Tokugawa Ieyasu, the founder of the Tokugawa Shogunate. In the seventeenth and eighteenth centuries, Japan reaped the rewards of peace. Steady economic growth and improved agricultural technology swelled the population to approximately 30 million. The samurai were transformed into peaceful city dwellers and civil bureaucrats. The wealth of the business classes grew, and the samurai, dependent on fixed agricultural rents or stipends in rice, fell into debt. The merchants created a lively urban culture, well-depicted in both fiction and the woodblock prints of the "floating world."

• *How did the sea link the countries of East Asia, and what happened when Europeans entered this maritime sphere?*

In the fifteenth through the eighteen centuries, maritime trade connected the countries of Asia. Trade between China and Japan was active. Piracy, however, was a perpetual problem. Early in this period, China sent out seven naval expeditions looking to promote diplomatic contacts and trade, which went as far as Africa. In the sixteenth century, European traders arrived in China and Japan. The first traders often acted like pirates, but profitable trading relationships

(continued on page 608)

Listening to the PAST

Keinen's Poetic Diary of the Korea Campaign

The Buddhist priest Keinen (1534?–1611) was ordered in 1597 to accompany the local daimyo on Hideyoshi's second campaign in Korea and spent seven months there. As a Buddhist, he did not revel in military feats but rather deplored the death and suffering that he observed. Adopting the time-honored form of the poetic diary, Keinen ends each day's entry with a short poem. The excerpt quoted here begins about six weeks after he left home.

Eighth month, 4th day. Every one is trying to be the first off the ship; no one wants to lag behind. They fall over each other in trying to get at the plunder, to kill people. It is a sight I cannot bear to see.

> A hubbub rises
> as from roiling clouds and mist
> where they swarm about
> in their rage for the plunder
> of innocent people's goods.

VIII.5. They are burning the houses. As I watched them go up in smoke, I thought that my own existence was like this and was seized by sympathy.

> The "Red Country" is
> what they call it, but black is
> the smoke that rises
> from the burning houses
> where you see flames flying high.

VIII.6. The very fields and hillsides have been put to the fire, not to speak of the forts. People are put to the sword, or they are shackled with chains and bamboo tubes choking the neck. Parents sobbing for their children, children searching for their parents—never before have I seen such a pitiable sight.

> The hills are ablaze
> with the cries of soldiers
> intoxicated
> with their pyrolatry—
> the battleground of demons.

VIII.7. Looking at the various kinds of plunder amassed by them all, I formed a desire for such things. Could I really be like this, I thought, and felt ashamed. How can I attain salvation like this, I thought.

> How ashamed I am!
> For everything that I see
> I form desires—
> a creature of delusions,
> my mind full of attachments.

On the same day, as I exerted myself in reflections on my spiritual state, I felt myself more and more ashamed. And yet the Buddha has vowed not to give weight to the weightiest of evil deeds, not to abandon the most abandoned and intemperate!

> Unless it be through
> reliance on the vow of
> Amida Buddha,
> who could obtain salvation
> with such wicked thoughts as mine?

VIII.8. They are carrying off Korean children and killing their parents. Never shall they see each other again. Their mutual cries—surely this is like the torture meted out by the fiends of hell.

> It is piteous;
> when the four fledglings parted,*
> it must have been thus—
> I see the parents' lament
> over their sobbing children.

VIII.11. As night fell, I saw people's houses go up in smoke. They have lost everything to the fire, all their grain and all their property.

> How wretched it is!
> Smoke lingers still where the grain
> was burned and wasted;
> so that is where I lay my
> head tonight: on the scorched earth.

*An allusion to the proverbial tale of a mother bird's sorrow at her fledglings' departure to the four directions.

VIII.13. His lordship has set up camp about five leagues this side of Namwon. Unless this fortress is taken, our prospects are dubious; so we are to close in and invest it this evening. The word is that fifty or sixty thousand soldiers from Great Ming are garrisoning the place.

We'll solve the challenge
posed even by this fortress
of the Red Country!—
The troops rejoice to hear this,
and they rest their weary feet.

VIII.14. Rain has been falling steadily since the evening. It comes down in sheets, like a waterfall. We have put up a makeshift tent covered with oil paper only, and it is frightening how the rain pours in. It is impossible to sleep. I had to think of the story "The Devil at One Gulp" in *Tales of Ise.*† The night described in that tale must have been just like this.

Inexorably,
fearsome torrents beating down
remind me of that
dreadful night when the devil
at one gulp ate his victim.

VIII.15. The fortress is to be stormed before dawn tomorrow. Fascines of bamboo have been distributed to the assault troops. The sun was about to set as they worked their way close in, right up against the edge of the castle's bulwarks, and gunfire opened up from the several siege detachments, accompanied by arrows shot from short-bows. Unthinkable numbers of men were killed. As I saw them dying:

From the fortress, too,
from their short-bows, too.
How many killed? Beyond count
is the number of the dead.

The castle fell to the assault in the course of the night. Lord Hishu's troops were the first inside the walls. Needless to say, he is to get a vermilion-seal letter of commendation.

VIII.16. All in the fortress were slaughtered, to the last man and woman. No prisoners were taken. To be sure, a few were kept alive for exchange purposes.

How cruel! This world
of sorrow and inconstancy
does have one constant—
men and women, young and old
die and vanish; are no more.

Although the Japanese invasion failed, some of the warriors who fought in it were celebrated, like Kato Kiyomasa, shown here fighting a tiger in the hills of Korea. *(Courtesy, Stephen Turnbull)*

VIII.17. Until yesterday they did not know that they would have to die; today, they are transformed into the smoke of impermanence, as is the way of this world of constant change. How can I be unaffected by this!

Look! Everyone, look!
Is this, then, to be called the human condition?—
a life with a deadline,
a life with a limit: today.

Questions for Analysis

1. Which of Keinen's responses can be identified as specifically Buddhist?

2. Does Keinen's use of poetry seem natural, or do you think it seems forced?

3. What would be the purpose of bringing a Buddhist priest opposed to killing on a military campaign?

Source: Sources of Japanese Tradition, by Wm. Theodore de Bary. Copyright © 2001 by Columbia University Press. Reproduced with permission of COLUMBIA UNIVERSITY PRESS in the format Textbook via Copyright Clearance Center.

†This is a story of an abduction that ends badly. The lady in question, sequestered in a broken-down storehouse to keep her safe from the elements on a dark and stormy night, is devoured "at one gulp" by an ogre who dwells there.

soon developed. The Chinese economy became so dependent on huge imports of silver acquired through this trade that when supplies were cut off, it caused severe hardship. Trade with Europe brought new world crops and new ideas as well as new trade possibilities. Many of the Catholic missionaries who began to arrive were highly educated and introduced Western science and learning as well as Christianity. Both in Japan and in China, however, the government authorities in the end banned missionary work. Although the shogunate severely restricted trade, some Western scientific ideas and technology entered Japan through the port of Nagasaki. Chinese, too, took an interest in those elements of Western technology and science that seemed superior, such as firearms, clockwork, astronomy, and oil painting.

Suggested Reading

Berry, Mary Elizabeth. *The Culture of Civil War in Kyoto.* 1994. Makes use of diaries and other records to examine how people made sense of violence and social change.

Elman, Benjamin. *A Cultural History of Civil Examinations in Late Imperial China.* 2000. Provides fascinating detail on how the examination system worked.

Elvin, Mark. *The Pattern of the Chinese Past.* 1973. Offers an explanation of China's failure to maintain its technological superiority in terms of a "high-level equilibrium trap."

Keene, Donald. *Yoshimasa and the Silver Pavilion: The Creation of the Soul of Japan.* 2003. A lively introduction to the aesthetic style associated with Zen and its connection to shogunate patrons.

Mote, Frederic *Imperial China* (1999). An overview that analyzes the strengths and weaknesses of both the Ming and Qing Dynasties.

Mungello, David. *The Great Encounter of China and the West, 1500–1800.* 1999. A short but stimulating examination of the various dimensions of the first phase of Chinese-European relations.

Pomeranz, Kenneth. *The Great Divergence: China, Europe, and the Making of the Modern World Economy.* 2000. Argues that the most advanced areas of China were on a par with the most advanced regions of Europe through the eighteenth century.

Totman, Conrad. *A History of Japan.* 2000. An excellent, well-balanced survey.

Vaporis, Constantine Komitos. *Breaking Barriers: Travel and the State in Early Modern Japan.* 1994. An examination of recreational and religious travel.

Waldron, Arthur. *The Great Wall of China: From History to Myth.* 1990. Places the construction of the current Great Wall in the context of Ming-Mongol relations.

Notes

1. L. J. Gallagher, trans., *China in the Sixteenth Century: The Journals of Matthew Ricci: 1583–1610* (New York: Random House, 1953), p. 23.

2. Quoted in D. H. Shively, "Bakufu Versus Kabuki," in *Studies in the Institutional History of Early Modern Japan,* ed. J. W. Hall (Princeton, N.J.: Princeton University Press, 1970), p. 236.

3. Quoted in G. B. Sansom, *A History of Japan, 1615–1867,* vol. 3 (Stanford, Calif.: Stanford University Press, 1978), p. 99.

4. W. T. de Bary et al., eds., *Sources of Japanese Tradition from Earliest Times to 1600* (New York: Columbia University Press, 2001), p. 467.

5. Pei-kai Cheng and M. Lestz, with J. Spence, ed., *The Search for Modern China: A Documentary History* (New York: W.W. Norton, 1999), p. 106

Liberty. The figure of Liberty bears a copy of the Declaration of the Rights of Man in one hand and a pike to defend them in the other, in this painting by the female artist Nanine Vallain. The painting hung in the Jacobin Club until its fall from power. *(Musée de la Revolution Française, Vizille/The Bridgeman Art Library)*

21 THE REVOLUTION IN POLITICS, 1775–1815

Chapter Preview

Background to Revolution
• *What social, political, and economic factors formed the background to the French Revolution?*

Revolution in Metropole and Colony (1789–1791)
• *What were the immediate events and ideas that sparked the Revolution in France and its Caribbean colony of Saint-Domingue?*

World War and Republican France (1791–1799)
• *How and why did the Revolution take a radical turn at home and in the colonies?*

The Napoleonic Era (1799–1815)
• *What factors explain the rise and fall of Napoleon Bonaparte and his loss of the colony of Saint-Domingue?*

The last years of the eighteenth century were a time of great upheaval. A series of revolutions and revolutionary wars challenged the old order of monarchs and aristocrats. The ideas of freedom and equality, ideas that continue to shape the world, flourished and spread. The revolutionary era began in North America in 1775. Then in 1789 France, the most influential country in Europe, became the leading revolutionary nation. It established first a constitutional monarchy, then a radical republic, and finally a new empire under Napoleon. Inspired by both the ideals of the Revolution and internal colonial conditions, the slaves of Saint-Domingue rose up in 1791. Their rebellion led to the creation of the new independent nation of Haiti in 1805.

The armies of France violently exported revolution beyond the nation's borders in an effort to establish new governments throughout much of Europe. The world of modern domestic and international politics was born.

BACKGROUND TO REVOLUTION

What social, political, and economic factors formed the background to the French Revolution?

The origins of the French Revolution have been one of the most debated topics in history. In order to understand the path to revolution, numerous interrelated factors must be taken into account. These include deep social changes in France, a long-term political crisis that eroded monarchical legitimacy, the impact of new political ideas derived from the Enlightenment, the emergence of a "public sphere" in which such opinions were formed and shared, and, perhaps most important, a financial crisis created by France's participation in expensive overseas wars.

Legal Orders and Social Change

As in the Middle Ages, France's 25 million inhabitants were still legally divided into three orders, or estates—the clergy, the nobility, and everyone else. As the nation's first estate, the clergy numbered about one hundred thousand and had important privileges, including exemption from regular taxes and the ability to tax landowners. The second estate consisted of some four hundred thousand nobles who owned about 25 percent of the land in France. The nobility also enjoyed special privileges associated with their exalted social position, including lighter taxes, exclusive hunting and fishing rights, monopolies on bread-baking and wine-pressing equipment, and the right to wear swords. The third estate was a conglomeration of very different social groups—prosperous merchants, lawyers, and officials along with poorer peasants, urban artisans, and unskilled day laborers—united only by their shared legal status as distinct from the nobility and clergy.

In discussing the origins of the French Revolution, historians long focused on growing tensions between the nobility and the comfortable members of the third estate, the *bourgeoisie* or upper middle class. In this formulation, the French bourgeoisie eventually rose up to lead the entire third estate in a great social revolution that destroyed feudal privileges and established a capitalist order based on individualism and a market economy.

In recent years, a flood of new research has challenged these accepted views. Above all, revisionist historians have questioned the existence of growing conflict between a capitalistic bourgeoisie and a reactionary feudal nobility in eighteenth-century France. Instead, they see both bourgeoisie and nobility as highly fragmented, riddled with internal rivalries. The ancient sword nobility, for example, was separated from the newer robe nobility by differences in wealth, education, and worldview. Differences within the bourgeoisie—between wealthy financiers and local lawyers, for example—were no less profound. Rather than standing as unified blocs against each other, nobility and bourgeoisie formed two parallel social ladders increasingly linked together at the top by wealth, marriage, and Enlightenment culture.

Revisionist historians note that the nobility and the bourgeoisie shared economic interests. Investment in land and government service were the preferred activities of both groups, and the goal of the merchant capitalist was to gain enough wealth to retire from trade, purchase an estate, and live nobly as a large landowner. At the same time, wealthy nobles often acted as aggressive capitalists, investing especially in mining, metallurgy, and foreign trade. In addition, until the Revolution actually began, key sections of both nobility and bourgeoisie were joined in opposition to the government.

Revisionists have clearly shaken the belief that the bourgeoisie and the nobility were locked in growing conflict before the Revolution. Yet they also make clear that the Old Regime had ceased to correspond with social reality by the 1780s. Legally, society was still based on rigid orders inherited from the Middle Ages. In reality, France had already moved far toward being a society based on wealth and education in which an

● **The Three Estates** In this political cartoon from 1789 a peasant of the third estate struggles under the crushing burden of a happy clergyman and a plumed nobleman. The caption—"Let's hope this game ends soon"—sets forth a program of reform that any peasant could understand. *(Réunion des Musées Nationaux/Art Resource, NY)*

A FAUT ESPERER Q'EU JEU LA FINIRA BEN TOT.

emerging elite that included both aristocratic and bourgeois notables was frustrated by a bureaucratic monarchy that continued to claim the right to absolute power.

The Crisis of Political Legitimacy

Overlaying these social changes was a century-long political and fiscal struggle between the monarchy and its opponents that was primarily enacted in the law courts. When Louis XIV died, his successor Louis XV (r. 1715–1774) was only five years old. The high courts of France—the parlements—regained the ancient right to evaluate royal decrees publicly in writing before they were registered and given the force of law. The parlements used this power to prevent the king from imposing taxes after a series of wars plunged France into fiscal crisis. The Parlement of Paris asserted that it was acting as the representative of the entire nation when it checked the king's power to levy taxes.

After years of attempting to compromise, Louis XV roused himself to defend his absolutist inheritance. His chancellor, René de Maupeou, abolished the existing parlements, exiled the vociferous members of the Parlement of Paris to the provinces, and began to tax privileged groups. Public opinion sided with the parlements, however, and there was widespread criticism of "royal despotism." The king also came under attack for his many mistresses and lost the sacred aura of God's anointed on earth.

Despite this progressive **desacralization** of the monarchy, its power was still great enough to quell opposition, and Louis XV would probably have prevailed if he had lived long enough, but he died in 1774. The new king, Louis XVI (r. 1774–1792), a shy twenty-year-old with good intentions, yielded in the face of vehement opposition from France's educated elite. He dismissed chancellor Maupeou and recalled the parlements. Louis also waffled on the economy, dismissing controller general Turgot when his attempts to liberalize the economy drew fire. A weakened but unreformed monarchy now faced a judicial opposition that claimed to speak for the entire French nation. The country was drifting toward renewed financial crisis and political upheaval.

The Impact of the American Revolution

Coinciding with the first years of Louis XVI's reign, the American Revolution had an enormous practical and ideological impact on France. French expenses to support the colonists bankrupted the Crown, while the ideals of liberty and equality provided heady inspiration for political reform.

Like the French Revolution, the American Revolution originated in struggles over taxes. The high cost of the Seven Years' War—fought with little financial contribution from the colonies—doubled the British national debt. When the government tried to recoup its losses in increased taxes on the colonies in 1765, the colonists reacted with anger.

Chronology

1775–1783	American Revolution
1786–1789	Financial crisis in France
1789	Feudalism abolished in France; ratification of U.S. Constitution; storming of the Bastille
1789–1799	French Revolution
1790	Burke, *Reflections on the Revolution in France*
1791	Slave insurrection in Saint-Domingue
1792	Wollstonecraft, *A Vindication of the Rights of Woman*
1793	Execution of Louis XVI
1793–1794	Economic controls to help poor in France; Robespierre's Reign of Terror
1794	Robespierre deposed and executed
1794–1799	Thermidorian reaction
1799–1815	Napoleonic era
1804	Haitian republic declares independence
1812	Napoleon invades Russia
1814–1815	Napoleon defeated and exiled

desacralization *The removal (during the reigns of Louis XV and Louis XVI) of the divine sanction that had undergirded the absolutism of Louis XIV.*

● **Toward Revolution in Boston** The Boston Tea Party was only one of many angry confrontations between British officials and Boston patriots. On January 27, 1774, an angry crowd seized a British customs collector and tarred and feathered him. This French engraving of 1784 commemorates the defiant and provocative action. *(The Granger Collection, New York)*

The key questions were political rather than economic. To what extent could the home government assert its power while limiting the authority of colonial legislatures? Accordingly, who should represent the colonies, and who had the right to make laws for Americans? The British government replied that Americans were represented in Parliament, albeit indirectly (like most British people themselves), and that the absolute supremacy of Parliament throughout the empire could not be questioned. Many Americans felt otherwise.

In 1773 the dispute reignited after the British government awarded a monopoly on Chinese tea to the East India Company, excluding colonial merchants from a lucrative business. In response, Boston men disguised as Indians held a rowdy "tea party" and threw the company's tea into the harbor. This led to extreme measures. The so-called Coercive Acts closed the port of Boston, curtailed local elections, and expanded the royal governor's power. County conventions in Massachusetts urged that the acts be "rejected as the attempts of a wicked administration to enslave America." Other colonial assemblies joined the protest. In September 1774 the First Continental Congress met in Philadelphia, where the more radical members argued successfully against concessions to the Crown. Compromise was also rejected by the British Parliament, and in April 1775 fighting began at Lexington and Concord.

The fighting spread, and the colonists moved slowly toward open rebellion. The uncompromising attitude of the British government and its use of German mercenaries dissolved long-standing loyalties to the home country. Many "Loyalists" who wished to remain within the empire emigrated to the northern colonies of Canada.

On July 4, 1776, the Second Continental Congress adopted the Declaration of Independence. Written by Thomas Jefferson, it boldly listed the tyrannical acts committed by George III (r. 1760–1820) and proclaimed the sovereignty of the American states. It also universalized the traditional rights of English people, stating that "all men are created equal, that they are endowed by their Creator with certain unalienable Rights, that among these are Life, Liberty, and the Pursuit of Happiness." By 1780, all thirteen states had adopted their own written constitutions.

On the international scene, the French wanted revenge for the humiliating defeats of the Seven Years' War. They sympathized with the rebels and supplied guns and gunpowder from the beginning. By 1777 French volunteers were arriving in Virginia, and a dashing young nobleman, the marquis de Lafayette (1757–1834), became one of Washington's most trusted generals. In 1778 the French government offered a formal alliance to the American ambassador in Paris, Benjamin Franklin, and in 1779 and 1780 the Spanish and Dutch declared war on Britain. Catherine the Great of Russia helped organize the League of Armed Neutrality in order to protect neutral shipping rights, which Britain refused to recognize.

Thus by 1780 Great Britain was at war with most of Europe as well as against the thirteen colonies. Outnumbered and suffering severe reverses, a new British government offered peace on generous terms. By the Treaty of Paris of 1783, Britain recognized the independence of the thirteen colonies and ceded vast territory between the

Primary Source:
The U.S. Declaration of Independence
Read a selection from Jefferson's famous text, which lays out the Enlightenment principles on which the United States was founded.

Allegheny Mountains and the Mississippi River to the Americans. In 1787 the Federal Convention met in Philadelphia to draft the new Constitution of the United States.

Europeans who dreamed of a new era were fascinated by the American Revolution. The Americans had begun with a revolutionary defense against tyrannical oppression, and they had been victorious. They had then shown how rational beings could assemble to exercise sovereignty and form a new social contract. All this gave greater reality to the concepts of individual liberty and representative government and reinforced a primary Enlightenment ideal: that a better world was possible.

No country felt the consequences of the American Revolution more directly than France. Hundreds of French officers were inspired by service in America, the marquis de Lafayette chief among them. French intellectuals engaged in passionate analysis of the new federal and state constitutions. Perhaps most importantly, the war's expenses provided the last nail in the coffin for the French treasury.

Financial Crisis

The French Revolution thus had its immediate origins in the king's financial difficulties. Thwarted in its efforts to reform the tax system, the royal government was forced to finance its contribution to the American Revolutionary with borrowed money. As a result, the national debt and the annual budget deficit soared.

By the 1780s, fully 50 percent of France's annual budget went for interest payments on the debt. Another 25 percent went to maintain the military, while 6 percent was absorbed by the king and his court at Versailles. Less than 20 percent of the national budget was available for productive functions, such as transportation and general administration. This was an impossible financial situation.

Louis XVI's minister of finance revived old proposals to impose a general tax on all landed property as well as to form provincial assemblies to administer the tax, and he convinced the king to call an **Assembly of Notables** to gain support for the idea. The notables, mainly important noblemen and high-ranking clergy, opposed the new tax. In exchange for their support, they demanded that control over government spending be given to the provincial assemblies. When the government refused, the notables responded that such sweeping reforms required the approval of the Estates General, the representative body of all three estates, which had not met since 1614.

Assembly of Notables *A consulting body of eminent nobles and clergymen that convened to advise the king of France in 1788 and 1789.*

Facing imminent bankruptcy, the king tried to reassert his authority. He dismissed the notables and established new taxes by decree. The Parlement of Paris promptly declared them null and void. When the king tried to exile the judges, a wave of protest erupted. Frightened investors also refused to advance more loans to the state. Finally, in July 1788, Louis XVI bowed to public opinion and called for a spring session of the Estates General.

REVOLUTION IN METROPOLE AND COLONY (1789–1791)

What were the immediate events and ideas that sparked the Revolution in France and its Caribbean colony of Saint-Domingue?

Although inspired by the ideals of the American Revolution, the French Revolution did not mirror the American example. It was more radical and more complex, more influential and more controversial, more loved and more hated. For Europeans and most of the rest of the world, it was the great revolution of the eighteenth century, *the revolution that opened the modern era in politics.* In turn, the slave insurrection in Saint-Domingue—which ultimately resulted in the second independent republic of the Americas—inspired liberation movements across the world.

The Formation of the National Assembly

Estates General *A legislative body in pre-revolutionary France made up of representatives of each of the three classes, or estates; it was called into session in 1789 for the first time since 1614.*

Once Louis had agreed to hold the **Estates General**, following precedent, he set elections for the three orders. Elected officials from the noble order were primarily conservatives from the provinces, but fully one-third of the nobility's representatives were liberals committed to major changes. The third estate elected lawyers and government officials to represent them, with few delegates representing business or the working poor.

As at previous meetings of the Estates General, local assemblies were to prepare a list of grievances for their representatives to bring to the next electoral level. The petitions for change coming from the three estates showed a surprising degree of consensus. There was general agreement that royal absolutism should give way to a constitutional monarchy in which laws and taxes would require the consent of the Estates General in regular meetings. All agreed that individual liberties should be guaranteed by law and economic regulations loosened. The striking similarities in the grievance petitions of the clergy, nobility, and third estate reflected a shared platform of basic reform among the educated elite.

Yet an increasingly bitter quarrel undermined this consensus: *how* would the Estates General vote, and *who* would lead political reorganization? The Estates General of 1614 had sat as three separate houses. Each house held one vote, despite the fact that the third estate represented the vast majority of France. Given the close ties between them, the nobility and clergy would control all decisions. As soon as the estates were called, the aristocratic Parlement of Paris ruled that the Estates General should once again sit separately. In response to protests from some reform-minded critics, the government agreed that the third estate should have as many delegates as the clergy and the nobility combined but then rendered this act meaningless by upholding voting by separate order.

Meeting in May 1789, the estates were almost immediately deadlocked. Delegates of the third estate refused to transact any business until the king ordered the clergy and nobility to sit with them in a single body. Finally, after a six-week war of nerves, a few parish priests began to go over to the third estate, which on June 17 voted to call itself the **"National Assembly."** On June 20 the delegates of the third estate, excluded from their hall because of "repairs," moved to a large indoor tennis court. There they swore the famous Oath of the Tennis Court, pledging not to disband until they had written a new constitution.

National Assembly *The first French revolutionary legislature, a constituent assembly made up primarily of representatives of the third estate and a few nobles and clergy who joined them, in session from 1789 to 1791.*

The king's response was ambivalent. On June 23 he made a conciliatory speech urging reforms to a joint session, and four days later he ordered the three estates to meet together. At the same time, the vacillating monarch apparently followed the advice of relatives and court nobles who urged him to dissolve the Estates General by force. Belatedly asserting his "divine right" to rule, the king called an army of eighteen thousand troops toward Versailles, and on July 11 he dismissed his finance minister and other liberal ministers.

The Revolt of the Poor and the Oppressed

While delegates of the third estate pressed for political rights, economic hardship gripped the common people. A poor grain harvest in 1788 caused the price of bread to soar, unleashing a classic economic depression of the preindustrial age. Demand for manufactured goods collapsed, and thousands were thrown out of work. By the end of 1789 almost half of the French people were in need of relief. In Paris perhaps 150,000 of the city's 600,000 people were unemployed in July 1789.

Against this background of political and economic crisis, the people of Paris entered decisively onto the revolutionary stage. They believed that they should have steady work and adequate bread at fair prices. They also feared that the dismissal of the king's moderate finance minister would put them at the mercy of aristocratic landowners and grain speculators. As rumors spread that the king's troops would sack the city, angry crowds formed and demanded action. On July 13 the people began to seize arms for the defense of the city, and on July 14 several hundred people marched to the Bastille in search of weapons.

The Bastille, once a medieval fortress, was a detested royal prison. Its panicked governor ordered his men to resist, killing ninety-eight people attempting to enter. Fighting continued until the prison surrendered. The next day a committee of citizens appointed the marquis de Lafayette commander of the city's armed forces. Paris was lost to the king, who was forced to recall the finance minister and disperse his troops. The popular uprising had saved the National Assembly. As the delegates resumed their debates, the countryside sent a radical message. Throughout France peasants began to rise against their lords, ransacking manor houses and burning feudal documents that recorded their obligations. In some areas peasants reinstated traditional village practices, undoing recent enclosures and reoccupying common lands. Fear of vagabonds and outlaws—called the **Great Fear** by contemporaries—seized the countryside and fanned the flames of rebellion. The long-suffering peasants were doing their best to free themselves from manorial rights and exploitation.

Great Fear *In the summer of 1789, the fear of vagabonds and outlaws that seized the French countryside and fanned the flames of revolution.*

In the end, they were successful. On the night of August 4, 1789, the delegates at Versailles agreed to abolish noble privileges—peasant serfdom where it still existed, exclusive hunting rights, fees for justice, village monopolies, and a host of other dues. Thus the French peasantry achieved an unprecedented victory in the early days of revolutionary upheaval. Henceforth, French peasants would seek mainly to protect their achievements. As the Great Fear subsided in the countryside, they became a force for order and stability.

A Limited Monarchy

The National Assembly moved forward. On August 27, 1789, it issued the Declaration of the Rights of Man, which stated, "Men are born and remain free and equal in rights." The declaration also maintained that mankind's natural rights are "liberty, property, security, and resistance to oppression" and that "every man is presumed innocent until he is proven guilty." As for law, "it is an expression of the general will; all citizens have the right to concur personally or through their representatives in its formation. . . . Free expression of thoughts and opinions is one of the most precious rights of mankind: every citizen may therefore speak, write, and publish freely." In short, this clarion call of the liberal revolutionary ideal guaranteed equality before the law, representative government for a sovereign people, and individual freedom. The declaration was disseminated throughout France and Europe and around the world.

Primary Source: The Declaration of Rights of Man and Citizen *This document, drafted by the National Assembly of France, is an Enlightenment cousin of Jefferson's Declaration.*

Moving beyond general principles to draft a constitution proved difficult. The questions of how much power the king should retain and whether he could veto legislation led to another deadlock. Once again the decisive answer came from the poor—in this instance, the poor women of Paris. Women customarily managed poor families' slender resources. The economic crisis worsened after the fall of the Bastille, as aristocrats fled the country and the luxury market collapsed. Foreign markets also shrunk, and unemployment grew.

On October 5 some seven thousand desperate women marched the twelve miles from Paris to Versailles to demand action. This great crowd invaded the Assembly, "armed with scythes, sticks and pikes." One tough old woman defiantly shouted into the debate, "Who's that talking down there? Make the chatterbox shut up. That's not the point: the point is that we want bread."[1] Hers was the genuine voice of the people, essential to any understanding of the French Revolution.

The women invaded the royal apartments, killed some of the royal bodyguards, and searched for the queen, Marie Antoinette, who was widely despised for her frivolous

a Versaille a Versaille. du 5. Octobre 1789.

● **The Women of Paris March to Versailles** On October 5, 1789, a large group of Parisian market women marched to Versailles to protest the price of bread. For the people of Paris, the king was the baker of last resort, responsible for feeding his people during times of scarcity. The crowd forced the royal family to return with them and to live in Paris, rather than remain isolated from their subjects at court. *(Erich Lessing/Art Resource, NY)*

and supposedly immoral behavior. The intervention of Lafayette and the National Guard saved the royal family from harm. But the only way to calm the disorder was for the king to live in Paris, as the crowd demanded.

The National Assembly followed the king to Paris, and the next two years, until September 1791, saw the consolidation of the liberal revolution. The National Assembly abolished the nobility as a legal order and pushed forward with the creation of a **constitutional monarchy,** which Louis XVI reluctantly accepted in July 1790. In the final constitution, the king remained the head of state, but lawmaking power was placed in the hands of the National Assembly. New laws broadened women's rights to seek divorce, to inherit property, and to obtain financial support for illegitimate children from fathers, but women were not allowed to hold political office or even vote. The men of the National Assembly believed that civic virtue would be restored if women focused on child rearing and domestic duties.

The National Assembly replaced the patchwork of historic provinces with eighty-three departments of approximately equal size. The jumble of weights and measures that varied from province to province was reformed, leading to the introduction of the metric system in 1793. Monopolies, guilds, and workers' associations were prohibited, and barriers to trade within France were abolished in the name of economic liberty. Thus the National Assembly applied the critical spirit of the Enlightenment in a thorough reform of France's laws and institutions.

The Assembly also imposed a radical reorganization on the country's religious life. It granted religious freedom to French Jews and Protestants. It nationalized the Catholic Church's property, used it as collateral to guarantee a new paper currency, the *assignats* and then sold the property in an attempt to put the state's finances on a solid footing.

Imbued with Enlightenment rationalism, delegates distrusted popular piety and "superstitious religion." Thus they established a national church with priests chosen

constitutional monarchy *A form of government in which the king retains his position as head of state, while the authority to tax and make new laws resides in an elected body.*

by voters. The National Assembly forced the Catholic clergy to take a loyalty oath to the new government. The pope formally condemned these actions, and only half of French priests swore the oath. Many sincere Christians, especially those in the countryside, were upset by these changes. The attempt to remake the Catholic Church, like the Assembly's abolition of guilds and workers' associations, sharpened the conflict between the educated classes and the common people that had been emerging in the eighteenth century.

Revolutionary Aspirations in Saint-Domingue

On the eve of the Revolution, French Saint-Domingue—the most profitable of all Caribbean colonies—was even more rife with social tensions than France itself. The island was composed of a variety of social groups who resented and mistrusted one another. The European population included French colonial officials, wealthy plantation owners and merchants, and poor immigrants. Greatly outnumbering the white population were the colony's five hundred thousand slaves, along with a sizable population of free people of African and mixed African European descent. This last group referred to it members as "free coloreds" or **"free people of color."**

free people of color *Free people of African or partly African descent living in the French isles of the Caribbean.*

The political turmoil of the 1780s, with its rhetoric of liberty, equality, and fraternity, raised new challenges and possibilities for each group. For slaves, abolitionist agitation in France and the royal government's attempts to rein in the abuses of slavery led to hope that the mother country might grant them freedom. Free people of color found in such rhetoric the principles on which to base claims for legal and political rights. They hoped for political enfranchisement and to regain legal rights that had been rescinded by colonial administrators. The white elite looked to revolutionary ideals of representative government for the chance to gain control of their own affairs, as had the American colonists before them. The meeting of the Estates General and the Declaration of the Rights of Man and Citizen raised these conflicting colonial aspirations to new levels.

The National Assembly, however, frustrated all of their hopes. It allowed each colony to draft its own constitution, with free rein over decisions on slavery and enfranchisement. After dealing this blow to the aspirations of slaves and free coloreds, the committee also reaffirmed French monopolies over colonial trade, thereby angering planters as well.

Following a failed revolt in Saint-Domingue led by Vincent Ogé, a free man of color, the National Assembly attempted a compromise. It granted political rights to free people of color born to two free parents who possessed sufficient property. The white elite of Saint-Domingue was furious, and the colonial governor refused to enact the legislation. Violence now erupted between groups of whites and free coloreds. The liberal revolution had failed to satisfy contradictory ambitions in the colonies.

WORLD WAR AND REPUBLICAN FRANCE (1791–1799)

How and why did the Revolution take a radical turn at home and in the colonies?

When Louis XVI accepted the National Assembly's constitution in September 1791, a young provincial lawyer and delegate named Maximilien Robespierre (1758–1794) concluded, "The Revolution is over." Robespierre was both right and wrong. He was right in the sense that the most constructive and lasting reforms were in place. Nothing substantial in the way of liberty and fundamental reform would be gained in the next generation. He was wrong in the sense that a much more radical stage lay ahead.

New heroes and new ideologies were to emerge in revolutionary wars and international conflict in which Robespierre himself would play a central role.

Foreign Reactions and the Beginning of War

Revolution in France produced great excitement and a sharp division of opinion in Europe and the United States. Liberals and radicals saw a mighty triumph of liberty over despotism. In Great Britain especially, they hoped that the French example would undo the landed elite's stronghold over Parliament. Conservative leaders, such as Edmund Burke (1729–1797), were deeply troubled by the Revolution. In 1790 Burke published *Reflections on the Revolution in France,* which defended inherited privileges in general and those of the English monarchy and aristocracy in particular. He predicted that thoroughgoing reform like that occurring in France would lead only to chaos and tyranny. Burke's work sparked much debate.

One passionate rebuttal came from a young writer in London, Mary Wollstonecraft (1759–1797). Incensed by Burke's book, Wollstonecraft wrote a blistering, widely read response, *A Vindication of the Rights of Man* (1790). Then she made a daring intellectual leap, developing for the first time the logical implications of natural-law philosophy in her masterpiece, *A Vindication of the Rights of Woman* (1792). To fulfill the still-unrealized potential of the French Revolution and to eliminate sexual inequality, she demanded that

the Rights of Women be respected . . . [and] JUSTICE for one-half of the human race. . . . It is time to effect a revolution in female manners, time to restore to them their lost dignity, and make them, as part of the human species, labor, by reforming themselves, to reform the world.

Wollstonecraft advocated rigorous coeducation, which would make women better wives and mothers, good citizens, and economically independent. Women could manage businesses and enter politics if only men would give them the chance. Wollstonecraft's analysis testified to the power of the Revolution to inspire outside of France. Paralleling ideas put forth independently in France by Olympe de Gouges (1748–1793), a self-taught writer and woman of the people (see the feature "Listening to the Past: Revolution and Women's Rights" on pages 638–639), Wollstonecraft's work marked the birth of the modern women's movement for equal rights.

European rulers, who had at first welcomed the revolution in France as weakening a competing monarchy, realized that their power was also threatened. In June 1791, Louis XVI and Marie-Antoinette were arrested and returned to Paris after trying unsuccessfully to slip out of France. The shock of this arrest led the monarchs of Austria and Prussia to issue the Declaration of Pillnitz in August 1791. This carefully worded statement declared their willingness to intervene in France in certain circumstances and was expected to prevent revolutionary excesses without causing war.

But the crowned heads of Europe misjudged France's revolutionary spirit. The representative body, known as the Legislative Assembly, that convened in October 1791 had new delegates and a different character. Most of the legislators were still prosperous and well-educated, but they were younger and less cautious than their predecessors. Many belonged to a political club called the **Jacobin club,** after the name of the former monastery in which they met. Such clubs had proliferated in Parisian neighborhoods since the beginning of the Revolution, drawing men and women to debate the burning political questions of the day.

The new Legislative Assembly representatives reacted with patriotic fury against the Declaration of Pillnitz. If the kings of Europe were attempting to incite war against France, then "we will incite a war of people against kings. . . . Ten million Frenchmen, kindled by the fire of liberty, armed with the sword, with reason, with eloquence

Jacobin club *In revolutionary France, a political club whose members were a radical republican group.*

● **The Capture of Louis XVI, June 1791**   This painting commemorates a dramatic turning point in the French Revolution, the midnight arrest of Louis XVI and the royal family as they tried to flee France in disguise and reach counter-revolutionaries in the Austrian Netherlands. Recognized and stopped at Varennes, the royal family was returned to house arrest in Paris. *(Bibliothèque nationale de France)*

would be able to change the face of the world and make the tyrants tremble on their thrones."[2] In April 1792 France declared war on Francis II, the Habsburg monarch.

France's crusade against tyranny went poorly at first. Prussian forces joined Austria against the French, who broke and fled at their first military encounter with this First Coalition. The road to Paris lay open, and it is possible that only conflict between the eastern monarchs over the division of Poland saved France from defeat.

The Legislative Assembly declared the country in danger, and volunteers rallied to the capital. In this supercharged atmosphere, rumors spread of treason by the king and queen. On August 10, 1792, a revolutionary crowd attacked the royal palace at the Tuileries, while the king and his family fled for their lives to the nearby Legislative Assembly. Rather than offering refuge, the Assembly suspended the king from all his functions, imprisoned him, and called for a new National Convention to be elected by universal male suffrage.

The Second Revolution

second revolution *From 1792 to 1795, the second phase of the French Revolution during which the fall of the French monarchy introduced a rapid radicalization of politics.*

The fall of the monarchy initiated a rapid radicalization of the Revolution, a phase often called the **second revolution**. Louis's imprisonment was followed by the September Massacres. Wild stories that imprisoned aristocrats and priests were plotting with the allied invaders seized the city. Angry crowds invaded the prisons of Paris and slaughtered half the men and women they found. In late September 1792 the new, popularly elected National Convention proclaimed France a republic.

The republic sought to create a new popular culture, fashioning symbols that broke with the past and glorified the new order. Its new revolutionary calendar eliminated saints' days and renamed the days and the months after the seasons of the year, while also adding secular holidays designed to instill a love of nation. These secular celebrations were less successful in villages, where Catholicism was stronger.

Girondists *A group contesting control of the National Convention in France; it was named after a department in southwestern France.*

All members of the National Convention were republicans, and at the beginning almost all belonged to the Jacobin club of Paris. But the Jacobins themselves were increasingly divided into two bitterly opposed groups—the **Girondists,** named after a department in southwestern France that was home to several of their leaders, and **the Mountain,** led by Robespierre and another young lawyer, Georges Jacques Danton. In Paris the National Convention was locked in a life-and-death political struggle between the Mountain and the more moderate Girondists. A majority of the indecisive Convention members, seated in the "Plain" below, floated back and forth between the rival factions.

the Mountain *The radical faction of the National Convention led by Robespierre. So called because its members sat in the uppermost benches on the left side of the assembly hall. The source of the modern division of political ideologies into "Left" and "Right."*

This division emerged clearly after the National Convention overwhelmingly convicted Louis XVI of treason. The Girondists accepted his guilt but did not wish to put the king to death. By a narrow majority, the Mountain carried the day, and Louis was executed on January 21, 1793, on the newly invented guillotine. Both the Girondists and the Mountain were determined to continue the "war against tyranny." The Prussians had been stopped at the Battle of Valmy in September 1792. French armies then invaded Savoy, moved into the German Rhineland, and by November 1792 were occupying the entire Austrian Netherlands (modern Belgium). Everywhere they went French armies of occupation chased the princes, abolished feudalism, and "liberated" the people.

But French armies also lived off the land, requisitioning supplies and plundering local treasures. The liberators looked increasingly like foreign invaders. International tensions mounted. In February 1793 the National Convention, at war with Austria and Prussia, declared war on Britain, Holland, and Spain as well. Republican France was now at war with almost all Europe, a great war that would last almost without interruption until 1815.

Conflict within France added to the turmoil. Peasants in western France revolted against being drafted into the army, and devout Catholics, royalists, and foreign agents encouraged their rebellion. In Paris the National Convention was locked in a life-and-death political struggle between the Girondists and the more moderate Mountain. With the political system bitterly divided, the laboring poor of Paris emerged as the decisive political factor. The laboring poor and the petty traders were often known as the **sans-culottes,** "without breeches," because their men wore trousers instead of the knee breeches of the aristocracy and bourgeoisie. The sans-culottes demanded radical political action to guarantee their daily bread. The Mountain joined with sans-culottes activists in the city government to engineer a popular uprising that forced the Convention to arrest thirty-one Girondist deputies for treason on June 2. All power passed to the Mountain.

sans-culottes *The name for the laboring poor of Paris, so called because the men wore trousers instead of the knee breeches of the aristocracy and middle class; it came to refer to the militant radicals of the city.*

The Convention also formed a Committee of Public Safety to deal with the threats to the Revolution. Led by Robespierre, the committee obtained dictatorial power. Moderates in leading provincial cities, such as Lyons and Marseilles, revolted against excessive central control. The peasant revolt also spread, and the republic's armies were driven back on all fronts. By July 1793 only the areas around Paris and on the eastern frontier were firmly held. Defeat seemed imminent.

The French Revolution

May 5, 1789	Estates General convene at Versailles.
June 17, 1789	Third estate declares itself the National Assembly.
June 20, 1789	Oath of the Tennis Court is sworn.
July 14, 1789	Storming of the Bastille occurs.
July–August 1789	Great Fear ravages the countryside.
August 4, 1789	National Assembly abolishes feudal privileges.
August 27, 1789	National Assembly issues Declaration of the Rights of Man.
October 5, 1789	Women march on Versailles and force royal family to return to Paris.
November 1789	National Assembly confiscates church lands.
July 1790	Civil Constitution of the Clergy establishes a national church. Louis XVI reluctantly agrees to accept a constitutional monarchy.
June 1791	Royal family is arrested while attempting to flee France.
August 1791	Austria and Prussia issue the Declaration of Pillnitz. Slave insurrections break out in Saint-Domingue.
April 1792	France declares war on Austria.
August 1792	Parisian mob attacks the palace and takes Louis XVI prisoner.
September 1792	September Massacres occur. National Convention declares France a republic and abolishes monarchy.
January 1793	Louis XVI is executed.
February 1793	France declares war on Britain, Holland, and Spain. Revolts take place in some provincial cities.
March 1793	Bitter struggle occurs in the National Convention between Girondists and the Mountain.
April–June 1793	Robespierre and the Mountain organize the Committee of Public Safety and arrest Girondist leaders.
September 1793	Price controls are instituted to aid the sans-culottes and mobilize the war effort. British troops invade Saint-Domingue.
1793–1794	Reign of Terror darkens Paris and the provinces.
February 1794	National Convention abolishes slavery in all French territories.
Spring 1794	French armies are victorious on all fronts.
July 1794	Robespierre is executed. Thermidorian reaction begins.
1795–1799	Directory rules.
1795	Economic controls are abolished, and suppression of the sans-culottes begins. Toussaint L'Ouverture named brigadier general.
1797	Napoleon defeats Austrian armies in Italy and returns triumphant to Paris.
1798	Austria, Great Britain, and Russia form the Second Coalition against France.
1799	Napoleon overthrows the Directory and seizes power.

Des Têtes !—du Sang !— la Mort ! —à la Lanterne !—à la Guillotine.—point de Reine !—Je suis la Deesse de la Liberté !— L'egalité !— que Londres soit brulé !— que Paris soit Libre !— Vive la Guillotine !—

Mfs Mary Stokes del.

A PARIS BELLE.

Pub. Feb.y 26.ᵗ 1794. by H. Humphrey Nᵒ 18. Old Bond Street

● **Contrasting Visions of the Sans-Culottes** The woman on the left, with her playful cat and calm simplicity, suggests how the French sans-culottes saw themselves as democrats and virtuous citizens. The ferocious sans-culotte harpy on the right, a creation of wartime England's vivid counter-revolutionary imagination, screams for more blood, more death: "I am the Goddess of Liberty! Long live the guillotine!" *(Bibliothèque nationale de France)*

Total War and the Terror

A year later, in July 1794, the Austrian Netherlands and the Rhineland were once again in the hands of French armies, and the First Coalition was falling apart. This remarkable reversal stemmed from the revolutionary government's success in harnessing, for perhaps the first time in history, the forces of a planned economy, revolutionary terror, and modern nationalism in a total war effort.

Robespierre and the Committee of Public Safety first collaborated with the fiercely patriotic sans-culottes to establish a **planned economy.** Rather than let supply and demand determine prices, the government set maximum allowable prices for key products. The most important was bread. Rationing was introduced, and bakers were permitted to make only the "bread of equality"—a brown bread made of a mixture of all available flours. The poor of Paris may not have eaten well, but at least they ate.

planned economy *In response to inflation and high unemployment, Robespierre and the government set maximum prices for products, rather than relying on supply and demand.*

They also worked, mainly to produce arms and munitions for the war effort. The government told craftsmen what to produce, nationalized many small workshops, and requisitioned raw materials and grain. The second revolution and the ascendancy of the sans-culottes had produced an embryonic emergency socialism, which thoroughly frightened Europe's propertied classes and had great influence on the subsequent development of socialist ideology.

Second, while radical economic measures supplied the poor with bread and the armies with weapons, the **Reign of Terror** (1793–1794) used revolutionary terror to solidify the home front. Special revolutionary courts tried "enemies of the nation" for political crimes. Some forty thousand French men and women were executed or died in prison. Another three hundred thousand suspects were arrested.

The third and perhaps most decisive element in the French republic's victory over the First Coalition was its ability to draw on the explosive power of patriotic dedication to a national mission. An essential part of modern **nationalism,** this commitment was something new in history. With their common identity newly reinforced by the ideas of popular sovereignty and democracy, large numbers of French people were stirred by a common loyalty. They developed an intense emotional commitment to the defense of the nation and saw the war as a life-and-death struggle between good and evil.

The fervor of nationalism combined with the all-out mobilization of resources made the French army virtually unstoppable. After August 1793 all unmarried young men were subject to the draft, resulting in the largest fighting force in the history of European warfare. French armed forces outnumbered their enemies almost four to one.[3] French generals used mass assaults at bayonet point to overwhelm the enemy. "No maneuvering, nothing elaborate," declared the fearless General Hoche. "Just cold steel, passion and patriotism."[4] By spring 1794 French armies were victorious on all fronts. The republic was saved.

Reign of Terror *The period from 1793 to 1794, during which Robespierre used revolutionary terror to solidify the home front of France. Some 40,000 French men and women were killed during this period.*

nationalism *Patriotic dedication to a national state and mission; it was a decisive element in the French republic's victory.*

● **Slave Revolt on Saint-Domingue** Starting in August 1791 the slaves of Saint-Domingue rose in revolt. (Giraudon/Art Resource, NY)

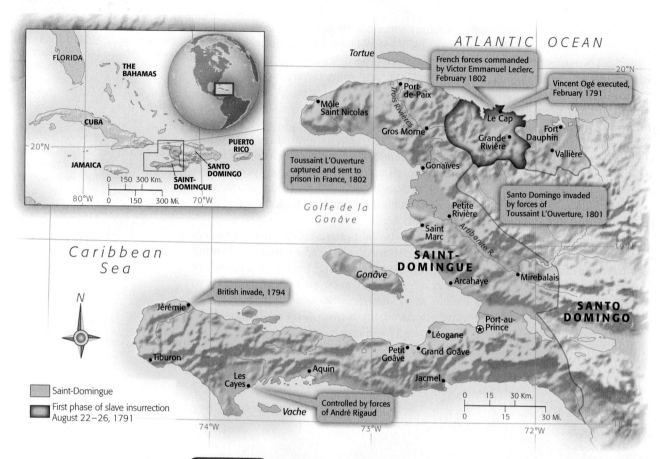

MAP 21.1   **The Haitian Revolution**   Neighbored by the Spanish colony of Santo Domingo, Saint-Domingue was the most profitable European colony in the Caribbean. In 1770 the French transferred the capital from Le Cap to Port-au-Prince, which became capital of the newly independent Haïti in 1804. Slave revolts erupted in the north, near Le Cap, in 1791.

Revolution in Saint-Domingue

The second stage of revolution in Saint-Domingue (see Map 21.1) also resulted from decisive action from below. In August 1791 groups of slaves organized a revolt that spread across much of the northern plain. By the end of August the uprising was "10,000 strong, divided into 3 armies, of whom 700 or 800 are on horseback, and tolerably well-armed."[5] During the next month slaves attacked and destroyed hundreds of sugar and coffee plantations.

On April 4, 1792, as war loomed with the European states, the National Assembly issued a decree enfranchising all free blacks and free people of color. This move was intended to gain loyalty against the slave rebellion and stabilize the colony, a vital source of income for the French state.

Less than two years later, on February 4, 1794, the Convention abolished slavery throughout its Caribbean colonies, and in 1795 granted former slaves full political rights. The National Convention was forced to make these concessions when Saint-Domingue came under siege from Spanish and British troops hoping to capture the profitable colony. With former slaves and free colored forces on their side, the French gradually regained control of the island in 1796.

The key leader in the French victory was General Toussaint L'Ouverture (1743–1803), who was named commander of the western province of Saint-Domingue. (See the feature "Individuals in Society: Toussaint L'Ouverture" on page 633.) The increasingly conservative nature of the French government, however, threatened to undo the gains made by former slaves and free people of color. As exiled planters gained a stronger voice in French policymaking, L'Ouverture and other local leaders grew ever more wary of what the future might hold.

The Thermidorian Reaction and the Directory (1794–1799)

With the French army victorious, Robespierre and the Committee of Public Safety relaxed emergency economic controls, but they extended the political Reign of Terror. In March 1794, he wiped out many of his critics as well as long-standing collaborators, including the famous orator Danton. A strange assortment of radicals and moderates in the Convention, knowing that they might be next, organized a conspiracy. They howled down Robespierre when he tried to speak to the National Convention on 9 Thermidor (July 27, 1794). The next day it was Robespierre's turn to face the guillotine.

As Robespierre's closest supporters were also put to death, France unexpectedly experienced a thorough reaction to the violence of the Reign of Terror. In a general way, this **Thermidorian reaction** recalled the early days of the Revolution. The middle-class professionals who had led the liberal revolution of 1789 reasserted their authority, drawing support from their own class, the provincial cities, and the better-off

Thermidorian reaction *The period after the execution of Robespierre in 1794; it was a reaction to the violence of the Reign of Terror.*

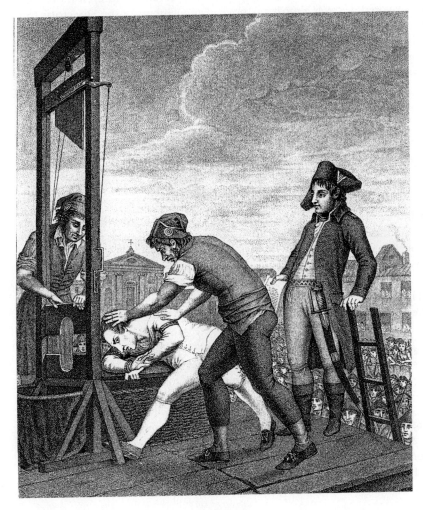

● **The Execution of Robespierre** The guillotine was painted red and was completely wooden except for the heavy iron blade. Large crowds witnessed the executions in a majestic public square in central Paris, then known as the Place de la Revolution and now called the Place de la Concorde (Harmony Square). *(Snark/Art Resource, NY)*

peasants. The National Convention abolished many economic controls, let prices rise sharply, and severely restricted the local political organizations where sans-culottes congregated.

The collapse of economic controls, coupled with runaway inflation, devastated the working poor. After the Convention used the army to suppress protest, the urban poor lost their revolutionary fervor. Excluded and disillusioned, they would have little interest in and influence on politics until 1830. The poor of the countryside turned toward religion as a relief from earthly cares. Rural women, especially, brought back the Catholic Church as the government began to soften its antireligious revolutionary stance.

As for the National Convention, in 1795 its members wrote yet another constitution that they believed would guarantee their economic position and political supremacy. As in previous elections, the mass of the population voted only for electors, whose number was cut back to men of substantial means. Electors then elected the members of a reorganized legislative assembly as well as key officials throughout France. The new assembly also chose a five-man executive—the Directory.

The Directory continued to support French military expansion abroad. War was no longer so much a crusade as a means to meet ever-present, ever-unsolved economic problems. Large, victorious French armies reduced unemployment at home and were able to live off the territories they conquered and plundered.

The unprincipled action of the Directory reinforced widespread disgust with war and starvation. This general dissatisfaction revealed itself clearly in the national elections of 1797, which returned a large number of conservative and even monarchist deputies who favored peace at almost any price. The members of the Directory, fearing for their skins, used the army to nullify the elections and began to govern dictatorially. Two years later Napoleon Bonaparte ended the Directory in a coup d'état and substituted a strong dictatorship for a weak one. The effort to establish stable representative government had failed.

THE NAPOLEONIC ERA (1799–1815)

What factors explain the rise and fall of Napoleon Bonaparte and his loss of the colony of Saint-Domingue?

For almost fifteen years, from 1799 to 1814, France was in the hands of a keen-minded military dictator of exceptional ability. One of history's most fascinating leaders, Napoleon Bonaparte (1769–1821) realized the need to put an end to civil strife in France in order to create unity and consolidate his rule. And he did. But Napoleon saw himself as a man of destiny, and the glory of war and the dream of universal empire proved irresistible. For years he spiraled from victory to victory, but in the end he was destroyed by a mighty coalition united in fear of his restless ambition.

Napoleon's Rule of France

In 1799 when he seized power, young General Napoleon Bonaparte was a national hero. Born in Corsica into an impoverished noble family in 1769, Napoleon left home and became a lieutenant in the French artillery. After a brief and unsuccessful adventure fighting for Corsican independence in 1789, he returned to France as a French patriot and a dedicated revolutionary. Rising rapidly in the new army, Napoleon was placed in command of French forces in Italy and won brilliant victories there in 1796 and 1797. His next campaign, in Egypt, was a failure, but Napoleon returned to France before the fiasco was generally known, and his reputation remained intact.

The Napoleonic Era

November 1799	Napoleon overthrows the Directory.
December 1799	French voters overwhelmingly approve Napoleon's new constitution.
1800	Napoleon founds the Bank of France.
1801	France defeats Austria and acquires Italian and German territories in the Treaty of Lunéville. Napoleon signs the Concordat with the pope.
February 1802	French forces arrive in Saint-Domingue.
March 1802	France signs the Treaty of Amiens with Britain.
August 1802	Napoleon restores slavery in French colonies.
April 1803	Toussaint L'Ouverture dies in France.
January 1804	Jean Jacques Dessalines declares Haitian independence.
March 1804	Napoleonic Code comes into force.
December 1804	Napoleon crowns himself emperor.
May 1805	First Haitian constitution promulgated.
October 1805	Britain defeats the French and Spanish fleet at the Battle of Trafalgar.
December 1805	Napoleon defeats Austria and Russia at the Battle of Austerlitz.
1807	Napoleon redraws the map of Europe in the treaties of Tilsit.
1810	The Grand Empire is at its height.
June 1812	Napoleon invades Russia with 600,000 men.
Fall–Winter 1812	Napoleon makes a disastrous retreat from Russia.
March 1814	Russia, Prussia, Austria, and Britain sign the Treaty of Chaumont, pledging alliance to defeat Napoleon.
April 1814	Napoleon abdicates and is exiled to Elba.
February–June 1815	Napoleon escapes from Elba and rules France until he is defeated at the Battle of Waterloo.

Napoleon soon learned that prominent members of the legislature were plotting against the Directory. Ten years of upheaval and uncertainty had convinced these disillusioned revolutionaries that a strong military ruler was needed to restore order. Together the conspirators and Napoleon organized a takeover. On November 9, 1799, they ousted the Directors, and the following day soldiers disbanded the legislature. Napoleon was named first consul of the republic, and a new constitution consolidating his position was overwhelmingly approved in a plebiscite in December 1799. Republican appearances were maintained, but Napoleon was the real ruler of France.

The essence of Napoleon's domestic policy was to use his great and highly personal powers to maintain order and end civil strife. He did so by working out unwritten agreements with powerful groups in France whereby the groups received favors in return for loyal service. Napoleon's bargain with the solid middle class was codified in the famous Civil Code of 1804, which reasserted two of the fundamental principles of the liberal revolution of 1789: equality of all male citizens before the law and absolute security of wealth and private property. Napoleon and the leading bankers of Paris established the privately owned Bank of France, which served the interests of both the state and the financial oligarchy. Peasants were also appeased when Napoleon defended the gains in land and status they had claimed during the revolution.

At the same time Napoleon perfected a thoroughly centralized state. He consolidated his rule by recruiting disillusioned revolutionaries for the network of ministers, prefects, and centrally appointed mayors that depended on him and came to serve him well. Only former revolutionaries who leaned too far to the left or to the right were excluded.[6] Nor were members of the old nobility slighted. In 1800 and 1802 Napoleon granted amnesty to one hundred thousand émigrés on the condition that they return to France and take a loyalty oath. Members of this returning elite soon occupied many high posts in the expanding centralized state. Napoleon also created a new imperial nobility to reward his most talented generals and officials.

Napoleon applied his diplomatic skills to healing the Catholic Church in France so that it could serve as a bulwark of order and social peace. Napoleon and Pope Pius VII (1800–1823) signed the Concordat of 1801. The pope gained the precious right for French Catholics to practice their religion freely, but Napoleon gained political power: his government now nominated bishops, paid the clergy, and exerted great influence over the church in France.

The domestic reforms of Napoleon's early years were his greatest achievement. Much of his legal and administrative reorganization has survived in France to this day. More generally, Napoleon's domestic initiatives gave the great majority of French people a welcome sense of stability and national unity.

Order and unity had a price: Napoleon's authoritarian rule. Women lost many of the gains they had made in the 1790s. Under the law of the new Napoleonic Code, women were dependents of either their fathers or their husbands, and they could not make contracts or even have bank accounts in their own names. Indeed, Napoleon and his advisers aimed at re-establishing a family monarchy, where the power of the husband and father was as absolute over the wife and the children as that of Napoleon was over his subjects.

Free speech and freedom of the press were continually violated. By 1811 only four newspapers were left, and they were little more than organs of government propaganda. The occasional elections were a farce. Later laws prescribed harsh penalties for political offenses, and people were watched carefully under an efficient spy system. There were about twenty-five hundred political prisoners in 1814.

Napoleon's Expansion in Europe

Napoleon was above all a military man, and a great one. After coming to power in 1799 he sent peace feelers to Austria and Great Britain, the two remaining members of the Second Coalition of 1798. When these overtures were rejected, French armies led by Napoleon decisively defeated the Austrians. In the Treaty of Lunéville (1801), Austria accepted the loss of almost all its Italian possessions, and German territory on the west bank of the Rhine was incorporated into France. The British agreed to the Treaty of Amiens in 1802, allowing France to remain in control of Holland, the Austrian Netherlands, the west bank of the Rhine, and most of the Italian peninsula. The Treaty of Amiens was a diplomatic triumph for Napoleon.

In 1802 Napoleon was secure but driven to expand his power. Aggressively redrawing the map of Germany so as to weaken Austria and encourage the secondary states of southwestern Germany to side with France, Napoleon tried to restrict British trade with all of Europe. He then plotted to attack Great Britain, but his Mediterranean fleet was virtually annihilated by Lord Nelson at the Battle of Trafalgar on October 21, 1805. Invasion of England was henceforth impossible. Renewed fighting had its

● **The Coronation of Napoleon, 1804 (detail)**   In this grandiose painting by Jacques-Louis David, Napoleon prepares to crown his wife, Josephine, in an elaborate ceremony in Notre Dame Cathedral. Napoleon, the ultimate upstart, also crowned himself. Pope Pius VII, seated glumly behind the emperor, is reduced to being a spectator. *(Louvre/Réunion des Musées Nationaux/Art Resource, NY)*

advantages, however, for the first consul used the wartime atmosphere to have himself proclaimed emperor in late 1804.

Austria, Russia, and Sweden joined with Britain to form the Third Coalition against France shortly before the Battle of Trafalgar. Actions such as Napoleon's assumption of the Italian crown had convinced both Alexander I of Russia and Francis II of Austria that Napoleon was a threat to their interests and to the European balance of power. Yet they were no match for Napoleon, who scored a brilliant victory over them at the Battle of Austerlitz in December 1805. Alexander I decided to pull back, and Austria accepted large territorial losses in return for peace as the Third Coalition collapsed.

Napoleon then proceeded to reorganize the German states. In 1806 he abolished many of the tiny German states as well as the ancient Holy Roman Empire and established by decree the German Confederation of the Rhine, a union of fifteen German states minus Austria, Prussia, and Saxony. Naming himself "protector" of the confederation, Napoleon firmly controlled western Germany.

Napoleon's intervention in German affairs alarmed the Prussians, who mobilized their armies after more than a decade of peace with France. Napoleon attacked and won two more brilliant victories in October 1806 at Jena and Auerstädt, where the Prussians were outnumbered two to one. The war with Prussia, now joined by Russia, continued into the following spring. After Napoleon's larger armies won another victory, Alexander I of Russia was ready to negotiate the peace. In the subsequent treaties of Tilsit, Prussia lost half of its population, while Russia accepted Napoleon's reorganization of western and central Europe and promised to enforce Napoleon's economic blockade against British goods.

The War of Haitian Independence

Another strong military leader was emerging in the French colonies. Toussaint L'Ouverture increasingly acted as an independent ruler of the western province of Saint-Domingue. This provoked another general, André Rigaud, to set up his own government in the southern peninsula, which had long been more isolated from France than the rest of the colony. Civil war broke out between the two sides in 1799, when L'Ouverture's forces, led by his lieutenant Jean Jacques Dessalines, invaded the south. Victory over Rigaud gave Toussaint control of the entire colony. (See the feature "Individuals in Society: Toussaint L'Ouverture.")

L'Ouverture's victory was soon challenged, however, by Napoleon's arrival in power. Napoleon intended to re-invigorate the Caribbean plantation economy as a basis for expanding French power. He ordered his brother-in-law General Charles-Victor-Emmanuel Leclerc to crush the new regime. In 1802 Leclerc landed in Saint-Domingue. Although Toussaint L'Ouverture cooperated with the French and turned his army over to them, he was arrested and deported, along with his family, to France, where he died in 1803. Jean Jacques Dessalines united the resistance under his command and led them to a crushing victory over the French forces. Of the fifty-eight thousand French soldiers, fifty thousand were lost in combat and to disease. On January 1, 1804, Dessalines formally declared the creation of the new sovereign nation of Haiti, the name used by the pre-Columbian inhabitants of the island. (France's other Caribbean colonies were not granted independence. Napoleon re-established slavery in 1802, and it remained in force until 1848.)

Haiti, the second independent state in the Americas and the first in Latin America, was thus born from the first successful large-scale slave revolt in history. As one recent historian of the Haitian revolution commented:

The insurrection of Saint-Domingue led to the expansion of citizenship beyond racial barriers despite the massive political and economic investment in the slave system at the time. If we live in a world in which democracy is meant to exclude no one, it is in no small part because of the actions of those slaves in Saint-Domingue who insisted that human rights were theirs too.[7]

The Grand Empire and Its End

Grand Empire *Napoleon's name for the European empire over which he intended to rule. This Grand Empire would consist of France, a number of lesser dependent states ruled by his relations, and several major allied states (Austria, Prussia, and Russia).*

Napoleon resigned himself to the loss of Saint-Domingue, but he still maintained imperial ambitions in Europe. Increasingly, he saw himself as the emperor of Europe and not just of France. The so-called **Grand Empire** he built had three parts. The core was an ever-expanding France, which by 1810 included Belgium, Holland, parts of northern Italy, and much German territory on the east bank of the Rhine. Beyond French borders Napoleon established the second part: a number of dependent satellite kingdoms ruled by members of his large family. The third part comprised the independent but allied states of Austria, Prussia, and Russia. After 1806 both satellites and allies were expected to support Napoleon's continental system and to cease trade with Britain.

The impact of the Grand Empire on the peoples of Europe was considerable. In the areas incorporated into France and in the satellites (see Map 21.2), feudal dues and serfdom were abolished. Yet Napoleon put the prosperity and special interests of France first in order to safeguard his power base. Levying heavy taxes in money and men for his armies, he came to be regarded more as a conquering tyrant than as an enlightened liberator. Thus French rule encouraged the growth of reactive

Toussaint L'Ouverture

Equestrian portrait of Toussaint L'Ouverture. *(Réunion des Musées Nationaux/Art Resource, NY)*

Little is known of the early life of the brilliant military and political leader Toussaint L'Ouverture. He was born in 1743 on a plantation outside Le Cap owned by the Count de Bréda. According to tradition, Toussaint was the eldest son of a captured African prince from modern-day Benin. Toussaint Bréda, as he was then called, occupied a privileged position among slaves. Instead of performing backbreaking labor in the fields, he served his master as a coachman and livestock keeper. He also learned to read and write French and some Latin, but he was always more comfortable in the Creole dialect.

During the 1770s the plantation manager emancipated Toussaint. After being freed, he leased his own small coffee plantation, worked by slaves. A devout Catholic who led a frugal and ascetic life, L'Ouverture impressed others with his enormous physical energy, intellectual acumen, and air of mystery. He married Suzanne Simone, who already had one son, and the couple had another son during their marriage.

Toussaint L'Ouverture entered history in 1791 when he joined the slave uprisings that swept Saint-Domingue. (At some point he took on the cryptic *nom de guerre* "l'ouverture" meaning "the opening.") Toussaint rose to prominence among rebel slaves allied with Spain and by early 1794 controlled his own army. In 1794 he defected to the French side and led his troops to a series of victories against the Spanish. In 1795 France's National Convention promoted L'Ouverture to brigadier general.

Over the next three years L'Ouverture successively eliminated rivals for authority on the island. First he freed himself of the French commissioners sent to govern the colony. With a firm grip on power in the northern province, Toussaint defeated General André Rigaud in 1800 to gain control in the south. His army then marched on the capital of Spanish Santo Domingo on the eastern half of the island, meeting little resistance. The entire island of Hispaniola was now under his command.

With control of Saint-Domingue in his hands, L'Ouverture was confronted with the challenge of building a post-emancipation society, the first of its kind. The task was made even more difficult by the chaos wreaked by war, the destruction of plantations, and bitter social and racial tensions. For L'Ouverture the most pressing concern was to re-establish the plantation economy. Without revenue to pay his army, the gains of the rebellion could be lost. He therefore encouraged white planters to return and reclaim their property. He also adopted harsh policies toward former slaves, forcing them back to their plantations and restricting their ability to acquire land. When they resisted, he sent troops across the island to enforce submission.

In 1801 L'Ouverture convened a colonial assembly to draft a new constitution that reaffirmed his draconian labor policies. The constitution named L'Ouverture governor for life, leaving Saint-Domingue as a colony in name alone. When news of the constitution arrived in France, an angry Napoleon dispatched General Leclerc to reestablish French control. In June 1802 Leclerc's forces arrested L'Ouverture and took him to France. He was jailed at Fort de Joux in the Jura Mountains near the Swiss border, where he died of pneumonia on April 7, 1803. It was left to his lieutenant, Jean Jacques Dessalines, to win independence for the new Haitian nation.

Questions for Analysis

1. Toussaint L'Ouverture was both slave and slave owner. How did each experience shape his life and actions?

2. Despite their differences, what did Toussaint L'Ouverture and Napoleon Bonaparte have in common? Why did they share a common fate?

MAP 21.2 Napoleonic Europe in 1810 Only Great Britain remained at war with Napoleon at the height of the Grand Empire. Many British goods were smuggled through Helgoland, a tiny but strategic British possession off the German coast.

Legend:
- French empire
- Dependent states
- Allied with Napoleon
- At war with Napoleon
- ★ Major battle

0 200 400 Km.
0 200 400 Mi.

ATLANTIC OCEAN

GREAT BRITAIN
London

North Sea

KINGDOM OF NORWAY AND DENMARK
Copenhagen

Baltic Sea

KINGDOM OF SWEDEN
Stockholm

St. Petersburg

RUSSIAN EMPIRE
Moscow
Borodino 1812 ★
Smolensk
Kiev

SWEDISH POMERANIA
Königsberg
Danzig
Tilsit
Friedland 1807 ★

PRUSSIA
Berlin

GRAND DUCHY OF WARSAW

Lübeck
Hamburg
Bremen
WESTPHALIA
Auerstädt 1806 ★
SAXONY
Jena 1806 ★

Rhine R.
Elbe R.
Neman R.

Brussels
Waterloo 1815 ★
Amiens
Paris
Lunéville

FRANCE

CONFEDERATION OF THE RHINE
BADEN
WÜRTTEMBERG
BAVARIA
Zurich
SWITZERLAND

Austerlitz 1805 ★
Wagram 1809 ★
Vienna
Pressburg
Buda Pest

AUSTRIAN EMPIRE

Danube R.

ILLYRIAN PROVINCES

Marseilles
Milan
Marengo 1800 ★
Genoa
KINGDOM OF ITALY

Corsica
Sardinia
Elba

Rome
Naples
KINGDOM OF NAPLES
Palermo
KINGDOM OF SICILY
Malta (Gr. Br.)

Mediterranean Sea

Ionian Is. (Gr. Br.)
Athens

OTTOMAN EMPIRE
Constantinople

Black Sea

PORTUGAL
Lisbon
Trafalgar 1805 ★

SPAIN
Madrid
GIBRALTAR (Gr. Br.)

10W
0
10E
20E
30E

● **The War in Spain**   This unforgettable etching by the Spanish painter Francisco Goya (1746–1828) comes from his famous collection "The Disasters of the War." A French firing squad executes captured Spanish rebels almost as soon as they are captured, an everyday event in a war of atrocities on both sides. Do you think these rebels are "terrorists" or "freedom fighters"? *(Foto Marburg/Art Resource, NY)*

nationalism, for individuals in different lands developed patriotic feelings of their own in opposition to Napoleon's imperialism.

The first great revolt occurred in Spain. In 1808 a coalition of Catholics, monarchists, and patriots rebelled against Napoleon's attempts to make Spain a French satellite with a Bonaparte as its king. Yet Napoleon pushed on, determined to hold his complex and far-flung empire together. In 1810, when the Grand Empire was at its height, Britain still remained at war with France, helping guerrillas in Spain and Portugal. The continental system, organized to exclude British goods from the continent and force that "nation of shopkeepers" to its knees, was a failure. Instead, it was France that suffered economically from Britain's counter-blockade. Perhaps looking for a scapegoat, Napoleon turned on Alexander I of Russia, who in 1811 openly repudiated Napoleon's war of prohibitions against British goods.

Napoleon's invasion of Russia began in June 1812 with a force that eventually numbered 600,000, probably the largest force yet assembled in a single army. Only one-third of this Great Army was French, however; nationals of all the satellites and allies were drafted into the operation. Napoleon reached Smolensk and recklessly pressed on toward Moscow. The great Battle of Borodino that followed was a draw, and the Russians retreated in good order. Alexander ordered the evacuation of Moscow, which then burned in part, and he refused to negotiate. Finally, after five weeks in the abandoned city, Napoleon ordered a retreat, one of the greatest disasters in military history. The Russian army, the Russian winter, and starvation cut Napoleon's army to pieces. When the frozen remnants staggered into Poland and Prussia in December, 370,000 men had died and another 200,000 had been taken prisoner.[8]

Leaving his troops to their fate, Napoleon raced to Paris to raise yet another army. Austria and Prussia deserted Napoleon and joined Russia and Great Britain in the Treaty of Chaumont in March 1814, by which the four powers pledged allegiance to defeat the French emperor. All across Europe patriots called for a "war of liberation" against Napoleon's oppression. Less than a month later, on April 4, 1814, a defeated Napoleon abdicated his throne. The victorious allies granted Napoleon the island of Elba off the coast of Italy as his own tiny state. Napoleon was even allowed to keep his imperial title, and France was required to pay him a yearly income of 2 million francs.

The allies also agreed to the restoration of the Bourbon dynasty under Louis XVIII (r. 1814–1824). The new monarch tried to gain support by issuing the Constitutional Charter, which accepted many of France's revolutionary changes and guaranteed civil liberties. Yet Louis XVIII—old, ugly, and crippled by gout—lacked the glory and magic of Napoleon. Sensing an opportunity, Napoleon staged a daring escape from Elba in February 1815. Landing in France, he issued appeals for support and marched on Paris with a small band of followers. Louis XVIII fled, and once more Napoleon took command. But Napoleon's gamble was a desperate long shot, for the allies were united against him. At the end of a frantic period known as the Hundred Days, they crushed his forces at Waterloo on June 18, 1815, and imprisoned him on the rocky island of St. Helena, off the western coast of Africa. Louis XVIII recommenced his reign. The allies now dealt more harshly with the apparently incorrigible French. As for Napoleon, he took revenge by writing his memoirs, skillfully nurturing the myth that he had been Europe's revolutionary liberator, a romantic hero whose lofty work had been undone by oppressive reactionaries. An era had ended.

Chapter Summary

Key Terms

desacralization
Assembly of Notables
Estates General
National Assembly
Great Fear
constitutional monarchy
free people of color
Jacobin club
second revolution
Girondists
the Mountain
sans-culottes
planned economy
Reign of Terror
nationalism
Thermidorian reaction
Grand Empire

To assess your mastery of this chapter, go to
bedfordstmartins.com/mckayworld

• *What social, political, and economic factors formed the background to the French Revolution?*

The French Revolution was forged by multiple and complex factors. French society had undergone significant transformations during the eighteenth century, which dissolved many economic and social differences among elites without removing the legal distinction between them. These changes were accompanied by political struggles between the monarchy and its officers, particularly in the high law courts. Emerging public opinion focused on the shortcomings of monarchical rule in political and personal terms. With their sacred royal aura severely tarnished, Louis XV and his successor Louis XVI found themselves unable to respond to the financial crises generated by war and public debt. Louis XVI's half-hearted efforts to redress the situation were quickly overwhelmed by demands for fundamental reform.

• *What were the immediate events and ideas that sparked the Revolution in France and its Caribbean colony of Saint-Domingue?*

Forced to call a meeting of the Estates General for the first time since 1614, Louis XVI fell back on the traditional formula of one vote for each of the three orders of society. Debate over the composition of the assembly called forth a bold new paradigm: that the Third Estate in itself constituted the French nation. By 1791 the National Assembly had eliminated Old Regime privileges and had established a constitutional monarchy. Talk in France of liberty, equality, and fraternity raised contradictory aspirations among the wealthy white planters, free people of color, and African slaves of the colony of Saint-Domingue. All looked to the Revolution for a better future, a promise that could not be fulfilled for all.

• How and why did the Revolution take a radical turn at home and in the colonies?

With the execution of the royal couple and the declaration of terror as the order of the day, the French Revolution took an increasingly radical turn from the summer of 1792. Fears of counter-revolutionary conspiracy combined with the outbreak of war convinced many that the Revolution was vulnerable and must be defended against its multiple enemies. In a spiraling cycle of accusations and executions, the Jacobins eliminated political opponents and then factions within their own party. The Directory government that took power after the fall of Robespierre restored political equilibrium at the cost of his platform of social equality. In the colonies, slave revolt and the pressure of war led to the abolition of slavery and the enfranchisement of free people of color and former slaves.

• What factors explain the rise and fall of Napoleon Bonaparte and his loss of the colony of Saint-Domingue?

Wearied by the Directory's weaknesses, conspirators gave Napoleon Bonaparte control of France. His military brilliance, his charisma and determination made him seem ideal to lead France to victory over its enemies. As is so often the case in history, Napoleon's relentless ambitions ultimately led to his downfall. His story is paralleled by that of Toussaint L'Ouverture, another soldier who emerged to the political limelight from the chaos of revolution only to endure exile and defeat.

As complex as its origins are, the legacies of the French Revolution included liberalism, assertive nationalism, radical democratic republicanism, embryonic socialism, self-conscious conservatism, abolitionism, decolonization, and movements for racial and sexual equality. The Revolution also left a rich and turbulent history of electoral competition, legislative assemblies, and even mass politics. Thus the French Revolution presented a range of political options and alternative visions of the future. For this reason, it was truly the revolution in modern European politics.

Suggested Reading

Bell, David A. *The Cult of the Nation in France: Inventing Nationalism, 1680–1800.* 2001. Traces early French nationalism through its revolutionary culmination.

Blanning, T. C. W. *The French Revolutionary Wars (1787–1802).* 1996. A masterful account of the revolutionary wars that also places the French Revolution in its European context.

Broers, Michael. *Europe Under Napoleon.* 2002. Probes Napoleon's impact on the territories he conquered.

Connelly, Owen. *The French Revolution and Napoleonic Era.* 1991. An excellent introduction to the French Revolution and Napoleon.

Desan, Suzanne. *The Family on Trial in Revolutionary France.* 2004. Studies the effects of revolutionary law on the family, including the legalization of divorce.

Dubois, Laurent. *Avengers of the New World: The Story of the Haitian Revolution.* 2004. An excellent and highly readable account of the revolution that transformed the French colony of Saint-Domingue into the independent state of Haiti.

Englund, Steven. *Napoleon: A Political Life.* 2004. A good biography of the French emperor.

(continued on page 640)

Listening to the PAST

Revolution and Women's Rights

The 1789 Declaration of the Rights of Man was a revolutionary call for legal equality, representative government, and individual freedom that excluded women from its manifesto. Among those who saw the contradiction in granting supposedly universal rights to only half the population was Marie Gouze (1748–1793), known to history as Olympe de Gouges. The daughter of a provincial butcher and peddler, she pursued a literary career in Paris after the death of her husband. De Gouges's great work was her "Declaration of the Rights of Woman" (1791). Excerpted here, it called on males to end their oppression of women and to give women equal rights. A radical on women's issues, de Gouges sympathized with the monarchy and criticized Robespierre in print. Convicted of sedition, she was guillotined in November 1793.

. . . Man, are you capable of being just? . . . Tell me, what gives you sovereign empire to oppress my sex? Your strength? Your talents? Observe the Creator in his wisdom . . . and give me, if you dare, an example of this tyrannical empire. Go back to animals, consult the elements, study plants . . . and distinguish, if you can, the sexes in the administration of nature. Everywhere you will find them mingled; everywhere they cooperate in harmonious togetherness in this immortal masterpiece.

Man alone has raised his exceptional circumstances to a principle. . . . [H]e wants to command as a despot a sex which is in full possession of its intellectual faculties; he pretends to enjoy the Revolution and to claim his rights to equality in order to say nothing more about it.

DECLARATION OF THE RIGHTS OF WOMAN AND THE FEMALE CITIZEN

. . . Mothers, daughters, sisters and representatives of the nation demand to be constituted into a national assembly. Believing that ignorance, omission, or scorn for the rights of woman are the only causes of public

misfortunes and of the corruption of governments, [the women] have resolved to set forth in a solemn declaration the natural, inalienable, and sacred rights of woman. . . .

I. Woman is born free and lives equal to man in her rights. Social distinctions can be based only on the common utility.

II. The purpose of any political association is the conservation of the natural and imprescriptible rights of woman and man; these rights are liberty, property, security, and especially resistance to oppression.

III. The principle of all sovereignty rests essentially with the nation, which is nothing but the union of woman and man. . . .

IV. Liberty and justice consist of restoring all that belongs to others; thus, the only limits on the exercise of the natural rights of woman are perpetual male tyranny; these limits are to be reformed by the laws of nature and reason.

V. Laws of nature and reason proscribe all acts harmful to society. . . .

VI. The law must be the expression of the general will; all female and male citizens must contribute either personally or through their representatives to its formation; it must be the same for all: male and female citizens, being equal in the eyes of the law, must be equally admitted to all honors, positions, and public employment according to their capacity and without other distinctions besides those of their virtues and talents. . . .

IX. Once any woman is declared guilty, complete rigor is [to be] exercised by the law.

X. No one is to be disquieted for his very basic opinions; woman has the right to mount the scaffold; she must equally have the right to mount the rostrum, provided that her demonstrations do not disturb the legally established public order.

XI. The free communication of thoughts and opinions is one of the most precious rights of woman, since that liberty assures the recognition of children by their fathers. Any female citizen thus may say freely, I am the mother of a child which belongs to you, without being forced by a barbarous prejudice to hide the truth. . . .

XIII. For the support of the public force and the expenses of administration, the contributions of woman and man are equal; she shares all the duties . . . and all the painful tasks; therefore, she must have the same share in the distribution of positions, employment, offices, honors, and jobs. . . .

XVI. No society has a constitution without the guarantee of rights and the separation of powers; the constitution is null if the majority of individuals comprising the nation have not cooperated in drafting it.

XVII. Property belongs to both sexes whether united or separate; for each it is an inviolable and sacred right.

Olympe de Gouges in 1784; aquatint by Madame Aubry (1748–1793). *(Musée de la Ville de Paris, Musée Carnavalet, Paris, France/The Bridgeman Art Library)*

Questions for Analysis

1. On what basis did de Gouges argue for gender equality? Did she believe in natural law?

2. What consequences did "scorn for the rights of woman" have for France, according to de Gouges?

3. Did de Gouges stress political rights at the expense of social and economic rights? If so, why?

Source: Olympe de Gouges, "Declaration of the Rights of Woman," in *Women in Revolutionary Paris, 1789–1795: Selected Documents Translated with Notes and Commentary*. Translated with notes and commentary by Darline Gay Levy, Harriet Branson Applewhite, and Mary Durham Johnson. Copyright © 1979 by the Board of Trustees, University of Illinois. Used with permission of the editors and the University of Illinois Press.

Hunt, Lynn. *Politics, Culture and Class in the French Revolution,* 2d ed. 2004. A pioneering examination of the French Revolution as a cultural phenomenon that generated new festivals, clothing, and songs and even a new calendar.

Landes, John B. *Visualizing the Nation: Gender, Representation, and Revolution in Eighteenth-Century France.* 2001. Analyzes images of gender and the body in revolutionary politics.

Schechter, Ronald. *Obstinate Hebrews: Representations of Jews in France, 1715–1815.* An illuminating study of Jews and attitudes toward them in France from Enlightenment to emancipation.

Sutherland, Donald. *France, 1789–1815.* 1986. An overview of the French Revolution that emphasizes its many opponents as well as its supporters.

Tackett, Timothy. *When the King Took Flight.* 2003. An exciting re-creation of the royal family's doomed effort to escape from Paris.

Notes

1. G. Pernoud and S. Flaisser, eds., *The French Revolution* (Greenwich, Conn.: Fawcett, 1960), p. 61.

2. Quoted in L. Gershoy, *The Era of the French Revolution, 1789–1799* (New York: Van Nostrand, 1957), p. 150.

3. T. Blanning, *The French Revolutionary Wars, 1787–1802* (London: Arnold, 1996), pp. 116–128.

4. 10. Quoted ibid., p. 123.

5. Quoted in Laurent Dubois, *Avengers of the New World: The Story of the Haitian Revolution* (Cambridge: Harvard University Press, 2004), p. 97.

6. I. Woloch, *Napoleon and His Collaborators: The Making of a Dictatorship* (New York: W. W. Norton, 2001), pp. 36–65.

7. Quoted in Laurent Dubois, *Avengers of the New World: The Story of the Haitian Revolution* (Cambridge: Harvard University Press, 2004), p. 3.

8. D. Sutherland, France, *1789–1815: Revolution and Counterrevolution* (New York: Oxford University Press, 1986), p. 420.

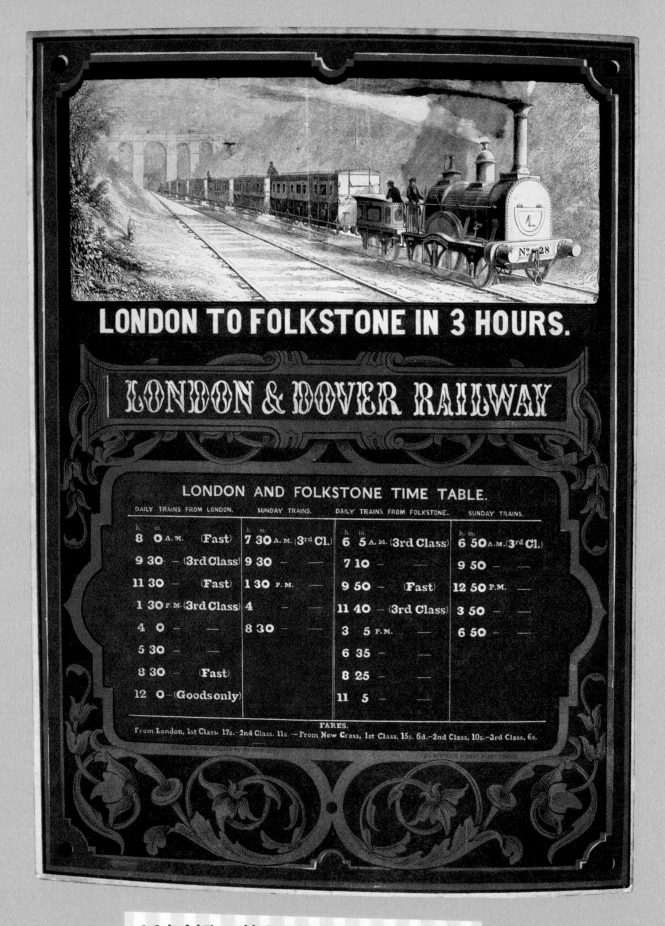

A Colorful Timetable Poster lists the trains from London to Folkstone, the English Channel's gateway port to the European continent, and proudly proclaims the speed of the journey. *(The Bridgeman Art Library)*

22 THE INDUSTRIAL REVOLUTION IN EUROPE, CA. 1780–1860

Chapter Preview

The Initial Breakthrough in England
• *What were the origins of the Industrial Revolution in England?*

Energy and Transportation
• *What changes in England revolutionized the provision of energy and transportation?*

Industrialization in Continental Europe
• *How after 1815 did continental countries respond to the challenge of industrialization?*

Capital and Labor
• *How did the Industrial Revolution affect social classes, the standard of living, and working conditions?*

While the Revolution in France was opening a new political era, another revolution was transforming economic and social life. The Industrial Revolution, which began in England around the 1780s, started to influence continental Europe and the rest of the world after 1815. Because the Industrial Revolution was less dramatic than the French Revolution, some historians see industrial development as basically moderate and evolutionary. From a long-term global perspective, however, it was rapid and brought about radical changes. Perhaps only the development of agriculture during Neolithic times had a similar impact and significance.

The Industrial Revolution profoundly modified much of human experience. It changed patterns of work, transformed the social class structure, and altered the international balance of political and military power, giving added impetus to ongoing Western expansion into non-Western lands. The Industrial Revolution also helped ordinary people gain a higher standard of living.

Unfortunately, improvement in the European standard of living was quite limited until about 1850, for at least two reasons. First, even in England only a few key industries experienced a technological revolution. Many more industries continued to use old methods, especially on the European continent, and this held down the increase in total production. Second, the increase in Europe's total population, which began in the eighteenth century, continued as the era of the Industrial Revolution unfolded. As a result, the rapid growth in population threatened—quite literally—to eat up the growth in production and to leave individuals poorer than ever. Chapter 23 will examine accompanying changes in urban living, and Chapters 24 and 25 will probe the consequences of industrialization in Europe for world history.

THE INITIAL BREAKTHROUGH IN ENGLAND

What were the origins of the Industrial Revolution in England?

The Industrial Revolution began in England. It was something new in history, and it was quite unplanned. With no models to copy and no idea of what to expect, England had to pioneer not only in industrial technology but also in social relations and urban living. Between 1793 and 1815 almost constant war with France complicated these formidable tasks.

Eighteenth-Century Origins

Although many aspects of the Industrial Revolution are still matters for scholarly debate, it is generally agreed that the industrial changes that did occur grew out of a complex combination of factors. These factors came together in eighteenth-century England and initiated a decisive breakthrough that many place in the 1780s.

In analyzing the causes of the late-eighteenth-century acceleration in the English economy, historians have paid particular attention to dramatic changes in agriculture, foreign trade, technology, energy supplies, and transportation. Although this chapter focuses on those issues, one must first understand that England had other, less conspicuous assets that favored the long process of development that culminated in industrial breakthrough.

Relatively good government was one such asset. The monarchy and the aristocratic oligarchy, which jointly ruled the country after the constitutional settlement of 1688, provided stable and predictable government. Neither civil strife nor invading armies threatened peace. Thus the government let the domestic economy operate fairly freely and with few controls, encouraging personal initiative, technological change, and a free market.

A related asset was an experienced business class with modern characteristics. This business class, which traced its origins to the Middle Ages, eagerly sought to make profits and to accumulate capital. England also had a large class of hired agricultural laborers. These rural wage earners were relatively mobile—compared with village-bound peasants in France and western Germany, for example—and along with cottage workers they formed a potential labor force for capitalist entrepreneurs.

Several other assets supporting English economic growth stand out. First, unlike its rival France as well as most other countries, England had an effective central bank and well-developed credit institutions. Second, although England may seem a rather small country today, it undoubtedly enjoyed the largest effective domestic market in eighteenth-century Europe. In an age when shipping goods by water was much cheaper than shipping goods by land, no part of England was more than twenty miles from navigable water. Beginning in the 1770s a canal-building boom greatly enhanced this natural advantage. Nor were there any tariffs within the country to hinder trade, as there were in France before 1789 and in politically fragmented Germany and Italy. Finally, only in Holland did the lower classes appear to live as well as in England. The ordinary English family did not have to spend almost everything it earned just to buy bread. It could spend more on other items, thereby adding significantly to the growing demand for manufactured goods that was a critical factor in initiating England's industrial breakthrough.

All these factors combined to bring about the **Industrial Revolution,** a term coined in the 1830s by awed contemporaries to describe the burst of major inventions and technical changes that they had witnessed in certain industries. This technical revolution went hand in hand with an impressive quickening in the annual rate of industrial

Industrial Revolution *A term coined in the 1830s to describe the burst of major inventions and technical changes in certain industries.*

growth in England. Thus industry grew at only 0.7 percent per year between 1700 and 1760—before the Industrial Revolution—but it grew at the much higher rate of 3 percent between 1801 and 1831, when industrial transformation was in full swing.[1] The decisive quickening of growth probably came in the 1780s, after the American War of Independence and just before the French Revolution.

The economic and political revolutions that shaped the modern world occurred almost simultaneously. The Industrial Revolution, however, was a longer process. It was not complete in England until about 1850, and it had no real impact on continental European countries until after the Congress of Vienna (see page 676) ended the era of revolutionary wars in Europe in 1815.

The Agricultural Revolution

A gradual but profound revolution in agricultural methods promoted accelerated economic growth. In essence, the **agricultural revolution** eliminated the traditional pattern of village agriculture found in northern and central Europe. It replaced the medieval **open-field system** and the annual fallowing of some fields with a new system of continuous rotation that resulted in more food for humans and their animals. The new agricultural system had profound implications, for it eliminated long-standing **common rights** as well as the fallow. But whereas peasants and rural laborers checked the spread of the new system on the continent of Europe in the eighteenth century, large landowners and powerful market forces overcame such opposition in England.

The new methods of agriculture originated in the Low Countries. The vibrant, dynamic middle-class society of seventeenth-century republican Holland was the most advanced in Europe in many areas of human endeavor, including agriculture. By 1650 intensive farming was well established throughout much of the Low Countries. Enclosed fields, continuous rotation, heavy manuring, and a wide variety of crops—all these innovations were present. Agriculture was highly specialized and commercialized. The Low Countries became "the Mecca of foreign agricultural experts who came . . . to see Flemish agriculture with their own eyes, to write about it and to propagate its methods in their home lands."[2]

The English were the best students. They learned about water control from Dutch experts, who made a great contribution to draining the extensive marshes, or fens, of wet and rainy England. Dutch practice also encouraged improvements in livestock through selective breeding. By 1740 agricultural improvement had become a craze among the English aristocracy.

By the mid-eighteenth century English agriculture was in the process of a radical and technologically desirable transformation. The eventual result was that by 1870 English farmers produced 300 percent more food than they had produced in 1700, although the number of people working the land had increased by only 14 percent. This great surge of agricultural production provided food for England's rapidly growing urban population. It was a remarkable achievement.

Chronology

ca. 1765	Hargreaves invents spinning jenny
1769	Watt creates modern steam engine
1775–1783	American Revolution
1780–1851	Population boom in England
1780s–1850	Industrial Revolution in England
1789–1799	French Revolution
1798	Malthus, *Essay on the Principle of Population*
1799	Combination Acts passed
1810	Strike of Manchester cotton spinners
1812	First Luddite attacks on factories
1824	Combination Acts repealed
1830	Stephenson's *Rocket,* first effective steam locomotive
1833	Factory Act
1842	Mines Act
1844	Engels, *The Condition of the Working Class in England*
1851	Great Exposition held at Crystal Palace

agricultural revolution *A gradual but profound change in agricultural methods that promoted accelerated economic growth.*

open-field system *A system of village farming developed by peasants where the land was divided into several large fields, which were in turn cut into strips.*

common rights *The shared use of agriculture land; it was abolished with the enclosure movement.*

enclosure *The enclosing of the individual shares of the pastures as a way of farming more effectively.*

Technological progress in agriculture had a cost. The impetus for enclosing the fields came mainly from the powerful ruling class—the English landowning aristocracy, who benefited directly from higher yields that could support higher rents. The large landowners controlled Parliament, which made the laws. They had Parliament pass hundreds of "enclosure acts," each of which authorized the fencing of open fields in a given village and the division of the common lands in proportion to one's property in the open fields. The division of the heavy legal and surveying costs of **enclosure** among the landowners meant that many peasants who had small holdings had to sell out to pay their share of the expenses. Similarly, landless cottagers lost their age-old access to the common pasture but received no compensation.

By eliminating common rights and greatly reducing the access of poor men and women to the land, the eighteenth-century enclosure movement marked the completion of two major historical developments in England: the rise of market-oriented estate agriculture and the emergence of a landless proletariat. By 1815 a tiny minority of wealthy English (and Scottish) landowners held most of the land and pursued profits aggressively, leasing their holdings through agents to middle-size farmers at competitive prices. These farmers produced mainly for cash markets and relied on landless laborers for their workforce. In strictly economic terms these landless laborers may have lived as well in 1800 as in 1700, but they had lost that bit of independence and self-respect that common rights had provided. They had become completely dependent on cash wages. In no other European country had this **proletarianization**—this transformation of large numbers of small peasant farmers into landless rural wage earners—gone as far as it had in England by the late eighteenth century. England's village poor found the cost of economic change and technological progress heavy and unjust.

proletarianization *The transformation of large numbers of small peasant farmers into landless rural wage earners.*

The Growth of Foreign Trade

In the eighteenth century Great Britain (formed in 1707 by the union of England and Scotland into a single kingdom) also became the leading maritime power, dominating long-distance trade, particularly intercontinental trade across the Atlantic. This foreign trade stimulated the economy.

Britain's commercial leadership in the eighteenth century had its origins in the mercantilism of the seventeenth century. European **mercantilism** was a system of economic regulations aimed at increasing the power of the state. It rested on the general premise that a nation's power and wealth were determined by its supply of precious metals, which were to be acquired by increasing exports (paid for with gold) and reducing imports to achieve domestic self-sufficiency. What distinguished English mercantilism was the unusual idea that government economic regulations could and should serve the private interests of individuals and groups as well as the public needs of the state.

mercantilism *The prevailing economic theory of European nations in the sixteenth and seventeenth centuries. Mercantilism remained the dominant theory until the Industrial Revelation and articulation of the theory of laissez faire.*

The seventeenth-century Navigation Acts reflected the desire of Great Britain to increase both its military power and its private wealth. The initial target of these instruments of economic warfare was the Netherlands, which was far ahead of the English in shipping and foreign trade in the mid-seventeenth century. By the later seventeenth century, after three Anglo-Dutch wars, the Netherlands was falling behind England in shipping, trade, and colonies. France then stood clearly as England's most serious rival in the competition for overseas empire. Thus from 1701 to 1763 Britain and France were locked in a series of wars to decide, in part, which nation would become Europe's leading maritime power and claim the lion's share of the profits of Europe's overseas expansion.

The first round was the War of the Spanish Succession, which resulted in major gains for Great Britain in the Peace of Utrecht (1713). France ceded Newfoundland, Nova Scotia, and the Hudson Bay territory to Britain. Spain was compelled to give

Britain control of the lucrative West African slave trade—the so-called *asiento*—and to let Britain send one ship of merchandise into the Spanish colonies annually.

The Seven Years' War (1756–1763) was the decisive round in the Franco-British competition for colonial empire. With the Treaty of Paris (1763) France lost all its possessions on the mainland of North America and gave up most of its holdings in India as well. By 1763 Britain had realized its goal of monopolizing a vast trade and colonial empire for its benefit.

This interconnected expansion of trade and empire marked a major step toward the Industrial Revolution, although people could not know it at the time. Protected colonial markets provided a great stimulus for many branches of English manufacturing. The value of the sales of manufactured products to the Atlantic economy—primarily the mainland colonies of North America and the West Indian sugar islands, with an important assist from West Africa and Latin America—soared from 1700 to 1773. English exports of manufactured goods to continental Europe grew hardly at all in these years.

English exports became much more balanced and diversified. To America and Africa went large quantities of metal items—axes to frontiersmen, firearms, chains for slave owners. Also exported were clocks and coaches, buttons and saddles, china and furniture, musical instruments and scientific equipment, and a host of other things. Thus the mercantile system established in the seventeenth century continued to shape trade in the eighteenth century, and the English concentrated in their hands much of the demand for manufactured goods from the growing Atlantic economy. Sales to other "colonies"—Ireland and India—also rose substantially in the eighteenth century. Nor was this all. Demand from the well-integrated home market was also rising. Thus growing demand from home and abroad put intense pressure on the whole system of production.

The First Factories

The pressure to produce more goods for a growing market was directly related to the first decisive breakthrough of the Industrial Revolution—the creation of the world's first large factories in the English cotton textile industry. Technological innovations in the manufacture of cloth led to a whole new pattern of production and social relationships. No other industry experienced such a rapid or complete transformation before 1830.

Although merchant-capitalists "put out" raw materials to cottage workers for processing and payment all across Europe in the late eighteenth century, this pattern of rural industry was most fully developed in England. Thus it was in England, under the pressure of growing demand for more production, that the putting-out system's shortcomings first began to outweigh its advantages—especially in the cottage textile industry after about 1760.

There was always a serious imbalance in this family enterprise: the work of four or five spinners was needed to keep one weaver steadily employed. The wife and the husband had constantly to try to find more thread and more spinners. Widows and unmarried women—"spinsters" who spun for their living—were recruited by the wife. Or perhaps the weaver's son went off on horseback to seek thread.

Deep-seated conflict between workers and employers complicated increased production. In "The Clothier's Delight, or the Rich Men's Joy and the Poor Men's Sorrow," an English popular song written about 1700, a merchant boasts of his countless tricks used to "beat down wages":

We heapeth up riches and treasure great store
Which we get by griping and grinding the poor.
And this is a way for to fill up our purse
Although we do get it with many a curse.[3]

● **Woman Working a Hargreaves's Spinning Jenny** The loose cotton strands on the slanted bobbins passed up to the sliding carriage and then on to the spindles in back for fine spinning. The worker, almost always a woman, regulated the sliding carriage with one hand and with the other she turned the crank on the wheel to supply power. By 1783 one woman could spin by hand a hundred threads at a time on an improved model. *(Mary Evans Picture Library)*

There were constant disputes over the weights of materials and the quality of the cloth. Merchants accused workers of stealing raw materials, and weavers complained that merchants delivered underweight bales. Both were right; each tried to cheat the other, even if only in self-defense.

There was another problem, at least from the merchant-capitalist's point of view. Scattered rural labor was cheap but hard to control. Cottage workers tended to work in spurts. After they got paid on Saturday afternoon, the men in particular tended to drink and carouse for two or three days. By the end of the week the weaver was probably working feverishly to make his quota. But if he did not succeed, there was little the merchant could do. The merchant-capitalist's search for more efficient methods of production intensified.

Attention focused on ways of improving spinning. Many a tinkering worker knew that a better spinning wheel promised rich rewards. It proved hard to spin the traditional raw materials—wool and flax—with improved machines, but cotton was different. Cotton textiles had first been imported into England from India by the East India Company, and by 1760 there was a tiny domestic industry in northern England. After many experiments over a generation, a gifted carpenter and jack-of-all-trades, James Hargreaves, invented his cotton-spinning jenny about 1765. At almost the same moment a barber-turned-manufacturer named Richard Arkwright invented another kind of spinning machine, the water frame. These breakthroughs produced an explosion in the infant cotton textile industry in the 1780s. By 1790 the new machines were producing ten times as much cotton yarn as had been made in 1770.

spinning jenny *A machine, invented by James Hargreaves, that enabled workers to spin cotton.*

Hargreaves's **spinning jenny** was simple and inexpensive. It was also hand operated. In early models from six to twenty-four spindles were mounted on a sliding carriage, and each spindle spun a fine, slender thread. The woman moved the carriage back and forth with one hand and turned a wheel to supply power with the other. Now it was the male weaver who could not keep up with the vastly more efficient female spinner.

Arkwright's **water frame** employed a different principle. It quickly acquired a capacity of several hundred spindles and demanded much more power—waterpower. The water frame thus required large specialized mills, factories that employed as many as one thousand workers from the very beginning. The water frame could spin only coarse, strong thread, which was then put out for respinning on hand-powered cottage jennies. After about 1790, all cotton spinning was gradually concentrated in factories.

The first consequences of these revolutionary developments were more beneficial than is generally believed. Cotton goods became much cheaper, and they were bought and treasured by all classes. In the past only the wealthy could afford the comfort and cleanliness of underwear, which was called **body linen** because it was made from expensive linen cloth. Now millions of poor people, who had earlier worn nothing underneath their coarse, filthy outer garments, could afford to wear cotton slips and underpants as well as cotton dresses and shirts.

Families using cotton in cottage industry were freed from their constant search for adequate yarn from scattered part-time spinners, for all the thread needed could be spun in the cottage on the jenny or obtained from a nearby factory. The wages of weavers, now hard-pressed to keep up with the spinners, rose markedly until about 1792. Weavers were among the best-paid workers in England. As a result, large numbers of agricultural laborers became hand-loom weavers, while mechanics and capitalists soon sought to invent a power loom to save on labor costs. This Edmund Cartwright achieved in 1785. But the power looms of the factories worked poorly at first, and hand-loom weavers continued to receive good wages until at least 1800.

Until the late 1780s most English factories were in rural areas, where they had access to waterpower. These factories employed a relatively small percentage of all cotton textile workers. Working conditions in the early factories were less satisfactory than the conditions of cottage weavers and spinners, and people were reluctant to work in them. Therefore, factory owners turned to young children who had been abandoned by their parents and put in the care of local officials. These local officials often "apprenticed" such unfortunate orphans to factory owners, who gained over them almost the authority of slave owners.

Both symbolically and substantially, the big new cotton mills marked the beginning of the Industrial Revolution in England. By 1831 the largely mechanized cotton textile industry towered above all others, accounting for fully 22 percent of the country's entire industrial production.

water frame   *Invented by Richard Arkwright, this machine used waterpower to spin coarse, strong thread in factories.*

body linen   *Another term for underwear, so called because it was made from expensive cloth.*

ENERGY AND TRANSPORTATION

What changes in England revolutionized the provision of energy and transportation?

The growth of the cotton textile industry might have been stunted or cut short if water from rivers and streams had remained the primary source of power for the new factories. But this did not occur. Instead, an epoch-making solution was found to the age-old problem of energy and power. The solution to the energy problem permitted continued rapid development in cotton textiles, the gradual generalization of the factory system, and the triumph of the Industrial Revolution in England and Scotland.

The Problem of Energy

Human beings, like all living organisms, require energy. Depending on the individual's level of physical activity, adult men and women need two thousand to four thousand calories (units of energy) daily simply to fuel their bodies, work, and survive.

Prehistoric people relied on plants and plant-eating animals as their sources of energy. With the development of agriculture, early civilizations were able to increase the number of useful plants and thus the supply of energy. Some plants could be fed to domesticated animals, such as the horse. Stronger than human beings, these animals converted the energy in the plants into work.

Human beings have used their toolmaking abilities to construct machines that convert one form of energy into another for their own benefit. In the common era people began to develop water mills to grind their grain and windmills to pump water and drain swamps. More efficient use of water and wind in the sixteenth and seventeenth centuries enabled human beings to accomplish more; intercontinental sailing ships were a prime example. Nevertheless, societies around the world continued to rely mainly on plants for energy, and human beings and animals continued to perform most work.

Lack of power lay at the heart of the poverty that afflicted the large majority of the world's people. The man behind the plow and the woman at the spinning wheel could employ only horsepower and human muscle in their labor. No matter how hard they worked, they could not produce very much.

The shortage of energy had become particularly severe in England by the eighteenth century. Wood was in ever-shorter supply, yet it remained tremendously important. In addition to serving as the primary source of heat for homes and industries and as a basic raw material, processed wood (charcoal) was the fuel that was mixed with iron ore in the blast furnace to produce pig iron. The iron industry's appetite for wood was enormous, and by 1740 the English iron industry was stagnating. Vast forests enabled Russia in the eighteenth century to become the world's leading producer of iron, much of which was exported to England.

The Steam Engine Breakthrough

As this early energy crisis grew worse, England looked toward its abundant and widely scattered reserves of coal as an alternative to its vanishing wood. By 1640 most homes in London were heated with it, and it also provided heat for making beer, glass, soap, and other products. Coal, however, was not used to make iron, to produce mechanical energy, or to power machinery. It was there that coal's potential was enormous, as a simple example shows.

A hard-working miner can dig out five hundred pounds of coal a day using hand tools, the equivalent of about one horsepower-hour of labor. Even an extremely inefficient converter, which transforms only 1 percent of the heat energy in coal into mechanical energy, will produce twenty-seven horsepower-hours of work from that five hundred pounds of coal. Early steam engines were just such inefficient converters.

As more coal was produced, mines were dug deeper and deeper and were constantly filling with water. Mechanical pumps, usually powered by animals walking in circles at the surface, had to be installed. At one mine fully five hundred horses were used in pumping. Such power was expensive and bothersome. In an attempt to overcome these disadvantages Thomas Savery in 1698 and Thomas Newcomen in 1705 invented the first primitive **steam engines.** Both engines burned coal to produce steam, which was then used to operate a pump. Both engines were extremely inefficient, but by the early 1770s hundreds of these steam engines were operating successfully in English and Scottish mines.

steam engines *A breakthrough invention by Thomas Savery in 1698 and Thomas Newcomen in 1705 in which coal was burned to produce steam, which was then used to operate a pump.*

In the early 1760s a gifted young Scot named James Watt (1736–1819) was drawn to a critical study of the steam engine. Watt was employed at the time by the University of Glasgow as a skilled craftsman making scientific instruments. Called on to repair a Newcomen engine being used in a physics course, Watt saw that the Newcomen engine's great waste of energy could be reduced by adding a separate condenser. This splendid invention, patented in 1769, greatly increased the efficiency of the steam engine.

● **Manchester, England, 1851**   The development of the steam engine enabled industry to concentrate in towns and cities. Manchester mushroomed from a town of 20,000 in 1750 into "Cottonopolis," cotton city, with 400,000 inhabitants in 1850. In this painting the artist contrasts the smoky city and its awesome power with the idealized beauty of the suburbs, where the new rich settled and built their mansions. *(The Royal Collection, © 2007 Her Majesty Queen Elizabeth II)*

Watt formed a partnership with a wealthy toymaker, who provided risk capital and a manufacturing plant. In England's craft tradition of locksmiths, tinsmiths, and millwrights, Watt found skilled mechanics who could install, regulate, and repair his sophisticated engines. This support and more than twenty years of constant effort allowed him to create and regulate a complex engine. By the late 1780s the steam engine had become a practical and commercial success in England.

The steam engine of Watt and his followers was the Industrial Revolution's most fundamental advance in technology. For the first time in history, humanity had, at least for a few generations and without much serious thought about the environmental consequences, almost unlimited power at its disposal. For the first time inventors and engineers could devise and implement all kinds of power equipment to aid people in their work. For the first time abundance was at least a possibility for the world's ordinary men and women.

The steam engine was quickly put to use in several industries in England. It drained mines and began to replace waterpower in the cotton-spinning mills during the 1780s, contributing greatly to that industry's phenomenal rise. Steam also took the place of waterpower in flour mills, in the malt mills used in breweries, in the flint mills supplying the china industry, and in the mills exported by England to the West Indies to crush sugar cane.

Steam power promoted important breakthroughs in other industries. The English iron industry was radically transformed. The use of powerful steam-driven bellows in blast furnaces helped ironmakers switch over rapidly from limited charcoal to unlimited **coke** (which is made from coal) in the smelting of pig iron after 1770. In the 1780s Henry Cort developed the puddling furnace, which allowed pig iron to be refined in turn with coke. Strong, skilled ironworkers—the puddlers—"cooked" molten pig iron in a great vat, raking off globs of refined iron for further processing. Cort also

coke *A form of coal that was unlimited in supply and therefore easier and better to use.*

● **James Nasmyth's Mighty Steam Hammer** Nasmyth's invention was the forerunner of the modern pile driver, and its successful introduction in 1832 epitomized the rapid development of steam power technology in Britain. In this painting by the inventor himself, workers manipulate a massive iron shaft being hammered into shape at Nasmyth's foundry near Manchester. *(Science & Society Picture Library, London)*

developed heavy-duty steam-powered rolling mills, which were capable of spewing out finished iron in every shape and form.

The economic consequence of these technical innovations was a great boom in the English iron industry. In 1740 annual British iron production was only 17,000 tons. With the spread of coke smelting and the first impact of Cort's inventions, production reached 68,000 tons in 1788, 125,000 tons in 1796, and 260,000 tons in 1806. In 1844 Britain produced 3 million tons of iron. This was a truly amazing expansion. Once scarce and expensive, iron became the cheap, basic, indispensable building block of the economy.

The Coming of the Railroads

Throughout western Europe the second half of the eighteenth century saw extensive construction of hard and relatively smooth roads, particularly in France before the Revolution. Yet it was passenger traffic that benefited most from this construction. Overland shipment of freight, relying solely on horsepower, was still quite limited and frightfully expensive. Shippers used rivers and canals for heavy freight whenever possible. It was logical, therefore, that inventors would try to apply steam power to transportation.

As early as 1800 an American ran a "steam engine on wheels" through city streets. Other experiments followed. In the 1820s English engineers created steam cars capable of carrying fourteen passengers at ten miles an hour—as fast as the mail coach. But the noisy, heavy steam automobiles frightened passing horses and damaged themselves as well as the roads with their vibrations. For the rest of the nineteenth century horses continued to reign on highways and city streets.

The coal industry had long been using plank roads and rails to move coal wagons within mines and at the surface. Thus once a rail capable of supporting a heavy locomotive was developed in 1816, all sorts of experiments with steam engines on rails went forward. In 1825 after ten years of work, George Stephenson built an effective locomotive. In 1830 his *Rocket* sped down the track of the just-completed Liverpool and Manchester Railway at sixteen miles per hour. The world's first important railroad, the line from Liverpool to Manchester was a financial as well as a technical success, and many private companies were quickly organized to build more rail lines. Within twenty years these companies had completed the main trunk lines of Great Britain. Other countries in Europe and North America were quick to follow.

The significance of the railroad was tremendous. The railroad dramatically reduced the cost and uncertainty of shipping freight overland. This advance had many economic consequences. Previously, markets had tended to be small and local. As the barrier of high transportation costs was lowered, markets became larger. These larger markets encouraged larger factories with more sophisticated machinery in a growing number of industries. Such factories could make goods more cheaply, and they gradually subjected most cottage workers and many urban artisans to severe competitive pressures.

In all countries the construction of railroads created a strong demand for unskilled labor and contributed to the growth of a class of urban workers. Many landless farm laborers and poor peasants went to build railroads. After the work was finished, many men drifted to towns in search of work. By the time they sent for their wives and sweethearts to join them, they had become urban workers.

The railroad changed the outlook and values of the entire society. The last and culminating invention of the Industrial Revolution, the railroad dramatically revealed the power and increased the speed of the new age. Racing down a track at sixteen miles per hour or, by 1850, at a phenomenal fifty miles per hour was a new and awesome experience. As a French economist put it after a ride on the Liverpool and Manchester in 1833, "There are certain impressions that one cannot put into words!"

Some great painters, notably Joseph M. W. Turner (1775–1851) and Claude Monet (1840–1926), succeeded in expressing this sense of power and awe. So did the

● **The Saltash Bridge**
Railroad construction presented innumerable challenges, such as the building of bridges to span rivers and gorges. Civil engineers responded with impressive feats, and their profession bounded ahead. This painting portrays the inauguration of I. K. Brunel's Saltash Bridge, where the railroad crosses the Tamar River into Cornwall in southwest England. The high spans allow large ships to pass underneath. *(Elton Collection, Ironbridge Gorge Museum Trust)*

● **The Crystal Palace** The Great Exhibition of 1851 attracted more than 6 million visitors, many of whom journeyed to London on the newly built railroads. Countries and companies from all over the world displayed their products and juries awarded prizes in the strikingly modern Crystal Palace, an architectural marvel built using the cheap iron and glass of the industrial age. In this illustration visitors stroll through the domed hall and peruse the 1,500 exhibits. *(British Museum/Laurie Platt Winfrey, Inc.)*

massive new train stations, the cathedrals of the industrial age. Leading railway engineers, whose tunnels pierced mountains and whose bridges spanned valleys, became public idols—the astronauts of their day. Everyday speech absorbed the images of railroading. After you got up a "full head of steam," you "highballed" along. And if you didn't "go off the track," you might "toot your own whistle." The railroad fired the imagination.

Industry and Population

Crystal Palace *The location of the Great Exhibition in 1851 in London; an architectural masterpiece made entirely of glass and iron, both of which were now cheap and abundant.*

In 1851 London was the site of a famous industrial fair. This Great Exhibition was held in the newly built **Crystal Palace**, an architectural masterpiece made entirely of glass and iron, both of which were now cheap and abundant. For the millions who visited, one fact stood out: the little island of Britain—England, Wales, and Scotland—was the "workshop of the world." It alone produced two-thirds of the world's coal and more than one-half of its iron and cotton cloth. More generally, it has been estimated that in 1860 Britain produced 20 percent of the entire world's output of industrial goods, whereas it had produced only about 2 percent of the world total in 1750.[4] Experiencing revolutionary industrial change, Britain became the first industrial nation (see Map 22.1).

As the British economy significantly increased its production of manufactured goods, the gross national product (GNP) rose roughly fourfold at constant prices between 1780 and 1851. In other words, the British people as a whole increased their wealth and their national income dramatically. At the same time, the population of Great Britain boomed, growing from about 9 million in 1780 to almost 21 million in 1851. Thus average consumption per person increased by only 75 percent between 1780 and 1851, as the growth in the total population ate up a large part of the four-fold increase in GNP in those years.[5]

Many economic historians now believe that rapid population growth in Great Britain was not harmful because it facilitated industrial expansion and provided a more mobile labor force. Contemporaries were much less optimistic. In his famous and influential *Essay on the Principle of Population* (1798), Thomas Malthus (1766–1834) argued that population would always tend to grow faster than the food supply. In Malthus's opinion the only hope of warding off harsh checks to population growth such as war, famine, and disease was "prudential restraint": young men and women

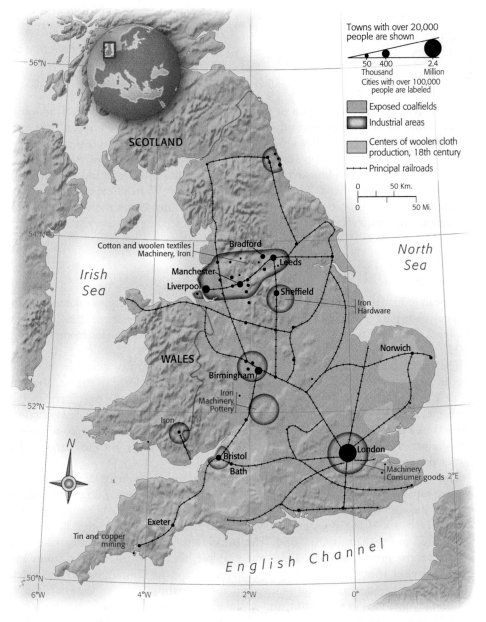

MAP 22.1 **The Industrial Revolution in England, ca. 1850** Industry concentrated in the rapidly growing cities of the north and the Midlands, where rich coal and iron deposits were in close proximity.

had to limit the growth of population by the old tried-and-true means of marrying late in life. But Malthus was not optimistic about this possibility. The powerful attraction of the sexes would cause most people to marry early and have many children.

Wealthy English stockbroker and leading economist David Ricardo (1772–1823) coldly spelled out the pessimistic implications of Malthus's thought. Ricardo's depressing **iron law of wages** posited that because of the pressure of population growth, wages would always sink to subsistence level—that is, wages would be just high enough to keep workers from starving. With Malthus and Ricardo setting the tone, economics was soon dubbed "the dismal science."

iron law of wages *The rule that because of the pressure of population growth, wages would always sink to subsistence level, meaning that wages would be just high enough to keep workers from starving.*

There was another problem with early industrialization. Perhaps workers, farmers, and ordinary people did not get their rightful share of the new wealth. Perhaps only the rich got richer while the poor got poorer or made no progress. We will turn to this great issue after looking at the process of industrialization in continental European countries in the nineteenth century.

INDUSTRIALIZATION IN CONTINENTAL EUROPE

How after 1815 did continental countries respond to the challenge of industrialization?

The new technologies developed in the British Industrial Revolution were adopted rather slowly by businesses in continental Europe, and there were uneven jerks and national (and regional) variations. Scholars are still struggling to explain these variations, especially since good answers may offer valuable lessons in our own time for poor countries seeking to improve their material condition through industrialization and economic development. The latest findings on the Western experience are encouraging. They suggest that there were alternative paths to the industrial world in the nineteenth century and that there was (and is) no need to follow a rigid, predetermined British model.

National Variations

European industrialization, like most economic developments, requires some statistical analysis as part of the effort to understand it. One important set of data compares the level of industrialization on a per capita basis in several countries from 1750 to 1913. These data are presented in Table 22.1 for closer study.

The table is a comparison of how much industrial product was available, on average, to each person in a given country in a given year. Therefore, all the numbers in Table 22.1 are expressed in terms of a single index number of 100, which equals the per capita level of industrial goods in Great Britain (and Ireland) in 1900. Every number is thus a percentage of the 1900 level in Great Britain and is directly comparable. The countries are listed in roughly the order in which they began to use large-scale, power-driven technology.

This quantitative overview of European industrialization confirms the primacy and relative rapidity of Britain's Industrial Revolution. In 1750 the leading countries of Europe and Asia were fairly close together. But by 1800 Britain had opened up a noticeable lead, and that gap progressively widened as the British Industrial Revolution accelerated to full maturity by 1860. The British level of per capita industrialization was twice the French level in 1830, for example, and more than three times the French level in 1860. All other large countries (except the United States) had fallen even further behind Britain than France had at both dates.

Second, variations in the timing and in the extent of industrialization in the continental powers and the United States are also apparent. Belgium, independent in 1831

Table 22.1 Per Capita Levels of Industrialization, 1750–1913

	1750	1800	1830	1860	1880	1900	1913
Great Britain	10	16	25	64	87	100	115
Belgium	9	10	14	28	43	56	88
United States	4	9	14	21	38	69	126
France	9	9	12	20	28	39	59
Germany	8	8	9	15	25	52	85
Austria-Hungary	7	7	8	11	15	23	32
Italy	8	8	8	10	12	17	26
Russia	6	6	7	8	10	15	20
China	8	6	6	4	4	3	3
India	7	6	6	3	2	1	2

Note: All entries are based on an index value of 100, equal to the per capita level of industrialization in Great Britain in 1900. Data for Great Britain are actually for the United Kingdom, thereby including Ireland with England, Wales, and Scotland.

Source: P. Bairoch, "International Industrialization Levels from 1750 to 1980," *Journal of European Economic History* 11 (Fall 1982): 294. Reprinted with permission.

and rich in iron and coal, led in adopting Britain's new technology. France developed factory production more gradually, although its pattern of early industrial growth was relatively good. In general, eastern and southern Europe began the process of modern industrialization later than northwestern and central Europe, as development in Austria-Hungary, Italy, and Russia suggests.

Third, Table 22.1 highlights the explosive rise of the United States and Germany to industrial prominence from 1880 to 1913, which is sometimes called the era of the Second Industrial Revolution. Thus in these years the United States and Germany led in the development of important new industries such as electricity, organic chemicals, petroleum, and automobiles. These new industries allowed the industrialized countries to continue rapid economic development as textiles and railroads became mature and slowed down.

Finally, all European states (as well as the United States, Canada, and Japan) managed to raise per capita industrial levels in the nineteenth century. These continent-wide increases stood in stark contrast to the large decreases that occurred at the same time in most non-Western countries, most notably China and India, as Table 22.1 shows. European countries industrialized to a greater or lesser extent even as most of the non-Western world *de*-industrialized. Thus differential rates of wealth- and power-creating industrial development greatly magnified growing inequalities between Europe and the rest of the world. We shall return to this momentous change in Chapters 24 and 25.

The Challenge of Industrialization

The different patterns of industrial development suggest that the process of industrialization was far from automatic. Indeed, building modern industry was an awesome challenge. When the pace of English industry began to accelerate in the 1780s, continental businesses began to adopt the new methods as they proved their profitability. English industry enjoyed clear superiority, but at first continental Europe was close behind. By 1815, however, the situation was quite different. In spite of wartime difficulties, English industry maintained the momentum of the 1780s and continued to grow and improve between 1789 and 1815. On the continent, the unending political and economic upheavals that began with the French Revolution disrupted trade, created runaway inflation, and impeded continental efforts to use new British machinery and technology. Thus economically and industrially France and the rest of Europe were further behind Britain in 1815 than in 1789.

This widening gap made it more difficult, if not impossible, for other countries to follow the British pattern in energy and industry after peace was restored in 1815. Above all, in the newly mechanized industries British goods were being produced very economically, and these goods had come to dominate world markets completely. Continental European firms had little hope of competing with mass-produced British goods in foreign markets for a long time. In addition, British technology had become so advanced and complicated that very few engineers or skilled technicians outside England understood it. Moreover, the technology of steam power had grown much more expensive. It involved large investments in the iron and coal industries and, after 1830, required the existence of railroads, which were very costly. Continental business people had great difficulty finding the large sums of money the new methods demanded, and there was a shortage of laborers accustomed to working in factories. Landowners and government officials were often so suspicious of the new form of industry and the changes it brought that they did little at first to encourage it. All these disadvantages slowed the spread of modern industry to continental Europe (see Map 22.2).

After 1815, however, continental countries also had at least three important advantages. First, most had a rich tradition of putting-out enterprise, merchant capitalists, and skilled urban artisans. Such a tradition gave firms in continental Europe the ability to adapt and survive in the face of new market conditions. Second, continental capitalists could simply "borrow" the advanced technology already developed in Great Britain, as well as engineers and some of the financial resources these countries lacked. European countries had a third asset that many non-Western areas lacked in the nineteenth century. They had strong independent governments that did not fall under foreign political control. These governments could fashion economic policies to serve their own interests.

Agents of Industrialization

The British realized the great value of their technical discoveries and tried to keep their secrets to themselves. Until 1825 it was illegal for artisans and skilled mechanics to leave Britain; until 1843 the export of textile machinery and other equipment was forbidden. Many talented, ambitious workers, however, slipped out of the country illegally and introduced the new methods abroad.

One such man was William Cockerill, a Lancashire carpenter. He and his sons began building cotton-spinning equipment in French-occupied Belgium in 1799. In 1817 the most famous son, John Cockerill, purchased the old summer palace of the deposed bishops of Liège in southern Belgium. Cockerill converted the palace into a large industrial enterprise that produced machinery, steam engines, and then railway locomotives. He also established modern ironworks and coal mines.

Many skilled British workers came illegally to work for Cockerill, and some went on to found their own companies throughout Europe. Newcomers brought the latest plans and secrets, so Cockerill could boast that ten days after an industrial advance occurred in Britain, he knew all about it in Belgium. Thus British technicians and skilled workers were a powerful force in the spread of early industrialization.

Talented entrepreneurs such as Fritz Harkort, a business pioneer in the German machinery industry, were a second agent of industrialization. Serving in England as a

Prussian army officer during the Napoleonic wars, Harkort concluded that Germany had to match English achievements as quickly as possible. Setting up shop in an abandoned castle in the still-tranquil Ruhr Valley, he felt an almost religious calling to build steam engines and become the "Watt of Germany."

Harkort's basic idea was simple but enormously difficult to carry out. Lacking skilled laborers to do the job, Harkort turned to England for experienced, though expensive, mechanics. He had to import from England the thick iron boilers that he needed at great cost. In spite of these problems, Harkort built and sold engines, winning fame and praise. His ambitious efforts over sixteen years also resulted in large financial losses for himself and his partners, and in 1832 his financial backers forced him out of his company. Harkort's career illustrates both the great efforts of a few important business leaders to duplicate the British achievement and the difficulty of the task.

Less famous entrepreneurs adopted factory technology slowly, and handicraft methods lived on. In France, for example, artisan production of luxury items grew, as the rising income of the international middle class created foreign demand for silk scarves, embroidered needlework, perfumes, and fine wines.

A third force for industrialization was government, which often helped business people in European countries to overcome some of their difficulties. **Tariff protection** was one such support. And after 1815 continental governments bore the cost of building roads and canals to improve transportation. They also bore to a significant

tariff protection *A government's way of supporting and aiding its own economy by laying high tariffs on the cheaper goods imported from another country.*

MAP 22.2 **Continental European Industrialization, ca. 1850** Although continental countries were beginning to make progress by 1850, they still lagged far behind Britain. For example, continental railroad building was still in an early stage, whereas the British rail system was essentially complete.

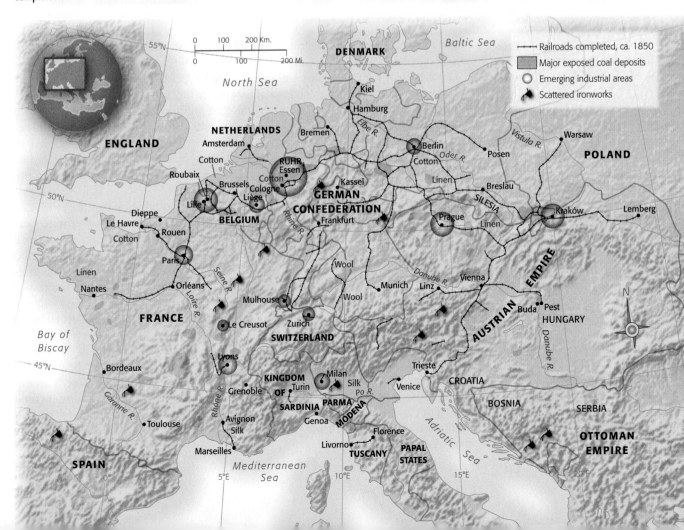

● **A German Ironworks, 1845** This big business enterprise, the Borsig ironworks in Berlin, mastered the new British method of smelting iron ore with coke. Germany, and especially the state of Prussia, was well endowed with both iron and coal, and the rapid exploitation of these resources after 1840 transformed a poor agricultural country into an industrial powerhouse. *(akg-images)*

economic nationalism *The idea that countries should protect and foster their own businesses by imposing high protective tariffs on imported goods as well as eliminating tariffs within the country.*

extent the cost of building railroads, the all-important leading sector in continental industrialization.

The career of German journalist and thinker Friedrich List (1789–1846) reflects government's greater role in industrialization on the European continent than in England. List considered the growth of modern industry of the utmost importance because manufacturing was a primary means of increasing people's well-being and relieving their poverty. Moreover, List was a dedicated nationalist who believed that an agricultural nation was not only poor but also weak, increasingly unable to defend itself and maintain its political independence. To promote industry was to defend the nation.

The practical policies that List focused on were railroad building and the tariff. List supported the formation of a customs union, or *Zollverein,* among the separate German states. Such a tariff union came into being in 1834. It allowed goods to move without tariffs between the German member states. A single uniform tariff was erected against all other nations to help infant industries to develop. List denounced the English doctrine of free trade as little more than England's attempt "to make the rest of the world, like the Hindus, its serfs in all industrial and commercial relations." By the 1840s List's **economic nationalism** had become increasingly popular in Germany, the United States, and elsewhere.

Banks, like governments, also played a larger and more creative role in continental countries than in England. Previously, almost all banks in Europe had been private partnerships. All the active partners were liable for all the debts of the firm. This unlimited liability meant that in the event of a disastrous bankruptcy each partner could lose all of his or her personal wealth. Such banks were content to deal with a few rich clients and a few big merchants. They generally avoided industrial investment as being too risky.

In the 1830s two important Belgian banks pioneered in a new direction, establishing themselves as corporations enjoying limited liability. A stockholder in these two banks could lose only his or her original investment in the bank's common stock. Able to attract many shareholders, large and small, because of the reduced risk, these Belgian banks mobilized impressive resources for investment in big industrial companies. They became industrial banks and successfully promoted industrial development.

Similar corporate banks became important in France and Germany in the 1850s and 1860s. Usually working in collaboration with governments, they established and developed many railroads and many companies working in heavy industry, which were increasingly organized as limited-liability corporations.

The combined efforts of skilled workers, entrepreneurs, governments, and industrial banks meshed successfully between 1850 and the financial crash of 1873. In Belgium, Germany, and France, key indicators of modern industrial development—railway mileage, iron and coal production, and steam-engine capacity—increased at average annual rates ranging from 5 to 10 percent compounded. In the early 1870s Britain was still Europe's most industrial nation, but a select handful of countries was closing the gap that had been opened up by the Industrial Revolution.

• • • • • • • • • • • •

CAPITAL AND LABOR

How did the Industrial Revolution affect social classes, the standard of living, and working conditions?

Industrial development brought new social relations and intensified long-standing problems between capital and labor. A new group of factory owners and industrial capitalists arose. These men and women and their families strengthened the wealth and size of the middle class, which had previously been made up mainly of merchants and professional people. The nineteenth century became the golden age of the European middle class. Modern industry also created a much larger group: the factory workers. For the first time large numbers of men, women, and children came together under one roof to work with complicated machinery for a single owner or a few partners in large companies.

The growth of new occupational groups in industry stimulated new thinking about social relations. It was argued, with considerable success, that individuals were members of economically determined classes that had conflicting interests. Accordingly, the comfortable, well-educated "public" of eighteenth-century Europe came increasingly to see itself as the backbone of the middle class (or the middle classes), and the "people" gradually transformed themselves into the modern working class (or working classes). The new class interpretation appealed to many because it seemed to explain what was happening. Thus conflicting classes came into being in part because many individuals came to believe that they existed and developed an appropriate sense of class feeling—what Marxists call **class-consciousness.**

The New Class of Factory Owners

Early industrialists operated in a highly competitive economic system in which success and large profits were by no means certain. Manufacturers waged a constant battle to cut their production costs and stay afloat. "Dragged on by the frenzy of this terrible life," according to one of the dismayed critics, the struggling manufacturer had "no time for niceties. He must conquer or die, make a fortune or drown himself."[6]

The early industrialists came from a variety of backgrounds. Many, such as Harkort, were from well-established merchant families, but artisans and skilled workers of exceptional ability had unparalleled opportunities. The ethnic and religious groups that had been discriminated against in the traditional occupations controlled by the landed

class-consciousness *Conflicting classes existed, in part, because many individuals came to believe they existed and developed an appropriate sense of class feeling.*

aristocracy jumped at the new chances. Quakers and Scots were tremendously important in England; Protestants and Jews dominated banking in Catholic France.

As factories grew larger, opportunities declined, at least in well-developed industries. It became considerably harder for a gifted but poor young mechanic to end up as a wealthy manufacturer. Formal education became more important as a means of advancement, and formal education at the advanced level was expensive. In England by 1830 and in France and Germany by 1860, leading industrialists were more likely to have inherited their well-established enterprises, and they were financially much more secure than their fathers and grandfathers had been. They also had a greater sense of class-consciousness, fully aware that ongoing industrial development had widened the gap between themselves and their workers.

The wives and daughters of successful businessmen also found fewer opportunities for active participation in Europe's increasingly complex business world. Rather than contributing as vital partners in family-owned enterprises, as so many middle-class women such as Elizabeth Strutt had done (see the feature "Individuals in Society: The Strutt Family"), these women were increasingly valued for their ladylike gentility. By 1850 some influential women writers and most businessmen assumed that middle-class wives and daughters should steer clear of undignified work in offices and factories. Rather, a middle-class lady should protect and enhance her femininity, concentrating on her proper role as wife and mother.

The New Factory Workers

The social consequences of the Industrial Revolution have long been hotly debated. The condition of English workers during the transformation has always generated the most controversy among historians because England was the first country to industrialize and because the social consequences seemed harshest there. Before 1850 other countries had not proceeded very far with industrialization, and almost everyone agrees that the economic conditions of European workers improved after 1850. Thus the experience of English workers to about 1850 deserves special attention. (Industrial growth also promoted rapid urbanization, with its own awesome problems, as will be shown in Chapter 23.)

From the beginning the Industrial Revolution in England had its critics. Among the first were the romantic poets. William Blake (1757–1827) called the early factories "satanic mills" and protested against the hard life of the London poor. William Wordsworth (1770–1850) lamented the destruction of the rural way of life and the pollution of the land and water. Some handicraft workers—notably the **Luddites,** who attacked whole factories in northern England in 1812 and after—smashed the new machines, which they believed were putting them out of work. Doctors and reformers wrote eloquently of problems in the factories and new towns, and Malthus and Ricardo concluded that workers would earn only enough to stay alive.

Friedrich Engels (1820–1895), the future revolutionary and colleague of Karl Marx, accepted and reinforced this pessimistic view. After studying conditions in northern England, this young middle-class German published in 1844 *The Condition of the Working Class in England.* "At the bar of world opinion," he wrote, "I charge the English middle classes with mass murder, wholesale robbery, and all the other crimes in the calendar." The new poverty of industrial workers was worse than the old poverty of cottage workers and agricultural laborers, according to Engels, and the culprit was industrial capitalism. Engels's extremely influential charge of middle-class exploitation and increasing worker poverty was embellished by Marx and later socialists.

Meanwhile, other observers believed that conditions were improving for the working people. Edwin Chadwick, a conscientious government official well acquainted with the problems of the working population, concluded that the "laboring community" was increasingly able "to buy more of the necessities and minor luxuries of life."[7] Nevertheless, if all the contemporary assessments had been counted up, those

Luddites *Followers of Ned Ludd; a social movement in protest against the industrial revolution that began in northern England in 1812. These handicraft workers attacked the new machines being brought in by the factory owners, which they believed were taking their jobs.*

The Strutt Family

For centuries economic life in Europe revolved around hundreds of thousands of small family enterprises. These family enterprises worked farms, crafted products, and traded goods.

They built and operated the firms and factories of the early industrial era, with the notable exceptions of the capital-hungry railroads and a few big banks. Indeed, until late in the nineteenth century, close-knit family groups continued to control most successful businesses, including those organized as corporations.

One successful and fairly well-documented family enterprise began with the marriage of Jedediah Strutt (1726–1797) and Elizabeth Woollat (1729–1774) in Derbyshire in northern England in 1755. The son of a farmer, Jedediah fell in love with Elizabeth when he was apprenticed away from home as a wheelwright and lodged with her parents. Both young people grew up in the close-knit dissenting Protestant community, which did not accept the doctrines of the state-sponsored Church of England, and the well-educated Elizabeth worked in a local school for dissenters and then for a dissenter minister in London. Indecisive and self-absorbed, Jedediah inherited in 1754 a small stock of animals from an uncle and finally married Elizabeth the following year.

Aided by Elizabeth, who was "obviously a very capable woman" and who supplied some of the drive her husband had previously lacked, Jedediah embarked on a new career.* He invented a machine to make handsome, neat-fitting ribbed silk stockings, which had previously been made by hand. He secured a patent, despite strong opposition from competitors, and went into production. Elizabeth helped constantly in the enterprise, which was nothing less than an informal partnership between husband and wife.†

In 1757, for example, when Jedediah was fighting to uphold his patent in the local court, Elizabeth left her son of nine months and journeyed to London to seek a badly needed loan from her former employer.

Jedediah Strutt (ca. 1790), by Joseph Wright of Derby. *(Derby Museum & Art Gallery/The Bridgeman Art Library)*

She also canvassed her London relatives and dissenter friends for orders for stockings and looked for sales agents and sources of capital. Elizabeth's letters reveal a detailed knowledge of ribbed stockings and the prices and quality of different kinds of thread. The family biographers, old-line economic historians writing without a trace of feminist concerns, conclude that her husband "owed much of his success to her energy and counsel." Elizabeth was always "active in the business—a partner in herself."‡ Historians have often overlooked such invaluable contributions from wives like Elizabeth, partly because the legal rights and consequences of partnership were denied to married women in Britain and Europe in the eighteenth and nineteenth centuries.

The Strutt enterprise grew and gradually prospered, but it always retained its family character. The firm built a large silk mill and then went into cotton spinning in partnership with Richard Arkwright, the inventor of the water frame (see page 648). The brothers of both Jedediah and Elizabeth worked for the firm, and their eldest daughter worked long hours in the warehouse. Bearing three sons, Elizabeth fulfilled yet another vital task because the typical family firm looked to its own members for managers and continued success. All three sons entered the business and became cotton textile magnates. Elizabeth never saw these triumphs. The loyal and talented wife in the family partnership died suddenly at age forty-five while in London with Jedediah on a business trip.

Questions for Analysis

1. How and why did the Strutts succeed?
2. What does Elizabeth's life tell us about the role of British women in the early Industrial Revolution?

*R. Fitton and A Wadsworth, *The Strutts and the Arkwrights, 1758–1830: A Study of the Early Factory System* (Manchester, England: Manchester University Press, 1958), p. 23.

†See the excellent discussion by C. Hall, "Strains in the 'Firm of Wife, Children and Friends'? Middle-Class Women and Employment in Early Nineteenth-Century England," in P. Hudson and W. Lee, eds., *Women's Work and the Family Economy in Historical Perspective* (Manchester, England: Manchester University Press, 1990), pp. 106–132.

‡Fitton and Wadsworth, *The Strutts,* pp. 110–111.

who thought conditions were getting worse for working people would probably have been the majority.

Scholarly statistical studies have weakened the idea that the condition of the English working class got much worse with industrialization. But more recent studies also confirm the view that the early years of the Industrial Revolution were hard ones for British workers. From about 1780 to about 1820 there was little or no increase in the purchasing power of the average British worker's wages. The years from 1792 to 1815, a period of almost constant warfare with France, were particularly difficult. Food prices rose faster than wages, and the living conditions of the laboring poor declined. Only after 1820, and especially after 1840, did real wages rise substantially. The average worker earned and consumed roughly 50 percent more in real terms in 1850 than in 1770.[8] In short, there was considerable economic improvement for workers throughout Great Britain by 1850, but that improvement was hard won and slow in coming.

At the same time the hours in the average workweek increased. To a large extent, workers earned more simply because they worked more. Thus England nonagricultural workers labored about 250 days per year in 1760 as opposed to 300 days per year in 1830, while the normal workday remained an exhausting eleven hours throughout the entire period. In 1760 nonagricultural workers still observed many religious and public holidays by not working. However, these days of leisure and relaxation declined rapidly after 1760, and by 1830 nonagricultural workers had generally joined landless agricultural laborers in toiling six rather than five days a week.[9]

Another way to consider the workers' standard of living is to look at the goods they purchased. Again the evidence is somewhat contradictory. Speaking generally, workers ate somewhat more food of higher nutritional quality as the Industrial Revolution progressed, except during wartime, and diets became more varied. Clothing improved, but housing for working people probably deteriorated somewhat. In short, per capita use of specific goods supports the position that the standard of living of the English working classes rose, at least moderately, after the long wars with France.

Conditions of Work

What about working conditions? Did workers eventually earn more only at the cost of working longer and harder? Were workers exploited harshly by the new factory owners? The first factories were cotton mills, which began functioning along rivers and streams in the 1770s. Cottage workers were reluctant to work in factories even when they received relatively good wages. In the factory, workers had to keep up with the machine and follow its tempo. They had to show up every day and work long, monotonous hours, adjusting their daily lives to the shrill call of the factory whistle. Cottage workers were not used to that kind of life and discipline. All members of the family worked hard and long, but in spurts, setting their own pace. They could interrupt their work when they wanted to. Women and children could break up their long hours of spinning with other tasks.

Also, early factories resembled English poorhouses, where totally destitute people went to live at public expense. Some poorhouses were industrial prisons where the inmates had to work in order to receive their food and lodging. The similarity between large brick factories and large stone poorhouses increased the cottage workers' fear of factories and their hatred of factory discipline.

It was cottage workers' reluctance to work in factories that prompted the early cotton mill owners to turn to abandoned and pauper children for their labor. These owners contracted with local officials to employ large numbers of these children, who were apprenticed as young as five or six years of age and who were forced by law to labor for their "master" for as many as fourteen years. Housed, fed, and locked up nightly in factory dormitories, the young workers received little or no pay. Hours were appalling—commonly thirteen or fourteen hours a day, six days a week. Harsh

● **Ford Maddox Brown: Work** This midcentury painting provides a rich visual representation of the new concepts of social class that became common by 1850. The central figures are the colorful laborers, endowed by the artist with strength and nobility. Close by, a poor girl minds her brother and sister for her working mother. On the right, a middle-class minister and a social critic observe and do intellectual work. What work does the couple on horseback perform? *(Birmingham Museums and Art Gallery/The Bridgeman Art Library)*

physical punishment maintained strict discipline. This unprecedented wholesale exploitation ultimately stirred the conscience of reformers and encouraged more humanitarian attitudes toward children and their labor.

By 1790 the early pattern was rapidly changing. The use of pauper apprentices was in decline, and in 1802 it was forbidden by Parliament. Many more factories were being built, mainly in urban areas, where they could use steam power rather than waterpower and attract a workforce more easily than in the countryside. People came from near and far to work in the cities, both as factory workers and as laborers, builders, and domestic servants. Yet as they took these new jobs, working people did not simply give in to a system of labor that had formerly repelled them. Rather, they helped modify the system by carrying over old, familiar working traditions.

For one thing, they often came to the mills and the mines as family units. This was how they had worked on farms and in cottage industry. The mill or mine owner paid the head of the family for the work of the whole family. In the cotton mills children worked for their mothers or fathers, collecting wastes and "piecing" broken threads together. In the mines children sorted coal, mothers pulled coal wagons through narrow tunnels, and fathers hewed with pick and shovel at the face of the seam.

The preservation of the family as an economic unit in the factories from the 1790s on made the new surroundings more tolerable, both in Great Britain and in other countries. Parents disciplined their children and directed their upbringing. The presence of the whole family meant that children and adults worked the same long hours (twelve-hour shifts were normal in cotton mills in 1800). Only when technical changes threatened to place control and discipline in the hands of impersonal managers and foremen did adult workers protest against inhuman conditions in the name of their children.

Some enlightened employers and social reformers in Parliament definitely felt otherwise. They argued that more humane standards were necessary, and they used widely circulated parliamentary reports to influence public opinion. (See the feature "Listening to the Past: The Testimony of Young Mine Workers" on pages 672–673.) For example, Robert Owen (1771–1858), a very successful manufacturer in Scotland, testified in 1816 before an investigating committee on the basis of his experience. He stated that "very strong facts" demonstrated that employing children under ten years of age as factory workers was "injurious to the children, and not beneficial to the proprietors."[10] Workers also provided graphic testimony at such hearings as the reformers pressed Parliament to pass corrective laws. They scored some important successes.

Factory Act of 1833 *An act that limited the factory workday for children between nine and thirteen years of age to eight hours and that of adolescents between fourteen and eighteen years of age to twelve hours.*

Their first major accomplishment was the **Factory Act of 1833.** It limited the factory workday for children between the ages of nine and thirteen to eight hours and that of adolescents between fourteen and eighteen to twelve hours, although the act made no effort to regulate the hours of work for children at home or in small businesses. The law also prohibited the factory employment of children under nine; they were to be enrolled in the elementary schools that factory owners were required to establish. The employment of children declined rapidly. Thus the Factory Act broke the pattern of whole families working together in the factory.

The Sexual Division of Labor

The era of the Industrial Revolution witnessed major changes in the sexual division of labor. In preindustrial Europe certain jobs were traditionally defined by gender—women and girls for milking and spinning, men and boys for plowing and weaving—but many tasks might go to either sex as particular circumstances dictated. Family employment carried over into early factories and subcontracting, but it collapsed as child labor was restricted and new attitudes emerged. A different sexual division of labor gradually arose to take its place. The man emerged as the family's primary wage earner, and the woman found only limited job opportunities. Generally denied good jobs at good wages in the growing urban economy, women were expected to concentrate on unpaid housework, child care, and craftwork at home.

This new pattern of "separate spheres" had several aspects. First, married women were much less likely to work full-time for wages outside the house after the first child arrived, although they often earned small amounts doing putting-out handicrafts at home and taking in boarders. Second, married women who did work for wages outside the house usually came from the poorest families, where the husbands were poorly paid, sick, unemployed, or missing. Third, these poor married (or widowed) women were joined by legions of young unmarried women, who worked full-time but only in certain jobs. Fourth, all women were generally confined to low-paying, dead-end jobs. Virtually no occupation open to women paid a wage sufficient for a person to live independently. Evolving gradually but largely in place by 1850, the new sexual division of labor in Britain constituted a major development in the history of women and of the family.

Although the reorganization of paid work along gender lines is widely recognized, there is as yet no agreement on its causes. One school of scholars sees little connection with industrialization and finds the answer in the deeply ingrained sexist attitudes of a "patriarchal tradition," which predated the economic transformation. These scholars stress the role of male-dominated craft unions in denying women access to good jobs

● **Workers at a Large Cotton Mill**   This 1833 engraving shows adult women operating power looms under the supervision of a male foreman, and it accurately reflects both the decline of family employment and the emergence of a gender-based division of labor in many English factories. The jungle of belts and shafts connecting the noisy looms to the giant steam engine on the ground floor created a constant din. *(Time Life Pictures/Getty Images)*

and relegating them to unpaid housework. Other scholars, stressing that the gender roles of women and men can vary enormously with time and culture, look more to a combination of economic and biological factors to explain the emergence of a sex-segregated division of labor.

Three ideas stand out in this more recent interpretation. First, the new and unfamiliar discipline of the clock and the machine was especially hard on married women. Above all, relentless factory discipline conflicted with child care in a way that labor on the farm or in the cottage had not done. A woman operating ear-splitting spinning machinery could mind a child of seven or eight working beside her (until such work was outlawed), but she could no longer pace herself through pregnancy or breast-feed her baby on the job. Thus a working-class woman had strong incentives to concentrate on child care within her home if her family could afford for her to do so.

Second, running a working-class household in conditions of primitive urban poverty was an extremely demanding job in its own right. There were no supermarkets or public transportation. Everything had to be done on foot. Shopping and feeding the family constituted a never-ending challenge. The woman marched from one tiny shop to another, dragging her tired children and struggling valiantly with heavy sacks and tricky shopkeepers. Yet another brutal job outside the house—a "second shift"—had limited appeal for the average married woman. Thus women might well have accepted the emerging division of labor as the best available strategy for family survival in the industrializing society.[11]

Third, why were the women who did work for wages outside the home segregated and confined to certain "women's jobs"? No doubt the desire of men to monopolize the best opportunities and hold women down provides part of the answer. But as some feminist scholars have argued, sex-segregated employment was also a collective response to the new industrial system. The growth of factories and mines brought unheard-of opportunities for girls and boys to mix on the job, free of familial supervision. Continuing to mix after work, they were "more likely to form liaisons, initiate courtships, and respond to advances."[12] Such intimacy also led to more unplanned pregnancies and fueled the illegitimacy explosion that had begun in Europe in the late eighteenth-century and that gathered force until at least 1850. Thus segregation of jobs by gender was partly an effort by older people to help control the sexuality of working-class youths.

Investigations into the British coal industry before 1842 provide a graphic example of this concern.(See the feature "Listening to the Past: The Testimony of Young Mine Workers" on pages 672–673). The middle-class men leading the inquiry often failed to appreciate the physical effort of the girls and women who dragged the carts of coal along narrow underground passages. But they professed horror at the sight of girls and women working without shirts, which was a common practice because of the heat, and they quickly assumed the prevalence of licentious sex with the male miners, who also wore very little clothing. In fact, most girls and married women worked in the coal mines for related males in a family unit that provided considerable protection and restraint. Yet many witnesses from the working class also stressed particularly the danger of sexual aggression in letting girls work past puberty. As one miner explained, "I consider it a scandal for girls to work in the pits. Till they are 12 or 14 they may work very well but after that it's an abomination. . . . The work of the pit does not hurt them, it is the effect on their morals that I complain of."[13] The **Mines Act of 1842** prohibited underground work for all women as well as for boys under ten.

Mines Act of 1842 *The act that prohibited underground work for all women as well as for boys under ten.*

Some women who had to support themselves protested against being excluded from coal mining, which paid higher wages than most other jobs open to women. But the girls and the women who had worked underground were generally pleased with the law if they were part of families that could manage economically. In explaining her satisfaction in 1844, one mother of four provided real insight into why many women accepted the emerging sexual division of labor:

While working in the pit I was worth to my [miner] husband seven shillings a week, out of which we had to pay 2½ shillings to a woman for looking after the younger children. I used to take them to her house at 4 o'clock in the morning, out of their own beds, to put them into hers. Then there was one shilling a week for washing; besides, there was mending to pay for, and other things. The house was not guided. The other children broke things; they did not go to school when they were sent; they would be playing about, and get ill-used by other children, and their clothes torn. Then when I came home in the evening, everything was to do after the day's labor, and I was so tired I had no heart for it; no fire lit, nothing cooked, no water fetched, the house dirty, and nothing comfortable for my husband. It is all far better now, and I wouldn't go down again.[14]

The Early Labor Movement

Many kinds of employment changed slowly during and after the Industrial Revolution in Great Britain. In 1850 more British people still worked on farms than in any other occupation. The second largest occupation was domestic service, with more than a million household servants, 90 percent of whom were women. Thus many old, familiar jobs outside industry lived on and provided alternatives for individual workers. This helped ease the transition to industrial civilization.

Within industry itself the pattern of artisans working with hand tools in small shops remained unchanged in many trades, even as technological change revolutionized some others. For example, as in the case of cotton and coal, large-scale capitalist firms completely dominated the British iron industry by 1850. Yet the firms that fashioned iron into small metal goods—such as tools, tableware, and toys—employed on average fewer than ten wage workers, who used time-honored handicraft skills. The survival of small workshops in some handicraft industries gave many workers an alternative to factory employment.

In Great Britain and in other countries later on, workers gradually built a labor movement to improve working conditions and to serve their needs. In 1799, partly in panicked reaction to the French Revolution, Parliament had passed the Combination Acts outlawing unions and strikes. These acts were widely disregarded by workers. Societies of skilled factory workers organized unions, as printers, papermakers, carpenters, and other such craftsmen had long since done. The unions sought to control the number of skilled workers, limit apprenticeship to members' own children, and bargain with owners over wages. They were not afraid to strike; there was, for example, a general strike of adult cotton spinners in Manchester in 1810. In the face of widespread union activity Parliament repealed the Combination Acts in 1824, and unions were tolerated though not fully accepted after 1825.

The next stage in the development of the British trade-union movement was the attempt to create a single large national union. This effort was led not so much by working people as by social reformers such as Robert Owen. Owen, the self-made cotton manufacturer quoted earlier, had pioneered in industrial relations by combining firm discipline with concern for the health, safety, and hours of his workers. After 1815 he experimented with cooperative and socialist communities, including one at New Harmony, Indiana. Then in 1834 Owen organized one of the largest and most visionary of the early national unions, the **Grand National Consolidated Trades Union**. When this and other grandiose schemes collapsed, the British labor movement moved once again after 1851 in the direction of craft unions. The most famous of these "new model unions" was the Amalgamated Society of Engineers. These unions won real benefits for members by fairly conservative means and thus became an accepted part of the industrial scene.

British workers also engaged in direct political activity in defense of their own interests. After the collapse of Owen's national trade union, many working people went into the Chartist movement, whose goal was political democracy. The key Chartist demand—that all men be given the right to vote—became the great hope of millions of aroused people. Workers were also active in campaigns to limit the workday in factories to ten hours and to permit duty-free importation of wheat into Great Britain to secure cheap bread. Thus working people developed a sense of their own identity and played an active role in shaping the new industrial system. Clearly, they were neither helpless victims nor passive beneficiaries.

● **Celebrating Skilled Labor** This handsome engraving embellished the membership certificate of the British carpenters union, one of the "new model unions" that represented skilled workers effectively after 1850. The upper panel shows carpenters building the scaffolding for a great arch; the lower panel captures the spirit of a busy workshop. *(HIP/Art Resource, NY)*

Grand National Consolidated Trades Union *Organized by Owen in 1834, this was one of the largest and most visionary early national unions.*

Chapter Summary

Key Terms

Industrial Revolution
agricultural revolution
open-field system
common rights
enclosure
proletarianization
mercantilism
spinning jenny
water frame
body linen
steam engines
coke
Crystal Palace
iron law of wages
tariff protection
economic nationalism
class-consciousness
Luddites
Factory Act of 1833
Mines Act of 1842
Grand National
   Consolidated Trades Union

To assess your mastery of this chapter, go to
bedfordstmartins.com/mckayworld

• *What were the origins of the Industrial Revolution in England?*

England's industrial breakthrough grew out of a long process of economic and social change in which the rise of capitalism, overseas expansion, and the growth of rural industry stood out as critical preparatory developments. Profiting also from stable government, agricultural improvement, a flexible labor force, and a growing demand for its products, England created a new system of factory production for cotton textiles in the 1780s. In doing so, England launched an epoch-making transformation known as the Industrial Revolution.

• *What changes in England revolutionized the provision of energy and transportation?*

Building on Watt's invention and development of the modern steam engine, England obtained abundant energy for the first time in history. Abundant energy encouraged factory production, transformed the iron and coal industries, and powered the railroads that revolutionized transportation. The island of Britain—England, Scotland, and Wales—became the "workshop of the world," producing 20 percent of the world's industrial goods in 1860.

• *How after 1815 did continental countries respond to the challenge of industrialization?*

In 1815 continental European countries lagged well behind Britain in industrialization, and they faced major obstacles to catching up. Only gradually did business initiatives, protective tariffs, economic nationalism, and industrial banks combine to bring major results. Only in the 1840s did railroad construction begin to create the strong demand for iron, coal, and railway equipment that speeded up the process of industrial growth in the 1850s and 1860s.

• *How did the Industrial Revolution affect social classes, the standard of living, and working conditions?*

The rise of modern industry intensified long-standing problems between capital and labor and promoted class feeling. Improvements in the average standard of living came slowly, but they were substantial by 1850. Industrialization fostered new attitudes toward child labor, encouraged protective factory legislation, and called forth an assertive labor movement with a strong sense of class consciousness. The era of industrial transformation also promoted within the family a more rigid division of roles and responsibilities that severely restricted women socially and economically, another gradual but profound change of revolutionary proportions.

Suggested Reading

Cameron, Rondo, and Larry Neal. *A Concise Economic History of the World,* 4th ed. 2003. Provides an introduction to key issues related to global industrialization and has a carefully annotated bibliography.

Davidoff, Leonore, and Catherine Hall. *Family Fortunes: Men and Women of the English Middle Class, 1750–1850,* rev. ed. 2003. Examines both economic and cultural beliefs with great skill.

Fuchs, Rachel G. *Gender and Poverty in Nineteenth Century Europe.* 2005. Provides a broad comparative perspective.

Gaskell, Elizabeth. *Mary Barton.* 1848. Gaskell's famous novel, which offers a realistic contemporary portrayal of social conflicts in the new industrial society.

Goodman, Jordan, and Katrina Honeyman. *Gainful Pursuits: The Making of Industrial Europe, 1600–1914.* 1988. An excellent general treatment of European industrial growth in long-term perspective.

Landes, David. *Dynasties: Fortunes and Misfortunes of the World's Great Family Businesses.* 2006. Fascinating and insightful histories of famous enterprises and leading capitalists in global perspective.

Pomeranz, Kenneth. *The Great Divergence: China, Europe, and the Making of the Modern World Economy.* 2000. A sophisticated reconsideration of why western Europe underwent industrialization and China did not.

Stearns, Peter N. *The Industrial Revolution in World History,* 3d ed. 2007. A helpful short survey.

Valenze, Deborah. *The First Industrial Woman.* 1995. A lively gender study that reinvigorates the debate about the consequences of industrialization for women in Great Britain.

Wrigley, E. A. *Continuity, Chance and Change: The Character of the Industrial Revolution in England.* 1994. An important reconsideration stressing resources and population growth.

Notes

1. N. F. R. Crafts, *British Economic Growth During the Industrial Revolution* (Oxford: Oxford University Press, 1985), p. 32. These estimates are for Great Britain as a whole.
2. B. H. Slicher van Bath, *The Agrarian History of Western Europe,* A.D. *500–1850* (New York: St. Martin's Press, 1963), p. 240.
3. Quoted in P. Mantoux, *The Industrial Revolution in the Eighteenth Century* (New York: Harper & Row, 1961), p. 75.
4. P. Bairoch, "International Industrialization Levels from 1750 to 1980," *Journal of European Economic History* 11 (Spring 1982): 269–333.
5. Crafts, *British Economic Growth During the Industrial Revolution,* pp. 45, 95–102.
6. J. Michelet, *The People,* trans. with an introduction by J. P. McKay (Urbana: University of Illinois Press, 1973; original publication, 1846), p. 64.
7. Quoted in W. A. Hayek, ed., *Capitalism and the Historians* (Chicago: University of Chicago Press, 1954), p. 126.
8. Crafts, *British Economic Growth During the Industrial Revolution,* p. 95.
9. H.-J. Voth, *Time and Work in England, 1750–1830* (Oxford: Oxford University Press, 2000), pp. 268–270; also pp. 118–133.
10. Quoted in E. R. Pike, *"Hard Times": Human Documents of the Industrial Revolution* (New York: Praeger, 1966), p. 109.
11. See especially J. Brenner and M. Rama, "Rethinking Women's Oppression," *New Left Review* 144 (March–April 1984): 33–71, and sources cited there.
12. J. Humphries, ". . . 'The Most Free from Objection' . . . : The Sexual Division of Labor and Women's Work in Nineteenth-Century England," *Journal of Economic History* 47 (December 1987): 948.
13. Ibid., p. 941; Pike, *"Hard Times,"* p. 266.
14. Quoted in Pike, *"Hard Times,"* p. 208.

Listening to the PAST

The Testimony of Young Mine Workers

The use of child labor in British industrialization quickly attracted the attention of humanitarians and social reformers. This interest led to investigations by parliamentary commissions, which resulted in laws limiting the hours and the ages of children working in large factories. Designed to build a case for remedial legislation, parliamentary inquiries gave large numbers of workers a rare chance to speak directly to contemporaries and to historians.

The moving passages that follow are taken from testimony gathered in 1841 and 1842 by the Ashley Mines Commission. Interviewing employers and many male and female workers, the commissioners focused on the physical condition of the youth and on the sexual behavior of workers far underground. The subsequent Mines Act of 1842 sought to reduce immoral behavior and sexual bullying by prohibiting underground work for all women (and for boys younger than ten).

Mr. Payne, coal master:

That children are employed generally at nine years old in the coal pits and sometimes at eight. In fact, the smaller the vein of coal is in height, the younger and smaller are the children required; the work occupies from six to seven hours per day in the pits; they are not ill-used or worked beyond their strength; a good deal of depravity exists but they are certainly not worse in morals than in other branches of the Sheffield trade, but upon the whole superior; the morals of this district are materially improving; Mr. Bruce, the clergyman, has been zealous and active in endeavoring to ameliorate their moral and religious education. . . .

Ann Eggley, hurrier, 18 years old:

I'm sure I don't know how to spell my name. We go at four in the morning, and sometimes at half-past four. We begin to work as soon as we get down. We get out after four, sometimes at five, in the evening. We work the whole time except an hour for dinner, and sometimes we haven't time to eat. I hurry [move coal wagons underground] by myself, and have done

so for long. I know the corves [small coal wagons] are very heavy, they are the biggest corves anywhere about. The work is far too hard for me; the sweat runs off me all over sometimes. I am very tired at night. Sometimes when we get home at night we have not power to wash us, and then we go to bed. Sometimes we fall asleep in the chair. Father said last night it was both a shame and a disgrace for girls to work as we do, but there was naught else for us to do. I began to hurry when I was seven and I have been hurrying ever since. I have been 11 years in the pits. The girls are always tired. I was poorly twice this winter; it was with headache. I hurry for Robert Wiggins; he is not akin to me. . . . We don't always get enough to eat and drink, but we get a good supper. I have known my father go at two in the morning to work . . . and he didn't come out till four. I am quite sure that we work constantly 12 hours except on Saturdays. We wear trousers and our shifts in the pit and great big shoes clinkered and nailed. The girls never work naked to the waist in our pit. The men don't insult us in the pit. The conduct of the girls in the pit is good enough sometimes and sometimes bad enough. I never went to a day-school. I went a little to a Sunday-school, but I soon gave it over. I thought it too bad to be confined both Sundays and week-days. I walk about and get the fresh air on Sundays. I have not learnt to read. I don't know my letters. I never learnt naught. I never go to church or chapel; there is no church or chapel at Gawber, there is none nearer than a mile. . . . I have never heard that a good man came into the world who was God's son to save sinners. I never heard of Christ at all. Nobody has ever told me about him, nor have my father and mother ever taught me to pray. I know no prayer; I never pray.

Patience Kershaw, aged 17:

My father has been dead about a year; my mother is living and has ten children, five lads and five lasses; the oldest is about thirty, the youngest is four; three lasses go to mill; all the lads are colliers, two getters and three hurriers; one lives at home and does nothing; mother does nought but look after home.

This illustration of a girl dragging a coal wagon was one of several that shocked public opinion and contributed to the Mines Act of 1842. *(© British Library Board. All rights reserved.)*

All my sisters have been hurriers, but three went to the mill. Alice went because her legs swelled from hurrying in cold water when she was hot. I never went to day-school; I go to Sunday-school, but I cannot read or write; I go to pit at five o'clock in the morning and come out at five in the evening; I get my breakfast of porridge and milk first; I take my dinner with me, a cake, and eat it as I go; I do not stop or rest any time for the purpose; I get nothing else until I get home, and then have potatoes and meat, not every day meat. I hurry in the clothes I have now got on, trousers and ragged jacket; the bald place upon my head is made by thrusting the corves; my legs have never swelled, but sisters' did when they went to mill; I hurry the corves a mile and more under ground and back; they weigh 300; I hurry 11 a day; I wear a belt and chain at the workings to get the corves out; the putters [miners] that I work for are *naked* except their caps; they pull off all their clothes; I see them at work when I go up; sometimes they beat me, if I am not quick enough, with their hands; they strike me upon my back; the boys take liberties with me, sometimes, they pull me about; I am the only girl in the pit; there are about 20 boys and 15 men; all the men are naked; I would rather work in mill than in coal-pit.

Isabel Wilson, 38 years old, coal putter:

When women have children thick [fast] they are compelled to take them down early. I have been married 19 years and have had 10 bairns [children]; seven are in life. When on Sir John's work was a carrier of coals, which caused me to miscarry five times from the strains, and was gai [very] ill after each. Putting is no so oppressive; last child was born on Saturday morning, and I was at work on the Friday night.

Once met with an accident; a coal brake my cheek-bone, which kept me idle some weeks.

I have wrought below 30 years, and so has the guid man; he is getting touched in the breath now.

None of the children read, as the work is no regular. I did read once, but no able to attend to it now; when I go below lassie 10 years of age keeps house and makes the broth or stir-about.

Questions for Analysis

1. To what extent are the testimonies of Ann Eggley and Patience Kershaw in harmony with that of Payne?

2. Describe the work of Eggley and Kershaw. What do you think of their work? Why?

3. What strikes you most about the lives of these workers?

4. The witnesses were responding to questions from middle-class commissioners. What did the commissioners seem interested in? Why?

Source: J. Bowditch and C. Ramsland, eds., *Voices of the Industrial Revolution* (Ann Arbor, Mich.: University of Michigan Press, 1961), pp. 86–90. Copyright © 1961, 1989 by the University of Michigan. Reprinted by permission.

Revolutionaries in Transylvania. Ana Ipatescu was a member
of the first group of revolutionaries in Transylvania against
Russia, 1848. *(National Historical Museum, Bucharest/The Art Archive)*

23

THE TRIUMPH OF NATIONALISM IN EUROPE, 1815–1914

Chapter Preview

Peace, Radical Ideas, and Romanticism

• How did the allies make peace in 1815, and what radical ideas emerged between 1815 and 1848?

Reforms and Revolutions (1815–1850)

• Why did revolutions break out in 1848, and why did they fail?

Nation Building in Italy, Germany, and Russia

• How did strong leaders and nation building transform Italy, Germany, and Russia?

Life in Urban Society

• What was the impact of urban growth on cities, social classes, families, and ideas?

The National State and the Socialist Movement (1871–1914)

• How did governments gain popular support and deal with the socialist movement?

Europe's momentous economic and political transformation of modern times began in the late eighteenth century with the Industrial Revolution in England and then the French Revolution. Until about 1815 these economic and political revolutions were separate, involving different countries and activities and proceeding at very different paces. After peace returned in 1815, the situation changed. Economic and political changes tended to fuse, reinforcing each other and bringing about what historian Eric Hobsbawm incisively called the **dual revolution.** For instance, the growth of the industrial middle class encouraged the drive for representative government, and the demands of French workers in 1793 and 1794 eventually inspired socialists in many countries. Gathering strength, the dual revolution transformed Europe and had a powerful impact on the rest of the world.

Revolutionary changes in economics and politics posed a tremendous intellectual challenge. The changes that were occurring fascinated observers and stimulated the growth of new ideas and powerful ideologies. The most important of these were revitalized conservatism and three ideologies of change—liberalism, nationalism, and socialism.

In the midst of the intellectual and economic upheaval after 1815, popular political revolutions welled up again in 1848 throughout most of Europe. These revolutions failed, however, and gave way to more sober—and more successful—nation building in the 1860s. Redrawing the political geography of central Europe and uniting first Italy and then Germany, European political leaders and middle-class nationalists also began to deal effectively with some of the problems posed by the burgeoning of urban society. European leaders also encouraged their peoples to put their faith in a responsive national state. Identification with the national state gradually enlisted widespread support, and in many European countries ordinary citizens developed a sense of belonging to a large and beloved national community. At the same time, the triumph of nationalism promoted bitter rivalries between states and peoples, and in the twentieth century it would bring an era of tragedy and decline in Europe.

dual revolution *The term that historian Eric Hobsbawn used for the economic and political changes that tended to fuse, reinforcing each other.*

Congress of Vienna *The peace settlement that attempted to redraw Europe's political map after the defeat of Napoleonic France.*

Holy Alliance *An alliance formed by Austria, Russia, and Prussia in September 1815 that became a symbol of the repression of liberal and revolutionary movements all over Europe.*

● **Metternich** This portrait by Sir Thomas Lawrence reveals much about Metternich the man. Handsome, refined, and intelligent, Metternich was a great aristocrat who was passionately devoted to the defense of his class and its interests. *(The Royal Collection, © 2007 Her Majesty Queen Elizabeth II)*

PEACE, RADICAL IDEAS, AND ROMANTICISM

How did the allies make peace in 1815, and what radical ideas emerged between 1815 and 1848?

The triumph of revolutionary economic and political forces was by no means certain as the Napoleonic era ended. Quite the contrary. The aristocratic monarchies of Russia, Prussia, Austria, and Great Britain had finally defeated France, and they were determined to reestablish a stable conservative order. This meant holding France in line and preventing political revolutions and radical change. Thus the allies agreed to meet at the **Congress of Vienna** to fashion a general peace settlement and reinforce conservative forces. The allies succeeded in constructing a settlement that did not sow the seeds of another great war, thereby contributing to a century unmarred by destructive generalized war in Europe (see Map 23.1).

Efforts to shore up conservatism were much less successful after 1815. Intellectuals and social observers articulated ideas that still live in today's world. Almost all of these basic ideas were radical. In one way or another they rejected the old conservatism, with its stress on tradition, a hereditary monarchy, and a strong landowning aristocracy. Instead, radicals developed and refined alternative visions—alternative ideologies—and tried to convince society to act on them. With time, they were very successful.

The Peace Settlement

The allied powers were most concerned with the defeated enemy, France. Agreeing to the restoration of the Bourbon dynasty (see page 636), the allies were quite lenient toward France after Napoleon's abdication. France was given the boundaries it possessed in 1792, and France did not have to pay any war reparations. Thus the victorious powers did not foment a spirit of injustice and revenge in the defeated country.

When the four allies of the Quadruple Alliance—Austria, Britain, Prussia, and Russia—met together at the Congress of Vienna, assisted in a minor way by a host of delegates from the smaller European states, they also agreed to raise a number of formidable barriers against renewed French aggression. For example, Prussia received considerably more territory on France's eastern border so as to stand as the "sentinel on the Rhine" against France.

In their moderation toward France, the allies were motivated primarily by self-interest and traditional ideas about the balance of power. To the peacemakers, and especially to Klemens von Metternich, Austria's all-important foreign minister, the European balance of power meant an international equilibrium of political and military forces that would discourage aggression by any single state or any combination of states. Unfortunately for France, in February 1815 Napoleon suddenly escaped from the island of Elba. Yet the peace concluded after Napoleon's final defeat at Waterloo was still relatively moderate toward France.

The rest of the settlement already concluded at the Congress of Vienna was left intact. Of considerable importance, the members of the Quadruple Alliance did agree to meet periodically to discuss their common interests and to consider appropriate measures for the maintenance of peace in Europe. This agreement marked the beginning of the European "congress system," which lasted long into the nineteenth century and peacefully settled many international crises through international conferences and balance-of-power diplomacy.

The domestic side of the peace settlement was much less moderate. In 1815 under Metternich's leadership, Austria, Prussia, and Russia embarked on a crusade against the ideas and politics of the dual revolution. This crusade lasted until Metternich fell from power in 1848. The first step was the **Holy Alliance,** formed by Austria, Prussia, and Russia in September 1815. First proposed by Russia's Alexander I, the alliance soon became a symbol of the repression of liberal and revolutionary movements all over Europe.

Metternich's policies dominated not only Austria and the Italian peninsula but also the entire German Confederation, which the peace settlement of Vienna had called into being (see Map 23.1). The confederation was composed of thirty-eight independent German states and was dominated by Austria, with Prussia a willing junior partner in the planning and execution of repressive measures. It was through the German Confederation that Metternich had the repressive **Carlsbad Decrees** issued in 1819. These decrees required the thirty-eight German member states to root out subversive ideas in their universities and newspapers, while a permanent committee was established to investigate and punish any liberal or radical organizations.

Born into the landed nobility, Metternich was a zealous defender of his class and its privileges. Like many European conservatives of his time, he firmly believed that liberalism, as embodied in revolutionary America and France, had been responsible for a generation of war with untold bloodshed and suffering. He blamed liberal revolutionaries for stirring up the lower classes, which he believed desired nothing more than peace and quiet.

The threat of liberalism appeared doubly dangerous to Metternich because liberals believed that each national group had a right to establish its own independent government. Such national self-determination posed a grave threat to the vast Austrian Empire of the Habsburgs, for it was a dynastic state made up of many national groups. The Germans had long dominated the empire, yet they accounted for only one-fourth of the population. The Magyars (Hungarians), a substantially smaller group, dominated the kingdom of Hungary, though even they did not account for a majority of the population in that part of the Austrian Empire. Czechs formed the third major group. There were also large numbers of Italians, Poles, and Ukrainians as well as smaller groups of Slovenes, Croats, Serbs, Ruthenians, and

Chronology

1790s–1840s	Romantic movement in literature and other arts
1814–1815	Congress of Vienna
1815	Revision of Corn Laws in Britain
1819	Carlsbad Decrees issued by German Confederation
1830–1848	Reign of Louis Philippe in France
1832	Reform Bill in Britain
1840s–1890s	Realism in literature
1845–1851	Great Famine in Ireland
1847	Ten Hours Act in Britain
1848	Revolutions in France, Austria, and Prussia; Marx and Engels, *The Communist Manifesto*
1850–1914	Modernization of cities; condition of working classes improves
1859	Darwin, *On the Origin of Species*
1859–1870	Unification of Italy
1861	Freeing of serfs in Russia
1866–1871	Unification of Germany
1870	France's Third Republic founded
1881	Assassination of Russian tsar Alexander II
1883–1889	Social security laws in Germany
1889–1914	Second Socialist International
1905	Revolution in Russia

Carlsbad Decrees *Issued in 1819, these decrees required the thirty-eight German member states to root out subversive ideas in their universities and newspapers.*

MAP 23.1 **Europe in 1815** Europe's leaders re-established a balance of political power after the defeat of Napoleon. Prussia gained territory on the Rhine and in Saxony and consolidated its position as a Great Power.

Romanians. Moreover, different ethnic groups often lived in the same provinces and even in the same villages.

The multinational state that Metternich served was both strong and weak. It was strong because of its large population and vast territories; it was weak because of its many and potentially dissatisfied nationalities. In these circumstances, Metternich virtually had to oppose liberalism and nationalism, for Austria was simply unable to accommodate those ideologies of the dual revolution.

In his efforts to hold back liberalism and nationalism Metternich was supported by the Russian Empire and, to a lesser extent, by the Ottoman Empire. Bitter enemies, these far-flung empires were, like Austria, absolutist states with powerful armies and long traditions of expansion and conquest. Both were multinational empires made up of many peoples, languages, and religions, but in each case most of the ruling elite came from a dominant ethnic group—the Orthodox Christian Russians and the Muslim Ottoman Turks. After 1815, both states worked with Austria to preserve their respective conservative orders.

Liberalism

The principal ideas of liberalism—liberty and equality—were by no means defeated in 1815. Liberalism demanded representative government as opposed to autocratic monarchy, equality before the law as opposed to legally separate classes. The idea of liberty also continued to mean specific individual freedoms: freedom of the press, freedom of speech, freedom of assembly, and freedom from arbitrary arrest. In Europe only France with Louis XVIII's Constitutional Charter and Great Britain with its Parliament and historic rights of English men and women had realized much of the liberal program in 1815. Even in those countries, liberalism had not fully succeeded.

Although liberalism retained its cutting edge, many considered it a somewhat duller tool than it had been. The reasons for this opinion were that liberalism faced more radical ideological competitors in the early nineteenth century. Opponents of classical liberalism especially criticized its economic principles, which called for unrestricted private enterprise and no government interference in the economy. This philosophy was popularly known as the doctrine of **laissez faire**. (This form of liberalism is often called "classical" liberalism in the United States to distinguish it sharply from modern American liberalism, which usually favors more government programs to meet social needs and to regulate the economy.)

laissez faire *Economic liberalism that believes in unrestricted private enterprise and no government interference in the economy.*

The idea of a free economy had first been persuasively formulated by Scottish philosophy professor Adam Smith, whose *Inquiry into the Nature and Causes of the Wealth of Nations* (1776) founded modern economics. Smith was highly critical of eighteenth-century mercantilism and its attempt to regulate trade and economic activity. Far preferable, he believed, were free competition and the "invisible hand" of the self-regulating market, which would give all citizens a fair and equal opportunity to do what they did best. Everyone would benefit, not just the rich.

In the early nineteenth century in Britain this economic liberalism was embraced most enthusiastically by business groups and became a doctrine associated with business interests. Businessmen used the doctrine to defend their right to do as they wished in their factories. Labor unions were outlawed because they supposedly restricted free competition and the individual's "right to work."

In the early nineteenth century liberal political ideals also became more closely associated with narrow class interests. Early-nineteenth-century liberals favored representative government, but they generally wanted property qualifications attached to the right to vote. In practice this meant limiting the vote to well-to-do males—aristocratic landowners, substantial businessmen, and successful members of the professions. Workers and peasants as well as the lower middle class of shopkeepers, clerks, and artisans did not own the necessary property and so could not vote.

As liberalism became increasingly identified with the middle class after 1815, some intellectuals and foes of conservatism felt that liberalism did not go nearly far enough. Inspired by memories of the French Revolution and the young American republic, they called for universal voting rights, at least for males, and for democracy. These democrats and republicans were more radical than the liberals.

Nationalism

Nationalism was a second radical idea in the years after 1815—an idea destined to have an enormous influence in the modern world. Early advocates of the "national idea" argued that each people had its own genius and its own *cultural* unity, which manifested itself especially in a common language, history, and territory. In fact, within each ethnic grouping only an elite spoke a standardized written language, and a variety of ethnic groups shared the territory of most states.

Nevertheless, European nationalists usually sought to turn the cultural unity that they perceived into a *political* reality, so that each people lived in an independent nation-state. It was this political goal that made nationalism so explosive in central

● **Building German Nationalism** As popular upheaval in France spread to central Europe in March 1848, Germans from the solid middle classes came together in Frankfurt to draft a constitution for a new united Germany. This colored woodcut commemorates the solemn procession of delegates entering Saint Paul's Cathedral in Frankfurt, where the delegates would have their deliberations. Festivals, celebrations, and parades helped create a feeling of belonging to a large unseen community, a nation binding millions of strangers together. *(akg-images)*

and eastern Europe after 1815, when there were either too few states (Austria, Russia, and the Ottoman Empire) or too many (the Italian peninsula and the German Confederation) and when different peoples overlapped and intermingled.

The nationalist vision, often fitting poorly with existing conditions, triumphed in the long run partly because the epoch-making development of complex industrial and urban society required much better communication between individuals and groups.[1] These communication needs promoted the use of a standardized national language within many countries, creating at least a superficial cultural unity as it eventually encompassed the entire population through mass education.

Nation-states also emerged because those who believed in the new ideology wanted to create "imagined communities," communities seeking to bind millions of strangers together around the abstract concept of an all-embracing national identity. Thus nationalist intellectuals and leaders brought citizens together with emotionally charged symbols and ceremonies, such as ethnic festivals and flag-waving parades, which celebrated the imagined nation of spiritual equals.[2]

Between 1815 and 1850 most people who believed in nationalism also believed in either liberalism or radical, democratic republicanism. A common faith in the creativity and nobility of the people was perhaps the single most important reason for the linking of these two concepts. Liberals and especially democrats saw the people as the ultimate source of all good government.

Early nationalists usually believed that every nation, like every citizen, had the right to exist in freedom and to develop its character and spirit. They were confident that a symphony of free nations would promote the harmony and ultimate unity of all peoples. Thus the liberty of the individual and the love of a free nation overlapped greatly in early-nineteenth-century Europe.

Yet early nationalists also stressed the differences among peoples. Even early nationalism developed a strong sense of "we" and "they," and the "they" was often the enemy. Thus early nationalism in Europe was ambiguous. Its main thrust was liberal and democratic. But below the surface lurked ideas of national superiority and national mission that could lead to aggression and conflict.

Socialism

socialism *A backlash against the emergence of individualism and fragmentation of society, it was a move toward cooperation and a sense of community; the key ideas were planning, greater economic equality, and state regulation of property.*

Socialism, the new radical doctrine after 1815, began in France, despite the fact that France trailed Great Britain in developing modern industry. These French thinkers were acutely aware that the political revolution in France, the rise of laissez faire, and the emergence of factory industry in England were transforming society. They were disturbed because they saw these trends as fomenting selfish individualism and splitting the community into isolated fragments. There was, they believed, an urgent need for a further reorganization of society to establish cooperation and a new sense of community.

Early French socialists believed in economic planning. Inspired by the emergency measures of 1793 and 1794 in France, they argued that the government should rationally organize the economy. Early socialists also shared an intense desire to help the poor. Finally, socialists believed that private property should be strictly regulated by the government or even abolished. Planning, greater economic equality, and state control of property—these were the key ideas of early French socialism and of all socialism since.

One of the most influential early socialist thinkers was Henri de Saint-Simon (1760–1825). Saint-Simon optimistically proclaimed the tremendous possibilities of industrial development: "The age of gold is before us!" The key to progress was proper social organization. Such an arrangement of society required the **parasites**— the court, the aristocracy, lawyers, churchmen—to give way, once and for all, to the **doers**—the leading scientists, engineers, and industrialists. The doers would carefully plan the economy, guide it forward, and improve conditions for the poor.

Charles Fourier (1772–1837), another influential French thinker, envisaged a socialist utopia of self-sufficient communities. An early proponent of the total emancipation of women, Fourier also called for the abolition of marriage, free unions based only on love, and sexual freedom. To many middle-class men and women, these ideas were shocking and immoral and made the socialist program appear doubly dangerous and revolutionary.

The message of French utopian socialists interacted with the experiences of French urban workers. Workers cherished the memory of the French Revolution, and they became violently opposed to laissez-faire laws that denied them the right to organize. Developing a sense of class in the process, workers favored collective action and government intervention in economic life. Thus the aspirations of workers and utopian theorists reinforced each other, and a genuine socialist movement emerged in Paris in the 1830s and 1840s.

It was left to Karl Marx (1818–1883) to establish firm foundations for modern socialism. The son of a Jewish lawyer who had converted to Christianity, the atheistic young Marx had studied philosophy at the University of Berlin before turning to journalism and economics. In 1848 the thirty-year-old Karl Marx and the twenty-eight-year-old Friedrich Engels (1820–1895) published *The Communist Manifesto*, which became the bible of socialism.

Early French socialists often appealed to the middle class and the state to help the poor. Marx ridiculed such appeals as naive. He argued that the interests of the middle class and those of the industrial working class were inevitably opposed to each other. Indeed, according to the *Manifesto*, the "history of all previously existing society is the history of class struggles." In Marx's view one class had always exploited the other, and with the advent of modern industry society was split more clearly than ever before: between the middle class (the **bourgeoisie**) and the modern working class (the **proletariat**).

Just as the bourgeoisie had triumphed over the feudal aristocracy, the proletariat, Marx predicted, would conquer the bourgeoisie in a violent revolution. While a tiny minority owned the means of production and grew richer, the ever-poorer proletariat was constantly growing in size and in class-consciousness. The critical moment, Marx thought, was very near. "The proletarians have nothing to lose but their chains. They have a world to win. WORKING MEN OF ALL COUNTRIES, UNITE!" So ends *The Communist Manifesto*.

Marx was strongly influenced by England's classical economists, who taught that labor was the source of all value. Marx went on to argue that profits were really wages stolen from the workers. Moreover, Marx incorporated Engels's account of the terrible oppression of the new class of factory workers in England; thus Marx's doctrines seemed to be based on hard facts. Forced to flee Germany after the revolutions of 1848, Marx settled in England and worked tirelessly to build an international socialist movement (see page 708).

parasites *In Saint-Simon's thought, these were the social groups that did not contribute directly to the industrial development of the state—the lawyers, clergymen, court, and aristocracy.*

doers *In Saint-Simon's thought, these were the social groups that led the way in the industrial development of the state—the scientists, engineers, and industrialists.*

Primary Source: "Working Men of All Countries, Unite!" *Read these excerpts from* The Communist Manifesto *and find out why "the proletarians have nothing to lose but their chains."*

bourgeoisie *A term for well-educated, prosperous, middle-class groups.*

proletariat *The Marxian term for the modern working class.*

Romanticism

Radical concepts of politics and society were accompanied by comparable changes in literature and other arts during the dual revolution. The early nineteenth century marked the acme of the romantic movement, which profoundly influenced the arts and enriched European culture immeasurably. The romantic movement was in part a revolt against classicism and the Enlightenment. The classicists believed that the ancient Greeks and Romans had discovered eternally valid aesthetic rules; that these rules fit with the Enlightenment's belief in rationality, order, and restraint; and that playwrights and painters should continue to follow them.

Forerunners of the romantic movement appeared from about 1750 on. Of these, Rousseau—the passionate advocate of feeling, freedom, and natural goodness—was the most influential. Romanticism then crystallized fully in the 1790s, primarily in England and Germany. The French Revolution kindled the belief that radical reconstruction was also possible in cultural and artistic life, and romanticism gained strength until the 1840s.

Romanticism was characterized by a belief in emotional exuberance, unrestrained imagination, and spontaneity in both art and personal life. In Germany early romantics of the 1770s and 1780s called themselves the **Sturm und Drang** (Storm and Stress), and many romantic artists of the early nineteenth century lived lives of tremendous emotional intensity. Suicide, duels to the death, madness, and strange illnesses were not uncommon among leading romantics. Great individualists, they believed the full development of each person's unique human potential to be the supreme purpose in life.

The French painter Eugène Delacroix (1798–1863) was a romantic master of dramatic, colorful scenes that stirred the emotions. He was fascinated with remote and exotic subjects, whether lion hunts in Morocco or the languishing, sensuous women of a sultan's harem. He was also a passionate spokesman for freedom, celebrating popular revolution in general and revolution in France in particular.

It was in music that romanticism realized most fully and permanently its goals of free expression and emotional intensity. Whereas the composers of the eighteenth century had remained true to well-defined structures, the great romantics used a great range of forms. Romantic composers also transformed the small classical orchestra, tripling its size by adding wind instruments, percussion, and more brass and strings. No composer ever surpassed its first great master, Ludwig van Beethoven (1770–1827). As the contemporary German novelist Ernst Hoffmann (1776–1822) wrote, "Beethoven's music sets in motion the lever of fear, of awe, of horror, of suffering, and awakens just that infinite longing which is the essence of Romanticism."

Nowhere was the break with classicism more apparent than in romanticism's general con-

Sturm und Drang *Literally "Storm and Stress," the German early romantics of the 1770s and 1780s who lived lives of tremendous emotional intensity; suicides, duels, madness, and strange illnesses were common.*

● **Nature and the Meaning of Life** Caspar David Friedrich (1774–1840) was Germany's greatest romantic painter, and his *Traveler Looking over a Sea of Fog* (1815) is a representative masterpiece. Friedrich's paintings often focus on dark silhouetted figures silently contemplating an eerie landscape. Friedrich came to believe that humans were only an insignificant part of an all-embracing higher unity. *(Bildarchiv Preussischer Kulturbesitz/Art Resource, NY)*

ception of nature. Eighteenth-century classicism was not particularly interested in nature. The romantics, in contrast, were enchanted by nature. Sometimes fascinated by its awesome and tempestuous side, at other times they saw nature as a source of spiritual inspiration. Most romantics saw the growth of modern industry as an ugly, brutal attack on their beloved nature and on the human personality.

Fascinated by color and diversity, the romantic imagination turned toward history with a passion. For romantics, history was beautiful and exciting. And it was the art of change over time—the key to a universe that was now perceived to be organic and dynamic. Historical studies supported the development of national aspirations and encouraged entire peoples to seek in the past their special destinies.

Victor Hugo (1802–1885) was France's greatest romantic master in both poetry and prose. His powerful novels exemplified the romantic fascination with fantastic characters, strange settings, and human emotions. The hero of Hugo's famous *Hunchback of Notre Dame* (1831) is the great cathedral's deformed bell-ringer, a "human gargoyle" overlooking the teeming life of fifteenth-century Paris.

In central and eastern Europe, literary romanticism and early nationalism often reinforced each other. Seeking a unique greatness in every people, well-educated romantics plumbed their own histories and cultures. Like modern anthropologists, they turned their attention to peasant life and transcribed the folk songs, tales, and proverbs that the cosmopolitan Enlightenment had disdained. The brothers Jacob and Wilhelm Grimm were particularly successful at rescuing German fairy tales from oblivion. In the Slavic lands romantics played a decisive role in converting spoken peasant languages into modern written languages. The greatest of all Russian poets, Aleksander Pushkin (1799–1837), used his lyric genius to mold the modern literary language of Russia.

REFORMS AND REVOLUTIONS (1815–1850)

Why did revolutions break out in 1848, and why did they fail?

While the romantic movement was developing, liberal, national, and socialist forces battered against the conservatism of 1815. In a few countries change occurred gradually and peacefully. Elsewhere pressure built up like steam in a pressure cooker without a safety valve. Then in 1848 revolutionary political and social ideologies combined with economic crisis and the romantic impulse to produce a vast upheaval. National independence, liberal-democratic constitutions, and social reform—the lofty aspirations of a generation seemed at hand. Yet in the end the revolutions failed, and the lofty aspirations were shattered.

Liberal Reform in Great Britain

Eighteenth-century British society was dominated by the landowning aristocracy, but that class was neither closed nor rigidly defined. Basic civil rights were guaranteed, but only about 8 percent of the population could vote for representatives to Parliament. The French Revolution then threw the British aristocracy into a panic for a generation, and after 1815 it was determined to defend its ruling position.

The first step in this direction began in 1815 with revision of the **Corn Laws** dealing with foreign grain imports. Fearing peace would bring a resumption of imports and lower prices for wheat, the aristocracy rammed through Parliament a new law that prohibited the importation of foreign grain unless the price at home rose to very high levels. More broadly, the landed aristocracy opposed the new manufacturing and

Corn Laws *The laws revised in 1815 that prohibited the importation of foreign grain into Great Britain unless the price at home rose to improbable levels.*

commercial groups that were insisting on a much greater place in the framework of political power and social prestige. Thus the House of Lords successfully blocked the reform of voting rights and representation in Parliament as long as possible. Only in 1832 did a surge of popular protest convince the king and lords to give in.

The Reform Bill of 1832 had profound significance. First, the House of Commons had emerged as the all-important legislative body. Second, the new industrial areas of the country gained representation in the Commons. Third, the number of voters increased by about 50 percent. Comfortable middle-class groups in the urban population, as well as some substantial farmers, received the vote. Thus the pressures building in Great Britain were temporarily released without revolution or civil war.

The principal radical program was embodied in the "People's Charter" of 1838 and the Chartist movement (see page 669), with its core demand for universal male (but not female) suffrage. In three separate campaigns hundreds of thousands of people signed gigantic petitions calling on Parliament to grant all men the right to vote. Parliament rejected the petitions, but the working poor learned a valuable lesson in mass politics.

While calling for universal male suffrage, many working-class people also joined with middle-class manufacturers in the Anti–Corn Law League. Mass participation made possible a popular crusade led by fighting liberals who argued that lower food prices and more jobs in industry depended on repeal of the Corn Laws. After Ireland's potato crop failed in 1845 and famine prices for food seemed likely in England, a minority of Tory aristocrats joined with the Whigs to repeal the Corn Laws in 1846 and allow free imports of grain. England escaped famine.

The following year the Tories passed the Ten Hours Act of 1847, which limited the workday for women and young people in factories to ten hours. Tory aristocrats continued to champion legislation regulating factory conditions. They were competing vigorously with the middle class for the support of the working class. This healthy competition between a still-vigorous aristocracy and a strong middle class was a crucial factor in Great Britain's peaceful evolution in the nineteenth century.

The people of Ireland did not benefit from this political competition. Long ruled as a conquered people, the great mass of the population (outside the northern counties of Ulster, which were partly Presbyterian) were Irish Catholic peasants who rented their land from a tiny minority of Church of England Protestants, many of whom lived in England. Ruthlessly exploited and growing rapidly in numbers, Irish peasants had come to depend on the potato crop.

The potato crop failed in 1845, 1846, 1848, and 1851 in Ireland and throughout much of Europe. Blight attacked the young plants, and the tubers rotted. The general result in Europe was high food prices, widespread suffering, and, frequently, social upheaval. In Ireland the result was widespread starvation and mass fever epidemics. Total losses of population were staggering. Fully 1 million emigrants fled the famine between 1845 and 1851, going primarily to the United States and Great Britain.

Revolutions in France

Louis XVIII's Constitutional Charter of 1814 protected the economic and social gains made by sections of the middle class and the peasantry in the French Revolution, and it permitted great intellectual and artistic freedom. The charter was anything but democratic, however. Only a tiny minority of males had the right to vote for the legislative deputies, who, with the king and his ministers, made the laws of the nation. The old aristocracy, with its pre-1789 mentality, was a minority within the voting population.

It was this situation that Louis's successor, his brother Charles X (r. 1824–1830), could not abide. A true reactionary who wanted to re-establish the old order in France, Charles finally repudiated the Constitutional Charter in an attempted coup in July 1830. He issued decrees stripping much of the wealthy middle class of its voting

● **The Triumph of Demo-cratic Republics** This French illustration constructs a joyous, optimistic vision of the initial revolutionary breakthrough in 1848. The peoples of Europe, joined together around their respective national banners, are achieving republican freedom, which is symbolized by the statue of liberty and the discarded crowns. The woman wearing pants (*front left*)—very radical attire—represents feminist hopes for liberation. (*Archives Charmet/The Bridgeman Art Library*)

rights, and he censored the press. The immediate reaction, encouraged by journalists and lawyers, was an insurrection in the capital by printers, other artisans, and small traders. In "three glorious days" the revolution of 1830 brought down the government. Charles fled. Then the upper middle class skillfully seated Charles's cousin, Louis Philippe, duke of Orléans, on the vacant throne.

Louis Philippe (r. 1830–1848) accepted the Constitutional Charter of 1814 and admitted that he was merely the "king of the French people." Yet the situation in France remained fundamentally unchanged. The vote was extended only from 100,000 to 170,000 citizens. Republicans, democrats, social reformers, and the poor of Paris were bitterly disappointed.

These disappointments in France grew in the 1840s, which were economically hard and politically tense throughout Europe. The government's stubborn refusal to consider electoral reform heightened a sense of class injustice among shopkeepers and urban working people, and it eventually touched off a popular revolt in Paris in February 1848. Barricades went up and Louis Philippe quickly abdicated.

The revolutionaries were firmly committed to a truly popular and democratic republic so that the healthy, life-giving forces of the common people—the peasants and the workers—could reform society with wise legislation. In practice, building such a republic meant giving the right to vote to every adult male, and this was quickly done. Revolutionary compassion and sympathy for freedom were expressed in the freeing of all slaves in French colonies, the abolition of the death penalty, and the establishment of **national workshops** for unemployed workers in Paris.

Yet there were profound differences within the revolutionary coalition in Paris. The moderate liberal republicans of the middle class viewed universal male suffrage as the ultimate reform, and they strongly opposed any further radical social measures. The radical republicans were committed to some kind of socialism. Thus when the French

national workshops *A system established to offer Parisians constant work at fair wages.*

masses went to the election polls for the first time in late April, they elected a majority of moderate republicans to the new Constituent Assembly. Socialism frightened not only the middle and upper classes but also the peasants, many of whom owned land.

After the elections this clash of ideologies—of liberal capitalism and socialism—became a clash of classes and arms. When the government dissolved the national workshops in Paris, workers rose in a spontaneous and violent uprising. Barricades sprang up in the narrow streets of Paris, and a terrible class war began. Working people fought with courage, but the government had the army and the support of peasant France. After three terrible "June Days" and the death or injury of more than ten thousand people, the republican army stood triumphant in a sea of working-class blood and hatred.

The revolution in France thus ended in spectacular failure. The February coalition of the middle and working classes had in four short months become locked in mortal combat. In place of a generous democratic republic, the Constituent Assembly completed a constitution featuring a strong executive. This allowed Louis Napoleon, nephew of Napoleon Bonaparte, to win a landslide victory in the election of December 1848.

Elected to a four-year term, President Louis Napoleon at first shared power with a conservative National Assembly. But in 1851 Louis Napoleon dismissed the Assembly and seized power in a coup d'état. A year later he called on the French to make him hereditary emperor, and 97 percent voted to do so in a national plebiscite. Louis Napoleon—proclaimed Emperor Napoleon III—then ruled France until 1870. Gradually his government became less authoritarian as he liberalized his empire. In 1870, on the eve of a disastrous war with Prussia, Louis Napoleon was still seeking with some success to reconcile a strong national state with universal male suffrage and an independent National Assembly with real power.

The Revolutions of 1848 in Central Europe

Throughout central Europe news of the upheaval in France evoked feverish excitement and eventually revolution. Liberals demanded written constitutions, representative government, and greater civil liberties from authoritarian regimes. When governments hesitated, popular revolts followed. Urban workers and students served as the shock troops, but they were allied with middle-class liberals and peasants. In the face of this united front, monarchs collapsed and granted almost everything. The popular revolutionary coalition then broke down as it had in France. Conflicting national aspirations played a key role. This permitted the traditional forces—the monarchy, the aristocracy, and the regular army—to recover their nerve, reassert their authority, and take back many, though not all, of the concessions. Reaction was everywhere victorious.

The revolution in the Austrian Empire began in Hungary, where nationalistic Hungarians demanded national autonomy, full civil liberties, and universal suffrage. When Viennese students and workers also took to the streets and peasant disorders broke out, the Habsburg emperor capitulated and promised reforms and a liberal constitution. However, the peasants soon lost interest in the political and social questions agitating the cities, for they quickly won a great victory when the monarchy abolished the harsh serfdom that still existed in the Austrian Empire.

Above all, the coalition was weakened and destroyed by conflicting national aspirations. In March the Hungarian revolutionary leaders pushed through an extremely liberal, almost democratic, constitution. But the Hungarian revolutionaries also sought to transform the mosaic of provinces and peoples that was the kingdom of Hungary into a unified, centralized Hungarian nation. To the minority groups that formed half of the population—the Croats, Serbs, and Romanians—such unification was completely unacceptable. Each felt entitled to political autonomy and cultural independence. The Habsburg monarchy in Vienna exploited the fears of the minority groups, and they were soon locked in armed combat with the new Hungarian government. In a somewhat similar way Czech nationalists based in the city of Prague and elsewhere in Bohemia came into conflict with German nationalists.

The monarchy's first breakthrough came in June when the army bombarded Prague and savagely crushed a working-class revolt. Subsequently, the well-equipped, predominantly peasant troops of the regular Austrian army attacked the student and working-class radicals in Vienna and retook the city.. Thus the determination of Austria's aristocracy and the loyalty of its army were the final ingredients in the triumph of reaction and the defeat of revolution.

Finally, another determined conservative, Nicholas I of Russia (r. 1825–1855), obligingly lent his iron hand. In June 1849, 130,000 Russian troops poured into Hungary and subdued the country after bitter fighting. For a number of years the Habsburgs ruled Hungary as a conquered territory.

After Austria, Prussia was the largest and most influential German kingdom. Prior to 1848, the goal of middle-class Prussian liberals had been to transform absolutist Prussia into a liberal constitutional monarchy that would transform the thirty-eight states of the German Confederation into a unified nation. Following the fall of Louis Philippe in France, artisans and factory workers in Berlin exploded in March 1848 and joined with the middle-class liberals in the struggle against the monarchy. The autocratic yet paternalistic Frederick William IV (r. 1840–1861) caved in and promised to grant Prussia a liberal constitution and to merge Prussia into a new national German state.

A self-appointed committee of predominantly middle-class liberals from various German states also began writing a federal constitution for a unified German state. Meeting in Frankfurt, the National Assembly soon became absorbed in a battle with Denmark over the provinces of **Schleswig and Holstein.** The provinces were inhabited primarily by Germans, but the new nationalistic king of Denmark was trying to integrate both provinces into the rest of his state. Hypnotized by this conflict, the National Assembly at Frankfurt finally called on the Prussian army to oppose Denmark in the name of the German nation. Prussia responded and began war with Denmark. As the Schleswig-Holstein issue demonstrated, the national ideal was the crucial factor motivating the German middle classes in 1848.

In March 1849 the slow moving National Assembly finally completed its drafting of a liberal constitution and elected King Frederick William of Prussia emperor of the new German national state. By early 1849, however,. Frederick William had reasserted his royal authority and granted his subjects a conservative constitution. Reasserting that he ruled by divine right, Frederick William contemptuously refused to accept the "crown from the gutter." Preoccupied with nationalist issues, the middle-class revolutionaries in Frankfurt had waited too long and acted too timidly.

When Frederick William tried to get the small monarchs of Germany to elect him emperor with authoritarian power, Austria balked. Supported by Russia, Austria forced Prussia to renounce all its schemes of unification in late 1850. The German Confederation was re-established. Attempts to unite the Germans—first in a liberal national state and then in a conservative Prussian empire—had failed completely.

In conclusion, political, economic, and social pressures building after 1815 exploded in 1848, but the upheavals were abortive, and very few revolutionary goals were realized. The moderate, nationalistic middle classes were unable to consolidate their initial victories in France or elsewhere in Europe. Instead, they drew back when artisans, factory workers, and radical socialists rose up to present their own much more revolutionary demands. This retreat made possible the crushing of Parisian workers by a coalition of solid bourgeoisie and landowning peasantry in France, and it facilitated the efforts of dedicated aristocrats in central Europe. By 1850, a sea of blood and disillusion had washed away the lofty ideals and utopian visions of a generation.

Schleswig and Holstein
Provinces that were inhabited primarily by Germans, but ruled by the king of Denmark; they revolted at the prospect of being integrated into the Danish state by the new Danish king, Frederick VII.

NATION BUILDING IN ITALY, GERMANY, AND RUSSIA

How did strong leaders and nation building transform Italy, Germany, and Russia?

The revolutions of 1848 closed one era in the West and opened another. In thought and culture exuberant romanticism gave way to hardheaded realism. In the Atlantic economy the hard years of the 1840s were followed by good times and prosperity throughout most of the 1850s and 1860s. In international politics the repressive peace and diplomatic stability of Metternich's time were replaced by a period of war and rapid change. Above all, Western society progressively found, for better or worse, a new and effective organizing principle capable of coping with the many-sided challenges of the dual revolution and the emerging urban civilization. That principle was nationalism—dedication to and identification with the nation-state.

The triumph of modern nationalism in Europe was an enormously significant historical development. A powerful force since at least 1789, nationalism became an almost universal faith in Western society after 1850, evolving away from a narrow appeal to predominately middle-class liberals to an intoxicating creed moving the broad masses. Many leaders and peoples throughout the world eventually embraced large parts of the doctrine of nationalism and the nation-state.

Cavour, Garibaldi, and the Unification of Italy

Italy had never been a united nation prior to 1860. Part of Rome's great empire in ancient times, the Italian peninsula was divided in the Middle Ages into competing city-states, and it became a battleground for foreign powers after 1494. Italy was reorganized in 1815 at the Congress of Vienna. The rich northern provinces of Lombardy and Venetia were taken by Metternich's Austria. Sardinia and Piedmont were under the rule of an Italian monarch, and Tuscany shared north-central Italy with several smaller states. Central Italy and Rome were ruled by the papacy. Naples and Sicily were ruled by a branch of the Bourbons. Metternich was not wrong in dismissing Italy as "a geographical expression" (see Map 23.2).

After 1815 the goal of a unified Italian nation captured the imaginations of increasing numbers of Italians, but there was no agreement on how it could be achieved. In 1848, revolutionary efforts to form a democratic Italian republic failed completely, and a thoroughly frightened Pope Pius IX (r. 1846–1878) turned against most modern trends, including a federation of existing Italian states under his presidency. At the same time, the king of independent Sardinia, Victor Emmanuel, retained the moderate liberal constitution granted under duress in March 1848. To the Italian middle classes Sardinia appeared to be a liberal, progressive state ideally suited to achieve the goal of national unification.

Sardinia had the good fortune of being led by a brilliant statesman, Count Camillo Benso di Cavour. Cavour came from a noble family and embraced the economic doctrines and business activities associated with the prosperous middle class. Cavour's national goals were limited and realistic. Until 1859 he sought unity only for the states of northern and perhaps central Italy in a greatly expanded kingdom of Sardinia.

In the 1850s Cavour worked to consolidate Sardinia as a liberal constitutional state capable of leading northern Italy. He worked out a secret diplomatic alliance with Napoleon III, and in July 1858 he goaded Austria into attacking Sardinia. The combined Franco-Sardinian forces were victorious, but Napoleon III decided on a compromise peace with the Austrians in July 1859. Sardinia would receive only Lombardy, the area around Milan. Cavour resigned in a rage.

Popular revolts and Italian nationalism salvaged Cavour's plans. While the war against Austria had raged in the north, dedicated nationalists in central Italy had risen

SWITZERLAND

AUSTRIAN EMPIRE

SAVOY
(to France 1860)

LOMBARDY
(from Austria)

VENETIA
(from Austria 1866)

Trieste

Magenta ★ ● Milan

Turin ●

Villafranca

Solferino ★

Venice

PIEDMONT   PARMA

Po R.

FRANCE   Genoa ●

ROMAGNA

MODENA

● Bologna

NICE
(to France 1860)

THE MARCHES

OTTOMAN EMPIRE

Marseilles ●   Nice ●

Pisa ●   ● Florence

TUSCANY

Adriatic Sea

Elba

PAPAL STATES
(1870)

Corsica
(France)

● Rome

Bari ●

Naples ●

Taranto ●

Sardinia

40°N

Tyrrhenian
Sea

KINGDOM OF
THE TWO SICILIES

Palermo ●

Sicily

Strait of
Messina

Kingdom of Sardinia before 1859

To Kingdom of Sardinia, 1859

To Kingdom of Sardinia, 1860

To Kingdom of Italy, 1866, 1870

★ Major battle

Boundary of Kingdom of Italy after unification

0   50   100 Km.

0   50   100 Mi.

MAP 23.2 **The Unification of Italy, 1859–1870** The leadership of Sardinia-Piedmont and nationalist fervor were decisive factors in the unification of Italy.

and driven out their rulers. Nationalist fervor seized the urban masses, and the leaders of the nationalist movement called for fusion with Sardinia. Cavour returned to power in early 1860, and the people of central Italy voted overwhelmingly to join a greatly enlarged kingdom of Sardinia. Cavour had achieved his original goal of a north Italian state (see Map 23.2).

For superpatriots such as Giuseppe Garibaldi (1807–1882), the job of unification was still only half done. The son of a poor sailor, Garibaldi personified the romantic revolutionary nationalism of 1848. Leading a corps of volunteers against Austria in 1859, Garibaldi emerged in 1860 as a powerful independent force in Italian politics. (See the feature "Individuals in Society: Giuseppe Garibaldi.")

Secretly supported by Cavour, Garibaldi had a bold plan to "liberate" the kingdom of the Two Sicilies. Landing on the shores of Sicily in May 1860, Garibaldi's guerrilla band of a thousand **Red Shirts** captured the imagination of the Sicilian peasantry. Outwitting the twenty-thousand-man royal army, the guerrilla leader took Palermo, crossed to the mainland, and prepared to attack Rome and the pope. But the wily Cavour quickly sent Sardinian forces to occupy most of the Papal States (but not

Red Shirts *The guerrilla army of Giuseppe Garibaldi, who invaded Sicily in 1860 in an attempt to "liberate" it and won the hearts of the Sicilian peasantry.*

Rome) and to intercept Garibaldi. When Garibaldi and Victor Emmanuel rode through Naples to cheering crowds, they symbolically sealed the union of north and south, of monarch and people.

Cavour had succeeded. He had controlled Garibaldi and had turned popular nationalism in a conservative direction. The new kingdom of Italy, which did not include Venice until 1866 or Rome until 1870, was a parliamentary monarchy under Victor Emmanuel, neither radical nor democratic. Only a small minority of Italian males had the right to vote. Despite political unity, the propertied classes and the common people were divided. A great social and cultural gap separated the progressive industrializing north from the stagnant agrarian south.

Bismarck and German Unification

Primary Source: Extracts from History of Germany in the Nineteenth Century *A nineteenth-century German historian proclaims a racist and militarist ideology.*

In the aftermath of 1848 the German states were locked in a political stalemate. Tension grew between Austria and Prussia as each power sought to block the other within the German Confederation. Stalemate and reaction also prevailed in the domestic politics of the individual German states in the 1850s.

At the same time, powerful economic forces were undermining the political status quo. Modern industry was growing rapidly within the German customs union (*Zollverein*), founded in 1834 to stimulate trade. By the end of 1853 all the German states except Austria had joined the customs union, and a new Germany excluding Austria was becoming an economic reality.

The national uprising in Italy in 1859 made a profound impression in Prussia. Great political change and war—perhaps with Austria, perhaps with France—seemed quite possible. Along with his top military advisers, the tough-minded William I of Prussia (r. 1861–1888) was convinced of the need for major army reforms and wanted to double the size of the regular army. Army reforms meant a bigger defense budget and higher taxes.

Prussia had emerged from 1848 with a parliament of sorts, the Prussian Assembly, which was in the hands of the liberal middle class by 1859. Above all, the middle-class representatives wanted to establish once and for all that the parliament, not the king, had the ultimate political power and that the army was responsible to Prussia's elected representatives. These demands were popular. After the parliament rejected the military budget in 1862, the liberals triumphed completely in new elections. King William then called on Count Otto von Bismarck to head a new ministry and defy the parliament. This was a momentous choice.

The most important figure in German history between Luther and Hitler, Otto von Bismarck (1815–1898) was above all a master of politics. Born into the Prussian landowning aristocracy, Bismarck loved power, but he was also extraordinarily flexible and pragmatic in pursuing his goals.

When Bismarck took office as chief minister in 1862, he declared that the government would rule without parliamentary consent. He lashed out at the middle-class opposition and ordered the Prussian bureaucracy to go on collecting taxes even though the Prussian parliament refused to approve the budget. He reorganized the army. And for four years, from 1862 to 1866, the voters of Prussia supported the opposition and sent large liberal majorities to the parliament.

Opposition at home spurred the search for success abroad. When the Danish king tried again, as in 1848, to bring the provinces of Schleswig and Holstein into a centralized Danish state, Prussia joined Austria in a short and successful war against Denmark in 1864. Then, determined to expel Austria from German politics, Bismarck launched another war of aggression.

The Austro-Prussian War of 1866 lasted only seven weeks. Utilizing railroads to mass troops, the reorganized Prussian army defeated Austria decisively at the Battle of Sadowa in Bohemia. Granting Austria realistic, even generous, peace terms, Bismarck forced Austria to withdraw from German affairs. The mainly Protestant states north

Giuseppe Garibaldi

When Giuseppe Garibaldi (1807–1882) visited England in 1864, he received the most triumphant welcome ever given to any foreigner. Honored and feted by politicians and high society, he also captivated the masses. An unprecedented crowd of a half-million people cheered his carriage through the streets of London. These ovations were no fluke. In his time, Garibaldi was probably the most famous and most beloved figure in the world.* How could this be?

A rare combination of wild adventure and extraordinary achievement partly accounted for his demigod status. Born in Nice, Garibaldi went to sea at fifteen and sailed the Mediterranean for twelve years. At seventeen his travels took him to Rome, and he was converted in an almost religious experience to the "New Italy, the Italy of all the Italians." As he later wrote in his best-selling *Autobiography,* "The Rome that I beheld with the eyes of youthful imagination was the Rome of the future—the dominant thought of my whole life."

Sentenced to death in 1834 for his part in a revolutionary uprising in Genoa, Garibaldi barely escaped to South America. For twelve years, he led a guerrilla band in Uruguay's struggle for independence from Argentina. "Shipwrecked, ambushed, shot through the neck," he found in a tough young woman, Anna da Silva, a mate and companion in arms. Their first children nearly starved in the jungle while Garibaldi, clad in his long red shirt, fashioned a legend as a fearless freedom fighter.

Returning to Italy in 1848, the campaigns of his patriotic volunteers against the Austrians in 1848 and 1859 mobilized democratic nationalists. The stage was set for his volunteer army to liberate Sicily against enormous odds, astonishing the world and creating a large Italian state. Garibaldi's achievement matched his legend.

A brilliant fighter, the handsome and inspiring leader was an uncompromising idealist of absolute integrity. He never drew any personal profit from his exploits, continuing to milk his goats and rarely possessing more than one change of clothing. When Victor Emmanuel offered him lands and titles after

Giuseppe Garibaldi, the charismatic leader, shown in an 1856 engraving based on a photograph. *(Corbis)*

his great victory in 1861, even as the left-leaning volunteers were disbanded and humiliated, Garibaldi declined, saying he could not be bought off. Returning to his farm on a tiny rocky island, he denounced the government without hesitation when he concluded that it was betraying the dream of unification with its ruthless rule in the south. Yet even after a duplicitous Italian government caused two later attacks on Rome to fail, his faith in the generative power of national unity never wavered. Garibaldi showed that ideas and ideals count in history.

Above all, millions of ordinary men and women identified with Garibaldi because they believed that he was fighting for them. They recognized him as one of their own and saw that he remained true to them in spite of his triumphs, thereby ennobling their own lives and aspirations. Welcoming runaway slaves as equals in Latin America, advocating the emancipation of women, introducing social reforms in the south, and pressing for free education and a broader suffrage in the new Italy, Garibaldi the national hero fought for freedom and human dignity. The common people understood and loved him for it.

Questions for Analysis

1. Why was Garibaldi so famous and popular?

2. Nationalism evolved and developed in the nineteenth century. How did Garibaldi fit into this evolution? What kind of a nationalist was he?

*Denis Mack Smith, *Garibaldi: A Great Life in Brief* (New York: Alfred A. Knopf, 1956), pp. 136–147; and Denis Mack Smith, "Giuseppe Garibaldi," *History Today,* August 1991, pp. 20–26.

North German Confederation *A new government structure created by Bismarck after the Austro-Prussian War of 1866; it put the federal government in control of the army and military affairs, but created a legislature with two houses that shared equally in the making of laws.*

of the Main River were grouped in the new **North German Confederation,** led by an expanded Prussia (see Map 23.3). Each state retained its own local government, but the federal government—William I and Bismarck—controlled the army and foreign affairs. There was also a legislature with delegates to the confederation's lower house elected by universal male suffrage, giving Bismarck the possibility of going over the head of the middle class directly to the people.

Long convinced that the old order should make peace with the liberal middle class and the nationalist movement Bismarck asked the Prussian parliament to approve after the fact all of the government's "illegal" spending between 1862 and 1866. Most of the liberals snatched at the chance to cooperate. With German unity in sight, they repented their "sins" and legalized the government's spending. The constitutional struggle in Prussia was over, and the German middle class was accepting respectfully the monarchical authority and aristocratic superiority that Bismarck represented.

The final act in the drama of German unification followed quickly with a patriotic war with France. The apparent issue—whether a distant relative of Prussia's William I might become king of Spain—was only a diplomatic pretext. By 1870 the French leaders of the Second Empire, alarmed by their powerful new neighbor on the Rhine, had decided on a war to teach Prussia a lesson.

As soon as war against France began in 1870, Bismarck had the wholehearted support of the south German states. With other European governments remaining neutral, German forces under Prussian leadership decisively defeated Louis Napoleon's armies at Sedan on September 1, 1870. Three days later French patriots in Paris proclaimed yet another French republic (the third) and vowed to continue fighting. But after five months, in January 1871, a starving Paris surrendered, and France went on to accept Bismarck's harsh peace terms. By this time the south German states had agreed to join a new German Empire. As in the 1866 constitution, the king of Prussia

● **Proclaiming the German Empire, January 1871** This commemorative painting by Anton von Werner testifies to the nationalistic intoxication in Germany after the victory over France. William I of Prussia stands on a platform surrounded by princes and generals in the famous Hall of Mirrors in the palace of Versailles, while officers from all the units around a besieged Paris cheer and salute him with uplifted swords as emperor of a unified Germany. Bismarck, like a heroic white knight, stands between king and army. *(akg-images)*

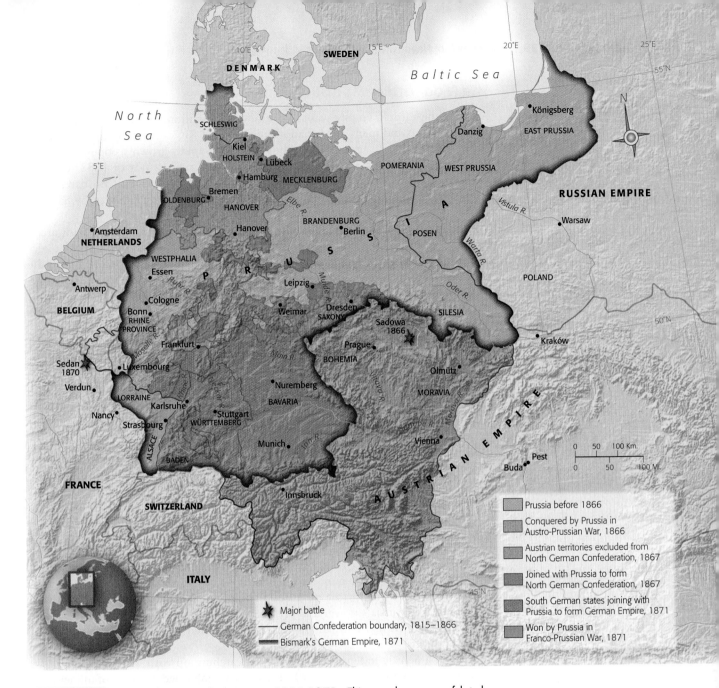

MAP 23.3 **The Unification of Germany, 1866–1871** This map deserves careful study. Note how Prussian expansion, Austrian expulsion from the old German Confederation, and the creation of a new German Empire went hand in hand. Austria lost no territory, but Prussia's neighbors in the north suffered grievously or simply disappeared. The annexation of Alsace-Lorraine turned France into a lasting enemy of Germany before 1914.

and his ministers had ultimate power in the new German Empire, and the lower house of the legislature was elected by universal male suffrage.

The Franco-Prussian War, which Europeans generally saw as a test of nations in a pitiless Darwinian struggle for existence, released an enormous surge of patriotic feeling in Germany. Bismarck's genius, the invincible Prussian army, the solidarity of king and people in a unified nation—these and similar themes were trumpeted endlessly during and after the war. The new German Empire had become the most powerful state in Europe, and most Germans were enormously proud, blissfully imagining themselves the fittest and best of the European species. Semi-authoritarian nationalism and a "new conservatism," which was based on an alliance of the propertied classes and sought the active support of the working classes, had triumphed in Germany.

The Modernization of Russia

In 1850, the Russian empire was an enormous multinational state, containing all the ethnic Russians and many other nationalities as well. Russia was also a poor agrarian society with backward agricultural techniques and a rapidly growing population. Serfdom was still the basic social institution. Then the Crimean War of 1853 to 1856, arising out of a dispute with France over who should protect certain Christian shrines in the Ottoman Empire, brought crisis. France and Great Britain, aided by Sardinia and the Ottoman Empire, inflicted a humiliating defeat on Russia.

modernization *The changes that enable a country to compete effectively with the leading countries at a given time.*

Military defeat showed that Russia had fallen behind western Europe in many areas. Russia's leaders realized that they had to embrace the process of **modernization,** defined narrowly as the changes that enable a country to compete effectively with the leading countries at a given time. At the very least, Russia needed railroads, better armaments, and reorganization of the army if it was to maintain its international position. Military disaster thus forced the new tsar, Alexander II (r. 1855–1881), and his ministers along the path of rapid social change and general modernization.

The first and greatest of the reforms was the freeing of the serfs in 1861. Human bondage was abolished forever, and the emancipated peasants received, on average, about half of the land. But the peasants had to pay fairly high prices for their land, which was owned collectively by peasant villages. Thus the effects of the reform were limited. More successful was reform of the legal system, which established independent courts and equality before the law. Education was also liberalized somewhat, and censorship was relaxed but not removed.

Russia made great strides toward economic modernization in the reform era. Rapid railroad construction to 1880 enabled agricultural Russia to export grain and thus earn money for further industrialization. Industrial suburbs grew up around Moscow and St. Petersburg, and a class of modern factory workers began to take shape.

In 1881 a small group of terrorists assassinated Alexander II, and the era of reform came to an abrupt end. Political modernization remained frozen until 1905, but economic modernization sped forward in the massive industrial surge of the 1890s. Nationalism played a decisive role, as it had after the Crimean War. The key leader was Sergei Witte, the energetic minister of finance. Witte subscribed to the economic nationalism of Friedrich List (see page 660) and believed that industrial backwardness was threatening Russia's power and greatness. Under Witte's leadership the government built state-owned railroads rapidly and promoted Russian industry with high protective tariffs.

By 1900 a fiercely independent Russia was catching up with western Europe and expanding its empire in Asia. By 1903 Russia had established a sphere of influence in Chinese Manchuria and was casting greedy eyes on northern Korea. When the diplomatic protests of equally imperialistic Japan were ignored, the Japanese launched a surprise attack in February 1904. To the amazement of self-confident Europeans, Japan scored repeated victories, and Russia was forced in August 1905 to accept a humiliating defeat.

Military disaster in East Asia brought the revolution of 1905. Beginning in January 1905, a wave of strikes, peasant uprisings, and troop mutinies swept the country. The revolutionary surge culminated in October 1905 in a paralyzing general strike, which forced the government to capitulate. The tsar issued the **October Manifesto,** which granted full civil rights and promised a popularly elected *Duma* (parliament) with real legislative power.

October Manifesto *The result of a great general strike in October 1905, it granted full civil rights and promised a popularly elected Duma (parliament) with real legislative power.*

Under the new constitution the tsar retained great powers and the Duma had only limited authority. The middle-class liberals, the largest group in the newly elected Duma, were badly disappointed, and efforts to cooperate with the tsar's ministers soon broke down. In 1907, the tsar and his reactionary advisers rewrote the electoral law to increase greatly the weight of the wealthy classes at the expense of workers, peasants, national minorities, and middle-class professionals.

● **The Fruits of Terrorism**
In the late 1870s a small group of revolutionaries believed that killing the tsar could destroy the Russian state. Succeeding in blowing up the reforming Alexander II after several near misses, the five assassins, including one woman, were quickly caught and hanged. Russia entered an era of reaction and harsh authoritarian rule. *(Visual Connection Archive)*

The new law had the intended effect. With landowners assured half of the seats in the Duma, the government reestablished semi-authoritarian rule. On the eve of World War I, Russia was partially modernized, a conservative constitutional monarchy with a peasant-based but industrializing economy.

LIFE IN URBAN SOCIETY

What was the impact of urban growth on cities, social classes, families, and ideas?

After 1850, as identification with the nation-state was becoming a basic organizing principle of Western society, the growth of towns and cities rushed forward with undiminished force. In 1900 Western society was urban and industrial as surely as it had been rural and agrarian in 1800. This rapid urbanization, both a result of the Industrial Revolution and a key element in its enormous long-term impact, posed pressing practical problems that governments had to deal with. Eventual success with urban problems encouraged people to look to government as a problem solver and put their faith in a responsive national state.

Taming the City

Since the Middle Ages European cities had been centers of government, culture, and large-scale commerce. They had also been congested, dirty, and unhealthy. Nonetheless, as the Industrial Revolution took hold and the steam engine freed industrialists from dependence on the energy of fast-flowing streams and rivers, there was by 1800 a powerful incentive to build new factories in cities, which grew rapidly in Europe in the nineteenth century (see Map 23.4). There were also many hands wanting work in the cities, for cities drew people like a magnet.

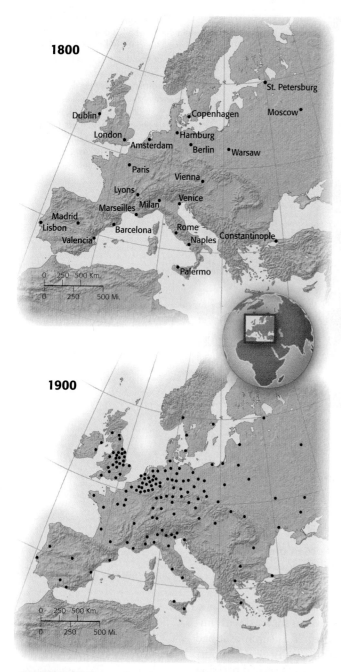

1800

St. Petersburg

Dublin Copenhagen Moscow

London Hamburg

Amsterdam Berlin Warsaw

Paris

Lyons Vienna

Marseilles Milan Venice

Madrid

Lisbon Barcelona Rome

Valencia Naples Constantinople

Palermo

0 250 500 Km.
0 250 500 Mi.

1900

0 250 500 Km.
0 250 500 Mi.

MAP 23.4 **European Cities of 100,000 or More, 1800 and 1900** There were more large cities in Great Britain in 1900 than in all of Europe in 1800. Northwestern Europe was the most urbanized area.

Benthamite *Followers of the radical philosopher Jeremy Bentham, they believed in the "greatest good for the greatest number."*

miasmatic theory *The belief that people contract disease by breathing bad odors and decay and putrefying excrement.*

In the 1820s and 1830s people in Britain and France began to worry about the condition of their cities. Everyone could agree that, except on the outskirts, each town or city was using every scrap of land to the full extent. Parks and open areas were almost nonexistent, and narrow houses were usually built wall to wall in long rows.

These highly concentrated urban populations lived in extremely unsanitary and unhealthy conditions. Open drains and sewers flowed alongside or down the middle of unpaved streets. Toilet facilities were primitive in the extreme. In parts of industrial Manchester as many as two hundred people shared a single outhouse.

The urban challenge eventually brought an energetic response from a generation of reformers. The most famous was Edwin Chadwick, a British official. Chadwick was a good **Benthamite**—that is, a follower of radical British philosopher Jeremy Bentham (1748–1832). Bentham had taught that public problems ought to be dealt with on a rational, scientific basis and according to the "greatest good for the greatest number." Applying these principles, Chadwick became convinced that disease and death actually caused poverty and that disease could be prevented by cleaning up the urban environment. That was his "sanitary idea."

Collecting detailed reports from local officials and publishing his findings in 1842, Chadwick correctly believed that the stinking excrement of communal outhouses could be carried off by water through cheap iron pipes at less than one-twentieth the cost of removing it by hand. In 1848, Britain created a national health board and gave cities broad authority to build modern sanitary systems. The public health movement won dedicated supporters in the United States, France, and Germany from the 1840s on. By the 1860s and 1870s European cities were making real progress toward adequate water supplies and sewerage systems, and city dwellers were beginning to reap the reward of better health.

Early reformers were seriously handicapped by the prevailing **miasmatic theory** of disease—the belief that people contract disease when they breathe the bad odors of decay and putrefying excrement. In the 1840s and 1850s keen observation suggested that contagion was *spread through* filth and not caused by it, thus weakening the miasmatic idea.

The theoretical breakthrough was the development of the **germ theory** of disease by Louis Pasteur (1822–1895), a French chemist who found that the growth of living organisms could be suppressed by heating a beverage—by **pasteurization.** By 1870 the work of Pasteur and others had clearly demonstrated the general connection between germs and disease. When, in the middle of the 1870s, Robert Koch and his German coworkers developed pure cultures of harmful bacteria and described their life cycles, the dam broke. Over the next twenty years researchers identified the organisms responsible for disease after disease. These discoveries led to the development of a number of effective vaccines. Surgeons also applied the germ theory in hospitals, sterilizing not only the wound but also everything—hands, instruments, clothing—that entered the operating room.

The achievements of the bacterial revolution coupled with the ever-more-sophisticated public health movement saved millions of lives, particularly after about 1890. In England, France, and Germany death rates declined dramatically from a range of twenty-one to twenty-seven per thousand inhabitants in the 1860s to a range of fourteen to eighteen per thousand in 1913. The awful death sentences of the past—diphtheria, typhoid, typhus, cholera, yellow fever—became vanishing diseases in the industrializing nations.

More effective urban planning after 1850 also improved the quality of urban life. France took the lead during the rule of Napoleon III (1848–1870), who believed that rebuilding much of Paris would provide employment, improve living conditions, and glorify his empire. In the baron Georges Haussmann (1809–1884), an aggressive, impatient Alsatian whom he placed in charge of Paris, Napoleon III found an authoritarian planner capable of bulldozing both buildings and opposition. In twenty years Paris was transformed by slum clearance, new streets and housing, small neighborhood parks and open spaces, and good fresh water. The rebuilding Paris stimulated modern urbanism throughout Europe, particularly after 1870.

The development of mass public transportation was also of great importance in the improvement of urban living conditions. In the 1870s many European cities authorized private companies to operate horse-drawn streetcars. Then in the 1890s countries in North America and Europe adopted another transit innovation, the electric streetcar. Electric streetcars were cheaper, faster, more dependable, and more comfortable than their horse-drawn counterparts. Service improved dramatically. Millions of riders—workers, shoppers, schoolchildren—hopped on board during the workweek. And on weekends and holidays, streetcars carried city people on happy outings to parks and the countryside, racetracks and music halls.[3] Electric streetcars also gave people of modest means access to improved housing, as the still-crowded city was able to expand and become less congested.

germ theory *The idea, contrary to miasmatic theory, that disease was spread through filth and not caused by it.*

pasteurization *The process developed by Louis Pasteur that suppressed the activity of living organisms in a beverage by heating it.*

A COURT FOR KING CHOLERA.

● **Filth and Disease** This 1852 drawing from *Punch* tells volumes about the unhealthy living conditions of the urban poor. In the foreground children play with a dead rat and a woman scavenges a dungheap. Cheap rooming houses provide shelter for the frightfully overcrowded population. (© *British Library Board. All rights reserved.)*

Social Structure and the Middle Classes

With general improvements in health and in the urban environment, the almost-completed journey to an urban industrialized world was bringing beneficial consequences for all kinds of people. The first great change was a substantial increase in the standard of living for the average person. The real wages of British workers, for example, almost doubled between 1850 and 1906. Similar increases occurred in continental European countries, reinforcing efforts to improve many aspects of human existence.

However. greater economic rewards for the average person did *not* eliminate hardship and poverty, nor did they significantly narrow the wealth and income gap separating the rich and the poor. In almost every industrialized country around 1900 the richest 20 percent of households received anywhere from 50 to 60 percent of all national income, whereas the bottom 30 percent of households received 10 percent or less of all income. Thus the gap between rich and poor remained enormous in western countries. It was probably almost as great in 1900 as it had been in the age of agriculture and aristocracy before the Industrial Revolution.

The great gap between rich and poor endured, in part, because industrial and urban development made society more diverse and less unified. By no means did society split into two sharply defined opposing classes, as Marx had predicted. Instead, economic specialization created more new social groups than it destroyed. There developed an almost unlimited range of jobs, skills, and earnings; one group or subclass shaded off into another in a complex, confusing hierarchy.

Certainly the diversity and range within the urban middle class were striking at the beginning of the twentieth century. Indeed, it is more meaningful to think of a confederation of middle classes loosely united by occupations requiring primarily mental, rather than physical, skill.

At the top stood the upper middle class, composed mainly of the most successful business families. As people in the upper middle class gained in income and progressively lost all traces of radicalism after the trauma of 1848, they were almost irresistibly drawn toward the aristocratic lifestyle. For although the genuine hereditary aristocracy constituted only a tiny minority in every European country, it retained imposing wealth, unrivaled social prestige, and substantial political influence. Thus the upper middle class purchased lavish country places or built beach houses for weekend and summer use. A large number of servants also indicated wealth and standing, while fancy carriages were sure signs of high social status.

Below the wealthy upper middle class were much larger, much less wealthy, and increasingly diversified middle-class groups. Here one found the moderately successful industrialists and merchants as well as professionals in law and medicine. This was the middle middle class, solid and quite comfortable but lacking great wealth. Below it were independent shopkeepers, small traders, and tiny manufacturers—the lower middle class.

The expansion of industry and technology created a growing demand for experts with specialized knowledge, and the most valuable of the specialties became solid middle-class professions. Engineers, architects, chemists, accountants, and surveyors first achieved professional standing in this period. Management of large public and private institutions also emerged as a kind of profession as governments provided more services and as very large corporations such as railroads came into being.

Industrialization and urbanization also diversified the lower middle class and expanded the number of white-collar employees. White-collar employees were propertyless, but generally they were fiercely committed to the middle class and to the ideal of moving up in society.

Well fed and well served, the middle classes were also well housed by 1900 and were quite clothes conscious. Education was another growing expense, as middle-class parents tried to provide their children with ever-more-crucial advanced education. The keystones of culture and leisure were books, music, and travel.

The middle classes were loosely united by a shared code of expected behavior and morality. Strict and demanding, this code laid great stress on hard work, self-discipline, and personal achievement. Men and women who fell into crime or poverty were generally assumed to be responsible for their own circumstances. In short, the middle-class person was supposed to know right from wrong and to act accordingly.

The Working Classes

About four out of five people belonged to the European working classes at the turn of the twentieth century. Many members of the working classes—that is, people whose livelihoods depended on physical labor and who did not employ domestic servants—were still small landowning peasants and hired farm hands. This was especially true in eastern Europe.

The urban working classes were even less unified and homogeneous than the middle classes. In the first place, economic development and increased specialization expanded the traditional range of working-class skills, earnings, and experiences. In the second place, skilled, semiskilled, and unskilled workers developed widely divergent lifestyles and cultural values, and their differences contributed to a keen sense of social status and hierarchy within the working classes. The result was great variety and limited class unity.

Highly skilled workers, who made up about 15 percent of the working classes, became a real **labor aristocracy.** The most "aristocratic" of the highly skilled workers were construction bosses and factory foremen, men who had often risen from the ranks and were fiercely proud of their achievement. The labor aristocracy also included members of the traditional highly skilled handicraft trades that had not yet been placed in factories, as well as new kinds of skilled workers such as shipbuilders and railway locomotive engineers. Thus the labor elite remained in a state of flux as individuals and whole crafts moved in and out of it.

labor aristocracy *Highly skilled workers who made up about 15 percent of the working classes at the turn of the twentieth century.*

To maintain this precarious standing, the upper working class adopted distinctive values and strait-laced, almost puritanical behavior. Like the middle classes, the labor aristocracy was strongly committed to the family and to economic improvement. Yet skilled workers viewed themselves primarily not as aspirants to the middle class but as the pacesetters and natural leaders of all the working classes. They practiced self-discipline and generally frowned on heavy drinking and sexual permissiveness.

Below the labor aristocracy stood the complex world of semiskilled and unskilled urban workers. A large number of the semiskilled were factory workers who earned highly variable but relatively good wages and whose relative importance in the labor force was increasing. Below the semiskilled workers was a larger group of unskilled workers that included day laborers such as longshoremen, wagon-driving teamsters, maids, teenagers, and every kind of "helper." Many of these people had real skills and performed valuable services, but they were unorganized and divided, united only by the common fate of meager earnings. The same lack of unity characterized street vendors and market people—self-employed workers who competed savagely with each other and with the established shopkeepers of the lower middle class.

Many a poor wife and mother joined the broad ranks of working women in the "sweated industries." These industries resembled the old putting-out and cottage industries of earlier times. The women normally worked at home and were paid by the piece.

The urban working classes sought fun and recreation, and they found both. Across the face of Europe drinking remained unquestionably the favorite leisure-time activity of working people. Generally, however, heavy "problem" drinking declined in the late nineteenth century as drinking became more public and social. Cafés and pubs became increasingly bright, friendly places.

The two other leisure-time passions of the working classes were sports and music halls. A great decline in "cruel sports," such as bullbaiting and cockfighting, led to the rise of modern spectator sports, of which racing and soccer were the most popular. There was a great deal of gambling on sports events. Music halls and vaudeville theaters, the working-class counterparts of middle-class opera and classical theater, were enormously popular throughout Europe.

The Changing Family

Industrialization and the growth of modern cities brought great changes to the lives of European women. These changes were particularly consequential for married women, and most women did marry in the nineteenth century.

After 1850 the work of most wives continued to become increasingly distinct and separate from that of their husbands (see pages 712–714). Husbands became wage earners in factories and offices; wives tended to stay home and manage households and care for children. As economic conditions improved, only married women in poor families tended to work outside the home. The ideal became **separate spheres**, the strict division of labor by sex: the wife as mother and homemaker, the husband as wage earner. This rigid division meant that married women faced great injustice if they tried to move into the men's world of employment outside the home.

separate spheres *A rigid gender division of labor, with the wife as mother and homemaker and the husband as wage earner.*

Middle-class women lacked legal rights and faced severe discrimination in education and employment. Thus organizations founded by middle-class feminists campaigned for legal equality as well as access to higher education and professional employment. In the later nineteenth century middle-class women scored some significant victories, such as the 1882 law giving English married women full property rights. Socialist women leaders usually took a different path. They argued that the liberation of working-class women would come only with the liberation of the entire working class through revolution. In the meantime they championed the cause of working women and won some practical improvements. In a general way these different approaches to women's issues reflected the diversity of classes in urban society.

As the ideology and practice of rigidly separate spheres narrowed women's horizons, their control and influence in the home became increasingly strong throughout Europe in the later nineteenth century. Among the English working classes, for example, it was the wife who generally determined how the family's money was spent. All the major domestic decisions, from the children's schooling and religious instruction to the selection of new furniture or a new apartment, were hers.

The woman's guidance of the household went hand in hand with the increased emotional importance of home and family. The home she ran was idealized as a warm shelter in a hard and impersonal urban world.

Married couples also developed stronger emotional ties to each other. Even in the comfortable classes, marriages in the late nineteenth century were increasingly based on sentiment and sexual attraction as money and financial calculation gradually declined in importance. Affection and eroticism became more central to the couple after marriage. Many French marriage manuals of the late 1800s stressed that women had legitimate sexual needs, such as the "right to orgasm."

One sign of deepening emotional ties within the family was the growing love and concern that mothers gave their tiny infants. Thus whereas the typical mother in pre-industrial Western society was frequently indifferent toward her baby because the child was so likely to die, ordinary women became better mothers as the nineteenth century progressed. For example, mothers increasingly breast-fed their infants, which saved lives. The surge of maternal feeling also gave rise to a wave of specialized books on child rearing and infant hygiene.

There was also greater concern for older children and adolescents. They, too, were wrapped in the strong emotional ties of a more intimate and protective family. For one thing, European women began to limit the number of children they bore in order

SUNDAY MORNING
WORKMANS HOME
LEATHER LANE

to care adequately for those they had. Indeed, many parents, especially in the middle classes, probably became *too* concerned about their children. The result was that many children and especially adolescents came to feel trapped and in need of greater independence.

The working classes probably had more avenues of escape from such tensions than did the middle classes. Unlike their middle-class counterparts, who remained economically dependent on their families until a long education was finished or a proper marriage secured, working-class boys and girls went to work when they reached adolescence. Earning wages on their own, they could bargain with their parents for greater independence within the household, or they could leave home to live cheaply as paying lodgers in other working-class homes. Thus the young person from the working classes broke away from the family more easily when emotional ties became oppressive.

● **A Working-Class Home, 1875** Emotional ties within ordinary families grew stronger in the nineteenth century. Parents gave their children more love and better care. *(Illustrated London News Library/ Mary Evans Picture Library)*

Science and Culture

Major changes in Western thought and culture accompanied the emergence of urban society. Two aspects of these complex developments stand out as especially significant. Scientific knowledge expanded rapidly and came to influence the Western worldview more profoundly than ever before. And between about the 1840s and the 1890s, European literature underwent a shift from soaring romanticism to tough-minded realism.

The intellectual achievements of the scientific revolution in the seventeenth century had resulted in few practical benefits, and theoretical knowledge had also played a relatively small role in the Industrial Revolution in England. But breakthroughs in industrial technology enormously stimulated basic scientific inquiry as researchers sought to explain theoretically how such things as steam engines and blast furnaces actually worked. The result from the 1830s onward was an explosive growth of fundamental scientific discoveries that were increasingly transformed into material improvements for the general population.

MR. BERGH TO THE RESCUE.

THE DEFRAUDED GORILLA. *"That Man wants to claim my Pedigree. He says he is one of my Descendants."*

Mr. BERGH. *"Now, Mr. DARWIN, how could you insult him so?"*

● **Satirizing Darwin's Ideas** The heated controversies over Darwin's theory of evolution also spawned innumerable jokes and cartoons. This cartoon is by Darwin's contemporary, the American Thomas Nast. *(Culver Pictures)*

thermodynamics *A branch of physics built on Newton's laws of mechanics that investigated the relationship between heat and mechanical energy.*

evolution *The idea, applied by thinkers in many fields, that stresses gradual change and continuous adjustment.*

Social Darwinists *A group of thinkers who saw the human race as driven forward to ever-greater specialization and progress by the unending economic struggle, which would determine "the survival of the fittest."*

A perfect example of the translation of better scientific knowledge into practical human benefits was the work of Louis Pasteur and his followers in biology and the medical sciences (see page 696). Another was the development of the branch of physics known as **thermodynamics,** the relationship between heat and mechanical energy. By mid-century physicists had formulated the fundamental laws of thermodynamics, which were then applied to mechanical engineering, chemical processes, and many other fields.

The triumph of science and technology had at least three significant consequences. First, though ordinary citizens continued to lack detailed scientific knowledge, everyday experience and innumerable popularizers impressed the importance of science on the popular mind.

Second, as science became more prominent in popular thinking, the philosophical implications of science formulated in the Enlightenment spread to broad sections of the population. Natural processes appeared to be determined by rigid laws, leaving little room for either divine intervention or human will.

Third, the methods of science acquired unrivaled prestige after 1850. Thus many thinkers tried to apply the objective methods of science to the study of society from the 1830s onward. Leading nineteenth-century social scientists resembled the eighteenth-century philosophes, but they were more all-encompassing and dogmatic. Marx was a prime example (see page 681).

Living in an era of rapid change, nineteenth-century thinkers in Europe were fascinated with the idea of **evolution** and dynamic development. The most influential of all nineteenth-century evolutionary thinkers was Charles Darwin (1809–1882). Darwin came to doubt the general belief in a special divine creation of each species of animal. Instead, he concluded, all life had gradually evolved from a common ancestral origin in an unending "struggle for survival." Darwin's theory is summarized in the title of his work *On the Origin of Species by the Means of Natural Selection* (1859). He argued that chance differences among the members of a given species help some survive while others die. Thus the variations that prove useful in the struggle for survival are selected naturally and spread gradually to the entire species through reproduction.

Darwin's theory had a powerful and many-sided influence on European thought and the European middle classes. His findings reinforced the teachings of secularists such as Marx, who scornfully dismissed religious belief in favor of agnostic or atheistic materialism. Many writers also applied the theory of biological evolution to human affairs. Herbert Spencer (1820–1903), an English philosopher, saw the human race as driven forward to ever-greater specialization and progress by a brutal economic struggle that efficiently determines the "survival of the fittest." According to Spencer and other **Social Darwinists,** the poor are the ill-fated weak, the prosperous the chosen strong.

In literature, the key themes of realism emerged in the 1840s and continued to dominate Western culture and style until the 1890s. Realist writers believed that literature should depict life exactly as it is. Forsaking poetry for prose and the personal, emotional viewpoint of the romantics for strict scientific objectivity, the realists simply observed and recorded—content, they said, to let the facts speak for themselves.

The major realist writers focused their extraordinary powers of observation on contemporary everyday life. Beginning with a dissection of the middle classes, from which most of them sprang, many realists eventually focused on the working classes, especially the urban working classes, which had been neglected in imaginative literature before this time. The realists put a microscope to many unexplored and taboo subjects—sex, strikes, violence, alcoholism—and hastened to report that slums and factories teemed with savage behavior.

The realists' claims of objectivity did not prevent the elaboration of a definite worldview. Unlike the romantics, who had gloried in individual freedom and an unlimited universe, realists such as the famous French novelist Emile Zola (1840–1902) were strict determinists. They believed that human beings, like atoms, are components of the physical world and that all human actions are caused by unalterable natural laws: heredity and environment determine human behavior; good and evil are merely social conventions.

• •

THE NATIONAL STATE AND THE SOCIALIST MOVEMENT (1871–1914)

How did governments gain popular support and deal with the socialist movement?

After 1871 the heartland of Europe was organized into strong national states, and the common themes within that framework were the emergence of mass politics and growing mass loyalty toward the national state. On the borders of Europe—in Ireland and Russia, in Austria-Hungary and the Balkans—the dynamics were different. Subject peoples there were still striving for political unity and independence. National aspirations created tensions, and mass politics often undermined existing states.

There were good reasons why ordinary people—the masses of an industrializing, urbanizing society—felt increasing loyalty to their governments in central and western Europe. More people could vote. By 1914 universal male suffrage had become the rule rather than the exception. This development had as much psychological as political significance. Ordinary men felt that they were becoming "part of the system."

Women also began to demand the right to vote. The women's suffrage movement achieved its first success in the western United States, and by 1913 women could vote in twelve states. In Europe, Norway gave the vote to most women in 1914. Elsewhere women generally failed before 1914, but they prepared the way for the triumph of the women's suffrage movement in many countries immediately after World War I.

As the right to vote spread, politicians and parties in national parliaments usually represented the people more responsively. The multiparty system prevailing in most countries meant that parliamentary majorities were built on shifting coalitions, which gave political parties leverage to obtain benefits for their supporters. Governments also passed laws to alleviate general problems, thereby acquiring greater legitimacy and appearing more worthy of support.

Less positively, governments found that they could manipulate national feeling to create a sense of unity and to divert attention away from the growing socialist movement. Therefore, after 1871 governing elites frequently channeled national sentiment in an antiliberal and militaristic direction, tolerating anti-Semitism and waging wars in nonwestern lands. This policy helped manage domestic conflicts, but only at the expense of increasing the international tensions that erupted in 1914 in cataclysmic war and revolution (see Chapter 27).

The German Empire

Politics in Germany after 1871 reflected many of the general developments. The new German Empire was a federal union of Prussia and twenty-four smaller states. Much of the everyday business of government was conducted by the separate states, but

Reichstag *The popularly elected lower house of government of the new German Empire after 1871.*

Kulturkampf *Bismarck's attack on the Catholic Church within Germany, also known as the "struggle for civilization."*

there was a strong national government with a chancellor—until 1890 Bismarck—and a popularly elected parliament called the **Reichstag.** Although Bismarck refused to be bound by a parliamentary majority, he tried nonetheless to maintain one. This situation gave the political parties opportunities. Until 1878 Bismarck relied mainly on the National Liberals, who had rallied to him after 1866 and represented the solid middle class. They supported legislation useful for further economic and legal unification of the country.

Less wisely, they backed Bismarck's attack on the Catholic Church, the so-called **Kulturkampf,** or "struggle for civilization." Like Bismarck, the middle-class National Liberals were particularly alarmed by Pius IX's declaration of papal infallibility in 1870. That dogma seemed to ask German Catholics to put loyalty to their church above loyalty to their nation. The Kulturkampf had limited success because German Catholics generally voted for the Catholic Center party, which blocked passage of national laws hostile to the church. Finally, in 1878 Bismarck abandoned his attack and entered into an uneasy but mutually advantageous alliance with the Catholic Center party. The reasons on both sides were largely economic.

Bismarck moved to enact high tariffs on cheap grain from the United States, Canada, and Russia, against which less efficient European producers could not compete. This won over not only the Catholic Center, whose supporters were small farmers in western and southern Germany, but also the Protestant Junkers, who had large landholdings in the east. With the tariffs, then, Bismarck won Catholic and conservative support. His use of tariffs was typical of other European governments of the late 1800s, which tried to protect national industries in response to popular pressure.

As for socialism, Bismarck tried to stop its growth in Germany, and in 1878 he forced through a law outlawing the Social Democrats. He genuinely feared their revolutionary language and allegiance to a movement transcending the nation-state. Unable to force socialism out of existence, Bismarck's essentially conservative nation-state pioneered social measures designed to win the support of working-class people. In 1883 he pushed through the Reichstag the first of several modern social security laws to help wage earners. Henceforth sick, injured, and retired workers could look forward to some regular benefits from the state. This national social security system, paid for through compulsory contributions by wage earners and employers as well as grants from the state, was the first of its kind anywhere.

In 1890 the new emperor, the young, idealistic, and unstable William II (r. 1888–1918), opposed Bismarck's attempt to renew the law outlawing the Social Democratic party. Eager to rule in his own right and to earn the support of the workers, William II forced Bismarck to resign. The government did pass new laws to aid workers and to legalize socialist political activity, but German foreign policy changed profoundly and mostly for the worse.

Yet William II was no more successful than Bismarck in getting workers to renounce socialism, and more and more Social Democrats were elected to the Reichstag in the 1890s. Yet the "revolutionary" socialists were actually becoming less and less revolutionary in Germany. In the years before World War I, the Social Democratic party broadened its base and adopted a more patriotic tone. Thus even German socialists identified increasingly with the German state, and they concentrated on gradual social and political reform.

Republican France

Although Napoleon III's reign made some progress in reducing antagonisms between classes, the war with Prussia undid these efforts, and in 1871 France seemed hopelessly divided once again. The patriotic republicans who proclaimed the Third Republic in Paris after the military disaster on the battlefield refused to admit defeat. They defended Paris with great heroism for weeks, living off rats and zoo animals until they were starved into submission by German armies in January 1871. When national elections then sent a large majority of conservatives and monarchists to the National Assembly, the traumatized Parisians exploded in patriotic frustration and proclaimed the Paris Commune in March 1871. Vaguely radical, the leaders of the Commune wanted to govern Paris without interference from the conservative French countryside. The National Assembly, led by aging conservative politician Adolphe Thiers, would hear none of it. The Assembly ordered the French army into Paris and brutally crushed the Commune. Twenty thousand people died in the fighting. As in June 1848, it was Paris against the provinces, French against French.

Out of this tragedy France slowly formed a new national unity before 1914. How is one to account for this? Luck played a part. Until 1875 the monarchists in the "republican" National Assembly had a majority but could not agree about who should be king. Thiers's destruction of the radical Commune and his other firm measures showed the fearful provinces and the middle class that the Third Republic might be moderate and socially conservative. France therefore retained the republic, though reluctantly.

Another stabilizing factor was the skill and determination of the moderate republican leaders in the early years. The most famous of these was Léon Gambetta, the son of an Italian grocer, a warm, easygoing lawyer who had turned professional politician. By 1879 the great majority of members of the upper and lower houses of the National Assembly were republicans, and the Third Republic had firm foundations after almost a decade.

● **Captain Alfred Dreyfus** Leaving an 1899 reconsideration of his original court martial, Dreyfus receives an insulting "guard of dishonor" from soldiers whose backs are turned. Top army leaders were determined to brand Dreyfus as a traitor. *(Roger-Viollet/Getty Images)*

The moderate republicans sought to preserve their creation by winning the hearts and minds of the next generation. Trade unions were fully legalized, and France acquired a colonial empire. More important, a series of laws between 1879 and 1886 established free compulsory elementary education for both girls and boys, thereby greatly reducing the role of parochial Catholic schools that had long been hostile to republics and to much of secular life. In France and elsewhere the general expansion of public education served as a critical nation-building tool in the late nineteenth century.

Many French Catholics rallied to the republic in the 1890s, and tensions between church and state eased. Unfortunately, the **Dreyfus affair** changed all that. Alfred Dreyfus, a Jewish captain in the French army, was falsely accused and convicted of treason. His family never doubted his innocence and fought to reopen the case, enlisting the support of prominent republicans and intellectuals. In 1898 and 1899 the case split France apart. On one side was the army, which had manufactured evidence against Dreyfus, joined by anti-Semites and most of the Catholic establishment. On the other side stood the civil libertarians and most of the more radical republicans.

This battle, which eventually led to Dreyfus's being declared innocent, revived militant republican feeling against the church. Between 1901 and 1905 the government severed all ties between the state and the Catholic Church after centuries of close relations, and the state school system's power of indoctrination was greatly strengthened. In France only the growing socialist movement, with its very different but thoroughly secular ideology, stood in opposition to the dominant faith in patriotic republican nationalism.

Dreyfus affair *A divisive case in which a Jewish captain in the French army was falsely accused and convicted of treason.*

Great Britain and the Austro-Hungarian Empire

The development of Great Britain and Austria-Hungary, two leading but quite different powers, throws a powerful light on the dynamics of nationalism in Europe before 1914. Britain in the late nineteenth century has often been seen as a shining example of peaceful and successful political evolution, where an effective two-party parliament skillfully guided the country from classical liberalism to full-fledged democracy with hardly a misstep. This view of Great Britain is not so much wrong as incomplete. After the right to vote was granted to males of the solid middle class in 1832, opinion leaders and politicians wrestled with the uncertainties of a further extension of the franchise. In 1867 Benjamin Disraeli and the Conservatives extended the vote to all middle-class males and the best-paid workers in the Second Reform bill, in order to broaden the Conservative party's traditional base of aristocratic and landed support. After 1867 English political parties and electoral campaigns became more modern, and the "lower orders" appeared to vote as responsibly as their "betters." Hence the Third Reform Bill of 1884 gave the vote to almost every adult male.

While the House of Commons was drifting toward democracy, the House of Lords, between 1901 and 1910, tried and ultimately failed to reassert itself. Aristocratic conservatism yielded to popular democracy once and for all. The result was that extensive social welfare measures, slow to come to Great Britain, were passed in a spectacular rush between 1906 and 1914. During those years the Liberal party substantially raised taxes on the rich as part of the so-called People's Budget. This income helped the government pay for national health insurance, unemployment benefits, old-age pensions, and a host of other social measures. The state was integrating the urban masses socially as well as politically.

This record of accomplishment was only part of the story, however. On the eve of World War I the question of Ireland brought Great Britain to the brink of civil war. The Irish famine in the 1840s (see page 684) fueled an Irish revolutionary movement. Thereafter the English slowly granted concessions, but refused to give Ireland self-government. After two decades of relative quiet, Irish nationalists in the British Parliament saw their chance. They supported the Liberals in their battle for the People's Budget and in 1913 received a home-rule bill for Ireland in return.

Ireland, however, was composed of two peoples. The Irish Catholic majority in the southern counties wanted home rule, but the Irish Protestants in the northern counties of Ulster vowed to resist it in northern Ireland with a hundred thousand armed volunteers. Ireland and Britain faced the prospect of civil war. Unable to resolve the conflicting nationalisms in Ireland as all Europe was suddenly overtaken by World War I in August 1914, the British government decided to postpone indefinitely the whole question of home rule for Ireland.

The dilemma of conflicting nationalisms in Ireland also helps one appreciate how desperate the situation in the Austro-Hungarian Empire had become by the early twentieth century. In 1849 Magyar nationalism had driven Hungarian patriots to declare an independent Hungarian republic, which was savagely crushed by Russian and Austrian armies (see pages 686–687). Throughout the 1850s Hungary was ruled as a conquered territory, and Emperor Francis Joseph (r. 1848–1916) and his bureaucracy tried hard to centralize the state and Germanize the language and culture of the different nationalities.

Then in the wake of defeat by Prussia in 1866, a weakened Austria was forced to strike a compromise and establish the so-called dual monarchy. The empire was divided in two, and the nationalistic Magyars gained virtual independence for Hungary. The two states were joined only by a shared monarch and common ministries for finance, defense, and foreign affairs. After 1867 the disintegrating force of competing nationalisms continued unabated, for both Austria and Hungary had several "Irelands" within their borders.

In Hungary the Magyar nobility in 1867 restored the constitution of 1848 and used it to dominate both the Magyar peasantry and the minority populations until 1914. Only the wealthiest one-fourth of adult males had the right to vote, making the parliament the creature of the Magyar elite. Laws promoting use of the Magyar (Hungarian) language in schools and government were rammed through and bitterly resented, especially by the Croatians and Romanians. While Magyar extremists campaigned loudly for total separation from Austria, the radical leaders of the subject nationalities dreamed in turn of independence from Hungary. Unlike most major European countries, which harnessed nationalism to strengthen the state after 1871, the Austro-Hungarian Empire was progressively weakened and eventually destroyed by the conflicting national aspirations of its different ethnic groups.

Jewish Emancipation and Modern Anti-Semitism

Revolutionary changes in political principles and the triumph of the nation-state brought equally revolutionary changes in Jewish life in western and central Europe. Beginning in France in 1791, Jews gradually gained their civil rights, although early progress was slow and uneven. In the 1850s and 1860s liberals in Austria, Italy, and Prussia pressed successfully for legal equality. In 1871 the constitution of the new German Empire consolidated the process of Jewish emancipation in central Europe. It abolished all restrictions on Jewish marriage, choice of occupation, place of residence, and property ownership. Exclusion from government employment and discrimination in social relations remained. However, according to one leading historian, by 1871 "it was widely accepted in Central Europe that the gradual disappearance of anti-Jewish prejudice was inevitable."[4]

The process of emancipation presented Jews with challenges and opportunities. Traditional Jewish occupations, such as court financial agent, village moneylender, and peddler, were undermined by free-market reforms, but careers in business, the professions, and the arts were opening to Jewish talent. Many Jews responded energetically and successfully. By 1871 a majority of Jewish people in western and central Europe had improved their economic situations and entered the middle classes. Most Jewish people also identified strongly with their respective nation-states and with good reason saw themselves as patriotic citizens.

Vicious anti-Semitism reappeared after the stock market crash of 1873, beginning in central Europe. Drawing on long traditions of religious intolerance, ghetto exclusion, and periodic anti-Jewish riots and expulsions, this anti-Semitism was also a modern development. It built on the general reaction against liberalism and its economic and political policies. Modern anti-Semitism whipped up resentment against Jewish achievement and Jewish "financial control," while fanatics claimed that the Jewish race (rather than the Jewish religion) posed a biological threat to the German people. Anti-Semitic beliefs were particularly popular among conservatives, extremist nationalists, and people who felt threatened by Jewish competition.

Anti-Semites also created modern political parties to attack and degrade Jews. In 1893, the prewar electoral high point in Germany, small anti-Semitic parties secured 2.9 percent of the votes cast. However, in Austrian Vienna in the early 1890s, Karl Lueger and his "Christian socialists" won striking electoral victories. This spurred a Jewish journalist named Theodor Herzl (1860–1904) to turn from German nationalism and advocate Jewish political nationalism, or **Zionism**, and the creation of a Jewish state. Lueger, the popular mayor of Vienna from 1897 to 1910, combined fierce anti-Semitic rhetoric with municipal ownership of basic services, and he appealed especially to the German-speaking lower middle class—and to an unsuccessful young artist named Adolf Hitler.

Before 1914 anti-Semitism was most oppressive in eastern Europe, where Jews also suffered from terrible poverty. In the Russian empire, where there was no Jewish

Primary Source:
Leo Pinsker, a Jewish Intellectual, Proposes a "Jewish Homeland," 1882
Noting that they are "at home everywhere, and nowhere at home," Pinsker argues that in order to be truly free, Jews need a homeland.

Zionism *The movement toward Jewish political nationhood started by Theodor Herzl.*

Primary Source:
Ahad Ha-Am's "The Jewish State and the Jewish Problem"
Ha-Ams provides a different, more cautious, perspective on Zionism.

Primary Source:
The Jews' State
The organizer of the first World Zionist Congress argues for the creation of a Jewish state in Palestine.

emancipation and 4 million of Europe's 7 million Jewish people lived in 1880, officials used anti-Semitism to channel popular discontent away from the government and onto the Jewish minority. Russian Jews were denounced as foreign exploiters, and in 1881–1882 a wave of violent pogroms commenced in southern Russia. The police and the army stood aside for days while peasants looted Jewish property and injured and killed many Jewish people. Official harassment and discrimination continued in the following decades. As a result, some Russian Jews turned toward self-emancipation and the vision of a Zionist settlement in the Ottoman province of Palestine. Large numbers also emigrated to western Europe and the United States. About 2.75 million Jews left eastern Europe between 1881 and 1914.

The Socialist Movement

Nationalism served, for better or worse, as a new unifying principle. But what about socialism? Did the rapid growth of socialist parties, which were generally Marxian parties dedicated to an international proletarian revolution, mean that national states had failed to gain the support of workers? This question requires close examination.

Certainly socialism appealed to large numbers of working men and women in the late nineteenth century, and the growth of socialist parties after 1871 was phenomenal. (See the feature "Listening to the Past: The Making of a Socialist" on pages 712–713.) By 1912, the German Social Democratic party, which espoused Marxian ideology, had millions of followers and was the largest party in the Reichstag. Socialist parties also grew in other countries, and Marxian socialist parties were linked together in an international organization.

The bookish Marx showed a rare flair for combining theorization with both lively popular writing and organizational ability. In 1864 he played an important role in founding the First International of socialists, and he used its annual meetings as a means of spreading his realistic, "scientific" doctrines of inevitable socialist revolution.

The First International collapsed, but in 1889 socialist leaders came together to form the Second International, which lasted until 1914. The International had a great psychological impact. Every three years delegates from the different parties met to interpret Marxian doctrines and plan coordinated action by a permanent executive. Many feared and many others rejoiced in the growing power of socialism and the Second International.

Yet socialism was not as radical and revolutionary in these years as it sometimes appeared. Indeed, as socialist parties grew and attracted large numbers of members, they looked more and more toward gradual change and steady improvement for the working class and less and less toward revolution. Workers themselves were progressively less inclined to follow radical programs for several reasons. As workers gained the right to vote and won real benefits, their attention focused more on elections than on revolutions. Workers were also not immune to patriotic education, drum-beating parades, and aggressive foreign policy as they loyally voted for socialists. Nor were workers a unified social group. Perhaps most important of all, workers' standard of living rose gradually but substantially after 1850, and the quality of life improved substantially in urban areas. Thus workers tended to become militantly moderate: they demanded gains, but they were less likely to take to the barricades in pursuit of them.

The growth of labor unions reinforced this trend toward moderation. In the early stages of industrialization modern unions were considered subversive bodies and were generally prohibited by law. In Great Britain new unions formed for skilled workers after 1850 avoided radical politics and concentrated on winning better wages and hours for their members through collective bargaining and compromise. After 1890, unions for unskilled workers developed in Britain.

● **"Greetings from the May Day Festival"** Workers participated enthusiastically in the annual one-day strike on May 1 to honor internationalist socialist solidarity, as this postcard from a happy woman visitor to her cousin suggests. Speeches, picnics, and parades were the order of the day, and workers celebrated their respectability and independent culture. Picture postcards developed with railroads and mass travel. *(akg-images)*

German unions were not granted important rights until 1869, and until the antisocialist law was repealed in 1890 the government frequently harassed them as socialist fronts. Then, with German industrialization still storming ahead and almost all legal harassment eliminated, union membership skyrocketed from only about 270,000 in 1895 to roughly 3 million in 1912. Genuine collective bargaining, long opposed by socialist intellectuals as a "sellout," was officially recognized as desirable by the German Trade Union Congress in 1899.

The German trade unions and their leaders were in fact, if not in name, thoroughgoing revisionists. **Revisionism** was an important effort by various socialists to update Marxian doctrines to reflect the realities of the time. The socialist Edward Bernstein (1850–1932) argued in 1899 in his *Evolutionary Socialism* that Marx's predictions of ever-greater poverty for workers had been proved false. Therefore, Bernstein suggested, socialists should reform their doctrines and win gradual evolutionary gains for workers through legislation, unions, and further economic development. The Second International denounced these views as heresy. Yet the revisionist, gradualist approach continued to gain the tacit acceptance of many German socialists, particularly in the trade unions.

Moderation found followers elsewhere. In France the great socialist leader Jean Jaurès (1859–1914) formally repudiated revisionist doctrines in order to establish a unified socialist party, but he remained at heart a gradualist. Questions of revolutionary versus gradualist policies split Russian Marxists.

Socialist parties in other countries also had clear-cut national characteristics. Russians and socialists in the Austro-Hungarian Empire tended to be the most radical. In Great Britain the socialist Labour party was non-Marxian and formally committed to gradual reform. In Spain and Italy anarchism, seeking to smash the state rather than the bourgeoisie, dominated radical thought and action. In short, socialist policies and doctrines varied from country to country. Socialism itself was to a large extent "nationalized" behind the imposing façade of international unity. This helps explain why almost all socialist leaders supported their governments when war came in 1914.

revisionism *An effort by various socialists to update Marxian doctrines to reflect the realities of the time.*

Chapter Summary

Key Terms

dual revolution
Congress of Vienna
Holy Alliance
Carlsbad Decrees
laissez faire
socialism
parasites
doers
bourgeoisie
proletariat
Sturm und Drang
Corn Laws
national workshops
Schleswig and Holstein
Red Shirts
North German
  Confederation
modernization
October Manifesto
Benthamite
miasmatic theory
germ theory
pasteurization
labor aristocracy
separate spheres
thermodynamics
evolution
Social Darwinists
Reichstag
Kulturkampf
Dreyfus affair
Zionism
revisionism

To assess your mastery of this chapter, go to
bedfordstmartins.com/mckayworld

• *How did the allies make peace in 1815, and what radical ideas emerged between 1815 and 1848?*

In 1814 the victorious allied powers came together to restore peace and stability in Europe. Dealing moderately with France and wisely settling their own differences, the allies laid the foundations for beneficial international cooperation throughout much of the nineteenth century. Led by Metternich, the conservative powers also sought to prevent the spread of subversive ideas and radical changes in domestic politics. Yet European thought has seldom been more powerfully creative than after 1815, and ideologies of liberalism, nationalism, and socialism all developed to challenge the existing order. The romantic movement reinforced the spirit of change and revolutionary anticipation.

• *Why did revolutions break out in 1848, and why did they fail?*

All of these forces culminated in the liberal and nationalistic revolutions of 1848, but these upheavals failed to realize their goals. The moderate middle classes were unable to consolidate their initial victories. Instead, they drew back in fear when artisans, factory workers, and radical socialists rose up to present their own much more revolutionary demands. This retreat facilitated a resurgence of conservative forces that crushed revolution all across Europe.

• *How did strong leaders and nation building transform Italy, Germany, and Russia?*

These conservative forces, led by Cavour in Sardinia and by Bismarck in Prussia, then took the lead in the unification of Italy and of Germany after 1850. In both countries nation building relied on strong rule that was fortified by popular nationalism at critical moments. By 1871 larger, more unified, and more popular states had emerged in the West. Responding to military defeat, Russia also built a stronger country as it modernized partially by freeing the serfs, industrializing rapidly, and establishing a conservative constitutional monarchy after 1905.

• *What was the impact of urban growth on cities, social classes, families, and ideas?*

As urban civilization also came to prevail in Europe, governments took effective action in public health and developed badly needed urban services. Family life became more stable and more loving, although a sharp separation of gender roles tended to lock women into subordinate and stereotypical roles. While the quality of urban and family life improved, the class structure became more complex and diversified. Urban society featured many distinct social groups, and the complexity of social relations was a favorite theme of realist novelists. More generally, literary realism reflected Western society's growing faith in science, material progress, and evolutionary thinking.

• How did governments gain popular support and deal with the socialist movement?

Western society became increasingly nationalistic as well as urban and industrial in the late nineteenth century. Nation-states became more responsive, and they enlisted widespread support as peaceful political participation expanded, educational opportunities increased, and social security systems took shape. More broadly, nation-states may be seen as providing a stabilizing response to the profoundly unsettling challenges of the dual revolution. Even socialism became increasingly national in orientation, gathering strength as a champion of working-class interests in domestic politics. Yet even though nationalism served to unite peoples, it also drove them apart—not only in Austria-Hungary and Ireland but also throughout Europe and the rest of the world. The national faith, which reduced social tensions within states, promoted a bitter, almost Darwinian competition between states and thus threatened the progress and unity it had helped to build, as we shall see in Chapter 27.

Suggested Reading

Anderson, Bonnie S., and Judith P. Zinsser. *A History of Their Own: Women in Europe from Prehistory to the Present,* vol. 2, rev. ed. 2000. An excellent, wide-ranging survey.

Berend, Ivan T. *History Derailed: Central and Eastern Europe in the Long Nineteenth Century.* 2003. Focuses on industrialization and its consequences.

Coontz, Stephanie. *Marriage, A History: From Obedience to Intimacy, or How Love Conquered Marriage.* 2005. A lively inquiry into the historical background to current practice.

Gildea, Robert. *Barricades and Borders: Europe, 1800–1914,* 2d ed. 1996. A recommended general study.

Gottlieb, Beatrice. *The Family in the Western World.* 1993. A wide-ranging synthesis.

Malia, Martin, and Terrence Emmons. *History's Locomotives: Revolutions and the Making of the Modern World.* 2006. An ambitious comparative work of high quality.

Mann, Thomas. *Buddenbrooks.* 1901. A wonderful historical novel that traces the rise and fall of a prosperous German family over three generations.

Rubinstein, W. D. *Britain's Century: Political and Social History, 1815–1905.* 1998. An excellent history with strong coverage of social questions.

Tombs, Robert. *France, 1814–1914,* 1996. An impressive survey with a useful bibliography.

Vital, David. *A People Apart: The Jews in Europe, 1789–1939.* 1999. An engaging and judicious investigation.

Notes

1. E. Gellner, *Nations and Nationalism* (Oxford: Basil Blackwell, 1983), pp. 19–39.
2. B. Anderson, *Imagined Communities: Reflections on the Origins and Spread of Nationalism,* rev. ed. (London/New York: Verso, 1991).
3. J. McKay, *Tramways and Trolleys: The Rise of Urban Mass Transport in Europe* (Princeton, N.J.: Princeton University Press, 1976), p. 81.
4. R. Seltzer, *Jewish People, Jewish Thought: The Jewish Experience in History* (New York: Macmillan, 1980), p. 533.

Listening to the PAST

The Making of a Socialist

Nationalism and socialism appeared locked in bitter competition in Europe before 1914, but they actually complemented each other in many ways. Both faiths were secular as opposed to religious, and both fostered political awareness. A working person who became interested in politics and developed nationalist beliefs might well convert to socialism at a later date.

This was the case for Adelheid Popp (1869–1939), a self-taught working woman who became an influential socialist leader. Born into a desperately poor working-class family in Vienna and remembering only a "hard and gloomy childhood," she was forced by her parents to quit school at age ten to begin full-time work. She struggled with low-paying piecework for years before she landed a solid factory job, as she recounts in the following selection from her widely read autobiography.

Always an avid reader, Popp became the editor of a major socialist newspaper for German working women. She then told her life story so that all working women might share her truth: "Socialism could change and strengthen others, as it did me."

[Finally] I found work again; I took everything that was offered me in order to show my willingness to work, and I passed through much. But at last things became better. [At age fifteen] I was recommended to a great factory which stood in the best repute. Three hundred girls and about fifty men were employed. I was put in a big room where sixty women and girls were at work. Against the windows stood twelve tables, and at each sat four girls. We had to sort the goods which had been manufactured, others had to count them, and a third set had to brand on them the mark of the firm. We worked from 7 A.M. to 7 P.M. We had an hour's rest at noon, half-an-hour in the afternoon. . . . I had never yet been paid so much. . . .

I seemed to myself to be almost rich. . . . [Yet] from the women of this factory one can judge how sad and full of deprivation is the lot of a factory worker. In none of the neighbouring factories were the wages so high; we were envied everywhere. Parents considered themselves fortunate if they could get their daughters of fourteen in there on leaving school. . . . And even

here, in this paradise, all were badly nourished. Those who stayed at the factory for the dinner hour would buy themselves for a few pennies a sausage or the leavings of a cheese shop. . . . In spite of all the diligence and economy, every one was poor, and trembled at the thought of losing her work. All humbled themselves, and suffered the worst injustice from the foremen, not to risk losing this good work, not to be without food. . . .

I did not only read novels and tales; I had begun . . . to read the classics and other good books. I also began to take an interest in public events. . . . I was not democratically inclined. I was full of enthusiasm then for emperors, and kings and highly placed personages played no small part in my fancies. . . . I bought myself a strict Catholic paper, that criticised very adversely the workers' movement, which was attracting notice. Its aim was to educate in a patriotic and religious direction. . . . I took the warmest interest in the events that occurred in the royal families, and I took the death of the Crown Prince of Austria so much to heart that I wept a whole day. . . . Political events [also] held me in suspense. The possibility of a war with Russia roused my patriotic enthusiasm. I saw my brother already returning from the battlefield covered with glory. . . .

When a particularly strong anti-Semitic feeling was noticeable in political life, I sympathised with it for a time. A broad sheet, "How Israel Attained Power and Sovereignty over all the Nations of the Earth," fascinated me. . . .

About this time an Anarchist group was active. Some mysterious murders which had taken place were ascribed to the Anarchists, and the police made use of them to oppress the rising workmen's movement. . . . I followed the trial of the Anarchists with passionate sympathy. I read all the speeches, and because, as always happens, Social Democrats, whom the authorities really wanted to attack, were among the accused, I learned their views. I became full of enthusiasm. Every single Social Democrat . . . seemed to me a hero. . . .

There was unrest among the workers . . . and demonstrations of protest followed. When these

1890 engraving of a meeting of workers in Berlin. *(Bildarchiv Preussischer Kulturbesitz/ Art Resource, NY)*

were repeated the military entered the "threatened" streets. . . . In the evenings I rushed in the greatest excitement from the factory to the scene of the disturbance. The military did not frighten me; I only left the place when it was "cleared."

Later on my mother and I lived with one of my brothers who had married. Friends came to him, among them some intelligent workmen. One of these workmen was particularly intelligent, and . . . could talk on many subjects. He was the first Social Democrat I knew. He brought me many books, and explained to me the difference between Anarchism and Socialism. I heard from him, also for the first time, what a republic was, and in spite of my former enthusiasm for royal dynasties, I also declared myself in favour of a republican form of government. I saw everything so near and so clearly, that I actually counted the weeks which must still elapse before the revolution of state and society would take place.

From this workman I received the first Social Democratic party organ. . . . I first learned from it to understand and judge of my own lot. I learned to see that all I had suffered was the result not of a divine ordinance, but of an unjust organization of society. . . .

In the factory I became another woman. . . . I told my [female] comrades all that I had read of the workers' movement. Formerly I had often told stories when they had begged me for them. But instead of narrating . . . the fate of some queen, I now held forth on oppression and exploitation. I told of accumu-

lated wealth in the hands of a few, and introduced as a contrast the shoemakers who had no shoes and the tailors who had no clothes. On breaks I read aloud the articles in the Social Democratic paper and explained what Socialism was as far as I understood it. . . . [While I was reading] it often happened that one of the clerks passing by shook his head and said to another clerk: "The girl speaks like a man."

Questions for Analysis

1. How did Popp describe and interpret work in the factory?

2. To what extent did her socialist interpretation of factory life fit the facts she described?

3. What were Popp's political interests before she became a socialist?

4. How and why did she become a Social Democrat?

5. Was this account likely to lead other working women to socialism? Why?

Source: Slightly adapted from A. Popp, *The Autobiography of a Working Woman,* trans. E. C. Harvey (Chicago: F. G. Browne, 1913), pp. 29, 34–35, 39, 66–69, 71, 74, 82–90.

Ottoman Sultan Abdulaziz
(r. 1861–1876), supporter of vigorous modernizing reform.
(Topkapi Saray Museum/Dagli Orti/The Art Archive)

24

AFRICA, SOUTHWEST ASIA, AND WESTERN IMPERIALISM, 1800–1914

W hile industrialization and nationalism were transforming urban life and Western society, Western society had a profound impact on non-Western countries and regions. An ever-growing stream of products, people, and ideas flowed out of Europe at this time. The most spectacular manifestation of this many-sided Western expansion came in the late nineteenth century when the leading European nations established or enlarged their far-flung political empires.

Western industrialization and imperialism posed a profound challenge to the many, highly diverse peoples of Africa and Asia. Economic relationships changed, as Europe consolidated its industrial lead and urged Africa and Asia to sell more commodities and raw materials. Political independence and established cultural and religious values also were threatened by Western penetration. It is little wonder, therefore, that African and Asian states and peoples often tried to repel the foreigners with military force and searched for other methods when they were defeated. Stretching over two centuries, the timing of these encounters with the West certainly contributed to the great diversity of historical experiences in Africa and Asia in the years before World War I. This chapter will consider the Islamic heartland and Africa, and Chapter 25 will turn to South Asia and East Asia.

The Western challenge in the land of Islam emerged in the late seventeenth century, when the Ottoman Empire began to suffer military reversals. The Ottomans eventually responded with a series of reforms designed to modernize the army and protect the empire, but these efforts were only partly successful. The Ottoman Empire continued to lose territory throughout the nineteenth century. Its Egyptian province became increasingly independent and launched its own campaign of westernization until it went bankrupt and was conquered by Britain. Yet both the Ottoman Empire and Egypt also made real progress and laid the foundations of modern Turkey and Egypt.

In sub-Saharan Africa the slow decline of the transatlantic slave trade in the nineteenth century accompanied a great expansion of commodity exports, a shift that marked the beginning of modern economic development in this vast and diverse region. At the same time, powerful movements of Islamic revival extended the sway of Islam in West and central Africa and made Islam a more important part of everyday life and culture. In southern Africa competing groups of white settlers pressed northward and eastward after 1800, foreshadowing European conquest and empire building in the whole continent after 1880. In short, in the nineteenth century Africa experienced greater and more far-reaching changes than ever before.

INDUSTRIALIZATION AND THE WORLD ECONOMY

What were the global consequences of European industrialization between 1800 and 1914?

The Industrial Revolution created, first in Great Britain and then in continental Europe and North America, a growing and dynamic economic system. In the course of the nineteenth century that system expanded and transformed economic relations across the face of the earth. As a result the world's total income grew as never before, international trade boomed, and millions of migrants settled in distant lands. Thus Western industrialization had profound consequences for the global economy and the world's peoples.

The Rise of Global Inequality

The Industrial Revolution in Europe marked a momentous turning point in human history. From a global perspective, the ultimate significance of the Industrial Revolution was that it allowed those regions of the world that industrialized in the nineteenth century to increase their wealth and power enormously in comparison with those that did not. Moreover, this pattern of uneven global development became institutionalized, or built into the structure of the world economy, and the **lopsided world**—a world of rich lands and poor—evolved.

lopsided world *A world of rich lands and poor lands and global inequality.*

Figure 24.1 depicts the gap between the industrializing regions (mainly Europe and North America) and the non-industrializing ones (mainly Africa, Asia, and Latin America) that opened up in the late eighteenth and the nineteenth centuries. In 1750 the average standard of living was no higher in Europe as a whole than in the rest of the world. By 1970, however, the average person in the wealthiest countries had an income fully twenty-five times as great as the income received by the average person in the poorest countries of Africa and Asia. The rise in average income and well-being, first in Great Britain and then in the other developed countries, reflected the rising level of industrialization (see pages 656–657). Thus average income per person stagnated in the Third World before 1913. Only after 1945, in the era of political independence and decolonization, did the developing countries of Africa, Asia, and Latin America as a whole make real economic progress and begin the critical process of industrialization.

The rise of these enormous income disparities, which are poignant indicators of disparities in food and clothing, health

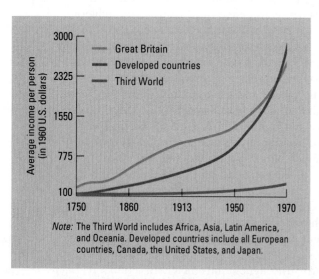

Note: The Third World includes Africa, Asia, Latin America, and Oceania. Developed countries include all European countries, Canada, the United States, and Japan.

● FIGURE 24.1 **The Growth of Average Income per Person in the Third World, Developed Countries, and Great Britain, 1750–1970** (Source: P. Bairoch and M. Lévy-Leboyer, eds., *Disparities in Economic Development Since the Industrial Revolution,* published 1981, Macmillan Publishers. Reproduced with permission of Palgrave Macmillan.)

and education, life expectancy and general material well-being, has generated a great deal of debate. One school of interpretation stresses that the West used science, technology, capitalist organization, and even its critical worldview to create its wealth and greater physical well-being. Another school argues that the West used its political and economic power to steal much of its riches, continuing in the nineteenth (and twentieth) century the rapacious colonialism born of the era of European expansion.

These issues are complex, and there are few simple answers. As noted in Chapter 22, the wealth-creating potential of technological improvement and more intensive capitalist organization was indeed great. At the same time, the initial breakthroughs in the late eighteenth century rested in part on Great Britain's having already used political force to dominate a substantial part of the world economy. In the nineteenth century other industrializing countries joined with Britain to extend Western dominion over the entire world economy. Unprecedented wealth was indeed created, but the lion's share of that new wealth flowed to the West and its propertied classes and to a tiny non-Western elite of cooperative rulers, landowners, and merchants.

The World Market

World trade was a powerful stimulus to economic development in the nineteenth century. In 1913 the value of world trade was about twenty-five times what it had been in 1800, even though prices of manufactured goods and raw materials were lower in 1913 than in 1800. In a general way, the enormous increase in international commerce summed up the growth of an interlocking world economy centered in Europe.

Great Britain played a key role in using trade to tie the world together economically. In 1815 Britain already had a colonial empire, for India, Canada, Australia, and other scattered areas remained British possessions after American independence. The technological breakthroughs of the Industrial Revolution encouraged British manufacturers to seek export markets around the world. After the repeal of the Corn Laws in 1846 (see page 684), Britain also became the world's leading importer of foreign goods. Free access to Britain's market stimulated the development of mines and plantations in Africa and Asia.

The growth of trade was facilitated by the conquest of distance. The earliest railroad construction occurred in Europe and in America north of the Rio Grande; other parts of the globe saw the building of rail lines after 1860. By 1920 about a quarter of the world's railroads were in Latin America, Asia, Africa, and Australia. Wherever railroads were built, they drastically reduced transportation costs, opened new economic opportunities, and called forth new skills and attitudes.

Much of the railroad construction undertaken in Africa, Asia, and Latin America connected seaports with inland cities and regions, as opposed to linking and developing

Chronology

1780s–1860	Industrial Revolution
1808–1839	Mahmud II rules Ottoman state and enacts reforms
1809	Usuman founds Sokoto caliphate
1810–1855	Palm oil becomes "legitimate" commerce in West Africa
1830	France begins conquest of Algeria
1839–1876	Ottoman statesmen enact reforms (Tanzimat)
1863–1879	Reign of Ismail in Egypt
1871–1879	Al-Afghani preaches Islamic regeneration
1875	Ottoman state declares partial bankruptcy; European creditors take over
1876	Europeans take financial control in Egypt
1880	Western and central Sudan united under Islam
1880–1902	Europeans scramble for Africa
1880–1914	Height of Western imperialism in Asia and Africa
1884–1885	Berlin Conference
1899	Kipling, "The White Man's Burden"; Amin, *The Liberation of Women*
1899–1902	South African War
1902	Conrad, *Heart of Darkness;* Hobson, *Imperialism*
1908	Young Turks seize power in Ottoman state

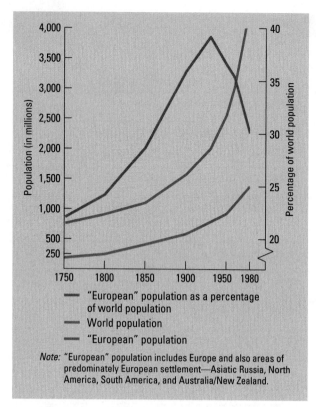

● FIGURE 24.2 **The Increase of European and World Populations, 1750–1980** (Sources: W. Woodruff, *Impact of Western Man: A Study of Europe's Role in the World Economy.* St. Martin's Press, New York, 1967, p. 103; United Nations, *Statistical Yearbook, 1982*, pp. 2–3.)

cities and regions within a given country. Thus railroads dovetailed with Western economic interests, facilitating the inflow and sale of Western manufactured goods and the export and development of local raw materials.

The power of steam also revolutionized transportation by sea. Steam power, long used to drive paddle wheelers on rivers, particularly in Russia and North America, finally began to supplant sails on the oceans of the world in the late 1860s. Lighter, stronger, cheaper steel replaced iron, which had replaced wood. Passenger and freight rates tumbled, and the shipment of low-priced raw materials from one continent to another became feasible.

The revolution in land and sea transportation helped European settlers take vast, thinly populated territories and produce agricultural products and raw materials there for sale in Europe. Improved transportation enabled Asia, Africa, and Latin America to export not only the traditional tropical products—spices, dyes, tea, sugar, coffee—but also new raw materials for industry, such as jute, rubber, cotton, and coconut oil. (See the feature "Global Trade: Indigo" on pages 720–721.)

Intercontinental trade was enormously facilitated by the Suez and Panama Canals. Of great importance, too, was large and continual investment in modern port facilities, which made loading and unloading cheaper, faster, and more dependable. Finally, transoceanic telegraph cables inaugurated rapid communications among the financial centers of the world and linked world commodity prices in a global network.

The growth of trade and the conquest of distance encouraged Europeans to make massive foreign investments beginning about 1840. Most of the capital exported did not go to European colonies or protectorates in Asia and Africa. About three-quarters of total European investment went to other European countries, the United States and Canada, Australia and New Zealand, and Latin America. Europe found its most profitable opportunities for investment in construction of the railroads, ports, and utilities that were necessary to settle and develop the lands of extensive European expansion. Much of this investment was peaceful and mutually beneficial for lenders and borrowers. The victims were Native American Indians and Australian Aborigines, who were displaced and decimated by the diseases, liquor, and weapons of an aggressively expanding Western society (see Chapter 26).

The Great Migration

A poignant human drama was interwoven with economic expansion: millions of people pulled up stakes and left their ancestral lands in one of history's greatest migrations. In the early eighteenth century the world's population entered a period of rapid growth, which continued unabated through the nineteenth and twentieth centuries, as Figure 24.2 shows. The population of Europe (including Asiatic Russia) more than doubled, from approximately 188 million in 1800 to roughly 432 million in 1900. More than 60 million people left Europe, primarily for the rapidly growing "areas of European settlement"—North and South America, Australia, New Zealand, and Siberia (see Chapter 26).

Between 1750 and 1900 the population of Asia followed the same general trend. China, by far the world's most populous country in the middle of the eighteenth century, increased from about 143 million in 1741 to a little more than 400 million in the 1840s, although total numbers grew more slowly in the turbulent late nineteenth century. Since population increased more slowly in Africa and Asia than in Europe, Europeans and peoples of predominately European origin jumped from about 22 percent of the world's total in 1850 to a high of about 38 percent in 1930.

The growing number of Europeans was a driving force behind emigration and Western expansion. The rapid increase in numbers led to relative overpopulation in area after area in Europe. Thus millions of country folk went abroad as well as to nearby cities in search of work and economic opportunity. European emigration crested in the first decade of the twentieth century, when more than five times as many men and women departed as in the 1850s.

The European migrant was most often a small peasant landowner or a village craftsman whose traditional way of life was threatened by too little land, estate agriculture, and cheap factory-made goods. Determined to maintain or improve their precarious status, the vast majority of migrants were young and very often unmarried. Many European migrants returned home after some time abroad. One in two migrants to Argentina and probably one in three to the United States eventually returned to their native lands.

Ties of family and friendship played a crucial role in the movement of peoples. Many people from a given province or village settled together in rural enclaves or tightly knit urban neighborhoods thousands of miles away. Very often a strong individual—a businessman, a religious leader—would blaze the way and others would follow, forming a **migration chain**.

migration chain   *The movement of peoples in which one strong individual would blaze the way and others would follow.*

Many young European men and women were spurred to leave by a spirit of revolt and independence. In Sweden and Norway, in Jewish Russia and Italy, these young people felt frustrated by the small privileged classes that often controlled both church and government and resisted demands for change and greater opportunity. Migration slowed when people won basic political and social reforms, such as the right to vote and social security.

A substantial number of Asians—especially Chinese, Japanese, Indians, and Filipinos—also responded to population pressure and rural hardship with temporary or permanent migration. At least 3 million Asians (in contrast to more than 60 million Europeans) moved abroad before 1920. Most went as indentured laborers to work under incredibly difficult conditions on the plantations or in the gold mines of Latin America, southern Asia, Africa, California, Hawaii, and Australia (see Chapter 25). White estate owners very often used Asians to replace or supplement blacks after the suppression of the Atlantic slave trade.

Such migration from Asia would undoubtedly have grown to much greater proportions if planters and mine owners in search of cheap labor had had their way. But usually they did not. Asians fled the plantations and gold mines as soon as possible, seeking greater opportunities in trade and towns. There they came into conflict with white settlers in areas of European settlement. These settlers demanded a halt to Asian immigration. By the 1880s Americans and Australians were building **great white walls**—discriminatory laws designed to keep Asians out.

great white walls   *Discriminatory laws that appeared in the 1880s in the United States and Australia and were designed to keep Asians out.*

The general policy of "whites only" in the lands of large-scale European settlement meant that Europeans and people of European ancestry reaped the main benefits of the great migration. By 1913 people in Australia, Canada, and the United States all had higher average incomes than people in Great Britain, still Europe's wealthiest nation. This, too, was part of Western dominance in the increasingly lopsided world.

Within Asia and Africa the situation was different. Migrants from south China frequently settled in Dutch, British, and French colonies of Southeast Asia, where they established themselves as peddlers and small shopkeepers (see Chapter 25). These "overseas Chinese" gradually emerged as a new class of entrepreneurs and officeworkers. Traders from India and modern-day Lebanon performed the same function in much of sub-Saharan Africa after the European seizure in the late nineteenth century.

GLOBAL TRADE

INDIGO

Few items shed more light on issues of production and on the prodigious growth of world trade in the nineteenth century than indigo, the oldest and most important natural colorant. The extract of leaves from a small bush that are carefully fermented in vats and processed into cakes of pigment, indigo has been highly prized since antiquity. It dyes all fabrics, does not fade with time, and yields tints ranging from light blue to the darkest purple-blue. Used primarily today as a dye for blue jeans, indigo has been used throughout history as a dye for textiles, as a pigment for painting, and for medicinal and cosmetic purposes. Global trade in the famous blue dye expanded after 1500 and was repeatedly restruc-

tured until, in the late nineteenth century, it was revolutionized by an industrializing Europe.

Indigo for local consumption could be obtained from many plants in tropical climates, but the best-known species for trade came from India. Widely grown and used in Asia, indigo trickled into Europe from western India in the High Middle Ages but was very expensive. Woad—an inferior homegrown product—remained Europe's main blue dye until the opening of a direct sea route to India by the Portuguese in 1498 reconfigured the intercontinental trade in indigo, as it did for many Asian products. Bypassing Muslim traders in the Indian Ocean and gradually overcoming the opposition of the woad interests in Europe, first Portuguese and then Dutch and English merchants and trading companies supplied European dyers and consumers with cheaper, more abundant indigo.

The Indigo Trade

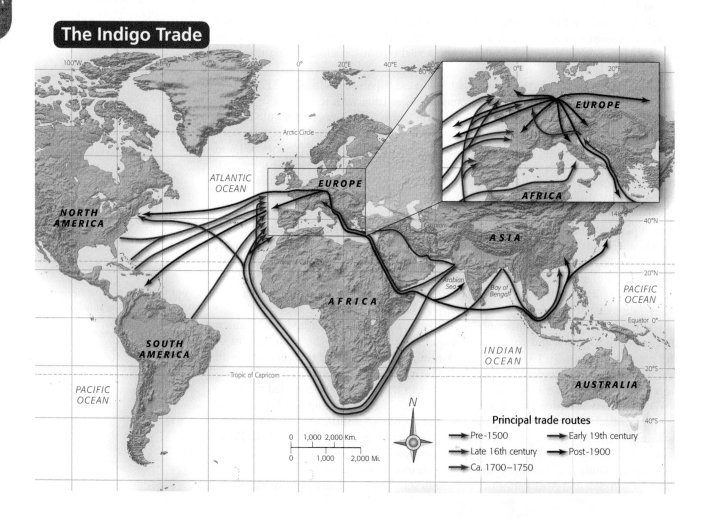

Principal trade routes

→ Pre-1500
→ Late 16th century
→ Ca. 1700–1750
→ Early 19th century
→ Post-1900

Squatting next to a dye pit in northern Nigeria, a man soaks clothing in natural indigo dye, which is still used locally in parts of Africa and South Asia. (Corbis)

In the early seventeenth century, indigo became one of the British East India Company's chief articles of trade, and it was exported from India to Europe more than ever before. However, as European governments adopted mercantilist policies, they tried to control trade and limit the flow of gold and silver abroad for products like indigo. The result was a second transformation in the global trade in indigo.

Europeans established indigo plantations in their American colonies, and by the first half of the eighteenth century only small quantities of indigo continued to reach Europe from peasant producers in western India. Indigo plantations in Brazil, Guatemala, Haiti and the Caribbean, and South Carolina were big, capitalistic operations and frequently very profitable. They depended on slaves brought from Africa, as did the entire Atlantic economy in the eighteenth century.

In the late eighteenth century the geography of the indigo trade shifted dramatically once again: production returned to India, now largely controlled by the British. Why did this happen? Political upheaval in the revolutionary era played a key role. American independence left South Carolina outside Britain's mercantilist system; slave rebellion in Haiti in 1791 decimated some of the world's richest indigo producers; and Britain's continental blockades cut off Spain and France from their colonies. On the economy side, the takeoff in the British textile industry created surging demand for indigo. Thus in the 1780s, the British East India Company hired experienced indigo planters from the West Indies to develop indigo production in Bengal. Leasing lands from Indian *zemindars* (landlords who doubled as tax collectors), British planters coerced Bengali peasants into growing indigo, which the planters processed in their "factories." Business expanded rapidly, as planters made—and lost—fortunes in boom-and-bust cycles characteristic of commodity production in the nineteenth century.

In 1859 Bengali peasants revolted and received unexpected support from British officials advocating free-market contracts and recourse to the courts to settle disputes. As peasants pressed their case against the outraged planters, Indian professionals and intellectuals joined their cause. Winning freer and more equitable contracts, the rural-urban alliance created in the "Indigo Disturbances" marked a key step in the growth of nationalism in Bengal, a leading force in the subsequent drive for Indian independence.

Even as the "Indigo Disturbances" agitated Bengal, industrializing Europe discovered on its doorstep a completely new source of colorants—thick, black coal tar. This residue, a noxious byproduct from the destructive distillation of soft coal for the gas used in urban lighting and heating, was emerging as the basic material for the chemistry of carbon compounds and a new synthetic dye industry. Building on early theoretical and experimental work, British, German, and French chemists synthesized a small number of dyes between 1856 and 1869, when the first synthetic dye replaced a natural dye. Thereafter German researchers and Germany's organic chemical companies, protected by effective international patent laws after 1877, built up an interlocking global monopoly that produced more than 90 percent of the world's synthetic dyes.

Indigo was emblematic of this resounding success. Professor Adolf Bayer first synthesized indigo in 1880. But an economically viable process required many years of costly, systematic research before two leading German companies working together achieved their objective in 1897. Producers' groups in India slashed indigo prices drastically but to no avail. Indian exports of natural indigo plummeted from nineteen thousand tons in 1895 to only one thousand tons in 1913. Synthetic indigo claimed the global market, German firms earned super profits, and Indian peasants turned to different crops. Today, nearly all of the indigo produced in the world is synthetic, although limited production of natural indigo still occurs in India, as well as in parts of Africa and South America.

● **An Italian Custom in Argentina**   Italian immigrants introduced the game of *boccia* to Argentina, where it took hold and became a popular recreation for men. Dressed up in their Sunday best, these Argentinean laborers are totally focused on the game, which is something like horseshoes or shuffleboard. *(Hulton Archive/Getty Images)*

Thus in some parts of Asia and Africa the business class was both Asian and foreign, protected and tolerated by Western imperialists who found them useful.

While migration from Europe, and to a lesser extent Asia, increased in the nineteenth century, the total flow of enslaved men and women out of Africa declined very gradually after 1800. The decline began in the 1830s and continued at an accelerating pace until the 1890s, when the export of African slaves had been greatly reduced. The gradual passing of the long-standing and massive forced migration of Africans to the Americas had many far-reaching consequences for African societies, as we shall see.

WESTERN IMPERIALISM (1880–1914)

What were the causes and consequences of European empire building after 1880?

Western expansion into Asia and Africa reached its apex between about 1880 and 1914. In those years the leading European nations continued to send streams of money and manufactured goods to both continents, and they also rushed to create or enlarge vast political empires abroad. This frantic political empire building contrasted sharply with the economic penetration of non-Western territories between 1816 and 1880, which, albeit by naked military force, had left a China or a Japan "opened" but politically independent (see Chapter 25). By contrast, the empires of the late nineteenth century recalled the old European colonial empires of the seventeenth and eighteenth centuries and led contemporaries to speak of the "new imperialism."

The most spectacular manifestation of the new imperialism was the seizure of almost all of Africa, which broke sharply with previous patterns and fascinated contemporary Europeans and Americans, as we shall see later in this chapter. Although the sudden division of Africa was more striking, Europeans also extended their political control in Asia. The British expanded from their base in India, and in the 1880s the

French took Indochina (modern Vietnam, Cambodia, and Laos). India and China also experienced a profound imperialist impact (see Chapter 25).

Causes of the New Imperialism

Many factors contributed to the West's late-nineteenth-century rush for territory in Africa and Asia, and it is little wonder that controversies have raged over interpretation of the new imperialism. But despite complexity and controversy, basic causes are clearly identifiable.

Economic motives played an important role in the extension of political empires, especially the British Empire. By the late 1870s France, Germany, and the United States were industrializing rapidly behind rising tariff barriers. Great Britain was losing its industrial leadership and facing increasingly tough competition in foreign markets. In this new economic situation Britain came to value more highly its old possessions, especially its vast and highly profitable colony in India, which it had exploited most profitably for more than a century. When in the 1880s European continental powers began to grab unclaimed territories, the British followed suit immediately. They feared France and Germany would seal off their empires with high tariffs and that future economic opportunities would be lost forever.

Actually, the overall economic gains of the new imperialism proved limited before 1914. The new colonies were too poor to buy much, and they offered few immediately profitable investments. Nonetheless, colonies became important for political and diplomatic reasons. Each leading European country saw colonies as crucial to national security, military power, and international prestige.

Colonial rivalries reflected the increasing aggressiveness of European Social Darwinian theories of brutal competition among races. Thus European nations, which were seen as racially distinct parts of the dominant white race, had to seize colonies to show they were strong and virile. Moreover, the conquest of inferior peoples was just. Social Darwinism and harsh racial doctrines fostered imperialist expansion.

Ongoing industrial and technological advances, accelerating after 1880 with new industries based on scientific research (see page 702), gave Western countries unprecedented military superiority and greatly facilitated Western imperialism. Three aspects were crucial. First, the rapidly firing machine gun became an ultimate weapon in many an unequal battle. Second, newly discovered **quinine** proved effective in controlling attacks of malaria, which had previously decimated Europeans in the tropics whenever they left breezy coastal enclaves and dared to venture into mosquito-infested interiors. Third, the combination of the steamship and the international telegraph permitted Western powers to quickly concentrate their firepower in a given area when it was needed. Never before—and never again after 1914—would the technological gap between the West and non-Western regions of the world be so great.

Social tensions and domestic political conflicts also contributed to overseas expansion. Conservative political leaders often manipulated colonial issues in order to divert popular attention from domestic conflicts and to create a false sense of national unity. Thus imperial propagandists relentlessly stressed that colonies benefited workers as well as capitalists, and they encouraged the masses to savor foreign triumphs and glory in the supposed increase in national prestige.

Special-interest groups in each country were powerful agents of expansion. White settlers wanted more land, and humanitarians wanted to stop the slave trade. Military men and colonial officials foresaw rapid advancement and high-paid positions in growing empires.

Imperialists did not rest the case for empire solely on naked conquest and a Darwinian racial struggle or on power politics and the need for naval bases on every ocean. Imperialists developed additional arguments to satisfy their consciences and answer their critics. A favorite idea was that Europeans and Americans could and should "civilize" supposedly primitive non-Western peoples. According to this view,

quinine *An agent that proved effective in controlling attacks of malaria, which had previously decimated Europeans in the tropics.*

Africans and Asians would receive the benefits of modern economies, cities, advanced medicine, and higher standards of living and eventually might be ready for self-government and Western democracy.

Another argument was that imperial government protected colonized peoples from ethnic warfare and the slave trade within Africa, as well as from cruder forms of exploitation by white settlers and business people. Thus the French spoke of their sacred "civilizing mission." Similarly, Rudyard Kipling (1865–1936), who wrote extensively on Anglo-Indian life and was perhaps the most influential British writer of the 1890s, exhorted Westerners to provide humanitarian service in imperial possessions. There they should "take up the White Mans's Burden" and work for the betterment of their "new-caught sullen peoples."[1]

Imperialists claimed that peace and stability under European control would permit the spread of Christianity. In Africa Catholic and Protestant missionaries competed with Islam south of the Sahara, seeking converts and building schools. Many Africans' first real contact with Europeans and Americans was in mission schools. Some peoples, such as the Ibo in Nigeria, became highly Christianized. Such occasional successes in black Africa contrasted with the general failure of missionary efforts in the Islamic world and in much of Asia.

Western Critics of Imperialism

The expansion of empire aroused sharp, even bitter, Western critics. A forceful attack was delivered in 1902, after the unpopular South African War, by radical English economist J. A. Hobson (1858–1940) in his *Imperialism,* a work that influenced Lenin and others. Hobson contended that the rush to acquire colonies was due to the economic needs of unregulated capitalism. Moreover, Hobson argued, the quest for empire diverted popular attention away from domestic reform and the need to reduce the great gap between rich and poor at home. These and similar arguments had limited appeal because most people were sold on the idea that imperialism was economically profitable for the homeland.

Hobson and many Western critics struck home, however, with their moral condemnation of whites imperiously ruling nonwhites. Kipling and his kind were lampooned as racist bullies whose rule rested on brutality, racial contempt, and the Maxim machine gun. Polish-born novelist Joseph Conrad (1857–1924), in *Heart of Darkness* (1902), castigated the "pure selfishness" of Europeans in "civilizing" Africa. The main character in the novel, once a liberal European scholar, is corrupted by power in Africa and turns into a savage brute.

Critics charged Europeans with applying a degrading double standard and failing to live up to their own noble ideals. At home Europeans had won or were winning representative government, individual liberties, and a certain equality of opportunity. In their empires Europeans imposed military dictatorships on Africans and Asians; forced them to work involuntarily; and discriminated against them shamelessly. Only by renouncing imperialism and giving captive peoples the freedom idealized in Western society would Europeans be worthy of their traditions.

African and Asian Resistance

Primary Source:

His Story

Read a firsthand account of the hardships suffered by the Ndebele, a people of southeastern Africa, in their dealings with European colonists.

To peoples in Africa and Asia, Western expansion represented a disruptive, many-sided assault with many consequences. Everywhere it threatened traditional ruling classes, economies, and ways of life. Christian missionaries and European secular ideologies challenged established beliefs and values. African and Asian societies experienced a crisis of identity and a general pattern of reassertion, although the details of each people's story varied substantially.

● A Missionary School
A Swahili schoolboy leads his class-mates in a reading lesson in Dar es Salaam in German East Africa before 1914, as portraits of Emperor William II and his wife look down on the classroom. Europeans argued that they were spreading the benefits of a superior civilization with schools like this one, which is unusually solid because of its strategic location in the capital city. *(Ullstein Bilderdienst/ The Granger Collection, New York)*

Often the initial response of African and Asian rulers was to try driving the unwelcome foreigners away, as in China and Japan (see Chapter 25). Violent antiforeign reactions exploded elsewhere again and again, but the superior military technology of the industrialized West almost invariably prevailed. Beaten in battle, many Africans and Asians concentrated on preserving their cultural traditions at all costs. Others found themselves forced to reconsider their initial hostility. Some concluded that the West was indeed superior in certain ways and that it was therefore necessary to reform their societies and copy some European achievements. Thus it is possible to think of responses to the Western impact as a spectrum, with **traditionalists** at one end, westernizers or **modernizers** at the other, and many shades of opinion in between. The struggles among these groups were often intense. With time, however, the modernizers tended to gain the upper hand.

When armed resistance to European domination was thoroughly shattered by superior force, the great majority of Asians and Africans accepted imperial rule. Political participation in non-Western lands was historically limited to small elites, and the masses were used to doing what their rulers told them to do. In these circumstances Europeans governed effectively. They received considerable support from both traditionalists (local chiefs, landowners, and religious leaders) and modernizers (Western-educated professional classes and civil servants).

Nevertheless, imperial rule was in many ways an imposing edifice built on sand. Support for European rule among the conforming and accepting millions was shallow and weak. Thus the conforming masses came to follow with greater or lesser enthusiasm a few determined personalities who came to oppose the Europeans. Such leaders always arose, both when Europeans ruled directly and when they manipulated native governments, for at least two basic reasons.

First, the nonconformists—the eventual anti-imperialist leaders—developed a burning desire for human dignity. They came to feel that such dignity was incompatible

traditionalists *Those native to a colony who focused on preserving their traditional culture against imperialists at all costs.*

modernizers *Those native to a colony who believed that Western impact had affected their society in some positive ways and who wanted to reform their country in a similar manner.*

with foreign rule. Second, potential leaders found in the Western world the ideologies and justification for their protest. Thus they discovered liberalism, with its credo of civil liberty and political self-determination. They echoed the demands of anti-imperialists in Europe and America that the West live up to its own ideals.

More important, they found themselves attracted to the nineteenth-century Western ideology of nationalism, which asserted that every people—or at least every European people—had the right to control its own destiny. After 1917 anti-imperialist revolt would find another weapon in Lenin's version of Marxian socialism.

● ● ● ● ● ● ● ● ● ● ● ● ● ● ● ● ●

THE ISLAMIC HEARTLAND UNDER PRESSURE

How did the Ottoman Empire and Egypt try to revitalize themselves, and what were the most important results?

Stretching from West Africa into southeastern Europe and across Southwest Asia all the way to the East Indies, Islamic civilization competed successfully and continuously with western Europe for centuries. Thus from the seventh to the seventeenth centuries, Muslim forces conquered and ruled many lands, while Muslim economies generally equaled or surpassed those in Europe. Muslim societies were also proud and self-confident because they believed in the truth and the superiority of their faith.

Beginning in the late seventeenth century, the rising absolutist states of Austria and Russia began to challenge the greatest Muslim state, the vast Ottoman Empire, and gradually to reverse Ottoman rule in southeastern Europe. In the nineteenth century European industrialization and nation building further altered the long-standing balance of power, and Western expansion eventually posed a serious challenge to Muslims everywhere. In the words of a leading historian, "Muslim states and societies could no longer live in a stable and self-sufficient system of inherited culture; their need was now to generate the strength to survive in a world dominated by others."[2]

In close contact with Europe and under constant European pressure, the ruling elites both in the Ottoman Empire and in Egypt, a largely independent Ottoman province, led the way in trying to generate the strength to survive. The ongoing military crisis required, first of all, wrenching army reforms on Western lines in order to defend and preserve the state. These military reforms then snowballed into a series of innovations in education, which created modern schools and skilled specialists as well as army officers and had a powerful cultural impact on Ottoman and Egyptian elites. Western interests and governments also pushed for the adoption of the entire Western liberal creed—that is, the West demanded free trade, constitutional government, civil liberties, and equal rights for all religious groups. Western ideas challenged the superiority of Islam and undermined the traditional Muslim self-confidence.

The results of all these pressures and the momentous changes they brought were profound and paradoxical. On the one hand, the Ottoman Empire and Egypt did achieve considerable modernization on Western lines. On the other hand, these impressive accomplishments never came fast enough to offset the growing power and appetite of the West. The Islamic heartland in Southwest Asia and North Africa fell increasingly under foreign control. Only in the twentieth century did parts of the Islamic world escape Western economic and political domination.

Decline and Reform in the Ottoman Empire

Although the Ottoman Empire began to decline slowly after Suleiman the Magnificent in the sixteenth century (see pages 568–569), the relationship between the Ottomans and the Europeans in about 1750 was still one of roughly equal strength.

● **Pasha Halim Receiving Archduke Maximilian of Austria**   As this painting suggests, Ottoman leaders became well versed in European languages and culture. They also mastered the game of power politics, playing one European state off against another and securing the Ottoman Empire's survival. The black servants on the right may be slaves from the Sudan. *(Miramare Palace Trieste/Dagli Orti/ The Art Archive)*

However, in the later eighteenth century this situation began to change quickly and radically. The Ottomans fell behind western Europe in science, industrial skill, and military technology. At the same time, absolutist Russia pushed southward between 1768 and 1774. The danger that the Great Powers of Europe would gradually conquer the Ottoman Empire and divide up its vast territories was real.

Caught up in the Napoleonic wars and losing more territory to Russia, the Ottomans were forced in 1816 to grant Serbia local autonomy. In 1821 the Greeks revolted against Ottoman rule, and in 1830 they won their national independence. Facing uprisings by their Christian subjects in Europe, the Ottomans also failed to defend their Islamic provinces in North Africa. In 1830 French armies began their long and bloody conquest of the Arabic-speaking province of Algeria. By 1860, two hundred thousand French, Italian, and Spanish colonists had settled among the Muslim majority, which had been reduced to about 2.5 million by the war against the French and related famines and epidemics.

Ottoman weakness reflected the decline of the sultan's "slave army," the so-called **janissary corps.** In the sixteenth century the Ottoman sultans levied an annual slave tax of one to three thousand male children on the conquered Christian provinces in the Balkans. The boys and other slaves were raised in Turkey as Muslims, trained to

> **Primary Source:**
> **Imperial Rescript**
> *In this proclamation, Abdul Mejid announces plans to reform and modernize the Ottoman Empire, while protecting the rights of non-Muslims.*

janissary corps   *The Ottoman sultan's slave army; its members soon became a corrupt and privileged hereditary caste.*

fight and administer, and joined the elite corps of the Ottoman infantry. With time, however, the janissaries became a corrupt and privileged hereditary caste. They zealously pursued their own interests and refused any military innovations that might undermine their high status.

A transformation of the army was absolutely necessary to battle the Europeans more effectively and enhance the sultanate's authority within the empire. The empire was no longer a centralized military state. Instead, local governors were becoming increasingly independent, pursuing their own interests and even seeking to establish their own governments and hereditary dynasties.

The energetic sultan Selim III (r. 1789–1807) understood these realities, but when he tried to reorganize the army, the janissaries refused to use any "Christian" equipment. In 1807 they revolted, and Selim was quickly executed in a palace revolution, one of many that plagued the Ottoman state. The reform-minded Mahmud II (r. 1808–1839) proceeded cautiously, picking loyal officers and building up his dependable artillery corps. In 1826 his council ordered the janissaries to drill in the European manner. As expected, the janissaries revolted and charged the palace, where they were mowed down by the waiting artillery corps.

The destruction and abolition of the janissaries cleared the way for building a new army, but it came too late to stop the rise of Muhammad Ali, the Ottoman governor in Egypt (see below). In 1831 his French-trained forces occupied the Ottoman province of Syria and appeared ready to depose Mahmud II. The Ottoman sultan survived, but only by begging Europe for help. Britain, Russia, and Austria responded and forced Muhammad Ali to stop his military campaign. Succeeding in reestablishing direct rule over the province of Iraq, the overconfident Ottomans were saved again in 1839 after their forces were routed trying to drive Muhammad Ali from Syria. Britain and Russia forced Muhammad Ali to return Syria to the Ottomans. European powers preferred a weak and dependent Ottoman state to a strong and revitalized Muslim entity under a dynamic leader such as Muhammad Ali.

Tanzimat *Radical reforms to the Ottoman Empire that were designed to remake the empire on a western European model.*

Realizing their precarious position, liberal Ottoman statesmen launched in 1839 an era of radical reforms, which lasted with fits and starts until 1876 and culminated in a constitution and a short-lived parliament. Known as the **Tanzimat** (literally, regulations or orders), these reforms were designed to remake the empire on a western European model. The new decrees called for the equality of Muslims, Christians, and Jews before the law and in business, security of life and property, and a modernized administration and military. New commercial laws allowed free importation of foreign goods, as British advisers demanded, and permitted foreign merchants to operate freely throughout an economically dependent empire. Under heavy British pressure, slavery in the empire was drastically curtailed, though not abolished completely. Of great significance, growing numbers among the elite and the upwardly mobile embraced Western education, adopted Western manners and artistic styles, and accepted secular values to some extent.

Intended to bring revolutionary modernization such as that experienced by Russia under Peter the Great (see pages 479–480) and Japan in the Meiji era (see pages 764–766), the Tanzimat permitted partial recovery. Yet the Ottoman state and society failed to regain its earlier strength, for several reasons. First, implementation of the reforms required a new generation of well-trained and trustworthy officials, and that generation did not exist. Second, the liberal reforms failed to halt the growth of nationalism among Christian subjects in the Balkans (see Chapter 27), which resulted in crises and defeats that undermined all reform efforts. Third, the Ottoman initiatives did not curtail the appetite of Western imperialism, and European bankers gained a usurious stranglehold on Ottoman finances. In 1875 the Ottoman state had to declare partial bankruptcy and place its finances in the hands of European creditors.

Primary Source:
An Ottoman Government Decree Defines the Official Notion of the "Modern" Citizen
This document reveals a striking prejudice against communities of nomadic pastoralists, in favor of "civilized" urban folk.

Finally, the elaboration—at least on paper—of equal rights for citizens and religious communities did not create greater unity within the state. Indeed, religious disputes increased, worsened by the relentless interference of the Great Powers. This development embittered relations between the religious communities, distracted the government from its reform mission, and split Muslims into secularists and religious conservatives. Many conservative Muslims detested the religious reforms, which they saw as an impious departure from Islamic tradition and holy law. These Islamic conservatives became the most dependable support of Sultan Abdülhamid (r. 1876–1909), who abandoned the model of European liberalism in his long and repressive reign.

The combination of declining international power and conservative tyranny eventually led to a powerful resurgence of the modernizing impulse among idealistic Turkish exiles in Europe and young army officers in Istanbul. These fervent patriots, the so-called **Young Turks,** seized power in the revolution of 1908, and they forced the sultan to implement reforms. Failing to stop the rising tide of anti-Ottoman nationalism in the Balkans, the Young Turks helped to prepare the way for the birth of modern secular Turkey after the defeat and collapse of the Ottoman Empire in World War I (see pages 818–819).

Young Turks *Idealistic Turkish exiles in Europe and young army officers in Istanbul who seized power in the revolution of 1908 and helped pave the way for the birth of modern secular Turkey.*

Egypt: From Reform to British Occupation

The ancient land of the pharaohs had been ruled by a succession of foreigners since 525 B.C.E. and was most recently conquered by the Ottoman Turks in the early sixteenth century. In 1798 French armies under the young General Napoleon Bonaparte invaded Egypt and occupied the territory for three years as part of the war with Britain. Into the power vacuum left by the French withdrawal stepped an extraordinary Albanian-born Turkish general, **Muhammad Ali** (1769–1849).

First appointed governor of Egypt by the Turkish sultan, Muhammad Ali set out to build his own state on the strength of a large, powerful army organized along European lines. In 1820–1822 the Egyptian leader conquered much of the Sudan to secure slaves for his army, and thousands of African slaves were brought to Egypt during his reign. Because many slaves died in Egyptian captivity, Muhammad Ali turned to drafting Egyptian peasants. He also reformed the government and promoted modern industry. (See the feature "Individuals in Society: Muhammad Ali.") For a time Muhammad Ali's ambitious strategy seemed to work, but it eventually floundered when he was defeated by his Ottoman overlords and their British allies. Nevertheless, by the time of his death in 1849, Muhammad Ali had established a strong and virtually independent Egyptian state to be ruled by his family on a hereditary basis within the Turkish empire.

Muhammad Ali *The Turkish general who established a modernized and virtually independent Egyptian state.*

To pay for a modern army and industrialization, Muhammad Ali encouraged the development of commercial agriculture geared to the European market. This development had profound social implications. Egyptian peasants had been poor but largely self-sufficient, growing food on state-owned land allotted to them by tradition. Offered the possibility of profits from export agriculture, high-ranking officials and members of Muhammad Ali's family began carving large private landholdings out of the state domain, and they forced the peasants to grow cash crops for European markets. Ownership of land became very unequal. By 1913, 12,600 large estates owned 44 percent of the land and 1.4 million peasants owned only 27 percent. Estate owners "modernized" agriculture, but to the detriment of the peasants' well-being.

Muhammad Ali's policies of modernization attracted growing numbers of Europeans to the banks of the Nile. By 1863, when Muhammad Ali's grandson Ismail began his sixteen-year rule as Egypt's *khedive,* or prince, the port city of Alexandria had more than fifty thousand Europeans. Europeans served as army officers, engineers, doctors, government officials, and police officers. Others worked in trade, finance, and shipping. Above all, Europeans living in Egypt combined with landlords and officials to continue the development of commercial agriculture geared to exports. By 1900 about two hundred thousand Europeans lived in Egypt and accounted for 2 percent

● **The Opening of the Suez Canal** A long procession of eighty ships passed through the Suez Canal when it was opened in November 1869, and thousands of spectators lined the shores and joined in the celebrations. The building of the hundred-mile canal was a momentous event, cutting in half the length of the journey between Europe and Asia. *(Archives Charmet/The Bridgeman Art Library)*

of the population. As throughout the Ottoman Empire, Europeans enjoyed important commercial and legal privileges and formed an economic elite.

Ismail (r. 1863–1879) was a westernizing autocrat. Educated at France's leading military academy, he dreamed of using European technology and capital to modernize Egypt and build a vast empire in northeastern Africa. He promoted cotton production, and exports to Europe soared. Ismail also borrowed large sums and with his support the Suez Canal was completed by a French company in 1869. The canal shortened the voyage from Europe to Asia by thousands of miles. Traffic boomed. A new Cairo with long straight boulevards and modern apartment buildings grew up alongside the medieval maze of twisting lanes and beautiful historic mosques.

Major cultural and intellectual changes accompanied the political and economic ones. The Arabic of the masses, rather than the Turkish of the conquerors, became the official language, and young Egyptians educated in Europe helped spread new skills and ideas in the bureaucracy. A host of writers, intellectuals, and religious thinkers responded to the novel conditions with innovative ideas that had a powerful impact in Egypt and in other Muslim societies.

Three influential figures, who represented broad families of thought, were especially significant. The teacher and writer Jamal al-Din al-Afghani (1838/39–1897), who lived in Cairo from 1871 to 1879, preached Islamic regeneration and defense against Western/Christian aggression. Regeneration, he argued, required the purification of religious belief, the unity of all Muslim peoples, and a revolutionary overthrow of corrupt Muslim rulers and foreign exploiters. The more moderate Muhammad

Muhammad Ali

Muhammad Ali, the Albanian-born ruler of Egypt, in 1839. (Mary Evans Picture Library)

The dynamic leader Muhammad Ali (1769–1849) stands across the history of modern Egypt like a colossus. Yet the essence of the man remains a mystery, and historians vary greatly in their interpretations of him. Sent by the Ottomans, with Albanian troops, to oppose the French occupation of Egypt in 1799, Muhammad Ali maneuvered skillfully after the French withdrawal in 1802. In 1805 he was named *pasha,* or Ottoman governor, of Egypt. Only the Mamluks remained as rivals. Originally an elite corps of Turkish slave-soldiers, the Mamluks had become a semifeudal military ruling class living off the Egyptian peasantry. In 1811 Muhammad Ali offered to make peace, and he invited the Mamluk chiefs and their retainers to a banquet in Cairo's Citadel. As the unsuspecting guests processed through a narrow passage, his troops opened fire, slaughtering all the Mamluk leaders.

After eliminating his foes, Muhammad Ali embarked on a program of radical reforms. He reorganized agriculture and commerce, reclaiming most of the cultivated land for the state domain, which he controlled. He also established state agencies to monopolize, for his own profit, the sale of agricultural goods. Commercial agriculture geared to exports to Europe developed rapidly, especially after the successful introduction of high-quality cotton in 1821. Canals and irrigation systems along the Nile were rebuilt and expanded.

Muhammad Ali used his growing revenues to recast his army along European lines. He recruited French officers to train the soldiers. As the military grew, so did the need for hospitals, schools of medicine and languages, and secular education. Young Turks and some Egyptians were sent to Europe for advanced study. The ruler boldly financed factories to produce uniforms and weapons, and he prohibited the importation of European goods so as to protect Egypt's infant industries. In the 1830s state factories were making one-fourth of Egypt's cotton into cloth. Above all, Muhammad Ali drafted Egyptian peasants into the military for the first time, thereby expanding his army to 100,000 men. It was this force that conquered the Ottoman province of Syria, threatened the sultan in Istanbul, and triggered European intervention. Grudgingly recognized by his Ottoman overlord as Egypt's hereditary ruler in 1841, Muhammad Ali nevertheless had to accept European and Ottoman demands to give up Syria and abolish his monopolies and protective tar-

iffs. The old ruler then lost heart; his reforms languished, and his factories disappeared.

In the attempt to understand Muhammad Ali and his significance, many historians have concluded that he was a national hero, the "founder of modern Egypt." His ambitious state-building projects—hospitals, schools, factories, and the army—were the basis for an Egyptian reawakening and eventual independence from the Ottomans' oppressive foreign rule. Similarly, state-sponsored industrialization promised an escape from poverty and Western domination, which was foiled only by European intervention and British insistence on free trade.

A growing minority of historians question these views. They see Muhammad Ali primarily as an Ottoman adventurer. This disobedient Turkish general, they say, did not aim for national independence for Egypt, but rather "intended to carve out a small empire for himself and for his children after him."* Paradoxically, his success, which depended on heavy taxes and brutal army service, did lead to Egyptian nationalism among the Arabic-speaking masses, but that new nationalism was directed *against* Muhammad Ali and his Turkish-speaking entourage. Continuing research into this leader's life will help to resolve these conflicting interpretations.

Questions for Analysis

1. Which of Muhammad Ali's actions support the interpretation that he was the founder of modern Egypt? Which actions support the opposing view?

2. After you have studied Chapter 25, compare Muhammad Ali and the Meiji reformers in Japan. What accounts for the similarities and differences?

*K. Fahmy, *All the Pasha's Men: Mehmed Ali, His Army, and the Making of Modern Egypt* (Cambridge: Cambridge University Press, 1997), p. 310.

Abduh (1849–1905) also searched for Muslim rejuvenation and launched the modern Islamic reform movement, which became very important in the twentieth century. Abduh concluded that Muslims should return to the purity of the earliest, most essential doctrines of Islam and reject later additions that could limit Muslim creativity. This would permit a flexible, reasoned approach to change, social questions, and foreign ideas.

Finally, the writer Qasim Amin (1863–1908) represented those who found inspiration in the West in the late nineteenth century. In his influential book *The Liberation of Women* (1899), Amin argued forcefully that superior education for European women had contributed greatly to the Islamic world's falling far behind the West. The rejuvenation of Muslim societies required greater equality for women.

Egypt changed rapidly during Ismail's rule but his projects were reckless and enormously expensive. By 1876 the Egyptian government could not pay the interest on its colossal debt. Rather than let Egypt go bankrupt and repudiate its loans, France and Great Britain intervened politically to protect the European investors who held the Egyptian bonds. They forced Ismail to appoint French and British commissioners to oversee Egyptian finances so that the Egyptian debt would be paid in full. This meant that Europeans were going to determine the state budget and in effect rule Egypt.

Foreign financial control evoked a violent nationalistic reaction among Egyptian religious leaders, intellectuals, and army officers. In 1879, under the leadership of Colonel Ahmed Arabi, they formed the Egyptian Nationalist Party. Continuing diplomatic pressure, which forced Ismail to abdicate in favor of his weak son, Tewfiq (r. 1879–1892), resulted in bloody anti-European riots in Alexandria in 1882. A number of Europeans were killed, and Tewfiq and his court had to flee to British ships for safety. The British fleet then bombarded Alexandria, and a British expeditionary force decimated Arabi's forces and occupied all of Egypt.

The British said that their occupation was temporary, but British armies remained in Egypt until 1956. They maintained the façade of the khedive's government as an autonomous province of the Ottoman Empire, but the khedive was a mere puppet. The British consul, General Evelyn Baring, later Lord Cromer, ruled the country after 1883. Baring was a paternalistic reformer, and his rule did result in tax reforms and somewhat better conditions for peasants. Foreign bondholders received their interest payments, and Egyptian nationalists chaffed under foreign rule.

In Egypt the British abandoned what some scholars have called the "imperialism of free trade," which was based on economic penetration and indirect rule. They accepted a new model for European expansion in the densely populated lands of Africa and Asia. Such expansion was based on military force, political domination, and a self-justifying ideology of beneficial reform. This model was to predominate from the 1880s until 1914.

SUB-SAHARAN AFRICA: FROM THE SLAVE TRADE TO EUROPEAN RULE

What were the most significant changes in sub-Saharan Africa, and why did they occur?

From the beginning of the nineteenth century to the global depression of the 1930s, the different regions of sub-Saharan Africa experienced gradual but monumental change. The long-standing transatlantic slave trade declined and practically disappeared by the late 1860s. In the early nineteenth century Islam expanded its influence in a long belt south of the Sahara, but Africa generally remained free of European political control. After about 1880 further Islamic expansion to the south stopped, but the pace of change accelerated as France and Britain led European nations in the "scramble for Africa." Africa was divided and largely conquered by Europeans, and by 1900 the foreigners were consolidating their authoritarian empires.

African Trade and Social Change (1800–1880)

The most important development in West Africa before the European conquest was the decline of the Atlantic slave trade and the simultaneous rise of the export of palm oil and other commodities. A major break with the past, the shift in African foreign trade marked the beginning of modern economic development in sub-Saharan Africa.

Although the trade in African people was a worldwide phenomenon, the Atlantic slave trade became the most extensive and significant portion of it. The forced migration of millions of Africans—so cruel, unjust, and tragic—intensified after 1700, and especially after 1750. By the 1780s, shipments of black men and women averaged eighty thousand a year, in an attempt to satisfy the constantly rising demand for labor—and slave owner profits—in the Americas. Increasing demand resulted in rising prices for African slaves in the eighteenth century. Some African merchants and rulers who controlled exports profited, and some Africans secured foreign products that they found appealing. But the negative consequences of the expanding trade predominated in Africa, because warfare increased and enslavement spread.

Until 1700, and perhaps even 1750, almost all Europeans considered the African slave trade a legitimate business activity. After 1775 a broad campaign to abolish slavery developed in Britain. This campaign grew into one of the first peaceful mass political movements based on the mobilization of public opinion in British history. British women played a critical role in this movement, denouncing the immorality of human bondage and stressing the cruel treatment of female slaves and slave families. In 1807 Parliament declared the slave trade illegal. Britain then used its navy to seize the ships of the slave runners, liberating the captives and settling them in the British port of Freetown, in Sierra Leone.

British action had a limited impact at first. The transatlantic slave trade regained its previous massive level after peace returned to Europe in 1815, and it declined only gradually. Britain's African squadron intercepted fewer than 10 percent of all slave ships, and the demand for slaves remained high on the expanding sugar and coffee plantations of Cuba and Brazil until the 1850s and 1860s. (The United States prohibited the importation of slaves in 1808, and natural increase accounted mainly for the subsequent growth of the African American slave population there before the Civil War.) Strong incentives remained for Portuguese slave traders, as well as for those African rulers who relied on profits from the trade for power and influence.

As more nations joined Britain in outlawing the slave trade, the shipment of human cargo slackened along the West African coast. The decline began on the long stretch from Guinea and Senegal to the Gold Coast and present-day Nigeria by the 1830s and occurred thereafter in west-central Africa, in present-day Congo and Angola (see Map 24.1). At the same time the ancient but limited shipment of slaves across the Sahara and from the East African coast into the Indian Ocean and through the Red Sea expanded dramatically. Only in the 1860s did this expanding trade begin to decline rapidly. As a result of these shifting currents, exports of slaves from all of West Africa across the Atlantic declined from an estimated 5.6 million persons in the eighteenth century to 3.5 million in the nineteenth century. Yet total exports of slaves from all regions of sub-Saharan Africa declined less than half as fast in the same years, from 7.4 million to 6.1 million.[3] The abolitionist vision of "legitimate" commerce in tropical products quickly replacing illegal slave exports was not realized.

Nevertheless, beginning in West Africa, trade in tropical products did make steady progress, for several reasons. First, the oil and kernels of naturally growing palm trees already provided food for coastal populations. With Britain encouraging palm tree

● **Palm Oil for Soap and Power** Europeans, led by the British, encouraged West Africans to stop exporting slaves and start selling palm oil from naturally growing palm trees, as seen on the left. In Europe palm oil was made into soap, which was heavily advertised and endowed with symbols and hidden messages. In this 1890s ad (*right*), the Lifebuoy soap given to British travelers becomes a lifesaving charm warding off danger in foreign lands. *(left: Corbis; right: Mary Evans Picture Library)*

palm oil *A West African tropical product, often used to make soap; the British encouraged its cultivation as an alternative to the slave trade.*

cultivation as an alternative to the slave trade, **palm oil** sales from West Africa to Britain surged from only one thousand tons in 1810 to more than forty thousand tons in 1855. Second, the sale of palm oil admirably served the self-interest of industrializing Europe. From palm oil, manufacturers made the first good, cheap soap and mass-produced candles to light people's homes. Third, the production of peanuts for export also grew rapidly, in part because small, independent African farmers and their families could compete effectively with large-scale producers in growing peanuts.

Finally, powerful West African rulers and warlords who had benefited from the Atlantic slave trade succeeded in redirecting some of their slaves into the production of "legitimate" goods for world markets. This was possible because slavery and slave markets remained strong in sub-Saharan Africa, as local warfare and slave raiding continued to enslave large numbers of men, women, and children for many uses. Enslaved captives were sold abroad, and they became wives, concubines, and servants. They transported goods, mined gold, grew crops, and served in slave armies. For example, after the collapse of the Oyo empire, Yoruba warlords in present-day Nigeria developed palm oil plantations worked by slaves. By the 1860s and 1870s, 104 families in the city of Ibadan owned fifty thousand slaves, an average of five hundred per family.[4] As the experience of the Yoruba suggests, the slow decline of the transatlantic slave trade coincided with the most intensive use of slaves within Africa.

At the same time, a new group of African merchants—often liberated slaves from Freetown who had received some Western education—did rise to handle legitimate trade, and some grew rich. By the 1850s and 1860s legitimate African traders, flanked

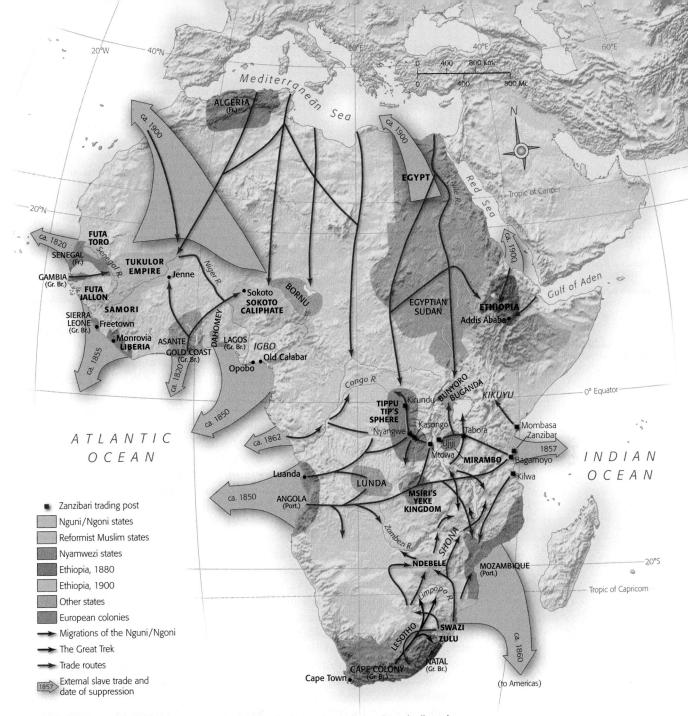

MAP 24.1 **Africa, 1800–1878** The export of African slaves declined gradually in the early nineteenth century, and by 1860 it was greatly reduced. Islamic reformers forged stronger states in West Africa, and Arab traders and Nyamwezi elites built informal empires in central Africa. In 1878 European settlement was limited to Algeria, southern Africa, and a few scattered outposts on the Atlantic coast.

by Western-educated African lawyers, teachers, and journalists, formed an emerging middle class in the coastal towns of West Africa. This tiny middle class provided new leadership that augured well for the region's future. Unfortunately for West Africans, in the 1880s and 1890s African business leadership then gave way to imperial subordination.

Islamic Revival and Expansion

In the early eighteenth century Islam had been practiced throughout the Sudanic Savanna—that vast belt of flat grasslands that stretches across Africa below the southern fringe of the Sahara from Senegal and Gambia in the west to the mountains of Ethiopia in the east—for five hundred to a thousand years, depending on the area. The cities, political rulers, and merchants in many small states were Muslim. Yet the peasant farmers and migratory cattle raisers—the vast majority of the population—generally remained true to traditional animist practices, worshiping ancestors, local shrines, and protective spirits. Many Muslim rulers shared some of these beliefs and did not try to convert their subjects in the countryside or enforce Islamic law.

Beginning in the eighteenth century and gathering strength in the early nineteenth century, a powerful Islamic revival brought reform and revolutionary change from within to the western and eastern Sudan, until this process was halted by European military conquest at the end of the nineteenth century. In essence, Muslim scholars and fervent religious leaders arose to wage successful **jihads,** or religious wars, against both animist rulers and Islamic states that they deemed corrupt. The new reformist rulers believed that African cults and religious practice could no longer be tolerated, and they often effected mass conversions of animists to Islam.

The most important of these revivalist states, the enormous **Sokoto caliphate,** illustrates the general pattern. It was founded by Usuman dan Fodio (1754–1817), an inspiring Muslim teacher who first won zealous followers among both the Fulani herders and the Hausa peasants in the Muslim state of Gobir in the northern Sudan. After his religious community was attacked by Gobir's rulers, Usuman launched the jihad of 1804, one of the most important events in nineteenth-century West Africa. Usuman claimed that the Hausa rulers of Muslim Gobir "worshipped many places of idols, and trees, and rocks, and sacrificed to them," killing and plundering their subjects without any regard for Islamic law.[5] Young religious students and discontented Fulani cattle raisers formed the backbone of the fighters, who succeeded in overthrowing the Hausa rulers and inspired more jihads in the Sudan. In 1809 Usuman founded the new Sokoto caliphate, which was ably consolidated by his son Muhammad Bello as a vast and enduring decentralized state (see Map 24.1).

The triumph of the Sokoto caliphate had profound consequences for Africa and the Sudan. First, the caliphate was based on Islamic history and law, which gave sub-Saharan Africa a sophisticated written constitution that earlier preliterate states had never achieved. This government of laws, not men, provided stability and made Sokoto one of the most prosperous regions in tropical Africa. Second, because of Sokoto and other revivalist states, Islam became much more widely and deeply rooted in sub-Saharan Africa than ever before. By 1880 the entire western and central Sudan was united in Islam. In this vast expanse Islam became an unquestioned part of everyday life and culture. Women gained greater access to education, even as veiling and seclusion became more common. Finally, Islam had always approved of slavery for non-Muslims and Muslim heretics, and "the *jihads* created a new slaving frontier on the basis of rejuvenated Islam."[6] In 1900 the Sokoto caliphate had 1 million and perhaps as many as 2.5 million slaves. Of all modern slave societies, only the American South had more, about 4 million in 1860.

Islam also expanded in East Africa, in large part because of the efforts of Sayyid Said (r. 1804–1856), the energetic imam of Oman. Reviving his family's lordship of the African island of Zanzibar and eventually moving his capital from southern Arabia to Zanzibar in 1840, Said and his Baluchi mercenaries (from present-day Pakistan) gained control of most of the Swahili-speaking East African coast. Said concentrated the shipment of slaves to the Ottoman Empire and Arabia through Zanzibar. In addition, he successfully encouraged Indian merchants to develop slave-based clove plantations in his territories. Thus from the 1820s on, Arab merchants and adventurers pressed far into the interior in search of slaves and ivory, converting and intermarrying with local Nyamwezi elites and establishing small Muslim states. The Arab immigrants brought literacy, administrative skills, and increased trade and international contact, as well as the intensification of slavery, to East Africa. In 1870, before Christian mission-

jihads *Religious wars waged by Muslim scholars and religious leaders against both animist rulers and Islamic states that they deemed corrupt.*

Sokoto caliphate *Founded in 1809 by Usuman dan Fodio, this African state was based on Islamic history and law.*

● **Celebrating the Sokoto Caliphate**   The Sokoto Caliphate still exists in modern northern Nigeria, and the Sultan of Sokoto remains an extremely influential force as the spiritual leader of Nigeria's large Muslim population. This crowd of Muslim believers is standing on a podium in 2004 to participate in bicentennial celebrations commemorating the Caliphate's foundation by Usuman dan Fodio. *(Pius Utomi Ekpei/Getty Images)*

aries and Western armies began to arrive in force, it appeared that most of the East African population would accept Islam within a generation.[7]

The Seizure of Africa (1880–1902)

Between 1880 and 1900 Britain, France, Germany, and Italy scrambled for African possessions as if their national livelihoods were at stake. By 1902 only Ethiopia in northeast Africa and Liberia on the West African coast remained independent (see Map 24.2).

In addition to the general causes underlying Europe's imperialist burst after 1880 (see pages 723–724), certain events and individuals stand out. First, as the antislavery movement succeeded in shutting down the Atlantic slave trade by the late 1860s, the persistence of slavery elsewhere attracted growing attention in Europe. Through the publications of Protestant missionaries such as David Livingstone and the fiery eye-witness accounts of the Catholic White Fathers, Europeans learned of the horrors of slave raids and the suffering of thousands of innocent victims sold within Africa and through East African ports. The public was led to believe that European rule would end this human tragedy, as well-meaning Protestants and Catholics "provided a moral justification for the conquest of Africa."[8]

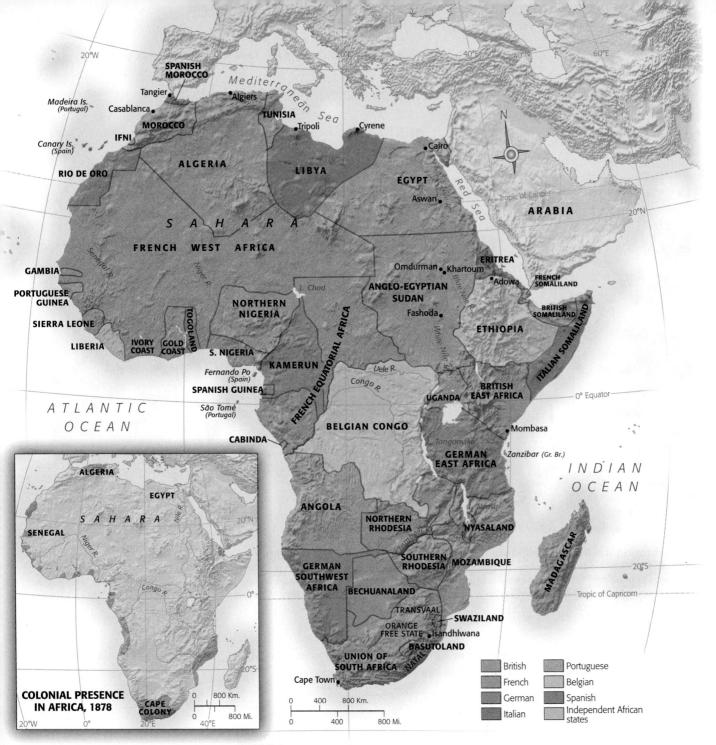

MAP 24.2 **Africa in 1878 and 1914** European nations carved up Africa after 1878 and built vast political empires. Britain and France took the most territory. Which African states remained independent?

Leopold II *The king of Belgium who colonized the Congo and sent expeditions into central Africa.*

Berlin Conference *Held in 1884 and 1885 in order to lay down some basic rules for imperialist competition in sub-Saharan Africa, it established the principle that European claims to African territory had to rest on "effective occupation" in order to be recognized by other states.*

Second, **Leopold II** of Belgium (r. 1865–1909) played a crucial role. His agents signed "treaties" with African chiefs and planted Leopold's flag along the Congo River. The French reacted by establishing a French protectorate on the north bank of the Congo River. By 1883 Europe had caught "African fever," and the race for territory was on.

To lay down some rules for this imperialist competition, Premier Jules Ferry of France and Chancellor Otto von Bismarck of Germany arranged an international conference on Africa in Berlin in 1884–1885. The **Berlin Conference,** at which no Africans were present (nor had any been invited), established the principle that European claims to African territory had to rest on "effective occupation" in order to be recognized by other states. This meant that Europeans would push relentlessly into interior regions from all sides and that no single European power would be able to claim the entire continent. The conference recognized Leopold's rule over a neutral Congo state and agreed to work to stop slavery and the slave trade in Africa.

The Berlin Conference coincided with Germany's emergence as an imperial power. In 1884 and 1885 Bismarck's Germany established protectorates over a number of small African kingdoms and societies in Togo, Cameroons, southwest Africa, and, later, East Africa (see Map 24.2). In acquiring colonies, Bismarck cooperated with France's Jules Ferry against the British. (See the feature "Listening to the Past: A French Leader Defends Imperialism" on pages 746–747.) The French expanded into West Africa and formed a protectorate on the Congo River. As for the British, they began enlarging their West African enclaves and pushed northward from the Cape Colony and westward from the East African coast.

Pushing southward from Egypt, the British were blocked in the eastern Sudan by fiercely independent Muslims, who had felt the full force of Islamic revival. In 1881 a pious local leader, Muhammad Ahmad (1844–1885), led a revolt against foreign control of Egypt. In 1885 his army massacred a British force and took the city of Khartoum, forcing the British to retreat to Cairo. Ten years later a British force returned, building a railroad to supply arms and reinforcements as it went. Finally, in 1898, these troops met their foe at Omdurman, where Sudanese Muslims armed with spears charged time and time again, only to be cut down by the recently invented machine gun. In the end eleven thousand brave but poorly armed Muslim tribesmen lay dead. Only twenty-eight Britons had been killed.

The British conquest of the Sudan exemplified the general process of empire building in Africa. The fate of the Muslim force at Omdurman was eventually inflicted on most colonized peoples who resisted European rule: they were crushed by vastly superior military force.

Southern Africa in the Nineteenth Century

The development of southern Africa diverged from the rest of sub-Saharan Africa in important ways. Whites settled in large numbers, modern capitalist industry took off, and British imperialists had to wage all-out war.

In 1652 the Dutch East India Company established a supply station at Cape Town for Dutch ships sailing between Amsterdam and Indonesia. The healthy, temperate climate and the sparse Nguni population near the Cape resulted in the colony's gradual expansion. When the British took possession in the Napoleonic wars, the Cape Colony included about twenty thousand free Dutch citizens and twenty-five thousand African slaves, with substantial mixed-race communities on the northern frontier of white settlement.

After 1815 powerful African chiefdoms, Dutch settlers—first known as Boers, and then as **Afrikaners**—and British colonial forces waged a complicated, three-cornered battle to build strong states in southern Africa. Of critical importance, the talented Zulu leader Shaka (r. 1818–1828) revolutionized African warfare between 1818 and his death in 1828, and he managed to create "the largest and most powerful African society in southern Africa in the nineteenth century."[9] Drafted by age groups and placed in highly disciplined regiments, Shaka's warriors perfected the use of a new, short stabbing spear in deadly hand-to-hand combat. Shaka's Zulu armies often destroyed their African enemies completely, sowing chaos and sending refugees fleeing in all directions. Shaka's wars also led to the consolidation of the Zulu, Swazi, and Sotho peoples into stronger states in southern Africa. By 1880 these states were largely subdued by Dutch and British invaders, but only after many hard-fought frontier wars.

Beginning in 1834, the British gradually abolished slavery in the Cape Colony and introduced colorblind legislation to protect African labor. In 1836 these measures led

Afrikaners *The descendants of the Dutch in the Cape Colony.*

● **Diamond Mining in South Africa** At first, both black and white miners could own and work claims at the diamond diggings, as this early photo suggests. However, as the industry expanded and was monopolized by European financial interests, white workers claimed the supervisory jobs and blacks were limited to dangerous low-wage labor. Mining revolutionized the South African economy. *(Royal Commonwealth Society. By permission of the Syndics of Cambridge University Library)*

about ten thousand Afrikaner cattle ranchers and farmers to make their so-called Great Trek northward into the interior (see Map 24.1). In 1845 another group of Afrikaners joined the other trekkers north of the Orange River. Over the next thirty years Afrikaner and British settlers, who often fought and usually detested each other, reached a mutually advantageous division of southern Africa. The British ruled strategically valuable coastal colonies, and the Afrikaners controlled their ranch-land republics in the interior. The Zulu, Xhosa, and other African peoples lost much of their land but remained the majority—albeit an exploited majority.

The discovery of incredibly rich deposits of diamonds in 1867 and later gold revolutionized the economy of southern Africa, making possible large-scale industrial capitalism and transforming the lives of all its peoples. Small white and black diamond diggers soon gave way to Cecil Rhodes and the powerful financiers behind his De Beers mining company, which reaped fabulous profits monopolizing the world's diamond industry. The regular, deep-level gold deposits discovered in 1886 in the Afrikaners' Transvaal republic required big foreign investment, European engineering expertise, and an enormous labor force. The "color bar" system of the diamond fields gave whites—often English-speaking immigrants—the well-paid skilled positions and put black Africans in the dangerous, low-wage jobs far below the surface. Whites lived with their families in subsidized housing. African workers lived in all-male dormitories like men in prison, closely watched by company guards. Southern Africa became the world's leading gold producer and pulled in migratory workers from all over the region.

The mining bonanza whetted the appetite of British imperialists led by the powerful Rhodes. Between 1889 and 1893 he used missionaries and a front company chartered by the British government to force African chiefs to accept British protectorates and managed to add Southern and Northern Rhodesia (modern-day Zimbabwe and Zambia) to the British Empire (see Map 24.2). Rhodes and the imperialist clique then succeeded in starting the South African War of 1899–1902 (also known as the Anglo-Boer War), Britain's greatest imperial campaign on African soil. The British needed 450,000 to crush the Afrikaners.

The long and bitter war divided whites in South Africa, but South Africa's blacks were the biggest losers. The British had promised the Afrikaners representative government in return for surrender in 1902, and they made good on their pledge. In 1910 the Cape Colony, Natal, and the two Afrikaner republics formed a new self-governing Union of South Africa. Because whites—21.5 percent of the total population in 1910—held almost all political power and because the Afrikaners outnumbered the English-speakers, following the peace settlement the Afrikaners began to regain what they had lost on the battlefield. South Africa, under a joint British-Afrikaner government within the British Empire, began the creation of a modern, segregated society that culminated in an even harsher system of racial separation, or apartheid, after World War II.

The Imperial System (1900–1930)

By 1900 most of black Africa had been conquered—or, as Europeans preferred to say, "pacified"—and a system of imperial administration was taking shape. In general, this system weakened or shattered the traditional social order and challenged accepted values.

The self-proclaimed political goal of the French and the British—the principal foreign powers—was to provide good government for their African subjects, especially after World War I. "Good government" meant, above all, law and order. It meant strong, authoritarian government, which maintained a small army and built up an African police force to put down rebellion, suppress ethnic warfare, and protect life and property. Good government required a modern bureaucracy capable of taxing and governing the population. Many African leaders and their peoples had chosen not to resist the invaders' superior force, and most others had stopped fighting after experiencing crushing military defeat. Thus the goal of law and order was widely achieved.

Colonial governments demonstrated much less interest in providing basic social services. Expenditures on education, public health, hospitals, and other social services increased after the First World War but still remained small. Europeans feared the political implications of mass education and typically relied instead on the modest efforts of state-subsidized mission schools. Moreover, they tried to make even their poorest colonies pay for themselves. Thus salaries for government workers normally absorbed nearly all tax revenues.

Economically, the imperialist goal was to draw the African interior into the world economy on terms favorable to the dominant Europeans. The key was railroads linking coastal trading centers to outposts hundreds of miles in the interior. Cheap, dependable transportation facilitated easy shipment of raw materials out and manufactured goods in. Most African railroads were built after 1900; fifty-two hundred miles were in operation by 1926, when attention turned to road building for trucks. Railroads and roads had two other important outcomes: they allowed the quick movement of troops to put down any local unrest, and they allowed many African peasants to earn wages for the first time.

● **The Governor's Arrival** This painting by an African artist depicts the landing of a high British official at a port on the East African coast. African soldiers stand at attention, ready to do the governor's bidding and maintain imperial order. *(National Museums, Tanzania)*

The focus on economic development and low-cost rule explained why colonial governments were reluctant to move decisively against slavery within Africa. Officials feared that an abrupt abolition of slavery where it existed would disrupt production and lead to costly revolts by powerful slaveholding elites, especially in Muslim areas. Thus colonial regimes settled for halfway measures designed to satisfy humanitarian groups in Europe and also make all Africans, free or slave, participate in a market economy and work for wages. Even this cautious policy was enough for many slaves to boldly free themselves by running away, and it facilitated a rapid decline of slavery within Africa. At the same time, colonial governments often imposed head taxes, payable in money or labor, to compel Africans to work for their white overlords. No aspect of imperialism was more despised by Africans than forced labor, widespread until about 1920. In some regions, particularly in West Africa, African peasants continued to respond freely to the new economic opportunities by voluntarily shifting to export crops on their own farms. Overall, the result of these developments was an increase in wage work and production geared to the world market and a decline in traditional self-sufficient farming and nomadic herding.

In sum, the imposition of bureaucratic Western rule and the gradual growth of a world-oriented cash economy between 1900 and 1930 had a revolutionary impact on large parts of Africa. The experiences of Ghana and Kenya, two very different African countries, dramatically illustrate variations on the general pattern.

Present-day Ghana (see Map 32.4 on page 1008), which takes its name from one of West Africa's famous early kingdoms, had a fairly complex economy well before British armies smashed the powerful Asante kingdom in 1873 and established the crown colony that they called the Gold Coast. Precolonial local trade was vigorous and varied, and palm oil exports were expanding. Into this sophisticated economy British colonists subsequently introduced the production of cocoa beans for the world's chocolate. Output rose spectacularly, from a few hundred tons in the 1890s to 305,000 tons in 1936. Independent peasants and energetic African business people (many of the traders were women) were mainly responsible for the spectacular success of cocoa-bean production. Creative African entrepreneurs even went so far as to build their own roads, and they sometimes reaped big profits.

The Gold Coast also showed the way politically and culturally. The westernized elite—relatively prosperous and well-educated lawyers, professionals, and journalists—and business people took full advantage of opportunities provided by the fairly enlightened colonial regime. The black elite was the main presence in the limited local elections permitted by the British, for few permanent white settlers ventured to hot and densely populated West Africa.

Across the continent in the British East African colony of Kenya, events unfolded differently. Before the arrival of Western imperialists, East African peoples were more self-sufficient, less numerous, and less advanced commercially and politically than Africans in the Gold Coast. Once the British had built their strategic railroad from the Indian Ocean across Kenya to Uganda, foreigners from Great Britain and India moved in to exploit the situation. Indian settlers became shopkeepers, clerks, and laborers in the towns. British settlers dreamed of turning the cool, beautiful, and fertile Kenyan highlands into a "white man's country" like Southern Rhodesia or the Union of South Africa. They dismissed the local population of peasant farmers as "barbarians," fit only to toil as cheap labor on their large estates and plantations. Kenya's Africans thus experienced much harsher colonial rule than did their fellow Africans in the Gold Coast.

Chapter Summary

To assess your mastery of this chapter, go to
bedfordstmartins.com/mckayworld

• *What were the global consequences of European industrialization between 1800 and 1914?*

Between 1800 and 1914 European industrialization opened up a growing gap in average income between people in the West and people in Africa, Asia, and Latin America. This new, lopsided world—a world of rich lands and poor—experienced a prodigious increase in international trade, but the lion's share of the gains from trade went to the Western nations. Millions of Europeans also moved to sparsely populated areas of European settlement, while similar migration from Asia was generally quite limited.

• *What were the causes and consequences of European empire building after 1880?*

After 1880 a handful of Western nations seized most of Africa (and parts of Asia) and rushed to build authoritarian empires. The reasons for this empire

Key Terms

lopsided world
migration chain
great white walls
quinine
traditionalists
modernizers
janissary corps
Tanzimat
Young Turks
Muhammad Ali
palm oil
jihads
Sokoto caliphate
Leopold II
Berlin Conference
Afrikaners

building included trade rivalries, competitive nationalism in Europe, and self-justifying claims of a "civilizing mission." Above all, European states had acquired unprecedented military superiority, which they used to crush resistance and impose their will.

• How did the Ottoman Empire and Egypt try to revitalize themselves, and what were the most important results?

In the Muslim heartland both the Ottoman Empire and Egypt introduced reforms to improve the military, provide technical and secular education, and expand personal liberties. In so doing, both countries prepared the way for modern nation-states in the twentieth century, but they failed to defend themselves from Western imperialism. The Ottoman Empire survived as an economic colony and groped for unity. Egypt went bankrupt and was conquered and ruled by Britain. Western domination was particularly bitter for most Muslims because they saw it profaning their religion as well as taking away their political independence.

• What were the most significant changes in sub-Saharan Africa, and why did they occur?

In sub-Saharan Africa European pressure contributed to the reorientation of the economy, which gradually turned from a focus on the Atlantic slave trade to the production of commodities for export. Islam revived and expanded until about 1870. The European conquest of Africa after 1880 led to colonial empires that improved internal security and built bureaucracies, but also treated Africans as racial inferiors. Government based on racial discrimination, which was most thoroughly developed in southern Africa, set the stage for a new anti-imperialist struggle for equality and genuine independence after the First World War.

Suggested Reading

Bagachi, Amiya Kumar. *Perilous Passage: Mankind and the Ascendancy of Capital.* 2005. A spirited radical critique of Western imperialism.

Conklin, Alice. *A Mission to Civilize: The French Republican Ideal and West Africa, 1895–1930.* 1997. An outstanding examination of French imperialism.

Cook, Scott B. *Colonial Encounters in the Age of High Imperialism.* 1996. A stimulating and very readable overview.

Curtin, P., et al. *African History: From Earliest Times to Independence,* 2d ed. 1995. An excellent discussion of Africa in the nineteenth century.

Findley, C. *The Turks in World History.* 2005. An exciting reconsideration of the Turks in long-term perspective.

Headrick, D. *Tools of Empire.* 1991. Stresses technological superiority in Western expansion.

Hourani, A. *A History of the Arab Peoples.* 1991. Brilliant on developments in the nineteenth century.

Iliffe, J. *Africans: The History of a Continent.* 1995. Outstanding and original, stressing environmental developments.

Lovejoy, P. *Transformation in Slavery: A History of Slavery in Africa,* 2d ed. 2000. A fine synthesis of current knowledge.

Mahfouz, H. *Palace of Desire.* 1991. A great novelist's portrait of an Egyptian family before 1914.

Notes

1. Rudyard Kipling, *The Five Nations* (London,1903).

2. A. Hourani, *A History of the Arab Peoples* (Cambridge, Mass.: Harvard University Press, 1991), p. 263.

3. P. Lovejoy, *Transformations in Slavery: A History of Slavery in Africa,* 2d ed. (Cambridge: Cambridge University Press, 2000), p. 142.

4. Ibid., p. 179.

5. Quoted in J. Iliffe, *Africans: The History of a Continent* (Cambridge: Cambridge University Press, 1995), p. 169.

6. Lovejoy, *Transformations in Slavery,* p. 15.

7. R. Oliver, *The African Experience* (New York: Icon Editions, 1991), pp. 164–166.

8. S. Miers and R. Roberts, eds., *The End of Slavery in Africa* (Madison: University of Wisconsin Press, 1988), p. 16.

9. R. Beck, *The History of South Africa* (Westport, Conn.: Greenwood Press, 2000), p. 63.

Listening to the PAST

A French Leader Defends Imperialism

Although Jules Ferry (1832–1893) first gained political prominence as an ardent champion of secular public education, he was most famous for his empire building. While he was French premier in 1880–1881 and again in 1883–1885, France occupied Tunisia, extended its rule in Indonesia, seized Madagascar, and penetrated the Congo. Criticized by conservatives, socialists, and some left-wing republicans for his colonial expansion, Ferry defended his policies before the French National Assembly and also elaborated a philosophy of imperialism in his writings.

In a speech to the Assembly on July 28, 1883, portions of which follow, Ferry answered his critics and summarized his three main arguments with brutal honesty. Note that Ferry adamantly insisted that imperial expansion did not weaken France in its European struggle with Germany, as some opponents charged, but rather that it increased French grandeur and power. Imperialists needed the language of patriotic nationalism to be effective.

M. Jules Ferry: Gentlemen, . . . I believe that there is some benefit in summarizing and condensing, in the form of arguments, the principles, the motives, and the various interests by which a policy of colonial expansion may be justified; it goes without saying that I will try to remain reasonable, moderate, and never lose sight of the major continental interests which are the primary concern of this country. What I wish to say, to support this proposition, is that in fact, just as in word, the policy of colonial expansion is a political and economic system; I wish to say that one can relate this system to three orders of ideas: economic ideas, ideas of civilization in its highest sense, and ideas of politics and patriotism.

In the area of economics, I will allow myself to place before you, with the support of some figures, the considerations which justify a policy of colonial expansion from the point of view of that need, felt more and more strongly by the industrial populations of Europe and particularly those of our own rich and hard working country: the need for export markets. Is this some kind of chimera? Is this a view of the future

or is it not rather a pressing need, and, we could say, the cry of our industrial population? I will formulate only in a general way what each of you, in the different parts of France, is in a position to confirm. Yes, what is lacking for our great industry, drawn irrevocably on to the path of exportation by the [free trade] treaties of 1860, what it lacks more and more is export markets. Why? Because next door to us Germany is surrounded by barriers, because beyond the ocean, the United States of America has become protectionist, protectionist in the most extreme sense. . . .

Gentlemen, there is a second point, . . . the humanitarian and civilizing side of the question. On this point the honorable M. Camille Pellatan has jeered in his own refined and clever manner; he jeers, he condemns, and he says "What is this civilization which you impose with cannonballs? What is it but another form of barbarism? Don't these populations, these inferior races, have the same rights as you? Aren't they masters of their own houses? Have they called upon you? You come to them against their will, you offer them violence, but not civilization." There, gentlemen, is the thesis; I do not hesitate to say that this is not politics, nor is it history: it is political metaphysics. (*"Ah, Ah" on far left.*)

. . . Gentlemen, I must speak from a higher and more truthful plane. It must be stated openly that, in effect, superior races have rights over inferior races. (*Movement on many benches on the far left.*)

M. Jules Maigne: Oh! You dare to say this in the country which has proclaimed the rights of man!

M. de Guilloutet: This is a justification of slavery and the slave trade! . . .

M. Jules Ferry: I repeat that superior races have a right, because they have a duty. They have the duty to civilize inferior races. . . . (*Approval from the left. New interruptions from the extreme left and from the right.*)

. . . M. Pelletan . . . then touched upon a third point, more delicate, more serious, and upon which I ask your permission to express myself quite frankly. It is the political side of the question. The honorable M. Pelletan, who is a distinguished writer, always comes up with remarkably precise formulations. I will borrow

Jules Ferry, French politician and ardent imperialist. *(Corbis)*

from him the one which he applied the other day to this aspect of colonial policy.

"It is a system," he says, "which consists of seeking out compensations in the Orient with a circumspect and peaceful seclusion which is actually imposed upon us in Europe."

I would like to explain myself in regard to this. I do not like this word, "compensation," and, in effect, not here but elsewhere it has often been used in a treacherous way. If what is being said or insinuated is that any government in this country, any Republican minister could possibly believe that there are in any part of the world compensations for the disasters which we have experienced [in connection with our defeat in the Franco-Prussian War of 1870–1871], an injury is being inflicted . . . and an injury undeserved by that government. *(Applause at the center and left.)* I will ward off this injury with all the force of my patriotism! *(New applause and bravos from the same benches.)*

Gentlemen, there are certain considerations which merit the attention of all patriots. The conditions of naval warfare have been profoundly altered. ("Very true! Very true!")

At this time, as you know, a warship cannot carry more than fourteen days' worth of coal, no matter how perfectly it is organized, and a ship which is out of coal is a derelict on the surface of the sea, abandoned to the first person who comes along. Thence the necessity of having on the oceans provision stations, shelters, ports for defense and revictualling. *(Applause at the center and left. Various interruptions.)* And it is for this that we needed Tunisia, for this that we needed Saigon and the Mekong Delta, for this that we need Madagascar, that we are at Diégo-Suarez and Vohemar [two Madagascar ports] and will never leave them! *(Applause from a great number of benches.)* Gentlemen, in Europe as it is today, in this competition of so many rivals which we see growing around us, some by perfecting their military or maritime forces, others by the prodigious development of an ever growing population; in a Europe, or rather in a universe of this sort, a policy of peaceful seclusion or abstention is simply the highway to decadence! Nations are great in our times only by

means of the activities which they develop; it is not simply "by the peaceful shining forth of institutions" *(interruptions on the extreme left and right)* that they are great at this hour.

. . . [The Republican Party] has shown that it is quite aware that one cannot impose upon France a political ideal conforming to that of nations like independent Belgium and the Swiss Republic; that something else is needed for France: that she cannot be merely a free country, that she must also be a great country, exercising all of her rightful influence over the destiny of Europe, that she ought to propagate this influence throughout the world and carry everywhere that she can her language, her customs, her flag, her arms, and her genius. *(Applause at center and left.)*

Questions for Analysis

1. What was Jules Ferry's economic argument for imperial expansion? Why had colonies recently gained greater economic value?

2. How did Ferry's critics attack the morality of foreign expansion? How did Ferry try to claim the moral high ground in his response?

3. What political arguments did Ferry advance? How would you characterize his philosophy of politics and national development?

Source: Speech before the French National Assembly, July 28, 1883. Reprinted in R. A. Austen, ed., *Modern Imperialism: Western Overseas Expansion and Its Aftermath, 1776–1965* (Lexington, Mass.: D. C. Heath, 1969), pp. 70–73.

Western Warehouses and Offices in Guangzhou (Canton) Harbor, nineteenth century (detail). *(Photograph courtesy Peabody Essex Museum, Neg #M3156)*

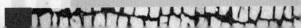

chapter

25 ASIA IN THE ERA OF IMPERIALISM, 1800–1914

Chapter Preview

India and the British Empire in Asia
• In what ways did India change as a consequence of British rule?

Competition for Southeast Asia
• Why were some Southeast Asian societies reduced to colonies and others not?

China Under Pressure
• Was China's decline in the nineteenth century due more to internal problems or Western imperialism?

Japan's Rapid Transformation
• How was Japan able to quickly master the challenges posed by the West?

The Movement of Peoples
• Why did people move much more in this period, and where did they go?

During the nineteenth century, the societies of Asia underwent enormous changes—the results of population growth, social unrest, and the looming presence of Western imperialist powers. In this period half the people of the world lived in the region from India east to the Pacific Ocean, but they were very unevenly distributed. In the temperate zones of East Asia the old established monarchies of China, Japan, and Korea were all densely populated and boasted long literary traditions. India was just as densely populated but politically and culturally more diverse, with several major languages and dozens of independent rulers reigning in kingdoms large and small. What Britain and later the other Western powers initially wanted from the more developed Asian societies was to refashion trading relations to the West's benefit. At the other extreme were thinly populated and relatively primitive areas without literate cultures and sometimes even without agriculture, such as some of the islands of the Philippines and Indonesia. They could not provide manufactured goods such as porcelain or silk, but they offered opportunities for Western development, much as the Americas had earlier.

The economics of industrialization and the political rivalries among the European powers all shaped the steps taken by Western nations to gain power in Asia, and these influences changed over the course of the century. Western science and technology were making rapid advances, which gave European armies progressively greater advantages in weaponry. The Industrial Revolution made it possible for early industrializers such as Britain to produce huge surpluses of goods for which they had to find markets, shifting their interest in Asia from a place to buy goods to a place to sell goods. Britain had been able to profit from its colonization of India, and this profit both encouraged it to consolidate its rule and invited its European rivals to look for their own colonies.

The societies of Asia varied enormously at the beginning of the century, but the common encounter with the expanding West gradually gave them more in common. Often the initial response of Asian leaders was to try to drive the unwelcome foreigners away. This was seen in China, Japan, and Korea in particular. Violent antiforeign reactions exploded again and again, but the superior military technology of the industrialized West almost invariably prevailed. After suffering humiliating defeats, some Asian leaders insisted on the need to preserve their cultural traditions at all costs. Others came to the opposite conclusion that the West was indeed superior in some ways and that they would have to adopt European ideas or techniques for their own purposes. The struggles between the traditionalists and the westernizers were often intense. As nationalism took hold in the West (see Chapter 23), it found a receptive audience among the educated elites in Asia. How could the assertion that every people had the right to control its own destiny not appeal to the colonized?

By the end of the nineteenth century, most of the southern tier of Asia, from India to the Philippines, had been made colonies of Western powers. Many of these areas became major exporters of agricultural products or raw materials, including timber, rubber, tin, sugar, tea, cotton, and jute. New knowledge and new technologies spread rapidly. Railroads, telegraphs, modern sanitation, and a wider supply of inexpensive manufactured goods brought fundamental changes in everyday life. To a much greater extent than in any earlier time, Europeans were living in Asia and learning its languages and cultures, and Asians were studying Western languages or emigrating abroad. Still, cultural barriers between the colonizers and the colonized were huge. The West relied on force to conquer and rule, and it treated non-Western peoples as racial inferiors.

Not all the countries in Asia became victims of Western imperialism. Japan became the first non-Western country to use an ancient love of country to transform itself and thereby meet the many-sided challenge of Western expansion. Japan came out of the nineteenth-century crisis stronger than any other Asian nation. It became the first non-Western country to industrialize successfully and by the end of this period had become an imperialist power itself, making Korea and Taiwan its colonies.

• • • • • • • • • • • • • •

INDIA AND THE BRITISH EMPIRE IN ASIA

In what ways did India change as a consequence of British rule?

Arriving in India on the heels of the Portuguese in the seventeenth century, the British East India Company outmaneuvered French and Dutch rivals and was there to pick up the pieces as the Mughal Empire decayed during the eighteenth century (see pages 553–554). By 1757, the company had gained control over much of India. During the nineteenth century, the British government took over, progressively unified the subcontinent, and harnessed its economy to British interests.

Communication between Britain and India became much faster, safer, and more predictable in this period. Clipper ships with their huge sails cut the voyage from Europe to India from six to three months. By the 1850s steamships were competing with clipper ships, and they made ocean travel more predictable. After the Suez Canal was opened in 1869, the voyage by steamship from England to India took only three weeks. In the 1860s cables were laid on the ocean floor, allowing telegrams to be sent from England to India. Whereas at the beginning of the nineteenth century someone in England had to wait a year or more to get an answer to a letter sent to India, by 1870 it took only a couple of months—or, if the matter was urgent, only a few hours by telegraph.

In 1818 the British East India Company controlled territory occupied by 180 million Indians—more people than lived in all of western Europe and fifty times the number of people the British had lost after the American Revolution. The British ruled with the cooperation of Indian princely allies, whom they could not afford to offend. Still, the British disbanded and disarmed local armies, introduced simpler private property laws, and enhanced the powers of local princes and religious leaders, both Hindu and Muslim. The British administrators, backed by British officers and native troops, were on the whole competent and concerned about the welfare of the Indian peasants. Slavery was outlawed and banditry suppressed. New laws designed to improve women's position in society were introduced. Sati (widow immolation) was outlawed in 1829, legal protection of widow remarriage was extended in 1856, and infanticide was banned in 1870.

The last armed resistance to British rule occurred in 1857. By that date the British military presence in India had grown to include two hundred thousand Indian sepoy troops and thirty-eight thousand British officers. The sepoys were well trained and armed with modern rifles. In 1857 groups of them, especially around Delhi, revolted in what the British called the **Great Mutiny** and the Indians called the **Great Revolt**. Their grievances were many, ranging from the use of animal grease on their rifles to the incorporation of low-caste soldiers into the army and high tax rates. The insurrection spread rapidly throughout northern and central India before it was finally crushed, primarily by native troops from other parts of India loyal to the British. Thereafter, although princely states were allowed to continue, Britain ruled India much more tightly. Moreover, the British in India were more aware that they were an occupying power and mixed less with the Indian elite.

After 1858 India was ruled by the British Parliament in London and administered by a civil service in India, the upper echelons of which were all white. In 1900 this elite consisted of fewer than thirty-five hundred top officials for a population of 300 million. In 1877 Queen Victoria adopted the title **Empress of India**, and her image became a common sight in India.

The impact of British rule on the Indian economy was multifaceted. In the early stages, the British East India Company expanded agricultural production, creating large plantations. Early crops were opium to export to China (see page 758) and tea to substitute for imports from China. India gradually replaced China as the leading exporter of tea to Europe. During the nineteenth century India also exported cotton fiber, silk, sugar, jute, coffee, and other agricultural commodities to be processed elsewhere. Clearing land for tea and coffee plantations, along with massive commercial logging operations, led to extensive deforestation.

The colonial administration invested heavily in India's infrastructure. By 1855 India's major cities had all been linked by telegraph and railroads, and postal service was being extended to local villages. By 1870 India had the fifth-largest rail network in the world—4,775 miles, carrying more than 18 million passengers a year. By 1900 the rail

Chronology

1825	Government of Japan orders foreign vessels to be turned away from Japanese ports; King Minh Mang outlaws teaching of Christianity in Vietnam
1830	Dutch institute Culture System in Indonesia
1842	Treaty of Nanjing ends Opium War
1851–1864	Taiping Rebellion in China
1853	Commodore Perry opens Japanese ports to foreign trade
1857	Great Mutiny/Great Revolt by Indian sepoys against British rule
1858	British Parliament begins to rule India
1859–1885	Vietnam becomes a colony of France
1860s	Rise of Tonghak movement in Korea
1867	Meiji Restoration in Japan
1869	Suez Canal opens
1872	Universal public schools established in Japan
1885	Foundation of Indian National Congress
1894–1895	Japan defeats China in Sino-Japanese War and gains control of Taiwan
1898	United States takes control of Philippines from Spain
1900	Boxer Rebellion in China
1904	Japan attacks Russia and starts Russo-Japanese War
1910	Korea becomes a province of Japan
1912	China's monarchy is replaced by a republic

Great Mutiny/Great Revolt *The terms used by the British and the Indians to describe the last armed resistance to British rule in India, which occurred in 1857.*

Empress of India *The title adopted by Queen Victoria in 1877 to reflect the British rule of India.*

● **British and Sikh Leaders at Lahore** The Sikh kingdom in the Punjab fell to the British in a brief war in 1845–1846. This painting depicts the British and Sikh representatives who negotiated the resulting treaty, which gave Britain control of the region. *(Courtesy of the Trustees of the British Museum)*

network had increased fivefold to 25,000 miles, and the number of passengers had increased tenfold to 188 million. By then over 370,000 Indians worked for the railroads. Irrigation also received attention, and by 1900 India had the world's most extensive irrigation system.

At the same time, Indian production of textiles suffered a huge blow. Britain imported India's raw cotton but exported machine-spun yarn and machine-woven cloth, displacing millions of Indian hand-spinners and hand-weavers. By 1900 India was buying 40 percent of Britain's cotton exports. Not until 1900 were there small steps toward industrializing India. Local Gujaratis set up textile mills in Bombay, and the Tata family started the first steel mill in Bihar in 1911. By 1914 about a million Indians worked in factories.

The standard of living of the poor did not see much improvement. Tenancy and landlessness increased with the growth in plantation agriculture. Increases in production were eaten up by increases in population, which reached approximately 300 million by 1900. There was also a negative side to improved communication. As Indians traveled more widely on the convenient trains, disease spread, especially cholera, which is transmitted by exposure to contaminated water. Pilgrims' bathing in and drinking from sacred pools and rivers worsened this problem. New sewerage and water supply systems were installed in Calcutta in the late 1860s, and the death rate there decreased, but in 1900 four out of every one thousand residents of British India still died of cholera each year.

The Indian middle class probably gained more than the poor from British rule. The British built a large educational establishment in India with instruction in English. In the words of the member of Parliament who proposed it, Thomas Macaulay, this system would form "a class of persons Indian in blood and color, but English in taste, in opinions, in morals, and in intellect."[1] Missionaries also established schools with Western curricula, and by 1870, 790,000 Indians were attending some 24,000 schools. High-caste Hindus came to form a new elite profoundly influenced by Western thought and culture.

By creating a well-educated, English-speaking Indian elite and a bureaucracy based on a modern communication system, the British laid the groundwork for a unified, powerful state. Britain placed under the same general system of law and administration the various Hindu and Muslim peoples of the subcontinent who had resisted one another for centuries. It was as if Europe, with its many states and varieties of Christianity, had been conquered and united in a single great empire. University graduates tended to look on themselves as Indians more than as residents of the separate states and kingdoms, a necessary step for the development of Indian nationalism.

In spite of these achievements, British rule rankled the educated elite. Some Indian intellectuals sought to reconcile the values of the modern West and their own traditions. Rammohun Roy (1772–1833), who had risen to the top of the native ranks in the British East India Company, founded the Hindu College in Calcutta in 1816, which offered instruction in Western languages and subjects. A few years later he founded a society to reform certain Hindu customs, especially child marriage, the caste system, and restrictions on widows. He espoused a modern Hinduism founded on the *Upanishads,* the ancient sacred texts of Hinduism.

The more that Western-style education was developed in India, the more the inequalities of the system became apparent to educated Indians. Indians were eligible to take the examinations for entry into the elite **Indian Civil Service,** but the exams were given in England, and in 1870 only 1 of the 916 members of the service was Indian. In other words, no matter how Anglicized the educated classes became, they could never become the white rulers' equals. The top jobs, the best clubs, the modern hotels, and even certain railroad compartments were sealed off to brown-skinned men and women. Most of the British elite considered the jumble of Indian peoples and castes to be racially inferior. For example, when the British Parliament in 1883 was considering a bill to allow Indian judges to try white Europeans in India, the British community rose in protest and defeated the measure. The idea of being judged by Indians was inconceivable to the Europeans, for it was clear to them that the empire in India rested squarely on racial inequality. As Lord Kitchener, one of the most distinguished British military commanders in India, stated:

It is this consciousness of the inherent superiority of the European which has won for us India. However well educated and clever a native may be, and however brave he may prove himself, I believe that no rank we can bestow on him would cause him to be considered an equal of the British officer.[2]

The peasant masses might accept such inequality as the latest version of age-old class and caste hierarchies, but the well-educated, English-speaking elite eventually could not. They had studied not only Milton and Shakespeare but also English traditions of democracy, liberty, and national pride.

In the late nineteenth century the colonial ports of Calcutta, Bombay, and Madras, now all linked by railroads, became centers of intellectual ferment. In these and other cities, newspapers in English and in regional languages gained influence. Lawyers trained in English law began agitating for Indian independence. By 1885, when educated Indians came together to found the **Indian National Congress,** demands were increasing for the equality and self-government that Britain enjoyed and had already granted white-settler colonies such as Canada and Australia (see Chapter 26). Members of the congress called for more opportunities for Indians in the Indian

Indian Civil Service *The bureaucracy that administered the government of India. Entry into its elite ranks was by examinations that Indians were eligible to take but that were offered only in England.*

Indian National Congress *A political association formed in 1885 that worked for Indian self-government.*

● **Imperial Complexities in India** Britain permitted many native princes to continue their rule if they accepted British domination. This photo shows a road-building project designed to facilitate famine relief in a southern native state. Officials of the local Muslim prince and their British "advisers" watch over workers drawn from the Hindu majority. (*Nizam's Good Works Project–Famine Relief: Road Building, Aurangabad 1895–1902, from Judith Mara Gutman,* Through Indian Eyes. *Courtesy, Private Collection)*

Civil Service and reallocation of the government budget from military expenditures to the alleviation of poverty. They advocated unity across religious and caste lines, but most members were upper-caste, Western-educated Hindus.

Defending its possessions in India became a key element of British foreign policy during the nineteenth century and led to steady expansion of the territory Britain controlled in Asia. The kingdom of Burma, to India's east, also was trying to expand, which led the British to annex Assam (located between India and Burma) in 1826, then all of Burma by 1852. Burma was then administered as a province of India. British trade between India and China went through the Strait of Malacca, making that region strategically important. Britain had taken over several Dutch territories in this region during the Napoleonic occupation of the Netherlands, including Java. After returning them to the Netherlands in 1814, Britain created its own base in the area at Singapore, later expanding into Malaya (now Malaysia) in the 1870s and 1880s. In both Burma and Malaya, Britain tried to foster economic development. Railroads were built, and trade was promoted. Burma became a major exporter of timber and rice, Malaya of tin and rubber. So many laborers were brought into Malaya for the expanding mines and plantations that its population came to be approximately one-third Malay, one-third Chinese, and one-third Indian.

COMPETITION FOR SOUTHEAST ASIA

Why were some Southeast Asian societies reduced to colonies and others not?

At the beginning of the nineteenth century, only a small part of Southeast Asia was under direct European control. Spain administered the Philippines, and the Dutch controlled Java. By the end of the century, most of the region would be in foreign hands.

The Dutch East Indies

Although Dutch forts and trading posts in the East Indies dated back to the seventeenth century, in 1816 the Dutch ruled little more than the island of Java. Thereafter they gradually brought almost all of the 3,000-mile-long archipelago under their political authority. In extending their rule, the Dutch, like the British in India, brought

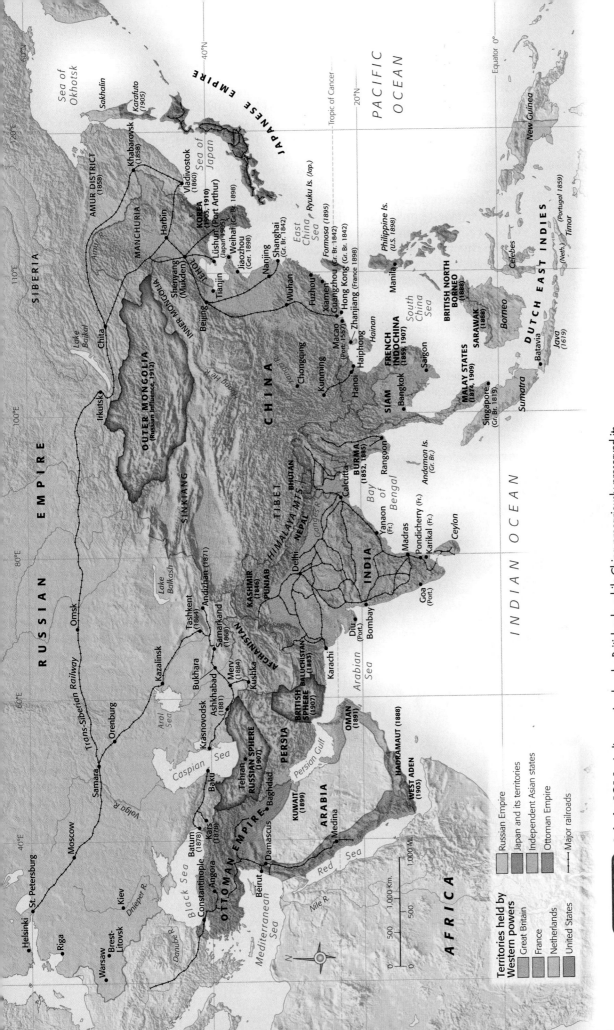

MAP 25.1 **Asia in 1914** India remained under British rule, while China precariously preserved its political independence. The Dutch empire in modern-day Indonesia was old, but French control of Indochina was a product of the new imperialism.

diverse peoples with different languages and distinct cultural traditions into a single political entity (see Map 25.1). Thus they inadvertently created the foundations of modern-day Indonesia—the world's fourth most populous nation.

Taking over the Dutch East India Company in 1799, the Dutch government modified the company's loose control of Java and gradually built a modern bureaucratic state. Javanese resistance led to the bloody **Java War** (1825–1830). In 1830, after the war, the Dutch abolished the combination of tribute from rulers and forced labor from peasants that they had used to obtain spices, and they established instead a particularly exploitive policy called the **Culture System**. Indonesian peasants were forced to plant a fifth of their land in export crops, especially coffee and sugar, to turn over to the Dutch as their taxes. The Culture System proved highly profitable for the Dutch and brought Dutch shipping and intercontinental commerce back to life. In 1870 Dutch liberals succeeded in eliminating some of the system's most coercive elements, but the practical effects were limited because Dutch and Javanese officials still worked together to make sure the flow of goods continued.

At the end of the nineteenth century the Dutch began to encourage Western education in the East Indies. The children of local rulers and privileged elites, much like their counterparts in India, encountered new ideas in Dutch-speaking schools. They began to question the long-standing cooperation of local elites with Dutch colonialism, and they searched for a new identity. Thus anticolonial nationalism began to take shape in the East Indies in the early twentieth century, and it would blossom after World War I.

Java War *The 1825–1830 war between the Dutch government and the Javanese, fought over the extension of Dutch control of the island.*

Culture System *The Dutch policy that required Indonesian peasants to plant a fifth of their land in export crops, which were then turned over to the Dutch as taxes.*

Nguyen Dynasty *The last Vietnamese ruling house, which lasted from 1802 to 1945.*

Mainland Southeast Asia

Unlike India and Java, mainland Southeast Asia had escaped European rule through the eighteenth century. In 1802 the new **Nguyen Dynasty** came to power in Vietnam, putting an end to thirty years of peasant rebellion and civil war. For the first time in the country's history, a single Vietnamese monarchy ruled the entire country, and Vietnam's future appeared bright. Working through a centralizing scholar bureaucracy fashioned on the Chinese model, the dynasty energetically built irrigation canals, roads and bridges, and impressive palaces in Hue, the new capital city. In 1821 a European who had lived in India, Java, and Siam (Thailand) wrote that Hue had a "neatness, magnitude, and perfection" that made other Asian achievements look "like the works of children."[3] Yet construction placed a heavy burden on the peasants drafted to do the work, and it contributed to a resurgence of peasant uprisings.

Roman Catholic missionaries from France posed a second, more dangerous threat to Vietnam's Confucian ruling elite. The king and his advisers believed that Christianity would undermine Confucian moral values and the unity of the Vietnamese state. In 1825 King Minh Mang (r. 1820–1841) outlawed the teaching of Christianity, and soon his government began executing Catholic missionaries and Vietnamese converts. As many as thirty thousand Vietnamese Christians were executed in the 1850s. In response, in 1859–1860 a French naval force seized Saigon

● **The French Governor General and the Vietnamese Emperor** The twelfth emperor of the Nguyen Dynasty, Khai Dinh (1885–1925) had to find ways to get along with the French governor general (in this picture, Albert Sarraut) if he wished to preserve his dynasty. Seen here in 1917 or 1918, he had adopted Western leather shoes but otherwise tried to keep a distinct Vietnamese identity in his dress. *(Roger Viollet/Getty Images)*

Individuals IN SOCIETY

José Rizal

In the mid-seventeenth century, a Chinese merchant immigrated to the Philippines and married a woman who was half Chinese, half Philippine. Because of anti-Chinese animosity, he changed his name to Mercado, Spanish for "merchant."

Mercado's direct patrilineal descendant, José Rizal (1861–1896), was born into a well-to-do family that leased a plantation from Dominican friars. Both of his parents were educated, and he was a brilliant student himself. In 1882, after completing his studies at the Jesuit-run college in Manila, he went on to Madrid to study medicine. During his ten years in Europe, not only did he earn a medical degree in Spain and a Ph.D. in Germany, but he also found time to learn several European languages and make friends with scientists, writers, and political radicals.

While in Europe, Rizal became involved with Philippine revolutionaries and contributed numerous articles to their newspaper, *La Solidaridad,* published in Barcelona. Rizal advocated making the Philippines a province of Spain, giving it representation in the Spanish parliament, replacing Spanish friars with Filipino priests, and making Filipinos and Spaniards equal before the law. He spent a year at the British Museum doing research on the early phase of the Spanish colonization of the Philippines. He also wrote two novels.

The first novel, written in Spanish, was fired by the passions of nationalism. In satirical fashion, it depicts a young Filipino of mixed blood who studies for several years in Europe before returning to the Philippines to start a modern secular school in his hometown and marry his childhood sweetheart. The church stands in the way of his efforts, and the colonial administration proves incompetent. The novel ends with the hero gunned down after the friars falsely implicate him in a revolutionary conspiracy. Rizal's own life ended up following this narrative surprisingly closely.

In 1892 Rizal left Europe, stopped briefly in Hong Kong, then returned to Manila to help his family with a lawsuit. Though he secured his relatives' release from jail, he ran into trouble himself. Because his writings were critical of the power of the church, he made many enemies, some of whom had him arrested. He was sent into exile to a Jesuit mission town on the relatively primitive island of Mindanao. There he founded a school and a hospital, and the Jesuits tried to win him back to the church. He kept busy during his four years in exile, not only teaching English, sci-

After his death, Rizal's portrait was used to inspire patriotism. *(Cover of "The Filipino Teacher," December 1908. Museo Santisima Trinidad)*

ence, and self-defense, but also maintaining his correspondence with scientists in Europe. When a nationalist secret society rose in revolt in 1896, in an effort to distance himself, he volunteered to go to Cuba to help in an outbreak of yellow fever. Although he had no connections with the secret society and was on his way across the ocean, Rizal was arrested and shipped back to Manila.

Tried for sedition by the military, Rizal was found guilty. When handed his death certificate, Rizal struck out the words "Chinese half-breed" and wrote "pure native." He was publicly executed by a firing squad in Manila at age thirty-five, making him a martyr of the nationalist cause.

Questions for Analysis

1. Did Rizal's comfortable family background contribute to his becoming a revolutionary?

2. How would Rizal's European contemporaries have reacted to his opposition to the Catholic Church?

French Indochina *The name given the French colonial state that ruled the region of the modern countries of Vietnam, Laos, and Cambodia.*

and three surrounding provinces in southern Vietnam, making that part of Vietnam a French colony. In 1884–1885 France launched a second war against Vietnam and conquered the rest of the country. Laos and Cambodia were added to **French Indochina** in 1887. In all three countries the local rulers were left on their thrones, but France dominated and tried to promote French culture.

After the French conquest, Vietnamese patriots continued to resist with a combination of loyalty to Confucian values and intense hatred of foreign rule. After Japan's victory over Russia in 1905 (see page 767–768), a new generation of nationalists saw Japan as a model for Vietnamese revitalization and freedom. They went to Japan to study and planned for anticolonial revolution in Vietnam.

In all of Southeast Asia, only Siam succeeded in preserving its independence. Siam was sandwiched between the British in Burma (and India) and the French in Indochina. Thus geography enabled its very able King Chulalongkorn (r. 1868–1910) to balance the two competitors against each other and to escape the smothering embrace of both. Chulalongkorn had studied Greek and Latin and Western science and kept up with Western news by reading British newspapers from Hong Kong and Singapore. He outlawed slavery and implemented modernizing reforms that centralized the government so that it could more effectively control outlying provinces coveted by the imperialists. Independent Siam gradually developed a modern centralizing state similar to the states constructed by Western imperialists in their Asian possessions.

The Philippines

The United States became one of the imperialist powers in Asia when it took the Philippines from Spain in 1898.

When the Spanish established rule in the Philippines in the sixteenth century, the islands had no central government or literate culture; order was maintained by village units dominated by local chiefs. Under the Spanish, Roman Catholic churches were established, and Spanish priests able to speak the local languages became the most common intermediaries between local populations, who rarely could speak Spanish, and the new rulers. The government of Spain encouraged Spaniards to colonize the Philippines through the **encomienda system:** Spaniards who had served the Crown were rewarded with grants giving them the exclusive right to control public affairs and collect taxes in a specific locality. A local Filipino elite also developed, aided by the Spanish introduction of private ownership of land. Given the great distance between Madrid and Manila, the governor general, appointed by Spain, had almost unlimited powers over the courts and the military. Manila developed into an important entrepôt in the galleon trade between Mexico and China, and this trade also attracted a large Chinese community, which handled much of the trade within the Philippines.

encomienda system *The system under which Spanish colonists were given the exclusive right to control public affairs in the Philippines and collect taxes in a specific locality.*

Spain did not do much to promote education in the Philippines, and few Filipinos could read, write, or speak Spanish. In the late nineteenth century, however, wealthy Filipinos began to send their sons to study abroad, and a movement to press Spain for reforms emerged. When the Spanish cracked down on critics, a rebellion erupted in 1896 (see Individuals in Society: José Rizal). It was settled in 1897 with Spanish promises to reform.

In 1898, war between Spain and the United States broke out on the coast of Cuba (see page 791), and in May the American naval officer Commodore George Dewey sailed into Manila Bay and sank the Spanish fleet anchored there. Dewey called on the Philippine rebels to help defeat the Spanish forces, but when the rebels declared independence, the U.S. government refused to recognize them, despite protests by American anti-imperialists. U.S. forces fought the Philippine rebels, and by the end of the insurrection in 1902, the war had cost the lives of 5,000 Americans and about 200,000 Filipinos. In the following years, the United States introduced a form of colonial rule that included public works and economic development projects, improved education and medicine, and, in 1907, an elected legislative assembly.

CHINA UNDER PRESSURE

Was China's decline in the nineteenth century due more to internal problems or Western imperialism?

In 1800 most Chinese had no reason to question the conception of China as the central kingdom: no other country had so many people, Chinese products were in great demand in foreign countries, and the borders had recently been expanded. A century later, all that had changed. In 1900 foreign troops marched into China's capital, and more and more Chinese had come to think that their government, society, and cultural values needed to be radically changed.

The Opium War

Seeing little to gain from trade with European countries, the Qing (Manchu) emperors, who had been ruling China since 1644 (see pages 585–588), permitted Europeans to trade only at the port of Guangzhou (Canton) and only through licensed Chinese merchants. Initially, the balance of trade was in China's favor, as Great Britain and the other Western nations used silver to pay for tea. By the 1820s, however, the British had found something the Chinese would buy—opium. Grown legally in British-occupied India, opium was smuggled into China, where its use and sale were illegal. Huge profits and the cravings of addicts led to rapid increases in sales, from 4,500 chests a year in 1810 to 10,000 in 1830 and to 40,000 in 1838. At this point it was China that suffered a drain of silver.

To deal with this crisis, the Chinese government dispatched Lin Zexu to Guangzhou in 1839. He dealt harshly with Chinese who purchased opium and seized the opium stores of British merchants. Lin even wrote to Queen Victoria: "Suppose there were people from another country who carried opium for sale to England and seduced your people into buying and smoking it; certainly your honorable ruler would deeply hate it and be bitterly aroused."[4] When Lin pressured the Portuguese to expel the uncooperative British from their trading post at Macao, the British settled on the barren island of Hong Kong.

Although for years the little community of foreign merchants had accepted Chinese rules, by 1839 the British, the dominant group, were ready to flex their muscles. British merchants wanted to create a market for their goods in China and get tea more cheaply by trading closer to its source in central China. They also wanted a diplomatic system more on the European model, with envoys and ambassadors, commercial treaties, and published tariffs. With the encouragement of their merchants in China, the British sent an expeditionary force from India with forty-two warships, many of them leased from the major opium trader, Jardine, Matheson, and Company.

With its control of the seas, the British easily shut down key Chinese ports and forced the Chinese to negotiate. Dissatisfied with the resulting agreement, the British sent a second, larger force, which took even more coastal cities, including Shanghai. This **Opium War** was settled at gunpoint in 1842. The resulting **Treaty of Nanjing** (Nanking) opened five ports to international trade, fixed the tariff on imported goods at 5 percent, imposed an indemnity of 21 million ounces of silver on China to cover Britain's war expenses, and ceded the island of Hong Kong to Britain. Through the clause on **extraterritoriality**, British subjects in China became answerable only to British law, even in disputes with Chinese. The treaty also had a "most-favored nation" clause, which meant that whenever one nation extracted a new privilege from China, it was extended automatically to Britain.

This treaty satisfied neither side. China continued to refuse to accept foreign diplomats at its capital in Beijing, and the expansion of trade fell far short of Western expectations. Between 1856 and 1860 Britain and France renewed hostilities with China. Seventeen thousand British and French troops occupied Beijing and set the

Primary Source: Letter to Queen Victoria, 1839
On behalf of the emperor, Lin Zexu implores Queen Victoria to halt the British opium trade in China.

Opium War *The 1839–1842 war between the British and the Chinese over limitations on trade and the importation of opium into China.*

Treaty of Nanjing *The treaty ending the Opium War; it opened five ports to international trade, fixed the tariff on imported goods, imposed an indemnity on China to cover Britain's war expenses, and ceded the island of Hong Kong to Britain, among other measures.*

extraterritoriality *The legal principle that exempts individuals from local law; it was included in the Treaty of Nanjing so that British subjects in China would be answerable only to British law.*

● **Mixed Court** In the treaty ports, beginning in 1864, disputes between Chinese and Westerners were heard by two judges, one Chinese and one representing the Western powers. These "mixed courts" applied Western law for offenses that occurred within the concessions. *(John Hillelson Agency)*

emperor's summer palace on fire. Another round of harsh treaties gave European merchants and missionaries greater privileges and forced the Chinese to open several more cities to foreign trade. Large areas in some of the treaty ports were leased in perpetuity to foreign powers; these were known as **concessions**.

concessions *Large areas of Chinese treaty ports that were leased in perpetuity to foreign powers.*

Internal Problems

China's problems in the nineteenth century, however, were not all of foreign origin. By 1850 China, for centuries the world's most populous country, had more than 400 million people. As the population grew, farm size shrank, forests were put to the plow, and surplus labor suppressed wages. When the best parcels of land were all occupied, conflicts over rights to water and tenancy increased. Hard times also led to increased female infanticide, as families felt that they could not afford to raise more than two or three children and saw sons as necessities. A shortage of marriageable women resulted, reducing the incentive for young men to stay near home and do as their elders told them. Some became bandits, others boatmen, carters, sedan-chair carriers, or, by the end of the century, rickshaw pullers.

Taiping Rebellion *A massive rebellion by the believers in the religious teachings of Hong Xiuquan, begun in 1851 and not suppressed until 1864.*

These economic and demographic circumstances led to some of the most destructive rebellions in China's history. The worst was the **Taiping Rebellion** (1851–1864), in which some 20 million people lost their lives, making it one of the bloodiest wars in world history.

This rebellion was initiated by Hong Xiuquan (1814–1864), a man from South China who had studied for the civil service examinations but never passed. His career as a religious leader began with visions of a golden-bearded old man and a middle-aged man who addressed him as younger brother and told him to annihilate devils. After reading a Christian tract given to him by a missionary, Hong interpreted his visions to mean he was Jesus' younger brother. He soon gathered followers, whom he instructed to destroy idols and ancestral temples, give up opium and alcohol, and renounce foot binding and prostitution. In 1851 he declared himself king of the Heavenly Kingdom of Great Peace (Taiping), an act of open insurrection. By 1853 the

Taipings had moved north and established their capital at the major city of Nanjing, which they held onto for a decade. From this base they set about creating a utopian society based on the equalization of landholdings and the equality of men and women. Christian missionaries quickly concluded that the Christian elements in Taiping doctrines were heretical and did not help them. To suppress the Taipings, the Manchus had to turn to Chinese scholar-officials, who raised armies on their own, revealing that the Manchus were no longer the mighty warriors they had been when they had conquered China two centuries earlier.

The Self-Strengthening Movement

After the various rebellions were suppressed, forward-looking reformers began addressing the Western threat. Under the slogan **"self-strengthening,"** they set about modernizing the military along Western lines. Arsenals and dockyards were established, and envoys were sent abroad. Recognizing that guns and ships were merely the surface manifestations of the Western powers' economic strength, some of the most progressive reformers also initiated new industries, which in the 1870s and 1880s included railway lines, steam navigation companies, coal mines, telegraph lines, and cotton spinning and weaving factories. These were the same sorts of initiatives that the British were introducing in India, but China lagged behind, especially in railroads.

These measures drew resistance from conservatives, who thought copying Western practices was compounding defeat. The highly placed Manchu official Woren objected that "from ancient down to modern times" there had never been "anyone who could use mathematics to raise a nation from a state of decline or to strengthen it in times of weakness."[5] Yet knowledge of the West gradually improved with more translations and travel in both directions. Newspapers covering world affairs began publication in Shanghai and Hong Kong. By 1880 China had embassies in London, Paris, Berlin, Madrid, Washington, Tokyo, and St. Petersburg.

Despite the enormous effort put into trying to catch up, China was humiliated yet again at the end of the nineteenth century. First came the discovery that Japan had so

"self-strengthening" *The goal of the reform movement in late-nineteenth-century China that sought to master Western technology in order to better resist Western pressure.*

● **China's First Railroad**   Soon after this railroad was constructed near Shanghai in 1876, the provincial governor bought it in order to tear it out. Many Chinese of the period saw railroads as harmful not only to the balance of nature but also to people's livelihoods, since the railroads eliminated jobs in transport like dragging boats along canals or driving pack horses. *(Private Collection)*

● **Hong Kong Tailors** In 1872 the newspaper *Shenbao* was founded in Shanghai, and in 1884 it added an eight-page weekly pictorial supplement. Influenced by the pictorial press then popular in Europe, it depicted both news and human interest stories, both Chinese and foreign. In this scene we are shown a tailor shop in Hong Kong, where Chinese tailors use sewing machines and make women's clothes in current Western styles. To Chinese readers, men making women's clothes and placing them on bamboo forms would have seemed as peculiar as the style of the dresses. *(From* Dianshizhai huabao, *a Shanghai picture magazine, 1885 or later)*

Sino-Japanese War *The 1894–1895 war between Japan and China, fought over Japanese efforts to separate Korea from Chinese influence.*

successfully modernized that it posed a threat to China (see pages 764–768). In 1894 Japanese efforts to separate Korea from Chinese influence led to the brief **Sino-Japanese War** in which China was decisively defeated, even though much of its navy had been purchased abroad at great expense. In the peace negotiations, China ceded Taiwan to Japan, agreed to a huge indemnity, and gave Japan the right to open factories in China. China's helplessness in the face of aggression led to a scramble among the European powers for concessions and protectorates in China. At the high point of this rush in 1898, it appeared that the European powers might actually divide China among themselves, the way they had recently divided Africa.

The End of Monarchy in China

China's humiliating defeat in 1895 led to a renewed drive for reform. In 1898 a group of educated young reformers gained access to the twenty-seven-year-old Qing emperor. They warned him of the fate of Poland (divided by the European powers in the eighteenth century) and regaled him with the triumphs of the Meiji reformers in Japan. They proposed redesigning China as a constitutional monarchy with modern financial and educational systems. For three months the emperor in fact issued a series of reform decrees. The Manchu establishment and the empress dowager, who had dominated the court for the past quarter century, felt threatened and not only suppressed the reform movement but imprisoned the emperor. Hope for reform from the top was dashed.

A period of violent reaction swept the country, reaching its peak in 1900 with the uprising of a secret society that foreigners dubbed the **Boxers**. The Boxers blamed China's ills on foreigners, especially the missionaries who traveled throughout China telling the Chinese that their beliefs were wrong and their customs backward. After the Boxers laid siege to the legation quarter in Beijing, a dozen nations including Japan sent twenty thousand troops to lift the siege. In the negotiations that followed, China had to accept a long list of penalties, including canceling the civil service examinations for five years (punishment for gentry collaboration) and a staggering indemnity of 450 million ounces of silver, almost twice the government's annual revenues.

After this defeat gradual reform lost its appeal. More and more Chinese were studying abroad and learning about Western political ideas, including democracy and revolution. The most famous of them was Sun Yatsen (1866–1925). Sent by his peasant family to Hawai'i, he learned English there and continued his education in Hong Kong. From 1894 on, he spent his time abroad organizing revolutionary societies and seeking financial support from overseas Chinese. He later joined forces with Chinese student revolutionaries studying in Japan, and together they attempted several times to spark rebellion. The plot that finally triggered the collapse of China's imperial system is known as the **1911 Revolution.** Army officers fearful that their connections to the revolutionaries would be exposed staged a coup and persuaded the provincial governments to secede. The powers behind the child emperor (who had ascended to the throne at the age of three in 1908) agreed to his abdication, and at the beginning of 1912 China's long history of monarchy came to an end, to be replaced by a republic modeled on Western political ideas. China had escaped direct foreign rule but would never be the same again.

Boxers *A Chinese secret society that blamed the country's ills on foreigners, especially missionaries, and rose in rebellion in 1899–1900.*

Primary Source: The Three People's Principles and the Future of the Chinese People *Decrying the gulf between rich and poor in Europe and America, Sun Yat-Sen calls for a revolution in China that will ensure prosperity and social justice.*

1911 Revolution *The uprising that brought China's monarchy to an end.*

JAPAN'S RAPID TRANSFORMATION

How was Japan able to quickly master the challenges posed by the West?

During the nineteenth century, while China's standing in the world plummeted, Japan's was rising.

European traders and missionaries first arrived in Japan in the sixteenth century, but in the early seventeenth century, in part because of the remarkable success of Catholic missionaries (see pages 602–603), the Japanese government expelled them. During the eighteenth century, Japan much more effectively than China kept foreign merchants and missionaries at bay. It limited trade to a single port (Nagasaki), where only the Dutch were allowed, and forbade Japanese to travel abroad. Because Japan's land and population were so much smaller than China's, the Western powers never expected much from Japan as a trading partner and did not press it as urgently.

The "Opening" of Japan

Wanting to play a greater role in the Pacific, the United States decided to force the Japanese to share their ports and behave as a "civilized" nation. In 1853 Commodore Matthew Perry steamed into Edo (now Tokyo) Bay and demanded diplomatic negotiations with the emperor. Some Japanese samurai urged resistance, but senior officials knew what had happened in China and how defenseless their cities would be against naval bombardment. After consulting with the daimyo (major lords), they signed a treaty with the United States that opened two ports and permitted trade.

gunboat diplomacy *The imposition of treaties and agreements under threat of military violence, such as the opening of Japan to trade after Commodore Perry's demands.*

When Japan was "opened" by **gunboat diplomacy,** it was a complex society. The emperor in Kyoto had no effective powers. For more than two hundred years real power had been in the hands of the Tokugawa shogun in Edo (see pages 591–593). The country was divided into numerous domains, each under a daimyo. Each daimyo had under him samurai, who had hereditary stipends and privileges, such as the right to wear a sword. Peasants and merchants were also legally distinct classes, and in theory social mobility from peasant to merchant or merchant to samurai was impossible. After two centuries of peace, there were many more samurai than were needed to administer or defend the country, and many lived very modestly. They were proud, however, and felt humiliated by the sudden American intrusion and the unequal treaties that the Western countries imposed. Some began agitating against the shogunate under the slogan "Revere the emperor and expel the barbarians."

When foreign diplomats and merchants began to settle in Yokohama after 1858, radical samurai reacted with a wave of antiforeign terrorism and antigovernment assassinations. The Western imperialist response was swift and unambiguous. Much as the Western powers had sent troops to Beijing a few years before, they now sent an allied fleet of American, British, Dutch, and French warships to demolish key Japanese forts, further weakening the power and prestige of the shogun's government.

The Meiji Restoration

In 1867 a coalition of reform-minded domains led a coup that ousted the Tokugawa Shogunate. The samurai who led this coup declared a return to direct rule by the emperor, not practiced in Japan for more than six hundred years. This emperor is called the Meiji emperor and this event the **Meiji Restoration,** a great turning point in Japanese history.

Meiji Restoration *The 1867 ousting of the Tokugawa Shogunate that "restored" the power of the Japanese emperors.*

Meiji Oligarchs *The leaders who organized the ouster of the Tokugawa Shogunate and then ran the government in the name of the emperor.*

The domain leaders who organized the coup, called the **Meiji Oligarchs,** moved the boy emperor to Tokyo castle (previously the seat of the shogun, now the imperial palace). They used the young sovereign to win over both the lords and the commoners. During the emperor's first decade on the throne, the leaders carried him around in hundreds of grand imperial processions so that he could see his subjects and they him. The emerging press also worked to keep its readers informed of the young emperor's actions and their obligations to him. Real power, however, remained in the hands of the oligarchs.

"strong army, rich nation" *The slogan of the Meiji reformers who did not want the Western powers to be able to intimidate Japan.*

The battle cry of the Meiji reformers had been **"strong army, rich nation."** But how were these goals to be accomplished? In an about-face that is one of history's most remarkable chapters, the determined but flexible leaders of Meiji Japan dropped their antiforeign attacks. Convinced that they could not beat the West until they mastered the secrets of its military and industrial might, they initiated a series of measures to reform Japan along modern, Western lines. One even proposed that "Japan must be reborn with America its mother and France its father."[6] In 1868 an imperial declaration promised representative government and that "knowledge shall be sought throughout the world so as to strengthen the foundations of imperial rule."[7] Within four years a delegation was traveling the world to learn what made the Western powers strong. They examined everything from the U.S. Constitution to the factories, shipyards, and railroads that made the European landscape so different from Japan's.

Primary Source: Anniversary Statement *Read the political platform, published in 1930, of the militarist and nationalist Black Dragon Society of Japan.*

Japan under the shoguns had been decentralized, with most of the power over the population in the hands of the daimyos. By elevating the emperor, the oligarchs were able to centralize the government. In 1871 they abolished the domains and merged the domain armies. Following the example of the French Revolution, they dismantled the four-class legal system and declared everyone equal. This amounted to stripping the samurai (7 to 8 percent of the population) of its privileges. First the samurai's stipends were reduced; then in 1876 the stipends were replaced by one-time grants of income-bearing bonds. Most samurai had to find work or start businesses, as the value of the bonds declined with inflation. Samurai no longer were to wear their swords, long the symbols of their status. Even their monopoly on the use of force was eliminated: the new army recruited commoners along with samurai. Not surprisingly, some samurai rose to protest their loss of privileges. In one extreme case, the rebels refused to use guns in a futile effort to retain the mystique of the sword. None of these uncoordinated uprisings deflected the transition.

Several leaders of the Meiji Restoration, in France on a fact-finding mission during the Franco-Prussian War of 1870–1871, were impressed by the active participation of French citizens in the defense of Paris. This contrasted with the indifference of most Japanese peasants during the battles that led to the Meiji Restoration. For Japan to survive in the hostile international environment, they concluded, ordinary people had to be trained to fight. A conscription law, modeled on the French law, was issued in 1872. Like French law, it exempted first sons. The new War College was organized along German lines, and German instructors were recruited to teach there. Young samurai were trained to form the new professional officer corps. The success of this approach was demonstrated first in 1877, when the professionally led army of draftees crushed a major rebellion by samurai.

Many of the new institutions established in the Meiji period reached down to the local level. Universal public schools were rapidly introduced after 1872. Teachers were trained in newly established normal schools, where they learned to inculcate discipline, patriotism, and morality. Another modern institution that reached down to the local level was a national police force. In 1884 police training schools were established in every prefecture, and within a few years one- or two-man police stations were set up throughout the country. These policemen came to act as local agents of the central government. They not only dealt with crime but also enforced public health rules, conscription laws, and codes of behavior.

● **Japan's Modernized Army** A set of woodblock prints depicting the new sights of Tokyo included this illustration of a military parade ground. The soldiers' brightly colored Western-style uniforms undoubtedly helped make this a sight worth seeing. *(Ryogoku Tsuneo Tamba Collection/Laurie Platt Winfrey, Inc.)*

Those measures in time brought benefits, but at the local level they were often perceived as oppressive. Protests became very common against everything from conscription and the Western calendar to the new taxes for the compulsory schools.

In 1889 Japan became the first non-Western country to adopt the constitutional form of government. Prefectural assemblies, set up in the 1870s and 1880s, gave local elites some experience in debating political issues. The constitution, however, was handed down from above, drafted by the top political leaders and issued in the name of the emperor. A commission sent abroad to study European constitutional governments had come to the conclusion that the German constitutional monarchy would provide the best model for Japan, rather than the more democratic governments of the British, French, and Americans. The new government had a two-house parliament,

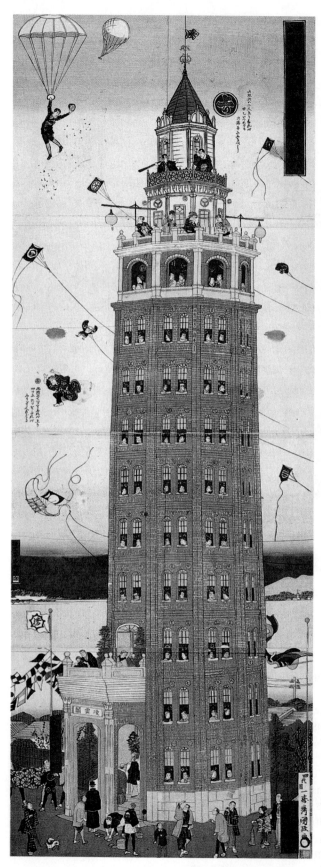

called the Diet. The upper house of lords was drawn largely from former lords and nobles, and the lower house was elected by a limited electorate (about 5 percent of the adult male population in 1890). Although Japan now had a government based on laws, it was authoritarian rather than democratic. The emperor was declared "sacred and inviolable," and he was sovereign. He had the right to appoint the prime minister and cabinet. He did not have to ask the Diet for funds, because wealth assigned to the imperial house was entrusted to the Imperial Household Ministry, which was outside the government's control.

Cultural change during the Meiji period was just as profound as political change. For more than a thousand years China had provided the major source of ideas and technologies introduced into Japan, ranging from the writing system to Confucianism and Buddhism, tea and silk, chopsticks and soy sauce. But in the late nineteenth century China, beset by Western pressure, had become an object lesson in the dangers of stagnation rather than a model to follow. The influential author Fukuzawa Yukichi began urging Japan to pursue **"civilization and enlightenment,"** by which he meant Western civilization. (See the feature "Listening to the Past: Escape from Asia" on pages 774–775.) Fukuzawa advocated learning Western languages and encouraged Japan to learn from the West in order to catch up with it. Soon Japanese were being told to conform to Western taste, eat meat, wear Western-style clothes, and drop customs that Westerners found odd, such as married women blackening their teeth.

Industrialization

The leaders of the Meiji Restoration, wanting to strengthen Japan's military capacity, promoted industrialization. The government paid large salaries to attract foreign experts to help with industrialization, and Japanese were encouraged to go abroad to study science and engineering.

The government played an active role in getting railroads, mines, and factories started. Japan's coal mines had produced only 390,000 tons in 1860, but by 1900 this had risen to 5 million tons. Early on the Japanese government decided to compete with China in the export of tea and silk to the West. Introducing the mechanical reeling of silk gave Japan a strong advantage, and Japan's total foreign trade increased tenfold from 1877 to 1900. The next stage was to develop heavy industry. The huge indemnity exacted from

● **Japan's First Skyscraper** Meiji Japan's fascination with things Western led to the construction of Western-style buildings. Japan's first elevator made possible this twelve-story tower built in Tokyo in 1890. Built in the entertainment district, it was filled with shops, theaters, bars, and restaurants. *(Department of Historical Documents, National Institute of Japanese Literature.)*

China in 1895 was used to establish the Yawata Iron and Steel Works. A third step would today be called import substitution. Factories such as cotton mills were set up to help cut the importation of Western consumer goods. By 1912 factory output accounted for 13 percent of the national product, even though only 3 percent of the labor force worked in factories, mostly small ones with fewer than fifty workers.

Most of the great Japanese industrial combines, known as *zaibatsu*, got their start in this period, often founded by men with government connections. Sometimes the government set up plants that they then sold to private investors at bargain prices. Successful entrepreneurs were treated as patriotic heroes.

As in Europe, the early stages of industrialization brought hardship to the countryside. Farmers often rioted as their incomes failed to keep up with prices or their tax burdens grew. In 1898 railroad workers went on strike for better working conditions and overtime pay. Still, rice production increased, death rates dropped as public health was improved, and the population grew from about 33 million in 1868 to about 45 million in 1900.

Japan as an Imperial Power

During the course of the Meiji period, Japan became an imperial power, making Taiwan and Korea into its colonies. Taiwan had been a part of China for two centuries; Korea had been an independent country with a unified government since 668. The conflicts that led to Japanese acquisition of them revolved around Korea.

The Choson Dynasty had been on the throne in Korea since 1392. Chinese influence had grown over this period as the Korean elite enthusiastically embraced Confucian teachings and studied for Chinese-style civil service examinations.

In the second half of the nineteenth century Korea found itself caught between China, Japan, and Russia, each trying to protect or extend its sphere of influence. Added to this, Westerners also began demanding that Korea be "opened." Korea's first response was to insist that its foreign relations be handled through Beijing. Matters were complicated by the rise of a religious cult in the 1860s that had strong xenophobic elements. Although the government executed the cult founder in 1864, this cult continued to gain support, especially among impoverished peasants. Thus, like China in the same period, the Korean government faced simultaneous internal and external threats.

In 1871 the U.S. minister to China took five warships to try to "open" Korea but left after exchanges of fire resulted in 250 Koreans dead without any progress in getting the Korean government to make concessions. Japan tried next and in 1876 forced the Korean government to sign an unequal treaty and open three ports to Japanese trade. On China's urging, Korea also signed treaties with the European powers in an effort to counterbalance Japan.

Over the next couple of decades reformers in China and Japan tried to encourage Korea to adopt its own "self-strengthening" movement, but Korean conservatives, including the queen (regent for the child king), did their best to undo reform efforts. In 1894, when the religious cult rose in a massive revolt, both China and Japan sent military forces, claiming to come to the Korean government's aid. They ended up fighting each other instead. With Japan's decisive victory, it gained Taiwan from China and was able to make Korea a protectorate. Japan also arranged the assassination of the Korean queen in 1895.

Just a few years later, in 1900, Japan participated with the European powers in occupying Beijing to suppress the Boxer Rebellion. In this period Japan was competing aggressively with the leading European powers for influence and territory in China, particularly in the northeast (Manchuria). There Japanese and Russian imperialism met and collided. In 1904 Japan attacked Russian forces, and after this bloody

"civilization and enlightenment" *A slogan set forth by the influential author Fukuzawa Yukichi, who urged the Japanese to abandon their ancient ways and learn the ways of the West.*

Primary Source:
Two Proclamations of the Boxer Rebellion
The secret society known as "The Righteous and Harmonious Fists" announces its intention to kill the "foreign devils" plaguing China.

Russo-Japanese War *The 1904–1905 war between Russia and Japan, fought over imperial influence and territory in northeast China (Manchuria).*

Russo-Japanese War Japan emerged with a valuable foothold in China—Russia's former protectorate over Port Arthur (see Map 25.1).

Japan also steadily strengthened its hold on Korea. In 1907, when the Korean king proved less than fully compliant, the Japanese forced him to abdicate in favor of his feeble-minded son. Korean resistance was suppressed in bloody fighting, and in 1910 Korea was formally annexed as a province of Japan.

Japan's victories over China and Russia changed the way European nations looked at Japan. Through negotiations Japan was able to eliminate extraterritoriality in 1899 and gain control of its own tariffs in 1911. Within Japan, the success of the military in raising Japan's international reputation added greatly to its political influence.

THE MOVEMENT OF PEOPLES

Why did people move much more in this period, and where did they go?

The nineteenth century was marked by extensive movement of people into, across, and out of Asia. In no earlier period had so many Europeans lived in Asia or so many Asians taken up residence in other countries. This vast migration both resulted from and helped accelerate the increasing integration of the world economy. Improvements in shipping and the digging of the Suez and Panama Canals made crossing the oceans faster and safer. Foreigners could survive tropical climates more easily after 1850 when the effects of malaria could be limited by taking the medicine quinine. Knowledge of foreign languages improved dramatically, and translations of works from Western to Asian languages and vice versa made the understanding of alien cultures much easier to acquire, at least for the literate.

Westerners to Asia

Imperialism brought Europeans to Asia in unprecedented numbers. By the early 1900s there were significant expatriate communities of European and American businessmen, missionaries, and colonial civil servants in many countries. The most extreme case was India. By 1863 there were already sixty-five thousand British troops in India and many more British in the civil service and commercial companies. Especially after the opening of the Suez Canal in 1869, British working in India were accompanied by their wives and children, who would return to Britain every few years on leave. By the eve of World War I, hundreds of thousands of expatriates lived in India, many since birth.

Beginning in 1809, British recruits to the British East India Company and subsequently to the Indian Civil Service were required to learn at least one Indian language fluently, but the trend, especially after the Great Revolt of 1857 (see page 751), was for the British to live separately from the Indians in their own enclaves. Houses were adapted to the local climate, with wide, well-shaded porches and large lawns. Houses and grounds were tended by Indian servants, who also minded the colonists' children, did their shopping, and handled most of their dealings with local Indians. British colonists who were curious about India and wanted to make Indian friends found social intercourse difficult, especially with Muslims and higher-caste Hindus, whose social contact with outsiders was restricted by traditional rules.

China was not under colonial occupation and so did not have so many foreign civil servants and soldiers in its cities, but it did attract more missionaries than any other Asian country. After 1860, when China agreed to allow missionaries to proselytize throughout the country, missionaries came in large numbers. Unlike the British civil servants in India, missionaries had no choice but to mix with the local population, finding the best opportunities for conversion among ordinary poor Chinese. Although the majority of missionaries devoted themselves to preaching, over the course of the nineteenth century more and more worked in medicine and education. By 1905 about three hundred fully qualified physicians were doing medical missionary work, and 250 mission hospitals and dispensaries served about 2 million patients. Missionary hospitals in Hong Kong also ran a medical school, which trained hundreds of Chinese as physicians.

Missionaries helped spread Western learning at their schools. For their elementary schools, missionaries produced textbooks in Chinese on a full range of subjects. They also translated dozens of standard works into Chinese, especially in the natural sciences, mathematics, history, and international law. By 1906 nearly sixty thousand Chinese students were attending twenty-four hundred Christian schools. Most of this activity was supported by contributions sent from America and Britain.

Missionaries in China had more success in spreading Western learning than in gaining converts. By 1900 fewer than a million Chinese were Christians. Ironically, although Western missionaries paid much less attention to Korea—the first missionary arrived there in 1884—Christianity took much stronger root there, and today about 25 percent of the Korean population is Christian. Missionaries also had some success in Vietnam, where Catholic missionaries were protected by the French government.

Asian Emigration

In the nineteenth century Asians, like Europeans, left their native countries in unprecedented numbers. As in Europe, both push and pull factors prompted people to leave home. Between 1750 and 1900 world population grew rapidly, in many places tripling. China and India were extremely densely populated countries—China with about 400 million people in the mid-nineteenth century, India with more than 200 million. Not surprisingly, these two giants were the leading exporters of people. On the pull side were the new opportunities created in part by the flow of development capital into previously underdeveloped areas. In many of the European colonies in Asia and Africa the business class came to consist of both Asian and European migrants, the Asians protected and tolerated by the Western imperialists who found them useful.

In China voluntary migration in search of opportunity had been going on for centuries. Chinese from the southern coastal regions had formed key components of the mercantile communities throughout Southeast Asia, from Siam south to Java and east to the Philippines. Chinese often assimilated in Siam and Vietnam, but they rarely did so in Muslim areas such as Java, Catholic areas such as the Philippines, and primitive tribal areas such as northern Borneo. In these places, distinct Chinese communities emerged, usually dominated by speakers of a single Chinese dialect.

With the growth in trade that accompanied the European expansion, Chinese began to settle in insular Southeast Asia in larger numbers. After Singapore was founded by the British in 1819, Chinese rapidly poured in, soon to become its dominant ethnic group. In British-controlled Malaya, some Chinese built great fortunes in the tin business, while others worked in the mines. There the Chinese community included both old overseas families long settled in the Portuguese city of Malacca, who spoke Malay, and a much larger number of more recent immigrants, most of whom spoke Cantonese. In the Spanish-controlled Philippines and Dutch-controlled Indonesia, however, the Chinese suffered repeated persecutions. Early in the nineteenth century in Borneo, the Dutch expropriated the mines that the Chinese had worked for generations. Elsewhere, however, the Dutch made use of the Chinese. In Java, for instance, Chinese merchants were used as tax collectors. Moreover, after the Dutch conquered southern Sumatra in 1864, Chinese were recruited to work in the sugar and tobacco plantations. By 1900 more than five hundred thousand Chinese were living in the Dutch East Indies.

● **Chinese Street Opera in Singapore** In Singapore there were so many Chinese people that they were able to maintain their traditional forms of entertainment, such as the opera shown here in a photograph from the 1890s. Although most of the men were still wearing the Manchu-imposed queue hairstyle, many concealed them under Western-style hats. *(Courtesy, National Museum of Singapore)*

Discovery of gold in California in 1848, Australia in 1851, and Canada in 1858 encouraged Chinese to book passage to those places (see Chapter 26). In California few arrived soon enough to strike gold, but they soon found other work. Thousands worked laying railroad tracks, and others took up mining in Wyoming and Idaho. In 1880 more than a hundred thousand Chinese men and three thousand Chinese women were living in the western United States.

Indian entrepreneurs were attracted by the burgeoning commerce of Southeast Asia, though not in quite so large numbers as Chinese. Indian migrants also moved outside Asia, especially to areas under British control. The bulk of Indian emigrants were **indentured laborers,** recruited under contract. The rise of indentured labor from Asia was a direct result of the outlawing of the African slave trade in the early nineteenth century. Sugar plantations in the Caribbean and elsewhere needed new sources of workers. In the British colonies, planters discovered that they could recruit Indian laborers to replace blacks. By 1870 more than half a million Indians had migrated to Mauritius (in the southern Indian Ocean, east of Madagascar) and to the British

indentured laborers *Laborers who in exchange for passage agreed to work for a number of years, specified in a contract.*

Caribbean, especially Trinidad. After the French abolished slavery in 1848, they recruited workers from India as well, with nearly eighty thousand Indians making the trip to the French Caribbean over the next half century. Later in the century, many Indians emigrated to British colonies in Africa, the largest numbers to South Africa. Indentured Indian laborers built the railroad in East Africa. Malaya, Singapore, and Fiji also received many emigrants from India.

Indentured laborers secured as substitutes for slaves were often treated little better than slaves, both on the ships that delivered them and on the plantations and in the mines where they worked. After abuses of this sort were exposed, the Indian government established regulations stipulating a maximum indenture period of five years, after which the migrant would be entitled to passage home. Even though government "protectors" were appointed at the ports of embarkation, exploitation of indentured workers continued largely unchecked. Few of the indentured workers were women, so the community failed to reproduce itself, and emigration had to be continued to maintain the workforce. Still, many of the migrants stayed on after their indenture.

In areas outside the British Empire, China offered the largest supply of ready labor. Starting in the 1840s, contractors arrived at Chinese ports to recruit labor for plantations and mines in Cuba, Peru, Hawai'i, Sumatra, and elsewhere. In the 1840s, for example, the Spanish government actively recruited Chinese laborers for the plantations of Cuba. They came under eight-year contracts, were paid about twenty-five cents a day, and were fed potatoes and salted beef. Between 1853 and 1873 more than 130,000 Chinese laborers went to Cuba, the majority spending their lives as virtual slaves.

Chinese laborers did not have the British government to protect them and seem to have suffered even more than Indian workers. Some of the worst abuses were in Peru, where nearly 100,000 Chinese had arrived by 1875, lured by promoters who promised them easy riches. Instead, they were set to laying railroad tracks or working on cotton plantations or in dangerous guano pits. Those who tried to flee were forced to work in chains.

India and China sent more people abroad than any other Asian countries during this period, but they were not alone. As Japan started to industrialize, its cities could not absorb all those forced off the farms, and people began emigrating in significant numbers, many to Hawai'i and later to South America. Emigration from the Philippines also was substantial, especially after it became a U.S. territory in 1898.

Asian migration to the United States, Canada, and Australia—the primary destinations of European emigrants—would undoubtedly have been greater if it had not been so vigorously resisted by the white settlers in those regions. On the West Coast of the United States, friction between Chinese and white settlers was fed by racist rhetoric that depicted Chinese as opium-smoking heathens. In 1882 Chinese were barred from becoming American citizens, and the immigration of Chinese laborers was suspended. In 1888 President Grover Cleveland declared the Chinese "impossible of assimilation with our people, and dangerous to our peace and welfare."[8]

Most of the Asian migrants discussed so far were illiterate peasants or business people, not members of the traditional educated elites. By the beginning of the twentieth century, however, another group of Asians was going abroad in significant numbers: students. Indians and others in the British colonies usually went to Britain, Vietnamese and others in the French colonies to France, and so on. Chinese eager to master modern learning most commonly went to Japan, but others went to Europe and the United States, as did Japanese students. Most of these students traveled abroad to learn about Western science, law, and government in the hope of strengthening their own countries. On their return they contributed enormously to the intellectual life of their societies, increasing understanding of the modern Western world but also becoming the most vocal advocates of overthrowing the old order and driving out the colonial masters.

Primary Source: Memorandum to Lord Selborne, High Commissioner of Transvaal
An Indian in Transvaal answers criticisms of Indian merchants made by a white merchants' group, the Anti-Asiatic Vigilance Society.

Chapter Summary

Key Terms

Great Mutiny/Great Revolt
Empress of India
Indian Civil Service
Indian National Congress
Java War
Culture System
Nguyen Dynasty
French Indochina
encomienda system
Opium War
Treaty of Nanjing
extraterritoriality
concessions
Taiping Rebellion
"self-strengthening"
Sino-Japanese War
Boxers
1911 Revolution
gunboat diplomacy
Meiji Restoration
Meiji Oligarchs
"strong army, rich nation"
"civilization and
  enlightenment"
Russo-Japanese War
indentured laborers

To assess your mastery of this chapter, go to
bedfordstmartins.com/mckayworld

• In what ways did India change as a consequence of British rule?

In the nineteenth century, Britain extended its rule to all of India, though often the British ruled indirectly, through local princes. Britain brought many modern advances to India, such as railroads, schools, and hospitals. Slavery was outlawed, as was widow suicide and infanticide. Resistance to British rule took several forms. In 1857 Indian soldiers in the employ of the British rose in a huge revolt, which was put down only at huge cost. Indians who received English educations turned English ideas of liberty and representative rule against the British and founded the Indian National Congress, which called for Indian independence.

• Why were some Southeast Asian societies reduced to colonies and others not?

By the end of the nineteenth century, most of Southeast Asia, from Burma to the Philippines, had been made colonies of Western powers, which developed them as exporters of agricultural products or raw materials including timber, rubber, tin, sugar, tea, cotton, and jute. The principal exception was Siam (Thailand), whose king was able to play the English and French off against each other and institute centralizing reforms. In the Philippines, more than three centuries of Spanish rule came to an end, but the United States took over control.

• Was China's decline in the nineteenth century due more to internal problems or Western imperialism?

In the nineteenth century China faced unprecedented population pressure, popular revolts, and the aggression of the Western powers. The government's efforts to suppress the opium trade led to military confrontation with Britain and numerous concessions that opened China to trade on Britain's terms. Uprisings in several parts of the country reflected worsening economic situations and proved very difficult to suppress. Further humiliations by the Western powers led to concerted efforts to modernize the military and learn other secrets of Western success, but China never quite caught up. The dynasty, humiliated by its defeat by Japan in 1895 and the occupation of Beijing by foreign powers in 1900, finally was overthrown in 1911.

• How was Japan able to quickly master the challenges posed by the West?

Japan was the one Asian country to quickly transform itself when confronted by the military strength of the West. It did this by overhauling its power structure. The Meiji reformers deprived the samurai of their privileges, wrote a constitution, instituted universal education, and created a modern army. At the same time they guided Japan toward rapid industrialization. By the early twentieth century Japan had become an imperialist power itself with colonies in Korea and Japan.

• **Why did people move much more in this period, and where did they go?**

The rapid pace of political and economic change in the nineteenth century led to people moving across national borders much more frequently than before. Major cities in Asia developed expatriate communities of Westerners. Asian students traveled to foreign countries, including Japan, to continue their educations. And millions more left in search of work. With the end of the African slave trade, labor recruiters from the Americas and elsewhere went to India and China to secure labor on indentured contracts. In other cases, ambitious young men who heard of gold strikes or other chances to get rich funded their own travels. As a consequence, Asian diasporas formed in many parts of the world, with the majority in Asia itself, especially Southeast Asia.

Suggested Reading

Bayly, C. A. *Indian Society and the Making of the British Empire.* 1990. A synthesis of recent research that provides a complex portrait of the interaction of Indian society and British colonial administration.

Bose, Sugata, and Ayesha Jalal. *Modern South Asia: History, Culture, Political Economy.* 1998. Incorporates recent scholarship with postcolonial perspective in a wide-ranging study.

Duus, Peter. *The Abacus and the Sword: The Japanese Penetration of Korea, 1895–1910.* 1995. Analyzes the interplay of business interests (the abacus) and military interests (the sword) in Japan's push for colonial possessions.

Fairbank, John King, and Merle Goldman. *China: A New History,* 2d ed. 2006. A treatment of China's experiences in the nineteenth century that is rich in interesting detail.

Hane, Mikiso. *Peasants, Rebels, Women and Outcastes: The Underside of Modern Japan,* 2d ed. 2003. Draws on wide-ranging sources to provide a fuller picture of Japanese history.

Irokawa, Daiichi. *The Culture of the Meiji Period.* 1988. Makes excellent use of letters, diaries, and songs to probe changes in the ways ordinary people thought during a crucial period of political change.

Masselos, Jim. *Indian Nationalism: A History,* 5th ed. 2004. A detailed account of the political movement for independence in nineteenth- and twentieth-century India.

Pruitt, Ida. *A Daughter of Han: The Autobiography of a Chinese Working Woman.* 1967. A highly revealing glimpse of Chinese society fashioned by journalist Ida Pruitt in the 1930s based on what a Chinese woman born in 1867 told Pruitt of her life.

Spence, Jonathan. *God's Chinese Son.* 1997. Tells the story of the Taipings as much as possible from their own perspective.

Steinberg, David Joel, ed. *In Search of Southeast Asia: A Modern History,* rev. ed. 1987. An impressive work on Southeast Asia by seven specialists.

Walthall, Anne. *Japan: A Cultural, Social, and Political History.* 2006. A concise overview with good coverage of local society and popular culture.

Notes

1. Quoted in S. Wolpert, *A New History of India* (New York: Oxford University Press, 1993), p. 215.
2. Quoted in K. M. Panikkar, *Asia and Western Dominance: A Survey of the Vasco da Gama Epoch of Asian History* (London: George Allen & Unwin, 1959), p. 116.
3. Quoted in D. J. Steinberg, ed., *In Search of Southeast Asia: A Modern History,* rev. ed. (Honolulu: University of Hawaii Press, 1987), p. 129.
4. Ssu-yu Teng and J. K. Fairbank, *China's Response to the West: A Documentary Survey* (New York: Atheneum, 1971), p. 26.
5. Ibid., p. 76, modified.
6. Quoted ibid., p. 289.
7. R. Tsunoda, W. T. de Bary, and D. Keene, eds., *Sources of Japanese Tradition,* vol. 2 (New York: Columbia University Press, 1964), p. 137.
8. Quoted in J. D. Spence, *The Search for Modern China* (New York: W. W. Norton, 1990), p. 215.

Listening to the
PAST

Escape from Asia

Fukuzawa Yukichi was one of the most prominent intellectuals and promoters of westernization in Meiji Japan. His views on domestic policy were decidedly liberal, but he took a hard-line approach to foreign affairs. His ruthless criticism of Korea and China, published on March 16, 1885, can be read as inviting colonialism. In 1895, ten years after writing this call to action, he rejoiced at Japan's victory over China in their conflict over Korea.

Civilization is like an epidemic of measles. The current measles in Tokyo, which has advanced eastwards from Nagasaki in western Japan, seems to have begun to claim more victims with the arrival of springtime. Will we be able now to find a means of checking this epidemic? It is obvious that we have no way to do so. We cannot put up effective resistance, even against an epidemic that carries with it only harm; much less against civilization, which is always accompanied by both harm and good, but by more good than harm.

Though our land of Japan is situated on the Eastern edge of Asia, the spirit of its people has already shaken off the backwardness of Asia to accept the civilization of the West. Unfortunately, however, we have two neighboring countries, one being called China, the other called Korea. The people of these two countries are no different from us Japanese people in having been brought up since olden times in the Asian culture and customs, and yet, whether because they are of another racial origin, or because, while similar in culture and customs, differ from us in the main lines of their traditional education, a comparison of the three countries, Japan, China, and Korea, reveals that the latter two resemble each other more closely than they do Japan. The people of those two countries do not know how to go about reforming and making progress, whether individually or as a country. It is not that they have not seen or heard of civilized things in the present world of facile communication; yet what their eyes and ears perceive have failed to stimulate their minds, and their emotional attachment to ancient

manners and customs has changed little for the past hundreds and thousands of years. In this lively theater of civilization, where things change daily, they still speak of education in terms of Confucianism, cite humanity, justice, civility, and wisdom as their principles of school education, are completely obsessed only with outward appearance, are in reality not only ignorant of truths and principles but so extreme in their cruelty and shamelessness that for them morality is completely non-existent, and yet are as arrogant as if they never gave a thought to self-examination.

In our view, these countries have no likelihood of maintaining their independence in the current tide of civilization's eastward advance. Let there not be the slightest doubt that, unless they are fortunate enough to have motivated men appear in their lands who, as a first step to improve the condition of their countries will plan such a great enterprise of overall reform of their governments as our Restoration was, and succeed in altering their people's minds through political reforms, those countries will meet their doom in but a few years, with their territories divided among the civilized countries of the world. The reason is that China and Korea, confronted by an epidemic of civilization comparable to measles, are impossibly trying to ward it off, despite its inevitability, by shutting themselves up in a room, with the result being that they are cutting off their supply of fresh air and asphyxiating themselves. Though mutual help between neighboring countries has been likened to the relationship between the lips and the teeth, China and Korea of today cannot be of any assistance at all to our country of Japan.

Civilized western man is not without a tendency to regard all three countries as identical because of their geographic proximity and to apply his evaluation of China and Korea to Japan also. For example, when he finds that the governments of China and Korea are old-fashioned autocracies without abiding laws, the western man will suppose Japan too to be a lawless country. When he finds that the gentlemen of China and Korea are too deeply infatuated to know what science is, the western scholar will think that Japan too is a land of Yin-Yang and the Five Elements. When the Chinese display their servility and shamelessness, they obscure the chivalrous spirit of the Japanese. When the Koreans employ cruel means of physical punishment, the Japanese too are surmised to be just as inhuman. Such examples are too numerous to count. This may be compared to the case in which most of those in a string of houses within a village or town are foolish, lawless, cruel, and inhuman; an occasional family that heeds what is just and right will be eclipsed by the other's evil and its virtue will never be noticed. It is indeed not infrequent that something similar happens in our foreign relations and indirectly interferes with them. This should be regarded a great misfortune for our country of Japan.

To plan our course now, therefore, our country cannot afford to wait for the enlightenment of our neighbors and to cooperate in building Asia up. Rather, we should leave their ranks to join the camp of the civilized countries of the West. Even when dealing with China and Korea, we need not have special scruples simply because they are our neighbors, but should behave toward them as the westerners do. One who befriends an evil person cannot avoid being involved in his notoriety. In spirit, then, we break with our evil friends of Eastern Asia.

Fukuzawa Yukichi. *(Fukuzawa Memorial Center for Modern Japanese Studies, Keio University)*

Questions for Analysis

1. What does Fukuzawa mean by "civilization"?

2. How does Fukuzawa's justification of colonialism compare to Europeans' justification of the same period?

Source: Centre for East Asian Cultural Studies, comp., *Meiji Japan Through Contemporary Sources,* Vol. 3, 1869–1894 (Tokyo: Centre for East Asian Cultural Studies, 1972), pp. 129–133, modified.

Portrait of Skikellany. The clothing worn by this important Oneida Indian of upstate New York identifies him as a member of the Northeast Woodlands Indians. *(Unknown artist, American, Portrait of a Native American Man of the Northeast Woodlands. Philadelphia Museum of Art, The Collection of Edgar William Bernice Chrysler Garbisch, 1966 [1966-219-3])*

chapter

26 NATION BUILDING IN THE WESTERN HEMISPHERE AND AUSTRALIA

Chapter Preview

Latin America (1800–1929)
• *Why and how did the Spanish and Portuguese colonies of North and South America shake off European domination and develop into national states?*

The United States (1789–1929)
• *How does nation building in the United States look from a world history perspective?*

Canada, from French Colony to Nation
• *What geographical, economic, and political conditions shaped the development of Canada?*

Australia, from Penal Colony to Nation
• *What circumstances shaped the development of Australia?*

The New Countries in Comparative Perspective
• *How and why did the new countries treated in this chapter develop differently?*

n the Western Hemisphere and in Australia, as in Europe, the nineteenth century was a period of nation building and industrial and commercial growth. Unlike in Europe, the century was also a time of geographic expansion and large-scale in-migration.

At the end of the eighteenth century, Canada and the countries of South America remained colonies. Their European mother countries looked on the democratic experiment of the infant United States with suspicion and scorn. The island continent of Australia, remote from Europe and economically undeveloped, served as a dumping ground for English criminals. The nineteenth century brought many challenges—including revolutions, civil wars, and foreign invasions. In some countries abolishing slavery was achieved with great difficulty. Yet by 1914 all of the countries were not only politically independent but also stronger and richer than they had been in 1800.

Many issues cross-cut all the histories of these countries in the long nineteenth century—nation building, nationalism, urbanization, racism, regional separatism, new technologies, new lands to open, new trading patterns, and new constitutional governments, to name just a few. Yet the outcomes by 1914 were strikingly different. The United States had become a major industrial power and a stable democracy with a standard of living comparable to western Europe. Canada and Australia also had stable democratic governments and high standards of living, but their economies remained predominantly agricultural. Most of the countries of Latin America suffered political instability, and their economies did not fare as well in the emerging world trade system.

LATIN AMERICA (1800–1929)

Why and how did the Spanish and Portuguese colonies of North and South America shake off European domination and develop into national states?

In 1800 the Spanish Empire in the Western Hemisphere stretched from the head-waters of the Mississippi River in present-day Minnesota to the tip of Cape Horn in the Antarctic (see Map 26.1). In addition to large regions of South America, the Spanish Empire included large parts of the present-day United States, including California. Mexico's silver mines were the richest in the world, and Mexico City had a larger population than any city in Spain. Spain believed that the great wealth of the Americas existed for its benefit, and Spanish policies fostered bitterness and the desire for independence in the colonies. Between 1806 and 1825, the Spanish colonies in Latin America were convulsed by upheavals that ultimately resulted in their separation from Spain. Until 1898 Spain did, however, retain its colonies in the Caribbean: Cuba and Puerto Rico.

The **Creoles**—people of Spanish descent born in America—resented the economic and political dominance of the **peninsulares,** as the colonial officials and other natives of Spain or Portugal were called. In 1800 there were about thirty thousand peninsulares and 3.5 million Creoles. Peninsulares controlled the rich export-import trade, intercolonial trade, and mining industries. The Creoles wanted to free themselves from Spain and Portugal and also to supplant the peninsulares as the ruling class. They had little interest in improving the lot of the Indians or the *mestizos* of mixed Spanish and Indian background and *mulattos* of mixed Spanish and African heritage.

Over the course of the nineteenth century, the countries of Latin America developed into national states. The predominant factors in this evolution were the heritage of colonial exploitation, a neocolonial economic structure, massive emigration from Europe and Asia, and the fusion of Amerindian, Caucasian, African, and Asian peoples.

The Origins of the Revolutions

The Latin American movements for independence grew out of recent colonial grievances. By the eighteenth century, the Spanish colonies had become self-sufficient producers of foodstuffs, wine, textiles, and consumer goods. What was not produced domestically was secured through a healthy intercolonial trade. In Peru, for example, domestic agriculture supported the large mining settlements, and the colony did not have to import food. Craft workshops owned by the state or by private individuals produced consumer goods for the working class; what was not manufactured locally was bought from Mexico and transported by the Peruvian merchant marine. By 1700 Mexico and Peru were sending shrinking percentages of their revenues to Spain and retaining more for public works, defense, and administration.

Creoles *People of Spanish descent born in America.*

peninsulares *A term for natives of Spain or Portugal.*

● **Don Juan Joachin Gutierrez Altamirano Velasco, ca. 1752** In this painting by Miguel Cabrera, the pleated cuffs on Velasco's shirt, the richly embroidered and very expensive coat, the knee breeches, the tricorn hat, and the coat of arms on the wall all attest to the proud status of this member of the peninsulares, the most powerful element in colonial Mexican society. *(Miguel Cabrera, Mexican, 1695–1768, oil on canvas, 81⁵⁄₁₆ x 53½. Brooklyn Museum of Art, Museum Collection Fund, and the Dick S. Ramsay Fund 52.166.1)*

Spain's humiliating defeat in the War of the Spanish Succession (1701–1713) prompted demands for sweeping reform of all of Spain's institutions, including colonial policies and practices. To improve administrative efficiency, the enlightened monarch Charles III (r. 1759–1788) carved the region of modern Colombia, Venezuela, and Ecuador out of the vast viceroyalty of Peru; it became the new viceroyalty of New Granada with its capital at Bogotá. The Crown also created the viceroyalty of Rio de la Plata (present-day Argentina) with its capital at Buenos Aires (see Map 26.1). Far more momentous was Charles III's radical overhaul of colonial trade policies to enable Spain to compete with Great Britain and Holland in the great eighteenth-century struggle for empire. The Spanish crown intended the colonies to serve as sources of raw materials and as markets for Spanish manufactured goods. Charles III's free-trade policies cut duties and restrictions drastically for Spanish merchants. In Latin America, these actions stimulated the production of crops in demand in Europe: coffee in Venezuela; sugar in the Caribbean; hides, leather, and salted beef in the Rio de la Plata viceroyalty. The volume of Spain's trade with the colonies soared, possibly as much as 700 percent between 1778 and 1788.[1]

Colonial manufacturing, which had been growing steadily, suffered severely. Colonial textiles, china, and wine, for example, could not compete with cheap Spanish products. For one thing, Latin American free laborers were paid more than European workers in the eighteenth century; this disparity helps explain the great numbers of immigrants to the colonies. Also, intercolonial transportation costs were higher than transatlantic costs. In the Rio de la Plata region, for example, heavy export taxes and light import duties shattered the wine industry. Geographical obstacles—mountains, deserts, jungles, and inadequate natural harbors—also frustrated colonial efforts to promote economic integration.

After 1789 the French Revolution and Napoleonic wars isolated Spain from Latin America. Foreign traders, especially from the United States, swarmed into Spanish-American ports. In 1796 the Madrid government lifted the restrictions against neutrals trading with the colonies, thus acknowledging Spain's inability to supply the colonies with needed goods and markets.

At the end of the eighteenth century, colonists also complained bitterly that only peninsulares were appointed to the colonies' highest judicial bodies and to other positions in the colonial governments. From 1751 to 1775, only 13 percent of appointees to the judicial bodies were Creoles.[2] According to the nineteenth-century Mexican statesman and historian Lucas Alamán (1792–1853),

This preference shown to Spaniards in political offices and ecclesiastical benefices has been the principal cause of the rivalry between the two classes; add to this the fact that Europeans possessed great wealth, which although it may have been the just reward of

Chronology

1770   Cook lands in Australia and claims land for British crown

1774   Quebec Act grants religious freedom to French Canadians

1778–1788   Height of Spain's trade with colonies

1780–1781   Tupac Amaru II leads rebellion in Peru

1786   British government establishes a penal colony at Botany Bay, Australia

1791   Constitution Act in Canada

1803   United States purchases Louisiana Territory from France

1804   Haiti achieves independence from France

1806–1825   Wars of independence in Latin America

1845   First use of term *manifest destiny* in United States; Texas and Florida admitted into United States

1861–1865   U.S. Civil War

1865–1877   U.S. Reconstruction

1867   Dominion of Canada formed

1883–1894   Mexican land laws put most land into the hands of a few individuals

1898   Spanish-American War

1901   Commonwealth of Australia formed

1904   United States takes control of Panama Canal

1914–1918   World War I

NEW FRANCE
(Conquered by England, 1760)

Mississippi R.

ENGLISH COLONIES
(Independence declared, 1776)

40°W

40°N

Effective frontier
of Spanish settlement

Silver
Silver **COAHUILA**

Rio Grande

FLORIDA
(Ceded to England, 1763–1783)

Gulf of Mexico

A T L A N T I C
O C E A N

Sugar cane
Beef
Tobacco

VICEROYALTY OF NEW SPAIN (1535)

BAJIO LEÓN

Guadalajara
✕ Zacatecas
✕ Guanajuato

Havana

HAITI [SAINT-DOMINGUE]
(Ceded to France, 1697)

Mexico City
Silver
Veracruz

Sugar cane
Indigo

Sugar cane

Beef

20°N

Cacao

BRITISH HONDURAS

Sugar cane
Cochineal

Guatemala

Silver

JAMAICA
(Conquered by England, 1655)

SANTO DOMINGO

PUERTO RICO

Sugar cane

Sugar cane

Caribbean Sea

Cochineal
Cacao
Indigo

Sugar cane

N

Pearls

Caracas
Cacao

GUIANA

Gold

Magdalena R.

Orinoco R.

Bogotá

VICEROYALTY OF NEW GRANADA
(Separated from Viceroyalty of Peru, 1717, 1739)

Equator 0°

Amazon R.

Quito

Forest
products

VICEROYALTY OF PERU
(1590s)

Sugar cane

P A C I F I C
O C E A N

Lima

Cuzco

VICEROYALTY OF BRAZIL
(1720)

Sugar
cane
Pernambuco

Sugar
cane
Salvador

Cacao

A
N
D
E
S

Sugar
cane

La Paz

Chuquisaca
(La Plata; Sucre)

Potosí

Diamonds
Gold

Rio de Janeiro
(Capital, 1763)

20°S

Yerba
Tobacco

São Paulo

Paraná R.

VICEROYALTY OF LA PLATA
(Separated from Viceroyalty of Peru, 1776)

Wheat

AUDIENCIA OF CHILE
(Retained by Viceroyalty of Peru, 1776)

Santiago

Beef and
hides

Buenos Aires

Montevideo

0   500   1,000 Km.

0   500   1,000 Mi.

Beef and
hides

Claimed but not
settled by Spain

Islas Malvinas
(Falkland Islands)

Cape Horn

80°W

60°W

Spanish colonies

Viceroyalty of New Spain

Viceroyalty of New Granada

Viceroyalty of Peru and Audiencia of Chile

Viceroyalty of Rio de la Plata

Portuguese colonies

Viceroyalty of Brazil

✕ Silver mine

MAP 26.1 **Latin America Before Independence** Consider the factors that led to the boundaries of the various Spanish and Portuguese colonies in North and South America.

effort and industry, excited the envy of Americans and was considered as so much usurpation from them; consider that for all these reasons the Spaniards had obtained a decided preponderance over those born in the country; and it will not be difficult to explain the increasing jealousy and rivalry between the two groups which culminated in hatred and enmity.[3]

Madrid's tax reforms also aggravated discontent. Like Great Britain, Spain believed its colonies should bear some of the costs of their own defense. Accordingly, Madrid raised the prices of its monopoly products, tobacco and liquor, and increased sales taxes on many items. As in the thirteen North American colonies a decade earlier, protest movements in Latin America claimed that the colonies were being unfairly taxed.

Other burdens fell on the Indians, many of whom were still subject to the *mit'a* and the *repartimiento*. The law of repartimiento required Indians to buy goods solely from local tax collectors. *Mit'a* means a turn or rotation. The practice was that every seventh household in the region between Huancavelica and Potosí in the Andes took a turn working in the silver mines, with the duration of service varying. Some historians have called this forced labor. But the Indians took their wives and other family members, who pilfered on the side, usually were not caught, and often made tidy incomes for themselves.

The racial complexion of Latin American societies is one of the most complicated in the world. Because few European women immigrated to the colonies, Spanish men formed relationships with Indian and African women. African men deprived of black women sought Indian women. The result was a population composed of every possible combination of Indian, Spanish, and African blood.

Demographers estimate that Indians still accounted for between 60 and 75 percent of the population of Latin America at the end of the colonial period, in spite of the tremendous population losses caused by the introduction of diseases in the sixteenth and seventeenth centuries. The colonies that became Peru and Bolivia had Indian majorities; the regions that became Argentina and Chile had European majorities. Indians and black slaves toiled in the silver and gold mines of Mexico, Colombia, and Peru; in the wheat fields of Chile; in the humid, mosquito-ridden cane-brakes of Mexico and the Caribbean; and in the diamond mines and coffee and sugar plantations of Brazil. Almost 40 percent of all slaves shipped from Africa went to the Caribbean, where the white elite formed a tiny minority.

Spanish theories of racial purity rejected people of mixed blood, particularly those of African descent. Peninsulares and Creoles reinforced their privileged status by showing contempt for people who were not white. Moreover, owners of mines, plantations, and factories had a vested interest in keeping blacks and Indians in servile positions. Nevertheless, nonwhites in Latin America did experience some social mobility in the colonial period, certainly more than nonwhites in North America experienced. A few mulattos rose in the army, some as high as the rank of colonel. The army and the church seem to have offered the greatest opportunities for social mobility. Many black slaves gained their freedom by fleeing to the jungles or mountains, where they established self-governing communities. Around the year 1800, Venezuela counted 2,400 fugitive slaves in a total population of 87,000.

For decades the Enlightenment ideas of Voltaire, Rousseau, and Montesquieu had been trickling into Latin America. North American ships calling at South American ports introduced the subversive writings of Thomas Paine and Thomas Jefferson. In 1794 the Colombian Antonio Nariño translated and published the French Declaration of the Rights of Man and the Citizen (Spanish authorities sentenced him to ten years in an African prison, but he lived to become the father of Colombian independence). By 1800 the Creole elite throughout Latin America was familiar with liberal Enlightenment political thought, and the Creoles wanted the "rights of man" extended to themselves.

**Primary Source:
The Problems of the Indian and the Problem of the Land**
Read a Marxist's analysis of the oppression of Peru's Indians, and his prescription for political change.

Resistance and Rebellion

The middle years of the eighteenth century witnessed frequent Andean Indian rebellions against the Spaniards' harsh exploitation. Five uprisings occurred in the 1740s, eleven in the 1750s, twenty in the 1760s, and twenty in the 1770s. In 1780, under the leadership of a descendant of the Inca rulers who took the name Tupac Amaru II, a massive insurrection exploded. Indian chieftains from the Cuzco region gathered a powerful force of Indians and people of mixed race. Rebellion swept across highland Peru, where many Spanish officials were executed. Before peace was restored two years later, a hundred thousand people lay dead, and vast amounts of property were destroyed. Although Spanish rule was not ended, the government abolished the repartimiento system and established assemblies in Cuzco. The revolts also raised elite fears of racial and class warfare.

As news of the rebellion of Tupac Amaru II trickled northward, it helped stimulate the Comunero Revolution in the New Granada viceroyalty (see Map 26.2). An Indian peasant army commanded by Creole captains marched on Bogotá. Dispersed by the government that made promises it did not intend to keep, the revolt in the end did little to improve the Indians' lives.

Much more than the Peruvian and Colombian revolts, the successful revolution led by Toussaint L'Ouverture (ca. 1744–1803) in Haiti aroused elite fears of black revolt and class warfare (see pages 626–627 and Map 21.1). In the seventeenth century Haiti, the western third of the island of Hispaniola, offered a haven for French and English pirates. By the end of the century Spain ceded Haiti to France and in the eighteenth century French settlers established sugar plantations there and imported African slaves to work them. Haiti soon became France's most prosperous colony and the world's chief producer of sugar and coffee.

In Haiti the French maintained a rigid social stratification of French, Creoles, freed blacks, and black slaves. When the Creoles refused the mulattos' representation in the local assemblies and in the French National Assembly of 1789, the mulattos revolted. Blacks formed guerrilla bands under the self-educated freed slave Toussaint L'Ouverture. In 1793, as part of their campaign against Napoleon, the British invaded Haiti and took all of its coastal cities. L'Ouverture, with his widespread support, soon retook the cities. In 1801 he declared himself emperor of the entire island of Hispaniola, abolished slavery, and instituted reforms. Napoleon dispatched a large army to restore French control, but the French could not take the interior. The U.S. president Thomas Jefferson, fearing that the French would use the island to invade Louisiana, aided the rebels. Weakened by yellow fever, the French withdrew. L'Ouverture negotiated peace with France, but French officials

● **Toussaint L'Ouverture, Haitian Patriot** The freed slave Toussaint L'Ouverture joined the slave rebellion in 1791 and quickly became its leader and organizing genius. A man of enormous strength and determination, L'Ouverture devoted his life to freedom for his people. He is shown here negotiating with French officials during the war with Britain. *(Getty Images)*

MAP 26.2 **Latin America in 1830** By 1830 almost all of Central America, South America, and the Caribbean islands had won independence. Note that the many nations that now make up Central America were unified when they first won independence from Mexico. Similarly, modern Venezuela, Colombia, and Ecuador were still joined in Gran Colombia.

tricked him and took him to France, where he died in prison. Still, in 1804 Haiti became the second nation (after the United States) in the Western Hemisphere to achieve independence. The revolt was also the first successful uprising of a non-European people against a colonial power, and it sent waves of fear through the upper classes in both Europe and Latin America.

Independence

In 1808 Napoleon Bonaparte deposed the Spanish king Ferdinand VII and placed his own brother on the Spanish throne (see page 635). Since everything in Spanish America was done in the name of the king, the Creoles in Latin America argued that the removal of the legitimate king shifted sovereignty to the people—that is, to themselves.

The Creoles who led the various movements for independence did not intend a radical redistribution of property or reconstruction of society. They merely rejected the authority of the Spanish crown. A distinguished scholar has described the movement for independence as

a prolonged, confused, and in many ways contradictory movement. In Mexico it began as a popular social movement and ended many years later as a conservative uprising against a liberal Spanish constitution. In Venezuela it came to be a war unto the death; in other places it was a war between a small Creole minority and the Spanish authorities. It was not an organized movement with a central revolutionary directorate. It had no Continental Congress. . . . If there was no central direction, no centrally recognized leadership, likewise there was no formally accepted political doctrine.[4]

The great hero of the movement for independence was Simón Bolívar (1783–1830), a very able general who is considered the Latin American George Washington. (See the feature "Listening to the Past: Simón Bolívar's Speculation on Latin America" on pages 812–813.) Bolívar's victories over the royalist armies won him the presidency of Gran (Greater) Colombia in 1819. He dreamed of a continental union and in 1826 summoned a conference of the American republics at Panama. The meeting achieved little. The territories of Gran Colombia splintered, and a sadly disillusioned Bolívar went into exile, saying, "America is ungovernable." Under Spain, Mexico had been united with Central America as the Viceroyalty of New Spain. In the 1830s, after independence, regional separatism resulted in its breakup into five separate countries. In South America, too, the old colonies were divided, not amalgamated. The failure of Pan-Americanism isolated individual countries, prevented collective action, and later paved the way for the political and economic intrusion of the United States and other powers.

Brazil followed a different path to independence from Portugal. When Napoleon's troops entered Portugal, the royal family fled to Brazil and made Rio de Janeiro the capital of the Portuguese Empire. The new government immediately lifted the old mercantilist restrictions and opened Brazilian ports to the ships of all friendly nations. The king returned to Portugal in 1821, leaving his son Pedro in Brazil as regent. Under popular pressure, Pedro proclaimed Brazil's independence in 1822, issued a constitution, and even led resistance against Portuguese troops. He accepted the title Emperor Pedro I (r. 1822–1834). Even though Brazil was a monarchy, Creole elites dominated society as they did elsewhere in Latin America. The reign of his successor, Pedro II (r. 1831–1889), witnessed the expansion of the coffee industry, the beginnings of the rubber industry, and massive immigration.

The Latin American wars of independence, over by 1825, differed from the American Revolution in important ways. They lasted much longer, and outside powers provided no help, leaving those involved weary and divided. Many of the peninsulares returned to Europe. Following the example of the United States, the Creole elites

Latin America, ca. 1760–1900

1764–1780	Charles III of Spain's administrative and economic reforms
1781	Comunero Revolution in New Granada
1806–1825	Latin American wars of independence against Spain
1822	Proclamation of Brazil's independence by Portugal
1825–ca. 1870	Political instability in most Latin American nations
1826	Call by Simón Bolívar for Panama conference on Latin American union
ca. 1870–1929	Latin American neocolonialism
1876–1911	Porfirio Díaz's control of Mexico
1880–1914	Massive emigration from Europe and Asia to Latin America
1888	Emancipation of slaves in Brazil; final abolition of slavery in Western Hemisphere
1898	Spanish-American War End of Spanish control over Cuba Transfer of Puerto Rico and the Philippines to the United States

wrote constitutions for their new governments, but the governments created in Latin America excluded much of the population from political participation. To a large degree the local elites took over exploiting the peasantry from the old colonial elites. Small independent farmers of the sort that became common in the United States and Canada did not gain a comparable place in Latin America. The new governments also largely confirmed the wealth and authority of the Roman Catholic Church.

The newly independent nations had difficulty achieving political stability when the wars of independence ended. The Creole leaders of the revolutions had no experience in government, and the wars left a legacy of military, not civilian, leadership. Throughout the continent, idealistic but impractical leaders proclaimed republics governed by representative assemblies. Mexico lost half its territory to the United States between 1836 and 1848, and other countries, too, had difficulty defending themselves from their neighbors.

The wars of liberation disrupted the economic life of most Latin American countries. Mexico and Venezuela in particular lost large percentages of their populations and suffered great destruction of farmland and animals. Even areas that saw relatively little violence, such as Chile and New Granada, experienced a weakening of economic life. Armies were frequently recruited by force, and when the men were demobilized, many did not return home. The consequent population dislocation hurt agriculture and mining. Guerrilla warfare disrupted trade and communications. Forced loans and the seizure of private property for military use ruined many people.

Cuba and Brazil, which had large slave populations, did not free their slaves until 1886 and 1888. Elsewhere, however, independence speeded the abolition of slavery. The destruction of agriculture in countries such as Mexico and Venezuela caused the collapse of the plantation system, and fugitive slaves could not be recaptured. Also, generals on both sides offered slaves their freedom in exchange for military service.

Although the edifice of racism persisted in the nineteenth century, Latin America offered Negroes greater economic and social mobility than did the United States. One reason for the relative racial permeability of Latin America is that the Creole elite in Latin America approved of "whitening"—that is, they viewed race mixture as a civilizing process that diminished and absorbed the dark and "barbarous" blood of

Africans and Indians. In Latin America, light-skinned colored people could rise economically and socially in a way not available to those with darker skins.

In many Latin American countries, generals ruled. In Argentina, Juan Manuel de Rosas (r. 1835–1852) assumed power amid widespread public disorder and ruled as dictator. In Mexico, liberals declared a federal republic, but incessant civil strife led to the rise of the dictator Antonio López de Santa Anna in the mid-nineteenth century. Likewise in Venezuela, strongmen, dictators, and petty aristocratic oligarchs governed from 1830 to 1892. Some countries suffered constant coups d'état; in the course of the century, Bolivia had sixty and Venezuela fifty-two.

On occasion, the ruling generals were charismatic military leaders who were able to attract mass support for their governments. Páez in Venezuela was able to present himself as a patron of the common man and maintain his popularity even though his economic policies favored the elite and he built up a personal fortune. Some, in fact, were of common origins. In Mexico, Benito Juarez, an Indian who had risen from poverty, led efforts to reduce the power of the Catholic Church and later led resistance to the "emperor" imposed by Napoleon III in 1862. He became president and served until his death in 1872.

Neocolonialism

At first, political instability discouraged foreign investment in Latin America's newly independent nations. With the general expansion of world trade after 1870 and the development of stable dictatorships, foreign investors developed Latin America as a source of raw materials and basic commodities to supply industrializing Europe and the United States. Modern business enterprises, often owned by foreign capitalists, led the way. These firms usually specialized in a single product that could be shipped through the growing international network of railroads, ports, and ocean freighters.

In Mexico, for example, North American capital supported the production of hemp, sugar, bananas, and rubber, frequently on American-owned plantations. British and American interests backed the development of tin, copper, and gold mining. By 1911 Mexico had taken third place among the world's oil producers. British financiers built Argentina's railroads, meatpacking industry, and utilities; Chile's copper and nitrate industries (nitrate is used in the production of pharmaceuticals and fertilizers); and Brazil's coffee, cotton, and sugar production. By 1904 Brazil produced 76 percent of the world's coffee.

neocolonialism *A way of referring to the political and economic systems that perpetuated Western economic domination after political independence.*

Thus, by the turn of the century, the Latin American nations were active participants in the international economic order, but foreigners controlled most of their industries and would use force to defend their economic interests. This form of economic domination is often called **neocolonialism**. The United States intervened in Latin American affairs whenever it felt its economic interests threatened. Americans secured control of the Panama Canal in 1904 on their own terms; in 1912 and 1926 U.S. Marines interfered in Nicaragua to bolster conservative governments; and the Marines who were sent to Haiti in 1915 to protect American property stayed until 1934. Another distinctive feature of neocolonialism was that each country's economy revolved around only one or two products: sugar in Cuba, nitrates and copper in Chile, meat in Argentina, coffee in Brazil. A sharp drop in the world market demand for a product could devastate the export sector and with it the nation's economic well-being. The outbreak of the First World War in 1914 drastically reduced exports of Latin American raw materials and imports of European manufactured goods, provoking a general economic crisis.

haciendas *Large landed estates.*

Many of those who worked on the plantations producing export products were Indians or mestizos. In the United States and Canada, Indians were pushed out of the way when their land was taken from them. In Latin America, many more of them were kept in place and incorporated into the social system as subordinated workers, especially on large plantations called **haciendas**.

● **Rivera: Sugar Cane**   Diego Rivera (1886–1957) used art to convey messages of social protest. Here Indians and blacks labor in the sugar-cane fields, while a white man relaxes in a hammock. *(Diego Rivera, Sugar Cane, 1931. Philadelphia Museum of Art, Gift of Mr. and Mrs. Herbert Cameron Morris [1943-46-2])*

The late nineteenth century witnessed ever-greater concentrations of land in ever fewer hands. In places like the Valley of Mexico in southern Mexico, a few large haciendas controlled all the land. Under the dictatorship of General Porfirio Díaz, the Mexican government in 1883 passed a law allowing real estate companies (controlled by Díaz's political cronies) to survey public and "vacant" lands and to retain one-third of the land they surveyed. An 1894 law provided that land could be declared vacant if legal title to it could not be produced. Since few Indians had deeds to the land that their ancestors had worked for centuries, the door swung open to wholesale expropriation of small landowners and entire villages. Indians who dared armed resistance were crushed by government troops and carried off to virtual slave labor. Vast stretches of land came into the hands of private individuals—in one case, 12 million acres. Stripped of their lands, the Indians were an easily exploitable labor supply. Debt peonage became common: landowners paid their laborers not in cash but in vouchers redeemable only at the company store, where high prices and tricky bookkeeping kept the **peons** permanently in debt.

peons   *Low-status laborers*

Although some hacienda owners were indolent and technologically backward, scholars generally believe that most haciendas were efficient enterprises whose owners sought to maximize profits on invested capital. The Sanchez Navarro family of northwestern Mexico, for instance, engaged in a wide variety of agricultural and commercial pursuits, exploiting their lands and resources as fully as possible. With lands about the size of West Virginia, they had vast cattle ranches and sheep runs containing as many as 250,000 sheep, as well as maize, wheat, and cotton fields. Keeping their peons in debt was another way they maximized profits.

● **Business District in Mexico, 1921** Business signs in several languages—such as those here in Spanish, English, and Chinese—indicate the pluralistic, multicultural character of many Latin American cities in the early twentieth century. *(Courtesy of the photographer, C. B. Williams)*

The Impact of Immigration

In 1852 the Argentine political philosopher Juan Bautista Alberdi published *Bases and Points of Departure for Argentine Political Organization,* arguing that the development of his country—and, by extension, all of Latin America—depended on immigration. Indians and blacks, Alberdi maintained, lacked basic skills, and it would take too long to train them. Thus he pressed for massive immigration from the "advanced" countries of northern Europe and the United States. Alberdi's ideas won immediate acceptance and were even incorporated into the Argentine constitution, which declared that "the Federal government will encourage European immigration." Other Latin American countries adopted similar policies promoting immigration.

Europe had plenty of people to send. After 1880, Ireland, Great Britain, Germany, Italy, Spain, and the central European nations experienced greater population growth than their labor markets could absorb. Immigrants from Asia also flowed into South America and the Caribbean islands. For example, in the late nineteenth and early twentieth centuries, large numbers of Japanese arrived in Brazil, most settling in urban areas, especially in São Paulo. By 1920 Brazil had the largest Japanese community in the world outside of Japan. From the Middle East, Lebanese, Turks, and Syrians also entered Brazil. Between 1850 and 1880, 144,000 East Indian laborers went to Trinidad, 39,000 to Jamaica, and smaller numbers to the islands of St. Lucia, Grenada, and St. Vincent as indentured servants under five-year contracts. Perhaps one-third returned to India, but the rest stayed, saved money, and bought small businesses or land. Cuba, the largest of the Caribbean islands (about the size of Pennsylvania), had received 500,000 African slaves between 1808 and 1865. When slavery was abolished in 1886, some of the work in the sugar-cane fields was done by Chinese indentured servants, who followed the same pattern as the South Asian migrants who had gone to Trinidad. Likewise, the abolition of slavery in Mexico led to the arrival of thousands of Chinese bonded servants.

Immigration helped fuel urbanization. Buenos Aires, Rio de Janeiro, Mexico City, Montevideo, Santiago, and Havana also experienced spectacular growth. Portuguese, Italian, French, Chinese, and Japanese immigrants gave an international flavor and a more vigorous tempo to Latin American cities.

By 1914 Buenos Aires had emerged as one of the most cosmopolitan cities in the world, with a population of 3.6 million. As Argentina's political capital, the city housed all its government bureaucracies and agencies. The meatpacking, food-processing, flour-milling, and wool industries were concentrated there as well. Half of all overseas tonnage passed through the city, which was also the heart of the nation's railroad network. Elegant shops near the Plaza de Mayo catered to the expensive tastes of the elite upper classes, who constituted about 5 percent of the population. By contrast, the thousands of immigrants who toiled twelve hours a day, six days a week, on docks and construction sites and in meatpacking plants were crowded into the city's one-room tenements, furnished with a few iron cots, a table and chairs, and maybe an old trunk.

Immigrants' dreams of rapid economic success in the New World often came true. The first generation almost always did manual labor, but its sons often advanced to upper-blue-collar or white-collar jobs. The sons of successful Genoese or Neapolitan immigrants typically imitated the dress, style, and values of the Creole elite.

Immigrants brought wide-ranging skills that helped develop industry and commerce. Italian and Spanish settlers in Argentina stimulated the expansion of the cattle industry and the development of the wheat and shoe industries. In Brazil, Swiss immigrants built the cheese business, Italians gained a leading role in the coffee industry, and Japanese pioneered the development of the cotton industry. In Peru, Italians became influential in banking and the restaurant business, while the French dominated jewelry, dressmaking, and pharmaceuticals. Chinese laborers built the railroads, and in sections of large cities such as Lima, the Chinese came to dominate the ownership of shops and restaurants. European immigrants also brought anarchist and socialist ideas and became involved in union organizing.

The vast majority of migrants were unmarried males; seven out of ten people who landed in Argentina between 1857 and 1924 were single males between thirteen and forty years old. There, as in other South American countries, many of those who stayed sought out Indian or other low-status women, leading to further racial mixing.

Independence per se did little to improve the position of the poor in Latin America. Property changed hands and haciendas expanded, reflecting the concentration of wealth and greater Creole social mobility, often at the expense of the Indians. Spanish and Portuguese merchants who returned to the Iberian Peninsula were replaced by British and U.S. businessmen. Just as the United States waged wars against the Indians (see page 791–792) and pushed its frontier westward, so Brazil, Venezuela, Ecuador, Peru, and Bolivia expanded into the Amazonian frontier at the expense of indigenous peoples. Likewise, Mexico, Chile, and Argentina had their "Indian wars" and frontier expansion. Neocolonialism's modernizing influence on commerce and industry strengthened the position of the elite and allowed it to use capitalistic values and ideals as a shield against demands for fundamental socioeconomic reforms. European styles in art, clothing, housing, and literature became highly popular, particularly among members of the elite as they sought acceptance and approval by their economic masters.

Racial prejudice kept the vast bulk of the South American black population in a wretched socioeconomic position until the Second World War. European immigrants, rather than black plantation workers, gained the urban jobs. In 1893, 71.2 percent of the working population of São Paulo was foreign-born. Blacks continued to work cutting sugar cane and picking coffee.

THE UNITED STATES (1789–1929)

How does nation building in the United States look from a world history perspective?

The victory of the North American colonies and the founding of the United States seemed to validate the Enlightenment idea that a better life on earth was possible. Americans carried over into the nineteenth and twentieth centuries an unbounded optimism about the future. Although most eastern states retained a property or tax-paying qualification for the vote down to 1860, suffrage was gradually expanded to include most adult white males. The movement toward popular democracy accelerated as the young nation, confident of its "manifest destiny," pushed relentlessly across the continent. The industrializing North and the agricultural South came into conflict over extending slavery. The ensuing Civil War cost six hundred thousand American lives—more than any other war the nation has fought. The victory of the North preserved the federal system and strengthened the United States as a nation.

The years between 1865 and 1917 witnessed the building of a major industrial power. Immigrants settled much of the West, put the prairies to the plow, provided the labor to exploit the country's mineral resources, turned small provincial towns into sophisticated centers of ethnic and cultural diversity, and built the railroads that tied the country together. Most of the social and cultural changes seen in western Europe in this period (see Chapter 23)—such as improved sanitation, mass transit, faith in science, and strong identification with the nation—occurred also in the United States.

Manifest Destiny

In an 1845 issue of the *United States Magazine and Democratic Review,* editor John L. O'Sullivan boldly declared that foreign powers were trying to prevent American annexation of Texas in order to impede "the fulfillment of our manifest destiny to overspread the continent allotted by Providence for the free development of our yearly multiplying millions." O'Sullivan was articulating a sentiment prevalent in the United States since early in its history: that God had foreordained the nation to cover the entire continent. After a large-circulation newspaper picked up the phrase **manifest destiny,** it was used on the floor of Congress and soon entered the language as a catchword for and justification of expansion.

manifest destiny *Catchword for the belief that God had foreordained Americans to cover the entire continent.*

When George Washington took office in 1789, fewer than 4 million people inhabited the thirteen states on the eastern seaboard. By the time Abraham Lincoln became the sixteenth president in 1861, the United States stretched across the continent and had 31 million inhabitants.

During the colonial period, pioneers had pushed westward to the Appalachian Mountains. After independence, westward movement accelerated. The eastern states claimed all the land from the Atlantic Ocean to the Mississippi River, but two forces blocked immediate expansion. The Indians, trying to save their lands, allied with the British in Canada to prevent further American encroachment. In 1794, however, Britain agreed to evacuate border forts in the Northwest Territory, roughly the area north of the Ohio River and east of the Mississippi, and thereby end British support for the Indians. A similar treaty with Spain paved the way for southeastern expansion.

Events in Europe and the Caribbean led to a massive increase in American territory. In 1800 Spain ceded the Louisiana Territory—the land between the Mississippi River and the Rocky Mountains—to France. Three years later, Napoleon sold it to the United States for only $12 million. Spain, preoccupied with rebellions in South America, sold the Florida Territory to the U.S. government, and beginning in 1821 American settlers poured into the Mexican territory of Texas, whose soil proved excellent for the production of cotton and sugar. Southern politicians, fearing that Texas would become a refuge for fugitive slaves, pressured President John Tyler to admit Texas to the United States in 1845. The admission of Texas as the twenty-eighth state and Florida as the twenty-seventh state (also in 1845) meant the absorption of large numbers of Hispanic people into the United States. Many of them had lived in those regions since the sixteenth century, long before Anglo immigration.

The acquisition of Texas's 267,339 square miles (France, by comparison, covers 211,200 square miles) whetted American appetites for the rest of the old Spanish Empire in North America. Some expansionists even dreamed of taking Cuba and Central America.

Exploiting Mexico's political instability, President James Polk goaded Mexico into war. Mexico suffered total defeat and in the **Treaty of Guadalupe Hidalgo (1848)** surrendered its remaining claims to Texas, yielded New Mexico and California, and recognized the Rio Grande as the international border. A treaty with Great Britain in 1846 had already recognized the American settlement in the Oregon Territory. The continent had been acquired. Then, in 1898, a revolt in Cuba against an incompetent Spanish administration had consequences beyond "manifest destiny." Inflamed by press reports of Spanish atrocities, public opinion swept the United States into war. The Spanish-American War—the "splendid little war," as Secretary of State John Hay called it—lasted just ten weeks and brought U.S. control over Cuba, the Philippine Islands, and Puerto Rico. The United States had become a colonial power.

The only people who were native to this vast continent fared poorly under manifest destiny. Government officials sometimes manipulated the Indians by gathering a few chiefs, plying them with cheap whiskey, then inducing them to hand over the tribes' hunting grounds. Sometimes officials exploited rivalries among tribes or used bribes. By these methods, William Henry Harrison, superintendent of the Indians of the Northwest Territory and a future president, got some Native Americans to cede 48 million acres (see Map 26.3). He had the full backing of President Jefferson.

Treaty of Guadalupe Hidalgo (1848) *The 1848 treaty between the United States and Mexico in which Mexico ceded large tracts of land to the United States in exchange for 15 million U.S. dollars.*

MAP 26.3 **Indian Cession of Lands to the United States** Forced removal of the Creeks, Cherokees, and Chickasaws to reservations in Oklahoma led to the deaths of thousands of Native Americans on the Trail of Tears, as well as to the destruction of their cultures.

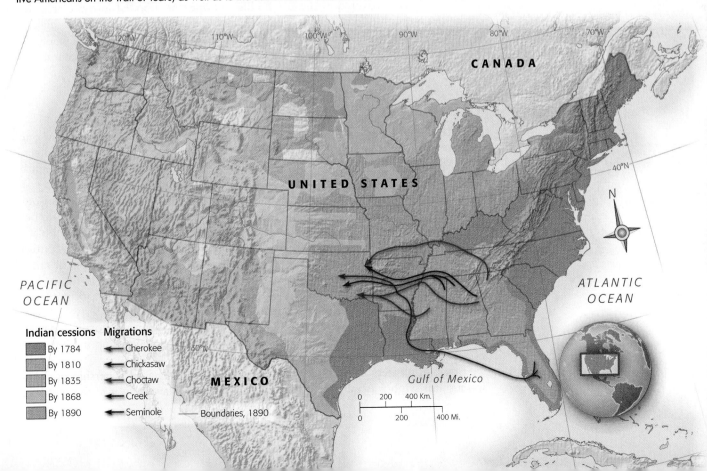

Indian cessions
- By 1784
- By 1810
- By 1835
- By 1868
- By 1890

Migrations
- Cherokee
- Chickasaw
- Choctaw
- Creek
- Seminole
- Boundaries, 1890

PACIFIC OCEAN

CANADA

UNITED STATES

ATLANTIC OCEAN

MEXICO

Gulf of Mexico

0   200   400 Km.
0   200   400 Mi.

The policy of pushing the Indians westward across the Mississippi accelerated during Andrew Jackson's presidency (1829–1837). Thousands of Delawares, Shawnees, and Wyandots, tricked into moving from east of the Mississippi River to reservations west of Missouri, died of cholera and measles during the journey. The survivors found themselves hopelessly in debt for supplies and farming equipment. The state of Georgia, meanwhile, was nibbling away at Cherokee lands, which were theoretically protected by treaty with the U.S. government. Then gold was discovered on the Cherokee lands, and a gold rush took place. The Creek, Cherokee, and other tribes were rounded up, expelled, and sent beyond the western boundaries of Missouri and Arkansas.

The two decades before and after the Civil War saw a steady flow of white settlers westward to the Great Plains, where Indians hunted on horseback using rifles. The U.S. Army, in the name of protecting the migrants, fought the Indians, destroyed their lodges and horses, and slaughtered the buffalo on which they depended for food, shelter, and clothing. The federal government's policy was to confine indigenous people to reservations, where malnutrition and disease took a terrible toll.

Cultural differences aggravated conflict between white and Native Americans. Indians did not think of land in terms of private property; they believed that land, like other resources such as air and water, belonged to everyone, that individuals or groups might hold temporary stewardship over the land but that it should be respected and treasured for future generations. Americans, because they had a commander in chief (the president) who could give orders and expect them to be carried out, assumed that a respected Native American chief could make agreements binding on all tribes. But no chief could command all the Sioux, let alone all the Plains Indians. When a tribe or group of tribes opposed or disregarded a treaty made by a particular chief, the whites then claimed that the Indians as a whole had broken the treaty.

In 1868, after pursuing a policy of total war on the Plains Indians, General W. T. Sherman brokered the Treaty of Fort Laramie. This treaty promised that the United States would close western forts and grant the Sioux and Cheyenne permanent control of their ancestral lands in the Dakotas, the Black Hills, as well as the area between the Platte River and the Bighorn Mountains. A few chiefs signed; many did not. In 1874 gold was discovered in the Black Hills. Prospectors flooded into the area. By 1875 whites outnumbered Indians there. Disaster ensued. (See the feature "Individuals in Society: Crazy Horse.") During the course of the nineteenth century when the number of white residents skyrocketed from 4.3 million to 66.8 million, the number of Indians steadily declined, to a recorded 237,196 in 1900.

Black Slavery in the South

In 1619 Dutch traders brought the first black people to Virginia as prisoners as one solution to the chronic shortage of labor in North America (white indentured servants who worked for a term of years was another solution). In the early eighteenth century, as rice cultivation expanded in the Carolinas and tobacco in Virginia and Maryland, planters demanded more laborers. Between 1720 and 1770, black prisoners poured into the Southern colonies. In South Carolina, they came to outnumber whites by almost two to one. In the decades 1730 through 1760, white fears of black revolts pushed colonial legislatures to pass laws that established tight white control and blacks' legal position as slaves, enshrining the slave system in law. Racist arguments of blacks' supposed inferiority were used to justify slavery.

The American Revolution did not bring liberty to slaves. The framers of the Constitution treated private property as sacrosanct and viewed slaves as property. Antislavery sentiment was growing, however, and states from Delaware north outlawed slavery. In 1809 the United States followed Britain's lead in outlawing the importation of slaves.

For white planters and farmers, slavery proved lucrative, and ownership of slaves was a status symbol as well as a means of social control. Slavery "was at the center of

Crazy Horse

On June 25, 1876, in the valley of the Little Bighorn in southern Montana, Colonel George Armstrong Custer attacked an encampment of Sioux Indians. Custer had been warned that his regiment of 647 men faced a superior force of perhaps 2,500 Sioux warriors; he was specifically ordered not to attack until reinforcements arrived. Nevertheless, Custer recklessly divided his men, sending one group to scout along the left side of the valley while he led troops along the right side. In the ensuing battle Custer and his greatly outnumbered soldiers were surrounded and slaughtered by the Indians under the Sioux leader Crazy Horse (1842?–1877).

Our only verifiable evidence about Crazy Horse derives from two sources: the 1906–1907 interviews by Nebraska judge Eli Ricker of about fifty people (only ten of them Indians) and the 1930–1931 interviews by journalist Eleanor Hinman and Nebraska writer Mari Sandoz of Crazy Horse's lifelong friend, He Dog, a man then in his nineties. In both sets of interviews, most of the questions related to the last four months of Crazy Horse's life, meaning that we know nothing of his first thirty-four years. But an enormous legend has grown up around him, reflecting "a broken people's need to remember and believe in unbroken heroes . . . who remained true to the precepts of their fathers and to the ways of the culture and traditions which bred them."

The Sioux people, one of many Plains Indian tribes, scarcely knew Crazy Horse; they called him "Our Strange Man" and "Our Mystery." Short Buffalo described him as of medium build and height, with hair and complexion lighter than that of other Indians. Legend held him to be a genius at war but a lover of peace, a dreamer and a mystic who spent long periods alone on the plains. He avoided people, especially white men, and detested reservations. His people respected and loved him as much for the charity he showed the poor and oppressed as for his courage in battle.

When the Indians realized that the U.S. government intended to take back the Black Hills (see page 792), they knew that their old ways of life were ending and that they would have to yield to the white men's plans for them (life on reservations) or die opposing them. In the spring of 1876 vast numbers of Indians moved north to an encampment of the Sioux chief Sitting Bull in the region of the Little Bighorn River, creating the last great gathering of native peoples on the Great Plains. The U.S. Army followed.

Crazy Horse refused to be photographed, so this portrait is probably an idealization. *(Corbis)*

Precisely what happened at Little Bighorn we will never know. With at least two thousand horses milling and charging, the battleground would have been a hell of dust and gunsmoke, making visibility very poor. Custer received wounds in the chest and head, either of which would have been fatal. But his head was not scalped nor his body mutilated. Crazy Horse survived; the huge force of Indians melted away on the plains.

Though not a traditional chief, Crazy Horse had about nine hundred followers who looked to him for protection and provision. The long winter of 1876–1877, with bitter cold and little food, wore them down. For their sake, having been promised the army's respect, his own agency, and a buffalo hunt for his people, Crazy Horse laid down his arms at Fort Robinson, Nebraska, in May 1877. He still enjoyed the respect of his people and had moral authority over them. That influence provoked jealousy among other Indians at Fort Robinson. For their part, whites feared that he would become a symbol of resistance and lead another war.

The fort's commander ordered Crazy Horse's arrest. The moment he saw, or smelled, the filthy cells where chained Indians were held, he tried to escape. In a brief melee, his Sioux enemies shouted, "Kill the son of a bitch." A white private, William Gentles, bayoneted him twice, one thrust piercing his kidneys. Crazy Horse fell to the ground, mortally wounded. Receiving no medical attention, he died that night, September 6, 1877.

Questions for Analysis

1. Being such a "loner" all his life, was Crazy Horse an "individual in society"?

2. Why would some Sioux be against Crazy Horse?

Sources: L. McMurtry, *Crazy Horse* (New York: Penguin Books, 1999); J. Keegan, *Fields of Battle: The Wars for North America* (New York: Vintage Books, 1997).

● **Slave Auction, 1850s** In a scene outside a country tavern near a river with a Mississippi-type steamer on it, an auctioneer extols a biracial girl's qualities to a group of planters *(center)*, while another dealer with a whip *(at left)* brutally separates a mother from her children. The picture was intended to send an abolitionist message. *(Carnegie Museum of Art, Pittsburgh. Gift of Mrs. W. Fitch Ingersoll)*

a well-established way of life to which [slave owners] were accustomed and attached, and the disruption or demise of which they feared above all else."[5] Since the possession of slaves brought financial profit *and* conferred social status and prestige, struggling small farmers had a material and psychological interest in maintaining black bondage. Slavery provided the means by which they might rise and the floor beneath which they could not fall.

Between 1820 and 1860, as new lands in the South and West—in Arkansas, Mississippi, Texas, and Louisiana—were put to the production of cotton and sugar, the demand for labor skyrocketed. The upper South—Maryland and Virginia—where decades of tobacco farming had reduced the fertility of the soil, supplied the slaves. Slave traders worked either independently or from firms in Charleston, Natchez, or New Orleans, the largest slave market in the United States. This period witnessed the forced migration of about 650,000 people, in many cases causing the breakup of slave families.

What impact did slavery have on the black family? A study of the entire adult slave population of North Carolina in 1860 has shown that most slave women spent their entire adult lives in settled unions with the same husband. Planters encouraged slave

MAP 26.4 **Slavery in the United States, 1861** Although many issues contributed to the tension between North and South, slavery was the fundamental, enduring force that underlay all others. Lincoln's prediction, "I believe this government cannot endure, permanently half *slave* and half *free*," tragically proved correct.

marriages because large slave families were in their economic interest, especially after the end of the Atlantic slave trade. As one owner put it, "marriage adds to the comfort, happiness, and health of those entering upon it, besides insuring a greater increase."[6] Evidence from all parts of the South reveals that, in spite of illiteracy, separated spouses tried to remain in touch with one another and, once slavery had been abolished, went to enormous lengths to reunite their families. Typically, a slave woman had her first child around the age of nineteen. On the Good Hope plantation in South Carolina, 80 percent of slave couples had at least four children. Almost all women had all their children by one husband, and most children grew to their teens in households with both parents present.

Freed blacks often went north in search of better opportunities. James Forten, a free black man (d. 1842) from Philadelphia, built a large sailmaking business that employed an integrated workforce. He had a reputation as a businessman of integrity and acquired considerable wealth. But most whites of the city refused to accept him as a citizen and subjected him to verbal and physical assaults.[7]

The Civil War

In the 1850s westward expansion, not moral outrage, brought the controversy over slavery to a head. As Congress created new territories, the question of whether slavery would be extended arose again and again (see Map 26.4). For years elaborate compromises were worked out, but tensions rose, and the North and South were growing increasingly different. The South was overwhelmingly agricultural on the eve of the Civil War; 90 percent of the country's industrial capacity was in the North.

Abraham Lincoln, committed to checking the spread of slavery, was elected president in 1860. To protest his victory in the presidential election of 1860, South Carolina seceded from the Union in December 1860. Ten Southern states soon followed South Carolina's example and formed the **Confederacy.** Its capital was at Richmond, Virginia.

Lincoln declared their actions illegal and to preserve the Union declared war. Only after the war had dragged on and the slaughter had become frightful on both sides, and only when it had been proved that the Southern war effort benefited considerably from slave labor, did Lincoln, reluctantly, resolve on emancipation.

Confederacy *The eleven Southern states that seceded from the United States and bonded together with a capital at Richmond, Virginia.*

The Emancipation Proclamation became effective on January 1, 1863 (two years after the abolition of serfdom in Russia; see page 694). The proclamation freed slaves only in states and areas that were in rebellion against the United States. It preserved slavery in states that were loyal to the United States or under military jurisdiction. It allowed slavery for convicted felons. The Emancipation Proclamation nevertheless spelled the doom of North American slavery. It transformed the Civil War from a political struggle to preserve the Union into a moral crusade for the liberty of Americans.

chattel slavery *Absolute legal ownership of another person, including the right to buy or sell that person.*

European and English liberals greeted the proclamation with joy. A gathering of working people in Manchester, England, wrote President Lincoln: "The erasure of that foul blot upon civilization and Christianity—**chattel slavery**—during your Presidency will cause the name of Abraham Lincoln to be honoured and revered by posterity."[8] As Lincoln acknowledged, this was a magnanimous statement, for the Civil War hurt working people in Manchester, whose factories had shut when importation of cotton from the South stopped.

The war also had important political consequences in Europe. In 1861 British and European opinion had divided along class lines. The upper classes sympathized with the American South; the commercial classes and working people sided with the North. The English people interpreted the Northern victory as a triumph of the democratic experiment over aristocratic oligarchy. Thus the United States gave a powerful stimulus to those in Britain and elsewhere who supported the cause of political democracy. When parliaments debated the extension of suffrage, the American example was frequently cited.

In April 1865, the Confederate general Robert E. Lee surrendered his army at Appomattox Court House in Virginia, ending the war. Lincoln had called for "malice toward none and charity for all" in his second inaugural address in 1864 and planned a generous policy toward the defeated South. The bullet that killed him brought on a different kind of reconstruction.

During Reconstruction (1865–1877), the vanquished South adjusted to a new social and economic order without slavery. Former slaves wanted land to farm, but, lacking cash, they soon accepted the sharecropping system: farmers paid landowners about half of a year's crops at harvest time in return for a cabin, food, mules, seed, and tools the rest of the year. Believing that education was the key to economic advancement, blacks flocked to country schools and to colleges supported by Northern religious groups. Although the Fifteenth Amendment to the U.S. Constitution forbade states to deny anyone the vote "on account of race, color, or previous condition of servitude," whites used violence, terror, and, between 1880 and 1920, so-called Jim Crow laws to prevent blacks from voting and to enforce rigid racial segregation. Lacking strong Northern support, blacks did not gain legal equality or suffrage in many parts of the old Confederacy until the 1960s. Racist assumptions and attitudes thwarted their legal, social, and economic advance.

In the construction of a black community, no institution played a larger role than the black Protestant churches. Local black churches provided hope, education, and a forum for the spread of political ideas and platforms. During Reconstruction, black preachers esteemed for their oratorical skill, organizational ability, and practical judgment held important positions in black politics. In a racist and exploitative society, the black church gave support, security, and a sense of solidarity.

Industrialization and Immigration

From the beginning, the United States attracted immigrants. Before the Civil War, the majority came from England, Ireland, and Germany. When the Irish potato crop was destroyed by a fungal disease leading to a horrific famine in 1845–1859, a million people fled overseas, the majority heading to the United States. Immigrants who arrived with nothing had to work as laborers for years, but many in time were able to acquire farms, especially if they were willing to move west as the country expanded. The Homestead Act of 1862 made land available to anyone willing to work it. From then until the end of the century, 500 million acres were put into production.

As new lands were opened, food production soared. Grain elevators, introduced in 1850, made it possible to store much more grain, which could be transported by the growing rail system as needed. The new practice of canning meant that food did not have to be eaten immediately. The development of refrigeration meant that meat could be shipped long distances. Food processing became industrial. Factories turned out crackers, cookies, and breakfast cereals.

The West also held precious metals. The discovery of gold and silver in California, Colorado, Arizona, and Montana, and on the reservations of the Sioux Indians of South Dakota (see page 792), precipitated huge gold and silver rushes. Even before 1900, miners had extracted $1.24 billion in gold and $901 million in silver from western mines. Many miners settled down to farm. By 1912 the West had been won.

Generally speaking, the settlers' lives blurred sex roles. It fell to women to make homes out of crude log cabins that had no windows or doors or out of tarpaper shacks with mud floors. Lacking cookstoves, they prepared food over open fireplaces, using all kinds of substitutes for ingredients easily available back east. Before they could wash clothes, women had to make soap out of lye and carefully saved household ashes.

Considered the carriers of "high culture," women organized whatever educational, religious, musical, and recreational activities the settlers' society possessed. Women also had to defend their homes against prairie fires and Indian attacks. These burdens were accompanied by frequent pregnancies and, often, the need to give birth without medical help or even the support of other women. The death rate for infants and young children ran as high as 30 percent in the mid-nineteenth century. Even so, these women had large families.

Influenced by ideas then circulating in England, some women began promoting the idea of rights for women. At the Seneca Falls Convention in 1848, women demanded equal political and economic rights. Others promoted women's education and opened women's colleges. It was not until 1920, however, that women in the United States got the right to vote.

England remained an important cultural influence in other spheres besides women's rights and abolition. Many books published in London were quickly reprinted in the United States once copies arrived. Popular English novelists such as Charles Dickens were popular in the United States as well. Education beyond the elementary level usually involved reading classics of English literature.

At the beginning of the nineteenth century, the place of the United States in global trade was as a producer of raw materials—cotton, tobacco, whale oil, pelts, and skins. By the end of the century the United States had become a major manufacturing power, due in part to extensive British investment in U.S. enterprises. The flow of British funds was a consequence of Britain's own industrialization, which generated enormous wealth.

Industrialization was aided by an abundance of raw materials. Huge iron ore deposits were found near the Great Lakes in 1844. Coal was widely available; oil was discovered in Pennsylvania in 1859, and oil drilling soon began. The fossil fuels coal and oil provided energy in very concentrated forms. A few pounds of coal can replace an acre of timber as a source of heat. Coal and oil are much better fuels to power steam engines and to smelt iron and other metals.

The federal government turned over vast amounts of land and mineral resources to industry for development. The railroads—the foundation of industrial expansion—received 130 million acres. By 1900 the U.S. railroad system was 193,000 miles long, connected every part of the nation, and represented 40 percent of the railroad mileage of the entire world. Immigrant workers built it.

Between 1880 and 1920, industrial production soared. By the 1890s, the United States was producing twice as much steel as Britain. New inventions such as the steam engine, the dynamo (generator), and the electric light were given industrial and agricultural applications. Large factories replaced small ones. In the automobile industry, Henry Ford of Detroit set up assembly lines. Each person working on the line performed only one task instead of assembling an entire car. In 1910 Ford sold 10,000 cars; in 1914, a year after he inaugurated the first moving assembly line, he sold 248,000 cars. The automobile increased opportunities for travel, general mobility, and change. Other new machines also had a pervasive impact. Sewing machines made cheap, varied, mass-produced clothing available to city people in department stores and to country people through mail-order catalogues.

The national economy experienced repeated cycles of boom and bust in the late nineteenth century. Serious depressions in 1873, 1884, and 1893 slashed prices and threw many people out of work. Leading industrialists responded by establishing larger corporations and consolidated companies into huge conglomerates. As a result of the merger of several small oil companies, John D. Rockefeller's Standard Oil Company controlled 84 percent of the nation's oil and most American pipelines in 1898. J. P. Morgan's United States Steel monopolized the iron and steel industries, and Swift & Co. of Chicago controlled the meat-processing industry.

Many of those who worked in the new factories were immigrants. Between 1860 and 1900, 14 million immigrants arrived in the United States, and during the peak years between 1900 and 1914, another 14 million immigrants passed through the U.S. customs inspection station at Ellis Island in New York City. Chinese, Scandinavian, and Irish immigrants laid thirty thousand miles of railroad tracks between 1867 and 1873 and another seventy-three thousand miles in the 1880s. At the Carnegie Steel Corporation, Slavs and Italians produced one-third of the world's total steel supply in 1900. Lithuanians, Poles, Croats, Scandinavians, Irish, and blacks entered the Chicago stockyards and built the meatpacking industry. Irish immigrants continued to operate the spinning frames and knitting machines of New England's textile mills. Industrial America developed on the sweat and brawn—the cheap labor—of its immigrant millions.

As in South America, immigration fed the growth of cities. In 1790 only 5.1 percent of Americans were living in centers of twenty-five hundred or more people. By 1860 this figure had risen to 19.9 percent, and by 1900 almost 40 percent were living in cities. By 1900, three of the largest cities in the world were in the United States—New York City with 3.4 million people, Chicago with 1.7 million, and Philadelphia with 1.4. In 1800, New York City had had only sixty thousand people. As in Europe (see Chapter 23), cities themselves were being transformed. By the early twentieth century, cities had electricity, sewer systems that had curbed the spread of infectious diseases, and streetcars that allowed the cities to expand, thus reducing crowding.

Still, the working conditions that these new immigrants found were often deplorable. Industrialization had created a vast class of wage workers who depended totally on their employers for work. To keep labor costs low, employers paid workers piecemeal for the number of articles they made. They hired women and children who could be paid much less than men. Some women textile workers earned as little as

THE COMING MAN—JOHN CHINAMAN.
Uncle Sam introduces Eastern Barbarism to Western Civilization.

● **Racism Rampant**
Nineteenth-century immigrants encountered terrible prejudice, as "respectable" magazines and newspapers spewed out racism, such as this cartoon from an 1869 issue of *Harper's Weekly.* The Irishman (identifiable by the shillelagh or blackthorn club, supposedly a sign of his tendency toward violence) and the Chinese man (identifiable by the pigtail, supposedly a sign of his devious obsequiousness) are both satirized as "barbarians." Well into the twentieth century, being "American" meant being of Anglo-Saxon descent. *(Harper's Weekly, August 28, 1869. Private Collection)*

$1.56 for seventy hours of work, while men received from $7 to $9 for the same work. Owners fought in legislatures and courts against the installation of costly safety devices, so working conditions in mines and mills were frightful. In 1913, even after some safety measures had been taken, twenty-five thousand people died in industrial accidents. Between 1900 and 1917, seventy-two thousand railroad worker deaths occurred. Workers responded with strikes, violence, and, gradually, unionization.

In *How the Other Half Lives* (1890), Jacob Riis, a newspaper reporter and recent immigrant from Denmark, drew national attention to what he called "the foul core of New York's slums." Riis estimated that three hundred thousand people inhabited a single square mile on New York's Lower East Side. Overcrowding, poor sanitation, and lack of health services caused frequent epidemics. The blight of slums increased crime, prostitution, alcoholism, and other drug-related addictions.

Nationalism carried different meanings in the United States than it did in Europe (see pages 679–680). It did not refer to an ancient people whose unique culture was tied to its language. Immigrants were expected to learn English and identify with their new country. As in Europe, however, much was done to promote patriotism and bring people together through flag-waving parades and other emotionally charged symbols and ceremonies. The negative side of identification with the nation was nativist sentiment—that is, intense hostility to foreign and "un-American" looks, behavior, and loyalties—among native-born Americans. Some of this antagonism sprang from deep-rooted racism. Some grew out of old Protestant suspicions of Roman Catholicism, the faith of many of the new arrivals. Long-standing anti-Semitism also played a part. A great deal of the dislike of the foreign-born sprang from fear of economic competition. To most Americans, the Chinese with their exotic looks and willingness to work for very little seemed the most dangerous. Increasingly violent agitation against Asians led to race riots in California and finally culminated in the Chinese Exclusion Act of 1882, which denied Chinese laborers entrance to the country.

In the 1890s, the nation experienced a severe economic depression. Faced with overproduction, the rich and politically powerful owners of mines, mills, and factories fought the organization of labor unions, laid off thousands of workers, slashed wages, and ruthlessly exploited their workers. Workers in turn feared that immigrant labor would drive salaries lower. The frustrations provoked during the depression boiled over into savage attacks on the foreign-born. One of the bloodiest incidents took place in western Pennsylvania in 1897, when about 150 unarmed Polish and Hungarian coal miners persuaded others to join their walkout. The mine owners convinced the local sheriff that the strike was illegal. He panicked and ordered his deputies to shoot at the strikers. Twenty-one immigrants died, and forty were wounded. The sheriff declared that the miners were only "infuriated foreigners . . . like wild beasts." Local people agreed that if the strikers had been American-born, no blood would have been shed.[9]

After the First World War, labor leaders lobbied Congress for restrictions on immigration because they feared losing the wage gains achieved during the war. In the 1920s, Congress responded with laws that set severe quotas—2 percent of resident nationals as of the 1890 census—on immigration from southern and eastern Europe. The Japanese were completely excluded (as the Chinese had been earlier). These racist laws remained on the books until 1965.

• • • • • • • • • • • • • • •

CANADA, FROM FRENCH COLONY TO NATION

What geographical, economic, and political conditions shaped the development of Canada?

In 1608 the French explorer Samuel de Champlain (1567–1635) sailed down the St. Lawrence River and established a trading post on the site of present-day Quebec. Thus began the permanent colony of New France. The fur-trading monopolies subsequently granted to Champlain by the French crown attracted settlers, and Jesuit missionaries to the Indians further increased the French population. The British, however, vigorously challenged French control of the lucrative fur trade. The mid-eighteenth-century global struggle for empire between the British and the French, known in Europe as the Seven Years' War and in North America as the French and Indian Wars, spilled into North America. In 1759, on a field next to the city of Quebec, the English defeated the French and ended the French empire in North America. By the Treaty of Paris of 1763, France ceded Canada to Great Britain.

For the French Canadians, who in 1763 numbered about ninety thousand, the British conquest was a tragedy and the central event in their history. British governors replaced the French; English-speaking merchants from Britain and the thirteen American colonies to the south took over the colony's economic affairs. The Roman Catholic Church remained and until about 1960 played a powerful role in the political and cultural, as well as the religious, life of French Canadians. Most French Canadians were farmers, though a small merchant class sold furs and imported manufactured goods.

In 1774 the British Parliament passed the Quebec Act, which granted religious freedom to French Canadians and recognized French law in civil matters, but it denied Canadians a legislative assembly, a traditional feature of British colonial government. Parliament placed power in the hands of an appointed governor and an appointed council composed of both English and French Canadians. English Canadian businessmen protested that they were being denied a basic right of Englishmen—representation.

During the American Revolution, about forty thousand Americans demonstrated their loyalty to Great Britain and its empire by moving to Canada. These "loyalists" not only altered the French-English ratio in the population but also pressed for a representative assembly. In 1791 Parliament responded with the Constitution Act, which divided the province of Quebec in two and provided for an elective assembly in each province.

MAP 26.5 **The Dominion of Canada, 1871** Shortly after the Dominion of Canada came into being in 1867 as a self-governing nation within the British Empire, new provinces were added. Vast areas of Canada were too sparsely populated to achieve provincial status. Alberta and Saskatchewan did not become part of the Dominion until 1905, Newfoundland only in 1949.

Not wanting to repeat the errors made in 1776, the British gradually extended home rule in stages between 1840 and 1867. During the American Civil War, English-American relations were severely strained, and fear of American aggression led to **confederation.** The provinces of New Brunswick and Nova Scotia joined Ontario and Quebec to form the Dominion of Canada (see Map 26.5). The Dominion Cabinet received complete jurisdiction over internal affairs, while Britain retained control over foreign policy. (In 1931 the British Statute of Westminster officially recognized Canadian autonomy in foreign affairs.)

Believing that the American constitution left the states too strong and helped to bring on the Civil War, the framers of the Canadian constitution created a powerful central government. The first prime minister, John A. Macdonald, vigorously pushed Canada's "manifest destiny" to absorb all the northern part of the continent. In 1869 his government purchased the vast Northwest Territories of the Hudson's Bay Company for $1.5 million. Fearful that the sparsely settled colony of British Columbia would join the United States, Macdonald lured British Columbia into the confederation with a subsidy to pay its debts and the promise of a transcontinental railroad. Likewise, the debt-ridden little maritime province of Prince Edward Island was drawn into confederation with a large subsidy. In five short years, between 1868 and 1873, through Macdonald's imagination and drive, Canadian sovereignty stretched from coast to coast. The completion of the Canadian Pacific Railroad in 1885 led to the formation of two new prairie provinces, Alberta and Saskatchewan, which in 1905 entered the Dominion. (Only in 1949 did the island of Newfoundland renounce colonial status and join the Dominion.)

Canada was thinly populated in the nineteenth century, and by 1900 still had only a little over 5 million people. As in the United States, the native peoples were pushed

confederation *A relatively loose form of union, leaving the separate units with substantial powers.*

801

● **Russian Immigrant Women in Saskatchewan** These women were Duokhobors, a religious sect that came to Canada seeking religious freedom from tsarist persecution. While most of the men took railroad jobs, the women planted the vast plains with rye, wheat, oats, and flax. Their farms and orchards flourished, and the Duokhobors played an important role in the development of western Canada. (*Saskatchewan Archives Board, photo no. R-B 1964*)

aside by Canada's development plans and their population dropped by about half during the century, to only about one hundred thousand in 1900. French Canadians remained the largest minority in the population. Distinctively different in language, law, and religion, and fiercely proud of their culture, they resisted assimilation.

Immigration picked up in the 1890s. Between 1897 and 1912, 961,000 people entered Canada from the British Isles, 594,000 from Europe, and 784,000 from the United States. Some immigrants went to work in the urban factories of Hamilton, Toronto, and Montreal. Most immigrants from continental Europe—Poles, Germans, Scandinavians, and Russians—flooded the midwestern plains and soon transformed the prairies into one of the world's greatest grain-growing regions. Between 1891 and 1914, wheat production rocketed from 2 million bushels per year to 150 million bushels. Mining also was expanded. British Columbia, Ontario, and Quebec produced large quantities of wood pulp, much of it sold to the United States. Canada's great rivers were harnessed to supply hydroelectric power for industrial and domestic use. But Canada remained a predominantly agricultural country, with less than 10 percent of its population engaged in manufacturing (and a third of them processing timber or food).

In 1914 the British government still controlled the foreign policy of all parts of the empire. When Britain declared war on Germany, Canada unhesitatingly followed.

More than six hundred thousand Canadian soldiers served with distinction in the army, some of them in the bloodiest battles in France. Canadian grain and foodstuffs supplied much of the food of the Allied troops, and Canadian metals were in demand for guns and shells. Canadian resentment, therefore, over lack of voice in the formulation of Allied war policies was understandable. In 1918 Canada demanded and received—over the initial opposition of Britain, France, and the United States—the right to participate in the Versailles Peace Conference and in the League of Nations. Since 1939 Canada has been a member of the British Commonwealth of Nations.

AUSTRALIA, FROM PENAL COLONY TO NATION

What circumstances shaped the development of Australia?

In April 1770 James Cook, the English explorer, navigator, and captain of HMS *Endeavor,* dropped anchor in a wide bay about ten miles south of the present city of Sydney on the coast of eastern Australia. Because the young botanist on board the ship, Joseph Banks, subsequently discovered thirty thousand specimens of plant life in the bay, sixteen hundred of them unknown to European science, Captain Cook called the place **Botany Bay.** Totally unimpressed by the flat landscape and its few naked inhabitants—the Aborigines, or native people—Cook sailed north along the coast (see Map 26.6). On August 21, on a rock later named Possession Island, Cook formally claimed the entire land south of where he stood for King George III, sixteen thousand miles away. Cook called the land **New South Wales.** In accepting possession, the British crown acted on the legal fiction that Australia was *Terra Nullius,* completely unoccupied, thus entirely ignoring the native people.

The world's smallest continent, Australia is about half the size of Europe and almost as large as the United States (excluding Alaska and Hawai'i). It has a temperate climate and little intense cold. Three topographical zones roughly divide the continent. The Western Plateau, a vast desert and semidesert region, covers almost two-thirds of the continent. The Central Eastern Lowlands extend from the Gulf of Carpentaria in the north to western Victoria in the south. The Eastern Highlands are a complex belt of tablelands.

When Cook arrived in Australia, about three hundred thousand Aborigines lived there. A peaceful and nomadic people who had emigrated from southern Asia millennia earlier, the Aborigines lived entirely by food gathering, fishing, and hunting. They had no agriculture. Although they used spears and bows and arrows in hunting, they never practiced warfare as it was understood by more technologically advanced peoples such as the Aztecs of Mexico or the Mandinke of West Africa. When white settlers arrived, they occupied the Aborigine lands unopposed. Like the Indians of Central and South America, the Aborigines fell victim to the white peoples' diseases and to a spiritual malaise caused by the breakdown of their tribal life. Today only about forty-five thousand pureblood Aborigines survive.

The victory of the thirteen North American colonies in 1783 inadvertently contributed to the establishment of a colony in Australia five years later. Crime in England was increasing in the 1770s and 1780s, and the transportation of felons "beyond the seas" seemed the answer to the problem of overcrowded prisons. Before 1775 the British government had shipped about one thousand convicts annually to Georgia. After that became impossible, the prisons were so full that old transport ships in southern naval ports were being used to house criminals, and pressure on the government to do something was intense. Finally, in August 1786, the British Cabinet

Botany Bay   *A bay on the coast of eastern Australia in which numerous specimens of plant life were discovered. It later became home to a penal colony.*

New South Wales   *The name given to Australia by James Cook, the English explorer; today it is the name of the most populous of the six states of Australia.*

● **Governor Arthur's Proclamation** To communicate to Aborigines the idea of equal justice for all, the governor of Van Dieman's land (modern Tasmania) in 1830 had picture boards displayed. This one shows an Aborigine being hung for killing a settler with a spear, and a settler being hung for shooting an aborigine with a rifle. *(Mitchell Library, State Library of New South Wales)*

approved the establishment of a penal colony at Botany Bay to serve as "a remedy for the evils likely to result from the late alarming and numerous increase of felons in this country, and more particularly in the metropolis (London)."[10] The name "Botany Bay" became a byword for the forced and permanent exile of criminals. In May 1787, a fleet of eleven ships packed with one thousand felons and their jailers sailed for Australia. After an eight-month voyage, it landed in Sydney Cove on January 28, 1788.

Mere survival in an alien world was the first challenge. Because the land at Botany Bay proved completely unsuited for agriculture and lacked decent water, the first governor, Arthur Phillip, moved the colony ten miles north to Port Jackson, later called Sydney. Announcing that those who did not work would not eat, Phillip set the prisoners to planting seeds. Coming from the slums of London, the convicts knew nothing of agriculture, and some were too ill or old to work. Moreover, the colony lacked draft animals and plows. For years the colony of New South Wales tottered on the brink of starvation.

Up until the penal colony system was abolished in 1869, a total of 161,000 convicts were transported to Australia. Transportation rested on two premises: that criminals should be punished and that they should not be a financial burden on the state. Convicts became free when their sentences expired or were remitted. Few returned to England.

For the first thirty years, men far outnumbered women. Because the British government refused to allow wives to accompany their convict-husbands, prostitution flourished. Many women convicts, if not professional prostitutes when they left England, became such during the long voyage south. Army officers, government officials, and free immigrants chose favorite convicts as mistresses.

Officers and jailers, though descended from the middle and lower middle classes, tried to establish a colonial gentry and to impose the rigid class distinctions that they had known in England. Known as **exclusionists,** this self-appointed colonial gentry tried to exclude from polite society all freed or emancipated persons, called **emancipists.** Deep and bitter class feeling took root.

Governor Phillip and his successors urged the Colonial Office to send free settlers to Australia, not just prisoners. After the end of the Napoleonic wars in 1815, a steady stream of people relocated. The end of the European wars also released capital for potential investment. But investment in what? What commodity could be developed and exported to England?

exclusionists *The officers and jailers who tried to establish a colonial gentry and impose rigid class distinctions from England.*

emancipists *The lower strata of the Australian social order in the mid-nineteenth century, made up of former convicts.*

Immigrants explored several possibilities. In the last decade of the eighteenth century, for example, sealing seemed a good prospect. Sealing merchants hired Aborigine women to swim out to the seal rocks, lie down among the seals until their suspicions were dulled, and then at a signal rise up and club the seals to death. In 1815 a single ship carried sixty thousand sealskins to London (a normal cargo contained at least ten thousand skins). Such destruction rapidly depleted the seals.

Credit for the development of the product that was to be Australia's staple commodity for export—wool—goes to John Macarthur (1767–1834). Granted a large tract of Crown lands and assigned thirty convicts to work for him, Macarthur conducted experiments in the production of fine merino wool. In 1800 he sent sample fleeces to England to determine their quality. He also worked to attract the financial support of British manufacturers.

The report of J. T. Bigge, an able lawyer sent out in 1819 to evaluate the colony, proved decisive. Persuaded by large landowners like Macarthur, Bigge reported that wool was the country's future staple. He recommended that convicts be removed from the temptations of towns and seaports and dispersed to work on the estates of men of capital. He also urged that British duties on colonial wool be suspended. The

MAP 26.6 **Australia** Because of the vast deserts in western Australia, cities and industries developed mainly in the east. Australia's early geographical and cultural isolation bred a sense of inferiority. Air travel, the communications revolution, and the massive importation of Japanese products and American popular culture have changed that.

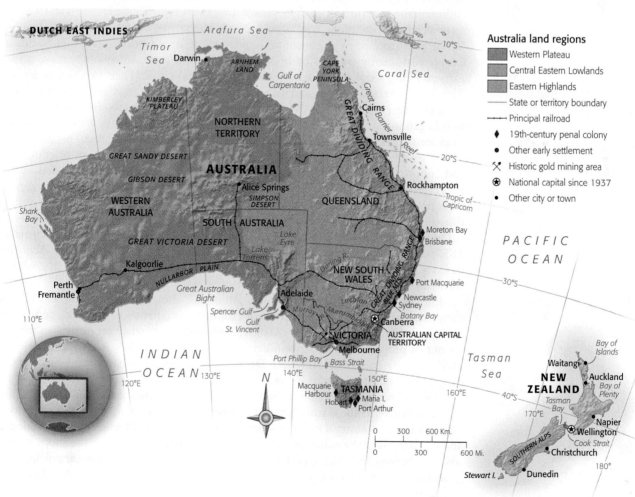

Colonial Office accepted this advice, and the pastoral economy of Australia, as the continent was beginning to be called, began.

Australia's temperate though capricious climate is ideally suited to sheep farming. Moreover, wool production requires much land and little labor—precisely the situation in Australia. In 1830 the sheep population reached a half million. After 1820 the commercial importance of Australia exceeded its significance as a penal colony, and wool exports steadily increased, from 75,400 pounds in 1821, to 2 million pounds in 1830, to 24 million pounds in 1845.

Settlers also experimented with wheat farming. Soil deficiencies and the dry climate slowed early production, but farmers eventually developed a successful white-grained winter variety. By 1900 wheat proved Australia's second most valuable crop.

Population shortage remained a problem through the nineteenth century. In the quest for British immigrants, Australia could not compete with North America. The twelve-thousand-mile journey to Australia cost between £20 and £25 and could take five weary months. By contrast, the trip to Canada or the United States cost only £5 and lasted just ten weeks. To reduce the financial disincentives, immigrants were offered free passage by the government. Still, over 2.5 million British immigrants went to North America and only 223,000 to Australia.

Population in the early nineteenth century concentrated on the eastern coast of the continent. The growth of sheep farming led to the opening of the interior. The Ripon Land Regulation Act of 1831, which provided land grants, attracted free settlers. By 1850 Australia had five hundred thousand inhabitants. The discovery of gold in Victoria in 1851 quadrupled that number in a few years. Gold fever convulsed Australia. Although the government charged prospectors a very high license fee, men and women from all parts of the globe flocked to Australia to share in the fabulous wealth.

The gold rush led to an enormous improvement in transportation within Australia. People customarily traveled by horseback or on foot and used two-wheel ox-drawn carts to bring wool from inland ranches to coastal cities. Then two newly arrived Americans, Freeman Cobb and James Rutherford, built sturdy four-wheel coaches capable of carrying heavy cargo and of negotiating the bush tracks. Railroad construction began in the 1870s, and by 1890, nine thousand miles of track were laid. Railroad construction, financed by British investors, stimulated agricultural production.

The gold rush also provided the financial means for the promotion of education and culture. Public libraries, museums, art galleries, and universities opened in the thirty years after 1851. In keeping with the overwhelmingly British ethnic origin of most immigrants to Australia, these institutions dispensed a distinctly British culture, though a remote and provincial version.

On the negative side, the large numbers of Asians in the goldfields—in Victoria in 1857, one adult male in seven was Chinese—sparked bitter racial prejudice. Scholars date the "white Australia policy" to the hostility, resentment, and fear that whites showed the Chinese.

Although Americans numbered only about five thousand in Victoria and Asians forty thousand, Americans, with their California gold-rush experience, aggressive ways, and "democratic" frontier outlook, exercised an influence on Australian society far out of proportion to their numbers. On the Fourth of July in 1852, 1854, and 1857 (anniversaries of the American Declaration of Independence), anti-Chinese riots occurred in the goldfields of Victoria.

"Colored peoples" (as all nonwhites were called in Australia) adapted more easily than the British to the warm climate and worked for lower wages. Thus they proved essential to the country's economic development in the nineteenth century. Chinese and Japanese built the railroads and ran the market gardens near, and the shops in, the towns. Filipinos and Pacific Islanders did the hard work in the sugar-cane fields. Afghanis and their camels controlled the carrying trade in some areas. But fear that

● **The Life of Emigration**   Some of the advertising designed to attract people to move to Australia was aimed at children. This wooden box contains a 38-piece wooden puzzle of scenes of the life of a family moving from Britain to Australia, from their departure to clearing ground and sheering sheep. It dates to about 1840. *(Photograph courtesy of the State Library of South Australia, SA Memory Website)*

colored labor would lower living standards and undermine Australia's distinctly British culture triumphed. The Commonwealth Immigration Restriction Act of 1901 closed immigration to Asians and established the "white Australia policy," which remained on the books until the 1970s.

In 1850 the British Parliament had passed the Australian Colonies Government Act, which allowed the four most populous colonies—New South Wales, Tasmania, Victoria, and South Australia—to establish colonial legislatures, determine the franchise, and frame their own constitutions. By 1859 all but one colony was self-governing. The provincial parliament of South Australia was probably the most democratic in the world, since it was elected by universal manhood suffrage and by secret ballot. Other colonies soon adopted the secret ballot. In 1902 Australia became one of the first countries in the world to give women the vote.

The Commonwealth of Australia came into existence on January 1, 1901. From the British model, Australia adopted the parliamentary form of government in which a cabinet is responsible to the House of Commons. From the American system, Australia took the concept of decentralized government, whereby the states and the federal government share power.

Deep loyalty to the mother country led Australia to send 329,000 men and vast economic aid to Britain in the First World War. The issue of conscription, however, bitterly divided the country, partly along religious lines. About one-fourth of Australia's population was (and is) Irish and Roman Catholic. Although the Catholic population, like the dominant Anglican one, split over conscription, the powerful, influential, and long-lived Catholic archbishop of Melbourne, Daniel Mannix (1864–1963), publicly supported Irish nationalism and denounced the English and the European war. Twice submitted to public referendum, conscription twice failed.

Australia's staggering 213,850 casualties in World War I exerted a traumatic effect on Australian life and society. With the young men died the illusion that remote Australia could escape the problems and sins of the Old World. But the experience of the Great War forged a sense of national identity among the states of Australia.

At the Paris Peace Conference in 1919, Australian delegates succeeded in excluding recognition of the principle of racial equality in the League of Nations Covenant. Australians did not want Asian immigrants. The treaties that followed the war allowed Australia a mandate over German New Guinea and the equatorial island of Nauru. Nauru had vast quantities of phosphates that Australian wheat fields needed as fertilizer. The former penal colony had become a colonial power.

- - - - - - - - - - - -

THE NEW COUNTRIES IN COMPARATIVE PERSPECTIVE

How and why did the new countries treated in this chapter develop differently?

Looked at from the perspective of world history, there was much that the new countries of the Western Hemisphere and Australia had in common. All of them began as European colonies. All had indigenous populations who suffered from the arrival of Europeans. For all of them the nineteenth century was a period of nation building, and all had achieved self-rule by the end of the century. In all of them, the languages of the colonial powers—English, French, Spanish, and Portuguese—became the languages of government after independence. All provided European financiers with investment opportunities, not only in the expansion of agricultural enterprises, but also in mines, transportation, and manufacturing. By the end of the nineteenth century, all of the countries had become connected to the rest of the world through global trade. Another global current they all felt was nationalism, which in these countries meant mass identification with the country rather than identification with an ancient people and its language. All at one time or another allowed or encouraged immigration, and many had also imported slaves from Africa. Discrimination on the basis of ethnic origin and race was pervasive in all of them.

Despite so many similarities, the countries covered in this chapter were already very different by 1914. By then the United States had become one of the half-dozen richest and most powerful countries in the world. That could not be said of any of the others. The United States had built a strong industrial base; the economies of most of the other countries were still predominantly agricultural. The three English-speaking countries had established strong democratic traditions; most of the countries of Latin America were controlled by narrow elites or military strongmen, with much of the population excluded from the political process. Of the countries of Latin America, only Argentina, with its temperate climate, fertile prairies, and large influx of European immigrants approached the prosperity of the United States, Canada, or Australia.

What accounts for these differences in outcomes? That the three countries that began as British colonies ended up as stable democracies strongly suggests that their common origins mattered. Even though they obtained independence in different ways, the British tradition of representative government shaped the political culture of each of the new states. By the time they achieved independence, their citizens were already accustomed to elections and local self-government. That was not true of any of the former Spanish or Portuguese colonies.

The United States also benefited from its size. That a single country was formed by the original thirteen colonies in North America and preserved through the Civil War, gave the United States the advantages of substantial size from the beginning. In addition it had room to expand west into territory with many advantages—temperate climate, navigable rivers, and abundant arable land and mineral resources. The expansion of the United States was made possible by the willingness of France and Spain to sell it large territories in the early years and its own willingness to aggressively pursue expansion at the expense of the Indians and Mexico. As a consequence of its original size and subsequent expansion, the United States became the largest of the new countries in population. The only country that had more land was Canada, and much of Canada's land was too far north to be of high value. If Simón Bolívar had succeeded in forming a union of the Spanish-speaking countries of South America, it might have shared some of the advantages of size that the United States had

Certainly it was important that the United States did not long remain a supplier for Europe of raw materials and basic commodities, but was quick to industrialize. Why did the United States industrialize in the nineteenth century at a much more rapid rate than any of the other countries of the Western Hemisphere? Many reasons can be suggested. It had ample resources such as iron, coal, petroleum, and fertile land. Its political policies helped. The government put few obstacles in the way of those who built the great enterprises. Through much of the nineteenth century, the United States placed high tariffs on imports in order to discourage importing European goods and to foster its own industries. It had no difficulty attracting both capital and immigrants from abroad. The United States developed a social structure that rewarded self-made men and encouraged innovation. At the beginning of the nineteenth century, the most crucial advances in industrial technology were made in Europe, but by the beginning of the next century, they were just as likely to come from the United States. It was the United States that introduced streetcars and Henry Ford who developed the assembly line.

Once the United States became an industrialized country, its economic advantages accelerated, as its citizens had more money to buy the products of its industries, its capitalists had more income to invest, educational levels rose as the advantages of learning became clearer, it attracted more immigrants, and so on. Countries further behind could not easily catch up. Another way to put this is that the United States escaped the neocolonial situation. Because its economy diversified early, when world trade quickened after 1870, the United States was in just as advantageous a position as Britain, France, and Germany.

Chapter Summary

Key Terms

Creoles
peninsulares
neocolonialism
haciendas
peons
manifest destiny
Treaty of Guadalupe
  Hidalgo (1848)
Confederacy
chattel slavery
confederation
Botany Bay
New South Wales
exclusionists
emancipists

To assess your mastery of this chapter, go to
bedfordstmartins.com/mckayworld

• Why and how did the Spanish and Portuguese colonies of North and South America shake off European domination and develop into national states?

In Latin America dissatisfaction with Spanish colonial rule grew over the course of the eighteenth century, both on the part of the Indians and mestizos and on the part of the Creoles of European ancestry who resented the privileges granted those from Spain. The wars of independence that lasted from 1805 to 1825 ended colonial status but also led to fragmentation into more than a dozen separate countries. Frequently, military dictators gained political power. Many Indians and mestizos worked on haciendas, often constrained by debt peonage. Many of the large plantations produced basic commodities for the international market, dominated by foreign powers.

• How does nation building in the United States look from a world history perspective?

The United States was the first of the European colonies in the New World to gain its independence, and it remained a step ahead during the nineteenth century both in attracting immigrants and in industrializing. The North's victory in the bloody Civil War, fought over the issues of slavery and union, assured the permanence of the Union, but racial equality remains the American dilemma. Domestic matters preoccupied the country through most of the nineteenth century, as it subdued the continent, linked it with railroads, and built gigantic steel, oil, textile, food-processing, and automobile industries. Nationalist sentiment grew, and after 1898, the United States became a colonial power and a major player in international affairs.

• What geographical, economic, and political conditions shaped the development of Canada?

The development of Canada was shaped by the emergence of the United States to its south, not only because many loyalists fled to Canada after the American Revolution, but also because Britain did not want to repeat its experience with its earlier American colonies. Adopting the British model of cabinet government and utilizing rich natural resources, the provinces of Canada formed a strong federation with close economic ties to the United States. French separatism, centered in Quebec, remains the Canadian dilemma.

• What circumstances shaped the development of Australia?

Australia is much farther from Britain than North America is, and it was colonized later. The first European settlers were forcibly transported to Australia as convicts, but by the mid-nineteenth century Australia was attracting large numbers of Irish and English immigrants and smaller numbers from other countries. As in the United States and Canada, the discovery of gold quickened the pace of immigration. Because of Australia's dry climate, farming concentrated on sheep raising and wheat. After 1850 Australia was largely self-governing and in 1901 drafted a constitution that utilized political features of both the British and the American political systems.

• How and why did the new countries treated in this chapter develop differently?

Of all the new countries of the Western Hemisphere and Australia, only one had become a great power by 1914—the United States. Like the other countries that had begun as British colonies, it developed a stable democracy based on representative government and an expanding electorate. Political stability aided its rapid industrialization, which was also fostered by its rich endowment of natural resources and its ability to attract capital and immigrants. By the beginning of the twentieth century, many of the countries of Latin America, by contrast, seemed trapped in neocolonial systems that kept much of their population poor.

Suggested Reading

Bayly, C. A. *The Birth of the Modern World.* 2003. Useful for viewing the countries of the Western Hemisphere in the context of global developments.

Berlin, Ira. *Many Thousands Gone: The First Two Centuries of Slavery in North America.* 1998. An excellent study that shows how varied slavery was in different times and places.

Burkholder, Mark A., and Lyman Johnson. *Colonial Latin America,* 6th ed. 2007. A broad, comprehensive survey of Latin American history in the colonial period.

Foner, Eric. *Reconstruction: America's Unfinished Revolution, 1863–1877.* 1988. A lucidly written social history that gives attention to the role of former slaves in remaking their world.

Howe, Irving. *World of Our Fathers.* 1976. Brilliant account of the lives of Jews and other immigrants in American cities.

Hughes, Robert. *The Fatal Shore.* 1987. Beautifully written account of the origins of Australia as a penal colony, drawing on diaries and letters.

Morton, Desmond. *A Short History of Canada,* 6th ed. 2006. Well-written popular history.

Rodriguez O., J. E. *The Independence of Spanish America.* 1998. An up-to-date treatment focusing on nation building.

Stampp, K. M. *America in 1857: A Nation on the Brink.* 1990. The best comprehensive treatment of the pre–Civil War years.

Terrill, Ross. *The Australians.* 1987. Offers an attractive appreciation of the Australian people and the society they made, from the first settlers to the present.

White, Richard. *"It's Your Misfortune and None of My Own": A History of the American West.* 1991. Includes environmental, urban, ethnic, and women's history, as well as the more familiar story.

Notes

1. See B. Keen and M. Wasserman, *A Short History of Latin America* (Boston: Houghton Mifflin, 1980), pp. 109–115.
2. M. Burkholder and D. S. Chandler, *From Impotence to Authority: The Spanish Crown and the American Audiencias, 1687–1808* (Columbia: University of Missouri Press, 1977), p. 145.
3. Quoted in J. Lynch, *The Spanish-American Revolutions, 1808–1826* (New York: Norton, 1973), p. 18.
4. F. Tannenbaum, *Ten Keys to Latin America* (New York: Random House, 1962), pp. 69–71.
5. See P. J. Parish, *Slavery: History and Historians* (New York: Harper & Row, 1989), pp. 45–46.
6. H. G. Gutman, *The Black Family in Slavery and Freedom, 1750–1925* (New York: Random House, 1977).
7. See J. Winch, *A Gentleman of Color: The Life of James Forten* (New York: Oxford University Press, 2002), passim.
8. Quoted in S. E. Morison, *The Oxford History of the American People* (New York: Oxford University Press, 1965), p. 654.
9. Quoted in J. Higham, *Strangers in the Land: Patterns of American Nativism, 1860–1925* (New York: Atheneum, 1971), pp. 89–90.
10. Quoted in R. Hughes, *The Fatal Shore* (New York: Knopf, 1987), p. 66.

Listening to the PAST

Simón Bolívar's Speculation on Latin America

Descended from a wealthy Venezuelan family, Simón Bolívar (1783–1830) was educated privately by tutors, who instilled in him the liberal and republican ideals of the French Enlightenment. He traveled to Europe and in 1805, while in Rome, dedicated himself to liberating his country from Spanish rule. Returning to Venezuela, Bolívar worked as a diplomat, a statesman, and, above all, the general who defeated the Spaniards and liberated northern regions of the continent. When he entered Caracas, the citizens called him "the Liberator," and the name stuck.

Almost two generations earlier, on July 4, 1776, the Second Continental Congress had adopted the Declaration of Independence, justifying the thirteen colonies' independence and appealing for European support with a long diatribe against King George III's supposedly tyrannical acts. It was a document of propaganda. In 1815 Simón Bolívar addressed a letter to the governor of Jamaica responding to the latter's request for Bolívar's views on prospects for Latin American liberation and the establishment of one unified nation. Bolívar's "Letter from Jamaica" expresses Latin American ideals and came to serve purposes comparable to those served by the Declaration of Independence.

Kingston, Jamaica, September 6, 1815.

My dear Sir:

. . . With what a feeling of gratitude I read that passage in your letter in which you say to me: "I hope that the success which then followed Spanish arms may now turn in favor of their adversaries, the badly oppressed people of South America." I take this hope as a prediction. . . . The hatred that the Peninsula [Spain and Portugal] has inspired in us is greater than the ocean between us. . . .

Europe could do Spain a service by dissuading her from her rash obstinacy, thereby at least sparing her the costs she is incurring and the blood she is expending. And if she will fix her attention on her own precincts she can build her prosperity and power

upon more solid foundations than doubtful conquests, precarious commerce, and forceful exactions from remote and powerful peoples. Europe herself, as a matter of common sense policy, should have prepared and executed the project of American independence, not alone because the world balance of power so necessitated, but also because this is the legitimate and certain means through which Europe can acquire overseas commercial establishments. . . .

It is even more difficult to foresee the future fate of the New World, to set down its political principles, or to prophesy what manner of government it will adopt. . . . We are a young people. We inhabit a world apart, separated by broad seas. We are young in the ways of almost all the arts and sciences, although, in a certain manner, we are old in the ways of civilized society. . . . We are, moreover, neither Indian nor European, but a species midway between the legitimate proprietors of this country and the Spanish usurpers. In short, though Americans by birth we derive our rights from Europe, and we have to assert these rights against the rights of the natives, and at the same time we must defend ourselves against the invaders. This places us in a most extraordinary and involved situation. Notwithstanding that it is a type of divination to predict the result of the political course which America is pursuing, I shall venture some conjectures which, of course, are colored by my enthusiasm and dictated by rational desires rather than by reasoned calculations. . . .

We have been harassed by a conduct which has not only deprived us of our rights but has kept us in a sort of permanent infancy with regard to public affairs. If we could at least have managed our domestic affairs and our internal administration, we could have acquainted ourselves with the processes and mechanics of public affairs. We should also have enjoyed a personal consideration, thereby commanding a certain unconscious respect from the people, which is so necessary to preserve amidst revolutions. That is why I say we have even been deprived of an active tyranny, since we have not been permitted to exercise its functions.

The Liberator: Simón Bolívar. *(akg-images)*

Americans today, and perhaps to a greater extent than ever before, who live within the Spanish system occupy a position in society no better than that of serfs destined for labor, or at best they have no more status than that of mere consumers. Yet even this status is surrounded with galling restrictions, such as being forbidden to grow European crops, or to store products which are royal monopolies, or to establish factories of a type the Peninsula itself does not possess. To this add the exclusive trading privileges, even in articles of prime necessity, and the barriers between American provinces, designed to prevent all exchange of trade, traffic, and understanding. In short, do you wish to know what our future held?—simply the cultivation of the fields of indigo, grain, coffee, sugar cane, cacao, and cotton; cattle raising on the broad plains; hunting wild game in the jungles; digging in the earth to mine its gold—but even these limitations could never satisfy the greed of Spain. . . .

More than anyone, I desire to see America fashioned into the greatest nation in the world, greatest not so much by virtue of her area and wealth as by her freedom and glory. Although I seek perfection for the government of my country, I cannot persuade myself that the New World can, at the moment, be organized as a great republic. Since it is impossible, I dare not desire it; yet much less do I desire to have all America a monarchy because this plan is not only impracticable but also impossible. Wrongs now existing could not be righted, and our emancipation would be fruitless. The American states need the care of paternal governments to heal the sores and wounds of despotism and war. . . .

From the foregoing, we can draw these conclusions: The American provinces are fighting for their freedom, and they will ultimately succeed. Some provinces as a matter of course will form federal and some central republics; the larger areas will inevitably establish monarchies, some of which will fare so badly that they will disintegrate in either present or future revolutions. To consolidate a great monarchy will be no easy task, but it will be utterly impossible to consolidate a great republic.

It is a grandiose idea to think of consolidating the New World into a single nation, united by pacts into a single bond. It is reasoned that, as these parts have a common origin, language, customs, and religion, they ought to have a single government to permit the newly formed states to unite in a confederation. But this is not possible. . . . Would to God that some day we may have the good fortune to convene . . . an august assembly of representatives of republics, kingdoms, and empires to deliberate upon the high interests of peace and war with the nations of the other three-quarters of the globe. This type of organization may come to pass in some happier period of our regeneration. But any other plan . . . would be meaningless.

When success is not assured, when the state is weak, and when results are distantly seen, all men hesitate; opinion is divided, passions rage, and the enemy fans these passions in order to win an easy victory because of them. As soon as we are strong and under the guidance of a liberal nation which will lend us her protection, we will achieve accord in cultivating the virtues and talents that lead to glory. Then will we march majestically toward that great prosperity for which South America is destined.

Questions for Analysis

1. Compare the arguments in the Declaration of Independence (see page 614) and the "Letter from Jamaica."

2. For Bolívar, what are the prospects for Latin American unity as one nation?

Source: A. J. Andrea and J. H. Overfield, eds., *The Human Record,* vol. 2, rev. ed. (Boston: Houghton Mifflin, 1994).

In the Trenches. French soldiers in a trench man a machine gun, the weapon that killed so many, in this chilling work by Christopher Nevinson. *(Art Resource, NY/© Tate, London, 2008)*

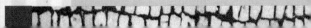

chapter 27
THE GREAT BREAK: WAR AND REVOLUTION

Chapter Preview

The First World War
• How did Europe's system of alliances contribute to the outbreak of World War I?

The Home Front
• How did total war impact the home fronts of the major European combatants?

The Russian Revolution
• How and why did the war lead to the Russian Revolution?

The Peace Settlement
• Why is the peace settlement following World War I considered by most historians to have been a terrible failure?

In the summer of 1914 the nations of Europe went willingly to war. They believed they had no other choice. Moreover, both peoples and governments confidently expected a short war leading to a decisive victory. Such a war, they believed, would "clear the air," and then European society could go on as before. They were wrong. The First World War was long, indecisive, and tremendously destructive. It quickly degenerated into a senseless military stalemate lasting four years. To the shell-shocked generation of survivors, it became simply the Great War.

THE FIRST WORLD WAR
How did Europe's system of alliances contribute to the outbreak of World War I?

The First World War clearly marked a great break in the course of world history. The war accelerated the growth of nationalism in Asia (see Chapter 28), and it consolidated America's position as a global power. Yet the war's greatest impact was on Europe. A noted British political scientist contends that even in victorious Great Britain, the First World War was *the* great turning point in government and society, "as in everything else in modern British history. . . . There's a much greater difference between the Britain of 1914 and, say, 1920, than between the Britain of 1920 and today."[1] This strong statement was as true for all Europe as for Britain.

The Bismarckian System of Alliances

France's defeat in 1871 (see page 692) and the founding of the German Empire opened a new era in international relations. In just ten years, from 1862 to 1871, Bismarck had made Prussia-Germany—traditionally the weakest of the Great Powers—the most powerful nation in Europe. Yet, Bismarck declared Germany a "satisfied" power, having no territorial ambitions within Europe and desiring only peace.

But how to preserve the peace? Bismarck needed first to keep an embittered France diplomatically isolated and without military allies. His second concern was the threat to peace posed by Austria-Hungary and Russia. These two enormous multinational empires had many conflicting interests, particularly in the Balkans, where the Ottoman Empire was losing its grip. To avoid Germany's being dragged into a great war between the two rival empires, Bismarck devised an alliance system to restrain both Russia and Austria-Hungary, to prevent conflict between them, and to isolate a hostile France.

Three Emperors' League *A conservative alliance that linked the monarchs of Austria-Hungary, Germany, and Russia against radical movements.*

First, Bismarck created the **Three Emperors' League** in 1873 to link the conservative monarchs of Austria-Hungary, Germany, and Russia. In 1877 and 1878, when Russia's victories over the Ottoman Empire threatened the balance of Austrian and Russian interests in the Balkans and the balance of British and Russian interests in the Middle East, Bismarck played sincere peacemaker at the Congress of Berlin in 1878 (see page 817). But his balancing efforts infuriated Russian nationalists, leading Bismarck to conclude a defensive military alliance with Austria against Russia in 1879. Motivated by tensions with France, Italy joined Germany and Austria to form the Triple Alliance in 1882.

Bismarck's foreign policy accomplishments after 1871 were impressive. He maintained good relations with Britain and Italy while encouraging France in Africa but keeping France isolated in Europe. In 1887 Bismarck brokered the Russian-German Reinsurance Treaty, by which both states promised neutrality if the other was attacked. For almost a generation he maintained German leadership in international affairs, working successfully for peace by managing conflicts and by restraining Austria-Hungary and Russia with defensive alliances.

The Rival Blocs

In 1890 the young, impetuous German emperor William II forced Bismarck to resign. William then adamantly refused to renew the Russian-German Reinsurance Treaty. This prompted long-isolated republican France to court absolutist Russia, offering loans, arms, and friendship. In 1894 France and Russia became military allies, pledging to remain so as long as the Triple Alliance of Austria, Germany, and Italy existed. Continental Europe was now dangerously divided into two rival blocs.

Great Britain's foreign policy became increasingly crucial. Long content with "splendid isolation" and no permanent alliances, Britain after 1891 found itself the only uncommitted Great Power. Alliance with France or Russia seemed highly unlikely. With a vast and rapidly expanding empire, Britain was often in serious conflict with these countries around the world.

Britain also squabbled with Germany, but many Germans and some Britons felt that a "natural alliance" united the advanced, racially related Germanic and Anglo-Saxon peoples. However, the generally good relations that had prevailed between Prussia and Great Britain since the mid-eighteenth century, and certainly under Bismarck, gave way after 1890 to a bitter Anglo-German rivalry.

There were several reasons for this tragic development. Commercial rivalry between Germany and Great Britain in world markets, William II's tactless public statements, and Germany's pursuit of world power all unsettled the British. Above all, Germany's decision in 1900 to expand greatly its battle fleet challenged Britain's long-standing naval supremacy. This decision coincided with the hard-fought South African War (1899–1902) between the British and the Afrikaner republics of South Africa, which convinced British leaders that Britain was overextended around the world. The South African War also revealed widespread anti-British feeling across Europe. Thus British leaders prudently set about shoring up their exposed position with alliances and agreements.

Britain began by improving its often-strained relations with the United States and then concluded a formal alliance with Japan in 1902. Next, Britain responded favorably to the advances of France's skillful foreign minister Théophile Delcassé, who offered to accept British rule in Egypt if the British supported French plans to dominate Morocco. The resulting Anglo-French Entente of 1904 settled all outstanding colonial disputes between Britain and France.

Frustrated by Britain's turn toward France in 1904, Germany's leaders decided to test the entente's strength and foolishly insisted in 1905 on an international conference on the whole Moroccan question. Germany's crude bullying forced France and Britain closer together, and Germany left the resulting Algeciras Conference of 1906 empty-handed and isolated (except for Austria-Hungary).

The Moroccan crisis and the Algeciras Conference led to something of a diplomatic revolution. Britain, France, Russia, and even the United States began to view Germany as a potential threat that might seek to dominate all Europe. At the same time, German leaders began to suspect sinister plots to "encircle" Germany and block its development as a world power. In 1907 Russia, battered by its disastrous war with Japan and the 1905 revolution, agreed to settle its quarrels with Great Britain in Persia and Central Asia with a special Anglo-Russian Agreement. Germany's blustering paranoia only increased after this agreement, as did Britain's thinly disguised hostility.

Germany's decision to add an enormously expensive fleet of big-gun battleships to its already expanding navy also heightened tensions after 1907. German nationalists saw a large navy as the legitimate mark of a great world power. But British leaders such as David Lloyd George considered it a detestable military challenge that forced them to spend the "People's Budget" (see page 706) on battleships rather than social welfare. In 1909 the *London Daily Mail* hysterically informed its readers that "Germany is deliberately preparing to destroy the British Empire."[2] By then Britain was psychologically, if not officially, in the Franco-Russian camp. Europe's leading nations were divided into two hostile blocs, both ill-prepared to deal with upheaval on Europe's southeastern frontier.

Chronology

1879–1918 Alliance between Austria and Germany (the "Central Powers")

1891–1917 Alliance between Russia and France

1912 First Balkan War

1914 Assassination of Archduke Francis Ferdinand; formation of Triple Entente (Great Britain, France, Russia); Ottoman Empire joins Central Powers

1914–1918 World War I

1916 Britain crushes Irish Easter Rebellion; Auxiliary Service Law requires German males aged seventeen to sixty to work for war effort; Rasputin murdered

1916–1918 Growth of antiwar sentiment throughout Europe

1917 United States declares war on Germany; Bolshevik Revolution in Russia

1919 Treaty of Versailles

The Outbreak of War

In the early twentieth century, a Balkans war was as inevitable as anything can be in human history. The reason was simple: nationalism was destroying the Ottoman Empire in Europe and threatening to break up the Austro-Hungarian Empire. Greece had long before led the struggle for national liberation, winning its independence in 1830. In 1875 widespread nationalist rebellion in the Ottoman Empire resulted in Turkish repression, Russian intervention, and Great Power tensions. With Bismarck's help, delegates at the 1878 Congress of Berlin worked out the partial division of Turkish possessions in Europe. Austria-Hungary obtained the right to "occupy and administer" Bosnia and Herzegovina. Serbia and Romania won independence, and a part of Bulgaria won local autonomy. But the Ottoman Empire retained important Balkan holdings (see Map 27.1).

By 1903 Balkan nationalism was asserting itself once again. Serbia led the way, becoming openly hostile toward both Austria-Hungary and the Ottoman Empire. The Slavic Serbs looked to Slavic Russia for support of their national aspirations. To block

● **German Warships Under Full Steam** As suggested by these impressive ships engaged in battle exercises in 1907, Germany did succeed in building a large modern navy. But Britain was equally determined to maintain its naval superiority, and the spiraling arms race helped poison relations between the two countries. *(Archives Charmet/The Bridgeman Art Library)*

Serbian expansion and to take advantage of Russia's weakness after the 1905 revolution, Austria in 1908 formally annexed Bosnia and Herzegovina, with their large Serbian, Croatian, and Muslim populations. Serbia erupted in rage but could do nothing without Russian support.

Then two nationalist wars, the First and Second Balkan Wars in 1912 and 1913, finally destroyed the centuries-long Ottoman presence in Europe (see Map 27.2). This sudden but long-awaited event elated the Balkan nationalists and dismayed Austria-Hungary's multinational leaders. The former hoped and the latter feared that Austria might be next to be broken apart.

Within this tense context Archduke Francis Ferdinand, heir to the Austrian and Hungarian thrones, and his wife, Sophie, were assassinated by ultranationalist Serbian revolutionaries on June 28, 1914, during a state visit to the Bosnian capital of Sarajevo. Austria-Hungary's leaders held Serbia responsible and presented Serbia with an unconditional ultimatum on July 23. The Serbs had just forty-eight hours to agree to demands that amounted to Austrian control of the Serbian state. When Serbia replied moderately but evasively, Austria began to mobilize and then declared war on Serbia on July 28. Austria-Hungary had deliberately chosen war in a last-ditch attempt to stem the rising tide of hostile nationalism within its borders and to save its empire. The "Third Balkan War" had begun.

Of prime importance in Austria-Hungary's fateful decision was Germany's unconditional support. Emperor William II and his chancellor, Theobald von Bethmann-Hollweg, gave Austria-Hungary a "blank check," although realizing that war between Austria and Russia was the likely result. A resurgent Russia could not simply stand by and watch the Serbs be crushed. Yet Bethmann-Hollweg apparently hoped that while

Russia (and therefore France) would go to war, Great Britain would remain neutral, unwilling to fight for "Russian aggression" in the distant Balkans.

Military plans and timetables, rather than diplomacy, soon began to dictate policy, however. On July 28, as Austrian armies bombarded Belgrade, Tsar Nicholas II ordered a partial mobilization against Austria-Hungary, but almost immediately found this was impossible. The Russian general staff had assumed a war with both Austria and Germany: Russia could not mobilize against one without mobilizing against the other. Therefore, on July 29 Russia ordered full mobilization and in effect declared general war.

Germany faced the same conundrum. The German general staff had only prepared for a two-front war: first knocking out France with a lightning attack through neutral Belgium before turning on Russia. So on August 2, 1914, General Helmuth von Moltke demanded that Belgium permit German armies to pass through its territory. Belgium, whose neutrality had been solemnly guaranteed in 1839 by all the great states including Prussia, refused. Germany attacked. Thus, Germany's response to a war in the Balkans was an all-out invasion of France by way of neutral Belgium on August 3. Great Britain reacted by joining France and declaring war on Germany the following day. The First World War had begun.

MAP 27.1 **The Balkans After the Congress of Berlin, 1878** The Ottoman Empire suffered large territorial losses but remained a power in the Balkans.

MAP 27.2 **The Balkans in 1914** Ethnic boundaries did not follow political boundaries, and Serbian national aspirations threatened Austria-Hungary.

● **Nationalist Opposition in the Balkans** This band of well-armed and determined guerrillas from northern Albania was typical of groups fighting against Ottoman rule in the Balkans. Balkan nationalists succeeded in driving the Ottoman Turks out of most of Europe, but their victory increased tensions with Austria-Hungary and among the Great Powers. *(Roger-Viollet/Getty Images)*

In reflecting on the Great War's origins, it seems clear that Austria-Hungary deliberately started a conflict. The Third Balkans War was Austria-Hungary's desperate response to the revolutionary drive of Serbian nationalists to unify all Serbs in a single state. Moreover, in spite of Russian intervention, Germany was clearly most responsible for turning a third war in the Balkans into the Great War by its attack on Belgium and France. Why Germany was so aggressive in 1914 is less certain.

Diplomatic historians stress that after Bismarck's resignation in 1890 German leaders lost control of the international system. The Germans felt increasingly that their new country's status as a world power was declining, while the status of Britain, France, Russia, and the United States was growing. Indeed, the **Triple Entente** powers—Great Britain, France, and Russia—were checking Germany's vague but real aspirations and working to strangle Austria-Hungary, Germany's only real ally. Germany's aggression in 1914 reflected the failure of all European leaders, not just those in Germany, to incorporate Bismarck's mighty empire permanently and peacefully into the international system.

A more controversial interpretation argues that while Germany industrialized and urbanized rapidly after 1870 and had a popularly elected parliament, political power remained concentrated in the hands of the monarchy, army, and nobility. Frightened by the socialist movement and a wave of strikes in 1914, the German ruling class was

Triple Entente *The alliance of Great Britain, France, and Russia in the First World War.*

determined to hold on to power and willing to gamble on a diplomatic victory or even war as the means of rallying the masses to its side and preserving the existing system.

Above all, the triumph of nationalism was a crucial underlying precondition of the Great War. Nationalism was at the heart of the Balkan wars, and it drove the spiraling arms race. In each country the great majority of the population rallied to defend their nation and enthusiastically embraced war in August 1914. Patriotic nationalism brought unity in the short run.

In all of this, Europe's governing classes fatally underestimated the risk of war to themselves in 1914. They had forgotten that great wars and great social revolutions very often go hand in hand. Metternich's alliance of conservative forces in support of international peace and the social status quo had become a distant memory.

Stalemate and Slaughter

When the Germans invaded Belgium in August 1914, everyone believed the war would be short: "The boys will be home by Christmas." The Belgian army heroically defended its homeland, however, and then fell back to join a rapidly landed British army corps near the Franco-Belgian border. Instead of quickly capturing Paris in a vast encircling movement, dead-tired German soldiers by the end of August were advancing along an enormous front in the scorching summer heat. On September 6 the French attacked a gap in the German line at the Battle of the Marne. For three days France threw everything into the attack. At one point the French government desperately requisitioned all the taxis of Paris to rush reserves to the troops at the front. Finally, the Germans fell back. Paris and France had been miraculously saved (see Map 27.3).

The two stalled armies now began to dig trenches to protect themselves from machine-gun fire. Eventually an unbroken line of parallel trenches stretched over four hundred miles from the Belgian ports to the Swiss frontier. By November 1914 the defenders on both sides had dug in behind rows of trenches, mines, and barbed wire, and the slaughter on the western front had begun in earnest. For days and even weeks ceaseless shelling by heavy artillery supposedly "softened up" the enemy in a given area (and also signaled the coming attack). Then young draftees and their junior officers went "over the top" of the trenches in frontal attacks on the enemy's line.

The human cost was staggering; territorial gains were minuscule. The massive French and British offensives during 1915 never gained more than three miles of blood-soaked earth from the enemy. In the Battle of the Somme in the summer of 1916, the British and French gained an insignificant 125 square miles at the cost of 600,000 dead or wounded, and the Germans lost 500,000 men. In that same year the unsuccessful German campaign against Verdun cost 700,000 lives on both sides. British poet Siegfried Sassoon (1886–1967) wrote of the Somme offensive, "I am staring at a sunlit picture of Hell."

The year 1917 was equally terrible. The hero of Erich Remarque's great novel *All Quiet on the Western Front* (1929) describes a typical attack:

● **"Never Forget!"** This 1915 French poster with its passionate headline dramatizes Germany's brutal invasion of Belgium in 1914. Neutral Belgium is personified as a traumatized mother, assaulted and ravished by savage outlaws. The "rape of Belgium" featured prominently—and effectively—in anti-German propaganda. *(Mary Evans Picture Library)*

MAP 27.3 The First World War in Europe The trench war on the western front was concentrated in Belgium and northern France, while the war in the east encompassed an enormous territory.

We see men living with their skulls blown open; we see soldiers run with their two feet cut off. . . . Still the little piece of convulsed earth in which we lie is held. We have yielded no more than a few hundred yards of it as a prize to the enemy. But on every yard there lies a dead man.

Such was war on the western front.

Trench warfare shattered an entire generation of young men. Millions who could have provided political creativity and leadership after the war were forever missing. Millions were killed, and millions more who lived through the holocaust were maimed, shell-shocked, embittered, and profoundly disillusioned. The young soldiers went to war believing in the world of their leaders and elders—the pre-1914 world of order, progress, and patriotism. Then, in Remarque's words, the "first bombardment showed us our mistake, and under it the world as they had taught it to us broke in pieces."

trench warfare *Fighting behind rows of trenches, mines, and barbed wire; the cost in lives was staggering and the gains in territory minimal.*

The Widening War

On the eastern front slaughter did not degenerate into suicidal trench warfare. With the outbreak of war, the "Russian steamroller" immediately moved into eastern Germany but suffered appalling losses against the Germans under General Paul von Hindenburg and General Erich Ludendorff at the Battle of Tannenberg and the Battle of the Masurian Lakes in August and September 1914. Russia never threatened Germany again (see Map 27.3). On the Austrian front enormous armies seesawed back and forth. But with the help of German forces, the Austrians reversed the Russian advances of 1914 and forced the Russians to retreat deep into their own territory in the 1915 eastern campaign. A staggering 2.5 million Russians were killed, wounded, or taken prisoner that year.

These changing tides of victory and hopes of territorial gains brought neutral countries into the war. Italy, a member of the Triple Alliance since 1882, had declared its neutrality in 1914 on the grounds that Austria had launched a war of aggression. Then, in May 1915, Italy joined the Triple Entente of Great Britain, France, and Russia in return for promises of Austrian territory. In October 1914 the Ottoman Empire joined with Austria and Germany, by then known as the Central Powers. The following September Bulgaria followed the Ottoman Empire's lead in order to settle old scores with Serbia (see Map 27.3).

The entry of the Ottoman Turks carried the war into the Middle East, a momentous development. In 1915 British forces tried to take the Dardanelles and Constantinople from Turkey but were badly defeated. The British were more successful at inciting the Arabs to revolt against their Turkish overlords. An enigmatic British colonel, soon known to millions as Lawrence of Arabia, helped lead the Arab revolt in early 1917. In 1918 British armies totally smashed the old Ottoman state, drawing primarily on imperial forces from Egypt, India, Australia, and New Zealand. Thus war brought revolutionary change to the Middle East (see pages 848–857).

War also spread to some parts of Africa and East Asia. Instead of revolting as the Germans hoped, French and British colonial subjects supported their foreign masters, providing critical supplies and fighting in Europe and in the Ottoman Empire. They also helped local British and French commanders seize Germany's colonies around the globe. More than a million Africans served in the various armies of the warring powers, with more than double that number serving as porters to carry equipment. The opportunity to fight against and kill Europeans, and the spectacle of Europeans fighting each other to protect their nations' freedom and their individual rights, had a profound impact on these soldiers. African American soldiers serving in France also gained a new sense of dignity and self-worth from their experiences in the war. The Japanese, allied in Asia with the British since 1902, similarly used the war to grab German outposts in the Pacific Ocean and on the Chinese mainland, infuriating Chinese patriots and heightening long-standing tensions between China and Japan.

Another crucial development in the expanding conflict came in April 1917 when the United States declared war on Germany. American intervention grew out of the war at sea, sympathy for the Triple Entente, and the increasing desperation of total war. At the beginning of the war Britain and France had established a total naval blockade to strangle the Central Powers. No neutral ship was permitted to sail to Germany with any cargo. The blockade annoyed Americans, but effective propaganda about German atrocities in occupied Belgium as well as lush profits from selling war supplies to Britain and France blunted American indignation.

Moreover, in early 1915 Germany launched a counter-blockade using the murderously effective submarine, a new weapon that sank ships without the traditional niceties of fair warning under international law. In May a German submarine sank the British passenger liner *Lusitania,* which was also carrying arms and munitions. More than a thousand people, including 139 Americans, died. President Woodrow Wilson protested vigorously. Germany was forced to restrict its submarine warfare for almost two years, or face almost certain war with the United States.

Early in 1917 the German military command—confident that improved submarines could starve Britain into submission before the United States could come to its

Lusitania *The name of the British passenger liner sunk by a German submarine that claimed more than a thousand lives.*

● **The Tragic Absurdity of Trench Warfare** As soldiers charged across a scarred battlefield and overran an enemy trench, the dead defender on the right would fire no more. But this was only another futile charge that would yield much blood and little land. A whole generation was being decimated by the slaughter. *(By courtesy of the Trustees of the Imperial War Museum)*

● **Otto Dix: War (detail)** Returning to Germany after the war, Dix was haunted by the horrors he had seen. This vivid expressionist masterpiece, part of a triptych painted in 1929–1932, probes the tormented memory of endless days in muddy trenches and dugouts, living with rats and lice and the constant danger of exploding shells, snipers, and all-out attack. Many who escaped death or dismemberment were mentally wounded forever by their experiences. *(Staatliche Kunstsammlungen Dresden. © 2002 Artists Rights Society [ARS], New York/ VG Bild-Kunst, Bonn)*

rescue—resumed unrestricted submarine warfare. Like the invasion of Belgium, this was a reckless gamble. "German submarine warfare against commerce," President Wilson told a sympathetic Congress and people, "is a warfare against mankind." Thus the last uncommitted great nation, as fresh and enthusiastic as Europe had been in 1914, entered the world war in April 1917. The United States eventually tipped the balance in favor of the Triple Entente and its allies.

• • • • • • • • • • • •

THE HOME FRONT

How did total war impact the home fronts of the major European combatants?

Before looking at the Great War's final year, let us turn our attention to the people on the home front. War's impact on them was no less massive than on the men crouched in the trenches.

Mobilizing for Total War

In August 1914 most Europeans greeted the outbreak of hostilities enthusiastically, believing their own nation was in the right and defending itself from aggression. Except for a few extreme left-wingers, even socialists supported the war. Everywhere the support of the patriotic masses and working class contributed to national unity and an energetic war effort.

● **Hair for the War Effort** Blockaded and cut off from overseas supplies, Germany mobilized effectively to find substitutes at home. This poster calls on German women—especially young women with long flowing tresses—to donate their hair, which was used to make rope. Children were organized by their teachers into garbage brigades to collect every scrap of useful material. *(akg-images)*

total war *In each country during the First World War, a government of national unity that began to plan and control economic and social life in order to make the greatest possible military effort.*

War Raw Materials Board *Masterminded by Walter Rathenau, this was set up by the German government to ration and distribute raw materials.*

Auxiliary Service Law *A German law requiring all males between the ages of seventeen and sixty to work only at jobs considered critical to the war effort.*

By mid-October generals and politicians began to realize that, with no end in sight, more than patriotism would be needed to win the war. Every country experienced a relentless, desperate demand for men and weapons. In each country change had to come, and fast, to keep the war machine from sputtering to a stop.

The change came through national unity governments that began to plan and control economic and social life in order to wage **total war.** Governments imposed rationing, price and wage controls, and even restrictions on workers' freedom of movement. These total war economies involved entire populations, blurring the old distinction between soldiers on the battlefield and civilians at home. Based on tremendously productive industrial economies, total war yielded an effective—and therefore destructive—war effort on all sides. (See the feature "Listening to the Past: The Experience of War" on pages 842–843.)

However awful the war was, the ability of central governments to manage and control highly complicated economies increased and strengthened their powers, often along socialist lines. With the First World War socialism for the first time became a realistic economic blueprint rather than a utopian dream. Germany went furthest in developing a planned economy to wage total war.

As soon as war began, the Jewish industrialist Walter Rathenau convinced the German government to set up the **War Raw Materials Board** to ration and distribute raw materials. Under Rathenau's direction every useful material from foreign oil to barnyard manure was inventoried and rationed. Moreover, the board launched successful attempts to produce substitutes, such as synthetic rubber and synthetic nitrates, needed to make explosives and essential to the blockaded German war machine. An aggressive recycling campaign augmented these efforts. Food was also rationed, with men and women doing hard manual work receiving extra rations. During the war's final two years only children and expectant mothers received milk rations. Many people were living on less than a thousand calories a day. At the same time, Germany's failure to tax the war profits of private firms heavily enough contributed to massive deficit financing, inflation, the growth of a black market, and the eventual re-emergence of class conflict.

Following the terrible Battles of Verdun and the Somme in 1916, military leaders Hindenburg and Ludendorff became Germany's real rulers. They decreed the ultimate mobilization for total war: all agriculture, industry, and labor must be "used exclusively for the conduct of War."[3] In December 1916 military leaders rammed through the Reichstag the **Auxiliary Service Law,** which required all males between seventeen and sixty to work only at jobs considered critical to the war effort. Many more women also followed those already working into war factories, mines, and steel mills. Thus in Germany total war led to history's first "totalitarian" society.

Great Britain mobilized for total war less rapidly and less completely than Germany, for it could import materials from its empire and from the United States. In June 1915, however, a serious shortage of shells led to the establishment of the Ministry of Munitions under David Lloyd George. The ministry organized private industry to

● **Waging Total War** A British war plant strains to meet the insatiable demand for trench-smashing heavy artillery shells. Quite typically, many of these defense workers are women. *(By courtesy of the Trustees of the Imperial War Museum)*

produce for the war, controlled profits, allocated labor, fixed wage rates, and settled labor disputes. By December 1916 the British economy was largely planned and regulated directly by the state.

The Social Impact

The social impact of total war was no less profound than the economic impact, though again there were important national variations. The military's insatiable needs created a tremendous demand for workers. This situation—seldom, if ever, seen before 1914, when unemployment and poverty had been facts of urban life—brought about momentous changes.

One such change was greater power and prestige for labor unions. Having proved their loyalty in August 1914, labor unions cooperated with war governments on work rules, wages, and production schedules in return for real participation in important decisions. This entry of labor leaders into policymaking councils paralleled the entry of socialist leaders into the war governments.

Women's roles also changed dramatically. In every country large numbers of women, displaying a growing sense of independence, left home and domestic service to work in industry, transportation, and offices. Moreover, women became highly visible—not only as munitions workers but as bank tellers, mail carriers, even police officers. Women also served as nurses and doctors at the front. (See the feature "Individuals in Society: Vera Brittain.") In general, the war greatly expanded the range of women's activities and changed attitudes toward women. As a direct result of women's many-sided war effort, Britain, Germany, and Austria granted women the right to vote immediately after the war.

War promoted social equality, blurring class distinctions and lessening the gap between rich and poor. Greater equality was reflected in full employment, rationing according to physical needs, and a sharing of hardships. Society became more uniform and more egalitarian, in spite of some war profiteering.

Death itself had no respect for traditional social distinctions. It savagely decimated both the young aristocratic officers who led the charge and the mass of drafted peasants and unskilled workers who followed. Death, however, often spared the aristocrats of labor—the skilled workers and foremen. Their lives were too valuable to squander at the front, for they were needed to train the newly recruited women and older unskilled men laboring valiantly in war plants at home.

Growing Political Tensions

> **Primary Source:**
> **Mud and Khaki, Memoirs of an Incomplete Soldier**
> *Read from the memoirs of a British soldier, and imagine the horrors of trench warfare and poison gas in World War I.*

During the war's first two years most soldiers and civilians supported their governments. Even in Austria-Hungary—the most vulnerable of the belligerents with its competing nationalities—loyalty to the state and monarchy remained astonishingly strong through 1916. Belief in a just cause, patriotic nationalism, the planned economy, and a sharing of burdens united peoples behind their various national leaders.

Each government employed rigorous censorship to control public opinion, and each used propaganda to maintain popular support. German propaganda pictured black soldiers from France's African empire raping German women. The French and British ceaselessly recounted and exaggerated German atrocities in Belgium and elsewhere. Patriotic posters and slogans, slanted news, and biased editorials inflamed national hatreds and helped sustain superhuman efforts.

By spring 1916, however, people were beginning to crack under the strain of total war. In April 1916 Irish nationalists in Dublin tried to take advantage of this situation and rose up against British rule in an Easter Rebellion. The rebels were crushed after a week of bitter fighting and their leaders executed. Strikes and protest marches over inadequate food flared up on every home front. Soldiers' morale began to decline. Italian troops mutinied. Numerous French units refused to fight for a time after the disastrous French offensive of May 1917. War-weariness and defeatism also swept France's civilian population before Georges Clemenceau emerged as a ruthless and effective wartime leader in November 1917. Clemenceau (1841–1929) established a virtual dictatorship, pouncing on strikers and jailing without trial anyone who dared to suggest a compromise peace with Germany.

The Central Powers experienced the most strain. In October 1916 a young socialist crying "Down with Absolutism! We want peace!" assassinated Austria's chief minister.[4] When the feeble old Emperor Francis Joseph died the following month a unifying symbol disappeared. Conflicts among nationalities grew, and both Czech and Yugoslav leaders demanded autonomous democratic states for their peoples. The strain of total war and of the Auxiliary Service Law was also evident in Germany. By 1917 national political unity was collapsing and prewar social conflicts re-emerging. Some socialists in the Reichstag voted against war credits, and in July 1917 a coalition of socialists and Catholics passed a resolution calling for a compromise "peace without annexations or reparations." Conservatives and military leaders found such a peace unthinkable. Thus militaristic Germany, like its ally Austria-Hungary (and its enemy France), began to crack in 1917. But it was Russia that collapsed first and saved the Central Powers—for a time.

Vera Brittain

Although the Great War upended millions of lives, it struck Europe's young people with the greatest force. For Vera Brittain (1893–1970), as for so many in her generation, the war became life's defining experience, which she captured forever in her famous autobiography, *Testament of Youth* (1933).

Brittain grew up in a wealthy business family in northern England, bristling at small-town conventions and discrimination against women. Very close to her brother Edward, two years her junior, Brittain read voraciously and dreamed of being a successful writer. Finishing boarding school and beating down her father's objections, she prepared for Oxford's rigorous entry exams and won a scholarship to its women's college. Brittain also fell in love with Roland Leighton, an equally brilliant student from a literary family and her brother's best friend. All three, along with two more close friends, Victor Richardson and Geoffrey Thurlow, confidently prepared to enter Oxford in late 1914.

When war suddenly approached in July 1914, Brittain shared with millions of Europeans a thrilling surge of patriotic support for her government, a pro-war enthusiasm she later played down in her published writings. She wrote in her diary that her "great fear" was that England would declare its neutrality and commit the "grossest treachery" toward France.* She seconded Roland's decision to enlist, agreeing with her sweetheart's glamorous view of war as "very ennobling and very beautiful." Later, exchanging anxious letters in 1915 with Roland in France, Vera began to see the conflict in personal, human terms. She wondered if any victory or defeat could be worth Roland's life.

Struggling to quell her doubts, Brittain redoubled her commitment to England's cause and volunteered as an army nurse. For the next three years she served with distinction in military hospitals in London, Malta, and northern France, repeatedly torn between the vision of noble sacrifice and the reality of human tragedy. She lost her sexual inhibitions caring for mangled male bodies, and she longed to consummate her love with Roland. Awaiting his return on leave on Christmas Day in 1915, she was greeted instead with a telegram: Roland had been killed two days before.

Roland's death was the first of the devastating blows that eventually overwhelmed Brittain's idealistic patriotism. In 1917, first Geoffrey and then Victor died from gruesome wounds. In early 1918, as the last great German offensive covered the floors of her war-zone hospital with maimed and dying German prisoners, the bone-weary Vera felt a common humanity and saw only more victims. A few weeks later brother Edward—her last hope—died in action. When the war ended, she was, she said, a "complete automaton," with "my deepest emotions paralyzed if not dead."

Returning to Oxford and finishing her studies, Brittain gradually recovered. She formed a deep, restorative friendship with another talented woman writer, Winifred Holtby, published novels and articles, and became a leader in the feminist campaign for gender equality. She also married and had children. But her wartime memories were always there. Finally, Brittain succeeded in coming to grips with them in *Testament of Youth,* her powerful antiwar autobiography. The unflinching narrative spoke to the experiences of an entire generation and became a runaway bestseller. Above all, perhaps, Brittain captured the ambivalent, contradictory character of the war, when millions of young people found excitement, courage, and common purpose but succeeded only in destroying their lives with their superhuman efforts and futile sacrifices. Becoming ever more committed to pacifism, Brittain opposed England's entry into World War II.

Vera Brittain, marked forever by her wartime experiences. *(Vera Brittain Archive, William Ready Division of Archives and Research Collections, McMaster University Library)*

Questions for Analysis

1. What were Brittain's initial feelings toward the war? How did they change as the conflict continued? Why did they change?

2. Why did Brittain volunteer as a nurse, as many women did? How might wartime nursing have influenced women of her generation?

3. In portraying the ambivalent, contradictory character of World War I for Europe's youth, was Brittain describing the contradictory character of all modern warfare?

*Quoted in the excellent study by P. Berry and M. Bostridge, *Vera Brittain: A Life* (London: Virago Press, 2001), p. 59; additional quotes are from pp. 80 and 136. This work is highly recommended.

THE RUSSIAN REVOLUTION

How and why did the war lead to the Russian Revolution?

The 1917 Russian Revolution, directly related to the Great War, had a significance far beyond the wartime agonies of a single European nation. The Russian Revolution opened a new era, with a radically new prototype of state and society.

The Fall of Imperial Russia

Like their allies and their enemies, Russians embraced war with patriotic enthusiasm in 1914. At the Winter Palace, while kneeling throngs sang "God Save the Tsar," Tsar Nicholas II (r. 1894–1917) vowed never to make peace as long as the enemy stood on Russian soil. For a moment Russia was united. But soon the war began to take its toll.

Unprecedented artillery barrages quickly exhausted Russia's supplies of shells and ammunition, and better-equipped German armies inflicted terrible losses—one and a half million casualties and nearly another million captured in 1915 alone. In that year substantial numbers of Russian soldiers were sent to the front without rifles; they were told to find their arms among the dead. Nevertheless, Russia's battered peasant army continued to fight courageously. The Duma, (the lower house of the Russian parliament) and local governments led the effort toward full mobilization, setting up special committees to coordinate defense, industry, transportation, and agriculture. Although these efforts improved the military situation some, there were many failures, and Russia mobilized less effectively for total war than did the other warring nations.

The great problem was leadership. Under the constitution resulting from the 1905 revolution (see pages 694–695), the tsar retained complete control over the bureaucracy and the army. A kindly, slightly stupid man, Nicholas failed to form a close partnership with his citizens in order to fight the war more effectively. He relied instead on the old bureaucratic apparatus, distrusting the moderate Duma, rejecting popular involvement, and resisting calls to share power. As a result, the Duma, the educated middle classes, and the masses became increasingly critical of the tsar's leadership. In response, Nicholas announced in September 1915 that he was traveling to the front to lead Russia's armies.

His departure was a fatal turning point, as the hysterical German-born empress, Tsarina Alexandra, now took control of the government. She tried to rule absolutely in her husband's absence with an uneducated Siberian preacher, appropriately nicknamed "Rasputin" (Russian for the "Degenerate"), as her most trusted adviser. Rasputin gained her trust by miraculously stopping the bleeding, perhaps through hypnosis, of her hemophiliac son Alexis, Alexandra's fifth child and heir to the throne. In this atmosphere of unreality the government slid steadily toward revolution.

In a desperate attempt to right the situation, three members of the high aristocracy murdered Rasputin in December 1916, sending the empress into semipermanent shock. In the meantime, food shortages worsened and morale declined. On March 8 a women's bread march in Petrograd (formerly St. Petersburg) started riots, which spread throughout the city. The tsar ordered troops to restore order, but discipline broke down, and the soldiers joined the revolutionary crowd. The Duma declared a provisional government on March 12, 1917. Three days later Nicholas abdicated.

The Provisional Government

The March revolution was joyfully accepted throughout the country. After generations of arbitrary authoritarianism, the provisional government quickly established equality before the law; freedom of religion, speech, and assembly; the right of unions to organize and strike; and other classic liberal measures. But both moderate socialist and liberal leaders of the provisional government rejected social revolution. The government formed in May 1917, which included the socialist Alexander Kerensky, refused to confiscate large landholdings and give them to peasants, fearing that such drastic action in the countryside would only complete the disintegration of Russia's peasant army. For the patriotic Kerensky, who became prime minister in July, as for other moderate socialists, the continuation of war was still the all-important national duty. There would be plenty of time for land reform later; for now all the government's efforts were directed toward a last offensive in July. Meanwhile human suffering and war-weariness grew, sapping the provisional government's limited strength.

From its first day the provisional government had to share power with a formidable rival—the **Petrograd Soviet** (or council) of Workers' and Soldiers' Deputies. Modeled on the revolutionary soviets of 1905, the Petrograd Soviet was a huge, fluctuating mass meeting of two thousand to three thousand workers, soldiers, and socialist intellectuals. This counter- or half-government issued its own radical orders, further weakening the provisional government. Most famous of these was **Army Order No. 1** (March 1917), which stripped officers of their authority and gave power to elected committees of common soldiers.

Army Order No. 1 led to a total collapse of army discipline and the summary execution of many an officer. Meanwhile, masses of peasant soldiers began "voting with their feet," to use Lenin's graphic phrase. They returned to their villages to get a share of the land, which peasants were simply seizing from landowners in a great agrarian upheaval. Liberty was turning into anarchy in the summer of 1917, offering an unparalleled opportunity for the most radical and most talented of Russia's many socialist leaders, Vladimir Ilyich Lenin (1870–1924).

● **"The Russian Ruling House"** This wartime cartoon captures the ominous, spellbinding power of Rasputin over Tsar Nicholas II and his wife, Alexandra. Rasputin's manipulations disgusted Russian public opinion and contributed to the monarchy's collapse. (*Stock Montage*)

Lenin and the Bolshevik Revolution

Lenin's whole life had been dedicated to the revolutionary cause. Born into the middle class, Lenin became an implacable enemy of imperial Russia when his older brother was executed for plotting to kill the tsar in 1887. As a law student Lenin began searching for a revolutionary faith and found it in Marxian socialism. Exiled to Siberia for three years because of socialist agitation, Lenin studied Marxian doctrines with religious ferocity. After his release he lived for seventeen years in western Europe and developed his own revolutionary interpretations of Marxian thought.

Three interrelated ideas were central for Lenin. First, turning to the early fire-breathing Marx of 1848 and *The Communist Manifesto* for inspiration, Lenin stressed that only violent revolution could destroy capitalism. Lenin's second, more original idea was that a socialist revolution was possible even in a country like Russia, where capitalism was not fully developed. There the industrial working class was small, but the poor peasants were also potential revolutionaries.

Petrograd Soviet
A counter-government that was a huge, fluctuating mass meeting of two to three thousand workers, soldiers, and socialist intellectuals.

Army Order No. 1 *A radical order of the Petrograd Soviet that stripped officers of their authority and placed power in the hands of elected committees of common soldiers.*

● Lenin Rallies Worker and Soldier Delegates At a midnight meeting of the Petrograd Soviet, the Bolsheviks rise up and seize power on November 6, 1917. This painting from the 1940s idealizes Lenin, but his great talents as a revolutionary leader are undeniable. In this re-creation Stalin, who actually played only a small role in the uprising, is standing behind Lenin, already his trusty right-hand man. *(Sovfoto)*

Bolsheviks *The "majority group"; this was Lenin's camp of the Russian party of Marxian socialism.*

Lenin believed that at a given moment revolution was determined more by human leadership than by vast historical laws. Thus was born his third basic idea: the necessity of a highly disciplined workers' party, strictly controlled by a dedicated elite, a vanguard, of intellectuals and full-time revolutionaries like Lenin himself. This elite would not stop until revolution brought it to power.

Lenin's theories and methods did not go unchallenged by other Russian Marxists. At a Social Democratic Labor Party congress in London in 1903, Lenin demanded a small, disciplined, elitist party; his opponents wanted a more democratic party with mass membership. The Russian party of Marxian socialism was divided then into two rival factions. Lenin's camp was called **Bolsheviks,** or "majority group"; his opponents were *Mensheviks,* or "minority group." Lenin's majority did not last, but he kept the Bolshevik name and developed the party he wanted anyhow: tough, disciplined, revolutionary.

Lenin, from neutral Switzerland, saw the war as a product of imperialistic rivalries and as a marvelous opportunity for class war and socialist upheaval. After the March revolution the German government provided safe passage for Lenin, his wife, and about twenty trusted colleagues across Germany and back into Russia in April 1917. The Germans hoped that Lenin would undermine Russia's sagging war effort. They were not disappointed.

Arriving triumphantly at Petrograd's Finland Station on April 3, Lenin attacked at once. To the great astonishment of the local Bolsheviks, he rejected all cooperation with the "bourgeois" provisional government of the liberals and moderate socialists. His slogans were radical in the extreme: "All power to the soviets"; "All land to the peasants"; "Stop the war now." Never a slave to Marxian determinism, Lenin was a superb tactician and realized his moment had come.

Throughout the summer the Bolsheviks markedly increased their popular support, while Prime Minister Kerensky's unwavering support for the war lost him all credit with the army, the only force that might have saved him and democratic government in Russia. In October the Bolsheviks gained a fragile majority in the Petrograd Soviet. It was Lenin's supporter Leon Trotsky (1879–1940), an independent radical Marxist, who brilliantly executed the Bolshevik seizure of power. On the night of November 6, militant Trotsky followers from the Petrograd Soviet joined with trusty Bolshevik soldiers to seize government buildings and arrest provisional government members. At the congress of soviets a Bolshevik majority—roughly 390 of 650 turbulent delegates—then declared that all power had passed to the soviets and named Lenin head of the new government.

The Bolsheviks came to power for three key reasons. First, by late 1917 democracy had given way to anarchy, leaving a power vacuum. Second, in Lenin and Trotsky the Bolsheviks had an utterly determined and truly superior leadership. Third, in 1917

The Russian Revolution

1914	Russia enthusiastically enters the First World War.
1915	Russia suffers one and a half million casualties. Progressive bloc calls for a new government responsible to the Duma rather than to the tsar. Tsar Nicholas adjourns the Duma and departs for the front; Alexandra and Rasputin exert a strong influence on the government.
December 1916	Rasputin is murdered.
March 8, 1917	Bread riots take place in Petrograd (St. Petersburg).
March 12, 1917	Duma declares a provisional government.
March 15, 1917	Tsar Nicholas abdicates without protest.
April 3, 1917	Lenin returns from exile and denounces the provisional government.
May 1917	Reorganized provisional government, including Kerensky, continues the war. Petrograd Soviet issues Army Order No. 1, granting military power to committees of common soldiers.
Summer 1917	Agrarian upheavals: peasants seize estates; peasant soldiers desert the army to participate.
October 1917	Bolsheviks gain a majority in the Petrograd Soviet.
November 6, 1917	Bolsheviks seize power; Lenin heads the new "provisional workers' and peasants' government."
November 1917	Lenin accepts peasant seizure of land and worker control of factories; all banks are nationalized.
January 1918	Lenin permanently disbands the Constituent Assembly.
February 1918	Lenin convinces the Bolshevik Central Committee to accept a humiliating peace with Germany in order to safeguard the revolution.
March 1918	Treaty of Brest-Litovsk: Russia loses one-third of its population. Trotsky as war commissar begins to rebuild the Russian army.
Summer 1918	White armies oppose the Bolshevik Revolution.
1918–1922	Great civil war takes place.
1919	White armies are on the offensive but divided politically; they receive little benefit from Allied intervention.
1922	Lenin and the Red Army are victorious.

the Bolsheviks appealed to many soldiers and urban workers, people who were exhausted by war and eager for socialism.

Dictatorship and Civil War

History is full of short-lived coups and unsuccessful revolutions. The truly monumental accomplishment of Lenin, Trotsky, and the rest of the Bolsheviks was not taking power but keeping it and conquering the chaos they had helped create. How was this done?

Lenin had the genius to profit from developments over which he and the Bolsheviks had no control. Since summer 1917 an unstoppable peasant revolution had been sweeping across Russia as peasants seized and divided among themselves the estates of the landlords and the church. Thus Lenin's first law, which supposedly gave land to

● **"You! Have You Volunteered?"** A Red Army soldier makes a compelling direct appeal to the ordinary citizen and demands all-out support for the Bolshevik cause in this 1920 poster by Dmitri Moor, a popular Soviet artist. Lenin recognized the importance of visual propaganda in a vast country with limited literacy, and mass-produced posters like this one were everywhere during the civil war of 1918–1922. *(Stephen White, University of Glasgow)*

Constituent Assembly *A freely elected assembly promised by the Bolsheviks that was permanently disbanded after one day on Lenin's orders after Bolshevik delegates won fewer than one-fourth of the seats.*

war communism *The application of the total-war concept to a civil conflict; the Bolsheviks seized grain from peasants, introduced rationing, nationalized all banks and industry, and required everyone to work.*

the peasants, actually merely approved what peasants were already doing. Lenin then met urban workers' greatest demand with a decree in November 1917 giving direct control of individual factories to local workers' committees.

Lenin also acknowledged that Russia had lost the war with Germany and that the only realistic position was peace at any price. That price was very high. Germany demanded in December 1917 that the Soviet government give up all its western territories. These areas were inhabited by Poles, Finns, Lithuanians, and other non-Russians. The Bolsheviks surrendered a third of old Russia's population in the Treaty of Brest-Litovsk in March 1918. With peace, however, Lenin had escaped the certain disaster of continued war and could pursue his goal of absolute political power for the Bolsheviks—now renamed Communists—within Russia.

In November 1917 the Bolsheviks had cleverly proclaimed their regime only a "provisional workers' and peasants' government," promising that a freely elected **Constituent Assembly** would draw up a new constitution. But after Bolshevik delegates won fewer than one-fourth of the seats, the Constituent Assembly met for only one day, on January 18, 1918. Bolshevik soldiers acting under Lenin's orders then permanently disbanded it.

The destruction of the democratically elected Constituent Assembly revealed the Bolsheviks' true intentions, and people who had risen up for self-rule in November realized they were again getting dictatorship from the capital. For the next three years "Long live the [democratic] soviets; down with the Bolsheviks" was a popular slogan. Officers of the old army organized the so-called White opposition to the Bolsheviks in southern Russia, Ukraine, Siberia, and west of Petrograd. The Whites came from many social groups united only by their hatred of the Bolsheviks—the Reds. By the end of 1918 White armies were on the attack. In October 1919 it appeared they might triumph as they closed in on Lenin's government from three sides. Yet they did not. Intense fighting continued through 1920, and the tide turned. Although some White forces held out until 1923, the Red Army captured Vladivostok in October 1922 and that effectively marked the end of the civil war. Lenin had won.

Lenin and the Bolsheviks won for several reasons. Strategically, they controlled the center, while the Whites were always on the fringes and disunited. Moreover, the poorly defined political program of the Whites was vaguely conservative, and it did not unite all the foes of the Bolsheviks under a progressive, democratic banner. Most important, the Communists quickly developed a better army, an army for which the divided Whites were no match.

The Bolsheviks also mobilized the home front. Establishing **war communism**—the application of the total-war concept to a civil conflict—they seized grain from peasants, introduced rationing, nationalized all banks and industry, and required everyone to work. Although these measures contributed to a breakdown of normal economic activity, they also served to maintain labor discipline and to keep the Red Army supplied.

"Revolutionary terror" also contributed to the Communist victory. The old tsarist secret police was reestablished as the **Cheka,** which hunted down and executed thousands of real or supposed foes, such as the tsar and his family and other "class enemies." The terror caused by the secret police became a tool of the government. The Cheka sowed fear, and fear silenced opposition.

Finally, foreign military intervention in the civil war ended up helping the Communists. The Allies (the Americans, British, and Japanese) sent troops to Archangel and Vladivostok to prevent war materiel that they had sent to the provisional government from being captured by the Germans. After the Soviet government nationalized all foreign-owned factories without compensation and refused to pay all of Russia's foreign debts, Western governments, particularly France, began to support White armies. While these small and halfhearted efforts did little to help the Whites' cause, they did permit the Communists to appeal to the patriotic nationalism of ethnic Russians.

Together, the Russian Revolution and the Bolshevik triumph were one reason why the First World War was such a major turning point in modern history. A radically new government, based on socialism and one-party dictatorship, came to power in a great European state, maintained power, and eagerly encouraged worldwide revolution. Although Russia was undoubtedly headed for some kind of political crisis before 1914, it is hard to imagine the triumph of the most radical proponents of change and reform except in a situation of total collapse. That was precisely what happened to Russia in the First World War.

Cheka   *The re-established tsarist secret police, which hunted down and executed thousands of real or suspected foes, sowing fear and silencing opposition.*

THE PEACE SETTLEMENT

Why is the peace settlement following World War I considered by most historians to have been a terrible failure?

Victory over revolutionary Russia temporarily boosted sagging German morale. In spring 1918 the Germans launched their last major attack against France. It failed. With breathtaking rapidity, the United States, Great Britain, and France then decisively defeated Germany militarily. Austria-Hungary and the Ottoman Empire broke apart and ceased to exist. The guns of world war finally fell silent. Then, as civil war spread in Russia and as chaos engulfed much of eastern Europe, the victorious Western Allies came together in Paris to establish a lasting peace.

Expectations were high; optimism almost unlimited. Laboring intensively, the allies soon worked out terms for peace with Germany and for the creation of the peacekeeping **League of Nations.** The 1919 peace settlement, however, turned out to be a failure and only sowed the seeds of another war. Surely this was the ultimate tragedy of the Great War that cost $332 billion and left 10 million people dead and another 20 million wounded. How did this tragedy happen? Why was the peace settlement unsuccessful?

League of Nations   *A permanent international organization established during the peace conference in Paris in January 1919; it was designed to protect member states from aggression and avert future wars.*

The End of the War

After the March 1917 Russian Revolution, there were major strikes in Germany. To quell these demonstrations and counter a growing peace movement, the German military established a virtual dictatorship and exploited the collapse of Russian armies in the harsh Treaty of Brest-Litovsk. With victory in the east quieting German moderates, General Ludendorff and company fell on France once more in the great spring offensive of 1918. For a time German armies pushed forward, coming within thirty-five miles of Paris, but they never broke through. They were decisively stopped in July at the second Battle of the Marne, where 140,000 fresh American soldiers saw action.

Adding 2 million men in arms to the war effort by August, the late but massive American intervention decisively tipped the scales in favor of Allied victory.

By September British, French, and American armies were advancing steadily on all fronts. On October 4 the emperor formed a new, more liberal German government to sue for peace. As negotiations over an armistice dragged on, an angry and frustrated German people finally rose up. On November 3 sailors in Kiel mutinied, and throughout northern Germany soldiers and workers established revolutionary councils on the Russian soviet model. Austria-Hungary surrendered to the Allies the same day. With army discipline collapsing, the German emperor abdicated and fled to Holland. Socialist leaders in Berlin proclaimed a German republic on November 9 and simultaneously agreed to tough Allied terms of surrender. The armistice went into effect at 11 A.M. on November 11, 1918. The war was over.

The German Revolution of November 1918 resembled the Russian Revolution of March 1917. In both countries a popular uprising toppled an authoritarian monarchy, and moderate socialists took control of the government. But when Germany's radical socialists tried to seize power, the moderate socialists called on the army to crush the attempted coup. Thus Germany had a political revolution, but without a communist second installment. It was Russia without Lenin's Bolshevik triumph.

Military defeat brought political revolution to Austria-Hungary, as it had to Germany, Russia, and the Ottoman Empire (see pages 848–854). In Austria-Hungary the revolution was primarily nationalistic and republican in character. Independent Austrian, Hungarian, and Czechoslovak republics were proclaimed. A greatly expanded Serbian monarchy united the South Slavs and took the name Yugoslavia. The prospect of firmly establishing the new national states overrode class considerations for most people in east-central Europe.

The Treaty of Versailles

Primary Source:
Comments of the German Delegation to the Paris Peace Conference on the Conditions of Peace, October 1919
Read Germany's response to the Treaty of Versailles, which deprived it of its colonies, 13 percent of its land, and 10 percent of its population.

The peace conference opened in the Versailles Palace near Paris in January 1919 with seventy delegates representing twenty-seven victorious nations. There were great expectations. A young British diplomat later wrote that the victors "believed in nationalism, we believed in the self-determination of peoples." Indeed, "we were journeying to Paris . . . to found a new order in Europe. We were preparing not Peace only, but Eternal Peace."[5] This general optimism and idealism had been greatly strengthened by President Wilson's January 1918 peace proposal, the Fourteen Points, which stressed national self-determination and the rights of small countries.

The real powers at the conference were the United States, Great Britain, and France. Germany was not allowed to participate, and Russia was locked in civil war and did not attend. Italy was considered one of the Big Four, but its role was quite limited. Almost immediately the three Allies began to quarrel. President Wilson insisted that the first order of business be the creation of the League of Nations, for he passionately believed that only a permanent international organization could protect member states from aggression and avert future wars. Wilson had his way, although Lloyd George of Great Britain and especially Clemenceau of France were unenthusiastic. They were primarily concerned with punishing Germany.

Playing on British nationalism, Lloyd George had already won a smashing electoral victory in December on the popular platform of making Germany pay for the war. Although personally inclined to make a somewhat moderate peace with Germany, Lloyd George was a captive of demands for a total victory worthy of the sacrifices of total war against a totally depraved enemy. As Rudyard Kipling summed up the general British feeling at war's end, the Germans were "a people with the heart of beasts."[6]

France's Georges Clemenceau, like most French people, also wanted old-fashioned revenge. In addition, he wanted lasting security for France, which, he believed, required the creation of a buffer state between France and Germany, the permanent demilitarization of Germany, and vast German reparations. Otherwise, he feared, Germany would sooner or later attack France again. Moreover, France had no English Channel (or Atlantic Ocean) as a reassuring barrier against German aggression. Wilson, supported by Lloyd George, would hear none of this. Clemenceau's demands seemed vindictive, violating morality and the principle of national self-determination. By April the conference was deadlocked on the German question, and Wilson packed his bags to go home.

In the end, Clemenceau agreed to a compromise. He gave up the French demand for a Rhineland buffer state in return for a formal defensive alliance with the United States and Great Britain. Both Wilson and Lloyd George also promised their countries would come to France's aid if attacked. Thus Clemenceau appeared to win his goal of French security, as Wilson had won his of a permanent international organization.

The terms of the **Treaty of Versailles** between the Allies and Germany were not unreasonable as a first step toward re-establishing international order. Germany's colonies were given to France, Britain, and Japan as League of Nations mandates. Germany's territorial losses within Europe were minor, thanks to Wilson. Alsace-Lorraine was returned to France. Parts of Germany inhabited primarily by Poles were ceded to the new Polish state, in keeping with the principle of national self-determination. The treaty limited Germany's army to one hundred thousand men and allowed no new military fortifications in the Rhineland (see Map 27.4).

● **The Allied Leaders at Versailles**   The old tiger, Clemenceau of France, gestures with his walking stick to the scholarly Woodrow Wilson, as the strong-willed Lloyd George strides forward on the left. The negotiations at Versailles were difficult and often bitter, but the Allies reached a compromise agreement and imposed it on Germany. *(Corbis)*

More harshly, the Allies declared that Germany (with Austria) was responsible for the war and had therefore to pay reparations equal to all civilian damages caused by the war. These much-criticized "war-guilt" and "reparations" clauses expressed inescapable popular demands for German blood. The actual reparations figure was not set, however, and there was the clear possibility it might be set at a reasonable level in the future when tempers had cooled.

When presented with the treaty, the German government protested vigorously, but there was no alternative. On June 28, 1919, German representatives of the ruling moderate Social Democrats and Catholic parties signed the treaty in the Hall of Mirrors at Versailles.

The Allies concluded separate peace treaties with the other defeated powers—Austria, Hungary, Bulgaria, and Turkey. For the most part these treaties merely ratified the existing situation in east-central Europe following the breakup of the Austro-Hungarian Empire (see Map 27.4). Like Austria, Hungary was a particularly big loser, as its "captive" nationalities (and some interspersed Hungarians) were ceded to Romania, Czechoslovakia, Poland, and Yugoslavia. Italy acquired some Austrian territory. The Ottoman Empire was broken up. France received Lebanon and Syria. Britain took Iraq and Palestine, which was to include a Jewish national homeland first

Treaty of Versailles   *The World War I treaty that declared Germany responsible for the war; it limited Germany's army to one hundred thousand men and forced Germany to pay reparations equal to all civilian damages caused by the war.*

Primary Source: The Zionist Organization's Memorandum to the Peace Conference in Versailles
See how the Zionist Organization promoted the idea of a Jewish state in Palestine to the Allies meeting in Versailles.

MAP 27.4 **Territorial Changes in Europe After World War I** The Great War brought tremendous changes to eastern Europe. Empires were shattered, and new nations were established. A dangerous power vacuum was created between Germany and Soviet Russia.

Map legend:
- Boundaries of German, Russian, and Austro-Hungarian Empires in 1914
- Areas lost by Austro-Hungarian Empire
- Areas lost by Russian Empire
- Areas lost by German Empire
- Areas lost by Bulgaria
- Demilitarized Zones
- Boundaries of 1926

promised by Britain in 1917. Officially League of Nations mandates, these Allied acquisitions were one of the most imperialistic elements of the peace settlement. Another was mandating Germany's holdings in China to Japan (see page 862). The age of Western, and Eastern, imperialism lived on.

American Rejection of the Versailles Treaty

The 1919 peace settlement was not perfect, but for war-shattered Europe it was an acceptable beginning. The organizing framework was national self-determination, which had played such a critical role in starting the war. Germany was punished but not dismembered. A new world organization complemented a traditional defensive alliance of victorious powers. The serious remaining problems could be worked out in the future. Moreover, Allied leaders wanted a quick settlement for another reason: they detested Lenin and feared his Bolshevik Revolution might spread. The best answer to Lenin's unending calls for worldwide upheaval, they realized, was peace and tranquility for war-weary peoples.

There were, however, two great interrelated obstacles to such peace: Germany and the United States. Plagued by communist uprisings, reactionary plots, and popular disillusionment with losing the war, Germany's moderate socialists and their liberal and Catholic supporters faced an enormous challenge. They needed time (and luck) if they were to establish firmly a peaceful and democratic republic. Progress in this direction required understanding yet firm treatment of Germany by the victorious Western Allies.

In the United States, there was a quick reversion to prewar preferences for isolationism and no entangling alliances, which caused the U.S. Senate and, to a lesser extent, the American people to reject Wilson's handiwork. Republican senators led by Henry Cabot Lodge refused to ratify the Treaty of Versailles without changes in the articles creating the League of Nations. The key issue was the League's power—more apparent than real—to require member states to take collective action against aggression. Opponents believed this requirement gave away Congress's constitutional right to declare war. In failing health, Wilson rejected all attempts at compromise, and thereby ensured the treaty would never be ratified by the United States in any form and the United States would never join the League of Nations. Moreover, the Senate refused to ratify Wilson's defensive alliance with France and Great Britain. America turned its back on Europe.

The Wilson-Lodge fiasco and return to isolationism represented a tragic and cowardly renunciation of America's responsibility. Using America's action as an excuse, Great Britain, too, refused to ratify its defensive alliance with France. Betrayed by its allies, France would very shortly take actions against Germany that fed the fires of German resentment and seriously undermined democratic forces in the new German republic. The great hopes of early 1919 had turned to ashes by year's end. The Western alliance had collapsed, and a grandiose plan for permanent peace had given way to a fragile truce. For this and for what came later, the United States must share a large part of the blame.

Chapter Summary

To assess your mastery of this chapter, go to
bedfordstmartins.com/mckayworld

• How did Europe's system of alliances contribute to the outbreak of World War I?

Following the Franco-Prussian War of 1870–1871, the German Chancellor Otto van Bismarck sought to maintain peace in Europe by negotiating a series of alliances among the various nations. When Kaiser William II became German emperor in 1888, however, he forced Bismarck to resign, refused to renew the Russian-German Reinsurance Treaty, and raised tensions across Europe. He caused France and Russia to join together against the Triple Alliance of Germany, Austria, and Italy, and he also alienated Great Britain, which later joined France and Russia in an alliance known as the Triple Entente. Commercial rivalry between Great Britain and Germany and Germany's challenge to Great Britain's long-standing naval supremacy also drove the two great powers further apart. Europe's leaders allowed extreme nationalism and militarism to dictate

Key Terms

Three Emperors' League
Triple Entente
trench warfare
Lusitania
total war
War Raw Materials Board
Auxiliary Service Law
Petrograd Soviet
Army Order No. 1
Bolsheviks
Constituent Assembly
war communism
Cheka
League of Nations
Treaty of Versailles

political decisions and foreign policy. Austria's attack on Serbia in July 1914 seemed to set the two great alliances in motion, like giant machines, blindly fulfilling their security obligations to their allies and moving inexorably to war.

• How did total war impact the home fronts of the major European combatants?

The Great War as a total war caused an administrative revolution that continues to influence European governments today. This revolution, born of the need to mobilize entire societies and economies for total war, greatly increased government power in the West. After the guns grew still, government planning of highly complicated economies and wholesale involvement in daily social life did not disappear. Liberal market capitalism and a well-integrated world economy were among the many casualties of the administrative revolution, and greater social equality, particularly for women and workers, was everywhere one of its results. Thus even in European countries where a communist takeover never came close to occurring, society still experienced a great revolution, and socialism became a realistic economic blueprint that many countries adopted.

• How and why did the war lead to the Russian Revolution?

After three years of horrible slaughter on the eastern front, the Russian people were tired of the autocratic rule of Tsar Nicholas II and wanted change. In March 1917 the Tsar abdicated, and the reins of government were taken over by a provisional government controlled by moderate social democrats under the leadership of Alexander Kerensky. Kerensky refused to pull Russia out of the war, however, and the massive waste of Russian lives continued until army discipline completely collapsed in resistance to the war. This opened the way for a second Russian revolution, this time led by Vladimir Lenin and his communist Bolshevik party, in November 1917. The Bolsheviks established a radical regime, smashed existing capitalist institutions, and stayed in power with a new kind of authoritarian rule. Whether the new Russian regime was truly Marxian or socialist was questionable, but it indisputably posed a powerful, ongoing revolutionary challenge to Europe and its colonial empires.

• Why is the peace settlement following World War I considered by most historians to have been a terrible failure?

Finally, the "war to end war" brought not peace but only a fragile truce. Over President Woodrow Wilson's protests, France and Great Britain viewed the Versailles Treaty as an opportunity to take revenge on Germany for the war and to ruin it. The treaty denied Germany an empire by taking away its colonies; militarily the treaty forced Germany to destroy its army and navy; and economically the victors demanded exorbitant war reparations. The Allies also took control of key Germany industries and raw material producing regions. And the Germans were humiliated by a key article in the treaty that forced them to take full responsibility for causing the war. While the Allies failed to maintain their wartime solidarity, Germany remained unrepentant and soon had more grievances to nurse. The vengeful treaty allowed Adolf Hitler to rally the German people around him, to promise to restore Germany to its former greatness, and to lead them into World War II with visions of national (and Germanic) glory.

Suggested Reading

Ecksteins, Modris. *Rites of Spring: The Great War and the Birth of the Modern Age*. 1989. An imaginative cultural investigation that has won critical acclaim.

Ellis, John. *Eye-Deep in Hell*. 1976. A vivid account of trench warfare.

Fromkin, David. *Europe's Last Summer: Who Started the Great War?* 2004. Well-argued, compulsively readable discussion of responsibility for the war by a master historian.

Fussell, Paul. *The Great War and Modern Memory*. 1975. Probes all the powerful literature inspired by the war.

Gilbert, Martin. *The First World War: A Complete History*. 1994. Comprehensive in one volume by a major military historian.

Gorham, Deborah. *Vera Brittain: A Feminist Life*. 1996. A major study of Brittain's life.

Hobsbawm, Eric. *The Age of Extremes: A History of the World, 1914–1991*. 1996. Offers a provocative interpretation of the "short twentieth century," with a good description of war and revolution.

Macmillan, Margaret. *Paris, 1919: Six Months That Changed the World*. 2001. A masterful account of the negotiations and the issues at the Versailles Peace Conference.

Massie, Raymond. *Nicholas and Alexandra*. 1971. A moving popular biography of Russia's last royal family and the terrible health problem of the heir to the throne.

Ousby, Ian. *The Road to Verdun: World War I's Most Momentous Battle and the Folly of Nationalism*. 2002. A moving reconsideration of the famous siege.

Pasternak, Boris. *Doctor Zhivago*. 1958. A justly celebrated, great historical novel of the Russian Revolution era, including the civil war that followed, by a Nobel Prize–winning author.

Read, Christopher. *From Tsar to Soviets: The Russian People and Their Revolution, 1917–1921*. 1996. A social history of the revolution focusing on ordinary Russian men and women.

Reed, John. *Ten Days That Shook the World*. 1919. The classic eyewitness account of the Russian Revolution by a young, pro-Bolshevik American.

Strachan, Hew. *The First World War*. 2004. Thorough one-volume history by one of the premier Great War historians.

Tuchman, Barbara. *The Guns of August*. 1962. A marvelous account of the dramatic first month of the war and the beginning of the military stalemate.

Volkogonov, Dmitri. *Lenin: A New Biography*. 1994. A lively study with some new revelations by a well-known postcommunist Russian historian.

Wade, Rex. *The Russian Revolution, 1917*. 2000. Comprehensive and accessible history of the revolution.

Wall, Richard, and Jay Winter, eds. *The Upheaval of War: Family, Work, and Welfare in Europe, 1914–1918*. 1988. An excellent collection of essays that probes the enormous consequences of the war for people and society.

Notes

1. M. Beloff, quoted in *U.S. News & World Report,* March 8, 1976, p. 53.
2. Quoted in J. Remak, *The Origins of World War I* (New York: Holt, Rinehart & Winston, 1967), p. 84.
3. Quoted in F. P. Chambers, *The War Behind the War, 1914–1918* (London: Faber & Faber, 1939), p. 168.
4. Quoted in R. O. Paxton, *Europe in the Twentieth Century* (New York: Harcourt Brace Jovanovich, 1975), p. 109.
5. H. Nicolson, *Peacemaking 1919* (New York: Grosset & Dunlap Universal Library, 1965), pp. 8, 31–32.
6. Quoted ibid., p. 24.

Listening to the PAST

The Experience of War

World War I was a total war: it enlisted the efforts of men, women, adults, and children, both at home and on the battlefield. It was a terrifying and painful experience for all those involved. To be sure, it was not the romantic endeavor it was purported to be. The documents below offer two different wartime experiences. The first excerpt is from a letter written by a German soldier fighting in the trenches. The second is from the diary of a Viennese woman. As you read both passages, think about the different ways war and its consequences were made real for these two people.

A German Soldier Writes from the Trenches, March 1915

Souchez, March 11th, 1915
"So fare you well, for we must now be parting," so run the first lines of a soldier-song which we often sang through the streets of the capital. These words are truer than ever now, and these lines are to bid farewell to you, to all my nearest and dearest, to all who wish me well or ill, and to all that I value and prize.

Our regiment has been transferred to this dangerous spot, Souchez. No end of blood has already flowed down this hill. A week ago the 142nd attacked and took four trenches from the French. It is to hold these trenches that we have been brought here. There is something uncanny about this hill-position. Already, times without number, other battalions of our regiment have been ordered here in support, and each time the company came back with a loss of twenty, thirty or more men. In the days when we had to stick it out here before, we had 22 killed and 27 wounded. Shells roar, bullets whistle; no dugouts, or very bad ones; mud, clay, filth, shell-holes so deep that one could bathe in them.

This letter has been interrupted no end of times. Shells began to pitch close to us—great English 12-inch ones—and we had to take refuge in a cellar. One such shell struck the next house and buried four men, who were got out from the ruins horribly mutilated. I saw them and it was ghastly!

Everybody must be prepared now for death in some form or other. Two cemeteries have been made up here, the losses have been so great. I ought not to write that to you, but I do so all the same, because the newspapers have probably given you quite a different impression. They tell only of our gains and say nothing about the blood that has been shed, of the cries of agony that never cease. The newspaper doesn't give any description either of *how* the "heroes" are laid to rest, though it talks about "heroes' graves" and writes poems and such-like about them. Certainly in Lens I have attended funeral-parades where a number of dead were buried in one large grave with pomp and circumstance. But up here it is pitiful the way one throws the dead bodies out of the trench and lets them lie there, or scatters dirt over the remains of those which have been torn to pieces by shells.

I look upon death and call upon life. I have not accomplished much in my short life, which has been chiefly occupied with study. I have commended my soul to the Lord God. It bears His seal and is altogether His. Now I am free to dare anything. My future life belongs to God, my present one to the Fatherland, and I myself still possess happiness and strength.

A Viennese Woman Remembers Home Front Life

Ten dekagrammes [3½ ounces] of horse-flesh per head are to be given out to-day for the week. The cavalry horses held in reserve by the military authorities are being slaughtered for lack of fodder, and the people of Vienna are for a change to get a few mouthfuls of meat of which they have so long been deprived. Horse-flesh! I should like to know whether my instinctive repugnance to horse-flesh as food is personal, or whether my dislike is shared by many other housewives. My loathing of it is based, I believe, not on a physical but on a psychological prejudice.

I overcame my repugnance, rebuked myself for being sentimental, and left the house. A soft, steady rain was falling, from which I tried to protect myself with galoshes, waterproof, and umbrella. As I left the house before seven o'clock and the meat distribution

A ration coupon used in the city of Eisenberg showing Germans waiting in line for their meager rations. *(akg-images)*

did not begin until nine o'clock, I hoped to get well to the front of the queue.

No sooner had I reached the neighbourhood of the big market hall than I was instructed by the police to take a certain direction. I estimated the crowd waiting here for a meagre midday meal at two thousand at least. Hundreds of women had spent the night here in order to be among the first and make sure of getting their bit of meat. Many had brought with them improvised seats—a little box or a bucket turned upside down. No one seemed to mind the rain, although many were already wet through. They passed the time chattering, and the theme was the familiar one: What have you had to eat? What are you going to eat? One could scent an atmosphere of mistrust in these conversations: they were all careful not to say too much or to betray anything that might get them into trouble.

At length the sale began. Slowly, infinitely slowly, we moved forward. The most determined, who had spent the night outside the gates of the hall, displayed their booty to the waiting crowd: a ragged, quite freshly slaughtered piece of meat with the characteristic yellow fat. [Others] alarmed those standing at the back by telling them that there was only a very small supply of meat and that not half the people waiting would get a share of it. The crowd became very uneasy and impatient, and before the police on guard could prevent it, those standing in front organized an attack on the hall which the salesmen inside were powerless to repel. Everyone seized whatever he could lay his hands on, and in a few moments all the eatables had vanished. In the confusion stands were overturned, and the police forced back the aggressors and closed the gates. The crowds waiting outside, many of whom had been there all night and were soaked through, angrily demanded their due, whereupon the mounted police made a little charge, provoking a wild panic and much screaming and cursing. At length I reached home, depressed and disgusted, with a broken umbrella and only one galosh.

We housewives have during the last four years grown accustomed to standing in queues; we have also grown accustomed to being obliged to go home with empty hands and still emptier stomachs. Only very rarely do those who are sent away disappointed give cause for police intervention. On the other hand, it happens more and more frequently that one of the pale, tired women who have been waiting for hours collapses from exhaustion. The turbulent scenes which occurred to-day inside and outside the large market hall seemed to me perfectly natural. In my dejected mood the patient apathy with which we housewives endure seemed to me blameworthy and incomprehensible.

Questions for Analysis

1. How does the soldier see the war he is in? Is it a grand patriotic effort? Or is it a story of senseless bloodshed and loss of life?

2. How did the soldiers cope with the reality of war in the trenches?

3. How does the experience of the Viennese woman differ from the soldier's?

4. Were the women who pillaged the food hall "blameworthy" or "incomprehensible," as the Viennese woman put it?

Sources: Alfons Ankenbrand, in *German Students' War Letters,* ed. A. F. Wedd (London: Methuen, 1929), pp. 72–73; *Blockade: The Diary of an Austrian Middle-Class Woman, 1914–1924,* trans. Winifred Ray (New York: Ray Long & Richard Smith, 1932), pp. 63–68.

Victory at Smyrna. Turks celebrate victory over Greek forces at Smyrna in October 1922. This was one of the final battles in the Turkish War for Independence that led to establishing the Republic of Turkey in 1923. *(Price/Getty Images)*

chapter

28 NATIONALISM IN ASIA, 1914–1939

From Asia's perspective the First World War was largely a European civil war that shattered Western imperialism's united front and convulsed prewar relationships throughout Asia. Most crucially, the war speeded the development of modern nationalism in Asia. Before 1914 the nationalist gospel of anti-imperialist political freedom and racial equality had already won converts among Asia's westernized, educated elites. In the 1920s and 1930s it increasingly won the allegiance of the masses. As in nineteenth-century Europe, nationalism in Asia between 1914 and 1939 became a mass movement with potentially awesome power.

There were at least three reasons for the upsurge of nationalism in Asia. First and foremost, nationalism provided the most effective means of organizing the anti-imperialist resistance both to direct foreign rule and to indirect Western domination. Second, nationalism called for fundamental changes and challenged old political and social practices and beliefs. Thus modernizers used it to contest the influence and power of conservative traditionalists. Third, nationalism offered a vision of a free and prosperous future, and provided an ideology to ennoble the sacrifices the struggle would require.

Nationalism also had a dark side. As in Europe (see page 679), Asian nationalists developed a strong sense of "we" and "they." "They" were often the enemy—the oppressor. European imperialists were just such a "they," and nationalist feeling generated the power to destroy European empires and challenge foreign economic domination. But, as in Europe, Asian nationalism also stimulated bitter conflicts and wars between peoples, in two different ways.

First, it stimulated conflicts between relatively homogeneous peoples in large states, rallying, for example, Chinese against Japanese and vice versa. Second, nationalism often heightened tensions between ethnic (or religious) groups within states, especially states with diverse populations, like British India and the Ottoman Empire. Such states had been formed by authoritarian rulers and their armies and bureaucracies, very much like the Austro-Hungarian and Russian empires before 1914. When their rigid rule declined or snapped, the different nationalistic peoples might easily quarrel, seeking to divide the existing state or to dominate the enemy "they" within its borders.

The modern nationalism movement has never been monolithic. In Asia especially, where the new and often narrow ideology of nationalism was grafted onto old, rich, and complex civilizations, the range of historical experience has been enormous. Between the outbreak of the First and Second World Wars each Asian country developed a distinctive national movement rooted in its own unique culture and history. Each nation's people created their own national reawakening, which renovated thought and culture as well as politics and economics.

THE FIRST WORLD WAR AND WESTERN IMPERIALISM

How did modern nationalism—the dominant force in most of the world in the twentieth century—develop in Asia between the First and Second World Wars?

Every Asian national movement sought genuine freedom from foreign imperialism. The First World War profoundly affected these aspirations by altering relations between Asia and Europe. In the words of a distinguished Indian historian, "the Great War of 1914–1918 was from the Asian point of view a civil war within the European community of nations."[1] For four years Asians watched Kipling's haughty bearers of "the White Man's Burden" (see page 724) vilifying and destroying each other. Japan's defeat of imperial Russia in 1904 (see page 768) had shown that an Asian power could beat a European Great Power; now for the first time Asians saw the entire West as divided and vulnerable.

In China and Japan few people particularly cared who won the distant war in Europe. In British India and French Indochina enthusiasm was also limited, but the war's impact was unavoidably greater. Total war required that the British and the French draft their colonial subjects into the conflict, uprooting hundreds of thousands of Asians to fight the Germans and the Ottoman Turks. This too had major consequences. An Indian or Vietnamese soldier who fought in France and came in contact there with democratic and republican ideas was less likely to accept foreign rule when he returned home.

The British and the French also made rash promises to gain the support of colonial peoples during the war. British leaders promised Europe's Jewish nationalists a homeland in Palestine, while promising Arab nationalists independence from the Ottoman Empire. In India the British were forced in 1917 to announce a new policy of self-governing institutions in order to counteract Indian popular unrest fanned by wartime inflation and heavy taxation. After the war the nationalist genie the colonial powers had called on refused to slip meekly back into the bottle.

President Wilson's war aims also raised the hopes of peoples under imperial rule. In January 1918 Wilson proposed his Fourteen Points (see page 836), whose key idea was national self-determination for the peoples of Europe and the Ottoman Empire. Wilson also recommended that in all colonial questions "the interests of native populations be given equal weight with the desires of European governments," and he seemed to call for national self-rule. This subversive message had enormous appeal for educated Asians, fueling their hopes of freedom.

Military service and Wilsonian self-determination also fired the hopes of some Africans and some visionary African American supporters of African freedom. The First World War, however, had less impact on European imperialism in sub-Saharan Africa than in Asia and the Arab world. For sub-Saharan Africa, the Great Depression and the Second World War were much more influential in the growth of nationalist movements (see pages 1000–1004).

After winning the war, the Allies tried to re-establish or increase their political and economic domination in Asia and Africa. Although fatally weakened, Western imperialism remained very much alive in 1918, partly because President Wilson was no revolutionary. At the Versailles Peace Conference he compromised on colonial questions in order to achieve some of his European goals and the creation of the League of Nations. Also, Allied statesmen and ordinary French and British citizens quite rightly believed their colonial empires had contributed to their ultimate victory over the Central Powers. They would not give up such valuable possessions voluntarily. If pressed, Europeans said their administration was preparing colonial subjects for eventual self-rule, but only in the distant future.

The compromise at Versailles between Wilson's vague, moralistic idealism and the European preoccupation with "good administration" was a system of League of Nations mandates over Germany's former colonies and the old Ottoman Empire. Article 22 of the League of Nations Covenant, which was part of the Treaty of Versailles, assigned territories "inhabited by peoples incapable of governing themselves" to various "developed nations." "The well-being and development of such peoples" was declared "a sacred trust of civilization." The **Permanent Mandates Commission,** whose members came from European countries with colonies, was created to oversee the developed nations' fulfillment of their international responsibility. Thus the League elaborated a new principle—development toward the eventual goal of self-government—but left its implementation to the colonial powers themselves.

The mandates system demonstrated that Europe was determined to maintain its imperial power and influence, leaving patriots throughout Asia bitterly disappointed after the First World War. They saw France, Great Britain, and other nations—industrialized Japan was the only Asian state to obtain mandates—grabbing Germany's colonies as spoils of war and extending the existing system of colonial rule in Muslim North Africa into the territories of the old Ottoman Empire. Yet Asian patriots did not give up. They preached national self-determination and struggled to build mass movements capable of achieving freedom and independence.

In this struggle Asian nationalists were encouraged by Soviet communism. After seizing power in 1917, Lenin declared that the Asian inhabitants of the new Soviet Union were complete equals of the Russians with a right to their own development. (In actuality this equality hardly existed, but the propaganda was effective nonetheless.) The Communists also denounced European and American imperialism and

Chronology

1914–1918   World War I

1915   Japan seizes German holdings in China and expands into southern Manchuria

1916   Sykes-Picot Agreement divides Ottoman Empire between Britain and France

1916–1917   Arab revolt against Turkish rule grows

1917   Balfour Declaration establishes Jewish homeland in Palestine

1919   Amritsar Massacre in India; May Fourth Movement in China; Treaty of Versailles

1920   Faisal proclaimed king of Syria but quickly deposed by French, who establish their mandate in Syria

1920s   New Culture Movement challenges traditional Chinese values

1920s–1930s   Large numbers of Jews immigrate to Palestine; Hebrew becomes common language there

1923   Sun Yatsen allies Nationalist Party with Chinese Communists; Kita Ikki advocates ultranationalism in Japan

1923–1938   Mustafa Kemal imposes Western reforms to modernize and secularize Turkey

1925–1941   Reign of Reza Shah Pahlavi in Iran

1927   Jiang Jieshi, leader of Nationalist Party, purges his Communist allies

1930   Gandhi leads Indians on march to the sea to protest the British salt tax

1931   Japan occupies Manchuria

1932   Iraq gains independence in return for military alliance with Great Britain

1934   Mao leads Chinese Communists on Long March; Philippines gain self-governing commonwealth status from United States

1935   Turkish National Assembly introduces family names on European model; Mustafa Kemal granted the surname Atatürk

1937   Japanese militarists launch general attack on China; Rape of Nanjing

Permanent Mandates Commission *A commission created by the League of Nations to oversee the developed nations' fulfillment of their international responsibility.*

pledged to support revolutionary movements in all colonial countries, even when they were primarily movements of national independence led by "middle-class" intellectuals instead of by revolutionary workers. Foreign political and economic exploitation was the immediate enemy, they said, and socialist revolution could wait until Western imperialism had been defeated. The example, ideology, and support of Soviet communism exerted a powerful influence in the 1920s and 1930s, particularly in China and French Indochina.

Nationalism's appeal in Asia was not confined to territories under direct European rule. The extraordinary growth of international trade after 1850 had drawn millions of Asian peasants and shopkeepers into the Western-dominated world economy, disrupting local markets and often creating hostility toward European businessmen. Moreover, Europe and the United States had forced even the most solid Asian states, China and Japan, to accept unequal treaties and humiliating limitations on their sovereignty. Thus the nationalist promise of genuine economic independence and true political equality with the West appealed as powerfully in old but weak states like China as in colonial territories like British India.

Finally, as in Russia after the Crimean War or in Japan after the Meiji Restoration, the nationalist creed after World War I went hand in hand with acceptance of modernization by the educated elites. Modernization promised changes that would enable old societies to compete effectively with the world's leading nations.

THE MIDDLE EAST

How did the collapse of the Ottoman Empire in World War I shape the history of the Middle East for the rest of the century?

The most flagrant attempt to expand Western imperialism occurred in the Middle East, or, more accurately, Southwest Asia—the vast expanse that stretches eastward from the Suez Canal and Turkey's Mediterranean shores across the Tigris-Euphrates Valley and the Iranian Plateau to the Arabian Sea and the Indus Valley. There the

● **Prince Faisal and His British Allies** On board a British warship on route to the Versailles Peace Conference in 1919, Prince Faisal is flanked on his right by the British officer T. E. Lawrence—popularly known as Lawrence of Arabia because of his daring campaign against the Turks. Faisal failed to win political independence for the Arabs, as the British backed away from the vague pro-Arab promises they had made during the war. *(Rowley Atterbury)*

British and the French successfully encouraged an Arab revolt in 1916 and destroyed the Ottoman Empire. Europeans then sought to replace Turks as principal rulers throughout the region, even in Turkey itself. Turkish, Arab, and Iranian nationalists, as well as Jewish nationalists arriving from Europe, reacted violently. They struggled to win dignity and nationhood, and as the Europeans were forced to make concessions, they sometimes came into sharp conflict with each other, most notably in Palestine.

The First World War and the Arab Revolt

Long subject to European pressure, the Ottoman Empire failed to reform and modernize in the late nineteenth century (see pages 726–729). Declining international stature and domestic tyranny led to revolutionary activity among idealistic exiles and young army officers who wanted to seize power and save the Ottoman state. These patriots, the so-called **Young Turks,** succeeded in the 1908 revolution, and subsequently they were determined to hold together the remnants of the vast multiethnic empire. Defeated by Bulgaria, Serbia, and Greece in the Balkan War of 1912, and stripped of practically all territory in Europe, the Young Turks redoubled their efforts in Southwest Asia. The most important of their possessions were Syria—consisting of modern-day Lebanon, Syria, Israel, and Jordan—and Iraq. The Ottoman Turks also claimed the Arabian peninsula but exercised only loose control there.

For centuries the largely Arabic populations of Syria and Iraq had been tied to their Ottoman rulers by their common faith in Islam (though there were Christian Arabs as well). Yet beneath the surface, ethnic and linguistic tensions simmered between Turks and Arabs, who were as different as Chinese and Japanese.

Young Turk actions after 1908 made the embryonic "Arab movement" a reality. The majority of Young Turks promoted a narrow Turkish nationalism. They further centralized the Ottoman Empire and extended the sway of the Turkish language, culture, and race. In 1909 the Turkish government brutally slaughtered thousands of Armenian Christians, a prelude to the wholesale massacre of more than a million Armenians during the First World War. Meanwhile, Arab discontent grew.

In late 1914 the Turks willingly joined forces with Germany and Austria-Hungary. The Young Turks were pro-German because the Germans had helped reform the Ottoman armies before the war and had built important railroads, like the one to Baghdad. Alliance with Germany permitted the Turks to renounce the limitations on Ottoman sovereignty that the Europeans had imposed in the nineteenth century and also to settle old scores with Russia, the Turks' historic enemy.

The Young Turks' fatal alliance with the Central Powers pulled the entire Middle East into the European civil war and made it truly a global conflict. While Russia attacked the Ottomans in the Caucasus, the British protected their rule in Egypt and the Suez Canal, the lifeline to India. Thus Arab leaders opposed to Ottoman rule suddenly found an unexpected ally in Great Britain. The foremost Arab leader was Hussein ibn-Ali (1856–1931), a direct descendant of the prophet Muhammad. As the **sharif,** or chief magistrate, of Mecca, the Muslim world's holiest city, Hussein governed much of the Ottoman Empire's territory along the Red Sea, an area known as the Hejaz (see Map 28.1). Basically anti-Turkish, Hussein refused the Turkish sultan's call for a holy war against the Triple Entente. His refusal pleased the British, who feared a Muslim revolt in India.

In 1915 Hussein won vague British commitments for an independent Arab kingdom. When the British attempt to take the Dardanelles and capture Constantinople in 1915 failed miserably, Britain (and Russia) badly needed a new ally on the Ottoman front. In 1916 Hussein revolted against the Turks, proclaiming himself king of the Arabs. Hussein joined forces with the British under T. E. Lawrence, who in 1917 led Arab tribesmen and Indian soldiers in a highly successful guerrilla war against the Turks on the Arabian peninsula. In September 1918 British armies and their Arab allies rolled into Syria and occupied Damascus.

Young Turks *Idealistic Turkish exiles in Europe and young army officers in Istanbul who seized power in the revolution of 1908 and helped pave the way for the birth of modern secular Turkey.*

**Primary Source:
Letter from Turkey,
Summer 1915**
Read an eyewitness account of the Armenian genocide, by a U.S. missionary from Massachusetts.

sharif *A term for the chief magistrate of Mecca.*

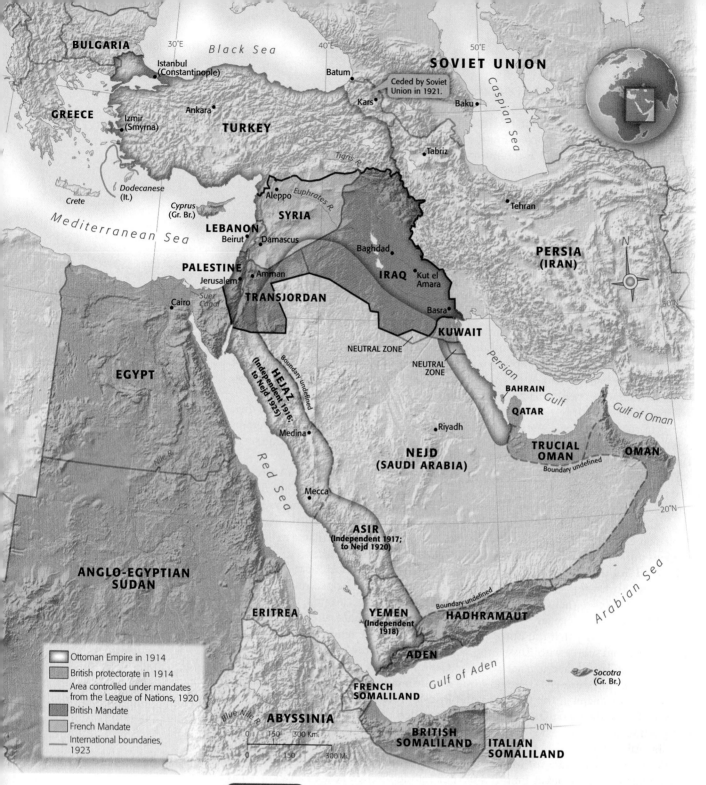

MAP 28.1 **The Partition of the Ottoman Empire, 1914–1923** The decline of the mighty Ottoman Empire began in 1699, when the Habsburgs conquered Hungary, and it accelerated after 1805, when Egypt became virtually independent. By 1914 the Ottoman Turks had been pushed out of the Balkans, and their Arab provinces were on the edge of revolt. That revolt erupted in the First World War and contributed greatly to the Ottomans' defeat. When the Allies then attempted to implement their plans, including independence for the Armenian people, Mustafa Kemal arose to forge in battle the modern Turkish state.

In the Ottoman province of Iraq, Britain occupied Basra in 1914 and captured Baghdad in 1917. Arabs rejoiced, and many patriots expected a large, unified Arab state to rise from the dust of the Ottoman collapse. Within two years, however, Arab nationalists felt bitterly betrayed by Great Britain and its allies, and this bitterness left a legacy of distrust and hatred toward the West.

Arab bitterness was partly directed at secret wartime treaties between Britain and France to divide and rule the old Ottoman Empire. In the 1916 **Sykes-Picot Agreement,** Britain and France secretly agreed that France would receive modern-day Lebanon, Syria, and much of southern Turkey, and Britain would receive Palestine, Jordan, and Iraq. The Sykes-Picot Agreement contradicted British (and later Wilsonian) promises concerning Arab independence after the war, and left Arab nationalists feeling cheated and betrayed.

A related source of Arab bitterness was Britain's wartime commitment to a Jewish homeland in Palestine. The **Balfour Declaration** of November 1917, made by the British foreign secretary Arthur Balfour, declared that

His Majesty's Government views with favor the establishment in Palestine of a National Home for the Jewish People, and will use their best endeavors to facilitate the achievement

Sykes-Picot Agreement *The 1916 secret agreement between Britain and France that divided up the Arab lands of Lebanon, Syria, southern Turkey, Palestine, Jordan, and Iraq.*

Balfour Declaration *A 1917 statement by British foreign secretary Arthur Balfour that supported the idea of a Jewish homeland in Palestine.*

● **The Armenian Atrocities** When in 1915 some Armenians welcomed Russian armies as liberators after years of persecution, the Ottoman government ordered a genocidal mass deportation of its Armenian citizens from their homeland in the empire's eastern provinces. This photo, taken in Kharpert in 1915 by a German businessman from his hotel window, shows Turkish guards marching Armenian men off to a prison, where they will be tortured to death. A million Armenians died from murder, starvation, and disease during World War I. *(Armenian Library and Museum of America Archives)*

Primary Source:
The Balfour Declaration, Stating the British Government's Support for a Jewish Homeland in Palestine
Learn which questions were considered—and which were ignored—as Britain prepared to support the Zionist movement.

of this object, it being clearly understood that nothing shall be done which may prejudice the civil and religious rights of existing non-Jewish communities in Palestine, or the rights and political status enjoyed by Jews in any other country.

As careful reading reveals, the Balfour Declaration made contradictory promises to European Jews and Middle Eastern Arabs.

Some British Cabinet members apparently believed the Balfour Declaration would appeal to German, Austrian, and American Jews and thus help the British war effort. Others sincerely supported the Zionist vision of a Jewish homeland, but also believed that this homeland would then be grateful to Britain and help maintain British control of the Suez Canal.

In 1914 Jews were about 11 percent of the predominantly Arab population in the Ottoman territory that became, under British control, Palestine. The "National Home for the Jewish People" mentioned in the Balfour Declaration implied to the Arabs—and to the Zionist Jews as well—some kind of Jewish state that would be incompatible with majority rule. Moreover, a state founded on religious and ethnic exclusivity was out of keeping with both Islamic and Ottoman tradition, which had historically been more tolerant of religious diversity and minorities than had the Christian monarchs or nation-states in Europe.

Despite strong French objections, Hussein's son Faisal (1885–1933) attended the Versailles Peace Conference, but his efforts to secure Arab independence came to nothing. President Wilson wanted to give the Arab case serious consideration, but the British and the French were determined to rule Syria, Iraq, and Palestine as League of Nations mandates, and accept only the independence of Hussein's kingdom of Hejaz. In response, Arab nationalists met in Damascus as the General Syrian Congress in 1919 and unsuccessfully called again for political independence. (See the feature "Listening to the Past: Arab Political Aspirations in 1919" on pages 874–875.) Brushing aside Arab opposition, the British mandate in Palestine formally incorporated the Balfour Declaration and its commitment to a Jewish national home. In March 1920 Faisal's followers met as the Syrian National Congress and proclaimed Syria independent, with Faisal as king. A similar congress declared Iraq an independent kingdom.

Western reaction to events in Syria and Iraq was swift and decisive. A French army stationed in Lebanon attacked Syria, taking Damascus in July 1920. Faisal fled, and the French took over. Meanwhile, the British put down an uprising in Iraq with bloody fighting and established effective control there. Western imperialism appeared to have replaced Turkish rule in the Middle East (see Map 28.1).

The Turkish Revolution

In November 1918 the Allied fleet entered Constantinople, the Ottoman capital. A young English official wrote that he found the Ottoman Empire "utterly smashed." The Turks were "worn out," and without bitterness they awaited the construction of a "new system."[2] The Allies' new system was blatant imperialism, which proved harsher for the defeated Turks than for the "liberated" Arabs. A treaty forced on the helpless sultan dismembered Turkey and reduced it to a puppet state. Great Britain and France occupied parts of Turkey, and Italy and Greece claimed shares as well. There was a sizable Greek minority in western Turkey, and Greek nationalists cherished the "Great Idea" of a modern Greek empire modeled on long-dead Christian Byzantium. In 1919 Greek armies carried by British ships landed on the Turkish coast at Smyrna, met little resistance from the exhausted Turkish troops, and advanced into the interior. Turkey seemed finished.

But Turkey produced a great leader and revived to become an inspiration to the entire Middle East. Mustafa Kemal (1881–1938), the father of modern Turkey, was a military man, and sympathetic to the Young Turk movement. Kemal had distinguished himself in the Great War by directing the successful defense of the Dardanelles against

British attack. After the armistice, Mustafa Kemal watched with anguish the Allies' aggression and the sultan's cowardice. In early 1919 he began working to unify Turkish resistance.

The sultan, bowing to Allied pressure, initially denounced Kemal, but the cause of national liberation proved more powerful. The catalyst was the Greek invasion and attempted annexation of much of western Turkey. A young Turkish woman described feelings she shared with countless others:

After I learned about the details of the Smyrna occupation by Greek armies, I hardly opened my mouth on any subject except when it concerned the sacred struggle. . . . I suddenly ceased to exist as an individual. I worked, wrote and lived as a unit of that magnificent national madness.[3]

Treaty of Lausanne *The 1923 treaty that ended the Turkish war and recognized the territorial integrity of a truly independent Turkey.*

Refusing to acknowledge the Allied dismemberment of their country, the Turks battled on through 1920 despite staggering defeats. The next year the Greeks advanced almost to Ankara, the nationalist stronghold in central Turkey. There Mustafa Kemal's forces took the offensive and won a great victory. The Greeks and their British allies sued for peace. The resulting **Treaty of Lausanne** (1923) solemnly abolished the hated capitulations, which gave Europeans special privileges in the Ottoman Empire (see page 563), and recognized a truly independent Turkey. Turkey lost only its former Arab provinces.

Mustafa Kemal believed Turkey should modernize and secularize along Western lines. His first moves were political. Drawing on his prestige as a war hero, Kemal called on the National Assembly to depose the sultan and establish a republic. He had himself elected president and moved the capital from cosmopolitan Constantinople (now Istanbul) to Ankara in the Turkish heartland. Kemal savagely crushed the demands for independence of ethnic minorities like the Armenians and the Kurds, but he realistically abandoned all thought of winning back lost Arab territories. He then created a one-party system—partly inspired by the Bolshevik example—in order to work his will.

Kemal's most radical changes pertained to religion and culture. For centuries most believers' intellectual and social activities had been regulated by Islamic religious authorities. Profoundly influenced by the example of western Europe, Mustafa Kemal set out, like the philosophes of the Enlightenment, to limit religious influence in daily affairs. But, like Russia's Peter the Great, he employed dictatorial measures rather than reason to reach his goal. Kemal simply decreed a revolutionary separation of church and state. Secular law codes inspired by European models replaced religious courts. State schools replaced religious schools and taught such secular subjects as science, mathematics, and social sciences.

Mustafa Kemal also struck down many entrenched patterns of behavior. Women, traditionally secluded and inferior to males in Islamic society, received the right to vote. Civil law on a European model, rather than the Islamic code, now governed marriage. Women could seek divorces, and no man could have more than one wife at a time. Men were forbidden to wear the tall red fez of the Ottoman era as headgear; government employees were ordered to wear business suits and felt hats, erasing the visible differences between Muslims and "infidel"

● **Mustafa Kemal** Surnamed Atatürk, meaning "father of the Turks," Mustafa Kemal and his supporters imposed revolutionary changes aimed at modernizing and westernizing Turkish society and the new Turkish government. Dancing here with his adopted daughter at her high-society wedding, Atatürk often appeared in public in elegant European dress—a vivid symbol for the Turkish people of his radical break with traditional Islamic teaching and custom. *(Hulton Archive/Getty Images)*

Europeans. The old Arabic script was replaced with a new Turkish alphabet based on Roman letters, which facilitated massive government efforts to spread literacy after 1928. Finally, in 1935, family names on the European model were introduced. The National Assembly granted Mustafa Kemal the surname **Atatürk,** which means "father of the Turks."

By his death in 1938, Atatürk and his supporters had consolidated their revolution. Government-sponsored industrialization was fostering urban growth and new attitudes, encouraging Turks to embrace business and science. Poverty persisted in rural areas, as did some religious discontent among devout Muslims. But like the Japanese after the Meiji Restoration, the Turkish people had rallied around the nationalist banner to repulse European imperialism and were building a modern secular nation-state.

Iran and Afghanistan

In Persia (renamed Iran in 1935), strong-arm efforts to build a unified modern nation ultimately proved less successful than in Turkey. In the late nineteenth century Iran had also been subject to extreme foreign pressure, which stimulated efforts to reform the government as a means of reviving Islamic civilization. In 1906 a nationalistic coalition of merchants, religious leaders, and intellectuals revolted. The despotic shah was forced to grant a constitution and establish a national assembly, the **Majlis.** Nationalist hopes ran high.

Yet the 1906 Iranian revolution was doomed to failure, largely because of European imperialism. Without consulting Iran, Britain and Russia in 1907 simply divided the country into spheres of influence. Britain's sphere ran along the Persian Gulf; the Russian sphere encompassed the whole northern half of Iran (see Map 28.1). Thereafter Russia intervened constantly. It blocked reforms, occupied cities, and completely dominated the country by 1912. When Russian power collapsed in the Bolshevik Revolution, British armies rushed into the power vacuum. By bribing corrupt Iranians, Great Britain in 1919 negotiated a treaty allowing the installation of British "advisers" in every government department.

The Majlis refused to ratify the treaty, and the blatant attempt to make Iran a British satellite aroused the national spirit. In 1921 reaction against the British brought to power a military dictator, Reza Shah Pahlavi (1877–1944), who proclaimed himself shah in 1925 and ruled until 1941.

Inspired by Turkey's Mustafa Kemal, the patriotic, religiously indifferent Reza Shah had three basic goals: to build a modern nation, to free Iran from foreign domination, and to rule with an iron fist. The challenge was enormous. Iran was a vast, undeveloped country of deserts, mountain barriers, and rudimentary communications. The rural population was mostly poor and illiterate, and among the Persian majority were sizable ethnic minorities with their own aspirations. Furthermore, Iran's powerful religious leaders hated Western (Christian) domination but were no less opposed to a more secular, less Islamic society.

To realize his vision of a strong Iran, the energetic shah created a modern army, built railroads, and encouraged commerce. He won control over ethnic minorities such as the Kurds in the north and Arab tribesmen on the Iraqi border. He reduced the privileges granted to foreigners and raised taxes on the powerful Anglo-Persian Oil Company, which had been founded in 1909 to exploit the first great oil strike in the Middle East. Yet Reza Shah was less successful than Atatürk.

Because the European-educated elite in Iran was smaller than the comparable group in Turkey, the idea of re-creating Persian greatness on the basis of a secularized society attracted relatively few determined supporters. Many powerful religious leaders turned against Reza Shah, and he became increasingly brutal, greedy, and tyrannical, murdering his enemies and lining his pockets. His support of Hitler's Nazi Germany also exposed Iran's tenuous and fragile independence to the impact of European conflicts.

Atatürk *The name bestowed on the Turkish president Mustafa Kemal; it means "father of the Turks."*

Majlis *The national assembly established by the despotic shah of Iran in 1906.*

Primary Source:
The Link Between the Education of Girls and the Advancement of Iranian Society, 1907, 1909
Two articles argue that, if Iran is to become truly "civilized," it must recognize the virtues of educating women.

Afghanistan, meanwhile, was nominally independent in the nineteenth century, but the British imposed political restrictions and constantly meddled in the country's affairs. In 1919 the violently anti-British amir Amanullah (1892–1960) declared a holy war on the British government in India and won complete independence for the first time. Amanullah then decreed revolutionary reforms designed to hurl his primitive country into the twentieth century. The result was tribal and religious revolt, civil war, and retreat from reform. Islam remained both religion and law. A powerful but primitive patriotism enabled Afghanistan to win political independence from the West, but not to build a modern society.

The Arab States and Palestine

French and British mandates established at gunpoint forced Arab nationalists to seek independence by gradual means after 1920. Arab nationalists were indirectly aided by Western taxpayers, who wanted cheap—that is, peaceful—empires. As a result, Arabs won considerable control over local affairs in the mandated states, except Palestine, though the mandates remained European satellites in international and economic affairs.

In Iraq, the wily British chose Faisal, whom the French had deposed in Syria, as king. Faisal obligingly gave British advisers broad behind-the-scenes control. The king also accepted British ownership of Iraq's oil fields, consequently giving the West a stranglehold on the Iraqi economy. Given the severe limitations imposed on him, Faisal (r. 1921–1933) proved to be an able ruler, gaining the support of his people and encouraging moderate reforms. In 1932 he secured Iraqi independence at the price of a restrictive long-term military alliance with Great Britain.

Egypt had been occupied by Great Britain since 1882 (see page 732) and a British protectorate since 1914. Following intense nationalist agitation after the Great War, Great Britain in 1922 proclaimed Egypt formally independent but continued to occupy the country militarily and control its politics. In 1936, the British agreed to restrict their troops to their bases in the Suez Canal Zone.

The French were less compromising in Syria. They practiced a policy of divide-and-rule, carving out a second mandate in Lebanon and generally playing off ethnic and religious minorities against each other. Lebanon eventually became a republic, dominated by a very slender Christian majority and under French protection. Arab nationalists in Syria finally won promises of Syrian independence in 1936 in return for a treaty of friendship with France.

In short, the Arab states gradually freed themselves from Western political mandates but not from the Western military threat or from pervasive Western influence. Of great importance, large Arab landowners and urban merchants increased their wealth and political power after 1918, and they often supported the Western hegemony, from which they benefited greatly. Western control of the newly discovered Arab oil fields helped to convince radical nationalists that economic independence and genuine freedom had not yet been achieved.

Relations between the Arabs and the West were complicated by the tense situation in the British mandate of Palestine, and that situation deteriorated in the interwar years. Both Arabs and Jews denounced the British, who tried unsuccessfully to compromise with both sides. Arab nationalist anger, however, was aimed primarily at Jewish settlers. The key issue was Jewish migration from Europe to Palestine.

A small Jewish community had survived in Palestine ever since the dispersal of the Jews in Roman times. But Jewish nationalism, known as **Zionism,** took shape in Europe in the late nineteenth century under the leadership of Theodor Herzl (see page 707). Herzl believed that only a Jewish state could guarantee Jews dignity and security. The Zionist movement encouraged the world's Jews to settle in Palestine, but until 1921 the great majority of Jewish emigrants preferred the United States.

Zionism *The movement toward Jewish political nationhood started by Theodor Herzl.*

After 1921 the situation changed radically. An isolationist United States drastically limited immigration from eastern Europe, where war and revolution had kindled anti-Semitism. Moreover, the British began honoring the Balfour Declaration despite Arab protests. Thus Jewish immigration to Palestine from turbulent Europe grew rapidly. In the 1930s German and Polish persecution created a mass of Jewish refugees. By 1939 the Jewish population of Palestine had increased almost fivefold since 1914 and accounted for about 30 percent of all inhabitants.

Jewish settlers in Palestine faced formidable difficulties. Although much of the land purchased by the Jewish National Fund was productive, the sellers of such land were often wealthy absentee Arab landowners who cared little for their Arab tenants' welfare. When the new Jewish owners subsequently replaced those age-old Arab tenants with Jewish settlers, Arab farmers and intellectuals burned with a sense of injustice. Moreover, most Jewish immigrants came from urban backgrounds and preferred to establish new cities like Tel Aviv or to live in existing towns, where they competed with the Arabs. The land issue combined with economic and cultural friction to harden Arab protest into hatred. Anti-Jewish riots and even massacres ensued.

The British gradually responded to Arab pressure and tried to slow Jewish immigration. This effort satisfied neither Jews nor Arabs, and by 1938 the two communities were engaged in an undeclared civil war. On the eve of the Second World War, the frustrated British proposed an independent Palestine with the number of Jews permanently limited to only about one-third of the total population. Zionists felt themselves in grave danger.

In the face of adversity Jewish settlers from many different countries gradually succeeded in forging a cohesive community. Hebrew, for centuries used only in religious worship, was revived as a living language to bind the Jews in Palestine together. Despite its slow beginnings, rural development achieved often remarkable results. The key unit of agricultural organization was the **kibbutz,** a collective farm on which each member shared equally in the work, rewards, and defense of the farm. An egalitarian socialist ideology also characterized industry, which grew rapidly. By 1939 a new but old nation was emerging in the Middle East.

kibbutz *A Jewish collective farm on which each member shared equally in the work, rewards, and defense of the farm.*

Reuven Rubin: First Fruits (or First Pioneers) (1923)   Whereas Jerusalem was the center of Jewish religious culture and conservative art in the 1920s, the new coastal city of Tel Aviv sprang up secular, and it gloried in avant-garde modern art (see pages 884–886). In this painting Rubin, a leader of Tel Aviv's modernist school, depicts Jewish pioneers in a stark, two-dimensional landscape and conveys an exotic "Garden of Eden" flavor. Arriving from Romania, Rubin was bowled over by Palestine. "The world about me became clear and pure: life was formless, blurred, primitive." *(Reuven Rubin,* First Fruits, *1922, Coll. Rubin Museum, Tel-Aviv, Israel)*

● ● ● ● ● ● ● ● ● ● ● ● ● ● ● ● ●

TOWARD SELF-RULE IN INDIA

What role did Gandhi and his campaign of militant nonviolence play in leading India to independence from the British?

The national movement in British India grew out of two interconnected cultures, Hindu and Muslim, which came to see themselves as fundamentally different in rising to challenge British rule. Nowhere has modern nationalism's power both to unify and to divide been more strikingly demonstrated than in India.

Promises and Repression (1914–1919)

Indian nationalism had emerged in the late nineteenth century (see page 753), and when the First World War began, the British feared revolt. Instead, Indians supported the war effort. About 1.2 million Indian soldiers and laborers voluntarily served in Europe, Africa, and the Middle East. The British government in India and the native Indian princes sent large supplies of food, money, and ammunition. In return, the British opened more good government jobs to Indians and made other minor concessions.

As the war in distant Europe ground on, however, inflation, high taxes, food shortages, and a terrible influenza epidemic created widespread suffering and discontent. The prewar nationalist movement revived, stronger than ever, and moderates and radicals in the Indian National Congress joined forces. Moreover, in 1916 Hindu leaders in the Congress Party hammered out an alliance—the **Lucknow Pact**—with India's Muslim League. The League was founded in 1906 to uphold Muslim

Lucknow Pact *A 1916 alliance between Hindus leading the Indian National Congress and the Muslim League.*

Jallianwala Bagh Massacre This is a highly dramatized painting of the massacre in the Jallian-wala Bagh (Garden) in Amritsar on April 13, 1919. Having banned gatherings of five persons or more, General Dyer ordered the fifty British Indian Army troops under his command to open fire on unarmed men, women, and children who had gathered on a Sunday to celebrate the Sikh festival of *Baisakhi*. The soldiers fired 1,650 rounds of ammunition (until they ran out of bullets), killing nearly 400 and wounding some 1,100 others. The terror-stricken people had no means of escape for the Indian troops blocked the only exit from the Bagh. *(Courtesy, Indialog Publications Pvt. Ltd., Delhi. Photo: Amrit and Rabindra Dingh, Fine Arts, U.K.)*

Primary Source:
An Indian Nationalist Condemns the British Empire

In this excerpt from a speech, an Indian nationalist and feminist accuses the British Empire of betraying its ideals and losing its soul.

interests, as, under British rule, the once-dominant Muslim minority had fallen behind the Hindu majority. The Lucknow Pact forged a powerful united front of Hindus and Muslims and called for putting India on equal footing with self-governing British dominions like Canada, Australia, and New Zealand.

The British response was contradictory. On the one hand, the secretary of state for India made the unprecedented announcement in August 1917 that British policy in India called for the "gradual development of self-governing institutions and the progressive realization of responsible government." In late 1919 the British established a dual administration: part Indian and elected, part British and authoritarian. Such uncontroversial activities as agriculture and health were transferred from British to Indian officials who were accountable to elected provincial assemblies. More sensitive matters like taxes, police, and the courts remained solely in British hands.

Old-fashioned authoritarian rule seriously undermined the positive impact of this reform. Despite the unanimous opposition of the elected Indian members, the British in 1919 rammed the repressive Rowlatt Acts through India's Imperial Legislative Council. These acts indefinitely extended wartime "emergency measures" designed to curb unrest and root out "conspiracy." The result was a wave of rioting across India.

Under these tense conditions a crowd of some ten thousand gathered to celebrate a Sikh religious festival in an enclosed square in the Sikh holy city of Amritsar in the northern Punjab province. Unknown to the crowd, the local English commander, General Reginald Dyer, had banned all public meetings that very day. Dyer marched his native Gurkha troops into the square and, without warning, ordered them to fire into the unarmed mass at point-blank range until the ammunition ran out. Offical British records of the Amritsar Massacre list 379 killed and 1,137 wounded, but these figures remain hotly contested for being too low. India stood on the verge of more violence and repression and, sooner or later, terrorism and guerrilla war. That India took a different path to national liberation was due largely to Mohandas "Mahatma" Gandhi (1869–1948), the most influential Indian of modern times.

The Roots of Militant Nonviolence

By the time of Gandhi's birth in 1869, the Indian subcontinent was firmly controlled by the British. Part of the country was ruled directly by British (and subordinate Indian) officials, answerable to the British Parliament in London. In each of the so-called protected states, the native prince—usually known as the *maharaja*—remained the titular ruler, although he was bound to the British by unequal treaties and had to accept the "advice" of the British resident assigned to his court.

Gandhi grew up in one of the small protected states north of Bombay. Gandhi's father was the well-to-do head of a large extended family. Gandhi's mother was devoted but undogmatic in religious matters, and she exercised a strong influence on her son.

After his father's death, Gandhi went to study law in England. After passing the English bar and returning to India, he decided in 1893 to try a case for some wealthy Indian merchants in South Africa. It was a momentous decision.

In South Africa, Gandhi took up the plight of the expatriate Indian community. White plantation owners there imported poor Indians as indentured laborers on five-year renewable contracts. When some Indians completed their terms and remained in South Africa as free persons and economic competitors, the Dutch and British settlers passed brutally discriminatory laws. Poor Indians had to work on plantations or return to India; rich Indians lost the vote. Gandhi undertook his countrymen's legal defense, and in 1896 a white mob almost lynched the "coolie lawyer."

Meanwhile, Gandhi was searching for a spiritual theory of social action. He studied Hindu and Christian teachings, and gradually developed a weapon for the weak that he called **Satyagraha**. Gandhi conceived of Satyagraha, loosely translated as "Soul Force," as a means of striving for truth and social justice through love, suffering, and conversion of the oppressor. Its tactic is active nonviolent resistance.

As the undisputed leader of South Africa's Indians before the First World War, Gandhi put his philosophy into action. When South Africa's white government severely restricted Asian immigration and internal freedom of movement, Gandhi organized a nonviolent mass resistance campaign. Thousands of Indian men and women marched in peaceful protest and withstood beatings, arrest, and imprisonment.

In 1914, South Africa's exasperated whites agreed to many of the Indians' demands. They passed a law abolishing discriminatory taxes on Indian traders, recognizing the legality of non-Christian marriages, and permitting the continued immigration of free Indians. Satyagraha—militant nonviolence in pursuit of social justice—proved itself a powerful force in Gandhi's hands.

Satyagraha *Loosely translated as "Soul Force," which Gandhi believed was the means of striving for truth and social justice through love, suffering, and conversion of the oppressor.*

Gandhi Leads the Way

In 1915 Gandhi returned to India. His reputation had preceded him: the masses hailed him as a *Mahatma*, or "Great Soul"—a Hindu title of veneration for a man of great knowledge and humanity. Drawing on his South African experience, Gandhi in 1920 launched a national campaign of nonviolent resistance to British rule. Denouncing British injustice, he urged his countrymen to boycott British goods, jobs, and honors. He told peasants not to pay taxes or buy English cloth or the heavily taxed liquor. Gandhi electrified the people, initiating a revolution in Indian politics.

The nationalist movement had previously touched only the tiny, prosperous, Western-educated elite. Now both the illiterate masses of village India and the educated classes

● Gandhi Arrives in Delhi, October 1939 A small frail man, Gandhi possessed enormous courage and determination. His campaign of nonviolent resistance to British rule inspired the Indian masses and mobilized a nation. Here he arrives for talks with the British viceroy after the outbreak of World War II. *(Corbis)*

heard Gandhi's call for militant nonviolent resistance. It particularly appealed to the masses of Hindus who were not members of the warrior caste or the so-called military races and who were traditionally passive and nonviolent. The British had regarded ordinary Hindus as cowards. Gandhi told them that they could be courageous and even morally superior:

What do you think? Wherein is courage required—in blowing others to pieces from behind a cannon, or with a smiling face to approach a cannon and be blown to pieces? Who is the true warrior—he who keeps death always as a bosom-friend, or he who controls the death of others? Believe me that a man devoid of courage and manhood can never be a passive resister.[4]

Gandhi made Congress into a mass political party, welcoming members from every ethnic group and cooperating closely with the Muslim minority.

In 1922 some Indian resisters turned to violence, murdering twenty-two policemen. Savage riots broke out, and Gandhi abruptly called off his campaign. Arrested for fomenting rebellion, Gandhi told the British judge that he had committed "a Himalayan blunder to believe that India had accepted nonviolence." Released from prison after two years, Gandhi set up a commune, established a national newspaper, and set out to reform Indian society and improve the lot of the poor. He welcomed the outcaste untouchables, worked to help child widows, and promoted native cottage industry production. For Gandhi moral improvement, social progress, and the national movement went hand in hand. Above all, Gandhi nurtured national identity, self-respect, and courage in India's people.

The 1920–1922 resistance campaign left the British severely shaken, but the commission formed in 1927 to consider further steps toward self-rule included no Indian members. Indian resentment was intense. In 1929 the radical nationalists, led by the able and aristocratic Jawaharlal Nehru (1889–1964), pushed through the National Congress a resolution calling for virtual independence within a year. The British stiffened, and Indian radicals talked of a bloody showdown.

Into this tense situation Gandhi masterfully reasserted his leadership, taking a hard line toward the British, but insisting on nonviolent methods. He organized a massive resistance campaign against the hated salt tax, which affected every Indian family. Gandhi himself led fifty thousand people in a spectacular march to the sea where he made salt in defiance of the law. A later demonstration at the British-run Dhrasana salt works resulted in many of the 2,500 nonviolent marchers being beaten senseless by policemen in a brutal and well-publicized encounter. Over the next months the British arrested Gandhi and sixty thousand other protesters for making and distributing salt. In 1931 the frustrated and unnerved British released Gandhi from jail and sat down to negotiate with him, as an equal, over Indian self-rule. Negotiations resulted in a new constitution in 1935, which greatly strengthened India's parliamentary representative institutions. It was practically a blueprint for independence, which came quickly after World War II.

Despite his best efforts, Gandhi failed to heal a widening split between Hindus and Muslims. Indian nationalism, based largely on Hindu symbols and customs, increasingly disturbed the Muslim minority. Tempers mounted and both sides committed atrocities. By the late 1930s Muslim League leaders were calling for the creation of a Muslim nation in British India, a "Pakistan" or "land of the pure." As in Palestine, the rise of conflicting nationalisms in India would lead to tragedy (see pages 990–994).

• • • • • • • • • • • •

TURMOIL IN EAST ASIA

Why did some of the Asian nationalist movements come into brutal conflict?

Because of the efforts of the Meiji reformers, nationalism and modernization were well developed in Japan by 1914. Japan competed politically and economically with the world's leading nations, building its own empire and proclaiming its special mission in Asia. China lagged far behind, but after 1912 the pace of nationalist development there began to quicken.

In the 1920s the Chinese nationalist movement managed to win a large measure of political independence from the imperialist West and promoted extensive modernization. These achievements were soon undermined, however, by internal conflict and war with an expanding Japan. Nationalism also flourished elsewhere in Asia, scoring a major victory in the Philippine Islands.

The Rise of Nationalist China

The 1911 Revolution, which overthrew the Qing Dynasty (see page 763), opened an era of unprecedented change for Chinese society. Before the revolution many progressive Chinese realized that fundamental technological and political reforms were necessary to save the Chinese state, but most hoped to preserve the traditional core of Chinese civilization and culture. The fall of the ancient dynastic system shattered such hopes. If the emperor himself was no longer sacred, what was?

The central figure in the revolution was a crafty old military man, Yuan Shigai (Yüan Shih-k'ai). Called out of retirement to save the dynasty, Yuan (1859–1916) betrayed the Manchus and convinced the revolutionaries that he could unite the country peacefully and prevent foreign intervention. Once elected president of the republic, however, Yuan concentrated on building his own power. In 1913 he used military force to dissolve China's parliament and ruled as a dictator. China's first modern revolution had failed.

The extent of the failure became apparent only after Yuan's death in 1916. The central government in Beijing almost disintegrated. For more than a decade power resided in a multitude of local military leaders, the so-called warlords. Their wars, taxes, and corruption created terrible suffering.

● **Students Demonstrating in Tiananmen Square, Beijing, Summer 1919** The news that the Versailles Peace Conference left China's Shandong Peninsula in Japanese hands brought an explosion of student protest on May 4, 1919. Student demonstrations in the capital's historic Tiananmen Square continued through June, as the May Fourth Movement against foreign domination took root and grew. (Photo from Kautz Family YMCA Archives. Reproduced with permission.)

May Fourth Movement *A nationalist movement against foreign imperialists; it began as a student protest against the decision of the Versailles Peace Conference to leave the Shandong Peninsula in the hands of Japan.*

Foreign imperialism intensified the agony of warlordism. Although China declared its neutrality in 1914, Japan used the Great War as an opportunity to seize Germany's holdings on the Shandong (Shantung) Peninsula and in 1915 forced China to accept Japanese control of Shandong and southern Manchuria (see Map 28.2). Japan's expansion angered China's growing middle class and enraged China's young patriots. On May 4, 1919, five thousand students in Beijing exploded against the decision of the Versailles Peace Conference to leave the Shandong Peninsula in Japanese hands. This famous incident launched the **May Fourth Movement**, which opposed both foreign domination and warlord government.

The May Fourth Movement and the anti-imperialism of Bolshevik Russia renewed Chinese nationalist hopes. In 1923 Sun Yatsen (1866–1925) decided to ally his Nationalist Party, or Guomindang (Kuomintang), with the Communist Third International and the newly formed Chinese Communist Party. The result was the first of many so-called national liberation fronts, in keeping with Lenin's blueprint for temporarily uniting all anticonservative, anti-imperialist forces in a common revolutionary struggle.

Sun, however, was no Communist. In his *Three Principles of the People,* elaborating on the official Nationalist Party ideology—nationalism, democracy, and people's livelihood—nationalism remained of prime importance:

Compared to the other peoples of the world we have the greatest population and our civilization is four thousand years old; we should be advancing in the front rank with the nations of Europe and America. But the Chinese people have only family and clan solidarity, they do not have national spirit. . . . If we do not earnestly espouse nationalism and weld together our four hundred million people into a strong nation, there is a danger of China's

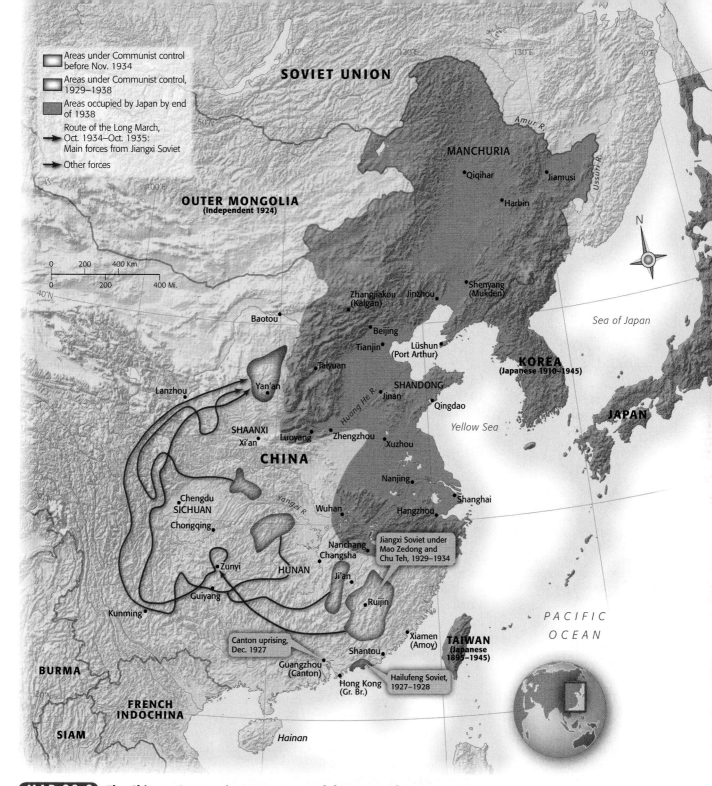

Areas under Communist control
before Nov. 1934

Areas under Communist control,
1929–1938

Areas occupied by Japan by end
of 1938

Route of the Long March,
Oct. 1934–Oct. 1935:
Main forces from Jiangxi Soviet

Other forces

SOVIET UNION

MANCHURIA

Qiqihar
Jiamusi
Harbin

OUTER MONGOLIA
(Independent 1924)

Shenyang
(Mukden)

Baotou

Zhangjiakou
(Kalgan)
Jinzhou

Beijing

Tianjin
Lüshun
(Port Arthur)

KOREA
(Japanese 1910–1945)

Taiyuan

Sea of Japan

JAPAN

Yan'an

SHANDONG
Jinan

SHAANXI
Xi'an
Luoyang
Zhengzhou

Qingdao

Yellow Sea

CHINA
Xuzhou

Lanzhou

Huang He R.

Chengdu
SICHUAN
Chongqing

Nanjing

Shanghai

Wuhan

Hangzhou

Yangzi R.

Nanchang
Changsha

Jiangxi Soviet under
Mao Zedong and
Chu Teh, 1929–1934

Zunyi
HUNAN

Ji'an

Guiyang

Ruijin

PACIFIC
OCEAN

Kunming

Canton uprising,
Dec. 1927

Xiamen
(Amoy)

Shantou

TAIWAN
(Japanese
1895–1945)

BURMA

Guangzhou
(Canton)

Hailufeng Soviet,
1927–1928

Hong Kong
(Gr. Br.)

FRENCH
INDOCHINA

SIAM

Hainan

MAP 28.2 **The Chinese Communist Movement and the War with Japan,**
1927–1938   After urban uprisings ordered by Stalin failed in 1927, Mao Zedong succeeded in
forming a self-governing Communist soviet in mountainous southern China. Relentless Nationalist attacks between 1930 and 1934 finally forced the Long March to Yenan, where the Communists were
well positioned for guerrilla war against the Japanese.

being lost and our people being destroyed. If we wish to avert this catastrophe, we must espouse nationalism and bring this national spirit to the salvation of the country.[5]

Democracy, in contrast, had a less exalted meaning. Sun equated it with firm rule by the Nationalists, who would improve people's lives through land reform and welfare measures.

Sun planned to use the Nationalist Party's revolutionary army to crush the warlords and reunite China under a strong central government. When Sun unexpectedly died in 1925, Jiang Jieshi (Chiang Kai-shek), the young Japanese-educated director of the party's army training school, took his place. In 1926 and 1927 Jiang (1887–1975) led Nationalist armies in a successful attack on warlord governments in central and northern China. In 1928 the Nationalists established a new capital at Nanjing (Nanking). Foreign states recognized the Nanjing government, and superficial observers believed China to be truly reunified.

In fact, national unification was only skin-deep. China remained a vast agricultural country plagued by foreign concessions, regional differences, and a lack of modern communications. Moreover, the uneasy alliance between the Nationalist Party and the Chinese Communist Party had turned into a bitter, deadly rivalry. Justifiably fearful of Communist subversion of the Nationalist government, Jiang decided in April 1927 to liquidate his left-wing "allies" in a bloody purge. Chinese Communists went into hiding and vowed revenge.

China's Intellectual Revolution

Nationalism was the most powerful idea in China between 1911 and 1929, but it was only one aspect of a complex intellectual revolution, generally known as the **New Culture Movement,** that hammered at traditional Chinese thought and custom, advocated cultural renaissance, and pushed China into the modern world.

The New Culture Movement was founded by young Western-oriented intellectuals in Beijing during the May Fourth era. These intellectuals fiercely attacked China's ancient Confucian ethics, which subordinated subjects to rulers, sons to fathers, and wives to husbands. As modernists, they provocatively advocated new and anti-Confucian virtues: individualism, democratic equality, and the critical scientific method. They also promoted the use of simple, understandable written language as a means to clear thinking and mass education. China, they said, needed a whole new culture, a radically different worldview.

Many intellectuals thought the radical worldview China needed was Marxian socialism. It too was Western in origin, "scientific" in approach, and materialist in its denial of religious belief and Confucian family ethics. But while liberalism and individualism reflected the bewildering range of Western thought since the Enlightenment, Marxian socialism offered the certainty of a single all-encompassing creed. As one young Communist intellectual exclaimed, "I am now able to impose order on all the ideas which I could not reconcile; I have found the key to all the problems which appeared to me self-contradictory and insoluble."[6]

Though undeniably Western, Marxism provided a means of criticizing Western dominance, thereby salving Chinese pride. Chinese Communists could blame China's pitiful weakness on rapacious foreign capitalistic imperialism. Thus Marxism, as modified by Lenin and applied by the Bolsheviks in the Soviet Union, appeared as a means of catching up with the hated but envied West. For Chinese believers, it promised salvation soon.

Chinese Communists could and did interpret Marxism-Leninism to appeal to the masses—the peasants. Mao Zedong (Mao Tse-tung) in particular quickly recognized the impoverished Chinese peasantry's enormous revolutionary potential. A member of a prosperous, hard-working peasant family, Mao (1893–1976) converted to Marx-

New Culture Movement *An intellectual revolution, sometimes called the Chinese Renaissance, that attacked traditional Chinese, particularly Confucian, culture and promoted Western ideas of science, democracy, and individualism, from around 1916 to 1923.*

Primary Source: Our Attitude Toward Modern Civilization of the West *A Chinese professor rejects the idea that Eastern civilization is more "spiritual" than the "materialistic" West.*

● **Mao Zedong** Adapting Marxian theory to Chinese reality, Mao concentrated on the revolutionary potential of the peasantry. In this propagandistic painting, typical of Chinese art after the Communist takeover in 1949, the young Mao speaks to a group of worshipful peasant soldiers on the Long March, while Lenin and Marx look down with approval. *(Library of Congress)*

ian socialism in 1918. He began his revolutionary career as an urban labor organizer. In 1925 protest strikes by Chinese textile workers against their Japanese employers unexpectedly spread from the big coastal cities to rural China, prompting Mao to reconsider the peasants. Investigating the rapid growth of radical peasant associations in Hunan province, Mao argued passionately in a 1927 report that

the force of the peasantry is like that of the raging winds and driving rain. It is rapidly increasing in violence. No force can stand in its way. The peasantry will tear apart all nets which bind it and hasten along the road to liberation. They will bury beneath them all forces of imperialism, militarism, corrupt officialdom, village bosses and evil gentry.[7]

Mao's first experiment in peasant revolt—the Autumn Harvest Uprising of September 1927—was not successful, but Mao learned quickly. He advocated equal distribution of land and broke up his forces into small guerrilla groups. After 1928 he and his supporters built up a self-governing Communist soviet, centered at Ruijin (Juichin) in southeastern China, and dug in against Nationalist attacks.

China's intellectual revolution also stimulated profound changes in popular culture and family life. After the 1911 Revolution Chinese women enjoyed increasingly greater freedom and equality. Foot binding was outlawed and attacked as cruel and uncivilized. Arranged marriages and polygamy declined. Women gradually gained unprecedented educational and economic opportunities. Thus rising nationalism and the intellectual revolution interacted with monumental changes in Chinese family life. (See the feature "Individuals in Society: Ning Lao, a Chinese Working Woman.")

From Liberalism to Ultranationalism in Japan

The efforts of the Meiji reformers (see page 764) to build a powerful nationalistic state and resist Western imperialism were spectacularly successful and deeply impressed Japan's fellow Asians. The Japanese, alone among Asia's peoples, had mastered modern industrial technology by 1910 and fought victorious wars against both China and Russia. The First World War brought more triumphs. In 1915 Japan easily seized Germany's Asian holdings and held on to most of them as League of Nations mandates. The Japanese economy expanded enormously. Profits soared as Japan won new markets that wartime Europe could no longer supply.

In the early 1920s Japan seemed to make further progress on all fronts. Most Japanese nationalists believed that Japan had a semidivine mission to enlighten and protect Asia, but some were convinced that they could achieve their goal peacefully. In 1922 Japan signed a naval arms limitation treaty with the Western powers and returned some of its control over the Shandong Peninsula to China. These conciliatory moves reduced tensions in East Asia. At home Japan seemed headed toward genuine democracy. The electorate expanded twelvefold between 1918 and 1925 as all males over

● **Japanese Suffragists** In the 1920s Japanese women pressed for political emancipation in demonstrations like this one, but they did not receive the right to vote until 1946. Like these suffragists, some young women adopted Western fashions. Most workers in modern Japanese textile factories were also women. *(Time Life Pictures/Getty Images)*

Ning Lao, a Chinese Working Woman

The tough and resilient Ning Lao (*right*) with Ida Pruitt. *(Reproduced with permission of Eileen Hsu-Belzer)*

The voice of the poor and uneducated is often muffled in history. Thus *A Daughter of Han,* a rare autobiography of an illiterate working woman as told to an American friend, offers unforgettable insights into the evolution of ordinary Chinese life and family relations.

Ning Lao was born in 1867 to poor parents in the northern city of Penglai on the Shandong Peninsula. Her foot binding was delayed to age nine, "since I loved so much to run and play." When the bandages were finally drawn tight, "my feet hurt so much that for two years I had to crawl on my knees."* Her arranged marriage at age fourteen was a disaster. She found that her husband was a drug addict ("in those days everyone took opium to some extent") who sold everything to pay for his habit. Yet "there was no freedom then for women," and "it was no light thing for a woman to leave her house" and husband. Thus Ning Lao endured her situation until her husband sold their four-year-old daughter to buy opium. Taking her remaining baby daughter, she fled.

Taking off her foot bandages, Ning Lao became a beggar. Her feet began to spread, quite improperly, but she walked without pain. And the beggar's life was "not the hardest one," she thought, for a beggar woman could go where she pleased. To care better for her child, Ning Lao became a servant and a cook in prosperous households. Some of her mistresses were concubines (secondary wives taken by rich men in middle age), and she concluded that concubinage resulted in nothing but quarrels and heartache. Hot tempered and quick to take offense and leave an employer, the hard-working woman always found a new job quickly. In time she became a peddler of luxury goods to wealthy women confined to their homes.

The two unshakable values that buoyed Ning Lao were a tough, fatalistic acceptance of life—"Only fortune that comes of itself will come. There is no use to seek for it"—and devotion to her family. She eventually returned to her husband, who had mellowed, seldom took opium, and was "good" in those years. "But I did not miss him when he died. I had

*Ida Pruitt, *A Daughter of Han: The Autobiography of a Chinese Working Woman* (New Haven, Conn.: Yale University Press, 1945), p. 22. Other quotations are from pages 83, 62, 71, 182, 166, 235, and 246.

my newborn son and I was happy. My house was established. . . . Truly all my life I spent thinking of my family." Her lifelong devotion was reciprocated by her son and granddaughter, who cared for her well in her old age.

Ning Lao's remarkable life story encompasses both old and new Chinese attitudes toward family life. Her son moved to the capital city of Beijing, worked in an office, and had only one wife. Her granddaughter, Su Teh, studied in missionary schools and became a college teacher and a determined foe of arranged marriages. She personified the trend toward greater freedom for Chinese women.

Generational differences also highlighted changing political attitudes. When the Japanese invaded China and occupied Beijing in 1937, Ning Lao thought that "perhaps the Mandate of Heaven had passed to the Japanese . . . and we should listen to them as our new masters." Her nationalistic granddaughter disagreed. She urged resistance and the creation of a new China, where the people governed themselves. Leaving to join the guerrillas in 1938, Su Teh gave her savings to her family and promised to continue to help them. One must be good to one's family, she said, but one must also work for the country.

Questions for Analysis

1. Compare the lives of Ning Lao and her granddaughter. In what ways were they different and similar?

2. In a broader historical perspective, what do you find most significant about Ning Lao's account of her life? Why?

twenty-five won the vote. Two-party competition was intense. Japanese living standards were the highest in Asia. Literacy was universal.

Japan's remarkable rise, however, was accompanied by serious problems. Japan had a rapidly growing population, but scarce natural resources. As early as the 1920s Japan was exporting manufactured goods in order to pay for imports of food and essential raw materials. Deeply enmeshed in world trade, Japan was vulnerable to every boom and bust. These economic realities broadened support for Japan's colonial empire. Before World War I, Japanese leaders saw colonial expansion primarily in terms of international prestige and national defense. They believed that control of Taiwan, Korea, and Manchuria provided an essential "outer ring of defense" to protect the home islands from Russian attack and Anglo-American imperialism. Now, in the 1920s, Japan's colonies also seemed essential for markets, raw materials, and economic growth.

Japan's rapid industrial development also created an imbalanced "dualistic" economy. The modern sector consisted of a handful of giant conglomerate firms, the **zaibatsu,** or "financial combines." Zaibatsu firms like Mitsubishi employed thousands of workers and owned banks, mines, steel mills, cotton factories, shipyards, and trading companies, all of them closely interrelated. Zaibatsu firms wielded enormous economic power and dominated the other sector of the economy, an unorganized multitude of peasant farmers and craftsmen. The result was financial oligarchy, corruption of government officials, and a weak middle class.

Behind the façade of party politics, the old and new elites—the emperor, high government officials, big businessmen, and military leaders—were jockeying savagely for the real power. Cohesive leadership, which had played such an important role in Japan's modernization by the Meiji reformers, had ceased to exist. By far the most serious challenge to peaceful progress, however, was fanatical nationalism. As in Europe, ultranationalism first emerged in Japan in the late nineteenth century but did not flower fully until the First World War and the 1930s.

Though often vague, Japan's ultranationalists shared several fundamental beliefs. They were violently anti-Western. They rejected democracy, big business, and Marxian socialism, which they blamed for destroying the older, superior Japanese practices they wanted to restore. Reviving old myths, they stressed the emperor's godlike qualities and the samurai warrior's code of honor and obedience. Despising party politics, they assassinated moderate leaders and plotted armed uprisings to achieve their goals. Above all else, the ultranationalists preached foreign expansion. Like Western imperialists shouldering "the White Man's Burden," Japanese ultranationalists thought their mission was a noble one. "Asia for the Asians" was their anti-Western rallying cry. As the famous ultranationalist Kita Ikki wrote in 1923, "Our seven hundred million brothers in China and India have no other path to independence than that offered by our guidance and protection."[8]

The ultranationalists were noisy and violent in the 1920s, but it took the Great Depression of the 1930s to tip the scales decisively in their favor. The worldwide depression, which had dire consequences for many countries (see Chapter 29), hit Japan like a tidal wave in 1930. Exports and wages collapsed; unemployment and raw suffering soared. Starving peasants ate the bark off trees and sold their daughters to brothels. The ultranationalists blamed the system, and people listened.

Japan Against China

Among those who listened with particular care were young Japanese army officers in Manchuria, the underpopulated, resource-rich province of northeastern China controlled by the Japanese army since its victory over Russia in 1905. Many junior Japanese officers in Manchuria came from the peasantry and were distressed by the stories

zaibatsu *Giant conglomerate firms in Japan.*

● **Japanese Atrocities in China**   In December 1937, after the fall of the Chinese capital Nanjing, Japanese soldiers went on a horrifying rampage. These Japanese recruits are using Chinese prisoners of war as live targets in a murderous bayonet drill. Other Chinese prisoners were buried alive by their Japanese captors. *(Hulton Archive/Getty Images)*

of rural suffering they heard from home. They also knew the Japanese army's budget and prestige had declined in the prosperous 1920s.

The rise of Chinese nationalism worried the young officers most. This new political force, embodied in the Guomindang unification of China, challenged Japanese control over Manchuria. In response, junior Japanese officers in Manchuria, in cooperation with top generals in Tokyo, secretly manufactured an excuse for aggression in late 1931. They blew up some Japanese-owned railroad tracks near the city of Shenyang (Mukden) and then with reinforcements rushed in from Korea quickly occupied all of Manchuria in "self-defense."

In 1932 Japan proclaimed Manchuria an independent state and installed a member of the old Qing Dynasty as puppet emperor. When the League of Nations condemned its aggression in Manchuria, Japan resigned in protest. Japanese aggression in Manchuria showed that the army, though reporting directly to the Japanese emperor, was clearly an independent force subject to no outside control.

The Japanese puppet state named Manchukuo in northeast China became the model for the subsequent conquest and occupation of China and then Southeast Asia. Throughout the 1930s, the Japanese worked to integrate Manchuria (and Korea and

Taiwan) into a large, self-sufficient economic bloc that provided resources, markets, and investment opportunities safe from Western power in East Asia. While exporting raw materials, state-sponsored Japanese companies in Manchuria also built steel mills and heavy industry to supply vital military goods. At home, newspapers and newsreels glorified Japan's efforts and mobilized public support for colonial empire.

For China the Japanese conquest of Manchuria was disastrous. Japanese aggression in Manchuria drew attention away from modernizing efforts. The Nationalist government promoted a massive boycott of Japanese goods but lost interest in social reform. Above all, the Nationalist government after 1931 completely neglected land reform and the Chinese peasants' grinding poverty.

As in many poor agricultural societies throughout history, Chinese peasants paid roughly half of their crops to their landlords as rent. Land ownership was very unequal. One study estimated that a mere 4 percent of families, usually absentee landlords living in cities, owned fully half the land. Poor peasants and farm laborers—70 percent of the rural population—owned only one-sixth of the land. As a result, peasants were heavily in debt and chronically underfed. A contemporaneous Chinese economist spelled out the revolutionary implications: "It seems clear that the land problem in China today is as acute as that of eighteenth-century France or nineteenth-century Russia." Mao Zedong certainly agreed.

Having abandoned land reform, partly because they themselves were often landowners, the Nationalists under Jiang Jieshi devoted their energies between 1930 and 1934 to great campaigns of encirclement and extermination against the Communists' rural power base in southeastern China. In 1934 they closed in for the kill, but, in one of the most incredible sagas of modern times, the main Communist army broke out, beat off attacks, and retreated 6,000 miles in twelve months to a remote region on the northwestern border (see Map 28.2). Of the estimated 100,000 men and women who began the **Long March,** only 8,000 to 10,000 reached the final destination. There Mao built up his forces once again, established a new territorial base, and won local peasant support by undertaking land reform.

Long March *The 6,000-mile retreat of the Communist army to a remote region on the northwestern border of China, during which tens of thousands lost their lives.*

In Japan politics became increasingly chaotic. In 1937 the Japanese military and the ultranationalists were in command. Unable to force China to cede more territory in northern China, they used a minor incident near Beijing as a pretext for a general attack. This marked the beginning of World War II in Asia, although Japan issued no declaration of war. The Nationalist government, which had just formed a united front with the Communists, fought hard, but Japanese troops quickly took Beijing and northern China. Taking the great port of Shanghai after ferocious combat, the Japanese launched an immediate attack up the Yangzi River (see Map 28.2).

Foretelling the horrors of World War II, the Japanese air force bombed Chinese cities and civilian populations with unrelenting fury. Nanjing, the capital, fell in December 1937. Entering the city, Japanese soldiers went berserk and committed dreadful atrocities over seven weeks. Tens of thousands of Chinese were killed, and many thousands of women were raped. The "Rape of Nanjing" combined with other Japanese atrocities to outrage world opinion. The Western Powers denounced Japanese aggression but, with tensions rising in Europe, took no action.

By late 1938 Japanese armies occupied sizable portions of coastal China (see Map 28.2). But the Nationalists and the Communists had retreated to the interior, and both refused to accept defeat. In 1939, as Europe edged toward another great war, the undeclared war between China and Japan bogged down in a savage stalemate. The bloody undeclared war provided a spectacular example of conflicting nationalisms.

Southeast Asia

The tide of nationalism was also rising in Southeast Asia. Like their counterparts in India, China, and Japan, nationalists in French Indochina, the Dutch East Indies, and the Philippines urgently wanted genuine political independence and freedom from foreign rule. In both French Indochina and the Dutch East Indies, they ran up against an imperialist stone wall. The obstacle to Filipino independence came from America and Japan.

In the words of one historian, "Indochina was governed by Frenchmen for Frenchmen, and the great liberal slogans of liberty, equality, and fraternity were not considered to be export goods for overseas dominions."[9] This uncompromising attitude stimulated the growth of an equally stubborn communist opposition under Ho Chi Minh, which despite ruthless repression emerged as the dominant anti-French force.

In the East Indies—modern Indonesia—the Dutch made some concessions after the First World War, establishing a people's council with very limited lawmaking power. But in the 1930s the Dutch cracked down hard, jailing all the important nationalist leaders. Like the French, the Dutch were determined to hold on.

In the Philippines, however, a well-established nationalist movement achieved greater success. As in colonial Latin America, the Spanish in the Philippines had been indefatigable missionaries. By the late nineteenth century the Filipino population was 80 percent Catholic. Filipinos shared a common cultural heritage and a common racial origin. Education, especially for girls, was quite advanced for Southeast Asia, and already in 1843 a higher percentage of people could read in the Philippines than in Spain itself. Economic development helped to create a westernized elite, which turned first to reform and then to revolution in the 1890s. As in Egypt and Turkey, long-standing intimate contact with Western civilization created a strong nationalist movement at an early date.

Filipino nationalists were bitterly disillusioned when the United States, having taken the Philippines from Spain in the Spanish-American War of 1898, ruthlessly beat down a patriotic revolt and denied the universal Filipino desire for independence. The Americans claimed the Philippines were not ready and might be seized by Germany or Britain. As the imperialist power in the Philippines, the United States encouraged education and promoted capitalistic economic development. As in British India, an elected legislature was given some real powers. In 1919 President Wilson even promised eventual independence, though subsequent Republican administrations saw it as a distant goal.

As in India and French Indochina, demands for independence grew. One important contributing factor was American racial attitudes. Americans treated Filipinos as inferiors and introduced segregationist practices borrowed from the American South. American racism made passionate nationalists of many Filipinos. However, it was the Great Depression that had the most radical impact on the Philippines.

As the United States collapsed economically, the Philippines suddenly appeared to be a liability rather than an asset. American farm groups lobbied for protection from cheap Filipino sugar. To protect American jobs, labor unions demanded an end to Filipino immigration. In 1934 Congress made the Philippines a self-governing commonwealth and scheduled independence for 1944. Sugar imports were reduced, and immigration limited to only fifty Filipinos per year.

Like Britain and France in the Middle East, the United States was determined to hold on to its big military bases in the Philippines as it permitted increased local self-government and promised eventual political independence. Some Filipino nationalists denounced the continued presence of U.S. fleets and armies. Others were less certain that the American presence was the immediate problem. Japan was fighting in China and expanding economically into the Philippines and throughout Southeast Asia. By 1939 a new threat to Filipino independence appeared to come from Asia itself.

Chapter Summary

To assess your mastery of this chapter, go to
bedfordstmartins.com/mckayworld

• *How did modern nationalism—the dominant force in most of the world in the twentieth century—develop in Asia between the First and Second World Wars?*

The Asian nationalist revolt against the West began before the First World War. But only after 1914 did Asian nationalist movements broaden their bases sufficiently to challenge Western domination effectively. These mass movements sought human dignity as well as political freedom. Generally speaking, Asian nationalists favored modernization and adopted Western techniques and ideas even as they rejected Western rule. Everywhere Asian nationalists had to fight long and hard, though their struggle gained momentum from growing popular support and the encouragement of the Soviet Union.

• *How did the collapse of the Ottoman Empire in World War I shape the history of the Middle East for the rest of the century?*

The collapse of the Ottoman Empire in World War I left a power vacuum that both Western imperialists and Turkish, Arab, Persian, and Jewish and other nationalists sought to fill. The Turks, who had ruled the old Ottoman Empire, created the modern secular state of Turkey under the leadership of Mustafa Kemal. He brutally crushed the budding nationalism of the Kurds and Armenians. A nationalist movement in Iran, led by the military dictator Reza Shah Pahlavi, gained independence from British control, as did Afghanistan under the anti-British amir Amanullah. The British made promises to both the Palestinians and Jewish Zionists regarding independent homelands in Palestine, creating an impasse that has yet to be settled. France and England had divided areas of the Middle East between them during the war, and then claimed jurisdiction over them as League of Nations mandates. The British and French maintained various degrees of control over the Arab states of Iraq, Syria, Lebanon, Egypt, and Arabia after the war but lost much of their influence over the next two decades as Arab nationalists pushed for complete independence.

• *What role did Gandhi and his campaign of militant nonviolence play in leading India to independence from the British?*

In facing the might of the British Empire Gandhi knew that the Indian people were not capable of fighting a military campaign against the British without suffering hundreds of thousands, perhaps millions, of deaths. But he realized that a few thousand British could do nothing if 350 million Indians refused to cooperate or obey British laws. By employing active, nonviolent resistance, which he called Satyagraha, Gandhi and his millions of Hindu and Muslim followers were able to bring British colonial rule in India to a standstill, leading to Indian independence in 1947. Regrettably, however, Gandhi was not able to control the extreme religious nationalism of the Muslims and Hindus following independence. After bloody massacres on both sides, Muslim Pakistan and Bangladesh split off from predominantly Hindu India (see Chapter 32).

• Why did some of the Asian nationalist movements come into brutal conflict?

Asia's nationalist movements arose out of separate historical experiences and distinct cultures. Variations on the common theme of nationalism were evident in China, Japan, and the Philippines. This diversity helps explain why Asian peoples became defensive in their relations with one another while rising against Western rule. Like earlier nationalists in Europe, Asian nationalists developed a strong sense of "we" and "they"; "they" included other Asians as well as Europeans. Nationalism meant freedom, modernization, and cultural renaissance, but it nonetheless proved to be a mixed blessing.

Suggested Reading

Chang, Jung, and Jon Halliday. *Mao: The Unknown Story.* 2006. New, and very controversial, biography of the Chinese leader.

Chow, Tse-tung. *The May Fourth Movement: Intellectual Revolution in Modern China.* 1960. The classic study of the Chinese intellectual revolution that began in 1919.

Erikson, Eric. *Gandhi's Truth: On the Origins of Militant Nonviolence.* 1969. A classic study of Gandhi's life and the origins of Satyagraha.

Fromkin, David. *A Peace to End All Peace: The Fall of the Ottoman Empire and the Creation of the Modern Middle East.* 2001. A very thorough but very readable introduction to the Middle East in the early twentieth century.

Hourani, Albert, and Malise Ruthven. *History of the Arab Peoples.* 2003. One of the best single volume histories of the Arab peoples.

Hsü, Immanuel C.Y. *The Rise of Modern China,* 6th ed. 1999. Sixth edition of a classic history of modern China.

Irokawa, Daikichi. *The Age of Hirohito: In Search of Modern Japan.* 1995. An excellent brief account by a leading Japanese historian.

Lacqueur, Walter. *A History of Zionism. From the French Revolution to the Establishment of the State of Israel.* 1972. Good general history of Zionism and the founding of Israel.

Mango, Andrew. *Atatürk.* 2000. Rich, well-researched biography of this complex Turkish leader.

Myers, Ramon H., and M. Peattie, eds. *The Japanese Colonial Expansion, 1895–1945.* 1984. Broad collection of essays covering all of Japan's colonial empire, both formal and informal.

Osborne, Milton. *Southeast Asia: An Introductory History,* 9th ed. 2005. Ninth edition of the classic introduction to the region's history.

Owen, Norman, David Chandler, and William R. Roff. *The Emergence of Southeast Asia: A New History.* 2004. New history looking at both individual countries and social and economic themes, including gender and ecology.

Reischauer, Edwin O. *Japan: The Story of Nation,* 4th ed. 1991. The classic history in its fourth edition by America's leading historian on Japan.

Spence, Jonathan. *The Search for Modern China.* 1990. Important study of modern China by a leading Chinese scholar.

Wolpert, Stanley. *India.* 2005. An excellent introduction to India's history.

Young, Louise. *Japan's Total Empire: Manchuria and the Culture of Wartime Imperialism.* 1998. A fascinating pioneering work on Japanese imperialism.

Notes

1. K. M. Panikkar, *Asia and Western Dominance: A Survey of the Vasco da Gama Epoch of Asian History* (London: George Allen & Unwin, 1959), p. 197.

2. H. Armstrong, *Turkey in Travail: The Birth of a New Nation* (London: John Lane, 1925), p. 75.

3. Quoted in Lord Kinross, *Atatürk: A Biography of Mustafa Kemal, Father of Modern Turkey* (New York: Morrow, 1965), p. 181.

4. Quoted in E. Erikson, *Gandhi's Truth: On the Origins of Militant Nonviolence* (New York: W. W. Norton, 1969), p. 225.

5. Quoted in W. T. deBary, W. Chan, and B. Watson, *Sources of Chinese Tradition* (New York: Columbia University Press, 1964), pp. 768–769.

6. Quoted in J. F. Fairbank, E. O. Reischauer, and A. M. Craig, *East Asia: Tradition and Transformation* (Boston: Houghton Mifflin, 1973), p. 774.

7. Quoted in B. I. Schwartz, *Chinese Communism and the Rise of Mao* (Cambridge, Mass.: Harvard University Press, 1951), p. 74.

8. Quoted in W. T. deBary, R. Tsunoda, and D. Keene, *Sources of Japanese Tradition,* vol. 2 (New York: Columbia University Press, 1958), p. 269.

9. Quoted in W. Bingham, H. Conroy, and F. Iklé, *A History of Asia,* vol. 2, 2d ed. (Boston: Allyn and Bacon, 1974), p. 480.

Listening to the PAST

Arab Political Aspirations in 1919

Great Britain and France had agreed to divide up the Arab lands, and the British also had made conflicting promises to Arab and Jewish nationalists. However, President Wilson insisted at Versailles that the right of self-determination should be applied to the conquered Ottoman territories, and he sent an American commission of inquiry to Syria, even though the British and French refused to participate. The commission canvassed political views throughout greater Syria, and its long report with many documents reflected public opinion in the region in 1919.

To present their view to the Americans, Arab nationalists from present-day Syria, Lebanon, Israel, and Jordan came together in Damascus as the General Syrian Congress, and they passed the following resolution on July 2, 1919. In addition to the Arab call for political independence, the delegates addressed the possibility of French rule under a League of Nations mandate and the establishment of a Jewish national home.

We the undersigned members of the General Syrian Congress, meeting in Damascus on Wednesday, July 2nd, 1919, . . . provided with credentials and authorizations by the inhabitants of our various districts, Moslems, Christians, and Jews, have agreed upon the following statement of the desires of the people of the country who have elected us to present them to the American Section of the International Commission; the fifth article was passed by a very large majority; all the other articles were accepted unanimously.

1. We ask absolutely complete political independence for Syria within these boundaries. [Describes the area including the present-day states of Syria, Lebanon, Israel, and Jordan.]

2. We ask that the Government of this Syrian country should be a democratic civil constitutional Monarchy on broad decentralization principles, safeguarding the rights of minorities, and that the King be the Emir Faisal, who carried on a glorious struggle in the cause of our liberation and merited our full confidence and entire reliance.

3. Considering the fact that the Arabs inhabiting the Syrian area are not naturally less gifted than other more advanced races and that they are by no means less developed than the Bulgarians, Serbians, Greeks, and Roumanians at the beginning of their independence, we protest against Article 22 of the Covenant of the League of Nations, placing us among the nations in their middle stage of development which stand in need of a mandatory power.

4. In the event of the rejection by the Peace Conference of this just protest for certain considerations that we may not understand, we, relying on the declarations of President Wilson that his object in waging war was to put an end to the ambition of conquest and colonization, can only regard the mandate mentioned in the Covenant of the League of Nations as equivalent to the rendering of economical and technical assistance that does not prejudice our complete independence. And desiring that our country should not fall a prey to colonization and believing that the American Nation is farthest from any thought of colonization and has no political ambition in our country, we will seek the technical and economical assistance from the United States of America, provided that such assistance does not exceed 20 years.

5. In the event of America not finding herself in a position to accept our desire for assistance, we will seek this assistance from Great Britain, also provided that such assistance does not infringe the complete independence and unity of our country and that the duration of such assistance does not exceed that mentioned in the previous article.

6. We do not acknowledge any right claimed by the French Government in any part whatever of our Syrian country and refuse that she should assist us or have a hand in our country under any circumstances and in any place.

7. We oppose the pretensions of the Zionists to create a Jewish commonwealth in the southern part of Syria, known as Palestine, and oppose Zionist migration to any part of our country; for we do not acknowledge their title but consider them a grave peril to our people from the national, economical, and political points of view. Our Jewish compatriots shall enjoy our common rights and assume the common responsibilities.

Palestinian Arabs protest against large-scale Jewish migration into Palestine. *(Roger-Viollet/Getty Images)*

8. We ask that there should be no separation of the southern part of Syria, known as Palestine, nor of the littoral western zone, which includes Lebanon, from the Syrian country. We desire that the unity of the country should be guaranteed against partition under whatever circumstances.

9. We ask complete independence for emancipated Mesopotamia [today's Iraq] and that there should be no economical barriers between the two countries.

10. The fundamental principles laid down by President Wilson in condemnation of secret treaties impel us to protest most emphatically against any treaty that stipulates the partition of our Syria country and against any private engagement aiming at the establishment of Zionism in the southern part of Syria; therefore we ask the complete annulment of these conventions and agreements.

The noble principles enunciated by President Wilson strengthen our confidence that our desires emanating from the depths of our hearts, shall be the decisive factor in determining our future; and that President Wilson and the free American people will be our supporters for the realization of our hopes, thereby proving their sincerity and noble sympathy with the aspiration of the weaker nations in general and our Arab people in particular.

We also have the fullest confidence that the Peace Conference will realize that we would not have risen against the Turks, with whom we had participated in all civil, political, and representative privileges, but for their violation of our national rights, and so will grant us our desires in full in order that our political rights may not be less after the war than they were before, since we have shed so much blood in the cause of our liberty and independence.

We request to be allowed to send a delegation to represent us at the Peace Conference to defend our rights and secure the realization of our aspirations.

Questions for Analysis

1. What kind of state did the delegates want?

2. How did the delegates want to modify an unwanted League of Nations mandate to make it less objectionable?

3. Did the delegates view their "Jewish compatriots" and the Zionists in different ways? Why?

Source: "Resolution of the General Syrian Congress at Damascus, 2 July 1919," from the *King-Crane Commission Report, in Foreign Relations of the United States: Paris Peace Conference, 1919,* 12: 780–781.

Outside and Inside. This detail of George Grosz's *Draussen und Drinnen* (Outside and Inside) captures the uncertainty and anxiety of the 1920s. *(Estate of George Grosz/ Licensed by VAGA, New York, NY. Photo: akg-images)*

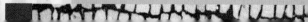

29 THE AGE OF ANXIETY IN THE WEST

Allied diplomats meeting in Paris in early 1919 had optimistic plans for building a lasting peace. Most held high hopes for happier times and looked forward to life returning to normal after the terrible trauma of total war—life in the familiar prewar terms of peace, prosperity, and progress. These hopes were in vain. The Great Break—the First World War and the Russian Revolution—had mangled too many things beyond repair. Thus in the 1920s and 1930s, as Asians developed renewed self-confidence and forged powerful nationalist movements directed against Western domination (see Chapter 28), many in the West felt themselves increasingly adrift in a strange, uncertain, and uncontrollable world. They saw themselves living in an age of anxiety, an age of continual crisis (which would last until the early 1950s). In almost every area of human experience, they went searching for ways to put meaning back into life.

UNCERTAINTY IN MODERN THOUGHT

What was the nature of the uncertainty in modern thought in Europe at the beginning of the twentieth century, and what did the doubts and searching mean for Western thought, art, and culture?

A complex revolution in thought and ideas was under way in Western society before the First World War, but relatively few people were aware of it. After the war new and upsetting ideas began to spread through the entire population. Western society began to question and even abandon many cherished values and beliefs that had guided it since the eighteenth-century Enlightenment and the nineteenth-century triumph of industrial development, scientific advances, and evolutionary thought.

● **Kollwitz: The Grieving Parents** After the renowned German artist Kathe Kollwitz learned in October 1914 that her son Peter had died in battle, the heartbroken mother conceived of a sculpture to honor his memory. Yet her efforts were repeatedly overwhelmed by sorrow. Only in 1931 could she complete this graveside memorial in a military cemetery, a telling indication of the war's ongoing devastation for millions. The grieving father and mother are finally reunited with their son, and they beg forgiveness for the mad war their generation inflicted on its children. *(John Parker, Photographer/© Artists Rights society (ARS), New York/VG Bild-Kunst, Bonn)*

Before 1914 most people in the West still believed in progress, reason, and individual rights. Progress was a daily reality, apparent in the rising standard of living, the taming of the city, and the steady increase in popular education. Such developments also encouraged the comforting belief in the logical universe of Newtonian physics and faith that a rational human mind could understand that universe through intellectual investigation. There were also laws of society, like the laws of science, which rational human beings could discover and then wisely act on. At the same time, individual rights were actually increasing. Well-established rights were gradually spreading to women and workers, and new "social rights," such as old-age pensions, were emerging. In short, before World War I most Europeans and North Americans had a moderately optimistic view of the world, and with good reason.

Nevertheless, since the 1880s a small band of serious thinkers and creative writers had been attacking these optimistic ideas. These critics rejected the general faith in progress and the power of the rational human mind. Their numbers expanded after the experience of history's most destructive war—a war that suggested to many that human beings were a pack of violent, irrational animals quite capable of tearing the individual and his or her rights to shreds. Disorientation and pessimism were particularly acute in the 1930s, when harsh dictatorships and the Great Depression transformed old certainties into bitter illusions.

In the early 1920s no one expressed this state of uncertainty better than French poet and critic Paul Valéry (1871–1945): "We think of what has disappeared, and we are almost destroyed by what has been destroyed; we do not know what will be born, and we fear the future, not without reason."[1] Above all, Valéry saw the "cruelly injured mind" besieged by doubts and suffering from anxieties. New ideas and discoveries in philosophy, physics, psychology, and literature contributed to this general intellectual crisis of the twentieth century.

Modern Philosophy

Among those thinkers in the late nineteenth century who challenged the belief in progress and the general faith in the rational human mind, German philosopher Friedrich Nietzsche (1844–1900) was particularly influential. A Lutheran minister's son, Nietzsche utterly rejected Christianity. In 1872 he argued that ever since classical Athens, the West had overemphasized rationality and stifled the passion and animal instinct that drive human activity and true creativity. Nietzsche questioned all values. He claimed that Christianity embodied a "slave morality" that glorified weakness, envy, and mediocrity. In Nietzsche's most famous line, a wise fool proclaims that "God is dead," murdered by lackadaisical modern Christians who no longer truly believe in Him. Nietzsche regarded the pillars of conventional morality—reason, democracy, progress, respectability—as outworn social and psychological constructs that suffocated self-realization and excellence. Little read during his lifetime, Nietzsche attracted growing attention in the early twentieth century, and his influence remains enormous to this day.

French philosophy professor Henri Bergson (1859–1941) also expressed growing dissatisfaction with established ideas before 1914. Bergson argued that immediate experience and intuition were as important as rational and scientific thinking for understanding reality. Rejecting democracy, French socialist Georges Sorel (1847–1922) frankly characterized Marxian socialism as an inspiring but unprovable religion rather than a rational scientific truth. Socialism would come to power, he believed, through a great, violent strike of all working people, which would miraculously shatter capitalist society.

The First World War accelerated the revolt against established certainties in philosophy, but that revolt went in two very different directions. In English-speaking countries, logical empiricism (or logical positivism) gained acceptance in university circles. In continental Europe the primary development in philosophy was existentialism.

Logical empiricism was truly revolutionary. It rejected most concerns of traditional philosophy, from God's existence to the meaning of happiness, as nonsense. Austrian philosopher Ludwig Wittgenstein (1889–1951), who spent much of his life at Cambridge, is primarily responsible for this postulation.

Wittgenstein argued in his pugnacious *Tractatus Logico-Philosophicus* (*Essay on Logical Philosophy*) in 1922 that philosophy is only the logical clarification of thoughts. It therefore becomes the study of language, which expresses thoughts. In Wittgenstein's opinion the great philosophical issues of the ages—God, freedom, morality, and so on—are quite literally senseless, for statements about them can be neither tested by scientific experiments nor demonstrated by the logic of mathematics. Logical empiricism drastically reduced the scope of philosophical inquiry. Anxious people could find few, if any, answers in this direction.

Some looked to **existentialism** for answers. Highly diverse and even contradictory, existential thinkers were loosely united in a courageous search for moral values in a world of terror and uncertainty. Theirs were the age of anxiety's true voices.

Most existential thinkers in the twentieth century were atheists. Often inspired by Nietzsche, they did not believe a Supreme Being had established humanity's fundamental nature and given life its meaning. In the words of the famous French existentialist Jean-Paul Sartre (1905–1980), human beings simply exist: "They turn up, appear on the scene." Only then do they seek to define themselves. Honest human beings are terribly alone, hounded by despair and the meaningless of life, for there is no God to help them. The crisis of the existential thinker epitomized the modern intellectual crisis—the shattering of traditional beliefs in God, reason, and progress.

Existentialists did recognize that human beings, unless they kill themselves, must act. Indeed, in Sartre's words, "man is condemned to be free." There is therefore the possibility—indeed, the necessity—of giving life meaning through actions, of defining

Chronology

1919 Treaty of Versailles; Keynes, *Economic Consequences of the Peace;* Rutherford splits the atom; Freudian psychology gains popular attention; Gropius founds the Bauhaus

1920s Existentialism gains prominence

1920s–1930s Dadaism and surreal artistic movements

1922 Wittgenstein writes on logical empiricism; Woolf, *Jacob's Room;* Joyce, *Ulysses;* Eliot, *The Waste Land*

1923 French and Belgian armies occupy the Ruhr

1924 Dawes Plan

1925 Hitler, *Mein Kampf*

1926 Germany joins League of Nations

1928 Kellogg-Briand Pact

1929 Faulkner, *The Sound and the Fury*

1929–1939 Great Depression

1932 Franklin Roosevelt elected U.S. president

1934 Riefenstahl, *The Triumph of the Will,* documentary film on Nazi rally

1935 Creation of Works Progress Administration as part of New Deal

1936–1937 Popular Front government in France

logical empiricism *A revolt against established certainties in philosophy that rejected most of the concerns of traditional philosophy, from the existence of God to the meaning of happiness, as nonsense and hot air.*

existentialism *A highly diverse and even contradictory system of thought that was loosely united in a courageous search for moral values in a world of terror and uncertainty.*

oneself through choices. To do so, individuals must become "engaged," choose their own actions courageously and consistently and be fully aware of their responsibility for their own behavior.

Existentialism came of age in France during and immediately after World War II. With Hitler's barbarous wartime regime, people had to choose whether to join the resistance or abet the murderous Nazis. Sartre himself was active in the resistance; he and his colleagues offered a powerful answer to the profound moral issues of the day.

The Revival of Christianity

The loss of faith in human reason and in continual progress also led to a renewed interest in Christianity. Christianity and religion in general had been on the defensive in intellectual circles since the Enlightenment. In the years before 1914 some theologians, especially Protestant ones, interpreted Christian doctrine and the Bible so they did not seem to contradict science, evolution, and common sense. Christ became primarily the greatest moral teacher, and his divine "supernatural" aspects were strenuously played down.

Especially after World War I, several thinkers and theologians began to revitalize Christian fundamentals. Sometimes described as Christian existentialists because they shared the loneliness and despair of atheistic existentialists, they stressed human beings' sinful nature, the need for faith, and the mystery of God's forgiveness. The revival of fundamental Christian belief was fed by rediscovery of the work of nineteenth-century Danish religious philosopher Søren Kierkegaard (1813–1855). Rejecting formalistic religion, Kierkegaard resolved his personal anguish over his imperfect nature by making a total religious commitment to a remote and majestic God.

Similarly, Swiss Protestant theologian Karl Barth (1886–1968) maintained that religious truth is made known to human beings only through God's grace. As sinful creatures whose reason and will are hopelessly flawed, people must accept God's Word and the supernatural revelation of Jesus Christ with awe, trust, and obedience. Lowly mortals should not expect to "reason out" God and his ways.

After 1914 religion became much more relevant and meaningful than it had been before the Great War, and many illustrious individuals turned to religion between about 1920 and 1950. Though often of a despairing, existential variety, religion was one meaningful answer to terror and anxiety. In the words of a famous Roman Catholic convert, English novelist Graham Greene, "One began to believe in heaven because one believed in hell."[2]

The New Physics

By the late nineteenth century science was one of the main pillars supporting Western society's optimistic and rationalistic worldview. Darwin's concept of evolution had been accepted and assimilated in most intellectual circles. Progressive minds believed science was based on hard facts and controlled experiments, producing an unerring and almost completed picture of reality. Unchanging natural laws seemed to determine physical processes and permit useful solutions to more and more problems. All this was comforting, especially to people no longer committed to traditional religious beliefs. And all this was challenged by the new physics.

An important first step toward the new physics was the discovery at the end of the nineteenth century that atoms were not like hard, permanent little billiard balls. They were actually composed of many far-smaller, fast-moving particles, such as electrons and protons. Polish-born physicist Marie Curie (1867–1934) and her French husband Pierre (1859–1906) discovered that radium constantly emits subatomic particles and thus does not have a constant atomic weight. German physicist Max Planck (1858–1947) showed in 1900 that subatomic energy is emitted in uneven little spurts, which Planck called "quanta," and not in a steady stream, as previously believed.

Planck's discovery called into question the old sharp distinction between matter and energy and challenged the old view of atoms as the stable, basic building blocks of nature.

In 1905 German-born Jewish genius Albert Einstein (1879–1955) further undermined Newtonian physics. His famous theory of special relativity postulated that time and space are relative to the observer's viewpoint and that only the speed of light is constant for all frames of reference in the universe. To make his revolutionary and paradoxical idea somewhat comprehensible to the nonmathematical layperson, Einstein used analogies involving moving trains. For example, if a woman in the middle of a moving car gets up and walks forward to the door, she has moved a half car length relative to the train. But relative to an observer on the embankment, she has moved farther. The closed framework of Newtonian physics was quite limited in comparison with the framework of Einsteinian physics, which unified an apparently infinite universe with the incredibly small, fast-moving subatomic world. Moreover, Einstein's theory stated that matter and energy are interchangeable and that even a particle of matter contains enormous levels of potential energy.

The 1920s opened the "heroic age of physics," in the apt words of one of its leading pioneers, Ernest Rutherford (1871–1937). Breakthrough followed breakthrough. In 1919 Rutherford first split the atom. By 1944 seven subatomic particles had been identified, of which the most important was the **neutron.** The neutron's capacity to pass through other atoms allowed for even more intense experimental bombardment of matter, leading to chain reactions of unbelievable force. This was the road to the atomic bomb.

● **Unlocking the Power of the Atom** Many of the fanciful visions of science fiction came true in the twentieth century, although not exactly as first imagined. This 1927 cartoon satirizes a professor who has split the atom and unwittingly destroyed his building and neighborhood in the process. In the Second World War professors harnessed the atom in bombs and decimated faraway cities and their inhabitants. *(Mary Evans Picture Library)*

Although few nonscientists understood this revolution in physics, its implications as presented by newspapers and popular writers were disturbing to millions of men and women in the 1920s and 1930s. The new universe was strange and troubling, seemingly lacking any absolute objective reality. Everything was "relative"—that is, dependent on the observer's frame of reference. Moreover, science appeared distant from human experience and human problems. When, for example, Planck was asked what science could contribute to resolving conflicts of values, he responded simply, "Science is not qualified to speak to this question."

neutron *The most important of the subatomic particles because its capacity to pass through other atoms allowed for intense experimental bombardment of matter, leading to chain reactions of unbelievable force.*

Freudian Psychology

With physics presenting an uncertain universe so unrelated to ordinary human experience, questions about the human mind's power and potential assumed special significance. The findings and speculations of psychologist Sigmund Freud (1856–1939) were particularly disturbing.

Before Freud, most professional, "scientific" psychologists assumed that human behavior was the result of rational calculation—of "thinking"—by the single, unified conscious mind. By analyzing dreams and hysteria, Freud developed a very different view of the human psyche.

According to Freud, human behavior is basically irrational. The key to understanding the mind is the primitive, irrational unconscious, which he called the **id**. The unconscious is driven by sexual, aggressive, and pleasure-seeking desires and is locked in constant battle with the mind's two other parts: the rationalizing conscious (the **ego**), which mediates what a person *can* do, and ingrained moral values (the **superego**), which specify what a person *should* do. Human behavior is a product of a fragile compromise between instinctual drives and the controls of rational thinking and moral values. Since the instinctual drives are extremely powerful, the ever-present danger for individuals and whole societies is that unacknowledged drives will overwhelm the control mechanisms in a violent, distorted way. Yet Freud also agreed with Nietzsche that the mechanisms of rational thinking and traditional moral values can be too strong. They can repress sexual desires too effectively, crippling individuals and entire peoples with guilt and neurotic fears.

Freudian psychology and clinical psychiatry had gained international scholarly attention by 1910, but only after 1918 did they receive popular attention. Many interpreted Freud as saying the first requirement for mental health is an uninhibited sex life. This popular interpretation reflected and encouraged growing sexual experimentation, particularly among middle-class women. For more serious students, Freudian psychology drastically undermined the old easy optimism about the rational and progressive nature of the human mind.

id *Freudian term for the primitive, irrational unconscious.*

ego *Freudian term for the rationalizing conscious that mediates what a person can do.*

superego *Freudian term for the ingrained moral values, which specify what a person should do.*

Twentieth-Century Literature

Literature also reflected the general intellectual climate of pessimism, relativism, and alienation. The great nineteenth-century novelists had typically written as all-knowing narrators, describing realistic characters in an understandable, if sometimes harsh, society. In the twentieth century most major writers adopted the limited, often confused viewpoint of a single individual. Like Freud, these novelists focused on the complexity and irrationality of the human mind, where feelings, memories, and desires are forever scrambled. For example, the great French novelist Marcel Proust (1871–1922), in his semi-autobiographical *Remembrance of Things Past* (1913–1927), tried to discover the innermost meaning of his childhood memories as he withdrew from the present to dwell on the past.

Serious novelists also used the **stream-of-consciousness technique** to explore the psyche. In *Jacob's Room* (1922) Virginia Woolf (1882–1941) created a novel made up of a series of internal monologues. William Faulkner (1897–1962), perhaps America's greatest twentieth-century novelist, used the same technique in *The Sound and the Fury* (1929), much of whose intense drama is confusedly seen through an idiot's eyes. The most famous stream-of-consciousness novel is *Ulysses,* which Irish novelist James Joyce (1882–1941) published in 1922. Into an account of an ordinary day in the life of an ordinary man, Joyce weaves an extended ironic parallel between his hero's aimless wanderings through Dublin's streets and pubs and the adventures of Homer's hero Ulysses on his way home from Troy. Abandoning conventional grammar and blending foreign words, puns, bits of knowledge, and scraps of

● **Virginia Woolf** Her novels captured sensations like impressionist paintings, and her home attracted a circle of artists and writers known as the Bloomsbury Group. Many of Woolf's essays dealt with women's issues and urged greater opportunity for women's creativity. *(Gisèle Freund/Photo Researchers, Inc.)*

memory together in bewildering confusion, the language of *Ulysses* is intended to mirror modern life itself: a gigantic riddle waiting to be unraveled.

Creative writers rejected the idea of progress. Some even described "anti-utopias," nightmare visions of things to come. In 1918 Oswald Spengler (1880–1936) published *The Decline of the West,* in which he argued that every culture experiences a life cycle of growth and decline. Western civilization, in Spengler's opinion, was in its old age, and death was approaching in the form of conquest by the yellow race. T. S. Eliot (1888–1965) depicts a world of growing desolation in his famous poem *The Waste Land* (1922). Franz Kafka's (1883–1924) novels *The Trial* (1925) and *The Castle* (1926) portray helpless individuals crushed by inexplicably hostile forces.

Englishman George Orwell (1903–1950) had witnessed the nightmarish reality of the Nazi state and its Stalinist counterpart by 1949 when he wrote perhaps the ultimate in anti-utopian literature: *1984.* In a future world, Big Brother—the dictator—and his totalitarian state use a new kind of language, sophisticated technology, and psychological terror to strip a weak individual of his last shred of human dignity. The supremely self-confident chief of the Thought Police tells the tortured and broken Winston Smith, "If you want a picture of the future, imagine a boot stamping on a human face—forever."[3] A phenomenal bestseller, *1984* spoke to millions of people in the age of anxiety.

stream-of-consciousness technique *A literary technique in which James Joyce and others used interior monologue to explore the human psyche.*

- - - - - - - - - - - -
MODERN ART AND MUSIC

What new forms did art and music take during the age of anxiety?

Throughout the twentieth and early twenty-first centuries, there has been considerable unity in the arts. The "modernism" of the immediate prewar years and the 1920s is still strikingly modern. Like scientists, creative artists rejected old forms and old values. Modernism in art and music has meant constant experimentation and a search for new kinds of expression. And though many people find the varied modern visions of the arts strange, disturbing, and even ugly, the twentieth century will probably stand as one of history's great artistic eras.

Architecture and Design

Modernism in the arts was loosely unified by a revolution in architecture. This revolution intended to transform the physical framework of urban society according to a new principle: **functionalism.** Buildings, like industrial products, should be useful and "functional"—that is, they should serve the purpose for which they were made. Franco-Swiss genius Le Corbusier (1887–1965) insisted that "a house is a machine for living in."[4]

The United States, with its rapid urban growth and lack of rigid building traditions, pioneered in the new architecture. In the 1890s the Chicago school of architects, led by Louis H. Sullivan (1856–1924), used cheap steel, reinforced concrete, and electric elevators to build skyscrapers and office buildings lacking almost any exterior ornamentation.

In Europe architectural leadership centered in German-speaking countries until Hitler took power in 1933. In 1911 twenty-eight-year-old Walter Gropius (1883–1969) broke sharply with the past in his design of the Fagus shoe factory at Alfeld, Germany—a clean, light, elegant building of glass and iron. After the First World War Gropius merged the schools of fine and applied arts at Weimar into a single interdisciplinary school, the Bauhaus. Throughout the 1920s the Bauhaus, with its stress on functionalism and good design for everyday life, attracted enthusiastic students from all over the world. It had a great and continuing impact.

functionalism *The principle that buildings, like industrial products, should serve the purpose for which they were made as well as possible.*

Modern Painting and Music

Modern painting grew out of a revolt against French impressionism. The *impressionism* of such French painters as Claude Monet (1840–1926), Pierre Auguste Renoir (1841–1919), and Camille Pissarro (1830–1903) was, in part, a kind of "superrealism." Leaving exact copying of objects to photography, these artists sought to capture the momentary overall feeling, or impression, of light falling on a real-life scene before their eyes. By 1890, when impressionism was finally established, a few artists known as *postimpressionists,* or sometimes as *expressionists,* were already striking out in new directions. After 1905 art increasingly took on a nonrepresentational, abstract character, a development that reached its high point after World War II.

Though individualistic in their styles, postimpressionists were united in their desire to know and depict unseen, inner worlds of emotion and imagination. In *The Starry Night* (1889), for example, the great Dutch expressionist Vincent van Gogh (1853–1890) painted the moving vision of his mind's eye. Paul Gauguin (1848–1903), the French stockbroker-turned-painter, pioneered in expressionist techniques, though he used them to infuse his work with tranquility and mysticism. In 1891 Gauguin fled to the South Pacific, where he found inspiration in Polynesian forms, colors, and legends and painted his greatest works. Gauguin believed the picture's form and design were important in themselves and the painter need not try to represent objects on canvas as the eye actually saw them.

Fascination with form, as opposed to light, was characteristic of postimpressionism and expressionism. Paul Cézanne (1839–1906), who profoundly influenced twentieth-

● **Van Gogh: The Starry Night** Van Gogh absorbed impressionism in Paris, but under the burning sun of southern France he went beyond the portrayal of external reality. In *The Starry Night* (1889) flaming cypress trees, exploding stars, and a comet-like Milky Way swirl together in one great cosmic rhythm. Painting an inner world of intense emotion and wild imagination, van Gogh contributed greatly to the rise of expressionism in modern art. *(Digital image © The Museum of Modern Art/Licensed by Scala/Art Resource, NY)*

century painting, was particularly committed to form and ordered design. He told a young painter, "You must see in nature the cylinder, the sphere, and the cone."[5] As Cézanne's later work became increasingly abstract and nonrepresentational, it also moved away from the traditional three-dimensional perspective toward the two-dimensional plane, which has characterized much of modern art.

In 1907 a young Spaniard in Paris, Pablo Picasso (1881–1973), founded another movement—*cubism*. In his first great cubist work, *Les Demoiselles d'Avignon* (1907), Picasso sought to create a new visual reality and provoked a revolutionary upheaval in art. Since the Renaissance, artists had represented objects from a single viewpoint and created unified human forms. Yet Picasso's female figures appear broken into large, flat planes with heads that are twisted, fractured dislocations (see the illustration on the next page). The faces of three figures resemble large wooden African masks, as the artist reinforced his radical new view of reality with a strikingly non-Western depiction of the human form. Cubism concentrated on a complex geometry of zigzagging lines and sharply angled, overlapping planes, but the distorted subjects generally remained at least vaguely recognizable.

The influence of Polynesian art on Gauguin and of carved African masks on Picasso reflected the growing importance of non-Western artistic traditions in Europe in the late nineteenth and early twentieth centuries. Japanese woodcuts had fascinated the great early impressionist Edouard Manet (1832–1883), for example, and he incorporated certain Japanese techniques into his painting. The work of many other European artists revealed comparable non-Western inspiration.

About 1910 came the ultimate stage in the development of abstract, nonrepresentational art. Artists such as the Russian-born Wassily Kandinsky (1866–1944) turned away from nature completely. "The observer," said Kandinsky, "must learn to look at [my] pictures . . . as form and color combinations . . . as a representation of mood and not as a representation of *objects*."[6]

In the 1920s and 1930s prewar artistic movements were extended and consolidated. The most notable new developments were *dadaism* and *surrealism*. Dadaism attacked all accepted standards of art and behavior, delighting in outrageous conduct. After 1924 many dadaists were attracted to surrealism, which became very influential in art in the late 1920s and 1930s. Surrealists, such as Salvador Dali (1904–1989), painted fantastic worlds of wild dreams and complex symbols, where watches melted and giant metronomes beat time in precisely drawn but impossible alien landscapes.

Refusing to depict ordinary visual reality, surrealist painters made powerful statements about the age of anxiety. Picasso's twenty-six-foot-long mural *Guernica* was inspired by the fascist bombing of the ancient Spanish town of Guernica during the Spanish civil war. Using only the mournful colors of black, white, and gray, the painting combines the free distortion of expressionism, cubism's overlapping planes, and the surrealist fascination with grotesque subject matter. Picasso hoped it would be an unforgettable attack on "brutality and darkness."

Developments in modern music were strikingly parallel to those in painting. Composers, too, were attracted by the emotional intensity of expressionism. The pulsating, dissonant rhythms and the dancers' earthy representation of lovemaking in the ballet *The Rite of Spring* by composer Igor Stravinsky (1882–1971) practically caused a riot when first performed in Paris in 1913 by Sergei Diaghilev's famous Russian dance company.

After the experience of the First World War, when irrationality and violence seemed to pervade the human psyche, expressionism in opera and ballet flourished. Some composers turned their backs on long-established musical conventions. As abstract painters arranged lines and color but did not draw identifiable objects, so modern composers arranged sounds without creating recognizable harmonies. Accustomed to the harmonies of classical and romantic music, audiences generally resisted modern atonal music.

● **Picasso: Les Demoiselles d'Avignon** Originating in memories of a brothel scene in Barcelona, this is one of the twentieth century's most influential paintings. Picasso abandoned unified perspective and depicted instead fragmented figures and distorted forms in his search for the magical violence of a pictorial breakthrough. The three faces on either side were inspired by African masks. *(Digital image © The Museum of Modern Art/Licensed by Scala/Art Resource, NY/© Estate of Pablo Picasso/Artists Rights Society [ARS], New York)*

Primary Source:
U.S. Senate Speech,
June 29, 1922
Find out why a U.S. Senator called for a national board of film censorship.

MOVIES AND RADIO

How did the movies and the radio affect society when they first appeared?

Until after World War II at the earliest, the revolutionary changes in art and music appealed mainly to a minority of "highbrows" and not to the general public. That public was primarily and enthusiastically wrapped up in movies, radio, and advertising. Standardized commercial entertainment replaced the long-declining traditional arts and amusements of people in villages and small towns.

Moving pictures were first shown as a popular novelty in naughty peepshows—"What the Butler Saw"—and penny arcades in the 1890s, especially in Paris. The first movie houses, dating from an experiment in Los Angeles in 1902, showed short silent action films such as the eight-minute *Great Train Robbery* of 1903. On the eve of the First World War, full-length feature films such as the Italian *Quo Vadis* and the American *Birth of a Nation,* coupled with improvements in picture quality, suggested the screen's vast possibilities.

During the First World War the United States became the dominant force in the rapidly expanding silent-film industry, and Charlie Chaplin (1889–1978), a funny little Englishman working in Hollywood, was unquestionably the king of the "silver screen." In his enormously popular role as a lonely tramp, complete with baggy trousers, battered derby, and an awkward, shuffling walk, Chaplin symbolized the "gay spirit of laughter in a cruel, crazy world."[7] Chaplin also demonstrated that in the hands of a genius the new medium could combine mass entertainment and artistic accomplishment.

The early 1920s were also the great age of German films. Protected and developed during the war, the large German studios excelled in bizarre expressionist dramas, beginning with *The Cabinet of Dr. Caligari* in 1919. Unfortunately, their period of creativity was short-lived. By 1926 American money was drawing the leading German talents to Hollywood and consolidating America's international domination. European producers remained at a great disadvantage until "talkies" permitted a revival of national film industries in the 1930s, particularly in France.

Whether foreign or domestic, motion pictures became the main entertainment of the masses until after the Second World War. Motion pictures, featuring glittering stars such as Ginger Rogers and Fred Astaire, and fanciful cartoons of Mickey Mouse, offered ordinary people a temporary escape from the hard realities of international tensions, uncertainty, unemployment, and personal frustrations. Escapist entertainment was especially appealing during the Great Depression.

Radio became possible with the transatlantic "wireless" communication of Guglielmo Marconi (1874–1937) in 1901 and the development of the vacuum tube in 1904, which permitted the transmission of speech and music. Only in 1920, however, were the first major public broadcasts made in Great Britain and the United States. Singing from London in English, Italian, and French, "the world's very best, the soprano Nellie Melba,"[8] was heard simultaneously all over Europe on June 16, 1920. This historic event captured the public's imagination, and radio's meteoric career was launched.

Every major country quickly established national broadcasting networks. In the United States these were privately owned and financed by advertising. In Great Britain Parliament set up an independent public corporation, the British Broadcasting Corporation (BBC), supported by licensing fees. Elsewhere in Europe the typical pattern was direct government control. Radio quickly became popular and influential. By the late 1930s more than three-fourths of the households in both democratic Great Britain and dictatorial Germany had at least one cheap, mass-produced radio.

Radio was particularly well suited for political propaganda. Dictators such as Mussolini and Hitler controlled the airwaves and could reach enormous national audiences with their frequent, dramatic speeches. In democratic countries politicians such as President Franklin Roosevelt and Prime Minister Stanley Baldwin effectively used informal "fireside chats" to bolster their support.

Motion pictures also became powerful tools of indoctrination, especially in countries with dictatorial regimes. Lenin encouraged the development of Soviet film making and beginning in the mid-1920s a series of epic films, the most famous of which were directed by Sergei Eisenstein (1898–1948), brilliantly dramatized the communist view of Russian history.

● **The Great Dictator** In 1940 the renowned actor and director Charlie Chaplin abandoned the little tramp to satirize the "great dictator," Adolf Hitler. Chaplin had strong political views and made a number of films with political themes as the escapist fare of the Great Depression gave way to the reality of the Second World War. *(The Museum of Modern Art/Still Film Archives)*

In Germany Hitler turned to a young and immensely talented woman film maker, Leni Riefenstahl (1902–2003), for a masterpiece of documentary propaganda, *The Triumph of the Will*. Based on the Nazi Party rally at Nuremberg in 1934, her film was a brilliant and all-too-powerful depiction of Germany's "Nazi rebirth." Mass culture's new media were potentially dangerous instruments of political manipulation.

● ● ● ● ● ● ● ● ● ● ● ● ● ● ● ● ● ● ●

THE SEARCH FOR PEACE AND POLITICAL STABILITY

How did leaders deal with the political dimensions of uncertainty and try to re-establish real peace and prosperity between 1919 and 1939?

As established patterns of thought and culture were challenged and mangled by the ferocious impact of World War I, so also was the political fabric stretched and torn by the consequences of the great conflict. The Versailles settlement had established a shaky truce, not a solid peace.

The pursuit of real and lasting peace proved difficult for many reasons. Germany hated the Treaty of Versailles. France was fearful and isolated. Britain was undependable, and the United States had turned its back on European problems. Eastern Europe was in ferment, and no one could predict the future of communist Russia. In addition, the international economic situation was poor and greatly complicated by war debts and disrupted patterns of trade. Yet for a time, from 1925 to late 1929, it appeared that peace and stability were within reach.

Germany and the Western Powers

Germany held the key to lasting peace, yet all Germans believed the Treaty of Versailles represented a harsh, dictated peace and should be revised or repudiated as soon as possible. The treaty had neither broken nor reduced Germany, potentially still the strongest country in Europe. Thus the treaty had fallen between two stools: too harsh for a peace of reconciliation, too soft for a peace of conquest.

Moreover, France and Great Britain disagreed over Germany. By the end of 1919 France wanted to stress the harsh elements in the Treaty of Versailles. The war on the western front had been fought mainly on French soil, and the expected costs of reconstruction, as well as of repaying war debts to the United States, were staggering. Thus French politicians believed that massive reparations from Germany were a vital economic necessity. America's failure to ratify the treaty left many French leaders believing that strict implementation of all the treaty's provisions was France's last best hope. Large reparation payments could hold Germany down indefinitely, and France would realize its goal of security.

The British soon felt differently. Prewar Germany had been Great Britain's second-best market in the entire world, and after the war a healthy, prosperous Germany appeared to be essential to the British economy. Indeed, many English people agreed with the analysis of the young English economist John Maynard Keynes (1883–1946). In his famous *Economic Consequences of the Peace* (1919) Keynes argued that astronomical reparations and harsh economic measures would impoverish Germany and increase economic hardship in all countries. Only a complete revision of the foolish treaty could save Germany—and Europe. Keynes's attack stirred deep guilt feelings about Germany in the English-speaking world, feelings that often paralyzed English and American leaders in their relations with German leaders between the First and Second World Wars.

The British were suspicious of France's army—the largest in Europe—and the British and French were also at odds over their League of Nations mandates in the Middle

Primary Source: An Economist Analyzes the Versailles Treaty and Finds It Lacking
Read how an American economist condemned the Allies for ignoring, in the provisions of the Versailles Treaty, "the economic rehabilitation of Europe."

East (see page 847). While France and Britain drifted in different directions, the Allied reparations commission completed its work. In April 1921 it announced that Germany had to pay the enormous sum of 132 billion gold marks ($33 billion) in annual installments of 2.5 billion gold marks. Facing possible occupation of more of its territory, the young German republic—known as the Weimar Republic—made its first payment in 1921. Then in 1922, wracked by rapid inflation and political assassinations and motivated by hostility and arrogance as well, the Weimar Republic announced its inability to pay more and proposed a reparations moratorium for three years.

The British were willing to accept a moratorium, but the French were not. Led by their prime minister, Raymond Poincaré (1860–1934), they decided they had to either call Germany's bluff or see the entire peace settlement dissolve to France's great disadvantage. So, despite strong British protests, in January 1923 armies of France and its ally Belgium occupied the Ruhr district, industrial Germany's heartland, creating the most serious international crisis of the 1920s.

Strengthened by a wave of patriotism, the German government ordered the people of the Ruhr to stop working and to nonviolently resist the French occupation. The coal mines and steel mills of the Ruhr grew silent, leaving 10 percent of Germany's total population in need of relief. The French responded by sealing off not only the Ruhr but also the entire Rhineland from the rest of Germany, letting in only enough food to prevent starvation.

By summer 1923 France and Germany were engaged in a great test of wills. French armies could not collect reparations from striking workers at gunpoint. But French occupation was paralyzing Germany and its economy and had turned rapid German inflation into runaway inflation. Needing to support the striking Ruhr workers and their employers, the German government began to print money to pay its bills. Prices soared. German money rapidly lost all value, and so did anything else with a stated fixed value.

Runaway inflation brought about a social revolution. Many retired and middle-class people saw their savings wiped out. Catastrophic inflation cruelly mocked the old middle-class virtues of thrift, caution, and self-reliance. Many Germans felt betrayed. They hated and blamed the Western governments, their own government, big business, the Jews, the workers, and the communists for their misfortune. The crisis left them psychologically prepared to follow radical leaders.

In August 1923, as the mark fell and political unrest grew throughout Germany, Gustav Stresemann (1878–1929) became German chancellor. Stresemann adopted a compromising attitude. He called off the peaceful resistance campaign in the Ruhr and in October agreed in principle to pay reparations but asked for a re-examination of Germany's ability to pay. Poincaré accepted. His hard line was becoming increasingly unpopular with French citizens, and was hated in Britain and the United States. (See the feature "Individuals in Society: Gustav Stresemann.")

● "Hands Off the Ruhr"   The French occupation of the Ruhr to collect reparations payments raised a storm of patriotic protest in Germany. This anti-French poster of 1923 turns Marianne, the personification of French republican virtue, into a vicious harpy. (International Instituut voor Sociale Geschiedenis)

More generally, in both Germany and France power was finally passing to the moderates, who realized that continued confrontation was a destructive, no-win situation. Thus after five years of hostility and tension, Germany and France decided to try compromise and cooperation. The British, and even the Americans, were willing to help. The first step was a reasonable compromise on the reparations question.

Hope in Foreign Affairs (1924–1929)

The reparations commission appointed an international committee of financial experts headed by American banker Charles G. Dawes to re-examine reparations. The resulting **Dawes Plan** (1924) was accepted by France, Germany, and Britain. Germany's yearly reparations were reduced and depended on the level of German economic prosperity. Germany would also receive large loans from the United States to promote German recovery. In short, Germany would get private loans from the United States and pay reparations to France and Britain, thus enabling those countries to repay the large sums they owed the United States.

Dawes Plan *The product of the reparations commission, accepted by Germany, France, and Britain, that reduced Germany's yearly reparations, made payment dependent on German economic prosperity, and granted Germany large loans from the United States to promote recovery.*

This circular flow of international payments was complicated and risky, but for a while it worked. Germany experienced a spectacular economic recovery. By 1929 its wealth and income were 50 percent greater than in 1913. With prosperity and large, continual inflows of American capital, Germany easily paid about $1.3 billion in reparations in 1927 and 1928, enabling France and Britain to pay the United States. Thus, America belatedly played a part in the general economic settlement that facilitated the worldwide recovery of the late 1920s.

This economic settlement was matched by a political settlement in 1925 among European leaders meeting in Locarno, Switzerland. Germany and France solemnly pledged to accept their common border, and both Britain and Italy agreed to fight either France or Germany if one invaded the other. Stresemann also agreed to settle boundary disputes with Poland and Czechoslovakia by peaceful means, and France promised those countries military aid if Germany attacked them. For years a "spirit of Locarno" gave Europeans a sense of growing security and stability in international affairs.

Other developments also strengthened hopes. In 1926 Germany joined the League of Nations, where Stresemann continued his "peace offensive." In 1928 fifteen countries signed the Kellogg-Briand Pact, initiated by French prime minister Aristide Briand and U.S. secretary of state Frank B. Kellogg. This multinational pact "condemned and renounced war as an instrument of national policy." The signing states agreed to settle international disputes peacefully. The pact fostered the cautious optimism of the late 1920s and also encouraged the hope that the United States would accept its international responsibilities.

Domestic politics also offered reason to hope. During the Ruhr occupation and the great inflation, Germany's republican government appeared ready to collapse. In 1923 communists momentarily entered provincial governments, and in November an obscure nobody named Adolf Hitler proclaimed a "national socialist revolution" in a Munich beer hall. Hitler's plot to seize government control was poorly organized, however, and easily crushed. Hitler was sentenced to prison, where he outlined his theories and program in his book **Mein Kampf** (*My Struggle*, 1925). Throughout the 1920s, Hitler's National Socialist Party attracted support only from a few fanatical anti-Semites, ultranationalists, and disgruntled former servicemen.

Mein Kampf *A book written by Adolf Hitler in which he outlines his theories and program for a "national socialist revolution."*

The moderate businessmen who tended to dominate the various German coalition governments believed that economic prosperity demanded good relations with the Western Powers, and they supported parliamentary government at home. Elections were held regularly, and as the economy boomed, republican democracy appeared to have growing support among a majority of Germans.

Gustav Stresemann

Foreign Minister Gustav Stresemann of Germany (*right*) leaves a meeting with Aristide Briand, his French counterpart. *(Corbis)*

The German foreign minister Gustav Stresemann (1878–1929) is a controversial historical figure. Hailed by many as a hero of peace, he was denounced as a traitor by radical German nationalists and then by Hitler's Nazis. After World War II, revisionist historians stressed Stresemann's persistent nationalism and cast doubt on his peaceful intentions. Weimar Germany's most renowned leader is a fascinating example of the restless quest for convincing historical interpretation.

Stresemann's origins were modest. His parents were Berlin innkeepers and retailers of bottled beer, and only Gustav of their five children was able to attend high school. Attracted first to literature and history, Stresemann later turned to economics, earned a doctoral degree, and quickly reached the top as a manager and director of German trade associations. A highly intelligent extrovert with a knack for negotiation, Stresemann entered the Reichstag in 1907 as a business-oriented liberal and nationalist. When World War I erupted, he believed, like most Germans, that Germany had acted defensively and was not at fault. He emerged as a strident nationalist and urged German annexation of conquered foreign territories. Germany's collapse in defeat and revolution devastated Stresemann. He seemed a prime candidate for the hateful extremism of the far right.

Yet although Stresemann opposed the Treaty of Versailles as an unjust and unrealistic imposition, he turned back toward the center. He accepted the new Weimar Republic and played a growing role in the Reichstag as the leader of his own small probusiness party. His hour came in the Ruhr crisis, when French and Belgian troops occupied the district. Named chancellor in August 1923, he called off passive resistance and began talks with the French. His government also quelled communist uprisings; put down rebellions in Bavaria, including Hitler's attempted coup; and ended runaway inflation with a new currency. Stresemann fought to preserve German unity, and he succeeded.

Voted out as chancellor in November 1923, Stresemann remained as foreign minister in every government until his death in 1929. Proclaiming a policy of peace and agreeing to pay reparations, he achieved his greatest triumph in the Locarno agreements of 1925 (see page 890). But the interlocking guarantees of existing French and German borders (and the related agreements to resolve peacefully all disputes with Poland and Czechoslovakia) did not lead the French to make any further concessions that might have disarmed Stresemann's extremist foes. Working himself to death, he made little additional progress in achieving international reconciliation and sovereign equality for Germany.

Stresemann was no fuzzy pacifist. Historians debunking his "legend" are right in seeing an enduring love of nation in his defense of German interests. But Stresemann, like his French counterpart Aristide Briand, was a statesman of goodwill who wanted peace through mutually advantageous compromise. A realist trained by business and politics in the art of the possible, Stresemann also reasoned that Germany had to be a satisfied and equal partner if peace was to be secure. His unwillingness to guarantee Germany's eastern borders (see Map 27.4 on page 838), which is often criticized, reflects his conviction that keeping some Germans under Polish and Czecho-slovak rule created a ticking time bomb in Europe. Stresemann was no less convinced that war on Poland would almost certainly recreate the Allied coalition that had crushed Germany in 1918.* His insistence on the necessity of peace in the east as well as the west was prophetic. Hitler's 1939 invasion of Poland resulted in an even mightier coalition that almost annihilated Germany in 1945.

Questions for Analysis

1. What did Gustav Stresemann do to promote reconciliation in Europe? How did his policy toward France differ from that toward Poland and Czechoslovakia?

2. What is your interpretation of Stresemann? Does he arouse your sympathy or your suspicion and hostility? Why?

*Robert Grathwol, "Stresemann: Reflections on His Foreign Policy," *Journal of Modern History* 45 (March 1973): 52–70.

● **An American in Paris** The young Josephine Baker suddenly became a star in 1925 when she brought an exotic African eroticism to French music halls. American blacks and Africans had a powerful impact in Europe in the 1920s and 1930s. *(Hulton Archive/Getty Images)*

There were, however, sharp political divisions in the country. Many unrepentant nationalists and monarchists populated the right and the army. Members of Germany's Communist Party received directions from Moscow, and they endlessly accused the Social Democrats of betraying the revolution. The working classes were divided politically, but most supported the socialist, but nonrevolutionary, Social Democrats.

The situation in France had numerous similarities to that in Germany. Communists and socialists battled for the workers' support. After 1924 the democratically elected government rested mainly in the hands of moderate coalitions, and business interests were well represented. France's great accomplishment was rapid rebuilding of its wartorn northern region, and good times prevailed until 1930.

France attracted artists and writers from all over the world in the 1920s. Much of the intellectual and artistic ferment of the times flourished in Paris. As writer Gertrude Stein (1874–1946), a leader of the large colony of American expatriates living in Paris, later recalled, "Paris was where the twentieth century was."[9]

Britain, too, faced challenges after 1920. The wartime trend toward greater social equality continued, however, helping maintain social harmony. The great problem was unemployment, which throughout the 1920s hovered around 12 percent. The state provided unemployment benefits and supplemented those payments with subsidized housing, medical aid, and increased old-age pensions. These and other measures kept living standards from seriously declining, defused class tensions, and pointed the way toward the welfare state Britain established after World War II.

Relative social harmony was accompanied by the Labour Party's rise as a determined champion of the working classes and of greater social equality. Committed to moderate, "revisionist" socialism, the Labour Party under Ramsay MacDonald (1866–1937) governed the country in 1924 and 1929. Yet Labour moved toward socialism gradually and democratically, so that the middle classes were not overly frightened as the working classes won new benefits.

The Conservatives under Stanley Baldwin (1867–1947) showed the same compromising spirit on social issues, and Britain experienced only limited social unrest in the 1920s and 1930s. In 1922 Britain granted southern, Catholic Ireland full autonomy after a bitter guerrilla war, thereby removing another source of prewar friction. Thus developments in both international relations and domestic politics gave the leading democracies cause for cautious optimism in the late 1920s.

THE GREAT DEPRESSION (1929–1939)

Why did democratic leaders fail to effectively address problems created by the depression?

Like the Great War, the Great Depression must be spelled with capital letters. Economic depressions occurred regularly throughout the nineteenth century, but this depression was exceptionally long and severe. It struck the entire world with ever-greater intensity from 1929 to 1933, and recovery was uneven and slow. Only with the Second World War did the depression disappear in much of the world.

Everywhere the social and political consequences of prolonged economic collapse were enormous. Economic depression was a major factor in Japan's fatal turn from peaceful trade and foreign investment in the 1920s to aggressive empire building and militarism in the 1930s (see pages 868–870). Elsewhere in Asia, agricultural depression devastated millions of peasants and small farmers. The price of rice—Asia's staff of life and main cash crop—fell by two-thirds between 1929 and 1932. With debts to local moneylenders fixed in value and taxes to colonial governments hardly ever reduced, peasants in the 1930s struggled under crushing debt and suffered severely.

In Latin America and Africa agricultural producers also suffered greatly from the collapse in prices, while urban workers faced pay cuts and high unemployment. Several Latin American countries tried to turn away from export economies based on agriculture and instead promoted state-sponsored industrialization and national self-sufficiency. In West Africa anticolonial nationalism attracted widespread support for the first time in the 1930s, setting the stage for strong independence movements after World War II. Chapter 32 examines the powerful, many-sided impact of the Great Depression in Latin America and Africa.

In Europe and the United States the depression shattered the fragile optimism of political leaders in the late 1920s. Mass unemployment made insecurity a reality for millions of ordinary people. In desperation, people looked for leaders who would "do something." They willingly supported radical attempts to deal with the crisis by both democratic leaders and dictators.

The Economic Crisis

Though economic activity was already declining moderately in many countries by early 1929, the U.S. stock market crash in October of that year really started the Great Depression. The American stock market boom, which had seen stock prices double between early 1928 and September 1929, was built on borrowed money. Wealthy investors, speculators, and people of modest means had bought stocks by paying only a small fraction of the total purchase price and borrowing the remainder from their stockbrokers. Such buying "on margin" was extremely dangerous. When prices started falling, the hard-pressed margin buyers started selling to pay their debts. The result was a financial panic. Countless investors and speculators were wiped out in a matter of days or weeks.

The financial panic in the United States triggered a worldwide financial crisis, and that crisis resulted in a drastic decline in production in country after country. Throughout the 1920s American bankers and investors had lent large sums to many countries, and as panic broke, New York bankers began recalling their short-term loans. Frightened Europeans began to withdraw their savings from banks, leading to general financial chaos. The recall of American loans also accelerated the collapse in world prices, as business people dumped goods in a frantic attempt to get cash to pay what they owed.

The financial chaos led to a general crisis of production. Between 1929 and 1933 world output of goods fell by an estimated 38 percent. As this happened, each country turned inward and tried to go it alone. Country after country followed the example of the United States, which raised protective tariffs to their highest levels ever in 1930 and tried to seal off shrinking national markets for American producers only.

Although opinions differ, two factors probably best explain the relentless slide to the bottom from 1929 to early 1933. First, the international economy lacked a leadership able to maintain stability when the crisis came. The seriously weakened British, the world economy's traditional leaders, "couldn't and the United States wouldn't" stabilize the international economic system in 1929.[10] Instead, the United States cut back its international lending and erected high tariffs.

The second factor was national economic policy. In almost every country, governments cut their budgets and reduced spending when they should have run large deficits in an effort to stimulate their economies. After World War II such a "counter-cyclical policy," advocated by John Maynard Keynes, became a well-established weapon against depression. But in the 1930s orthodox economists generally regarded Keynes's prescription with horror.

Mass Unemployment

The need for large-scale government spending was tied to mass unemployment. As the financial crisis led to production cuts, workers lost their jobs and had little money to buy goods. This led to still more production cuts and still more unemployment, until millions were out of work. In Britain unemployment had averaged 12 percent in the 1920s; between 1930 and 1935 it averaged more than 18 percent. In Japan 3 million people were out of work. Far worse was the case of the United States. In the 1920s unemployment there had averaged only 5 percent; in 1932 it soared to about 33 percent of the entire labor force: 14 million people were out of work. Only by pumping new money into the economy could the government increase demand and break the vicious cycle of decline.

Along with economic effects, mass unemployment posed a great social problem. Poverty increased dramatically, although in most industrialized countries unemployed workers generally received some kind of meager unemployment benefits or public aid that prevented starvation. (See the feature "Listening to the Past: Life on the Dole in Great Britain" on pages 900–901.) Millions of people lost their spirit, condemned to an apparently hopeless search for work or to idle boredom. Homes and ways of life were disrupted in millions of personal tragedies. In 1932 workers in Manchester, England, appealed to their city officials—a typical appeal echoed throughout the Western world:

We tell you that thousands of people . . . are in desperate straits. We tell you that men, women, and children are going hungry. . . . We tell you that great numbers are being rendered distraught through the stress and worry of trying to exist without work. . . .

If you do not do this—if you do not provide useful work for the unemployed—what, we ask, is your alternative? Do not imagine that this colossal tragedy of unemployment is going on endlessly without some fateful catastrophe. Hungry men are angry men.[11]

Only strong government action could deal with mass unemployment, a social powder keg preparing to explode.

The New Deal in the United States

Of all the major industrial countries, only Germany was harder hit by the Great Depression, or reacted more radically to it, than the United States. Depression was so traumatic in the United States because the 1920s had been a period of complacent prosperity. The Great Depression and the response to it marked a major turning point in American history.

President Herbert Hoover (1874–1964) and his administration initially reacted to the stock market crash and economic decline with dogged optimism and limited action. But when the full force of the financial crisis struck Europe in the summer of 1931 and boomeranged back to the United States, people's worst fears became reality. Banks failed; unemployment soared. In 1932 industrial production fell to about 50 percent of its 1929 level. In these tragic circumstances Franklin Delano Roosevelt (1882–1945), an inspiring wheelchair-bound aristocrat previously crippled by polio, won a landslide electoral victory in 1932 with grand but vague promises of a "**New Deal** for the forgotten man."

Roosevelt's basic goal was to preserve capitalism by reforming it. Rejecting socialism and government ownership of industry, Roosevelt undertook capitalist reform through forceful government intervention in the economy. In this choice Roosevelt was flexible, pragmatic, and willing to experiment. Roosevelt and his "brain trust" of advisers adopted policies echoing the American experience in World War I, when the American economy had been thoroughly planned and regulated.

New Deal *Franklin Delano Roosevelt's plan to reform capitalism through forceful government intervention in the economy.*

● **Isaac Soyer: Employment Agency (1937)** The frustration and agony of looking for work against long odds are painfully evident in this American masterpiece. The time-killing, pensive resignation, and dejection seen in the four figures are only aspects of the larger problem. One of three talented brothers born in Russia and trained as artists in New York, Isaac Soyer worked in the tradition of American realism and concentrated on people and the influence of their environment. *(Oil on canvas, 34¼ x 45 in. Whitney Museum of American Art, New York, Purchase 37.44)*

Innovative programs promoted agricultural recovery, a top priority. As in Asia, Africa, and Latin America, American farmers were hard hit by the Great Depression. Roosevelt's decision to leave the gold standard and devalue the dollar was designed to raise American prices and save farmers. The Agricultural Adjustment Act (1933) aimed at raising prices and farm income by limiting production. For a while, these measures worked.

Roosevelt then attacked the key problem of mass unemployment. New agencies were created to undertake a vast range of public works projects so that the federal government could employ directly as many people as financially possible. The most famous of these was the **Works Progress Administration (WPA),** set up in 1935. One-fifth of the entire labor force worked for the WPA at some point in the 1930s, constructing public buildings, bridges, and highways. The WPA was enormously popular, and the prospect of a government job helped check the threat of social revolution in the United States.

Such relief programs were part of the New Deal's fundamental commitment to use the federal government to provide for the welfare of all Americans. This commitment marked a profound shift from the traditional stress on family support and community responsibility. Embraced by a large majority in the 1930s, this shift proved to be one of the New Deal's most enduring legacies.

Other social measures aimed in the same direction. Following the path blazed by Germany's Bismarck in the 1880s (see page 704), the U.S. government in 1935 established a national social security system, with old-age pensions and unemployment benefits, to protect workers against some of life's uncertainties. The National Labor Relations Act of 1935 gave union organizers the green light by declaring collective bargaining to be U.S. policy. Union membership more than doubled, from 4 million in 1935 to 9 million in 1940. In general, between 1935 and 1938 government rulings and social reforms chipped away at the privileges of the wealthy and tried to help ordinary people.

Yet despite undeniable accomplishments in social reform, the New Deal was only partly successful as a response to the Great Depression. At the height of the recovery in May 1937, 7 million workers were still unemployed, in contrast to a high of 15 million in 1933. The economic situation then worsened seriously in the recession of 1937 and 1938, and unemployment was still a staggering 10 million when war broke out in Europe in September 1939. The New Deal brought fundamental reform, but it never did pull the United States out of the depression.

Works Progress Administration (WPA) *The most famous of Roosevelt's New Deal programs, it employed one-fifth of the entire labor force at some point in the 1930s, constructing public buildings, bridges, and highways.*

The Scandinavian Response to the Depression

Of all the Western democracies, the Scandinavian countries under socialist leadership responded most successfully to the challenge of the Great Depression. After the First World War the socialists became the largest political party in Sweden and then in Norway. In the 1920s they passed important social reform legislation for both peasants and workers, gained practical administrative experience, and developed a unique kind of socialism. Flexible and nonrevolutionary, Scandinavian socialism grew out of a strong tradition of cooperative community action. Even before 1900, Scandinavian agricultural cooperatives had shown how individual peasant families could join together for everyone's benefit. Labor leaders and capitalists were also inclined to work together.

When the economic crisis struck in 1929, socialist governments in Scandinavia built on this pattern of cooperative social action. Sweden pioneered the use of large-scale deficits to finance public works and thereby maintain production and employment. Scandinavian governments also increased social welfare benefits, from old-age pensions and unemployment insurance to subsidized housing and maternity allowances. All this spending required a large bureaucracy and high taxes, first on the rich and then on practically everyone. Yet both private and cooperative enterprise thrived, as did democracy. Some observers saw Scandinavia's welfare socialism as an appealing "middle way" between sick capitalism and cruel communism or fascism.

Recovery and Reform in Britain and France

In Britain MacDonald's Labour government and then, after 1931, the Conservative-dominated coalition government followed orthodox economic theory. The budget was balanced, but unemployed workers received barely enough welfare to live. Despite government lethargy, the economy recovered considerably after 1932. By 1937 total production was about 20 percent higher than in 1929. In fact, for Britain the years after 1932 were actually somewhat better than the 1920s had been, quite the opposite of the situation in the United States and France.

This recovery reflected the gradual reorientation of the British economy. After abandoning the gold standard in 1931 and establishing protective tariffs in 1932, Britain concentrated increasingly on the national, rather than the international, market. The Industrial Revolution's old export industries, such as textiles and coal, continued to decline, but new industries, such as automobiles and electrical appliances, grew in response to British home demand. These developments encouraged Britain to look inward and avoid unpleasant foreign questions.

Because France was relatively less industrialized and more isolated from the world economy, the Great Depression came there late. But once the depression hit France, it stayed and stayed. Decline was steady until 1935, and a short-lived recovery never brought production or employment back up to predepression levels. Economic stagnation both reflected and heightened an ongoing crisis of political instability. As before 1914, the French parliament consisted of many political parties that could never cooperate for very long. In 1933, for example, five coalition cabinets formed and fell in rapid succession.

The French lost the underlying unity that had made government instability bearable before 1914. Fascist-type organizations agitated against parliamentary democracy and looked to Mussolini's Italy and Hitler's Germany for inspiration. In February 1934 French fascists rioted and threatened to overturn the republic. At the same time, the Communist Party and many workers looked to Stalin's Russia for guidance. Moderate republicanism's vital center was sapped from both sides.

Frightened by the fascists' growing strength at home and abroad, French Communists, Socialists, and Radicals formed an alliance—the **Popular Front**—for the May 1936 national elections. Their clear victory reflected the trend toward polarization. The number of Communists in parliament jumped dramatically, and the Socialists, led by Léon Blum, became the strongest party in France. The really quite moderate Radicals slipped badly, and the conservatives lost ground to the semifascists.

In the next few months Blum's Popular Front government made the first and only real attempt to deal with France's social and economic problems during the 1930s. Inspired by Roosevelt's New Deal, the Popular Front encouraged the union movement and launched a far-reaching program of social reform, complete with paid vacations and a forty-hour workweek. Popular with workers and the lower middle class, these measures were quickly sabotaged by rapid inflation and cries of revolution from fascists and frightened conservatives. Wealthy people sneaked their money out of the country, labor unrest grew, and France entered a severe financial crisis. Blum was forced to announce a "breathing spell" in social reform.

The Spanish civil war also fanned the fires of political dissension. Communists demanded that France support the Spanish republicans, while many French conservatives would gladly have joined Hitler and Mussolini in aiding the Spanish fascists. Extremism grew, and France itself verged on civil war. Blum was forced to resign in June 1937, and the Popular Front quickly collapsed. An anxious and divided France drifted aimlessly once again, preoccupied by Hitler and German rearmament.

Popular Front   *A New Deal–inspired party in France led by Léon Blum that encouraged the union movement and launched a far-reaching program of social reform, complete with paid vacations and a forty-hour workweek.*

Chapter Summary

Key Terms

logical empiricism
existentialism
neutron
id
ego
superego
stream-of-consciousness
  technique
functionalism
Dawes Plan
Mein Kampf
New Deal
Works Progress
  Administration (WPA)
Popular Front

• *What was the nature of the uncertainty in modern thought in Europe at the beginning of the twentieth century, and what did the doubts and searching mean for Western thought, art, and culture?*

After the First World War, Western society entered a complex and difficult era—truly an age of anxiety. Intellectual life underwent a crisis marked by pessimism, uncertainty, and fascination with irrational forces. Scientists continued to make previously unimaginable discoveries. Einstein's theory of relativity and Marie Curie's work with protons and electrons are but two of the discoveries that totally changed our understanding of the universe. Sigmund Freud revolutionized the field of psychology with his methods of psychoanalysis and his studies of human behavior.

• *What new forms did art and music take during the age of anxiety?*

Ceaseless experimentation and rejection of old forms characterized art and music. Architects abandoned the excessive ornamentation of the past and turned to functionalism. This new principle dictated that buildings be designed to be functional and useful. The Bauhaus movement in Germany drew students from all over the world to study functionalism in fine and applied arts. Art seemed to be in a constant state of change, with the Spanish artist Pablo Picasso making a revolutionary break with the past when he introduced the style of art known as cubism. This was followed by abstract art, as exemplified by such artists as Wassily Kandinsky. Musical compositions, such as the works of Igor Stravinsky, were strikingly parallel to the expressionist developments in art.

• *How did the movies and the radio affect society when they first appeared?*

Motion pictures and radio provided a new, standardized entertainment for the masses. Intellectual and artistic developments that before 1914 had been confined to small avant-garde groups gained wider currency, as did the insecure state of mind they expressed. The first movie stars, such as Charlie Chaplin, became familiar household names. Radio and movies allowed political leaders such as Adolf Hitler and Franklin Roosevelt to reach mass audiences instantly for the first time. These new wonders of modern mass communication became political propaganda tools, for bad or for good.

• *How did leaders deal with the political dimensions of uncertainty and try to re-establish real peace and prosperity between 1919 and 1939?*

The death and destruction caused by World War I led to political and economic disruption across Europe in the years following the war. In the 1920s moderate political leaders replaced the World War I generation and groped to create an enduring peace and rebuild prewar prosperity. The Dawes Plan was one example of how Europe and America worked to create financial stability in Europe. For a brief period late in the decade they seemed to have succeeded.

• Why did democratic leaders fail to effectively address problems created by the depression?

The Great Depression shattered the fragile stability briefly achieved after World War I. Uncertainty returned with redoubled force in the 1930s. The international economy collapsed, and unemployment affected millions worldwide. The democracies turned inward as they sought to cope with massive domestic problems and widespread disillusionment. Generally speaking, they were not very successful. The old liberal ideals of individual rights and responsibilities, elected government, and economic freedom, even when they managed to survive, seemed ineffective and outmoded to many. In many countries these ideals were abandoned completely.

Suggested Reading

Andelman, David A. *A Shattered Peace: Versailles 1919 and the Price We Pay Today.* 2007. Clearly written history of the Versailles peace conference and how it has shaped world history to the present day.

Arnason, Harvey H., and Peter Kalb. *History of Modern Art.* 2003. Classic history of modern art, including painting, sculpture, architecture, and photography.

Burrow, J. W. *The Crisis of Reason: European Thought, 1848–1914.* 2000. Elegantly explores transformations in European thought in the decades before the Great War.

Camus, Albert. *The Stranger,* 1942, and *The Plague,* 1947. The greatest existential novelist at his unforgettable best in these two novels.

Cantor, Norman, and Mindy Cantor. *The American Century: Varieties of Culture in Modern Times.* 1998. Pugnacious and stimulating survey.

Gay, Peter. *Modernism: The Lure of Heresy.* 2007. A personal perspective on twentieth-century high culture by a leading intellectual and cultural historian.

Issacson, Walter. *Einstein: His Life and Universe.* 2007. New, well-received introduction to Einstein's life and work.

Jacobson, Jon. *Locarno Diplomacy: Germany and the West, 1925–1929.* 1972. Superb study of Stresemann and enduring tensions after the Locarno breakthrough.

Judt, Tony. *The Burden of Responsibility: Blum, Camus, Aron, and the French Twentieth Century.* 1998. Probes the moral and intellectual issues of the modern age.

Kindleberger, Charles P. *The World in Depression, 1929–1939.* 1986. Perhaps the best analytical account of the global origins, events, and aftermath of the Great Depression.

Martin, Benjamin. *France and the Après Guerre: Illusions and Disillusionments.* 1999. Solid work with masterful portraits of key figures.

Mazower, Mark. *Dark Continent: Europe's Twentieth Century.* 2000. Provocative history of the forces of communism, fascism, and liberal democracy at war.

Orwell, George, *The Road to Wigan Pier.* 1937. A nonfiction study of poverty among the English working class by one of the century's greatest novelists.

Smith, Bernard. *Modernism's History: A Study in Twentieth-Century Thought and Ideas.* 1998. Admirably straightforward with a global perspective.

Solomon, Robert C. *Existentialism.* 2004. Accessible and comprehensive introduction to existentialist thought.

Weitz, Eric D. *Weimar Germany: Promise and Tragedy.* 2007. Intellectually stimulating introduction to the Weimar world.

Winders, James A. *European Culture Since 1848: From Modernism to Postmodern and Beyond.* 1998. Lively and accessible mosaic of cultural and intellectual history.

Winter, Jay. *Sites of Memory, Sites of Meaning: The Great War in European Cultural History.* 1995. Excellent study of the war's influence on literature, art, and society.

Wolfe, Tom. *From Bauhaus to My House.* 1981. Lively critique of modern architecture.

Notes

1. P. Valéry, *Variety,* trans. M. Cowley (New York: Harcourt Brace, 1927), pp. 27–28.
2. G. Greene, *Another Mexico* (New York: Viking Press, 1939), p. 3.
3. G. Orwell, *1984* (New York: New American Library, 1950), p. 220.
4. C. E. Jeanneret-Gris (Le Corbusier), *Towards a New Architecture* (London: J. Rodker, 1931), p. 15.
5. Quoted in A. H. Barr, Jr., *What Is Modern Painting?* 9th ed. (New York: Museum of Modern Art, 1966), p. 27.
6. Quoted ibid., p. 25.
7. R. Graves and A. Hodge, *The Long Week End: A Social History of Great Britain, 1918–1939* (New York: Macmillan, 1941), p. 131.
8. Quoted in A. Briggs, *The Birth of Broadcasting,* vol. 1 (London: Oxford University Press, 1961), p. 47.
9. Quoted in R. J. Sontag, *A Broken World, 1919–1939* (New York: Harper & Row, 1971), p. 129.
10. C. P. Kindleberger, *The World in Depression, 1929–1939* (Berkeley: University of California Press, 1973), p. 292.
11. Quoted in S. B. Clough et al., eds., *Economic History of Europe: Twentieth Century* (New York: Harper & Row, 1968), pp. 243–245.

Life on the Dole in Great Britain

Periodic surges in unemployment were an old story in capitalist economies, but the long-term joblessness of millions in the Great Depression was something new and unexpected. In Britain especially, where the depression followed a weak postwar recovery, large numbers suffered involuntary idleness for years at a time. Whole families lived "on the dole," the weekly welfare benefits paid by the government.

One of the most insightful accounts of unemployed workers was written by the British journalist and novelist George Orwell (1903–1950), who studied the conditions in northern England and wrote The Road to Wigan Pier *(1937), excerpted here. An independent socialist who distrusted rigid Marxism, Orwell believed that socialism could triumph in Britain if it came to mean "justice and liberty" for a commonsense majority. Orwell's disillusionment with authoritarian socialism and communism pervades his most famous work,* 1984 *(1949).*

When you see the unemployment figures quoted at two millions, it is fatally easy to take this as meaning that two million people are out of work and the rest of the population is comparatively comfortable. . . . [Adding in the destitute,] you might take the number of underfed people in England (for *everyone* on the dole or thereabouts is underfed) as being, at the very most, five millions.

This is an enormous under-estimate, because, in the first place, the only people shown on unemployment figures are those actually drawing the dole—that is, in general, heads of families. An unemployed man's dependants do not figure on the list unless they too are drawing a separate allowance. . . . In addition there are great numbers of people who are in work but who, from a financial point of view, might equally be unemployed, because they are not drawing anything that can be described as a living wage. Allow for these and their dependants, throw in as before the old-age pensioners, the destitute and other nondescripts, and you get an *underfed* population of well over ten millions. . . .

Take the figures for Wigan, which is typical enough of the industrial and mining districts. . . . The total population of Wigan is a little under 87,000; so that at any moment more than one person in three out of the whole population—not merely the registered workers—is either drawing or living on the dole. . . .

Nevertheless, in spite of the frightful extent of unemployment, it is a fact that poverty—extreme poverty—is less in evidence in the industrial North than it is in London. Everything is poorer and shabbier, there are fewer motor-cars and fewer well-dressed people; but also there are fewer people who are obviously destitute. . . . In the industrial towns the old communal way of life has not yet broken up, tradition is still strong and almost everyone has a family—potentially, therefore, a home. In a town of 50,000 or 100,000 inhabitants there is no casual and as it were unaccounted-for population; nobody sleeping in the streets, for instance. Moreover, there is just this to be said for the unemployment regulations, that they do not discourage people from marrying. A man and wife on twenty-three shillings a week are not far from the starvation line, but they can make a home of sorts; they are vastly better off than a single man on fifteen shillings. . . .

But there is no doubt about the deadening, debilitating effect of unemployment upon everybody, married or single, and upon men more than upon women. . . . Everyone who saw Greenwood's play *Love on the Dole* must remember that dreadful moment when the poor, good, stupid working man beats on the table and cries out, "O God, send me some work!" This was not dramatic exaggeration, it was a touch from life. That cry must have been uttered, in almost those words, in tens of thousands, perhaps hundreds of thousands of English homes, during the past fifteen years.

But, I think not again—or at least, not so often. . . . When people live on the dole for years at a time they grow used to it, and drawing the dole, though it remains unpleasant, ceases to be shameful. Thus the old, independent, workhouse-fearing tradition is undermined. . . .

So you have whole populations settling down, as it were, to a lifetime of the P.A.C. . . . Take, for instance, the fact that the working class think nothing of getting

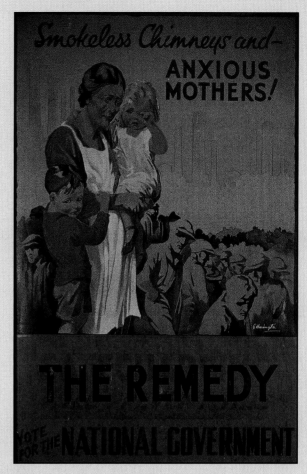

married on the dole. . . . Life is still fairly normal, more normal than one really has the right to expect. Families are impoverished, but the family-system has not broken up. The people are in effect living a reduced version of their former lives. Instead of raging against their destiny they have made things tolerable by lowering their standards.

But they don't necessarily lower their standards by cutting out luxuries and concentrating on necessities; more often it is the other way about—the more natural way, if you come to think of it. Hence the fact that in a decade of unparalleled depression, the consumption of all cheap luxuries has increased. The two things that have probably made the greatest difference of all are the movies and the mass-production of cheap smart clothes since the war. The youth who leaves school at fourteen and gets a blind-alley job is out of work at twenty, probably for life; but for two pounds ten on the hire-purchase system he can buy himself a suit which, for a little while and at a little distance, looks as though it had been tailored in Saville Row. The girl can look like a fashion plate at an even lower price. . . . You can stand on the street corner, indulging in a private daydream of yourself as Clark Gable or Greta Garbo, which compensates you for a great deal. . . .

Trade since the war has had to adjust itself to meet the demands of underpaid, underfed people, with the result that a luxury is nowadays almost always cheaper than a necessity. One pair of plain solid shoes costs as much as two ultra-smart pairs. . . . And above all there is gambling, the cheapest of all luxuries. Even people on the verge of starvation can buy a few days' hope ("Something to live for," as they call it) by having a penny on a sweepstake. . . . Twenty million people are underfed but literally everyone in England has access to a radio. What we have lost in food we have gained in electricity. Whole sections of the working class who have been plundered of all they really need are being compensated, in part, by cheap luxuries which mitigate the surface of life.

Do you consider all this desirable? No, I don't. But it may be that the psychological adjustment which the working class are visibly making is the best they could make in the circumstances. They have neither turned revolutionary nor lost their self-respect; merely they have kept their tempers and settled down to make the best of things on a fish-and-chip standard. The alternative would be God knows what continued agonies of despair; or it might be attempted insurrections which, in a strongly governed country like England, could only lead to futile massacres and a régime of savage repression.

Questions for Analysis

1. According to Orwell, "extreme poverty" was less visible in the northern industrial towns than in London. Were family relations important in this regard?

2. What were the consequences of long-term unemployment for English workers? Were some of the consequences surprising?

3. From Orwell's description, did radical revolution seem likely in England in the depression?

A Crowd of Enthusiastic Hitler Supporters, in a photograph by Hugo Jaeger. *(Time Life Pictures/Getty Images)*

30 DICTATORSHIPS AND THE SECOND WORLD WAR

Chapter Preview

Authoritarian States
• *What was the nature of twentieth-century dictatorships and authoritarian rule?*

Stalin's Soviet Union
• *How were the five-year plans part of the totalitarian order in the Soviet Union?*

Mussolini and Fascism in Italy
• *How was Italian fascism a halfway house between conservative authoritarianism and modern totalitarianism?*

Hitler and Nazism in Germany
• *Why were Hitler and his Nazi regime initially so popular?*

The Second World War
• *How did Hitler's actions lead to another world war?*

The era of anxiety and economic depression was also a time of growing strength for political dictatorship. Popularly elected governments and basic civil liberties declined drastically. In Europe on the eve of the Second World War, liberal democratic governments were surviving only in Great Britain, France, the Low Countries, the Scandinavian nations, and neutral Switzerland. Dictatorship seemed the wave of the future worldwide. Thus the intellectual and economic crisis discussed in Chapter 29 and the decline in liberal political institutions and the rise of dictatorships discussed in this chapter were interrelated elements of a global crisis.

The mid-twentieth-century era of dictatorship is a highly disturbing chapter in the history of civilization. The key development was not only the resurgence of authoritarian rule but also the rise of a particularly ruthless and dynamic tyranny that reached its full realization in the Soviet Union and Nazi Germany in the 1930s. Stalin and Hitler mobilized their peoples for enormous undertakings and ruled with unprecedented severity. Hitler's mobilization was ultimately directed toward racial aggression and territorial expansion, and his sudden attack on Poland in 1939 started World War II. Hitler's successes then encouraged the Japanese to expand their stalemated Chinese campaign into a vast Pacific war by attacking Pearl Harbor and advancing into South Asia.

Nazi and Japanese armies were defeated by a great coalition, and today we want to believe that the era of totalitarian dictatorship was a terrible accident, that Stalin's slave labor camps and Hitler's gas chambers "can't happen again." But the cruel truth is that horrible atrocities continue to plague the world in our time. The Khmer Rouge inflicted genocide on its people in Kampuchea, and civil war led to ethnically motivated atrocities in Bosnia, Rwanda, Burundi, and Sudan, recalling the horrors of the Second World War. And there are other examples. A deeper understanding of these brutal dictatorships will help us guard against their recurrence.

AUTHORITARIAN STATES

What was the nature of twentieth-century dictatorships and authoritarian rule?

Both conservative and radical dictatorships arose in the 1920s and the 1930s. Although they sometimes overlapped in character and practice, they were in essence profoundly different. Conservative authoritarian regimes were an old story in world history. Radical, totalitarian dictatorships were a new and frightening development.

Conservative Authoritarianism

The traditional form of antidemocratic government in world history was conservative authoritarianism. Like Russia's tsars and China's emperors, the leaders of such governments tried to prevent major changes that would undermine the existing social order. To do so, they relied on obedient bureaucracies, vigilant police departments, and trustworthy armies. They forbade popular participation in government or else severely limited it to natural allies such as landlords, bureaucrats, and high church officials. They persecuted liberals, democrats, and socialists as subversive radicals, often consigning them to jail, exile, or death.

Yet old-fashioned authoritarian governments were limited in their power and in their objectives. They had neither the ability nor the desire to control many aspects of their subjects' lives. Preoccupied with the goal of mere survival, these governments largely limited their demands to taxes, army recruits, and passive acceptance. As long as the people did not try to change the system, they often had considerable personal independence.

After the First World War, this kind of authoritarian government revived, especially in Latin America and in the less-developed eastern part of Europe. In eastern Europe parliamentary regimes founded on the wreckage of empires in 1918 fell one by one. By early 1938 only Czechoslovakia remained true to liberal political ideals. Conservative dictators also took over in Spain and Portugal.

There were several reasons for this development. These lands lacked strong traditions of self-government, with its necessary restraint and compromise. Moreover, many of these new states, such as Yugoslavia, were torn by ethnic conflicts that threatened their very existence. Dictatorship appealed to nationalists and military leaders as a way to repress such tensions and preserve national unity. Large landowners and the church were still powerful forces in these predominantly agrarian areas, and they often looked to dictators to save them from progressive land reform or communist agrarian upheaval. Finally, the Great Depression delivered the final blow to fragile democracies in Austria, Bulgaria, Romania, Greece, Estonia, and Latvia.

Although some of the conservative authoritarian regimes adopted certain Hitlerian and fascist characteristics in the 1930s, their general aims were limited. They were concerned more with maintaining the status quo than with mobilizing the masses or forcing society into rapid change or war. This tradition continued into the late twentieth century, especially in some of the Latin American military dictatorships.

Radical Totalitarian Dictatorships

By the mid-1930s a new kind of radical dictatorship had emerged in the Soviet Union, Germany, and, to a lesser extent, Italy. Scholars generally agree that these radical dictatorships violently rejected liberal values and exercised unprecedented control over the masses. Further interpretation of these regimes, however, has caused heated controversy and debate.

One extremely useful approach relates the radical dictatorships to the rise of modern totalitarianism. The concept of **totalitarianism** emerged in the 1920s and 1930s.

totalitarianism *A dictatorship that exercises unprecedented control over the masses and seeks to mobilize them for action.*

In 1924 Benito Mussolini spoke of the "fierce totalitarian will" of his movement in Italy. In the 1930s observers linked Italian and especially German fascism with Soviet communism in "a 'new kind of state' that could be called totalitarian." "All doubts" about the totalitarian nature of both dictatorships "were swept away for most Americans,"[1] following the Hitler-Stalin alliance in 1939.

Some scholars argue that modern totalitarian dictatorship burst on the scene with the revolutionary total war effort of 1914–1918. The war called forth a tendency to subordinate all institutions and all classes to the state in order to achieve one supreme objective: victory. As the French thinker Elie Halévy put it in 1936 in his influential *The Era of Tyrannies,* the varieties of modern totalitarian tyranny—fascism, Nazism, and communism—could be thought of as "feuding brothers" with a common father: the nature of modern war.[2]

Halévy and others believed Lenin and the Bolsheviks carried the crucial experience of World War I further during the Russian civil war. Lenin showed how a dedicated minority could achieve victory over a less determined majority and subordinate institutions and human rights to the needs of a single group—the Communist Party—and its leader. Lenin's model of single-party dictatorship inspired imitators, including Adolf Hitler. The modern totalitarian state reached maturity in the 1930s in the Stalinist U.S.S.R. and Nazi Germany.

Scholars have also argued that the totalitarian state used modern technology and communications to exercise complete political power, and then complete control over the economic, social, intellectual, and cultural aspects of people's lives as well. Deviation from the norm, even in art or family behavior, could become a crime.

This vision of total state represented a radical revolt against liberalism. Classical liberalism (see page 679) sought to limit state power and protect individual rights. Moreover, liberals stood for rationality, peaceful progress, economic freedom, and a strong middle class. All of that disgusted totalitarians. They believed in willpower, preached conflict, and worshiped violence. The individual was infinitely less valuable than the state.

Unlike old-fashioned authoritarianism, modern totalitarianism was based not on an elite but on people who had already become engaged in the political process, most notably through commitment to nationalism and socialism. Thus totalitarian societies were fully mobilized societies moving toward some goal and possessing boundless dynamism. As soon as one goal was achieved, another arose at the leader's command. As a result totalitarianism was a *permanent* revolution, an *unfinished* revolution, in which rapid, profound change imposed from on high went on forever.

There were major differences between Stalin's communist U.S.S.R. and Hitler's Nazi Germany. Soviet communism, growing out of Marxian socialism, seized all private property (except personal property) for the state and crushed the middle classes.

Chronology

1921	New Economic Policy in Soviet Union
1922	Mussolini seizes power in Italy
1924–1929	Buildup of Nazi Party in Germany
1927	Stalin comes to power in Soviet Union
1928	Stalin's first five-year plan
1929	Start of collectivization in Soviet Union; Lateran Agreement
1929–1939	Great Depression
1932–1933	Famine in Ukraine
1933	Hitler appointed chancellor in Germany; Nazis begin to control intellectual life and blacklist authors
1934	Sergei Kirov, Stalin's number-two man, is murdered
1935	Mussolini invades Ethiopia
1936	Start of great purges under Stalin
1939	Germany occupies Czech lands; Germany invades Poland; Britain and France declare war on Germany
1940	Japan signs formal alliance with Germany and Italy
1941	SS stops Jewish emigration from Europe; Germany invades Soviet Union; bombing of Pearl Harbor; United States enters war
1941–1945	Six million Jews killed in death camps
1944	Allied invasion at Normandy
1945	Atomic bombs dropped on Japan; end of war

● **Nazi Mass Rally, 1936** This picture captures the essence of the totalitarian interpretation of dynamic modern dictatorship. The uniformed members of the Nazi Party have willingly merged themselves into a single force and await the command of the godlike leader. *(AP/Wide World Photos)*

Nazi Germany, growing out of extreme nationalism and racism, criticized big landowners and industrialists, but both private property and the middle classes survived. This difference in property and class relations led some scholars to speak of "totalitarianism of the left"—Stalinist Russia—and "totalitarianism of the right"—Nazi Germany.

A second group of observers in the 1930s approached radical dictatorships outside the Soviet Union through the concept of **fascism**. These writers severely criticized fascism, linking it to decaying capitalism and domestic class conflict. Mussolini and Hitler, however, proudly used the term to describe their movements' supposedly "total" and revolutionary character. Orthodox Marxists argued that powerful capitalists used fascist ideology to create a mass movement capable of destroying the revolutionary working class and thus protect their enormous profits.

fascism *A movement characterized by extreme, often expansionist nationalism, an antisocialism aimed at destroying working-class movements, alliances with powerful capitalists and landowners, a dynamic and violent leader, and glorification of war and the military.*

Comparative studies of European fascist movements show that they shared many characteristics, including extreme nationalism, an antisocialism aimed at destroying working-class movements, alliances with powerful capitalists and landowners, a dynamic and violent leader, and glorification of war and the military. These studies also highlight how fascist movements generally failed to gain political power.

In recent years, many historians have tended to adopt a third approach, emphasizing the uniqueness of developments in each country. This is especially true for Hitler's Germany, where some elements of the totalitarian interpretation have been nuanced and revised. A similar revaluation of Stalin's U.S.S.R. is in progress now that communism's collapse has opened the former Soviet Union's archives to new research.

In summary, despite conflicting interpretations the concept of totalitarianism remains a valuable tool for historical understanding. It correctly highlights that both Hitler's Germany and Stalin's Soviet Union made an unprecedented "total claim" on the beliefs and behaviors of their respective citizens.[3] As for fascism, antidemocratic, antisocialist fascist movements sprang up all over Europe, but only in Italy and Germany (and some would say Spain) were they able to take power. Finally, it is important to remember that the problem of Europe's radical dictatorships is complex, with few easy answers.

STALIN'S SOVIET UNION

How were the five-year plans part of the totalitarian order in the Soviet Union?

Lenin's harshest critics claim that he established the basic outlines of a modern totalitarian dictatorship after the Bolshevik Revolution and during the Russian civil war. If this is so, then Joseph Stalin (1879–1953) certainly finished the job. A master of political infighting, Stalin cautiously consolidated his power and eliminated his enemies in the mid-1920s. Then in 1928, as the ruling Communist Party's undisputed leader, he launched the first **five-year plan**—the "revolution from above," as he so aptly termed it.

Extremely ambitious, the five-year plans marked the beginning of a renewed attempt to mobilize and transform Soviet society along socialist lines. The means Stalin and the small Communist Party elite chose in order to do so were constant propaganda, enormous sacrifice, and unlimited violence and state control. Thus many historians argue that the Soviet Union in the 1930s became a dynamic, modern totalitarian state.

five-year plan *Launched by Stalin and termed "revolution from above," its ultimate goal was to generate new attitudes, new loyalties, and a new socialist humanity.*

From Lenin to Stalin

By spring 1921 Lenin and the Bolsheviks had won the civil war, but they ruled a shattered and devastated land. Many farms were in ruins, and food supplies were exhausted. Drought and war in southern Russia combined to produce the worst famine in generations. Industrial production also broke down completely. The Bolsheviks had destroyed the economy as well as their foes.

In the face of economic disintegration, riots by peasants and workers, and an open rebellion by previously pro-Bolshevik sailors at Kronstadt, Lenin changed course. In March 1921 he announced the **New Economic Policy (NEP)**, which re-established limited economic freedom in an attempt to rebuild agriculture and industry. Peasant producers could sell their surpluses in free markets, as could private traders and small handicraft manufacturers. Heavy industry, railroads, and banks, however, remained wholly nationalized.

New Economic Policy (NEP) *Lenin's policy of re-establishing limited economic freedom in an attempt to rebuild agriculture and industry in the face of economic disintegration.*

The NEP was shrewd and successful both politically and economically. Politically, it was a necessary but temporary compromise with the Soviet Union's overwhelming peasant majority, which Lenin realized was the only force capable of overturning his government. Economically, the NEP brought rapid recovery. In 1926 industrial output surpassed the level of 1913, and Soviet peasants were producing almost as much grain as before the war.

As the economy recovered, an intense power struggle began in the Communist Party's inner circles, for Lenin left no chosen successor when he died in 1924. The principal contenders were the stolid Stalin and the flamboyant Trotsky.

Joseph Dzhugashvili—later known as Stalin—was a shoemaker's son. He studied for the priesthood but was expelled from his theological seminary. By 1903 he was a Bolshevik revolutionary in southern Russia. Stalin was a good organizer but had no experience outside Russia. Trotsky, an inspiring leader who had planned the 1917 takeover (see page 832) and created the victorious Red Army, appeared to have all the advantages. Yet it was Stalin who succeeded Lenin, because he gained the all-important support of the party, the only genuine source of power in the one-party state. Rising to general secretary of the party's Central Committee just before Lenin's first stroke in 1922, Stalin used his office to win friends and allies with jobs and promises.

With cunning skill Stalin gradually achieved absolute power between 1922 and 1927. Stalin used the moderates to crush Trotsky, then he turned against the moderates and destroyed them as well. Stalin's final triumph came at the party congress of December 1927, which condemned all "deviation from the general party line"

● **Kazimir Malevich: Suprematism, ca. 1917**
Russian artists occupied a prominent position in the international avant-garde in the early twentieth century, and the Ukrainian-born Malevich is widely recognized as a leading figure in the development of modern abstract art. Malevich originated the theory of suprematism, whereby he abandoned images from nature and painted pure forms that were beautiful in themselves, as in this outstanding example. When the Bolsheviks condemned abstraction and demanded "socialist realism," Malevich returned to more recognizable forms and taught design. *(Erich Lessing/Art Resource, NY)*

formulated by Stalin. He then launched his revolution from above—the real revolution for millions of ordinary citizens.

The Five-Year Plans

The 1927 party congress marked the end of the NEP and the beginning of the era of socialist five-year plans. The first five-year plan had staggering economic objectives. In just five years, total industrial output was to increase by 250 percent and agricultural production by 150 percent, and one-fifth of the peasants were to give up their private plots and join socialist collective farms. By 1930 economic and social change was sweeping the country.

Stalin unleashed his "second revolution" for a variety of interrelated reasons. First, like Lenin, Stalin and his militant supporters were deeply committed to socialism as they understood it. Second, there was the old problem of catching up with the advanced and presumably hostile Western capitalist nations. "We are fifty or a hundred years behind the advanced countries," Stalin said in 1931, "We must make good this distance in ten years. Either we do it, or we shall go under."[4]

Domestically, there was the peasant problem. For centuries peasants had wanted to own the land, and finally they had it. Sooner or later, the communists reasoned, the peasants would become conservative little capitalists and threaten the regime. Therefore, Stalin decided on a preventive war against the peasantry in order to bring it under the state's absolute control.

That war was **collectivization**—the forcible consolidation of individual peasant farms into large, state-controlled enterprises. Beginning in 1929 peasants were ordered to give up their land and animals and become members of collective farms. As for the **kulaks,** the better-off peasants, Stalin instructed party workers to "liquidate them as a class." Stripped of land and livestock, the kulaks were generally not even permitted to join the collective farms. Many starved or were deported to forced-labor camps for "re-education."

Since almost all peasants were in fact poor, the term *kulak* soon meant any peasant who opposed the new system. Whole villages were often attacked. One conscience-stricken colonel in the secret police confessed to a foreign journalist,

I am an old Bolshevik. I worked in the underground against the Tsar and then I fought in the Civil War. Did I do all that in order that I should now surround villages with machine guns and order my men to fire indiscriminately into crowds of peasants? Oh, no, no![5]

Forced collectivization led to disaster. Many peasants slaughtered their animals and burned their crops in sullen, hopeless protest. Between 1929 and 1933 the number of horses, cattle, sheep, and goats in the Soviet Union fell by at least half. Nor were the state-controlled collective farms more productive. Grain output barely increased between 1928 and 1938. Collectivized agriculture made no substantial financial contribution to Soviet industrial development during the first five-year plan.

The disaster's human dimension was absolutely staggering. Stalin himself confided to Winston Churchill at Yalta in 1945 that 10 million people had died in the course of collectivization. In Ukraine the drive against peasants snowballed into a general assault on Ukrainians as reactionary nationalists and enemies of socialism. The result was a terrible man-made famine in Ukraine in 1932 and 1933, which probably claimed 6 million lives.

Collectivization was a cruel but real victory for communist ideologues. By 1938, 93 percent of peasant families had been herded onto collective farms. Regimented as state employees and dependent on the state-owned tractor stations, the collectivized peasants were no longer even a potential political threat to the regime.

The industrial side of the five-year plans was more successful—indeed, quite spectacular. Soviet industry produced about four times as much in 1937 as in 1928. No other major country had ever achieved such rapid industrial growth. Heavy industry led the way; consumer industry grew quite slowly. Urban development accelerated, and more than 25 million people migrated to cities during the 1930s.

The sudden creation of dozens of new factories (and the increasingly voracious military) demanded tremendous resources purchased at enormous sacrifice. The money was collected from the people by means of heavy, hidden sales taxes. Firm labor discipline and foreign engineers also made important contributions to rapid industrialization. Trade unions lost most of their power, and individuals could not move without police permission. When factory managers needed more hands they were sent millions of "unneeded" peasants from collective farms over the years.

Foreign engineers were hired to plan and construct many of the new factories. Highly skilled American engineers, hungry for work in the depression years, were particularly important until newly trained Soviet experts began to replace them after 1932. Siberia's new gigantic steel mills were modeled on America's best. Thus Stalin's planners harnessed even the skill and technology of capitalist countries to promote the surge of socialist industry.

Life and Culture in Soviet Society

Stalin's five-year plans aimed also to create a new kind of society and human personality. The utopian vision of a new humanity floundered, but Stalin did build a new society whose broad outlines existed into the mid-1980s.

collectivization *The forcible consolidation of individual peasant farms into large, state-controlled enterprises.*

kulaks *Better-off peasants who were stripped of land and livestock under Stalin. They generally were not permitted to join the collective farms, and many of them starved or were deported to forced-labor camps for "re-education."*

● **"Let's All Get to Work, Comrades!"** Art in the Stalinist era generally followed the official doctrine of socialist realism, representing objects in a literal style and celebrating Soviet achievements. Characteristically, this poster glorifies the working class, women's equality (in hard labor at least), mammoth factories, and the Communist Party (represented by the hammer and sickle by the woman's foot). Assailed by propaganda, Soviet citizens often found refuge in personal relations and deep friendships. *(From Art of the October Revolution, Mikhail Guerman [Aurora Publishers, Leningrad]. Reproduced by permission)*

Primary Source:
Letters to Izvestiya on the Abortion Issue, May–June 1936
Find out what some citizens of the Soviet Union thought about a proposed ban on abortion.

Life was hard in Stalin's Soviet Union. Because consumption was reduced to pay for investment, there was no improvement in the average standard of living. The masses lived primarily on black bread and wore old, shabby clothing. Stores experienced constant shortages, although very heavily taxed vodka was always readily available. Housing shortages were a particularly serious problem. A relatively lucky family received one room for all its members and shared both a kitchen and a toilet with others on the floor. Less fortunate people built scrap-lumber shacks in shantytowns.

Despite the hardships, idealism and ideology had real appeal for many communists, who saw themselves heroically building the world's first socialist society while capitalism crumbled and fascism rose in the West. This optimistic belief in the Soviet Union's future also attracted many disillusioned Westerners to communism in the 1930s.

On a more practical level Soviet workers did receive some important social benefits, such as old-age pensions, free medical services, free education, and child day-care centers. Unemployment was almost unknown. Finally, there was the possibility of personal advancement.

The keys to improving one's position were specialized skills and technical education. Rapid industrialization required massive numbers of trained experts, such as skilled workers, engineers, and plant managers. Thus the Stalinist state broke with the egalitarian policies of the 1920s and provided tremendous incentives to those who could serve its needs. A growing technical and managerial elite joined with the political and artistic elites in a new upper class, whose members were rich, powerful, and insecure. Thus millions struggled for an education.

Soviet society's radical transformation profoundly affected women's lives. Marxists traditionally believed that both capitalism and middle-class husbands exploited women. The Russian Revolution of 1917 immediately proclaimed complete equality of rights for women. In the 1920s divorce and abortion were made easily available, and women were urged to work outside the home and liberate themselves sexually. After Stalin came to power, sexual and familial liberation was played down, and the most lasting changes for women involved work and education.

While many peasant women continued to work on farms, millions of women now toiled in factories and heavy construction. The more determined women entered the ranks of the better-paid specialists in industry and science. Medicine practically became a woman's profession. By 1950, 75 percent of all doctors in the Soviet Union were women. The massive mobilization of women was a striking characteristic of the Soviet state.

Culture lost its autonomy in the 1930s and became thoroughly politicized through constant propaganda and indoctrination. Party activists lectured workers in factories and peasants on collective farms, while newspapers, films, and radio broadcasts endlessly recounted socialist achievements and capitalist plots. Writers and artists who could effectively combine genuine creativity and political propaganda became the darlings of the regime.

Stalinist Terror and the Great Purges

In the mid-1930s the great offensive to build socialism and a new socialist personality culminated in ruthless police terror and a massive purging of the Communist Party. In late 1934 Stalin's number-two man, Sergei Kirov, was suddenly and mysteriously murdered. Although Stalin himself probably ordered Kirov's murder, he used the incident to launch a reign of terror.

In August 1936 sixteen prominent Old Bolsheviks confessed to all manner of plots against Stalin in spectacular public show trials in Moscow. Then in 1937 the secret police arrested a mass of lesser party officials and newer members, also torturing them and extracting more confessions for more show trials. In addition to the party faithful, union officials, managers, intellectuals, army officers, and countless ordinary citizens were struck down. In all at least 8 million people were probably arrested, and millions of these were executed or never returned from prisons and forced-labor camps.

Stalin recruited 1.5 million new members to take the place of those purged. Thus more than half of all Communist Party members in 1941 had joined since the purges. "These new men were 'thirty-something' products of the Second Revolution of the 1930s, Stalin's upwardly mobile yuppies, so to speak."[6] This new generation of Stalin-formed Communists served the leader effectively until his death in 1953, and then governed the Soviet Union until the early 1980s.

Stalin's mass purges remain baffling, for almost all historians believe that those purged posed no threat and confessed to crimes they had not committed. Revisionist historians have challenged the long-standing interpretation that blames the great purges on Stalin's cruelty or madness. They argue that Stalin's fears were exaggerated but genuine and were shared by many in the party and in the general population who were bombarded daily with ideology and political slogans. Investigations and trials snowballed into a mass hysteria, a new witch-hunt.[7] In short, a popular but deluded Stalin found large numbers of willing collaborators for crime as well as for achievement.

MUSSOLINI AND FASCISM IN ITALY

How was Italian fascism a halfway house between conservative authoritarianism and modern totalitarianism?

Mussolini's movement and his seizure of power in 1922 were important steps in the rise of dictatorships between the two world wars. Like all the future dictators, the young Mussolini hated liberalism and wanted to destroy it in Italy. He and his supporters were the first to call themselves "fascists"—revolutionaries determined to create a certain kind of totalitarian state. Few scholars today would argue that Mussolini succeeded. His dictatorship was brutal and theatrical, but it remained a halfway house between conservative authoritarianism and modern totalitarianism.

The Seizure of Power

In the early twentieth century Italy was a liberal state with civil rights and a constitutional monarchy. On the eve of the First World War the parliamentary regime finally granted universal male suffrage. But there were serious problems. Poverty was widespread, and many peasants were more attached to their villages and local interests than to the national state. Moreover, the papacy, many devout Catholics, conservatives, and landowners remained strongly opposed to the middle-class lawyers and politicians who ran the country largely for their own benefit. Church-state relations were often tense. Class differences were also extreme, and by 1912 the Socialist Party's radical wing led the powerful revolutionary socialist movement.[8]

● **Hitler and Mussolini in Italy, May 1938**   At first Mussolini distrusted Hitler, but Mussolini's conquest of Ethiopia in 1936 and Hitler's occupation of the Rhineland brought the two dictators together in a close alliance. State visits by Mussolini to Berlin in 1937 and by Hitler to Rome in 1938 included gigantic military reviews, which were filmed to impress the whole world. Uniformed Italian fascists accompany this motorcade. *(Time Life Pictures/Getty Images)*

The war worsened the political situation. Having fought on the Allied side almost exclusively for purposes of territorial expansion, the parliamentary government bitterly disappointed Italian nationalists with Italy's modest gains at Versailles. Workers and peasants also felt cheated: to win their support during the war, the government had promised social and land reform, which it did not deliver after the war.

The Russian Revolution inspired and energized Italy's revolutionary socialist movement, and radical workers and peasants began occupying factories and seizing land in 1920. These actions scared and mobilized the property-owning classes. Thus by 1921 revolutionary socialists, antiliberal conservatives, and frightened property owners were all opposed—though for different reasons—to the liberal parliamentary government.

Into these crosscurrents of unrest and fear stepped the blustering, bullying Benito Mussolini (1883–1945). Son of a village schoolteacher and a poor blacksmith, Mussolini began his political career as a Socialist Party leader and radical newspaper editor before World War I. Expelled from the Italian Socialist Party for supporting the war and wounded in 1917, Mussolini returned home and began organizing bitter war veterans into a band of fascists—from the Italian word for "a union of forces."

At first Mussolini's program was a radical combination of nationalist and socialist demands, including territorial expansion, workers' benefits, and land reform for peasants. It competed directly with the well-organized Socialist Party and failed to get off the ground. When Mussolini saw that his violent verbal assaults on rival Socialists won him growing support from conservatives and the frightened middle classes, he shifted gears in 1920. In thought and action Mussolini was a striking example of the turbulent uncertainty of the age of anxiety.

Black Shirts   *A private army under Mussolini that destroyed Socialist newspapers, union halls, and Socialist Party headquarters, eventually pushing Socialists out of the city governments of northern Italy.*

Mussolini and his private army of **Black Shirts** began to grow violent, attacking Socialist organizers and meetings. Few people were killed, but Socialist newspapers, union halls, and local Socialist Party headquarters were destroyed. A skillful politician, Mussolini allowed his followers to convince themselves that they were not just opposing the "Reds" but were also making a real revolution of their own, helping the little people against the established interests.

With the government breaking down in 1922, largely because of the chaos created by his direct-action bands, Mussolini stepped forward as the savior of order and property, demanding the existing government's resignation and his own appointment by the king. In October 1922 a large group of fascists marched on Rome to threaten the king and force him to call on Mussolini. The threat worked. Victor Emmanuel III (r. 1900–1946), who had no love for the old liberal politicians, asked Mussolini to form a new cabinet. Thus, after widespread violence and a threat of armed uprising, Mussolini seized power "legally." The king and parliament immediately granted Mussolini dictatorial authority for one year.

The Regime in Action

Mussolini became dictator on the strength of Italians' rejection of parliamentary government coupled with fears of Soviet-style revolution. In 1924 he declared his desire to "make the nation Fascist," and imposed a series of repressive measures. Press freedom was abolished, elections were fixed, and the government ruled by decree. Mussolini arrested his political opponents, disbanded all independent labor unions, and put dedicated Fascists in control of Italy's schools. He created a fascist youth movement, fascist labor unions, and many other fascist organizations. He trumpeted his goal in a famous slogan of 1926: "Everything in the state, nothing outside the state, nothing against the state." By year's end Italy was a one-party dictatorship under Mussolini's unquestioned leadership.

Mussolini, however, did not complete the establishment of a modern totalitarian state. His Fascist Party never destroyed the old power structure. Interested primarily in personal power, Mussolini was content to compromise with the old conservative classes that controlled the army, the economy, and the state. He never tried to purge these classes or even move very vigorously against them. He controlled labor but left big business to regulate itself, profitably and securely. There was no land reform.

Mussolini also drew increasing support from the Catholic Church. In the **Lateran Agreement** of 1929, he recognized the Vatican as a tiny independent state and agreed to give the church heavy financial support. The pope urged Italians to support Mussolini's government.

Nothing better illustrates Mussolini's unwillingness to harness everyone and everything for dynamic action than his treatment of women. He abolished divorce and told women to stay at home and produce children. In 1938 women were limited by law to a maximum of 10 percent of the better-paying jobs in industry and government. Italian women appear not to have changed their attitudes or behavior in any important way under fascist rule.

Mussolini's government passed no racial laws until 1938 and did not persecute Jews savagely until late in the Second World War, when Italy was under Nazi control. Nor did Mussolini establish a truly ruthless police state. Only twenty-three political prisoners were condemned to death between 1926 and 1944. In spite of much pompous posing by the chauvinist leader, Mussolini's fascist Italy, though repressive and undemocratic, was never really totalitarian.

Lateran Agreement *A 1929 agreement that recognized the Vatican as a tiny independent state, with Mussolini agreeing to give the church heavy financial support. In turn, the pope expressed his satisfaction and urged Italians to support Mussolini's government.*

HITLER AND NAZISM IN GERMANY

Why were Hitler and his Nazi regime initially so popular?

The most frightening dictatorship developed in Nazi Germany. A product of Hitler's evil genius, as well as of Germany's social and political situation and the general attack on liberalism and rationality in the age of anxiety, the Nazi movement shared some of the characteristics of Mussolini's Italian model and fascism. But Nazism asserted an unlimited claim over German society and proclaimed the ultimate power of its endlessly aggressive leader—Adolf Hitler. Nazism's aspirations were truly totalitarian.

The Roots of Nazism

Nazism grew out of many complex developments, of which the most influential were extreme nationalism and racism. These two ideas captured the mind of the young Hitler, and it was he who dominated Nazism for as long as it lasted.

Nazism *A movement born of extreme nationalism and racism and dominated by Adolf Hitler for as long as it lasted.*

Born the fourth child of a successful Austrian customs official and an indulgent mother, Adolf Hitler (1889–1945) spent his childhood in small towns in Austria. He did poorly in high school and dropped out at age sixteen. He then headed to Vienna, where he found most of the perverted beliefs that guided his life.

In Vienna Hitler soaked up extreme German nationalism, which was particularly strong there. Austro-German nationalists believed Germans to be a superior people and central Europe's natural rulers. They often advocated union with Germany and violent expulsion of "inferior" peoples as the means of maintaining German domination of the Austro-Hungarian Empire. Hitler was deeply impressed by Vienna's mayor, Karl Lueger (1844–1910). With the help of the Catholic trade unions, Lueger had won the support of Vienna's lower classes, and he showed Hitler the enormous potential of anticapitalist and antiliberal propaganda.

From Lueger and others Hitler eagerly absorbed virulent anti-Semitism, racism, and hatred of Slavs. He developed an unshakable belief in the crudest, most exaggerated distortions of the Darwinian theory of survival, the superiority of Germanic races, and the inevitability of racial conflict. Anti-Semitism and racism became Hitler's most passionate convictions, his explanation for everything. The Jews, he claimed, directed an international conspiracy of finance capitalism and Marxian socialism against German culture, German unity, and the German race. Hitler's belief was totally irrational, but he never doubted it.

Hitler greeted the outbreak of the Great War as a salvation. The struggle and discipline of war gave his life meaning, and when Germany was suddenly defeated in 1918, Hitler's world was shattered. Convinced that Jews and Marxists had "stabbed Germany in the back," he vowed to fight on.

In late 1919 Hitler joined a tiny extremist group in Munich called the German Workers' Party, which promised a uniquely German "national socialism" that would abolish the injustices of capitalism and create a mighty "people's community." By 1921 Hitler had gained absolute control of this small but growing party. Already a master of mass propaganda and political showmanship, his most effective tool was the mass rally, where he often worked his audience into a frenzy with wild attacks on the Versailles treaty, the Jews, war profiteers, and Germany's Weimar Republic.

In late 1923 the Weimar Republic seemed on the verge of collapse, and Hitler, inspired by Mussolini's recent easy victory, attempted an armed uprising in Munich. Despite the failure of the poorly organized plot and Hitler's arrest, Nazism had been born.

Hitler's Road to Power

At his trial Hitler violently denounced the Weimar Republic, and he gained enormous publicity and attention. Moreover, he learned from his unsuccessful revolt. Hitler concluded that he had to undermine, rather than overthrow, the government and come to power legally through electoral competition. He also used his brief prison term to dictate *Mein Kampf.* There he expounded on his basic themes: "race," with a stress on anti-Semitism; "living space," with a sweeping vision of war and conquered territory; and the leader-dictator, called the **Führer,** with unlimited, arbitrary power.

Führer *"Leader-dictator" with unlimited, arbitrary power; this title was bestowed upon Adolf Hitler.*

In the years of prosperity and relative stability between 1924 and 1929, Hitler concentrated on building his National Socialist German Workers' Party, or Nazi Party. The Nazis remained a small splinter group, however, until the 1929 Great Depression shattered economic prosperity and presented Hitler with a fabulous opportunity. By the end of 1932 an incredible 43 percent of the labor force was unemployed. Industrial production fell by one-half between 1929 and 1932. No factor contributed more to Hitler's success than the economic crisis. Hitler began promising German voters economic as well as political and international salvation.

Hitler rejected free-market capitalism and advocated government programs to bring recovery. He pitched his speeches especially to middle- and lower-middle-class groups and to skilled workers striving for middle-class status. As the economy collapsed, great numbers of these people "voted their pocketbooks"[9] and deserted the conservative and moderate parties for the Nazis. In the 1930 election the Nazis won 6.5 million votes and 107 seats, and in July 1932 the Nazis gained 14.5 million votes—38 percent of the total—and became the largest party in the Reichstag.

Hitler and the Nazis also appealed strongly to German youth. Indeed, in some ways the Nazi movement was a mass movement of young Germans. Hitler himself was only forty in 1929, and he and most of his top aides were much younger than other leading German politicians. "National Socialism is the organized will of the youth," proclaimed the official Nazi slogan. In 1931 almost 40 percent of Nazi Party members were under thirty, compared with 20 percent of Social Democrats. National recovery, exciting and rapid change, and personal advancement made Nazism appealing to millions of German youths.

Hitler also came to power because normal democratic government broke down. Germany's economic collapse in the Great Depression convinced many voters that the country's republican leaders were stupid and corrupt, thereby adding to Hitler's appeal. Disunity on the left was another nail in the republic's coffin. The Communists refused to cooperate with the Social Democrats, even though the two parties together outnumbered the Nazis in the Reichstag, even after the 1932 elections. German Communists (and the still complacent Stalin) believed that Hitler's fascism represented the last agonies of monopoly capitalism and that a communist revolution would soon follow his taking power.

Finally, Hitler excelled in dirty backroom politics. In 1932 he succeeded in gaining support from key people in the army and big business who thought they could use him to their own advantage. Many conservative and nationalistic politicians thought similarly. Thus in January 1933 Hindenburg legally appointed Hitler, leader of Germany's largest party, chancellor of Germany.

The Nazi State and Society

Hitler quickly and skillfully established an unshakable dictatorship. When the Reichstag building was partly destroyed by fire, Hitler blamed the Communist Party, and he convinced President Hindenburg to sign dictatorial emergency acts that practically abolished freedom of speech and assembly and most personal liberties. He also called for new elections.

When the Nazis won only 44 percent of the votes, Hitler immediately outlawed the Communist Party and arrested its parliamentary representatives. Then on March 23, 1933, the Nazis forced through the Reichstag the so-called **Enabling Act,** which gave Hitler absolute dictatorial power for four years. Hitler and the Nazis took over the government bureaucracy intact, installing many Nazis in top positions.

Enabling Act *The act pushed through the Reichstag by the Nazis that gave Hitler absolute dictatorial power for four years.*

Hitler next outlawed strikes and abolished independent labor unions, which were replaced by the Nazi Labor Front. Professional people—doctors and lawyers, teachers and engineers—also saw their previously independent organizations swallowed up in Nazi associations. Publishing houses and universities were put under Nazi control, and passionate students and pitiful professors burned forbidden books in public squares. Modern art and architecture were ruthlessly prohibited. Life became violently anti-intellectual. As the cynical Joseph Goebbels, later Nazi minister of propaganda, put it, "When I hear the word 'culture' I reach for my gun."[10] By 1934 a brutal dictatorship characterized by frightening dynamism and total obedience to Hitler was already largely in place.

In June 1934 Hitler ordered his elite personal guard—the SS—to arrest and shoot without trial roughly a thousand long-time Nazi storm troops. Shortly thereafter army leaders surrendered their independence and swore a binding oath of "unquestioning obedience . . . to the Leader of the German State and People, Adolf Hitler." The SS grew rapidly. Under its methodical, inhuman leader, Heinrich Himmler

Ganz Deutschland hört den Führer

mit dem Volksempfänger

● **Reaching a National Audience** This poster ad promotes the VE-301 receiver, "the world's cheapest radio," and claims that "All Germany listens to the Führer on the people's receiver." Constantly broadcasting official views and attitudes, the state-controlled media also put the Nazis' favorite entertainment—gigantic mass meetings that climaxed with Hitler's violent theatrical speeches—on an invisible stage for millions. (*Bundesarchiv Koblenz Plak 003-022-025*)

Primary Source:
Speech to the National Socialist Women's Association, September 1935
Learn what the Nazis believed were the proper roles for women in society—from the woman appointed to disseminate their beliefs.

(1900–1945), the SS joined with the political police, the Gestapo, to expand its network of special courts and concentration camps. Nobody was safe.

From the beginning Jews were a special object of Nazi persecution. By late 1934 most Jewish lawyers, doctors, professors, civil servants, and musicians had lost their jobs and the right to practice their professions. In 1935 the infamous Nuremberg Laws classified as Jewish anyone having one or more Jewish grandparents and deprived Jews of all rights of citizenship. By 1938 roughly one-quarter of Germany's half million Jews had emigrated, sacrificing almost all their property in order to leave Germany.

In late 1938 the attack on the Jews accelerated. A well-organized wave of violence destroyed homes, synagogues, and businesses, after which German Jews were rounded up and made to pay for the damage. It became very difficult for Jews to leave Germany. Some Germans privately opposed these outrages, but most went along or looked the other way. Although this lack of response reflected the individual's helplessness in a totalitarian state, it was more certainly a sign of the strong popular support Hitler's government enjoyed.

Hitler's Popularity

Hitler had promised the masses economic recovery—"work and bread"—and he delivered, launching a large public works program to pull Germany out of the depression. Work began on superhighways, offices, gigantic sports stadiums, and public housing. In 1935 Germany turned decisively toward rearmament. Unemployment dropped steadily, and by 1938 everyone had work. The average standard of living increased moderately. Business profits rose sharply. For millions of people economic recovery was tangible evidence that Nazi promises were more than show and propaganda.

For the masses of ordinary German citizens who were not Jews, Slavs, Gypsies, Jehovah's Witnesses, communists, or homosexuals, Hitler's government meant greater equality and more opportunities. In 1933 class barriers in Germany were generally high. Hitler's rule introduced changes that lowered these barriers. For example, stiff educational requirements favoring the well-to-do were relaxed. The new Nazi elite included many young and poorly educated dropouts, rootless lower-middle-class people like Hitler who rose to the top with breathtaking speed. More generally, the Nazis tolerated privilege and wealth only as long as they served party needs.

Yet few historians today believe that Hitler and the Nazis brought about a real social revolution, as an earlier generation of scholars often argued. The well-educated classes held on to most of their advantages, and only a modest social leveling occurred in the Nazi years. Significantly, the Nazis shared with the Italian fascists the stereotypical view of women as housewives and mothers. Only under the relentless pressure of war did they reluctantly mobilize large numbers of German women for office and factory work.

Not all Germans supported Hitler, however, and a number of German groups actively resisted him after 1933. Tens of thousands of political enemies were imprisoned, and thousands were executed. In the first years of Hitler's rule, the principal resisters were trade union communists and socialists. The expansion of the SS system of terror after 1935 smashed most of these leftists. Catholic and Protestant churches produced a second group of opponents. Their efforts were directed primarily at preserving genuine religious life, however, not at overthrowing Hitler. Finally in 1938 (and again from 1942 to 1944) some high-ranking army officers, who feared the consequences of Hitler's reckless aggression, plotted, unsuccessfully, against him.

Aggression and Appeasement (1933–1939)

Although economic recovery and somewhat greater opportunity for social advancement won Hitler support, the guiding and unique concepts of Nazism remained space and race—the territorial expansion of the superior German race. As we shall see, German expansion was facilitated by the uncertain, divided, pacific Western democracies, which tried to buy off Hitler to avoid war.

Hitler realized that his aggressive policies had to be carefully camouflaged at first, for the Treaty of Versailles limited Germany's army to only a hundred thousand men. As Hitler told some army commanders in February 1933, the early stages of his policy of "conquest of new living space in the East and its ruthless Germanization" had serious dangers. If France had real leaders, Hitler said, it would "not give us time but attack us, presumably with its eastern satellites."[11] Thus while Hitler loudly proclaimed his peaceful intentions, Germany's withdrawal from the League of Nations in October 1933 indicated its determination to rearm. When in March 1935 Hitler established a general military draft and declared the "unequal" Versailles treaty disarmament clauses null and void, some European leaders appeared to understand the danger and warned him against future aggressive actions.

But the emerging united front against Hitler quickly collapsed. Britain adopted a policy of appeasement, granting Hitler everything he could reasonably want (and more) in order to avoid war. The last chance to stop the Nazis came in March 1936 when Hitler suddenly marched his armies into the demilitarized Rhineland, brazenly violating the Treaties of Versailles and Locarno. An uncertain France would not move without British support, however, and Britain refused to act (see Map 30.1).

British appeasement, which practically dictated French policy, lasted far into 1939. It was motivated by British feelings of guilt toward Germany and the pacifism of a population still horrified by the memory of the Great War. As in Germany, many powerful British conservatives underestimated Hitler. They also believed that Soviet communism was the real danger and that Hitler could be used to stop it. Such strong anticommunist feelings made an alliance between the Western Powers and Stalin unlikely.

As Britain and France opted for appeasement and the Soviet Union watched all developments suspiciously, Hitler found powerful allies. In 1935 the bombastic Mussolini attacked the independent African kingdom of Ethiopia. The Western Powers and the League of Nations piously condemned Italian aggression, but Hitler supported Italy energetically. In 1936 Italy and Germany signed an agreement on close cooperation, the so-called Rome-Berlin Axis. Japan, which wanted support for its occupation of Manchuria, soon joined the Axis alliance.

At the same time, Germany and Italy intervened in the Spanish civil war (1936–1939). Their support eventually

Primary Source: The Centerpiece of Nazi Racial Legislation: The Nuremberg Laws *These laws defined who was a Jew, forbade marriage between Germans and Jews, and paved the way for the Holocaust.*

● **Hitler's Success with Aggression** This biting criticism of appeasing leaders by the cartoonist David Low appeared shortly after Hitler remilitarized the Rhineland. Appeasement also appealed to millions of ordinary citizens in Britain and France who wanted to avoid another great war at any cost. *(Solo Syndication/Associated Newspapers)*

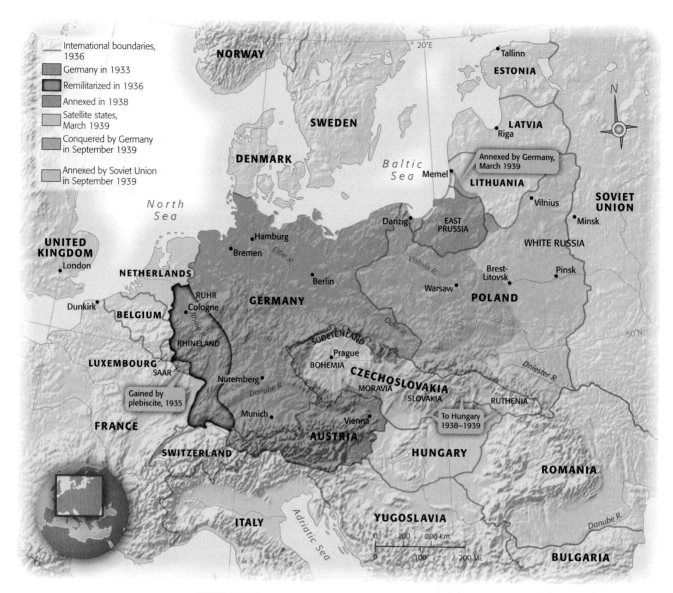

MAP 30.1 **The Growth of Nazi Germany, 1933–1939** Until March 1939, Hitler brought ethnic Germans into the Nazi state; then he turned on the Slavic peoples, whom he had always hated. He stripped Czechoslovakia of its independence and prepared for an attack on Poland in September 1939.

helped General Francisco Franco's fascist movement defeat republican Spain. Spain's only official aid came from the Soviet Union, for public opinion in Britain and especially in France was hopelessly divided on the Spanish question.

In late 1937 Hitler moved forward with his plans to crush Austria and Czechoslovakia as the first step in his long-contemplated drive to the east for living space. By threatening Austria with invasion, Hitler forced the Austrian chancellor in March 1938 to put local Nazis in control of the government. The next day German armies moved in unopposed, and Austria became two provinces of Greater Germany (see Map 30.1).

Simultaneously, Hitler began demanding that the pro-Nazi, German-speaking minority of western Czechoslovakia—the Sudetenland—be turned over to Germany. Democratic Czechoslovakia, however, was prepared to defend itself. Moreover, France had been Czechoslovakia's ally since 1924, and if France fought, the Soviet Union was pledged to help. War appeared inevitable, but appeasement triumphed again. In September 1938 Prime Minister Chamberlain flew to Germany three times in fourteen days. In these negotiations, to which the Soviet Union was deliberately not invited, Chamberlain and the French agreed with Hitler that the Sudetenland should be ceded to Germany immediately. Returning to London from the Munich Conference, Chamberlain told cheering crowds that he had secured "peace with honor . . . peace for our time." Sold out by the Western Powers, Czechoslovakia gave in.

Hitler's armies occupied the remainder of Czechoslovakia in March 1939. The effect on Western public opinion was electrifying. For the first time, there was no possible rationale of self-determination for Nazi aggression, because Hitler was treating the Czechs and Slovaks as captive peoples. When Hitler used the question of German minorities in Danzig as a pretext to confront Poland, a suddenly militant Chamberlain declared that Britain and France would fight if Hitler attacked his eastern neighbor. Hitler did not take these warnings seriously and decided to press on.

In an about-face that stunned the world, Hitler offered and Stalin signed a ten-year Nazi-Soviet nonaggression pact in August 1939. Each dictator promised to remain neutral if the other became involved in war. An attached secret protocol ruthlessly divided eastern Europe into German and Soviet zones "in the event of a political territorial reorganization." The British and French felt betrayed for they, too, had been negotiating with Stalin. But Stalin had remained distrustful of Western intentions, and Hitler had offered territorial gain.

For Hitler, everything was set. He told his generals on the day of the nonaggression pact, "My only fear is that at the last moment some dirty dog will come up with a mediation plan." On September 1, 1939, German armies and warplanes smashed into Poland from three sides. Two days later Britain and France, finally true to their word, declared war on Germany. The Second World War had begun.

THE SECOND WORLD WAR

How did Hitler's actions lead to another world war?

War broke out in both western and eastern Europe because Hitler's ambitions were essentially unlimited. On both war fronts Nazi soldiers scored enormous successes until late 1942, establishing a horrifyingly vast empire of death and destruction. Hitler's victories increased tensions in Asia between Japan and the United States and prompted Japan to attack the United States and overrun much of Southeast Asia. Yet reckless German and Japanese aggression also raised a mighty coalition determined to smash the aggressors. Led by Britain, the United States, and the Soviet Union, the Grand Alliance—to use Winston Churchill's favorite term—functioned quite effectively in military terms. Thus the Nazi and Japanese empires proved short-lived.

Hitler's Empire in Europe (1939–1942)

Using planes, tanks, and trucks in the first example of a **blitzkrieg,** or "lightning war," Hitler's armies crushed Poland in four weeks. The Soviet Union quickly took its part of the booty—the eastern half of Poland and the Baltic states of Lithuania, Estonia, and Latvia. In the west French and British armies dug in; they expected another war of attrition and economic blockade. But in spring 1940 the lightning war struck again. After occupying Denmark, Norway, and Holland, German motorized columns broke through southern Belgium and into France.

blitzkrieg *"Lightning war" using planes, tanks, and trucks, the first example of which Hitler used to crush Poland in four weeks.*

Events Leading to World War II

1919	Treaty of Versailles is signed; J. M. Keynes publishes *Economic Consequences of the Peace.*
1919–1920	U.S. Senate rejects the Treaty of Versailles.
1921	Germany is billed $33 billion in reparations.
1922	Mussolini seizes power in Italy; Germany proposes a moratorium on reparations.
January 1923	France and Belgium occupy the Ruhr; Germany orders passive resistance to the occupation.
October 1923	Stresemann agrees to reparations based on Germany's ability to pay.
1924	Dawes Plan: German reparations are reduced and put on a sliding scale; large U.S. loans to Germany are recommended to promote German recovery; Adolf Hitler dictates *Mein Kampf.*
1924–1929	Spectacular German economic recovery occurs; circular flow of international funds enables sizable reparations payments.
1925	Treaties of Locarno promote European security and stability.
1926	Germany joins the League of Nations.
1928	Kellogg-Briand Pact renounces war as an instrument of international affairs.
1929	U.S. stock market crashes.
1929–1939	Great Depression rages.
1931	Japan invades Manchuria.
1932	Nazis become the largest party in the Reichstag.
January 1933	Hitler is appointed chancellor of Germany.
March 1933	Reichstag passes the Enabling Act, granting Hitler absolute dictatorial power.
October 1933	Germany withdraws from the League of Nations.
1935	Nuremberg Laws deprive Jews of all rights of citizenship.
March 1935	Hitler announces German rearmament.
June 1935	Anglo-German naval agreement is signed.
October 1935	Mussolini invades Ethiopia and receives Hitler's support.
March 1936	German armies move unopposed into the demilitarized Rhineland.
July 1936	Civil war breaks out in Spain.
1937	Japan invades China; Rome-Berlin Axis in effect.
March 1938	Germany annexes Austria.
September 1938	Munich Conference: Britain and France agree to German seizure of the Sudetenland from Czechoslovakia.
March 1939	Germany occupies the rest of Czechoslovakia; appeasement ends in Britain.
August 1939	Nazi-Soviet nonaggression pact is signed.
September 1, 1939	Germany invades Poland.
September 3, 1939	Britain and France declare war on Germany.

As Hitler's armies poured into France, aging marshal Henri-Philippe Pétain formed a new French government—the so-called Vichy government—and accepted defeat. By July 1940 Hitler ruled practically all of western continental Europe; Italy was an ally, the Soviet Union a friendly neutral (see Map 30.2). Only Britain, led by the uncompromising Winston Churchill (1874–1965), remained unconquered.

To mount an amphibious invasion of Britain, Germany first needed to gain control of the air. In the Battle of Britain, up to a thousand German planes attacked British airfields and key factories in a single day, dueling with British defenders high in the skies. In September Hitler angrily began indiscriminately bombing British cities in an attempt to break British morale. British aircraft factories increased production, and the heavily bombed people of London defiantly dug in. In September and October 1940 Britain was beating Germany three to one in the air war. There was no possibility of an immediate German invasion of Britain.

Hitler now allowed his lifetime obsession with a vast eastern European empire for the "master race" to dictate policy. In June 1941 German armies suddenly attacked the Soviet Union along a vast front. By October Leningrad was practically surrounded, Moscow was besieged, and most of Ukraine had been conquered. But the Soviets did not collapse, and when a severe winter struck German armies outfitted in summer uniforms, the invaders were stopped.

Stalled in Russia, Hitler had come to rule an enormous European empire stretching from the outskirts of Moscow to the English Channel. He and the top Nazi leadership began building their **New Order.** In doing so, they showed what Nazi victory would have meant.

Hitler's New Order was based firmly on the guiding principle of Nazi totalitarianism: racial imperialism. Within this New Order the Nordic peoples—the Dutch, Norwegians, and Danes—received preferential treatment, for they were racially related to the Germans. The French, an "inferior" Latin people, occupied the middle position.

New Order *Hitler's program, based on the guiding principle of racial imperialism that gave preferential treatment to the Nordic peoples.*

● **London, 1940** Hitler believed that his relentless terror bombing of London—the "blitz"—could break the will of the British people. He was wrong. The blitz caused enormous destruction, but Londoners went about their business with courage and calm determination, as this unforgettable image of a milkman in the rubble suggests. *(Hulton-Deutsch Collection/Corbis)*

Slavs in the conquered eastern territories were treated with harsh hatred as "subhumans." Hitler envisioned a vast eastern colonial empire where Poles, Ukrainians, and Russians would be enslaved and forced to die out, while Germanic peasants resettled the resulting abandoned lands. Hitler needed countless helpers, however, and these accomplices came forth. Himmler and the elite SS corps shared Hitler's ideology of barbarous racial imperialism. Supported (or condoned) by military commanders and German policemen in the occupied territories, the SS corps pressed relentlessly to implement the program of destruction and to create a "mass settlement space" for Germans. Many Poles, captured communists, Gypsies, and Jehovah's Witnesses were murdered in cold blood.

MAP 30.2 **World War II in Europe** The map shows the extent of Hitler's empire at its height, before the Battle of Stalingrad in late 1942 and the subsequent advances of the Allies until Germany surrendered on May 7, 1945.

Finally, the Nazi state condemned all European Jews to extermination in the **Holocaust**. After the fall of Warsaw the Nazis began deporting all German Jews to occupied Poland, and in 1941 expulsion spiraled into extermination on the Russian front. Himmler's SS killing squads and regular army units forced Soviet Jews to dig giant pits, which became mass graves as the victims were lined up on the edge and cut down by machine guns. Then in late 1941 Hitler and the Nazi leadership, in some still-debated combination, ordered the SS to stop all Jewish emigration from Europe and speeded up planning for mass murder. All over the Nazi empire Jews were systematically arrested, packed like cattle onto freight trains, and dispatched to extermination camps.

Arriving at their destination, small numbers of Jews were sent to nearby slave labor camps, where they were starved and systematically worked to death. (See the feature "Individuals in Society: Primo Levi.") But most victims were taken by force or deception to "shower rooms," which were actually gas chambers. For fifteen to twenty minutes came the terrible screams and gasping sobs of men, women, and children choking to death on poison gas. Then, only silence. Special camp workers quickly yanked the victims' gold teeth from their jaws, and the bodies were then cremated, or sometimes boiled for oil to make soap. The extermination of European Jews was the ultimate monstrosity of Nazi racism and racial imperialism. By 1945, 6 million Jews had been murdered.

Who was responsible for this terrible crime? An older generation of historians usually laid most of the guilt on Hitler and the Nazi leadership. Ordinary Germans had little knowledge of the extermination camps, it was argued, and those who cooperated had no alternative given the brutality of Nazi terror and totalitarian control. But in recent years many studies have revealed a much broader participation of German people in the Holocaust and popular indifference (or worse) to the Jews' fate.

In most occupied countries, local non-German officials also cooperated in the arrest and deportation of Jews. As in Germany, only a few exceptional bystanders did not turn a blind eye. Thus some scholars have concluded that the key for most Germans (and most people in occupied countries) was that they felt no personal responsibility for Jews and therefore were not prepared to help them. This meant that many individuals, conditioned by Nazi racist propaganda but also influenced by peer pressure and brutalizing wartime violence, were psychologically prepared to perpetrate ever-greater crimes, from mistreatment to arrest to mass murder.

Holocaust *The attempted extermination of all European Jews by the Nazi state.*

> **Primary Source: Memoirs**
> *Read what the man responsible for administering and overseeing the Holocaust thought and felt about his "work."*

● **Prelude to Murder** This photo captures the terrible inhumanity of Nazi racism. Frightened and bewildered families from the soon-to-be-destroyed Warsaw Ghetto are being forced out of their homes by German soldiers for deportation to concentration camps. There they face murder in the gas chambers. *(Hulton Archive/Getty Images)*

Japan's Asian Empire

By late 1938, 1.5 million Japanese troops were bogged down in China, holding a great swath of territory but unable to defeat the Nationalists and the Communists (see pages 868–870). Nor had Japan succeeded in building a large, self-sufficient Asian economic zone, for it still depended on oil and scrap metal from the Netherlands East Indies and the United States. Thus Japanese leaders followed events in Europe closely, looking for alliances and actions that might improve their position in Asia. At home they gave free rein to the anti-Western ultranationalism that had risen in the 1920s and 1930s (see pages 866, 868): proclaiming Japan's liberating mission in Asia; glorifying the warrior virtues of honor and sacrifice; and demanding absolute devotion to the semidivine emperor. (See the feature "Listening to the Past: Radical Nationalism for Japanese Students" on pages 934–935).

The outbreak of war in Europe in 1939 and Hitler's early victories opened up opportunities for the Japanese in Asia. In China the Japanese redoubled their brutal efforts to crush peasant support for the Nationalists and the Communists. Implementing a brutal "three-alls" policy—"kill all, burn all, destroy all"—Japanese troops massacred whole villages, torched buildings, slaughtered farm animals, and committed shocking atrocities. In March 1940 the Japanese set up a Chinese puppet government in Nanjing, but the fighting—and the atrocities—continued until the war ended.

In Southeast Asia European empires appeared vulnerable. In September 1940 Japan signed a formal alliance with Germany and Italy and forced the French to accept Japanese domination of northern French Indochina. The United States had repeatedly condemned Japanese aggression in China. Now the United States also opposed Japanese expansion, because it feared that embattled Britain would collapse if it lost the support of its Asian colonies. Applying economic sanctions in October 1940, the United States stopped scrap iron sales to Japan and later froze all Japanese assets in the United States.

Japan's invasion of southern Indochina in July 1941 further worsened relations with the United States. President Franklin Roosevelt demanded that Japan withdraw from China, keeping only Manchuria. Japan refused. The United States responded by cutting off U.S. oil sales to Japan and thereby reducing Japan's oil supplies by 90 percent. Japanese leaders now increasingly believed that war with the United States was inevitable, for Japan's battle fleet would run out of fuel in eighteen months and its industry would be crippled. After much debate Japanese leaders decided to launch a surprise attack on the United States. They hoped to cripple their Pacific rival, gain time to build a defensible Asian empire, and eventually win an ill-defined compromise peace.

The Japanese attack on the U.S. naval base at Pearl Harbor in the Hawaiian Islands was a complete surprise but a limited success. On December 7, 1941, the Japanese sank or crippled every American battleship, but by chance all the American aircraft carriers were at sea and escaped unharmed. This enabled rapid American recovery, because aircraft carriers dominated the Pacific war. More important, most Americans felt superior to the Japanese, and they were humiliated by this unexpected defeat. Pearl Harbor overwhelmed American isolationism and brought Americans together in a spirit of anger and revenge.

Hitler immediately declared war on the United States. Simultaneously, Japanese armies successfully attacked European and American colonies in Southeast Asia. Japanese armies were small (because most soldiers remained in China), but they were well trained, well led, and highly motivated. They defeated larger Dutch and British armies to seize the Netherlands East Indies and its rich oil fields, and the British colonies of Hong Kong, Malaya, and Singapore. After American forces surrendered the Philippines in May 1942, Japan held a vast empire in Southeast Asia and the western Pacific (see Map 30.3).

Primo Levi

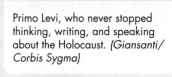

Most Jews deported to Auschwitz were murdered as soon as they arrived, but the Nazis made some prisoners into slave laborers and a few of these survived. Primo Levi (1919–1987), an Italian Jew, became one of the most influential witnesses to the Holocaust and its death camps.

Like much of Italy's small Jewish community, Levi's family belonged to the urban professional classes. The young Primo graduated in 1941 from the University of Turin with highest honors in chemistry. But since 1938, when Italy introduced racial laws, he had faced growing discrimination, and two years after graduation he joined the antifascist resistance movement. Quickly captured, he was deported to Auschwitz with 650 Italian Jews in February 1944. Stone-faced SS men picked only ninety-six men and twenty-nine women to work in their respective labor camps. Primo was one of them.

Nothing prepared Levi for what he encountered. The Jewish prisoners were kicked, punched, stripped, branded with tattoos, crammed into huts, and worked unmercifully. Hoping for some sign of prisoner solidarity in this terrible environment, Levi found only a desperate struggle of each against all and enormous status differences among prisoners. Many stunned and bewildered newcomers, beaten and demoralized by their bosses—the most privileged prisoners—simply collapsed and died. Others struggled to secure their own privileges, however small, because food rations and working conditions were so abominable that ordinary Jewish prisoners perished in two to three months.

Sensitive and noncombative, Levi found himself sinking into oblivion. But instead of joining the mass of the "drowned," he became one of the "saved"—a complicated surprise with moral implications that he would ponder all his life. As Levi explained in *Survival in Auschwitz* (1947), the usual road to salvation in the camps was some kind of collaboration with German power.* Savage German criminals were released from prison to become brutal camp guards; non-Jewish political prisoners competed for jobs entitling them to better conditions; and, especially troubling for Levi, a small number of Jewish men plotted and struggled

*Primo Levi, *Survival in Auschwitz: The Nazi Assault on Humanity,* rev. ed. 1958 (London: Collier Books, 1961), pp. 79–84, and *The Drowned and the Saved* (New York: Summit Books, 1988). These powerful testimonies are highly recommended.

for the power of life and death over other Jewish prisoners. Though not one of these Jewish bosses, Levi believed that he himself, like almost all survivors, had entered the "gray zone" of moral compromise. Only a very few superior individuals, "the stuff of saints and martyrs," survived the death camps without shifting their moral stance.

Primo Levi, who never stopped thinking, writing, and speaking about the Holocaust. *(Giansanti/Corbis Sygma)*

For Levi, compromise and salvation came from his profession. Interviewed by a German technocrat for the camp's synthetic rubber program, Levi performed brilliantly in scientific German and savored his triumph as a Jew over Nazi racism. Work in the warm camp laboratory offered Levi opportunities to pilfer equipment that could then be traded for food and necessities with other prisoners. Levi also gained critical support from three saintly prisoners who refused to do wicked and hateful acts. And he counted "luck" as essential for his survival: in the camp infirmary with scarlet fever in February 1945 as advancing Russian armies prepared to liberate the camp, Levi was not evacuated by the Nazis and shot to death like most Jewish prisoners.

After the war Primo Levi was forever haunted by the nightmare that the Holocaust would be ignored or forgotten. Always ashamed that so many people whom he considered better than himself had perished, he wrote and lectured tirelessly to preserve the memory of Jewish victims and guilty Nazis. Wanting the world to understand the Jewish genocide in all its complexity so that never again would people tolerate such atrocities, he grappled tirelessly with his vision of individual choice and moral compromise in a hell designed to make the victims collaborate and persecute each other.

Questions for Analysis

1. Describe Levi's experience at Auschwitz. How did camp prisoners treat each other? Why?

2. What does Levi mean by the "gray zone"? How is this concept central to his thinking?

3. Will a vivid historical memory of the Holocaust help prevent future genocide?

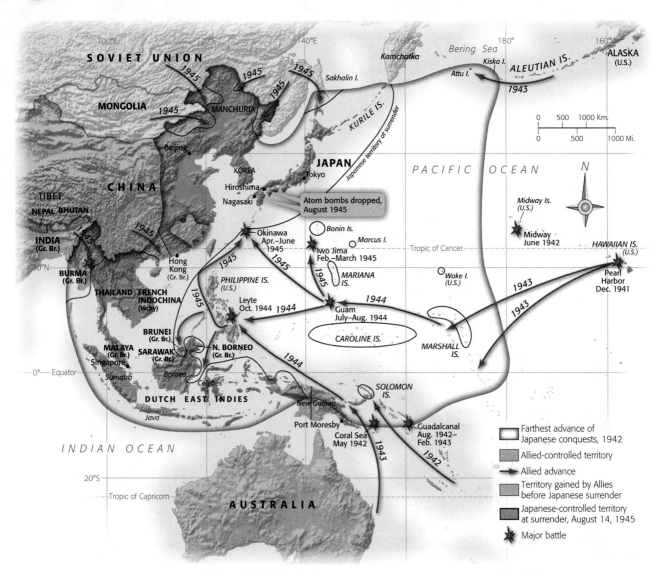

MAP 30.3 **World War II in the Pacific** Japanese forces overran an enormous amount of territory in 1942, which the Allies slowly recaptured in a long, bitter struggle. As this map shows, Japan still held a large Asian empire in August 1945, when the unprecedented devastation of atomic warfare suddenly forced it to surrender.

The Japanese claimed they were freeing Asians from Western imperialism, and they called their empire the Greater East Asian Co-prosperity Sphere. Some, perhaps many, Japanese army officers and officials sincerely believed that they were creating a mutually advantageous union for Asia's long-term development. Initially they tapped currents of nationalist sentiment, and most local populations were glad to see the Western Powers go. But Asian faith in "co-prosperity" and support for Japan steadily declined as the war went on. Why was this so?

A key factor was that although the Japanese set up anticolonial governments and promised genuine independence, real power always rested with Japanese military commanders and their superiors in Tokyo. The "independent" governments established in the Philippines, French Indochina, Burma, and the Netherlands East Indies were basically shams. Moreover, the Japanese never treated local populations as equals.

● **The War in the Philippines** U.S. and Philippine forces held out on the Bataan peninsula until April 1942, when seventy-six thousand soldiers surrendered to the Japanese military. Most of the prisoners were sick, wounded, or suffering from malnutrition, and the Japanese systematically executed many of them. Other prisoners, such as those pictured here, were marched to exhaustion without water in the blazing sun on the infamous Bataan Death March, and many were bayoneted or beaten to death. (Bettmann/Corbis)

As Japanese living standards plummeted and heavy industry sputtered, the Japanese occupiers exploited local peoples for Japan's wartime needs. They cut wages, imposed supply quotas on raw materials, and drafted local people for military and labor service. Ships left for Japan laden with rice, oil, and raw materials, but they returned empty, if they returned at all.

The Japanese often exhibited great cruelty toward prisoners of war and civilians, as they had toward the Chinese since 1937. After the fall of Hong Kong in December 1941, for example, wounded prisoners there were murdered and burned, and there was a mass rape of nurses. Elsewhere Korean, Dutch, and Indonesian women were forced into sexual bondage, providing sex for Japanese soldiers as "comfort women." Recurring cruel behavior also aroused local populations against the invaders.

The Grand Alliance

While the Nazis and the Japanese built their savage empires, the Allies faced the hard fact that chance, rather than choice, had brought them together. Stalin had been cooperating fully with Hitler between August 1939 and June 1941, and only the Japanese attack on Pearl Harbor in December 1941 had overwhelmed powerful isolationism in the United States.

As a first step toward building an unshakable alliance, U.S. president Franklin D. Roosevelt accepted the policy of **"Europe first"** as proposed by Winston Churchill (Chamberlain's successor as British prime minister). Only after Hitler was defeated would the United States turn toward the Pacific for an all-out attack on Japan, the lesser threat. The Americans and the British also put immediate military needs first, consistently postponing tough political questions relating to the eventual peace settlement that might have split the alliance.

To further encourage mutual trust, the Allies adopted the principle of the "unconditional surrender" of Germany and Japan. This policy cemented the Grand Alliance because it denied Germany and Japan any hope of dividing their foes.

"Europe first" *The military strategy, set forth by Churchill and adopted by Roosevelt, that called for the defeat of Hitler in Europe before the United States launched an all-out strike against Japan in the Pacific.*

The Grand Alliance's military resources were awesome. The United States possessed a unique capacity to wage global war with its mighty industry, large population, and national unity. These were all harnessed in 1942 to gear up rapidly for all-out war. In 1943 America out produced not only Germany, Italy, and Japan but also all of the rest of the world combined.[12]

Britain continued to make a great contribution as well. The British economy was totally and effectively mobilized, and the sharing of burdens through rationing and heavy taxes on war profits maintained social harmony. Britain, the impregnable floating fortress, became a gigantic frontline staging area for the decisive blow to the heart of Germany.

As for the Soviet Union, so great was its strength that it might well have defeated Germany without Western help. In the face of the German advance, whole factories and populations were successfully evacuated to eastern Russia and Siberia. There war production was reorganized and expanded, and the Red Army was increasingly well supplied and well led. Above all, Stalin drew on the massive support and heroic determination of the Soviet people, especially those in the central Russian heartland. Broad-based Russian nationalism, as opposed to narrow communist ideology, became the powerful unifying force in what the Soviet people appropriately called the "Great Patriotic War of the Fatherland."

Finally, the United States, Britain, and the Soviet Union had the resources of much of the world at their command. They were also aided by a growing resistance movement against the Nazis throughout Europe, even in Germany. After the Soviet Union was invaded in June 1941, communists throughout Europe took the lead in the underground resistance, joined by a growing number of patriots, Christians, and agents sent by governments-in-exile in London.

The War in Europe (1942–1945)

Barely halted at the gates of Moscow and Leningrad in 1941, the Germans renewed their offensive against the Soviet Union in 1942 and attacked the southern city of Stalingrad in July. In November 1942 Soviet armies counterattacked, quickly surrounding the entire German Sixth Army of 300,000 men. By late January 1943 only 123,000 soldiers were left to surrender. Hitler, who had refused to allow a retreat, suffered a catastrophic defeat. In summer 1943 the larger, better-equipped Soviet armies took the offensive and began moving forward (see Map 30.2).

Not yet prepared to attack Germany directly through France, the Western Allies saw heavy fighting in North Africa (see Map 30.2). In summer 1942 British forces finally defeated combined German and Italian armies at the Battle of El Alamein, only seventy miles from Alexandria. Almost immediately thereafter an Anglo-American force landed in Morocco and Algeria. These French possessions, which were under the control of Pétain's Vichy French government, quickly went over to the Allied side.

Having driven the Axis powers from North Africa by spring 1943, Allied forces invaded Italy. War-weary Italians deposed Mussolini, and the new Italian government publicly accepted unconditional surrender in September 1943. Italy, it seemed, was liberated. But then German commandos in a daring raid rescued Mussolini and put him at the head of a puppet government. German armies seized Rome and all of northern Italy. Fighting continued in Italy.

Indeed, bitter fighting continued in Europe for almost two years. Germany, less fully mobilized for war than Britain in 1941, applied itself to total war in 1942 and enlisted millions of German women and millions of prisoners of war and slave laborers from all across occupied Europe in that effort. Between early 1942 and July 1944 German war production actually tripled in spite of heavy bombing by the British and American air forces. Terrorized at home and frightened by the prospect of unconditional surrender, the Germans fought on with suicidal stoicism.

On June 6, 1944, American and British forces under General Dwight Eisenhower landed on the beaches of Normandy, France, in history's greatest naval invasion. In a hundred dramatic days more than 2 million men and almost a half million vehicles pushed inland and broke through German lines. Rejecting proposals to strike straight at Berlin in a massive attack, Eisenhower moved forward cautiously on a broad front. Not until March 1945 did American troops cross the Rhine and enter Germany.

The Soviets, who had been advancing steadily since July 1943, reached the outskirts of Warsaw by August 1944. On April 26, 1945 the Red Army met American forces on the Elbe River. The Allies had closed their vise on Nazi Germany and overrun Europe. As Soviet forces fought their way into Berlin, Hitler committed suicide in his bunker, and on May 7 the remaining German commanders capitulated.

● **The Normandy Invasion, Omaha Beach, June 6, 1944** Airborne paratroopers landed behind German coastal fortifications around midnight, and U.S. and British forces hit several beaches at daybreak as Allied ships and bombers provided cover. U.S. troops secured full control of Omaha Beach by nightfall, but at a price of three thousand casualties. Allied air power prevented the Germans from bringing up reserves and counterattacking. *(Naval Historical Foundation, Washington, D.C.)*

The War in the Pacific (1942–1945)

While gigantic armies clashed on land in Europe, the greatest naval battles in history decided the fate of warring nations in Asia. In April 1942 the Japanese devised a complicated battle plan to take Port Moresby in New Guinea and also destroy U.S. aircraft carriers in an attack on Midway Island (see Map 30.3). Having broken the secret Japanese code, the Americans skillfully deployed the small number of ships at their disposal and won decisive naval victories. First, in the Battle of the Coral Sea in May 1942, an American carrier force halted the Japanese advance on Port Moresby and relieved Australia from the threat of invasion. Then, in the Battle of Midway in June 1942, American carrier-based pilots sank all four of the attacking Japanese aircraft carriers and established overall naval equality with Japan in the Pacific.

● **"Follow Me!"** This painting by Charles McBarron, Jr., shows the action at Red Beach on October 20, 1944, in the Battle of Leyte Gulf in the Philippine Islands. It captures the danger and courage of U.S. troops, which had to storm well-fortified Japanese positions again and again in their long island-hopping campaign. The officer exhorts his men, and death is all around. *(The Granger Collection, New York)*

Badly hampered in the ground war by the Europe first policy, the United States gradually won control of the sea and air as it geared up massive production of aircraft carriers, submarines, and fighter planes. By 1943 the United States was producing one hundred thousand aircraft a year, almost twice as many as Japan produced in the entire war. By 1944 hundreds of American submarines were hunting in "wolf packs," decimating shipping and destroying economic links in Japan's far-flung, overextended empire. In July 1943 the Americans and their Australian allies opened an "island-hopping" campaign toward Japan. Pounding Japanese forces on a given island with saturation bombing, American army and marine units would then hit the beaches with rifles and flamethrowers and secure victory in hand-to-hand combat.

The Pacific war was brutal—a "war without mercy," in the words of a leading American scholar—and atrocities were committed on both sides.[13] Aware of Japanese atrocities in China and the Philippines, the U.S. Marines and Army troops seldom took Japanese prisoners after the Battle of Guadalcanal in August 1942, killing even those rare Japanese soldiers who offered to surrender. American forces moving across the central and western Pacific in 1943 and 1944 faced unyielding resistance and this resistance hardened American hearts as American casualties kept rising. A product of spiraling violence, mutual hatred, and dehumanizing racial stereotypes, the war without mercy intensified as it moved toward Japan.

In June 1944 giant U.S. bombers began a relentless bombing campaign of the Japanese home islands. In October 1944 American forces under General Douglas MacArthur landed on Leyte Island in the Philippines. The Japanese believed they could destroy MacArthur's troops and transport ships before the main American fleet arrived. The result was the four-day Battle of Leyte Gulf, the greatest battle in naval history, with 282 ships involved. The Japanese lost 13 large warships, including

Primary Source:
The Decision to Use the Atomic Bomb
Learn why President Truman was advised to drop atomic bombs on Japan—from the chairman of the committee that gave him that advice.

4 aircraft carriers, while the Americans lost only 3 small ships in their great triumph. The Japanese navy was practically finished.

In spite of massive defeats, Japanese troops continued to fight with enormous courage and determination. Indeed, the bloodiest battles of the Pacific war took place on Iwo Jima in February 1945 and on Okinawa in June 1945. MacArthur and his commanders believed the conquest of Japan might cost a million American casualties and possibly 10 million to 20 million Japanese lives. In fact, Japan was almost helpless, its industry and dense, fragile wooden cities largely destroyed by incendiary bombing and uncontrollable hurricanes of fire. Yet the Japanese seemed determined to fight on, if only with bamboo spears, ever ready to die for a hopeless cause.

On August 6 and 9, 1945, the United States dropped atomic bombs on Hiroshima and Nagasaki in Japan. Mass bombing of cities and civilians, one of the terrible new practices of World War II, had led to the final nightmare—unprecedented human destruction in a single blinding flash. On August 14, 1945, the Japanese announced their surrender. The Second World War, which had claimed the lives of more than 50 million soldiers and civilians, was over.

● **A Hiroshima Survivor Remembers** Yasuko Yamagata was seventeen when she saw the brilliant blue-white "lightning flash" that became a fiery orange ball consuming everything that would burn. Thirty years later Yamagata painted this scene, her most unforgettable memory of the atomic attack. An incinerated woman, poised as if running with her baby clutched to her breast, lies near a water tank piled high with charred corpses. (Courtsey, Hiroshima Peace Memorial Museum)

Chapter Summary

To assess your mastery of this chapter, go to
bedfordstmartins.com/mckayworld

• *What was the nature of twentieth-century dictatorships and authoritarian rule?*

The Second World War marked the climax of the tremendous practical and spiritual maladies of the age of anxiety, which led in many lands to the rise of dictatorships. Many of these dictatorships were variations on conservative authoritarianism, but there was also a fateful innovation—a new kind of radical dictatorship that was exceptionally dynamic and theoretically unlimited in its actions. The totalitarian regimes formed in the 1920s and 1930s—specifically in Hitler's Germany and Stalin's Russia, and to a lesser extent in Mussolini's Italy, Franco's Spain, Hirohito's Japan, and Salazar's Portugal—were violent, dynamic, and profoundly antiliberal. They all, to a greater or lesser extent, asserted a total claim on the lives of their citizens, posed ambitious goals, and demanded popular support. Stalin's Russia and Hitler's Germany in particular

Key Terms

totalitarianism
fascism
five-year plan
New Economic Policy (NEP)
collectivization
kulaks
Black Shirts
Lateran Agreement
Nazism
Führer
Enabling Act
blitzkrieg
New Order
Holocaust
"Europe first"

exuded tremendous dynamism and awesome power. That dynamism, however, was channeled in quite different directions. Stalin and the Communist Party aimed at building their kind of socialism and the new socialist personality at home. Hitler and the Nazi elite aimed at unlimited territorial and racial aggression on behalf of a "master race"; domestic recovery was only a means to that end.

• How were the five-year plans part of the totalitarian order in the Soviet Union?

The five-year plans initiated in the Soviet Union in 1928 were a critical part of Stalin's efforts to totally control the Russian economy and society. Meant to introduce a "revolution from above," the plans were extremely ambitious efforts to modernize and industrialize the U.S.S.R. along socialist lines and to create a new socialist humanity. They set staggering industrial and agricultural objectives and replaced private lands with (often forced) collectivization. Labor unions were severely weakened, and foreign experts from Europe and America were brought in to lend their skill and expertise to the building of new factories and machinery in order to catch up with the more advanced capitalist nations of the West.

• How was Italian fascism a halfway house between conservative authoritarianism and modern totalitarianism?

In Italy Mussolini's hatred of liberalism led him to set up the first fascist government. Although brutal in its methods, it was never truly a totalitarian state on the order of Hitler's Germany or Stalin's Soviet Union. Mussolini did create a one-party dictatorship by abolishing press freedoms, disbanding independent trade unions, rigging elections, and ruling by decree. Mussolini allowed the old conservative classes to retain control of the economy, army, and the state bureaucracy. He gained the support of the Roman Catholic Church by recognizing the Vatican as a tiny independent state in 1929. Racial laws were never a very significant aspect of Mussolini's rule, as they were for Hitler, and Jews were not severely persecuted until Italy came under Nazi control toward the end of World War II. Thus, though repressive and undemocratic, fascist Italy was never really a totalitarian state.

• Why were Hitler and his Nazi regime initially so popular?

Hitler created a model totalitarian state in Germany, initially with the support of most of the German people. Hitler began by drawing on the anger and sense of betrayal many Germans felt after losing the Great War, and the humiliation of the terms of the Versailles Treaty. The war was followed by a period of astronomical inflation and unemployment. He added to the economic and patriotic discontent by drawing on the racist sentiments about "inferior" peoples, such as the Jews and the Slavs, which had deep roots in German history and culture. He convinced many Germans that Jews and Marxists had caused Germany to lose the war, and that a worldwide Jewish conspiracy continued to harm German culture, German unity, and the German race. Hitler was also a master of mass propaganda and political showmanship and effectively used the new propaganda tools of the movies and the radio to reach mass audiences. When the Great Depression struck, Hitler appealed to people's economic welfare, and made great promises that caused voters to desert the old leaders and turn to this dynamic new voice. Finally, Hitler was successful in gaining the support of Germany's young people by directly answering their needs and concerns, by appointing young party members to positions of power, and by emphasizing rapid change, national recovery, and personal advancement.

• *How did Hitler's actions lead to another world war?*

Hitler and his Nazi followers' genocidal racism and unlimited aggression made war inevitable, first with the western European democracies, then with hated eastern neighbors, and finally with the United States. Plunging Europe into the ultimate nightmare, unlimited aggression unwittingly forged a mighty coalition that smashed the racist Nazi empire and its leader. In the words of the ancient Greeks, he whom the gods would destroy, they first make mad.

Suggested Reading

Applebaum, Anne. *Gulag.* 2004. An excellent survey of Stalin's labor-death camps.

Arendt, Hannah. *The Origins of Totalitarianism.* 1951. Controversial, classic philosophical-historical study.

Brendon, Piers. *The Dark Valley. A Panorama of the 1930s.* Masterful, sweeping account of this tumultuous decade.

Brooker, Paul. *Twentieth Century Dictatorships: The Ideological One-Party State.* 1995. Comparative analysis.

Fitzpatrick, Sheila. *Everyday Stalinism: Ordinary Life in Extraordinary Times.* 1999. Social and cultural history.

Gilbert, Martin. *The Second World War: A Complete History,* rev. ed. 2004. Massively detailed global survey.

Glantz, David M. *When Titans Clashed: How the Red Army Stopped Hitler.* 1995. Authoritative account of the Eastern Front in World War II.

Hasegawa, Tsuyoshi. *Racing the Enemy: Stalin, Truman and the Surrender of Japan.* 2005. Masterful diplomatic history with controversial new account of the end of the war.

Hillberg, Raul. *The Destruction of the European Jews, 1933–1945,* rev. ed. 3 vols. 1985. A monumental classic.

Hsiung, James C., and Seven Levine, eds. *China's Bitter Victory: The War with Japan, 1937–1945.* 1992. Investigates various aspects of the long struggle.

Keegan, John. *The Second World War.* 1990. Broad survey by a distinguished military historian.

Kershaw, Ian. *The Nazi Dictatorship, Problems and Perspectives of Interpretation,* 2nd ed. 1989. Interpretive, historiographical.

Levi, Primo. *Survival at Auschwitz.* 1947. First published in English as *If This Is a Man;* memoir and meditation on the meaning of survival.

Lewin, Moshe. *The Making of the Soviet System.* 1985. Social history, especially agrarian.

Marrus, Michael. *The Holocaust in History.* 1987. Classic interpretive survey.

Weinberg, Gerhard. *World at Arms: A Global History of World War II.* 1994. Global survey with political-diplomatic emphasis.

Wright, Gordon. *The Ordeal of Total War,* rev. ed. 1997. Explores scientific, psychological, and economic dimensions of the war.

Notes

1. A. Gleason, *Totalitarianism: The Inner History of the Cold War* (New York: Oxford University Press, 1995), p. 50.

2. E. Halévy, *The Era of Tyrannies* (Garden City, N.Y.: Doubleday, 1965), pp. 265–316, esp. p. 300.

3. I. Kershaw, *The Nazi Dictatorship: Problems and Perspectives of Interpretation,* 2d ed. (London: Edward Arnold, 1989), p. 34.

4. Quoted in A. G. Mazour, *Soviet Economic Development: Operation Outstrip, 1921–1965* (Princeton, N.J.: Van Nostrand, 1967), p. 130.

5. Quoted in I. Deutscher, *Stalin: A Political Biography,* 2d ed. (New York: Oxford University Press, 1967), p. 325.

6. M. Malia, *The Soviet Tragedy: A History of Socialism in Russia* (New York: Free Press, 1994), p. 248.

7. R. Thurston, *Life and Terror in Stalin's Russia, 1934–1941* (New Haven, Conn.: Yale University Press, 1996), esp. pp. 16–106; and Malia, *The Soviet Tragedy,* pp. 227–270.

8. R. Vivarelli, "Interpretations on the Origins of Fascism," *Journal of Modern History* 63 (March 1991): 41.

9. W. Brustein, *The Logic of Evil: The Social Origins of the Nazi Party, 1925–1933* (New Haven, Conn.: Yale University Press, 1996), pp. 52, 182.

10. Quoted in R. Stromberg, *An Intellectual History of Modern Europe* (New York: Appleton-Century-Crofts, 1966), p. 393.

11. Quoted in K. D. Bracher, *The German Dictatorship: The Origins, Structure and Effects of National Socialism* (New York: Praeger, 1970), p. 289.

12. H. Willmott, *The Great Crusade: A New Complete History of the Second World War* (New York: Free Press, 1989), p. 255.

13. J. Dower, *War Without Mercy: Race and Power in the Pacific War* (New York: Pantheon, 1986).

Listening to the PAST

Radical Nationalism for Japanese Students

In August 1941, only four months before Japan's coordinated attack on Pearl Harbor and colonial empires in Southeast Asia, Japan's Ministry of Education issued "The Way of Subjects." Required reading for high school and university students, this twenty-page pamphlet summed up the basic tenets of Japanese ultranationalism, which had become dominant in the 1930s.

As this selection suggests, ultranationalism in Japan combined a sense of mission with intense group solidarity and unquestioning devotion to a semidivine emperor. Thus Japanese expansion into Manchuria and the war in China were part of Japan's sacred calling to protect the throne and to free Asia from Western exploitation and misrule. Of course, an unknown percentage of students (and adults) did not believe that the myths of Japan's state religion were literally true. Nevertheless, they were profoundly influenced by extremist nationalism: Japanese soldiers' determination to fight to the death was a prime indicator of that influence.

The way of the subjects of the Emperor issues from the policy of the Emperor and is to guard and maintain the Imperial Throne coexistent with the Heavens and the Earth. This is not an abstract principle but a way of daily practices based on history. The life and activities of the nation are all attuned to the task of strengthening the foundation of the Empire. . . .

Modern history, in a nutshell, has been marked by the formation of unified nations in Europe and their contests for supremacy in the acquisition of colonies. . . . Their march into all parts of the world paved the way for their subsequent world domination politically, economically, and culturally and led them to believe that they alone were justified in their outrageous behavior. . . .

The thoughts that have formed the foundation of Western civilization since the early modern period are individualism, liberalism, materialism, and so on. These thoughts regard the strong preying on the weak as reasonable, unstintedly promote the pursuit of luxury and pleasure, encourage materialism, and stimulate competition for acquiring colonies and

securing trade, thereby leading the world to a veritable hell of fighting and bloodshed [in the First World War]. . . . [Thereafter] a vigorous movement was started by Britain, France, and the United States to maintain the status quo by any means. Simultaneously, a movement aiming at social revolution through class conflict on the basis of thoroughgoing materialism like Communism also vigorously developed. On the other hand, Nazism and Fascism arose with great force. The basic principles of the totalitarianism in Germany and Italy are to remove the evils of individualism and liberalism.

That these [totalitarian] principles show great similarity to Eastern culture and spirit is a noteworthy fact that suggests the future of Western civilization and the creation of a new culture. Thus, the orientation of world history has made the collapse of the old world order a certainty. Japan has hereby initiated the construction of a new world order based on moral principles.

The Manchurian Affair [the Japanese invasion of Manchuria in 1931] was a violent outburst of Japanese national life long suppressed. Taking advantage of this, Japan in the glare of all the Powers made a step toward the creation of a world based on moral principles and the construction of a new order. This was a manifestation of the spirit, profound and lofty, embodied in the founding of Empire, and an unavoidable action for its national life and world mission. . . .

The general tendency of world domination by Europe and America has begun to show signs of a change since the Russo-Japanese War of 1904–05. Japan's victory attracted the attention of the entire world, and this caused a reawakening of Asiatic countries, which had been forced to lie prostrate under British and American influence, with the result that an independence movement was started.

Hopes to be free of the shackles and bondage of Europe and America were ablaze among the nations of India, Turkey, Arabia, Thailand, Vietnam, and others. This also inspired a new national movement in China. Amid this stormy atmosphere of Asia's reawakening,

Japan has come to be keenly conscious of the fact that the stabilization of East Asia is her mission, and that the emancipation of East Asian nations rests solely on her efforts. . . .

Japan has a political mission to help various regions in the Greater East Asian Co-prosperity Sphere [the Japanese term for Japan's Asian empire], which are reduced to a state of quasi-colony by Europe and America, and rescue them from their control. Economically, this country will have to eradicate the evils of their exploitation and then set up an economic structure for coexistence and co-prosperity. Culturally, Japan must strive to fashion East Asian nations to abandon their following of European and American culture and to develop Eastern culture for the purpose of contributing to the creation of a just world. The East has been left to destruction for the past several hundred years. Its rehabilitation is not an easy task. It is natural that unusual difficulties attend the establishment of a new order and the creation of a new culture. Overcoming these difficulties will do much to help in establishing a world dominated by morality, in which all nations can co-operate and all people can secure their proper positions. . . .

In Japan, the Emperors of a line unbroken for ages eternal govern and reign over it, as the Heavens and the Earth endure, since the Imperial Foundress, Amaterasu-o-Mikami, . . . caused Her grandson Ninigi-no-Mikoto to descend on the eight great countries and She commanded him, saying: "This country, fruitful and abounding in rice, is the land over which Our descendants shall rule. Go you, therefore, down and reign over it. Under you and your offspring it shall prosper as long as the Heavens and the Earth endure." . . .

The Imperial Family is [therefore] the fountain source of the Japanese nation, and national and private lives issue from this. In the past, foreign nationals came to this country only to enjoy the benevolent rule of the Imperial Family, and became Japanese subjects spiritually and by blood. The Imperial virtues are so great and boundless that all are assimilated into one.

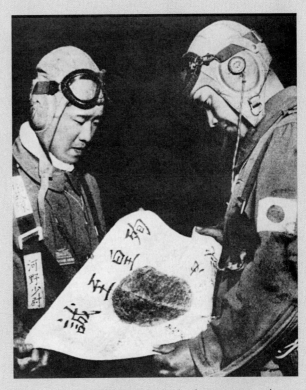

Kamikaze pilots ponder the message on the flag that they will take on their suicide mission: "All for the Emperor, we are happy to die for him." *(Archives Mondadori, Milan)*

Here is the reason for the present glorious state, in which the Emperor and his subjects are harmonized into one great unit. That the myriad subjects with one mind are glad to be unified in their devotion to the Throne is the substance of the Imperial subjects.

The way of the subjects is to be loyal to the Emperor in disregard of self. . . . To serve the Emperor is its key point. Our lives will become sincere and true when they are offered to the Emperor and the state. . . . All must be unified under the Emperor. Herein lies the significance of national life in Japan.

Questions for Analysis

1. How does "The Way of Subjects" interpret modern history? In what ways do Western thought and action threaten Japan?

2. What is Japan's mission in Asia?

3. What is the basis of Japanese sovereignty? What is the individual's proper role in society?

Source: "The Way of Subjects," in *Tokyo Record,* copyright 1943 by Otto D. Tolischus and renewed 1970 by Naya G. Tolischus. Reprinted by permission of Houghton Mifflin Harcourt Publishing Company.

Duck and Cover. These American schoolchildren in the 1950s practice the "duck and cover" drill in the event of a nuclear attack from the Soviet Union. *(Bettmann/Corbis)*

chapter

31

GLOBAL RECOVERY AND DIVISION BETWEEN SUPERPOWERS

After the defeat of the Axis powers in Europe and of Japan in Asia, recovery began around the world from this most devastating war. Hopes of world peace quickly faded, however, when differences in Allied economic and political ideologies set aside during wartime came to the fore. A three-part global division soon developed. The democratic and capitalist "First World"—the United States and its allies, including Japan—confronted the Marxist communist "Second World"—the Soviet Union and its allies. The "Third World," the often newly independent and so-called nonaligned nations of Latin America, Africa, and Asia, were forced to negotiate with the other two. This chapter discusses the First and Second Worlds and the cold war they fought for forty years.

After World War II, a battered western Europe once again had to dig itself out from under rubble. Having avoided wartime destruction and occupation, the United States, Canada, Australia, and New Zealand quickly converted their economies to peacetime production. After seven years of Allied occupation, Japan began the economic recovery and social transformation that by the 1960s made it one of the world's leading economic powers. Having experienced massive death and destruction in two world wars, the Soviet Union sought to protect itself from future attacks from the west by occupying eastern Europe and establishing communist dictatorships there. Although the U.S.S.R. became more humane and less totalitarian after Stalin's death in 1953, his successors continued to rule eastern European countries as though they were imperial colonies.

In the early 1970s the global economic boom of the early cold war years—the 1950s and 1960s—finally came to an end. Domestic political stability and social harmony evaporated, and several countries experienced major crises. Serious economic difficulties returned with distressing regularity to Europe, Asia, and the Americas in the 1980s and 1990s. These difficulties encompassed much of the globe, a trend that accelerated the knitting together of peoples and regions.

The spectacular collapse of communism in eastern Europe in 1989 and the end of the cold war reinforced global integration. The result was monumental change, especially in postcommunist eastern Europe. A similar though less dramatic transformation also occurred in the nations of western Europe as they moved toward greater unity within the European Union.

THE DIVISION OF EUROPE

What were the causes of the cold war?

In 1945 triumphant American and Russian soldiers embraced along the Elbe River in the heart of vanquished Germany. At home the soldiers' loved ones erupted in joyous celebration. Yet victory was flawed. The Allies could not cooperate politically in peacemaking. The United States and the Soviet Union soon found themselves at loggerheads. By the end of 1947 Europe was rigidly divided, West versus East, in a cold war eventually waged around the world.

The Origins of the Cold War

Almost as soon as the unifying threat of Nazi Germany disappeared, the Soviet Union and the United States began to quarrel. Hostility between the Eastern and Western superpowers was the sad but logical outgrowth of military developments, wartime agreements, and long-standing political and ideological differences dating back to World War I.

In the early phases of the Second World War, the Americans and the British made military victory their highest priority. They consistently avoided discussion of Stalin's war aims and the shape of the eventual peace settlement, fearing that hard bargaining

● **The Big Three** In 1945 a triumphant Winston Churchill, an ailing Franklin Roosevelt, and a determined Joseph Stalin met at Yalta in southern Russia to plan for peace. Cooperation soon gave way to bitter hostility. *(F.D.R. Library)*

might encourage Stalin to make a separate peace with Hitler. They focused instead on the policy of unconditional surrender to solidify the alliance.

By late 1943 decisions that would affect the shape of the postwar world could no longer be postponed. Stalin, Roosevelt, and Churchill met in Teheran, Iran, in November 1943, and there the **Big Three** reaffirmed their determination to crush Germany and searched for the appropriate military strategy. Churchill argued that American and British forces should attack Germany's "soft underbelly" through the Balkans. Roosevelt, however, agreed with Stalin that a joint American-British frontal assault through France would be better. Soviet, rather than American and British armies, would then liberate eastern Europe.

The Big Three met again in February 1945 at Yalta on the Black Sea in southern Russia. By then, the Red Army had occupied most of eastern Europe and advancing Soviet armies were within a hundred miles of Berlin. American and British forces had yet to cross the Rhine into Germany. Moreover, the United States was far from defeating Japan. In short, the Soviet Union's position was strong and America's weak. The increasingly sick and apprehensive Roosevelt could do little but double his bet on Stalin's peaceful intentions. At Yalta the Big Three agreed that Germany would be divided into zones of occupation and would pay the Soviet Union heavy reparations. At American insistence Stalin agreed to declare war on Japan after Germany's defeat. As for Poland and eastern Europe—"that Pandora's Box of infinite troubles," according to American secretary of state Cordell Hull—the Big Three reached an ambiguous compromise: eastern European governments were to be freely elected but pro-Russian.

Almost immediately this compromise broke down. Even before the Yalta Conference, communists arriving home with the Red Army controlled Bulgaria and Poland. Elsewhere in eastern Europe pro-Soviet "coalition" governments of several parties were formed, but key ministerial posts were reserved for Moscow-trained communists.

At the postwar Potsdam Conference in July 1945, long-avoided differences over eastern Europe were finally debated. When the compromising Roosevelt died in April, the more assertive Harry Truman became U.S. president, and he now demanded immediate free elections throughout eastern Europe. Stalin refused point-blank. "A freely elected government in any of these East European countries would be anti-Soviet," he admitted simply, "and that we cannot allow."[1]

Here, then, is the key to the much-debated origins of the cold war. American ideals, pumped up by the crusade against Hitler, and American politics, heavily influenced by millions of U.S. voters of eastern European heritage, demanded free elections in Soviet-occupied eastern Europe. Stalin, who had lived through two enormously destructive German invasions, wanted absolute military security from Germany and its

Chronology

1945–1952	Allied occupation of Japan
1945–early 1960s	Decolonization of Asia and Africa
1947	Truman Doctrine; Marshall Plan
1949	Formation of NATO
1950–1970	Enormous growth rate in Japanese economy
1953–1964	De-Stalinization of Soviet Union
1957	Formation of Common Market
1961	Building of Berlin Wall
1962	Solzhenitsyn, *One Day in the Life of Ivan Denisovich*; Cuban missile crisis
1964	Civil Rights Act in United States
1964–1973	Principal years of U.S. involvement in Vietnam War
1973	OPEC oil embargo
1985	Glasnost leads to greater freedom of speech and expression in the Soviet Union
November 1989	Collapse of Berlin Wall
1989–1991	Fall of communism in Soviet Union and eastern Europe
1990–1992	Collapse of Japanese stock market
1991–2000	Resurgence of nationalism and ethnic conflict in eastern Europe
1993	Formation of European Union
May–June 2005	France and Holland vote against ratification of the European Union constitution

Big Three *Stalin, Roosevelt, and Churchill.*

potential eastern European allies once and for all. He believed only communist states could be truly dependable allies. By the middle of 1945 the United States had no way to determine political developments in eastern Europe short of war, and war was out of the question. Stalin would have his way.

West Versus East

America's response to Stalin's exaggerated conception of security was to "get tough." In May 1945 Truman abruptly cut off all aid to Russia. In October he declared that America would never recognize any government established by force against the free will of its people. His declaration, however, applied only to Europe and to countries threatened by communism, not to British and French colonies in Asia and Africa, for example, or to Latin American right-wing dictatorships. In March 1946 former British prime minister Churchill ominously informed an American audience that an "iron curtain" had fallen across the European continent, dividing Germany and all of Europe into two antagonistic camps. Yet the United States also responded to the popular desire to "bring the boys home" and demobilized with great speed. America had 12 million men in uniform when the war against Japan ended in September 1945; by 1947 there were only 1.5 million, in contrast to 6 million in the Soviet Union. Some historians have argued that American leaders believed the atomic bomb gave the United States all the power it needed and that "getting tough" really meant "talking tough."

Stalin's agents quickly renewed the "ideological struggle against capitalist imperialism." France's and Italy's large, well-organized Communist parties challenged their own governments with violent criticisms and large strikes. The Soviet Union also put pressure on Iran, Turkey, and Greece, and a bitter civil war raged in China. By spring 1947 many Americans believed Stalin was determined to export communism throughout Europe and around the world.

Truman Doctrine *The U.S. plan to contain communism to areas already occupied by the Red Army.*

The United States responded with the **Truman Doctrine,** which aimed at "containing" communism. Truman told Congress in March 1947, "I believe it must be the policy of the United States to support free people who are resisting attempted subjugation by armed minorities or by outside pressure." Truman asked Congress for military aid for Greece and Turkey. Then, in June, Secretary of State George C. Marshall offered Europe economic aid—the **Marshall Plan**—to help it rebuild. Stalin refused Marshall Plan assistance for all of eastern Europe, where he had established Soviet-style, one-party communist dictatorships.

Marshall Plan *The plan of economic aid to Europe to help it rebuild, which Stalin refused for all of eastern Europe.*

On July 24, 1948, Stalin blocked all highway traffic through the Soviet zone of Germany to Berlin. The Western allies responded by flying hundreds of planes over the Soviet roadblocks to supply provisions to the West Berliners. After 324 days the Soviets backed down: containment seemed to work. In 1949, therefore, the United States formed an anti-Soviet military alliance of Western governments: the North Atlantic Treaty Organization (NATO). Stalin countered by tightening his hold on his satellites, later united in the Warsaw Pact. Europe was divided into two hostile blocs.

As tensions rose in Europe, the cold war spread to Asia. In 1945 as the defeated Japanese surrendered, Korea, like Germany, was divided into Soviet and American zones of occupation, which became in 1948 a communist North Korea and an anti-communist South Korea. In late 1949 the Communists triumphed in China (see page 983), frightening and angering many Americans, who saw new evidence of a powerful worldwide communist conspiracy. When the Russian-backed communist forces of North Korea invaded South Korea in spring 1950, President Truman acted swiftly. American-led United Nations forces under U.S. general Douglas MacArthur intervened.

The Korean War was bitterly fought and extremely bloody. Initially, the well-equipped North Koreans almost conquered the entire peninsula, but the South

Koreans and the Americans rallied and drove their foes north to the Chinese border. At that point China intervened, and its armies pushed the South Koreans and Americans back south. The war then seesawed back and forth near where it had begun. President Truman rejected General MacArthur's call to attack China and fired him. In 1953 a fragile truce was finally negotiated, and the fighting stopped. Thus the United States extended its policy of containing communism to Asia but drew back from invading communist China and possible nuclear war.

RENAISSANCE AND CRISIS IN WESTERN EUROPE

How and why, despite the cold war, did western Europe recover so successfully from the ravages of war and Nazism?

As the cold war divided Europe into two blocs, the future appeared bleak on both sides of the iron curtain. Yet western Europe recovered to enjoy unprecedented economic prosperity and peaceful social transformation. Then, in the early 1970s, the cycle turned abruptly. A downturn in the world economy hit western Europe hard with serious social and psychological consequences.

The Postwar Challenge

After the war economic conditions in western Europe were terrible. Runaway inflation and black markets testified to severe shortages and hardships. Many questioned whether Europe would ever recover.

Suffering was most intense in defeated Germany. The major territorial change of the war had moved the Soviet Union's border far to the west. Poland was in turn compensated for this loss to the Soviets with land taken from Germany (see Map 31.1). To solidify these boundary changes, 13 million people were driven from their homes throughout eastern Europe and forced to resettle in a greatly reduced Germany. By spring 1947 refugee-clogged, hungry, prostrate Germany verged on total collapse and threatened to drag down the rest of Europe.

Yet western Europe began to recover. New groups and leaders with new ideas came forward. Progressive Catholics and their Christian Democrat political parties were particularly influential. In Italy antifascist Alcide De Gasperi and in Germany anti-Nazi Konrad Adenauer took power, steadfastly rejecting totalitarianism and narrow nationalism and placing their faith in democracy and cooperation. Socialists and communists active in the resistance against Hitler emerged from the war with increased power and prestige, especially in France and Italy. In the immediate postwar years welfare measures such as family allowances, health insurance, and increased public housing were enacted throughout much of continental Europe. Social reform complemented political transformation, creating solid foundations for a great European renaissance.

There were many reasons for this amazing recovery. The United States speeded the process by providing western Europe with massive economic aid through the Marshall Plan and with ongoing military protection through NATO, which featured American troops stationed permanently in Europe, and the American nuclear umbrella. As Marshall Plan aid poured in, western Europe's battered economies began to turn the corner in 1948, and Europe entered a period of unprecedented economic progress lasting into the late 1960s.

Western European governments also adopted a variety of imaginative and successful economic and social strategies. Postwar West Germany adopted a free-market economy while maintaining the extensive social welfare network inherited from the

MAP 31.1 **The Results of World War II in Europe** Millions of refugees fled westward because of war and territorial changes. The Soviet Union and Poland took land from Germany, which the Allies partitioned into occupation zones. Those zones subsequently formed the basis of the East and West German states as the iron curtain fell to divide both Germany and Europe. Austria was detached from Germany, but the Soviets subsequently permitted Austria to reunify as a neutral state.

Legend

Postwar national boundaries, to 1989

Allied occupation of Germany and Austria, 1945–1955

Territory lost by Germany

Territory gained by Soviet Union

1945 Year communist control of government gained

"Iron curtain" to 1989

Refugee movements

Baltic
Czech
Finns
Germans
Poles
Russians
Peoples settled by International Refugee Organization

Berlin inset

BERLIN

EAST GERMANY

East Berlin — Soviet Sector

French Sector
British Sector — West Berlin
U.S. Sector

Potsdam

Berlin Wall (1961–1989)

Map labels

ATLANTIC OCEAN

North Sea

Baltic Sea

Mediterranean Sea

Black Sea

Adriatic Sea

Caspian Sea

PORTUGAL — Lisbon
SPAIN — Madrid
IRELAND — Dublin
UNITED KINGDOM — London
FRANCE — Paris
NORWAY — Oslo
SWEDEN — Stockholm
FINLAND — Helsinki
DENMARK — Copenhagen
NETHERLANDS — Amsterdam
BELGIUM — Brussels
LUX.
Bonn
WEST GERMANY 1949
EAST GERMANY 1949 — Berlin
Bremen
Munich
SWITZ. — Bern
AUSTRIA — Vienna
Prague
CZECHOSLOVAKIA 1948
POLAND 1947 — Warsaw, Brest
HUNGARY 1949 — Budapest
ITALY — Rome, Milan
YUGOSLAVIA 1945 — Belgrade
ROMANIA 1947 — Bucharest
BULGARIA 1946 — Sofia
ALBANIA 1944 — Tiranë
GREECE — Athens
TURKEY — Ankara, Istanbul
SOVIET UNION 1917 — Moscow, Leningrad
UKRAINE

Corsica
Sardinia
Sicily
Balearic Is.
Cyprus

U.S. Zone
British Zone
French Zone
Soviet Zone

Soviet Zone
U.S. Zone
French Zone
British Zone (Austria)

ESTONIA to U.S.S.R. 1940
LATVIA to U.S.S.R. 1940
LITHUANIA to U.S.S.R. 1940
Incorp. into U.S.S.R. 1945
Incorporated into Poland, 1945
From Poland, 1940–1947
From Czechoslovakia, 1945–1947
From Romania, 1940–1947
From Romania, 1940
From Finland, 1940–1956
From Italy, 1945
BESSARABIA

Volga R.
Don R.
Dnieper R.
Danube R.

Yalta

0° 20°E 40°E
60°N

400 Mi.
400 Km.
200
0

● **Affair of the Scarves**   Muslim women protest France's September 2004 ban on the wearing of all "conspicuous" religious apparel by the country's 12 million schoolchildren, including Jewish skullcaps, Sikh turbans, large Christian crosses, and Islamic veils and scarves. The ban is meant to enforce France's tradition, going back to the French Revolution, of a strict separation between church and state. *(AP Photo/ Wide World Photos)*

Hitler era. The French established a new kind of planning commission that set ambitious but flexible goals for the French economy, using the nationalized banks to funnel money into key industries. France achieved the most rapid economic development in its long history.

European workers also deserve some credit for the economic turnaround. They worked hard for low wages in hopes of a better future. Moreover, during the Great Depression, few Europeans had been able to afford many of the new consumer products. Thus in 1945 the electric refrigerator, the washing machine, and the automobile were rare luxuries, and there was great potential demand, which manufacturers moved to satisfy.

Migrant laborers from the Mediterranean basin (southern Italy, North Africa, Turkey, Greece, and Yugoslavia) also played a key role in Europe's postwar recovery. They accepted the most menial and least desirable jobs for the lowest pay. Europeans assumed that rising birthrates among the majority population would eventually fill the labor shortages, so at first they labeled the migrants "guest workers" to signal their temporary status. By the 1980s, however, as millions more migrants arrived from Europe's former colonies and settled in every European nation, it was clear their presence would be permanent. Their full integration into the economic, political, and social life of these countries has been incomplete, creating a backlash against them by the majority populations and a simmering anger within the immigrant communities. Immigrants resent what seems a second-class citizenship, poor working conditions and wages, a perceived lack of respect for ethnic and religious traditions, and alleged mistreatment by police.

Finally, western European nations abandoned protectionism and gradually created a large, unified market. This historic action, which certainly stimulated the economy, was part of a larger search for European unity.

"Building Europe" and Decolonization

Western Europe's political recovery in the generation after 1945 was unprecedented. Republics were re-established in France, West Germany, and Italy. Constitutional monarchs were restored in Belgium, the Netherlands, and Norway. Democratic governments took root again and thrived in an atmosphere of civil liberties and individual freedom.

A similarly extraordinary achievement was the march toward a united Europe. Many Europeans believed that only unity could forestall future European conflict and that only a new "European nation" could reassert western Europe's influence in world affairs dominated by the United States and the Soviet Union.

The experience of close cooperation among European states for Marshall Plan aid led European federalists to turn toward economics as a way of attaining genuine unity. On May 9, 1950 (now "Europe Day"), French foreign minister Robert Schuman proposed an international organization to control and integrate all European steel and coal production. France, West Germany, Italy, Belgium, the Netherlands, and Luxembourg joined together in 1952. In 1957 the six nations of the Coal and Steel Community signed the Treaty of Rome, creating the European Economic Community, generally known as the **Common Market**. The treaty's primary goal was a gradual reduction of all tariffs among the six in order to create a single market almost as large as that of the United States.

Common Market *The European Economic Community created in 1957.*

● **African Independence** Britain's Queen Elizabeth II pays an official visit in 1961 to Ghana, the former Gold Coast colony. Accompanying the queen at the colorful welcoming ceremony is Ghana's popular Kwame Nkrumah, who was educated in black colleges in the United States and led Ghana's breakthrough to independence in 1957. *(Bettmann/Corbis)*

The Common Market was a great success, encouraging hopes of rapid progress toward political as well as economic union in western Europe. In the 1960s, however, a resurgence of more traditional nationalism in France led by Charles de Gaulle, French president from 1958 to 1969, frustrated these hopes. Viewing the United States as the main threat to genuine French (and European) independence, he withdrew all French military forces from the "American-controlled" NATO command as France developed its own nuclear weapons. Within the Common Market de Gaulle refused to permit majority rule. Thus throughout the 1960s the Common Market thrived economically but remained a union of sovereign states.

As Europe moved toward greater economic unity in the postwar era, its centuries-long overseas expansion was dramatically reversed. Between 1945 and the early 1960s almost every colonial territory gained formal independence. This rolling back of Western expansion—or **decolonization**—marks one of world history's great turning points. The basic cause of imperial collapse was the rising demand by Asian and African peoples for national self-determination and racial equality (see Chapter 32). Yet decolonization also involved the imperial powers, and considering the process from their perspective helps explain why independence came so quickly and why a kind of neocolonialism subsequently evolved in some former colonies.

European empires had been sustained by an enormous imbalance of power between the rulers and the ruled. By 1945 that imbalance had almost vanished. Moreover, most

Europeans viewed their empires after 1945 very differently than they had before 1914. Empires had rested on self-confidence and self-righteousness; Europeans had believed their superiority to be not only technical and military but also spiritual and moral. The horrors of the Second World War destroyed such complacent arrogance and gave imperialism's opponents much greater influence in Europe. After 1945 many Europeans were willing to let go of their colonies more or less voluntarily and to concentrate on rebuilding at home.

European political and business leaders still wanted some ties with the former colonies, however. As a result, western European countries actually managed to increase their economic and cultural ties with their former African colonies in the 1960s and 1970s. This situation led many Third World leaders and scholars to charge that western Europe (and the United States) had imposed a system of **neocolonialism** designed to perpetuate Western economic domination and undermine political independence, just as the United States had subordinated the new nations of Latin America in the nineteenth century (see Chapter 26).

decolonization *The reversal of Europe's overseas expansion caused by the rising demand of Asian and African peoples for national self-determination, racial equality, and personal dignity.*

neocolonialism *A system designed to perpetuate Western economic domination and undermine the promise of political independence.*

The Changing Class Structure

A more mobile and more democratic European society developed after World War II as old class barriers relaxed and class distinctions became fuzzier. Most noticeably, the structure of the middle class changed. In the nineteenth and early twentieth centuries the model for the middle class had been the independent, self-employed property owner who ran a business or practiced a liberal profession such as law or medicine. After 1945 a new breed of managers and experts required by large corporations and government agencies replaced traditional property owners as leaders of the middle class. They tried to give their children the all-important advanced education, but only rarely could they pass on the positions they had attained. Thus the new middle class, based largely on specialized skills and high levels of education, was more open, democratic, and insecure than the old propertied middle class.

The structure of the lower classes also became more flexible and open. There was a mass exodus from farms and the countryside. Meanwhile, the industrial working class ceased to expand, but job opportunities for white-collar and service employees grew rapidly. Such employees bore a greater resemblance to the new middle class of salaried specialists than to industrial workers, who themselves were also better educated and more specialized.

European governments also reduced class tensions with a series of social reforms. Many of these reforms—such as increased unemployment benefits and more extensive old-age pensions—simply strengthened social security measures first pioneered in Bismarck's Germany. Other programs were new, such as state-run, comprehensive national health systems. Most countries introduced family allowances—direct government grants to parents to help them raise their children—that helped many poor families make ends meet. Maternity grants and inexpensive public housing for low-income families and individuals were also common. These and other social reforms provided a humane floor of well-being and promoted greater equality.

Economic and Social Dislocation (1970–1990)

For twenty years after 1945 most Europeans were preoccupied with economic progress and consumerism. In the late 1960s a new era of uncertainty and crisis dawned as radical European college students joined a global wave of demonstrations and protests by young people challenging authority, questioning tradition, and voicing their opposition to consumerism, politics, racism, sexism, and war. The year 1968 marked the high point of this loud, sometimes violent, but brief movement for political and social change. An economic crisis in the 1970s, however, brought more serious challenges for the average person.

The crisis had two main causes. First, the postwar international monetary system was based on the U.S. dollar. In 1971 its value fell sharply, and inflation accelerated worldwide. Fixed rates of exchange were abandoned, and uncertainty replaced predictability in international trade and finance.

Even more damaging was the dramatic reversal in the price and availability of energy. Cheap oil fueled the postwar boom. (See the feature "Global Trade: Oil" on pages 948–949.) In 1971 the Arab-led Organization of Petroleum Exporting Countries—**OPEC**—decided to reverse the decline in the crude oil price by presenting a united front against the oil companies. After the Arab-Israeli war in October 1973, OPEC placed an embargo on oil exports, and crude oil prices quadrupled in a year. The rapid price rise was economically destructive, but the world's big powers did nothing. The Soviet Union, itself an oil exporter, benefited directly; the United States was immobilized by the Watergate crisis in politics (see page 961). Thus governments, companies, and individuals could only deal piecemeal with the so-called oil shock—which was really an earthquake.

Following the upheaval in the international monetary system, the revolution in energy prices plunged the world into its worst economic decline since the 1930s. Unemployment rose; productivity and living standards declined. By 1976 a modest recovery was in progress, but when Iranian oil production collapsed during Iran's fundamentalist Islamic revolution (see page 999), crude oil prices doubled again in 1979. In summer 1985, unemployment rates in western Europe rose to their highest levels since the Great Depression. Global recovery was painfully slow until late 1993.

Western Europe's welfare system, fashioned in the postwar era, prevented mass suffering through extended benefits for the unemployed, free medical care, and special allowances for the needy. But increased government spending was not matched by higher taxes, causing a rapid growth of budget deficits, national debts, and inflation. By the late 1970s a powerful reaction against government's ever-increasing role had set in. Growing voter dissatisfaction helped bring Conservative Margaret Thatcher (b. 1925) to power in Britain in 1979. Prime Minister Thatcher slowed government spending and privatized industry by selling off state-owned companies to private investors. Of great social significance, her government encouraged low- and moderate-income renters in state-owned housing projects to buy their apartments at rock-bottom prices. This step created a whole new class of property owners, thereby eroding the

OPEC *An Arab-led organization of countries that export oil that helps set policies and prices on its trade.*

● **Sharjah Archaeological Museum, United Arab Emirates** Like other major cities in the oil-rich United Arab Emirates such as Dubai and Abu Dhabi, Sharjah possesses some of the most interesting and beautiful modern architecture in the world. The Archaeological Museum shown here is located in a complex of buildings devoted to the sciences, arts, history, and Islam near the Cultural (or Qur'an) Roundabout. *(Courtesy, Fotogalerie SAE)*

electoral base of Britain's socialist Labour Party. Other Western governments introduced austerity measures to slow the seemingly inexorable growth of public spending and the welfare state.

Individuals felt the impact of austerity at an early date. Indeed, the very real threat of unemployment—or "underemployment" in a dead-end job—seemed to shape the outlook of a whole generation. Students in the 1980s were serious, practical, and often conservative. As one young woman at a French university told a reporter in 1985, "Jobs are the big worry now, so everyone wants to learn something practical."[2] In France as elsewhere, the shift away from the romantic visions and political activism of the late 1960s was remarkable.

Harder times also meant that more women entered or remained in the workforce after they married. Although attitudes related to personal fulfillment were one reason for the continuing increase—especially for well-educated upper-middle-class women— many wives in poor and middle-class families worked outside the home because of economic necessity. As in preindustrial Europe, the wives' earnings provided the margin of survival for millions of hard-pressed families.

THE SOVIET UNION AND EASTERN EUROPE (1945–1991)

Why did a reform movement eventually triumph in eastern Europe in 1989 and bring an end to the cold war?

While western Europe surged ahead economically after World War II, postwar economic recovery in eastern Europe proceeded along Soviet lines, and changes in the Soviet Union strongly influenced political and social developments. That trend remained true more than forty years later, when radical reform in the Soviet Union opened the door to popular revolution in the eastern European satellites—and ultimately to the collapse of the Soviet Union itself.

Stalin's Last Years

Americans were not the only ones who felt betrayed by Stalin's postwar actions. The "Great Patriotic War of the Fatherland" had fostered Russian nationalism and a relaxation of totalitarian terror. Having made a heroic war effort, the vast majority of the Soviet people hoped in 1945 that a grateful party and government would grant greater freedom and democracy. Such hopes were soon crushed.

Even before war's end, Stalin was moving his country back toward rigid dictatorship. As early as 1944 Communist Party members received a new motivating slogan: "The war on Fascism ends, the war on capitalism begins."[3] Stalin's new Western foe provided him with an excuse for re-establishing a harsh dictatorship. He purged thousands of returning soldiers and ordinary civilians in 1945 and 1946, and he revived the terrible forced-labor camps of the 1930s. Culture and art were purged in violent campaigns that reimposed rigid anti-Western ideological conformity. Orthodox Christianity again came under attack and anti-religion policies were reimplemented. In 1949 Stalin launched a savage verbal attack on Soviet Jews, accusing them of being pro-Western and antisocialist.

In the political realm Stalin reasserted the Communist Party's complete control of the government and his absolute mastery of the party. Five-year plans were reintroduced to cope with the enormous task of economic reconstruction. Once again heavy and military industry were given top priority, and consumer goods, housing, and collectivized agriculture were neglected. Everyday life was very hard. In short, it was the 1930s all over again in the Soviet Union, although police terror was less intense.

GLOBAL TRADE

OIL

Crude oil is a liquid hydrocarbon that is located in certain rocks below the earth's crust. Although it is found throughout the world, the Persian Gulf and Caspian Sea areas contain about three-quarters of the world's proven reserves. The uses of crude oil are limited, but it may be refined into valuable products such as kerosene, gasoline, and fuel oil.

Oil has been used throughout history, although it did not become a worldwide commodity until the nineteenth century. In antiquity, the Sumerians and Babylonians mixed evaporated oil from tar pits with sand to make asphalt for waterproofing ships and paving roads. Islamic societies in the Middle East used small quantities of oil for lighting, although cooking fires were probably the main source of light.

In Europe, lamp oil—from animal fats and plants—was a luxury. The nineteenth century brought revolutionary changes in lighting—the "industrialization of light." By the 1840s manufacturers in coal-rich Europe were distilling coal into crude oil and gas, which were sold for lighting. North America followed suit. Thus when E. L. Drake drilled the first successful oil well in Pennsylvania in 1859, a growing demand for lamp oil already existed. The production of kerosene, easily distilled from the light oils of Pennsylvania, took off as American consumers accepted the bright, clean-burning, and relatively inexpensive oil for use in their lamps.

The modern oil industry operated on a global scale from the beginning. After the late 1860s the United States exported two-thirds of its kerosene, first in wooden barrels, then in large tin cans, and finally in tankers for bulk distribution. The leading producer was John D. Rockefeller's Standard Oil, which held a monopoly on kerosene until the U.S. government broke the corporation into separate companies in 1911. Most kerosene went to Europe at first, but other markets grew rapidly.

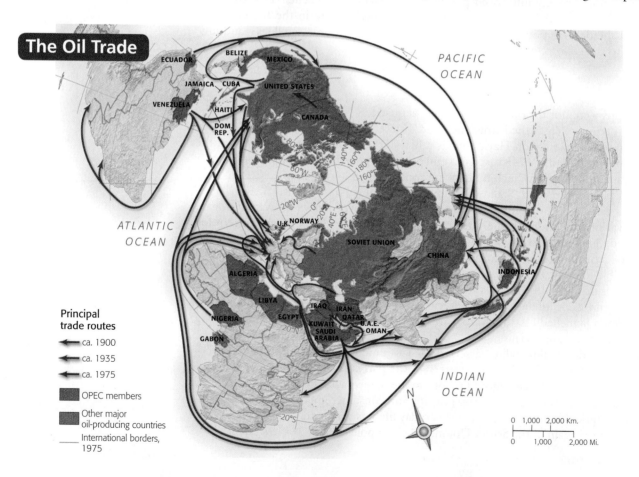

The Oil Trade

Principal trade routes

← ca. 1900
← ca. 1935
← ca. 1975

OPEC members

Other major oil-producing countries

International borders, 1975

PACIFIC OCEAN

ATLANTIC OCEAN

INDIAN OCEAN

0   1,000   2,000 Km.
0   1,000   2,000 Mi.

China's growing middle class is adopting the automobile culture of the West, which will only put more pressure on the world's dwindling supply of fossil fuels. (© 2005 Bob Englehart, *The Hartford Courant*)

"FIRST WE'LL VACATION AT THE SHORE, THEN WE'LL GO TO THE MOUNTAINS, THEN UP TO THE LAKE....."

In the 1870s the Baku region on the Caspian Sea, home of an ancient artisan oil industry, introduced drilling, brought in fabulous gushers, and created a Russian refining industry. Russian capitalists fought well-publicized "oil wars" with Standard Oil for world kerosene markets.

International differences were significant. In the United States and western Europe kerosene appealed especially to farmers and urban working people, who had previously lacked decent lighting. The affluent urban classes generally continued to use coal-distilled gas until the 1880s, when electricity from central power stations began to replace gas in elegant neighborhoods. In China peasants rejected bulk distribution and insisted on kerosene in tin cans, recycling them into valuable all-purpose containers. Russia pioneered in using oil as fuel, as the refining of heavy Baku crude yielded abundant thick "leftovers"—an excellent power source for riverboats, railroads, and factories.

During the twentieth century oil became a major fuel source as kerosene production declined. Until 1941 the explosive growth of automobiles in the United States was easily outpaced by the development of domestic oil fields, enabling the United States to sell one-third of all the oil consumed beyond its borders. In oil-poor Europe (Russia excepted), fuel oil loomed large as a strategic material. After 1919 the British government took control of the two oil companies in Iran and Iraq to guarantee supplies for Britain's military and industrial needs. Germany distilled coal into synthetic gasoline, and Hitler relentlessly pushed production of this very expensive alternative to free his war machine from dependence on foreign oil.

The international oil trade shifted dramatically after 1945. The United States, previously producing half the world's oil, became the world's largest importer. The Middle East, producing very modestly in the 1920s and 1930s, became the world's leading exporter. At the same time, western Europe and Japan shifted from coal to oil to drive their factories and fuel their automobiles. Nevertheless, the American and British oil companies in the Middle East expanded output so rapidly—sixteen times between 1948 and 1972—that the inflation-adjusted price for Middle Eastern oil actually fell substantially in these years.

Increasingly dissatisfied with their share of the profits, the main exporting countries—Iran, Iraq, Kuwait, Saudi Arabia, and Venezuela—organized OPEC (Organization of Petroleum Exporting Countries) in 1960 to gain control of their oil resources. In 1973, during the Arab-Israeli war, OPEC engineered a fourfold price increase with enormous global consequences. The exporting states also nationalized their oil industries, reducing foreign companies to simple buyers and transporters. The oil exporters used their financial windfalls to improve health and living standards somewhat, but vast sums went for lavish spending by the elite and for overly ambitious development projects. Above all, money went for expensive military hardware from the industrialized countries, which increased tensions and prolonged the terrible war between Iraq and Iran in the 1980s (see page 999).

A price collapse followed the upward price revolution of the 1970s. In the 1980s and early 1990s conservation, greater efficiency, recession, environmental concerns, and significant new oil discoveries outside the Middle East eliminated much of the inflation-adjusted price increases of the 1970s. By 2002 some argued that oil was really "just another commodity." The outbreak of the Iraq War in 2003, however—followed by natural disasters such as Hurricane Katrina; instability in Nigeria, Venezuela, and other major oil-producing countries; and skyrocketing demand for oil from China and India—sent oil to nearly $150 per barrel by July 2008, creating another global energy crisis.

Stalin then exported the Stalinist system to eastern Europe. Rigid ideological in-doctrination, attacks on religion, and a lack of civil liberties were soon facts of life in the region's one-party states. Industry was nationalized and the middle class stripped of its possessions. Only Yugoslavia's Josip Tito (1892–1980), the popular resistance leader and Communist Party chief, could resist Soviet domination successfully, be-cause there was no Russian army in Yugoslavia.

Limited De-Stalinization and Stagnation

In 1953 the aging Stalin died. Even as his heirs struggled for power, they realized that reforms were necessary because of the widespread fear and hatred induced by Stalin's political terrorism. They curbed secret police powers and gradually closed many forced-labor camps. Change was also necessary for economic reasons. Agriculture was in bad shape, and shortages of consumer goods were discouraging hard work and ini-tiative. Moreover, Stalin's belligerent foreign policy had led directly to a strong West-ern alliance, isolating the Soviet Union.

The Communist Party leadership was badly split on just how much change to per-mit. Conservatives wanted few changes. Reformers, led by Nikita Khrushchev (1894–1971), argued for major innovations and won. Khrushchev launched an all-out attack on Stalin and his crimes. At a Twentieth Party Congress closed session in 1956, he described in gory detail to startled delegates how Stalin had tortured and murdered thousands of loyal Communists, bungled the country's defense by trusting Hitler, and "supported the glorification of his own person." Khrushchev's "secret speech" strengthened the reform movement.

de-Stalinization *The liberal-ization of the post-Stalin Soviet Union, led by reformer Nikita Khrushchev.*

The liberalization of the Soviet Union—labeled **de-Stalinization** in the West—was genuine. The Communist Party jealously maintained its monopoly on political power, but Khrushchev shook up the party and brought in new members. Some resources were shifted from heavy industry and the military toward consumer goods and agri-culture, and controls over workers were relaxed. The Soviet Union's very low stan-dard of living finally began to improve and continued to rise substantially throughout the booming 1960s.

De-Stalinization created great ferment among writers and intellectuals who hun-gered for cultural freedom. The writer Aleksandr Solzhenitsyn (b. 1918) created a sensation when his *One Day in the Life of Ivan Denisovich* was published in the Soviet Union in 1962. Solzhenitsyn's novel portrays life in a Stalinist concentration camp in grim detail and is a damning indictment of the Stalinist past.

Khrushchev also de-Stalinized Soviet foreign policy. "Peaceful coexistence" with capitalism was possible, he argued, and great wars were not inevitable. Between 1955 and 1957 cold war tensions relaxed.

De-Stalinization stimulated rebelliousness in the eastern European satellites, where communist reformers and the masses sought greater liberty and national indepen-dence. Poland won greater autonomy in 1956 when extensive rioting brought in a new government. Hungary experienced a real and tragic revolution. Led by students and workers—the classic urban revolutionaries—the people of Budapest installed a liberal communist reformer as their new chief in October 1956. After the new govern-ment promised free elections and renounced Hungary's military alliance with Mos-cow, Russian leaders ordered an invasion and crushed the revolution. When the United States did not come to their aid, Hungarians and most eastern Europeans concluded that their only hope was to strive for small domestic gains while following Russia obediently in foreign affairs.

By late 1962 there was strong opposition in Soviet party circles to Khrushchev's policies. De-Stalinization posed a dangerous threat to Stalin's still living and still pow-erful former henchmen, to party authority, and to the whole system. What is more, Khrushchev's policy toward the West was erratic and ultimately unsuccessful. When

● **Czechs Protest Soviet Invasion in 1968** A young Czech girl shouts "Ivan go home" at Russian soldiers sitting on tanks in Prague during the Soviet invasion of Czechoslovakia in August 1968. *(Bettmann/Corbis)*

Khrushchev ordered missiles with nuclear warheads installed in Fidel Castro's communist Cuba in 1962, U.S. president John F. Kennedy countered with a naval blockade of Cuba. After a tense diplomatic crisis Khrushchev agreed to remove the missiles, and looked like a bumbling buffoon. Within two years of the Cuban missile crisis he was gone in a bloodless palace revolution.

After Leonid Brezhnev (1906–1982) and his supporters took over in 1964, they talked quietly of Stalin's "good points," stopped further liberalization, and launched a massive arms buildup, determined never to suffer Khrushchev's humiliation in the face of American nuclear superiority.

In the wake of Khrushchev's reforms, the 1960s brought modest liberalization and more consumer goods to eastern Europe, as well as somewhat greater national autonomy. In January 1968 reform elements in the Czechoslovakian Communist Party gained a majority and replaced a long-time Stalinist leader with Alexander Dubček (1921–1992), whose new government launched dramatic reforms. The determination of the Czech reformers to build what they called "socialism with a human face" frightened hard-line Communists. Thus in August 1968, five hundred thousand Russian and eastern European troops occupied Czechoslovakia, and the Czech experiment in humanizing communism came to an end. Shortly afterward, Brezhnev declared the so-called **Brezhnev Doctrine**, according to which the Soviet Union and its allies could intervene in any socialist country whenever they saw the need.

The aftermath of intervention in Czechoslovakia also brought a certain re-Stalinization of the U.S.S.R. Free expression and open protest disappeared. Dissidents were blacklisted or quietly imprisoned in jails or mental institutions. Unlike in the Stalinist era, though, dictatorship was collective rather than personal, and coercion replaced uncontrolled terror. This compromise seemed to suit the leaders and a majority of the people, and the Soviet Union appeared stable in the 1970s and early 1980s.

Brezhnev Doctrine *The doctrine created after the Soviet invasion of Czechoslovakia in 1968, according to which the Soviet Union and its allies had the right to intervene in any socialist country whenever they saw the need.*

A rising standard of living for ordinary people contributed to stability, although the economic crisis of the 1970s greatly slowed the rate of improvement, and long lines and shortages persisted. The exclusive privileges enjoyed by the Communist Party elite also reinforced the system. Ambitious individuals had tremendous incentive to do as the state wished in order to gain access to special, well-stocked stores, attend superior schools, and travel abroad.

Another source of stability was the enduring nationalism of ordinary Russians. Party leaders successfully identified themselves with Russian patriotism, stressing their role in saving the motherland during the Second World War and protecting it now from foreign foes, including eastern European "counter-revolutionaries." Moreover, the politically dominant Great Russians, only half of the total Soviet population, held the top positions in the Soviet Union's non-Russian republics.

Beneath this stability, however, the Soviet Union was experiencing a social revolution. Three aspects of this revolution were particularly significant. First, the urban population continued its rapid growth in the 1960s and 1970s. In 1985 two-thirds of all Soviet citizens lived in cities, and one-fourth lived in big cities. This expanding urban population abandoned its old peasant ways, exchanging them for more education, better job skills, and greater sophistication. Second, the number of highly trained scientists, managers, and specialists expanded prodigiously, jumping fourfold between 1960 and 1985. Third, the education that created expertise also helped foster the growth of Soviet public opinion. Educated people read, discussed, and formed definite ideas about social questions from environmental pollution to urban transportation. They increasingly saw themselves as worthy of having a voice in society's decisions, even its political decisions. These changes set the stage for the dramatic reforms of the Gorbachev era.

The Gorbachev Era

The Soviet Union's Communist Party elite seemed safe in the early 1980s from any challenge from below. The party's long-established system of centralized control reached down to factories, neighborhoods, and villages. The party hierarchy continued to manipulate every aspect of national life. Organized opposition was impossible, and average people simply left politics to the bosses.

The country had serious problems, however. The massive state and party bureaucracy discouraged personal initiative and promoted economic inefficiency and apathy among the masses and the rapidly growing class of well-educated urban experts. Therefore, when Brezhnev died in 1982, efforts were made to improve economic performance and to combat worker absenteeism and high-level corruption. These efforts set the stage for the emergence in 1985 of Mikhail Gorbachev (b. 1931), the most vigorous Soviet leader since Stalin.

Smart, charming, and tough, Gorbachev believed in communism, but realized it was failing. Gorbachev also realized full well that success at home required better relations with the West, for the wasteful arms race had had a disastrous impact on Soviet Union living standards. Gorbachev attempted to save the Soviet system by reforming it. He elaborated a series of reform policies he labeled democratic socialism, or "socialism with a democratic face," which were designed to revive and even remake the vast Soviet Union.

The first set of reforms was intended to transform and restructure the economy. This economic restructuring, or **perestroika**, permitted freer prices, more independence for state enterprises, and the setting up of some profit-seeking private cooperatives. The reforms were rather timid, however, and when the economy stalled, Gorbachev's popular support gradually eroded.

Gorbachev's bold and far-reaching campaign of openness, or **glasnost**, was much more successful. Where censorship, dull uniformity, and outright lies had long char-

perestroika *The economic "restructuring" reform implemented by Gorbachev that permitted an easing of government price controls on some goods, more independence for state enterprises, and the setting up of profit-seeking private cooperatives to provide personal services for consumers.*

glasnost *"Openness," part of Gorbachev's campaign to "tell it like it is," marked a break from the past; long-banned writers sold millions of copies of their works, and denunciations of Stalin and his terror were standard public discourse.*

acterized public discourse, the new frankness led rather quickly to something approaching free speech and free expression, a veritable cultural revolution.

Democratization was the third of Gorbachev's reforms, and it led to the first free elections in the Soviet Union since 1917. Gorbachev and the party remained in control, but a minority of critical independents was elected in April 1989 to a revitalized Congress of People's Deputies, and many top-ranking Communists were defeated.

Democratization also encouraged demands for greater autonomy by non-Russian minorities, especially in the Baltic region and in the Caucasus. These demands certainly went beyond what Gorbachev had envisaged. But whereas China's Communist Party leaders brutally massacred similar pro-democracy demonstrators in Beijing (Peking) in June 1989 (see page 986), Gorbachev drew back from repression. Thus nationalist demands continued to grow.

Finally, the Soviet leader brought "new political thinking" to foreign affairs. He withdrew Soviet troops from Afghanistan and sought to reduce East-West tensions. Of enormous historical importance, Gorbachev repudiated the Brezhnev Doctrine, pledging to respect the political choices of eastern Europe's peoples. By 1989 it seemed the tragic Soviet occupation of eastern Europe might gradually wither away.

The Revolutions of 1989

Instead of gradually changing, history accelerated. In 1989 a series of largely peaceful revolutions swept across eastern Europe. These revolutions overturned existing communist regimes and led to the formation of governments dedicated to democratic elections, human rights, and national rejuvenation. Eastern Europe changed dramatically almost overnight.

The Poles led the way. Poland had been an unruly satellite from the beginning. After widespread riots in 1956, Polish communists dropped their efforts to impose Soviet-style collectivization on the peasants and to break the Roman Catholic Church. Faced with an independent agriculture and a vigorous church, the communists failed to monopolize society. They also failed to manage the economy effectively and instead sent it into a nosedive by the mid-1970s. Then the "Polish miracle" occurred: Cardinal Karol Wojtyla, archbishop of Cracow, was elected pope, and in June 1979 he returned to his native land to preach the love of Christ and country and the "inalienable rights of man." Pope John Paul II electrified the Polish nation, and the economic crisis became a spiritual crisis as well.

In August 1980 scattered strikes snowballed into a working-class revolt. Led by a feisty electrician and devout Catholic named Lech Walesa, the workers organized an independent trade union they called **Solidarity.** In response, Communist Party leader General Wojciech Jaruzelski proclaimed martial law in December 1981 and arrested Solidarity's leaders. (See the feature "Listening to the Past: A Solidarity Leader Speaks from Prison" on pages 974–975.) Though outlawed and driven underground, Solidarity maintained its organization and strong popular support. By 1988 widespread labor unrest and raging inflation had brought Poland to the brink of economic collapse. Solidarity pressured Poland's frustrated Communist Party leaders into legalizing Solidarity and allowing free elections in June 1989 for some seats in the Polish parliament. Solidarity won every contested seat. A month later the editor of Solidarity's weekly newspaper was sworn in as the first noncommunist leader in eastern Europe in a generation. Soon Poland was not alone in its revolution.

In Czechoslovakia communism died in ten days in December 1989 during the so-called **Velvet Revolution** that peacefully ousted Communist leaders. It grew out of massive street protests led by students and intellectuals, and led to Václav Havel's election as president in 1989. (See the feature "Individuals in Society: Václav Havel.")

In Romania revolution was violent and bloody. There the iron-fisted communist dictator Nicolae Ceauşescu, alone among eastern European bosses, ordered his

Primary Source: The Last Heir of Lenin Explains His Reform Plans: Perestroika and Glasnost
Read President Gorbachev's analysis of the Soviet Union's decline, and his prescriptions for reform.

Solidarity   *Led by Lech Walesa, this group of Polish workers organized a free and democratic trade union that quickly became the union of a nation.*

Velvet Revolution   *The moment when communism died in 1989 with an ousting of Communist bosses in only ten days; it grew out of popular demonstrations led by students, intellectuals, and a dissident playwright.*

● **Fall of the Berlin Wall** A man stands atop the partially destroyed Berlin Wall flashing the V for victory sign as he and thousands of other Berliners celebrate the opening of the Berlin Wall in November 1989. Within a year the wall was torn down, communism collapsed, and the cold war ended. *(AP Photo/Wide World Photos)*

ruthless security forces to slaughter thousands, thereby sparking an armed uprising. After Ceauşescu's forces were defeated, the tyrant and his wife were captured and executed by a military court.

In Hungary growing popular resistance forced the Communist Party to renounce one-party rule and schedule free elections for early 1990. Hungarians gleefully tore down the barbed-wire "iron curtain" that separated Hungary and Austria (see Map 31.1) and opened their border to refugees from East Germany.

As thousands of dissatisfied East Germans passed through Czechoslovakia and Hungary on their way to thriving West Germany, a protest movement arose in East Germany. Desperately hoping to stabilize the situation, East Germany's Communist Party leaders opened the Berlin Wall in November 1989, then were swept aside. In general elections in March 1990 a conservative-liberal "Alliance for Germany" won and quickly negotiated an economic union with West Germany.

Three factors contributed to this rapid reunification. First, the opening of the Berlin Wall was critically important. In the first week alone almost 9 million East Germans—roughly half the country's population—poured across the border into West Germany. Although almost all returned home, the joy of warm welcomes from long-lost friends and family aroused long-dormant hopes of unity among ordinary citizens. Second, West German chancellor Helmut Kohl moved skillfully to reassure American, Soviet, and European leaders they need not fear a reunified Germany. At the same time, he promised the ordinary people of bankrupt East Germany an immediate economic bonanza—a one-for-one exchange of all East German marks held in savings accounts and pensions into much more valuable West German marks. Finally, Kohl and Gorbachev signed a historic agreement in July 1990 in which United Germany solemnly affirmed its peaceful intentions and pledged never to develop nuclear, biological, or chemical weapons. On October 3, 1990, East and West Germany merged, forming a single nation under West Germany's constitution and laws.

Cold War Finale and Soviet Disintegration

Germany's peaceful reunification accelerated the pace of agreements to reduce armaments and liquidate the cold war. In November 1990 delegates from twenty-two European countries joined those from the United States and the Soviet Union in Paris and agreed to a scaling down of all their armed forces. The **Paris Accord** was for all practical purposes a general peace treaty, bringing an end to World War II and the cold war.

Peace in Europe encouraged the United States and the Soviet Union to scrap a significant portion of their nuclear arsenals. In September 1991 President George H. W. Bush unilaterally declared another major cut in American nuclear weapons. He also canceled the around-the-clock alert status for American bombers outfitted with atomic bombs. Gorbachev quickly followed suit. For the first time in four decades Soviet and American nuclear weapons were no longer standing ready to destroy capitalism, communism, and life itself.

Paris Accord *A general peace treaty that brought an end to World War II and the cold war that followed; it called for a scaling down of all armed forces and the acceptance of all existing borders as legal and valid.*

Václav Havel

On the night of November 24, 1989, the revolution in Czechoslovakia reached its climax. Three hundred thousand people had poured into Prague's historic Wenceslas Square to continue the massive protests that had erupted a week earlier after the police savagely beat student demonstrators. Now all eyes were focused on a high balcony. There an elderly man with a gentle smile and a middle-aged intellectual wearing jeans and sport jacket stood arm in arm and acknowledged the cheers of the crowd. "Dubček-Havel," the people roared. "Dubček-Havel!" Alexander Dubček, who represented the failed promise of reform communism in the 1960s (see page 951), was symbolically passing the torch to Václav Havel, who embodied the uncompromising opposition to communism that was sweeping the country. That very evening, the hard-line Communist government resigned, and soon Havel was the unanimous choice to head a new democratic Czechoslovakia. Who was this man to whom the nation turned in 1989?

Born in 1936 into a prosperous, cultured, upper-middle-class family, the young Havel was denied admission to the university because of his class origins. Loving literature and philosophy, he gravitated to the theater, became a stagehand, and emerged in the 1960s as a leading playwright. His plays were set in vague settings, developed existential themes, and poked fun at the absurdities of life and the pretensions of communism. In his private life, Havel thrived on good talk, Prague's lively bar scene, and officially forbidden rock 'n' roll.

In 1968 the Soviets rolled into Czechoslovakia, and Havel watched in horror as a tank commander opened fire on a crowd of peaceful protesters in a small town. "That week," he recorded, "was an experience I shall never forget."* The free-spirited artist threw himself into the intellectual opposition to communism and became its leading figure for the next twenty years. The costs of defiance were enormous. Purged and blacklisted, Havel lifted barrels in a brewery and wrote bitter satires that could not be staged. In 1977 he and a few other dissidents publicly protested Czechoslovakian violations of the Helsinki Accord on human rights, and in 1989 this Charter '77 group became the inspiration for Civic Forum, the democratic coalition that toppled communism. Havel spent five years in prison and was constantly harassed by the police.

Havel's thoughts and actions focused on truth, decency, and moral regeneration. In 1975, in a famous open letter to Czechoslovakia's Communist boss, Havel wrote that the people were indeed quiet, but only because they were "driven by fear. . . . Everyone has something to lose and so everyone has reason to be afraid." Havel saw lies, hypocrisy, and apathy undermining and poisoning all human relations in his country: "Order has been established—at the price of a paralysis of the spirit, a deadening of the heart, and a spiritual and moral crisis in society."†

Václav Havel, playwright, dissident leader, and the first postcommunist president of the Czech Republic. (Chris Niedenthal/stockphoto.com)

Yet Havel saw a way out of the Communist quagmire. He argued that a profound but peaceful revolution in human values was possible. Such a revolution could lead to the moral reconstruction of Czech and Slovak society, where, in his words, "values like trust, openness, responsibility, solidarity and love" might again flourish and nurture the human spirit. Havel was a voice of hope and humanity who inspired his compatriots with a lofty vision of a moral postcommunist society. As president of his country (1989–2003), Havel continued to speak eloquently on the great questions of our time.

Questions for Analysis

1. Why did Havel oppose Communist rule? How did his goals differ from those of Dubček and other advocates of reform communism?

2. Havel has been called a "moralist in politics." Is this a good description of him? Why? Can you think of a better one?

*Quoted in M. Simmons, *The Reluctant President: A Political Life of Václav Havel* (London: Methuen, 1991), p. 91.

†Quoted ibid., p. 110.

The great question then became whether the Soviet Union would also experience a popular anticommunist revolution. In February 1990 the Communist Party suffered stunning defeats in local elections throughout the country. Democrats and anticommunists won clear majorities in the Russian Federation's major cities. Separating himself further from Communist Party hardliners, a hard-pressed Gorbachev asked Soviet citizens to ratify a new constitution, which formally abolished the Communist Party's monopoly of political power and expanded the power of the Congress of People's Deputies. Gorbachev then convinced a majority of deputies to elect him president of the Soviet Union.

Gorbachev's eroding power and unwillingness to risk a popular election for the presidency strengthened his rival, Boris Yeltsin (b. 1931). A radical reform communist, Yeltsin became the most prominent figure in the democratic movement in the Russian Federation. In May 1990, as leader of the Russian parliament, Yeltsin boldly announced that Russia would declare its independence from the multiethnic Soviet Union. This move broadened the base of the anticommunist movement by skillfully joining the patriotism of ordinary Russians with the democratic aspirations of big-city intellectuals.

In August 1991 Gorbachev survived an attempted coup by Communist Party hardliners who wanted to preserve Communist Party power and the multinational Soviet Union; they succeeded only in destroying both. An anticommunist revolution swept the Russian Federation as the Communist Party was outlawed and its property confiscated. Yeltsin and his liberal allies declared Russia independent and withdrew from the Soviet Union. All the other Soviet republics followed suit; the Soviet Union—and Gorbachev's job as its president—ceased to exist on December 25, 1991 (see Map 31.2).

● **Celebrating Victory, August 1991** A Russian soldier flashes the victory sign in front of the Russian parliament, as the last-gasp coup attempt of Communist hardliners is defeated by Boris Yeltsin and an enthusiastic public. The soldier has cut the hammer and sickle out of the Soviet flag, consigning those famous symbols of proletarian revolution to what Trotsky once called the "garbage can of history." *(Filip Horvat/Corbis Saba)*

MAP 31.2 **Russia and the Successor States** After the attempt in August 1991 to depose Gorbachev failed, an anticommunist revolution swept the Soviet Union. Led by Russia and Boris Yeltsin, the republics that formed the Soviet Union declared their sovereignty and independence. Eleven of the fifteen republics then formed a loose confederation called the Commonwealth of Independent States, but the integrated economy of the Soviet Union dissolved into separate national economies, each with its own goals and policies.

THE UNITED STATES: CONFRONTATION AND TRANSFORMATION

What cold war tradeoffs between anticommunism and anticolonialism did the United States make?

After World War II, superpower status forced the United States to play a leading role on the world stage in the second half of the twentieth century. America had no other option, however, as long as another superpower held political and economic ideologies diametrically opposed to democracy and capitalism. Confrontation with the Soviet Union dominated U.S. foreign policy throughout the cold war. The Soviet Union's collapse in 1991 left Americans grappling with questions about the United States' new position in the world as the only superpower.

After 1945, members of America's World War II generation had babies, built houses, bought cars, and created the largest economy in the world. They also started to face up to the contradictions inherent in the promotion of democracy abroad and the denial of civil rights at home, and in calling for self-determination in eastern Europe while fighting what many considered a colonial war in Vietnam. As America tried to contain communism around the globe, it underwent an internal transformation that gave African Americans, women, and other minorities the social, political, and economic rights promised in the U.S. Constitution, and America's young gained a new voice in society and politics.

America's Economic Boom and Civil Rights Revolution

The Second World War ended the Great Depression in the United States, bringing about a great economic boom. Unemployment practically vanished, and Americans' well-being increased dramatically. As in western Europe, the U.S. economy advanced fairly steadily for a generation.

Prosperity helps explain why postwar domestic politics consisted largely of modest adjustments to the status quo until the 1960s. Truman's upset victory in 1948 demonstrated that Americans had no interest in undoing Roosevelt's social and economic reforms. In 1952 American voters turned to General Dwight D. Eisenhower (1890–1969), a national hero and self-described moderate. In 1960 young John F. Kennedy (1917–1963) captured the popular imagination. He revitalized the old Roosevelt coalition and modestly expanded existing liberal legislation before being struck down by an assassin's bullet in 1963.

Civil Rights Act *A 1964 act that prohibited discrimination in public services and on the job.*

Belatedly and reluctantly, complacent postwar America did experience a genuine social revolution: after a long struggle African Americans (and their white supporters) threw off a deeply entrenched system of segregation and discrimination. This civil rights movement advanced on several fronts. Eloquent lawyers from the National Association for the Advancement of Colored People (NAACP) challenged school segregation in the courts. In 1954 they won a landmark decision in the Supreme Court, which ruled in *Brown v. Board of Education* that "separate educational facilities are inherently unequal." Blacks also effectively challenged institutionalized inequality by using Gandhian methods of nonviolent, peaceful resistance (see page 860), such as bus boycotts, sit-ins, and demonstrations. In describing his principles for change, the civil rights leader Martin Luther King, Jr. (1929–1968), said that "Christ furnished the spirit and motivation, while Gandhi furnished the method." He told the white power structure, "We will not hate you, but we will not obey your evil laws."[4]

● **The March on Washington, August 1963** The march marked a dramatic climax in the civil rights struggle. More than two hundred thousand people gathered at the Lincoln Memorial to hear the young Martin Luther King, Jr., deliver his greatest address, the "I have a dream" speech. *(Time Life Pictures/ Getty Images)*

With African American support in key Northern states, Democrat Lyndon Johnson (1908–1973) won the 1964 presidential election in a liberal landslide. He repaid liberals' support by getting enacted the 1964 **Civil Rights Act,** which prohibited discrimination in public services and on the job, and the 1965 Voting Rights Act, which firmly guaranteed all blacks the right to vote. By the 1970s substantial numbers of blacks held public office throughout the Southern states, proof of major changes in American race relations.

In the mid-1960s Americans also generally supported President Johnson's "unconditional war on poverty" and the new social legislation behind it. Congress and the administration created a host of antipoverty projects, such as medical care for the poor and aged, free preschools for poor children, and community-action programs. Thus the United States promoted the kind of fundamental social reform that western Europe had embraced immediately after the Second World War. It became more of a welfare state as government spending for social benefits rose dramatically, approaching European levels for some programs.

Youth and the Counterculture

Economic prosperity and a more democratic class structure had a powerful impact on youth throughout North America and western Europe. The "baby boomers" born after World War II developed a distinctive and very international youth culture. This youth culture became increasingly oppositional in the 1960s, interacting with leftist thought to create a counterculture that rebelled against parents, authority figures, and the status quo.

Young people in the United States took the lead. American college students in the 1950s were docile and were often dismissed as the "Silent Generation," but some young people did revolt against the conformity of middle-class suburbs. The "beat" movement of the late 1950s expanded on the theme of revolt, and this subculture quickly spread to major American and western European cities.

Rock music helped tie this international subculture together. Rock grew out of the black music culture of rhythm and blues, which was flavored with country and western music to make it more accessible to white teenagers. Artists Elvis Presley and the Beatles became enormously popular, while suggesting personal and sexual freedom many older people found disturbing. Bob Dylan, a young folksinger turned rock poet, captured the radical aspirations of some youth when he sang that "the times they are a'changing."

Several factors contributed to the emergence of the international youth culture in the 1960s. First, mass communications and youth travel linked countries and continents together. Second, the postwar baby boom meant that young people formed an unusually large part of the population and therefore exercised exceptional influence on society as a whole. Third, postwar prosperity and greater equality gave young people more purchasing power than ever before. This enabled them to set their own trends and fads in everything from music to fashion to chemical stimulants to sexual behavior. Finally, prosperity meant that good jobs were readily available.

The youth culture practically fused with the counterculture in opposition to the established order in the late 1960s. Student protesters embraced romanticism and revolutionary idealism, dreaming of complete freedom and simpler, purer societies. The materialistic West was hopelessly rotten, but better societies were being built in the newly independent countries of Asia and Africa, or so many young radicals believed. Thus the Vietnam War took on special significance. Many politically active students in the United States and Europe believed America was fighting an immoral and imperialistic war against a small and heroic people who wanted only national unity and human dignity. Worldwide student opposition increased as the Vietnam War intensified.

> **Primary Source:**
> **Feminist Manifestoes from the Late 1960s**
> *Learn why feminists in the United States opposed all forms of patriarch, and protested institutions like the Miss America Pageant.*

The United States in World Affairs (1964–1991)

American involvement in Vietnam was a product of the cold war and the ideology of containment (see page 940). After France's defeat in Indochina in 1954 (see page 989), the Eisenhower administration refused to sign the Geneva Accords, which temporarily divided the country into two zones pending national unification by means of free elections. President Eisenhower then acquiesced in the anticommunist South Vietnamese government's refusal to accept the verdict of elections and provided military aid to help that government resist communist North Vietnam. President Kennedy increased the number of American "military advisers" to sixteen thousand.

In 1964 and 1965 President Johnson greatly expanded America's role in the Vietnam conflict, declaring "I am not going to lose Vietnam. I am not going to be the President who saw Southeast Asia go the way China went."[5] American strategy was to "escalate" the war sufficiently to break the will of the North Vietnamese and their

● **Anti– and Pro–Vietnam War Protesters Clash**   America became a divided country as the Vietnam War dragged on and American casualties mounted. In May 1970 New York City hardhat construction workers and other prowar sympathizers break up an antiwar demonstration by several hundred young protesters on Wall Street. *(Bettmann/Corbis)*

southern allies without resorting to "overkill," which might risk war with the entire Communist bloc. Thus South Vietnam received massive military aid; American forces in the South grew to a half million men; and the United States bombed North Vietnam with ever-greater intensity. But there was no invasion of the North or naval blockade. In the end the American strategy of gradual escalation backfired. It was the Americans who grew weary and the American leadership that cracked.

The undeclared war in Vietnam, visible every night on American television, eventually divided the nation. At first, support was strong. The politicians, the media, and the population as a whole saw the war as part of a legitimate defense against communist totalitarianism in all poor countries. But an antiwar movement quickly emerged on college campuses, partly because of the military draft. In October 1965 student protesters joined forces with old-line socialists, New Left intellectuals, and pacifists in antiwar demonstrations in fifty American cities. By 1967 a growing number of critics denounced the war as a criminal intrusion into a complex and distant civil war.

Criticism reached a crescendo after the Vietcong Tet Offensive against major South Vietnamese cities in January 1968. The attack was a military failure, but it resulted in heavy losses on both sides, and it belied Washington's claims that victory in South Vietnam was in sight. In March 1968 President Johnson announced he would not stand for re-election, and in October he called for negotiations with North Vietnam.

Elected by a razor-slim margin in 1968, Richard Nixon (1913–1994) sought to disengage America gradually from Vietnam and the accompanying national crisis. He intensified the continuous bombardment of the enemy while simultaneously pursuing peace talks with the North Vietnamese. He also began a slow process of withdrawal from Vietnam in a process called "Vietnamization," cutting American forces there from 550,000 to 24,000 in four years. Moreover, he launched a flank attack in diplomacy. He journeyed to China in 1972 and reached a spectacular if limited reconciliation with the People's Republic of China.

Re-elected in 1972, Nixon and Secretary of State Henry Kissinger finally reached a peace agreement with North Vietnam in 1973, which allowed the remaining American forces to complete their withdrawal. Fighting declined markedly in South Vietnam. The storm of crisis in the United States seemed to have passed.

On the contrary, the country reaped the **Watergate** whirlwind. Nixon had authorized special units to conduct domestic spying activities that went beyond the law. One such group broke into Democratic Party headquarters in Washington's Watergate building in June 1972 and was promptly arrested. Facing the threat of impeachment for trying to cover up the affair, a beleaguered Nixon resigned in disgrace in 1974.

The renewed political crisis flowing from the Watergate affair had profound consequences. First, Watergate resulted in a major power shift away from the presidency and toward Congress, especially in foreign affairs. Therefore, as an emboldened North Vietnam launched a general invasion against South Vietnamese armies in early 1974, Congress refused to permit any American military response. After more than thirty-five years of battle, the Vietnamese communists unified their country in 1975 as a harsh dictatorial state—a second consequence of the U.S. crisis. Third, South Vietnam's fall shook America's postwar confidence and left Americans divided and uncertain about America's proper role in world affairs.

One alternative to containing communism was **détente,** or progressive relaxation of cold war tensions. Détente reached its high point in 1975 when all European nations (except isolationist Albania), the United States, and Canada signed the Helsinki Accord. These nations agreed that Europe's existing political frontiers could not be changed by force, and they solemnly guaranteed the human rights and political freedoms of their citizens. Optimistic hopes for détente faded quickly, however, when Brezhnev's Soviet Union ignored the human rights provisions of the Helsinki Accord and in December 1979 invaded Afghanistan to save an unpopular Marxist regime. Thus, once again, many alarmed Americans looked to NATO to thwart communist expansion. Jimmy Carter (b. 1924), elected president in 1976, pushed the Western alliance to apply economic sanctions to the Soviet Union, but among the European allies only Great Britain supported Carter's plan. Some observers felt the alliance had lost its cohesiveness.

Yet the Western alliance endured. The U.S. military buildup launched by Jimmy Carter was greatly accelerated by Ronald Reagan (1911–2004). The Reagan administration concentrated especially on nuclear arms and an expanded navy as keys to American power in the renewed crusade against the Soviet Union—which the president anathematized as the "evil empire."

Reagan found invaluable conservative allies in Britain's strong-willed Margaret Thatcher (see page 946) and in West Germany's distinctly pro-American Helmut Kohl (see page 954). Together they also gave indirect support to ongoing efforts to liberalize communist eastern Europe and probably helped convince Mikhail Gorbachev that endless cold war conflict was foolish and dangerous. With the Soviet Union's collapse, the United States emerged as the world's lone superpower.

In 1991 the United States used its military superiority on a grand scale in a quick war in southwestern Asia after Iraq's strongman, Saddam Hussein (1937–2006), invaded Kuwait in August 1990 (see page 999). Reacting vigorously, the United States called on the United Nations to turn back Iraqi aggression. With United Nations General Assembly and Security Council consent, a U.S.-led military coalition smashed Iraqi forces in a lightning-quick desert campaign when a defiant Hussein refused to withdraw from Kuwait.

The Gulf War demonstrated the awesome power of the rebuilt and revitalized U.S. military. In the flush of victory President Bush spoke of a "new world order," apparently meaning the United States and a cooperative United Nations working together to impose peace and security throughout the world.

Watergate *The scandal in which Nixon's assistants broke into Democratic Party headquarters in July 1972.*

détente *The progressive piecemeal relaxation of cold war tensions.*

JAPAN'S RESURGENCE AS A FIRST WORLD POWER

How did Japan recover so quickly after its total defeat in World War II to become an economic superpower?

In 1945 Japan and China, East Asia's two great powers, lay exhausted and devastated. Japanese aggression had sown extreme misery in China and reaped an atomic whirlwind at Hiroshima and Nagasaki. The future looked bleak. Yet both nations recovered even more spectacularly than western Europe. In the course of recovery the two countries went their separate ways. Japan under American occupation turned from military expansion to democracy. It experienced extraordinarily successful economic development until the 1990s and in the process joined the ranks of First World nations both politically and economically. China under Mao Zedong (Mao Tse-tung) transformed itself into a strong, one-party Communist state. Although Mao initially sought a working relationship with Stalin and the Soviet Union, he soon led China off on its own as a nonaligned nation. Not until the late 1970s did the reborn giants begin moving closer together, as China retreated from Maoist communism and moved toward capitalism. China is discussed in Chapter 32.

● **Ancient Shinto Practices in Modern Japan** Ancient religious practices and modern technology come together as Shinto priests perform a ceremony of purification in front of a reactor pressure chamber in Japan. *(Yoshitaka Nakatani/ PLUS ONE, Inc., Tokyo)*

Japan's American Revolution

When American occupation forces landed in the Tokyo-Yokohama area after Japan's surrender in August 1945, they found only smokestacks and giant steel safes standing amid miles of rubble in what had been the heart of industrial Japan. Japan lay helpless before its conqueror.

Japan, like Nazi Germany, was formally occupied by all the Allies, but real power resided in American hands. General Douglas MacArthur (1880–1964), the five-star hero of the Pacific, exercised almost absolute authority. MacArthur and the Americans had a revolutionary plan for defeated Japan, introducing fundamental reforms designed to make Japan a free, democratic society along American lines. The exhausted, demoralized Japanese, who had feared a worse fate, accepted passively. Long-suppressed liberal leaders emerged to offer crucial support and help carry the reforms forward.

Japan's sweeping American revolution began with demilitarization and a systematic purge. A special international tribunal tried and convicted as war criminals twenty-five top government leaders and army officers. Other courts sentenced hundreds to death and sent thousands to prison. Over 220,000 politicians, businessmen, and army officers were declared ineligible for office.

The American-dictated, British-style constitution of 1946 allowed the emperor to remain the "symbol of the State." Real power, however, resided in the Japanese Diet, whose members were popularly elected by all adults. A bill of rights granted basic civil liberties and freed all political prisoners, including communists. Article 9 of the new constitution also abolished all Japanese armed forces and declared that Japan forever renounced war. Japan's resurrected liberals enthusiastically supported this American move to destroy militarism.

The American occupation left Japan's powerful bureaucracy largely intact and used it to implement the fundamental social and economic reforms that were rammed through the Japanese Diet. Many had a New Deal flavor. The occupation promoted the Japanese labor movement and introduced American-style antitrust laws. The American reformers proudly "emancipated" Japanese women, granting them equality before the law. The occupation also imposed revolutionary land reform. This reform strengthened the small, independent peasant, who became a staunch defender of postwar democracy.

America's efforts to remake Japan in its own image were powerful but short-lived. By 1948, as China went communist, American leaders began to see Japan as a potential ally, not as an object of social reform. The American command began purging leftists and rehabilitating prewar nationalists. The occupation ended in 1952. Under the treaty terms Japan regained independence, and the United States retained its vast military complex in Japan. Japan became America's chief Asian ally in the fight against communism. With American encouragement Japan also developed an effective "Defense Force." A sophisticated modern army in everything but name, it was never deployed in a conflict area until a tiny contingent was sent to Iraq in 2004.

"Japan, Inc."

Japan's economic recovery, like Germany's, proceeded painfully slowly immediately after the war. During the Korean War, however, the economy took off and grew with spectacular speed for a whole generation. Japan served as a base for American military operations during the Korean War, and billions of dollars in military contracts and aid poured into the Japanese economy. Between 1950 and 1970 the real growth rate of Japan's economy—adjusted for inflation—averaged a breathtaking 10 percent a year. Already by the 1960s Japan had the third-largest economy in the world. Even after the shock of much higher energy prices in 1973, the petroleum-poor Japanese did considerably better than most other peoples. In 1975 Japan joined France, West Germany, Italy, Great Britain, and the United States to form the G6, the world's six leading industrialized nations. In 1986 Japan's average per capita income exceeded that in the United States for the first time.

Japan's emergence as an economic superpower fascinated outsiders. Many Asians and Africans looked to Japan for the secrets of successful modernization, but some of Japan's Asian neighbors again feared Japanese exploitation. And in the 1970s and 1980s some Americans and Europeans bitterly accused **"Japan, Inc."** of an unfair alliance between government and business and urged their own governments to retaliate.

Japan's remarkable economic surge had deep roots in Japanese history, culture, and national character. When Commodore Perry arrived in the mid-nineteenth century, Japanese agriculture, education, and material well-being were advanced even by European standards. Moreover, a culturally homogeneous Japanese society put group needs before individual needs. The Meiji reformers who redefined Japan's primary task as catching up with the West, had the support of a sophisticated and disciplined people (see pages 764–766). By 1952, this tight-knit, group-centered society had reassessed its future and worked out a new national consensus. Japan's new task was to build its economy and compete efficiently in world markets. Improved living standards emerged as a related goal after the initial successes of the 1950s.

In a system of managed capitalism, the government decided which industries were important, then made loans and encouraged mergers to create powerful firms in those industries. Antitrust regulations introduced by the Americans were quickly scrapped, and the home market was protected from foreign competition by various measures. Big business was valued and respected in postwar Japan because it served the national goal and mirrored Japanese society. Workers were hired for life immediately after they

"Japan, Inc." *A nickname developed in the 1980s to describe the intricate relationship of the business world of Japan and its government. Many European nations believed that this collusion gave the Japanese an unfair trading advantage and urged their own governments to retaliate.*

● **Searching for Work** Japanese young people, who once could expect many first job offers after leaving school, have suffered severely from the recession that began in 2001. These job seekers, like many others, have headed to Young Hellowork in Tokyo, the nation's first employment center designed specifically for young men and women. *(Kazuhiro Nogi/AFP/Corbis)*

finished school, and employees' social lives revolved around the company. (Discrimination against women remained severe: their wages and job security were strikingly inferior to men's.) Most unions became moderate, agreeable company unions. The social and economic distance between salaried managers and workers was slight and often breached. *Efficiency, quality,* and *quantity* were the watchwords.

Japan in the Post–Cold War World

The 1990s brought a sharp reversal in Japan's economic performance and a decade of frustration. Financial problems were critical. Driven to great heights by excessive optimism, the Japanese stock market dropped by 65 percent from 1990 to 1992. The bursting of the speculative bubble crippled Japanese banks, stymied economic growth, and led to record postwar unemployment of 4.5 percent in 1998. Unemployment remained around that number through 2007. Japan also faced increasingly tough competition from its industrializing neighbors in Asia (see Chapter 32), especially in the important American market. In the early twentieth-first century the economy has fluctuated between recovery and recession, with economic growth occurring from 2005 through 2007, and then declining again in 2008.

Postwar Japanese society, with its stress on discipline and cooperation as opposed to individualism and competition, has generally proved well adapted to meet the challenges of modern industrial urban society. For example, Japan, almost alone among industrial nations, has experienced a marked decrease in crime over the past generation. Similarly, since the 1970s the Japanese have addressed such previously neglected problems as serious industrial pollution and limited energy resources. Unemployment rates, though high by Japanese standards, remain below those for most other industrialized countries, which have averaged around 5 to 7 percent in the 2000s. Long-term problems that have to be addressed include a massive government debt, a declining population, the aging of the population, and dependence on foreign sources for energy, forest products, and minerals needed for modern industry.

THE POST–COLD WAR ERA IN EUROPE (1991 TO THE PRESENT)

What have been the consequences of the collapse of the Soviet Union and the end of communism there and in eastern Europe for Europe as a whole?

The end of the cold war and the Soviet Union's collapse ended the division of Europe into two opposing camps. Thus, although Europe in the 1990s was a collage of diverse peoples with their own politics, cultures, and histories, the entire continent now shared a commitment to capitalism and democracy (see Map 31.3).

Common Patterns and Problems

In economic affairs European leaders embraced, or at least accepted, a large part of the neoliberal, free-market vision of capitalist development. This vision differed markedly from western Europe's still-dominant welfare capitalism.

Two factors were particularly important in explaining the shift to tough-minded capitalism. First, Europeans were following practices and ideologies revived and enshrined in the 1980s by Ronald Reagan in the United States and Margaret Thatcher in Great Britain. Western Europeans especially took free-market prescriptions more seriously during the presidency of Bill Clinton (1993–2001) because U.S. prestige and power were so high after the cold war ended and because the U.S. economy outperformed its western European counterparts. Second, market deregulation and the privatization of state-controlled enterprises in different European countries were integral parts of the momentous trend toward a wide-open, wheeler-dealer global economy. The rules of this global economy, laid down by powerful Western governments, multinational corporations, and big banks and international financial organizations such as the International Monetary Fund (IMF), called for the free movement of capital and goods and services, low inflation, and limited government deficits. Accepting these rules and attempting to follow them was the price of participating in the global economy.

The freer global economy had powerful social consequences. Millions of ordinary citizens in western Europe were wary of global capitalism and freer markets as they challenged hard-won social achievements. As in the United States and Great Britain in the 1980s, many Europeans generally opposed the unemployment that accompanied corporate downsizing, the efforts to reduce the power of labor unions, and, above all, government plans to reduce social benefits. The reaction was particularly intense in France and Germany, where unions remained strong and socialists championed a minimum of change in social policies.

In the 1990s political developments across Europe were also loosely unified by common patterns and problems. Most obviously, the demise of European communism brought the apparent triumph of liberal democracy everywhere. All countries embraced genuine electoral competition, with elected presidents and legislatures, and they guaranteed basic civil liberties. For the first time since before the French Revolution almost all of Europe followed the same general political model, although the variations were endless.

Recasting Eastern Europe and Russia Without Communism

With Soviet-style communism in ruins, eastern Europeans experienced continued rapid change. In Russia politics and economics were closely intertwined as President Boris Yeltsin sought to create conditions that would prevent a return to communism and right the faltering economy. Following the example of some postcommunist governments in eastern Europe, Yeltsin opted in January 1992 for breakneck liberalization.

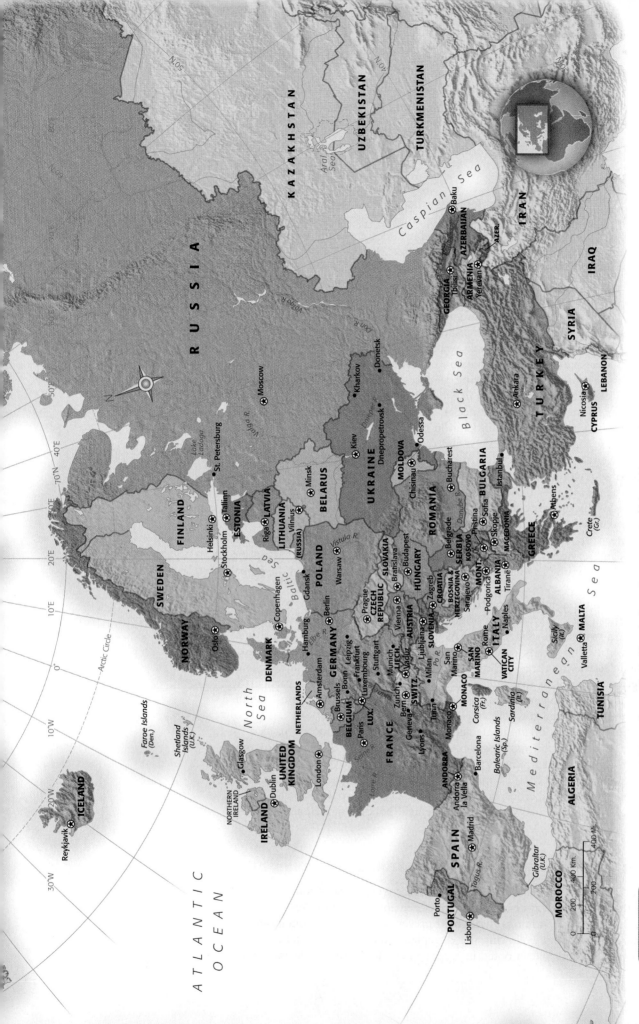

MAP 31.3 **Contemporary Europe** No longer divided by ideological competition and the cold war, today's Europe features a large number of independent states. Several of these states were previously part of the Soviet Union and Yugoslavia, both of which broke into many different countries. Czechoslovakia also divided on ethnic lines, while a reunited Germany emerged, once again, as the dominant nation in central Europe.

This shock therapy freed prices on 90 percent of all Russian goods, with the exception of bread, vodka, oil, and public transportation. The government also launched a rapid privatization of industry and turned thousands of factories and mines over to new private companies. However, control of the privatized companies usually remained in their old bosses' hands.

Yeltsin and his advisers believed shock therapy would revive production and bring prosperity after a brief period of hardship. The results were quite different. Prices soared and production fell sharply. The expected months of hardship stretched into years. By 1996 the Russian economy produced at least one-third and possibly one-half less than in 1991. From 1992 to 2001 the Russian economy fell by almost 30 percent—roughly equivalent to the United States during the Great Depression. In 2005 Russia's GDP (gross domestic product) was still lower than in 1991, but it has been growing sharply, averaging around 6.5 to 7 percent from 2003 through 2007.

Rapid economic liberalization worked poorly in Russia for several reasons. With privatization, powerful state industrial monopolies simply became powerful private monopolies, which cut production and raised prices to limit losses and maximize profits. Powerful managers forced Yeltsin's government to hand out enormous subsidies and credits to reinforce the positions of big firms or avoid bankruptcies. The managerial elite also combined with criminal elements to intimidate would-be rivals, preventing the formation of new firms. In addition, many Russians—told for decades that all capitalists were "speculators" and "exploiters"—were not interested in starting new businesses.

Runaway inflation and poorly executed privatization brought a profound social revolution to Russia. A new capitalist elite acquired great wealth and power. Managers, former officials, and financiers who came out of the privatization process with large shares of the old state monopolies stood at the top of Russian society.

At the other extreme the vast majority saw their savings become practically worthless. Pensions lost much of their value, and people sold personal goods to survive. The quality of public services and health care declined precipitously—so far that the average Russian male's life expectancy dropped from sixty-nine years in 1991 to fifty-nine years in 2007. In 2003 Russia's per capita income was lower than at any time since 1978, meaning essentially that there had been no economic progress for twenty-five years.

Political problems remained as well. Either the tsar or the Communist Party had dominated Russian politics for four hundred years. Newly formed political parties were naturally weak and inexperienced. Russia also had no law or court system that could deal with crime and corruption. Yet all politicians looked to the ballot box for legitimacy, as the election of President Vladimir Putin, Yeltsin's handpicked successor, clearly indicated in 2000. Putin's stress on public order and economic reform was popular.

During his seven and a half years in office, however, Putin became progressively more authoritarian, harking back even to the days of Communist Party rule. Under Putin, significant restrictions were placed on media freedoms, regional elections were abolished, and the distinction between judicial and executive authority collapsed. Putin consolidated the power and authority of the state around himself and his closest advisers, closing off the development of democratic pluralism and an independent legal system in Russia. Putin also supported renationalization of some industries and more state regulation of energy policy and economic planning in general. As Marshall Goldman observed, Putin's "increased involvement in economic matters is worrisome. It means that, under Putin, Russia is reversing some of the most important economic and political reforms it adopted after freeing itself from the yoke of communism."[6]

Putin's illiberal tendencies were also evident in his brutal military campaign against the separatist movement in Chechnya, a tiny republic of 1 million Muslims in southern Russia (see Map 31.2). Putin used the excuse of the global war on terror to try to destroy all Chechen opposition to Russian domination. An estimated two hundred thousand Chechen civilians have died in the war, many more have become refugees, and the country's infrastructure has been destroyed. Chechen resistance to Russian domination continues.

Putin's increasingly authoritarian rule drew criticism from many quarters, both within and outside Russia. He came under increasing pressure from the European Union countries and even from the United States to back away from some of his most undemocratic positions. Though economically now only a middle-tier country, Russia still retains the world's second-largest nuclear arsenal. That requires the rest of the world to acknowledge and negotiate with Russia.

Developments in eastern Europe shared important similarities with those in Russia, as many problems were the same. First, the postcommunist states worked to replace state planning and socialism with market mechanisms and private property. Second, Western-style electoral politics took hold, and as in Russia these politics were marked by intense battles between presidents and parliaments and by weak political parties. Third, ordinary citizens and the elderly were the big losers, while the young and former Communist Party members were the big winners. Regional inequalities persisted. Capital cities such as Warsaw, Prague, and Budapest concentrated wealth, power, and opportunity while provincial centers stagnated and industrial areas declined.

The postcommunist era saw more than a difficult transition to market economies and freely elected governments in eastern Europe, however. Eastern Europeans had never fully accepted communism, which the opposition of 1989 linked to Russian imperialism and the loss of national independence. The joyous crowds that toppled communist regimes believed they were liberating the nation as well as the individual. Thus as communism died, nationalism was reborn, as had occurred when authoritarian multinational empires had broken apart after World War I.

● **Putin and Democracy**   After the Soviet Union's collapse in 1991, Russia's new leaders instituted a number of democratic reforms. After taking office in 2000, however, Russian President Vladimir Putin, who worked as a KGB agent during the Soviet era, was accused of rolling back many of these measures, including weakening the power of the Russian parliament, curbing the freedom of the media, restricting individual freedoms, using the war on terrorism to attack opponents, and centralizing and concentrating power in the president's office. It remains to be seen whether Dmitry Medvedev, who succeeded Putin as president in May 2008, will continue Putin's policies. Medvedev appointed Putin as prime minister of Russia the day after his inauguration. (Robert Ariail/© The State/distributed by Newspaper Enterprise Association, Inc.)

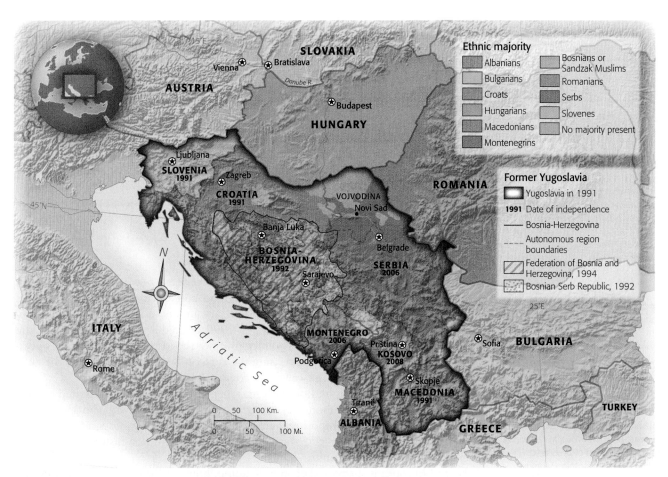

MAP 31.4 **The Breakup of Yugoslavia** Yugoslavia had the most ethnically diverse population in eastern Europe. The Republic of Croatia had substantial Serbian and Muslim minorities. Bosnia-Herzegovina had large Muslim, Serbian, and Croatian populations, none of which had a majority. In June 1991 Serbia's brutal effort to seize territory and unite all Serbs in a single state brought a tragic civil war to the region. Six new states have now emerged from parts of the old Yugoslavia— Serbia (2006), Montenegro (2006), Bosnia-Herzegovina (1992), Croatia (1991), Macedonia (1991), and Slovenia (1991). In February 2008 Kosovo declared its independence from Serbia but ethnic conflict between the majority Albanian population and the Serbian minority (who oppose independence) continues.

The response to this opportunity was varied. Poland, the Czech Republic, and Hungary were the most successful in making the transition. They managed to control national and ethnic tensions that might have destroyed their postcommunist reconstruction. The popular goal of "rejoining the West" also was a powerful force for moderation in these countries. They hoped to find security in NATO membership, which came in 1997, and prosperity by joining western Europe's economic union (see pages 970–971).

The great postcommunist tragedy was Yugoslavia, which under Josip Tito had been a federation of republics and regions. After Tito's death in 1980, power passed increasingly to the sister republics. This decentralization encouraged a revival of regional and ethnic conflicts, made worse by charges of ethnically inspired massacres during World War II and by a dramatic economic decline in the mid-1980s.

The revolutions of 1989 accelerated the breakup of Yugoslavia. When Serbian president Slobodan Milosevic attempted to grab land from other republics and unite all Serbs in a "greater Serbia," a civil war broke out that eventually involved Kosovo, Slovenia, Croatia, and Bosnia-Herzegovina (see Map 31.4). The civil war unleashed ruthless brutality, with murder, rape, the destruction of villages, the herding of refugees into concentration camps, and charges of "ethnic cleansing"—genocide—against opposing ethnic groups.

Serbian aggression appalled the Western nations. From March to June 1999 the Western powers, led by the United States, carried out heavy bombing attacks on the Serbian capital, Belgrade, on Serbian strategic sites, and on Serbian military forces. They were demanding that Milosevic withdraw Serbian armies. The impoverished Serbs eventually voted the still-defiant Milosevic out of office in September 2000, and in July 2001 a new pro-Western Serbian government turned him over to a war crimes tribunal in the Netherlands to stand trial for crimes against humanity. The civil wars in the former Yugoslavia were a monument to human cruelty. But ongoing efforts to preserve peace, repatriate refugees, and try war criminals also testified to the regenerative power of liberal values and human rights.

Unity and Identity in Western Europe

The movement toward western European unity received a powerful second wind in the 1990s. French president François Mitterrand and German chancellor Helmut Kohl took the lead in pushing for the monetary union of European Community members, and the Maastricht Agreement of 1992 created a single EU currency, the euro. In 1993 the European Community proudly rechristened itself the **European Union (EU).** Financial markets began using the euro on January 1, 1999, and the euro replaced national currencies in twelve EU countries in January 2002.

Western European elites and opinion makers generally supported this step toward economic union. They saw monetary union as a means of coping with Europe's ongoing economic problems, imposing financial discipline, cutting costs, and reducing high unemployment. These elites also saw monetary union as a historic, irreversible step toward basic political unity.

Not all Europeans supported economic union, however. Many people resented the unending flow of rules handed down by the EU's growing bureaucracy, which sought to standardize everything from cheeses to day care. Moreover, many people feared that more power in the hands of distant bureaucrats would undermine popular sovereignty and democratic control. Above all, ordinary citizens feared that the new Europe was being created at their expense. Joining the monetary union required governments to meet stringent fiscal standards and impose budget cuts and financial austerity. The resulting reductions in health care and social benefits hit ordinary citizens and did nothing to reduce western Europe's high unemployment rate.

The movement toward union also raised profound questions about the meaning of European unity and identity. Would the EU remain an exclusive Western club, or would it expand to include the postcommunist nations of eastern Europe? If some of them were included, how could Muslim Turkey's long-standing application for membership be ignored? Conversely, how could a union of twenty-five to thirty countries have any real unity?

Western Europeans proceeded cautiously at first in considering new requests for EU mem-

European Union (EU) *The new name given to the European Community in 1993.*

● **Srebrenica** When Bosnia officially declared its independence in 1992, a brutal three-year civil war broke out between Bosniaks and Croats on the one hand and Bosnian Serbs on the other. Supported by Serbia, Bosnian Serb militias practiced ethnic cleansing in those areas under their control. In July 1995 Bosnia Serb militiamen slaughtered more than 8,000 Muslim men and boys in the town of Srebrenica, Bosnia. Here a Bosnian woman weeps over the coffins of 335 newly discovered bodies found in a mass grave in 2004. *(AFP/Getty Images)*

bership. Sweden, Finland, and Austria, with strong capitalist economies, were admitted. The highly successful introduction of the euro in January 2002, however, encouraged the EU to accelerate plans for an ambitious enlargement to the east. On May 1, 2004, ten new members joined the EU: Cyprus, the Czech Republic, Slovakia, Slovenia, Latvia, Lithuania, Estonia, Hungary, Malta, and Poland. The additions brought the EU's population to 450 million, making it the world's largest trading bloc. Future candidates for membership include countries in the Balkans, former members of the old Soviet Union, and Turkey.

A proposed EU constitution binding EU member states even closer together was scheduled to go into effect in 2007. First, however, it needed approval by voters in all twenty-five countries. In late May and early June 2005 voters in two EU founding member states, France and Holland, voted overwhelmingly against the constitution and threw the entire process into confusion. Dutch officials cancelled a September 2007 referendum to approve a nearly identical reform treaty, intended to replace the original constitution treaty, when it became clear Dutch voters would reject it. An Irish "no" vote in June 2008 on the Libson Treaty, the most recent attempt at a European constitution, halted the process again. A united Europe under a common constitution remains a dream for the foreseeable future.

Chapter Summary

To assess your mastery of this chapter, go to
bedfordstmartins.com/mckayworld

• *What were the causes of the cold war?*

Ideological, political, and security differences going back to the years following the Great War began pulling the United States and the Soviet Union apart before World War II ended. A critical difference was over the future of eastern Europe after the war. Stalin refused, in his meetings with Churchill, Roosevelt, and Truman, to consider free elections in eastern Europe that might put in place anti-Soviet governments. The Western allies, and especially the United States, pushed hard for free elections, but there was little they could do to stop the Soviet occupying forces from installing pro-Soviet communist leaders in these countries. Forty years of political and military standoffs followed.

• *How and why, despite the cold war, did western Europe recover so successfully from the ravages of war and Nazism?*

In western Europe the massive aid provided by the Marshall Plan gave a quick jump-start to recovery. These countries focused all their resources on economic recovery and growth. Keynesian economic policies that encouraged governments to increase spending, even while incurring large deficits, were adopted by most western European countries. Workers, including many migrant laborers from the Mediterranean basin, advanced the economic turnaround by working hard for low wages. Pent-up demand for basic consumer products, like automobiles, refrigerators, and washing machines, encouraged full-blown economic production. Efforts to unite western Europe into a single large market helped as well to stimulate European economies.

Key Terms

Big Three
Truman Doctrine
Marshall Plan
Common Market
decolonization
neocolonialism
OPEC
de-Stalinization
Brezhnev Doctrine
perestroika
glasnost
Solidarity
Velvet Revolution
Paris Accord
Civil Rights Act
Watergate
détente
"Japan, Inc."
European Union (EU)

• *Why did a reform movement eventually triumph in eastern Europe in 1989 and bring an end to the cold war?*

The communist system in eastern Europe and the U.S.S.R. was tightened up in the Brezhnev years (1964–1982). Then, in the 1980s, public opposition to Soviet domination spread throughout the Soviet-bloc countries, eventually leading to the revolutions of 1989 and to free elections, the restoration of civil liberties, and the institution of capitalist economies in eastern Europe.

• *What cold war tradeoffs between anticommunism and anticolonialism did the United States make?*

At the beginning of the cold war the United States was faced with a difficult dilemma: to support anticolonial movements around the world, or to stand by France and Great Britain, its two major allies in World War II and potentially in the cold war, but also the two largest colonial powers. American leaders generally viewed the Soviet Unions and the spread of communism as the greatest dangers they faced, and therefore turned their back on Third World liberation movements in order to gain the support of Great Britain and France in the cold war. This stance had its most tragic consequences when the United States went to the aid of France in its efforts to hold onto its colony of Vietnam.

• *How did Japan recover so quickly after its total defeat in World War II to become an economic superpower?*

Before World War II Japan was one of the world's leading industrial nations. By the end of the war Japan lay exhausted and devastated, facing what seemed a bleak future. Allied occupation forces, however, under the direction of General Douglas MacArthur, set about helping Japan rebuild economically and develop a stable democratic government. Social and economic reforms were pushed through a new, and popularly elected, Diet (Japanese parliament). Article 9 of the new Japanese constitution abolished the military and renounced war. Eager to have a stable capitalist ally against communism in Asia, the United States guaranteed Japanese security with its own forces. America also poured billions of dollars into the Japanese economy, particularly during the Korean War when Japan served as a military operations base for American forces. Japan's economic growth skyrocketed in the 1950s and 1960s, surpassing even western Europe's success in postwar recovery.

• *What have been the consequences of the collapse of the Soviet Union and the end of communism there and in eastern Europe for Europe as a whole?*

The collapse of the Soviet Union and of communism there and across eastern Europe left little option for these countries but to adopt liberal democracy and free market capitalism. Europe was no longer divided, and differences in political organization, human rights, and economic philosophy became less pronounced in the 1990s than at any time since 1914. Eastern Europe especially struggled to rejoin the West and replace the bankrupt communist order with efficient capitalist democracies. Results varied greatly, and ordinary citizens often experienced real hardships. But in the early twenty-first century there appeared to be few attractive alternatives to global liberalism, and no effort was made to restore economic planning or one-party rule. This outcome suggests that the anticommunist revolutions of 1989 marked a major turning point in world history.

Suggested Reading

Ash, Timothy Garton. *The Polish Revolution: Solidarity,* 3d ed. 2002. A definitive account of the role of the Solidarity movement in the Polish revolution and its subsequent fate.

Dobbs, Michael. *Down with Big Brother: The Fall of the Soviet Empire.* 1997. A superb account by a journalist who covered eastern Europe.

Eksteins, Modris. *Walking Since Daybreak: A Story of Eastern Europe, World War II, and the Heart of Our Century.* 1999. A powerful, partly autobiographical account that is highly recommended.

Gaddis, John Lewis. *The Cold War. A New History.* 2005. A concise, authoritative, and accessible account of the cold war by one of its leading historians.

Grass, Günter. *The Tin Drum.* 1963. Nobel prize winner explores the spiritual dimension of West German recovery in his world-famous novel.

Halberstam, David. *The Coldest Winter. America and the Korean War.* 2007. One of America's finest journalist-historian's last, and perhaps best, history.

Hughes, H. Stuart. *Sophisticated Rebels: The Political Culture of European Dissent, 1968–1987.* 1988. Provocatively analyzes the culture and politics of protest in Europe.

Kagan, Robert. *Of Paradise and Power: America and Europe in the New World Order.* 2004. Controversial but brilliant analysis of the post–cold war world.

Karnow, Stanley. *Vietnam. A History,* 2d ed. 1997. One of the best and most comprehensive accounts of all sides in the war.

Kingston, Jeffrey. *Japan's Quiet Transformation: Social Change and Civil Society in the 21st Century. Politics, Economics and Society.* 2004. Leading scholar considers Japan's economic problems in the 1990s and their effects on Japanese politics and society.

Lampe, J. *Yugoslavia as History: Twice There Was a Country,* 2d ed. 2000. Considers judiciously and insightfully the history and violent collapse of Yugoslavia.

Laqueur, Walter. *Europe in Our Time: A History, 1945–1992.* 1992. Excellent, comprehensive study of postwar Europe, with extensive bibliography.

Sheehan, Neil. *A Bright and Shining Lie: John Paul Vann and America in Vietnam.* 1988. Classic account of the Vietnam War built around a biography of one of its harshest critics, Lieutenant Colonel Vann.

Urwin, Derek W. *The Community of Europe. A History of European Integration since 1945,* 2d ed. 1995. Eloquent history of all aspects of European attempts at economic and political union since 1945.

Wapshott, Nicholas. *Ronald Reagan and Margaret Thatcher: A Political Marriage.* 2007. Particularly good analysis of their policies of economic conservatism and anticommunism in the 1980s.

Notes

1. Quoted in N. Graebner, *Cold War Diplomacy, 1945–1960* (Princeton, N.J.: Van Nostrand, 1962), p. 17.
2. *Wall Street Journal,* June 25, 1985, p. 1.
3. Quoted in D. Treadgold, *Twentieth Century Russia,* 5th ed. (Boston: Houghton Mifflin, 1981), p. 442.
4. Regarding Gandhi's methods: see M. L. King, Jr., *Stride Toward Freedom: The Montgomery Story* (New York: Perennial Library, 1964), p. 67. Regarding evil laws: quoted in S. E. Morison et al., *A Concise History of the American Republic* (New York: Oxford University Press, 1977), p. 697.
5. Quoted in Morison, *Concise History,* p. 735.
6. M. Goldman, "Putin and the Oligarchs," *Foreign Affairs* 83 (November/December 2004): 44.

Listening to the PAST

A Solidarity Leader Speaks from Prison

Solidarity built a broad-based alliance of intellectuals, workers, and the Catholic Church. That alliance was one reason that Solidarity became such a powerful movement in Poland. Another reason was Solidarity's commitment to social and political change through non-violent action. That commitment enabled Solidarity to avoid a bloodbath in 1981 and thus maintain its structure after martial law was declared, although at the time foreign observers often criticized Lech Walesa's leadership for being too cautious and unrealistic.

Adam Michnik was one of Walesa's closest coworkers. Whereas Walesa was a skilled electrician and a devout Catholic, Michnik was an intellectual and disillusioned Communist. Their faith in nonviolence and in gradual change bound them together. Trained as a historian but banned from teaching because of his leadership in student strikes in 1968, Michnik earned his living as a factory worker. In 1977 he joined with others to found the Committee for the Defense of Workers (KOR), which supported workers fired for striking. In December 1981, Michnik was arrested with the rest of Solidarity's leadership. While in prison until July 1994, he wrote his influential Letters from Prison, *from which this essay is taken.*

Why did Solidarity renounce violence? This question returned time and again in my conversations with foreign observers. I would like to answer it now. People who claim that the use of force in the struggle for freedom is necessary must first prove that in a given situation it will be effective and that force, when it is used, will not transform the idea of liberty into its opposite.

No one in Poland is able to prove today that violence will help us to dislodge Soviet troops from Poland and to remove the communists from power. The U.S.S.R. has such enormous military power that confrontation is simply unthinkable. In other words, we have no guns. Napoleon, upon hearing a similar reply, gave up asking further questions. However, Napoleon was above all interested in military victories and not building democratic, pluralistic societies. We, by contrast, cannot leave it at that.

In our reasoning, pragmatism is inseparably intertwined with idealism. Taught by history, we suspect that by using force to storm the existing Bastilles we shall unwittingly build new ones. It is true that social change is almost always accompanied by force. But it is not true that social change is merely a result of the violent collision of various forces. Above all, social changes follow from a confrontation of different moralities and visions of social order. Before the violence of rulers clashes with the violence of their subjects, values and systems of ethics clash inside human minds. Only when the old ideas of the rulers lose this moral duel will the subjects reach for force—sometimes. This is what happened in the French Revolution and the Russian Revolution—two examples cited in every debate as proof that revolutionary violence is preceded by a moral breakdown of the old regime. But both examples lose their meaning when they are reduced to such compact notions, in which the Encyclopedists are paired with the destruction of the Bastille, and the success of radical ideologies in Russia is paired with the storming of the Winter Palace. An authentic event is reduced to a sterile scheme.

In order to understand the significance of these revolutions, one must remember Jacobin and Bolshevik terror, the guillotines of the sans-culottes, and the guns of the commissars. Without reflection on the mechanisms in victorious revolutions that gave birth to terror, it is impossible to even pose the fundamental dilemma facing contemporary freedom movements. Historical awareness of the possible consequences of revolutionary violence must be etched into any program of struggle for freedom. The experience of being corrupted by terror must be imprinted upon the consciousness of everyone who belongs to a freedom movement. [Or], as Simone Weil wrote, freedom will again become a refugee from the camp of the victors. . . .

Solidarity's program and ethos are inextricably tied to this strategy. Revolutionary terror has always been justified by a vision of an ideal society. In the name of this vision, Jacobin guillotines and Bolshevik execution squads carried out their unceasing, gruesome work.

Solidarity activist Adam Michnik in 1984, appearing under police guard in the military court that sentenced him to prison. *(Wide World Photos)*

The road to God's Kingdom on Earth led through rivers of blood.

Solidarity has never had a vision of an ideal society. It wants to live and let live. Its ideals are closer to the American Revolution than to the French. . . . The ethics of Solidarity, with its consistent rejection of the use of force, has a lot in common with the idea of nonviolence as espoused by Gandhi and Martin Luther King, Jr. But it is not an ethic representative of pacifist movements.

Pacifism as a mass movement aims to avoid suffering; pacifists often say that no cause is worth suffering or dying for. The ethics of Solidarity are based on an opposite premise: that there are causes worth suffering and dying for. Gandhi and King died for the same cause as the miners in Wujek who rejected the belief that it is better to remain a willing slave than to become a victim of murder [and who were shot down by police for striking against the imposition of martial law in 1981]. . . .

But ethics cannot substitute for a political program. We must therefore think about the future of Polish-Russian relations. Our thinking about this key question must be open; it should consider many different possibilities. . . .

The Soviet state has a new leader; he is a symbol of transition from one generation to the next within the Soviet elite. This change may offer an opportunity, since Mikhail Gorbachev has not yet become a prisoner of his own decisions. No one can rule out the possibility that an impulse for reform will spring from the top of the hierarchy of power. This is exactly what happened in the time of Alexander II and, a hundred years later, under Khrushchev. Reform is always possible, even in the face of resistance by the old apparatus. . . .

So what can now happen [in Poland]?

The "fundamentalists" say, no compromises. Talking about compromise, dialogue, or understanding demobilizes public opinion, pulls the wool over the eyes of the public, spreads illusions. Walesa's declarations about readiness for dialogue were often severely criticized from this point of view. I do not share the fundamentalist point of view. . . . The logic of fundamentalism precludes any attempt to find compromise, even in the future. It harbors not only the belief that communists are ineducable but also a certainty that they are unable to behave rationally, even in critical situations—that, in other words, they are condemned to suicidal obstinacy.

This is not so obvious to me. Historical experience shows that communists were sometimes forced by circumstances to behave rationally and to agree to compromises. Thus the strategy of understanding must not be cast aside. We should not assume that a bloody confrontation is inevitable and, consequently, rule out the possibility of evolutionary, bloodless change. This should be avoided all the more inasmuch as democracy is rarely born from bloody upheavals. We should be clear in our minds about this: The continuing conflict may transform itself into either a dialogue or an explosion. The TKK [the underground Temporary Coordinating Committee of outlawed Solidarity] and [Lech] Walesa are doing everything in their power to make dialogue possible. Their chances of success will be greater if the level of self-organization of independent Polish society increases. For street lynchings, angry crowds are enough; compromise demands an organized society.

Questions for Analysis

1. Are Michnik's arguments for opposing the government with nonviolent actions convincing?

2. How did Michnik's study of history influence his thinking? What lessons did he learn?

3. Analyze Michnik's attitudes toward the Soviet Union and Poland's Communist leadership. What policies did he advocate? Why?

Source: Adam Michnik, *Letters from Prison and Other Essays,* trans. Maya Latynski (Berkeley and Los Angeles: University of California Press, 1985), pp. 86–89, 92, 95, by permission of the University of California Press. Copyright © 1985 by The Regents of the University of California.

African Market. This bustling market in Monrovia, Liberia, reflects the vibrant diversity of modern Africa. *(Tim Hetherington/ Panos Pictures)*

chapter

32 LATIN AMERICA, ASIA, AND AFRICA IN THE CONTEMPORARY WORLD

Chapter Preview

Historians often describe the cold war era as "bipolar," consisting of (1) the United States and its allies in the West and East and (2) the Soviet Union and its allies in the West and East. Of course, the world was not truly bipolar. Two-thirds of the world's people were certainly influenced by the two superpowers' actions and were often willing or unwilling participants in their global power struggle. Just as often, they simply watched anxiously from the sidelines, hoping the two giants would not destroy them and the planet with nuclear weapons. While the United States and the Soviet Union faced each other in a deadly confrontation, people in the so-called Third World went about their daily lives.

The term *Third World* has its origins in the 1950s, when many thinkers, journalists, and politicians viewed Africa, Asia, and Latin America as a single entity, different from both the capitalist, industrialized "First World" and the communist, industrialized "Second World." Or, in contemporary scholarly jargon, they imagined and "constructed" Africa, Asia, and Latin America as a unit for effective analysis and action. Despite differences in history and culture, African, Asian, and Latin American countries—for a generation—did share many characteristics linking them together that encouraged a common consciousness and ideology.

First, nearly all African, Asian, and Latin American countries had experienced political or economic domination, nationalist reaction, and a struggle for genuine independence. Precisely because of their shared sense of past injustice and continued exploitation, many influential Latin Americans identified with the Third World, despite their countries' greater affluence.

Second, Asian, African, and most Latin American countries had—many still do—predominately agricultural economies, earning the majority of their revenues from one or two cash crops whose production was frequently controlled and exploited by First World countries or by multinational agribusinesses. In the second half of the twentieth century they became united by their growing awareness of their common poverty and dependency on First World markets to set prices and buy their raw materials.

Third, in the 1950s and 1960s a majority of people in most poor countries lived in the countryside and depended on agriculture for a living. By contrast, most First World people lived in cities and depended mainly on industry and urban services for employment. Not everyone in the Third World was poor; a small elite were quite wealthy. But the average standard of living was low, and massive poverty was ever present.

Finally, Third World peoples were united in their opposition to political and economic oppression in all its forms, particularly colonialism, neocolonialism, and racism. Their leaders believed genuine independence and social justice were the real challenges before them, and they worked in the United Nations for a restructuring of the world economic system (see page 1023).

LATIN AMERICA: MOVING TOWARD DEMOCRACY

How was Latin America similar to, and different from, the other Third World nations?

After the Second World War Latin America experienced a many-faceted recovery, somewhat similar to that of Europe, though beginning earlier. After a generation, Latin America also experienced its own period of turbulence and crisis. Many Latin American countries responded by establishing authoritarian military regimes until, in the late 1980s, Latin America copied eastern Europe by electing civilian governments and embracing economic liberalism for the first time since the 1920s.

Economic Nationalism in Latin America

The growth of economic nationalism was a common development throughout Latin America in much of the twentieth century. Just as Spanish and Portuguese colonies won political independence in the early nineteenth century, much of recent history has witnessed a quest for genuine economic independence. To understand the rise of economic nationalism, one must remember that Latin American countries developed as producers of foodstuffs and raw materials exported to Europe and the United States in return for manufactured goods and capital investment. This exchange brought considerable economic development but exacted a heavy price: neocolonialism (see pages 786–787). Latin America became dependent on foreign markets, products, and investments. Industry did not develop, and large landowners profited the most from economic development, using their advantage to enhance their social and political power.

The Great Depression made matters worse. Prices and exports of Latin American commodities collapsed as Europe and the United States drastically reduced their purchases and raised tariffs to protect domestic products. With their foreign sales plummeting, Latin American countries could not buy the industrial goods they needed from abroad. The global depression provoked a profound shift toward economic nationalism after 1930, as popularly based governments worked to reduce foreign influence and gain control of their own economies and natural resources. These efforts were fairly successful. By the late 1940s factories in Argentina, Brazil, and Chile could generally satisfy domestic consumer demand for the products of light industry. In the 1950s some countries began moving into heavy industry. Economic nationalism and the rise of industry are particularly striking in the two largest and most influential countries, Mexico and Brazil, which account for half of Latin America's population.

Primary Source:
Speech to the Nation
In this excerpt from a radio address given in 1938, President Lázaro Cárdenas announces his decision to nationalize the Mexican oil industry.

The Mexican Revolution of 1910 overthrew the elitist, upper-class rule of the tyrant Porfirio Díaz, culminating in 1917 in a new constitution. This radical nationalistic document called for universal suffrage, massive land reform, benefits for labor, and strict control of foreign capital. Progress was modest until 1934, when a charismatic young Indian from a poor family, Lázaro Cárdenas, became president and dramatically revived the languishing revolution. Under Cárdenas many large estates were divided among small farmers or were returned undivided to Indian communities. Meanwhile, state-supported Mexican businessmen built many small factories to meet domestic needs. In 1938 Cárdenas nationalized the petroleum industry. Also, the 1930s saw the flowering of a distinctive Mexican culture that proudly embraced the long-despised Indian past.

In the 1940s and 1950s more moderate Mexican presidents used the state's power to promote industrialization, and the Mexican economy grew rapidly until the late 1960s. The upper and middle classes reaped the lion's share of the benefits.

Brazilian politics was dominated by the coffee barons and by regional rivalries after the fall of Brazil's monarchy in 1889. Regional rivalries and deteriorating economic conditions allowed a military revolt led by Getúlio Vargas to seize control of the federal government in 1930. Vargas established a mild dictatorship that lasted until 1945. His rule was generally popular, combining effective economic nationalism and moderate social reform.

Modernization continued for the next fifteen years, and Brazil's economy boomed. Economic nationalism was especially vigorous under the flamboyant President Juscelino Kubitschek. Between 1956 and 1960 the government borrowed heavily from international bankers to promote industry and build the new capital of Brasília in the midst of a wilderness. Kubitschek's slogan was "Fifty Years' Progress in Five." By the late 1950s economic and social progress seemed to be bringing less violent, more democratic politics to Latin America. These expectations were shaken by the Cuban Revolution.

Authoritarianism and Democracy in Latin America

Achieving nominal independence in 1898 as a result of the Spanish-American War, Cuba was practically an American protectorate until the 1930s. Cuba's political institutions were weak and its politicians corrupt. Yet Cuba was one of Latin America's most prosperous countries by the 1950s, although enormous differences remained between rich and poor.

Fidel Castro (b. 1927) and his guerrilla forces overthrew the Cuban government in late 1958. Castro had promised a "real" revolution, and it soon became clear that

Chronology

1946–1964 Decolonization in Africa and Asia

1947 Separation of India and Pakistan

1948 End of British mandate in Palestine; Jews proclaim state of Israel

1949–1954 Mass arrests, forced-labor camps, and Communist propaganda in China

1949–present Harsh restrictions against religion and speech in China

1956 Nasser nationalizes Suez Canal Company

1964–1973 Vietnam War

1965 Cultural Revolution in China; intellectuals are exiled and art is destroyed

1967 Six-Day War in Israel

1975–present Slower population growth in Asia and Latin America

Late 1970s–present Revival of Islamic fundamentalism

1978 Islamic revolution in Iran

1980–1988 Iran-Iraq War

1989 Chinese military puts down student revolt in Tiananmen Square

1991 Congress Party in India embraces Western capitalist reforms; Gulf War

1994 Nelson Mandela becomes president of South Africa

1995 Assassination of Israeli prime minister Yitzhak Rabin

2004 Death of PLO leader Yasir Arafat

2008 Retirement of Cuban president Fidel Castro after 49 years as ruler

● **Brasília: Metropolitan Cathedral** The Metropolitan Cathedral at night in Brazil's capital city, Brasília. The cathedral was inaugurated in 1970, ten years after the inauguration of the planned city that replaced Rio de Janeiro as Brazil's capital. *(Augusto C. B. Real)*

"real" meant "communist." Middle-class Cubans began fleeing to Miami. Cuban relations with the Eisenhower administration deteriorated rapidly. In April 1961 the U.S. president, John Kennedy, tried to use Cuban exiles to topple Castro, but Kennedy abandoned the exiles as soon as they landed ashore at the Bay of Pigs.

After routing the Bay of Pigs forces, Castro moved to build an authoritarian communist society: an alliance with the Soviet bloc; a Communist Party dictatorship; state ownership; a Castro cult; prisons and emigration to silence opposition; and the exportation of communist revolutions throughout Latin America. Fearing Castro would succeed, the United States in 1961 funded the new hemispheric Alliance for Progress, intended to promote long-term economic development and social reform.

U.S. aid contributed modestly to continued Latin American economic development in the 1960s, but democratic social reforms—the other half of the Alliance for Progress formula—stalled. Conflict between leftist movements and ruling elites grew, won most often by the elites and their military allies, but at the cost of imposing a new kind of conservative authoritarianism. By the late 1970s only Costa Rica, Venezuela, Colombia, and Mexico retained some measure of democratic government. Brazil, Argentina, and Chile represented the general trend.

In Brazil, intense political competition in the early 1960s prompted President João Goulart to swing to the left to gain fresh support. When Goulart appeared ready to use force to break up landed estates and extend the vote to Brazil's many illiterates, army leaders staged a coup in 1964. Industrialization and urbanization went forward under right-wing military rule, but social inequalities increased.

In Argentina the military ousted the dictatorial populist and economic nationalist Juan Perón in 1955 and restored elected democratic government. Then, worried by a Peronist revival and following the Brazilian example, the army took control in 1966 and again in 1976 after a brief civilian interlude. Repression escalated following each military takeover. Though culturally and economically advanced, Argentina became a brutal military dictatorship.

Events in Chile were truly tragic, given its long tradition of democracy and moderate reform. When Salvador Allende, a doctor and the Marxist head of a coalition of communists, socialists, and radicals, won a plurality in 1970, he was duly elected president by the Chilean Congress. Allende completed the nationalization of the American-owned copper companies and proceeded to socialize private industry, accelerate the breakup of landed estates, and radicalize the poor. Marxism in action evoked a powerful backlash. In 1973, with widespread conservative support and U.S. backing, the traditionally impartial army struck in a well-organized coup. Allende died, probably murdered, and thousands of his supporters were arrested, or worse. As in Argentina, the military imposed a harsh despotism.

The military governments that revived antidemocratic authoritarianism in Latin America blocked not only Marxist and socialist programs but most liberal and moderate reforms as well. The new authoritarians were, however, determined modernizers, deeply committed to nationalism, industrialization, technology, and some modest social progress. They even promised free elections in the future.

That time came in the 1980s, when another democratic wave gained momentum throughout Latin America. In Argentina the military government of General Leopoldo Galtieri gradually lost almost all popular support because of its "dirty war" against its own citizens, in which thousands arbitrarily accused of opposing the regime were imprisoned, tortured, and murdered. In 1982, in a desperate gamble to rally the people, Argentina's military rulers seized the Falkland (or Malvinas) Islands (see Map 26.2 on page 783) from Great Britain. The British rout of Argentina's poorly led

● **Justice for the Victims of Chile's General Pinochet** With their faces covered with death masks, demonstrators outside Britain's High Court in 2000 hold up crosses carrying pictures of the "Disappeared"—the thousands kidnapped and allegedly murdered between 1973 and 1988 under the military dictatorship of General Pinochet. The High Court ruled against extraditing Pinochet to Spain to stand trial, but he was finally charged with torture and murder when he returned to Chile. *(Dan Chung/Reuters New-Media Inc./Corbis)*

troops forced the humiliated generals to schedule national elections. The democratically elected government prosecuted the former military rulers for their crimes and laid solid foundations for liberty and political democracy.

The Brazilian military was relatively successful in its industrialization effort, but proved unable (or unwilling) to improve the social and economic position of the masses. In 1985, after twenty-one years of rule, the military leaders allowed civilian politicians to have a try. Chile also turned from right-wing military dictatorship to elected government. Thus by the late 1980s, 94 percent of Latin Americans lived under regimes that guaranteed elections and civil liberties.

The most dramatic developments in Central America occurred in Nicaragua. In 1979 the Sandinistas, a broad coalition of liberals, socialists, and Marxist revolutionaries, drove long-time dictator Anastasio Somoza from power. The new leaders wanted genuine political and economic independence from the United States, as well as thoroughgoing land reform, some nationalized industry, and friendly ties with communist countries. These policies infuriated the Reagan administration, which sought to overthrow the Sandinista government by creating a counterrevolutionary mercenary army, the Contras, and supplying it with military aid funded illegally through military weapons sales to Iran. After years of civil war, the Nicaraguan economy collapsed, and the Sandinista government's popularity eventually declined. The Sandinistas surrendered power when they were defeated in free elections by a coalition of opposition parties.

The Reagan administration also helped engineer a 1986 coup in Haiti, where "Papa Doc" Duvalier, followed by his son, "Baby Doc," had for decades ruled in one of the most repressive dictatorships in the Americas, with U.S. support. Although "Baby Doc" was forced into exile, the country experienced a period of violence and disorder until semi-fair elections were held in 1994 with the help of U.S. military intervention. More than thirteen years later, however, Haiti remained not only the Western Hemisphere's poorest country but also in political turmoil with no improvement in sight.

Latin America in the 1990s

In the 1990s Latin America's popularly elected governments relaxed economic relations with other countries, moving decisively from tariff protection and economic nationalism toward free markets and international trade. In so doing, they revitalized their economies and registered solid gains. In 1994 Mexico joined with the United States and Canada in the North American Free Trade Agreement (NAFTA). Hoping to copy the success of the European Union, twelve South American countries (Brazil, Argentina, Paraguay, Uruguay, Venezuela, Bolivia, Colombia, Ecuador, Peru, Guyana, Suriname, and Chile) met in Cuzco, Peru, in December 2004 and signed the Cuzco Declaration, announcing the formation of the Union of South American Nations. The Constitutive Treaty formally establishing the union was signed on May 23, 2008, in Brasília, Brazil. The union will provide a free-trade zone for its members and compete economically with the United States and the European Community.

- - - - - - - - - - - - - -

THE RESURGENCE OF EAST ASIA

How did the defeat of Japan lead to East Asian resurgence after World War II?

Except for Japan, most Asian countries recovered slowly after World War II. In the early 1950s the two Koreas and China were at war in the Korean peninsula, and the Vietnamese were fighting among themselves and against the French. The Nationalist Chinese in Taiwan were adjusting to life in exile from the mainland. Hong Kong, Singapore, Indonesia, South Korea, and the Philippines were recovering from years of colonial rule and Japanese occupation. Over the next forty years, China and the "Asian Tigers" developed some of the largest and fastest-growing economies in the world, but liberal democracy remained elusive.

The Communist Victory in China

Communism triumphed in China for many reasons. As a noted historian forcefully argued, however, "Japanese aggression was . . . the most important single factor in Mao's rise to power."[1] Half of Japan's overseas armies were pinned down in China in 1945, in a long war that exhausted the established government and its supporters. Jiang Jieshi's Nationalists had mobilized 14 million men, and a staggering 3 million Chinese soldiers had been killed or wounded. The war created massive Chinese deficits and runaway inflation, hurting morale and ruining lives. Mao and the Communists had avoided pitched battles and concentrated on winning peasant support and forming a broad anti-Japanese coalition. By reducing rents, promising land redistribution, enticing intellectuals, and spreading propaganda, Mao and the Communists emerged in peasant eyes as the true patriots, the genuine nationalists.

When Japan suddenly collapsed in August 1945, Communists and Nationalists both rushed to seize evacuated territory. Heavy fighting broke out in Manchuria, and civil war began in earnest in April 1946. By 1948 the demoralized Nationalist forces were disintegrating before the better-led, more determined Communists. The following year Jiang Jieshi and 2 million mainland Chinese fled to Taiwan, and in October 1949 Mao Zedong proclaimed the People's Republic of China.

Within three years the Communists consolidated their rule. The Communist government seized the holdings of landlords and rich peasants—10 percent of the farm population had owned between 70 and 80 percent of the land—and distributed it to 300 million poor peasants and landless laborers. This revolutionary land reform was extremely popular. Meanwhile, as Mao admitted in 1957, eight hundred thousand "class enemies" were summarily liquidated between 1949 and 1954; the true figure is probably much higher. All visible opposition from the old ruling groups was destroyed.

Finally, Mao and the Communists reunited China's 550 million inhabitants in a strong centralized state. Claiming a new Mandate of Heaven, they set out to prove that China was once again a great power. This was the real significance of China's participation in the Korean War. From 1950 to 1953, the Chinese army's ability to fight the American "imperialists" to a bloody standstill on the Korean peninsula mobilized the masses and increased Chinese self-confidence.

Mao's China

Wanting to assert Chinese power and prestige in world affairs, Mao and the party looked to the Soviet Union for inspiration in the early 1950s. Along with the gradual collectivization of agriculture, China adopted a typical Soviet-style five-year plan to develop large factories and heavy industry rapidly. Russian specialists built many Chinese plants. Soviet economic aid was also considerable. The first five-year plan was successful, as undeniable economic growth followed the Communists' social revolution.

In the cultural and intellectual realms, too, the Chinese followed the Soviet example. Basic civil and political rights, which the Nationalists had seriously curtailed, were now simply abolished. Temples and churches were closed, and press freedom died. Soviet-style puritanism took hold, as the Communists quickly eradicated prostitution and drug abuse, which they had long regarded as humiliating marks of exploitation and national decline. They enthusiastically promoted Soviet-Marxian ideas concerning women and the family. Full equality, work outside the home, and state-supported child care became primary goals.

Great Leap Forward *Mao Zedong's acceleration of development in which industrial growth was to be based on small-scale backyard workshops run by peasants living in gigantic self-contained communes.*

Great Proletarian Cultural Revolution *A movement launched by Mao Zedong that attempted to purge the party of time-serving bureaucrats and recapture the revolutionary fervor of his guerrilla struggle.*

Red Guards *Radical cadres formed by young people who would attack anyone identified as an enemy of either the Communist Party or Chairman Mao.*

By the mid-1950s China seemed to be firmly set on the Marxist-Leninist course of development, but in 1958 it began to go its own way. Mao proclaimed a spectacular acceleration of development, a **Great Leap Forward** in which soaring industrial growth would be based on small-scale backyard workshops run by peasants living in gigantic self-contained communes. The creation of a new socialist personality that rejected individualism and traditional Confucian family values, such as filial piety and acceptance of parental authority, was a second goal.

The intended great leap produced an economic disaster, for frantic efforts with primitive technology often resulted only in chaos. In the countryside land went untilled as peasants turned to industrial production. As many as 20 million to 30 million people died in famines that swept the country in 1960–1961, one of the greatest human disasters in world history. When Soviet premier Nikita Khrushchev criticized Chinese policy in 1960, Mao condemned him and his Russian colleagues as detestable "modern revisionists." The Russians abruptly cut off economic and military aid, splitting the communist world apart.

Mao lost influence in the party after the Great Leap Forward fiasco and the Sino-Soviet split, but in 1965 the old revolutionary staged a dramatic comeback. Fearing that China was becoming bureaucratic, capitalistic, and "revisionist" like the Soviet Union, Mao launched the **Great Proletarian Cultural Revolution**. He sought to purge the party and to recapture the revolutionary fervor of his guerrilla struggle (see pages 864–865). The army and the nation's young people, especially students, responded enthusiastically, organizing themselves into radical cadres called **Red Guards**. The young people denounced their teachers and practiced rebellion in the name of revolution. One Red Guard manifesto exulted that "Revolution is rebellion, and rebellion is the soul of Mao Tse-tung's thought."[2]

The Red Guards sought to erase all traces of "feudal" and "bourgeois" culture and thought. Ancient monuments and countless works of art, antiques, and books were destroyed. Party officials, professors, and intellectuals were exiled to remote villages to purify themselves with heavy labor. Universities were shut down for years. Thousands of people died, many of them executed, and millions more were sent to rural forced-labor camps. The Red Guards attracted enormous worldwide attention and served as an extreme model for the student rebellions in the West in the late 1960s (see page 959).

The Limits of Reform

Mao and the Red Guards succeeded in mobilizing the masses, shaking up the party, and creating greater social equality. But the Cultural Revolution also created growing chaos and a general crisis of confidence, especially in the cities. Persecuted intellectuals, technicians, and purged party officials launched a counterattack on the radicals and regained much of their influence by 1969. Thus China shifted to the right at the same time that Europe and the United States did. This shift in China opened the door to a limited but lasting reconciliation between China and the United States in 1972.

The moderates were led by Deng Xiaoping (1904–1997), a long-time member of the Communist elite who had been branded a dangerous capitalist agent during the Cultural Revolution. After Mao's death in 1976, Deng and his supporters initiated a series of new policies, embodied in the ongoing campaign of the "Four Modernizations"—agriculture, industry, science and technology, and national defense.

China's 800 million peasants experienced the greatest and most beneficial change from this modernization campaign, what Deng proudly called China's "second revolution." At first glance this may seem surprising. Peasant support had played a major role in the 1949 Communist victory. After 1949 land reform and rationing undoubtedly improved the diet of poor peasants. Subsequently, literacy campaigns taught rural people how to read, and "barefoot doctors"—local peasants trained to do simple

● **Shaming of Enemies During the Cultural Revolution**　During the Chinese Cultural Revolution in the 1960s, young Chinese militants and Red Guards attacked people identified as enemies of the Communist Party and Chairman Mao. Many of these "enemies" were intellectuals such as teachers and artists, but they could be neighbors and even parents who were considered bourgeoisie. Here a victim is paraded through the streets wearing a dunce cap with his crimes written on it. *(Wide World Photos)*

diagnosis and treatment—brought modern medicine to the countryside. But rigid collectivized agriculture failed to provide either the peasants or the country with adequate food. Levels of agricultural production and per capita food consumption were only slightly higher in the mid-1970s than in 1937, before the war with Japan.

Determined to modernize the economy, Deng looked to the peasants as natural allies. China's peasants were allowed to farm the land in small family units rather than in large collectives and to produce what they could produce best and "dare to be rich." Peasants responded enthusiastically, increasing food production by more than 50 percent between 1978 and 1984.

The successful use of free markets and family responsibility in agriculture encouraged further economic experimentation. Foreign capitalists were allowed to open factories in southern China, and they successfully exported Chinese products around the world. Chinese private enterprise was also permitted in cities, where snack shops, beauty parlors, and a host of small businesses sprang up. China's Communist Party leaders also drew on the business talent of wealthy "overseas" Chinese in Hong Kong and Taiwan who knew the world market, needed new sources of cheap labor, and played a key role in the emerging Greater China. The Chinese economy grew rapidly between 1978 and 1987, and per capita income doubled in these years.

Change, however, was also circumscribed. Most large-scale industry remained state owned, and cultural change proceeded slowly. Above all, the Communist Party zealously preserved its monopoly of political power. When the worldwide movement for greater democracy and political freedom in the late 1980s also took root in China, the government responded by banning all demonstrations and slowing the trend toward a freer economy. Inflation then soared to more than 30 percent a year. The economic

● **Chinese Students in 1989** These exuberant demonstrators in Tiananmen Square personify the idealism and optimism of China's prodemocracy movement. After some hesitation the Communist government crushed the student leaders and their supporters with tanks and executions, reaffirming its harsh, authoritarian character. *(Erika Lansner/stockphoto.com)*

Tiananmen Square *The site of a Chinese student revolt in 1989 at which Communists imposed martial law and arrested, injured, or killed hundreds of students.*

reversal, the continued lack of political freedom, and the conviction that Chinese society was becoming more corrupt led China's idealistic university students to spearhead demonstrations in April 1989.

The students evoked tremendous popular support, and more than a million people streamed into Beijing's central **Tiananmen Square** on May 17 supporting their demands. The government then declared martial law and ordered the army to clear the students. Masses of courageous Chinese citizens blocked the soldiers' entry into the city for two weeks, but in the early hours of June 4, 1989, tanks rolled into Tiananmen Square. At least 700 students died as a wave of repression, arrests, and executions descended on China. China's Communist leaders claimed they had saved the country from plots to destroy socialism and national unity.

In the months after Tiananmen Square communism fell in eastern Europe, the Soviet Union broke apart, and China's rulers felt vindicated. They believed their strong action had preserved Communist power, prevented chaos, and demonstrated the limits of permissible reform. After some hesitation Deng, and his successor Jiang Zemin, reaffirmed economic liberalization. Private enterprise and foreign investment boomed in the 1990s. Consumerism was encouraged, and the living standard rose. But critics of Communist rule were jailed, and every effort was made to ensure the People's Army would again crush the people if ordered. Thus China coupled growing economic freedom with continued political repression, embracing only one half of the trend toward global liberalization and rejecting the other.

These policies continued into the twenty-first century. In 2001, after long negotiations, China joined the World Trade Organization, giving it all the privileges and obligations of participation in the liberal global economy. Politically communist, China now has a full-blown capitalist economy. From 1978, when Deng Xiaoping took over and launched economic reforms, through 2008, the Chinese economy has grown at an average annual rate of over 9 percent; foreign trade at an average of 16 percent. Average per capita income in China has doubled every ten years.

But China continues to have a miserable human rights record. In 2002 Hu Jintao succeeded the aging Jiang Zemin, and introduced modest legal reforms. He remains clearly committed, however, to maintaining a strong authoritarian state. As China prepared to host the 2008 Summer Olympic Games, there was some hope that, as promised, China's Communist leaders would make significant human rights, labor rights, and press freedom reforms before the games began. In spring 2008, however, the Chinese harshly crushed demonstrations in Tibet (see the feature "Individuals in Society: The Dalai Lama" on page 1061), which sparked worldwide protest, including disruption of the Olympic torch global relay. As the Olympic Games opened in August 2008, the Chinese, with only perfunctory pressure from world leaders, had made no effort to institute democratic reforms.

The Asian "Economic Tigers"

China's exploding economy has replicated the rapid industrial progress that characterized first Japan and then Asia's "Economic Tigers" (or "Four Dragons")—Taiwan, Hong Kong, Singapore, and South Korea.

Both South Korea and Taiwan were typical underdeveloped countries in the early postwar years—poor, small, agricultural, densely populated, and lacking in natural resources. They also had suffered from Japanese imperialism and from destructive civil wars with communist foes. Yet they managed to make good. How was this possible?

First, economic development became a national mission in South Korea and Taiwan. Radical land reform expropriated large landowners and drew the mass of small farmers into a competitive market economy. Probusiness governments cooperated with capitalists, opposed strikes, and did nothing to improve the long hours and low wages of self-sacrificing workers. These governments protected their own farmers and industrialists from foreign competition while also securing almost free access to the large American market. Second, both countries succeeded in preserving many cultural fundamentals even as they accepted and mastered Western technology. Third, tough nationalist leaders—Park Chung Hee in South Korea and Jiang Jieshi in Taiwan—maintained political stability at the expense of genuine political democracy.

After a military coup overthrew Park in 1980, South Korea suffered under an even more authoritarian regime through the 1980s until democracy was restored at the end of the decade. South Korea's economy, however, continued to grow and expand. By the late 1990s South Korea had one of the largest economies in the world and is a world leader in shipbuilding and high-technology products. Its GDP is about twenty times larger than North Korea's.

In 1949 after Jiang Jieshi had fled to Taiwan with his Nationalist (Kuomintang) troops and around 2 million refugees, he re-established the Republic of China (ROC) in exile. Over the next fifty years, Taiwan created one of the world's most highly industrialized capitalist economies, becoming a world leader in high-technology and electronic manufacturing and design.

● **Lights in the Night in the Eastern Hemisphere** This NASA photo uniquely illustrates differences in wealth between the North and South. Human-made lights shine brightly from developed countries and heavily populated cities. Africa's continent-wide economic poverty is clearly evident, while North Korea sits in stark dark contrast to the blaze of light from South Korea and the other "Asian Tigers." *(Image by Craig Mayhew and Robert Simmons, NASA GSFC)*

A large threatening cloud hangs over the island, however. As one of the United Nations' founding members in 1945, Jiang's ROC government held one of the Security Council's five permanent seats. In 1971 the United Nations expelled the ROC, and its Security Council seat was given to the People's Republic of (mainland) China. This action left Taiwan in political limbo: should it remain the ROC or become an independent Republic of Taiwan? Meanwhile, mainland China claims authority over Taiwan, considers it part of "One China," and has threatened to attack if Taiwan declares its formal independence. Pro-independence candidate Chen Shui-bian defeated the Kuomintang candidate in 2000 to become the first non-Kuomintang president in Taiwan's postwar history. Though he adopted a somewhat more moderate stance, he still supported independence and remained defiant toward the mainland. On January 12, 2008, however, the Taiwanese people gave the Kuomintang Party (KMT) a landslide victory in parliamentary elections, and Chen immediately resigned as chairperson of his Democratic Progressive Party. The KMT won 81 of 113 seats in parliament. In March 2008 the KMT leader, Ma Ying-jeou, won the presidential elections with 58 percent of the vote. He has dropped talk of Taiwanese independence and is seeking closer relations with the mainland. Thus, the tension surrounding the standoff between China and Taiwan, potentially one of most explosive situations in the world, may have eased.

In 1965 the largely Chinese city of Singapore was pushed out of the Malayan-dominated Federation of Malaysia. The independent city-state of Singapore prospered on the hard work and inventiveness of its largely Chinese population. Singapore's government promoted education, private enterprise, high technology, and affordable housing for all citizens. Since the mid-1990s Singapore has enjoyed one of the highest per capita incomes in the world. The government, dominated by the People's Action Party since independence, forcefully promotes conservative family values and strict social discipline.

The British first occupied Hong Kong in 1841. Primarily a center of oceanic trade in the nineteenth century, Hong Kong turned to finance, such as banking and insurance, and to manufacturing in the twentieth. On July 1, 1997, the United Kingdom returned Hong Kong to Chinese control. Under the agreement Hong Kong became the Hong Kong Special Administrative Region (SAR) of China, and China promised that, under its "one country, two systems" formula, China's socialist economic system would not be imposed on Hong Kong. Hong Kong remains one of the most vibrant global economies. It is the world's tenth-largest trading entity and eleventh-largest banking center, and it continues to have one of the world's highest per capita GDPs.

Since recovering from a series of economic crises in the late 1990s, a vibrant, independent East Asia has emerged as an economic powerhouse, an event of enormous significance in long-term historical perspective.

Political and Economic Progress in Southeast Asia

While the Philippines and Indonesia gained independence quickly after 1945, the attainment of stable political democracy proved a more difficult goal. As ethnic conflicts and cold war battles divided their countries, Filipino and Indonesian leaders frequently turned to authoritarian rule and military power in an effort to impose order and unity. By the early twentieth-first century both the Philippines and Indonesia were moving toward more stable governments and growing economies.

During the Second World War the Philippine Islands suffered greatly under Japanese occupation. After the war the United States retained its large military bases (they were finally closed in 1992) but granted the Philippines independence in 1946. The Philippines pursued American-style two-party competition until 1965 when President Ferdinand Marcos (1917–1989) subverted the constitution and ruled as dictator. In 1986 a widespread popular rebellion forced him into exile and Corazón Aquino became president. Aquino and the presidents who have followed her have made some progress in improving the economy. Many Filipinos work abroad. Their remittances back home, plus rapid growth in exports to China and strong sales of semiconductor electronics, helped the Philippine economy grow at over 7 percent in 2007. Despite the growing economy, communist insurgents and Muslim separatists continue to threaten the Philippines' political stability.

The Netherlands East Indies emerged in 1949 as independent Indonesia under the nationalist leader Achmed Sukarno (1901–1970). Like the Philippines, the populous new nation encompassed a variety of peoples, islands, and religions (85 percent of the population practices Islam; see Map 32.2 on page 995). A military coup led by General Suharto forced Sukarno out in 1965. Suharto's authoritarian rule concentrated mainly on economic development. Blessed with large oil revenues, Indonesia achieved solid economic growth for a generation. Increasingly tied to the world economy, Indonesia in 1997 was suddenly devastated by financial crisis. Suharto was forced to resign in 1998.

After Suharto's fall, freely elected governments attacked corruption and reversed the economic decline. In 2000 Indonesia gave East Timor political independence. In 2004 in the first direct presidential elections ever held, the Indonesians elected Susilo Bambang Yudhoyono as president. Despite years of natural disasters—a 2004 Indian Ocean tsunami, earthquakes, severe floods, and outbreaks of the bird flu (avian influenza)—and militant Islamic terrorist acts, the economy grew at over 6 percent in 2007, its fastest pace in eleven years.

The Reunification of Vietnam

French Indochina experienced the bitterest struggle for independence in Southeast Asia. The French tried to reimpose imperial rule there after the communist and nationalist guerrilla leader Ho Chi Minh (1890–1969) declared an independent republic in 1945, but they were decisively defeated in the 1954 Battle of Dien Bien Phu. At the subsequent international peace conference, French Indochina gained independence. Laos and Cambodia became separate states, and Vietnam was "temporarily" divided into two hostile sections at the seventeenth parallel pending elections to select a single unified government within two years.

● **Capitalism in Today's Vietnam** Swarms of "angry bees" in the street of Hanoi, Vietnam, where there are an estimated four million people and two million bikes. Motorbikes make up 90 percent of all the vehicles on the road in this rapidly modernizing country, and their numbers will only increase as Vietnam adopts market capitalism and its citizens have more disposable income. An accident death rate of over one thousand per month caused the government to mandate safety helmets as of 2008. *(Maxim Marmur/Getty Images)*

The elections were never held, and a civil war soon broke out between the two Vietnamese governments, one communist and the other anticommunist. The United States invested tremendous military effort but fought its Vietnam War (1964–1973) as a deeply divided country (see pages 959–961). The tough, dedicated communists eventually proved victorious in 1975 and created a unified Marxist nation. In 1986 Vietnamese communists began to turn from central planning toward freer markets and private initiative with mixed results. The Vietnamese economy has grown 7 to 8 percent per year since 1990, but these numbers are deceiving because inflation and unemployment are also very high. Vietnam remains one of the poorest countries in the region. Still, Communist officials are committed to a market economy, and Vietnam became the World Trade Organization's 150th member on January 11, 2007. Vietnam's Communist leaders, however, continue to zealously guard their monopoly of political power.

NEW NATIONS AND OLD RIVALRIES IN SOUTH ASIA

How did Hindus and Muslims adjust to the end of British colonial rule?

The South Asian subcontinent has transformed itself no less spectacularly than China, Japan, and the "Asian Tigers." India's national independence movements triumphed decisively over weakened and demoralized British imperialism after the Second World War. The newly independent nations of India, Pakistan, and Bangladesh exhibited many variations on the dominant themes of national renaissance and modernization, especially as the struggle for political independence receded into the past. Ethnic and religious rivalries greatly complicated the process of renewal and development.

The End of British India

After the First World War, Mahatma Gandhi and the Indian Congress Party developed the philosophy of Satyagraha (militant nonviolence) to oppose British rule of India and to lessen oppression of the Indian poor by the Indian rich (see pages 857–861). Gradually and grudgingly, Britain's rulers introduced reforms culminating in limited self-government in 1937.

The Second World War accelerated the drive toward independence. In 1942 Gandhi called on the British to "Quit India" and threatened another civil disobedience campaign. He and the other Congress leaders were quickly arrested and jailed for most of the war. Thus, India's wartime support for hard-pressed Britain was substantial but not always enthusiastic. Meanwhile, the Congress Party's prime political rival skillfully seized the opportunity to increase its influence.

Muslim League *The rival to the Indian Congress, it argued for separate homelands for Muslims and Indians.*

That rival was the **Muslim League,** led by the English-educated lawyer Muhammad Ali Jinnah (1876–1948). Jinnah feared Hindu domination of an independent Indian state led by the Congress Party. Asserting in nationalist terms the right of Muslim areas to separate from the Hindu majority, Jinnah described the Muslims of India as "a nation with our distinct culture and civilization, . . . our own distinctive outlook on life and of life."[3] In March 1940 Jinnah called on the British government to grant the Muslim and Hindu peoples separate homelands by dividing India into autonomous national states. Gandhi regarded Jinnah's two-nation theory as simply untrue and as promising the victory of hate over love.

Britain's Labour government agreed to speedy independence for India after 1945, but conflicting Hindu and Muslim nationalisms and religious hatred led to murderous clashes between the two communities in 1946. When it became clear that Jinnah

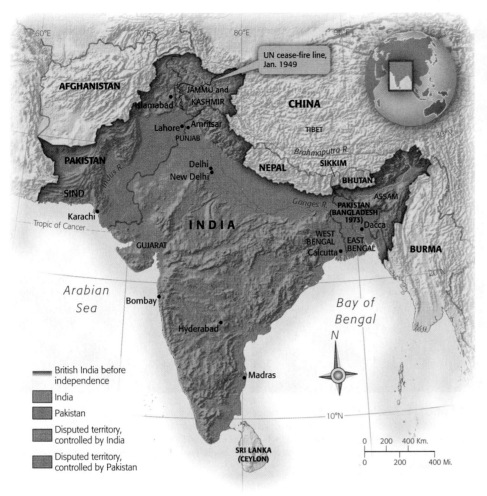

MAP 32.1 **The Partition of British India, 1947** Violence and fighting were most intense where there were large Hindu and Muslim minorities—in Kashmir, the Punjab, and Bengal. The tragic result of partition, which occurred repeatedly throughout the world in the twentieth century, was a forced exchange of populations and greater homogeneity on both sides of the border.

and the Muslim League would accept nothing less than an independent Pakistan, India's last viceroy—war hero Lord Louis Mountbatten (1900–1979)—proposed partition. Both sides accepted. At midnight on August 14, 1947, one-fifth of humanity gained political independence (see Map 32.1).

Yet independence through partition brought tragedy. In the weeks following independence communal strife exploded into an orgy of massacres and mass expulsions. Perhaps a hundred thousand Hindus and Muslims were slaughtered, and an estimated 5 million made refugees. Congress Party leaders were completely powerless to stop the wave of violence. "What is there to celebrate?" exclaimed Gandhi in reference to independence, "I see nothing but rivers of blood."[4] In January 1948, Gandhi himself was gunned down by a Hindu fanatic.

After the ordeal of independence, relations between India and Pakistan—both members of the British Commonwealth—remained tense. Fighting over the disputed area of Kashmir continued until 1949 and broke out again in 1965–1966, 1971, and 1999 (see Map 32.1).

Pakistan and Bangladesh

Pakistan's western and eastern provinces were separated by more than a thousand miles of Indian territory, as well as by language, ethnic background, and social custom. They shared only the Muslim faith. The Bengalis of East Pakistan constituted a

● **Bhutto's Assassination** Pakistani presidential candidate Benazir Bhutto stands up in her campaign van just moments before she was assassinated on December 27, 2007. In the initial confusion it was reported that an assassin fired at her with a pistol and then threw a bomb. Scotland Yard investigators later determined that she died when the force of the bomb explosion slammed her head into part of the open hatch. *(AP Images)*

majority of Pakistan's population as a whole but were neglected by the central government, which remained in the hands of West Pakistan's elite after Jinnah's death. In essence, East Pakistan remained a colony of West Pakistan.

Tensions came to a head in the late 1960s. Bengali leaders calling for virtual independence were charged with treason, and martial law was proclaimed in East Pakistan. In 1971 the Bengalis revolted. Despite savage repression the Bengalis won their independence as the new nation of Bangladesh in 1973. Bangladesh is the world's eighth most populous country, and also one of its poorest.

Emerging as completely separate states after 1973, Pakistan and Bangladesh both moved erratically from semi-authoritarian one-party rule toward competitive parliamentary systems with open elections. In the process each also experienced a series of military takeovers, restorations of civilian authority, political assassinations, and charges of official corruption. Each achieved some economic improvement but little social progress, especially for women.

India Since Independence

Jawaharlal Nehru (1889–1964) and the Congress Party ruled India for a generation after independence and introduced major social reforms. Hindu women and even young girls were granted legal equality, including the right to vote, to seek divorce, and to marry outside their castes. The constitution abolished the untouchable caste. In practice less discriminatory attitudes toward women and untouchables evolved slowly—especially in the villages, where 85 percent of the people lived.

The Congress Party leadership tried with modest success to develop the country economically by means of democratic socialism. But population growth of about 2.4 percent per year ate up much of the increase in output. Intense poverty remained the lot of most people and encouraged widespread corruption within the bureaucracy. The Congress Party maintained a moralizing neutrality in the cold war and sought to group India and other newly independent states in Asia and Africa into a "third force" of "nonaligned" nations. This effort culminated in the Afro-Asian Conference in Bandung, Indonesia, in 1955.

Nehru's daughter, Indira Gandhi (1917–1984), became prime minister in 1966. Mrs. Gandhi (whose deceased husband was no relation to Mahatma Gandhi) dominated Indian political life for a generation. In 1975 Mrs. Gandhi subverted parliamentary democracy and proclaimed a state of emergency. Attacking dishonest officials, black-marketeers, and tax evaders, she also threw the weight of the government behind a heavy-handed campaign of mass sterilization to reduce population growth. More than 7 million men were sterilized in 1976.

Many believed that Mrs. Gandhi's emergency measures marked the end of the parliamentary democracy and Western liberties introduced in the last phase of British rule. But Mrs. Gandhi—true to the British tradition—called for free elections. She suffered a spectacular electoral defeat, largely because of the vastly unpopular sterilization campaign and her subversion of democracy. Her successors, however, fell to fighting among themselves, and in 1980 Mrs. Gandhi won an equally stunning electoral victory. Her defeat and re-election undoubtedly strengthened India's democratic tradition.

Separatist ethnic nationalism plagued Mrs. Gandhi's last years in office. Democratic India remained a patchwork of religions, languages, and peoples, always threatening to further divide the country along ethnic or religious lines. Most notable among these were the 15 million Sikhs of the Punjab in northern India (see Map 32.1), who have their own religion—a blend of Islam and Hinduism—and a distinctive culture. Most Sikhs wanted greater autonomy for the Punjab, and by 1984 some Sikh radicals were fighting for independence. Mrs. Gandhi cracked down hard, and she was assassinated by Sikhs in retaliation. Violence followed as Hindu mobs slaughtered over a thousand Sikhs throughout India.

Elected prime minister in 1984 by a landslide sympathy vote, one of Mrs. Gandhi's sons, Rajiv Gandhi (1944–1991), showed considerable skill at effecting a limited reconciliation with a majority of the Sikh population. Under his leadership the Congress Party also moved away from the socialism of his mother and grandfather. In 1991 the Congress Party wholeheartedly embraced market reforms, capitalist development, and Western technology and investment. These reforms were successful, and since the 1990s India's economy has experienced explosive growth.

Holding power almost continuously from 1947, the Congress Party was challenged increasingly by Hindu nationalists in the 1990s. These nationalists argued forcefully that India was based, above all, on Hindu culture and religious tradition and that these values had been badly compromised by the Western secularism of Congress Party leaders and by the historical influence of India's Muslims. Campaigning also for a strong Indian military, the Hindu nationalist party finally gained power in 1998. The new government immediately exploded nuclear devices, asserting its vision of a militant Hindu nationalism. In 2004 a center-left coalition, the United Progressive Alliance (UPA), dominated by the Congress Party, regained control of the government.

Pakistan also exploded a nuclear weapon in 1998, and relations between Pakistan and India continued to worsen. In December 2001, the two nuclear powers had massive armies facing each other, poised for war, until intense diplomatic pressure forced them to step back from the abyss. In April 2005 both sides agreed to open business and trade relations and to work to negotiate a peaceful solution to the Kashmir dispute. Since then, although Islamic and Hindu chauvinism remain strong, this agreement has reduced the immense hostility that existed between the two countries.

● **Indira Gandhi's Funeral**   Covered with beautiful flower wreaths and carried to her funeral pyre by devoted friends, the body of the assassinated leader was then cremated in a solemn public ceremony according to Hindu religion and custom. Although the strong-willed Gandhi flirted with dictatorship, she nurtured and strengthened modern India's vibrant democratic tradition. *(David Turnley/Corbis)*

THE ISLAMIC HEARTLAND

What was the dual nature of nationalism in the Islamic heartland?

Throughout the vast *Ummah* ("world of Islam"; see Map 32.2), nationalism remained the primary political force after 1945. Anti-Western and anticommunist in most instances, Muslim nationalism generally combined a strong secular state with deep devotion to Islam. Cold war conflicts and enormous oil resources enhanced the region's global standing.

Nationalism in the Arab countries of North Africa and Southwest Asia wore two faces. The idealistic side focused on the Pan-Arab dream of uniting all Arabs in a single nation that would be strong enough to resist the West, defeat the new state of Israel, and achieve genuine independence. Despite political and economic alliances like the Arab League, this vision floundered on intense regional, ideological, and personal rivalries. Thus a more practical Arab nationalism focused largely on nation building within former League of Nations mandates and European colonies.

Subsequent one-party dictatorships, corruption, and continued daily hardship, however, caused some Islamic preachers and devoted laypeople in the late 1970s to charge that the model of modernizing, Western-inspired nationalism, had failed. These critics, labeled fundamentalists in the West, urged a return to strict Islamic principles and traditional morality. They evoked a sympathetic response among many educated Muslims as well as among villagers and city dwellers, and in Iran they gained power.

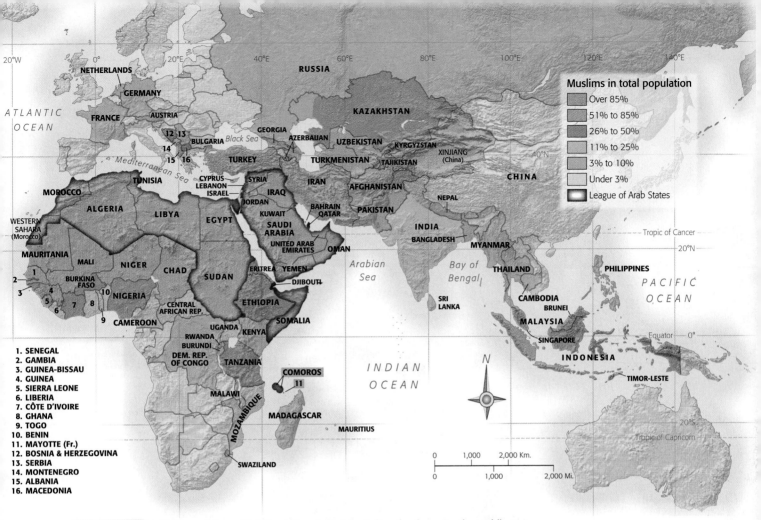

MAP 32.2 **Modern Islam, 2007** Although the Islamic heartland remains the Middle East and North Africa, Islam is growing steadily in Africa south of the Sahara and is the faith of heavily populated Indonesia. *(Source: Data from* CIA World Factbook, *2007)*

Legend — Muslims in total population:
- Over 85%
- 51% to 85%
- 26% to 50%
- 11% to 25%
- 3% to 10%
- Under 3%
- League of Arab States

1. SENEGAL
2. GAMBIA
3. GUINEA-BISSAU
4. GUINEA
5. SIERRA LEONE
6. LIBERIA
7. CÔTE D'IVOIRE
8. GHANA
9. TOGO
10. BENIN
11. MAYOTTE (Fr.)
12. BOSNIA & HERZEGOVINA
13. SERBIA
14. MONTENEGRO
15. ALBANIA
16. MACEDONIA

The Arab-Israeli Conflict

Before the Second World War, Arab nationalists were loosely united in their opposition to the colonial powers and to Jewish migration to Palestine. The British had granted independence to Egypt and Iraq before the war, and the French followed suit with Syria and Lebanon in 1945. Attention then focused even more sharply on British-mandated Palestine. The situation was volatile. Jewish settlement in Palestine was strenuously opposed by the Palestinian Arabs and the seven independent states of the newly founded Arab League (Egypt, Iraq, Jordan, Lebanon, Saudi Arabia, Syria, and Yemen). Murder and terrorism flourished, nurtured by bitterly conflicting Arab and Jewish nationalisms.

The British announced in 1947 their intention to withdraw from Palestine in 1948. The insoluble problem was dumped in the United Nations' lap. In November 1947 the United Nations General Assembly passed a plan to partition Palestine into two separate states—one Arab and one Jewish (see Map 32.3). The Jews accepted, but the Arabs rejected, partition of Palestine.

By early 1948 an undeclared civil war was raging in Palestine. When the British mandate officially ended on May 14, 1948, the Jews proclaimed the state of Israel. Arab countries immediately attacked the new Jewish state, but the Israelis drove off the invaders and conquered more territory. Roughly nine hundred thousand Arab refugees fled or were expelled from old Palestine. This war left an enormous legacy of Arab bitterness toward Israel and its political allies, Great Britain and the United

> **Primary Source:**
> **Arab and Israeli Soccer Players Discuss Ethnic Relations in Israel, 2000**
> *Learn how Arabs and Jews get along in the world of professional soccer in Israel.*

995

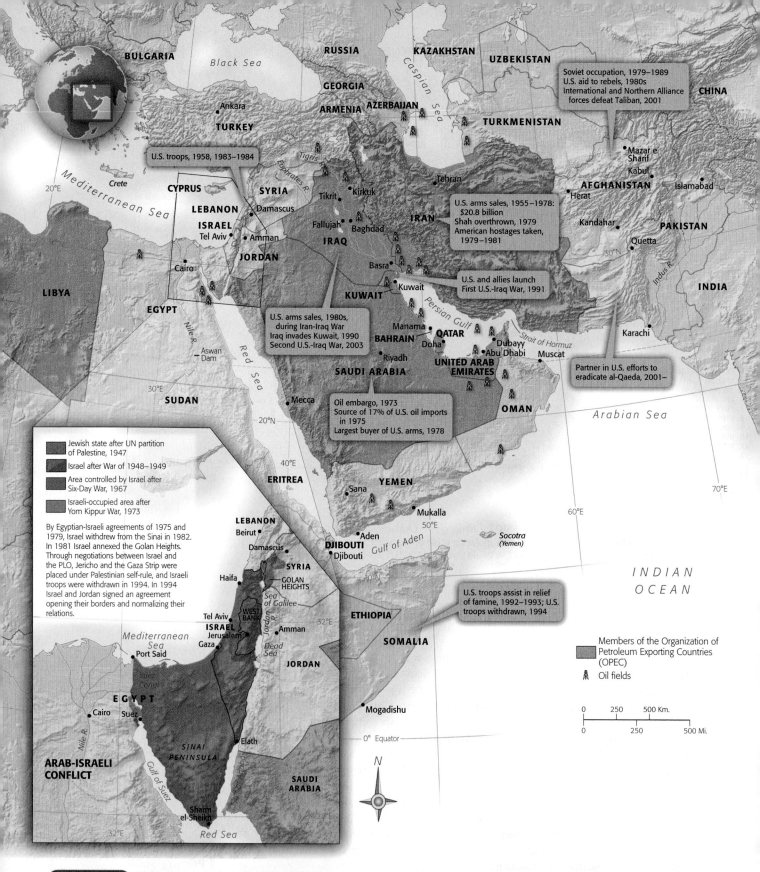

MAP 32.3 **Palestine, Israel, and the Middle East**

Since the British mandate expired on May 14, 1948, there have been five major wars and innumerable armed clashes in what was formerly Palestine. After winning the War of Independence in 1948, Israel achieved spectacular victories in 1967 in the Six-Day War, occupying the Sinai Peninsula, the Golan Heights, and the West Bank. The Yom Kippur War of 1973 eventually led to the Israeli evacuation of the Sinai and peace with Egypt. In 1993 Israel and the Palestine Liberation Organization agreed in principle to self-rule for Palestinian Arabs in the West Bank in five years, and in 1994 the Gaza Strip and Jericho were placed under the administration of the Palestinian Authority. Negotiations in Washington in 2000 failed to reach a final peace agreement, and armed conflict began again. The Israeli army reoccupied much of the West Bank, and the peace process collapsed. The election of Mahmoud Abbas as PLO leader following the death of Yasir Arafat in 2004 resulted in resumed negotiations and some concessions by both sides. These included, in July and August 2005, the removal of all Jewish settlers from the Gaza Strip.

States. It also led in 1964 to the creation of the **Palestine Liberation Organization (PLO),** a loose union of Palestinian refugee groups opposed to Israel.

The Development of Egypt

In Egypt the humiliation of Arab defeat triggered a nationalist revolution. A young army colonel named Gamal Abdel Nasser (1918–1970) drove out the corrupt and pro-Western king Farouk in 1952. Nasser enjoyed powerful influence in the Middle East and throughout Asia and Africa.

Nasser preached the gospel of neutralism in the Cold War, but accepted Soviet aid to demonstrate Egypt's independence of the West. Relations with Israel and the West worsened, and in 1956 Nasser nationalized the European-owned Suez Canal Company, Europe's last vestige of power in the Middle East. Outraged, the British and French joined forces with the Israelis and successfully invaded Egypt. The Americans, however, unexpectedly sided with the Soviets and forced the British, French, and Israelis to withdraw from Egypt. Nasser's great victory encouraged anti-Western radicalism, hopes of Pan-Arab political unity, and a vague "Arab socialism." Yet the Arab world remained deeply divided except in their bitter opposition to Israel and support for the right of Palestinian refugees to return to their homeland.

In late 1977 Egypt's president Anwar Sadat made a pathbreaking official visit to Israel, which led to direct negotiations between Israel and Egypt, effectively mediated by U.S. president Jimmy Carter, and a historic though limited peace settlement. Each country gained: Egypt got back the Sinai Peninsula, which Israel had taken in the 1967 Six-Day War (see Map 32.3), and Israel obtained peace and normal relations with Egypt. Israel also kept the Gaza Strip, taken from Egypt in 1967 and home to about 1 million Palestinians. Some Arab leaders denounced Sadat's initiative as treason.

After Sadat's assassination by Islamic radicals in 1981, Egypt's relations with Israel deteriorated badly. Yet Egypt and Israel maintained their fragile peace, and Sadat's successor as president, Hosni Mubarak (r. 1981 to present), concentrated on curbing fundamentalism and promoting economic development.

Israel and the Palestinians

In 1988 young Palestinians in the occupied territories began a prolonged campaign of rock throwing and civil disobedience against Israeli soldiers. Inspired increasingly by Islamic fundamentalists, the Palestinian uprising eventually posed a serious challenge not only to Israel but also to the secular Palestinian liberation movement, long led from abroad by Yasir Arafat (1929–2004). The result was an unexpected and mutually beneficial agreement in 1993 between Israel and the PLO. Israel agreed to recognize Arafat's organization and start a "peace process" that granted Palestinian self-rule in Gaza and Jericho and called for self-rule throughout the West Bank in five years. In return, Arafat renounced terrorism and abandoned the long-standing demand that Israel must withdraw from all land occupied in the 1967 war.

The 1993 agreement and the peace process were hotly debated in an increasingly divided Israel. In 1995 a right-wing Jewish extremist assassinated Prime Minister Yitzhak Rabin (r. 1992–1995). In 1996 a coalition of opposition parties won a slender majority, charging the Palestinian leadership with condoning anti-Jewish terrorism. The new Israeli government limited Palestinian self-rule where it existed and expanded Jewish settlements in the West Bank. On the Palestinian side, dissatisfaction with the peace process grew. Between 1993 and 2000 the number of Jewish settlers in the West Bank doubled to two hundred thousand and Palestinian per capita income declined by 20 to 25 percent. In addition, many Palestinians viewed Arafat's administration as corrupt and self-serving.

● **Israel's Wall of Separation** A Palestinian man waves as he walks across the hills near Jerusalem, where Israel's wall of separation divides Israeli and Palestinian territory. Israelis argue that the wall, made of concrete and covered with razor wire, protects them from Palestinian militants and suicide bombers. Increasingly it is described by Palestinians and others as a Berlin Wall–like structure, a symbol of Israelis forcing a separation, an Israeli version of apartheid, between the two peoples. *(AP Photo/ Wide World Photos)*

Nevertheless, in early 2000 Arafat, Israeli prime minister Ehud Barak, and U.S. president Bill Clinton met in Washington to negotiate a final peace agreement. The key Israeli proposal, however, did not offer what the Palestinians wanted—a sovereign and independent state—and they rejected it. The failed negotiations unleashed an explosion of tit-for-tat violence beginning in September 2000 in Israel and in the West Bank and Gaza Strip. In 2003 the Israelis began building a "fence" around the West Bank, which has met opposition from Israelis and Palestinians alike.

The death of Yasir Arafat, the PLO's long-time leader, in November 2004 marked a major turning point in the Israeli-Palestinian dispute. Mahmoud Abbas, Arafat's successor, is viewed as moderate and pragmatic. After taking office in January 2005, he immediately called for a peaceful solution to the conflict. Peace talks between the two sides have made very little progress, however, and in some ways matters have become worse. In January 2006 the militant Palestinian Islamist political party Hamas won elections in the Gaza Strip, seizing control from Abbas and the PLO. (See the Epilogue.) While Hamas remains isolated in Gaza, Abbas and the Israelis have been negotiating over the West Bank, with some renewed U.S. involvement by President George W. Bush and Secretary of State Condoleezza Rice in 2007–2008.

Nationalism, Fundamentalism, and Competition

The recent history of the non-Arab states of Turkey and Iran and of the Arab state of Iraq (see Map 32.2) testifies to the diversity of national development in the Muslim world. It also dramatically illustrates the intense competition between rival states and the growing strength of Islamic revival.

Turkey remained basically true to Atatürk's vision of a thoroughly modernized, secularized, Europeanized state (see pages 852–854). Islam continued to exert less influence in daily life and thought as Turkey joined NATO in 1952 and eventually sought full membership in the European Union (EU). Turkey, however, was not one of the ten eastern European countries admitted to the EU in 2004. Many Europeans questioned Turkey's dedication to the protection of human rights and feared that Turkish membership in the EU would result in a large inflow of unwanted Muslim immigrants. Turkey's long-running dispute with the Cyprian Greeks over Cyprus (which became an EU member in 2004) and continued refusal to take responsibility for its role in the Armenian genocide during World War I have further clouded its chances for membership.

After 1945 Iran tried again to follow Turkey's example, as it had before 1939 (see page 854). Once again its success was limited. The new shah—Muhammad Reza Pahlavi (r. 1941–1979), the son of Reza Shah Pahlavi—angered Iranian nationalists by courting Western powers and Western oil companies. In 1953, the freely elected prime minister Muhammad Mossaddeq tried to nationalize the British-owned Anglo-Iranian Oil Company, and the shah was forced to flee to Europe. But Mossaddeq's victory was short-lived. Loyal army officers, with the help of the American CIA, quickly restored the shah to his throne.

The shah set out to build a powerful modern nation to ensure his rule. Iran's gigantic oil revenues provided the necessary cash. The shah undermined the power bases of the traditional politicians—large landowners and religious leaders—by means of land reform, secular education, and increased power for the central government. Modernization surged forward, but at the price of ancient values, widespread corruption, and harsh dictatorship. The result was a violent reaction against modernization and secular values: an Islamic revolution in 1979 aimed at infusing strict Islamic principles into all aspects of personal and public life. Led by the Islamic cleric Ayatollah Ruholla Khomeini, the fundamentalists deposed the shah and tried to build their vision of a true Islamic state.

Iran's Islamic republic frightened its neighbors. Iraq, especially, feared that Iran—a nation of Shi'ite Muslims—would succeed in getting Iraq's Shi'ite majority to revolt against its Sunni leaders. Thus in September 1980 Iraq's strongman, Saddam Hussein (1937–2006), launched a surprise attack. With their enormous oil revenues and military machines, Iranians and Iraqis—Persians and Arabs—clashed in a savage eight-year conflict that killed hundreds of thousands of soldiers before finally grinding to a halt in 1988.

Emerging from the eight-year war with a big, tough army equipped by Western countries and the Soviet bloc, Hussein now eyed Kuwait's great oil wealth. In August 1990 he ordered his forces to overrun his tiny southern neighbor and proclaimed its annexation to Iraq. To Saddam's surprise, his aggression brought a vigorous international response and touched off the Gulf War. In early 1991 his troops were chased out of Kuwait by an American-led, United Nations–sanctioned military coalition, which included some Arab forces from Egypt, Syria, and Saudi Arabia.

Iraq and Iran went in different directions in the 1990s. The United Nations Security Council imposed stringent economic sanctions on Iraq as soon as it invaded Kuwait, and these sanctions remained after the Gulf War to force Iraq to destroy its weapons of mass destruction. United Nations inspectors destroyed many such weapons, but the United States charged Iraq with deceit and ongoing weapons development. An American-led invasion of Iraq in 2003 overthrew Saddam Hussein's regime (see pages 1025–1026).

As secular Iraq spiraled downward toward collapse and foreign occupation, Iran appeared to back away from fundamentalism. Following the constitution established by the Ayatollah Khomeini, executive power in Iran was divided between a Supreme Leader and twelve-member Guardian Council selected by high Islamic clerics, and a president and parliament elected by universal male and female suffrage. After 1990 the Supreme Leader remained a very conservative religious leader, but a growing reform movement pressed for a relaxation of strict Islamic decrees and elected a moderate, Mohammad Khatami, as president in 1997 and again in 2001. The Supreme

● **Iranian Elections, June 2005** This Iranian woman displays her support for the relatively moderate former Iranian president, Akbar Hashemi Rafsanjani, during an election rally in June 2005. To the surprise, shock, and dismay of Iranian moderates and many in the West, the ultraconservative mayor of Teheran, Mahmoud Ahmadinejad, won a landslide victory. With his election all the governing organs of the Iranian government were in the hands of ultraconservative Islamic hardliners. *(AP Photo/Wide World Photos)*

Leader, controlling the army and the courts, vetoed many of Khatami's reform measures and jailed some of the religious leadership's most vocal opponents.

Khatami had to step down in 2005, and elections were held in June. Dubious election returns gave the presidency to an ultraconservative Islamic hardliner, Mahmoud Ahmadinejad. His populist speeches and actions have made him quite popular among some elements of Iranian society. His calls for Israel's destruction; support of extremist groups in Iraq, Gaza, and Lebanon; and refusal to suspend Iran's nuclear program, however, have caused much anxiety and anger in the West. Despite this setback, many Iranians believe moderate, secular reform is inevitable, for, as one Iranian journalist observed, "Fundamentalism is good for protest, good for revolution, and good for war, but not so good for development. No country can organize its society on fundamentalism."[5]

Algeria and Civil War

The important North African country of Algeria also illustrated the development of nationalism and then fundamentalism. Nationalism in the French colony of Algeria was emboldened by Nasser's great triumph in Egypt and by France's defeat in Indochina. But Algeria's large European population—known as the *pieds noirs* ("black feet") because its members wore black shoes instead of sandals—was determined to keep Algeria part of France, and the Algerian war for independence was long, bitter, and bloody. Finally, in 1962, Algeria became an independent Arab state. The European population quickly fled.

The victorious anticolonial movement, known as the **National Liberation Front** (FLN), used revenues from Algeria's nationalized oil fields to promote state-owned industries, urban growth, and technical education. But the FLN also imposed a one-party state, crushing dissent. In the 1980s many dissatisfied Algerians looked to Islam for moral and social revival, and in the early 1990s the Islamic opposition swept municipal and national elections. The FLN called out the army, claiming the fundamentalists would "hijack" democracy and create an Islamic dictatorship. Military rule then led to growing violence and armed struggle between the government and the fundamentalist opposition that has lasted into the 2000s. Algeria's ruthless civil war placed in bold relief the cultural and ideological divisions simmering just below the surface in the Muslim world.

National Liberation Front *The name of the victorious anticolonial movement in Algeria.*

IMPERIALISM AND NATIONALISM IN SUB-SAHARAN AFRICA

How did Kwame Nkrumah represent the new leaders of independent Africa?

Most of sub-Saharan Africa won political independence fairly rapidly after World War II. Only Portugal's colonies and white-dominated southern Africa remained beyond the reach of African nationalists by 1964. The rise of independent states in sub-Saharan Africa resulted directly from both a reaction against Western imperialism and the growth of African nationalism.

The Growth of African Nationalism

Western intrusion was the critical factor in the development of African nationalism, as it had been in Asia and the Middle East. But two things were different about Africa. First, because the imperial system and Western education did not solidify in Africa until after 1900 (see pages 741–743), national movements began to come of age only in the 1920s and reached maturity after 1945. Second, Africa's multiplicity of ethnic groups, coupled with imperial boundaries that often bore no resemblance to existing ethnic boundaries, greatly complicated the development of political—as distinct from cultural—nationalism. Was a modern national state to be based on ethnic or clan loyalties (as it had been in France and Germany)? Was it to be a continent-wide union of all African peoples? Or would the multiethnic territories arbitrarily carved out by competing European empires become the new African nations? Only after 1945 did a tentative answer emerge.

A few educated West Africans in British colonies had articulated a kind of black nationalism before 1914. But the first real impetus came from the United States and the British West Indies. The most renowned participant in this "black nationalism" was W. E. B. Du Bois (1868–1963). The first black to receive a Ph.D. from Harvard, this brilliant writer and historian organized Pan-African congresses in Paris during the Versailles Peace Conference and in Brussels in 1921. **Pan-Africanists** sought black solidarity and, eventually, a vast self-governing union of all African peoples. The flamboyant Jamaican-born Marcus Garvey (1887–1940) was the most influential Pan-Africanist voice in Africa. Young, educated Africans rallied to his call of "Africa for the Africans" and European expulsion from Africa.

In the 1920s many educated French and British Africans experienced a strong surge of pride and cultural nationalism. African intellectuals in Europe formulated and articulated the rich idea of *négritude,* or blackness: racial pride, self-confidence, and joy in black creativity and the black spirit. This westernized African elite pressed for more equal access to government jobs, modest steps toward self-government, and an end to humiliating discrimination. They claimed the right to speak for ordinary Africans and denounced the government-supported chiefs as "Uncle Toms," yet their demands remained moderate.

The Great Depression was the decisive turning point in the development of African nationalism. For the first time unemployment was widespread among educated Africans. African peasants and small business people who had been drawn into world trade, and who sometimes profited from booms, also felt the agony of the decade-long bust, as did urban workers. In some areas the result was unprecedented mass protest. The Gold Coast **cocoa holdups** of 1930–1931 and 1937–1938 are the most famous examples.

Cocoa completely dominated the Gold Coast's economy. As prices plummeted after 1929, cocoa farmers refused to sell their beans to the large British firms that fixed prices and monopolized the export trade. Instead, the farmers organized cooperatives to cut back production and sell their crops directly to European and American chocolate manufacturers. The cocoa holdups succeeded in mobilizing much of the population against the foreign companies and demonstrated the power of mass organization and mass protest. Mass movements for national independence would not be far behind.

Achieving Independence with New Leaders

The repercussions of the Second World War in black Africa greatly accelerated the changes begun in the 1930s. Many African soldiers who served in India were powerfully impressed by Indian nationalism. As mines and plantations strained to meet wartime demands, towns mushroomed into cities where tin-can housing, inflation, and shortages of consumer goods created discontent and hardship.

Pan-Africanists *People, such as Marcus Garvey, who promoted solidarity among all blacks and the eventual self-governing union of all African peoples.*

cocoa holdups *A mass protest in the 1930s by Gold Coast producers of cocoa, who refused to sell their beans to British firms and instead sold them directly to European and American chocolate manufacturers.*

Nationalism in Black Africa

1919	Du Bois organizes first Pan-African congress.
1920s	Cultural nationalism grows among Africa's educated elites.
1929	Great Depression brings economic hardship and discontent.
1930–1931	Farmers in the Gold Coast organize first cocoa holdups.
1939–1945	World War II accelerates political and economic change.
1951	Nkrumah and Convention People's Party win national elections in Ghana.
1957	Nkrumah leads Ghana—former Gold Coast—to independence.
1958	De Gaulle offers commonwealth status to France's African territories; Guinea alone chooses independence.
1960	Nigeria becomes an independent state.
1966	Ghana's Nkrumah deposed in military coup.
1967	Ibos secede from Nigeria to form state of Biafra.
1979	Nigeria's military rulers permit elected civilian government.
1980	Blacks rule Zimbabwe—formerly Southern Rhodesia—after long civil war with white settlers.
1984	South Africa's whites maintain racial segregation and discrimination.
1989–1990	South African government begins process of reform; black leader Nelson Mandela freed from prison.
1994	Mandela elected president of South Africa.

Western imperialist attitudes also changed. Both the British and the French acknowledged the need for rapid social and economic improvement in their colonies; both began sending money and aid on a large scale for the first time. The principle of self-government was written into the United Nations charter and was supported by Great Britain's postwar Labour government. Thus the key question for African colonies became their rate of progress toward self-government. The British and the French were in no rush. But a new breed of African leader was emerging. Impatient and insistent, these modern African nationalists were remarkably successful: by 1964 almost all of western, eastern, and central Africa had achieved statehood, usually without much bloodshed.

These new postwar African leaders formed an elite by virtue of advanced European or American education, and they were profoundly influenced by Western thought. But compared with the interwar generation of educated Africans, they were more radical and humbler in social origin. Among them were former schoolteachers, union leaders, government clerks, and unemployed students, as well as lawyers and prize-winning poets.

Postwar African leaders accepted prevailing colonial boundaries to avoid border disputes and achieve freedom as soon as possible. Sensing a loss of power, traditional rulers sometimes became the new leaders' worst political enemies. Skillfully, the new leaders channeled postwar hope and discontent into support for mass political organizations. Eventually they came to power by winning the general elections that the colonial governments belatedly called to choose their successors.

Ghana Shows the Way

Perhaps the most charismatic of this generation of African leaders was Kwame Nkrumah (1909–1972). Nkrumah spent ten years studying in the United States, where he was deeply influenced by European socialists and Marcus Garvey. Nkrumah returned to the Gold Coast immediately after the Second World War and entered politics. Under his leadership the Gold Coast—which he rechristened "Ghana"— became the first independent African state to emerge from colonialism.

Nkrumah came to power by building a radical mass party appealing particularly to modern elements—former servicemen, market women, union members, urban toughs, and cocoa farmers. He and his party injected the joy and enthusiasm of religious revivals into their rallies and propaganda: "Self-Government Now" was their credo, secular salvation the promise.

Rejecting halfway measures—"We prefer self-government with danger to servitude in tranquility"—Nkrumah and his Convention People's Party staged strikes and riots. Arrested, the "Deliverer of Ghana" campaigned from jail and saw his party win a smashing victory in the 1951 national elections. Called from prison to head the transitional government, Nkrumah and his nationalist party defeated both westernized moderates and more traditional political rivals in free elections. By 1957 Nkrumah had achieved worldwide fame and influence as Ghana became independent.

> **Primary Source:**
> **Parable of the Eagle, Limbo, Prayer for Peace, Vultures**
> *The literature of four African writers expresses the traumatic effects of colonialism.*

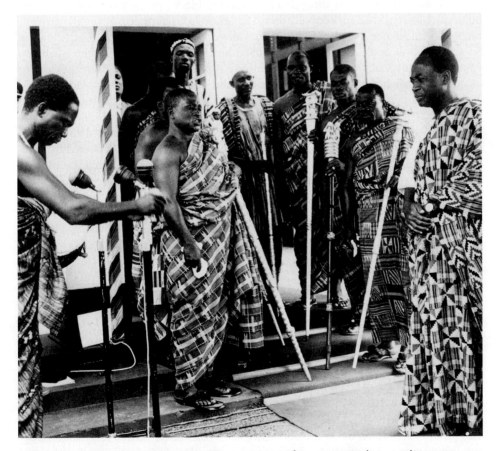

● **The Opening of Parliament in Ghana**   As part of an ancient ritual, two medicine men pour out sacred oil and call on the gods to bless the work of the Second Parliament and President Kwame Nkrumah, standing on the right. The combination of time-honored customs and modern political institutions was characteristic of African states after they secured independence. *(Wide World Photos)*

After Ghana's breakthrough, independence for other African colonies followed rapidly. As in Algeria, the main problem in some colonies was the permanent white settlers, as distinguished from the colonial officials. Wherever white settlers were numerous, as in Kenya, they sought to preserve their privileged position. But only in Southern Rhodesia and South Africa were whites numerous enough to prevail for long. Southern Rhodesian whites declared independence illegally in 1965 and held out until 1980, when black nationalists won a long liberation struggle and renamed the country Zimbabwe. Majority rule in South Africa took even longer.

French-Speaking Regions

Decolonization took a somewhat different course in French-speaking Africa. France tried hard to hold on to Indochina and Algeria after 1945. Thus although France upped its aid to its African colonies, independence remained a dirty word until Charles de Gaulle came to power in 1958. Seeking to head off radical nationalists and receiving the crucial support of moderate black leaders, de Gaulle chose a divide-and-rule strategy. He divided the French West Africa and French Equatorial Africa federations into thirteen separate governments, thus creating a "French commonwealth." Plebiscites were called in each territory to ratify the new arrangement. An affirmative vote meant continued ties with France; a negative vote signified immediate independence and a complete break with France.

De Gaulle's gamble was shrewd. The educated black elite—as personified by the influential poet-politician Léopold Sédar Senghor, who now led Senegal's government—loved France and dreaded a sudden divorce. (See the feature "Individuals in Society: Léopold Sédar Senghor, Poet and Statesman.") They also wanted French aid to continue. France, in keeping with its ideology of assimilation, had given the vote to its educated colonial elite after the Second World War, and about forty Africans held French parliamentary seats after 1946. For both cultural and practical reasons, therefore, French Africa's leaders tended to be moderate and in no rush for independence.

In Guinea, however, a young nationalist named Sekou Touré (1922–1984) led his people in overwhelming rejection of the new constitution in 1958. Inspired by Ghana's Nkrumah, Touré laid it out to de Gaulle face-to-face: "We have to tell you bluntly, Mr. President, what the demands of the people are. . . . We have one prime and essential need: our dignity. But there is no dignity without freedom. . . . We prefer freedom in poverty to opulence in slavery."[6]

The Belgians, long-time practitioners of paternalism coupled with harsh, selfish rule in their enormous Congo colony, had always discouraged the development of an educated elite. In 1959, therefore, when after wild riots they suddenly decided to grant independence, the fabric of government simply broke down. Independence was soon followed by violent ethnic conflict, civil war, and foreign intervention. The Belgian Congo was the great exception to black Africa's generally peaceful and successful transition to independence between 1957 and 1964.

• • • • • • • • • • • • • • • • • • •

SUB-SAHARAN AFRICA SINCE 1960

What are some of the common features of independent Africa since 1960?

The facility with which most of black Africa achieved independence stimulated buoyant optimism in the early 1960s. But within a generation democratic government and civil liberties gave way to one-party rule or military dictatorship and widespread corruption.

The rise of authoritarian government in Africa after independence must be viewed in historical perspective. Representative institutions on the eve of independence were

Léopold Sédar Senghor, Poet and Statesman

President Léopold Sédar Senghor in 1965. (Hulton Archive/Getty Images)

O f all the modern leaders in French-speaking Africa, Léopold Sédar Senghor (1906–2001) was the most famous and the most intriguing. His early years in a dusty village in southern Senegal were happy and varied. Later, in cold and lonely Paris, he would feast on memories of this "kingdom of childhood." Senghor's father, a successful peanut merchant, lived in the port city of Joal and had two dozen children and several wives. His last wife, Senghor's mother, remained in her village, where her extended family taught the boy the legends and mysteries of his people. In a famous poem, Senghor later wrote that his mother's brother, Uncle Waly the shepherd, could hear "what is beyond hearing," and that he lovingly explained to the wondering child "the signs that the Ancestors give in the calm seas of the constellations."*

Islam is Senegal's majority religion and the Wolof its dominant ethnic group. But Senghor's family was staunchly Christian and of the Serer people, and when he was seven, his practical father sent him to a French mission school near Joal. Learning French and Wolof, Senghor made rapid progress. When he was seventeen, his teachers sent him on to the colonial capital of Dakar, where he became the top student in the predominately white lycée. In 1928 he received a rare scholarship for advanced study in Paris. Working hard in elite schools and settling on a university career, Senghor became the first African to win the equivalent of a Ph.D. He then took a position as a classics teacher in a lycée near Paris. It was an extraordinary achievement.

Senghor's chance to pursue advanced education reflected French colonial policy in Africa. The French believed that most Africans deserved only a little practical schooling, but they also wanted to create a tiny elite of "black Frenchmen." This elite would link the French rulers and the African masses, who would need permanent French guidance. In the 1930s the brilliant Senghor seemed a model of elitist assimilation.

In fact, however, Senghor was experiencing a severe identity crisis. Who was he? How could he reconcile his complex African heritage with his French education and culture? Making close friends with other black intellectuals in Paris and strongly influenced by African

American music and literature, Senghor concluded that he would never be a "black Frenchman," for in European eyes the most accomplished African always remained exotic and inferior. He then found a new identity in racial pride and the idea of *négritude,* or blackness (see page 1001). Yet Senghor did not repudiate Europe. Instead, he reconciled his identity crisis—his being torn "between the call of the Ancestors and the call of Europe"—by striving to hold his "two sides" in equilibrium and "peaceful accord." He advocated "cross-fertilization" for Africa and Europe, which, he believed, would benefit both continents.†

Serving in the French army in World War II and turning to politics after 1945, Senghor was elected Senegal's deputy to the French National Assembly. Idolized in Senegal, he joined with other African deputies to press for greater autonomy, as well as for harmony between France and Africa. He led Senegal into Charles de Gaulle's "French commonwealth" in 1958 and then on to independence in 1960. All the major political parties in Senegal were merged to form a one-party government, with Senghor as president. Wisely avoiding dictatorship, ethnic conflict, and military rule, he led Senegal until 1980, when he retired voluntarily. Lionized in France as a great poet and statesman, Senghor was increasingly criticized by some young Senegalese, who grumbled that the aging leader had become too cooperative with France—a real "black Frenchman."

Questions for Analysis

1. What cultural and intellectual forces influenced Senghor's development? Why did he have difficulty reconciling these influences?

2. How did Senghor fit into the whole process of decolonization and African independence?

*Quoted in J. Vaillant, *Black, French, and African: A Life of Léopold Sédar Senghor* (Cambridge, Mass.: Harvard University Press, 1990), p. 18.

†Ibid., p. 146.

an imperial afterthought, and the new African countries faced tremendous challenges. Above all, ethnic divisions threatened civil conflicts that could tear the fragile states apart. Yet this did not happen. Strong leaders used nationalism, first harnessed to throw off foreign rule, to build one-party regimes and promote unity. Unfortunately, nation building by idealistic authoritarians often deteriorated into brutal dictatorships, frequent military coups, and civil strife. Then, in the early 1990s, a powerful reaction to this decline, inspired by the eastern European revolutions, resulted in a surge of democratic protest, which achieved major political gains and rekindled in part the optimism of the independence era.

Striving for National Unity

Africa's imperial legacy is more negative than positive. Although some countries left generally better legacies than others—Britain's was better than Belgium's or Portugal's, for example—overall the "civilizing mission" did more harm than good. On something of a positive note, the forty or so states (see Map 32.4 on page 1008) inherited varying degrees of functioning bureaucracies, some elected political leaders, and some modern infrastructure—transportation, schools, hospitals, and the like. And every country inherited the cornerstone of imperial power—a tough, well-equipped army to maintain order. But other features of the imperialist legacy served to torment independent Africa.

The disruption of traditional life had caused real suffering and resulted in unobtainable post-independence expectations. The prevailing export economies were weak, lopsided, and concentrated in foreign hands. Technical, managerial, and medical skills were in acutely short supply. Above all, the legacy of political boundaries imposed by foreigners without regard to ethnic and cultural groupings weighed heavily on post-independence Africa. Nearly every new state encompassed a variety of peoples who might easily develop conflicting national aspirations.

Great Britain and France had granted their African colonies democratic government as they prepared to depart. Yet belated Western-style democracy served the new multiethnic states poorly. After freedom from imperialism no longer provided a unifying common objective, political parties often coalesced along regional and ethnic lines. Many African leaders concluded that democracy threatened to destroy the existing states and prevent social and economic progress. Thus these leaders maintained the authoritarian tradition they inherited from the imperialists, and free elections often gave way to dictators and one-party rule.

After Ghana won its independence, for instance, Nkrumah jailed without trial his main opponents—chiefs, lawyers, and intellectuals—and outlawed opposition parties. Nkrumah worked to build a "revolutionary" one-party state and a socialist economy. By the mid-1960s his grandiose economic projects had almost bankrupted Ghana, and in 1966 the army suddenly seized power while he was visiting China.

The French-speaking countries also shifted toward one-party government to promote state unity and develop distinctive characteristics that could serve as the basis for statewide nationalism. Mali followed Guinea into Marxist radicalism. Senegal and the Ivory Coast stressed moderation and close economic and cultural ties with France.

Like Nkrumah, many of the initial leaders at the helm of one-party states were eventually overthrown by military leaders. The rise of would-be Napoleons was lamented by many Western liberals and African intellectuals, who often failed to note that military rule was also widespread in Latin America, Asia, and the Near East in the 1970s and 1980s.

As elsewhere, military rule in Africa was authoritarian and undemocratic. In Uganda, for instance, the brutal Idi Amin (1925?–2003) seized power in 1971, packed the army with his ethnic supporters, and terrorized the population for a decade. Yet military regimes generally did manage to hold their countries together, and many, like their Latin American counterparts (see pages 979–982), were committed to social and economic modernization. Drawing on an educated and motivated elite, they sometimes accomplished much. As economic and social conditions stagnated and often declined in African countries from the mid-1970s to the early 1990s, however, army leaders and dictators became more and more greedy and dishonest. By the late 1980s military rulers and one-party authoritarian regimes were coming under increasing pressure to hand over power to more democratic forces.

Nigeria, Africa's Giant

Nigeria's history illustrates just how difficult genuine nation building could be after independence was achieved. "Nigeria" was a name coined by the British to designate their nineteenth-century conquests in the Niger River basin, which encompassed many ancient kingdoms and hundreds of ethnic groups. Also, for administrative convenience, the British consolidated the northern Muslim territories and the southern Christian or animist areas. Despite this diverse population, by 1945 Nigeria had spawned a powerful independence movement, and independence was achieved in 1960 (see Map 32.4).

The key constitutional question was the relationship between the central government and the various regions. Ultimately Nigeria adopted a federal system, whereby the national government at Lagos shared power with three regional or state governments in

● **Nigerian Presidential and Parliamentary Elections, April 2003** In April 2003, Nigeria held its first presidential and parliamentary elections since the end of military rule in 1999. Over 60 million voters turned out across the country to choose for candidates from thirty political parties. Here federal police watch as election officials begin counting the ballots after sorting them by party. *(Corbis)*

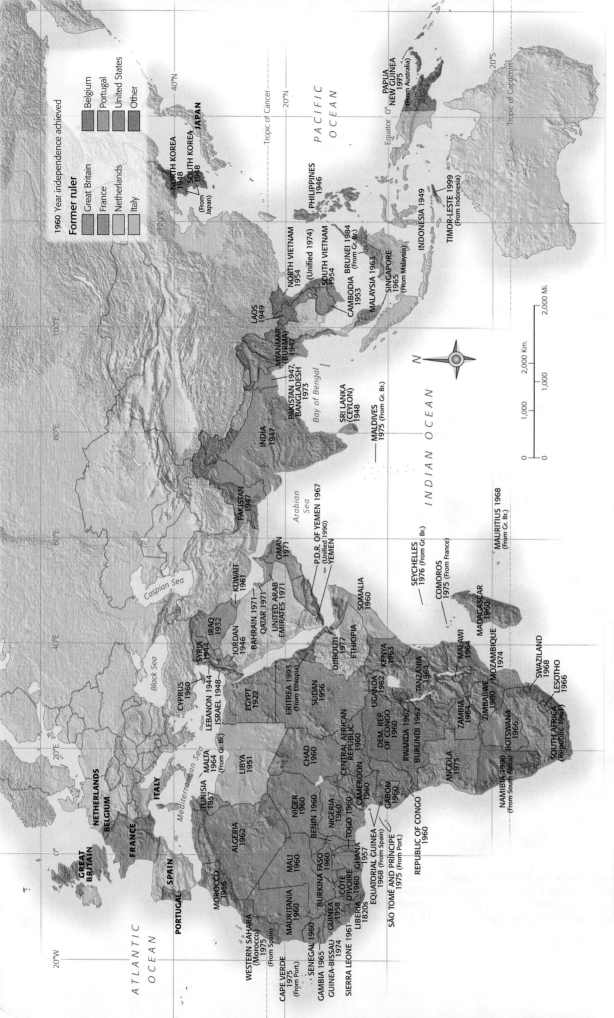

MAP 32.4 **The New States in Africa and Asia** Divided primarily along religious lines into two states, British India led the way to political independence in 1947. Most African territories achieved statehood by the mid-1960s, as European empires passed away, unlamented.

Former ruler
1960 Year independence achieved

- Great Britain
- France
- Netherlands
- Italy
- Belgium
- Portugal
- United States
- Other

ATLANTIC OCEAN

GREAT BRITAIN

NETHERLANDS
BELGIUM

FRANCE

SPAIN

PORTUGAL

ITALY

Mediterranean Sea

Black Sea

Caspian Sea

Arabian Sea

INDIAN OCEAN

Bay of Bengal

PACIFIC OCEAN

JAPAN

Equator 0°

Tropic of Cancer

Tropic of Capricorn

20°W · 0° · 20°E · 40°E · 60°E · 80°E · 100°E · 120°E

40°N · 20°N · 0° · 20°S

MOROCCO 1956
WESTERN SAHARA 1975 (Morocco) (From Spain)
CAPE VERDE 1975 (From Port.)
MAURITANIA 1960
SENEGAL 1960
GAMBIA 1965
GUINEA-BISSAU 1974
GUINEA 1958
SIERRA LEONE 1961
LIBERIA 1820s
CÔTE D'IVOIRE 1960
MALI 1960
BURKINA FASO 1960
GHANA 1957
TOGO 1960
BENIN 1960
NIGER 1960
NIGERIA 1960
EQUATORIAL GUINEA 1968 (From Spain)
SÃO TOMÉ AND PRÍNCIPE 1975 (From Port.)
GABON 1960
CAMEROON 1960
REPUBLIC OF CONGO 1960
ALGERIA 1962
TUNISIA 1957
MALTA 1964 (From Gr. Br.)
LIBYA 1951
CHAD 1960
CENTRAL AFRICAN REPUBLIC 1960
DEM. REP. OF CONGO 1960
ANGOLA 1975
NAMIBIA 1990 (From South Africa)
BOTSWANA 1966
SOUTH AFRICA (Republic 1961)
LESOTHO 1966
SWAZILAND 1968
ZIMBABWE 1980
MOZAMBIQUE 1974
ZAMBIA 1964
MALAWI 1964
TANZANIA 1964
RWANDA 1962
BURUNDI 1962
UGANDA 1962
KENYA 1963
SOMALIA 1960
ETHIOPIA
DJIBOUTI 1977
ERITREA 1993 (From Ethiopia)
SUDAN 1956
EGYPT 1922
CYPRUS 1960
LEBANON 1944
ISRAEL 1948
SYRIA 1944
JORDAN 1946
IRAQ 1932
KUWAIT 1961
BAHRAIN 1971
QATAR 1971
UNITED ARAB EMIRATES 1971
OMAN 1971
P.D.R. OF YEMEN 1967 (Unified 1990)
YEMEN
MADAGASCAR 1960
COMOROS 1975 (From France)
SEYCHELLES 1976 (From Gr. Br.)
MAURITIUS 1968 (From Gr. Br.)
MALDIVES 1975 (From Gr. Br.)
SRI LANKA (CEYLON) 1948
INDIA 1947
PAKISTAN 1947
PAKISTAN 1947, BANGLADESH 1973
MYANMAR (BURMA) 1947
LAOS 1949
NORTH VIETNAM 1954 (Unified 1974)
SOUTH VIETNAM 1954
CAMBODIA 1953
MALAYSIA 1963
BRUNEI 1984 (From Gr. Br.)
SINGAPORE 1965 (From Malaysia)
PHILIPPINES 1946
INDONESIA 1949
TIMOR-LESTE 1999 (From Indonesia)
PAPUA NEW GUINEA 1975 (From Australia)
NORTH KOREA 1948
SOUTH KOREA 1948 (From Japan)

N

0 · 1,000 · 2,000 Km.
0 · 1,000 · 2,000 Mi.

the north, west, and east. Each region had a dominant ethnic group and a corresponding political party. The parties were expected to cooperate in the national parliament, and the rights of minorities were protected by law.

After independence Nigerians' bright hopes gradually dimmed because of growing ethnic rivalries. In 1967 these intense rivalries erupted into a civil war. The crisis began in 1964 when some young military officers, many of whom were Ibos from the southeast, seized the government and executed its leaders.

At first the young officers were popular, but the Muslim northerners had long distrusted the hard-working, clannish, non-Muslim Ibos. When the Ibo-led military council proclaimed a centralized dictatorship, wild mobs in northern cities massacred thousands of Ibos. When a group of northern officers then seized the national government in a countercoup, the traumatized Ibos revolted and proclaimed the independent state of Biafra in 1967.

The Biafran war lasted three years. The Ibos fought with heroic determination, believing that political independence was their only refuge from genocide. Heavily outnumbered, the Ibos were gradually surrounded. Perhaps millions starved to death as Biafra became a symbol of monumental human tragedy.

Having preserved the state in the 1960s, Nigeria's military rulers focused on building a nation in the 1970s. Although the federal government held the real power, the country was divided into nineteen small, manageable units to handle local and cultural matters. The defeated Ibos were pardoned, and Iboland was rebuilt with federal oil revenues.

Except for a couple of brief periods of civilian rule, combinations of Hausa-Fulani Muslim army officers ruled until 1998, when the brutal military dictator General Sani Abacha suddenly died and gave Nigeria renewed hope for unity and democracy. In 1999 Nigerians voted in free elections and re-established civilian rule; the April 2003 elections marked the first civilian transfer of power in Nigeria's history.

Nigeria is the world's eleventh-largest oil producer and a member of OPEC. Oil provides about 20 percent of Nigeria's GDP, 95 percent of its foreign exchange earnings, and about 65 percent of its budgetary revenues. Nigeria still needs to diversify its economy, however, if it is to overcome massive poverty and become economically stable. Nigeria's leaders must also calm the religious strife that continues to divide the country. Since 2000, riots between Muslims and non-Muslims have left thousands dead in the predominately Muslim northern Nigerian states, where there is a movement to implement shari'a (Islamic law) as the law of the state.

The Struggle in Southern Africa

After the great rush toward political independence in the early 1960s, decolonization stalled. Southern Africa remained under white minority rule, largely because of the numerical strength and determination of its white settlers.

In Portuguese Angola and Mozambique, the white population actually increased from 70,000 to 380,000 between 1940 and the mid-1960s, as white settlers using forced native labor established large coffee farms. As economic exploitation grew, so did resentment. Nationalist liberation movements arose to wage unrelenting guerrilla warfare. After a coup overturned the long-established dictatorship in Portugal, African liberation forces seized control in Angola and Mozambique in 1975. Shortly thereafter a coalition of nationalist groups also won in Zimbabwe after a long struggle.

The battle in South Africa threatened to be still worse. The racial conflict in the white-ruled Republic of South Africa could be traced back in part to the outcome of the South African War (see page 816). After the British finally conquered the inland Afrikaner republics, they agreed to grant all of South Africa self-government—South

Africa became basically a self-governing British dominion, like Canada and Australia—as soon as possible. English and moderate Afrikaners ruled jointly and could also decide which nonwhites, if any, should vote.

In 1913 the new South African legislature passed the **Native Land Act**, which limited black ownership of land to native reserves encompassing a mere one-seventh of the country. Poor, overpopulated, and too small to feed themselves, the rural native reserves served as a pool of cheap, temporary black labor for white farms, gold mines, and urban factories. Legally, the black worker was only a temporary migrant who could be returned at will by the employer or the government. The native reserves system, combining racial segregation and indirect forced labor, formed the foundation of white supremacy in South Africa.

Native Land Act *A 1913 South African law that limited black ownership of land to native reserves encompassing only one-seventh of the country.*

Some extreme Afrikaner nationalists, however, refused to accept defeat and any British political presence. They elaborated an even more potently racist Afrikaner nationalist platform of white supremacy and racial segregation that between 1910 and 1948 gradually won them political power from their English-speaking settler rivals. After their decisive 1948 electoral victory, Afrikaner nationalists spoke increasingly for a large majority of South African whites.

Once in control, successive Afrikaner governments wove the somewhat haphazard early racist measures into an authoritarian fabric of racial discrimination and inequality. This system was officially known as **apartheid,** meaning "apartness" or "separation." The population was divided into four legally unequal racial groups: whites, blacks, Asians, and racially mixed "coloureds." Although Afrikaner propagandists claimed that apartheid served the interests of all racial groups by preserving separate cultures and racial purity, most observers saw it as a way of maintaining the lavish privileges of the white minority, which accounted for only one-sixth of the total population.

apartheid *The system of racial segregation and discrimination that was supported by the Afrikaner government.*

After 1940, South Africa became the most highly industrialized country in Africa. Rapid urbanization followed, changing the face of the country, but good jobs in the cities were reserved for whites. Whites lived in luxurious modern central cities. Blacks, as temporary migrants, were restricted to outlying black townships plagued by poverty, crime, and white policemen.

South Africa's harsh white supremacy elicited many black nationalist protests from the 1920s onward. By the 1950s blacks—and their coloured, white, and Asian allies—were staging large-scale peaceful protests. A turning point came in 1960, when police at Sharpeville fired into a crowd of demonstrators and killed sixty-nine blacks. The main black nationalist organization—the **African National Congress (ANC)**—was then outlawed but sent some of its leaders abroad to establish new headquarters. Other members, led by a young black lawyer named Nelson Mandela (b. 1918), stayed in South Africa to set up an underground army to oppose the government. Captured after seventeen months, Mandela was tried for treason and sentenced to life imprisonment. (See the feature "Listening to the Past: The Struggle for Freedom in South Africa" on pages 1018–1019.)

African National Congress (ANC) *The main black nationalist organization in South Africa; it was led by Nelson Mandela.*

By the late 1970s the white government had apparently destroyed the moderate black opposition within South Africa. Operating out of the sympathetic black states of Zimbabwe and Mozambique to the north, the militant ANC turned increasingly to armed struggle. South Africa struck back hard and forced its neighbors to curtail the ANC's guerrilla activities. Fortified by these successes, South Africa's white leaders launched in 1984 a program of cosmetic "reforms." For the first time, the 3 million coloureds and the 1 million South Africans of Asian descent were granted limited parliamentary representation. But no provision was made for any representation of the country's 22 million blacks, and laws controlling black movement and settlement were maintained.

The government's self-serving reforms provoked black indignation and triggered a massive reaction. In the segregated townships young black militants took to the

Primary Source: The Rivonia Trial Speech to the Court
Read how Nelson Mandela defended himself against charges of treason before an all-white South African court in 1964.

● **Men of Destiny** Nelson Mandela shakes hands with Frederik de Klerk following a televised presidential debate in the 1994 electoral campaign. Mandela won and replaced de Klerk as president of South Africa after 350 years of white supremacy. De Klerk became vice president. Both leaders vowed to build a multiracial democratic society. *(Mark Peters/Sipa Press)*

streets, attacking in particular black civil servants and policemen as agents of white oppression. Heavily armed white security forces clashed repeatedly with black protesters, who turned funerals for fallen comrades into mass demonstrations. Between 1985 and 1989 five thousand died and fifty thousand were jailed without charges because of the political unrest.

By 1989 the white government and the black opposition had reached an impasse. Black protesters had been bloodied but not beaten, and their freedom movement had gathered worldwide support. The U.S. Congress had applied strong sanctions against South Africa in October 1986, and the Common Market had followed. The white government still held power, but harsh repression of black resistance had failed.

The political stalemate ended in September 1989 with the election of a new state president, Frederik W. de Klerk, an Afrikaner lawyer and politician. A late-blooming reformer, de Klerk cautiously opened a dialogue with ANC leaders. Negotiating with Nelson Mandela, whose reputation had soared during his long years in prison, de Klerk lifted the state of emergency, legalized the ANC, and freed Mandela in February 1990. Mandela then courageously suspended the ANC's armed struggle and met with de Klerk for serious talks on South Africa's political future. They reached an agreement calling for universal suffrage, which meant black majority rule. They also guaranteed the civil and economic rights of minorities, including job security for white government workers.

Elected South Africa's first black president by an overwhelming majority in May 1994, Mandela told his jubilant supporters of his "deep pride and joy—pride in the ordinary, humble people of this country. . . . And joy that we can loudly proclaim from the roof tops—free at last!"[7] Heading the new "government of national unity," which included de Klerk as vice president, Mandela and the South African people set about building a democratic, multiracial nation. The new constitution guaranteed all political parties some legislative seats until 1998.

In an imaginative attempt to heal the wounds of apartheid, the new black majority government established the Truth and Reconciliation Commission. This commission let black victims speak out and share their suffering, and it also offered white perpetrators amnesty from prosecution in return for fully confessing their crimes. Mandela's ministers repudiated their earlier socialist beliefs and accepted global capitalism as the only way to develop the economy and reduce widespread black poverty.

In 1999 Thabo Mbeki succeeded Mandela as South Africa's president. The magnitude of the problems facing Mandela and Mbeki in availability of health care, housing, electricity, water, and the other amenities necessary for a decent standard of living in the twenty-first century were truly daunting, but significant progress has been made. Much still needs to be done, and all under the heavy burden of the worst AIDS crisis in the world (see pages 1055–1056). Still, South Africa at independence had a better education system, a more viable infrastructure, and a more diversified economy than any other African country. Many people across southern Africa, and even farther north, are looking to South Africa to be the economic engine that drives the continent.

Political Reform in Africa Since 1990

Democracy's triumph in South Africa was part of a broad trend toward elected civilian government that swept through sub-Saharan Africa after 1990. Political protesters rose up and forced one-party authoritarian regimes to grant liberalizing reforms and call national conferences, which often led to competitive elections and new constitutions. These changes occurred in almost all African countries; in the words of two leading scholars, "they amounted to the most far-reaching shifts in African political life since the political independence of thirty years earlier."[8]

Many factors contributed to this historic watershed. The anticommunist revolutions of 1989 in eastern Europe were extremely important. They showed Africans that even the most well-entrenched one-party regimes could be opposed, punished for prolonged misrule, and replaced with electoral competition and even democracy. The decline of military rule in Latin America and the emerging global trend toward political and economic liberalism worked in the same direction.

The end of the cold war also transformed Africa's relations with Russia and the United States. Both superpowers had viewed Africa as an important cold war battleground, and both had given large-scale military and financial aid to their allies, as well as to "uncommitted" African leaders who often played one side against the other. Communism's collapse in Europe brought an abrupt end to communist aid to Russia's African clients, leaving them weakened and much more willing to compromise with opposition movements.

American involvement in Africa also declined. During the cold war U.S. leaders had generally supported "pro-Western" African dictators, no matter how corrupt or repressive. This interventionist policy gave way to a less intense (and much cheaper) interest in free elections and civil rights in the 1990s. A striking example of this evolution was steadfast U.S. support for the "anticommunist" General Mobutu Sese Seko after he seized power in 1965 in Zaire (the former Belgian Congo, renamed the Democratic Republic of the Congo in 1997). Mobutu looted and impoverished his country for decades before the United States cut off aid in the early 1990s, thereby helping an opposition group topple the dying tyrant in 1997.

If events outside Africa established conditions favoring political reform, Africans themselves were the principal actors in the shift toward democracy. They demanded reform because long years of mismanagement and repression had delegitimized one-party rule.

Above all, the strength of the democratic opposition rested on a growing class of educated urban Africans, for post-independence governments had enthusiastically expanded opportunities in education, especially higher education. In the typical West African state of Cameroon, the number of students graduating from the French-speaking national university jumped from a minuscule 213 in 1961 to 10,000 in 1982 and 41,000 in 1992.⁹ The growing middle class of educated professionals—generally pragmatic, moderate, and open to new ideas—chafed at the ostentatious privilege of tiny closed elites and pressed for political reforms that would democratize social and economic opportunities. Thus after 1990 sub-Saharan Africa participated fully in the global trend toward greater democracy and human rights.

The world's media have generally focused on the African governments and economies that failed in the years since 1990. Eight years into the twenty-first century, however, many African countries continue to make significant progress in the consolidation of democracy and human rights. Even some of the countries that experienced horrible civil war and nearly complete disintegration in the 1990s and early 2000s—such as Sierra Leone, Liberia, Angola, the Central African Republic, and Guinea-Bissau—have begun to pull back from the abyss. Ivory Coast experienced years of civil war after its first-ever military coup in 1999. Rebels continue to control the country's northern half, but they and the government met and signed the Ouagadougou Agreement in March 2007, committing themselves to disarmament and reunification and the holding of elections sometime in 2008.

Democracy, however, is still a long struggle away in many African countries. All of North Africa remains under the control of one-party, authoritarian rulers, and Eritrea, Ethiopia, Equatorial Guinea, Zimbabwe, Swaziland, Cameroon, and Gambia have increasingly brutal dictatorships. Sudan's authoritarian Islamic rulers ended their long civil war with the Christians and animists in the south, only to have pro-government Arab militias attack Muslim ethnic Africans in the western Darfur region. The genocidal attacks have caused tens of thousands of deaths and an estimated 2 million refugees. Congo-Kinshasa, Rwanda, Burundi, and Somalia remain perilously close to the abyss of unimaginable violence they experienced in the 1990s. In Kenya, riots following the bitterly contested and questionable re-election of Mwai Kibaki as president on December 27, 2007, resulted in over 250 deaths in the first week after the election. Often considered one of Africa's most stable nations, Kenya unexpectedly erupted into chaos, with interethnic violence forcing hundreds of thousands to flee their homes.

Many of the most stable, democratic countries are in southern Africa: Botswana, South Africa, Zambia, and Namibia have all made the transition from colonialism to democracy. With a few stops and starts, Malawi, Nigeria, Niger, and Madagascar are also making good progress. Much of the political progress is closely linked to economic progress. As Zimbabwe's authoritarian regime under Robert Mugabe has created a corrupt, immoral, human rights nightmare, it has also suffered total economic collapse. More politically stable countries such as Ghana have seen their economies grow and foreign investments increase. Countries in western and central Africa may soon undergo revolutionary political and economic change as a result of the oil and natural gas boom in those regions. Chad, Mauritania, Angola, Nigeria, Gabon, São Tomé and Príncipe, Congo Brazzaville, and Equatorial Guinea could all benefit from complete economic turnarounds, and others will follow.

INTERPRETING THE EXPERIENCES OF THE EMERGING WORLD

How do the writings of Chinua Achebe represent the common experiences of peoples in the emerging world?

Having come of age during and after the struggle for political emancipation, numerous intellectuals embraced the vision of Third World solidarity, and some argued that genuine independence and freedom from outside control required a total break with the former colonial powers and a total rejection of Western values. This was the mes-

● **Nigeria's Conscience** Chinua Achebe's powerful novels focus on complex and believable individuals caught up in the unfolding drama of colonialism, independence, and nation building in Africa. Achebe is an intensely serious writer, a man who speaks for his people and believes in the high moral calling of literature and art. *(Photo, Chido Nangwu)*

sage of Frantz Fanon (1925–1961) in his powerful study of colonial peoples, *The Wretched of the Earth* (1961).

According to Fanon, a French-trained black psychiatrist from the Caribbean island of Martinique, decolonization is always a violent and totally consuming process whereby one "species" of men, the colonizers, is completely replaced by an absolutely different species—the colonized, the wretched of the earth. During decolonization the colonized masses mock colonial values, "insult them, and vomit them up" in a psychic purge.

Fanon believed that throughout Africa and Asia the former imperialists and their local collaborators—the "white men with black faces"—remained the enemy:

During the colonial period the people are called upon to fight against oppression; after national liberation, they are called upon to fight against poverty, illiteracy, and underdevelopment. The struggle, they say, goes on.

. . . We are not blinded by the moral reparation of national independence; nor are we fed by it. The wealth of the imperial countries is our wealth too. . . . Europe is literally the creation of the Third World. The wealth which smothers her is that which was stolen from the underdeveloped peoples.[10]

Fanon's passionate, angry work became a sacred text for radicals attacking imperialism and struggling for liberation.

As countries gained independence and self-rule, some writers looked beyond wholesale rejection of the industrialized powers. They too were "anti-imperialist," but often also activists and cultural nationalists who applied their talents to celebrating the rich histories and cultures of their peoples. Many did not hesitate to criticize their own leaders or fight against oppression and corruption.

The Nigerian writer Chinua Achebe (b. 1930) rendered these themes with acute insight and vivid specificity in his short, moving novels. Achebe sought to restore his people's self-confidence by reinterpreting the past. For Achebe the "writer in a new nation" had first to embrace the "fundamental theme":

This theme—quite simply—is that the African people did not hear of culture for the first time from Europeans; that their societies were not mindless but frequently had a philosophy of great depth and volume and beauty; that they had poetry and above all, they had dignity. It is this dignity that many African peoples all but lost in the colonial period, and it is this that they must now regain. The worst thing that can happen to any people is the loss of their dignity and self-respect. The writer's duty is to help them regain it by showing what happened to them, what they lost.[11]

In *Things Fall Apart* (1958) Achebe achieved his goal by vividly bringing to life the men and women of an Ibo village at the beginning of the twentieth century, with all their virtues and frailties. Woven into the story are the proverbs and wisdom of a sophisticated people and the beauty of a vanishing world. In later novels Achebe portrays the post-independence disillusionment of many writers and intellectuals, which reflected trends in many developing nations in the 1960s and 1970s: the rulers seemed increasingly corrupted by Western luxury and estranged from the rural masses.

From the 1970s onward Achebe was active in the struggle for democratic government in Nigeria. In his novel *Anthills of the Savannah* (1989), he calls upon Africa to stand on its own two feet, take responsibility, and realize that widespread corruption is frustrating hopes of progress and genuine independence. Yet in his recent essays and speeches he also returns to his earlier theme of the West's enduring low opinion of Africa—ever the "dark continent," the savage, non-Western "other world."

The Nobel Prize–winning novelist V. S. Naipaul, born in Trinidad in 1932 of Indian parents, also castigated governments in the developing countries for corruption, ineptitude, and self-deception. Another of Naipaul's recurring themes is the poignant loneliness and homelessness of people uprooted by colonialism and Western expansion.

Chapter Summary

To assess your mastery of this chapter, go to **bedfordstmartins.com/mckayworld**

• How was Latin America similar to, and different from, the other Third World nations?

Nearly all the countries of Central and South America had gained their independence by the mid-1800s. This was just the time when Europe initiated a second great period of colonization that resulted in the colonization of much of Africa, Asia, and the Middle East. Despite their independence, many Latin Americans still believed the West was economically exploiting their countries through a form of neocolonialism. Politically throughout most of the twentieth century, Latin American countries were ruled by conservative, authoritarian leaders, some of them harsh and cruel dictators supported by the West. Thus many Latin Americans felt closer ties to the colonized peoples of Asia and Africa than they did to Western colonizers. In the 1980s much of Latin America turned toward free elections, civil liberties, and freer markets, abandoning the long-standing commitment to economic nationalism.

• How did the defeat of Japan lead to East Asian resurgence after World War II?

When World War II ended with the Japanese defeat, long suppressed nationalist movements pushed for political independence across East Asia. Mao Zedong's Communist forces took over in China, and the pro-Western Nationalist leader Jiang Jieshi was defeated. Meanwhile, thirty-five years of Japanese occupation of the Korean peninsula ended only to have the country divided, with the northern half controlled by a communist government installed by Stalin. The North became one of the harshest dictatorships and poorest countries in the world, while the South became one of the "Asian tigers," a modern, industrial powerhouse with one of the highest standards of living in the world. The other Asian tigers—Taiwan, Hong Kong, and Singapore—also left the war and colonial rule behind them to develop vibrant global economies. Vietnam had to fight a long war of independence against the French and then the Americans before beginning an economic recovery.

Key Terms

Great Leap Forward
Great Proletarian Cultural Revolution
Red Guards
Tiananmen Square
Muslim League
Palestine Liberation Organization (PLO)
National Liberation Front
Pan-Africanists
cocoa holdups
Native Land Act
apartheid
African National Congress (ANC)

• How did Hindus and Muslims adjust to the end of British colonial rule?

The Hindu and Muslim populations of India threw off British colonial rule only to go to war among themselves. Mahatma Gandhi was unable to convince the two groups to remain united in an independent India, and the Muslims broke away to create two new countries, Bangladesh and Pakistan. Pakistan and India have remained at odds ever since, often violently, because of religious hatred and territorial disputes in the Kashmir region of northwest India.

• What was the dual nature of nationalism in the Islamic heartland?

The Muslim world was also rejuvenated after 1945, most notably under Nasser in Egypt. Nasser was respected throughout the Arab world for having stood up to the West and was a symbol of the pan-Arab, anti-Western movement. Pan-Arabism, the uniting of all Arabs into a single nation, was a dream of many Arabs, but regional, ideological, and personal rivalries made such unification impossible. Nationalism thus took a more traditional turn as individual states developed out of territories that had been League of Nations mandates and European colonies. Common to all these states was a deep devotion to Islam.

• How did Kwame Nkrumah represent the new leaders of independent Africa?

In black Africa a generation of nationalist leaders successfully guided colonial territories to self-rule by the middle of the 1960s. The father of independent Africa was Kwame Nkrumah, a Ghanaian who, like many African nationalists, had spent many years studying in the West. He returned to Ghana after World War II and led an independence movement against British rule. Again, like many other nationalist leaders, Nkrumah was arrested by the British after leading mass strikes and demonstrations and was elected while in jail to lead a transitional government. In 1957 Ghana became the first sub-Saharan country to gain independence from colonial rule.

• What are some of the common features of independent Africa since 1960?

By the mid-1960s nearly all African countries had won independence. The two largest colonial powers, Britain and France, had tried, although belatedly, to set up democratic governments in their former colonies. The new leaders of these countries, however, soon turned their backs on democracy and resorted to authoritarian, one-party rule. Opposition parties were outlawed, and political opponents were jailed, sent into exile, or killed. Many of these early dictators were overthrown by military juntas, as happened, for example, in Ghana and Nigeria. Despite the high expectations all Africans held after throwing off colonial rule, most have lived, and continue to live, under harsh and corrupt authoritarian governments.

• How do the writings of Chinua Achebe represent the common experiences of peoples in the emerging world?

There are many artists in the emerging world who have eloquently described the common experiences of peoples living under colonial rule and then in newly independent nations. One of the most famous of these artists is Chinua Achebe, a Nigerian writer whose novels have been translated into many languages because of their universal appeal. One of Achebe's primary themes is that Africans had their own cultures, philosophies, poetry, and dignity before the Europeans arrived and tried to force their own values on the peoples they colonized. This theme he fully developed in his first and most widely read novel, *Things Fall Apart.* In later novels Achebe described the disillusionment felt by many Africans (and peoples of Asia and Latin America as well) with the corruption and authoritarian rule of post-independence governments.

Suggested Reading

Beck, Roger B. *The History of South Africa.* 2000. Introduction to South African history with emphasis on the twentieth century.

Chang, Jung, and Jon Halliday. *Mao: The Unknown Story.* 2005. Controversial new biography of the Chinese communist leader.

Church, Peter. *A Short History of South-East Asia.* 4th ed. 2005. A concise but comprehensive survey of the region's history.

Collins, Robert O., and James M. Burns. *A History of Sub-Saharan Africa.* 2007. Clearly written introduction to the continent's history.

Davidson, Basil. *The Black Man's Burden: Africa and the Curse of the Nation State.* 1993. A thought-provoking reconsideration by a noted historian.

Du Bois, W. E. B. *The World and Africa.* 1947. A classic text by the distinguished American black thinker.

Jayakar, Pupul. *Indira Gandhi: An Intimate Biography.* 1993. Very readable narrative of the powerful and controversial Indian prime minister.

Guha, Ramachandra. *India After Gandhi: The History of the World's Largest Democracy.* 2007. In-depth study of the last sixty years of Indian history and development.

Kenyatta, Jomo. *Facing Mount Kenya.* 1953. Powerful commentary and autobiography by one of Africa's foremost revolutionary and political leaders.

Lowenthal, Abraham F., and Gregory F. Treverton, eds. *Latin America in a New World.* 1994. Analyzes the move toward regional cooperation and market economies.

Meredith, Robyn. *The Elephant and the Dragon: The Rise of India and China and What It Means for All of Us.* 2005. Useful and accessible introduction to these two economic giants.

Mahbubani, Kishore. *The New Asian Hemisphere: The Irresistible Shift of Global Power to the East.* 2008. A history and analysis of the rise of Asia in world politics and economics by one of Asia's leading intellectuals.

Nehru, Jawaharlal. *An Autobiography.* 1962. Classic personal account of India's history in the first half of twentieth century by its first president.

Osborne, Milton. *Southeast Asia: An Introductory History.* 9th rev. ed. 2005. Classic introduction to the region.

Wasserstrom, Jeffrey N., ed. *Twentieth Century China: New Approaches.* 2002. Collection of essays on cultural and national developments using recently released archives.

Notes

1. S. Schram, *Mao Tse-tung* (New York: Simon and Schuster, 1966), p. 151.
2. Quoted in P. B. Ebrey, ed., *Chinese Civilization and Society: A Source Book* (New York: Free Press, 1981), p. 393.
3. Quoted in W. Bingham, H. Conroy, and F. Iklé, *A History of Asia,* vol. 2, 2d ed. (Boston: Allyn and Bacon, 1974), p. 459.
4. Quoted in K. Bhata, *The Ordeal of Nationhood: A Social Study of India Since Independence, 1947–1970* (New York: Atheneum, 1971), p. 9.
5. Quoted in B. Baktiari and H. Vaziri, "Iran's Liberal Revolution?" *Current History,* January 2002, p. 21.
6. Quoted in R. Hallett, *Africa Since 1875: A Modern History* (Ann Arbor: University of Michigan Press, 1974), pp. 378–379.
7. *Chicago Tribune,* May 3, 1994, section 1, p. 5.
8. M. Bratton and N. van de Walle, *Democratic Experiments in Africa: Regime Transitions in Comparative Perspectives* (Cambridge: Cambridge University Press, 1997), p. 3.
9. D. Birmingham and P. Martin, eds., *History of Central Africa: The Contemporary Years Since 1960* (London: Routledge, 1998), p. 59.
10. F. Fanon, *The Wretched of the Earth* (New York: Grove Press, 1968), pp. 43, 93–94, 97, 102.
11. C. Achebe, *Morning Yet on Creation Day* (London: Heinemann, 1975), p. 81.

Listening to the PAST

The Struggle for Freedom in South Africa

Many African territories won political freedom in the mid-1960s, but in South Africa the struggle was long and extremely difficult. Only in 1990 did the white government release Nelson Mandela from prison and begin negotiations with the famous black leader and the African National Congress (ANC). Only in 1994 did Mandela and the ANC finally come to power and establish a new system based on majority rule and racial equality.

Born in 1918 into the royal family of the Transkei, Nelson Mandela received an education befitting the son of a chief. But he ran away to escape an arranged marriage, experienced the harsh realities of black life in Johannesburg, studied law, and became an attorney. A born leader with a natural air of authority, Mandela was drawn to politics and the ANC. In the 1950s the white government responded to the growing popularity of Mandela and the ANC with tear gas and repression.

In 1960 the ANC called a general strike to protest the shooting of peaceful protesters at Sharpeville. Acts of sabotage then shook South Africa, and Mandela led the underground opposition. Betrayed by an informer, he was convicted of treason in 1964 and sentenced to life imprisonment. Mandela defended all of the accused in the 1964 treason trial. The following selection is taken from Mandela's opening statement.

At the outset, I want to say that the suggestion made by the State in its opening that the struggle in South Africa is under the influence of foreigners or communists is wholly incorrect. I have done whatever I did, both as an individual and as a leader of my people, because of my experience in South Africa and my own proudly felt African background, and not because of what any outsider might have said.

In my youth in the Transkei I listened to the elders of my tribe telling stories of the old days. Amongst the tales they related to me were those of wars fought by our ancestors in defence of the fatherland. . . . I hoped then that life might offer me the opportunity to serve my people and make my own humble contribution to their freedom struggle. . . .

It is true that there has often been close cooperation between the ANC [African National Congress] and the Communist Party. But cooperation is merely proof of a common goal—in this case the removal of White supremacy—and is not proof of a complete community of interests. . . . What is more, for many decades communists were the only political group in South Africa who were prepared to treat Africans as human beings and their equals; who were prepared to eat with us, talk with us, live with us, and work with us. . . . Because of this, there are many Africans who today tend to equate freedom with communism. . . .

I turn now to my own position. I have denied that I am a communist. . . . [But] I am attracted by the idea of a classless society, an attraction which springs in part from Marxist reading and, in part, from my admiration of the structure and organization of early African societies in this country. The land, then the main means of production, belonged to the tribe. There were no rich or poor and there was no exploitation. . . .

[Unlike communists] I am an admirer of the parliamentary system of the West. . . . [Thus] I have been influenced in my thinking by both West and East. . . . [I believe] I should be absolutely impartial and objective. I should tie myself to no particular system of society other than of socialism. I must leave myself free to borrow the best from the West and from the East. . . .

Our fight is against real, and not imaginary, hardships or, to use the language of the State Prosecutor, "so-called hardships." . . . Basically, we fight against two features which are the hallmarks of African life in South Africa and which are entrenched by legislation which we seek to have repealed. These features are poverty and lack of human dignity, and we do not need communists or so-called "agitators" to teach us about these things.

South Africa is the richest country in Africa, and could be one of the richest countries in the world. But it is a land of extremes and remarkable contrasts. The Whites enjoy what may well be the highest standard of living in the world, while Africans live in poverty and

Nelson Mandela at the time of his imprisonment in 1964. (Mohamed Lounes/Gamma)

misery. . . . Poverty goes hand in hand with malnutrition and disease. . . .

The lack of human dignity experienced by Africans is the direct result of the policy of White supremacy. White supremacy implies Black inferiority. Legislation designed to preserve White supremacy entrenches this notion. . . . Because of this sort of attitude, Whites tend to regard Africans as a separate breed. They do not look upon them as people with families of their own; they do not realize that they have emotions. . . .

Africans want to be paid a living wage. Africans want to perform work which they are capable of doing, and not work which the Government declares them to be capable of. . . . Africans want a just share in the whole of South Africa; they want security and a stake in society.

Above all, we want equal political rights, because without them our disabilities will be permanent. I know this sounds revolutionary to the Whites in this country, because the majority of voters will be Africans. This makes the White man fear democracy.

But this fear cannot be allowed to stand in the way of the only solution which will guarantee racial harmony and freedom for all. It is not true that the enfranchisement of all will result in racial domination. Political division, based on color, is entirely artificial and, when it disappears, so will the domination of one color group by another. The ANC has spent half a century fighting against racialism. When it triumphs it will not change that policy.

This then is what the ANC is fighting. Their struggle is a truly national one. It is a struggle of the African people, inspired by their own suffering and their own experience. It is a struggle for the right to live.

During my lifetime I have dedicated myself to this struggle of the African people. I have fought against White domination, and I have fought against Black domination. I have cherished the ideal of a democratic and free society in which all persons live together in harmony and with equal opportunities. It is an ideal which I hope to live for and to achieve. But if need be, it is an ideal for which I am prepared to die.

Questions for Analysis

1. How does Nelson Mandela respond to the charge that he and the ANC are controlled by communists?

2. What factors influenced Mandela's thinking? In what ways has he been influenced by "both East and West" and by his African background?

3. According to Mandela, what is wrong with South Africa? What needs to be done?

4. What are Mandela's goals for South Africa? Are his goals realistic, idealistic, or both?

Source: Slightly adapted from Nelson Mandela, *No Easy Walk to Freedom: Articles, Speeches and Trial Addresses* (London: Heinemann, 1973), pp. 163, 179–185, 187–189. Reprinted by permission of Heinemann Publishers (Oxford) Ltd.

Forum on Cultures. The May 2004 opening ceremony of the five-month Forum on Cultures in Barcelona, Spain, which addressed issues of peace, cultural diversity, and sustainable development on earth. *(AP Photo/Wide World Photos)*

chapter

33 A NEW ERA IN WORLD HISTORY

Chapter Preview

Global Unity or Continued Division?
• What is the global political situation in the early twenty-first century, and how do competing nation-states address common problems?

Global Interdependence
• How are the United Nations and multinational corporations representative of increasing globalization?

The Growth of Cities (1945 to the Present)
• What factors spurred the growth of cities in Africa, Asia, and Latin America, and what were some of the main consequences of urbanization in the late twentieth century?

Science and Technology: Changes and Challenges
• What key technological and scientific developments have had the greatest impact on life at the beginning of the new millennium?

Social Reform and Progress
• What social problems are the focus of reformers in the new millennium?

ommunism's collapse in Europe in 1991 opened a new era in world history—one that arrived with promises of peace, democracy, and economic prosperity. Millions of people still living under repressive, authoritarian, corrupt regimes were inspired to start pressing their governments for political and human rights. Certainly for most Europeans the end of the cold war has had positive consequences. For many people in Africa, Asia, and Latin America, however, the results have been mixed. What is more, the post-1991 optimism soon faded as new tensions, conflicts, and divisions arose.

In the first part of this chapter we look at the global political and economic systems, formal and informal, with which we enter the twenty-first century. These are the broad systems under which the peoples of the world live and work. The latter part of the chapter takes a closer look at the global issues directly affecting ordinary people's lives. We live in a global age. Economic cycles, international treaties and agreements, multinational organizations, and global threats connect the world's citizens in complex networks. Every day around the world billions of individuals are confronted with similarly complex global issues that impact each of them in an immediate and personal way. As we bring our history of the world's societies to a close, let us look at our interconnected planet once again, this time focusing on ordinary people and the global changes and challenges they face.

Because people living in developing nations make up at least two-thirds of the earth's population, many of the people discussed here live in the so-called Third World, where the changes and challenges of the new millennium are perhaps greatest. We should not forget, though, that there really is no "Third World." There is only a set of conditions—such as poverty, disease, hunger, and unemployment—that are at their worst in the poorest or developing countries but exist in all countries.

GLOBAL UNITY OR CONTINUED DIVISION?

What is the global political situation in the early twenty-first century, and how do competing nation-states address common problems?

The end of the cold war superpower confrontation brought dramatic changes to the global political situation. Yet nation-states, the traditional building blocks of global politics, continued to exist. An astonishing aspect of recent scientific and technological achievements is the lack of any corresponding change in the way the human race governs—or fails to govern—itself. Sovereign nation-states continue to reign supreme, reinforced by enormous military power. The embryonic growth of an effective global political organization, of a government that could protect nations from themselves, appears permanently arrested, although efforts to control weapons of mass destruction, global warming, and other universal threats have sometimes led to global agreements. The tension generated by powerful, independent nation-states in a fragile and interdependent world remains one of the most striking and dangerous characteristics of our small planet.

Nation-States and the United Nations

The rise of the nation-state and the global triumph of nationalism have been grand themes of modern world history. The independent territorial nation-state—sometimes containing separatist ethnic groups striving for nationhood in their own right—remains the fundamental political organization in the early twenty-first century. Yet surely from a global perspective the nation-state as the basic building block of political organization can no longer be taken so easily for granted.

Has the nation-state system, with its apparently inevitable conflicts, become a threat to life on the planet? Some historians have thought so. In *Mankind and Mother Earth* (1976), the renowned British historian Arnold Toynbee (1889–1975) expressed the post-1914 disillusionment of many European and American intellectuals. Borrowing a term from the ancient Greeks, he explained that the spread of the western European political idea of the national state, first to eastern Europe and then to Asia and Africa, had created a fatal discrepancy:

the discrepancy between the political partition of the Oikoumené [the habitat of the human race] into local sovereign states and the global unification of the Oikoumené on technological and economic planes. This misfit is the crux of mankind's present plight. Some form of global government is now needed for keeping the peace . . . and for reestablishing the balance between Man and the rest of the biosphere.[1]

Some members of Toynbee's generation gave this question of world government serious consideration and came up with the League of Nations. Although the League had only a short life, the idea of a global authority transcending sovereign states remained alive. The World War II generation revived the idea and founded the **United Nations** in San Francisco in 1945. President Franklin D. Roosevelt and Democrats in the Wilsonian tradition pushed its creation, believing America's failure to join the League of Nations had contributed to the tragic breakdown of "collective security" in the 1930s.

The United Nations' main purpose is "to maintain international peace and security." The U.N. charter prohibits any member nation from using armed force except for self-defense. At the same time, the charter gives the organization's **Security Council** the authority to examine any international conflict, impose economic and political penalties on an aggressor, and "take such action by air, sea, or land forces as may be necessary to restore international peace and security." In theory, the Security Council

United Nations *Founded in 1945 as a resurrected League of Nations, its main purpose is to "maintain international peace and security."*

Security Council *The United Nations body that has the authority to examine international conflicts, impose economic and political penalties on an aggressor, and even use force, if necessary, to restore international peace and security.*

has the power to police the world. In practice, however, this power is severely restricted. The Security Council's five permanent members—China, Great Britain, France, Russia (formerly the Soviet Union), and the United States—have to agree on any peacekeeping action. But none of them, and certainly not the United States, is willing to surrender sovereign power to a global organization.

The United Nations charter affirms and reinforces the primacy of the national state in world politics. Every "peace-loving" state is eligible to join the organization and to participate in its **General Assembly.** Founded with 50 members, the General Assembly comprises 192 members in 2008. Each member state, whatever its size, has one voice and one vote on all General Assembly resolutions, but General Assembly resolutions become legally binding on states only if all five permanent members of the Security Council agree to them.

The founders of the United Nations acknowledged the expanded scope of government since the late nineteenth century and gave voice to an emerging vision of global interdependence. According to its charter, the United Nations is "to achieve international cooperation in solving international problems of an economic, social, cultural, or humanitarian character, and in promoting and encouraging respect for human rights and for fundamental freedom for all without distinction as to race, sex, language, or religion."

During the cold war, the original hopes for the creation of an effective world body were stymied by Security Council members, most often the Soviet Union, using their veto power to block actions they felt would harm their own or their allies' national interests. With the Security Council often deadlocked, the General Assembly claimed ever-greater authority. As decolonization picked up speed and the number of member states grew, a nonaligned, anticolonial African-Asian bloc emerged. Reinforced by sympathetic Latin American countries, by the mid-1960s the bloc succeeded in organizing within the General Assembly a Third World majority that concentrated on economic and social issues.

With a large numerical majority, the developing nations succeeded in broadening the organization's economic, social, and cultural mission. By the 1970s an alphabet soup of United Nations committees, specialized agencies, and affiliated international organizations were studying and promoting health, labor, agriculture, industrial development, and world trade, not to mention disarmament, control of narcotics, and preservation of the great whales and other endangered species. Today, these United Nations agencies continue to serve their main constituency—the overwhelming majority of developing nations in both the General Assembly and the world's total population. Without directly challenging national sovereignty, they exert a steady pressure for international cooperation in dealing with specific global issues, and the world's major powers sometimes go along.

Chronology

1945	United Nations founded
1945–1960s	Decolonization in Africa and Asia
1945–present	Explosive growth of cities; rapid urbanization; increasing gap in wealth between rich and poor nations
1950s	Beginning of Green Revolution
1970	Non-Proliferation of Nuclear Weapons treaty
1973	OPEC raises price of crude oil and causes panic in industrialized countries
1980s–present	HIV/AIDS global epidemic
1989	United Nations Convention on the Rights of the Child; fall of communism in eastern Europe
1997	Asian currencies collapse; International Monetary Fund provides emergency loans; Kyoto Protocol on global warming
1998	India and Pakistan explode nuclear weapons
2000	United Nations Millennium Project initiated
2001	Al-Qaeda attacks on World Trade Center and U.S. Pentagon
2003	North Korea withdraws from 1970 nonproliferation treaty; U.S.-led coalition invades Iraq; Human Genome Project completes sequencing of human genome
2004	Bombing of train station in Madrid; tsunami kills thousands in South Asia
2005	Bombing of London subway and bus systems
2007	Assassination of Pakistani politician Benazir Bhutto

General Assembly *The second main body of the United Nations; each "peace-loving" state is eligible to join and participate in it.*

● **The United Nations in Action** These soldiers are part of a French battalion serving in a United Nations peacekeeping operation in Cambodia (Kampuchea), a country wracked by war and civil conflict since 1970. United Nations forces usually provide humanitarian aid as they try to preserve fragile cease-fires after warring armies agree to stop fighting. (J. F. Roussier/Sipa Press)

The United Nations became the central forum for the ongoing debate about the relations between rich and poor countries. In 2000, the United Nations issued the "Millennium Declaration," which created the Millennium Project, a plan of action identifying eight goals for the United Nations and member nations to reach by 2015. Millennium goals focus on global poverty and hunger, disease, education, the environment, maternal health, child mortality, gender equality, and global partnerships. (See the feature "Listening to the Past: The United Nations Millennium Project Report" on pages 1068–1069.)

Throughout the 1970s and 1980s the United Nations played a role in establishing peace in conflicts that did not directly involve the superpowers. Then, as the cold war ended, the United Nations participated in the largest joint military action taken since the Korean conflict in the early 1950s. In 1990 the five permanent members of the Security Council agreed to repel the Iraqi invasion of Kuwait, and in 1991 they required the defeated Saddam Hussein to destroy all his weapons of mass destruction. Success in Iraq led some leaders and observers to believe the United Nations could fulfill its original purpose and guarantee peace throughout the world.

Such hopes were immediately tested in 1992, when American armed forces landed on the beaches of Somalia to stop a savage civil war and allow United Nations soldiers to maintain peace thereafter. The operation failed, as Somali fighters attacked and killed some of their would-be benefactors. United Nations negotiators also failed to stop the savage civil war in Bosnia in the mid-1990s. In response to these and other setbacks, the United Nations scaled back its peacekeeping ambitions and concentrated on helping warring factions that wanted to make peace. Even this proved to be an awesome task. On average since the mid-1990s, around sixty-seven thousand United

Nations soldiers have been stationed in hot spots around the world. United Nations peacekeeping efforts have been imperfect, but they have also been indispensable.

In 2002 another crisis over Iraq brought the United Nations to the center of the world's political stage. U.S. president George W. Bush accused Iraq of rebuilding its weapons of mass destruction and ominously warned that Saddam Hussein might give them to anti-American terrorists, although he produced no evidence linking the secular Iraqi dictator with Osama bin Laden or other Islamic extremists. Bush made clear his intention to drive Saddam Hussein from power, claiming this outcome would promote democracy in Iraq and peace in the Middle East. He legitimized his attack against Hussein by claiming that the United States had the right to act preemptively to forestall or prevent a hostile attack. This claim, however, was at odds with the United Nations charter, which grants the Security Council the sole authority to use armed force except in self-defense; and Iraq, impoverished by a decade of tough United Nations sanctions, gave no indication of plans to attack any of its neighbors or the United States. Moreover, large numbers of Americans shared the world's doubts about the legality—and wisdom—of a U.S. attack on Iraq. Thus the Bush administration reluctantly agreed to new Security Council resolutions requiring Iraq to destroy any remaining prohibited weapons and to agree to the return of United Nations weapons inspectors. Iraq accepted, declaring it had destroyed all prohibited weapons.

As 2002 ended, UN inspectors operated freely in Iraq and found no weapons of mass destruction. The United States and Britain denounced Iraq's lukewarm cooperation, however, dismissed the inspections as a fraud, moved armies to the Middle East, and lobbied for a new resolution authorizing immediate military action against Iraq. France, Russia, China, Germany, and a majority of the smaller states argued for continued weapons inspections, and France in particular threatened to veto any resolution authorizing an invasion of Iraq. Rather than risk this veto, the United States and Britain claimed that earlier Security Council resolutions provided ample authorization and, with the almost token aid of about thirty other countries, they invaded Iraq.

Although all parties in the crisis recognized the United Nations as a key source of international legality, in the end American and British leaders and their coalition allies ignored the wishes of the majority of the international community and large numbers of their own populations, and went to war. What is more, America's declaration of its right to stage a unilateral "preemptive strike" to prevent attack seemed to set a dangerous precedent. It also raised questions about when and how the United Nations charter's stipulations about the use of armed force for self-defense apply.

The Iraq invasion began on March 20, 2003. President Bush announced an "end" to the war on May 1, 2003. Saddam Hussein was captured in December 2003. Although the war brought an end to Saddam's brutal rule, Iraq remained one of the most dangerous places on earth. Relatively free national elections were held in January 2005, but they were boycotted by one of the three main groups in Iraq, the Sunni Muslims. The other two groups, the Shi'ite Muslims and the Kurds, formed a government and tried, with mixed success, to include the Sunnis. Civil war remained a very real possibility. So-called insurgents carried out daily attacks on Iraqi police, members of the military, government officials, religious leaders, and civilians. Estimates of Iraqi deaths since the war began ranged from one hundred thousand to over 1 million. Many observers warned that Iraq was becoming a breeding ground for terrorists.

Meanwhile, the United States, Britain, and their coalition allies maintained their forces in Iraq. In the spring of 2004 stories and photographs surfaced in the world press of American soldiers abusing and torturing prisoners and even causing their deaths at Abu Ghraib and other detention centers in Iraq, at the Guantánamo Bay naval base in Cuba, and at prisons in Afghanistan. Some soldiers were prosecuted, but no high-ranking U.S. military officers or government officials were implicated. Questions were raised about the willingness of the United States to abide by the Geneva Convention on prisoners of war and by the United Nations convention against torture.

● **U.S. Army Humvee Burning in Baghdad** Although President Bush declared an end to the Iraq War with his "mission accomplished" speech on May 1, 2003, attacks on U.S. soldiers increased, resulting in over 4,100 U.S. deaths and over 60,000 wounded by July 2008. Here an Iraqi man throws gasoline on a destroyed Army Humvee. *(AP Photo/Wide World Photos)*

Disregarding opposition to the Iraq War in the United States and around the world, President Bush and the U.S. Congress by July 2008 had spent nearly $650 billion in Iraq, a number that roughly equaled the entire cost of the Vietnam War. An earthquake in world affairs, the Iraqi war split the West and seemed likely to reorient relations between Western and Islamic peoples in new and unpredictable directions.

Complexity and Violence in a Multipolar World

> **Primary Source:**
> **Selection from a Roundtable Discussion of Globalization and Its Impact on Arab Culture, October 26, 2000**
> *An Arab intellectual discusses the challenges and opportunities of globalization for Arab culture.*

middle powers *Those countries not considered part of either the First World or the developing world; they became increasingly assertive after the cold war.*

Alongside territorial nation-states and international organizations that focus on specific problems stretch a wide range of alliances, blocs, and partnerships. For several reasons, it is often difficult to make sense of this tangle of associations.

First, the end of the cold war removed one of the planet's most enduring political realities. During the cold war the hostile superpowers dominated and curbed their allies and clients and were in turn restrained by them. The sudden end of the cold war shattered these interlocking restraints, removing a basic principle of global organization and order.

Second, the cold war division had contributed to the ideology of Third World solidarity (see Chapter 32). Then in the 1980s and 1990s wide differences in economic performance in countries and regions undermined the whole idea of Third World solidarity, and developing countries increasingly went their own ways.

A striking third development was the growing "multipolar" nature of world politics. Calling on nationalism as a mobilizing force, increasingly assertive **middle powers** jockeyed for regional leadership and sometimes came into conflict. Brazil, with more than 140 million people, vast territory and resources, and a rapidly industrializing economy, emerged as the dominant nation-state in South America. Mexico emerged as the natural leader of the Spanish-speaking Americas. France and West Germany had re-emerged as strong regional powers in western Europe by the early 1960s. Nigeria and South Africa were unquestionably the leading powers in sub-Saharan Africa. Heavily populated Egypt and much smaller Israel were also regional powerhouses. Iran and Iraq competed and fought for dominance in the Persian Gulf. China, India, and Japan were all leading regional powers, and several other Asian countries—notably South Korea, Indonesia, Vietnam, and Pakistan—were determined to join them. The rise of these middle powers reflected the fact that most countries were small and weak, with fewer than 20 million people. Very few countries had the resources necessary to wield real power on even a regional scale.

Conflict and violence often bedeviled the emerging multipolar political system, leading to several major wars and many small ones. In the 1990s civil wars in Bosnia, Kosovo, Rwanda, and Afghanistan killed over a million people and sent many hundreds of thousands of refugees running for their lives. Since the new century began, new or continuing wars have caused millions more deaths and new refugees, particularly in Sierra Leone, Liberia, the Democratic Republic of the Congo, Uganda, Afghanistan, Burundi, Somalia, Iraq, Sudan, and Angola.

Rivalries between ethnic groups are often at the heart of the civil wars that produce so many deaths and refugees. Different ethnic groups compete among themselves for power, or they fight against a majority population to overturn entrenched discrimination and oppression. Ethnic competition can turn violent and lead to **separatism**— radical demands for ethnic autonomy or political independence.

separatism *Radical demands for ethnic autonomy or political independence.*

Only about twenty states, representing about 10 percent of the world's population, are truly homogeneous. If common language were the only basis for national identity—and, of course, it is not—the number of countries in the world could explode to six thousand.[2] The goal of a separate state for each self-defined people—the classic nationalist goal—could lead to endless battles and to tragedy on a global scale. The peaceful reconciliation of existing states with widespread separatist aspirations stood as a mighty challenge in the early twenty-first century. The challenge of separatism seemed especially great in light of the fact that civil war and terrorism often had gone hand in hand in the previous century.

terrorism *The use of force or violence by a person or organized group with the intention of intimidating societies or governments, often for political purposes.*

The Terrorist Threat

Beginning in the 1920s and peaking in the 1960s, many nationalist movements used **terrorism** to win nationhood and political independence. This was the case in Ireland, Israel, Cyprus, Yemen, and Algeria.[3] Those fighting for independence often targeted police forces for assassination campaigns, thereby breaking down confidence in colonial governments and provoking counteratrocities that generated increased support for independence.

In the Vietnam War era, some far-left supporters of the communist Vietnamese, such as the Weathermen in the United States, the Red Army Faction in West Germany, and the Red Brigades in Italy, engaged in "revolutionary terror" in an effort to cripple the United States and western Europe. These groups carried out deadly bombings, assassinations, plane hijackings, and kidnappings. This wave of terrorism receded in the 1980s as painstaking police work and international cooperation defeated the "revolutionaries" in country after country.

● **A Casualty of the Rwandan Civil War** A Red Cross worker helps an injured victim of the Rwandan civil war between Hutu and Tutsis, the two major ethnic groups in the country. In a three-month period beginning in April 1994, five hundred thousand to 1 million Tutsis were slaughtered by the majority Hutu, while up to 2 million Hutu became refugees, fleeing to Zaire (the Congo) or Tanzania. *(David Turnley/Corbis)*

Generally successful in keeping ethnic nationalism under control in the West in the 1990s, many Europeans and most Americans believed that terrorism was primarily a problem for the developing countries of Asia, Africa, and Latin America. In fact, terrorism had become part of a complex global pattern of violence and political conflict. In northwestern Spain the Basque separatist organization used assassinations and car bombings in its bloody campaign to obtain a breakaway state from the Spanish government. In Northern Ireland Protestant and Catholic extremists turned to bombs and killings in their bitter conflict. As the new century opened, the global dimension of terrorism was revealed most dramatically in the United States.

On the morning of September 11, 2001, two hijacked passenger planes from Boston crashed into and destroyed the World Trade Center in New York City. Shortly thereafter a third plane crashed into the Pentagon, and a fourth, believed to be headed for the White House or the U.S. Capitol, crashed into a field in rural Pennsylvania. These terrorist attacks took the lives of almost three thousand people from many countries. The United States, led by President George W. Bush, launched a military campaign to destroy the perpetrators of the crime, Saudi-born millionaire Osama bin Laden's **al-Qaeda** network of terrorists and Afghanistan's reactionary Muslim government, the Taliban. Building a broad international coalition that included western Europe, Russia, and Pakistan, the United States joined its tremendous airpower with the faltering Northern Alliance in Afghanistan, which had been fighting the Taliban for years. In mid-November 2001 the Taliban collapsed, and jubilant crowds in the capital of Kabul welcomed Northern Alliance soldiers as liberators.

In trying to make sense of this latest wave of terrorism, many commentators were quick to stress the role of extreme Islamic fundamentalism as a motivating factor. But the most perceptive scholars noted that recent heinous crimes had been committed by terrorists inspired by several religious faiths and sects and were by no means limited to Islamic extremists.[4] These scholars also noted that different terrorist movements needed to be examined in the context of underlying political conflicts and civil wars for meaningful understanding.

When this perspective is brought to the study of Osama bin Laden and al-Qaeda members, two stages of their activities stand out. First, in the long, bitter fighting against the Soviet Union and the local communists in Afghanistan, bin Laden and like-minded "holy warriors" developed terrorist skills and a narrow-minded, fanatical Islamic puritanism. They also developed a hatred of most existing Arab governments, which they viewed as corrupt, un-Islamic, and unresponsive to the needs of ordinary Muslims. The objects of their hostility included the absolute monarchy of oil-rich Saudi Arabia (bin Laden's own country of origin), pro-Western but undemocratic Egypt, and the secular, one-party dictatorship of Saddam Hussein.

Second, when these Islamic extremists returned home and began to organize, they met the fate of many earlier Islamic extremists and were jailed or forced into exile, often in tolerant Europe. There they blamed the United States for being the supporter and corrupter of existing Arab governments, and they organized murderous plots against the United States—a despised proxy for the Arab rulers they could not reach. Bin Laden's network also blamed the United States for steadfastly supporting Israel and denying the claims of the Palestinians, although attempts to exploit the Israeli-Palestinian tragedy generally came later and operated mainly as a recruiting tool. These developments set the stage for the 1998 bombing of the U.S. embassy in Nairobi, Kenya, which claimed nearly two hundred lives, and for the September 11 atrocity in 2001.

Although U.S.-led forces subsequently decimated al-Qaeda camps in Afghanistan and overthrew the Taliban government that protected them, many analysts have since argued that the war on terrorism may have become more difficult as a result. On March 11, 2004, multiple bombs were set off in a Madrid train station, killing 191 people and wounding over 1,800. The Madrid bombings were carried out by Islamic extremists with only loose ties to al-Qaeda. In London on July 7, 2005, 56 people

al-Qaeda *A terrorist network led by Osama bin Laden; it claimed responsibility for the September 11 attacks and other terrorist acts.*

Primary Source:
Islamic Fundamentalist Osama Bin Laden Calls on Muslims to Take Up Arms Against America, 1998
Learn why Osama bin Laden and his associates declared war against the United States.

were killed and more than 700 were injured by bombs detonated on three subway trains and a double-decker bus. In this instance, at least three of the bombers were British citizens of Pakistani descent with some unclear links to al-Qaeda. Since then terrorist acts linked in some way to al-Qaeda have killed dozens of people in Indonesia, Jordan, Iraq, Pakistan, Algeria, Scotland, and elsewhere. A suicide bomber perhaps with links to Al-Qaeda has also been blamed for the most significant terrorist act since the London bombing: the assassination of Pakistani presidential candidate, Benazir Bhutto, on December 27, 2007. Thus, the war on terrorism is no longer against just one global network—al-Qaeda. Many loosely connected cells and movements have emerged around the world, and these groups share many of the same goals but are not answerable to Osama bin Laden or to anyone else.

Weapons of Mass Destruction

President George W. Bush justified the U.S.-led attack on Iraq by saying that the world needed to disarm Saddam Hussein and destroy his stockpiles of weapons of mass destruction. As it turned out, Hussein had no weapons of mass destruction. Still, the fear that terrorists or rogue governments might acquire such weapons reflects global concern about the enduring menace of nuclear proliferation and nuclear war, as well as the danger of chemical and biological attacks. How did this frightening situation arise? And what is being done to find solutions? (See the feature "Global Trade: Arms" on pages 1030–1031.)

Having let the atomic genie out of the bottle at Hiroshima and Nagasaki in 1945, a troubled United States immediately proposed that it be recaptured through effective international control of all atomic weapons. The Soviets rejected the American idea and exploded their first atomic bomb in 1949. The United States responded by exploding its first hydrogen bomb in 1952, and within ten months the Soviet Union did the same. Further American, Soviet, and then British tests aroused worldwide fear that radioactive fallout

● **New York, September 11, 2001** Pedestrians race for safety as the World Trade Center towers collapse after being hit by jet airliners. Al-Qaeda terrorists with box cutters hijacked four aircraft and used three of them as suicide missiles to perpetrate their unthinkable crime. Heroic passengers on the fourth plane realized what was happening and forced their hijackers to crash the plane in a field. *(AP Photo/Wide World Photos)*

would enter the food chain and cause leukemia, bone cancer, and genetic damage. Concerned scientists called for an international agreement to stop all testing of atomic bombs.

Partly in response to worldwide public pressure, the United States, the Soviet Union, and Great Britain agreed in 1958 to stop testing for three years. In 1963 these three powers signed an agreement, eventually signed by more than 150 countries, banning nuclear tests in the atmosphere. A second step toward control was the 1970 Treaty on the Non-Proliferation of Nuclear Weapons, designed to halt their spread to non-nuclear states and to reduce stockpiles of existing bombs held by the nuclear powers. It seemed that the nuclear arms race might yet be reversed.

This outcome did not come to pass. De Gaulle's France and Mao's China, seeing themselves as great world powers, simply disregarded the test ban and continued their development of nuclear weapons, although they later signed the nonproliferation

ARMS

On April 16, 1953, U.S. president Dwight Eisenhower spoke about the tremendous sums the Soviet Union and the United States were spending on cold war weapons:

Every gun that is made, every warship launched, every rocket fired signifies, in the final sense, a theft from those who hunger and are not fed, those who are cold and are not clothed. The world in arms is not spending money alone. It is spending the sweat of its laborers, the genius of its scientists, the hopes of its children. . . . This is not a way of life at all, in any true sense. Under the cloud of threatening war, it is humanity hanging from a cross of iron.

In the fifty-plus years since Eisenhower's speech, the spending has never stopped, not even after the cold war's end. In 2004 global military spending exceeded $1 trillion; the United States accounted for nearly half of that total. Globally, in 2003, the value of all conventional arms transfer agreements was more than $25.6 billion, and deliveries totaled $28.7 billion. Although both of those numbers have been dropping since the early 1990s, global arms manufacturing and trade remains big business.

Three different categories of arms are available on the world market. The category that generally receives the most attention is nuclear, biological, and chemical weapons. After the Soviet Union collapsed, there was widespread fear that former Soviet scientists would sell nuclear technology, toxic chemicals, or harmful biological agents from old, poorly guarded Soviet labs and stockpiles to the highest bidders. Recognizing the horrific danger such weapons represent, the world's nations have passed numerous treaties and agreements limiting their production, use, and stockpiling. The most important of these are the Treaty on the Non-Proliferation of Nuclear Weapons (1970), the Biological and Toxin Weapons Convention (1972), and the Chemical Weapons Conventions (1993).

A second category of arms is so-called heavy conventional weapons, such as tanks, heavy artillery, jet planes, missiles, and warships. In general, worldwide demand for these weapons declined significantly after the cold

The Arms Trade

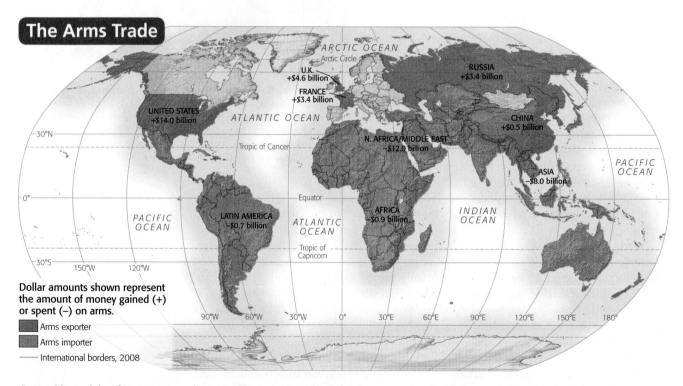

Dollar amounts shown represent the amount of money gained (+) or spent (−) on arms.

- ■ Arms exporter
- ■ Arms importer
- — International borders, 2008

Source: Map and data from www.controlarms.org/the_issues/movers_shakers.htm, reproduced with the permission of Oxfam GB, Oxfam House, John Smith Drive, Cowley, Oxford OX4 2JY, UK, www.oxfam.org.uk. Oxfam GB does not necessarily endorse any text or activities that accompany the materials.

Amnesty International and Oxfam put up mock gravestones in central London in 2003 to represent the more than a half million people killed on average each year by conventional light weapons. (Jim Watson/AFP/Getty Images)

war ended. Only a few companies, located in the largest industrialized nations, have the scientists, the funding, and the capacity to produce them. Because the major Soviet- and Western-bloc nations had large weapon surpluses in 1991, most of the new weapons produced in this category have been made for export. In 1995 the United States for the first time produced more combat aircraft for export sales than for U.S. military use. New demand comes mainly from developing nations that are not technologically or financially capable of producing such weapons, such as Chile, which purchased ten F-16 jet aircraft worth $660 million from the United States in 2002, and Pakistan, which announced plans in March 2005 to buy a minimum of twenty-four F-16s. Another significant market for the United States, Great Britain, France, and Germany has been new or potential NATO member states. In 2003, for example, the United States sold forty-eight F-16 fighter aircraft worth $3.5 billion to Poland, while Germany received $1 billion from Greece for 170 battle tanks. Many of the former Soviet-bloc countries of eastern Europe have illegally served as points of origin or transfer points for sales to embargoed nations such as North Korea and to terrorist groups such as al-Qaeda.

The third category is small arms and light conventional weapons (SALWs). These are almost any remotely portable weapon including automatic rifles, machine guns, pistols, antitank weapons, small howitzers and mortars, Stinger missiles and other shoulder-fired weapons, grenades, plastic explosives, land mines, machetes, small bombs, and ammunition. SALWs make up the majority of weapons exchanged in the global arms trade. They also do the most harm. In the 1990s, the weapons of choice in forty-seven of forty-nine major conflicts were small arms. Every year, they are responsible for over a half million deaths.

SALWs are popular because they have relatively long lives and are low-maintenance, cheap, easily available, highly portable, and easily concealable. Many can be used by child soldiers. Globally, there are around 650 million guns, about 60 percent of them owned by private citizens. Fifteen billion to twenty billion or more rounds of ammunition are produced annually. Despite widespread concern about terrorists obtaining nuclear or chemical weapons, terrorists on the whole favor such small conventional weapons as truck and car bombs and automatic rifles and pistols for assassinations, sniping, armed attacks, and massacres. One of the most deadly SALWs is the land mine. Over 110 million of them still lie buried in Afghanistan, Angola, Iran, and other former war zones, and they continue to kill or injure fifteen thousand to twenty thousand people a year.

Over ninety countries manufacture and sell SALWs, but the five permanent members of the UN Security Council—France, Britain, the United States, China, and Russia—dominate. The United States and Britain account for nearly two-thirds of all conventional arms deliveries, and these two nations plus France sometimes earn more income from arms sales to developing countries than they provide in aid. The total legal international trade in SALWs is estimated at about $8 billion a year; the illegal total is about $1 billion. Of course, every legal weapon can easily become an illegal one.

In 2000 UN Secretary-General Kofi Annan observed that "the death toll from small arms dwarfs that of all other weapons systems—and in most years greatly exceeds the toll of the atomic bombs that devastated Hiroshima and Nagasaki. In terms of the carnage they cause, small arms, indeed, could well be described as 'weapons of mass destruction.'"*

*Kofi A. Annan, "Freedom from Fear," in *"We the Peoples": The Role of the United Nations in the 21st Century,* ch. 4, p. 52.

treaty. By 1968 they too had hydrogen bombs. Reversing its previous commitment to nuclear arms limitations, India also developed weapons and in 1974 exploded an atomic device. Meanwhile, the nuclear arms race between the Soviet Union and the United States surged ahead after 1968. The Strategic Arms Limitation Talks (SALT) in the 1970s only limited the rate at which the two superpowers produced more nuclear warheads. As of 2008 these two nations possess 95 percent of the world's nuclear warheads.

India developed its atomic capability partly out of fear of China, which had manhandled India in a savage border war in 1962. India's nuclear blast in 1974 in turn frightened Pakistan, which after 1947 regarded India as a bitter enemy. Pakistan's president Zulfikar Ali Bhutto (1928–1979) set up a nuclear weapons program after having reportedly said that Pakistan must have the bomb even if its people had to eat grass. By the mid-1980s Pakistan had the ability to produce nuclear weapons. In 1998 both India and Pakistan set off nuclear devices within weeks of each other, becoming the world's sixth and seventh nuclear powers. The two countries came to the brink of full-scale war in 2002, and there was some official and popular support on both sides for the use of nuclear weapons. Pakistan did not sign the nonproliferation treaty, nor did it accept the "no-first-use doctrine," by which it would agree not to be the first to use a nuclear weapon. Just as ominously, the father of Pakistan's nuclear weapons program, Abdul Qadeer Khan, was charged in 2004 with passing on nuclear weapons expertise and technology to Iran, Libya, and North Korea. An agreement in April 2005 to normalize political and trade relations between the two nuclear powers and to negotiate a peaceful solution to the Kashmir problem eased tensions somewhat.

As of 2008, Israel had never confirmed or denied having nuclear weapons. In the 1950s, however, Israel began a nuclear weapons development program, and it was generally believed that Israel had had an arsenal of nuclear weapons since the 1980s. Israel's apparent nuclear superiority was profoundly humiliating and threatening to the Arabs. When Iraq attempted, with help from France, to develop nuclear capability in the 1980s, Israel responded suddenly, attacking and destroying the Iraqi nuclear reactor in June 1981.

Fortunately, Israel's attack on Iraq was an isolated event, but the possibility of other similar attacks and the continuing proliferation of nuclear weapons helped mobilize the international community and contributed to positive developments through the 1980s and 1990s. Argentina (1983), Romania (1989), Brazil (1998), South Africa (1990s), and Libya (2003) all abandoned their nuclear weapons programs. Several of the former Soviet republics possessing nuclear arsenals, including Belarus and Kazakhstan, returned their nuclear weapons to Russia. Nuclear watch-guard agencies monitored exports of nuclear material, technology, and missiles that could carry atomic bombs. These measures encouraged confidence in global cooperation and in the nonproliferation treaty, which was extended indefinitely in 1995. The treaty has been signed by 189 countries as of 2008, including America, France, Russia, China, and the United Kingdom. Pakistan, India, and Israel, all of whom have the bomb, have not signed it. North Korea ratified the treaty in 1985 but withdrew in January 2003, making it the first nation ever to withdraw from the agreement.

Still, serious challenges remained in the early twenty-first century besides the nuclear confrontation between India and Pakistan. First, top-secret efforts by Iraq to build a bomb before the Gulf War almost succeeded, highlighting the need for better ways to detect cheating. Second, Russia and the United States had promised vaguely to cut their nuclear weapons drastically, but in 2002 they were stalled at about six thousand each, with no hope of quick progress. In May 2005 a month-long meeting of the nonproliferation treaty members failed to make any progress in strengthening the treaty. Members were particularly concerned that the Bush administration talked of modernizing the U.S. nuclear forces and that America would not reaffirm its commitment to disarmament as promised at the 1995 and 2000 meetings. Third, although Iran is a signatory to the 1970 treaty, it developed a nuclear energy program

● **South Korean Protests Against North Korea** North Korea's development of nuclear weapons has sparked angry demonstrations in the major cities of its Asian neighbors. Here a South Korean protester burns a North Korean flag and a mock atomic bomb during a rally in Seoul. *(Reuters/Corbis)*

to generate power. In 2003 the United States demanded that Iran be held accountable for seeking to produce nuclear weapons and also accused Iran of building nuclear missiles. Despite intense scrutiny, as of July 2008 no country, including the United States, had produced any evidence to support the claim that Iran had a nuclear weapons program.

Fourth, there is the threat that enriched nuclear materials will fall into the hands of terrorist organizations. In 2001, three Pakistani nuclear scientists were arrested following allegations they had met with Taliban and al-Qaeda representatives. And in early 2005 it was estimated that half of Russia's nuclear materials could not be accounted for because of widespread corruption in that country and its inability to guard its nuclear arsenal.

Finally, in early 2003 long-standing tensions between North Korea and the United States, which had never signed a peace treaty ending the 1950–1953 Korean War, reached crisis proportions over the question of nuclear arms on the Korean peninsula. As each side accused the other of failing to live up to a 1994 agreement, North Korea announced its intention to withdraw from the 1970 nonproliferation treaty, and in October 2006 North Korea tested its first nuclear device. George W. Bush insisted on six-party talks (rather than one-on-one) involving North Korea and the United States, China, Japan, South Korea, and Russia to get the North Koreans to abandon their nuclear program. In February 2007 North Korea agreed to shut down its major nuclear facility at Yöngbyön in exchange for thousands of tons of heavy fuel oil from the West, and the release of $25 million in frozen North Korean funds, and it fulfilled its promise in July 2007. U.S., Russian, and Chinese inspectors toured the site in September 2007, and America's top Korean specialist, Sung Kim, was given eighteen thousand secret papers about activities at the reactor during a visit to North Korea in May 2008. As negotiations continue, this confrontation, like the one between India and Pakistan, illustrates the danger of atomic war in a multipolar world of intense regional rivalries.

Chemical and biological weapons of mass destruction created similar anxieties. For many years the use of chemical weapons had been outlawed by international agreement, but the manufacture of these terrible weapons was nonetheless permitted. In 1997 most of the world's nations signed a convention banning the production of chemical weapons and requiring the destruction of those in existence. Inspectors received the right to make surprise searches "anytime, anywhere." But complex practical questions relating to effective verification remained unanswered. Moreover, most Arab countries refused to sign the treaty, pointing to Israel's long-standing refusal to join the nuclear nonproliferation agreement. As of 2008, at least seventeen countries had active chemical weapons programs.

Building credible verification was an even greater problem for the experts monitoring the 1972 Biological and Toxin Weapons Convention, which outlawed the production of the tiny quantities sufficient to poison large populations. Iraq's attempts to develop biological weapons, discovered after the Gulf War, gave new urgency to formulating rules for surprise inspections and trade controls. Negotiations were held through the 1990s to develop a verification mechanism to carry out these inspections. In 2001, however, the Bush administration declared that the United States would not agree to any such protocol. Talks to develop a verification protocol acceptable to the United States were ongoing in 2008.

As far as terrorism was concerned, most weapons experts through the 1990s believed that terrorists were more likely to use chemical and biological weapons than to acquire and use nuclear arms because of the great complexity of construction of the latter and the need for missiles to deliver them. But there was growing concern that these experts might have underestimated the ability and willingness of terrorist groups to make and use nuclear devices. As early as 1978, Brian Jenkins, a RAND Corporation scholar, observed that

we are approaching an age in which national governments may no longer monopolize the instruments of major destruction. The instruments of warfare once possessed only by armies will be available to gangs. It will not be possible to satisfy the real or imagined grievances of all the little groups that will be capable of large-scale disruption and destruction, or to defend everyone against them. . . . In the future, warfare—highly destructive warfare—may be waged without the necessity for armies and governments, by people with little to lose.[5]

Jenkins's prescient vision appears more a possibility than ever before. Nations think in terms of preserving themselves while destroying their enemies. But terrorists willing to become martyrs with pounds of explosives strapped to their bodies have no need for a missile to deliver a nuclear device. They will deliver it personally.

In short, the terrible doomsday scenario of human-made plagues, lethal nerve gases, and mushroom clouds still haunts humanity, which seeks in turn to escape the threat of self-inflicted cataclysm.

● ● ● ● ● ● ● ● ● ● ● ● ● ● ● ●

GLOBAL INTERDEPENDENCE

How are the United Nations and multinational corporations representative of increasing globalization?

Alongside the political competition, war, and civil conflict in the twentieth century, a contradictory phenomenon unfolded: the nations of our small planet became increasingly interdependent both economically and technologically. Even the great continental states with the largest landmasses and populations and the richest natural resources found that they could not depend only on themselves. The United States required foreign oil, China needed foreign markets, and Russia needed foreign grain. All countries and peoples had need of each other.

Mutual dependence in economic affairs was often interpreted as a promising sign for the human race. Dependence promoted peaceful cooperation and limited the scope of violence. Yet the existing framework of global interdependence also came under intense attack. The poor countries of the developing world—frequently referred to now as the South—charged that the North (the industrialized countries) continued to receive far more than their rightful share from existing economic relationships, which had been forged unjustly to the South's disadvantage in the era of European political domination. The South demanded a new international economic order. Critics also saw strong evidence of neocolonialism in the growing importance of the North's huge global business corporations—the so-called multinationals—in world economic development. Thus global interdependence was widely acknowledged in principle and hotly debated in practice.

Multinational Corporations

A striking feature of global interdependence beginning in the early 1950s was the rapid emergence of **multinational corporations,** business firms that operate in a number of different countries and tend to adopt a global rather than a national perspective. Multinational corporations themselves were not new, but by 1971 they accounted for fully one-fifth of the noncommunist world's annual income, and they grew to be even more important in the 1980s and 1990s.

The rise of the multinationals was partly due to the general revival of capitalism after the Second World War (see Figure 33.1), relatively free international economic relations, and the worldwide drive for rapid industrialization. The multinationals also had three specific assets, which they used to their advantage. First, "pure" scientific knowledge unrelated to the military was freely available, but profitable industrial applications generally remained in the hands of the world's largest business firms. Second, the multinationals knew how to sell, as well as how to innovate and produce. They used modern advertising and marketing skills to push their products. Third, the multinationals developed new techniques to escape from political controls and

multinational corporations
Business firms that operate in a number of different countries and tend to adopt a global rather than a national perspective.

● **The Ubiquitous Multinational Corporations** Under one of the most recognized advertising symbols in the world, the Marlboro Man, Buddhist monks line up to wait for daily donations in Phnom Penh, Cambodia. *(AP Photo/ Wide World Photos)*

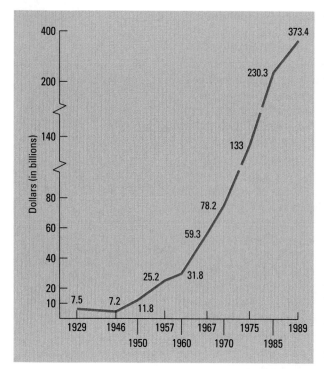

●FIGURE 33.1 **Total Investment by American Corporations in Foreign Subsidiaries, 1929–1989** (Source: Data from U.S. Department of Commerce, *Survey of Current Business*)

national policies. They treated the world as one big market, coordinating complex activities across many political boundaries.

The impact of multinational corporations, especially on Third World countries, was heatedly debated. From an economic point of view, the effects were mixed. The giant firms provided advanced technology, but the technology was expensive and often inappropriate for poor countries with widespread unemployment.

The social consequences were quite striking. The multinationals helped spread the products and values of consumer society to the developing world's elites. They fostered the creation of growing islands of Western wealth, management, and consumer culture around the world. After buying up local companies, multinational corporations often hired local business leaders to manage their operations abroad. Critics considered this practice an integral part of the process of neocolonialism, whereby local elites abandoned the national interest and made themselves willing tools of continued foreign domination. Global corporations often used aggressive techniques of modern marketing to sell products that were not well suited to Third World conditions, and they frequently came into sharp conflict with host countries.

Far from acting helpless in such conflicts, some poor countries found ways to assert their sovereign rights over the foreign multinationals. Many foreign mining companies, such as the extremely profitable U.S. oil companies in the Middle East, were simply nationalized by the host countries. More important, governments in the developing countries learned how to play Americans, Europeans, and Japanese off against each other and to make foreign manufacturing companies conform to some of their plans and desires. Increasingly, multinationals had to share ownership with local investors, hire more local managers, provide technology on better terms, and accept a variety of controls. Finally, having been denied the right to build manufacturing plants and industry as colonies, some newly independent countries also began to industrialize.

Industrialization and Modernization

industrialization strategy
The belief that the masses were impoverished because they were living in a primitive agricultural economy and that only modern factory industry would raise standards of living.

Throughout the 1950s and 1960s African, Asian, and Latin American leaders, pressed on by their European, American, and Soviet advisers, believed a vigorous **industrialization strategy** was the only answer to poverty and population growth. The masses, they concluded, were poor because they were imprisoned in a primitive, inefficient agricultural economy. Only modern factory industry appeared capable of creating wealth quickly enough to raise standards of living.

To Third World elites, the economic history of the West, Japan, and the Soviet Union seemed to validate this faith in industrialization. The wealthy countries had also been agricultural and "underdeveloped" until, one by one, the Industrial Revolution had lifted them out of poverty. It seemed this uneven progress of industrialization was primarily responsible for the great income gap between rich and poor countries in 1950.

modernization *A theory, popular in the 1960s, that assumed that all countries were following the path already taken by the industrialized nations and that the elites' task was to speed the trip.*

Modernization theories, popular in the 1960s, assumed that all countries were following the path already taken by the industrialized nations and that the elites' task was to speed the trip. Marxism, with its industrial and urban bias, preached a similar gospel. These ideas reinforced the desire of the newly independent countries to industrialize.

Nationalist leaders believed a successful industrialization strategy required state action and enterprise along socialist lines. Many were impressed by Stalin's forced industrialization in particular for its having won the Soviet Union international power and prominence. In Asia and Africa capitalists and private enterprise were often equated with the old rulers and colonial servitude. The reasoning was practical as well as ideological: socialism meant an expansion of steady government jobs for political and ethnic allies, and modern industry meant ports, roads, schools, and hospitals as well as factories. Only the state could afford such expensive investments.

The degree of state involvement varied considerably. A few governments, such as communist China, tried to control all aspects of economic life. A few one-party states in Africa, notably Zambia, Ghana, and Ethiopia, mixed Marxist-Leninist ideology and peasant communes in an attempt to construct a special "African socialism." At the other extreme the British colony of Hong Kong downgraded government control of the economy and emphasized private enterprise and the export of manufactured goods. Most governments assigned the state an important, even leading, role, but they also recognized private property and tolerated native (and foreign) business people. The **mixed economy**—part socialist, part capitalist—became the general rule in Africa and Asia.

mixed economy *An economy that is part socialist and part capitalist.*

Political leaders concentrated state investment in big, highly visible projects that proclaimed the country's independence and stimulated national pride. Enormous dams for irrigation and hydroelectric power were favored undertakings. Nasser's stupendous Aswan Dam harnessed the Nile, demonstrating that modern Egyptians could surpass even the pyramids of their ancient ancestors. These big projects testified to the prevailing faith in expensive advanced technology and modernization along European lines.

In many ways the Third World's first great industrialization drive was a success. Industry grew faster than ever before, though from an admittedly low base in Africa and most of Asia. Nevertheless, by the late 1960s disillusionment with relatively rapid industrialization was spreading. Asian, African, and Latin American countries did not as a whole match the "miraculous" concurrent advances of western Europe and Japan, and the great economic gap between rich and poor nations continued to widen.

Also, most leaders in the developing countries had genuinely believed that rapid industrial development would help the rural masses. Yet careful studies showed increasingly that the main beneficiaries of industrialization were business people, bureaucrats, skilled workers, and urban professionals. Peasants and agricultural laborers gained little or nothing. Moreover, the poorest countries—such as India and Indonesia in Asia, and Ethiopia and Sudan in Africa—were growing most slowly in per capita terms. Industrialization appeared least effective where poverty was most intense. Economic dislocations in the global economy after the 1973 OPEC oil embargo (see pages 946 and 949) accentuated this trend, visiting particularly devastating effects on the poorest countries.

Perhaps most serious, between 1950 and 1970, industrialization had provided jobs for only about one-fifth of the 200 million young men and women who had entered the exploding labor force in the developing countries in the same period. For the foreseeable future, it seemed, most people in these countries would have to remain on the farm or work in traditional handicrafts and service occupations. All-out modern industrialization had failed as a panacea. By the late 1960s widespread dissatisfaction with policies of all-out industrialization prompted a greater emphasis on rural development.

Agriculture and the Green Revolution

From the late 1960s onward the limitations of industrial development forced governments in the developing nations to take renewed interest in rural people and village life. At best this attention meant giving agriculture its due and coordinating rural development with industrialization and urbanization. At worst, especially in the very poorest countries, it deflated the optimistic vision that living standards would approach those of the wealthy industrialized nations.

Nationalist elites had neglected agriculture for various reasons. An agricultural economy represented colonial servitude, which they symbolically repudiated by embracing industrialization. To provide capital for industry, they squeezed agriculture and peasant producers, establishing artificially low food prices, which also subsidized their volatile urban supporters at the farmers' expense. In addition, the obstacles to more productive farming seemed overwhelming to unsympathetic urban elites and condescending foreign experts: farms were too small and fragmented for mechanization, peasants were too stubborn and ignorant to change their ways, and so on. Little wonder that only big farmers and some plantations received much government support. Wherever large estates and absentee landlords predominated—in large parts of Asia and in most of Latin America excluding Mexico, though not in sub-Saharan Africa—landless laborers and poor peasants who had no choice other than to rent land simply lacked the incentive to work harder. Any increased profits from larger crops went mainly to the absentee landowners.

Most honest observers were convinced that improved farm performance required land reform. Yet ever since the French Revolution, genuine land reform had been viewed as a profoundly radical measure, frequently bringing violence and civil war. Powerful landowners and their allies generally succeeded in blocking or subverting redistribution of land to benefit the poor. Land reform, unlike industrialization, was generally too hot for most politicians to handle.

Governments also neglected agriculture because feeding the masses was deceptively easy in the 1950s and early 1960s. Before 1939 the countries of Asia, Africa, and Latin America had collectively produced more grain than they consumed. After 1945, as their populations soared, they began importing ever-increasing but readily available quantities. Very poor countries, for example, received food from the United States at giveaway prices as part of a U.S. effort to dispose of enormous grain surpluses and help American farmers.

Although crops might fail in poor countries, starvation seemed a thing of the past. In 1965, when India was urged to build up its food reserves, one top Indian official expressed a widespread attitude: "Why should we bother? Our reserves are the wheat fields of Kansas."[6] In the short run, the Indian official was right. In 1966 and again in 1967, when famine gripped the land, the United States gave India one-fifth of the U.S. wheat crop. More than 60 million Indians lived exclusively on American grain. The effort required a food armada of six hundred ships, the largest fleet assembled since the Normandy invasion of 1944. The famine was ultimately contained, and instead of millions of deaths, there were only a few thousand.

That close brush with mass starvation sent a shiver down the world's spine. Complacency dissolved in Asia and Africa, and neo-Malthusian prophecies of disaster multiplied in wealthy nations. Paul Ehrlich, an American scientist, envisioned a grisly future in his polemical 1968 bestseller *The Population Bomb*:

The battle to feed all of humanity is over. In the 1970s the world will undergo famines— hundreds of millions of people are going to starve to death in spite of any crash programs embarked upon now. At this stage nothing can prevent a substantial increase in the world death rate.[7]

Countering such nightmarish visions was the hope offered by technological improvements. Plant scientists and agricultural research stations had already set out to develop new hybrid seeds genetically engineered to suit the growing conditions of tropical agriculture. Their model was the extraordinarily productive hybrid corn developed for the American Midwest in the 1940s. The first breakthrough came in Mexico in the 1950s, when an American-led team developed new strains of high-yielding dwarf wheat. These varieties enabled farmers to double their yields, though they demanded greater amounts of fertilizer and water for irrigation. Mexican wheat production soared. Thus began the transformation of agriculture in some poor countries—the so-called **Green Revolution.**

In the 1960s an American-backed team of scientists in the Philippines developed a new hybrid "miracle rice" that required more fertilizer and water but yielded more and grew much faster than ordinary rice. It permitted the revolutionary advent of year-round farming on irrigated land, making possible two, three, or even four crops a year. Asian scientists, financed by their governments, developed similar hybrids to meet local conditions.

Some Asian countries experienced rapid and dramatic increases in grain production. Farmers in India upped production more than 60 percent in fifteen years. By 1980 thousands of new grain bins dotted the Indian countryside, symbols of the agricultural revolution and the country's newfound ability to feed all its people. China followed with its own highly successful version of the Green Revolution under Deng Xiaoping.

The Green Revolution offered new hope to the developing nations, but it was no cure-all. Initially most of it benefits seemed to flow to large landowners and to substantial peasant farmers who could afford the necessary investments in irrigation and fertilizer. Subsequent experience in China and other Asian countries showed, however, that even peasant families with tiny farms could gain substantially. Indeed, the Green Revolution's greatest successes occurred in Asian countries with broad-based peasant ownership of land.

The technological revolution, however, shared relatively few of its benefits with the poorest villagers, who almost never owned the land. This helps explain why the Green Revolution failed to spread from Mexico throughout Latin America. As long as 3 to 4 percent of the rural population owned 60 to 80 percent of the land, as was still the case in many Latin American countries, the Green Revolution usually remained stillborn.

As the practice of genetically engineering or modifying foods grew in the late twentieth and early twenty-first centuries, global opposition to the practice and the foods also grew. Many people feared that such foods would have still-unknown effects on the human body. Several European and other countries placed bans on imports of genetically modified corn and soybeans from the United States, where the practice was most common.

The loss of biodiversity was also of growing concern. When one or two genetically engineered seeds replaced all of the local, naturally occurring seeds in a given area, as frequently happened when Green Revolution technologies became the norm, food security was threatened. As the world experiences a shrinking diversity of plants and animals, farmers will find it more difficult to respond and find alternatives if the dominant hybrid seed in use becomes susceptible to a particular disease or pest or there is a significant climate change. Corporate ownership of seeds through patents is another worrisome outcome of this shrinking diversity—farmers will be dependent on a few giant multinational agribusinesses for their seeds. And because seeds are being engineered that can be used for only one year, farmers will have to return to these companies each planting season for a complete stock of new seeds. Finally, economists worried that yet another gap would develop between the world's rich and poor over food. As mass-produced, genetically modified foods became cheaper, they would be eaten by the poor, while the rich would be able to afford organically grown, chemically free, but more expensive foods.

Green Revolution *The increase in food production stemming from the introduction of high-yielding wheat, hybrid seeds, and other advancements.*

The Economics and Politics of Globalization

After the 1960s there was dissatisfaction in Asia, Africa, and Latin America not only with the fruits of the industrialization drive but also with the world's economic system.

Scholars imbued with a Third World perspective and spokesmen for the United Nations majority declared that the international system was unjust and in need of radical change. Mahbub ul Haq, a Pakistani World Bank official and member of the international bureaucratic elite, sympathetically articulated this position in 1976:

The vastly unequal relationship between the rich and the poor nations is fast becoming the central issue of our time. The poor nations are beginning to question the basic premises of an international order which leads to ever-widening disparities between the rich and the poor countries and to a persistent denial of equality of opportunity to many poor nations. They are, in fact, arguing that in international order—just as much as within national orders—all distribution of benefits, credit, services, and decision-making becomes warped in favor of a privileged minority and that this situation cannot be changed except through fundamental institutional reforms.[8]

The subsequent demand of the developing nations for a "new international economic order" had many causes, both distant and immediate. Critics of imperialism such as J. A. Hobson (see page 724) and Third World writers on decolonization such as Frantz Fanon (see page 1014) had long charged that the colonial powers grew rich exploiting Asia, Africa, and Latin America. Beginning in the 1950s a number of writers, many of them Latin American Marxists, breathed new life into these ideas with their "theory of dependency."

The poverty and so-called underdevelopment of the South, they argued, were not the starting points but the deliberate and permanent results of exploitation by the capitalist industrialized nations in the modern era. Poor countries produced cheap raw materials for wealthy, industrialized countries and were conditioned to buy their expensive manufactured goods. As in the case of Latin America since the nineteenth

● **An International Labor Force** Since 2003 China has been the number one destination for foreign direct investment, with France and the United States ranking second and third. Although Chinese consumer goods—such as clothing or toys—dominate many world markets, China is also rapidly becoming a global leader in the production of high-tech products, such as personal computers. Here Chinese women assemble precision made parts on a factory production line. Beginning in 2007, problems with Chinese-made products—ranging from adulterated pharmaceuticals to tainted dog food to toys with high lead content—raised health and safety concerns in the United States and Europe. *(Peerpoint/Alamy)*

● **Indifference of Rich Nations to Poor** This cartoon expresses the opinion of many in the developing world that their suffering is being ignored by the more well-off residents of the developed world. The focus of their anger in 2005 was the huge debts of billions of dollars owed the rich nations. These debts were so large that many countries were paying more on their debts to the wealthiest nations than they were receiving in aid. European Union and G8 members pledged during the year to reduce the debts, but it remains to be seen what will come of the pledges. (The G8 consists of the original G6 members plus Canada and Russia.) *(Cam Cardow/The Ottawa Citizen)*

century, the industrialized nations perpetuated this neocolonial pattern after Third World countries gained political independence. Thus the prevailing economic interdependence was the unequal, unjust interdependence of dominant and subordinate, of master and peon. The international order needed a radical restructuring.

The OPEC oil coup of 1973–1974 ignited hopes in the developing countries of actually achieving a new system of economic interdependence. But generally the industrialized countries proved very tough bargainers when it came to basic changes. For example, in the late 1970s the developing nations hoped to formulate a new **Law of the Sea.** The proposed law was based on the principle that the world's oceans are "a common heritage of mankind" and should be exploited only for the benefit of all nations. In practice this would mean that a United Nations–sponsored authority would regulate and tax use of the sea. Some wealthy countries and their business firms were reluctant to accept such an infringement on what they judged to be their economic sovereignty and scope of action. The United States refused to sign the final draft of the law in 1982.

Law of the Sea *A proposed law based on the principle that the world's oceans are "a common heritage of mankind"; it would have allowed only a United Nations–sponsored authority to regulate and tax use of the sea.*

The great gap between the richest and poorest nations resulted from the coercive power of Western imperialism as well as from the wealth-creating effects of continuous technological improvement since the Industrial Revolution. In the face of bitter poverty, unbalanced economies, and local elites that often catered to Western interests, people of the developing countries had reason for frustration and anger.

But close examination of our small planet reveals a much more complex configuration than simply two sharply defined economic camps, a "North" and a "South." By the early 1990s there were several distinct classes of nations in terms of wealth and income (see Map 33.1). The former communist countries of eastern Europe formed something of a middle-income group, as did the major oil-exporting states, which still lagged behind the wealthier countries of western Europe and North America. Latin America was much better off than sub-Saharan Africa but contained a wide range of national per capita incomes. Some of the largest and fastest-growing economies, as well as highest standards of living, were found in South and East Asia. When one added global differences in culture, religion, politics, and historical development, the supposed clear-cut split between the rich North and the poor South broke down further. Moreover, the solidarity of the South had always been fragile, resting largely on the ideas of some Third World intellectuals and their supporters.

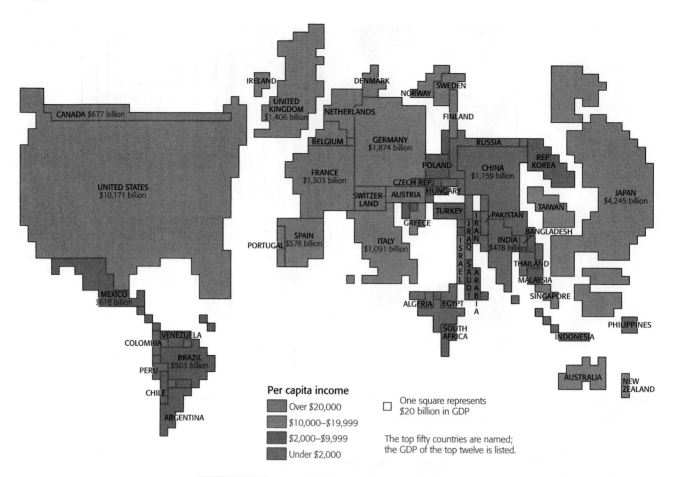

MAP 33.1 **The Global Distribution of Wealth** This size-comparison map, arranged according to global wealth distribution, vividly illustrates the gap in wealth between the Northern and Southern Hemispheres. The two small island nations of Japan and the United Kingdom have more wealth than all the nations of the Southern Hemisphere combined. As market capitalism expands in China, Vietnam and other Asian countries, and in Latin America and Africa, the relative size-ratios on the map will continue to change and evolve.

Thus a continuation of the global collective bargaining that first emerged in the 1970s seemed more likely than an international class war. The recurring international debt crisis illustrates the process of global bargaining. The economic dislocations of the 1970s and early 1980s worsened the problems of many developing countries, especially those that had to import oil. Growing unemployment, unbalanced budgets, and large trade deficits forced many poor countries to borrow rapidly from the wealthy industrialized nations. By the early 1980s much of the debt was short-term and could not be repaid as it came due, so it continued to build. By 2005 the world's poorest countries were spending more on debt repayments—$100 million a day—than on health care.

The wealthy lender nations generally were unwilling to cancel the debts. Seemingly only a major economic crisis that immediately threatened the lender nations themselves could get them to act. Such a crisis occurred in 1982 when Mexico appeared ready to default on its debts. The Reagan administration, consistently opposed to calls from the developing countries for a new international system, quickly organized a gigantic rescue operation to pump new money into Mexico. The reason was simple: Mexico's failure to service its foreign debt would cripple large American banks that had lent Mexico money and possibly cause a global financial panic and depression.

● **Run on the Banks** A security guard at Indonesia's Bank Harapan Santosa blocks the way of hundreds of depositors trying to get into the closed bank in Jakarta in November 1997. Most of Asia suffered a severe economic crisis in the late 1990s that had damaging ripple effects on the entire world economy. Indonesia closed ten banks during the crisis, setting off runs on banks by panicked depositors reminiscent of the Great Depression. *(AP Photo/Wide World Photos)*

Thus a series of international negotiations beginning in the 1980s reduced the debts of some developing countries, granted new loans, and encouraged economic liberalization. In 2000 the United Nations Millennium Project Report made debt relief a major goal.

While debt relief highlights the great wealth gap between the have and have-not countries, financial crises in the world's financial markets and networks threaten everyone. After the United States again saved Mexico (and American banks) from default in 1995, the world saw a new round of global financial crisis. In 1997 the rapidly growing economies of Thailand, Malaysia, South Korea, and Indonesia experienced a "run on the bank" when previously enthusiastic foreign investors panicked and withdrew their funds. As a result, the currencies of these Asian countries plunged, many Asian banks and companies could not repay their debts, and prices and unemployment soared. As in the 1980s, the industrialized countries and the International Monetary Fund (IMF) tried to stem the crisis with emergency loans and prescriptions for recovery. Yet the "Asian contagion" spread, bringing financial collapse in Russia and threatening to destroy Latin America's hard-won financial stability. Worried increasingly about the fate of their own economies, in late 1998 Japan, the United States, and the European Union, working with the IMF, redoubled their rescue operations and managed to stabilize international finances. The outcome benefited rich and poor countries. Global interdependence was clearly a fact of life.

Pressure on Vital Resources and Economic Development

A common theme in world history is the constant struggle of all living organisms to acquire the vital resources necessary for life. Indeed, one approach to studying any event in world history is simply to ask what, if any, vital resources were involved. Was a war fought over oil? Over land? Was a human migration in search of water or better grazing land for livestock? Were ocean voyages made in search of spices?

● **Gathering Firewood** These African women in Burkina Faso bring home headloads of wood, requiring a journey of one hour each way. In developing countries women (rarely men) make two or more such trips a week to provide fuel for cooking and heating, illustrating what has been called the "other energy crisis." As nearby forests are depleted they must travel farther and farther to find available wood, while the denuded land becomes open to soil erosion. Women and children spend another two to three hours every day or two hauling water. (Mark Edwards/Peter Arnold, Inc.)

During the postwar economic boom of the 1950s and 1960s nations became increasingly dependent on each other for vital resources. Yet resources also seemed abundant, and rapid industrialization was a worldwide article of faith. The situation changed suddenly in the 1970s. In a famous study aptly titled *The Limits to Growth* (1972), a group of American and European scholars argued that unlimited economic development is impossible on a finite planet. In the early twenty-first century, they predicted, the ever-increasing demands of too many people and factories would exhaust the world's mineral resources and destroy the fragile biosphere with pollution. Meanwhile, Japan imported 99 percent of its petroleum, western Europe 96 percent. When the Organization of Petroleum Exporting Countries (OPEC) increased the price of crude oil fourfold in 1973, there was panic in many industrial countries. Skyrocketing prices for oil and other raw materials in the 1970s seemed to confirm grim predictions that the world was exhausting its vital resources.

Of all the pressures on global resources, many observers believed that population growth was the most serious. Here recent experience offered room for optimism: population growth in the industrialized countries fell dramatically. In the 1950s women there had 2.8 children on average; in the late 1990s they had only 1.5. This level was not enough to maintain a stable population, and if that trend continued, total numbers in the developed countries would decline in the next generation. More important, equally dramatic declines in population growth were occurring throughout the developing world, and it was estimated that the world's population would level off at about 10 billion by 2100 (see pages 1054–1055).

Whatever the case may be, efforts to bring living standards in developing countries to levels approaching those in rich industrialized countries will put tremendous pressure on global resources. Jared Diamond, in his study of how societies succeed or fail, says it is therefore incumbent to ask how much of the traditional industrialized countries' consumer values and living standards we can afford to retain. He recognizes the seeming political impossibility of inducing consumer societies to lower their impact on the world's resources. But, he argues, "the alternative, of continuing our current impact, is more impossible." Diamond remains optimistic, however. He notes the decline in human fertility rates, and he argues that the strain on global resources could be lessened significantly if those with the highest standards of living accepted only a minimal reduction in their daily consumption of these resources. He is also encouraged because today humans have the advantage of a global communications network and a knowledge of human history that were not available to earlier generations.[9] Throughout its history, the human race has exhibited considerable skill in finding new resources and inventing new technologies. Perhaps we can learn from the achievements and mistakes made in the human past, and in the future share our finite global resources more equitably and wisely.

THE GROWTH OF CITIES (1945 TO THE PRESENT)

What factors spurred the growth of cities in Africa, Asia, and Latin America, and what were some of the main consequences of urbanization in the late twentieth century?

Perhaps no single phenomenon in the last hundred years has had a greater impact on individuals, families, and communities than the mass movement of peoples from rural areas to cities. The reasons for this migration are numerous, and the consequences for life on earth are profound.

Many of the most severe problems and most wonderful pleasures that humans experience are found in cities. Cities represent modernity, progress, and civilization. Countries newly free from colonial rule built shiny airports, international hotels, and massive government buildings, often next to tarpaper slums, as evidence of political independence and ongoing industrial development. Cities were also testimonials to increasing population, limited opportunities in the countryside, and neocolonial influence.

Rapid Urbanization

In 1945 when one thought of large cities, New York and London came to mind, followed by Tokyo and Paris. They were all soon overtaken, however, by cities in the developing world. Cities in Africa, Asia, and Latin America expanded at an astonishing pace after the Second World War. Many doubled or even tripled in size in a single decade. The population of the Algerian city of Algiers jumped from 300,000 to 900,000 between 1950 and 1960; Accra in Ghana, Lima in Peru, and Nairobi in Kenya grew just as fast. Moreover, rapid urban growth continued. In 1950 there were only eight **megacities** (5 million or more inhabitants), and just two were in developing countries. Estimates are that by 2015 there will be fifty-nine megacities, and forty-eight of them will be outside North America and Europe.

megacities *Cities with population of 5 million people or more.*

The urban explosion continued in the 1980s and 1990s, so that by 2000 more than 60 percent of the planet's city dwellers lived in the cities of Africa, Asia, and Latin America, according to United Nations estimates. Still, in Africa's and Asia's poorest countries urbanization is in its early stages. Thus if United Nations projections hold true, the urban population will triple from 1.4 billion persons in 1990 to 4.4 billion in 2025. Rapid urbanization in the developing countries represents a tremendous historical change. As recently as 1920, three out of every four of the world's urban inhabitants were concentrated in Europe and North America.

In the developing world, the capital city often emerged as an all-powerful urban center, encompassing all the important elite groups and dwarfing smaller cities as well as villages. Mexico City, for example, grew from 3 million to 12 million people between 1950 and 1975 and had an estimated 22 million people in 2000. In the 1980s and 1990s, an estimated 1.4 million Brazilian peasants were migrating annually to São Paulo, which also has over 20 million inhabitants, and to other Brazilian cities. The

● **Juan O'Gorman: Credit Transforms Mexico (1965)** Emerging as an important architect in the 1930s, O'Gorman championed practical buildings and then led the movement to integrate architecture with art in postrevolutionary Mexico. These panels from a fresco for a bank interior combine an optimistic view of economic development with many Mexican motifs. O'Gorman believed that Mexico had to preserve its cultural values in order to preserve its independence. (*Photos: Enrique Franco-Torrijos. Courtesy, Banco Bital, S.A., Mexico City*)

pattern of a dominant megalopolis has continued to spread from Latin America to Africa and Asia. Tokyo, in Japan, remains the largest city in the world with over 30 million inhabitants.

urban explosion *A rapid increase in the populations of world cities such as Mexico City.*

What caused this **urban explosion?** First, the general growth of population in the developing nations was critical. Urban residents gained substantially from a medical revolution that provided improved health care but only gradually began to reduce the size of their families. At the same time, the pressure of numbers in the countryside encouraged millions to set out for the nearest city. More than half of all urban growth has been due to rural migration.

Another factor was the desire to find jobs. Manufacturing jobs in the developing nations were concentrated in cities. In 1980 half of all the industrial jobs in Mexico were located in Mexico City, and the same kind of extreme concentration of industry occurred in many poor countries. Yet industrialization accounted for only part of the urban explosion.

urbanization without industrialization *A sociological phenomenon in which newcomers stream to cities seeking work even when no industrial jobs are available.*

Newcomers streamed to the cities even when there were no industrial jobs available, seeking any type of employment. Sociologists call this **urbanization without industrialization.** Many were pushed: they simply lacked enough land to survive. Large landowners found it more profitable to produce export crops, such as sugar or coffee, for wealthy industrialized countries, and their increasingly mechanized operations provided few jobs for agricultural laborers. The push factor was particularly strong in

Latin America, with its neocolonial pattern of large landowners and foreign companies exporting food and raw materials. More generally, much migration was seasonal or temporary. Many young people left home for the city to work in construction or serve as maids, expecting higher wages and steadier work and planning to return shortly with a modest nest egg.

Of course the magnetic attraction of cities was more than economic. It rested on the services and opportunities they offered, as well as on changing attitudes and the urge to escape from the traditional restraints of village life. Most of the modern hospitals, secondary schools, and transportation systems in less-developed countries were in the cities. So were most banks, libraries, movie houses, and basic conveniences. Safe piped water and processed food, for instance, were rare in rural areas, and village women by necessity spent much of their time carrying water and grinding grain.

Many of these developments were mirrored in the industrialized countries as well. But because industrialization had advanced in Europe and North America in the nineteenth and early twentieth centuries, people there had been drawn to urban areas at a much earlier date. By 1920, more Americans were already living in cities than in rural areas.

Overcrowding and Shantytowns

The late twentieth century saw a repeat of the problems associated with urbanization that had arisen in the cities of Europe and North America in an earlier era, but on a larger scale. Rapid population growth threatened to overwhelm urban social services; local authorities in many cities in the developing countries could not keep up with the demand. New neighborhoods often lacked running water, paved streets, electricity, and police and fire protection. As in the early days of Europe's industrialization, sanitation was minimal in poor sections of town. Outdoor toilets were shared by many, and raw sewage often flowed down streets and into streams.

Surging population growth had particularly severe consequences for housing. As in western Europe in the early nineteenth century, overcrowding reached staggering proportions in a great many Third World cities. Many old buildings were divided and redivided until population density reached the absolute saturation point.

Makeshift squatter settlements were another striking manifestation of the urban housing problem. These **shantytowns,** also known more positively as **self-help housing,** sprang up continuously, almost overnight, on the worst possible urban land. Typically, a group of urban poor "invaded" unoccupied land and quickly threw up tents or huts. Often beaten off by the police, they invaded again and again until the authorities gave up and a new squatter beachhead had been secured.

Shantytowns grew much faster than more prosperous urban areas. In the giant Brazilian city of Rio de Janeiro, for example, the population of the shantytowns grew four times faster than the rest of the city's population in the 1950s and 1960s. In most developing countries, self-help settlements came to house up to two-fifths of the urban population. Such settlements had occasionally grown up in American mining towns and in Europe, but never to the extent they did in Latin America, Asia, and Africa.

In the 1960s and 1970s efforts to bulldoze spontaneous communities out of existence were generally abandoned. Responding to pressure from these still-primitive neighborhoods and activists, some governments, particularly in Asia, agreed to make improvements—gradually installing piped water, public toilets, lighting, and some paved streets. Eventually, centrally located slums and old shantytowns attracted the attention of government planners and capitalists, who, under the guise of "urban renewal," sometimes joined forces to evict the poor and build new housing for the middle and upper classes. New self-help settlements continued to spring up on the urban fringes, but in the largest cities these settlements were less desirable because poor public transportation made getting to and from work a nightmare.

shantytowns *Areas of makeshift squatter settlements created by a group of the urban poor.*

self-help housing *A euphemism for shantytowns.*

Rich and Poor

At the beginning of the twenty-first century, differences in wealth between rich and poor countries, and often between rich and poor individuals within those countries, were truly staggering (see Table 33.1). American basketball star Michael Jordan received roughly $300,000 per game, as much as $10,000 per minute, when he played professionally in the late 1990s. Dividing his yearly income by the number of days in the year revealed that he earned about $178,000 per day whether he played or not. Still, he was far down on the list of the richest Americans. Microsoft founder and CEO Bill Gates had a net worth roughly 120 times greater than Jordan's in 2005. At the other end of the global income spectrum, there were sixty-one countries where the average person made less than $750 a year; half of the world's population—3 billion people—lived on less than $2 a day. The wealth of the world's three richest people was greater than the GDP of the poorest forty-eight nations combined.

Such disparities were not new. After World War II the gap in real income—income adjusted for differences in prices—between the industrialized world and the former colonies and dependencies of Africa, Asia, and Latin America was enormous. According to a leading historian, in 1950, when war-scarred Europe was in the early phase of postwar reconstruction,

● **Rich and Poor in Hong Kong** Global inequalities in wealth are evident in this photo of Hong Kong that shows refugee squatter housing in the foreground and modern, affluent apartment blocks behind. As a result of rapid urbanization and peasants' having to leave their land, this stark contrast between desperately poor and comfortably wealthy is found throughout the developing world. *(Brian Brake/ Photo Researchers, Inc.)*

the real income per capita of the Third World was five or six times lower than that of the developed countries. . . . In the developed countries, a century and a half of Industrial Revolution had resulted in a multiplication by more than five of the average standard of living in 1950. . . . For the average Third World countries the 1950s level was practically that of 1800 or, at best, only 10–20 percent above.[10]

The poor of these Third World countries were overwhelmingly concentrated in the countryside as small farmers and landless laborers.

Poverty meant, above all, not having enough to eat. For millions hunger and malnutrition were harsh facts of life. And in both developed and developing nations, even poor people who consumed enough calories often suffered from the effects of unbalanced high-starch diets and inadequate protein. Severe protein deficiency stunts the brain as well as the body, so many of the poorest children grew up mentally retarded.

Poor housing—crowded, often damp, and exposed to the elements—also contributed significantly to the less-developed world's high incidence of chronic ill health. So too did scanty education and lack of the fundamentals of modern public health: adequate and safe water, sewage disposal, immunizations, prenatal care, and control of communicable diseases. Infant mortality was savage, and chronic illness weakened and demoralized many adults, making them unfit for the hard labor their lives required. Generally speaking, people's health was better in Asia and Latin America than in the new states of sub-Saharan Africa.

After the developing countries achieved political independence, massive inequality continued, with few exceptions, to be the reality of life. A monumental gap separated rich and poor; it was most pronounced in the

Table 33.1 Urban Population as a Percentage of Total Population in the World and in Eight Major Areas, 1925–2025

AREA	1925	1950	1975	2000	2025 (EST.)
World Total	21	28	39	50	63
North America	54	64	77	86	93
Europe	48	55	67	79	88
Soviet Union	18	39	61	76	87
East Asia	10	15	30	46	63
Latin America	25	41	60	74	85
Africa	8	13	24	37	54

Note: Little more than one-fifth of the world's population was urban in 1925. In 2000 the urban proportion in the world total was about 50 percent. According to United Nations experts, the proportion should reach two-thirds by about 2025. The most rapid urban growth will occur in Africa and Asia, where the move to cities is still in its early stages.

exploding towns and cities. In Asia and Africa the rich often moved into the luxurious sections previously reserved for colonial administrators and foreign business people. Particularly in Latin America, upper-class and upper-middle-class people built fine mansions in exclusive suburbs, where they lived behind high walls with many servants and were protected from intruders by armed guards and fierce dogs.

Education also distinguished the wealthy from the masses. Children of the elite often attended expensive private schools, where classes were taught in English or French, and they had little in common with children in overcrowded public school classes taught in the national language. Subsequently, they often studied abroad at leading European and North American universities, or they monopolized openings at local universities. While absorbing the latest knowledge in prestigious fields such as civil engineering or economics, they also absorbed foreign customs and values. They mastered the fluent English or French that is indispensable for many top-paying jobs, especially with international agencies and giant multinational corporations. Thus elites in the developing countries often had more in common with the power brokers of the industrialized nations than with their own people, and they seemed willing tools of neocolonial penetration and globalization.

Too often the partnership formed among the wealthy elite of a developing country, multinational companies, and First World nations resulted in a developing country's experiencing **economic growth without economic development**. Enormous profits were being made from cash crop production or from industrial manufacturing, but few of these profits were used to build roads, schools, hospitals, or a more viable infrastructure, or to raise the standard of living of the common people. Multinational companies took the majority of the profits out of the country. The remainder often went directly into the private bank accounts of the wealthy elite, who also ruled the country, in return for their maintaining stability, keeping wages low and unions out, and allowing the companies to exploit the land and people as they wished.

In general, the majority of the exploding population of urban poor earned precarious livings in a modern yet traditional **bazaar economy** of petty traders and unskilled labor. Here regular salaried jobs were rare and highly prized, and a complex world of

economic growth without economic development *When large profits are made from cash crop production or from industrial manufacturing, few of these profits are put back into the construction of infrastructure or other efforts to raise the standard of living of the common people.*

bazaar economy *An economy with few salaried jobs and an abundance of tiny, unregulated businesses such as peddlers and pushcart operators.*

● **The Underground Economy** This Mexican woman sells fruit and other items along the roadside. In Latin America up to 60 percent of the workforce is part of the underground, or informal, economy. Throughout the developing world, millions of people eke out a daily living by selling their labor or crops. The government loses money because it receives no taxes from them. They nearly always earn less than a worker in the formal economy, and they are constantly harassed by corrupt police and government officials, blackmailers, and extortionists. *(Eric Nathan/Alamy Images)*

tiny, unregulated businesses and service occupations predominated. Peddlers and pushcart operators hawked their wares, and sweatshops and home-based workers manufactured cheap goods for popular consumption. This old-yet-new bazaar economy continued to grow prodigiously as migrants streamed to the cities, as modern industry provided too few jobs, and as the wide gap between rich and poor persisted.

Urban Migration and the Family

After 1945, large-scale urban migration had a massive impact on traditional family patterns in the developing countries, just as it had on families in industrialized countries earlier. Particularly in Africa and Asia, the great majority of migrants to the city were young men, married and unmarried; women tended to stay in the villages. The result was a sexual imbalance in both places. There were several reasons for this pattern. Much of the movement to cities (and to mines) remained temporary or seasonal. At least at first, young men left home to earn hard cash to bring back to their villages. Moreover, the cities were expensive, and prospects there were uncertain. Only after a man secured a genuine foothold did he marry or send for his wife and children.

For rural women the consequences of male out-migration were mixed. Asian and African women had long been treated as subordinates, if not inferiors, by their fathers and husbands. Rather suddenly, such women found themselves heads of households, faced with managing the farm, feeding the children, and running their own lives. In the East African country of Kenya, for instance, one-third of all rural households were headed by women in the late 1970s. African and Asian village women had to become unprecedentedly self-reliant and independent. As a result, the real beginnings of more equal rights and opportunities, of "women's liberation," became readily visible in Africa and Asia.

In Latin America the pattern of migration was different. Whole families migrated, very often to squatter settlements, much more commonly than in Asia and Africa. These families frequently belonged to the class of landless laborers, which was generally larger in Latin America than in Africa and Asia. Migration was also more likely to be once and for all. Another difference was that single women were as likely as single men to move to the cities, in part because women were in high demand there as domestic servants. The situation in Mexico in the late 1970s was typical:

They [women] leave the village seeking employment, often as domestic servants. When they do not find work in the cities, they have few alternatives. If they are young, they frequently turn to prostitution; if not, they often resort to begging in the streets. Homeless peasant women, often carrying small children, roam every quarter of Mexico City.[11]

Some women also left to escape the narrow, male-dominated villages. Even so, in Latin America urban migration seemed to have less impact on traditional family patterns and on women's attitudes than it did in Asia and Africa.

Urbanization and Agriculture

As we saw above, multinational agribusinesses, the Green Revolution, and various patterns of land transfer have dramatically altered the methods of global food production, the types of foods produced, and who produces it. These changes have also caused millions of small farmers and peasants to leave their land and migrate to the city. This is a global phenomenon, affecting farmers in developed and developing countries alike. The decline of the family farm in the United States is as representative as any of the consequences of modern agricultural production on small farmers.

A family farm is on land owned by the family; the majority of labor is done by family members; and the business is managed by the family in an open market system. In the United States, the number of family farms decreased from 7 million in the 1930s to fewer than 2 million in 2000. Since 1981, 750,000 farms and over a million jobs have been lost. Every week 330 farm operators leave the land. While the total number of farmers has decreased, total acreage under cultivation has increased. The average farm size increased from under 200 acres in 1940 to over 500 acres in 2000.

This transfer of land, from small family farmers to large operations owned by factory farmers or corporate agribusinesses, has dramatically altered the American labor force. Since the 1930s, the percentage of farmers in the workforce has shrunk from 21 percent to 2 percent. One half of all family farms now depend on off-farm income. Local economies and communities have also suffered because small farmers bought from local vendors, sold to local markets, received loans from local bankers, and shopped at local stores. The result has been the death of many small towns in America and the loss of many farm-related businesses and jobs.

Why has this happened? One simple reason is that the younger generation wants to move to the city—only 6 percent of American family farmers are under thirty-five. But there are other reasons as well. In 1980 an American farmer received 37 cents of every dollar spent on food; by 2000 he or she got only 20 cents. Even in the early 1980s, nominal net income, adjusted for inflation, was the same as during the Great Depression. As farm-related costs—land, equipment, fuel, seeds, fertilizer, irrigation—rise, it becomes more difficult for small farmers to compete with the large operations. Agribusinesses have the advantages of economy of scale and can afford larger machines to farm larger acreages as agriculture is industrialized. And, while the family farmer focuses simply on planting and harvesting a crop, the agribusiness is vertically integrated to control all phases of the process, from producing the hybrid seeds to marketing the final product, and can take advantage of international markets.

Peasants in developing countries leave the land for many of the same reasons. The major difference in developing countries, though, is that these peasant farmers, usually illiterate, are often producing subsistence crops and are simply forced off the land by government troops or thugs hired by large landowners or companies to make way for large cash crop production. The loss of land can also result from peasant families' possessing no documents proving ownership of the fields they have worked for generations. This inability to produce proof of ownership allows wealthy landowners, who obtain the proper documents, to claim the land and have the peasants legally evicted.

As we begin the twenty-first century, a few large agribusinesses threaten to fully industrialize, and then monopolize, global food production. At the same time, millions of small farmers around the world are leaving the land, willingly or unwillingly, and heading for the cities. In industrialized countries like the United States, the farmers and their children have educational and employment options. In developing countries, few options are available for illiterate peasants with no skills other than farming.

SCIENCE AND TECHNOLOGY: CHANGES AND CHALLENGES

What key technological and scientific developments have had the greatest impact on life at the beginning of the new millennium?

The twentieth century was a time of rapid urbanization, but it was equally an era of amazing advances in science and technology. These advances were not always positive. The great excitement over the telephone, the automobile, electricity, and the airplane was quickly tempered in 1914 by the killing machines invented and used in the Great War. Totalitarian regimes exploited new developments in mass communication for mass propaganda. And no sooner had the atom been harnessed than the United States released atomic bombs over Hiroshima and Nagasaki. Yet since the Enlightenment, scientists have believed that progress is possible and that no problem is unsolvable; whether their discoveries are used for good or evil is often out of their hands.

The Medical Revolution

medical revolution *The discovery of vaccines for many of the most deadly diseases during a period from the late 1800s through post–World War II.*

The **medical revolution** began in the late 1800s when Louis Pasteur made the case for a germ theory of disease and developed techniques for vaccine inoculation. The revolution continued after World War II. Scientists discovered vaccines for many of the most deadly diseases. Jonas Salk's development of the polio vaccine in 1952 was followed by the first oral polio vaccine (1962) and vaccines for measles (1964), mumps (1967), rubella (1970), chickenpox (1974), and hepatitis B (1981). Globally, these vaccines have saved millions of lives, especially those of children. According to the United Nations World Health Organization, medical advances reduced deaths from smallpox, cholera, and plague by more than 95 percent worldwide between 1951 and 1966.

Following independence, Asian and African countries increased the small numbers of hospitals, doctors, and nurses they had inherited from the colonial past. Sophisticated medical facilities became symbols of the commitment to a better life. In addition, local people were successfully trained as paramedics to staff rural outpatient clinics that offered medical treatment, health education, and prenatal and postnatal care. Many paramedics were women, for many health problems involved childbirth and infancy, and villagers the world over considered it improper for a man to examine a woman's body.

The medical revolution significantly lowered death rates and lengthened life expectancies. In particular, children became increasingly likely to survive their early years, although infant and juvenile mortality remained far higher in poor countries than in rich ones. By 1980 the average inhabitant of the developing countries could expect to live about fifty-four years; life expectancy at birth varied from forty to sixty-four years depending on the country. In industrialized countries life expectancy at birth averaged seventy-one years.

● **The Medical Revolution** A woman doctor in Yemen on the Arabian peninsula makes house calls by motorcycle, thereby carrying modern medicine to women in isolated desert communities. The doctor wears the veil traditionally required of women in public throughout parts of the Arab world. *(© Hans Bollinger/Pictures Press/Hamburg)*

Since the 1980s medical science has continued to make remarkable advances. In 1979 the World Health Organization announced the worldwide eradication of smallpox. By this time, transplants of such organs as hearts, lungs, eyes, and kidneys had become routine, and in 1982 an American man became the first recipient of an artificial heart. Also important were advances in our understanding of DNA made in the 1940s, 1950s, and 1960s that led to the Human Genome Project in the 1980s. Teams of scientists worked on this project until April 2003, when they announced they had successfully identified, mapped, and sequenced the entire genome, or hereditary information, of human beings. This knowledge gives health care providers immense new powers for preventing, treating, and curing diseases and makes the completion of the project one of the most important scientific developments in history. Embryonic stem cell research remains one of the most controversial areas of research in the early twenty-first century, but also one of the most promising. Proponents argue that it may offer cures for a range of illnesses from Parkinson's and Alzheimer's diseases to diabetes.

Still, despite these advances, the world continues to face a health care crisis because of the wide gap in health care availability and affordability between the rich and poor. Of the roughly $75 billion spent annually on health research, less than 10 percent is directed at 90 percent of the world's health problems. Thousands of people die every day from diseases and illnesses that are curable and easily treated. Between 1980 and 2000 the number of children under the age of five dying annually of diarrhea dropped by 60 percent, from 4.6 million to 1.8 million, through the global distribution of a cheap sugar-salt solution mixed in water. Still, over 1.5 million children worldwide continue to die each year from diarrhea. Malaria and tuberculosis also continue to be major killers of young and old alike, while deaths worldwide from HIV/AIDS are reaching epic proportions.

Population Change: Balancing the Numbers

A less favorable consequence of the medical revolution was the acceleration of population growth. As in nineteenth-century Europe, a rapid decline in death rates was not immediately accompanied by a similar decline in birthrates. Women in developing countries continued to bear five to seven children each, as their mothers and grandmothers had done. The combined populations of Asia, Africa, and Latin America, which had grown relatively modestly from 1925 to 1950, increased between 1950 and 1975 from 1.7 billion to 3 billion. It was an unprecedented explosion that promised to continue for many years.

The population explosion aroused fears of approaching famine and starvation. Thomas Malthus's gloomy late-eighteenth-century conclusion that population always tends to grow faster than the food supply (see page 655) was revived and updated by **neo-Malthusian** social scientists. Some governments began pushing family planning and birth control to slow population growth. These measures were not very successful in the 1950s and 1960s. In many countries Islamic and Catholic religious teachings were hostile to birth control. Moreover, widespread cultural attitudes dictated that a "real" man keep his wife pregnant. There were also economic reasons for preferring large families. Farmers needed the help of plenty of children at planting and harvest times, and sons and daughters were a sort of social security system for their elders. Thus a prudent couple wanted several children because some would surely die young. By the 1970s and 1980s, however, population growth in the industrialized countries had already begun to fall significantly. By the 1990s, some European leaders were bemoaning a birthrate in their countries that was below the 2.1 level needed to maintain a stable population.

Of much greater importance from a global perspective, the world's poor women began to bear fewer children. Small countries such as Barbados, Chile, Costa Rica, South Korea, Taiwan, and Tunisia led the way. Between 1970 and 1975 China followed, registering the fastest five-year birthrate decline in recorded history. Then other big countries, especially in Latin America and East Asia, experienced large declines in fertility. In 1970 the average Brazilian woman had close to 6 children; by 2005 she had 1.9. In 1970 the average woman in Bangladesh had more than 7 children; in 2005 she had 3.1.

There were several reasons for this decline in fertility among women in the developing world. Fewer babies were dying of disease or malnutrition, so couples needed fewer births to guarantee the survival of the number of children they wanted. Also, better living conditions, urbanization, and more education encouraged women to have fewer children. No wonder the most rapidly industrializing countries, such as Taiwan and South Korea, led the way in declining birthrates.

neo-Malthusian *Social science belief, based on the late-eighteenth-century works of Thomas Malthus, that population tends to grow faster than the food supply.*

● **Five Generations of the Yang Family** This group portrait suggests the enduring Chinese commitment to close family ties. It also puts a human face on social transformation, for the great-great-grandmother has bound feet and the baby she holds will be an only child. In the 1980s the Chinese government prohibited couples from having more than one child, a major factor in China's falling birthrate. *(Dermot Tatlow/Panos Pictures)*

In the early 1960s, the introduction of the birth control pill marked a revolution not only in birth control techniques but also in women taking control of their own fertility. "Family planning" was now truly possible; couples could make private decisions about how many children to have and when. In the early twenty-first century more than half of the world's couples practiced birth control, up from one in eight just forty years earlier, and that proportion continued to rise. Male chauvinism, religious teachings, and conservative government leaders combined in many countries to control the availability and distribution of birth control methods and abortion. Birth control and abortion were generally banned in predominately Roman Catholic countries, such as Ireland, Italy, Spain, and the countries of Latin America, and also in most Muslim countries. The practices were most accepted in North America, Protestant Europe, the Soviet Union, and East Asia, which explains why these regions had the lowest birthrates and population growth.

Although significant differences still exist between regions, projections of world population growth have declined sharply. By 2005 global birthrates had fallen to the lowest level in recorded history. The average woman in the developing world had 2.9 children, down from an average of nearly 6 babies in the 1970s. Fertility in most of the developing world could fall below the replacement level (2.1 children per woman) before 2100. The most recent estimates are that the world's population will "only" grow by 50 percent between 2000 and 2050, when it will reach about 9 billion. Over the next century it is then expected to level off at about 10 billion.

Global Epidemics

One of humanity's gravest fears in the early years of the new millennium comes from the threat posed by epidemic diseases. Outbreaks in Africa of the deadly Ebola and Marburg viruses; a worldwide outbreak of severe acute respiratory syndrome, or SARS, which began in 2002; ongoing avian, or bird, flu in Asia; and "mad-cow" disease, which has wreaked havoc with meat production in several countries, have all raised the frightening specter of a global recurrence of a modern Black Death. Tuberculosis (TB) has also made a comeback and kills one person every fifteen seconds, thus claiming millions of lives every year even though it is a curable disease. Malaria kills a million people a year worldwide, 90 percent of them in Africa.

But few diseases in world history have been more frightening, or caused more disruption of human society, than **HIV/AIDS.** In 2007 the Population Division of the United Nations calculated that 36 million persons globally were infected with HIV, the virus that causes AIDS. AIDS was the world's fourth-leading cause of death.

HIV/AIDS *A virus and a disease that infected more than 40 million persons worldwide by 2004; now the world's fourth leading cause of death.*

The global distribution of AIDS testifies to the existence of a lopsided, unequal world. About 90 percent of all persons who die from AIDS and 86 percent of those currently infected with HIV live in sub-Saharan Africa (see Map 33.2). In Africa HIV/AIDS has most commonly spread through heterosexual sex, and men and women frequently have failed to protect themselves against the disease in casual sexual relations. Widespread disease and poverty are also significant factors in that Africans already suffering from other illnesses such as malaria or tuberculosis have less resistance to HIV and less access to health care for treatment.

Another critical factor contributing to the spread of AIDS in Africa is the continued political instability of many countries—particularly those in the corridor running from Uganda to South Africa. This corridor was the scene of brutal civil or liberation wars that resulted in massive numbers of refugees, a breakdown in basic health care services, and the destruction of family and cultural networks. The countries along this corridor—Uganda, Rwanda, Burundi, Zaire/Congo, Angola, Zimbabwe, Mozambique, and South Africa—have had their populations decimated by HIV/AIDS. South Africa currently has the largest number of HIV/AIDS cases in the world. In 2007 around 10 percent of the South African population, about 5 million people, were

● **Fighting the AIDS Epidemic in Asia** A dramatic billboard warns people in Malaysia about the deadly dangers of AIDS. The billboard offers sound advice, focusing on the three primary ways by which the AIDS virus is spread. Can you "read" the three-part message? *(Robert Francis/The Hutchison Library/Eye Ubiquitous)*

living with HIV. Of these, 230,000 were children under fifteen years of age. An estimated 519,000 South Africans died of AIDS in 2005. As of 2005 medical health experts expected that Russia, India, China, Japan, and other countries in Asia might soon overtake South Africa in reported HIV/AIDS cases.

Although HIV/AIDS has had a devastating impact on Africa, globally the epidemic is still at a relatively early stage. Changes in behavior will be critical to slowing the spread of AIDS in the developing world. Although complicated treatments to contain the epidemic were available in 2008 in the wealthy industrialized countries, these treatments were still too expensive and too complicated for most national health services in the poor countries. Global interdependence increased in monitoring the spread of AIDS, but profound inequalities remained in its treatment.

Environmentalism

Many observers consider the publication in 1962 of Rachel Carson's *Silent Spring* as marking the beginning of the modern environmental movement. In the first pages, Carson (1907–1964) describes a "silent spring" in a nameless small American town. All the vegetation withers and turns brown. The townsfolk begin to fall ill. Birds make no sounds and are too weak to fly. No chicks hatch. Pig litters are small and soon die. There are no blossoms on the apple trees and no droning bees. Fishermen can catch no fish. Although her account is fictitious, Carson pointed out that some of these disasters had already befallen many real communities, and she warned that new chemicals released into the environment every year were responsible:

Along with the possibility of the extinction of mankind by nuclear war, the central problem of our age has therefore become the contamination of man's total environment with such substances of incredible potential for harm—substances that accumulate in the tissues of plants and animals and even penetrate the germ cells to shatter or alter the very material of heredity upon which the shape of the future depends.[12]

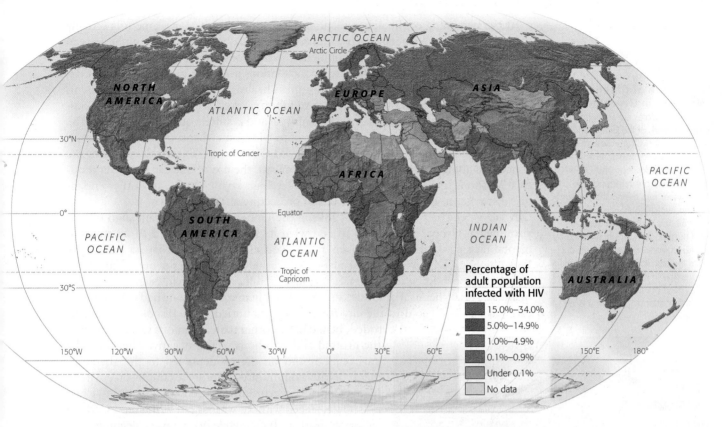

MAP 33.2 **People Living with HIV/AIDS Worldwide, 2007** As this map illustrates, Africa has been hit the hardest by the HIV/AIDS epidemic. It currently has fifteen to twenty times more identified cases than any other region of the world. AIDS researchers expect that in the coming decade, however, Russia and South and East Asia will overtake and then far surpass Africa in the number of infected people. (*Source: Data from World Health Organization, www.whosea.org*)

Carson was particularly concerned about pesticides, especially DDT, which was being utilized extensively and with much success to eradicate malaria. Her writings and campaigning, more than any other single cause, brought about the ban on DDT. Her work was a clarion call alerting people to the hazards present in all the chemicals they were using around their homes. Difficult decisions had to be made when weighing the advantages and disadvantages of using these often effective but highly toxic chemicals. At the time DDT was banned, for example, malaria had largely been wiped out; since the banning it has been making a deadly comeback.

Environmental history is one of the fastest-growing fields of study. Like disease, the environment knows no boundaries and therefore is an ideal topic for world historians. There have always been some voices expressing concern for the environment. In the eighteenth century, for example, governments became increasingly concerned about their forests as the great demand for lumber to build ships nearly destroyed the forests of Britain, Europe, the eastern United States, and later India. The United States created the first national park in the nineteenth century. "Wilderness areas" were viewed as refuges from industrialization and urbanization. The Sierra Club, today one of America's most famous environmental organizations, was founded in 1892. The modern environmental movement began with concerns about chemical waste, rapid consumption of energy and food supplies, massive global deforestation, environmental degradation caused in part by sprawling megacities, and threats to wildlife. By the 1970s citizens had begun joining together in organizations such as Greenpeace and Friends of the Earth to try to preserve, restore, or enhance the natural environment.

At the beginning of the new millennium, the environmental movement is actually several different movements, each with its own agenda. Rachel Carson might be seen as an early proponent of the environmental health movement. She and others were concerned about the effects of chemicals, radiation, pollution, waste, and urban development on the environment and on human health. The conservation movement, represented by the Sierra Club and the Audubon Society, seeks to protect the biodiversity of the planet and emphasizes the spiritual and aesthetic qualities of nature. The ecology movement consists of different groups with somewhat similar agendas, ranging from the politically active Green parties to Greenpeace. These organizations are concerned about global warming, toxic chemicals, the use of nuclear energy and nuclear weapons, genetically modified food, recycling, saving whales and other endangered species, sustainable agriculture, and protecting ancient forests.

A movement that began in the 1980s in the United States is the campaign for environmental justice, which seeks to end what its supporters consider to be environmental racism, classism, and sexism. The Love Canal tragedy in Niagara Falls, New York, highlighted environmental justice concerns. In 1978, residents of the Love Canal neighborhood learned that their houses and local school had been built on top of an industrial chemical dumpsite that Hooker Chemical Company had covered with earth in 1953 and sold to the city for a dollar. As buried waste disposal drums corroded, benzene and other toxic chemicals seeped through the ground and into homes. The negative effects on the environment and on the residents led to the abandonment of the community. Another example of environmental injustice occurred on December 3, 1984, when poison gas leaked without warning from a Union Carbide factory in Bhopal, India, while people were sleeping. The plant's safety systems were not working, so no warning sounded, and thousands soon died horrible deaths from breathing in the gas. Years after this tragedy, toxic chemicals abandoned at the plant continued to poison local drinking water. In 2004 the Indian Supreme Court ordered a cleanup. In 1986 the worst nuclear accident occurred: the explosion of a nuclear power plant at Chernobyl, in Ukraine. Estimated deaths from the accident range from hundreds to hundreds of thousands, and over two hundred thousand people had to be evacuated. Nuclear fallout landed in several European countries, and scientists are still studying the ongoing effects of the event.

At the beginning of the twenty-first century environmentalists are especially concerned about **global warming,** the increase of global temperatures over time. The 1990s was the warmest decade in recorded history. The majority of the world's scientists believe the increase began with the Industrial Revolution in the 1700s. The subsequent human-generated hydrocarbons produced through the burning of fossil fuels—coal, oil, natural gas—have caused a greenhouse effect.

Possible effects of global warming over the next century include a catastrophic rise in sea levels that would put many coastal cities and islands under water; ecosystem changes that may threaten various species of plants and animals; extreme and abnormal weather patterns; destruction of the earth's ozone layer, which shields the planet from harmful solar radiation; and a decline in agriculture

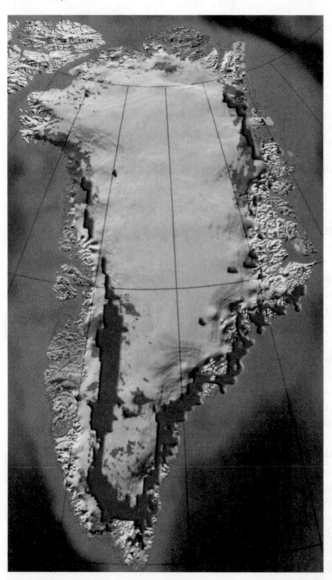

● **Evidence of Global Warming in Greenland** This graphic indicates the seasonal melt extent, in red, of the Greenland ice sheet in 2002. Of greatest immediate concern to scientists is that melting polar icecaps and Greenland glaciers are releasing cold, fresh water into the northern Atlantic Ocean, which could shut down the Gulf Stream that warms Europe and northeastern North America by bringing warm ocean currents up from the equator. This could produce an ice age in the northern Atlantic that would drastically affect global weather patterns. *(AP Photo/Wide World Photos)*

production. Although the exact causes and consequences of global warming are being debated, the world community is so concerned that in 1997 an amendment, the Kyoto Protocol, was added to the United Nations Framework Convention on Climate Change. Countries that ratify the protocol agree to try to reduce their emissions of carbon dioxide and five other greenhouse gases. Each country is assigned a certain limit of emission for each of these six gases, but countries may also trade emission amounts with one another if they want to maintain or increase gas emission for a particular gas. As of early 2008, 174 countries had ratified the protocol, including Russia in November 2004 and Australia in December 2007. The most notable exception was the United States.

global warming *The belief of the majority of the world's scientists that hydrocarbons produced through the burning of fossil fuels have caused a greenhouse effect that has increased global temperatures over time.*

Mass Communication

Between 1875 and 1900 the world witnessed the invention of the phonograph, the first moving pictures, the Kodak camera, the first dial telephone, the radio, magnetic recordings, and loudspeakers. These revolutionary new technologies prepared the way for a twentieth century of mass communications and the "information age." The radio and moving pictures dominated entertainment for the first half of the century and also served as propaganda tools for the era's dictators.

The global availability and affordability of transistorized radios and television sets in the 1950s introduced a second communications revolution. The transistor radio penetrated the most isolated hamlets of the developing world. Governments universally embraced radio broadcasting as a means of power, propaganda, and education. Relentlessly, the transistor radio propagated the outlooks and attitudes of urban elites and challenged old values.

Though less common, television use expanded into nearly every country, even if there was just one television in a village. Governments recognized the power of the visual image to promote their ideology or leader, and a state television network became a source of national pride. By the beginning of the twenty-first century, television was bringing the whole planet into the bars and meetinghouses of the world's villages and was having a profound, even revolutionary, impact everywhere. At the very least, alluring television images of high living standards and the excitement of urban life stirred powerful desires in young people, who copied Western materialism, migrated to the cities, and created a global youth culture.

The third, and perhaps greatest, communications revolution occurred with the first Apple personal computers in 1976. Mass communications have exploded since then. Some new technologies are obsolete by the time they reach the market. The computer and the cell phone have effected the greatest change in people's lives.

The first cell phones, in 1985, freed users from land lines and allowed individuals and nations in the developing world to bypass most of the stages of twentieth-century telephone development. Telephone lines, installation, and numerous other traditional obstacles to telephone use can be avoided with cell phones. Africa now has over 85 million cell phone users; equivalent land-line phone use would be impossible. Cell phone use has to overcome no barriers of gender, age, income, education, or even access to electricity. Cell phones have become one of the most widely owned consumer products worldwide.

Computers have revolutionized so many areas of human endeavor that it is impossible to enumerate them all. The Internet, or World Wide Web, has had the greatest impact on human communication. First made available in 1994 to the general public, the Internet and e-mail provide all human beings with the possibility of instantaneous communication with each other. They create a global coffeehouse where anything and everything may be discussed and debated. The possibilities for global access to information and knowledge are seemingly infinite. In the tradition of authoritarian regimes throughout history, dictators have quickly realized the threat the Internet poses to their power and control. The governments of China and North Korea have

● **Educational TV in South Africa** A South African TV crew films *Soul Buddyz,* a popular show for children that grapples honestly with everything from sexuality and AIDS to child abuse and physical disabilities. This show was inspired by *Soul City,* an award-winning soap opera for teenagers and young adults that includes practical information on safe sex and HIV infection. *(Louise Gubb/Corbis Saba)*

spent millions of dollars trying to restrict information traveling in and out of their countries over the Internet. For the first time in history, this type of censorship may prove impossible.

SOCIAL REFORM AND PROGRESS

What social problems are the focus of reformers in the new millennium?

Just as an end to slavery became the rallying cry for social reformers in the nineteenth century, modern social reformers have sought to end global inequality, racism, and sexism, and to improve human and civil rights for all. We have already described many of these developments, such as the victory of the democratic movement in eastern Europe and the end of the racist apartheid system in South Africa. Much remains to be achieved, however, and nowhere is more worldwide attention being focused than on the advancement of human and civil rights for women and children. Although significant progress has been made since 1945, women and children continue to enjoy fewer rights than men worldwide in nearly every category that might be measured.

Women: The Right to Equality

In September 1995 delegates from around the world met in Beijing, China, for the United Nations Fourth World Conference on Women. The meeting's final report called on the world community to take strategic action in twelve areas of critical concern to women: poverty, access to education and training, access to health care, violence against women, women and war, economic inequality with men, political inequality with men, creation of institutions for women's advancement, lack of

Individuals IN SOCIETY

The Dalai Lama

Shortly before he died in 1933, Thupten Gyatso (1876–1933), the "Great Thirteenth" Dalai Lama of Tibet, had a vision of the future. He predicted that if the Tibetans did not protect their territory, their spiritual leaders would be exterminated, their property and authority would be taken away, their political system would vanish, and their people would become slaves. For fifty-seven years he had ruled over a country treated like a pawn in the "Great Game" played by Russia, Britain, and China for territory and power. He feared the Chinese the most.

After his death, a mission of high officials went in search of his successor. Tibetans believe that each succeeding Dalai Lama is the reincarnation of the previous one. In 1937 the mission came to a peasant village in northeastern Tibet to question a two-year-old boy, Tenzin Gyatso. When he passed all their tests, they took him and his family to Lhasa, the Tibetan capital. There, in 1940, he was enthroned as His Holiness the Fourteenth Dalai Lama.

In Lhasa the boy spent much of his time studying, eventually earning a doctorate in Buddhist philosophy at age twenty-five. His youth ended abruptly in October 1950 when the thirteenth Dalai Lama's vision came true: eighty thousand Chinese soldiers invaded Tibet. In November the fifteen-year-old Dalai Lama assumed full political power. In 1954 he traveled to Beijing to meet for peace talks with Mao Zedong. Although he was impressed by Mao's promise to modernize Tibet and intrigued by socialism, he was stunned by Mao's last words to him: "But of course, religion is poison."*

This remark was deeply troubling because the Tibetans are an intensely religious people. For centuries they lived in near isolation, practiced Buddhism, and looked to the Dalai Lama as both their political and their spiritual leader. After returning to Tibet, the Dalai Lama tried to negotiate a peaceful settlement with the Chinese, to no avail. In March 1959 the Chinese army crushed a massive demonstration in Lhasa, and the Dalai Lama had to flee for his life. The Indian prime minister, Jawaharlal Nehru, gave him political asylum, and he established a Tibetan government-in-exile at Dharamsala, India. More than 120,000 Tibetan refugees live there today.

Since the Chinese occupation began, all but twelve of more than six thousand monasteries in Tibet have been destroyed, and thousands of sacred treasures have been stolen or sold. An estimated three thousand political or religious prisoners are in labor camps in Tibet, and the Chinese have been directly responsible for the deaths of 1.2 million Tibetans. Over 7 million Chinese settlers have poured into Tibet. Tibetan women are routinely forced to undergo sterilization or have abortions.

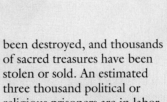

His Holiness the Dalai Lama in Germany promoting freedom for Tibet. *(AP Photo/ Wide World Photos)*

To counter this destruction, His Holiness the Dalai Lama has campaigned for Tibetan self-determination and basic human rights. He has established programs abroad to save the Tibetan culture and language and to shelter the refugees. There is a Tibetan educational system for refugee children, a Tibetan Institute of Performing Arts, and a university for Tibetan Studies. There are also agricultural settlements for refugees and over two hundred new monasteries to preserve Tibetan Buddhism and to train new monks. In his quest for justice, the Dalai Lama travels around the world seeking support from world leaders, institutions, and common citizens. Although he describes himself as a simple Buddhist monk, few individuals in human history have spoken for the downtrodden and oppressed and for universal justice and human dignity with such moral authority.

In December 1989 the Dalai Lama received the Nobel Peace Prize. In accepting, he said that he did so on behalf of all oppressed peoples—those who struggle for freedom and work for world peace—as well as for the people of Tibet. The prize, he said, "reaffirms our conviction that with truth, courage and determination as our weapons, Tibet will be liberated. Our struggle must remain nonviolent and free of hatred."†

Questions for Analysis

1. In what ways do Tibet's history and the Dalai Lama's life reflect many of the major issues and events of the twentieth century?

2. The world's response to China's occupation reflects what political and economic factors?

Source: Freedom in Exile: The Autobiography of the Dalai Lama (London: Little, Brown), 1990.

†http://nobelprize.org/peace/laureates/1989/lama-acceptance.html.

*Tenzin Gyatso, the Dalai Lama, *My Land and My People* (New York: McGraw-Hill, 1962), p. 117.

● **Kuwait's First Female Minister** Maasuma al-Mubarak, a leading women's rights activist and professor of international relations at Kuwait University, gives a thumbs-up during a session of the Kuwaiti parliament in June 2005. Al-Mubarak was the first woman in Kuwaiti history to be appointed as a cabinet minister in the government. She served as Health Minister until August 2007, when she resigned following a fire at a Kuwaiti hospital that killed two people. *(Yasser Al-Zayvat/AFP/Getty Images)*

feminization of poverty *The issue that those living in extreme poverty are disproportionately women.*

respect for women's rights, stereotyping of women, gender inequalities and the environment, and violation of girl children's rights.[13]

These are concerns that all women share, although degrees of inequality vary greatly from one country to another. Concerns over political inequality in the United States, for example, might focus on electing a woman president or electing as many women as men to the U.S. Senate. In countries where women are not allowed to vote, let alone hold political office, the concerns would be different. The type and extent of inequality varies greatly, and global progress in lessening it has been uneven. Generally the greatest advances have been in the leading industrialized nations, and there is some correlation between women's equality and economic prosperity.

The **feminization of poverty,** women living disproportionately in extreme poverty, is one of the greatest concerns among women activists in the new millennium. Unlike many other issues, it is as great a problem in the developed world as elsewhere. Even in the most developed countries, two out of every three poor adults are women. In the United States half of all poor families are supported by single mothers, who earn an average income 23 percent below the poverty line. There are many causes for this phenomenon. Having principal responsibility for child care, women have less time and opportunity for work, and because they have less access to health care they are often unable to work. As male labor migration worldwide increases, the number of households headed by women increases and thus the number of families living in poverty. Job restrictions and discrimination, plus limited education, result in women having few job options except in the "informal economy" as maids, street vendors, or prostitutes. These are generally the lowest-paid jobs; they require long hours to earn even a small amount of money; and they frequently involve violent and abusive treatment.

It is true that the declining global birthrate means that more women and couples are gaining control over their fertility through access to birth control. Women also benefit through improved overall health, longer life, and healthier children when they have fewer pregnancies. Even within developed countries, however, birthrates remain high among poor women, especially among poor adolescents, who make up an inordinate number of the estimated 585,000 women who die every year during pregnancy and childbirth. And it is the poorest women who usually suffer most from government policies, usually legislated by men, that restrict their access to reproductive health care.

Women have made some modest gains in the workplace, making up 38 percent of the nonfarm-sector global workforce in the early 2000s, as compared to 35 percent in 1990. But segregated labor markets remain the rule, with higher-paying jobs reserved for men. Gender equality in the workforce is critical if women are to become financially independent, have some financial security as they age, and contribute to the overall improvement of a country's economy. In the farm sector, women globally produce more than half of all the food that is grown, and up to 80 percent of subsistence crops grown in Africa. Because this is informal labor, and often unpaid, these women laborers are denied access to loans, and many of them cannot own the land they farm.

Some observers believe that violence against women is becoming worse rather than better. Although rape has always been a part of war, during the wars in the former Yugoslavia and in Rwanda in the early 1990s, rape and sexual violence became weapons of war. Both have been subsequently labeled crimes against humanity and are considered forms of torture and genocide. Still, rape and sexual violence have continued to be used as weapons of war in conflicts in Sierra Leone, Kosovo, Afghanistan, the Democratic Republic of the Congo, East Timor, and elsewhere. Domestic violence appears to be on the increase in many countries, including Russia, Pakistan, Peru, Uzbekistan, and South Africa. Forced prostitution and international female slave traffic is carried on by traffickers from such countries as Ukraine, Moldova, Nigeria, Burma, and Thailand. Perhaps five thousand women a year are killed in "honor killings," which occur when men kill their female relatives for bringing dishonor on the family's reputation, frequently because of some perceived misuse of their sexuality.

Some progress has been made toward equality for women. Just the fact that UN member nations have signed various human rights accords pertaining to women is a positive development. (See the feature "Listening to the Past: The United Nations Millennium Project Report" on pages 1068–1069.) New laws have been enacted, and more girls than ever before worldwide are receiving an education. More women are now allowed to vote and to hold office, and half of all the female heads of state elected since 1900 were elected after 1990. Women also are moving across and up in the workplace—holding a wider variety of jobs and more senior positions.

Children: The Right to Childhood

In 1989 the United Nations General Assembly adopted the Convention on the Rights of the Child, which spelled out a number of rights that member nations believed are due every child. These include civil and human rights and economic, social, and cultural rights. The convention has been ratified by more countries than any other human rights treaty in world history—192 countries as of 2005. The United States and Somalia are the only two countries that have not ratified it.

It is not difficult to see why such a document was necessary. Globally, a billion children live in poverty—one in every two children in the world. In the United States, 16 percent of children, more than 11 million girls and boys, live in poor families with parents who earn at or below the poverty line. Worldwide, 640 million children do not have adequate shelter, 400 million do not have safe water, and 270 million receive no health care. From 10 million to 11 million children die each year before age five.

Besides poverty, the convention addresses a number of other concerns. These include children making up half of the world's refugees, child labor and exploitation, sexual violence and sex trafficking, police abuse of street children, HIV/AIDS orphans, lack of access to education, and lack of access to adequate health care. Increasingly in the last decade, children have been recruited or kidnapped to become child soldiers, as many as 300,000 worldwide, 120,000 in Africa alone. Child sexual abuse and child soldiers have become such widespread problems that the United Nations wrote two additional protocols—one on the involvement of children in armed conflicts and the other on the sale of children, child pornography, and child prostitution—that were attached to the original convention and adopted in 2000.

● **Child Soldier in Sierra Leone** This eleven-year-old boy, with a rifle slung over his shoulder, is a member of the Sierra Leone army and stands guard at a checkpoint during his country's civil war. Tens of thousands of boys and girls under eighteen have been used by the militaries in more than sixty countries since 2000, either as armed combatants or informally in tasks such as spying, scouting, carrying messages, and cooking. *(AP Photo/Wide World Photos)*

Education

As the twenty-first century began, nearly a billion people were unable to read a book or sign their names. Of these, more than two-thirds were women. Of the 100 million children without access to primary education, 60 percent or more were girls. If less than 1 percent of the money allocated worldwide to military weapons every year were spent on education, every child in the world would be able to go to school.

There is a direct correlation between national rates of literacy and economic prosperity. Most of the global literacy problems are found in the developing world. The democracy movement of the early 1990s and increasing economic globalization have put pressure on all governments to improve literacy rates and to improve educational opportunities for young people. Since the 1990s more and more countries have recognized the importance of providing a minimum level of basic education and have made it compulsory. Globally, four in five children now participate in lower secondary education (U.S. ninth and tenth grades), but discrepancies remain wide. Many countries have 90 to 100 percent participation in at least lower secondary education, but in Africa the rate is closer to 45 percent and only 29 percent for upper secondary (U.S. eleventh and twelfth grades). Only when countries are stable and have prosperous economies will all children receive the education they deserve.

The most revolutionary advances in education in the developing world will come through access to the Internet. Despite the initial costs—significant for many countries—the benefits obtained from having even one computer connected to the Internet in each school are incalculable. Instantaneously, children get access to all the world's libraries, art galleries, museums, educational sites, and knowledge bases. Internet access does not make the playing field between rich and poor students exactly level, but it comes closer to doing so than any other development in history.

Chapter Summary

To assess your mastery of this chapter, go to
bedfordstmartins.com/mckayworld

Key Terms

United Nations
Security Council
General Assembly
middle powers
separatism
terrorism
al-Qaeda
multinational corporations
industrialization strategy
modernization
mixed economy
Green Revolution
Law of the Sea
megacities
urban explosion
urbanization without
  industrialization
shantytowns
self-help housing
economic growth without
  economic development
bazaar economy
medical revolution
neo-Malthusian
HIV/AIDS
global warming
feminization of poverty

• *What is the global political situation in the early twenty-first century, and how do competing nation-states address common problems?*

After forty years of superpower confrontation, the cold war's end brought renewed hope for global peace and prosperity. If we have learned anything since 1991, however, it is that neither peace nor prosperity come easily for the human race. New rifts and old animosities have set us at odds in ways that are just as dangerous and lethal as the cold war differences they replaced. Nation-states remained the primary building blocks of political organization as the world entered the twenty-first century. But increasing interdependency and globalization were forcing nations and peoples to come together, negotiate, and make joint global decisions more frequently than at any time in human history.

• *How are the United Nations and multinational corporations representative of increasing globalization?*

Increased globalization has created the need for public and private international organizations, such as the United Nations, to provide a forum and a vehicle for nation-states to come together to solve global problems. These organizations exert a steady pressure for international cooperation when dealing with global issues. Multinational corporations, however, have become perhaps the most important symbol of globalization. With capitalism's revival after World War II, relatively free international economic relations, and the need globally for swift industrialization, multinational corporations rapidly emerged in the early 1950s. They used advanced marketing and sales techniques to push their products around the world; they put huge sums of money into research and development; and they operated across political boundaries to create a single global marketplace.

• *What factors spurred the growth of cities in Africa, Asia, and Latin America, and what were some of the main consequences of urbanization in the late twentieth century?*

The phenomenal growth of cities over the past fifty years has had a tremendous impact on individuals, families, and communities. Megacities, in particular, have evolved at an astonishing pace. The reasons for this urban explosion include a tremendous spurt in population growth and people's desire to find jobs, particularly manufacturing jobs that were concentrated in the cities. People also left the countryside because they were pushed off their land or, if they were young, also for the excitement of the city.

The consequences of this rapid urbanization are similar to those associated with early-twentieth-century urbanization in Europe and North America, but on a larger scale. Overcrowding and shantytowns have been some of the most visible problems. Urban social services have been overwhelmed, and cities have been unable to provide the necessary police and fire protection and adequate sanitation, running water, and electricity services.

• *What key technological and scientific developments have had the greatest impact on life at the beginning of the new millennium?*

Science and technology also significantly changed global society in the twentieth century. A medical revolution has discovered vaccines to treat some of history's most deadly diseases; artificial hearts and organ transplants have become routine. The successful mapping of human DNA offers unimaginable possibilities for the prevention, treatment, and cure of diseases. As we learn more about the environment, global warming has drawn more attention from government leaders and private citizens. Mass communication is another area where advances have been revolutionary. Many people around the world now carry hand-held computers, phones, and other devices that make information exchange almost instantaneous.

• *What social problems are the focus of reformers in the new millennium?*

Social reformers continue to identify problems and inequalities in human society that need to be addressed. During the past hundred years these reformers have had some success in bringing an end to racial injustice in terms of political freedom, human and civil rights, and social and political equality. At the end of the twentieth century and the beginning of the twenty-first, social reformers have turned their attention to the advancement of human and civil rights for women and children.

The study of world history will put these and future events in perspective. Future developments on this small planet will surely build on the many-layered foundations hammered out in the past. Moreover, the study of world history, of mighty struggles and fearsome challenges, of shining achievements and tragic failures, imparts a strong sense of life's essence: the process of change over time. Again and again we have seen how peoples and societies evolve, influenced by ideas, human passions, and material conditions. Armed with the ability to think historically, students of history are prepared to comprehend this inexorable process of change in their own lifetimes, as the world races forward toward an uncertain destiny.

Suggested Reading

Allison, Graham. *Nuclear Terrorism: The Ultimate Preventable Catastrophe.* 2004. An assessment of the global nuclear threat.

Bales, Kevin. *Disposable People: New Slavery in the Global Economy.* 2004. Analysis of the economic exploitation of the world's poor.

Caircross, Frances. *The Death of Distance: How the Communications Revolution Is Changing Our Lives.* 2001. Discusses the global consequences of cell phones, satellites, and the Internet.

Chandler, Alfred D., and Bruce Mazlish. *Leviathans: Multinational Corporations and the New Global History.* 2005. A stimulating global perspective on multinational corporations and how they affect everyone's lives.

Das, Gurcharan. *India Unbound: The Social and Economic Revolution from Independence to the Global Information Age.* 2002. India's leap into the age of modern technology and computers and the consequences for its population and the world.

Drexler, Maeline. *Secret Agents: The Menace of Emerging Infections.* 2003. Provides an overview of the global threat from infectious diseases, old and new.

Fishman, Ted C. *China, Inc.: How the Rise of the Next Superpower Challenges America and the World.* 2006. Explains the profound consequences of China's becoming the next economic superpower.

Foer, Franklin. *How Soccer Explains the World: An Unlikely Theory of Globalization.* 2005. A unique but fascinating interpretation of globalization.

Friedman, Thomas L. *The Lexus and the Olive Tree: Understanding Globalization.* 2000. An interesting look at globalization and multinationals.

Gareis, Sven Bernhard, and Johannes Varwick. *The United Nations: An Introduction.* 2005. An up-to-date introduction to the United Nations.

Gore, Al. *An Inconvenient Truth: The Planetary Emergency of Global Warming and What We Can Do About It.* 2006. Reasoned discussion of the greatest threat to the planet in the twenty-first century, for which Gore won the Nobel Peace Prize.

Hobsbawm, Eric J. *On the Edge of the New Century: In Conversation with Antonio Polito.* 2000. An extraordinarily prescient commentary on the recent past and the near future by one of the premier historians of our time.

Johnson-Odim, Cheryl, and Margaret Strobel, eds. *Expanding the Boundaries of Women's History: Essays on Women in the Third World.* 1992. Groundbreaking essays on women's history outside of Europe and North America.

Jones, Geoffrey. *Multinationals and Global Capitalism: From the Nineteenth to the Twenty-first Century.* 2005. A historical overview of the development of multinational corporations and a global capitalist economy.

Kasarda, John, and Allan Parnell, eds. *Third World Cities: Problems, Policies and Prospects.* 1993. Discusses the prodigious growth of Third World cities in the second half of the twentieth century.

Kenney, Padraic, and Max Paul Friedman, eds. *Partisan Histories: The Past in Contemporary Global Politics.*

2005. An intriguing analysis of how nations are revising their histories to shape modern identities.

Klare, Michael T. *Resource Wars: The New Landscape of Global Conflict.* 2002. Analyzes the conflict over vital resources and the impact on national military and economic policies.

Moaddel, Mansoor. *Islamic Modernism, Nationalism, and Fundamentalism.* 2005. A scholarly historical introduction to society and politics in the Middle East.

O'Neill, Bard. E. *Insurgency and Terrorism: From Revolution to Apocalypse,* 2d ed. rev. 2005. An excellent introduction to the nature of modern war.

O'Neill, John Terence, and Nicholas Rees. *United Nations Peacekeeping in the Post–Cold War Era.* 2005. Discusses the problems associated with United Nations peacekeeping efforts.

Price, Monroe E. *Media and Sovereignty: The Global Information Revolution and Its Challenge to State Power.* 2004. Considers the challenges and threats posed by media and the communications revolution to the sovereignty of nation-states.

Notes

1. A. Toynbee, *Mankind and Mother Earth* (New York: Oxford University Press, 1976), pp. 576–577.
2. B. Barber, *Jihad vs. McWorld* (New York: Times Books, 1995), p. 9.
3. D. Rappaport, "The Fourth Wave: September 11 in the History of Terrorism," *Current History,* December 2001, pp. 419–424.
4. Ibid.
5. Quoted in J. Fallows, "Success Without Victory," in *The Atlantic Monthly* 295 (January/February 2005): 80.
6. Quoted in L. R. Brown, *Seeds of Change: The Green Revolution and Development in the 1970s* (New York: Praeger, 1970), p. 16.
7. P. Ehrlich, *The Population Bomb* (New York: Ballantine, 1968), p. 11.
8. M. ul Haq, *The Poverty Curtain: Choices for the Third World* (New York: Columbia University Press, 1976), p. 152.
9. J. Diamond, *Collapse: How Societies Choose to Fail or Survive* (New York: Viking, 2004), pp. 524–525.
10. P. Bairoch, *Economics and World History: Myths and Paradoxes* (Chicago: University of Chicago Press, 1993), p. 95.
11. P. Huston, *Third World Women Speak Out: Interviews in Six Countries on Change, Development, and Basic Needs* (New York: Praeger, 1979), p. 11.
12. R. Carson, *Silent Spring* (1962; repr., New York: Houghton Mifflin, 1994), pp. 1–3, 7–8.
13. United Nations, "Critical Areas of Concern," *Report of the Fourth World Conference on Women* (New York: United Nations Department for Policy Coordination and Sustainable Development, 1995), ch. 1, annex II, ch. 3, pp. 41–44; available at http://www.un.org/esa/gopher-data/conf/fwcw/off/a—20.en. See also Population Reference Bureau, *Women of Our World 2005* (Washington, D.C.: Population Reference Bureau, 2005), for the latest data and ten-year follow-up to the Beijing meeting.

Listening to the PAST

The United Nations Millennium Project Report

In September 2000, the United Nations issued a "Millennium Declaration"—a bold statement of values and an agenda of actions to be undertaken by the United Nations and its member nations to reach eight major goals relating to global poverty and hunger, disease, education, the environment, maternal health, child mortality, gender equality, and global partnerships by 2015. In the following speech delivered the previous April, Secretary-General Kofi Annan set out the broad framework for this plan of action, which became the United Nations Millennium Project. In January 2005, the United Nations issued a five-year report that summarized the results to date and offered strategies for meeting the goals by 2015.

If one word encapsulates the changes we are living through, it is "globalisation." We live in a world that is interconnected as never before. . . . This has its dangers, of course. Crime, narcotics, terrorism, disease, weapons—all these move back and forth faster, and in greater numbers, than in the past. . . .

But the *benefits* of globalisation are obvious too: faster growth, higher living standards, and new opportunities—not only for individuals but also for better understanding between nations, and for common action.

One problem is that, at present, these opportunities are far from equally distributed. . . . A second problem is that, even where the global market does reach, it is not yet underpinned, as national markets are, by rules based on shared social objectives. . . .

So, . . . the overarching challenge of our times is to make globalisation mean more than bigger markets. To make a success of this great upheaval we must learn how to govern better, and—above all—how to govern better together.

We need to make our States stronger and more effective at the national level. And we need to get them working together on global issues—all pulling their weight and all having their say.

What are these global issues? I have grouped them under three headings, each of which I relate to a fundamental human freedom—freedom from want, freedom from fear, and the freedom of future generations to sustain their lives on this planet.

First, *freedom from want*. How can we call human beings free and equal in dignity when over a billion of them are struggling to survive on less than one dollar a day, without safe drinking water, and when half of all humanity lacks adequate sanitation? Some of us are worrying about whether the stock market will crash, or struggling to master our latest computer, while more than half our fellow men and women have much more basic worries, such as where their children's next meal is coming from. . . .

Many of these problems are worst in sub-Saharan Africa, where extreme poverty affects a higher proportion of the population than anywhere else, and is compounded by a higher incidence of conflict, HIV/ AIDS, and other ills. I am asking the world community to make special provision for Africa's needs, and give full support to Africans in their struggle to overcome these problems. . . .

Within the next fifteen years, I believe we can halve the population of people living in extreme poverty; ensure that all children—girls and boys alike, particularly the girls—receive a full primary education; and halt the spread of HIV/AIDS. In twenty years, we can also transform the lives of one hundred million slum dwellers around the world. And I believe we should be able to offer all young people between 15 and 24 the chance of decent work. . . .

The second main heading in the Report is *freedom from fear*. Wars between States are mercifully less frequent than they used to be. But in the last decade *internal* wars have claimed more than five million lives, and driven many times that number of people from their homes. Moreover, we still live under the shadow of weapons of mass destruction.

Both these threats, I believe, require us to think of security less in terms of merely defending territory, and more in terms of protecting *people*. That means we must tackle the threat of deadly conflict at every stage in the process. . . .

A child is immunized against disease in a remote village in Thailand, advancing one of the United Nations Millennium Project's goals. *(Peter Charlesworth/OnAsia Images)*

[T]he best way to prevent conflict is to promote political arrangements in which all groups are fairly represented, combined with human rights, minority rights, and broad-based economic development. Also, illicit transfers of weapons, money or natural resources must be forced into the limelight, so we can control them better.

We must protect vulnerable people by finding better ways to enforce humanitarian and human rights law, and to ensure that gross violations do not go unpunished. National sovereignty offers vital protection to small and weak States, but it should not be a shield for crimes against humanity. In extreme cases the clash of these two principles confronts us with a real dilemma, and the Security Council may have a moral duty to act on behalf of the international community. . . .

Finally, we must pursue our disarmament agenda more vigorously. Since 1995 it has lost momentum in an alarming way. That means controlling the traffic in small arms much more tightly, but also returning to the vexed issue of nuclear weapons. . . .

The third fundamental freedom my Report addresses is one that is not clearly identified in the Charter, because in 1945 our founders could scarcely imagine that it would ever be threatened. I mean the freedom of future generations to sustain their lives on this planet. . . .

If I could sum it up in one sentence, I should say we are plundering our children's heritage to pay for our present unsustainable practices.

This must stop. We must reduce emissions of carbon and other "greenhouse gases," to put a stop to global warming. Implementing the Kyoto Protocol is a vital first step. . . .

We must face the implications of a steadily shrinking surface of cultivable land, at a time when every year brings many millions of new mouths to feed. Biotechnology may offer the best hope, but only if we can resolve the controversies and allay the fears surrounding it. . . .

We must preserve our forests, fisheries, and the diversity of living species, all of which are close to collapsing under the pressure of human consumption and destruction. In short, we need a new ethic of stewardship. We need a much better informed public, and we need to take environmental costs and benefits fully into account in our economic policy decisions. We need regulations and incentives to discourage pollution and overconsumption of nonrenewable resources,

and to encourage environment-friendly practices. And we need more accurate scientific data. . . .

But, you may be asking by now, what about the United Nations? . . .

[My] Report contains a further section on renewing the United Nations. . . . But let us not forget *why* the United Nations matters. It matters only to the extent that it can make a useful contribution to solving the problems and accomplishing the tasks I have just outlined.

Those are the problems and the tasks which affect the everyday lives of our peoples. It is on how we handle *them* that the utility of the United Nations will be judged. If we lose sight of that point, the United Nations will have little or no role to play in the twenty-first century.

Let us never forget . . . that our Organisation was founded in the name of "We, the Peoples." . . . We are at the service of the world's peoples, and we must listen to them. They are telling us that our past achievements are not enough. They are telling us we must do more, and do it better.

Source: Millennium Report, presented to the United Nations by Secretary-General Kofi Annan, April 3, 2000. Copyright © 2000 by the United Nations. Reproduced by permission.

THE MIDDLE EAST IN TODAY'S WORLD

Roger B. Beck

The focus of this update essay is a broad examination of the various crises in the Middle East and their global consequences.

ISRAEL, LEBANON, AND THE ISRAEL-HEZBOLLAH WAR

Following the collapse of the Ottoman Empire after World War I, the French designated Lebanon as one of several ethnic enclaves within a larger area that became part of the French mandate of Syria. Maronite Catholic Christians made up the majority of Lebanon's population, but there were also significant numbers of Muslims and Druzes. In 1926 Lebanon became a separate republic but remained under the control of the French mandate. During World War II, the French Vichy government allowed Germany to transport war materials and aircraft through Syria to Iraq to use against the British. The British then invaded Syria and Lebanon, and the Allies regained control, turning the area over to Charles de Gaulle and the Free French government in exile. In 1943 the Free French granted Lebanon independence.

In the ensuing decades, Lebanon has vacillated between periods of peace and prosperity and periods with wars of catastrophic destruction and death. Initially, despite its involvement in the 1948 Arab-Israeli War and a civil conflict in 1958, Lebanon prospered. In the 1950s, 1960s, and early 1970s, it was a favorite tourist destination; Beirut was referred to as the "Paris of the Middle East." The country became a regional center of banking and trade, and the economy thrived. A model primary, secondary, and university education system produced a population with one of the highest literacy rates in the Arab world.

In spring 1975, however, long-simmering dissatisfaction and anger over the dispersal of political power erupted into violence, setting off an utterly devastating fifteen-year civil war. A brief review of the civil war sheds light on events fifteen years after its end.

When Lebanon became an independent nation in 1943, the unwritten National Pact included agreement that the Lebanese president would be a Christian and the prime minister a Muslim. This arrangement was based on a 1932 census (still the last one taken in Lebanon) that showed a Christian majority. By the late 1960s, however, the Lebanese Muslim population had grown significantly, and Muslims were no longer content with a Christian-controlled government and military. The situation was exacerbated by the arrival after 1970 of thousands of Palestinian refugees into southern Lebanon following their expulsion by Jordan's King Hussein in an event known in the Arab world as Black September. Tensions came to a head in early 1975, starting with armed scrimmages between Christian and Muslim factions that resulted in the slaughter of many innocent civilians, and the escalating violence and reprisals led to all-out civil war.

In the course of the war the Lebanese army, whose soldiers represented all the various political and religious factions in the country, disintegrated as soldiers switched their allegiance from the national government to various sectarian militias. Eventually, besides the Lebanese army, there were five main militias. Four of them, the Christians, Sunnis, Shi'ites, and Druzes, were based on religious identity. In the early 1980s a hard-line faction broke away from the main Shi'ite militia to form a separate group known as Hezbollah, or Party of God, which had as one of its stated objectives the complete destruction of the state of Israel. A fifth group, the Palestinians, fought for a nationalist cause. In addition to these five militias, a number of loosely organized nonreligious groups fought for various causes, such as communism or a Greater Syria. The final major players in the civil war were Syria and Israel. Syria, which entered the war in 1976, eventually had over forty thousand soldiers stationed in the east and north of the country. The Arab League legitimized Syria's presence by giving Syria a mandate to provide the bulk of an Arab Deterrent Force charged with restoring peace. Concern over the Palestine Liberation Organization's control of southern Lebanon, and cross-border attacks that led to some Israeli civilian and military deaths, provoked Israel's first invasion of Lebanon in 1978. Although Israel withdrew later that year, the threat remained. In 1982 Israel invaded Lebanon again under the direction of the defense minister, Ariel Sharon. Israeli forces pushed deep into southern Lebanon to the outskirts of Beirut, intending to completely destroy the PLO and to establish southern Lebanon as a buffer zone to prevent future attacks against northern Israel.

The Lebanese civil war was brutal, massively destructive, and characterized by an utter disregard for human rights and human decency. War crimes and terrorist acts were committed by all sides. Car bombs became a particularly favorite weapon, and their perceived effectiveness has encouraged their continued use in terrorist acts to the present day. Extortion and mistreatment of civilians were common as militias set up Mafia-like control over their territories and supported their causes financially through smuggling—particularly of drugs as Lebanon became a major hashish producer—theft, ransom payments, and forcing travelers to pay "customs" as they passed through checkpoints. Altogether an estimated one hundred thousand people were killed and a like number injured. Close to a million people were forced out of their homes, and an estimated two hundred fifty thousand Lebanese left the country permanently. Tens of thousands of Lebanese, victims of kidnapping and wartime violence, are still missing. Lebanon's entire infrastructure was destroyed, and Beirut in 1990 looked like the bombed-out cities of Europe after World War II.

The beginning of the end to the civil war came with the Taif Agreement of 1989. The agreement provided for political reform, specifically a more balanced sharing of power between Lebanon's Maronite Christian and Muslim communities, provisions for a special cooperative relationship between Lebanon and Syria, and a framework for the complete withdrawal of Syrian troops from Lebanon. Maronite Christian general Michel Aoun, who directed a large militia in East Beirut and had been appointed prime minister illegally (the position was supposed to go to a Muslim), refused to recognize the agreement. As the violence continued into 1990, Syria launched a major offensive against Aoun's forces, destroying them and driving him into exile in France. By May 1991 the sectarian violence had generally ceased. With the critical exception of Hezbollah, all the militias were dissolved, and the Lebanese military tried to re-establish control over the country.

This proved an impossible task, however, as thousands of Syrian troops remained in the north and east of the country and Israel retained a large military presence in the south. Hezbollah, with significant diplomatic and financial backing from Iran, continued to attract thousands of followers, particularly among the rural and urban poor. Israeli forces finally left Lebanon in May 2000, but Syrian forces soon moved south to take their place. Following the assassinations of several prominent Lebanese politicians and journalists and massive protests in Beirut against the Syrian presence and influence in Lebanon, Syria was forced to withdraw its fifteen thousand troops from Lebanon. Thus a new beginning in Lebanon's history began on April 27, 2005, when the last Syrian troops departed, two months after Lebanon's Syrian-backed prime minister and cabinet were forced to resign. Lebanon was now free of Syrian occupiers for the first time in decades.

From the end of the civil war in 2006, Lebanon had slowly rebuilt its infrastructure. Schools and universities reopened; thousands of new buildings arose out of the war rubble; and new roads, bridges, hospitals, hotels, and restaurants served an increasingly prosperous population and foreign tourists who returned to the country once known as the "Switzerland of the Middle East."

But after the Israeli withdrawal in 2000, Hezbollah set about establishing a power base among the many villages and towns of the south and by 2004 had established virtual control over much of southern Beirut and southern Lebanon. Although it had abandoned its goal of transforming Lebanon into an Islamic republic, it continued to call for the complete destruction of Israel. Much to the chagrin of Washington and other Western capitals, Hezbollah won fourteen seats in the Lebanese legislature in parliamentary elections held in June 2005. It broadcast its message on its own radio and satellite television stations, and it set up massive charity and social programs that rivaled anything the government could provide. Hezbollah also developed a highly trained paramilitary army possessing some of the most advanced and sophisticated military hardware available through the international arms market. Hezbollah members adhere to a distinct brand of Islamic Shi'ite theology and ideology developed by the Shi'ite ayatollah Ruhollah Khomeini, leader of the Iranian Islamic Revolution in 1979. This connection explains the significant financial and military support that Iran provides and its powerful influence in shaping Hezbollah's policies, particularly toward Israel. Since coming to power in 2005 Iranian president Mahmoud Ahmadinejad has repeatedly called for the total annihilation of Israel, which is Hezbollah's primary goal.

That was the situation in July 2006, when Lebanon's years of reconstruction and hopes for peace were shattered once again. On July 12, 2006, Hezbollah began bombardment of northern Israeli military installations and towns while carrying out a cross-border raid that resulted in the capture of two Israeli soldiers and the killing of three others. An immediate rescue effort by Israel resulted in the deaths of five more Israelis. Hezbollah's intentions were to obtain Israeli prisoners to swap for Arab prisoners held by Israel. Israel responded with massive air strikes and artillery fire directed at what the Israeli military claimed were Hezbollah positions in southern and central Lebanon. Israel also instituted an air and naval blockade of the entire country and bombed runways at Beirut International Airport to render it impossible for planes to land or depart. Hezbollah retaliated with a rocket barrage launched into northern Israel, which Israel answered by invading southern Lebanon and thereby setting off a vicious war called the July War in Lebanon and the Second Lebanon War in Israel.

Israeli prime minister Ehud Olmert declared Hezbollah's attack an "act of war" and promised a "very painful and far-reaching response." In the ensuing weeks, Israeli

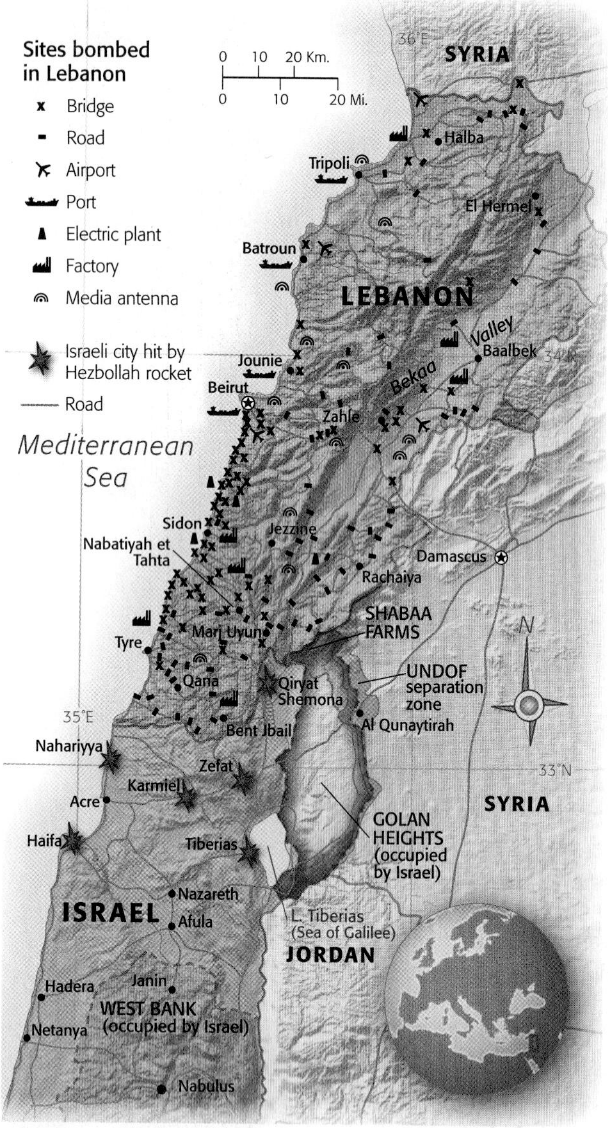

The 2006 Israel-Lebanon War The nation of Lebanon became the unwilling site of Israeli attacks directed at the political-religious movement Hezbollah following Hezbollah's shelling of northern Israel, abduction of two Israeli soldiers, and killing of eight others on July 12, 2006. In this Israel-Hezbollah war, the nation and people of Lebanon were the ones who suffered. This map shows the villages and cities in northern Israel struck by Hezbollah rockets and mortars, and the widespread damage done to Lebanon's infrastructure by Israeli shelling from the sea, land, and air.

forces hammered Lebanon from the land, sea, and air in what appeared to some as indiscriminate attacks on Hezbollah and non-Hezbollah targets alike. These attacks resulted in the destruction of large parts of Lebanon's civilian infrastructure, including schools, hospitals, sewage treatment plants, electrical facilities, roads, fuel stations and depots, commercial buildings, and homes. One attack by the Israeli air force on the Jiyeh power plant south of Beirut in mid-July ruptured oil tanks that spilled up to 110,000 barrels of fuel oil into the Mediterranean Sea, comparable in size to the 1989 *Exxon Valdez* oil spill in Alaska. The Jiyeh oil spill massively polluted beaches along the entire Lebanese coast, where the local economy is heavily dependent on the tourist and fishing industries.

Lebanese prime minister Fouad Siniora denied any knowledge of the Hezbollah raid, condemned it, and called for United Nations intervention. He and his government were forced to watch helplessly over the next few weeks, however, as Hezbollah and Israel fought. Hezbollah proved itself a formidable opponent to the much-vaunted Israeli Defense Force. Equipped with modern weaponry from Iran, China, Syria, and Russia, Hezbollah's well-organized and well-trained paramilitary units inflicted significant death and destruction on the invading Israeli forces. They also carried the attack into Israel itself, bombing more than eleven major cities in northern Israel along with dozens of kibbutzim and Druze and Arab villages. Over a half million civilians in northern Israel were forced to flee. Hezbollah forces destroyed at least twenty Israeli tanks, damaged an Israeli warship so severely that it had to be towed back to port, claimed credit for bringing down an Israeli helicopter, and on August 12 killed twenty-four Israeli soldiers, marking Israel's worst single-day loss. Environmentally, Hezbollah rockets ignited forest fires across northern Israel that are estimated to have destroyed as much as nine thousand acres of Israel's few forests.

United Nations organizations and various humanitarian agencies accused both sides of committing war crimes. Israel stood accused of indiscriminate and intentional attacks against civilians, the use of cluster bombs (that left more than one hundred thousand lethal unexploded bomblets) near civilian areas, and the reported use of white phosphorus, which is considered a chemical weapon when used in civilian areas. Hezbollah was condemned for indiscriminate and intentional shelling of civilian populations in cities and filling its shells with ball bearings to maximize harm to civilians. While Israeli forces dropped leaflets warning civilians to leave the southern Lebanon war zone, their destruction of roads and bridges into and out of the area made this impossible for many. Israel justified these attacks by claiming they were to prevent Hezbollah from rearming through Syria and Iran and smuggling out the captured Israeli soldiers. For its part, and as frequently happens in guerrilla wars, Hezbollah appeared to locate its rocket launchers and troops within populated residential areas. Israeli and some neutral reports charged that Hezbollah purposefully sought to draw Israeli fire on civilian targets in order to maximize civilian casualties and earn more sympathy for its cause.

● **Environmental Consequences of War**   Israeli attacks on the Jiyeh power plant south of Beirut during the Israel-Hezbollah war in July 2006 caused a massive oil spill of 10,000 to 15,000 barrels of oil, the worst environmental disaster in Lebanon's history. A hundred-mile stretch of Lebanon's shoreline was seriously affected, severely damaging the ecology and the local tourism economy. *(Ben Curtis/AP Images)*

Besides the release of the two captured Israeli soldiers, Israel appeared to have two goals: first, to destroy Hezbollah as a viable organization; and second, to send a clear signal to the Lebanese population and government that they would pay dearly if they continued to allow Hezbollah to control southern Lebanon and maintain a paramilitary presence that threatened Israel's peace and security. For its part, Hezbollah's leader, Hassan Nasrallah, said at one point during the war that Hezbollah would probably not have invaded Israel and captured the two soldiers if its leaders had known Israel's response would be so massive and destructive. Once at war, however, Hezbollah soldiers fought tenaciously and clearly did not intend to just slip away, abandoning Hezbollah's power base in southern Lebanon.

Diplomatic efforts to end the war involved, as is often the case, a flurry of diplomatic messages, diplomats shuttling back and forth between world capitals, solemn world leaders expressing profound concern, and little action. As the war intensified and civilian casualties mounted, there were calls from all quarters for an immediate and unconditional cease-fire—particularly from the Lebanese prime minister Fouad Siniora, who pleaded with the United States, Israel's closest ally, and with the United Nations to put an immediate stop to the war. Because the United States considers Hezbollah a terrorist organization, however, President George W. Bush and Secretary of State Condoleezza Rice continually refused to call for an immediate cease-fire, arguing that any agreement had to include the return of the two Israeli soldiers and Hezbollah's surrender of its weapons and return of control of southern Lebanon to the Lebanese government. Some observers argued that the U.S. refusal to demand an immediate and unconditional cease-fire was motivated by its desire to give Israel time to completely destroy Hezbollah.

Two events during the war drew particular condemnation from the world community and put greater pressure on Israel to end its invasion. First, there was what the

Israeli military described as a nondeliberate bombing of a UN observation post on July 26, 2006, that killed three UN observers. The Israelis argued that they were targeting Hezbollah fighters in the area. The second incident occurred on July 30, 2006, during an Israeli Air Force attack on a building in al'Khuraybah, near the village of Qana in southern Lebanon. The building collapsed, burying many Lebanese refugees who were sheltered in the basement. Although initial reports listed more than fifty casualties, the final count showed that at least twenty-eight people were killed, including sixteen children, and thirteen were missing. Although Israel argued it was responding to rockets launched from the village, the high number of women and children killed sparked outrage against Israel across the Muslim world and set off worldwide demonstrations protesting Israel's action and calling for peace.

Hezbollah's continued shelling of northern Israel and Israel's seeming inability to gain a quick military victory, while sustaining increasing numbers of civilian and military deaths itself, generated mounting discontent in Israel among soldiers and civilians alike about the handling and course of the war. By early August all sides clearly desired a way out, and on August 11, 2006, the United Nations Security Council unanimously approved UN Resolution 1701, which led to a cease-fire on August 14, 2006.

The resolution called for a full cessation of all hostilities. Israel was to withdraw its forces from southern Lebanon while Lebanese and UN forces took their place. Hezbollah was to be disarmed, and no paramilitary forces would be allowed in southern Lebanon. The Lebanese government was to have full control over the entire country, and the two Israeli soldiers were to be released. Hezbollah declared, however, that it would not disarm; Lebanon announced that it would not disarm Hezbollah; and Israel said it would not withdraw its forces until Hezbollah had been disarmed. Matters seemed at a stalemate, and Israel maintained its air and sea blockade of Lebanon, ostensibly to block illegal shipments of arms from Syria and Iran to resupply Hezbollah. Only four days after the cease-fire, on August 18, Hezbollah's famed network of humanitarian services attracted worldwide notice as the organization began distributing $12,000 (U.S. dollars) cash to every family in southern Beirut whose home had been destroyed. Hezbollah's largesse was an embarrassment to the Lebanese government, which could not match such funding, and to the international community, which was slow in responding to the war with humanitarian aid. Hezbollah's funds were thought to come from Syria and Iran.

As discontent with his conduct of the war continued to grow in Israel, Prime Minister Olmert lifted the aviation blockade on September 7 and the naval blockade the following day, and Israeli forces began to withdraw from southern Lebanon. On October 1, 2006, the last remaining Israeli soldiers in Lebanon crossed the border back into Israel. Hezbollah fighters had melted back into the population.

Opinions vary as to who won and who lost the war. Both the Syrian and Iranian presidents claimed victory for Hezbollah, although their countries may have gained more from the war than did Hezbollah. Certainly many in the Muslim world felt pride in Hezbollah's ability to stand up to the Israeli military machine and fight it toe to toe for thirty-four days. Many were also happy to see Israel under attack. This renewed Islamic pride would certainly rub off on the two leaders, Syrian president Bashar Assad and Iranian president Ahmadinejad, both of whom are seen as Islamic leaders in the forefront of the battle against Israel and its closest, and most unpopular, ally, the United States. Although Hezbollah's leaders declared victory over Israel, there can be no doubt that, other than perhaps the propaganda war, Hezbollah paid dearly. Even its leader, Hasan Nasrallah, admitted that given the opportunity he would not do it again. Hezbollah lost the elaborate infrastructure it had taken years to build in the south. Large amounts of its weaponry were used up, destroyed, or captured, and hundreds of its best fighters killed. The organization also lost the support of hundreds of thousands of Lebanese whose homes, lives, and livelihoods—and decades of painstaking rebuilding after the civil war—were destroyed by Hezbollah's actions. These

Lebanese deeply resented Hezbollah's crying "victory!" as they themselves sat among the rubble.

For its part, Israel claimed victory but was no better off. The two missing Israeli soldiers, Ehud Goldwasser and Eldad Regev, whose capture had sparked Israel's initial invasion of Lebanon, were not returned until July 16, 2008, in coffins. Many Israelis believe that Olmert's indecisive leadership cost Israel a rare opportunity to destroy Hezbollah, thereby ending its threat to Israeli security and its influence in Lebanese politics, and frustrating Iran's foreign policy. Israelis emerged from the war deeply troubled by a new sense of vulnerability. The Israeli government's Winograd Commission, tasked with investigating the war, issued reports in April 2007 and January 2008 highly critical of Olmert and his government's handling of the war. On July 30, 2008, Olmert announced he would resign as prime minister as soon as his Kadima Party picked his successor. His resignation has shaken up the peace process and created concern that Israeli hardliners, such as former prime minister and opposition Likud Party chair Benjamin Netanyahu, would win the next election. Netanyahu could be expected to take a much tougher stand against Hamas, Hezbollah, and Iran.

Meanwhile in Lebanon efforts have been ongoing to rebuild the country once again. The majority of Lebanese people appear to want nothing but peace. But in the last two years, Hezbollah has rearmed and reemerged as a political and military power. In May and June 2008 Hezbollah militia attacked Lebanese army units in Beirut and the Beqaa Valley. Furthermore, in May 2007 the worst internal fighting since the civil war broke out with a battle between the Lebanese armed forces and the militia of the Sunni extremist group Fatah al-Islam near Tripoli and the enormous Palestinian refugee camp of Nahr al-Bared in northern Lebanon. The fighting ended with the Lebanese army regaining control, but only after the death of several hundred soldiers, civilians, and Islamic militia members.

Lebanon perhaps pulled back from the brink of another civil war, however, when its politicians finally chose a successor to President Emile Lahoud, who had resigned in November 2007. On May 25, 2008, Lebanon's parliament elected army chief Michel Suleiman as the new head of state, ending months of government paralysis. Suleiman is expected to work for national unity, seek equal political relations with Syria, and try to integrate Hezbollah's militia into the Lebanese army.

• ———————————————

ISRAEL AND PALESTINE

While Israel was busy fighting Hezbollah in the north, the Israeli-Palestinian conflict remained unresolved. Prime Minister Ariel Sharon's successful execution of his unilateral plan for withdrawal of all Israeli settlers from the Gaza Strip in August and September 2005 resulted in a split in his ruling Likud party. Sharon left the party in November 2005 to found his own political party, Kadima, Hebrew for "forward." Despite changing his political allegiance, Sharon continued pressing for the completion of the West Bank barrier, or wall, which ostensibly is intended to protect Israel from attacks by armed Palestinian groups and suicide bombers. Despite worldwide criticism, the wall continues to be built, effectively annexing 9.5 percent of West Bank territory originally given to the Palestinians in the United Nations Partition Plan in 1947. Sharon also proceeded with his plan to build thirty-five hundred new Jewish settler homes in the West Bank, but his plans were cut short when he suffered a massive hemorrhagic stroke on January 4, 2006, that left him completely incapacitated and in a vegetative state with little hope of recovery. His place was taken by Ehud Olmert, who became acting prime minister and leader of the Kadima party. He and his party won national legislative elections in their own right in April 2006.

For their part, the Palestinians held legislative elections for the Palestinian National

Authority government in January 2006. To everyone's surprise, Hamas, a Sunni Muslim political party considered by many in the West to be a terrorist organization, won 76 of the 132 seats. Using suicide bombers as its primary weapon, Hamas has been best known for its attacks on Israeli civilians and military and security forces. Formed in 1987, its charter calls for Israel's destruction and its replacement with a Palestinian Islamic state. Not only does it share with Iran and Hezbollah a desire to destroy Israel, but like Hezbollah, Hamas has gained widespread support from many Palestinians for the extensive welfare programs it has established in the West Bank and Gaza Strip. While many Palestinians view the old ruling Palestine Liberation Organization as increasingly corrupt and impotent, they have watched as Hamas built health-care clinics, orphanages, shelters, and schools throughout the Gaza Strip and West Bank.

For President George Bush and other Western leaders who have called for the spread of democracy in the Middle East, the parliamentary victories in relatively free and fair elections by Hezbollah in Lebanon and Hamas among the Palestinians have caused embarrassment and concern. Immediately after the Hamas victory, Israel, the United States, the European Union, and several other leading European and Western donor nations cut off all aid to the Palestinian Authority. The United States and EU outlined "three principles" that they said Hamas and the Palestinians had to accept for funding to be renewed and diplomatic relations established. First, Hamas had to revise its charter and recognize Israel's right to exist as a sovereign nation, something Hamas has adamantly refused, through 2008, to do. Second, Hamas had to renounce violence and cease its support of suicide bombings. Third, it must fully support the Middle East peace process as outlined in the 1993 Oslo Accords. Hamas rejected these principles out of hand, calling them unfair and suggesting that it might agree to recognize Israel if Israel withdrew to its pre-1967 borders, which would mean pulling out of the West Bank, the Gaza Strip, the Golan Heights, and, most important, East Jerusalem. Hamas also demanded the right of return to their old homes and lands of all Palestinian refugees and their descendants.

Many political observers felt that once the Hamas members took their seats in the Palestinian legislature and formed a cabinet, the political realities of actually being responsible for the running of a government and the welfare of its citizens would force its leaders to abandon their most extreme positions. The new cabinet was announced on March 20, 2006. The old ruling PLO party, Fatah, refused to accept positions in the new cabinet, leaving the majority of the seats to Hamas and a few independents. It soon became clear that the new Hamas government would not back away from its call for the destruction of Israel.

The one moderate voice in the Palestinian Authority remains the president, Mahmoud Abbas, who is the chairman of the PLO Executive Committee. Elected president of the Palestinian Authority in January 2005 after the death of Yasir Arafat in November 2004. Abbas has found himself in a nearly impossible position. He has been blamed by the Israelis for not doing enough to stop attacks on Israeli civilians and military forces. Many of these attacks have been carried out by members of Hamas or by their allies in the Islamic Jihad movement. He has also failed in his efforts to form a government of national unity. Hamas refuses to join a coalition government if it means recognizing Israel and rejecting violence. In frustration, in December 2006 Abbas called for new elections for early 2007. Prime Minister Ismail Haniya, representing Hamas, dismissed the proposal, saying Abbas had no authority to call elections. In June 2007 Hamas seized control of the Gaza Strip, forcing Abbas and his followers out. Abbas then established an emergency Palestinian Authority government, which has been officially recognized by Israel and the West, in the West Bank. Abbas and Israeli prime minister Olmert met in Annapolis, Maryland, in November 2007 and set themselves the goal of reaching a final peace settlement by late 2008. Outbreaks of violence between the two sides continue, however, and little progress had been made through July 2008. Recent public opinion surveys of citizens on both sides suggest that attitudes are hardening against any compromise peace settlement.

If outgoing Prime Minister Ehud Olmert is succeeded by someone from the Likud Party, as appears likely, it will almost certainly mean Israel will take a more hardline stand toward any peace settlement with the Palestinians.

Meanwhile, economic and humanitarian conditions for average Palestinians, particularly in the Gaza Strip, continue to decline. The Palestinian Authority has no mechanism to raise tax revenues, but is dependent on Israel to forward an estimated $60 million in monthly tax revenues so that the government can pay its 165,000 civil employees. Israel stopped making these payments after Hamas took power and has only sporadically released some of these funds to Abbas and the West Bank Palestinian authorities. By late 2006, surveys suggested that more than 70 percent of the civil employees could no longer make ends meet and that more than 20 percent were considering emigrating. Health care has also deteriorated sharply, with drugs and medical supplies in critically short supply. Some hospitals and clinics have closed, and health-care providers, teachers, and other public employees have gone on strike, protesting having worked for months without pay or pay raises. The infrastructure in the Gaza Strip, already crippled by years of war, continues to deteriorate, with electrical power low and unreliable and water supplies irregular. Without reliable electricity, sewage treatment plants cannot operate efficiently, increasing the risk of disease spreading. Sixty-seven percent of Gazans live below the poverty line, and general lawlessness has risen sharply.

Making life even more difficult for average Palestinians, Hamas and Israel began an exchange of attacks in early June 2006 that have continued through early 2008. The refusal of Hamas to recognize Israel's right to exist has brought peace negotiations to a standstill and has delayed the formation of a viable, operative Palestinian government that will focus on protecting its citizens and providing for their needs. Nearly all the world powers have refused to recognize Hamas as a legitimate government until it renounces violence and recognizes Israel. It remains to be seen whether Hamas can continue to hold out, particularly as living and working conditions in the Gaza Strip and West Bank continue to deteriorate. Of course, the leaders of Hamas face the same problem that has caused many more-moderate leaders in the Middle East to hesitate to recognize Israel; when the Egyptian president Anwar Sadat formally recognized Israel in the late 1970s, he was assassinated by the Egyptian Islamic Jihad. Members of various radical groups have already threatened violence against the Hamas leaders if they back away from their call for Israel's destruction.

Thus, despite years of diplomacy, war, and stalemate, the main differences between the Israelis and the Palestinians remain unresolved. These include the nature of a future Palestinian state; the fate of Palestinian refugees and their "right of return"; Israel's establishment of Jewish settlements in the occupied territories and their ultimate fate; the status and future of the West Bank, East Jerusalem, and the Gaza Strip, which are the designated areas for a future Palestinian state; Israeli security and the recognition by all parties of Israel's right to exist; and, perhaps the most difficult question of all, who is to have sovereignty over Jerusalem and its holy sites, including the Temple Mount and Western Wall complex. For the moment at least, there appears to be no light at the end of the tunnel for one of the most complex human, religious, and ethnic dilemmas in world history.

IRAQ

One of the rationales for the overthrow of Saddam Hussein still put forward by the Bush administration is the desire to establish a stable democratic government in Iraq. To that goal, the Coalition Provisional Authority, established as a transitional government following Saddam Hussein's ouster, held executive, legislative, and judicial authority over the country from April 2003 to June 2004. On June 28 it handed over

● **Protecting Iraqi Oil** A U.S. soldier stands guard over an Iraqi oil field. Although Iraq is estimated to have the world's second largest oil deposits, about 11 percent of the world's total deposits, its oil production has been severely limited since the early 1990s—due first to UN sanctions and, from 2003, to the Iraqi war. Peak production of Iraqi oil was about 3.5 million barrels per day (bpd) in the late 1980s. In spring 2008 oil production was around 2 million bpd. Saudia Arabia's oil production, by comparison, was about 10 million bpd in May 2008. Still, with world oil prices at record levels, members of the U.S. Senate and House are pressing Iraq to accept a larger share of the war's costs. *(D. Hurst/Alamy)*

sovereignty to an Iraqi interim government, with Iyad Allawi serving as Iraq's acting prime minister until elections could be held in January 2005. Allawi immediately reintroduced capital punishment and, after assuming legal custody of Saddam Hussein, set in motion the trial of the former dictator. Insurgent attacks against coalition forces continued to mount, however, and the interim government failed to gain the support of large portions of the population, who viewed Allawi as a puppet of the United States. These factors, together with disputes and disorganization within the interim government itself, made the organizing of elections difficult at best.

Elections to select a 275-member Iraqi National Assembly that would draft a permanent Iraqi constitution were finally held on January 30, 2005. Many Sunni Arabs boycotted the elections, but most of the eligible Shi'ite and Kurdish population voted. Somewhat to Washington's embarrassment, the party of Prime Minister Allawi came in third, with just 14 percent of the vote. A party backed by the leading Shi'ite cleric, Ayatollah Ali al-Sistani, a frequent critic of the American-led war, received 48 percent of the votes, reflecting the Shi'ite majority in the country. A Kurdish party came in second with 26 percent of the votes.

After several delays, the draft of the new Iraqi constitution was approved in a nationwide referendum held on October 15, 2005. By permitting a compromise that allowed the first government working under the new constitution to make amendments to it at any time during the first four months, which would then have to be ratified by a similar referendum, the constitution received the important backing of the Sunni-majority Iraqi Islamic party. A new election was then held on December 15, 2005, to elect a permanent Iraqi National Assembly.

Disputes over vote rigging meant that the elections were not officially certified until February 10, 2006. Disagreements between all the various factions and parties in the legislative assembly over who should be the speaker, as well as who would be the first president and first prime minister, continued through the spring.

The current Iraqi government finally took office on May 20, 2006. The Kurdish leader Jalal Talabani was elected president, and the prime minister was Nouri al-Maliki, a Shi'ite Muslim whose Islamic Dawa party was a member of the United Iraqi Alliance, a coalition of primarily Shi'ite parties that had received the most votes in the election. Although by spring 2008 they had managed to hold a government together for two years, Iraq's leaders still faced essentially the same daunting problems as when they first took office. The most important challenge is to train national military and police forces that will restore order to the country and put an end to insurgency and sectarian violence without continued U.S. support. The government must also determine what the ongoing relationship will be with the United States and with a continued allied military presence that some Iraqis consider an occupation force. Government corruption must be ended, particularly relating to the illegal sale of Iraqi oil. Iraq's leaders have to convince all Iraqis that they are not favoring one faction—religious or ethnic—over another. Finally, the government must determine how the new constitution is to be

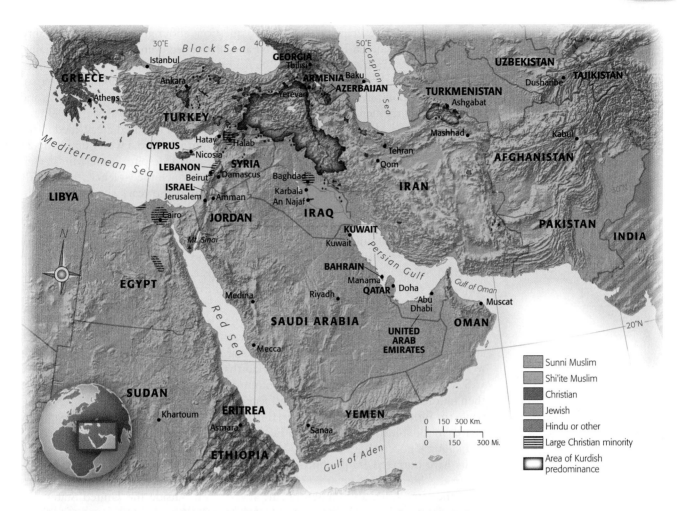

Abrahamic Religions in the Middle East and Surrounding Regions Although Islam is the majority religion throughout the Middle East, Judaism and Christianity, which also trace their origins back to the patriarch Abraham, still have significant populations, particularly in the modern Jewish state of Israel and in Lebanon. Though the Sunni branch of Islam has always dominated the Shi'ite branch, since the 1979 Iranian revolution Shi'ites throughout the region have become more strident in their demands for equality and power, and more militant. The Kurds, one of the largest stateless ethnic groups, who follow various religions, have become a major player in the politics of the region, especially in Iraq and Turkey, where they seek Kurdish independence.

implemented, whether it needs to be amended, and how much autonomy will be given to the various regions and factions within the country, especially the Kurds in the north.

As Iraqi politicians were writing a new constitution and attempting to form a new government, Iraqi judges and lawyers were trying Saddam Hussein for crimes against humanity. Specifically, Hussein was charged with the murder of 148 Shi'ite men in the town of Dujail after a 1982 assassination attempt against him. The trial began on October 19, 2005, with the defiant Hussein pleading not guilty, and adjourned in June 2006. On August 21 a second trial began, this time charging Hussein with war crimes against Iraqi Kurds, specifically for ordering poison gas to be dropped on Kurdish mountain villages. On September 19, 2006, the government appointed a new chief judge, Mohammed al-Ureybi, after sacking the old one, Abdullah al-Amin, allegedly for saying that Hussein was not a dictator. This action raised doubts in some legal circles about the freedom of the court from government interference in the trial.

On November 5, 2006, the court found Hussein guilty of crimes against humanity and condemned him to death by hanging. Rather than take the available thirty days to consider the Appeals Court decision, the Iraqi government determined that Hussein should be executed immediately, and the hanging took place on December 30,

2006. This "rush to execution" again raised questions about government impartiality. Many Sunnis considered Hussein a martyr and threatened even more reprisals against the Shi'ite-led government and the Shi'ite majority in the country. While these political and judicial deliberations were being held within the secure confines of the so-called Green Zone in downtown Baghdad, the violence in Baghdad's streets and across the country increased dramatically. In July and August 2006 alone, the United Nations reported, almost sixty-six hundred Iraqis, nearly a hundred a day, died in the sectarian violence. Attacks were averaging nearly eight hundred a week, up nearly 24 percent from the beginning of 2006. All this happened despite Prime Minister al-Maliki's repeated announcements of new initiatives to quell the violence, particularly in Baghdad. Instead, the violence increased throughout the year, with entire neighborhoods coming under the control of private militias. As the security situation grew worse, so too did the supply of basic services, such as sewage, electricity, and potable water, which remain intermittent at best. Outside Baghdad there were large areas of the country over which the Iraqi government had no control at all. In August 2006 the chief of intelligence for the U.S. Marine Corps concluded in a report that there was only a remote possibility that U.S. and Iraqi forces could secure al-Anbar Province, the heart of Sunni resistance.

The United States also seemed to be losing the battle for the "hearts and minds" of the Iraqi people in 2006. Most damaging were the various allegations of torture and abuse of prisoners, beginning with incidents at Abu Ghraib prison. American troops were also accused of killing civilians at Haditha in November 2005, and four of five U.S. soldiers accused of raping and then murdering a fourteen-year-old Iraqi girl and then murdering her mother, father, and sister on March 12, 2006, have pleaded guilty, while the fifth awaits trial. Blackwater, the American private security firm that supplies guards for diplomatic convoys and other security details, has been accused of harming and killing innocent Iraqi civilians while carrying out its duties. These and other incidents have outraged Iraqis and made innocent American soldiers the targets of revenge attacks.

At the same time, antiwar sentiment, always high outside the United States, has grown significantly within the United States since 2006 as the dollar cost of the war, estimated in spring 2008 at over $600 billion, mounts and the death toll continues to climb. On September 22, 2006, the number of U.S. soldiers killed in the Iraq and Afghanistan wars marked one more death than the 2,973 killed in the World Trade Center towers on September 11, 2001. U.S. deaths in Iraq passed 4,000 in March 2008. As the violence continues, the specter of an Iraqi civil war remains ever present—and some argue that Iraq is already experiencing a civil war. The Iraq War has also had a negative effect on the centerpiece of President Bush's foreign policy, the war on terror. A leaked U.S. intelligence report from April 2006, which pulled together intelligence information from sixteen American spy agencies, concluded that Islamic radicalism had mushroomed worldwide and that the Iraq War had contributed to a growth in the overall terrorist threat since 9/11.

Following the Republican loss of both houses of the U.S. Congress in the November 2006 elections, partly due to the unpopularity of the Iraq War, President Bush in January 2007 announced a new American strategy of sending an additional 20,000 American troops to Iraq and deploying the majority around Baghdad and in al-Anbar province. This new strategy has been called colloquially the "troop surge" (antiwar opponents refer to it as a "troop escalation") and has resulted in an increase of the American military presence in Iraq from 130,000 to over 160,000 troops. Whether this new strategy has been a success remains a matter of heated debate. Politically, most of the benchmarks set for the Iraqi government by the U.S. Congress have gone unmet. Militarily, there has been a decrease in violence across the country, but it is unclear whether this is due to the increased troop presence. Some mixed Sunni-Shi'ite neighborhoods that had experienced extreme factional violence have since been taken over by one or the other side, forcing the losers to flee from their homes. The Iraqi economy has shown some signs of recovery, with oil revenues increasing significantly, which has prompted both Democratic and Republican members of Congress to ask why Iraq is not paying a larger share of the cost of the war.

The Iraq War, as it has since its beginning in 2003, remains a complex affair that displays aspects of civil war, military occupation, religious and ethnic conflict, and holy war. With no end in sight after five long years, it appears that Bush's successor will have to find a solution that will bring peace and prosperity to Iraq while disengaging American troops and bringing them home.

IRAN

Prior to Iran's June 2005 elections many political observers felt that moderates were gaining an upper hand in revolutionary Iran and that Akbar Hashemi Rafsanjani, a relatively more moderate candidate in Iranian politics, would win the election. Certainly there was no expectation that he would be challenged by Mahmoud Ahmadinejad, the ultraconservative hard-line mayor of Tehran. Despite a series of protests prior to the election about the power of the Guardian Council, which has veto power over all political candidates in Iran and used that power to disqualify a number of more moderate ones, the elections went smoothly, with nearly 60 percent of eligible voters casting ballots. In a runoff, Ahmadinejad defeated Rafsanjani, winning 61 percent of the vote.

Mahmoud Ahmadinejad (b. 1956) holds bachelor's and master's degrees in civil engineering and a Ph.D. in traffic and transportation engineering and planning, which he received in 1987, after which he taught civil engineering at the prestigious Iran University of Science and Technology. He was appointed mayor of Tehran in May 2003 and served for three years before running for president. As mayor he reversed many of the more moderate and reformist regulations instituted by previous mayors, while implementing various social and welfare programs to help the poor. It is thought that this populist element in his governing style and rhetoric appeals to the masses and is partly responsible for his winning the presidency. Ahmadinejad has also enjoyed wide support among religious hardliners for his hostility to secular reforms and attacks on Western culture.

During the Iran-Iraq War in the 1980s Ahmadinejad was a member of the Revolutionary Guard, which operates parallel to the regular Iranian army. He served in the security and intelligence branch, and his role was to suppress dissidents in Iran and abroad. Although the evidence remains murky, a number of reports charge Ahmadinejad with involvement in the interrogation and execution of prisoners. He is also alleged to have been involved in a number of extraterritorial operations as part of an elite force that carried out assassinations in the Middle East and Europe.

Ahmadinejad is the sixth president of the Islamic Republic of Iran. He took office on August 3, 2005. During his campaign Ahmadinejad emphasized both his religious conservative views and his plans for helping the poorer economic classes, including a proposed monthly stipend to each citizen. He calls himself a "principalist" in reference to his strict adherence to his perceived version of the principles of Islam and of the Iranian Islamic Revolution. His most popular economic goal is a more even distribution of Iran's oil wealth among all its people, particularly the poor. After three years in office, however, Ahmadinejad has failed to repair Iran's ailing economy, and his support, even among conservatives, has eroded. In the March 2008 legislative elections, some reformers who want more democracy and closer ties with the West were allowed to run and won a few seats, but Ahmadinejad's party retained a large majority.

Ahmadinejad had not been in office long before he became the center of worldwide controversy. The debate over Iran's nuclear power program has stirred the most intense discussion, but Ahmadinejad's comments in speeches and interviews, particularly

about Israel and the Holocaust, have also drawn sharp criticism from many world political and religious leaders outside the Muslim world. Ahmadinejad has criticized the
arrangement of the United Nations Security Council and the veto power of the five
permanent members (Great Britain, United States, France, Russia, and China), arguing that the world's 1.5 billion Muslims are thereby denied a vote in the global policymaking process. Ahmadinejad is not staking out a particularly new or unusual
position here. All five veto-holding members of the Security Council are nuclear powers and have blocked any efforts to give other countries membership in this privileged
club. Germany, Japan, Brazil, and India have all sought permanent, veto-holding
membership on the Security Council.

Ahmadinejad's remarks regarding Israel have created a firestorm of controversy. In
a speech in October 2005 at a "World Without Zionism" conference held for students
in Tehran, he said that he accepted the position taken by the Ayatollah Khomeini that
Israel should be "wiped off the map" and that he expected Palestinians to soon "wipe
this disgraceful stain from the face of the Islamic world." Despite worldwide condemnation of these remarks, he has not backed away from them. Nor has he backed away
from statements first made on December 15, 2005, that seemed to deny the Holocaust. In subsequent remarks he has continued to voice doubts that the Holocaust
ever happened. In August 2006 a contest was held in Tehran to determine the best
Holocaust caricatures; the contest was presented as retaliation for the publication of
caricatures of Muhammad first published in Denmark in September 2005. In December 2006 a state-sponsored conference held in Tehran openly challenged the scale
and even the reality of the Holocaust.

Ahmadinejad has backed up his anti-Israel rhetoric with action. Iran's Shi'ite clergy
have long supported the Shi'ite population in Lebanon, and many Lebanese Shi'ite
clergy were trained in Iran before the 1979 revolution. After the revolution, Lebanon
was one of the first countries to which Iran's Shi'ite revolutionaries looked to export
their revolution. As we have seen, the immediate outcome of these efforts was the
formation of Hezbollah, whose stated goals were the creation of an Islamic Lebanese
state and the destruction of Israel. Lebanon is on the western end of what is becoming
known as the Shi'ite Crescent, a regional axis that stretches from Iran in the east
through Shi'ite communities in Bahrain, Iraq, eastern Saudi Arabia, and Syria (see the
map on page 1081). In Lebanon, Iran has provided both military and humanitarian
supplies and was probably responsible for the handout of $12,000 to each family that
lost its home after the war. There were even reports that some Iranian Revolutionary
Guard soldiers were training Hezbollah fighters in southern Lebanon. On June 16,
2006, a month before the Israel-Hezbollah war, Syria signed a defense pact with Iran
that would allow the stationing of Iranian troops in Syria and perhaps other support
from Iran if Syria were attacked. Iran has also supported Hamas with money, war materials, and humanitarian supplies.

The issue that has set Iran most at odds with the world's major powers, however, is
its determination to continue its nuclear energy program. The United States, the European Community, and other nations have accused Iran of developing nuclear power
in order to form a nuclear weapons arsenal. Iran has consistently denied that this is its
intention.

The Iranian nuclear technology program began during the reign of the Shah of Iran
in the 1950s with the help and support of the United States. It was abandoned temporarily after the 1979 revolution, but then revived. Although they have received only
limited Western assistance since then, primarily from Russia, the Iranians seem to have
developed a very sophisticated program and have several research sites. Iran has a uranium mine and uranium-processing facilities, including a uranium enrichment plant.
It also has a nuclear reactor. Russia is building Iran's first nuclear plant, Bushehr I,
which is expected to be operational by fall 2008. This program is the result of a compromise whereby Russia provides nuclear fuel and expertise to build the plant, thus

● **Iranian Nuclear Energy Program** Despite threats of sanctions from the United States, France, Germany, Great Britain, and Russia, Iran continues to develop its nuclear energy program. Here Iranian scientists move a container of radioactive uranium. Whether the uranium is being used for peaceful purposes, as Iran staunchly maintains, or to develop nuclear weapons, as the West argues, remains to be seen. *(Behrouz Mehri/AFP/Getty Images)*

alleviating international concerns over Iran's nuclear program, while still allowing Iran access to nuclear energy.

There is currently no evidence that Iran possesses any weapons of mass destruction, and the country is a signatory to most of the major agreements banning such weapons, such as the Biological Weapons Convention, the Chemical Weapons Convention, and the Nuclear Non-Proliferation Treaty. On March 6, 2006, despite continued accusations from the United States, Great Britain, France, Germany, and Russia, the International Atomic Energy Agency (IAEA) director general, Mohamed ElBaradei, stated that the agency had not found any evidence that Iran was diverting nuclear material to the production of weapons or nuclear explosive devices. The United Nations Security Council, however, passed a resolution on July 31, 2006, that demanded the suspension of Iran's uranium enrichment program by August 31 or face sanctions. These and later demands and ultimatums have had few teeth, however, as the world powers cannot agree on appropriate sanctions. Iran continues to take a hard line. On April 20, 2008, Ahmadinejad said he rejected any new incentives the world powers might offer in return for Iran's suspending its uranium enrichment program.

The debate over Iran's nuclear energy program has become a global issue that reaches far beyond the question of simply whether Iran has the ability to make, or intends to make, a nuclear weapon. By standing up to the West on this issue, Iran has garnered the support of many other nations that see the prohibition as another example of how the nations of the West want to deny to the rest of the world what they already enjoy—nuclear power and nuclear weapons. This support was most powerfully expressed in a resolution passed on September 16, 2006, at the meeting of the 118

Non-Aligned Movement members in Havana, Cuba. The resolution stated the developed countries should allow developing countries to participate in the development of nuclear energy for peaceful purposes, and that all countries had the inalienable right to produce and use nuclear energy for peaceful purposes without discrimination. In the Muslim world there is also the perception of hypocrisy on the part of the Western powers in allowing Israel to develop nuclear power and, it is generally agreed, possess nuclear weapons, while denying Iraq, Iran, and other Middle East countries that right.

Experts generally agree, however, that it will be at least ten to fifteen years before Iran has the capability to produce even one nuclear weapon. Thus, the immediate question of whether Iran intends to use its nuclear program to produce nuclear weapons is still open to debate. The larger question of who will determine which countries can produce nuclear energy programs in the future remains one to which the world community will have to return.

AFGHANISTAN

After the 2001 attack on the World Trade Center towers and the Pentagon, the United States declared a war on terrorism. Its first target was Afghanistan, where the accused mastermind of the September 11 attack, al-Qaeda leader Osama bin Laden, was being sheltered by the ultra-fundamentalist Sunni Muslim Taliban, which had ruled Afghanistan since 1996. With the help of the Afghan Northern Alliance, a loose coalition of Afghan groups that had been fighting the Taliban for some time, and U.S. and NATO member troops, the United States began Operation Enduring Freedom.

Taliban forces abandoned Kandahar, the birthplace of the movement and the last Taliban-controlled city, on December 7, 2001. The Taliban's leader, Mullah Mohammad Omar, managed to escape, however, with many of his troops and their weapons. Al-Qaeda forces meanwhile, with some Taliban allies, had concentrated their positions in a cave complex known as Tora Bora located to the southeast of the capital Kabul near the Pakistan border. The U.S.-led forces made a last assault on the al-Qaeda strongholds in the caves, where it is believed Osama bin Laden was also hiding. A temporary truce, however, appears to have allowed bin Laden, many other top al-Qaeda leaders, and many of their troops to escape across the mountains into Pakistan. This is the closest U.S. forces have ever been to capturing bin Laden. Through July 2008, bin Laden's whereabouts remain unknown.

When the fighting appeared to have ended, a grand council of the major Afghan factions and tribal leaders met in June 2002 to form an interim Afghan government. They selected Hamid Karzai, a politician almost from his birth in Kandahar in 1957. Karzai belongs to the influential Popalzai clan of the ethnic Pashtun, the second-largest ethnic group in Afghanistan. His father was a member of the Afghanistan parliament under the former king Mohammad Zahir Shah. Karzai was taking a postgraduate course in political science at a university in Shimla, India, when the Soviet Union invaded and occupied Afghanistan in 1979. During the resistance he served as an adviser, fundraiser, and diplomat. After the Soviets pulled out in 1989, Karzai was deputy foreign minister in the postwar government, but he resigned his post in 1994 as the country fell into civil war. When the Taliban came to power in 1996, Karzai went into exile in Pakistan, from where he organized anti-Taliban opposition.

After his father was murdered in Pakistan in July 1999, presumably by Taliban assassins, Karzai succeeded his father as clan chief, or khan, of the half-million Popalzai. He then organized a procession of tribal mourners that carried his father's body back to Kandahar, the Taliban stronghold but also the Popalzai home. The Taliban did not dare to halt the funeral or harm Karzai. This single act of courage and defiance earned Karzai recognition as the leader of Pashtun resistance to the Taliban.

When Karzai took power in 2002 his political base in the country was quite limited—so much so that people sometimes derided him as just the mayor of Kabul—and he ruled only through the presence of the coalition forces. When presidential elections were held in October 2004, however, Karzai won twenty-one of the thirty-four provinces to become the first democratically elected Afghanistani leader. After taking office, Karzai was expected to immediately set about initiating democratic and modernizing reforms in the country, but that has not been the case. In December 2004 he made major changes in his cabinet, removing many of the former Northern Alliance warlords but, reflecting his desire to proceed very cautiously, also fired his finance minister, Ashraf Ghani, who had instituted extensive economic, banking, credit, and customs reforms between 2002 and 2004 and had been recognized as the best finance minister in Asia in 2003.

Although the economy has been growing and government revenues increasing, this is partly the result of the harvest of the main crop in Afghanistan, the opium poppy, which in 2007 reached the highest levels ever recorded, up almost 60 percent from the 2005 harvest. The 2008 crop is already expected to be nearly as high. Total production was around sixty-five hundred metric tons of opium for the 2007 growing season, which equals 93 percent of the world's supply. Its estimated export value was $4 billion. Thirty-five percent of the country's gross domestic product now comes from the opium trade. This is despite the millions of dollars poured into eradication of the poppy crop by the Afghan government and international agencies.

Large areas of the country still under the control of warlords are increasingly coming back under the control of the Taliban, and the record harvest can be attributed in part to the resurgence of Taliban rebels in the prime opium-growing region in the

● **Afghanistan's Opium Poppy Fields**   An impoverished Afghan farmer inspects his opium poppy crop, which will bring him far greater profits than any other crop he can produce. The government's eradication program, poorly funded and facing much opposition from farmers and local officials, has had little success. The 2007 opium poppy harvest was the largest ever recorded, up nearly 60 percent from the 2005 harvest. *(Ahmad Sear/Corbis)*

south. The Karzai government exercises almost no control over these areas, and farmers have received virtually no incentives to plant alternative crops. The Taliban have stepped in, distributing seeds and fertilizers for new poppy crops and offering farmers protection, while receiving increased support, new recruits, and profits from the drug trade to fund their military operations.

The Bush administration has made opium poppy eradication one of the primary targets of its aid to Afghanistan, and it has been critical of the Karzai administration for not doing more. Karzai has been inconsistent in his efforts to deal with the opium problem. He rejected a U.S. proposal to eradicate production by aerial spraying with chemical herbicides, but he continues to reiterate his determination to eradicate the crops. He must tread a fine line, however, because he has neither the funds nor the worker capacity to effect much change or to initiate reforms beyond a very limited region around the capital of Kabul. Aerial spraying might get rid of the opium poppy, but it would win Karzai few allies among the warlords who profit from the drug trade and little political support from the farmers who depend on poppy production for their livelihood.

In a speech before the United Nations General Assembly on September 2006, Karzai said that terrorism is rebounding in Afghanistan, both from terrorists acting from within the country and from terrorists coming across from other countries to attack Afghanistani civilians. Since his speech, the situation has deteriorated even further. One estimate in February 2008 suggested that the Karzai government controlled only about 30 percent of the country and the Taliban about 10 percent, and that the remainder was under local tribal control. Suicide bombings have soared, and hundreds of civilians, aid workers, and Afghan security personnel have been killed despite an increased allied military presence. The United States has raised its troop level in Afghanistan from twenty-five thousand in 2004 to fifty thousand in 2008. Still, casualty figures have risen sharply in the last two years, and by August 2008 over 900 coalition troops, including over 500 Americans, had died since October 2001. Without the coalition forces, it is generally agreed that the Taliban would be in control of Kabul within a week, so ill-trained and ill-organized is the Afghanistani military. This would likely lead to another civil war as the warlords of the old Northern Alliance would defend their fiefdoms once again.

As the violence and death toll mount, President Karzai and the U.S.-led coalition are becoming increasingly unpopular. In 2007 and early 2008 the Bush administration took steps to more strongly support the war in Afghanistan, such as raising American troop levels there and encouraging other members of the coalition to do the same, but these efforts are still far short of U.S. military and monetary support for the Iraq War.

TURKEY

Turkey remains a country on the border—seeking membership in the European Union of the West, while acknowledging its Islamic heritage and historical connections with the East. It is a secular country, not ruled by Islamic law. Many of its citizens lead Western lifestyles, although the population is overwhelmingly Sunni Muslim. Despite concerted efforts by leaders to meet the economic, legal, and humanitarian standards set by the EU, Turkey's pace of reform has met with heavy EU criticism. The 1915–1917 Armenian massacres remain a major point of contention. In September 2006 a Turkish court acquitted a prizewinning Turkish author, Elif Shafak, of charges that she denigrated Turkish national identity by having characters in her novel *The Bastard of Istanbul* make statements about the Armenian massacres. Although this ruling saved Turkey short-term embarrassment, it did not seem to satisfy EU officials, who warned Turkey that it should purge its penal code of all restrictions on freedom of speech as a firm demonstration of its commitment to human rights and democracy.

The European Commission evaluating Turkey's application to join the EU has been highly critical of Turkey's accession progress, expressing concern over issues of access to ports and airports for EU member Cyprus, freedom of expression (especially in cases dealing with writers and journalists), and Kurdish minority rights. On December 7, 2006, Turkey announced it was opening one port and one airport to trade with Cyprus. It will be at least 2013, and the next round of EU membership admissions, before Turkey can be admitted into the EU, provided that it meets all of the EU's demands.

Although it is a major concern for Turkey's politicians and people, EU membership is not the only issue troubling the country. Turks are also deeply divided over the future of the secular state in Turkey, as well as the Kurdish question. To understand the first concern, we must remember that Turkey is the most secular of Islamic countries, going back to the presidency of Mustafa Kemal in the 1920s and 30s (see pages 853–854). Since that time Turks have closely guarded their secularism and maintained a strict separation of state and religion. In 2002 elections, however, the newly formed (1991) Justice and Development Party (or AKP) scored a stunning victory. Abdullah Gul became president of Turkey, and Recep Erdogan, head of the AKP, became prime minister. Although the AKP campaigned as a moderate, conservative, pro-Western party, supporting liberal market economics, many Turks are concerned that the AKP is really intent on doing away with Turkey's secular constitution and establishing an Islamic state. Although Erdogan has adamantly denied any secret agenda, laws such as the banning of alcoholic beverages, the lifting of the headscarf ban in all universities, the placing of antisecular individuals in government offices, the awarding of government contracts to Islamic businesses, and the arrest of several secular opponents of the government have been criticized by secular parties. Although the AKP won the 2007 elections by an even wider margin over its opponents, Turkey's chief prosecutor filed a lawsuit in March 2008, seeking to close down the AKP and ban Erdogan and Gul from holding any political office for five years. The AKP was charged with committing antisecularist actions that were banned by the constitution. On July 30, 2008, Turkey's Supreme Court fell one vote short of disbanding the party. The Court did, however, sharply criticize the party for its actions, and halved state funding for the party.

The second major problem facing Turkey is its handling of its minority Kurdish population, a problem that closely relates to the Iraq War. Many observers view the landslide victory of the AKP in the 2007 elections as prompted by a surge in Turkish nationalism and a resurgence of conservative Muslim influence since September 11, when the West, particularly the Bush administration in the United States, demanded an either-or, "with us or against us" position from Turkey, Pakistan, and other allies in the Middle East. When Turkey refused to participate in the invasion of Iraq in 2003 because it worried about destabilizing fragile relations with its Kurdish citizens, many in the Bush administration labeled the Turks as "against" the United States and the war on terrorism. As the situation in Iraq has continued to deteriorate and as the Kurds in northern Iraq continue to push for more autonomy, Kurdish nationalists within Turkey have increased their attacks against Turkish targets. In February and March 2008 the Turkish army began a military offensive against Kurds in eastern Turkey and also across the border in northern Iraq. These attacks have increased tensions between Turkey and the West.

Index

Death rates: in India, 752. *See also* Casualties

"Debate about women," 398–399

De Beers mining company, 740

Debts: national, 946; national repayment of, 1042

Debt slavery, 531

Deccan region, 30, 569; slaves in, 251

Decentralized government: in China, 60; in Japan, 764; in Australia, 808; in Yugoslavia, 969

Decimal mathematics system, 270

Declaration of Independence (U.S.), 614

Declaration of Pillnitz, 620–621

Declaration of the Rights of Man (France), 610(illus.), 617, 638

"Declaration of the Rights of Woman" (de Gouges), 638–639

Decline of the West, The (Spengler), 883

Decolonization, 1040; after Second World War, 944–945, 1023; in Algeria, 1000; in Africa, 1004, 1009; intellectual thought on, 1014

"Defense Force" (Japan), 963

Defensive alliances: of Bismarck, 816; after First World War, 837, 839. *See also* Alliance(s)

Deflation: in China, 584

Deforestation: in India, 751

De Gasperi, Alcide, 941

De Gaulle, Charles, 944, 1004, 1005, 1071

Deir el Bahri, 13

Deities, *see* Gods and goddesses; specific religions

De Klerk, Frederik, 1011, 1011(illus.)

Delacroix, Eugène, 682

Delaware Indians, 792

Delcassé, Théophile, 817

Delhi, India, 312, 557–558

Delhi Sultanate, 312, 314, 553; Mongols and, 300

Delian League, 83

Delphi: Pythian games at, 87

Deme (local unit), 82

Demesne (home farm), 366

Demilitarization: of Germany, 837; of Japan, 962

Democracy, 79; use of term, 79; in Athens, 82–83; in English-speaking countries, 809; in China, 864; before Second World War, 903; after Second World War, 944; Soviet Union and, 953; in Japan, 962; demise of communism and, 965; Putin and, 968(illus.); in Latin America, 980, 982; in India, 992–993; in Africa, 1006, 1012–1013

Democratic Progressive Party (Taiwan), 988

Democratic republicanism, 680

Democratic Republic of the Congo, 1012

Democritus (philosopher), 87

Demography: of Americas, 259–260; 17th century crisis in, 462–463

Deng Xiaoping (China), 984, 985, 986, 1039

Denmark: Vikings in, 354; in Enlightenment, 507; Schleswig and Holstein and, 687, 690; Nazis in, 919

Denmark-Norway: Protestantism and, 410

Depressions (economic): in U.S., 799–800; in 1929–1939, 893–897. *See also* Great Depression

Deregulation: in Europe, 965

Dervishes: Sufi, 220

Desacralization: of French monarchy, 613

Descartes, René, 498, 499, 501

Deserts: in Africa, 229

Deshima, Japan, 453

Design: modern, 883

Despotism: liberty vs., 620

Dessalines, Jean Jacques, 632, 633

De-Stalinization, 950–951

Détente policy, 961

Developing countries, 1021; income in, 716, 716(illus.); United Nations and, 1023; as global South, 1035; women in, 1044(illus.); urbanization in, 1045; capital cities in, 1045–1046; inequality in, 1048–1049; education in, 1064. *See also* Third World

Development: world market and, 717–718. *See also* Economy; Global economy

Devshirme: slave trade and, 550

Dewey, George, 758

Dharma, 42

Dhimmis (non-Muslims), 205

Di (god), 55

Diaghilev, Sergei, 885

Dialects: koine as, 91. *See also* Language(s); specific languages

Dialogue on the Two Chief Systems of the World (Galileo), 497

Diamond, Jared, 1044–1045

Diamond mines: in South Africa, 740–741, 740(illus.)

Diarbakr: Safavid capture of, 553

Diaspora, 166

Diaz, Bartholomew, 434, 437

Díaz, Bernal, 281

Díaz, Porfirio, 787, 979

Dickens, Charles, 797

Dictators and dictatorships: in Rome, 111–112; of Napoleon I, 628–636; in Latin America, 786, 787, 979, 980–982; in Russia, 834; in Germany, 835; Second World War and, 903–919; radical totalitarian, 904–906; in Italy, 913; Soviet, 947

Diderot, Denis, 508, 514–515, 515(illus.)

Dien Bien Phu: Battle of, 989

Diet (food): in Rome, 111(illus.); Mongol, 296; of medieval peasant households, 367, 367(illus.); in Southeast Asia, 429; in West Africa, 520; in China, 584. *See also* Food(s)

Diet (Japanese parliament), 766, 962, 963

Diet of Worms, 406

Digest (Justinian), 166

Dimitrash (Cossacks), 548

Dioceses: Roman and Christian, 170; in Scandinavia, 361

Diocletian (Rome), 121, 122–123, 170

Dionysus (god): cult of, 94

Diop, Cheikh Anta (Senegal), 230, 231

Diplomacy: Persian, 20–21; in Middle East, 1075

Directory (French Revolution), 628, 629

"Dirty war" (Argentina), 981

"Disappeared" (Chile), 981(illus.)

"Disasters of the War, The" (Goya), 635

Discovery: European, 433–443

Discrimination: in U.S., 958; toward women (Japan), 964

Diseases: in India, 33, 752; Hippocrates and, 87; Justinian plague as, 168; Muslim scholars on, 218; in Columbian Exchange, 259, 260, 444, 445; in Central Asia, 307; in China, 338–339, 586–587; urban conditions for, 376; in 17th century, 462; in West Africa, 520; of African slaves, 532; miasmatic theory of, 696; germ theory of, 696–697; medical revolution and, 1052–1053; global epidemics and, 1055–1056. *See also* Black Death (plague); Epidemics; HIV/AIDS; Medicine; specific diseases

Disraeli, Benjamin, 706

Dissidents: Soviet, 951; in Czechoslovakia, 955

Distribution of wealth: global, 1042(illus.)

Diversity: in Southeast Asia, 430; in Songhai, 523; in Americas, 778, 781; in Africa, 976(illus.), 1007

Divination texts: in China, 55, 56

Divine Office, 358

Divine right of kings: Louis XIV (France) and, 467–468; James I (England) and, 481; Louis XVI (France) and, 616

Division of labor, 3; sexual, 666–668

Divorce: in Muslim law, 208; in Southeast Asia, 429; in Japan, 597; in Turkey, 853; in Soviet Union, 910; in Italy, 913

Diwali festival: in Mughal India, 562

Diwān, 196, 200, 238

Dix, Otto, 825

Doctors, *see* Medicine; Physicians

Doers: Saint-Simon on, 681

Dogon region (Mali), 242(illus.)

Dole: in Britain, 900–901

Dome of the Rock mosque (Jerusalem), 195(illus.)

Domesday Book (England), 355–356

Domestic system, 565

Dominican Republic, *see* Hispaniola

Dominicans, 358, 445, 603

Dominion of Canada, 801, 801(illus.)

Donatello, 394

Don Cossacks, *see* Cossacks

Dongola, Nubia, 244

Don Juan Joachin Gutierrez Altamirano Velasco (Cabrera), 778(illus.)

Dorians, 78

Dowry: in Athens, 85; in China, 338

Draco (Athens), 82

Draft (military): in France, 625; in Nazi Germany, 917

Drainage: in Mohenjo-Daro and Harappa, 32

Drake, E. L., 948

Drama: Athenian, 83, 84; in China, 583–584; in Japan, 589. *See also* Theater

Draussen und Drinnen (Grosz), 876(illus.)

Dravidian-speaking peoples, 32, 34–35

Dreyfus, Alfred, 705(illus.)

Dreyfus affair, 705

Drinking, *see* Alcohol

Drug abuse: in China, 983

Drugs (medicine): Muslim, 217(illus.)

Druids, 4(illus.)

Druzes: in Lebanon, 1071

Dualism: Cartesian, 498

Dual monarchy: Austria-Hungary as, 706

Dual revolution, 675